Children
and Books

Children
and Books

Zena Sutherland
The University of Chicago

May Hill Arbuthnot

Chapters contributed by
Dianne L. Monson
The University of Minnesota

Part Four: Areas and Issues
edited by Peggy Sullivan

Cover, frontispiece,
and part opening illustrations
by David Macaulay

HarperCollins*Publishers*

The illustrator for this eighth edition of *Children and Books* is David Macaulay, who has won international acclaim for his distinctive books about architecture, including awards in several countries. His role as commentator for television adaptations for some of these books has made him a familiar figure to many. In 1989, he gave the annual Zena Sutherland Lecture. Mr. Macaulay teaches at the Rhode Island School of Design.

Sponsoring Editor: Christopher Jennison
Project Coordination: Proof Positive/Farrowlyne Associates, Inc.
Text and Cover Design: Kathleen Cunningham
Photo Research: Rosemary Hunter
Development: Anita Portugal
Compositor: Black Dot Graphics
Printer and Binder: R.R. Donnelley & Sons Company
Cover Printer: New England Book Components

Children and Books, Eighth Edition
Copyright © 1991 by HarperCollins Publishers, Inc.

ISBN 0-673-46357-5
Library of Congress Cataloging-in-Publication Data

Sutherland, Zena.
   Children and books/Zena Sutherland, May Hill Arbuthnot;
   chapters contributed by Dianne L. Monson.—8th ed.
     p.   cm.
   "Part four: areas and issues edited by Peggy Sullivan."
   Includes bibliographical references and index.
   ISBN (invalid) 0-673-46357-5
   1. Children's literature—History and criticism. 2. Children—
Books and reading.   I. Arbuthnot, May Hill, 1884–1969.
II. Monson, Dianne L.   III. Title
PN1009.A2S8 1991
809′.89282—dc20   90–21055
                CIP

93 9 8 7 6 5 4 3

Contents

Part Two
Exploring the Types of Literature

Part Three
Bringing Children and Books Together

Part Four
Areas and Issues–Children and Books

Preface

to the Eighth Edition

Children and Books is meant for all adults who are interested in bringing children and books together, but it is designed particularly for classes in children's literature in education and English departments and in library schools, in colleges and universities.

Since the first edition of *Children and Books* over forty years ago, children's books have achieved recognition and children's literature is being accorded a respect long overdue. The body of children's literature has grown enormously, courses in the subject have multiplied, and some of the best writers today are devoting all or part of their time to writing children's books. Realization that children's literature both reflects the values of our society and instills those values in children has made increasing numbers of adults aware that children's literature is a part of the mainstream of all literature and that, like adult literature, it is worthy of our respect both for what it is and for what it does.

The title suggests that dual nature of the book's approach. The emphases are on understanding children and their needs, on perspectives and background, on criteria and types of literature, and on artists and authors. In a sense, *Children and Books* has a *major-author* approach. It is impossible to describe all of the good books that have been written for children, but it is possible to introduce readers to the works of most of the major authors and artists of the past and present. The major-author emphasis should spare the reader, particularly the new student, from floundering in a sea of titles.

Children and Books is primarily about books; since the field is so broad, to include other media would mean giving them superficial treatment that would not do them justice. There are, however, some discussions of other media in Parts Three and Four; and the bibliographies for those parts, as well as the Adult References and Book Selection Aids in the appendices, refer the reader to articles and books on related media.

Organization and Revision

With each edition of *Children and Books,* the authors and the editors have been conscious of the need to reflect changes in our society by new emphases in the text, and to reorganize the text to reflect more accurately the changes in the ways in which children's literature is taught.

In this eighth edition, strikingly illustrated by David Macaulay, Part One, "Knowing Children and Books," is an overview of the range of books for children, types of children's literature, and an assessment of the criteria used to evaluate and choose children's books. It includes a consideration of children's emotional needs and reading interests, considering books in relation to needs and interests as well as to trends in publishing and to changes and conditions in our society. In this edition, the first two chapters of the previous edition have been combined. In a chapter on the history of children's books, charts on "Milestones in the History of Children's Literature" and "Twentieth Century Milestones" are included. Chapter Four focuses on the variety of books for very young children. Chapter Five is devoted to artists, and the gallery of examples of their work has been expanded.

Part Two, "Exploring the Types of Literature," considers books by genre, approaching them by emphasizing major authors, a process that makes it easier for readers of *Children and Books* to identify major contributors to a field in which identification is, by virtue of numbers, increasingly difficult. Individual chapters discuss folk tales, including tall tales; fables, myths, and epics; modern fantasy; poetry; modern fiction and historical fiction; and biography and informational books. In all these chapters, the text and bibliographies have been brought up to date, and the criteria for each genre are described at the beginning of the relevant chapter.

Part Three, "Bringing Children and Books Together," deals with methodology, discussing the role of the adult and some of the techniques that can be used in introducing children to literature and in evaluating and encouraging their responses to books. There are many additional suggestions for teachers, using ideas that emphasize literature in the curriculum.

Part Four, which considers areas and issues relating to children and their books, includes new articles on censorship, research, and internationalism, and other new articles on early literacy, the literature-based curriculum, and children's book awards. This section includes bibliographies and suggestions for further reading.

The Appendices are Book Selection Aids, Adult References, Publishers and Their Addresses, Children's Book Awards, and a Pronunciation Guide. There is a Subject Index in addition to the Author, Illustrator, and Title Index.

Special Features

Set off from the text are "Viewpoints," brief statements from books and articles that are germane to textual comments on authors, artists, books, and reading, not necessarily reflecting the author's viewpoint in *Children and Books* but suggesting some issues to explore.

The bibliographies are extensive, with books pertinent to chapter discussions listed by author and title under Adult References and Book Selection Aids at the end of each chapter, and books for children, separately listed and often divided into subcategories, in all the chapters on types of children's literature. Books mentioned in the text are not annotated; additional entries are. Some out-of-print books are included since they are still available in collections. Each reader undoubtedly will miss one or more favorite books; unfortunately, space limitations necessitate some omissions, even of books the authors would have liked to include. The age levels are suggestions only, as children of the same age often differ markedly in reading skills, interests, and social maturity. Since the text stresses the importance of books about minority groups, symbols are used in many of the bibliographies to denote books that emphasize African Americans, Hispanics, Native Americans, Asian Americans, and religious minorities, so that such books may be more accessible to readers.

To facilitate the finding of information sources, all adult references and book selection aids are listed, together with annotations and full bibliographic information, in Appendices A and B at the end of the book. To facilitate the finding of material about authors and artists, all references to major author or artist discussions are singled out in the index by the use of boldface type.

Acknowledgments

For various kinds of assistance in the preparation of the eighth edition of *Children and Books*, grateful acknowledgments are due to the following people:

For her writing of Chapters 14, 15, and 16: Dianne Monson, University of Minnesota.

For her editing of the Areas and Issues section: Peggy Sullivan, Northern Illinois University.

For her suggestions for revision throughout the book: Bette J. Peltola, University of Wisconsin–Milwaukee.

For her aid in bibliographic research as well as her contributions to the illustration program and the Viewpoints, Kathryn Pierson.

For her aid in the illustration program: Annice Jennison.

For her suggestions and contributions to the Viewpoints: Rebecca Rapport, University of Minnesota.

For their unfailing and cheerful patience and guidance: Chris Jennison and Anita Portugal, the editors.

For his sage counsel and continuing moral support: Alec Sutherland.

Zena Sutherland

The author and publisher would like to thank the following reviewers for their response to the revision plans and to the revised manuscript:

Richard F. Abrahamson
  University of Houston
Paulette C. Babner
  Cape Cod Community College
Sue A. Burgess
Arnold B. Cheyney
  University of Miami
Terri Christman
  Nova University
Patricia J. Cianciolo
  Michigan State University
Linda DeGroff
  University of Georgia

Rosalind Engel
  Iowa State University
Joan E. Gilley
  University of Missouri-St. Louis
Betsy Gray
  National College of Education
Deuel N. Griffin
  Clemson University
James Haskins
  University of Florida
Barbara Immroth
  University of Texas at Austin
Marilyn Kaye
  St. John's University
Eric A. Kimmel
  Portland State University
Rebecca Lukens
  Miami University of Ohio
Mary D. Manning
  East Tennessee State University
Wilma J. Pyle
  Florida Atlantic University
Sam Sebesta
  University of Washington, Seattle
Malcolm Usrey
  Clemson University
Stephen H. Voss
  Florida Atlantic University
Jerry Weiss
  Jersey City State College

Children and Books

Part One

Knowing Children and Books

Chapter One

Children and Books Today

Book lovers young and old know that there is no pleasure exactly like the moment when book and reader meet and are just right for each other. At the simplest level, that moment is what those of us who work with children and their books are working for. The sense of wonder and satisfaction may be instantaneous, as when a child recognizes, with delight, the familiar excitement of waiting for a visitor and the feeling of Beverly Cleary's Ramona, on the very first page, ". . . twirling around trying to make herself dizzy," or as when a child finds, deeply touched, that he or she cannot forget the poignant ending of *Charlotte's Web,* or even when an informational book is found to contain exactly the facts a child is looking for. The point is that the book has truly affected the reader. Most of us remember such books from our childhood. It isn't a ho-hum-isn't-that-interesting kind of experience; it's exciting, exhilarating.

While the roles of children have changed substantially in this century and the kinds of books published for them have also changed, the moment of enchantment when a child hears or reads for the first time about Ramona, or Charlotte, or Tom Sawyer, isn't very different from the moment of enchantment when children of long ago heard or overheard a grandmother or a tribal storyteller tell the story of the cleverness of Anansi or the magic of Mouse Woman. It is that moment of discovery that we hope to bring to all the children with whom we work. Their delight is our delight.

Adults working in the field of children's literature today find themselves involved with concerns about appropriate materials—questions of censorship, reading levels, fair representation of ethnic minorities and sex roles—and children's access to these materials and services, as well as other serious issues. However, we must not forget that the center of all such concerns is the meeting of a child and a book, an event that we want to make happen over and over again, for as many children as possible, and with as much satisfaction as possible.

That's basically what *Children and Books* is all about: gaining a knowledge of a broad variety of fine children's books, recognizing the diversity of children, and learning both children's changing preferences as they mature, and the ways in which we can bring children and books together—learning to help make the meeting a happy one.

One of the tenets upon which *Children and Books* is based is that love of literature can be a positive and enriching part of everyone's life. Learning to love reading and to enjoy good books in childhood can be the start of a lifelong habit that brings pleasure and knowledge. Many children do not have easy access to a wide range of good books, they do not necessarily encounter the best old and new authors, and often they do not know how to seek out books. Many children learn to read without learning to love reading. The recognition of children's literature may be greater today, and the number of books published may be larger than in 1947 when the first edition of *Children and Books* was published, but a whole new set of problems faces us in getting books into the hands of children, from financing to censorship or to the domination of television and computer games. Children are not born loving good books; neither are they born hating to read. They can be encouraged and influenced in either direction, and that is where we can hope to make a difference.

As adults who are involved with children and their books, and who are committed to bringing them together, we should ask and try to answer a number of questions:

First, what is children's literature? How can we define it?

Second, what is its present state and where does it seem to be going in the 1990s?

Third, what influences are shaping the books now being published?

Fourth, how can books help children as their needs, values, and skills grow?

What Is Children's Literature?

Is every book that children read a part of their literature? Their textbooks aren't, except for a language arts anthology here and there. Does children's literature consist, then, of books that children read of their own volition? Not comic books, and not the adult science fiction book borrowed from a parent. Nor is children's literature the same thing as young adult litera-ture, although the line dividing the two is hazy, and is at times crossed in either direction.

Today, publishing for children has become highly specialized, and there are separate bodies of literature for children and for young adults. Books written for younger adolescents are often popular with readers who have not yet reached their teens. Since those who make judgments may be swayed by either the popularity or the literary quality of such books, they may be assigned in reviews, book lists, or library collections, to both groups. Publishers usually designate in their catalogues and on book jackets whether a book is intended for children or for young adults, and the decisions of teachers, librarians, or reviewers may be based on the publishers' designations. The lack of sharpness in the dividing line between the two age groups is compounded by the fact that children's reading patterns are highly individual; two children of the same age may differ markedly in their tastes, their ability to comprehend, their reading interests, and their reading responses. One child may read and laugh or weep over *Charlotte's Web*, while the other may feel he or she has outgrown it and prefer a contemporary problem novel intended for older readers. In sum, it is easy to say where children's literature begins: with books for preschool children. It is not so easy to say where it ends and young adult literature begins, although the books themselves may have been published as distinctly labeled entities or shelved in separate parts of a school or public library.

Is there a way to define children's literature other than specifying what it is not? There are no rigid or absolute definitions and there are differences of opinion among the experts. Some maintain that anything children read and enjoy is a part of their literature. Most authorities in the field, however, hold that children's literature consists of books that are not only read and enjoyed, but also that have been written for children and that meet high literary and artistic standards. This second position is the one on which this book is based.

When we consider books that have been specifically written for children, it is clear that their literature has had a comparatively short history. Few children of the seventeenth or even the eighteenth century could read, but those

Viewpoint

Literature gives us an experience that stretches us vertically to the heights and depths of what the human mind can conceive, to what corresponds to the conceptions of heaven and hell in religion. In this perspective what I like or don't like disappears, because there's nothing left of me as a separate person: as a reader of literature I exist only as a representative of humanity as a whole. We'll see in the last talk how important this is.

No matter how much experience we may gather in life, we can never in life get the dimension of experience that the imagination gives us. Only the arts and sciences can do that, and of these, only literature gives us the whole sweep and range of human imagination as it sees itself.

Northrop Frye, *The Educated Imagination.* Bloomington: Indiana University Press, 1964, p. 101.

who could shared such adult delights as *Aesop's Fables* or Arthurian legends. These books were of course not designed for them; children's appointed reading fare of this period was, save for the rarity like *Mother Goose* or *Little Goody Two Shoes,* primarily educational. There were, therefore, two quite distinct kinds of books read by children: the useful, didactic books that were written to instruct them in manners and morals, and the adult books they read for pleasure. Because they have been loved by generations of children, some of these adult books, like *Robinson Crusoe* and *Gulliver's Travels,* have come to be regarded as a part of the literary heritage of children. Today, as in the past, some children enjoy reading adult books, particularly if the books are on a subject in which they have a special interest, or if such books are currently popular and much discussed.

There is today an amazing variety of material in print that is intended for children: picture books, some without text and some designed to clarify concepts or give information, some to tell a story; easy-to-read books, invaluable for the beginning reader and the poor reader; pop-up books and choose-your-own-adventure books; books written with a simple vocabulary but a sophisticated subject or plot, the so-called "high-low" books for the older reluctant reader. There is poetry for children; folk literature that includes tales, myths, fables, epics, and legends, many of which have appeared in handsomely illustrated single-tale editions for use with younger children; modern fantasy that includes imitations of folk tales, science fiction, and original, fanciful tales; historical fiction and biographies; animal stories, sports stories, and mysteries; family stories and problem novels; realistic fiction about people of almost every country or racial or ethnic group. There are informational books on hundreds of topics, and how-to-do-it, or make-it, or play-it books by the dozens. They are in every public and school

The vast amount of reading material available for children—including fiction, fantasy, poetry, and informational books—can provide many hours of adventure and enjoyment.

library, in bookstores and drugstores and airports, on supermarket racks and corner newsstands. There are reading kits, paperbacks and comic books, and children's magazines—and a great deal of print published for adults but read also by children. It is clearly important, therefore, that adults who want to encourage an appreciation of good books be able to discriminate, in this mass of print, between the pedestrian or ephemeral and the distinguished, and know what is going on today in the world of children's literature.

Where Is Children's Literature and Where Is It Going?

It was not until the twentieth century that children's literature was taken seriously enough to warrant a special place in the academic or publishing worlds. There had always been some advocates of its importance, as is evident from the books that were published in the nineteenth century, but it was not until the early 1900s that the first courses designed to train special children's librarians were established at the Carnegie Library School. While books for children had been published by major publishing houses, it was not until 1918 that the first separate children's department was established by Macmillan. Doubleday followed suit nine years later, and other publishers then rather quickly conformed and also set up separate children's sections under the aegis of children's book editors. Today, however, children's literature no longer needs to justify its existence. Although there are those who refuse to admit that children's literature is a part of the whole body of literature, considering it to be of lesser importance or quality, for most of the literary and educational world the immense importance of children's literature is clear.

Between 1900 and the 1990s, vast changes have taken place in our society and, as in the past, those changes have influenced children's books and are reflected in them. Our culture today has a greater awareness of the variety of children. They are bright, average, and slow;

Viewpoint

All our observations indicate that inner speech is an autonomous speech function. We can confidently regard it as a distinct plane of verbal thought. It is evident that the transition from inner to external speech is not a simple translation from one language into another. It cannot be achieved by merely vocalizing silent speech. It is a complex, dynamic process involving the transformation of the predicative, idiomatic structure of inner speech into syntactically articulated speech intelligible to others.

. . . Inner speech is not the interior aspect of external speech—it is a function in itself. It still remains speech, i.e., thought connected with words. But while in external speech thought is embodied in words, in inner speech words die as they bring forth thought. Inner speech is to a large extent thinking in pure meanings. It is a dynamic, shifting, unstable thing, fluttering between word and thought, the two more or less stable, more or less firmly delineated components of verbal thought. Its true nature and place can be understood only after examining the next plane of verbal thought, the one still more inward than inner speech.

That plane is thought itself. . . .

L. S. Vygotsky, *Thought and Language.* edited and translated by Eugenia Hanfmann and Gertrude Vakar. The Massachusetts Institute of Technology, 1962, pp. 148–149.

they are rural, urban, suburban, migrant, and small-town; they come from happy homes and homes torn by tension. African American, white, Native American, Appalachian, Hispanic, Asian American; loved and cherished, unloved and neglected; bookworms and nonreaders—boys and girls whose needs to identify, to develop, to feel pride in their heritage and acceptance in the community are being studied and served. The enormous range of books available today reflects an awareness of

From *Better With Two* by Barbara M. Joosse, illustrated by Catherine Stock.

the differences among children as well as of the similarities.

Children's literature also reflects much of the conflict and controversy in our society regarding moral standards and life-styles. Many of the enduring values of the past are reflected in books for children, but so are the values of a contemporary society that is less secure and more mobile than earlier generations knew. The children of the 1990s who watch television by the hour are familiar with the mores and the conflicts of the rest of the world, as well as with those of their own country. Television, to a greater extent than any of the other communications media, has made children more sophisticated. Some adults may deplore such sophistication in children and in their books, but the response of authors and publishers to children who are well aware of crime, violence, contemporary sex patterns, and other inescapably evident facets of our society has been to include these facets in books. They are not in all books, and there is a noticeable difference from genre

to genre, but there are few kinds of books that do not, today, give evidence of changing times.

While some of the changes have aroused controversy, in many ways children's books, taken as a whole, are better in this century—and even in the last few decades of this century—than they were in the past. They cover more subjects in which children have an interest; the informational books are more accurate and candid. The art in books today includes every medium and every style; while some illustrations are mediocre or awkward, there are also paintings and drawings of superlative quality. Despite the criticism from some adults, children have welcomed the candor that is evident in trends in contemporary publishing.

One of the subjects that is treated with frankness is death, both the process of dying and the adjustment of those bereaved. In books for younger children the focus tends to be on the death of a pet, as in *Better With Two*, by Barbara Joose, or on the death of an old person; in books for older children the emphasis may be on the death of a peer, on fatal illness or suicide, or on the range of emotions experienced by those who mourn.

There has also been a veritable flood of books dealing with the disabled, from such novels as Jan Slepian's *The Alfred Summer*, a touching story of the friendship between two boys, one having cerebral palsy and the other retarded, to *Different, Not Dumb*, Margot Marek's book about a second-grader with a learning disability. Factual books describe the range of mental, emotional, and physical handicaps, with the greatest number devoted to the latter, and there are novels about children who suffer from these handicaps and who adjust to or overcome them. There are photodocumentaries about real children, many of them expressing the child's desire for acceptance and understanding as well as giving information about a specific handicap. Not only do they help the handicapped child feel that a disability is not so onerous that it cannot be mentioned in children's books, they also help children who are not handicapped understand that their disabled classmates are children like themselves, sharing the same needs and pleasures and, above all, able to do many things for themselves.

The Changing View of Children in Illustration

From *British Workingwoman* (1874).

From *Under the Window*, illustrated by Kate Greenaway (1879).

"The Dangerous Cliff" from *Furze and Heather for Rainy Weather* in *Birdie's Book* (1880).

The illustrations of any period reflect the concepts of that time about the role of children and of the family, as well as what illustrations in children's books should depict. In the first drawing, all attention—even that of the dog—is centered on the father, reflecting the structure of the Victorian family. In Kate Greenaway's picture of children leaving school (1879), the children are prim; their behavior is decorous and their facial expressions serious. Books of this period were meant to buttress the strong role of the family in society, and to reinforce the idea that children were innocent little creatures easily led astray; stories were heavily didactic as well as moralistic. In the third illustration, the didacticism is paramount; although sentimentalized like the others, its message is stronger: children who ignore the guidance of adults are in grave danger.

"Rainy Day" from *Dream Blocks*, illustrated by Jesse Willcox Smith (1908).

From *Here, There, and Everywhere* by Dorothy Aldis, illustrated by Marjorie Flack (1927).

From *Told Under the Blue Umbrella*, illustrated by Marguerite Davis (1933).

From *Yonie Wondernose*, written and illustrated by Marguerite de Angeli (1944).

The same romanticized yet static quality is evidenced in the illustration of a mother reading to her child in "Rainy Day" by Jesse Willcox Smith (1908); however, this pose is more intimate and shows closeness between the two. The illustration from *Here, There, and Everywhere* (1927, 1928) has much of the same quality as the earlier pictures. The children are still from a white, conservative, middle-class background, still prim and obedient. The illustration from *Told Un-*der the Blue Umbrella* (1933) features a white, well-to-do child sedately playing with blocks, but the mother, although highlighted in a traditional role, is more casually posed at the child's level, and is participating in his play. The Amish children portrayed in *Yonie Wondernose* (1944) still depict an innocent rural life as they help their mother with the milking, although books of this period now begin to show children playing in boisterous activities.

Hello, Mrs. Piggle Wiggle (1957) goes one step further by focusing on mischief. Although each chapter offers a cure for some naughty behavior, the popularity of the series rested more on the humor of rascality than on the lesson. The world of children's books had become big business by this time, and adults were well aware that their audience wanted books that entertained as well as those that taught. *Alexander and the Terrible, Horrible, No Good, Very Bad Day* (1972) reflects a new awareness of children's problems and an honesty about some negative aspects of their lives. The knowledge gained from educational and psychological research had changed society's concept of children; they were no longer seen as cheerful products of a righteous adult world. *Ramona and Her Father* (1977) recognizes the importance of father–child interaction instead of the child's reliance on mother depicted in most family stories before this time. An important book counteracting what may be seen as the progress from the stiffness of the Victorian family to the natural, casual affection now important in children's illustration is the concern reflected in a book about the ultimate threat to families everywhere— nuclear holocaust, as experienced in *Hiroshima No Pika* (1980), which shows through dramatic paintings the effect of the August 6, 1945 atomic explosion on a child and her parents.

From *Hello, Mrs. Piggle Wiggle* by Betty MacDonald, illustrated by Hillary Knight (1957).

From *Alexander and the Terrible, Horrible, No Good, Very Bad Day* by Judith Viorst, illustrated by Ray Cruz (1972).

From *Ramona and Her Father* by Beverly Cleary, illustrated by Alan Tiegreen (1977).

From *Hiroshima No Pika*, written and illustrated by Toshi Maruki (1980).

From *Angel Mae: A Tale of Trotter Street*, written and illustrated by Shirley Hughes (1989).

From *I Hate English!* by Ellen Levine, illustrated by Steve Björkman (1989).

From *Ten, Nine, Eight,* written and illustrated by Molly Garrett Bang (1983).

Ten, Nine, Eight (1983), like *Ramona and Her Father*, underscores a new concept in family life, with a nurturant father assuming the child care role. In a warm bedtime scenario, an African-American father cuddles his sleepy child. Mae cannot wait for Mom's attention, so she tries a foot tickle in *Angel Mae: A Tale of Trotter Street* (1989). This humorous story focuses on an English family, but it has a universal appeal and it indicates contemporary attitudes in its depiction of the informality of a mother–child relationship. The influx of immigrant families and their children presents problems in acclimation to a new country and new customs. Helped by a sympathetic teacher, young Mei Mei gets over her fear of speaking a new language in *I Hate English!* (1989). The problem is serious, but the treatment, like that in *Angel Mae*, is light, and the students' animation a far cry from the decorous children of Greenaway's time.

In response to the feminist movement and a rising protest against sexism in children's books, there have been more biographies of women, more books in which female protagonists play active roles, more girls' sports stories, more reflections of women's careers that realistically parallel today's society, and less depiction of stereotypical sex roles for both males and females, young or old. Third world presses and feminist publishing houses have contributed to this growing trend.

With increased awareness of, and concern for, the rights of children, those who create and produce children's books have responded with books about child abuse, children's legal rights, the social agencies that deal with children, children as investors, and children's rights in personal relationships. Some of these books incorporate facts about children's rights into stories about the plight of children in foster homes—or, as in Katherine Paterson's touching story of a loving foster mother in *The Great Gilly Hopkins*, on the security found in some foster homes.

Certainly the many books by, for, and about black people have constituted one of the most significant trends in children's books. There were comparatively few such books earlier in the twentieth century, but from the 1960s on came a spate of them, long overdue—books that have faced the problems of black people with candor, fiction in which the characters are drawn with depth, nonfiction in which black history and contemporary issues are explored, and poetry in which black pride and black protest are expressed. Many of these books are produced by black authors and illustrators.

Books about other minority groups have also grown in number, although demand still exceeds supply. They are to some extent products of the trend in writing and publishing books about blacks that helped raise the consciousness—and perhaps the conscience—of the children's book world, but this movement has also been fed by the growing group consciousness of all minority racial and ethnic segments of the society. There have been increasing numbers of books about Latin Americans, Native Americans, and Asian Americans. Today, many more books are being written in, or translated into, Spanish. In a world in which pride in identity is stressed, it is especially important that no children feel that their family's customs or beliefs or language are unworthy of recognition and respect.

There are two significant trends in nonfiction today. The first is the inclusion of subjects that were formerly considered only of adult interest, subjects like pollution, international relations, AIDS, controversy over nuclear power plants, and other topics of concern to the knowledgeable children of our time. The second trend is seen in the care given to producing books that are accurate and authoritative, that provide sources and appendices, and that are written in a straightforward manner. Less often do we see

Viewpoint

The reading of books is not a natural activity for human beings; and even less, the reading of good books. But then, the natural proclivities of a human being are precisely what the civilizer hopes to subdue. A human being, by and large, is not the most likable of nature's productions. He has not the grace of the cat, the strength of the tiger, the dignity of the elephant, nor the honesty of the dog. He steals the fur he lacks and kills for sport; and his contributions to the well-being of the planet have been to destroy the ozone layer, poison the oceans, and invent the battery hen. But he has one saving grace. Unlike any other creature, he knows the depths of his own infamy, and, here and there, makes efforts to undo the harm he has done.

It is largely through books that he knows these things. It is through books that he discovers himself, and so discovers others. He is not born with self-knowledge, only with self-awareness. Self-knowledge may be acquired through experience, but that is a very chancy business. It is the rare soul who actually profits by experience. Most of us just keep up with the installments.

Leon Garfield, "The Outlaw," *Horn Book Magazine*, March/April, 1990, pp. 169–170.

the book that condescends to young readers; children are treated as a serious audience.

Almost all of these trends are combined in contemporary biographies: more representation of minorities, more varied depictions of women in a broad spectrum of careers, more candid portraits of prominent people as human beings with faults and foibles, and more careful documentation and accuracy in writing about all of them.

The United States is not alone in these trends. For example, an increasing number of the books originating in England are also concerned with minority group members and their participation in the society. The same group consciousness and search for identity can be seen in Canada, where increased numbers of books have reflected the Canadian multiethnic heritage and where a national children's book center, the establishment of several new book awards, and the founding of several journals devoted to children's literature all attest to a sense of growing pride in Canadian children's literature.

The burgeoning of international exchange and translation of children's books, sparked by such organizations as the International Board on Books for Young People and such events as the annual Children's Book Fair in Bologna, has waned in practice if not in principle. The numbers of books originating in other countries and later published in a new edition by a publisher in the United States has decreased since the 1970s, although adults seem no less committed, in articles and at international meetings, to the benefits of having children understand what life is like in other countries and how much children everywhere are alike in their basic needs. Clearly the attrition has been due in large measure to the financial problems of schools, publishers, and libraries; it is to be hoped that improved economic conditions will, in time, generate a resurgence of the trend. The need is still there.

There are, of course, differences among countries in their ideas of government, their philosophies, their customs, and their concepts of how children should be educated and how they should behave, and what should be in their books. We need to understand these differences, but we are concerned chiefly, in this book, with our own culture and our own children and their books, from wherever they originally came. To understand what is in our children's literature and why it is there, we must consider some of the factors that play a part in shaping the content of children's books.

Influences on Children's Literature

We have examined some of the trends, the kinds of books that are being published today, and some of the subjects and themes that they contain. The content of children's books is shaped by several factors: by what we know about children and about their needs and expectations, by the economic realities of publishing, and by the culture in which we all live and which, consciously or unconsciously, we reflect as authors, illustrators, editors, reviewers, and educators in the school, the library, and the home.

Children's book editors are eager to produce the best books they can, but they are also aware that their books must sell. If they don't sell, the publishing house stops producing children's books—and indeed, the vagaries of financial conditions in recent years led to the closing or the takeover of some children's book departments. While most adult books are sold directly to the consumer, the primary market for children's books has been the library, either school or public. However, there has been a marked increase in bookstore sales and in the establishment of children's bookstores. As federal subsidies for the purchase of books evaporated in the 1970s and 1980s publishers could not afford to carry old titles, however good, for which there was a lessening demand, with the result that many long-standing favorites went out of print. As production costs rose along with other costs in our economic system, so did book prices, and the market became increasingly competitive. One result is that editors can no longer afford to take chances on books that don't have a reasonably high profit potential. There are, of course, exceptions; nearly every editor will at times take a chance on a manuscript he or she thinks has unusual qualities

Parents reading to their preschool age children on a regular basis help their children realize that books and reading are sources of pleasure, even before they are ready to read.

even if it doesn't promise material rewards. On the whole, however, manuscripts tend to be chosen for publication because at least moderate success can be predicted—that is, because their authors have already been successful, or because they follow a successful pattern, or because they are on a topic which is of great current interest. This means, to a degree, repetition. There is also a tendency to emphasize, in promoting books, those that are most promising, especially those for which there may be lucrative motion picture or television tie-ins. Bookstores, always wary of overstocking, are cautious. The opinions of reviewers and of compilers of bibliographies and other book selection aids influence what goes into library collections and is, therefore, accessible to children. And, because the market is competitive and because critics are scrutinizing books more carefully than they did in the past, editors are turning more frequently to subject-matter experts to check and screen manuscripts. Thus informational books for children are more accurate and authoritative than they have been in the past. In sum, the economic influences at work in our society have had a profound impact on what is published for children as well as what older books stay in print.

Therefore, while the responses of authors and editors to the known needs and interests of children are influences on the content and the quality of books, some of the influences on the

authors and editors themselves stem, it is clear, from stresses that are part of the society. Publishing is affected by economic pressure, despite the fact that the total number of children's books published annually has remained fairly constant and that paperback publishing of children's books has risen dramatically.

Economic pressure is, however, only one of the ways in which our culture influences our books. Books are also affected by the sociopolitical atmosphere, by the causes and protest movements of our time, by the media that pervade our lives, and by the society's standards and mores. Children's books are affected, perhaps above all, by the society's concept of the roles of children: what and how they should learn, what their obligations and privileges should be, what rights they have, and what their books should contain. Not least, the content of books may be affected by what adults think they should *not* contain. What is, or is not, or ought to be, in children's books is and will undoubtedly continue to be one of the most controversial aspects of children's literature.

If we examine the whole phenomenon of the reflection of our culture in children's books, it is apparent that some of the values or the messages are deliberate, and that some are inherent, for all authors—differ as they may— are themselves products of the culture in which they live.

The influence of a society on books produced for children is nothing new. In colonial times, the sternly pietistic attitude of the culture and its belief that human beings, young as well as old, trembled always at the brink of corruption and damnation was forcefully conveyed in the material that was written for children. In Victorian times, children's books reflected the ornate language patterns of the era, the sanctity of the home and the near-sanctity of the parent, and the prevalent preoccupation with manners and strict morals. There were differences among authors, but taken as a whole, the body of children's literature mirrored the society. And so it does today.

The last several decades of the twentieth century have been marked by a changing sociopolitical environment. The demand for equality—given impetus by the civil rights movement—has been taken up by women, homosexuals,

Viewpoint

Our job, though it may, and probably will, prove difficult, bewildering, even painful in the doing, is essentially simple. We have only to figure out where the book is crying out to go—and then take it there. To me, this is equally true whether we are writing a picture book, a lighthearted story for the "fourth grade nothings," a realistic novel about a troubled boy hating life in a Junior High or a subtle, imagination-stretching fantasy. However magnificent or minimal our gifts are, we must try to write the best book we can.

While the publisher, the bookseller, the librarian, the educator may have to guard against all those "isms" and keep a weather eye out for emerging trends, writers must not let such concerns deflect them from their task. Once writers start leaving out vital scenes that may offend somebody or adding extraneous bits because they may help get the thing onto the Ministry of Education's list of approved books, the integrity of their work will be lost. Children will end up with diminished stories, bloodless, safe, and forgettable. Joy does not spring out of caution. Memorable, moving books are not written from a sense of duty.

Jean Little, "A Writer's Social Responsibility," *The New Advocate*, Volume 3, Number 2, Spring 1990, edited by Joel Taxel. Norwood, Massachusetts: Christopher-Gordon Publishers, 1990, p. 79.

Viewpoint

To be a good reader a person needs a number of tools: visual discrimination; the ability to see and hear differences and similarities; the ability to question; the ability to recognize and understand feelings; the ability to infer what is not specifically stated; the ability to recognize and understand individual words as well as concepts; the ability to use and understand figures of speech; the ability to compare, contrast, and classify; the ability to remember; and the ability to predict what words, ideas, or phrases will come next. Although these tools are vital, it is important to know that they will not suffice unless the reader has a solid base of experience and language pertaining to the written text. We understand, describe, and read best those things we know something about, and, ideally, have encountered as part of our life experience.

Masha Kabakow Rudman, Ed.D., and Anna Markus Pearce, Ed.D., *For Love of Reading.* Mount Vernon, New York: Consumers Union of United States, 1988, pp. 2–3.

older citizens, other ethnic minorities, and the disabled. Protest against the Vietnam War, and televised Watergate and Iran-Contra hearings have given a new tone to our political dialogue. Closer to "home," the divorce rate and the illegitimacy rate, especially among young adolescents, has climbed. So has drug addiction.

Many children today have seen more violence and more sexual titillation on television and in the news than children knew of in the past; almost every child has heard rough language that earlier generations never heard—or didn't hear until they were adults. Not all of these issues affect every child directly, but almost every child knows about them.

These facets of contemporary society have appeared in adult literature and, following a pattern of long standing, after a time, they began to appear in books for adolescents, then in books for younger children. Beginning in the late 1960s, one taboo after another was broken in children's literature.

Children's Needs

Accompanying the trend toward candor in children's literature has been a continuing recognition of the importance of reflecting and satisfying, in their books, the basic needs of children as they grow. Despite social change, certain basic needs—the need for security, the need to be loved, the need to achieve, among others—seem to be common to most peoples and most times. Such needs are at first intensely and narrowly personal but they should broaden and become more widely socialized as children mature. The direction these needs will take depends a great deal on the experience the child encounters in the critical early years before school. Struggling to satisfy their needs, children are forever seeking to maintain the precarious balance between personal happiness and social approval, and that is no easy task. Directly or indirectly, books may help, particularly if they are books written by sensitive, thoughtful adults who are percipient observers of children and who remember their own childhoods vividly. Such books not only may help children better understand themselves and others but also should help adults better understand and empathize with their own children and with the children in their classrooms and library centers. An understanding of how children learn—how they grow and develop social attitudes, cognitive abilities, moral precepts, and motor skills—helps in the selection of books that meet their interests, are appropriate for their ages, and reflect their developmental and emotional needs.

The Need for Security

A child's sense of physical security ordinarily begins in mother's or father's arms, includes routines of eating and sleeping, and comes gradually to embrace everything that gives a sense of comfort and well-being. For both children and adults, material satisfactions may become the chief symbols of security. The old fairy tales were told by peoples who seldom had enough food to eat or clothing to keep them warm. So their tales are full of brightly burning fires, sumptuous feasts, rich clothes, and splendid palaces. These are age-old symbols of security. Undoubtedly some of the appeal of the old *Elsie Dinsmore* stories and of Frances Hodgson Burnett's *The Secret Garden* lay in this same incredible affluence which the characters enjoyed.

Today, as in earlier times, material security is uncertain, and it continues to be one of people's most pressing needs. So in books as in life,

the lack of security and the hunger for it often supply the motive for the action and the theme of the story. In Betty Erwin's *Behind the Magic Line,* a black family leaves their crowded two-room city apartment to find security and a better life in a home of their own. In Ann Turner's *Grasshopper Summer,* a pioneer family of 1874 determines to stay in their sod house despite the harsh conditions of frontier life. In Vera and Bill Cleaver's *Where the Lilies Bloom,* the doughty young heroine struggles fiercely to keep her family together, lying about her father's death to prevent the authorities from separating the children, and outmaneuvering the landlord to keep the house in which they live.

In book after book, the search for security will spellbind young readers of the old fairy tales or of modern realistic books or biographies of heroes, all the way from Dick Whittington to *Tom Sawyer.*

The Need to Love and to Be Loved

Every human being wants to love and be loved. This need is so pressing that when it is frustrated in one direction it will provide its own substitutes, centering upon almost anything from lap dogs to antiques. Children, too, set up their own substitutes. A child who feels out-of-favor or rejected may lavish an abnormal amount of affection upon a stray cat, perhaps identifying with the unwanted animal. Two circus children, in Vivien Alcock's *Travelers by Night,* steal an aging elephant to save the gentle beast from the slaughterhouse. In John Donovan's *I'll Get There. It Better Be Worth the Trip,* Davy's whole devotion is directed to his dog, Fred, after his grandmother's death.

It is within the framework of the family that a child learns first lessons in affectionate relationships. Books, too, exemplify these relationships. In *Like Jake and Me* by Mavis Jukes, the theme is about the love and understanding between a boy and his stepfather. Not only does a child's sense of security develop from family patterns, but also his or her whole approach to other people.

From *Like Jake and Me* by Mavis Jukes, illustrated by Lloyd Bloom.

Sometimes stories about family life signify to fortunate children the aspects of their own experiences that might otherwise be taken for granted. Children may find traces of their own father in the father of Beverly Cleary's *Ramona,* and in the longing of the fatherless boy in Charlotte Zolotow's *A Father Like That,* or they may recognize their own mother in Mrs. March of *Little Women.* They may share the brother and sister fun of Lillian Hoban's many picture books about Arthur and his sister Violet, or feel the warmth of the love between Siebren and his grandfather in Meindert DeJong's *Journey from Peppermint Street.* Through reading books such as these, children may find that their own family will mean more to them. On the other hand, those children who have missed these happy experiences may find in family stories vicarious substitutes that will give them some satisfaction and supply them with new insight into family possibilities.

Out of family affection and trust grows a kind of *spiritual strength* that enables human beings to surmount dangers, failures, and even stark tragedies. Such books as Betsy Byars's stories of the Blossom family and the *Little House* books by Laura Ingalls Wilder leave children with the conviction that decent, kindly people can maintain an inner serenity even as they struggle with and master the problems that threaten them.

Another aspect of this need to love and to serve the beloved is the recognition of this same need in other creatures. Stories about wild animals defending their mates or their young or the herd are tremendously appealing. So, too, are stories of pets, steadfast not only in their affection for their own kind but for their human masters as well. Such stories as Sheila Burnford's *The Incredible Journey* have played upon this appeal. Fine animal stories of all kinds will undoubtedly contribute to breaking down the young child's unwitting cruelties toward animals and to building up the child's sensitivity to animals' needs.

Finally, the need to love and to be loved, which includes family affection, warm friendships, and devotion to pets, leads the child to look toward romance. In children's literature, romance begins early but remains impersonal. The fairy tales, with their long-delayed prince or their princess on a glass hill, are little more than abstract symbols of what is to come.

There are growing numbers of competent authors who supply realistic pictures of family life, with boys and girls looking away from their families to serious interest in the opposite sex. And many of these books deal frankly with some of the heartbreaking problems of young people. The establishment of a desirable romantic attachment is one of the important tasks of growing up. A well-written story that shows all the complications of romance, its pitfalls and disappointments as well as its happinesses, can provide young people with needed guidance in an approach to one of life's most vital concerns.

The Need to Belong

Growing out of the need for security is the need of every human being to belong, to be an accepted member of a group. "*My* daddy," or "*My* big sister," the young child says with pride. At first these experiences are merely egocentric extensions of children's self-love, but at least they are beginning to identify with family, and this acknowledgment of others marks a growing sense of belonging to a group. In time, these same children will identify with friends, school, later with city and country, and perhaps with a world group.

So the child's literature should reflect this expanding sense of the group. It should begin with stories about the family, the school, and the neighborhood in warm little books such as Martha Alexander, Ezra Jack Keats, and Charlotte Zolotow have written for the preschool child; Miriam Cohen for the primary age; and Beverly Cleary for the middle grades in her amusing *Henry Huggins* books. These stories represent happy group experiences. But there are also stories about children who must struggle anxiously to be liked by the people for whose acceptance they long. Orphaned Heidi in Johanna Spyri's book by the same name, and

From *Little Navajo Bluebird* by Ann Nolan Clark, illustrated by Paul Lantz.

From *Molly's Pilgrim* by Barbara Cohen, illustrated by Michael J. Deraney.

Mary in Frances H. Burnett's *The Secret Garden* are good examples. The story of a child who wins a respected place within the group that once rejected her or him follows a continuing, satisfying theme whether it is found in "Cinderella" or in *Fran Ellen's House* by Marilyn Sachs.

Current technology has brought people closer together through developments in communications and transportation. Exposed to the mass media and to the changing mores of the community, young readers are more aware of social injustices—and they need books that reflect their world, offering realistic and optimistic solutions in which minority characters gain acceptance, rather than mere tolerance. John Tunis, in his sports stories for the preadolescent and teenager, makes his young readers face fully the extra difficulties that beset youngsters of minority groups in winning a place on the team or in the community. This is also the general theme of Eleanor Estes's *The Hundred Dresses,* of Barbara Cohen's *Molly's Pilgrim,* and of Kristin Hunter's *The Soul Brothers and Sister Lou,* in which a group of black adolescents face prejudice toward and within themselves. Sometimes the problem is not one of winning acceptance but of accepting. For example, in Ann Nolan Clark's *Little Navajo Bluebird*, a Native American child passionately rejects the white man and all his ways and wants to belong only to her own tribal group. Books like these parallel the need of each individual not only to belong with pride to his or her own group, but to identify warmly and sympathetically with ever-widening circles of people. A good and honest book can strengthen the pride of the minority member and enrich all who read it.

The Need to Achieve

The need for competence—the "organism's capacity to interact effectively with its environment"[1]—is a strong motivating force in human behavior. The struggle to achieve competence begins with the infant's visual exploration, with crawling, grasping, and other primitive activities and grows into the complex physical or intellectual performances of the expert man or woman athlete, mathematician, musician, or scientist. Competence is as satisfying as inhibitions and frustrations are disruptive. To be happy or well adjusted, the child or the adult must have a satisfying sense of competence in one area or another.

In Mary J. Collier and Eugene L. Gaier's study "The Hero in the Preferred Childhood Stories of College Men,"[2] the important factor the book heroes had in common was that they performed their unique feats on their own. Whether it was Hänsel from the old fairy tale or the realistic Tom Sawyer, the hero's competence was achieved without help from adults, and his independence was the quality that made him memorable and admired. Achieving competence may become the compensation for rejection and a step toward acceptance. This is a frequent theme in stories for children—the lonely child or the shy teenager who develops competence in some field and so wins the

admiration and acceptance of the group. Eleanor Estes's *The Hundred Dresses*, Armstrong Sperry's *Call It Courage*, and Laurie Lawlor's *How to Survive Third Grade* are all built upon this theme.

The young child's first book heroes are doers, from Edward Ardizzone's Tim, who survives shipwreck and finds his lost parents, to David of the Old Testament, who slays the giant Goliath. In later childhood and adolescence young readers enjoy the competence of the heroes in adventure, mystery, and career stories, and the achievements of famous men and women in biographies. *Carry On, Mr. Bowditch* by Jean Latham, is a splendid, true record of competence independently achieved. More books are appearing that describe the accomplishments of men and women of ethnic minority groups: biographies of Matthew Henson, Henry Cisneros, Lena Horne, Maria Tallchief, Cesar Chávez, and many other Americans.

There is a stern, negative aspect to this hunger for achievement. The struggle for competence may involve failures and complete frustration. Physical and mental disabilities must be faced and accepted. In Jean Little's *Mine for Keeps*, a child with cerebral palsy comes home after five years in a residential school, feeling fear and self-pity; but adjusts to her own problems when she becomes involved in helping another child. In William Mayne's *Gideon Ahoy!* an English family loves Gideon, deaf and brain-damaged, and encourages him to get and keep a job. Emma Sterne's *Blood Brothers* tells the story of Charles Drew, a black ghetto child, who, despite discrimination, persists in his pursuit of a medical career and eventually becomes a distinguished pioneer in blood research. Stories of such heroes who refuse to accept defeat help children in the task of growing up.

The Need for Change

Play is sometimes classified as a part of the desire for change, which is one of the basic needs of the human organism. If we work hard, we need rest or play. If we are serious and intent, we need relaxation and gaiety. So, in our reading, after grave and factual books or books about everyday affairs, we like something light or imaginative. If we are beset with per-

[1]Robert H. White, "Motivation Reconsidered: The Concept of Competence." *Psychological Review*, Vol. 66, No. 5, 1959, p. 297.

[2]*American Imago*, Vol. 16, No. 2, 1959.

sonal anxieties, we may look for a book of adventure or mystery or romance, lose ourselves completely, and come back to our own problems refreshed.

Children, too, need such liberation. They suffer more than many adults realize from the pressure of routines, adult coercion and tensions, and the necessity of conforming to a code of manners and morals whose reasonableness they do not always understand. This is especially true today, when so many aspects of our present society are being challenged by the young. Some children suffer from school failures, feelings of social or physical inferiority, difficulty in communicating with their parents, and bewilderment or resentment about the strictures of cultural patterns.

Books of many kinds may be used to meet the child's need for healthy change. The old fairy tales have about them a dreamlike quality that is a welcome change from the everyday world of here and now. Modern fantasies provide laughter and imaginative adventures that are sometimes ribtickling nonsense and sometimes humor with overtones of beauty. These range from the fun of Dr. Seuss's rambunctious *Horton Hatches the Egg* to the compassionate self-sacrifice of *Charlotte's Web*.

There is bland burlesque of city problems in Jean Merrill's *The Pushcart War* and of the adolescents in Jill Pinkwater's affectionately satiric *Buffalo Brenda* in which a conservative teenager resists the influence of her beatnik parents. There is nonsense humor in the tall tales of Glen Rounds. Humor and suspense are combined in the *Encyclopedia Brown* series, Donald Sobol's stories of a boy detective. There are adventures in the world of the future in John Christopher's *The Guardians* and suspense in Lynn Hall's mystery story *A Killing Freeze*. All such stories afford children fun, pleasure, and respite. Fine poetry, too, that arrests the attention and stirs the emotions, light verse and nonsense jingles now and then—these may supply a child with the inspiration or laughter for which he or she hungers.

The Need to Know

Parents often complain about the bothersome curiosity of children. But this need to investi-

gate, to know for sure, is a sign of intelligence. In fact, the keener children are mentally, the wider and more persistent their curiosities will be. The need to know surely and accurately is a basic hunger and one which books help satisfy.

Books about Africa, nomadic tribes, birds, plants, stones, stars, rockets and jets, DNA, care of pets, and of course, dictionaries and encyclopedias properly gauged to the child's needs, are all available today. Adults need only discover children's particular interests to find books that will answer their questions reliably, stimulate new curiosities, and set them exploring further to satisfy their need to know and provide momentarily at least, a certain intellectual security.

Some books not only provide fascinating information but dramatically exemplify the human need to find out, to know for sure. For example, Thor Heyerdahl's *Kon-Tiki* tells the true story of five young men who set out on the flimsy raft *Kon-Tiki* to prove their theory of the origin and migrations of the Polynesian people. Nathan Aaseng's *The Problem Solvers* tells the stories of persistent men and women whose curiosity and determination led to the invention of many useful products.

The Need for Beauty and Order

There is still another human need that seems curiously at odds with man's more utilitarian search for competence and security of various kinds. It is the need for beauty and order.

A wealth of books is available today to satisfy a child's aesthetic needs—authentic poetry, fanciful tales with content and style perfectly suited, books that are beautiful in themselves, books that provide various kinds of aesthetically satisfying experiences, and books that help children grow in their appreciation of beauty and order. Shirley Glubok's books about art in various cultures (*The Art of Ancient Egypt, The Art of the North American Indian, The Art of Ancient Mexico*) are simply written and related to the way people lived. *Looking at Art* by Alice Elizabeth Chase, discusses the ways in which individual artists interpret landscapes, people, or spatial relations. Young children can enjoy and understand the concepts of artistic vision and sensibility in Cynthia Rylant's *All I See*, the

From *All I See* by Cynthia Rylant, illustrated by Peter Catalanotto.

ment of their taste depends not only on their initial capacities but also on the material they encounter and the way in which it is presented.

Understanding Children

In addition to providing books that are pertinent to the needs that have been discussed, adults who are responsible for planning educational experiences will find that knowledge of child development can be of use in selecting books that enhance the literary experience. Developmental psychologists seek to discover what children are like at various stages of maturity. We shall briefly survey those aspects of the developmental theories of Erik Erikson, Jean Piaget, Lawrence Kohlberg, and more

story of a painter who encourages a child's artistic efforts. *Ballet: A Pictorial History* by Walter Terry, and *The Wonderful World of Music* by Benjamin Britten and Imogen Holst, are fine examples of books about the performing arts written for children by experts in their fields.

Whether in music, dancing, drama, story, painting, or sculpture, the artist seizes upon some aspect of life and recreates it for us in a new form. We see it whole and understandable; people, events, and places assume a new dimension beyond the mere chronicling of facts. The artist can give us a long, clear view so that we see details in relation to the complete design. It is as if a kaleidoscope were held immovable. The colors and lines fall into a logical relationship and the design stands out in bold relief, not necessarily beautiful but complete and therefore satisfying.

Adults are continually seeking aesthetic satisfaction in one form or another and at varying levels of taste. One may find it in the songs of Tin Pan Alley. Another finds it in a symphony which exalts the sorrows of life to heroic proportions. Aesthetic satisfaction comes to small children as well as to adults, and the develop-

briefly, those of Abraham Maslow and Albert Bandura, that are most pertinent to experiences with literature.

Erikson's psychosocial theories are concerned with the development of individual identity and also with the individual's ability to function in society. Piaget has written most extensively about children's cognitive development, but his work deals with moral growth as well. Kohlberg's work is concentrated primarily on moral development, describing a succession of stages through which an individual moves with increased maturity. Maslow's great concern was for humanistic education and so his thinking focused on the individual's self-actualization as fulfillment of his or her potential. Bandura has studied the influence of social models on children's learning.

Such theories have implications for the selection of literature because they suggest something about children's interests and needs at various stages of development. They also help to identify cognitive and verbal skills which may influence an individual's ability to deal with such literary elements as point of view, flashback, and foreshadowing.

Erikson's Theory of Psychosocial Development

Erik Erikson's theory is based on the belief that development consists of a series of psychosocial crises that individuals must successfully resolve if they are to mature. Those conflicts involve the person's struggle to achieve individuality and, at the same time, to learn to function in society. According to Erikson, every individual moves through an orderly sequence of stages, with each successive stage being more complex. Maturation occurs as the individual ascends from one stage to another. At each stage, the individual is faced with a psychosocial conflict which must be resolved before moving on to the next stage of development. The first stage begins in infancy, with the crisis of *Trust versus Mistrust*. Erikson's second through fifth stages are of most interest to students of children's literature.

Early Childhood: Achieving Autonomy

Erikson's second stage of development described as *Autonomy versus Doubt,* generally takes place from about ages eighteen months to three years. During this stage, children are involved in a struggle to be independent, yet still need support from others, particularly from parents. Play is important for these children because it allows them a means for developing autonomy within their own set of rules. As children progress through this stage, they become more aware of adults other than parents. Children of this age seem to like books that deal with relationships between parent and child, like Helen Oxenbury's *The Important Visitor;* James Stevenson's *Are We Almost There?* a saga of restless children and patient parents; and Jill Murphy's plaintive wish of an elephant mother, *Five Minute's Peace.* (Erikson's concerns about the development of the individual in relationship to society might serve as a guideline in choosing stories to read aloud.)

Middle Childhood: Developing Initiative

The next stage, which takes place at about ages three to six, is that of *Initiative versus Guilt.* During these years, children are increasingly expected to be responsible. As independence develops, so does the realization that one's behavior may be in opposition to the behavior of others. Whenever there is conflict with another individual, a sense of guilt is likely to arise. Children also grow toward the cultural mores as their consciences develop. During this period, children ask many questions and begin to understand things which had previously been mysteries to them. Play takes on two forms: solitary daydreaming and play with other children in which life crises are enacted.

Erikson's description of children at this stage seems to suggest the importance of acquainting them with fiction in which characters, too, experience conflict when their actions throw them into opposition with others. Books will give children a chance to experience along with story characters what it is to take more respon-

From *Five Minutes' Peace,* written and illustrated by Jill Murphy.

sibility for their actions. This brings to mind books like Charles E. Martin's *For Rent,* in which a group of schoolchildren share the work of a project, or Rebecca Caudill's *Did You Carry the Flag Today, Charley?*

The quality of play is present in many books for children ages three to six. At times, children need to play alone, as does the small, imaginative girl in Judith Vigna's *Boot Weather;* at times they need the stimulation of such group play as the boys enjoy in Russell Hoban's *The Flight of Bembel Rudzuk.* Other concerns of the young child are reflected in the many picture books that should be included in read-aloud sessions, whether the material is folklore, fantasy, realism, poetry, or nonfiction.

Late Childhood: Becoming Industrious

Stage four in Erikson's scheme compares roughly to Piaget's concrete operational stage (p. 28) in terms of the ages involved. Reached during ages seven to eleven, it is a stage of *Industry versus Inferiority.* Children operating at this stage appear determined to master the tasks that are set for them. They cooperate with other children toward achieving a common goal and they are frequently engaged in activities that allow them to practice skills the culture requires of them. The conflict of industry versus inferiority emerges as a sense that they are inferior if they cannot show that they are competent and so these children are constantly comparing themselves with their peers.

Clearly, a good many of the books published for this age group pose situations in which children strive to be as successful as their peers. A number of books have also focused on the way in which children perceive their parents. *Harriet the Spy, Ramona and Her Father,* and books with one-parent families such as *Harry's Mom* make parents an important aspect of the story.

The growing determination of children in this group to master new tasks points to the importance of informational books in their lives. Some children may experience the conflict of industry versus inferiority vicariously, reading biographies of people who did succeed or realistic fiction about people who overcome hardships. These are representative of the kinds of books which appeal to children in this stage.

Adolescence: Establishing Identity

Erikson's stage of adolescence, ages eleven and upwards, is that of *Identity versus Role Diffusion*. The focal point now is a search for identity; the development of identity is linked with skill mastery. On a broader level, we might say that it includes cultural identity as well as personal identity, identity as a member of a community as well as identity as an individual. Adolescents grapple with the question of who they will become as well as the question of who they are. They often have a close attachment to their parents, yet are searching for other associations. Inevitably, the question arises of whether the parents still control them and that, of course, can create friction.

Play changes so that it is more likely to be role playing and experimentation with attitudes and behavior of adults in society. Adolescents baby-sit, they participate in sports, and they also belong to gangs and to in-groups. Literature for these readers includes a range of realistic fiction which can give them a chance to interact with situations in which other teenagers are searching for identity. That means

Stages in Child Development

Stage	Approximate Age Period	Major Features	Psychosocial Crisis (Erikson)	Cognitive Stage (Piaget)	Stages of Moral Reasoning (Kohlberg)
Infancy	Birth to 18 months	Locomotion established; rudimentary language; social attachment	Trust vs. mistrust	Sensorimotor	Premoral (Stage 0)
Early and Middle Childhood	18 months to 6 years	Language well established; sex typing; group play; ends with "readiness" for schooling	Autonomy vs. self-doubt Initiative vs. guilt	Preoperational	Pleasure-pain orientation (Stage 1) Cost-benefit orientation Reciprocity (Stage 2)
Late Childhood	6 to 13 years	Many cognitive processes become adult except in speed of operation; team play	Competence vs. inferiority	Concrete operational	Good child orientation (Stage 3)
Adolescence	13 to 20 years	Attainment of highest level of cognition; independence from parents; sexual relationships	Identity vs. role confusion	Formal operational	Law and order orientation (Stage 4)

Adapted from Philip G. Zimbardo and Floyd L. Ruch, *Psychology and Life*, 12th Edition (Scott, Foresman, 1985), pp. 77, 88, 90.

Viewpoint

Literature has long been seen not only as a mirror of life but as a means to illuminate the nature and meaning of one's existence. In the twentieth century, the nature of human existence has changed in a variety of ways, among which has been the emergence of adolescence as a widespread phenomenon of industrial, technological society. Adolescence has become a separate stage of life with its own concerns, distinct from, as well as linked to, other stages. Because literature speaks to concerns central to human existence and arises from a community with shared experience, a literature for adolescents was necessarily a recent development, having evolved in this century only after there had been a widespread, common experiencing of this new stage of life.

David A. Russell, "The Common Experience of Adolescence: A Requisite for the Development of Young Adult Literature," *Journal of Youth Services in Libraries*, Volume 2, Number 1, Fall 1988, pp. 58–59.

stories in which characterization is worked out with enough depth so that characters' fears and joys are evident throughout as they strive to discover themselves and to experience success. Walter Dean Myers's *The Young Landlords* and Katherine Paterson's *The Great Gilly Hopkins* are two such books. The psychosocial crises identified by Erik Erikson highlight the concerns likely to be shared by children within an age group.

Piaget's Developmental Levels

Jean Piaget's early training was in biology and so it is perhaps not surprising that his method of study depends to a large extent on observation and classification of behavior. He views intellect and affect as always together, like two sides of a coin, believing that human emotion, or affect, evolves from the same primary processes as cognitive development.

Much of Piaget's thinking about the child's cognitive development is based on four kinds of operations. They are assimilation and accommodation, conservation, and reversibility. The first two are closely related, for Piaget's theory is that the child develops units of knowledge about the world, called *schemata*. As the child takes note of new information about the environment, that information is *assimilated* into his or her thinking (schemata) and both thinking and behavior are *accommodated* (changed) to reflect those new perceptions. In assimilation the person adapts the environment to his or her own use, though that is limited by ability to consolidate the new experiences with previous experience. Accommodation, the reverse of assimilation, occurs when the individual modifies existing thought structures so as to incorporate the new experiences.

Conservation and reversibility are also related, in a sense. Conservation has to do with the child's ability to deal with the difference between making judgments on the basis of surface characteristics and being able to make inferences about the real characteristics that underlie the surface. Piaget's classic example is the young child who believes that a taller and thinner glass contains more liquid than a shorter, fatter glass, even though the child has watched as the water was poured from the short to the tall container. The tendency to deal with surface characteristics may extend, also, to social understanding so that the child forms ideas about people and social situations solely on the basis of outward appearance.

Both temporal and spatial factors are operating in the ability to deal with reversibility. Probably the clearest application to a child's response to literature lies in the ability to process flashbacks so that the child recognizes that the order in which events are described in a story is not necessarily the order in which they really occurred. Piaget's observations of children's behavior led him to believe that development proceeds in four major stages and that all children move through those stages in sequence, though not necessarily at the same pace. Although development is viewed as always proceeding forward, there is generally a stage of transition in which the child vacillates between earlier, less mature behavior and the newly gained competence.

The earliest of Piaget's stages is the period of *sensorimotor intelligence* from birth to about age two, or until the appearance of language. During this period, the child is particularly concerned with coordinating movement and action. Words come to represent objects and things. The second stage, the *period of preoperational thought,* spans the ages of about two up to eleven or twelve years. Within that stage, Piaget describes the first phase as *preconceptual.*

The Preconceptual Phase

During Piaget's preconceptual phase, ages two to four, children are busy discovering the environment. For that reason, concept books (Chapter 4) are important. Tana Hoban's *Look Again,* with photographs of familiar objects, or Shirley Hughes's stories about Alfie and the small events of his daily life reflect children's interest in the immediate environment.

The play of two- to four-year-olds centers on *how* and *why.* Activities that may seem fantastic to adults are realistic to these children. There is much imitation of the behavior of others, including the reading behavior of the adults around them. Imitative scenes in books like Robert McCloskey's *Blueberries for Sal* show story characters imitating the activities of their parents and that, in a sense, plays out the fantasy-into-reality.

Children in the preconceptual stage often explain things that happen by giving life to inanimate objects; for example, if they fall, saying that a toy reached out and tripped them. This delight in humanizing inanimate objects and animals is also related to a love for fantasy. Many children begin liking fantasy early, the interest persisting into succeeding stages of development.

The Intuitive Phase

As children move into the phase of intuitive thought, roughly ages four to seven, they shift from the egocentric "it's me" to "I see what's happening," becoming able to react realistically to the environment. They are moving toward conservation in terms of recognizing differences between how things *look* and how they *really are.*

During these ages, children begin to use language successfully to verbalize their mental activities and they are better able to generalize their experiences. They are becoming interested in realistic fiction, particularly fiction that gives them a chance to relate to one or more of the story characters, and to react realistically to the environment. Children have opportunity for that when they read books like *My Brother Tries to Make Me Laugh* by Andrew Glass.

At this stage, too, children become more able to project themselves into roles. They can relate to Charley in Rebecca Caudill's *Did You Carry the Flag Today, Charley?* and they can also begin to appreciate Charley's good and bad points. When they listen to books like Joan Fassler's *Howie Helps Himself,* or *Our Mom* by Kay Burns, they can begin to develop a sense of empathy for disabled people rather than stereotyping them as "different."

The growing ability to project themselves into other roles and to think as others think

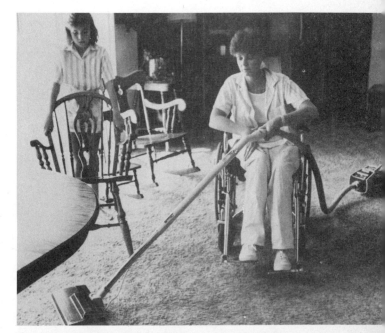

From *Our Mom* by Kay Burns, photographs by Rick Reil.

suggests a need for experiences with realism in literature. That means selecting books to read aloud and books for beginning readers that might give opportunity for talking about the feelings and motives of characters. Arnold Lobel's *Days with Frog and Toad* and James Marshall's *George and Martha,* for example, allow children to share experiences with animal characters. Some examples of realistic fiction for this age with more fully developed characters include Bernard Waber's *Ira Says Goodbye* and Evaline Ness's *Sam, Bangs and Moonshine.* Well-directed discussion can give a basis for perceiving conflict in the story from more than one character's point of view. Differences between how things *look* and how they *really are* have not been completely worked out by children in this stage; they should be allowed to read and enjoy fantasy without always worrying about whether or not a story is "real."

The older children in this group also enjoy nonfiction accounts and realistic fiction. Consider these forms along with classic fantasy and informational books and you have an idea of the range of interests these children have. Exposure to many kinds of literature allows children to test out some of their growing knowledge about the environment and continue to exercise their creative imaginations.

The Period of Concrete Operations

As children enter the period of concrete operations, approximately ages seven to eleven, they reach a new level of self-development that allows them to understand some of the ways they are related to other people and to better deal with conservation and reversibility. Through play and language, they seek to understand the social and physical world. This seems to imply the importance of realistic fiction which will encourage children to interact with story characters who are involved in some sort of conflict resolution. Paula Fox's *The Stone-faced Boy* and Lizi Boyd's *The Not-So-Wicked Stepmother* show conflict *within* self as well as conflict with others.

For children at this stage, concepts of time are more fully developed so that ideas about the past become important, and they grow in their capacity to appreciate historical fiction and the biographies of real-life heroes such as Daniel Boone or Rosa Parks. Historical fiction set in the United States, such as Carol Ryrie Brink's *Caddie Woodlawn,* Jean Fritz's *The Cabin Faced West,* and Patricia MacLachlan's *Sarah, Plain and Tall,* appeals to children at this stage.

During this period, children also begin to apply logic to concrete experiences, and they begin to move beyond one-dimensional thinking so that they are able to relate one event to a system of interrelated parts. They are now able to conceive of an event from beginning to end or, vice versa, perceive it backwards from conclusion to beginning. This would suggest the beginning of ability to handle flashbacks in literature or to think in terms of the future. That ability helps to prepare them not only for fantasy which may go back in time, but for science fiction, which generally goes forward in time. *Tom's Midnight Garden,* which moves between past and present, is often read by children at this stage. The more mature readers also enjoy Madeleine L'Engle's *A Wrinkle in Time* and John Christopher's *The White Mountains* trilogy, books which reach into the future.

From *George and Martha,* written and illustrated by James Marshall.

From *The Not-So-Wicked Stepmother,* written and illustrated by Lizi Boyd.

Piaget says that children who are in the concrete operational period internalize moral values and are interested in examining the rules that govern their lives. An examination of rules and what happens when rules and adult authority are rejected might be a logical topic for discussion with children who are moving toward the upper range of this concrete operational stage.

The Period of Formal Operations

From approximately age eleven to age fifteen, children progress through what Piaget terms the period of formal operations, making great gains in their ability to think beyond the present and to formulate theories about physical and social aspects of life. They develop the ability to examine another's point of view, which suggests the importance of encouraging interaction with literary characters and situations. Beyond basic communication, children at the formal operations stage are able to establish whether information is valid by comparing what they see and hear about things (their perceptions) with what they know and deduce about those things. In terms of literature, clearly there is a need to provide experience in contrasting fiction with nonfiction accounts, particularly contrasting historical and biographical fiction with historical material and real biography. There is an increase in ability to link parts and wholes, recognizing a sense of order and the rules that impose that order. This ability might make young people more aware of relationships within the structure of a story, for example the way that episodes build toward a climax and resolution.

Children at the eleven-plus stage are moving from stereotypical thinking to a greater ability to understand and empathize with others and to be more aware of their relationships within the family and within the community. Madeleine L'Engle's *Meet the Austins* gives readers a chance to be involved in situations that call upon their ability to interpret characters' needs and feelings in terms of their relations to one another. Brock Cole's story of two lonely children, *The Goats; Scorpions,* Walter Dean Myers's story of the pressures of the drug culture; and the tension of apartheid in Sheila Gordon's *Waiting for the Rain* are compelling stories for children who are ready to interact with the problems and emotions of the teenage characters, thus acquiring an expanded view of the world.

The Development of Moral Values and Social Behavior

Piaget's views of morality are mainly concerned with the individual's respect for the rules of the social order in which he or she lives and with the person's sense of justice. He has suggested that the bases of moral judgment change with the child's age, and he makes a number of predictions about reactions which might be expected at different ages. Intent is an important factor. A younger child considers a particular action to be "right" or "wrong" whereas an older child considers the behavior in its context. What is right in one situation may not be right in another. A younger child behaves correctly out of fear of punishment by others while the older child's proper behavior is a result of his or her own decision making. Piaget believed that there are two childhood moralities, one that is essentially governed by adult rules and regulations and the other representing mutual respect. He claimed that children under nine are primarily influenced by adult rules and that morality is acquired developmentally through imitation of and verbal interaction with adults.

Kohlberg's Stages of Moral Development

Lawrence Kohlberg has systematized Piaget's thinking and developed a hierarchy of moral development. His formulation is perhaps the most widely quoted of a number of value hierarchies that have been developed. It is important to note, however, that the stages are still changing in Kohlberg's conceptualization of moral development. His stages begin with preconventional levels of moral reasoning, oriented toward obedience and punishment. There is a progression to conventional levels similar to the moral judgment of adults, including conforming to majority behavior and maintaining law and order, and to the post-conventional levels of behavior, marked by rights of others and the conscience as a guide to moral conduct, levels which are reached by only a minority of adults.[3]

Value Formation

Essentially, all good literature deals with values. Children who read widely and hear stories read and told cannot help but interact with story characters involved in decision making, in formulating personal values, in learning to empathize with the difficulties of people the world over. We can help children select books that will give them some experience with the valuing process. Even beyond that, we can take note of their responses and can encourage young readers to observe the actions of story characters and to think through the motivations for, and consequences of, their actions. Children can then talk about similar situations in their own lives and determine whether the outcome was good or whether they would behave differently if given another chance.

Selecting literature that will play a role in value formation requires attention to characterization and to the kinds of situations that throw story characters into conflict with the values of their society. Such books as Madeleine L'Engle's *A Swiftly Tilting Planet* and Betty Sue Cummings's *Let a River Be* are powerful stories that give readers plenty of opportunity to consider their own values as well as those of the story characters.

Although it has not been established that value formation does occur as a result of experience with literature, the advantage of literature as an approach to developing moral values is that the dilemmas in well-chosen real and fanciful literature are realistic. At the same time, they are not as threatening to readers as they would be if they were part of their lives. That allows a degree of objectivity in deciding whether the characters acted morally and what alternative forms of behavior would have been more appropriate. More will be said about potential ways of dealing with moral development in Chapter 14.

Viewpoint

I became deeply dissatisfied with much of the literature intended to develop the child's mind and personality, because it fails to stimulate and nurture those resources he needs most in order to cope with his difficult inner problems. The pre-primers and primers from which he is taught to read in school are designed to teach the necessary skills, irrespective of meaning. The overwhelming bulk of the rest of so-called "children's literature" attempts to entertain or to inform, or both. But most of these books are so shallow in substance that little of significance can be gained from them. The acquisition of skills, including the ability to read, becomes devalued when what one has learned to read adds nothing of importance to one's life.

From *The Uses of Enchantment: Meaning and Importance of Fairy Tales* by Bruno Bettelheim. New York: Alfred A. Knopf, 1976, p. 4.

[3]See Michael Siegel, "Kohlberg versus Piaget: To What Extent Has One Theory Eclipsed the Other?" *Merrill-Palmer Quarterly* (October 1980), pp. 285–297.

Maslow's Hierarchy of Needs

Abraham Maslow's views about the education of children were firmly based in a humanistic philosophy of education. He was most concerned with the discovery of identity and humanness, believing that, as we go most deeply into ourselves, seeking individual identity, we also recognize more clearly the whole human species. When we become fully human, we learn not only how we are different from others, but how we are similar to others. Although Maslow worked largely with adults, he had much to say about children as well, applying his ideas to people of all ages. Maslow believed that human needs form a hierarchy, from basic physiological demands to the need for self-actualization. Needs at the lower levels must be reasonably well satisfied before the individual will turn his or her attention to those at the higher levels. For example, a child who is always hungry is not likely to develop much intellectual curiosity.

Maslow identified five levels of basic human needs: physiological, safety, belongingness and love, esteem, and self-actualization, as well as cognitive and aesthetic needs. These are comparable to the needs discussed earlier.

Bandura's Social Learning Theory

It is not possible, within this chapter, to deal with all of the theories of learning which may be useful background in book selection for children. The study of children's acquisition of social behavior has generated a good deal of interest, however, and warrants some comment even though it cannot be given full coverage.

Traditional learning theory has emphasized the viewpoint that behavior that is reinforced (rewarded) in some way will be learned. Albert Bandura, however, has shown that learning may occur when a child observes the behavior of others even when the child does not reproduce the responses made by them and does not receive any reinforcement. According to that

Viewpoint

Education must begin, as Dewey concluded his first article of belief, "with a psychological insight into the child's capacities, interests, habits," but a point of departure is not an itinerary. It is just as mistaken to sacrifice the adult to the child as to sacrifice the child to the adult. It is sentimentalism to assume that the teaching of life can be fitted always to the child's interests just as it is empty formalism to force the child to parrot the formulas of adult society. Interests can be created and stimulated. In this sphere it is not far from the truth to say that supply creates demand, that the provocation of what is available creates response. One seeks to equip the child with deeper, more gripping, and subtler ways of knowing the world and himself.

Jerome S. Bruner, *On Knowing*, Belknap Press of Harvard University Press, 1962, pp. 117–118.

theory of social learning, whether or not a child will imitate behavior depends not only on the type of behavior but also on the consequences of that behavior—that is, whether the model is rewarded or punished. Therefore, vicarious reinforcement plays a role in the theoretical framework.

The amount of vicarious learning may also be affected by differences between the sex of the child and the sex of a role model. The prestige the model has, in the eyes of the child, plays a part, too, with high prestige models more likely to be imitated than low prestige models. Furthermore, behavior is more likely to be imitated when it is rewarded by a high-prestige person than by one with low prestige.

There is a fairly obvious extension of social learning theory to selection of literature and literary experiences for children, for many books have models with whom young readers can identify. If the factors described above are indeed operating, then it would be important to provide books with admired role models and books in which the protagonist's behavior is reinforced by a high prestige person. For young children that might suggest books in which the models are parents and other adults in positions of authority. For older children and certainly for adolescents, it would suggest some books in which models are peers or cultural heroes such as athletes or people associated with popular culture. Further, it would seem to suggest the importance of characters and situations in the stories which are closely enough related to children's own lives so that they can identify closely with the motivations for behavior and the outcomes of the behavior.

Finally, it is important to remember that these are stages, not absolute age designations. Some children may enter a new stage earlier than others and there will be some overlap as children are moving from one stage to another.

Developmental Trends and Book Selection

Generally speaking, information from developmental studies may provide some guidelines for book selection. Caution is important, however, because groups and individuals differ and interest patterns appear to change somewhat over time. What does all of this information mean, then, to a person who is responsible for bringing children together with books? In book selection, it is as important to know about children as it is to know about literature. Considered from that standpoint, a knowledge of child development becomes a tool for book selection just as familiarity with literature is a tool. Information about developmental levels can help tell us something about children and also something about the types of literature they are likely to enjoy at a particular age.

A librarian or teacher responsible for guiding children's reading deals with individual children, the real meeting of child and book. The more generalized information about children's development and literature comes into sharper focus when a child appears and asks for a book.

Knowledge about characteristics of children at various developmental levels has an obvious value for professionals responsible for book

selection. Developmental characteristics can tell us what we need to keep in mind in ordering books for a typical elementary school population, taking into account individual interests and needs as well as group trends. In selecting books for groups of children or individuals, adults should know as much as possible about the particular children with whom they are working. Chapter 2 discusses in greater detail the business of guiding children's book selection. The adult should always keep in mind the goal: to make reading a pleasurable experience for children so that it will continue to be one of their leisure-time activities.

Like adults, children read for many reasons: to dream, to learn, to laugh, and to enjoy the familiar and explore the unknown. They read for sheer pleasure and they absorb, in their reading, those facets of books that reflect the developmental values appropriate to their particular stage of growth. Books may help children build a concept of the society in which they live and of their roles in that society; books may help shape and sharpen their concepts about other people and may contribute to their self-understanding. Like adults' books, children's books range from the inaccurate and the mediocre to the reliable, the beautifully written, and the permanently significant. Like adults' books, children's books have become more sophisticated and frank in their use of language and their treatment of subjects once considered taboo.

There are books that are timeless in their appeal and books that transcend age barriers. Children's literature in recent years has taken new directions, explored new themes, and opened up possibilities for developing new insight. In the chapters that follow, these changes will be discussed and the criteria for evaluation of individual books will be analyzed. Writers, artists, and editors have joined forces to make many of today's children's books so varied in content, beautiful to look at, and high in quality that adults as well as children enjoy them. The treasures must be sought for, but they are there, a wealth of fine books old and new.

The goals of *Children and Books* include helping concerned adults identify what is good and lasting in the vast array of children's books; describing the criteria by which books may be evaluated; clarifying the needs, interests, and stages of understanding in children; and suggesting ways in which children and books may be brought together to provide children not only with books they will enjoy reading but also with the best in children's literature.

Adult References and Book Selection Aids*

ALMY, MILLIE, E., and CELIA GENISHI. *Ways of Studying Children.*

*Complete bibliographic data are provided in Appendices A and B.

ANDERSON, CELIA, and MARILYN APSELOFF. *Nonsense Literature for Children: Aesop to Seuss.*

APPLEBEE, ARTHUR. *The Child's Concept of Story: Ages Two to Seventeen.*

ASSOCIATION OF HOSPITAL AND INSTITUTION LIBRARIES. *Bibliotherapy: Methods and Materials.*

BANDURA, ALBERT, and RICHARD H. WALTERS. *Social Learning and Personality Development.*

BRUNER, JEROME S. *Toward a Theory of Instruction.*

BUTLER, FRANCELIA, and RICHARD ROTERT, eds. *Reflections on Literature for Children.*

CARPENTER, HUMPHREY, and MARI PRITCHARD. *The Oxford Companion to Children's Literature.*

CHAMBERS, AIDAN. *Introducing Books to Children.*

————. *The Reluctant Reader.*

CHAMBERS, NANCY, ed. *The Signal Approach to Children's Books.*

CIONI, ALFRED J., ed. *Motivating Reluctant Readers.*

COLES, ROBERT. *Children of Crisis.*

COLES, ROBERT, and MARIA PIERS. *Wages of Neglect.*

COTT, JONATHAN. *Pipers at the Gates of Dawn: The Wisdom of Children's Literature.*

CULLINAN, BERNICE. *Literature and the Child.*

DUFF, ANNIS. *"Bequest of Wings": A Family's Pleasures with Books.*

————. *"Longer Flight": A Family Grows Up with Books.*

EGOFF, SHEILA. *Thursday's Child: Trends and Patterns in Contemporary Children's Literature.*

EGOFF, SHEILA, G. T. STUBBS, and L. F. ASHLEY, eds. *Only Connect: Readings on Children's Literature.* Article by Anthony Storr. "The Child and the Book."

ERIKSON, ERIK H. *Childhood and Society.*

FADER, DANIEL N., and ELTON B. MCNEIL. *Hooked on Books: Program and Proof.*

GERSONI-STAVN, DIANE, ed. *Sexism and Youth.* Part 3, "Books."

GESELL, ARNOLD, and FRANCES ILG. *Child Development: An Introduction to the Study of Human Growth.*

HARRISON, BARBARA, and GREGORY MAGUIRE, eds. *Innocence & Experience: Essays & Conversations on Children's Literature.*

HAZARD, PAUL. *Books, Children and Men.*

HEARNE, BETSY, and MARILYN KAYE, comps. *Celebrating Children's Books: Essays on Children's Literature in Honor of Zena Sutherland.*

HENTOFF, NAT. *Does Anybody Give a Damn?*

HOLT, JOHN. *How Children Fail.*

————. *How Children Learn.*

ILG, FRANCES L., and LOUIS BATES AMES. *Child Behavior.*

JAN, ISABELLE. *On Children's Literature.*

JENKINS, GLADYS G., and HELEN S. SHACTER. *These Are Your Children.*

KUJOTH, JEAN SPEALMAN. *Reading Interests of Children and Young Adults.*

MAIER, HENRY. *Three Theories of Child Development: The Contributions of Erik H. Erikson, Jean Piaget, and Robert R. Sears, and Their Applications.*

MAYERSON, CHARLOTTE LEON, ed. *Two Blocks Apart: Juan Gonzales and Peter Quinn.*

PATERSON, KATHERINE. *Gates of Excellence: On Reading and Writing Books for Children.*

PIAGET, JEAN. *Language and Thought of the Child.*

PIAGET, JEAN, and BARBEL INHELDER. *The Psychology of the Child.*

PURVES, ALAN C., and DIANNE L. MONSON. *Experiencing Children's Literature.*

RUDMAN, MASHA KABAKOW. *Children's Literature: An Issues Approach.*

SARAFINO, EDWARD P., and JAMES W. ARMSTRONG. *Child and Adolescent Development.*

SEBESTA, SAM L., and WILLIAM J. IVERSON. *Literature for Thursday's Child.*

SILBERMAN, CHARLES. *Crisis in the Classroom.*

SIMS, RUDINE. *Shadow & Substance: Afro-American Experience in Contemporary Children's Fiction.*

SINGER, DOROTHY G., and TRACEY A. REVENSON. *A Piaget Primer: How a Child Thinks.*

SMITH, LILLIAN. *The Unreluctant Years.*

TANYZER, HAROLD, and JEAN KARL, eds. *Reading, Children's Books, and Our Pluralistic Society.*

TUCKER, NICHOLAS. *The Child and the Book: A Psychological and Literary Exploration.*

————, ed. *Suitable for Children? Controversies in Children's Literature.*

TUROW, JOSEPH. *Getting Books to Children: An Exploration of Publisher-Market Relations.*

WILKIN, BINNIE TATE. *Survival Themes in Fiction for Children and Young People.*

WINN, MARIE. *Children Without Childhood.*

————. *The Plug-In Drug: Television, Children, and the Family.*

ZINSSER, WILLIAM, ed. *Worlds of Childhood: The Art and Craft of Writing for Children.*

Chapter Two

Guiding Children's Book Selection

Books are written for children, but adults buy them. Editors decide on manuscripts, reviewers make judgments, teachers and librarians exhibit books, recommend them, and otherwise guide children's reading. Parents, grandparents, uncles, and aunts select a choice volume for a favorite child. But how can adults know what book a child is going to enjoy?

Actually, they can't know with any degree of certainty. Moreover, they must face the fact that youngsters are skilled at rejecting what is not for them. A book may be judged a juvenile classic by experts in children's literature, but if it is beyond children's understanding or too subtle or sophisticated for their level of appreciation, they can turn it down with a stony indifference which leaves adults baffled and grieved. They need not mourn. Two years later a child may accept that very book with enthusiasm. It is the same with music. A simple melody may appeal to children, while a symphony may confuse them. But if their musical experiences increase as they mature, they hear parts of the symphony, its different movements, over and over, until they understand and enjoy them.

Finally, when they hear the whole symphony, they can follow it with pleasure, and its great melodies sing in their memories. So some poems must be heard repeatedly, and some stories must be talked over or listened to while someone who knows and loves them reads aloud.

Through this gradual induction into better and better literature, children catch the theme and savor the beauty or the subtle humor or the meaning that eluded them at first. Sometimes an adult has the privilege of seeing this discovery take place. The children's faces come suddenly alive; their eyes shine. They may be anticipating an amusing conclusion or a heroic triumph. There is a sudden chuckle, or breath is exhaled like a sigh. The book has moved them, perhaps even to laughter or tears, but in any case there is a deep inner satisfaction, and they will turn to books again with anticipation. It is through such anticipation and satisfaction that children become not just readers, but addicted readers. Once they have experienced the joy of reading, they have acquired a habit that will serve them all their lives. It is important, therefore, that those who guide their reading select wisely.

This chapter will discuss standards for evaluating books, the elements of literature (setting, viewpoint, characterization, plot, theme, and style), and the range of books for children.

Standards for Evaluating Books

In the evaluation of children's books there should be neither a casual, uncritical approach nor a rigid adherence to the standards for adult literature. The best in children's literature, as well as the best in adult literature, will meet those standards, but it is incumbent on critics (and this includes parents) to balance each book's strengths and weaknesses and to remember that each kind of book for children has its own requirements. As Lillian Smith points out in *The Unreluctant Years:*

A child's range of choice in his reading will always depend upon what is at hand, and this will largely depend upon his elders. Mistaken ideas among adults about what books a child likes, or should like, must prevent the very object they intend: a love for books and reading. If such misunderstanding is given widespread credence it will eventually affect what books are made generally available to children. (p. 13)[1]

Adults must be wary of pedestrian books, often oversize and profusely illustrated, the kind that bookstore clerks refer to as "grandmother books": slick, busy with detail, often coy, cute, or sentimental. They must try to distinguish between what appeals to some nostalgic adults and what appeals to children. They should guard against bias, preconception, or unevaluated loyalty to a childhood favorite.

Children's literature often reflects the values that adults think are important to encourage, and those who select books for children should be aware of the author's values and assumptions as well as of their own. If an author's attitude toward parent-child relationships, sex mores, civil rights, or any other issue is in agreement with our own, we may tend to approve of the book as a whole, but if the values and assumptions are at variance with our own, we may tend to dismiss it, regardless of its other qualities. For these reasons, it is particularly important for us to analyze books as carefully and objectively as we can. Each book must be judged on its own merits, but it is often illuminating to compare a book with the author's other books and with other authors' books on the same topic or in the same literary genre. The professional—teacher, librarian, reviewer, or editor—should know both the books themselves and the critical literature, since criticism entails making judgments that ought to be both informed and objective.

The special criteria for the various types of children's literature—poetry, folk tales, fables, myths, epics, modern fantasy, modern fiction, historical fiction, biography, and informational books—are discussed in succeeding chapters, and there are also evaluations of individual books, authors, and illustrators. Many different kinds of books can be judged by the criteria we will discuss for theme, plot, setting, characters, point of view, and style. Biography, for instance, may be so evaluated, but it should also be judged by other equally important criteria (see Chapter 12). One of the essential criteria for judging informational books (see Chapter 13) is accuracy, but style, too, is important. Information can, and should, be presented in an interesting, lively fashion.

Looking Closely at Books

Adults must know a great deal about books in choosing them for children and in guiding children to them. The chapters in this book will introduce many of the fine authors of the past and present, and will also suggest criteria for judging books in each genre. These chapters are, of course, guides only. In the end, you should choose books for children on the basis of your own first-hand knowledge of the child or groups of children you are working with and of the books themselves.

The best way to know books is to read them. Book selection guides can help and lists of award books are useful, but there is no substitute for reading. Using the lists of book selection aids and prize-winning books included later in this volume is only a first step. Many of the best books are published in paperback editions, and children can be encouraged to

[1]Lillian H. Smith, *The Unreluctant Years* (American Library Association, 1953).

Viewpoint

We read for delight. But at the same time we must read with a discerning eye and mind, with the intention of defining that delight. So on one hand or with one eye, we are reading with a receptive spirit, eagerly and nonjudiciously, unconsciously becoming the child that is still with us.

But with the other eye, we must go beyond our own delight to the nuts and bolts, the very basic hardware, of how and why this book delights us and what could make it a source of delight for child readers. Louise Rosenblatt writes, "Though a free, uninhibited emotional reaction to a work of art or literature is an absolutely necessary condition of sound literary judgment, it is not . . . a sufficient condition." Lillian Smith urges us to read with "mind and heart, interest and sympathy." And that means going beyond our emotional reaction to a critical analysis of the book. For some, perhaps it is possible to accomplish this in one reading, to experience the book on an emotional level, and to read critically at the same time. For others, several readings. But, in any case, how do we read a book in order to evaluate it? With two eyes, two minds.

Elizabeth Fitzgerald Howard, "Delight and Definition: The Nuts and Bolts of Evaluating Children's Books," *Top of the News*, Volume 43, Number 4, Summer 1987, p. 363.

start their own paperback libraries, especially if you can discuss books with knowledgeable enthusiasm. It really isn't enough to feel, "I like it," or "I don't like it." To make wise selections and to stimulate children's interest, one must know why. It is useful to keep records of such data as title, author, publisher, series, illustrator, availability in paperback, and of your opinion of plot, theme, style, characters, and so on. You may also want to note passages that would be particularly enticing as baits to reading. Publishers usually suggest the reading level, but this you will want to judge for yourself. (Would a fifth-grade class enjoy this book? Could a slow reader handle it? Will the subject interest a particular child who can read but seldom does?) While you will be careful to avoid the role of censor, you should know the book well enough to judge whether it should be given to special children or recommended to a class as a whole. If you have kept records of the books you have read, you may have the great satisfaction of being able to recommend another book when a child asks, "Is there any other book just like this one?"

In some classrooms, a teacher will have enthusiastic response to *The Wind in the Willows;* in others, no response at all. In some library story hours *Mary Poppins* may produce hilarity, in others boredom—in the same library. Think how differently you would select, say, for a fourth grade of bright, enthusiastic booklovers and a fourth grade of slow, apathetic readers. Or, in working with individual children, how differently you would choose a book for a child with a pronounced sense of humor and a child who is more literal.

You can turn to review sources for opinions of books, but in the end you must rely on your own judgment.[2] You should not feel restricted by children's immediate interests in choosing books because these are often narrower than they need to be and because they can change quite quickly. Children's reactions are often immediate and personal, and they often adhere conservatively to a known literary experience such as horse stories or science fiction. Teachers, parents, and librarians should keep children exploring both the best of the old books and the most promising of the new. Since new titles alone number over four thousand a year, you need some criteria to help you select wisely. To develop judgments that are reliable and useful, you need to look closely at a book, not only to appraise its total effect on you but to examine the elements that produce that effect.

[2]Obviously there are various ways to approach a book. Frederick C. Crews in *The Pooh Perplex* (Dutton, 1963) has produced a devastating satire of various literary approaches to criticism. As Orville Prescott remarked in the *New York Times,* "In twelve glittering, brightly malicious essays he has poleaxed and then neatly eviscerated twelve varieties of currently fashionable literary criticism."

The traditional literary elements we will be discussing are

1. setting   4. plot
2. point of view   5. theme
3. characters   6. style

In discussion of these elements, three books will be analyzed as examples, all realistic fiction for better comparison: Rebecca Caudill's *Did You Carry the Flag Today, Charley?* for the youngest children; Laura Ingalls Wilder's *Little House in the Big Woods* for the middle group; and Gillian Cross's *Roscoe's Leap* for older children.[3]

Setting

Where and when did the story take place?

The setting is the time and the place of the action. Its elements are the geographical location, which may be as broad as a country or city or as narrow as an isolated farm or a single classroom; and the time, which can be a historical period of several decades or more, a season, or a day. Other aspects of setting may be an occupational pattern or a general milieu or atmosphere, social or emotional. For some readers, or for some books, the setting of a story may be of paramount interest. For others, the action is all-absorbing, and the setting is of minor importance.

The limitations of young children's understanding of time and distance, a sense that expands as they grow older, must be taken into consideration in evaluating books meant for them. There are exceptions, but books for younger children are most comprehensible when their settings are familiar and within the child's limited experience. Fantasy that is set in an imaginary time or place demands careful structuring or it will lack cohesion and credibility. Lloyd Alexander's *Prydain* books are set in a wholly conceived world, with its own mores and language and topography; whether books of high fantasy or not, stories that are set in other worlds or invented countries or a future time

must be consistent within the parameters of their setting.

The setting of the story should be clear, believable, and, especially in the case of biography or historical fiction, authentic. A book like Irene Hunt's *Across Five Aprils* has strength in part because the author's research enabled her to reveal convincingly the tempo, the ideologies, and the language of the Civil War years—particularly in the conflict that existed in border-state families. Too often, in a mediocre book, the author substitutes for a subtly interwoven, authoritative treatment of a time or a place some laboriously detailed information awkwardly placed and often isolated from the characters and events. On the other hand, an author like Rosemary Sutcliff, who has a vast knowledge of British history, lets her characters give readers necessary details about customs, for example, or information about military leaders, in dialogue appropriate for the period in which the book is set. A less qualified writer might introduce into the dialogue an unnatural exchange of information that has the synthetic character of a travel brochure. A mediocre story with a hospital setting might have this ridiculous remark by one nurse to another: "Oh, did you know that one must go through decompression to enter a hyperbaric oxygen chamber?" Of course, the other nurse knows it, and the reader knows she knows it. The author simply hasn't been sufficiently skilled to bring in needed scientific details in a casual, natural way.

"To get to Charley Cornett's house, you turn left off the highway at Main Street, drive to the edge of town, and cross a bridge." So begins *Did You Carry the Flag Today, Charley?* and it goes on to place Charley's home in mountain country: a small house in which Charley lives with his parents, four brothers, and five sisters. Since this is a book for reading aloud to young children, it is quite fitting that there be no specific time, but the "highway" and "drive" make it clear that it is now. No confusion here. It is in the countryside, not the city; Charley is one of a large family. All of these interpretations are within the grasp of small children.

Little House in the Big Woods begins "once upon a time, sixty years ago, a little girl lived in the Big Woods of Wisconsin, in a little gray

---

[3]Rebecca Caudill, *Did You Carry the Flag Today, Charley?* (hardback, 1966; paperback, 1971—Holt, Rinehart & Winston). Laura Ingalls Wilder, *Little House in the Big Woods* (hardback, 1932, 1953; paperback, 1971—Harper & Row, Publishers). Gillian Cross, *Roscoe's Leap* (hardback, 1987, Holiday House).

From *Little House in the Big Woods* by Laura Ingalls Wilder, illustrated by Garth Williams.

house made of logs.'' Thus, deftly and simply, Wilder has made it clear not only that (at the time of writing) the story is set sixty years in the past, but that the little girl who was Laura Ingalls lived in pioneer fashion, in a log house. And how much more we learn about the setting because of the capitalization of "Big Woods." It immediately gives an impression of the isolation of the little gray house, and both the pinpointing of a past time and the expectation that readers will understand the locale are appropriate for the level of the readers.

In *Roscoe's Leap,* Cross introduces the dramatic setting that enhances and is part of the double-faceted mystery of the story, for Roscoe's Leap is a strange, gloomy mansion built over a waterfall. In the first paragraph, twelve-year-old Stephen is crossing a passage that connects the two parts of the house. The time is contemporary, but much of the aura of the story depends on the fact that the house had been built by Stephen's great-great-grandfather, an eccentric millionaire. Details like the glass roof, the smell of mold, and the noise of cascading water set the stage and form a backdrop for the comment that "it was No Man's Land, not belonging to either part of the house." Facts about the house and its first owner emerge naturally when a visitor comes to the door, and when Stephen introduces the man to his sister Hannah, age fifteen, readers learn that he has been given permission to explore the house and its contents by Uncle Ernest. Who is Uncle Ernest? Few first chapters achieve so strong an establishment of setting, and—for experienced readers—so much promise of a mystery.

Viewpoint

A good critic will indeed be aware of theme, plot, style, characterization, and many other considerations, some of them not previously spelled out but arising directly from the work; he will be sensitive; he will have a sense of balance and rightness; he will respond. Being only human he cannot possibly know all that it would be desirable for him to know; but he will have a wide knowledge of literature in general as well as of children and their literature, and probably a respectable acquaintance with cinema, theatre, television, and current affairs. That is asking a lot of him, but not too much. The critic (this is the heart of the matter) counts more than the criteria.

. . . If the book is for children, he should not let his mind be dominated by the fact, but neither, I believe, should he attempt to ignore it. Just as I feel the author must write for himself yet with awareness of an audience of children, so I feel the critic must write for himself with an awareness that the books he discusses are children's books.

. . . A book is a communication; if it doesn't communicate, does it not fail? True, it may speak to posterity, if it gets the chance; it may be ahead of its time. But if a children's book is not popular with children here and now, its lack of appeal may tell us something. It is at least a limitation, and it *may* be a sign of some vital deficiency which is very much the critic's concern.

Point of View

Who tells the story?

The author may write as an omniscient narrator, who simply describes the characters and gives their thoughts by direct exposition, perhaps at several points in the story. Or the narrator may make no comment and simply let the characters' actions speak for them. In a book in which the protagonist or an observer tells the story, readers see other characters only through the narrator's eyes and must remember that the view of them is therefore limited. The author must, to give a broader view, use other ways of telling the reader what other characters are like—perhaps through their actions and dialogue, perhaps through the reactions of other characters. Another device, less frequently used, is having different chapters told by different people. If the author uses a diary form or a monologue, the point of view is restricted and change only comes with changing attitudes of the speaker.

In *Did You Carry the Flag Today, Charley?* Rebecca Caudill's Charley is seen quite objectively, but the author identifies with him by making him the only character whose thoughts are given ("he remembered," or "he figured out"), so that the listening or reading audience tends to empathize with him.

In *Little House,* Wilder does the same thing; the story is told in third person (although it is based on her own childhood) and the emphasis is put on Laura as the main character both by introducing her first and by making the first comment on Laura from her viewpoint: "So far as the little girl could see. . . ."

In *Roscoe's Leap,* the author sees the viewpoints of both Stephen and Hannah, sometimes directly through their thoughts; but the fact that the first chapter begins, "Stephen walked along the gallery . . ." and the second chapter, "Stephen's skin prickled uncomfortably," are clear indications that it is he, rather than Hannah, who is the protagonist. Cross uses this shading of the authorial voice deftly, inviting an understanding of Stephen's timidity and Hannah's self-confidence and using these differences in personality to develop different aspects of the plot as well as to give a balanced picture of the action.

Characters

Who are the characters? How are they revealed? Do they grow and change?

It is clear from the discussion above that a major character is often distinguished by being the first person in the book to be introduced. Often, in a first-person narrative, the protagonist or narrator may start by a first-person introduction: "Here I am, Tom Bailey, sixteen years old, and I've never had a real date." The mythical Tom may go on to explain that he's shy, or that he's nervous about parental expectations. Characters may be defined by a conversation about them, or by the fact that they are people to whom others turn when there is a problem. Characters may thus be revealed by what is said, by what is done, or by what others say about them.

Characterization can be effected by physical description: If we read that a judge in colonial Salem has pursed lips and a frowning brow, that he is dressed in somber black and walks with stiff dignity, we anticipate his stern behavior. What characters say, what they do, how they react to others, how others talk about them are all clues to their personalities. If a character is a major character, he or she must play a dynamic role; if the character changes, the change should be logical for the sort of person the author has drawn. There should be depth of characterization, since to emphasize only one or two traits produces a one-dimensional portrait that is often more caricature than characterization.

Characters must be both believable and consistent. Children soon learn how superficial is the patterned mystery story in which no adult contributes to the solution, while an omniscient, persistent, superintelligent child adroitly sees all clues, pursues them, and solves the mystery single-handedly.

The characters should develop naturally and behave and talk in ways that are consistent with their age, sex, background, ethnic group, and education.

Whether the story is realistic or fantastic, the characters must be convincing. Although Mary Poppins is in a fanciful story, she is a very convincing character, a severe and crusty individual that no child ever forgets. When Michael asks anxiously, "Mary Poppins, you'll never leave us, will you?" the answer from his new nurse is a stern "One more word from that direction and I'll call the Policeman." Long after details of plot have been forgotten, children and adults will recall with a chuckle or a warm glow of affection such characters as Jo in *Little Women,* Long John Silver, Henry Huggins, Anastasia Krupnik, Arrietty in *The Borrowers,* and dozens of other salty book characters. It is through depth and perception in characterization that stories become memorable. And it is through such well-drawn individuals that children gain new insight into their own personal problems and into their ever widening relationships with other people.

As is appropriate for small children whose chief interest is the action in a story, Caudill's Charley is revealed more by what he does than by what he says. Cheerfully obstreperous, Charley, who is five and having his first school experiences, *has* to climb an apple tree to see how apples are attached, and when the class is playing "hoppity" like Christopher Robin, he hops right out the door. It is further revealing that when the teacher tells him to stay out in the rain, he happily pretends he is a rock and enjoys the rain. In all of his brothers' and sisters' daily inquiries about whether or not he has had the honor of being the flag-carrier, it is clear that they know their little brother and hardly expect it—yet they ask "anxiously," making it clear also that Charley is lovable and loved.

The theme of family love is strong in the *Little House* books, and the first thing we learn about Laura, as she lies in a trundle bed listening to a wolf howl, is the security she feels with Pa there to protect her. We also see in Laura's actions that she is a curious child, far less compliant than her sister Mary—and Wilder often uses Mary's behavior as a contrast to define Laura's livelier personality.

The characters that Cross develops are, as is appropriate for an older audience, more complex than Charley and Laura. Stephen's quiet and nervous agitation about some of the discoveries Nick makes as he explores the artifacts and papers from the past; Hannah's grim determination to save the decaying old house by making money enough for repairs; and the

From *Little Women* by Louisa May Alcott, illustrated by Barbara Cooney.

tense bullying by their mother, an icy and adamant woman; all lead to the question of how each is related to Uncle Ernest and to the inept Doug who takes care of him and who keeps to his own part of the house. Character is established by dialogue, by behavior, by comments or thoughts of each about the others, and by individual reactions to other people and to events. For older readers, there is little need for the author to give flat descriptions. *Roscoe's Leap* covers a short time span, and Cross deals deftly with changes in the characters, realistically using events as catalysts or establishing a change in behavior that is a logical response to change in another person; the children's stony mother, for example, alters her behavior when she learns that she has for years unjustly condemned the husband from whom she isolated herself.

Plot

What happens in the story?

Fiction for children usually focuses on what happens, what the action is. In some stream-of-consciousness novels or quiet character studies for adults, very little happens. While there are some children's books of which this is true, most of them are filled with action. Children want characters who have obstacles to overcome, conflicts to settle, difficult goals to win. It is the vigorous action in pursuit of these goals that keeps young readers racing along from page to page to find out how the central character achieves his or her ends. But achieve he or she must, in some way or other.

A plot is basically a series of actions that move in related sequence to a logical outcome; if there is no sequence or interaction, the book may have a series of episodes (in some books, particularly books of reminiscence, this can be very effective) rather than a plot or story line. Simple as it sounds, a story needs a beginning, a middle, and an end. First the author must set the stage. Then, to have development and momentum, a plot needs conflict, opposition, or a problem. Last, there should be a definitive ending: a climax of action, or even a strong indication of future resolution.

Linked to the development of the plot are the characters, who affect what happens by the sort of people they are and who are, in turn, affected by what happens to them. In stories for the very young, the plot is usually simple, with no subplot, whereas older readers can both understand and enjoy the complexity of a story with many threads.

In *Charley,* the story begins with the fact that a small boy going to school for the first time is told by his brothers and sisters that one child is honored each day by being allowed to carry the flag; as the story develops it becomes evident that Charley is an unlikely candidate. Then an understanding teacher acts—and Charley proudly carries the flag.

Little House is an episodic story; although the book and its sequels show the children growing, the separate incidents of the story might often be interchanged without affecting the outcome.

The dramatic quality of the setting of *Roscoe's Leap* would seem exaggerated were the plot insipid, but Cross has developed a story line that is strong and believable, yet sparse in structure. Adding to the mystery is Doug's identity. (He is the children's father, inept but loving, cast out by his wife for his part in an incident that had endangered his son's life years before. That is why mother and children live on one side of the house, father and

From *Did You Carry the Flag Today, Charley?* by Rebecca Caudill, illustrated by Nancy Grossman.

grouchy Uncle Ernest on the other.) This is the background for the arrival of a stranger whose probing (work on a thesis about the first owner, Samuel Roscoe) starts a chain of events that leads to Doug's exoneration and also clears up the mystery of Stephen's buried fears about the old automaton, a guillotine, that had terrified him years before. A final scene foreshadows some measure of rapprochement, so that every facet of plot development is smoothly observed.

Theme

What is the main idea of the story?

The theme of a story is its central core, its meaning, often its message. It is not the moral, although a moral can serve, as it does in Aesop, as a simpler form of theme. A moral can serve as the implication of a part of a story, while the theme is the implication of—or, if explicit, the commentary on—the whole story. It gives readers a vision, through fiction, of the author's perception of human experience.

In some fiction the author may be explicit or even didactic in stressing the theme, but the message is usually less effective if it is explicit; it is the implicit theme that is more often effective and memorable. A theme like the strength of family love, or the wisdom of accepting what we cannot change, especially if it emerges naturally through characters and events is far more likely to be absorbed and remembered than homilies on those themes by the author. If they are simply there, intrinsic to the story, readers discover themes for themselves and become involved rather than receiving a lecture.

Often in children's books the theme reflects those developmental values inherent in the process of growing up. The theme may be concerned with overcoming jealousy or fear, adjusting to a physical handicap, or accepting a stepparent. Books with developmental values can help the child who shares similar problems and also the child who does not but who needs to develop empathy and understanding.

Not all books have such themes; some are adventure stories, some written just for fun, and some historical fiction is intended only to highlight a person, a movement, or a period. Indeed, there can be no hard and fast rule about any of the elements of fiction, since there are good books in which almost any aspect may be omitted. The elements discussed here are those which exist in most books.

The theme in *Charley* is that of achieving status and acceptance: Charley has been told that carrying the flag is the signal of honor of the school day, and although he is really more excited, by the end of the story, by the fact that he owns his first book, he is well aware that the sign of approval has been carrying the flag. Although the *Little House* books are imbued with family love and pioneer courage, there really is no one underlying theme. In *Roscoe's Leap*, theme is overshadowed by plot, as is usually true in a mystery story. However, there are undercurrents of a thematic nature: the overcoming of fear or anger; the love of one's home; the fact that knowledge gives perspective; and perhaps the strongest of all, the tenacious paternal love that impels Doug to lead a life of lonely drudgery just so that he can be near the children who, cowed by their mother, never acknowledge him as their father.

Style

How is the story written? How are the ideas it contains expressed?

Style is very difficult to define. Whole books have been devoted to explaining and exemplifying it. There are many brief definitions—Jonathan Swift's "proper words in proper places make the true definition of style"; Lord Chesterton's "style is the dress of thoughts"; Comte de Buffon's "the style is the man." Style involves the author's choice of words, the sentence patterns (simple or involved structure, long or short sentences, arrangement of the words within the sentences), the imagery used, the rhythm of the sentences. There are many styles—as many styles as authors. As Thrall, Hibbard, and Holman say in *A Handbook to Literature*, "The best style, for any given purpose, is that which most nearly approximates a perfect adaptation of one's language to one's ideas."[4] Perhaps the best way to talk about style is simply to look at some passages. Read these excerpts from "The Three Little Pigs" and *Millions of Cats* aloud:

"Little pig, little pig, let me come in."
"No, not by the hair on my chinny-chin-chin."
"Then I'll huff and I'll puff and I'll blow your house in."

Hundreds of cats, thousands of cats, millions and billions and trillions of cats.

Bernard Evslin, in his retelling of the Finn McCool legend, *The Green Hero*, writes of high adventure in prose that has an epic sweep, but when he is describing small events, uses unexpectedly homely and amusing language. In listing the charms of the infant girl with whom the newly born Finn is smitten, he concludes (after rhapsodizing about her eyes and hair), "and teeth—a full set of them—so that she was able to bite Finn quite early."

Sid Fleischman's tall tales appeal to children because they are nonsensical, but it is his crisp, casual style that gives such tales as *McBroom's Ear* humor and flavor:

---

[4]William Thrall, Addison Hibbard, and C. Hugh Holman, *A Handbook to Literature* (Odyssey, 1960), p. 474.

I guess you've heard how amazing rich our farm was. Anything would grow in it quick. Seeds would burst in the ground and crops would shoot up right before your eyes. Why, just yesterday our oldest boy dropped a five-cent piece and before he could find it that nickel had grown to a quarter.

In style, as in the theme of a book, there should be appropriateness and integrity, the hallmarks of good writing. When they are absent, we often find pedestrian writing: flagrant repetitiveness, stiff dialogue, a gross exaggeration of humor or fantasy, conflict between realism and fantasy, didacticism, superciliousness ("Can YOU see the little duck in the tree?") or a use of language that is poorly chosen for the genre of the book or for the characters in it.

Rebecca Caudill's style in *Did You Carry the Flag Today, Charley?* is brisk and forthright, just as is Charley himself. Small children may not recognize the Appalachian setting, but they can hear the authenticity of the speech patterns and the fact that Charley's comments and observations sound the way a five-year-old's should:

Once inside Miss Amburgey's schoolroom, Charley looked around. Little chairs stood in a circle, with one big chair among them. Behind the big chair was a blackboard, and in a trough underneath lay pieces of chalk. Low tables stood at one side of the room. And there—there, fastened to the wall, was the white washbowl!

Notice how much like an inquisitive child's reaction this is—and how the exclamation point prepares the way for an episode in which Charley squirts water all over himself and several others. In contrast, note the quiet simplicity and the establishment of mood in Wilder's *Little House in the Big Woods:*

She looked at Ma, gently rocking and knitting. She thought to herself, "This is now." She was glad that the cozy house, and Pa and Ma and the firelight and the music, were now. They could not be forgotten, she thought because now is now. It can never be a long time ago.

Cross is equally adept at using style to establish mood and setting, as in the first paragraphs that open the story, establishing character by a blend of description and dialogue:

"We're cutting back the rhododendrons."
"Ah." Mrs. Roscoe relaxed slightly. "I wondered how Stephen was managing to get his shoes so dirty inside *the house."*
"Nick's giving us a hand too," Hannah went on blithely.
"He says it's restful when he's done a lot of work in the library."
That was a mistake. Stephen knew exactly what would come next, and he was not wrong. Mother stopped relaxing and looked distressed.

A third stylistic component is evident in the creation of suspense; there are no emotive words or exclamation marks in the passage in which a terrified Stephen, who does not understand the root of his terror, prepares to set fire to the guillotine, but the writing suddenly becomes staccato, echoing the agitation in Stephen's mind. Repetition of one phrase, italicized, adds to the cumulating fear: *"Get rid of the French Terror."*

An Analysis of *One-Eyed Cat*

As an example of analysis of the elements of a book (setting, point of view, characterization, plot, theme, and style) and the criteria used in assessing them, let's look at *One-Eyed Cat* by Paula Fox.

The setting and the background for Fox's story of Ned Wallis and the one-eyed cat emerge fluently and naturally in the first chapter. When they begin reading a new book, children are interested in such things as where the story takes place (a small village in the state of New York); who the protagonist is, and of what age (just about to turn eleven); and the protagonist's family situation. Fox's Ned is an only child whose father is a minister and whose mother is an invalid confined to bed, suffering from a severe case of rheumatoid arthritis. The reader learns that Papa prefers living in the rambling inherited homestead that's inconveniently far from the church rather than the parsonage just a hundred yards from the Congregational Church. Fox also introduces the self-important housekeeper, Mrs. Scallop, who is boastful and moody, but kind to mother.

The chapter goes on to describe a typical Sunday, including a dinner with two of Papa's congregation; Ned's reaction to this dinner and an unexpected visit with Uncle Hilary (Mama's brother) serve to show that he is a kind and sensitive child, and to forecast that, with the entrance of someone outside the immediate household, there may be change. Thus, in a single chapter, Fox has introduced her cast, set the stage, and subtly conveyed the focus of her story: It will be about Ned and how he feels; it will involve those close to him.

It is through Uncle Hilary that change comes to precipitate the problem that is the crux of the story. He has brought an air rifle as a gift for Ned's eleventh birthday, and Ned is thrilled. However, Papa feels Ned is too young to use the rifle, and puts the gun in the attic, telling his son that he knows it's disappointing, but that he trusts him not to try shooting until he is fourteen. This trust is betrayed.

Quietly, late at night, Ned goes to the attic, his heart thudding. He takes the gun out of the house, wanting only to feel its weight on his shoulder, to sight along the barrel, to taste the pleasure-to-come. "As he blinked and opened his right eye wide, he saw a dark shadow. . . . For a split second, it looked alive. Before he could think, his finger had pressed the trigger." There is a movement, then silence. Nothing. Dispirited, Ned plods home to put the gun away, sure that there is a face in the attic window. When a feral cat, one sightless eye still bloody, turns up near the home of an elderly neighbor, Ned is consumed by guilt and repentance. While other incidents and changes occur (Papa finds another job for Mrs. Scallop, the elderly neighbor has a stroke, the one-eyed cat recovers and—eventually—becomes independent), the plot is primarily a matrix for Ned's reactions to other people, to changes in his life, and to his internal anguish and ambivalence. Everything is seen from Ned's viewpoint. It is typical of Paula Fox's writing that a consistency of viewpoint is meshed with a delineation of characters so smoothly that one never feels the author is *telling* what a character is like or that events are seen from the protagonist's viewpoint. She respects readers' abilities to draw conclusions from what is shown.

Fox uses description, dialogue, and behavior

Cover illustration from *One-Eyed Cat* by Paula Fox.

to delineate character, particularly Ned's character, and most of the time the other characters are developed through his observations: "He . . . saw on his father's face an expression he didn't like. It was the sympathy that was often there when he said no to something Ned wanted. The *no* was bad enough; the sympathy was awful"; and "Ned didn't think he'd ever met anyone [Mrs. Scallop] who said so many nice things about herself." Ned's concern for his mother, his kindness to the elderly neighbor, and his persistent, nagging worry about the cat or his joy when it shows improvement, all underline the fact that he is a gentle and considerate human being and, therefore, make believable the extent of his guilt and shame.

For it is that guilt and shame that are the core and theme of the book. Ned has disobeyed his father in getting the gun out. He has lied to his father about his acts, and also to his mother. He had always been open with his parents:

What did matter was that he had a strange new life his parents knew nothing about and one that he must continue to keep hidden from them. Each

*lie he told them made the secret bigger, and that
meant even more lies. He didn't know how to
stop.*

One of the components of Fox's writing that
is most impressive is the fusion of the theme,
the plot, and the characters in her stories.
One-eyed Cat would make far less of an impact if
the author had told readers that Ned was a kind
boy rather than letting them discover this
through his words and thoughts and deeds.

If the plot consisted only of the sequence
of shooting-guilt-remorse-recovery, the story
might seem too serious or too internalized to
appeal to some readers. Fox introduces other
plot elements that provide contrast and also
make it possible to develop the theme and the
characters more fully. Through Ned's friendship with his neighbor, Mr. Scully, the reader
learns about the cat, when the old man and the
boy talk about the wounded animal. When Mr.
Scully is ill, unable to speak, Ned's hospital
visits create opportunity for a monologue that
becomes a confession. Scenes with Ned's peers
show how pervasive his concern for the cat is,
but they also lighten the mounting tension.
Similarly, Ned's secret shame impinges on his
ability to be frank with his invalid mother when
he spends time with her. Only after he has
confessed to Mr. Scully and then to Mama, and
after they have seen the one-eyed cat cavorting
in the moonlight, does Ned find peace. There
has been a problem; there is a solution.

Paula Fox is one of the finest stylists writing
for children today. She maintains the child's
viewpoint while writing with adult compassion
and literary grace. The writing flows smoothly;
the dialogue is realistic; the tension builds and
is defused in a logical way. Without excessive
use of adjectives, she achieves that almost-
poetic use of just the right word—in just the
right place—to make the reader see more
clearly. "Janet was as neat as a new pine
cone . . ." or, "I learned how nice it is to watch
an animal instead of pouncing on it and hug-
ging it every minute, covering up its nature with
your own." This is the essence of good style: a
distinctive use of words in a way that is both
memorable and unobtrusive, the ability to tell a
good story without ever coming between the
reader and the book.

The Range of Books for Children

Childhood should be a time of exploring many
kinds of books; adults who work with children
should know the different types, to prevent
children from falling into reading ruts and to
encourage them to try books of many varieties.

The books discussed in the following chapters are grouped variously—some according to
age level or setting (books for the very young,
historical fiction), some according to genre

Viewpoint

The . . . argument, "all taste is relative," must as a
matter of simple logic lead also to the conclusion
that no one book is inherently better than another.
If we accept this, then one of two things is true:
either all books are worthless, since if preference is
impossible all books are equal and therefore without *value* (for currency depends on varying stages
of value); alternatively, if preference is only possible in relative judgments, then discussion is point-
less, for everybody is as right as everybody else.

. . . Either some books *can* be dismissed out of
hand for reasons which can be precisely given, and
which depend on moral and literary principles, or
all judgment is purely personal, and there are no
grounds for saying that Shakespeare is better than
Noël Coward. All our experience and our most
valuable traditions uphold the first view: certain
books are good, others are bad, and a very large
number have something of both. The books are
good because they comment on experience with
profundity and intelligence, and occasionally with
genius; and these qualities lead us to some glimpse
of the truth about human experience.

Fred Inglis, *An Essential Discipline.* London: Methuen
Educational Ltd., 1968, pp. 3–5.

(poetry, biography), and so on. This kind of classification, though obviously mixed and inexact, is nonetheless useful, partly because it is based to some extent on the ways that children themselves describe their books.

One means of helping a child out of a reading rut—say, all animal stories or all fairy tales—is first to discover some common elements in the books he or she enjoys and then to use these as a stimulus to change. For example, if a child who reads only animal stories has enjoyed Vivien Alcock's *Travelers by Night,* he or she might be led to other books with some of the same elements—adventure, suspense, self-reliant runaways, or the saving of an animal whose life is endangered.

Picture Books

For prereaders and beginning readers, picture stories are enchanting. Significantly, the older stories which have lasted over the years are, for the most part, built around one or two general themes: love or reassurance, and achievement. *Peter Rabbit,* which is over eighty years old, has both. Peter has a daring adventure but returns safely to his home where his mother tucks him into bed with a justifiably punishing dose of camomile tea. Love and reassurance make Else Minarik's *Little Bear* books, and many other stories for the youngest, completely satisfying. And then, because the young child is always in an inferior position in relation to older children and adults, he or she yearns for independent achievement or competence. Hence the long life of *Mike Mulligan and His Steam Shovel,* the popularity of the *Madeline* books, and the success of the *Little Tim* stories, in which Tim triumphs gloriously over his many mishaps, such as shipwrecks and mislaying his parents—all books with themes of satisfying achievement.

In evaluating the various editions of the *Mother Goose* books or the many variations on alphabet books, the areas of decision are different. No need to wonder about the appeal of the former, since their rhyme, rhythm, and gay humor are established beyond controversy as appealing to the very young. The areas of decision lie primarily in the format of the book, the choice of rhymes included, and the illustrations (see Chapters 4 and 5). The latter are of

From *Little Bear* by Else Holmelund Minarik, illustrated by Maurice Sendak.

paramount importance, too, in ABC books and are, of course, all-important in wordless picture books.

To the picture book audience, illustrations are always important, whether or not they bear the burden of the story, as in wordless books, or the message, as in ABC books. Young children respond more easily to visual than auditory stimuli, and although they respond to a story, their first interest often is in the pictures. Anyone who reads aloud to a young child must be prepared to halt the reading repeatedly while the child points with pleasure or with a question to some pictorial detail. In picture books, the illustrations often do more than augment the story; often they contribute to its development.

Folk Tales

Challenge and achievement are the heart of the folk-tale themes. The heroes or heroines must perform stern tasks if they are to survive, but the fact that they deal competently with glass hills, giants, witches, wicked machinations, and come through modestly triumphant is both reassuring and encouraging. Stories such as "Cinderella," "The Three Little Pigs," "The

Bobby put the matchbox back in his pocket and curled his
fingers around it. He smiled a secret smile.

From *The Secret in the Matchbox* by Val Willis, illustrated
by John Shelley.

Three Billy-Goats Gruff," and "Molly
Whuppie" dramatize the stormy conflict of
good and evil. And they reiterate the old
verities that kindness and goodness will triumph over evil if they are backed by wisdom,
wit, and courage. These basic truths are the
folk tales' great contribution to the child's
social consciousness.

Fables, Myths, and Epics

Older children are the primary audience for
the pithy—if sometimes didactic—wisdom of
the fables, although many fables have been
skillfully used as single versions in picture-story
format. All of these forms of literature (fables,
myths, and epics) have a quality of universality,
and are part of the literary heritage with which
all children should become familiar. They may
not fully understand the complexity or symbolism of myths and legends, but they can appreciate the drama and beauty of the stories, and the
great epics can satisfy a child's reverence for
courage and high deeds.

Modern Fantasy

No genre so satisfies the child's boundless
imagination as does fantasy, from the adventures of Max in Maurice Sendak's *Where the
Wild Things Are* to the intricate depths of
Madeleine L'Engle's *A Wrinkle in Time*. It
encompasses happy little picture books about
friendly ghosts and little-girl witches, low-keyed
modern dragon stories like Val Willis' *The Secret
in the Matchbox*, the romantic adventure stories
by Lloyd Alexander, the picaresque books by
Joan Aiken, and the polished science fiction of
Peter Dickinson. All of them can extend the
reader's horizons, all of them have the action
that appeals to children, many of them provide
humor that ranges from daft nonsense to subtle
wit, and almost all of them have an ingredient
of durable attraction, magic.

Poetry

Poetry, too, extends children's imaginations,
although in a different way. Where fantasy
opens doors to things beyond belief, poetry
gives new inward vision and understanding.
The facile appeals of rhyme, rhythm, and repetition in simple verse and the quick humor of
nonsense poetry can lead to an appreciation of
the beauty of language and the crystallization
in poetry of a mood, an emotion, a relationship, or the loveliness of a scene. The storytelling appeal of narrative poetry makes it a good
choice for reading aloud as an introduction to
the genre, and children may be led from this to
lyric poetry and free verse. The increased
interest of children and young people in the
writing of poetry as well as in reading it is
evident in the many collections and anthologies
that have appeared and in the numbers of
poetry magazines and workshops that have
produced new young poets.

Modern Fiction

The themes of love, reassurance, and achievement are prominent in many stories of family
life. For the middle years, eight to ten, the
pleasant and amusing stories of *Ramona* and
Henry Huggins take place against a permissive
family background in suburbia, as does that

great family story for somewhat older readers, *Meet the Austins*. The children in these stories have their problems and difficulties, some funny, some grave; sometimes they meet these problems with the reassurance of family understanding and love, and sometimes it is missing and needed. This is also true of books about children like those in William Mayne's *Gideon Ahoy!* These books broaden children's social understanding and deepen their sympathies. It is significant that most of the realistic stories for today's children have gone beyond *The Bobbsey Twins* and *Nancy Drew* stories (although new formulaic series are available) and present real people confronted with real problems—from earning money for a bike to rebuilding a fairly normal life in a European city during wartime, as in Peter Härtling's *Crutches*.

This realistic fiction also acquaints children with a wider world than the city, suburbs, or regional groups of the United States. Books begin to introduce them to family life in other countries. Even in the picture-story stage, French *Madeline* is as familiar to American children as are the boys and girls of the United States in American children's books. The tens will enjoy the humor of Robin Klein's *Hating Alison Ashley*, and the twelves will find out what happens during wartime in Robert Westall's *The Machine Gunners*. Gone are fiesta stereotypes of foreign lands and gone are the stories about a country told by an author who has never seen it or who equates contemporary life with that of a hundred years ago. *Hans Brinker* has been supplemented by Hilda van Stockum's *The Borrowed House*. A contemporary picture of the Far East is created in Clive King's *The Night the Water Came*.

There is delightful humorous realism, too, as in Keith Robertson's *Henry Reed, Inc.* From the ingenuous absurdities of William Steig's *Spinky Sulks* to the sophisticated humor of Mary Rodgers' *Summer Switch*, the young of all ages can find amusing echoes of everyday life. Wherever laughter can be found, it is important that we search for it and relish it.

Historical Fiction

Children may know Paul Revere in story or verse, but do they also know children of Revere's time—the daughter of a free black man in James Lincoln and Christopher Collier's *War Comes to Willy Freeman* and Johnny in *Johnny Tremain*? Historical fiction today is both historically authentic and well written. Indeed, in such books we find some of the best contemporary writing for children and youth. The 1961, 1962, 1974, 1980, and 1986 Newbery Medals were awarded to books of historical fiction—*Island of the Blue Dolphins, The Bronze Bow, The Slave Dancer, A Gathering of Days,* and *Sarah, Plain and Tall,* five books readers should not miss. In each of the books mentioned in this brief sampling, the themes—from devotion to a cause to the message that it is only love, not hatred, that can bend a bow of bronze—speak strongly to children of today.

Biography

Realistic fiction, contemporary or historical, and biography may and should be used to reinforce each other. *Johnny Tremain* makes a biography of Paul Revere infinitely more real; Mary Benson's *Nelson Mandela* is a stirring example of the courage of adults and young people fighting apartheid; and the homespun

From *Spinky Sulks,* written and illustrated by William Steig.

From *War Comes to Willy Freeman* by James Lincoln Collier and Christopher Collier, illustrated by Gordon Crabb.

tional books give scant coverage or unbalanced treatment. This is an area in which the author's qualifications are important. The adult working with children should know those authors—and there are many—whose books are accurate, up-to-date, and written at the right level of complexity for their intended audience. Publishers are quick to respond to expressed needs, and the past years have seen an outpouring of books about pollution and ecology, oceanology and space science, and most of the reform and protest movements that stir our society, as well as books on the arts and sciences, humanity's past record, and our present environment. Handbooks and experiment books, reference books, do-it-yourself books, handsome art books—books by the hundreds —exist to fulfill the child's need to know. The adult can help children choose the best of these books by being aware of the accuracy of the contents, the thoroughness of the indexing (not all informational books need an index), the placement of maps and diagrams, and the organization of the material in a logical sequence.

frontier boys in William Steele's stories give vivid life to the scene and times of Daniel Boone. Both historical fiction and biography impress children with a sense of the reality of other days. Begin early to introduce children to these "real stories" we call biographies. Even the youngest readers can start with Ferdinand Monjo's simply written historical fiction and biographies, and can then progress to many excellent biographies suitable for children of each age level. Books about Paracelsus, Galileo, Joan of Arc, Columbus, Washington, Banneker, Sequoyah, Lincoln, Tubman, Bethune, Robeson, Gandhi, and many others are authentic and as fascinating as fiction.

Informational Books

The category of informational books is so broad and so diverse that almost any need a child has for facts about a subject can be satisfied. There is, however, a need for vigilance on the part of the adult to be familiar with the contents of such books, since some informa-

Viewpoint

Culture is a machine for conserving, discovering, and sharing knowledge. Knowledge is conveyed by two processes: teaching and learning.

Teaching requires a formal situation in which there is a clear distinction between the informed and the ignorant. Before we are old enough to defend ourselves, parents, preachers, teachers, and advertisers systematically teach us the myths, morals, and manners they believe we need to know in order to be civilized. But learning often takes place unconsciously and informally. Usually we learn best when we are enjoying ourselves most: songs, jokes, and stories told just for the fun of it worm their way into our imagination and nibble at the core of our more serious beliefs.

Sam Keen and Anne Valley-Fox, "To Tell a Story," *Storytelling*, Volume 1, Number 2, Fall 1989.

Children need books to widen their horizons, deepen their understandings, and give them broader social insights. They also need books that minister to their merriment and increase their appreciation of beauty. They need heroism, fantasy, and down-to-earth realism. They need information about themselves and their fast-changing world, and they need books to relieve the tensions of that world. Adults may think in terms of what the child will learn, how the book may improve an attitude, correct a misconception, or ease a fear. If books do this, fine, but—outside of school assignments— most children read primarily for pleasure. For many children, the right time for a book is fleeting, and gentle guidance may be needed to expand the interests of a child who is in a reading rut so that he or she may not miss a reading experience for which there may never be another time so right.

The analyses in this chapter are meant as guidelines, not as rigid specifications. There are fine books that do not measure up to every standard of good literature but that may have particular values for a particular child, or whose strengths outweigh their weaknesses. Each book should be judged on its own merits. Wide reading at all levels and careful observation of children's reactions to books and of their individual and special interests will also help adults make wise choices in guiding young readers.

Adult References and Book Selection Aids*

AIKEN, JOAN. *The Way to Write for Children.*
BATOR, ROBERT, comp. *Signposts to Criticism of Children's Literature.*
BECHTEL, LOUISE SEAMAN. *Books in Search of Children.*
BLISHEN, EDWARD, ed. *The Thorny Paradise.*
BUTLER, FRANCELIA, and RICHARD ROTERT. *Reflections on Literature for Children.*
CAMERON, ELEANOR. *The Green and Burning Tree.* Chapter, "Of Style and the Stylist."

*Complete bibliographic data are provided in Appendices A and B.

CARPENTER, HUMPHREY, and MARI PRICHARD. *The Oxford Companion to Children's Literature.*
CHAMBERS, AIDAN. *Introducing Books to Children.*
CHAMBERS, NANCY, ed. *The Signal Approach to Children's Books.*
COMMIRE, ANNE. *Something About the Author: Facts and Pictures About Contemporary Authors and Illustrators of Books for Young People.*
————. *Yesterday's Authors of Books for Children.*
COTT, JONATHAN. *Pipers at the Gates of Dawn: The Wisdom of Children's Literature.*
CULLINAN, BERNICE. *Literature and the Child.*
DONELSON, KENNETH L., and ALLEEN PACE NILSEN. *Literature for Today's Young Adults,* 3rd ed.
EGOFF, SHEILA. *The Republic of Childhood: A Critical Guide to Canadian Children's Literature in English.*
EGOFF, SHEILA, G. T. STUBBS, and L.F. ASHLEY, eds. *Only Connect: Readings on Children's Literature.*
ENGLAND, CLAIRE, and ADELE FASICK. *Childview: Evaluating and Reviewing Materials for Children.*
FENWICK, SARA INNIS, ed. *A Critical Approach to Children's Literature.* Papers by Rosenheim and Nesbitt.
FIELD, CAROLYN W., ed. *Special Collections in Children's Literature.*
FIELD, ELINOR WHITNEY, comp. *Horn Book Reflections: On Children's Books and Reading.*
FISHER, MARGERY. *Intent Upon Reading.*
————. *Who's Who in Children's Books.*
FOX, GEOFF, ed. *Writers, Critics and Children.*
HAVILAND, VIRGINIA. *Children's Literature: A Guide to Reference Sources.*
HEARNE, BETSY. *Choosing Books for Children: A Commonsense Guide.*
HEARNE, BETSY, and MARILYN KAYE, eds. *Celebrating Children's Books: Essays on Children's Literature in Honor of Zena Sutherland.*
HENDRICKSON, LINNEA. *Children's Literature: A Guide to the Criticism.*
HILDICK, WALLACE. *Children and Fiction.* Chapter, "Adult Responsibility: Authors' and Critics'."
HOFFMAN, MIRIAM, and EVA SAMUELS, eds. *Authors and Illustrators of Children's Books.*
HOLTZE, SALLY HOLMES, ed. *Sixth Book of Junior Authors & Illustrators.*
HUCK, CHARLOTTE S. *Children's Literature in the Elementary School.*
HUNTER, MOLLIE. *Talent Is Not Enough.*
JONES, DOLORES BLYTHE. *Children's Literature Awards and Winners: A Directory of Prizes, Authors and Illustrators.*
KIRKPATRICK, DANIEL, ed. *Twentieth Century Children's Writers.*
LANES, SELMA G. *Down the Rabbit Hole: Adventures and Misadventures in the Realm of Children's Literature.*

LEPMAN, JELLA. *A Bridge of Children's Books.*

LUKENS, REBECCA J. *A Critical Handbook of Children's Literature*, 4th ed.

MAHONY, BERTHA E., and ELINOR WHITNEY FIELD, eds. *Newbery Medal Books, 1922–1955.*

MEACHAM, MARY. *Information Sources in Children's Literature.*

MEEK, MARGARET, AIDAN WARLOW, and GRISELDA BARTON. *The Cool Web: The Pattern of Children's Reading.*

PATERSON, KATHERINE. *Gates of Excellence: On Reading and Writing Books for Children.*

PETERSON, LINDA and MARILYN SOLT, comps. *Newbery and Caldecott Medal and Honor Books: An Annotated Bibliography.*

POLETTE, NANCY, and MARJORIE HAMLIN. *Exploring Books with Gifted Children.*

PURVES, ALAN C., and DIANNE L. MONSON. *Experiencing Children's Literature.*

ROSENBLATT, LOUISE E. *Literature as Exploration.*

SAYERS, FRANCES CLARKE. *Summoned by Books: Essays and Speeches by Frances Clarke Sayers.*

SCHOOL LIBRARY JOURNAL/LIBRARY JOURNAL. *Issues in Children's Book Selection.*

SMITH, LILLIAN. *The Unreluctant Years.*

TOWNSEND, JOHN ROWE. *A Sense of Story.*

————. *A Sounding of Storytellers.*

WILSON, BARBARA KER. *Writing for Children: An English Editor and Author's Point of View.*

WYNDHAM, LEE. *Writing for Children and Teen-Agers.*

Chapter Three

The History of Children's Books

The flood of children's books being published today is so overpowering that it is important to remind ourselves that there are old books in children's literature as fresh and appealing today as they were a hundred years ago. There are also old books for children which have been discarded, and properly so. Age is no guarantee of a book's excellence, nor recency of its significance. Some of the discards we shall glance at briefly, only to know their kind and to be wary of their reappearance in modern dress—because that is what happens. Pedantic or moralistic stories still appear, although they are neither as frequently published nor as highly praised as they were in the past. The successors to the penny thrillers of decades ago are churned out today in patterned style in series books, such as the *Nancy Drew* stories or paperback romances, and as comic books, where they outdo the penny thrillers in superficiality of characterization and plethora of action. We have not arrived at our wealth of fine modern books for children without considerable trial and error, and the errors are difficult to eradi-

cate. We need perspective in judging children's books. We need to look at the past with modern eyes and view the present with the accumulated wisdom of the past. Where and how did children's literature begin? What has it grown out of and where is it going?

Before children can read, their acquaintance with literature begins, as it began for the race, through listening to the songs and stories of their people. All peoples had their explanations of the beginnings of the world, the coming of their own family or tribe, and the natural phenomena that delighted or terrified them. Mothers chanted or sang to their babies. In simpler days, old people told homely tales of the beasts and kept alive legends of strange events. Older people have always been the custodians of traditional tales, both of families and of the larger group, the tribe or the village. They told stories to the adults of daring exploits and great adventures, and we may be sure the children listened. The professional storytellers, the bards or minstrels, took these tales, embroidered and polished them, and made them into the ballads or the hero tales or the epics of the people. So unwritten folk literature grew and was passed on by word of mouth for centuries before the collectors gathered it together for printing. Much of it was bloody and terrible; some of it was romantic, some coarse and

Illustration for the William Caxton edition of *Aesop's Fables*.

humorous, told by adults to adults. Undoubtedly the children listened and loved many of these tales never intended for their ears and begged for them again and again. We say this with confidence because that is the way they have acquired much of their literature in every generation. Today, children watch adult television programs, take over adult songs, and read the same comics that adults read. They appropriate from adult material those things they understand and enjoy.

The Earliest Books

In the several centuries before the invention of movable type, all books for children were instructional, written by monastic teachers and chiefly intended for the children of wealthy families. These lesson books, often in Latin, began the tradition of didacticism that was to dominate children's books for hundreds of years and to persist as an influence into contemporary times.

Aldhelm (640?–709), abbot of Malmesbury, set the pattern used until the end of the sixteenth century of a text that was either rhymed or in question-and-answer form. In the eleventh century Anselm (1033–1109), archbishop of Canterbury, wrote an encyclopedia that treated such topics as manners and customs, natural science, children's duties, morals, and religious precepts. Such books were meant to instruct and to instill in children edifying

principles of belief and conduct; they were not meant to give delight to the young.

It has been argued that the first printed book intended to be read specifically by children, apart from elementary Latin grammars, was a French courtesy book on table manners that was published a few decades after the invention of printing. In about 1487, there appeared *Les Contenances de la Table,* possibly by Jean Du Pré, which contained rhyming quatrains and was apparently very popular, since several fifteenth-century editions survive.

For Adults: Fables, Romances, Adventures

William Caxton (1422–1491) was England's first printer. He issued a series of books which are still appearing in various versions on our publishers' book lists for children. Caxton's books included, among other titles, Sir Thomas Malory's *Morte d'Arthur, The Recuyell of the Historyes of Troye, The Boke of Histories of Jason, The Historye of Reynart the Foxe,* and *Aesop's Fables.* Tales of King Arthur still give the older child a fine introduction to romance, the story of Odysseus remains a popular adventure story, and the fables are enjoyed by young children even if they do skip the morals. Although Caxton intended his books for adults, children took many of them for themselves, and versions of these same collections continue to delight each generation.

For Children: Hornbooks and Battledores

While textbooks will not be discussed in detail, no account of children's books is complete without a word about the hornbooks and the battledores. The hornbooks, which first appeared in the 1440s, were not books at all but little wooden paddles on which were pasted lesson sheets of vellum or parchment. These sheets were covered with transparent horn and bound along the edges by strips of brass. Most of the hornbooks were two and three-fourths by five inches. The lesson sheets began with a cross followed by the alphabet (sometimes in both large and small letters) and by syllables: *ab, eb, ib,* and other vowel and consonant combinations. There would probably be "In the Name of the Father, the Son, and the Holy Ghost" and the Lord's Prayer. The hornbooks differed in content, but in general they were designed to teach the child letters and their combinations and to continue religious instruction. There is still in existence a little hornbook supposedly used by Queen Elizabeth I. We know that these first hornbooks made their way to the New World for the instruction of Puritan children.

The battledore, which was conceived by one of John Newbery's helpers, was in use from about 1746 to 1770. It had three folding cardboard leaves. Unlike the hornbook, it had no religious material but contained alphabets, easy reading, numerals, and woodcut illustrations. Neither the hornbook nor the battledore ever carried anything that was remotely entertaining, so children still sampled adult books.

And a Picture Book

In 1657 a Moravian bishop and educator, John Amos Comenius (1592–1671) put into practice his belief in better education for the young by preparing what is described today as the first picture book—*Orbis Pictus* (The World Illustrated).[1] Comenius's preface indicates the author's sensitivity to children's need for interesting material: "See then here a new help for Schooles, a Picture and Nomenclature of all the chief things in the World, and of mens Actions in their way of Living!" It would serve, he hoped, "to entice Witty Children to it . . . to stir up the Attention . . . by sport, and a merry pastime."

Pedlar's Treasury: A Tu'penny Treat

Then came the chapmen, the pedlars of the seventeenth and eighteenth centuries, with newssheets, ballads, broadsides, and chapbooks tucked in among their trinkets. Chapbooks were cheap little books that could be bought for as little as a penny. They had from sixteen to thirty-two or sixty-four pages, often not stitched but merely folded. F. J. H. Darton, in *Children's Books in England,* tells us that surviving copies have been found all carefully sewed with bits of silk or ribbon, perhaps by some young owner. The editors or compilers of these little books took the legends of antiquity, the old tales of the Middle Ages, elements of the fairy tales—any stories they could lay their hands on—and retold them in drastically condensed versions. All literary charm was lost; the grammar was often faulty, but what remained was a heightened sense of action with an adventure on almost every page. The educated upper classes of England may have frowned upon the chapbooks, but the common people loved them and bought them continually. Of course the children discovered them and became ardent patrons of the pedlar's treasures, too.

From a photograph in *A Little History of the Horn-Book* by Beulah Folmsbee. The Horn Book, 1942.

---

[1] An edition of *Orbis Pictus,* published in 1887 by C. W. Bardeen, has been reissued by the Singing Tree Press. See Chapter 5 for further discussion of *Orbis Pictus.*

The stories were the kind that children have always liked—adventure stories with heroes who do things. The account of their valiant deeds fills a book: *Chapbooks of the Eighteenth Century* by John Ashton. "The History of Valentine and Orson" is the story of twin brothers who were separated in infancy, Orson to be raised by a bear and Valentine to be reared by a king of France. Later, Valentine captured the wild Orson and they performed great deeds together, each winning the hand of a lovely princess. The bear child, Orson, is a forerunner of Mowgli in Kipling's *Jungle Books*.

One favorite, "Tom Hickathrift," is a kind of early English Paul Bunyan. "At ten years old he was six feet high and three in thickness, his hand was like a shoulder of mutton, and every other part proportionable." He pulled up trees, slew giants, and felled four highwaymen at a blow.

Tom Thumb.

How *Tom Thumb* fell into the Pudding-Bowl, and of his escape out of the Tinkers Budget.

He sat upon the pudding-bowl, the Candle for to hold,
A 4   Of

From the chapbook *Tom Thumb His Life and Death.*
Reproduced from an edition (circa 1665) in the John G.
White Collection, Cleveland Public Library.

In contrast to the colossal Tom Hickathrift, there is Tom Thumb, whose story is told in a chapbook rhymed version of "Tom Thumb His Life and Death." The woodcuts from 1630 show this tiny hero early in his career falling into a bowl of pudding but later riding valiantly into battle atop an enormous war horse.

The attitude of serious-minded adults of the day toward these crude, often vulgar little books was generally scornful. The clergy viewed them with alarm, but at least one man of letters spoke a good word for them. Richard Steele, in *The Tatler* (No. 95), tells how his young godson was "much turned in his studies" to these histories and adds:

He would tell you the mismanagements of John Hickerthrift, find fault with the passionate temper of Bevis of Southampton and loved St. George for being the champion of England: and by this means had his thoughts insensibly moulded into the notions of discretion, virtue, and honour.

This may be a charitable interpretation of the effects of chapbook reading, but Florence Barry, in *A Century of Children's Books*, adds a cheerful note also. She says:

John Bunyan was the first to reconcile the claims of religion and romance, and he could never have written The Pilgrim's Progress *if he had not been a good customer of the pedlar in his youth.* (pp. 6–7)

Badly written, crudely illustrated, unhonored though they were, the chapbooks preserved and popularized some of the precious elements of literature that children love. But their coarseness probably paved the way for the reaction against tales, stories, and jests—a reaction which produced children's books full of somber warnings and doleful examples.

The Puritans and Perdition

Even while the chapmen were peddling their lurid, lighthearted "Histories," the religious movement was under way that was to affect life on both sides of the Atlantic. Beginning in the late 1500s, about the middle of Queen Elizabeth's reign, the English had become "the people of a book, and that book was the Bible.'' In London people went daily, in great crowds, to St. Paul's to hear the Bible read aloud, and small Bibles were found in homes everywhere.

A group of deeply religious people whom we know as the Puritans read their Bibles with fervor. They venerated the victims of religious persecution and studied Foxe's *Book of Martyrs* (1563), with its details of death at the stake, and gave the book to their children.

As if this legacy of terror was not enough for small Puritans to endure, a clergyman, James Janeway, wrote in 1671 or 1672 a famous book that was long popular with the heaven-bent adults who ruled over Puritan nurseries. Its full title was:

A Token For Children: *being an Exact Account of the Conversion, Holy and Exemplary Lives, and Joyful Deaths of several young Children. To which is now added, Prayers and Graces, fitted for the use of little Children.*

There were thirteen good little children in this gloomy book, and, considering their lives, it is small wonder that they died young. They spent their time trying to reform, convert, and generally improve everyone they encountered. They brooded on sin and eternal torment and the state of their souls. Morbid and unnatural as this book was with its continual dwelling on death, it grew from the earnest desire of the Puritans to make children happy—not in our modern sense of the word, but in theirs. This meant being secure in the avoidance of Hell and the assurance of Heaven. Unfortunately their method of instilling religious ideas was chiefly through the use of fear—the fear of Hell.

Out of the Puritan world there emerged one great book for children—Bunyan's *Pilgrim's Progress* (Part I, 1678; Part II, 1684). This book was intended for adults and probably reached the children piecemeal as they listened to the adults read it aloud, or discuss it, or tell the more dramatic portions. Reviewing the story, we can easily understand why children enjoyed the book. It is told in the best tradition of the old fairy tales John Bunyan had enjoyed in chapbook form when he was a boy. Bunyan had published, also in 1678, *A Book for Boys and Girls or Country Rhymes for Children.*

Viewpoint

For, in spite of its seriousness of purpose and gravity of tone, the moral literature of the late eighteenth and early nineteenth centuries lacked a sense of urgency. It presupposed the stable society and the traditional parish organization. Its rational approach and dependence upon logical argument in the overworked form of dialogue precluded activity and humour. Child characters, with a few happy exceptions like Maria Edgeworth's Rosamond, were not childlike; present, like the young reader, to be instructed, they had the sameness of creatures of fable, obviously contrived to show the progression from ignorance to knowledge. The point of view in all this literature was that of the parent or mentor. Reason was exalted, and emotion either discouraged or directed into approved channels.

Margaret Nancy Cutt, *Ministering Angels: A Study of Nineteenth-Century Evangelical Writing for Children.* Five Owls Press, Ltd., 1979, p. 7.

John Bunyan (1628–1688), a humble tinker, confessed that one of the sins of his youth was his delight in the "History of the Life and Death of that Noble Knight Sir Bevis of Southampton." As he grew more and more religious, he put away all such light reading and turned to the Bible and to fear-inspiring books such as John Foxe's *Book of Martyrs.* He began to preach such fiery and fearsome sermons that he was locked up for nonconformity to the established Church of England. In jail for years with his Bible and his *Martyrs,* he began to write the story of a Christian soul on its troublesome pilgrimage through this world to everlasting life. Sir Bevis was not forgotten but was reborn as Christian; the giant Ascapart became the Giant Despair; and so, in good fairy-tale style, Christian fought monsters and enemies with properly symbolic names. But no chapbook tale was ever so somber and so dramatic as this progress of a Christian pilgrim. It begins as a dream:

As I went through the wild waste of this world, I came to a place where there was a den, and I lay down in it to sleep. While I slept, I had a dream, and lo! I saw a man whose clothes were in rags, and he stood with his face from his own house, with a book in his hand, and a great load on his back.

In its original form, with long interludes of theological moralizing, children would have difficulty reading this book, but when the dramatic story is cleared of these obstructions, it is a moving tale. In 1939 an edition abridged and illustrated by Robert Lawson was published.

The *Mayflower* reached our shores in 1620, but the great exodus of Puritans from England to the New World did not take place until around 1630. We can well imagine that those early years of colonization were too difficult for any excursions into book publishing for either children or adults, but the Puritans' passion for education could not long be submerged. The history of their activities in New England is alive with a deep and growing concern for schools and the tools of education, books. As

From *The New England Primer; or An Easy and Pleasant Guide to the Art of Reading.* Massachusetts Sabbath School Society.

early as 1632, there are references to hornbooks, brought from England with the crosses blotted out—crosses being at that time a religious symbol to which the Puritans objected.

The first book for children to be published in the New World appeared in 1646. It was written by John Cotton and its full title was:

Milk for Babes, Drawn out of the Breasts of Both Testaments, Chiefly for the Spirituall Nourishment of Boston Babes in either England, but may be of like Use for any Children.

Beneath this title it adds *A Catechism in Verse*, and begins:

> *Who is the Maker of all things?*
> *The Almighty God who reigns on high.*
> *He form'd the earth, He spread the sky.*

It continues with all the intricate details of Puritan theology.

Editions of the *New England Primer* published as early as 1691 have been found, although it is known to have been in print before that. Its famous rhyming alphabet begins:

> *In Adam's fall*
> *We sinned all.*
>
> *Thy life to mend*
> *God's Book attend.*

In addition, the book contains prayers, poems, the shorter catechism, the Ten Commandments, Bible verses, and pictures. One of these is a quaint woodcut of a Dame's school; another is the picture of a mournful figure contemplating a tombstone; and a third is a graphic illustration of the burning of Mr. John Rogers, with his wife and ten children looking on, while a jaunty man-at-arms holds them at bay. With tombs and torture, it is difficult to justify the subtitle, "An Easy and Pleasant Guide to the Art of Reading."

As late as 1832, Boston had its own descendant of Janeway's *Token*. It was written by Perkins and Marvin and the title page reads as follows:

> *Mary Lothrop*
> *Who Died In*
> *Boston*
> *1831*

The authors add in their preface that their Memoir was prepared "for the purpose of adding another to the bright pictures set before children to allure them into the paths of piety." This was a fairly large book for those days, about three by seven inches, and fully three fourths of it is devoted to the pious Mary's interminable death. The charming little frontispiece shows Mary and her little brother kneeling beside a chair, praying. The boy has struck his sister, and Mary is praying him into a state of repentance. Shortly after that, Mary becomes ill and begins her preparations for death. Gloom descends for the remaining pages. It is to be hoped that Boston children who were given this "bright picture" had recourse to the lusty nonsense of *Mother Goose*. For, despite the Puritans, a pirated edition of this cheerful volume was printed in the New World in 1785.

Fairy Tales and Fables in France

Paul Hazard in his delightful *Books, Children and Men* calls attention to the early portraits of children clad in long velvet skirts, heavily plumed hats, corsets, swords, and ornaments and he remarks, "If, for centuries, grownups did not even think of giving children appropriate clothes, how would it ever have occurred to them to provide children with suitable books?"

Yet around 1697 this miracle occurred in France with the publication of *Histoires ou contes du temps passé avec des moralités* (Histories or Tales of Long Ago with Morals), or, more familiarly, *Contes de ma Mère l'Oye* (Tales of Mother Goose). There is some question today as to whether the tales were written for adults or for children. But whatever the author's intention, they were loved by children. The stories were "La belle au bois dormant" (The Sleeping Beauty); "La petite chaperon rouge" (Little Red Riding Hood); "La Barbe Bleue" (Blue Beard); "Le Maître chat, ou le chat botté" (The Master Cat, or Puss in Boots); "Les fées" (Diamonds and Toads); "Cendrillon, ou la petite pantoufle de verre" (Cinderella, or the Little Glass Slipper); "Riquet à la houpe" (Riquet with the Tuft); and "Le petit poucet" (Little Thumb).

From *Beauty and the Beast*, illustrated by Eleanor Vere Boyle.

Did Charles Perrault (1628–1703), member of the French Academy and author of many serious but forgotten works, collect these traditional tales, or was it his eldest son, Pierre Perrault d'Armancour? "Today informed opinion in France . . . favours the son and we may very well leave it at that."[2] Perrault's Fairy Tales, we call them, and their immortality is due as much to the spontaneity and charm of the style as to the traditional content.[3]

Using Aesop and *The Fables of Bidpai* as sources, Jean de la Fontaine (1621–1695) wrote fables to amuse court circles, but they are savored by children today just as they were when they appeared as a series of twelve books in the years 1668–1694. Mme. d'Aulnoy (1650?–1705) turned the old folktale themes

[2]Percy Muir, *English Children's Books, 1600–1900* (Praeger, 1969), p. 49.

[3]For a fascinating account of the "lost manuscript" of 1695, see May Hill Arbuthnot, "Puss, the Perraults and a Lost Manuscript," *Elementary English*, October 1969, pp. 715–721.

into ornate novels for the court. "The Yellow Dwarf" and "Graciosa and Percinet" are sometimes adapted for modern collections but are rarely seen in their original form. Mme. de Beaumont (1711–1780), busy with the education of children, also took time to write some fairy tales for them. Of these, her "Beauty and the Beast" has survived deservedly. Still others took a hand at the fairy tales, but none with the freshness of Perrault.

John Newbery's Books

Meanwhile, in England, it was a happy day for children, steering a perilous course between the pedlar and the Puritan, when in 1729 R. Samber translated Perrault's *Tales of Mother Goose.* No chapbook was ever so thrilling as these eight tales, no "good Godly book" was ever so beloved. At the time, they must have attracted the attention of an English publisher by the name of John Newbery. Not only did his firm later use the title *Mother Goose,* but he may also have discovered through the popularity of the tales the importance of the child as a potential consumer of books.

John Newbery was what we would call today "a character." He dabbled in many things. He wrote; he published; he befriended indigent authors; he did a flourishing business manufacturing and dispensing medicines and a "Medicinal Dictionary." In 1744, along with Dr. James's Fever Powders, Newbery offered for sale his publication:

A LITTLE PRETTY
POCKET-BOOK
Intended for the
Instruction and Amusement
of
Little Master Tommy,
and
Pretty Miss Polly.
With Two Letters from
Jack the Giant-Killer;
As also
A Ball and a Pincushion;
The Use of which will infallibly make
Tommy
a good Boy and Polly a good Girl.

To which is added,
A Little Song-Book,
Being
A New Attempt to teach Children
the Use of the English Alphabet,
by way of Diversion.

For the *"amusement"* of Tommy and Polly, "by way of *diversion"*—here is a new approach to books for children and a momentous one. It marks the beginning of English books for their delight! Of course, Jack the Giant-Killer wrote two exceedingly moral letters to the readers of the *Pretty Pocket-Book.*[4] He had evidently reformed and settled down since the chapbook days, for his lectures are as mild as milk, with no threats anywhere. The letters are followed by a series of games with rhymed directions and morals: marbles, shuttle-cock, blindman's buff, thread the needle, leap frog, and many other old favorites. There are fables, proverbs, and rules of behavior, with a rhyming alphabet and a few poems thrown in for good measure. The morals to the fables are made more romantic and palatable by the signature of Jack the Giant-Killer. The success of the *Pocket-Book* evidently encouraged the publisher because other books for children followed rapidly.

In 1765 *The Renowned History of Little Goody Two Shoes, Otherwise Called Mrs. Margery Two Shoes,* appeared. This is a short juvenile novel, the first of its kind to be written expressly for children. Oliver Goldsmith is supposed to have written *Goody Two Shoes,* which tells the story of a virtuous and clever child, Margery *Meanwell.* At the opening of the book, Margery's father suffers "the wicked persecutions of Sir Timothy *Gripe* and Farmer *Graspall,"* who managed to ruin him and turn the whole family out of house and lands. The parents quickly die (evidently no Dr. James's Fever Powders available), leaving Margery and her brother Tommy destitute. Tommy goes to sea and Margery is rescued by charitable Clergyman Smith and his wife.

[4]No copies of the first English edition (1744) have survived. But in 1944, the two-hundredth anniversary of its first appearance, F. G. Melcher issued a reproduction of the first American edition, which was a reprint by Isaiah Thomas published in 1787 in Worcester, Mass. You can now examine the *Pocket-Book* gaily bedecked with a flowery gilt paper cover after Newbery's custom.

24   The *great* A Play.

CHUCK-FARTHING.

A S you value your Pence,
   At the *Hole* take your Aim;
Chuck all safely in,
   And you'll win the Game.

M O R A L.

Chuck-Farthing, like Trade,
   Requires great Care;
The more you observe,
   The better you'll fare.

The *little* a Play.   25

Flying the KITE

U PHELD in Air, the gaudy Kite,
   High as an Eagle takes her Flight;
But if the Winds their Breath restrain,
   She tumbles headlong down again.

RULE *of* LIFE.

Soon as thou seest the Dawn of Day,
To God thy Adoration pay.

From *The Original Mother Goose's Melody*. Reproduced in facsimile by W. H. Whitmore (Joel Munsell's Sons, 1899) from the edition reprinted by Isaiah Thomas of Worcester, Massachusetts, about 1785.

When they buy her two shoes, the child is so overcome with pleasure that she keeps crying out, "Two shoes, Madam, see my two shoes"— hence her name.

This happiness is short-lived, for Gripe forces Smith to turn her out of the house. Back to the hedgerows once more, Margery teaches herself to read with remarkable ease by studying the schoolbooks of more fortunate children. Soon she knows more than any of them and decides to advance their learning. She makes up an alphabet of wooden blocks or "rattle traps" with both small and large letters, puts them into a basket, and goes from house to house helping children to read. Her methods apparently work like a charm, for all her young pupils respond immediately with never a "retarded reader" in the whole countryside.[5]

Goody Two Shoes is full of sociological lessons; its characters are types rather than individuals. Nevertheless, it was entertaining and it was a child's book. Many adults, notably Charles Lamb, recalled the pleasure it gave them when they read it as children.

Between 1760 and 1766, John Newbery, according to many scholars, also published the first edition of *Mother Goose*,[6] but no trace of such a book remains and no contemporary reference to or advertisement of the book has ever been uncovered.[7] On the basis of their research, Jacques Barchilon and Henry Pettit[8] now assert that there was no such publication during those years. They assume that John Newbery may have planned such a book, but not until 1781 was there an advertisement announcing the first publication by his stepson, T. Carnan, of *Mother Goose's Melody*. John Newbery's firm remained in the family for many years and continued to publish books for children.

The first American edition of *Mother Goose* appeared about 1785 and was probably a pirated reprint of an early Newbery edition. It was published by Isaiah Thomas (1749–1831), of Worcester, Massachusetts, who cheerfully and not quite legally printed his own editions of Newbery's books, possibly for mercenary motives but certainly to the benefit of young Americans. W. H. Whitmore vouched for the

[6]Even the scholarly Opies give 1765–1766 in their *Oxford Dictionary of Nursery Rhymes* (Oxford, 1951), p. 33.

[7]See Chapter 4 for a discussion of *Mother Goose*. Other children's classics mentioned in this chapter are discussed more fully in later chapters. See the Index for relevant page references.

[8]*The Authentic Mother Goose Fairy Tales and Nursery Rhymes* (Denver: Alan Swallow, 1960), p. 11.

[5]*The Renowned History of Little Goody Two Shoes, Otherwise Called Mrs. Margery Two Shoes*. Attributed to Oliver Goldsmith. Edited by Charles Welsh.

fact that two copies of this Isaiah Thomas edition existed in his day, and in 1889 he reproduced the book in full, calling it *The Original Mother Goose's Melody.*[9] The little book is two and one-half by three and three-fourths inches. Preface, fifty-two jingles with maxims, sixteen songs of Shakespeare, and small wood-cuts are precisely the same as in the English edition. The maxims are surprising and often amusing, especially the one that follows "Margery Daw," which will surely be applauded by all bewildered readers of footnotes: "It is a mean and scandalous Practice in Authors to put Notes to Things that deserve no Notice."

It is fitting that John Newbery, this first English publisher of books for children, is honored annually when the Newbery Medal is presented for the year's most distinguished book for children written by an American citizen or resident and published in the United States.[10]

Robinson Crusoe

One book emerged from the Puritan world to mark not only the increase of cheerfulness but the beginning of contemporary adventure tales. It was Daniel Defoe's *Robinson Crusoe,* one of the most popular books in all English literature.

Defoe (1659–1731), with a wisdom far in advance of his times, wrote on banks, insurance companies, schools for women, asylums for the insane, and all sorts of social problems. He turned out bitter political and religious satires which landed him in the pillory. He rose to wealth and fame and sank to penury and prison more than once. Writing was his passion, and few men have written more continuously. His most famous book, *The Life and Strange Surprising Adventures of Robinson Crusoe,* appeared in 1719, when Defoe was sixty and nearing the end of his turbulent career. We are told four

editions of it were printed in four months, and for once the old fighter enjoyed fame with no unhappy repercussions of any kind.

Why has this book commended itself to children of each succeeding generation? It was addressed to adults and originally contained masses of moral ruminations that the children must have skipped with their usual agility in the avoidance of boredom. Most children's editions today omit these tiresome reflections and get on with the story.

Here is a book that satisfies children's hunger to achieve competence. Identifying with Robinson Crusoe, they win an ordered, controlled place in the world by their own efforts and foresight. With the coming of Friday, they have the love of a friend whom they in turn nurture and protect. The theme itself is irresistible: man pitted against nature, one man with a whole world to create and control. He must obtain food, provide himself with clothes and shelter, fight off wild animals, reckon time, keep himself civilized and sane.

The theme of the shipwrecked survivor was used in many books following publication of *Robinson Crusoe,* among them *The Swiss Family Robinson,* written by Johann David Wyss (1743–1818) and published in 1812. Despite its pedantic overtones, this story of a pious, energetic family on a desert island delighted worldwide audiences with its dramatic events.

Gulliver's Travels

Another remarkable book emerged from this period, a political satire not intended for children but read by them and known today as *Gulliver's Travels.* The author, Jonathan Swift (1667–1745), was born in Dublin and died there, Dean of the Cathedral. But between his birth and death, he spent considerable time in London and took an active part in the political life of the times. Recognized today as one of the greatest satirists in English literature, Swift wrote his book in Ireland to lampoon the follies of the English court, its parties, its politics, and its statesmen. Worried about the reception of the book, he published it anonymously in 1726 as *Travels into Several Remote Nations of the World,* in four parts, by Lemuel Gulliver. To Swift's surprise and relief, London society, the

---

[9]W. H. Whitmore, ed. *The Original Mother Goose's Melody* (Joel Munsell's Sons, 1889). It is reproduced in facsimile from the Isaiah Thomas edition (Worcester, Massachusetts, 1785). Whitmore's introduction gives many interesting facts about the early collections of *Mother Goose.*

[10]For the list of books which have been awarded the Newbery Medal, see Appendix D.

From *Gulliver's Travels* by Jonathan Swift, illustrated by Louis Rhead.

Poets and Children

About the time *Robinson Crusoe* and *Gulliver's Travels* were published, a gentle nonconformist preacher wrote a book of poetry for children. Isaac Watts (1674–1748) moralized in verse about busy bees and quarrelsome dogs, but he also wrote tender and beautiful hymns, many of which are found today in most hymnals. His *Divine and Moral Songs for Children* (1715) dwelt not on the fearful judgments of God, but on God "our refuge," and many a child must have been comforted by his tender "Cradle Hymn."

Toward the end of the seventeenth century, a major poet, William Blake (1757–1827), published a book of poems for and about children. In his *Songs of Innocence* (1789), each poem is illustrated with Blake's own decorative designs. Although it is now considered an epoch-making book, it caused no stir at the time of its publication. A companion volume, *Songs of Experience* (1794), followed. Although most of Blake's unique lyrics are geared for adult audiences, some of his other poetry appeals to children also.

Ann (1782–1866) and Jane (1783–1824) Taylor's *Original Poems for Infant Minds: By Several Young Persons* (1804) teaches lessons in the manner of Watts's *Moral Songs*, but with a difference. The vigorous, fun-loving Taylors usually tell good stories in their verse and reveal something of the simple, pleasant life of rural England. Unlike Blake's *Songs of Innocence*, the book by the Taylors' enjoyed immediate popularity and was translated into various languages, but it is best known today for the familiar "Twinkle, twinkle, little star."

The Butterfly's Ball, published in book form in 1807, was written by William Roscoe (1753–1831), a lawyer and member of Parliament, for the amusement of his little son. There is no story, but there are such fascinating details as a mushroom table with a water dock leaf tablecloth, and there are William Mulready's charming pictures of the insect guests at the ball. However, the verse is tame, and the long popularity of the poem must have been due in part to lack of better verse for children.

very society he was making fun of, was highly diverted. In these tall tales the humor sometimes overshadows the satire.

Children have always loved things in miniature, and they soon discovered the land of the Lilliputians. No one ever forgets Gulliver's waking to find six-inch people walking over him and Lilliputian ropes binding him. All the fascinating details are worked out to scale with logic and precision. Children are untroubled by any double meanings and like the fantasy for itself. The second journey, to the land of giants, Brobdingnag, is the next most popular, but is not so appealing as the omnipotent Gulliver in Lilliput. The remaining books most children never read.

If Gulliver's travels had not fascinated artists, the book might not have survived in children's reading as long as it has. An early edition illustrated by Charles E. Brock (1894) and later editions illustrated by Arthur Rackham and by Fritz Eichenberg would lure anyone into reading the story.

Didacticism in France, England, and the United States

A pervasive influence in his time, John Locke (1632–1704) was a political and educational philosopher who promulgated the idea that children were rational creatures with individual needs, not miniature adults to be taught by rote. Believing in the effectiveness of learning through play rather than force-fed inculcation of social values and mores, in the progression of observation, ideas, and concepts in a learning system, Locke affected both educators and authors through the ideas contained in *Some Thoughts Concerning Education* (1693). Many of his ideas: early childhood education, human development, and educational theory are again influential, but they were comparatively ignored in the nineteenth century, in part eclipsed by a revival of didacticism, and in part overshadowed by a lively response to the concepts advocated by the author of *Émile*.

In 1762 Jean Jacques Rousseau (1712–1778) proclaimed his theory of a new day for children through his book *Émile*. He believed in the joyous unfolding of a child's powers through a free, happy life. The child Émile was the companion of his tutor; he was free of all books except *Robinson Crusoe;* and he lived vigorously out of doors, learning from experiences and activities. Ideas similar to Rousseau's emphasis on experiences and activities are found in schools today.

In its day *Émile* effected a revolutionary change in people's attitudes toward both children and education. To some people, Rousseau seemed like a breeze blowing away the clouds of Puritan morbidity, and one would naturally expect the ardent Rousseau converts, if they wrote books for children, to write only the happiest ones. Instead, in France, in England, and even in the United States, they began to write painfully didactic stories, sometimes to teach religion, sometimes to inform and educate. The only thing these writers seemed to have carried over from Rousseau was the idea of following and developing the child's natural

interests. In practice, they went at the business hammer and tongs. If the poor children picked strawberries, the experience was turned into an arithmetic lesson. If they rolled a snowball, they learned about levers and proceeded from those to wedges. If they took a walk, they had to observe every bird, beast, stone, and human occupation. Day and night these ardent authors stalked their children, allowing them never a moment for play or fancy but instructing and improving on every page. No longer did they threaten children with the fear of Hell, but the pressure of Information hung almost as heavily over their hapless heads.

Here was a revival of didacticism with a vengeance—not the terrifying theological didacticism of the Puritans but the intellectual and moralistic variety. Those who wish to read more about this period should study the works of the French Mme. de Genlis (1746–1830) and Armand Berquin (1749–1791) and those of such English writers as Laetitia Barbauld (1743–1825), Sarah Trimmer (1741–1810), and Hannah More (1745–1833). For most readers, a few examples of this writing will probably suffice.

One of the classic examples of the new didacticism is *The History of Sandford and Merton* (1783–1789) in four volumes by Thomas Day (1749–1789). Tommy Merton was the spoiled, helpless, ignorant son of a rich gentleman, whereas Harry Sandford was the sturdy, industrious, competent child of an honest farmer. Harry was reared out of doors and trained to work and study; there was nothing he did not know and nothing he could not do. Father Merton, handicapped by wealth though he was, saw at once the advantage of having his young darling unspoiled and trained in the ways of the honest Harry. So poor Tommy, little knowing what was in store for him, was put in the charge of the same clerical tutor who had wrought such wonders with Harry. Mr. Barlow trained both boys, but Harry was always used as the perfect example to show up Tommy's ignorance, incompetence, and general orneriness. All day that worthy pair, the omniscient Barlow and the admirable Harry, instructed, disciplined, and uplifted poor Tommy. Through each of the volumes, he was plagued and polished into Rousseau-like simplicity and competence. At the end of four volumes, there he was at last—Tommy Merton remodeled, divested of all his fine apparel, his curls gone, and his life to be given over to study and philosophy forever. Could any reform go further?

Another and perhaps the most gifted exponent of didacticism in children's books was Maria Edgeworth (1767–1849), who told her moral tales with such dramatic realism that they are still remembered. She had an excellent laboratory for developing her stories as she was the second of twenty-two children. She not only helped her father with the education of the younger ones but wrote her stories in their midst, tried them out with the children, and modified them according to their suggestions. Thomas Day himself had a hand in Maria's early education, but her own father seems to have been a greater influence in her writings than anyone else.

Maria Edgeworth wrote many short stories, some deadly dull and unnatural. But at her best, she was a born storyteller. She developed real plots—the first in children's stories since the fairy tales—with well-sustained suspense and surprise endings that took some of the sting out of the inevitable morals. While she told an interesting story, her tales carry such a heavy and obvious burden of moral lessons that her characterizations and excellent plots are sacrificed to didacticism.

One writer of the period, however, not only deplored the pedantic stories written for children but tried to provide them with more entertaining fare. The best-known contribution to children's literature of Charles Lamb (1775–1835) and his sister Mary (1764–1847) is their *Tales from Shakespeare* (1806), in which they retold the plays from Shakespeare and made them more easily comprehensible and presumably more enjoyable for the young.

It was inevitable that the United States should develop its own brand of didacticism. Samuel G. Goodrich (1793–1860), who wrote under the name of Peter Parley and produced five or six volumes a year, wrote laudatory biographies of famous men and poured out a continuous stream of information in the fields of science, history, and geography. Jacob Abbott (1803–1879) launched a series in which a youth by the name of Rollo was dragged from one city and country to another, bearing up nobly under a steady barrage of travel talks and moralizing. Both men wrote well but pedantically. We shall detect some of their literary descendants in the books of today—information attractively sugared but oppressively informative nevertheless.

Our chief moralist was Martha Farquharson, pseudonym for Martha Finley (1828–1909), whose *Elsie Dinsmore* series began in 1868 and

Viewpoint

In the last quarter of the eighteenth century, the publication of children's books became a serious business—serious not merely because it was profitable but because it was taken for granted that children's books could greatly influence "the Minds of Children." The person who had discovered "the true Secret of Education," Locke wrote, was he who "found a way" to keep "a Child's Spirit, easy, active and free" while simultaneously restraining "him from many things he had a Mind to" and drawing "him to things" that were "uneasy to him." Instead of restraint, Newbery's books emphasized keeping children's spirits active and free. The shortest path to knowledge and proper conduct lay, he thought, across a landscape pepperminted with laughter. With smoke from the Gordon Riots, violent sectarian disturbances in London in 1780 that seemed to indicate instability within the nation, lingering on the horizon and with commercial growth and the spread of education beyond the upper and middle classes straining the oligarchic fabric of society, unrestrained merriment did not seem the ideal mate for wisdom in the 1780s. Although entertainment was recognized as a necessary ingredient of children's books, educators frequently pointed out the abuses of seductive playfulness.

Samuel F. Pickering, Jr., *John Locke and Children's Books in Eighteenth-Century England.* Knoxville, Tennessee: University of Tennessee Press, 1981, pp. 170–171.

ran to twenty-six volumes. This pious heroine had a way of bursting into tears or fainting with such effect that adult sinners were converted and even Elsie's worldly father was brought to a state of repentance. Most parents developed considerable resistance to Elsie but were baffled by her powers to charm their offspring. Elsie was a spellbinder, for her author had a sense of the dramatic. To this day sensible people remember weeping over Elsie's Sabbath sit-down strike at the piano, when she refused to play secular music for her erring father. She was made to sit on the piano stool until one of her best faints put an end to her martyrdom and Father repented. Elsie was a prig with glamor, and there is no telling how many more of her kind might have developed if certain pioneers had not appeared to clear away the artificiality and to bring laughter, fantasy, and realism to children's books.

Modern Books Begin

Even while Peter Parley was dispensing information, and Maria Edgeworth was teaching her heroines valuable lessons, and Martha Finley's heroine, Elsie Dinsmore, was piously swooning, epoch-making books in both England and the United States were appearing that were to modify the whole approach to children's literature. These children's classics, some as popular today as when they were first published, not only brought laughter, fantasy, and realism into stories for young people, but they began the trend toward better illustrations in children's books. Each of these books will be discussed in greater detail in later chapters; they are reviewed here because they are milestones in the development of children's literature.

Folk and Fairy Tales

Grimms' Popular Stories by Jacob (1785–1863) and Wilhelm (1786–1859) Grimm was translated into English by Edgar Taylor in 1823. Grimms' Fairy Tales, as they were called by the children, became as much a part of the literature of English-speaking children as the *Mother Goose* rhymes. These stories, some of them

gathered by the Grimm brothers from the lips of the old storytellers, were occasionally droll but often somber and harrowing.

The *Fairy Tales* of Hans Christian Andersen (1805–1875) appeared in England in 1846, translated by Mary Howitt. Many of these stories were Andersen's own adaptations of folk tales which he, too, had heard from the storytellers. But to these he added his own fanciful inventions and immeasurably enriched the child's world of the imagination. Andersen's stories have unusual literary and spiritual values, and they are, for the most part, in a minor key, melancholy and even tragic.

Joseph Jacobs (1854–1916) was the great compiler of English folk tales; and the folklorist Andrew Lang (1844–1912) began, in 1889, with the publication of *The Blue Fairy Book*, a series that is still deservedly popular.

Humor

One of the first notes of gaiety was a long story poem by an American professor, Clement Moore, entitled "A Visit from St. Nicholas" (1822), but known to children as "The Night Before Christmas." This fast-moving, humorous ballad, full of fun, fancy, and excitement, with never a threat or a dire warning to spoil the children's delight, is as beloved now as it was in Moore's day.

Under Queen Victoria, England's industrial age flourished and grew prosperous and pompous. Then suddenly two eminent men produced books that sent the children off into gales of laughter. One, Edward Lear (1812–1888), was an artist who earned his living by making scientific paintings of birds and reptiles. When he grew too bored with the drawing room, he took refuge with the children. For them he would write absurd limericks which he illustrated on the spot. His *Book of Nonsense* (1846) not only was an unprecedented collection of amusing verses and pictures but perhaps paved the way for another excursion into absurdity.

In 1865 a book appeared that is generally considered the first English masterpiece written for children. It was *Alice's Adventures in Wonderland*. The author was Charles Lutwidge Dodgson (1832–1898), an Oxford don, a lecturer in logic and mathematics, who used the pen name Lewis Carroll. *Alice* still remains a unique combination of fantasy and nonsense that is as logical as an equation. It was first told, and later written, solely for the entertainment of children, and neither it nor its sequel, *Through the Looking Glass,* has the faintest trace of a moral or a scrap of useful information or one improving lesson—only cheerful lunacy, daft and delightful. *Alice* launched the literature of nonsense and fantasy which is told so logically and reasonably that it seems entirely natural.

Two more books brought laughter to children. Written in Germany in 1844 and published the next year, *Struwwelpeter* (Slovenly Peter) by Heinrich Hoffmann (1809–1894) was a collection of merry, prankish rhyming stories intended only to entertain, although the verses are regarded by some people as brutal. It is still in print, having gone into dozens of editions in

From *The English Struwwelpeter* by Dr. Heinrich Hoffmann.

English. In America, children were captivated by the antics of the Peterkin family. Lucretia Hale (1820–1900) published a series of stories about the Peterkins in magazines, collected them in a book in 1880, and gave the young an unforgettable character: the Lady from Philadelphia.

Illustrations

Both Lear's and Carroll's laughter-provoking books have delightful illustrations—Lear's own outrageous caricatures for his *Book of Nonsense* and Sir John Tenniel's inimitable drawings for Carroll's *Alice.* Deservedly famous, too, are Walter Crane, Randolph Caldecott, and Kate Greenaway,[11] whose charming watercolors brightened the pages of children's books with decorative designs, appealing landscapes, and figures which hold their own with the best in modern books.

[11]See Chapter 5 for a fuller account of illustrators of children's books.

Frederic G. Melcher in 1938 proposed that the American Library Association institute a second award—this one for the most distinguished picture book for children published each year in the United States. At his suggestion, the new medal was named after Randolph Caldecott—a fitting memorial to the man who drew a picture of himself surrounded by children, and who left those children a delightful legacy of storytelling pictures.[12]

Myths: Hawthorne and Kingsley

In the United States Greek myths were introduced to children by a gifted novelist, Nathaniel Hawthorne (1804–1864). Around 1852 *A Wonder-Book for Girls and Boys* was published, followed in 1853 by *Tanglewood Tales for Girls and Boys.* These books contain stories of the Greek gods and heroes, supposedly told to a group of lively New England children by a young college student, Eustace Bright. Eustace talks down to the children; his gods lose much of their grandeur, and his heroes are often child-sized, but the style is delightful.

In England, Charles Kingsley (1819–1875), country parson, Victorian scholar, and poet, also retold the myths for children. His adaptations not only are closer to the original myths than Hawthorne's romantic versions, but convey the inner significance and grandeur of the myths in a style closer to the classic original. Here are dreams of greatness, presented with the sensitive perception of a poet. Interestingly, in Kingsley's own day these stories were less popular than his original fantasy, *The Water Babies* (1863), which is marred for us today by its moralizing.

Fantasy

Lewis Carroll's *Alice* was the great masterpiece of fantasy and nonsense, but the nineteenth century saw the publication of several other classics in fantasy for children. In 1841, John Ruskin (1819–1900) wrote *The King of the Golden River,* a long, serious fairy tale, and published it a decade later. In 1867, George

Macdonald (1824–1905), Scottish poet and novelist, published a delightfully playful tale, *The Light Princess,* and four years later, his most important children's fairy tale, the imaginative *At the Back of the North Wind.*

Some of the other great British writers of the period tried their hands at fantasy for children. William Makepeace Thackeray (1811–1863) contributed in 1855 *The Rose and the Ring,* a long fairy tale distinguished by its blithe humor; and in 1868, Charles Dickens (1812–1870) wrote, in the best fairy-tale tradition, *The Magic Fishbone.* Dickens's earlier story, *A Christmas Carol* (1843), is firmly ensconced in the list of hardy perennials of both Christmas literature and Victoriana. Rudyard Kipling (1865–1936), storyteller and poet, Nobel Prize winner and advocate of empire, wrote *The Jungle Books* (1894) and *Just So Stories* (1902) with a warmth and affection that make his animal characters part of the permanent heritage of children's lore, along with Beatrix Potter's *The Tale of Peter Rabbit* (1901) and Kenneth Grahame's *The Wind in the Willows* (1908).

From France came the stories of Jules Verne (1828–1905), who wrote for adults but whose books have fascinated children since the first,

From *At the Back of the North Wind* by George Macdonald, illustrated by Arthur Hughes.

---

[12]For a list of the books which have been awarded the Caldecott Medal, see Appendix D.

From the Earth to the Moon, was published in 1865. *Twenty Thousand Leagues Under the Sea* (1869) and *Around the World in Eighty Days* (1872) are still popular with both adults and children. In Verne's work, one sees the beginning of the new genre of science fiction.

From Italy came *Pinocchio* by C. Collodi (pseudonym for Carlo Lorenzini, 1826–1890). Published originally in a magazine, as so many books of this period were, the story was translated in 1892 to become an enduring classic.

Edith Nesbit (1858–1924) was one of the first and most skilled writers in combining realism and fantasy. Her first story, *The Story of the Treasure Seekers,* was published in 1899.

Realistic Fiction

During the Victorian period there was an increasing awareness of, and response to, children's needs. In England the awareness was most evident in the work of Charlotte Yonge (1823–1901), who wrote family stories based on her own happy childhood, and some school stories, sentimental in tone, moral in intent, and realistic in approach. Her prolific output (well over a hundred books) was read avidly by children of the period.

The epoch-making book in the United States was a modest story of family life. *Little Women,* like Charlotte Yonge's books, was based on the author's own family experiences. The author, Louisa May Alcott (1832–1888), submitted the manuscript hesitatingly, and her publisher told her as gently as possible how unacceptable it was. Fortunately, he felt some qualms about his judgment and allowed the children of his family to read the manuscript. They convinced him that he was wrong. Those astute little girls loved the book, and it has remained popular with children since its publication in 1867. The story is as genuine a bit of realism as we have ever had. Family life is there—from the kitchen to the sanctuary of the attic, from reading to giving amateur dramatics in which the home-made scenery collapses. But right as all the details are, the reason adults remember the book is the masterly characterizations of the four girls. No longer are people typed to represent Ignorance or Virtue; here are flesh-and-blood girls, as different from each other as they could well be, full of human folly and human courage, never self-righteous, sometimes irritable but never failing in warm affection for each other. This ability to make her characters vividly alive was Louisa May Alcott's gift to modern realism for children.

Lucy Maud Montgomery's *Anne of Green Gables* (1904), a Canadian story of a lively, independent orphan, was as popular in the United States as it was in Canada.

In his adventure stories for boys, England's George Henty (1832–1902) used his own experiences as a correspondent to furnish the backgrounds; in the same field in the United States, William Taylor Adams (1822–1897) wrote under the fetching pen name of Oliver Optic. That best of all purveyors of rags-to-riches books, Horatio Alger (1834–1899), captivated the young with *Ragged Dick* (1867) and all the succeeding stories that flowed out in the same pattern.

So far, on both sides of the Atlantic, realistic stories for children were primarily about eminently respectable characters. When Samuel Clemens (1835–1910), or Mark Twain as he signed himself, wrote *The Adventures of Tom Sawyer* in 1876, he carried realism further. In this book Huck Finn and his disreputable father were probably the child's first literary encounters with real people who were not considered respectable but who were likable anyway. Moreover, they were not typed to show the folly of being disreputable. Huckleberry won all hearts and so nearly stole the book from Tom that he had to appear in a book of his own—*The Adventures of Huckleberry Finn* (1884). Mark Twain in these two unsurpassed books not only gave us realism with humor—in itself a new development in literature for children—but also showed warm tolerance in his presentation of people then thought socially unacceptable.

Children's Literature Comes of Age

The Victorian period saw the stream of cheerfulness in children's literature rise steadily. Many of the books written then are still popular and will be considered in detail later. The list of "milestones" is a reminder of these and others that had a major impact on the development of children's literature from 1484 to 1908.

These are individual books that were turning points in children's literature. They not only carry us into the twentieth century with distinction, but their influence is discernible in the writing of today. Laura Richards continued the deft nonsense verses of Lear and Carroll in her *Tirra Lirra* (1932). A. A. Milne's skillful light verse, *When We Were Very Young* (1924), did as much to popularize poetry for young children in schools and homes as Robert Louis Stevenson had done earlier. The small, sweet lyrics of Christina Rossetti were followed by the exquisite poetry of Walter de la Mare and by poetry with the humor of David McCord, the arousing directness of Langston Hughes, the imagery of Lilian Moore, and the finely focused evocation of Valerie Worth's writing.

In the field of fairy tales and fantasy, *East o' the Sun and West o' the Moon* continued the interest in folklore that began with the Grimms. American children could share in the literary heritage of other lands with books like *Tales from a Finnish Tupa* (1936), Indian fables in the several versions of the Jataka stories, and Japanese folk tales in *The Dancing Teakettle* (1949). From Uncle Remus collections, there came a new consciousness of the United States as a repository of regional and racial folklore. This has been more recently continued in *Jump! The Adventures of Brer Rabbit* (1986) and its companion volumes. If the Italian fairy tale *Pinocchio* (1891) was a lively descendant in the tradition of Andersen's somber toy stories, so too was the young and equally lighthearted *Winnie-the-Pooh* (1926). Gulliver's Lilliput was not more fascinating than the miniature world of *The Borrowers* (1952). *Rabbit Hill* (1944) continued the great tradition of animal fantasy begun in *The Wind in the Willows,* to be followed by *Charlotte's Web* (1952), *The Cricket in Times Square* (1960), *Animal Family* (1965), and *Watership Down* (1974). And the daft world of *Alice's Adventures in Wonderland* grew perceptibly zanier in the fantastic dreams of Dr. Seuss.

True Americana began with *Little Women* and *Tom Sawyer* and continued to flourish in such descendants as *Little House in the Big Woods* (1932), *Caddie Woodlawn* (1935), the three early

From *East o' the Sun and West o' the Moon: Old Tales from the North*, illustrated by Kay Nielsen.

books about *The Moffats* (1941–1943), and *The Fighting Ground* (1984). It is there, too, in the fine animal story *Smoky* (1926), written in the vernacular of a cowboy, and in an excellent story of the South in the depression era, *The Rock and the Willow* (1963). And it is certainly alive in such regional stories as . . . *and now Miguel* (1953), *Child of the Owl* (1977), and *Borrowed Children* (1988).

The picture story so charmingly begun by Beatrix Potter continues in the varied books of Wanda Gág, Maurice Sendak, Russell Hoban, and many others. And if stories of other countries began auspiciously with *Hans Brinker* and *Heidi,* they have grown and strengthened in *The Good Master* (1935), *The Wheel on the School* (1954), *The Happy Orpheline* (1957), *Wildcat Under Glass* (1968), *Fly Away Home* (1975), *The Winter When Time Was Frozen* (1980), *Good Night, Mr. Tom* (1982), and *The Honorable Prison* (1988). So the types of books that were turning points in children's literature at an earlier period are alive and healthy today, although the kinship between the old and the new may sometimes seem remote.

Of the many good books that have been published in the twentieth century, some stand out. Probably no two people would agree on every one that merits inclusion in a list of landmark books; the older classics have proved themselves, the new ones have yet to do so. Still,

those listed here seem milestones either because they are distinguished of their kind or because they have broken new ground, or—as in the past—they are adult books that have been taken by children as their own.

Looking back at the past, it is evident that little today is completely new, but certainly some kinds of books are better written today than ever before and are enjoying such tremendous popularity that they seem to constitute a

Milestones in the History of Children's Literature

1484 *Aesop's Fables,* translated and printed by William Caxton

1646 *Spiritual Milk for Boston Babes,* John Cotton

1657 or 1658 *Orbis Pictus,* Comenius (original in Latin)

1678 *Pilgrim's Progress,* John Bunyan

1691 *The New England Primer*

1697 *Contes de ma Mère l'Oye,* Perrault

1715 *Divine and Moral Songs for Children,* Isaac Watts

1719 *Robinson Crusoe,* Daniel Defoe

1726 *Gulliver's Travels,* Jonathan Swift

1729 *Tales of Mother Goose,* Perrault (first English translation)

1744 *A Little Pretty Pocket-Book*

1765 *The Renowned History of Little Goody Two Shoes*

1781 *Mother Goose's Melody*

1785 *Mother Goose's Melodies* (Isaiah Thomas edition)

1789 *Songs of Innocence,* William Blake

1804 *Original Poems for Infant Minds,* Ann and Jane Taylor

1807 *The Butterfly's Ball,* William Roscoe

1822 *A Visit from St. Nicholas,* Clement C. Moore

1823 *Grimms' Popular Stories* (translated into English by Edgar Taylor)

1843 *A Christmas Carol,* Charles Dickens

1846 *Book of Nonsense,* Edward Lear

1846 *Fairy Tales,* Hans Christian Andersen (first English translation)

1848 *Struwwelpeter,* Heinrich Hoffmann (first English translation)

1852 *A Wonder-Book for Girls and Boys,* Nathaniel Hawthorne

1865 *Alice's Adventures in Wonderland,* Lewis Carroll (Charles Lutwidge Dodgson)

1865 *Hans Brinker, or the Silver Skates,* Mary Mapes Dodge

1867–1876 *Sing a Song of Sixpence,* and other toy books, illustrated by Walter Crane

1867 *Little Women,* Louisa May Alcott

1871 *At the Back of the North Wind,* George Macdonald

1872 *Sing-Song,* Christina Rossetti

1876 *The Adventures of Tom Sawyer,* Mark Twain (Samuel Clemens)

1878 *Under the Window,* Kate Greenaway

1878 *The House That Jack Built* and *The Diverting History of John Gilpin,* illustrated by Randolph Caldecott

1880 *The Peterkin Papers,* Lucretia Hale

1883 *Treasure Island,* Robert Louis Stevenson

1883 *Nights with Uncle Remus,* Joel Chandler Harris

1883 *The Merry Adventures of Robin Hood,* Howard Pyle

1884 *Heidi,* Johanna Spyri (first English translation)

1884 *The Adventures of Huckleberry Finn,* Mark Twain (Samuel Clemens)

1885 *A Child's Garden of Verses,* Robert Louis Stevenson

1889 *The Blue Fairy Book,* Andrew Lang

1891 *Pinocchio,* C. Collodi (Carlo Lorenzini) (first English translation)

1894 *The Jungle Books,* Rudyard Kipling

1899 *The Story of the Treasure Seekers,* E. Nesbit

1901 *The Tale of Peter Rabbit,* Beatrix Potter

1903 *Johnny Crow's Garden,* L. Leslie Brooke

1908 *The Wind in the Willows,* Kenneth Grahame

From *A Child's Garden of Verses* by Robert Louis
Stevenson, illustrated by Jessie Willcox Smith.

trend. The trends discussed in Chapter 1 make
it clear that many of today's books are about
serious subjects, deal with contemporary problems, and are designed for children whose
sophistication has grown with their exposure to

a media-dominated world—a world in which
the developmental stages and needs of children
are better understood and better reflected in
their books than in the past.

How do you spot a trend? Observe a pattern
long enough and you are looking backward; to
label a current change a trend is to make a
judgment about the importance of a development that may prove to be ephemeral. It is
within the context of the historic pattern that
you must decide. It is against the background
of the past—the changed concept of childhood, the establishment of universal education,
the growing numbers of libraries for children,
the evaluation of literary quality and trade-
book orientation of "whole language" programs in the elementary school classroom—
that publishers have established a broad program of special publishing for children. Despite the financial strictures of the 1980s, children's book publishing is still impressive by its
sheer weight; it has responded with sensitivity
to curricular needs and current interests; it has
made reading material more accessible by mass
distribution of inexpensively produced books
and by expanded production of paperback
editions of established books—one of the most
significant trends in bookmaking. Furthermore, many publishers are broadening their
programs to include book-oriented films, filmstrips, cassettes, and other audiovisual media;
and some have established flourishing book
clubs. Without any doubt, these are exciting
and productive times in the field of children's
literature.

Twentieth-Century Milestones

1921 *The Story of Mankind,* Hendrik Willem
Van Loon. A lively and readable history,
winner of the first Newbery Medal.

1926 *Winnie-the-Pooh,* A. A. Milne. An enduring fantasy about the lives of a small
boy's toy animals.

1928 *Millions of Cats,* Wanda Gág. Dramatic
illustrations flow with a story told in the
cadence of the oral tradition.

1928 *Abe Lincoln Grows Up,* Carl Sandburg.
Authoritative biography written in an
easy conversational style.

1932 *Little House in the Big Woods,* Laura
Ingalls Wilder. First of a series un-
matched for its warm picture of pioneer
life.

1934 *Mary Poppins,* P. L. Travers. Highly original fantasy with an unforgettable protagonist.

1937 *The Hobbit,* J. R. R. Tolkien. A classic
fantasy for adults and children.

1941 *George Washington's World,* Genevieve
Foster. Significant for its broad look at
people and events the world over.

Twentieth-Century Milestones (continued)

1941 *Paddle-to-the-Sea,* Holling C. Holling. A social geography uses a narrative framework for drama and cohesion.

1943 *Homer Price,* Robert McCloskey. Humor with which children can identify, and believable episodes with dramatic appeal.

1943 *Johnny Tremain,* Esther Forbes. Outstanding historical fiction set during the Revolutionary War period. Newbery Award

1944 *Rabbit Hill,* Robert Lawson. A cozy, engaging story about an animal community. Newbery Award

1947 *The Twenty-One Balloons,* William Pène du Bois. A fantasy adventure about the inventive people on a volcanic island. Newbery Award

1950 *The Lion, the Witch, and the Wardrobe,* C. S. Lewis. The first of seven intriguing fantasies about the mythical land of Narnia.

1952 *Anne Frank: Diary of a Young Girl.* The poignant diary of a Jewish adolescent who hid from the Nazis in the attic of a house in the Netherlands.

1952 *Charlotte's Web,* E. B. White. A touching, beautifully written fantasy about animal friendship.

1957 *The Cat in the Hat,* Dr. Seuss (pseudonym for Theodor Seuss Geisel). A pioneer easy-to-read book, with wordplay and nonsense humor that have made it a perennial favorite.

1959 *Tom's Midnight Garden,* Philippa Pearce. Polished style and perceptive characterization give depth to an imaginatively structured time-slip fantasy. Published in England in 1958. Carnegie Award

1960 *Island of the Blue Dolphins,* Scott O'Dell. A beautifully sustained story of a Native-American girl marooned on an island for eighteen years. Newbery Award

1961 *The Incredible Journey,* Sheila Burnford. A deftly sustained tale about three animals who trek through the Canadian wilderness.

1962 *The Snowy Day,* Ezra Jack Keats. Poster-simple composition in a picture book about a black child's imaginative play. Caldecott Award

1963 *Where the Wild Things Are,* Maurice Sendak. Superb illustrations complement a story in which a child consoles himself with dreams of power. Caldecott Award

1964 *Harriet the Spy,* Louise Fitzhugh. A boundary-breaking story, candid and perceptive, about an unhappy child.

1964 *The Pushcart War,* Jean Merrill. An adroit mock-history of the struggle against big truckers by the peddlers of New York City.

1964 *The Book of Three,* Lloyd Alexander. First of a five-book cycle of high fantasy in the Welsh tradition.

1969 *Where the Lilies Bloom,* Vera and Bill Cleaver. A trenchant and moving story about an orphaned family in Appalachia.

1970 *Blowfish Live in the Sea,* Paula Fox. Remarkable both for its fine writing style and its perceptive picture of the intricacies of familial relationships.

1974 *M. C. Higgins, the Great,* Virginia Hamilton. One of our great stylists, the author writes with grace and insight about an African-American family in the Cumberland Mountains. Newbery Award

1974 *Watership Down,* Richard Adams. A long, intricate, and absorbing fantasy about a rabbit community. First published in England in 1971. Carnegie Award

1977 *Bridge to Terabithia,* Katherine Paterson. A touching story of the friendship between two children, of the joy they have in the secret playland of Terabithia, and of the pain of one when the other dies. Newbery Award

1985 *Sarah, Plain and Tall,* Patricia MacLachlan. In a story set in pioneer times, a mail-order bride is instantly loved by her two new stepchildren. Newbery Award; Scott O'Dell Award

1988 *The Way Things Work,* David Macaulay. Remarkable for its range, its clarity, its usefulness as a reference source, and its wit—in both text and illustrations—a fine book on the principles and mechanics of machinery.

Adult References and Book Selection Aids*

ASHTON, JOHN. *Chap-Books of the Eighteenth Century.*

BARCHILON, JACQUES, and HENRY PETTIT. *The Authentic Mother Goose Fairy Tales and Nursery Rhymes.*

BARRY, FLORENCE V. *A Century of Children's Books.*

BINGHAM, JANE, ed. *Writers for Children: Critical Studies of the Major Authors Since the Seventeenth Century.*

BOSTON, LUCY. *Perverse and Foolish.*

CARPENTER, HUMPHREY. *Secret Gardens: A Study of the Golden Age of Children's Literature.*

CARPENTER, HUMPHREY, and MARI PRICHARD. *The Oxford Companion to Children's Literature.*

CHAMBERS, ROBERT. *Popular Rhymes of Scotland.*

COMENIUS, JOHANN AMOS. *The Orbis Pictus of John Amos Comenius.*

COMMIRE, ANNE, ed. *Yesterday's Authors of Books for Children.*

CROUCH, MARCUS. *Treasure Seekers and Borrowers: Children's Books in Britain, 1900–1960.*

DARLING, RICHARD L. *The Rise of Children's Book Reviewing in America, 1865–1881.*

DARTON, F. J. H. *Children's Books in England: Five Centuries of Social Life.*

DE VRIES, LEONARD. *Little Wide-Awake: An Anthology from Victorian Children's Books and Periodicals in the Collection of Anne and Fernand G. Renier.*

ELLIS, ALEC. *A History of Children's Reading and Literature.*

FIELD, ELINOR WHITNEY, comp. *Horn Book Reflections: On Children's Books and Reading.*

FIELD, LOUISE F. *The Child and His Book: Some Account of the History and Progress of Children's Literature in England.*

FOLMSBEE, BEULAH. *A Little History of the Horn-Book.*

FORD, PAUL LEICESTER, ed. *The New England Primer.*

FRASER, JAMES, ed. *Society and Children's Literature.*

FRYE, BURTON C., ed. *A St. Nicholas Anthology: The Early Years.*

GOTTLIEB, GERALD. *Early Children's Books and Their Illustration.*

GREEN, ROGER LANCELYN. *Tellers of Tales.*

HALSEY, ROSALIE V. *Forgotten Books of the American Nursery: A History of the Development of the American Story-Book.*

HAVILAND, VIRGINIA, and MARGARET COUGHLAN, comps. *Yankee Doodle's Literary Sampler of Prose, Poetry, & Pictures.*

HAZARD, PAUL. *Books, Children and Men.*

*Complete bibliographic data are provided in Appendices A and B.

HEWINS, CAROLINE M. *A Mid-Century Child and Her Books.*

JORDAN, ALICE M. *From Rollo to Tom Sawyer.*

KIEFER, MONICA. *American Children Through Their Books, 1700–1835.*

LANG, ANDREW, ed. *Perrault's Popular Tales.*

LYSTAD, MARY. *From Dr. Mather to Dr. Seuss: 200 Years of American Books for Children.*

McGUFFEY, WILLIAM HOLMES. *Old Favorites from the McGuffey Readers.*

MacLEOD, ANNE SCOTT. *A Moral Tale: Children's Fiction and American Culture 1820–1860.*

MEIGS, CORNELIA, ANNE EATON, ELIZABETH NESBITT, and RUTH HILL VIGUERS. *A Critical History of Children's Literature.*

MOORE, ANNE CARROLL. *My Roads to Childhood.*

MUIR, PERCY. *English Children's Books, 1600 to 1900.*

OPIE, IONA and PETER. *Children's Games in Street and Playground.*

————. *The Lore and Language of Schoolchildren.*

————. *A Nursery Companion.*

————, eds. *The Oxford Dictionary of Nursery Rhymes.*

The Original Mother Goose's Melody, As First Issued by John Newbery, of London, about A.D. 1760.

PICKERING, SAMUEL. *John Locke and Children's Books in Eighteenth-Century England.*

ROSELLE, DANIEL. *Samuel Griswold Goodrich, Creator of Peter Parley: A Study of His Life and Work.*

ROSENBACH, ABRAHAM S. W. *Early American Children's Books with Bibliographical Descriptions of the Books in His Private Collection.*

ST. JOHN, JUDITH. *The Osborne Collection of Early Children's Books 1566–1910: A Catalogue, Volumes 1 and 2.*

SMITH, IRENE. *A History of the Newbery and Caldecott Medals.*

STEWART, CHRISTINA. *The Taylors of Ongar: An Analytical Bio-Bibliography.*

TARG, WILLIAM, ed. *Bibliophile in the Nursery.*

THWAITE, MARY F. *From Primer to Pleasure in Reading.*

TOWNSEND, JOHN ROWE. *Written for Children: An Outline of English Language Children's Literature.*

TUER, ANDREW W. *Pages and Pictures from Forgotten Children's Books: Brought Together and Introduced to the Reader.*

VIGUERS, RUTH HILL, MARCIA DALPHIN, and BERTHA MAHONY MILLER, comps. *Illustrators of Children's Books, 1946–1956.*

WEISS, HARRY B. *A Book About Chapbooks: The People's Literature of Bygone Times.*

WELSH, CHARLES. *A Bookseller of the Last Century. Being some Account of the Life of John Newbery and of the Books he published with a Notice of the later Newberys.*

Chapter Four

Books for the Very Young

Young children are naturally receptive, responding with enthusiasm to new stimuli and experiences. The preschool years are ones during which it is first possible to instill a joy in books, to lead children to the realization that books and reading are sources of pleasure. Through the sharing of our own pleasure in books, we can not only help prepare children for learning to read but can also help them take the first steps toward the habit of reading, a habit that will provide lifelong pleasure.

Since children's first experiences with books and reading usually occur before they go to school, parents and other adults who are responsible for preschool children bear a large responsibility for creating an environment in which children can best develop language skills, formulate attitudes toward reading, and experience pleasure with books.

Studies of home environments of children in nursery schools show clearly the more advanced language skills in those children who have been sung to, read to, and talked with. In fact, there is evidence that their greatest response is to language. Infants may enjoy a mother's voice or a father's lap before they appreciate what's being read to them, but the association of books with pleasure can begin in infancy.

Children can make great discoveries about reading before learning to read for themselves. For one thing, seeing adults enjoy their own books can spur a positive attitude toward reading. Moreover, following the story as an adult reads and points out objects on the page, a child learns that the symbols in the book always go from left to right and, just as dependably, from the top to the bottom of the page. That's a big step. And then comes the marvelous realization that an "a" in one word is an "a" in another, that "c-a-t" in one book is exactly the same as "c-a-t" in another book; those are two more big steps, and they are learned most easily in a one-to-one situation when a small child and an adult, or an older child, share a book.

Interest in very young children and their intellectual development has increased remarkably in recent years. Scientific research suggests that 50 percent of a child's general intelligence is achieved between birth and age four, and an additional 30 percent by age eight. Children's speech and vocabulary development follow a similar pattern, with many of these skills achieved by the time they are six.

Small wonder, then, that there has been a corresponding flourishing of organizations concerned solely with young children and their education; of books, journals, and articles on myriad aspects of the subject; of special schools for early education; and of books written for this group. This chapter will examine the many kinds of books there are: *Mother Goose* and other books of nursery rhymes, alphabet books and counting books, concept books and picture books without text, toy books, picture story books to be read aloud, and simply written stories for beginning independent readers.

Books for young children are usually referred to en masse as "picture books." The true picture book is one in which the illustrations are the dominant feature with little or no text. *Brian Wildsmith's ABC* is an excellent example, with large-scale pictures of familiar objects a child can point to and gleefully recognize. An adult may get bored the tenth time a child points and says "dog," but to the child each repetition brings the delight of corroborating a known experience. The picture book affords opportunities for self-discovery experiences, while there is a greater component of sharing in listening to a picture story book being read aloud.

A picture story book has a structured, if minimal, plot; it really tells a story, while a picture book may not. In a picture story the illustrations are so integral a part of the content that the story can be "read" by the child from the pictures (Robert McCloskey's *Make Way for Ducklings,* for example). Pictures and text extend each other, reinforcing both the concepts and the forward movement of the story line, so that neither eye nor ear senses an interruption in the flow of the book.

The range of picture story books is enormous, but the criteria by which they can be judged are very much the same for all kinds. Whether the story is as simple as Helen Oxenbury's *The Important Visitor* or as profound psychologically as Maurice Sendak's *Where the Wild Things Are,* a story should be brief and straightforward if it is for young children; it should contain few concepts and none that are beyond comprehension if they are not familiar concepts; it should be written in a direct and simple style; and it should have illustrations that complement the text and are not in conflict with it. These criteria define the admirable and lasting qualities of *Peter Rabbit,* published over eighty years ago, as well as such treasures of the 1970s and 1980s as Arnold Lobel's *Frog and Toad Are Friends* or William Steig's *Spinky Sulks.*

Look at picture books, read picture story books aloud, take children to a public library and help them choose their books. Observe their reactions. If a television program is based on a book, follow it up by getting the book if you can; the average preschooler in the United States watches many hours of television each week, and any opportunity for capitalizing on that familiar medium should be seized. Talk about books you have read; tell stories if you possibly can (young children are not very demanding about technique). All of these are pleasurable shared activities, but they also prepare the child (as do street signs, magazines, and box tops) for reading independently. In Chapter 1 we discussed children's needs and the ways in which books can meet those needs; in Chapter 2 we described some of the criteria by which books can be evaluated. In considering books for young children, we should keep in mind those needs and those criteria as well as the limitations of experience and language of the very young. While this chapter focuses specifically on books for young children, many other books written for this age, and many of the authors and artists who excel in their creation, are discussed in the following chapter, "Artists and Children's Books," and in the later chapters on modern fantasy, modern and historical fiction, and informational books. You will probably find it useful to look at the following chapter on illustrators along with this chapter, since illustration is an essential element in books for the very young. The emphasis in this chapter is on the content of those books; the emphasis in the following chapter is on the artwork.

Mother Goose

Small children acquire a love for poetry as naturally as did people of early times, through hearing poems spoken or sung and through learning them, almost unconsciously, along with the speaker or singer. Favorite nursery ditties were easily remembered and passed on by word of mouth for generations before they achieved the permanency of print and became known as *Mother Goose.* Old folk rhymes are still important not only because children continue to enjoy them, but because many are skillfully composed, exuberant or dramatic, and lead naturally into modern nonsense verse and narrative poems.

Who was Mother Goose? The name *Mother Goose,* as we saw in Chapter 3, was first associated with the eight folk tales recorded by Perrault. Andrew Lang, in *Perrault's Popular Tales,* tells us that the frontispiece of *Histories ou contes du temps passé, avec des moralités* (Histories or Tales of Long Ago, with Morals) bore the words "Contes de ma Mère l'Oye" (Tales of Mother Goose). But the name *Mother Goose* has now become so completely associated with the popular verses that most English translations of the Perrault tales omit it from the title of the collection.

Lina Eckenstein, in *Comparative Studies in Nursery Rhymes,* said that the name *Mother Goose* was first used in England in connection with Robert Powell's puppet shows, exhibited in London between 1709 and 1711. What play did Powell present under the title of *Mother Goose?* It may have been one of Perrault's stories heard from a traveler. At any rate, Perrault's *Contes de ma Mère l'Oye* was translated into English in 1729, and the popularity of the eight tales undoubtedly helped establish still more firmly that delightful nonsense name, *Mother Goose.*

Early Editions of *Mother Goose*

The next mention of the name in England is in connection with John Newbery, whom we discussed in Chapter 3. At one time, Newbery was thought to have published an edition of *Mother Goose's Melody or Sonnets for the Cradle* between 1760 and 1765, but later research[1] suggests that he may have planned but did not publish such a book. In 1781 Newbery's stepson, T.

Carnan, who continued the Newbery publishing business, advertised in the *London Chronicle* for January 2, "The first publication of *Mother Goose's Melody.*"

The first American edition of *Mother Goose* was probably a pirated reprint of an early Newbery edition, published in about 1785 by Isaiah Thomas.[2] Two more notable American editions followed. Between 1824 and 1827, the Boston firm of Munroe and Francis published the *Mother Goose's Quarto, or Melodies Complete,* which contained many rhymes drawn from the Thomas reprint of Newbery's *Melody* but also many apparently old ones printed for the first time. In 1833 this firm made a reprint of the *Quarto* with the title *The Only True Mother Goose Melodies.* Both the *Quarto* and the 1833 edition are important sources for many of the later collections. These editions include, as many of our modern editions do, some poems that are not traditional, such as Shakespeare's "Jog on, jog on, the foot-path way," which are obviously out of place in a collection of folk rhymes.

Origins of the *Mother Goose* Verses

The *Mother Goose* verses underwent many changes during the years when they were passed on by word of mouth, and later when they traveled from one printed edition to another. As with the ballads, variants of the same verses were recited or sung in different places, and which ones were the originals no one can say. Certainly they have led to considerable speculation and to some careful research. Undoubtedly many of the rhymes are mere nonsense jingles, but many others reveal interesting bits of history, old customs, manners, and beliefs. Attempts to find historical characters to fit the people of *Mother Goose* have shown more imagination than documented research. Iona and Peter Opie, scholars of distinction in the field of nursery rhymes, comment in *The Oxford Dictionary of Nursery Rhymes:*

Much ingenuity has been exercised to show that certain nursery rhymes have had greater significance than is now apparent. They have been vested with mystic symbolism, linked with social and

---

[1] Jacques Barchilon and Henry Pettit, eds. *The Authentic Mother Goose Fairy Tales and Nursery Rhymes* (Swallow, 1960).

[2] See Chapter 3, p. 60.

HEAR WHAT MA'AM GOOSE SAYS!

My dear little Blossoms, there are now in this world, and always will be, a great many grannies besides myself, both in petticoats and pantaloons, some a deal younger to be sure; but all monstrous wise, and of my own family name. These old women, who never had chick nor child of their own, but who always know how to bring up other people's children, will tell you with very long faces, that my enchanting, quieting, soothing volume, my all-sufficient anodyne for cross, peevish, won't-be-comforted little bairns, ought to be laid aside for more learned books, such as *they* could select and publish. Fudge! I tell you that all their batterings can't deface my beauties, nor their wise pratings equal my wiser prattlings; and all imitators of my refreshing songs might as well write a new Billy Shakespeare as another Mother Goose — we two great poets were born together, and we shall go out of the world together.

No, no, my Melodies will never die,
While nurses sing, or babies cry.

From *The Only True Mother Goose Melodies*, an exact and full-size reproduction of the original edition published and copyrighted in Boston in the year 1833 by Munroe and Francis (Lothrop, Lee and Shepard, 1905).

political events, and numerous attempts have been made to identify the nursery characters with real persons. It should be stated straightway that the bulk of these speculations are worthless. Fortunately the theories are so numerous they tend to cancel each other out. The story of "Sing a song of sixpence," for instance, has been described as alluding to the choirs of Tudor monasteries, the printing of the English Bible, the malpractices of the Romish clergy, and the infinite workings of the solar system. The baby rocked on a tree top has been recognized as the Egyptian child Horus, the Old Pretender, and a New England Red Indian. Even when, by chance, the same conclusions are reached by two writers the reasons given are, as likely as not, antithetical. This game of "interpreting" the nursery rhymes has not been confined to the twentieth century, though it is curious that it has never been so overplayed as in the age which claims to believe in realism. (p. 27)

Children may not be interested in origins of rhymes, but teachers and librarians may find them a fascinating study.

Qualities That Appeal to Children

Children enjoy the variety of subject matter and mood that continually surprises them in *Mother Goose*.

The following list of examples, to which you can add dozens of others, suggests the variety in these verses:

People (a rich gallery of characters)
    Children—Little Miss Muffet
    Grownups—Old King Cole
    Imaginary—Old Mother Goose when she wanted to wander
    Grotesque—There was a crooked man
Children's pranks—Georgie, Porgie, pudding and pie
Animals—I had a little pony
Birds and fowl—Jenny Wren; Higgledy, piggledy, my black hen
Finger play—Pat-a-cake
Games—Ring a ring o' roses
Riddles—Little Nancy Etticoat
Counting rhymes—One, two, buckle my shoe
Counting out—Intery, mintery, cutery-corn
Alphabets—A, is an apple pie
Proverbs—Early to bed, early to rise
Superstitions—See a pin and pick it up
Time verses—Thirty days hath September
Days of the week—Solomon Grundy, born on Monday
Verse stories—The Queen of Hearts, she made some tarts
Dialogue—Who killed Cock Robin?
Songs—A frog he would a-wooing go
Street cries—Hot-cross Buns!
Weather—Rain, rain, go away
Tongue twisters—Peter Piper picked a peck of pickled peppers
Cumulative stories—This is the house that Jack built
Nonsense—Three wise men of Gotham

On the whole, descriptive nature poems, in the modern sense, are conspicuously lacking in these qualities, as are fairy poems.

Lured on by the variety of these rollicking jingles, children are also captivated by their musical quality. "Sing it again," they insist, when you finish reading or singing one of their favorites. They nod their heads or rock their bodies, marking time to the rhythm. They may suit the words to their own actions.

Saying these verses, children get a happy introduction to rhyme—perfect and imperfect—to alliteration, onomatopoeia, and other sound patterns. Happily they get these without the burden of their labels and so enjoy them lightheartedly. Alliteration, as in "Sing a song of sixpence," tickles their sound sense to a degree that astonishes us. They are also fascinated by the staccato in "Higgledy, piggledy, my black hen" and by the explosive -*tle* in "She lays eggs for gen*tle*men." Indeed, the brisk tune of this ditty turns upon its lively use of consonants, the *n* sounds making it ring delightfully. One of the many values of these melodious jingles is that they accustom the ear and the tongue to the musical aspects of the English language. All in all, the verses offer many opportunities for the development of a fine sense of the musical quality of language.

Still another characteristic of these verses that endears them to young children is their action: Jack and Jill fall down, Miss Muffet runs away, Mother Goose rides on her gander, the cow jumps over the moon, Polly puts the kettle on. Here are no meditations, no brooding introspections, no subtle descriptions. In these verses things happen as rapidly and riotously as youngsters would like to see them happening every day. The brevity of these verse stories makes them acceptable to children as young as two years old and they prepare children to enjoy longer and more involved prose and verse stories.

The sheer fun of *Mother Goose* keeps the verses alive in the hearts of every generation of children. What do children laugh at? It is hard to say; we can only watch and listen. Sometimes they laugh at the sound; often they laugh at the grotesque or the incongruous. Surprise and absurd antics amuse them, and broad horseplay delights them.

Finally, children love the pictures that illustrate their favorite book. Whether the edition is so small it can be tucked into a pocket, or so enormous it must be spread out on the floor, the numerous pictures enchant them. Just as there is endless variety in the stories, the moods, and the characters of these jingles, so there is a like variety in the size, the shape, the color, and the style of pictures that illustrate them. One adult prefers one edition, while a second adult greatly prefers another, but the children simply ask for *Mother Goose*—with colored pictures or black-and-white, simple or elaborate, commonplace or subtle.

Popular Editions

It is impractical to list all the fine editions of *Mother Goose,* but the following choices are popular with parents, teachers, librarians, and children for a variety of reasons.

Mother Goose: or, The Old Nursery Rhymes, illustrated by Kate Greenaway, is a tiny book to fit small hands and pockets. It contains forty-four of the brief rhymes, each with its own picture in the quaint Kate Greenaway style. The print is exceedingly small, but for nonreaders this does not matter. The illustrations are gently gay, the colors are soft, and the people exquisitely decorative.

Mother Goose: The Old Nursery Rhymes, illustrated by Arthur Rackham, one of England's great artists, is a splendid edition, brought back into print in 1978. The illustrations are of three types: pen-and-ink sketches, silhouettes, and full-page color. The silhouettes are amazingly effective, for example, the dripping bedraggled cat of "Ding, dong, bell." The color plates are Rackham at his best displaying many moods. These are pictures by an artist with imagination and a knowledge of folklore.

A good introduction to *Mother Goose* and her world is the tried and true *The Real Mother Goose,* illustrated by Blanche Fisher Wright. There are brightly colored pictures on every page; often one picture fills a whole page, or sometimes there are two or three small ones. The characters are dressed in period costumes and can be seen distinctly by a large group of children. The colors are clear washes, sometimes soft and pale but more often bright and lively. It is a big book with a wide selection of traditional verses which the illustrations really portray. This is more important than some artists have realized, because small children use pictures as clues to the meaning of the text.

In *Ring o' Roses,* Leslie Brooke provides an imaginative and broadly humorous pictorial interpretation of the traditional verses. The characters are in English period costumes and are utterly satisfying interpretations. Above all you will remember Leslie Brooke's pigs—after chuckling over them you will never again see pigs as plain pigs. This is, after all, the test of great illustrations: They do more than illustrate —they interpret the text so vividly that they become the embodiment of the words.

The Tall Book of Mother Goose, illustrated by Feodor Rojankovsky, is an elongated book, approximately five by twelve inches, which can be easily held. Rojankovsky was a master of color and realistic texture. His furry kittens, feathery chicks, and woolly mufflers have a depth that almost creates a tactual sensation. His children are husky, everyday youngsters, never beautiful and often very funny. This book, with its 150 rhymes and twice as many pictures, remains popular.

Marguerite de Angeli's *Book of Nursery and Mother Goose Rhymes* contains 376 jingles, 260 enchanting pictures, and innumerable decorations. It is a big book, and it must have been a labor of love for the artist. Children and animals dance and prance across the pages. The book is too big for small children to handle alone, but it is fine for children and adults to look at together. The verses are not arranged in any particular order, so a nursery jingle is often followed by a ballad to suit older children.

From the rich store of their scholarly study, Iona and Peter Opie have compiled *The Oxford Nursery Rhyme Book,* with eight hundred of the verses that have delighted children for generations. This vast collection is skillfully organized. It begins with the simplest ditties and progresses to more mature riddles, songs, and ballads. Almost every verse has a picture—small and black only, but amazingly effective. Many of the illustrations are taken from the old chapbooks and toy books. Students of early children's books will find this an invaluable edition, and parents will also enjoy the book. Designed as a companion volume to *The Oxford Nursery Rhyme Book* is the Opies' *A Family Book of Nursery Rhymes* (first published as *The Puffin Book of Nursery Rhymes*). Of its 358 rhymes, 200 are not included in the first book. Precise, delicate drawings by Pauline Baynes grace almost every page, and the notes at the back of the book are as entertaining as they are inform-

From *Tail Feathers from Mother Goose: The Opie Rhyme Book,* illustrated by Donald Carrick.

ative. *Tail Feathers from Mother Goose,* with little-known variants of nursery rhymes, has every rhyme illustrated by a different artist.

Brian Wildsmith's work is distinguished by its magnificent use of rich color, often in a patchwork of vibrant geometric figures. In his *Brian Wildsmith's Mother Goose,* the people are dressed in period clothing, and the almost theatrical quality of the pictures gives a sense of milieu as well as of the characters.

Another delightful collection is *A Book of Scottish Nursery Rhymes,* edited by Norah and William Montgomerie. Most of the selections are pure Scots, but anyone can recognize and enjoy such favorites as:

> *"Pussy, pussy baudrons*
> *Where have you been?"*
> *"I've been to London,*
> *To see the Queen!"*
>
> *"Pussy, pussy baudrons,*
> *What got you there?"*
> *"I got a good fat mousikie,*
> *Running up a stair!"*

One of the impressive collections of the 1960s is *The Mother Goose Treasury,* illustrated by Raymond Briggs. It contains over four hundred verses, most of them from the Opie

Popular *Mother Goose* Books

Old Mother Goose, when
She wanted to wander,
Would ride through the air
On a very fine gander.

"Old Mother Goose" from *Mother Goose: The Classic Volland Edition,* rearranged and edited by Eulalie Osgood Grover, illustrated by Frederick Richardson.

From *Sing a Song of Sixpence,* illustrated by Randolph Caldecott.

"Rub a Dub Dub" from *The Classic Mother Goose Nursery Rhymes,* first published by Ernest Nister under the title *Mother Goose's Nursery Rhymes.*

Mother Goose nursery rhymes, which appeared as a popular staple of children's books as early as the eighteenth century, persist today in a range of editions featuring ever-new, inventive, and original artistic interpretations, from literal to impressionistic. Graphic variations of humor and theme often enhance familiar verses, expanding children's visual perception as the words and rhythms in the various selections foster their language development.

HUMPTY DUMPTY

Humpty Dumpty sat on a wall,
Humpty Dumpty had a great fall;
All the King's horses, and all the
    King's men
Cannot put Humpty Dumpty together
    again.

"Little Miss Muffet" from *The Tall Book of Mother Goose*, illustrated by Feodor Rojankovsky.

"Humpty Dumpty" from *The Real Mother Goose*, illustrated by Blanche Fisher Wright.

From *London Bridge Is Falling Down!*, illustrated by Peter Spier.

"Little Jack Horner" from *Brian Wildsmith's Mother Goose*, illustrated by Brian Wildsmith.

From *The House That Jack Built: A Mother Goose Nursery Rhyme*, illustrated by Janet Stevens.

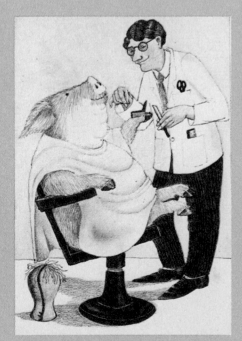

"Barber, Barber, Shave a Pig" from *Cakes and Custard*, selected by Brian Alderson, illustrated by Helen Oxenbury.

From *Chinese Mother Goose Rhymes*, selected and edited by Robert Wyndham, illustrated by Ed Young.

OLD King Cole was a merry old soul,
And a merry old soul was he;
He called for his pipe,
And he called for his bowl,
And he called for his fiddlers three.

"Old King Cole" from *Nicola Bayley's Book of Nursery Rhymes*, illustrated by Nicola Bayley.

"Jack Be Nimble" from *Mother Goose: A Collection of Classic Nursery Rhymes,* selected and illustrated by Michael Hague.

"Three Little Kittens" from *Tomie dePaola's Mother Goose,* illustrated by Tomie dePaola.

"This Little Pig" from *The Orchard Book of Nursery Rhymes,* selected by Zena Sutherland, illustrated by Faith Jaques.

collection, and each has at least one illustration. The verses and pictures, many of them small, are scattered over the pages with openhanded abandon. Occasionally there is a fullpage or a double-page spread in color. The pictures are greatly varied in mood and treatment: Some are bold, some delicate, some restrained, some grotesque, some humorous, but all have charm.

In *Mother Goose Lost,* Trevor Stubley's brightly colorful pictures illustrate a collection of unfamiliar rhymes found by Nicholas Tucker, a British psychologist, while doing research for an article. Another distinguished Englishman in the field of children's literature, Brian Alderson, includes some of his childhood favorites in addition to *Mother Goose* rhymes in *Cakes and Custard.* This handsomely designed book is illustrated by Helen Oxenbury with pictures that have wit, vigor, and superb draftsmanship. Arnold Lobel's *Gregory Griggs and Other Nursery Rhyme People* is also among the most entertaining new editions; as are his *Whiskers and Rhymes,* and his largest collection, *The Random House Book of Mother Goose.* Wallace Tripp's *Granfa' Grig Had a Pig and Other Rhymes Without Reason* from Mother Goose is filled with humorous details that both children and adults will find delightful. Compiled by Zena Sutherland and illustrated with bright, meticulously detailed paintings by Faith Jaques, *The Orchard Book of Nursery Rhymes* reflects the rural settings of the eighteenth century in its details. Susan Jeffers, in *If Wishes Were Horses and Other Rhymes,* uses ink and pastel pencil for strong, often comic pictures of rhymes only about horses.

Many attractive editions of single verses from *Mother Goose* have been published. Both Peter Spier and Ed Emberley illustrated *London Bridge Is Falling Down*—Emberley's fanciful version has an ornate bridge but little period detail; Spier's version has minutely and humorously detailed illustrations and notes on the history of the bridge. Barbara Cooney illustrated with delightful delicacy *Mother Goose in French,* ably translated by Hugh Latham. For the imaginative delicately detailed illustrations for *Three Jovial Huntsmen,* Susan Jeffers won the Golden Apple at the Bienniale of Illustrations in Bratislava, an international exhibit.

From *The Random House Book of Mother Goose,* selected and illustrated by Arnold Lobel.

It is clear that no single artistic interpretation is more appropriate than any other. Whether an edition is large in size or small, whether it contains a single verse or many, the illustrations should reflect the mood of the verses, should truly illustrate them rather than being merely decorative, and should be placed on the pages so that they relate to the verses, enabling children to relate words and pictures. The latter is especially important in *Mother Goose* books in which there are several verses and illustrations on a page; the layout of the page should leave no doubt as to which illustration fits each picture. Since such layout is difficult to achieve on a crowded page, adequate spacing is an important criterion in evaluating editions. Whether illustrations are delicate or robust, they should be realistic enough for young children to see the correlation between picture and verse.

From *The Tom Thumb Song Book*, J. Lumsden & Son, Glasgow (1815).

Variants of *Mother Goose*

In addition to the many editions of *Mother Goose* there are several collections of nursery rhymes which are fairly close in style and content to the old English jingles.

The American Mother Goose was compiled by Ray Wood and illustrated by Ed Hargis. Children studying frontier life are interested in and amused by this collection. The verses are both rougher and funnier than the English nursery rhymes and are as indigenous to America as a "possum up a gum stump." Here is such familiar doggerel as "I asked my mother for fifteen cents"; "How much wood would a woodchuck chuck"; and a final section of riddles, games, and finger play. The pen-and-ink sketches are full of hilarious touches that delight adults as much as they do children.

Maud and Miska Petersham's *The Rooster Crows: A Book of American Rhymes and Jingles* was awarded the Caldecott Medal in 1946. In spite of the inclusion of such American folk rhymes as "A bear went over the mountain" and "Mother, may I go out to swim," the subtitle is difficult to justify because the collection also contains such old-world rhymes as "Sally Waters" and "Oats, peas, beans and barley grows."

Lillian Morrison has made a delightful contribution to Americana with her small collections of riddles, auguries, school and playground chants, and amusing autograph album inscriptions. The three books in the last category—*Yours Till Niagara Falls, Remember Me When This You See,* and *Best Wishes, Amen*—are never on library shelves at commencement time.

A Rocket in My Pocket compiled by Carl Withers, carries the subtitle *The Rhymes and Chants of Young Americans.* Some four hundred ditties, tongue twisters, derisive chants, and bits of pure nonsense, together with Susanne Suba's line drawings, make this an unusually beguiling book.

Did You Feed My Cow? compiled by Margaret Burroughs, an authority on African-American culture, is a book of street games, chants, and rhymes in which traditional folk materials have been adapted by children.

Another collection of rhymes, street chants, games, and songs, *Sally Go Round the Sun,* is based on research by the compiler, Edith Fowke, an expert on Canadian folklore. A collection of Danish nursery rhymes, *It's Raining Said John Twaining,* translated and illustrated by N. M. Bodecker, has perky, rhythmic verses that have a humorous quality that is echoed in the illustrations. *The Prancing Pony,* translated by Charlotte De Forest, is a compilation of fifty-three favorite nursery song lyrics; the verses reflect Japanese culture but also have a universal appeal. Robert Wyndham's selections of Mandarin verses for *Chinese Mother Goose Rhymes* are beautifully illustrated by Ed Young on pages printed sideways and bordered by columns of Chinese calligraphy.

ABC Books

While most alphabet books are for young children and are useful in teaching the alphabet, they also make a contribution to visual literacy, helping the child organize graphic experiences. ABC books are not the only kinds of books that help children in identifying objects, but they do serve as identification books, usually comprising key words that label familiar objects or animals, less often identifying people.

Although early alphabet books like the *New England Primer* served not only to teach children letters but also to give moral instruction, the pictorial ABC books that followed *Mother Goose's* "A Apple Pie" are all variants on that

Popular *ABC* Books

Goat in a boat

L for Lizard – look how lazy

From *Ape in a Cape*, illustrated by Fritz Eichenberg. *(Top left)*

From *The ABC Bunny*, illustrated by Wanda Gág. *(Top right)*

From *Aster Aardvark's Alphabet Adventures*, illustrated by Steven Kellogg. *(Center)*

From *An Edward Lear Alphabet*, illustrated by Carol Newsom. *(Bottom)*

Alphabet books serve to combine entertainment with instruction. The simplicity and clarity basic to a concept book still allow an amazing range of artistic styles that satisfy aesthetic as well as informational requirements. The range of subjects used in ABC books is never-ending. These illustrations incorporate objects and figures good for identification as well as close scrutiny and even a few chuckles.

U u
U was once a little urn,
　Urny,
　Burny,
　Turny,
　Urny,
Bubbly, burny,
Little urn!

From *Anno's Alphabet*, illustrated by Mitsumasa Anno.

From *If There Were Dreams to Sell*, compiled by Barbara Lalicki, illustrated by Margot Tomes.

is for Circus wagon

From *ABC Americana from the National Gallery of Art*, selected by Cynthia Elyce Rubin.

Kk

K is for Killer Whale
In the deep blue sea,

From *The Wildlife ABC*, written and illustrated by Jan Thornhill.

From *The Ark in the Attic: An Alphabet Adventure*, text and painted backgrounds by Eileen Doolittle, photographs by Starr Ockenga.

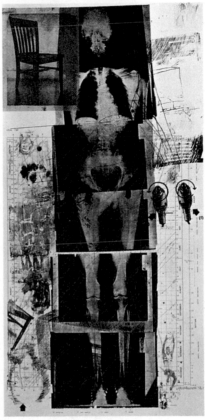

X-ray

Reprinted from *ABC: Museum of Modern Art, New York*, by Florence Cassen Mayers. Design copyright © 1986 Florence Cassen Mayers. Published 1986 by Harry N. Abrams, Inc., New York. All rights reserved.

From *A, B, See!*, illustrated by Tana Hoban.

theme. Edward Lear wrote one of the funniest, all in nonsense phonetics (*An Edward Lear Alphabet Book*), and it now appears in a delightful illustrated edition. Also working in the nineteenth century, Walter Crane made a charming *Baby's Own Alphabet*, Kate Greenaway turned *A Apple Pie* into a thing of beauty, and Tracey Pearson focuses on a huge apple pie in her hilarious pictures for a more recent *A—Apple Pie*.

Modern artists have also been intrigued by the austerity of a single letter and the possibilities of making it dramatic. Wanda Gág's *ABC Bunny* has a rhyming text with continuity unusual in such miscellanies. The dark woodcuts are relieved by large scarlet capital letters, which suggest the small child's ABC blocks. The pictures and story make it a favorite.

Bruno Munari's ABC depends for its charm on his masterful use of color and design to build interesting associations around each letter—"A Fly/ a Flower/ a Feather/ and a Fish" with "more Flies" at the top of the page to go buzzing on through the book. So arresting are his colors and use of space that the visual impact of each page is powerful.

Brian Wildsmith's ABC is a heady experience with color, an ABC book with the simplest of texts and the most glorious rainbow of subtle tints and hues. A fuchsia page displays "cat Cat" with letters in three colors, and opposite, against a muted blue, is a green-eyed black cat. *John Burningham's ABC* has upper- and lowercase letters and illustrative words on the left-hand pages, facing stunning pictures in bold compositions.

Some books are especially useful for environmental or spatial awareness. Francine Grossbart's *A Big City* has words which all start with oversize capital letters and are on colored pages with ample blank space: Antennas, Buildings, Cars, Doors, Elephant in a zoo, and so on. In Rachel Isadora's *City Seen from A to Z*, the focus is contemporary and multiethnic as well as urban. Tana Hoban uses photograms—white objects grouped against a black background—in *A, B, See!* and thereby stresses identification as well as the letters, always in a frieze at the bottom of the page, with the letter *for* that page in large, bold type, a device that emphasizes the whole alphabet and the sequence of letters.

Two of the most graphically outstanding ABC books are Dorothy Schmiderer's *The Alphabeast Book* in which each letter, framed, is reshaped in two other frames to end, in a fourth frame, as an object; and *Alphabatics* by Suse MacDonald, in which letters also change shapes to form pictures. This is useful for visual

From *Alphabatics*, illustrated by
Suse MacDonald.

conceptualizing as well as for learning the alphabet. *Still Another Alphabet Book,* by Seymour Chwast and Martin Stephen Moskof, is an unusual book, too, the pictures varied and inventive, and the entire alphabet used as a frieze on each page. Within each frieze, the letters used in the word for the pictured object are printed in a different color; for example, the *Q* page pictures a queenly figure and within the frieze of the alphabet the letters in "queen" are a different color from the other letters in the alphabet—a technique that intrigues children as a game and fosters reading readiness.

Among the more sophisticated ABC books is Arnold and Anita Lobel's *On Market Street,* in which Anita Lobel builds ingenious and decorative figures out of objects, like a man constructed of musical instruments for "M." The letters in Mitsumasa Anno's *Anno's Alphabet* are shown as pieces of roughly grained wood with intriguing objects surrounded by a delicate frame that differs on every page; and Muriel Feelings's *Jambo Means Hello,* a Swahili alphabet book illustrated by Tom Feelings with pictures in soft black and white, gives a vivid impression of East African life as well as words and word definitions for each letter in the Swahili alphabet.

There are many other ABC books and undoubtedly more to come, but these major examples illustrate some of the various types. Since alphabet books provide graphic experience, are used for identifying objects, and often include information and concepts as well as the letters *A–Z,* a primary requisite in choosing them is clarity. Objects should be easily identifiable, and illustrations, whether drawings or photographs, should be consistent with the theme of the book if a specific theme (*A Big City*) is presented. The typeface should be clean, rather than ornamented to the point of making the letter of the alphabet difficult to identify. Although there are successful exceptions, the use of an uncommon word as the key word is inadvisable in alphabet books intended for young children; it may pique the curiosity of some but is liable to frustrate many children who cannot name the object. The illustration should match the key word, and the word itself should use the starting letter in its most commonly pronounced way: It would be unwise, for

example, to use the word "children" to illustrate the letter *C.* Bruno Munari's *ABC* diverges from the practice but is both attractive and effective. Words, concepts, and facts are important, but children do need to know the letters of the alphabet in order to enjoy and learn from the ABC book.

Counting Books

Counting books range from those that present numbers—usually numerals from one to ten—in the simplest way, to books that have continuity, tell a story, or are used by an artist as a base for elaborately imaginative shapes or situations. One of the best of such books is Robert Allen's *Numbers: A First Counting Book* which uses color photographs of familiar objects and also introduces subtly the idea that size and location do not affect components of a numerical unit. After presenting numbers one through ten with facing pictures, the text goes on to show pictures in which there are two groups: apples in a circle, and the same number in a straight line, or pictures of two groups of tomatoes of varying sizes. Young children often confuse mass and numbers, or size and position, so this serves also as a concept book.

Other books that show only groups of objects are Mitsumasa Anno's *Anno's Counting Book* with handsome illustrations in which objects cumulate, and which incorporates concepts of times, seasons, and sets; Helen Oxenbury's *Numbers of Things,* a tall, narrow book in which the appeal lies chiefly in the deft, humorous illustrations; Dick Rowan's *Everybody In!,* which shows children of various ethnic backgrounds in a series of photographs, each with one more child joining the others in a swimming pool; and Demi's *Count the Animals 1, 2, 3.*

Some counting books use rhymes to add interest. In Beau Gardner's *Can You Imagine? . . . A Counting Book,* children enjoy a whale in a veil and ducks driving trucks. Also in verse, but with more story line, is Emilie McLeod's *One Snail and Me: A Book of Numbers and Animals and a Bathtub,* the gathering of assorted creatures in a huge old tub being an entertaining concept to the young child. John Burningham, in *Read One,* ingeniously uses the pages of a board book to help children associate number symbols and the words that represent them.

Something similar is *1 One Dancing Drum* by Gail Kredenser, with Stanley Mack's pictures showing a frenetic bandmaster amassing players and instruments in a small, circular bandstand: one dancing drum, two tinkling triangles —they all pile in, but each group is a different color, so it is easy to pick out the nine tootling trombonists, some of whom are perched on top of other musicians. There is a clutter of objects in Russell Hoban's *Ten What?* but as drawn by Sylvie Selig, it's an inspired clutter. The book is also a mystery story, and the baffled detective is surrounded on page 7, where "seven houses were searched," by seven police cars, seven oversize butterflies, seven chairs out on the sidewalk, and so forth.

Muriel Feelings's *Moja Means One* gives numerals from one to ten, the Swahili word for each numeral, phonetic pronunciation, and a sentence in which the names of objects that are to be counted are printed in red. While the geographic references may mean little to young children, the strong, soft pictures by Tom Feelings reinforce the concept of another culture.

Seymour Chwast and Martin Moskof, in *Still*

Another Number Book, do not use cumulation except for a reprise at the close, but use one page for 1, two for 2. Two children are pictured: $1 + 1 = 2$. Five dogs? $1 + 1 + 1 + 1 + 1 = 5$. The pictures are silly and lighthearted in contemporary, almost pop, style. Another interesting variant is Bruce McMillan's *Counting Wildflowers,* which presents numerals from one to twenty within a framework of botany and introduces, through photographs, color identification and wildflower recognition.

Many of the recent books move past a simple presentation of digits to expand arithmetical concepts for children who are already comfortable with numbers. John Burningham, in *The Shopping Basket,* tells the story of a boy who goes shopping for six eggs, five bananas, and so on, losing some of the items (subtraction) in a series of comic adventures. In *Ten, Nine, Eight,* Molly Bang uses a countdown as she pictures a small black child being put to bed by a loving father. Jane Miller's *Farm Counting Book* begins with color photographs of one kitten and two lambs, and then expands the concept of addition by including a picture with the caption "Here are three cows," facing it with separate pictures of three different animals, and the caption "3 animals altogether." In *Counting,* by

From *Anno's Counting Book*, illustrated by Mitsumasa Anno.

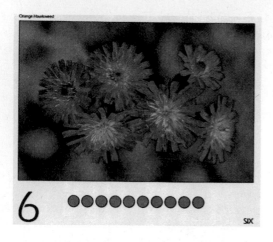

From *Counting Wildflowers*, photographs by Bruce McMillan.

Henry Pluckrose, text and excellent photographs present simple mathematical concepts.

Adults who are evaluating picture counting books should be wary of such pitfalls as the illustration that is out of pattern. In *The Sesame Street Book of Numbers*, for example, four objects follow the numeral 4, five follow 5, and so on—but the picture for 8 shows an octopus with eight tentacles rather than eight objects. This requires a visual sophistication that most young children have not yet achieved, although viewers of the television program on which the book is based may have no problem with it. In the same book, some of the numerals are so over-illustrated as to be difficult to read. Eve Merriam's *Project 1–2–3* is set in a large housing project, an interesting background but one that overshadows the counting function of the book, since the author gives a surfeit of information. For 7, for example, there are many signs on a basement wall ("Check faucets in building 7," "Check 7 incinerator hoppers," and others) and the text reads, "The maintenance men are busy fixing leaks and locks and lots of what gets broken. How many leaking faucets? Drip, drip, drip, drip, drip, drip, drip."

Two final counting books are delightful because of the beauty of the illustrations. Brian Wildsmith's *1, 2, 3's* has imperfections; when an arrow points to a geometric figure and the text asks "How many?", it isn't clear whether the question means green shapes or triangles. But the composition is handsome abstract art, and the colors are vividly beautiful. In Bert Kitchen's *Animal Numbers,* the large-scale paintings are marvelously effective, with animals twined about or perched on digits.

The same sort of clarity needed in ABC books is important in counting books: clear depiction of numerals, close relation of text to pictures, and easily identifiable objects if the objects are intended to be counted. A page crowded with vaguely drawn insects, among which are some intended to represent flies but not easily distinguishable from gnats, will only confuse the child if the text says "7—seven flies." It must be clear *what* is being counted. For very young children just beginning to familiarize themselves with the shapes of numerals and their relation to counting—often learned first by fingers—the best books are those that have plenty of open space to set off numerals and objects, those in which the numerals are large and clear.

Concept Books

In the early years of childhood, when the development of language skills is of paramount importance and when the young child's curiosity creates an interest in all the relationships and categories of a complex world, one of the more difficult areas to master is that of the abstract concept. How big is "big"? How far is "far"? Time, distance, size, mass, color, shape, and the difference between "between" and "through" need to be clarified and amplified in books as well as in conversation. Some concepts have to do with physical matter and can easily be depicted visually; some concepts—time, for example—can be described in words but cannot be shown by illustrations. Concepts like the nature of love or death are abstractions and are more difficult for young children to grasp; they cannot be drawn and they are not easy to explain. Through repeated experiences, explanations, and questions young children can be helped to grasp elusive concepts of their environment. Thus, in support of Piaget's theory, children develop *schemata,* units of knowledge about their world.

Small children are often fascinated by their own size and growth. In *The Growing Story,* Ruth Krauss explores a child's interest in his own growth, comparing that slow process with the more observable growth of plants and animals. When fall comes and the winter clothes that had been put away for him prove to be too small, the boy triumphantly discovers that he, too, is growing, though he sees no change when he looks in the mirror. Concept books explore differences and similarities in people. Ann McGovern's *Black Is Beautiful* praises the night-black sky, the rich earth, a black butterfly, and black faces; in Barbara Brenner's *Faces,* the photographs show not only how features vary but how they are alike in the ways they are used, incidentally presenting concepts about the senses.

Several concepts are combined in Helen Borten's *Do You Know What I Know?* It explores the senses, presents environmental concepts, and also touches on colors, size differences, and personal preferences, all illustrated with a dazzling variety of styles and techniques. Rachel Isadora, in *I See,* reflects the small world of a very young child. In three books, the versatile Marcia Brown uses stunning full-color photographs and poetic captions to encourage environmental awareness; *Listen to a Shape, Touch Will Tell,* and *Walk with Your Eyes* focus on sharpening children's observation of shapes and textures in nature.

Many concept books have no story line but depend upon accurate description, repetition, and comparison to convey ideas. Books about shapes usually deal with several shapes, as do *Let's Look for Shapes,* by Bill Gillham and Susan Hulme, and John Reiss's *Shapes.* The latter, illustrated in brilliant and effective color, goes past the familiar circle, square, and triangle to include solid forms (showing how squares form a cube) and to more complex ones like oval and rectangle. Examples of each shape are given; for oval, they are musical notes, plums, eggs, and spoons. Tana Hoban uses photographs also in *Shapes and Things* but these are much simpler—silhouettes in white against a black page. The objects are grouped so that children can

also perceive the concept of sets: kitchen utensils, tools, objects used at a desk, objects used in sewing. This book has the appeal of a simple game of identification and can be used with very young children.

In addition to his book about shapes, Reiss also has created one of the best of the books on color, with repetition of examples and—something lacking in other books on the subject—various shades of a color. A frog is in several shades of green, a pale green snake coils through the darker grass, and leaf shapes in a variety of forms are in several shades. Also noteworthy is Bruce McMillan's *Growing Colors,* with its use of fine color photographs to show fresh foods that even very young children can identify.

There are, of course, many books that are not written for the purpose of defining concepts that nevertheless do so; and there are also many books that could be placed as appropriately in one group as another. Some of Tana Hoban's books that illustrate concepts by making comparisons, for example, could be placed with wordless picture books like *Shapes and Things.* Her *Take Another Look* has no text but uses pages in which a cut-out circle challenges

From *Let's Look at Shapes* by Bill Gillham and Susan Hulme, photographs by Jan Siegieda.

the viewer to identify the portion of the picture shown and then, on another page, shows the picture in context.

The most effective uses of comparison are probably in those books that deal with elusive concepts: Hoban's *Push-Pull, Empty-Full* and *Over, Under, & Through;* Bruce McMillan's *Dry or Wet?* and Colin McNaughton's *At Home,* one of a series of board books about opposites for very young children. Hoban uses one set of pictures for each set of opposite terms, sharp and well-chosen photographs making the comparison very clear.

A lesser number of concept books are written with a narrative framework. Location and direction are emphasized in Betsy Maestro's *Where Is My Friend?* in which an elephant searches by going *through* a gate, peering *under* a rock, or looking *behind* her for the mouse which appears, beaming, *in front* of her nose. The concept of grouping is used in Rodney Peppe's *Odd One OuT,* the title giving a clue to the fact that there's one unit in each set that doesn't belong. A boy goes to school, window-shops, and visits a farm, a park, and a fair, in

From *School,* written and illustrated by Emily Arnold McCully.

each case seeing one thing that doesn't belong: a boat on the farm, a cash register in the park, a monkey in the classroom. While a strong story line is not evident, the book entertains while encouraging observation and the concept of appropriate placement.

Although there is little action in Walter Myers's *Where Does the Day Go?,* it has other strong values in addition to its exploration of the mystery of night and day. The discussion among a group of children shows some of the misconceptions that can arise. The book explains natural phenomena accurately, and it presents an exemplary father who takes an evening walk with his children and their friends, commenting on the fact that people are as different as night and day, and how wonderful that is.

It is, as all parents know, important for young children to learn that parental departure is not synonymous with parental desertion. There are two books that deal nicely, each in a different way, with the idea that separation need not be traumatic. Dorothy Corey's *You Go Away* addresses this concept by showing a baby playing peekaboo, a father tossing his child and catching him, children playing hide-and-seek, and so on. It ends with parents going off with luggage, and with the comforting "You are going far away . . . you will come back!" In Robert Welber's *Goodbye, Hello,* a series of small creatures leave their mothers happily: "A puppy goes sniffing down the road. Goodbye, Mother . . . (page turn) Hello, teacher." Emily Arnold McCully, in *School,* turns the tables, as the baby mouse of a large family follows siblings to school, enjoys participating, and is perfectly happy when rescued by a worried mother. McCully also uses the separation theme in *Picnic,* when the littlest mouse is jolted off the back of a truck, is missed, and is retrieved when a loving family returns for him—or maybe it's her. The story line is, in both of McCully's books, quite clear.

While concept books cannot be judged by exactly the same criteria as books that give importance to a story line, it is easy to determine the effectiveness of some. The best concept books reinforce ideas by reiterating the information but not boring readers, and they move from the familiar to the less familiar.

These books begin with simple ideas and pictures and move on to those that are slightly more complex. For example, books about shapes or colors can be evaluated for their pictorial success or failure, while books that deal with emotions must be assessed for the effectiveness of the text, and that involves making a subjective judgment. Concept books can help young children see relationships between objects, or see more than one aspect of an idea, or visualize changes, or become aware of similarities or differences.

Wordless Books

While there has been debate over whether wordless books are effective in preparing children for reading, there is little question that prereaders and readers enjoy them. Such books can predispose a young child to the attitude that books are a source of pleasure, can accustom them to the left-to-right pattern of reading, can accustom them to responding to the story told by the pictures, and can introduce them to the concept of sequential action as pages are turned. It must be kept in mind, when evaluating these books, that they are designed to encourage not reading, but reading readiness.

Some of these books are humorous, many are inventive, and a few—like Mitsumasa Anno's *Topsy-Turvies*—are beautifully illustrated. The best wordless books have pictures so clearly drawn that the child can easily follow the plot of the story, if there is a story line. In *Topsy-Turvies,* there is a series of pictures that play with perspective or position, presenting improbabilities to challenge the young imagination. Some wordless books give information, as does Iela and Enzo Mari's *The Apple and the Moth.* The illustrations in this book follow a moth through its egg, caterpillar, cocoon, and adult stages, beginning with the moth's egg in an apple and ending with the next generation's egg in an apple blossom. The child can supply the words, but the science lesson is clear.

Books without text that are informational are in the minority, but there are several good ones. Edward Koren's *Behind the Wheel* shows what you see from the driver's seat in a series of

Viewpoint

Until children are well into the school years, their attention is caught by objects or scenes that are strong and simple—big bold strokes, bright clear colors, sharp contrasts, and similar overstatements. They need more clues to what they're seeing, hearing, tasting, or touching than adults do. That is, much more of a building must be visible if they are going to recognize it—understandably, for they haven't seen many buildings and therefore aren't as able as adults to infer a church from a steeple or a service station from a revolving sign seen through some trees . . . . When children do become aware of details, they tend not to perceive them as parts-of-a-whole but as separate entities— smaller "wholes." This behavior was documented by William A. Miller, who tested the perception of third-graders by asking them to describe the pictures in their own school books. In each picture there were twenty to twenty-six constituent items whose perception was important to an understanding of the pictured scene. The children identified (on the average) fewer than a third of the items.

Muriel Beadle, *A Child's Mind; How Children Learn During the Critical Years from Birth to Age Five.* Garden City, New York: Doubleday & Company, 1970, pp. 151– 152.

vehicles and machines. Insets show labeled details of the controls, but there's no other text; it's an excellent book for the question and answer approach. In Donald Crews's *Trucks* the paintings of vehicles are bold, bright, and clear.

The increased awareness of the importance of language and books for the very young child has produced some excellent wordless books for infants. Helen Oxenbury's series of board books (*I Can, I Hear, I See, I Touch*) has captions on the pages, but no text, and each book focuses on one familiar concept, with deft and comic pictures that can be used for delighted identification. A second series (*Mother's Helper; Good Night, Good Morning*) is just right for the more sophisticated three-year-old. Two books by Jan Ormerod, *Sunshine* and *Moonlight,* have handsome pictures, framed in comic strip style, that show in detail the morning and evening routines in a child's day.

There are several wordless books that tell a realistic story. In Edward Ardizzone's *The Wrong Side of the Bed,* a scowling child has breakfast postponed while he is scrubbed, teases a little sister and is scolded, and goes outdoors and can't find anything to do; however, he comes home to a kiss and a cuddle on his mother's lap. In Tomie de Paola's *Pancakes for Breakfast,* the bucolic pictures vividly tell the story of a woman's problems in gathering ingredients to make pancakes.

Most animal stories are fanciful, but three of the better realistic stories of animals are John Hamberger's *The Lazy Dog,* in which a dog energetically chases a ball and then is so exhausted that a child has to rouse him; and *Pssst! Doggie* and *Kitten for a Day,* both by Ezra Jack Keats. In the first of these, a cat offers, "Pssst! Doggie—Wanna dance?" and a series of pas de deux follows, with the animals imagining themselves in costumes. In the second book, a friendly puppy joins a group of kittens and tries to do whatever they do (he's not very good at meowing), deciding at the end that next time they can all be puppies. There is some text, primarily "Lick, lick, lick," and "Slurp," so this isn't a true wordless book, but it is in the pattern. Boy meets dog in *Lucky Puppy, Lucky Boy* by Terry Morris, and boy loses and finds a favorite toy in Dieter Schubert's *Where's My Monkey?*. In *Bobo's Dream* by Martha Alexander, a boy rescues his dog's bone from a larger dog. Napping, the grateful pet dreams of protecting his boy; in the dream he is a large, fierce dog and when he wakes, he is still so confident that

Viewpoint

Since words are the separable parts of meaningful sentences, we can understand language only by understanding parts first, then building up to a whole that might in fact be an accurate combination of all the parts. But we see pictures all at once first and only then can begin to notice the potential relationships of their various parts. Our understanding of language starts with details and moves toward wholes; our understanding of pictures starts with wholes and breaks down into details. In terms of the halves of the brain, Jeremy Campbell suggests, "the right side tends to use a 'top-down' strategy, processing information as a whole, perceiving its full meaning rather than approaching it 'bottom-up,' using the parts to construct the whole, which is often more than the sum of its parts." We have to approach words bottom-up— one at a time, in the sequence in which they are given us. Consequently, words are best at describing relationships of details, pictures best at giving a sense of the whole. But each can eventually do both, and they can certainly help each other to do both.

Nevertheless, picture-book artists almost always convey information about the ways things look by means of pictures. While that may seem too obvious to be worth saying, the main difficulty facing neophyte writers of texts for picture books is understanding that they must leave such visual information in the hands of their illustrators. A good picture-book text does not tell us that the girl had brown eyes or that the room was gloomy—yet practitioners of literary art use exactly such visual details to establish character, mood, and atmosphere. Writers of picture books must imply character and mood without recourse to such details— and hope that illustrators sensitive to their stories will invent the right visual details to express the appropriate information.

Perry Nodelman, *Words About Pictures: The Narrative Art of Children's Picture Books.* Athens, Georgia: University of Georgia Press, 1988, p. 202.

he actually does frighten away a large dog. Alexander's pictures differentiate quite clearly between dream and reality.

Of the animal stories in which the creatures behave like animals but within an exaggerated or fanciful framework, the books about a boy and his frog by Mercer Mayer are among the most successful. *Frog Goes to Dinner,* for example, has bubbling humor and plenty of the action children enjoy, as the little stowaway hops out of his boy's pocket at an elegant restaurant and creates havoc. In *Hiccup,* Mayer bases the humor on an elephant's aggressive treatment of the hiccups suffered by Ms. Hippo, his lady love. José Aruego, in *Look What I Can Do,* gently and indirectly teases children's showoff instincts by having two animals compete in a follow-the-leader orgy; at the end, they are panting with fatigue but rouse themselves to sit on a third animal who says, "Look what I can do."

John Goodall's books use the device of half-pages inserted between each set of full pages, so that the turn of the half-page changes part of each illustration. In *The Ballooning Adventures of Paddy Pork,* an adventurous pig rescues a piglet in distress, braves storm and sea monster in his balloon, and returns from his voyage to the plaudits of a porcine crowd. (The adventures of this pig are continued in *Paddy Under Water.*) Goodall's unique format works particularly well in his version of *Little Red Riding Hood.*

One of the most ingenious wordless books is *Changes, Changes* by Pat Hutchins. Like *Topsy-Turvies,* it plays with transforming shapes, but it also tells a story as two stiff little wooden dolls shift and adapt the varied shapes of building blocks to make a house, transform it into a fire engine and then into other structures, ending with another house. This book has the full-circle action children find satisfying, aesthetic appeal, and the clarity of story line that marks the successful wordless book. The "changes" in Peter Collington's books are shifts between realism and fantasy—and they are so clearly demarcated by this author-illustrator that the changes can be followed without words. In *Little Pickle,* Collington portrays an amusingly obstreperous small girl who creates havoc but redeems herself in a dream sequence. In *The*

Viewpoint

Lillian Smith, in her book* about children's literature, designates the years of childhood as "the unreluctant years," and nowhere is this trait, this quick responsiveness, more noticeable than in the picture-book audience. The young child freely gives to writers and artists the benefit of his unprejudiced mind. Yet specific qualities in the book determine whether his reaction will be strong or weak, positive or negative. Notwithstanding initial "unreluctance," an inept or insipid book creates boredom in a child as surely as it does in anyone else and may instill suspicion about the value of books in general. On the other hand, a marked devotion occurs when strong literary or graphic elements are present, when there are illustrations, incidents, characters, or modes of expression which prove intriguing. Then the child quickly involves himself in the drama of the action, identifies with the hero, immerses himself in the setting, mimics comic characters, chants rhythmic words and phrases, and examines illustrations with an amazing awareness of mood and detail.

Donnarae MacCann and Olga Richard, *The Child's First Books; A Critical Study of Pictures and Texts,* H. W. Wilson Company, New York, 1973, p. 8.

*Lillian Smith. *The Unreluctant Years.* (Chicago: American Library Association), 1953.

Angel and the Soldier Boy, Collington creates a dramatic adventure shared by a child's toys while she sleeps.

Since the interpretation of books without words depends entirely on the pictures, it is of paramount importance that both the immediate action of each picture and the sequence of action in all the pictures be unequivocally clear. The story line should be distinct if there is a narrative, as in some of the Goodall books, and the development of any informational sequence should be clear, as in Mari's *The Apple and the Moth.* These books encourage children to interpret and embellish a story; they are a good

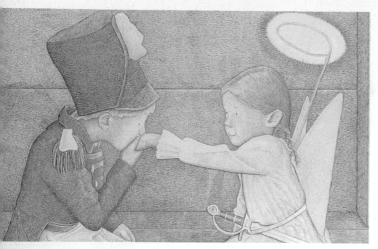

From *The Angel and the Soldier Boy*, illustrated by Peter Collington.

catalyst for discussion of the author's (or illustrator's) intent and for the child's creativity, encouraging the language skills that are so integral a part of reading readiness.

Books for Beginning Readers

Some children have learned to read through basal readers which include word repetition but lack a sense of narrative. The latter is one of the great assets of many of the fiction books published for first- and second-grade children today, or for those who learn to read before entering school. Since action and humor have strong appeal for young children, some of the contemporary books with these qualities are proving to be as popular as they are effective as reading materials for young children, and many of them have enough narrative flow to read aloud well also.

Whatever methods children have learned to read by, they have specific needs in the first books they read independently. The words must be simple enough for them to understand and the sentences brief enough so that the text does not appear formidable. Repetition helps the beginning independent reader, but it should be used with restraint and only when it would occur naturally, if it is used in dialogue. The print should be large and clear, with adequate space between words and between lines, and with not so much text on a page that the print seems discouragingly heavy to a child.

There have been books in the past that were suitable for the beginning reader, such as Du Bose Heyward's *The Country Bunny and the Little Gold Shoes* or even parts of Kate Greenaway's *Under the Window,* but both of these have more text on the page than would be used today, and the print of Greenaway's book is lamentably small. Two excellent books which appeared in the 1950s are Elizabeth Guilfoile's *Nobody Listens to Andrew* and *The Cat in the Hat* by Dr. Seuss. Nobody believes Andrew has anything important to say until he finally announces loudly and firmly that there is a bear in his bed; pandemonium ensues and is followed by a captured bear and a triumphantly vindicated boy. The story has a mild humor in the writing style, plenty of action, and a situation most children will find familiar: being ignored. It also fulfills all the physical requisites for a beginning reader's book. Seuss, a genre unto himself, uses rhyme, repetition, and nonsense humor in *The Cat in the Hat.* This fast-moving story uses a series of incidents rather than a smooth story line as the irrepressible cat turns a household into a shambles, zooms about on a machine with mechanical arms, and goes off leaving the scene looking as placid as it was before his entry.

Most of these short books have a continuous text, but some authors have divided their texts into short, separate episodes children can handle easily, giving them also the satisfaction of having "chapters" just as older children do. Notable among this group are the books by Else Minarik, by Arnold Lobel, and by James Marshall. Minarik's *Little Bear* has four stories about an ingenuous cub who makes himself some birthday soup, takes an imaginary trip to the moon, has a bedtime chat about the world's most fascinating topic (himself), and makes an interesting discovery about clothes. The warmth, tenderness, and humor of the story are echoed in Maurice Sendak's pictures. The illustrations for Lobel's books are his own, deft and direct and carefully placed on the pages so that they present no visual barrier to the print. His *Mouse Tales,* simply written and engaging, is a series of bedtime stories told by a father mouse to his young. However, it was with *Frog and Toad Are Friends* that Lobel established himself as master of this form. This book was a finalist for the National Book Award, and its sequel a Newbery Honor Book; this despite the fact that awards for distinguished literary contributions seldom come to books for beginning readers. What Lobel achieves in these and other books is a pervasive feeling of amused affection blended with a wry appreciation of the foibles of the characters in the stories. The pictures are appealing, but the smoothness of the writing and the establishment of personalities in so limited a space are the strongest aspects of these animal stories. James Marshall, in *Fox on the Job,* uses five episodes to show the hapless fox finally succeeding at making money —as a sleeper in a mattress display. The cartoon-like drawings are just right for the comic

From *Frog and Toad Are Friends*, written and illustrated by Arnold Lobel.

antics; the words are easy, and the humor makes the serious business of decoding easier.

Humor is a component of a wide variety of stories. There is the exaggeration in *The Case of the Double Cross* by Crosby Bonsall, whose stories have more suspense than most, and usually concern group activity. In Johanna Hurwitz's *Russell Sprouts,* a first-grader experiences the pleasure of role-reversal as he rates his parents on report card. In *There Is a Carrot in My Ear,* Alvin Schwartz has simplified six noodlehead stories, the humor of the writing echoed by the comical pictures; and in *Buggy Riddles,* by Katy Hall and Lisa Eisenberg, the funny answers are just right for primary grade readers.

In Joan Lexau's *The Homework Caper,* an interracial friendship is evident in the pictures as two boys hunt frantically for a lost homework paper, eventually discovering that the little sister of one of them had substituted her "homework" for her brother's. The dialogue is direct and brisk; the solution amicable; the story given warmth by an understanding teacher and by the boys' realization that they, too, had thought at little Susan's age that their scribbles were understandable communications. Leonard Kessler's *Old Turtle's Soccer Team* blends fantasy and realism in a story that presents some soccer facts within a fictional context of animal athletes making silly mistakes during a game. Kessler may have presented too many elements in the book for a smooth blending of fantasy and realism, yet the book is particularly notable because of the small number of sports stories for young children. However, it is significant that Kessler's book, like Lexau's and many of Bonsall's, shows both black and white children in the illustrations.

Some lively series books are geared to the young audience. Miriam Cohen's *First Grade Takes a Test* is one of a school-related series; Pat Ross's *M and M and the Bad New Babies,* part of the *M and M* series, describes the comic plight of two young friends as they try to gain the cooperation of the charges entrusted to their babysitting care. Children who have enjoyed one selection from a series will be likely to seek other books from the collection.

Informational books for beginning readers present a challenge to authors: They entail the arts of writing succinctly and sequentially and of knowing how to abridge material without omitting something of importance. Peggy Parish's *Dinosaur Time* satisfies young children's curiosity on this perennially popular subject, giving the names, their pronunciation, and a few salient facts about eleven kinds of dinosaurs. Except for the dinosaur names, the words are simple; the print is large; the information accurate. *Alligator* by Evelyn Shaw describes a life cycle in narrative form with no anthropomorphism. *Look at Your Eyes* by Paul Showers is a model of simplicity in the description of basic facts about the human eye. Harlow Rockwell offers a variety of easy projects in *I Did It,* a "how-to" book that incorporates adeptly repeated words. Photographs illustrate Millicent Selsam's *How Puppies Grow,* which follows newly born puppies through stages of development until they are old enough to be played with and become children's pets.

One of the foremost science writers for any age level, Selsam uses a fictional framework in *Tony's Birds* in which facts about birds are dispersed through a story of a father helping his son learn to become a bird watcher. Another natural science book in narrative form is Nathaniel Benchley's *The Several Tricks of Edgar Dolphin.* Benchley also achieves, in *George the Drummer Boy,* a comprehensible story about the American Revolution as seen from the viewpoint of a very young British soldier.

While some trade books for beginning independent readers use needed repetition in the unimaginative style of the basal readers, most trade books published today have a limited rather than a rigidly controlled vocabulary.

Viewpoint

Limited in the number of pages, a picture book often cannot afford the additional space necessary in order to focus on a detail for emphasis. Unlike film, a picture book with its still pictures cannot show movement itself. It is in such situations that the words can help to emphasize a detail, clarify an action, or link two pictures together. Unlike a storybook, which expresses sight and sound through words, a picture book separates the two, representing the sight by a picture and the sound by words. But since a picture book is read to the very young child, who doesn't know yet how to read, the child will *see* the pictures and *hear* the words.

In other words, the picture book is a return to an original premise: to see and to hear directly, without the intermediary of the printed word. By representing visually, instead of representing by words (describing), a picture book becomes naturally a *dramatic* experience: direct, immediate, vivid, moving. One can see the importance of reading the words aloud from a picture book: it is more important how the words will sound when heard than how they will be seen when read. The kinship between picture books and theater or film, the silent film in particular, becomes evident. The words in a picture book at times approach the quality of folk ballads or nursery rhymes, such as Caldecott's picture books. It is no mere coincidence that the picture book concept has been used to a greater extent by artists than by writers.

Uri Shulevitz, "What Is a Picture Book?", *The Five Owls,* Volume II, Number 4, March/April 1988, pp. 50–51.

From *Stanley and Rhoda,* written and illustrated by Rosemary Wells.

Several publishers (Harper & Row, Crowell, Greenwillow, and Random House, for example) have excellent series designed either for early readers or for readers in the primary grades. Harper & Row has a distinguished series of history books, and Crowell an impressive series of science books for very young readers. In 1990, both Harper and Crowell became HarperCollins Children's Books.

Although standards in series are usually maintained and we may expect a certain level of quality from the better series, still each book should be judged on its own merits and evaluated by the criteria that apply to all books for young readers and particularly to the first books they read alone.

Picture Story Books

While there were illustrated books for young children early in the history of children's books, the picture book really came into its own only when printing techniques made it possible to publish books illustrated in color at a reasonable price. Illustrators like Crane, Greenaway, and Caldecott became well known, and artists who followed them in the early and mid-twentieth century produced varied and intricately developed illustrations. Many artists from other countries came to the United States, and a flourishing exchange was established in translated editions and in copublication programs. The work of many major contributors in the first half of this century, as well as the work of today's illustrators, is discussed in Chapter 5, "Artists and Children's Books."

Most of the discussion here focuses on texts rather than on illustrations. It should be clear, however, that almost every artistic technique and medium has been used successfully in picture books for young children. In some books the pictures serve as elements of mood, as in Uri Shulevitz's *Dawn*, while in stories like Graham Oakley's adventure tales of the church mice and their friend the church cat, the illustrations are explicit representations of the setting and the action. One of the most important criteria for evaluating a picture story book is the degree to which pictures and text reinforce each other.

There is seldom enough time in a brief picture story book for full character development, although some may be shown by the illustrations. Many books with memorable characters, like Curious George or Ferdinand the Bull or the fractious Rhoda in Rosemary Wells's *Stanley and Rhoda,* achieve firm characterization by emphasis on one trait or behavior pattern. George is curious, Ferdinand likes to sit quietly and smell flowers, Rhoda is lazy and messy. Some stories focus on a one-to-one relationship, as do Lizi Boyd's *The Not-So-Wicked-Stepmother* and Kevin Henke's *Grandpa and Bo,* a quiet story of a warm affection. Characterization or individual relationships should be depicted without sentimentality; they should be believable and consistent.

The plot may be as simple as learning to tie a shoe, spending a first day at school or a first night away from home, or making the adjustment to the death of a pet, but it should have a structure: problem and solution, achievement of a new skill or a new experience, or the presentation of an event or an attitude that effects a change in a character or characters. There are always some books in which structure is lacking but is compensated for by the strength of some other aspect. An example is the Provensens's *Our Animal Friends at Maple Hill Farm,* in which the range of appealing creatures, lively illustrations, and witty captions carry the text along at a good pace.

Whether a picture story is realistic or fanciful, it will appeal to young children if it has humor or action. Again, some books lack these qualities but introduce a provocative concept or establish a mood so well that they appeal to children nevertheless. Although it is the text we are considering here, it should be kept in mind that in many picture story books, as in picture books, the illustrations may be so striking or so humorous as to rival the text and make the whole book appealing to children.

Sometimes the appealing element is the information given by the text, by the pictures, or by both. Children are always actively curious; they are intrigued when they find that another child's family has a pattern that differs from their own or when they learn from a book what it was like in their parents' time, which to them is in a misty past. They are at the same time reassured by similarities in pattern, and they need to identify with others as their circle enlarges, just as they need that first sense of identification with the family group. Children who live in the country find an urban setting fascinating, just as city children are interested in the details of farm life; each group receives a different kind of pleasure from books that have settings familiar to them. African-American children need to see themselves in books, as do members of other ethnic groups, and each group needs to see the others as a part of our society. They must feel both accepted and accepting. Recall Erikson's theory that as the child's ego develops, a major fact of psychosocial growth is his or her persistent need to identify with others, eventually achieving a sense of personal identity built on a firm base of trust and understanding.

This curiosity about people can be satisfied in part by books, as can children's curiosity about themselves, animals, weather, and other aspects of their lives. How does a mother know what to do when the toaster won't work? What is a cousin? What does "dead" mean? How does a dump truck work? Why doesn't the boy next door go to the same church or temple? What is that funny thing hanging around the doctor's neck? Children's questions are endless, their need to know insatiable. They have so much to learn in the early years, and they learn so quickly, that we cannot give them too many books.

Viewpoint

A young child shares with the primitive an extraordinary power to identify himself with the people, animals, and things of this world, and this power makes him extremely accessible to the magic power of symbol. This same power carried into adult life enables the artist to enter the feelings of his subjects and draw and paint them in such a way that not only do they look as if they felt a certain way, but they also make the spectator feel that same way. Young children have a profound sense of the mysterious, but if the mood of our work is to speak to them, it must relate to other realities they know. The child cannot gape forever at the juggler or shiver endlessly with the tightrope walker. After the circus is over the arc of his own ball in the air will be more beautiful, the sureness of his own foot as he walks the curb will give him pride. He contains his experience.

A picture book really exists only when a child and a book come together, when the stream that formed in the artist's mind and heart flows through the book and into the mind and heart of the child. Before starting to make the book, an artist must be sure the story is worth the time, his time and love spent in illustrating it, and the child's time to be spent in looking at it.

Reprinted with permission of Charles Scribner's Sons, an imprint of Macmillan Publishing Company from "Integrity and Intuition" in *Lotus Seeds* by Marcia Brown. Copyright © 1955, 1967, 1986 by Marcia Brown.

Family Life

Young children take pleasure in seeing the familiar relationships of home reflected in their books, whether the characters are human or animals. Children may recognize themselves and their families in a story as quiet and realistic as Cynthia Rylant's *Birthday Presents*— or in one as bouncy as Barrie Wade's *Little Monster.*

Very young children are most concerned with parents and their roles in respect to that center of the universe, the child. Books like Charlotte Zolotow's *When I Have a Little Girl,* in which a child announces how rules will be different when she is a parent, and Jill Murphy's *Five Minutes' Peace,* in which a mother elephant escapes briefly from her beloved but noisy young, project quite naturally a child's desire to have a world in which all wishes are granted by obliging parents. The arrival of a new baby in the family of a young child disturbs this world, and picture stories about sibling jealousy may help alleviate a child's feelings of guilt. In Ann Scott's *On Mother's Lap,* Michael is an Eskimo child who learns to share parental love, but his experience is universal; in Eloise Greenfield's *She Come Bringing*

From *Birthday Presents* by Cynthia Rylant, illustrated by Suçie Stevenson.

Me That Little Baby Girl, Kevin is African American; his feelings of resentment at the attention paid to the new baby are common to all children. John Steptoe explores similar feelings in *Stevie*, a boldly illustrated book in which a young boy is jealous of a child under the care of his mother. The tables are turned in Martha Alexander's *I'll Be the Horse If You'll Play With Me*, as Oliver (who had tried to give away baby Bonnie in *Nobody Asked Me If I Wanted a Baby Sister*) imposes on Bonnie, who learns that she, in turn, can now impose on the younger brother of whom she had been jealous. Jeanne Titherington, in *A Place for Ben*, explores the relationship between two small brothers.

One of the trends in books for children of all ages has been an increasing interest in grandparents. Tomie dePaola's *Nana Upstairs and Nana Downstairs* shows a small child's love for his great-grandmother and his adjustment to her death; this adjustment makes it easier for him to accept his grandmother's death years later. Alice's grandmother, Oma, in *Oma and Bobo* by Amy Schwartz, is a crusty critic of Alice's new dog, Bobo, but she's slowly won over. The range of books about grandparents fortunately includes some that are warm or humorous even when dealing with a serious subject matter, as each of these books does. Children need books that will help them adjust to the illness or the death of older persons and books that depict their older characters as vital parts of extended families.

Everyday Life Experiences

Closely allied to stories of home and family are books that picture children's experiences as they begin to extend their range of activities: sharing tasks and responsibilities in the home, making small forays into the outside world, becoming acquainted with neighbors. The family is still involved as the child grows toward independence—establishing an identity, gaining self-confidence through achievement, and satisfying curiosity.

Books about everyday experiences generally deal with the fulfillment of children's needs or their acquisition of new skills or attitudes; the treatment of these subjects ranges from light to serious. There is as much to be gained from a realistic story like *Storm in the Night*, by Mary Stolz, in which a grandparent helps a child conquer his fear, as there is from Lillian Hoban's *Arthur's Honey Bear*. When Arthur sells his old toys, he has to adjust to the fact that he really still wants the toy bear his little sister buys; this story not only shows a child's logic and a growing ability to compromise, but suggests the way in which young children can look back and see their own growth.

Small tasks loom large to young children, who take great pride in having their contribu-

From *Storm in the Night* by Mary Stolz, illustrated by Pat Cummings.

tions recognized, and who often look on with envy while older brothers and sisters are sent on errands. In a series of board books for very young children, Shigeo Watanabe shows achievement of tasks: *How Do I Put It On?* and *What a Good Lunch!* focus on dressing and on feeding oneself. In Rosemary Wells's *Shy Charles,* a mouse child saves the day in an emergency, but remains shy. The small boy in Lorenz Graham's *Song of the Boat* finds just the right tree for his father to use in making a canoe, taking pride in his father's pleasure at his discovery, and in the fact that he was able to keep up with his father on the long hunt for the perfect tree. Although the treatment of a child's first night away from home in Bernard Waber's *Ira Sleeps Over* is humorous, it touches on the child's very real need to have familiar objects about him, as well as on the importance of so sophisticated an event. In *Ira Says Goodbye,* Waber treats the trauma of having a friend move away with similar humor and insight.

Stories about play are significant because children learn by playing. For them it is an important task. There are rhyme and rhythm in the text of William Cole's *What's Good for a Three-Year-Old?* in which a group of romping children at a birthday party discovers that each of them has a slightly different idea of what is most enjoyable. The problem of sharing posses-sions is handled deftly in Beverly Cleary's *Janet's Thingamajigs.* There is no lesson in Petronella Breinburg's *Doctor Shawn,* only a modest, realistic picture of a group of children involved in imaginative play, as they take roles in the game of "playing hospital." (No sex stereotypes here: Shawn and his sister take turns being nurse and doctor.) The issues of self-image and admiration for a macho play-mate are dealt with nicely in Bob Graham's *Crusher is Coming!* when the school football hero stops to play with a baby. Traditional sex roles are challenged in Charlotte Zolotow's *William's Doll,* in which a small boy is teased because he wants to play with a doll; only his grandmother understands that a boy may want a doll so that he can imitate the role of a father in just the same way that a girl pretends to be a mother—that both are preparing for a future task.

School Stories

As more and more children participate in programs at kindergartens, nursery schools, daycare centers, or less formal group pro-grams, the need for books that will prepare them for such experiences becomes clear. One of the simplest presentations is Gwenda Turn-er's *Playbook,* which has a warm, motherly teacher in a cozy, friendly setting; the book gently insinuates the ideas of sharing toys and working together on projects. *Did You Carry the Flag Today, Charley?* (discussed at length in Chapter 2) gives a memorable picture of a free spirit adjusting to the strictures of the class-room. In *Annabelle Swift, Kindergartner,* by Amy Schwartz, a child takes her big sister's advice too literally and delays her own adjustment to the classroom.

Friends

Almost every aspect of friendship is explored in the many picture story books about the ups and downs of relationships: learning to share, plan-ning projects, being jealous, having a quarrel, exchanging confidences, and, above all, having fun. One such book, Arnold Lobel's *Frog and Toad Are Friends,* has become a minor classic, with the sequel, *Frog and Toad Together,* not far

From *Annabelle Swift, Kindergartner,* written and illustrated by Amy Schwartz.

behind. The stories are short and simple enough for a beginning reader but flow smoothly for reading aloud, and they have a humorous, ingenuous style.

Charlotte Zolotow's writing is notable for the combination of a loving and perceptive eye and a direct, quiet style. In *The Unfriendly Book,* she describes the problem of coping with a friend who carps and criticizes other people; the William Pène du Bois illustrations show each friend first as Bertha (the carper) sees them and then as Judy sees them, a valuable lesson in differing viewpoints. The anguish of quarreling is handled with a light touch in Marjorie Sharmat's *I'm Not Oscar's Friend Anymore,* in which a small, brooding boy imagines Oscar moping and desolate after their quarrel. It is, in fact, the boy himself who is downcast, and when he relents and telephones Oscar, he finds that his friend doesn't even remember the fight they had. There's no cautionary note, but the message is the more effective for its ruefully comic air.

As in the stories of Frog and Toad, James Marshall's George and Martha (hippos), in *George and Martha Round and Round,* survive tests of friendship with an affectionate tolerance that overcomes exasperation; Marshall has a sense of the ridiculous that particularly appeals to very young children. While most stories deal with same-age (and often same-sex) friendships, there are others that can broaden these concepts. Aliki, in *Overnight at Mary Bloom's,* explores the pleasure of having an adult friend who enjoys your company. Kevin Henkes shows how dear an imaginary friend can be in *Jessica.* In *Alfie Gives a Hand,* by Shirley Hughes, a small English boy makes a new friend when he overcomes his own shyness to help a girl who is even more bashful.

As is true of other kinds of books, those for young children often fit into more than one category. Take for example the series of books by Miriam Cohen about the children in a multiethnic first grade classroom. *See You in Second Grade!* is indeed a school story, but it gives the nicest kind of lesson in friendship—with no preaching—when one of the boys make a small sacrifice to enable a girl, who finds she has no swimsuit, to join the others at an end-of-the-year beach party.

From *My Brother Tries to Make Me Laugh,* written and illustrated by Andrew Glass.

Humor

While many stories about friendship, families, or school have humorous aspects, there are some books in which humor is the most important element. Many of these are fantasies, but some realistic picture stories use exaggeration or nonsense for primary appeal. In addition to exaggeration and nonsense, young children enjoy disaster humor, incongruity, absurdity, and humorous wordplay, whether it is in the form of invented words, silly rhymes, or misused words. They are amused by animals who behave like people, and seldom disturbed by the anthropomorphism that may perturb adults. Children enjoy these qualities in the story and in the illustrations, and often it is the contrast between a bland, straightforward text and nonsensical pictures that supplies the comic quality of a book. For example, in Norma Farber's *Where's Gomer?,* the humorous appeal is in the florid exaggeration of the rhyming text, as the crew of Noah's Ark bewails the boy who is missing at departure time: "O tempest and flood! O watery ways," his mother wails as she weeps into the stew she's cooking. The wordplay in Russell Hoban's *They Came from Aargh!* is part of the humor, as three small boys play at being space creatures. Role reversal is the key to the humor of *My Brother Tries to Make Me Laugh,* by Andrew Glass; here the protagonists are indeed space creatures, and their mother warns them to be polite to the odd-looking Earthlings they are going to visit.

Tall-tale humor is an appealing element in the cheerful story of *The Lady Who Saw the Good Side of Everything* by Pat Tapio. Her house washes away in a rainstorm? She needed a new house anyway. She drifts to sea on a log? She'd always wanted to see the ocean. Two other very funny books show that there are different ways of handling disaster humor. Helen Oxenbury, in *The Important Visitor,* uses bland understatement, both in the quiet writing and in tidy pastel illustrations, as she tells the story of a small girl who wreaks havoc while her mother tries (in vain) to conduct a business interview. Oxenbury counts on children to understand what *isn't* said. David Macaulay, on the other hand, uses lots of action and exaggeration for his version of *Why the Chicken Crossed the Road;* here the plot careens along at a wild pace but the style is controlled and sophisticated.

Exaggeration is inherent in William Steig's *Spinky Sulks;* there is no detail that is unrealistic, but by making Spinky obdurately sullen and unforgiving, and by making his family impressive in their stance of appeasement, the author invites listeners, and perhaps readers-aloud, to see the humor in the determined sulking some of them may have done. Exaggeration is blatant in *Bravo Minski* by Arthur Yorinks. Whatever it is, Minski either invented it, discovered it, or did it better than anyone else. Young children quickly appreciate the joke and can see how the pictures of adoring crowds add to the fun.

Bernard Waber's *I Was All Thumbs* has the double appeal of a situation in which the protagonist makes a series of errors and in which the dialogue plays with words. Children enjoy inventing disasters, and they find it more amusing than adults do if an octopus squirts ink in the wrong direction, as does Legs, the octopus-hero of this story.

One of the early classics of English drama, *The Ridiculous Story of Gammer Gurton's Needle,* has been adapted by David Lloyd for a picture book version of the slam-bang story of a clever rogue, Diccon the Bedlam, with all the appeal of any comic trickster tale. Even funnier is the adult who refuses to get out of the bathtub. In Audrey Wood's *King Bidgood's in the Bathtub,* a monarch includes a nighttime masquerade ball in his bathroom retreat. It's always fun to mock adults, especially if they are caught doing something for which children are often chided.

Animals

Almost all children are interested in animal stories—whether the creatures are animals that behave like human beings, animals that behave like animals but can talk, or animals that behave like animals whether there are people in the story or not. Most picture stories featuring animals fall in the first category and some have already been discussed in this chapter.

Viewpoint

The child needs somebody in a book with whom he can identify as a child. This accounts for the presence of many animals or children themselves in children's books and the comparative paucity of adults, especially parents—it is striking how parents are always got rid of so quickly. Although a child has parents he doesn't necessarily want to read about them, perhaps because he is experimenting with fantasy, with learning about himself, projecting himself into a book where he is not tied down to the fact that he has to go to bed at half past six and clean his teeth. A widespread mistake about children which is made very often by people who talk about social realism in children's books is to imagine that familiarity breeds content. It is not a question of having details which children can recognize but much more a question of having details which they want to recognize. If we have a picture of a school, children will certainly recognize it but they won't necessarily like it.

Nicholas Tucker, "How Children Respond to Fiction," *Children's Literature in Education 9,* pp. 51–52. Reprinted by permission of Agathon Press.

Because such stories parody the lives of human beings, it is in their perceptiveness about human foibles and emotions that their importance and appeal lie. It is not that Owl, in Arnold Lobel's *Owl at Home,* acts silly for an owl but because he acts like a silly human being as he tries frantically to be in two places at once, that children laugh at him. Nor is it because the mother, in Rosemary Wells's *Hazel's Amazing Mother,* is so powerful an animal that she is admirable, but because she symbolizes the importance of protective human love. Hans Rey's Curious George behaves as young children see themselves behave, and Russell Hoban's books about a small badger, Frances, will evoke empathy in small girls, and in those adults who care for them.

Arthur, in Graham Oakley's *The Church Mouse* and *The Church Mice Adrift,* behaves like a mouse some of the time, like a human other times, and the story is that much funnier by contrast when Arthur practices his crawl stroke in the baptismal font. Marjorie Sharmat takes a few digs at ambitious people in *Walter the Wolf,* in which an almost-perfect little wolf who writes poetry, practices violin without being reminded, and never bites, decides that he really doesn't have to be perfect. In *A Weekend with Wendell* by Kevin Henkes, a girl-mouse, Sophia, rebels at Wendell's bullying. When they play house, for example, Wendell makes the rules. "He was the father, the mother, and the five children. Sophia was the dog. . . ." The *Little Bear* stories by Else Minarik are for independent readers, but they should also be read aloud to younger children, for they reflect all the familial relations, friendships, and imaginative play of childhood.

Stories in which animals behave as animals except that they talk are usually rather placid, since they offer less opportunity for diversity of behavior or for humor, but they are eminently suitable for the very youngest children. In *Farmer Schultz's Ducks,* a lively story by Australian author Colin Thiele, a harried farmer thinks of a way to protect his ducks when growing traffic blocks a safe route to the river. The ducks don't talk. While surrounded by suspense and danger, they waddle placidly about, offering the same kind of humorous contrast to the setting that has made Robert

From *A Weekend with Wendell*, written and illustrated by Kevin Henkes.

McCloskey's *Make Way for Ducklings* a classic. The idea that one is never too old to learn is clear in Leo Lionni's *In the Rabbitgarden,* where two little rabbits disobey an injunction not to eat apples *or else* (or else the fox will get them). Children may take more satisfaction than adult readers-aloud in the inference that adults aren't invariably right. And in Munro Leaf's *The Story of Ferdinand,* a little bull behaves almost entirely like a real bull except for the fact that he prefers to sit under a cork tree and smell flowers, not to fight. Beestung, he rampages about, is thought fierce, and is taken to the bull ring. Part of the humor is in the illustrations, which show the matador weeping with frustration, and part in the writing, which uses understatement and refrain ("But not Ferdinand") to achieve its effect of placidity.

Stories in which animals are seen always behaving strictly like themselves usually have some human characters too, as a foil for the animals or as a viewpoint from which the animals are seen. *Our Animal Friends at Maple Hill Farm* by Alice and Martin Provensen has little story line but too much text to be called a picture book, since the long and very funny captions do tell stories about the highly

From *Owl Lake*, written and illustrated by Keizaburo
Tejima.

distinctive creatures of house and barn: the
greedy, grouchy geese; a coquettish hen; or a
languid Siamese who, in contrast to the other
cats, is beautiful but not interesting. An old
favorite is Lynd Ward's *The Biggest Bear,* in
which a boy's pet cub grows older and bigger
until the havoc he creates necessitates his being
sent to a zoo. Color woodcuts, stunningly dramatic, tell animal stories that do not have
human characters; in Keizaburo Tejima's *Fox's
Dream, Owl Lake,* and *Swan Sky,* wild creatures
hunt, or mate, or nest, or die. Here the bold
pictures emphasize the silent woods and the
cyclical pattern of animal life.

Adaptations of Folk Tales

In addition to the many contemporary stories
that are told with the cadence and in the
pattern of folk literature—stories like Wanda
Gág's *Millions of Cats*—there are many picture-
book versions of authentic folktales, stories that
exemplify the mores and morals of their cul-

tures, that teach a lesson or that explain the
natural phenomena of our world. Some are
humorous, like Dorothy Van Woerkom's version of a German folk tale, *The Queen Who
Couldn't Bake Gingerbread.* The monarch who
hunts for a perfect mate is a frequent theme,
but here the tables are turned twice; first,
Princess Calliope demands a husband who can
play a slide trombone, and second, when dreadful burning smells and noisy squawks pervade
the castle, it proves to be the king cooking and
the new queen practicing the trombone.
There's another kind of humor in a traditional
noodlehead story, *The Three Sillies,* Kathryn
Hewitt's adaptation of the tale of a foolish
bride and her equally foolish parents.

Why Mosquitoes Buzz in People's Ears, adapted
by Verna Aardema from a West African folk-
tale, is a "why" story, but it also carries a
message of justice meted out, the brilliant
illustrations adding to the humor. Gerald
McDermott's *Arrow to the Sun* is an adaptation
of a Pueblo Indian legend: A boy transforms
into an arrow and brings the spirit of the Lord
of the Sun (his father) back to the pueblo.
Mwenye Hadithi tells a variant of the trickster
tale in *Crafty Chameleon,* with bold pictures that
make it excellent for group use. Chameleon
fools a leopard and a crocodile into struggling
with each other instead of with him; this triumph of the smallest is very gratifying to young
children. Another familiar theme appears in
Llama and the Great Flood, Ellen Alexander's
retelling of a Peruvian folktale. Here, the llama
of an Andean family has a premonition in a
dream, and is able to forewarn his owner that
only by climbing to the top of the highest
mountain can catastrophe be averted. All of the
animals climb, too, only those on the mountain
surviving; this variant of the flood story common to many cultures is based on a Huarochiri
version as it was adapted by sixteenth-century
Spanish historians.

A favorite tale for storytellers is simply adapted by Cynthia Jameson in *The Clay Pot Boy,* the
story of a pot that comes to life and voraciously
devours everything in its path. Children enjoy
the frenzy of the chase, both in this story and in
Paul Galdone's version of *The Gingerbread Boy.*
Tomie dePaola's interpretation of Italian folklore, *Strega Nona,* is imbued with robust peasant

humor and stresses the poetic justice of the punishment meted out to a witch's greedy apprentice. In Patricia McKissack's *Nettie Jo's Friends,* a girl who wants to make her doll a dress turns to her animal friends for a needle, setting a pattern for the folklore tradition of animal helpers. The story of a small girl who outwits her kidnappers is deftly retold by Anita Lobel in *The Straw Maid,* giving a picture of an active, resourceful heroine. A picture book version of a tale by the brothers Grimm is illustrated by Maurice Sendak so that the disdainful princess of *King Grisly-Beard,* being taught humility by her husband, takes on the vitriolic mien of Shakespeare's Katharina in *The Taming of the Shrew.* It does espouse a traditional view of woman's role, but that is true of much folk literature.

Informational Books

Both in fiction and nonfiction, there have been numbers of books published that satisfy the young child's need to know. The best of such books deal with subjects that are within the child's experience, books like *Come to the Doctor, Harry* by Mary Chalmers, or *Going on an Airplane* by Fred Rogers, which inform, as well as assuage a young child's concerns. *Ferryboat,* by Betsy and Guilio Maestro, shows a family crossing the Connecticut River; an appended note gives additional facts about the ferry, established over two centuries ago. Alvin Tresselt's *The Dead Tree* gives information about the plants and animals that live in and on a fallen tree until it becomes part of the humus that nurtures the forest. The simple, poetic text is easily comprehended, yet it teaches a valuable lesson in ecology and the life cycle of all living things.

Although written in narrative form, such books as Tomie dePaola's *Charlie Needs a Cloak* describe actual procedures of manufacture or craft. The little shepherd in this story shears his sheep, cards and dyes the wool, and spins the cloth for a new red cloak. A book like this is an excellent springboard for a discussion about the origin of things that we use. Also by dePaola, *The Quicksand Book* provides information in a humorous story. Vaunda Nelson, in *Always Gramma,* gives facts about Alzheimer's disease from the viewpoint of a child narrator.

There are many books written about weather, seasons, and other aspects of the environment. The phenomena that are familiar to adults and to older children can amaze, delight, or baffle the very young. The art in writing such books involves being accurate, simple, vivid—knowing what to omit to gain simplicity without sacrificing accuracy. One of the best books that presents some facet of the natural environment is *Dawn* by Uri Shulevitz. Here, the quiet and beautiful pictures, the hushed tone of the text, and the slow, gradual pace of the writing build to a last burst of color as full sunlight fills the scene. *The Snowy Day* by Ezra Jack Keats captures the joy a small child feels when playing in a fresh, full fall of snow. Robert McCloskey's *Time of Wonder* not only portrays vividly the ominous feeling of an approaching hurricane, but also the way in which a family draws together to gain comfort and feelings of security when danger threatens.

The world, for young children, begins at home; they are concerned with small events which to them are of great importance, with the people in their immediate circle, and with what is happening here and now. As they grow older their horizons extend to include neighbors, relatives who are not part of the immediate family, classmates in nursery school or kindergarten, and friends. Their understanding of time, space, distance, and of relative sizes grows as they grow. Their books should take such conceptual limitations into account.

Toy Books

One type of book that cuts across all these lines is the toy book, which may be on any subject and of any genre. There are many types of toy books—pop-up, pull-tab, fold-out, and so forth. All depend on the craft of paper engineering, and the worth of the book may be judged in part by the delicacy, intricacy, and effectiveness of this ancient art.

Since most of the toy books depend on visual or tactile appeal, they tend to have a limited amount of text. One of the criteria for evaluating such books is the extent to which the paper engineering is used to extend the text rather

He washed the wool,

From *Charlie Needs a Cloak*, written and illustrated by Tomie dePaola.

than merely to embellish it. An excellent example of this is *Adding Animals* by Colin Hawkins, in which pull-tabs and sliding panels reinforce concepts of addition. More typical of this type of book is Eric Carle's *The Honeybee and the Robber* in which a butterfly springs from the page or a pull-tab causes a fish to snap at a bee; the paper engineering adds visual interest and appeal because of the game element, but it does not reinforce the words of the story.

This is an old art form which has regained popularity in recent years. Most of the toy books published today have little substance, little beauty, and a minimal amount of ingenuity. There are, however, reproductions of the work of such Victorian masters as Lothar Meggendorfer or Ernest Nister; antique books in reprint editions; and there are some books, like the many-layered pop-up version of an eighteenth-century creche in Neapolitan style, *The Nativity* or a three-dimensional *Leonardo da Vinci* by Alice and Martin Provensen that are stunningly effective.

As is true of books for older children, picture books reflect the culture from which they ema-nate as well as that culture's idea of the child's role. They also, at any period, reflect publishing trends. Thus we have today, much more than in the past, books that touch on social change, new family patterns, urban problems, and young children's potential ability to cope

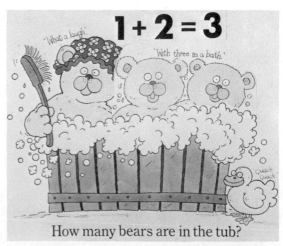

From *Adding Animals*, written and illustrated by Colin Hawkins.

with disappointment or responsibility, disabilities or abuse. The potential was always there, just as problems were always there; the difference is that now more is known about the capacity of young children to learn, to accept change, and to cope. The growing popularity, in the 1980s, of toy books and books with paper engineering, and of books based on films and television programs (Star Wars, Sesame Street, the Muppets) has been evident with young children as well as older readers.

Books for all ages mirror the changes in our society. In this review of the kinds of books that are appropriate for young children, some of those changes are evident. Such changes are of the utmost importance in showing young children a picture of their world, for it is in the early years that they learn most about that world.

Adult References and Book Selection Aids*

Books discussed in Chapter 5 which may also be considered books for early childhood are identified in this bibliography with a "5."

For help in locating books with special purposes or about minorities, see the section "Book Selection Aids" in the Adult References in the Appendices. In the following bibliography these symbols have been used to identify books about a particular religious or ethnic group:

§ African American
★ Hispanic
☆ Native American
○ Asian American
● Religious minority

ANDERSON, VERNA. *Reading and Young Children.*
BARCHILON, JACQUES, and HENRY PETTIT. *The Authentic Mother Goose Fairy Tales and Nursery Rhymes.*
BARING-GOULD, WILLIAM and CEIL. *The Annotated Mother Goose.*

BARSTOW, BARBARA, and JUDITH RIGGLE, comps. *Beyond Picture Books: A Guide to First Readers.* (See Appendix A.)
BATOR, ROBERT, comp. *Signposts to Criticism of Children's Literature.* Chapter 4, "Picture Books."
BUTLER, DOROTHY. *Babies Need Books.*
————. *Cushla and Her Books.*
CHUKOVSKY, KORNEI. *From Two to Five.*
CIANCIOLO, PATRICIA. *Picture Books for Children.*
COODY, BETTY. *Using Literature with Young Children.*
CRAGO, MAUREEN and HUGH. *Prelude to Literacy: A Preschool Child's Encounter with Picture and Story.*
CULLINAN, BERNICE, and CAROLYN CARMICHAEL, eds. *Literature and Young Children.*
ECKENSTEIN, LINA. *Comparative Studies in Nursery Rhymes.*
GESELL, ARNOLD, and others. *The First Five Years of Life: A Guide to the Study of the Preschool Child.*
GREEN, PERCY B. *A History of Nursery Rhymes.*
HALLIWELL-PHILLIPPS, JAMES O. *Popular Rhymes and Nursery Tales: A Sequel to The Nursery Rhymes of England.*
HEARNE, BETSY, and MARILYN KAYE, eds. *Celebrating Children's Books: Essays on Children's Literature in Honor of Zena Sutherland.* "A Good Picture Book Should . . ." by Arnold Lobel.
HÜRLIMANN, BETTINA. *Picture-Book World.*
JACOBS, LELAND, ed. *Using Literature with Young Children.*
JOHNSON, FERNE. *Start Early for an Early Start.*
JUSTEN, SUE, ed. *Opening Doors for Preschool Children and Their Parents.*
MACCANN, DONNARAE, and OLGA RICHARD. *The Child's First Books: A Critical Study of Pictures and Texts.*
MILLAR, SUSANNA. *The Psychology of Play.* Chapter entitled "Phantasy, Feeling, and Make-Believe Play."
MOORE, VARDINE. *Pre-School Story Hour.*
OPIE, IONA and PETER. *Children's Games in Street and Playground.*
————. *The Lore and Language of Schoolchildren.*
————, eds. *The Oxford Dictionary of Nursery Rhymes.*
POLETTE, NANCY. *Nancy Polette's E Is for Everybody: A Manual for Bringing Fine Picture Books into the Hands and Hearts of Children.*
————. *Picture Books for Gifted Programs.*
ROBERTS, PATRICIA. *Alphabet Books as a Key to Language Patterns: An Annotated Bibliography.* (See Appendix A.)
RUDMAN, MASHA, ANNA PEARCE, and the Editors of Consumer Report Books. *For Love of Reading: A Parent's Guide to Encouraging Young Readers from Infancy through Age 5.*

*Complete bibliographic data are provided in Appendices A and B.

THOMAS, KATHERINE ELWES. *The Real Personages of Mother Goose.*

WHITE, DOROTHY. *Books Before Five.*

YARDLEY, ALICE. *Young Children Thinking.*

Mother Goose Editions

ALDERSON, BRIAN, comp. *Cakes and Custard: Children's Rhymes Chosen by Brian Alderson,* ill. by Helen Oxenbury. Morrow, 1975.

————, ed. *The Helen Oxenbury Nursery Rhyme Book,* ill. by Helen Oxenbury. Morrow, 1987. Combined with colorful illustrations, the selected verses represent the best of Mother Goose, street rhymes, and childhood chants.

5 BRIGGS, RAYMOND, ill. *The Mother Goose Treasury.* Coward, 1966. Greenaway Medal.

BROOKE, L. LESLIE, ill. *Ring o' Roses: A Nursery Rhyme Picture Book.* Warne, 1922.

5 CALDECOTT, RANDOLPH, ill. *Hey Diddle Diddle Picture Book.* Warne, n.d. Some of Caldecott's finest pictures accompany favorite rhymes of the nursery.

5 DE ANGELI, MARGUERITE, ill. *Marguerite de Angeli's Book of Nursery and Mother Goose Rhymes.* Doubleday, 1954.

EMBERLEY, ED, ill. *London Bridge is Falling Down: The Song and Game.* Little, 1967.

5 FRASCONI, ANTONIO, ill. *The House That Jack Built.* Harcourt, 1958.

GALDONE, PAUL, ill. *Three Little Kittens.* Houghton/Clarion, 1986. Pen-and-wash drawings show the kittens in a variety of moods as they live through their famous adventure.

GREENAWAY, KATE, ill. *Mother Goose: Or, The Old Nursery Rhymes,* Warne, 1882.

5 JEFFERS, SUSAN, ill. *Three Jovial Huntsmen.* Bradbury, 1973.

LOBEL, ARNOLD, ill. *Gregory Griggs and Other Nursery Rhyme People.* Greenwillow, 1978.

————, comp. and ill. *The Random House Book of Mother Goose.* Random House, 1986.

————. *Whiskers and Rhymes.* Greenwillow, 1985.

MONTGOMERIE, NORAH and WILLIAM, comps. *A Book of Scottish Nursery Rhymes,* ill. by T. Ritchie and Norah Montgomerie. Oxford, 1965.

OPIE, IONA, ed. *Ditties for the Nursery,* ill. by Monica Walker. Walck, 1954.

OPIE, IONA and PETER, comps. *A Family Book of Nursery Rhymes,* ill. by Pauline Baynes. Oxford, 1964.

————, comps. *The Oxford Nursery Rhyme Book,* ill. from old chapbooks, with additional pictures by Joan Hassall. Walck, 1955.

————, comps. *Tail Feathers from Mother Goose.* Little, Brown, 1988.

PEARSON, TRACEY CAMPBELL, ill. *Sing a Song of Sixpence.* Dial, 1985. Comic illustrations of a flock of blackbirds and a hefty royal family spice up the old nursery song.

RACKHAM, ARTHUR, ill. *Mother Goose: The Old Nursery Rhymes.* Marathon, 1978.

ROJANKOVSKY, FEODOR, ill. *The Tall Book of Mother Goose.* Harper, 1942.

SPIER, PETER, ill. *London Bridge Is Falling Down!* Doubleday, 1967.

SUTHERLAND, ZENA, comp. *The Orchard Book of Nursery Rhymes,* ill. by Faith Jaques. Orchard, 1990.

TRIPP, WALLACE, ill. *Granfa' Grig Had a Pig and Other Rhymes Without Reason from Mother Goose.* Little, 1976.

TUCKER, NICHOLAS, comp. *Mother Goose Lost,* ill. by Tevor Stubley. T. Crowell, 1971.

WILDSMITH, BRIAN, ill. *Brian Wildsmith's Mother Goose.* Watts, 1965.

WRIGHT, BLANCHE FISHER, ill. *The Real Mother Goose.* Macmillan, 1916.

A Few Variants of *Mother Goose*

BODECKER, N.M., comp. *It's Raining Said John Twaining,* tr. and ill. by compiler, Atheneum, 1973.

BURROUGHS, MARGARET TAYLER, comp. *Did You Feed My Cow? Street Games, Chants, and Rhymes.* ill. by Joe DeValasco, rev. ed. Follett, 1969.

DEFOREST, CHARLOTTE B. *The Prancing Pony: Nursery Rhymes from Japan Adapted into English Verse for Children,* with "Kusa-e" ill. by Keiko Hida. Walker, 1968.

FOWKE, EDITH, comp. *Sally Go Round the Sun: Three Hundred Children's Songs, Rhymes and Games,* ill. by Carlos Marchiori. Doubleday, 1970.

LATHAM, HUGH, tr. *Mother Goose in French,* ill. by Barbara Cooney. T. Crowell, 1964.

LEACH, MARIA. *Riddle Me, Riddle Me, Ree,* ill. by William Wiesner. Viking, 1970. A collection of over two hundred riddles from folk materials the world over. Sources are given.

LOW, JOSEPH and RUTH. *Mother Goose Riddle Rhymes,* ill. by Joseph Low. Harcourt, 1953. Low has made a modern rebus from nursery rhymes that is beautiful in design and clever in conception—a brain teaser for young and old.

MORRISON, LILLIAN, comp. *Touch Blue,* ill. by Doris Lee. T. Crowell, 1958. "Signs and Spells, Love Charms and Chants, Auguries and Old Beliefs is Rhyme."

PETERSHAM, MAUD and MISKA. *The Rooster Crows: A Book of American Rhymes and Jingles.* Macmillan, 1945. Caldecott Medal.

POTTER, CHARLES FRANCIS, comp. *Tongue Tanglers,* ill. by William Wiesner. World, 1962.

REID, ALASTAIR, and ANTHONY KERRIGAN, trs. *Mother Goose in Spanish,* ill. by Barbara Cooney. T. Crowell, 1968.

WITHERS, CARL, comp. *A Rocket in My Pocket,* ill. by Susanne Suba. Holt, 1948.

WOOD, RAY. *The American Mother Goose,* ill. by Ed Hargis. Lippincott, 1940.

WYNDHAM, ROBERT, comp. *Chinese Mother Goose Rhymes,* ill. by Ed Young. World, 1968.

5 ZEMACH, HARVE. *Mommy, Buy Me a China Doll,* ill. by Margot Zemach. Follett, 1966.

5 ——————, ed. *The Speckled Hen: A Russian Nursery Rhyme,* ill. by Margot Zemach. Holt, 1966.

ABC Books

5 ANNO, MITSUMASA, ill. *Anno's Alphabet: An Adventure in Imagination.* T. Crowell, 1975.

——————. *Anno's Magical ABC: An Anamorphic Alphabet,* ill. by author. Philomel, 1981.

AZARIAN, MARY. *A Farmer's Alphabet,* ill. by author. Godine, 1981. Handsomely detailed woodcut prints picture aspects of rural life and farm-related objects.

BASKIN, LEONARD, ill. *Hosie's Alphabet,* words by Hosea, Tobias, and Lisa Baskin. Viking, 1972.

5 BROWN, MARCIA, ill. *All Butterflies: An ABC.* Scribner's, 1974.

5 BURNINGHAM, JOHN, ill. *John Burningham's ABC.* Bobbs, 1967.

CHWAST, SEYMOUR, and MARTIN STEPHEN MOSKOF, ills. *Still Another Alphabet Book.* McGraw, 1969.

CLEAVER, ELIZABETH, ill. *ABC.* Atheneum, 1985. Each letter is described through the mediums of collage and paint.

CRANE, WALTER. *An Alphabet of Old Friends and the Absurd ABC,* ill. by author. Metropolitan Museum of Art/Thames and Hudson, 1981. A reprinting of two humorous alphabet books originally published in 1874 by one of the first great illustrators of children's books.

——————, ill. *Baby's Own Alphabet.* Dodd, n.d.

DUVOISIN, ROGER, ill. *A for the Ark.* Lothrop, 1952.

FARBER, NORMA. *This Is the Ambulance Leaving the Zoo,* ill. by Tomie dePaola. Dutton, 1975. A lively alphabet book also tells about an Ambulance, Bus, Cars, Drivers in a busy story that has the cumulation young children enjoy.

5 FEELINGS, MURIEL. *Jambo Means Hello: Swahili Alphabet Book,* ill. by Tom Feelings. Dial, 1974.

5 GÁG, WANDA, ill. *The ABC Bunny.* Coward, 1933.

GREENAWAY, KATE, ill. *A Apple Pie.* Warne, n.d.

GROSSBART, FRANCINE, ill. *A Big City.* Harper, 1966.

HOBAN, TANA. *A, B, See!* photos by author. Greenwillow, 1982.

ISADORA, RACHEL, ill. *City Seen from A to Z.* Greenwillow, 1983. The multiethnic composition of urban areas is reflected in polished drawings that picture familiar activities and objects in a city setting.

KITCHEN, BERT, ill. *Animal Alphabet.* Dial, 1984. Animals are posed with each letter of the alphabet in these textured, wittily detailed paintings.

LEAR, EDWARD. *ABC,* penned and ill. by author. McGraw, 1965. Facsimile of a manuscript, this edition has the nonsense verses set in type at the back of the book.

——————. *An Edward Lear Alphabet,* ill. by Carol Newsome. Lothrop, 1983. Lear's nonsensical rhyming alphabet, with deliciously humorous watercolors of animal characters.

5 LOBEL, ARNOLD. *On Market Street,* ill. by Anita Lobel. Greenwillow, 1981.

MACDONALD, SUSE, ill. *Alphabatics.* Bradbury, 1987.

MCGINLEY, PHYLLIS. *All Around the Town,* ill. by Helen Stone. Lippincott, 1948.

MATTHIESEN, THOMAS. *ABC: An Alphabet Book,* photos by author. Platt, 1966.

MUNARI, BRUNO, ill. *Bruno Munari's ABC.* World, 1960.

§ 5 MUSGROVE, MARGARET. *Ashanti to Zulu,* ill. by Leo and Diane Dillon. Dial, 1976.

PEARSON, TRACEY CAMPBELL, ad. *A—Apple Pie,* ill. by adaptor. Dial, 1986.

POULIN, STEPHANE. *Ah! Belle Cité!/A Beautiful City ABC,* ill. by author. Tundra Books, 1985. Montreal is the setting for paintings with captions in both French and English.

PROVENSEN, ALICE and MARTIN, ills. *A Peaceable Kingdom: The Abecedarius.* Viking, 1978. First published in the Shaker Manifesto of 1882, this newly illustrated version adds appropriately quaint, prim people and an enchanting variety of animals to the original lilting rhyme.

SCHMIDERER, DOROTHY, ill. *The Alphabeast Book: An Abecedarium.* Holt, 1971.

SENDAK, MAURICE, ill. *Alligators All Around,* in *Nutshell Library.* Harper, 1962.

STEVENSON, JAMES. *Grandpa's Great City Tour,* ill. by author. Greenwillow, 1983.

TUDOR, TASHA, ill. *A is for Annabelle.* Walck, 1954.

5 VAN ALLSBURG, CHRIS. *The Z Was Zapped,* ill. by author. Houghton, 1987.

5 WILDSMITH, BRIAN, ill. *Brian Wildsmith's ABC.* Watts, 1963. Kate Greenaway Medal.

Counting Books

ANNO, MITSUMASA, ill. *Anno's Counting Book.* T. Crowell, 1977.

————, ill. *Anno's Counting House.* Philomel, 1982. Cut-out windows reveal and conceal the activities of ten small people who move between two houses in this innovative illustration of mathematical concepts.

§ BANG, MOLLY. *Ten, Nine, Eight,* ill. by author. Greenwillow, 1983. A warm bedtime countdown depicts a tender relationship between a black father and child.

BURNINGHAM, JOHN. *Read One,* ill. by author. Viking, 1983.

CARLE, ERIC, ill. *My Very First Book of Numbers.* T. Crowell, 1974. Board pages, spiral-bound, are cut horizontally so that the child can match top and bottom halves; one has a set of fruits (1 pineapple, 2 bananas) and the other has 1–10 black squares.

CHWAST, SEYMOUR, and MARTIN MOSKOF, ills. *Still Another Number Book.* McGraw, 1971.

DEMI. *Demi's Count the Animals 1, 2, 3,* ill. by author. Grosset, 1986.

ERNST, LISA CAMPBELL, ill. *Up to Ten and Down Again.* Lothrop, 1986. The activity in a quiet park increases as people, dogs, and ducks are added to the pages and then are subtracted by the appearance of a rainstorm.

§ FEELINGS, MURIEL. *Moja Means One: Swahili Counting Book,* ill. by Tom Feelings. Dial, 1971.

GARDNER, BEAU. *Can You Imagine . . . ? A Counting Book,* ill. by author. Dodd, 1987.

HOBAN, RUSSELL. *Ten What? A Mystery Counting Book,* ill. by Sylvie Selig. Scribner's, 1975.

HOBAN, TANA. *Count and See,* photos by author. Macmillan, 1972. Clear, sharp photos for a text that goes from 1–15, by tens to 50, and ends with 100 peas in their pods.

————, ill. *1, 2, 3.* Greenwillow, 1985. In board book format, crisp photographs illustrate each digit, the word for the digit, and the corresponding number of dots.

HOBZEK, MILDRED. *We Can A-Marching . . . 1, 2, 3,* ill. by William Pène du Bois. Parents' Magazine, 1978. The distinctive palette and engaging details of Pène du Bois's paintings add beauty to a rhyming narrative that teaches its young audience how to count 1, 2, 3 in twelve languages.

IPCAR, DAHLOV, ill. *Ten Big Farms.* Knopf, 1958.

KEATS, EZRA JACK, ill. *Over in the Meadow.* Four Winds, 1972.

KIRN, ANN. ill. *Nine in a Line.* Norton, 1966.

KITCHEN, BERT. *Animal Numbers,* ill. by author. Dial, 1987.

KREDENSER, GAIL. *1 One Dancing Drum,* ill. by Stanley Mack. Phillips, 1971.

5 LANGSTAFF, JOHN. *Over in the Meadow,* ill. by Feodor Rojankovsky. Harcourt, 1957.

MCMILLAN, BRUCE. *Counting Wildflowers,* photos by author. Lothrop, 1986.

§ MERRIAM, EVE. *Project 1–2–3,* ill. by Harriet Sherman. McGraw, 1971.

OXENBURY, HELEN, ill. *Numbers of Things.* Watts, 1968.

PETIE, HARRIS, ill. *Billions of Bugs.* Prentice, 1975.

PLUCKROSE, HENRY. *Counting,* photos by Chris Fairclough. Watts, 1988.

§ ROWAN, DICK. *Everybody In! A Counting Book,* ill. with photos. Bradbury, 1969.

SENDAK, MAURICE, ill. *One Was Johnny: A Counting Book,* in *Nutshell Library.* Harper, 1962. A rhyming text about a small boy's problem of too many visitors who appear one by one.

TAFURI, NANCY. *Who's Counting?* ill. by author. Greenwillow, 1986. A brown puppy is counting, as the illustrator makes dramatic use of a two-page spread for each number.

The Sesame Street Book of Numbers, by Children's Television Workshop and Preschool Press. Time-Life/Little, Brown, 1970.

WILDSMITH, BRIAN, ill. *1, 2, 3's.* Watts, 1965.

Concept Books

5 ANNO, MITSUMASA, ill., *The King's Flower.* World, 1979. A foolish king wants everything he possesses to be the biggest in the world—until his huge flowerpot produces an ordinary sized (but beautiful anyway) tulip.

ARUEGO, JOSÉ, and ARIANE DEWEY. *We Hide, You Seek,* ill. by authors. Greenwillow, 1979.

BORTEN, HELEN. *Do You Go Where I Go?* ill. by author. Abelard, 1972. Objects that can be seen at the park, the barbershop, etc., are grouped so that children may think in terms of clues and sets.

————. *Do You Know What I Know?* ill. by author. Abelard, 1970.

§ BRENNER, BARBARA. *Faces,* photos by George Ancona. Dutton, 1970.

BROWN, MARCIA. *Listen to a Shape.*

————. *Touch Will Tell.*

————. *Walk with Your Eyes.* All three are illustrated with photographs by the author. Watts, 1979.

CARLE, ERIC. *My Very First Book of Colors,* ill. by author. T. Crowell, 1974. Spiral-bound, board pages cut in half horizontally so that upper and lower can be matched. Here, each top half has a solid block of color, each bottom has a picture of a familiar object.

————. *My Very First Book of Shapes,* ill. by author. T. Crowell, 1974.

COLE, JOANNA. *A Chick Hatches,* ill. with photos. Morrow, 1976. A simply-written account of the development from egg to embryo to fetus to chick is made more meaningful by the accompanying photographs, some in color and almost all enlarged.

§ COREY, DOROTHY. *Tomorrow You Can,* ill. by Lois Axeman. Whitman, 1977. In a multiethnic book, young children are reassured about their potential for accomplishing tasks that are difficult at some stages of growth.

☆ § ————. *You Go Away,* ill. by Lois Axeman. Whitman, 1976.

CREWS, DONALD. *Freight Train.* Greenwillow, 1978. A pared-down description of the cars included in a small freight train also serves to identify black and the primary complementary colors.

————. *Parade.* Greenwillow, 1983. A parade's color, action, and music are captured in a bright frieze of pictures.

FISHER, LEONARD EVERETT. *Look Around! A Book About Shapes,* ill. by author. Viking Kestrel, 1987. The repeated use of squares, circles, triangles, and rectangles reinforces their concepts in a bold, clean design.

§ FUJIKAWA, GYO. *Let's Play!* ill. by author. Grosset, 1975. Pictures on board pages show everyday life experiences, with some stress on directional concepts.

GILLHAM, BILL, and SUSAN HULME. *Let's Look for Opposites,* ill. with photos by Jan Siegieda. Coward, 1984. Through simple text and good photographs, the idea of opposites comes across clearly on each two-page spread.

————. *Let's Look for Shapes,* ill. with photos by Jan Siegieda. Coward, 1984.

HAWKINS, COLIN. *Take Away Monsters,* ill. by author. Putnam, 1984. Monsters that disappear at the pull of a tab demonstrate subtraction in appealing form.

§ HOBAN, TANA. *Circles, Triangles and Squares.* Macmillan, 1974. Excellent photographs in which the three most familiar geometric forms occur. While a picture that has several different shapes is less explicit as a teaching tool than a page of triangles, there is an alternate value in letting the child discover forms that are not prominent.

————. *Is It Larger, Is It Smaller?* ill. with photos by author. Greenwillow, 1985. Color photographs of sets of large and small objects show contrasting size.

————. *Look Again!* Macmillan, 1971.

§ ————. *Over, Under & Through.* Macmillan, 1973.

————. *Push-Pull, Empty-Full.* Macmillan, 1972.

————. *Round and Round and Round.* Greenwillow, 1983.

————. *Shapes and Things.* Macmillan, 1970.

————. *Take Another Look.* Greenwillow, 1981.

————. *26 Letters and 99 Cents,* ill. with photos by author. Greenwillow, 1987. The book begins at both ends: the alphabet goes in one direction, coins are introduced in the other direction.

HUGHES, SHIRLEY. *All Shapes and Sizes,* ill. by author. Lothrop, 1986.

ISADORA, RACHEL. *I See,* ill. by author. Greenwillow, 1985.

KRAUSS, RUTH. *The Backward Day,* ill. by Marc Simont. Harper, 1950.

————. *The Growing Story,* ill. by Phyllis Rowand. Harper, 1947.

§ MCGOVERN, ANN. *Black Is Beautiful,* photos by Hope Wurmfeld. Four Winds, 1969.

MCMILLAN, BRUCE. *Dry or Wet?* photos by author. Lothrop, 1988.

————. *Growing Colors,* photos by author. Lothrop, 1988.

————. *Super Super Superwords,* photos by author. Lothrop, 1989. Good color photographs illustrate a series of captions (small, smaller, smallest or yellow, yellower, yellowest) to convey the concept of comparisons.

MCNAUGHTON, COLIN. *Autumn,* ill. by author. Dial, 1983. Sprightly pictures review activities of the season; companion volumes are *Spring, Summer,* and *Winter.*

MAESTRO, BETSY and GIULIO. *Where Is My Friend?* Crown, 1976.

§ MYERS, WALTER. *Where Does the Day Go?* ill. by Leo Carty. Parents' Magazine, 1969.

OXENBURY, HELEN, ill. *Dressing.* Wanderer/Simon & Schuster, 1981. Humorous illustrations enhance this delightful board book about a main event of a baby's day. Companion volumes include *Family, Friends, Playing,* and *Working.*

————, ill. *Shopping Trip.* Dial, 1982. A toddler's adventures on a shopping expedition are the subject of pictures drawn with simplicity, humor, and flair. *Beach Day; Good Night, Good Morning; Monkey See, Monkey Do;* and *Mother's Helper* are in the same series.

PEPPÉ, RODNEY. *Odd One OuT,* ill. by author. Viking, 1974.

PROVENSEN, ALICE. *The Year at Maple Hill Farm,* ill. by Alice and Martin Provensen. Atheneum, 1978.

PROVENSEN, ALICE and MARTIN. *Town and Country,* ill. by authors. Crown, 1984. Colorful, detailed drawings of interesting urban perspectives and rural landscapes combine in a book that shows both city and country are nice places to live.

REISS, JOHN J. *Colors,* ill. by author. Bradbury, 1969.

————. *Shapes,* ill. by author. Bradbury, 1974.

ROGERS, FRED. *Moving,* ill. with photos by Jim Judkis. Putnam, 1987. Mister Rogers narrates as a young boy relies on his parents for reassurance during the confusion of moving to a new home.

SIMON, NORMA. *The Saddest Time,* ill. by Jacqueline Rogers. Whitman, 1986. Soft pencil drawings illustrate three anecdotes that deal sensitively with the deaths of a young uncle, a classmate, and a grandparent.

TISON, ANNETTE, and TALUS TAYLOR. *The Adventures of the Three Colors.* World, 1971.

TRESSELT, ALVIN. *It's Time Now!* ill. by Roger Duvoisin. Lothrop, 1969. Reinforces concepts of seasons by describing seasonal activities. The tone is light, the illustrations bright and vigorous.

5 ————. *White Snow, Bright Snow,* ill. by Roger Duvoisin. Lothrop, 1947. Caldecott Medal.

UDRY, JANICE MAY. *A Tree Is Nice,* ill. by Marc Simont. Harper, 1956. Designed to give young children awareness of the varied uses and attractions of trees.

WATANABE, SHIGEO. *I Can Ride It!* ill. by Yasuo Ohtomo. Philomel, 1982. A bear-child rides a toy bus, uses a skateboard, and finally graduates from a tricycle to a two-wheeler with training wheels. Encouraging and supportive.

————. *I Can Take a Walk!* ill. by Yasuo Ohtomo. Philomel, 1984. Pride in learning self-reliance is the focus of this simple story.

————. *It's My Birthday!* ill. by Yasuo Ohtomo. Philomel, 1988. Bear receives a photo album filled with pictures of his young life triumphs: learning to take a bath, to dress, to walk.

WEISS, NICKI. *Where Does the Brown Bear Go?* ill. by author. Greenwillow, 1989.

WELBER, ROBERT. *Goodbye, Hello,* ill. by Cyndy Szekeres. Pantheon, 1974.

5 WELLS, ROSEMARY. *Max's Ride.* Dial, 1979.

WINTHROP, ELIZABETH. *That's Mine!* ill. by Emily McCully. Holiday, 1977. A boy and a girl, each building a block castle, discover after some boasting and fighting that they can build bigger and better things if they share and work together.

Wordless Books

§ ALEXANDER, MARTHA. *Bobo's Dream.* Dial, 1970.

ANNO, MITSUMASA, ill. *Anno's Britain.* Philomel, 1982. A blue-clad wayfarer tours the British Isles in scenes of fascinating pictorial detail that mingle period costume, anachronistic objects, and fictional characters.

5 ————. *Anno's Journey.* World, 1978.

————. *Anno's USA.* Philomel, 1983.

5 ————. *Topsy-Turvies: Pictures to Stretch the Imagination.* Walker/Weatherhill, 1970.

5 ARDIZZONE, EDWARD. *The Wrong Side of the Bed.* Doubleday, 1970.

ARUEGO, JOSE. *Look What I Can Do.* Scribner's, 1971.

BRIGGS, RAYMOND. *The Snowman,* ill. by author. Random House, 1978.

CARLE, ERIC. *Do You Want to Be My Friend?* T. Crowell, 1971.

COLLINGTON, PETER. *The Angel and the Soldier Boy,* ill. by author. Knopf. 1987.

————. *Little Pickle,* ill. by author. Dutton, 1986.

DEPAOLA, TOMIE, ill. *Pancakes for Breakfast.* Harcourt, 1978.

GOODALL, JOHN S. *The Ballooning Adventures of Paddy Pork.* Harcourt, 1969.

————. *Little Red Riding Hood,* ill. by author. McElderry, 1988.

————. *Paddy Pork's Holiday.* Atheneum, 1976. Like other Goodall books about a lively pig, this has half-pages inserted between each set of full pages. Here Paddy goes off on a hiking trip, has a few adventures, and eventually returns home in fine fettle.

————. *Paddy Under Water,* ill. by author. Atheneum, 1984.

HAMBERGER, JOHN. *The Lazy Dog.* Four Winds, 1971.

HOGROGIAN, NONNY. *Apples.* Macmillan, 1972.

HUTCHINS, PAT. *Changes, Changes.* Macmillan, 1971.

KEATS, EZRA JACK. *Kitten for a Day.* Watts, 1974.

————. *Pssst! Doggie—.* Watts, 1973.

KOREN, EDWARD, *Behind the Wheel.* Holt, 1972.

KRAHN, FERNANDO. *The Self-Made Snowman.* Lippincott, 1974.

MARI, IELA. *The Magic Balloon.* Phillips, 1969.

MARI, IELA and ENZO. *The Apple and the Moth.* Pantheon, 1970.

MAYER, MERCER. *Ah-Choo.* Dial, 1976.

————. *Frog Goes to Dinner.* Dial, 1974.

————. *The Great Cat Chase.* Four Winds, 1974.

————. *Hiccup.* Dial, 1976.

MCCULLY, EMILY ARNOLD. *Picnic,* ill. by author. Harper, 1984.

————. *School,* ill. by author. Harper, 1987.

ORMEROD, JAN, ill. *Sunshine.* Lothrop, 1981, ill. *Moonlight.* Lothrop, 1982.

OXENBURY, HELEN.

————. Series that begin with *Family.* Simon & Schuster, 1981.

_____. *I Can.*

_____. *I Hear.*

_____. *I See.*

_____. *I Touch.* All ill. by author. Random House, 1986.

SCHUBERT, DIETER. *Where's My Monkey?* ill. by author. Dial, 1987.

SIMMONS, ELLIE. *Family.* McKay, 1970.

VINCENT, GABRIELLE. *Breakfast Time, Ernest and Celestine,* ill. by author. Greenwillow, 1985. Ernest, a gentle bear, and Celestine, a young mouse, are an unlikely but loving family in this tale of a messy breakfast.

5 WARD, LYND. *The Silver Pony.* Houghton, 1973.

5 YOUNG, ED. *The Other Bone,* ill. by author. Harper, 1984.

Books for Beginning Readers

☆ BAKER, BETTY. *Partners,* ill. by Emily Arnold McCully. Greenwillow, 1978. Three native-American tales of the Southwest, retold with simplicity and understated humor, describe the trickery of Coyote whose wiles are usually matched by those of his partner Badger.

BENCHLEY, NATHANIEL. *George the Drummer Boy,* ill. by Don Bolognese. Harper, 1977.

5 _____. *Sam the Minute Man,* ill. by Arnold Lobel. Harper, 1969.

_____. *The Several Tricks of Edgar Dolphin,* ill. by Mamoru Funai. Harper, 1970.

☆ _____. *Snorri and the Strangers,* ill. by Don Bolognese. Harper, 1976. Set in America over a thousand years ago, this describes, from Snorri's viewpoint, the initial encounters between the people of Snorri's community (immigrant Norwegian descendants) and some native Americans.

§ BONSALL, CROSBY. *The Case of the Cat's Meow,* ill. by author. Harper, 1965. An amusing mystery story.

§ _____. *The Case of the Double Cross,* ill. by author. Harper, 1980.

§ _____. *The Case of the Scaredy Cats,* ill. by author. Harper, 1971. The staunch crew that coped with the cat's meow finds that girls can hold their own.

BUNTING, EVE. *Winter's Coming,* ill. by Howard Knotts. Harcourt, 1977. A quiet, cozy account of the natural signs of the advent of a hard winter and the preparations made by a family.

CHRISTIAN, MARY BLOUNT. *Penrod's Pants,* ill. by Jane Dyer. Macmillan, 1986. Penrod Porcupine and Griswald Bear's antics bring humor to five very short stories.

FRESCHET, BERNIECE. *Little Black Bear Goes for a Walk,* ill. by Glen Rounds. Scribner's, 1977. Little Black Bear makes his first solo trip while his mother naps. His actions are authentically bearlike and the underlying message (one learns by experience) will offer encouragement to beginning readers.

GAGE, WILSON. *Down in the Boondocks,* ill. by Glen Rounds. Greenwillow, 1977. The humorous rhyming text concerns a farmer who is deaf to the din surrounding him and a robber who isn't—and is frightened away by the racket.

GREENAWAY, KATE. *Under the Window.* Warne, n.d.

GRIFFITH, HELEN V. *Alex and the Cat,* ill. by Joseph Low. Greenwillow, 1982. Stories about an amicable dog, Alex, and his adventures with the family's other pet, a blase cat, are continued in a 1983 sequel, *More Alex and the Cat.*

GUILFOILE, ELIZABETH. *Nobody Listens to Andrew,* ill. by Mary Stevens. Follett, 1957.

HALL, KATY, and LISA EISENBERG. *Buggy Riddles,* ill. by Simms Taback. Dial, 1986.

HEYWARD, DU BOSE. *The Country Bunny and the Little Gold Shoes,* ill. by Marjorie Flack. Houghton, 1939.

HOBAN, LILLIAN. *Arthur's Honey Bear,* ill. by author. Harper, 1974.

_____. *Arthur's Prize Reader,* ill. by author. Harper, 1978. A third book about the small chimp Arthur who reluctantly comes to accept the fact that his little sister Violet has learned to read.

HOFF, SYD. *The Horse in Harry's Room,* ill. by author. Harper, 1970. Pictures in cartoon style illustrate a story in which a sympathetic teacher handles nicely Harry's belief in his imaginary horse.

HURWITZ, JOHANNA. *Russell Sprouts,* ill. by Lillian Hoban. Morrow, 1987.

§ KESSLER, LEONARD. *Old Turtle's Baseball Stories,* ill. by author. Greenwillow, 1982. A trio of simply written stories offers an irresistible blend of animal characters, baseball, and drollery.

_____. *Old Turtle's Soccer Team,* ill. by author. Greenwillow, 1988.

KRENSKY, STEPHEN. *Lionel at Large,* ill. by Susanna Natti. Dial, 1986. Five simply written stories about Lionel's everyday experiences are illustrated with cheerful vitality and humor.

§ LEXAU, JOAN M. *Don't Be My Valentine,* ill. by Syd Hoff. Harper, 1985. When it comes to making Valentines, Sam doesn't want Amy Lou's advice, but his attempt to let her know backfires when his insulting Valentine for Amy Lou gets delivered to the teacher.

§ _____. *The Homework Caper,* ill. by Syd Hoff. Harper, 1966.

§ _____. *The Rooftop Mystery,* ill. by Syd Hoff. Harper, 1968. Two boys cope with the traditional male embarrassment about dolls when they carry one to help on moving day. Despite the stereotypical sex role, an amusing story with problem-solution, humor, and an interracial friendship.

LOBEL, ARNOLD. *Days with Frog and Toad*, ill. by author. Harper, 1979.

————. *Frog and Toad All Year*, ill. by author. Harper, 1976. Lobel continues the saga of the devoted friendship of Frog and Toad, this time with five stories that focus on the seasons.

5 ————. *Frog and Toad Are Friends*, ill. by author. Harper, 1970.

5 ————. *Frog and Toad Together*, ill. by author. Harper, 1972. Short, short stories that are funnier than those of the first book and only a little less touching.

————. *Grasshopper on the Road*, ill. by author. Harper, 1978.

————. *Mouse Soup*, ill. by author. Harper, 1977.

————. *Owl at Home*, ill. by author. Harper, 1975.

5 MARSHALL, JAMES. *Fox on the Job*, ill. by author. Dial, 1988.

MARZOLLO, JEAN. *Amy Goes Fishing*, ill. by Ann Schweninger. Dial, 1980. An affectionate father/daughter relationship is at the heart of this pleasant story about Amy's first fishing trip.

MINARIK, ELSE HOLMELUND. *Father Bear Comes Home*, ill. by Maurice Sendak. Harper, 1959. The illustrations capture to perfection the ingenuous Little Bear and his loving parents in a story that has, for all its brevity, chapter divisions that look impressive to the beginning reader.

————. *A Kiss for Little Bear*, ill. by Maurice Sendak. Harper, 1968. Grandmothers do often send kisses, but seldom by as amusing a chain of helpers; Skunk breaks the chain when he finds another skunk so attractive he concentrates on kissing her rather than passing the kiss along.

5 ————. *Little Bear*, ill. by Maurice Sendak. Harper, 1957.

PARISH, PEGGY. *Dinosaur Time*, ill. by Arnold Lobel. Harper, 1974.

————. *Scruffy*, ill. by Kelly Oechsli. Harper, 1988. In a modest and appealing story, a boy gets his birthday wish: a kitten.

PORTE, BARBARA ANN. *Harry in Trouble*. Greenwillow, 1989.

————. *Harry's Dog*. Greenwillow, 1984.

————. *Harry's Mom*. Greenwillow, 1985. All ill. by Yossi Abolafia. Stories of Harry's troubles are written in a light style and with gentle humor as Harry loses his library card, begs his allergic father for a pet dog, and discusses his mother's death.

RICE, EVE. *Papa's Lemonade and Other Stories*, ill. by author. Greenwillow, 1976.

§ ROCKWELL, HARLOW. *I Did It*, ill. by author. Macmillan, 1974.

ROSS, PAT. *M and M and the Bad News Babies*, ill. by Marilyn Hafner. Pantheon, 1983. Inseparable friends Mandy and Mimi take care of rambunctious twin boys in order to earn some spending money.

RYLANT, CYNTHIA. *Henry and Mudge and the Forever Sea*. Bradbury, 1989.

————. *Henry and Mudge in Puddle Time*. Bradbury, 1987.

————. *Henry and Mudge in the Green Time*. Bradbury, 1987.

————. *Henry and Mudge: The First Book of Their Adventures*. Bradbury, 1987.

————. *Henry and Mudge under the Yellow Moon*. Bradbury, 1987. All ill. by Sucie Stevenson. The chapters of each book reveal Henry and Mudge in an idyllic boy/dog relationship, complete with mud-puddle jumping and leaf-pile kicking.

SCHWARTZ, ALVIN, ad. *There Is a Carrot in My Ear*. ill. by Karen Ann Weinhaus. Harper, 1982. Six lively noodlehead tales are offered in pared-down prose for beginning readers.

5 SELSAM, MILLICENT. *Benny's Animals and How He Put Them in Order*, ill. by Arnold Lobel. Harper, 1966.

————. *How Puppies Grow*, photos by Esther Bubley. Four Winds, 1972.

————. *Tony's Birds*. ill. by Kurt Werth. Harper, 1961.

SEUSS, DR. *The Cat in the Hat*, ill. by author. Random, 1957.

————. *The Cat in the Hat Comes Back*, ill. by author. Random, 1958. A sequel to the first book has 26 cats, A–Z, who help the Cat in the Hat in a series of the silly dilemmas he creates.

SHARMAT, MARJORIE. *Mitchell is Moving*, ill. by Jose Aruego and Ariane Dewey. Macmillan, 1978.

SHAW, EVELYN. *Alligator*, ill. by Frances Zweifel. Harper, 1972.

§ SHOWERS, PAUL. *Look at Your Eyes*, ill. by Paul Galdone. T. Crowell, 1962.

Picture Story Books

5 AARDEMA, VERNA. *Why Mosquitoes Buzz in People's Ears*, ill. by Leo and Diane Dillon. Dial, 1975. Caldecott Medal.

5 ACKERMAN, KAREN. *Song and Dance Man*, ill. by Stephen Gammell. Knopf, 1988. Grandpa, an old vaudeville dancer, entertains his grandchildren

with a magical performance in the attic. Caldecott Medal.

ADLER, DAVID A. *Bunny Rabbit Rebus,* ill. by Madelaine Gill Linden. T. Crowell, 1983. Sprightly rebus drawings add a game element to this story of a rabbit mother who goes to a series of animal friends to get food for her Little Rabbit. A glossary of rebus signs is included, along with a nonrebus telling.

★ ALEXANDER, ELLEN. *Llama and the Great Flood: A Folktale from Peru,* ill. by author. Crowell, 1989.

ALEXANDER, MARTHA. *I'll Be the Horse If You'll Play with Me,* ill. by author. Dial, 1975.

————. *Nobody Asked Me If I Wanted a Baby Sister,* ill. by author. Dial, 1971.

ALIKI. *At Mary Bloom's,* ill. by author. Greenwillow, 1976. A young child shares the joyous news of the birth of her pet mouse's babies with an older neighbor who has quite a menagerie of her own.

————. *Overnight at Mary Bloom's,* ill. by author. Greenwillow, 1987.

5 ALLARD, HARRY. *Miss Nelson Has a Field Day,* ill. by James Marshall. Houghton, 1985. Miss Nelson's dreadful Viola Swamp disguise comes in handy to spur the Horace B. Smedley School football team to victory.

ALLEN, PAMELA. *Mr. Archimedes' Bath,* ill. by author. Lothrop, 1980. A hilarious version of the scientist's discovery about water displacement includes a kangaroo and a wombat; the author-illustrator is Australian.

————. *Who Sank the Boat?* ill. by author. Coward, 1983. Comical repetition makes a point in this clever tale of four animals who capsize their boat.

5 AMBRUS, VICTOR. *A Country Wedding,* ill. by author. Addisons, 1975.

5 ANDERSEN, HANS CHRISTIAN. *The Steadfast Tin Soldier,* ill. by Marcia Brown. Scribner's, 1953.

5 ANDERSON, LONZO. *Two Hundred Rabbits,* ill. by Adrienne Adams. Viking, 1968.

5 ANNO, MITSUMASA. *Anno's Math Games,* ill. by author. Philomel, 1987.

————. *Anno's Medieval World,* ill. by author, ad. from translation by Ursula Synge. Philomel, 1980.

————. *Anno's Peekaboo,* ill. by author. Philomel, 1988. Partial pages alternate with full pages, each partial page consisting of a pair of hands covering an object that is fully revealed on the next complete page.

5 ARDIZZONE, EDWARD. *Little Tim and the Brave Sea Captain,* ill. by author. Walck, 1955.

5 ————. *Tim All Alone,* ill. by author. Oxford, 1957. Kate Greenaway Medal.

5 ————. *The Wrong Side of the Bed,* ill. by author. Doubleday, 1970.

5 BAKER, JEANNIE. *Where the Forest Meets the Sea,* ill. by author. Greenwillow, 1988. Striking relief collages of northeastern Australia illustrate a first-person narrative of a boy who boats with his father through a reef to the rainforest.

○ 5 BANG, MOLLY. *The Paper Crane,* ill. by author. Greenwillow, 1985. Paper cutout pictures accompany a tale about a paper crane that comes to life and dances as a reward for a poor restaurant owner's generosity to a weary traveler.

☆ § BARKIN, CAROL, and ELIZABETH JAMES. *Sometimes I Hate School,* photos by Heinz Kluetmeier. Raintree, 1975. Designed to help those who are not yet adjusted to the demands of a school environment.

5 BARNHART, PETER. *The Wounded Duck,* ill. by Adrienne Adams. Scribner's, 1979.

BATE, LUCY. *Little Rabbit's Loose Tooth,* ill. by Diane De Groat. Crown, 1975.

☆ 5 BAYLOR, BYRD. *The Desert Is Theirs,* ill. by Peter Parnall. Scribner's, 1975.

5 ————. *Everybody Needs a Rock,* ill. by Peter Parnall. Scribner's, 1974.

5 BEMELMANS, LUDWIG. *Madeline,* ill. by author. Viking, 1939.

BLAKE, QUENTIN. *Mister Magnolia,* ill. by author. Jonathan Cape, 1980. Ebullient rhymes and illustrations tell the nonsensical story of a man who has only one boot.

————. *The Story of the Dancing Frog,* ill. by author. Knopf, 1985. A preposterous show-biz story is set off by bland writing and lively pictures.

5 BLEGVAD, LENORE. *Anna Banana and Me,* ill. by Erik Blegvad. Atheneum, 1985.

BOYD, LIZI. *The Not-So-Wicked Stepmother,* ill. by author. Viking Kestrel, 1987.

BRANDENBERG, FRANZ. *I Wish I Was Sick, Too!* ill. by Aliki. Greenwillow, 1976.

§ BREINBURG, PETRONELLA. *Doctor Shawn,* ill. by Errol Lloyd T. Crowell, 1975.

5 BRIGGS, RAYMOND. *Father Christmas,* ill. by author. Coard, 1973. Kate Greenaway Medal.

5 ————. *Father Christmas Goes on Holiday,* ill. by author. Coward, 1975.

5 ————. *Jim and the Beanstalk,* ill. by author. Coward, 1970.

BROWN, MARC, and LAUREN KRASNY. *The Bionic Bunny Show,* ill. by Marc Brown. Little, 1984. This behind-the-scenes look at the filming of a television series is interwoven with an amusing story about a meek bunny cast in the role of a superhero.

5 BROWN, MARCIA. *Dick Whittington and His Cat,* ill. by author. Scribner's, 1950.

5 ———. *Once a Mouse,* ill. by author. Scribner's, 1961. Caldecott Medal.

——. *Stone Soup,* ill. by author. Scribner's, 1947.

5 BROWN, MARGARET WISE. *The Little Island,* ill. by Leonard Weisgard. Doubleday, 1946. Published under pseudonym of Golden MacDonald. Caldecott Medal.

——. *The Runaway Bunny,* ill. by Clement Hurd, rev. ed. Harper, 1962.

BROWN, MYRA BERRY. *First Night Away from Home,* ill. by Dorothy Marino. Watts, 1960.

5 BROWNE, ANTHONY. *Gorilla,* ill. by author. Knopf, 1985. Illustrations with a strong sense of design accompany a story about Hannah, who longs for her busy father and imagines a loving gorilla taking her to the zoo. Following the fantasy, father comes through with a real zoo trip.

5 ———. *Willy the Wimp,* ill. by author. Knopf, 1985. Willy, the scrawny chimpanzee, tires of being called a wimp and embarks on a massive body-building program.

5 BURNINGHAM, JOHN. *Avocado Baby,* ill. by author. T. Crowell, 1982. A baby fed on avocadoes becomes tremendously strong in this droll nursery tall tale.

——. *The Baby; The Rabbit; The School;* and *The Snow,* ill. by author. T. Crowell, 1975.

——. *The Blanket; The Cupboard; The Dog;* and *The Friend,* ill. by author. T. Crowell, 1976. Four more titles of the ''Little Books'' series perfectly scaled by their subjects, their brevity, and their direct simplicity to appeal to the young child.

5 ———. *Borka: The Adventures of a Goose with No Feathers,* ill. by author. Random, 1964. Kate Greenaway Medal.

5 ———. *Mr. Gumpy's Motor Car,* ill. by author. Crowell, 1976.

5 ———. *Mr. Gumpy's Outing,* ill. by author. Holt, 1971. Kate Greenaway Medal.

——. *Where's Julius?* ill. by author. Crown, 1986.

5 BURTON, VIRGINIA. *The Little House,* ill. by author. Houghton, 1942. Caldecott Medal.

5 ———. *Mike Mulligan and His Steam Shovel,* ill. by author. Houghton, 1939.

5 CARIGIET, ALOIS. *Anton and Anne,* tr. by Refna Wilkin, ill. by author. Walck, 1969.

CARLE, ERIC. *The Honeybee and the Robber,* ill. by author. Philomel, 1981.

CARLSON, NATALIE SAVAGE. *Marie Louise's Heyday,* ill. by Jose Aruego and Ariane Dewey. Scribner's, 1975.

CAUDILL, REBECCA. *Did You Carry the Flag Today, Charley?* ill. by Nancy Grossman. Holt, 1966.

5 ———. *A Pocketful of Cricket,* ill. by Evaline Ness. Holt, 1964.

§ 5 CENDRARS, BLAISE. *Shadow,* tr. and ill. by Marcia Brown. Scribner's, 1982. Caldecott Medal.

CHALMERS, MARY. *Come to the Doctor, Harry,* ill. by author. Harper, 1981. Despite his initial reluctance, cat-child Harry actually enjoys his visit to the doctor.

● CHAPMAN, CAROL. *The Tale of Meshka the Kvetch,* ill. by Arnold Lobel. Dutton, 1980. Meshka the kvetch (*complainer* in Yiddish) makes everyone around her miserable until a series of disasters changes her life.

CLEARY, BEVERLY. *Janet's Thingamajigs,* ill. by DyAnne DiSalvo-Ryan. Morrow, 1987.

§ CLIFTON, LUCILLE. *My Friend Jacob,* ill. by Thomas Digrazia. Dutton, 1980. A touching account of the loving friendship between a small black boy and his retarded adolescent neighbor, who is white.

§ 5 ———. *Some of the Days of Everett Anderson,* ill. by Evaline Ness. Holt, 1970.

○ § COHEN, MIRIAM. *First Grade Takes a Test,* ill. by Lillian Hoban. Greenwillow, 1980. When Anna Maria is moved to a class for the gifted, her jealous first-grade schoolmates begin to squabble.

○ § ———. *Lost in the Museum,* ill. by Lillian Hoban. Greenwillow, 1978. On a visit to the Museum of Natural History, several children follow Danny, who knows where the dinosaur skeleton is. In the process of relocating the class the children learn there are many different ways to be afraid—or brave.

§ ★ ———. *See You in Second Grade!* ill. by Lillian Hoban. Greenwillow, 1989.

§ ★ 5 ———. *Starring First Grade,* ill. by Lillian Hoban. Greenwillow, 1985. As their class rehearses for a production of ''The Three Billy Goats Gruff,'' Jim grows jealous of Paul, who plays the troll.

○ § ———. *When Will I Read?* ill. by Lillian Hoban. Greenwillow, 1977. A multiethnic classroom, a loving teacher, a child who yearns to read, amusing antics of the children in the class, natural-sounding dialogue: who could ask for anything more?

○ § ———. *Will I Have a Friend?* ill. by Lillian Hoban. Macmillan, 1967.

5 COLE, JOANNA. *Doctor Change,* ill. by Donald Carrick. Morrow, 1986. Clever Tom and his companion Kate trick Dr. Change, a shape-changing wizard, out of a fortune.

COLE, WILLIAM. *What's Good for a Three-Year-Old?* ill. by Lillian Hoban. Holt, 1974.

5 COONEY, BARBARA. *Island Boy,* ill. by author. Viking, 1988.

———. *Miss Rumphius,* ill. by author. Viking, 1982.

5 CRAFT, RUTH. *The Winter Bear,* ill. by Erik Blegvad. Atheneum, 1975.

5 CRESSWELL, HELEN. *Trouble,* ill. by Margaret Chamberlain. Dutton, 1988. Humorous line-and-wash pictures illustrate a three-generation story in which Grandma delights Emma by telling her of all the trouble Emma's mother caused as a child.

CROWE, ROBERT L. *Clyde Monster,* ill. by Kay Chorao. Dutton, 1976. A small, awkward, engaging monster is afraid of the dark—people might get him!

§ 5 DALY, NIKI. *Not So Fast Songololo,* ill. by author. Atheneum/Margaret K. McElderry, 1986. A warm story of a black South African child's trip to town with his grandmother concludes with the purchase of a pair of new red sneakers for the boy.

5 DAUGHERTY, JAMES. *Andy and the Lion,* ill. by author. Viking, 1938.

DEBRUNHOFF, JEAN. *The Story of Babar, the Little Elephant,* ill. by author. Random, 1937.

DELTON, JUDY. *Two Good Friends,* ill. by Giulio Maestro. Crown, 1974.

5 DEPAOLA, TOMIE. *The Art Lesson,* ill. by author. Putnam, 1989. First-grader and budding artist Tommy goes on strike when his art teacher tells him to copy a drawing from the board.

• ———. *Charlie Needs a Cloak,* ill. by author. Prentice, 1974.

5 ———. *Nana Upstairs and Nana Downstairs,* ill. by author. Putnam, 1973.

———. *The Quicksand Book.* Holiday, 1977.

5 ———, ad. *Strega Nona,* ill. by adapter. Prentice, 1975.

5 DEREGNIERS, BEATRICE SCHENK. *A Little House of Your Own,* ill. by Irene Haas. Harcourt, 1955.

5 ———. *May I Bring a Friend?* ill. by Beni Montresor. Atheneum, 1964. Caldecott Medal.

5 ———. *What Can You Do with a Shoe?* ill. by Maurice Sendak. Harper, 1955.

DICKINSON, MARY. *Alex and the Baby,* ill. by Charlotte Firmin. Deutsch, 1982. A toddler's envy of a visiting baby is explored in this fresh and engaging story.

DRAGONWAGON, CRESCENT. *When Light Turns into Night,* ill. by Robert Andrew Parker. Harper, 1975.

5 DUVOISIN, ROGER. *Snowy and Woody.* Knopf, 1979.

5 ELKIN, BENJAMIN. *How the Tsar Drinks Tea,* ill. by Anita Lobel. Parents' Magazine, 1971.

5 EMBERLEY, BARBARA, ad. *Drummer Hoff,* ill. by Ed Emberley. Prentice, 1967. Caldecott Medal.

★ 5 ETS, MARIE HALL. *Gilberto and the Wind,* ill. by author. Viking, 1963.

5 ———. *Talking Without Words,* ill. by author. Viking, 1968.

☆ 5 ———, and AURORA LABASTIDA. *Nine Days to Christmas,* ill. by Marie Hall Ets. Viking, 1959. Caldecott Medal.

FARBER, NORMA. *Where's Gomer?* ill. by William Pène du Bois. Dutton, 1974.

5 FATIO, LOUISE. *The Happy Lion,* ill. by Roger Duvoisin. Whittlesey, 1954.

5 FISHER, AILEEN. *Going Barefoot,* ill. by Adrienne Adams. T. Crowell, 1960.

5 ———. *Where Does Everyone Go?* ill. by Adrienne Adams. T. Crowell, 1961.

○ 5 FLACK, MARJORIE. *The Story About Ping,* ill. by Kurt Wiese. Viking, 1933.

FLEISCHMAN, SID. *The Scarebird,* ill. by Peter Sis. Greenwillow, 1988. Lonesome John learns that Sam, an orphan boy, makes a better companion than his silent scarecrow.

FREEMAN, DON. *Will's Quill,* ill. by author. Viking, 1975.

5 GÁG, WANDA. *Millions of Cats,* ill. by author. Coward, 1928.

GALDONE, PAUL. *The Gingerbread Boy,* ill. by author. Seabury, 1975.

———. *The Little Red Hen,* ill. by author. Seabury, 1973.

GERSTEIN, MORDICAI. *Arnold of the Ducks,* ill. by author. Harper, 1983. An infant boy is raised as a duckling until he is reunited with his own family in this whimsical fantasy.

GETZ, ARTHUR. *Hamilton Duck,* ill. by author. Golden Pr., 1972.

GLASS, ANDREW. *My Brother Tries to Make Me Laugh,* ill. by author. Lothrop, 1984.

5 GOUDEY, ALICE E. *The Day We Saw the Sun Come Up,* ill. by Adrienne Adams. Scribner's, 1961.

5 ———. *Houses from the Sea,* ill. by Adrienne Adams. Scribner's, 1959.

GRAHAM, BOB. *Crusher Is Coming!,* ill. by author. Viking, 1988.

§ GRAHAM, LORENZ. *Hongry Catch the Foolish Boy,* ill. by James Brown, Jr. T. Crowell, 1973.

§ ———. *Song of the Boat,* ill. by Leo and Diane Dillon. T. Crowell, 1975.

§ GRAY, GENEVIEVE. *Send Wendell,* ill. by Symeon Shimin. McGraw, 1974.

§ 5 GRAY, NIGEL. *A Balloon for Grandad,* ill. by Jane Ray. Orchard, 1988. When Sam's balloon blows away, Dad comforts him by describing the balloon's fantasy journey across continents to visit Grandad Abdulla.

§ GREENFIELD, ELOISE. *She Come Bringing Me That Little Baby Girl,* ill. by John Steptoe. Lippincott, 1974.

§ 5 GRIFALCONI, ANN. *The Village of Round and Square Houses,* ill. by author. Little, 1986. Set in a small west African village, the story explains why the women there live in round houses and the men in square ones.

GRIFFITH, HELEN V. *Grandaddy's Place,* ill. by James Stevenson. Greenwillow, 1987. City girl Janetta takes a while to warm up to her unfamiliar grandfather and his farm, but when she does, the two are in complete rapport.

5 GRIMM, JACOB and WILHELM. *King Grisley-Beard,* tr. by Edgar Taylor, ill. by Maurice Sendak. Farrar, 1973.

5 _____. *The Shoemaker and the Elves,* ill. by Adrienne Adams. Scribner's, 1960.

5 HADER, BERTA and ELMER. *The Big Snow,* ill. by authors. Macmillan, 1948. Caldecott Medal.

HADITHI, MWENYE. *Crafty Chameleon,* ill. by Adrienne Kennaway. Little, 1987.

§ 5 HALEY, GAIL E., ad. *A Story—A Story: An African Tale,* ill. by adapter. Atheneum, 1970. Caldecott Medal.

5 HALL, DONALD, *Ox-Cart Man,* ill. by Barbara Cooney. Viking, 1979. Caldecott Medal.

○ 5 HANDFORTH, THOMAS. *Mei Li,* ill. by author. Doubleday, 1938. Caldecott Medal.

§ 5 HAYES, SARAH. *Eat Up, Gemma.* Lothrop, 1988.

_____. *Happy Christmas, Gemma.* Lothrop, 1986. Both ill. by Jan Ormerod. Baby Gemma dismays her big brother by refusing to eat her food and amuses him by finding lots of chances to make big messes during her first Christmas celebration.

HENKES, KEVIN. *Grandpa and Bo,* ill. by author. Greenwillow, 1986.

_____. *Jessica,* ill. by author. Greenwillow, 1989.

_____. *A Weekend with Wendell,* ill. by author. Greenwillow, 1986.

HEWITT, KATHRYN, ad. *The Three Sillies,* ill. by adapter. Harcourt, 1986.

5 HOBAN, RUSSELL. *Bedtime for Frances,* ill. by Garth Williams. Harper, 1960.

_____. *Dinner at Alberta's,* ill. by James Marshall. T. Crowell, 1975.

_____. *The Flight of Bembel Rudzuk,* ill. by Colin McNaughton. Philomel, 1982. The three boys from Aargh share another imaginative, vigorously illustrated adventure.

_____. *They Came from Aargh!* ill. by Colin McNaughton. Philomel, 1981.

5 HODGES, MARGARET, ad. *Saint George and the Dragon,* ill. by Trina Schart Hyman. Little, 1984. Caldecott Medal.

5 HOGROGIAN, NONNY. *The Cat Who Loved to Sing,* ill. by author. Knopf, 1988.

5 _____. *The Contest,* ill. by author. Greenwillow, 1976.

§ 5 _____. *One Fine Day,* ill. by author. Macmillan, 1971. Caldecott Medal.

HOLL, ADELAIDE. *The Parade,* ill. by Kjell Ringi. Watts, 1975.

HUGHES, SHIRLEY. *Alfie Gets in First,* ill. by author. Lothrop, 1982. Warmly realistic ink and wash drawings picture the plight of a small boy who has locked himself in the house and his resourceful solution to the problem.

_____. *Alfie Gives a Hand,* ill. by author. Lothrop, 1984.

_____. *An Evening at Alfie's,* ill. by author. Lothrop, 1985. A babysitter copes with a domestic disaster.

§ 5 HUGHES, SHIRLEY. *Angel Mae,* ill. by author. Lothrop, 1989.

§ 5 _____. *The Big Alfie and Annie Rose Storybook,* ill. by author. Lothrop, 1989.

5 _____. *David and Dog,* ill. by author. Prentice, 1978. A child's attachment to a favorite toy, its loss, and its subsequent retrieval form the plot for this engaging tale. Published in England as *Dogger.* Kate Greenaway Medal.

HURWITZ, JOHANNA. *Busybody Nora,* ill. by Susan Jeschke. Morrow, 1976.

5 HUTCHINS, PAT. *Rosie's Walk,* ill. by author. Macmillan, 1968.

§ ISADORA, RACHEL. *Ben's Trumpet,* ill. by author. Greenwillow, 1979. A story of a small black boy who plays an imaginary trumpet is set off by black and white illustrations that are startling in their effectiveness.

5 JAMESON, CYNTHIA, ad. *The Clay Pot Boy,* ill. by Arnold Lobel. Coward, 1973.

§ 5 JOHNSON, ANGELA. *Tell Me a Story, Mama,* ill. by David Soman. Orchard, 1989. A small girl and her mother recall the child's favorite stories about Mama's childhood.

KAHL, VIRGINIA. *The Duchess Bakes a Cake,* ill. by author. Scribner's, 1955.

§ ★ KEATS, EZRA JACK. *Dreams,* ill. by author. Macmillan, 1974.

§ 5 _____. *Goggles!* ill. by author. Macmillan, 1969.

§ 5 _____. *Hi Cat!* ill. by author. Macmillan, 1970.

§ 5 _____. *Louie,* ill. by author. Greenwillow, 1975.

§ 5 _____. *Peter's Chair,* ill. by author. Harper, 1967.

§ 5 _____. *The Snowy Day,* ill. by author. Viking, 1962. Caldecott Medal.

§ 5 _____. *Whistle for Willie,* ill. by author. Viking, 1964.

5 KEEPING, CHARLES. *Charley, Charlotte and the Golden Canary,* ill. by author. Watts, 1967. Kate Greenaway Medal.

5 _____. *Joseph's Yard,* ill. by author. Watts, 1970.

KESSELMAN, WENDY ANN. *Time for Jody,* ill. by Gerald Dumas. Harper, 1975.

5 KINGMAN, LEE. *Peter's Long Walk,* ill. by Barbara Cooney. Doubleday, 1953.

5 KIPLING, RUDYARD. *How the Rhinoceros Got His Skin,* ill. by Leonard Weisgard. Walker, 1974.

KISMARIC, CAROLE, ad. *The Rumor of Pavel and Paali: A Ukranian Folktale,* ill. by Charles Mikolaycak. Harper, 1988.

KRAUSS, RUTH. *A Hole Is to Dig,* ill. by Maurice Sendak. Harper, 1952.

5 KUMIN, MAXINE, and ANNE SEXTON. *Joey and the Birthday Present,* ill. by Evaline Ness. McGraw, 1971.

KUSKIN, KARLA. *The Dallas Titans Get Ready for Bed,* ill. by Marc Simont. Harper, 1986. Reversing the concept of *The Philharmonic Gets Dressed,* here forty-five football players leave the playing field, undress and shower, and head home to bed.

_____. *The Philharmonic Gets Dressed,* ill. by Marc Simont. Harper, 1982. Witty illustrations and a straightforward text combine in a description of how members of the New York Philharmonic Orchestra prepare for a performance.

5 LANGSTAFF, JOHN. *Frog Went a-Courtin',* ill. by Feodor Rojankovsky. Harcourt, 1955. Caldecott Medal.

LAPSLEY, SUSAN. *I Am Adopted,* ill. by Michael Charlton. Bradbury, 1975. A small boy speaks of his adoption casually, he's so secure in the love of his family.

LASKER, JOE. *Mothers Can Do Anything,* ill. by author. Whitman, 1972.

LEAF, MUNRO. *The Story of Ferdinand,* ill. by Robert Lawson, Viking, 1936.

LENT, BLAIR. *John Tabor's Ride,* ill. by author. Atlantic/Little, 1966.

LIONNI, LEO. *In the Rabbitgarden,* ill. by author. Pantheon, 1975.

5 _____. *Inch by Inch,* ill. by author. Obolensky, 1960.

5 LIPKIND, WILL. *Chaga,* ill. by Nicolas Mordvinoff. Harcourt, 1955.

5 _____. *Finders Keepers,* ill. by Nicholas Mordvinoff. Harcourt, 1951. Caldecott Medal.

LLOYD, DAVID, ad. *The Ridiculous Story of Gammer Gurton's Needle,* ill. by Charlotte Voake. Potter, 1987.

5 LOBEL, ANITA. *King Rooster, Queen Hen,* ill. by author. Greenwillow, 1975.

5 _____. *The Pancake,* ill. by author. Greenwillow, 1978. In a version of the familiar folk tale aimed at beginning readers, a pancake hears that it is going to be eaten by the cook's seven hungry children and rolls off to escape its fate.

5 _____, ad. *The Straw Maid,* ill. by adapter. Greenwillow, 1983. Cheery paintings embellish this simply retold story of a peasant girl who outwits a band of robbers.

5 LOBEL, ARNOLD. *The Rose in My Garden,* ill. by Anita Lobel. Greenwillow, 1984. Cumulative verses and richly colored, likewise cumulative artwork about a garden romp.

5 _____. *The Turnaround Wind,* ill. by author. Harper, 1988.

5 _____. *A Zoo for Mr. Muster,* ill. by author. Harper, 1962.

○ LUENN, NANCY. *The Dragon Kite,* ill. by Michael Hague. Harcourt, 1982. A dragon kite used to steal gold ornaments from a rooftop later comes to the robber's rescue in magical style. Handsomely detailed paintings, oriental in mood, capture the setting of this three-hundred-year-old story.

5 MACAULAY, DAVID. *Black and White,* ill. by author. Houghton, 1990.

5 _____. *Why the Chicken Crossed the Road,* ill. by author. Houghton, 1987.

5 McCLOSKEY, ROBERT. *Blueberries for Sal,* ill. by author. Viking, 1948.

5 _____. *Burt Dow, Deep Water Man,* ill. by author. Viking, 1963.

5 _____. *Make Way for Ducklings,* ill. by author. Viking, 1941. Caldecott Medal.

5 _____. *Time of Wonder,* ill. by author. Viking, 1957. Caldecott Medal.

§ **5** McDERMOTT, GERALD. *Anansi the Spider,* ill. by author. Holt, 1972.

☆ **5** _____. *Arrow to the Sun,* ill. by author. Viking, 1974. Caldecott Medal.

§ McKISSACK, PATRICIA C. *Mirandy and Brother Wind,* ill. by Jerry Pinkney. Knopf, 1988.

§ _____. *Nettie Joe's Friends,* ill. by Scott Cook. Knopf, 1989.

MACLACHLAN, PATRICIA. *Mama One, Mama Two,* ill. by Ruth Lercher Bornstein. Harper, 1982. Softly crayoned pastel pictures establish the reassuring tone of this story about a small girl whose mother is in therapy and who lives with a foster parent, Mama Two.

MAESTRO, BETSY and GIULIO. *Ferryboat,* ill. by authors. Crowell, 1986.

MAHY, MARGARET. *The Boy Who Was Followed Home,* ill. by Steven Kellogg. Watts, 1975. The beguiled follower is a hippo.

————. *Jam: A True Story,* ill. by Helen Craig. Atlantic, 1986. While his wife is off working as an atomic scientist, Mr. Castle keeps house, tends the children, and makes hundreds and hundreds of jars of plum jam.

MANUSHKSIN, FRAN. *Bubblebath!* ill. by Ronald Himler. Harper, 1974.

MARSHALL, JAMES. *The Cut-Ups Cut Loose,* ill. by author. Viking, 1987. Spud and Joe can't resist cutting up on the first day of school, to the frustration and fury of their school principal, Lamar J. Spurgle.

————. *George and Martha,* ill. by author. Houghton, 1972.

————. *George and Martha Round and Round,* ill. by author. Houghton, 1988.

5 MERRIAM, EVE. *Mommies at Work,* ill. by Beni Montresor. Knopf, 1961.

5 MILNE, A. A. *When We Were Very Young,* ill. by Ernest H. Shepard. Dutton, 1924.

5 MIZAMURA, KAZUE. *If I Built a Village . . . ,* ill. by author. T. Crowell, 1971.

5 MONTRESOR, BENI. *House of Flowers, House of Stars,* ill. by author. Knopf, 1962.

5 ————. *The Witches of Venice,* ill. by author. Knopf, 1963.

5 MOSEL, ARLENE, ad. *The Funny Little Woman,* ill. by Blair Lent. Dutton, 1972. Caldecott Medal.

MURPHY, JILL. *Five Minutes' Peace,* ill. by author. Putnam, 1986.

NELSON, VAUNDA MICHEAUX. *Always Gramma,* ill. by Kimanne Uhler. Putnam, 1988.

NESS, EVALINE, *The Girl and the Goatherd,* ill. by author. Dutton, 1970.

5 ————. *Josefina February,* ill. by author, Scribner's 1963.

————. *Sam, Bangs & Moonshine,* ill. by author. Holt, 1966. Caldecott Medal.

————. *Tom Tit Tot,* ill. by author. Scribner's, 1965.

NIC LEODHAS, SORCHE. *All in the Morning Early,* ill. by Evaline Ness. Holt, 1963.

————. *Always Room for One More,* ill. by Nonny Hogrogian. Holt, 1965. Caldecott Medal.

OAKLEY, GRAHAM. *The Church Cat Abroad,* ill. by author. Atheneum, 1973.

————. *The Church Mice Adrift,* ill. by author. Atheneum, 1977.

————. *The Church Mice at Christmas,* ill. by author. Atheneum, 1980. A witty Christmas story in which the mice and their cat friend procure holiday goodies in an unexpected manner.

5 OLSEN, IB SPANG. *Smoke,* ill. by author. Coward, 1972.

OSBORN, LOIS. *My Dad Is Really Something,* ill. by Rodney Pate. Whitman, 1983. Harry George learns the sad truth about a boastful friend's father while his appreciation of his own understanding dad soars.

OXENBURY, HELEN. *The Birthday Party,* ill. by author. Dial, 1983. Affectionate humor and clean, clear illustrations are the hallmark of this splendidly realistic look at a child's first birthday party experience. Also on target for the preschool child and in the same vein are *The Dancing Class, Eating Out,* and *The Car Trip,* all ill. by author. Dial, 1983.

5 § ○ ————. *Clap Hands,* ill. by author. Aladdin, 1987. One of a series of board books, the simple yet poetic text describes babies at play.

§ ○ ————. *The Important Visitor,* ill. by author. Dial, 1984.

PARISH, PEGGY. *Merry Christmas, Amelia Bedelia,* ill. by Lynn Sweat. Greenwillow, 1986. Literal-minded Amelia Bedelia takes pruning shears to the Christmas tree and fills the stocking with turkey dressings when she is instructed to "trim" and "stuff."

5 PARNALL, PETER. *The Mountain,* ill. by author. Doubleday, 1971.

————. *Feet!* ill. by author. Macmillan, 1988.

5 ○ PATERSON KATHERINE. *The Tale of the Mandarin Ducks,* ill. by Leo and Diane Dillon. Lodestar/Dutton. 1990

5 PEARCE, PHILIPPA. *Emily's Own Elephant,* ill. by John Lawrence. Greenwillow, 1988. When a zookeeper tells Emily an elephant needs a home, she offers her family's empty shed and gets a new pet.

PEARSON, SUSAN, *Izzie,* ill. by Robert Andrew Parker. Dial, 1975.

5 PETERSON, HANS. *The Big Snowstorm,* ill. by Harald Wiberg. Coward, 1976.

POLITI, LEO. *Juanita,* ill. by author. Scribner's, 1948.

○ ————. *Moy Moy,* ill. by author. Scribner's, 1960. Two of Politi's stories that focus on American children of various ethnic backgrounds.

POTTER, BEATRIX. *The Tale of Peter Rabbit,* ill. by author. Warne, 1901.

5 PROVENSEN, ALICE. *The Buck Stops Here: The Presidents of the United States,* ill. by author. Harper, 1990.

5 PROVENSEN, ALICE and MARTIN. *The Glorious Flight,* ill. by authors. Viking, 1983. Caldecott Medal.

————. *My Little Hen,* ill. by authors. Random, 1973.

————. *Our Animal Friends at Maple Hill Farm,* ill. by authors. Random, 1974.

5 ————. *Shaker Lane,* ill. by authors. Viking, 1987.

5 RANSOME, ARTHUR. *The Fool of the World and the Flying Ship,* ill. by Uri Schulevitz. Farrar, 1968. Caldecott Medal.

REY, HANS. *Curious George,* ill. by author. Houghton, 1941. And its sequels.

ROCKWELL, HARLOW. *My Dentist,* ill. by author. Greenwillow, 1975.

————. *My Doctor,* ill. by author. Macmillan, 1973.

§ ————. *My Nursery School,* ill. by author. Greenwillow, 1976. Sharing work and play in a multiethnic classroom.

§ ○ ROGERS, FRED. *Going on an Airplane,* photos by Jim Judkis. Putnam, 1989.

ROSEN, WINIFRED. *Ralph Proves the Pudding,* ill. by Lionel Kalish. Doubleday, 1972.

RUSS, LAVINIA. *Alec's Sand Castle,* ill. by James Stevenson. Harper, 1972.

5 RYAN, CHELI DURAN. *Hildilid's Night,* ill. by Arnold Lobel. Macmillan, 1971.

RYLANT, CYNTHIA. *All I See,* ill. by Peter Catalanotto. Orchard, 1988. Charlie, a shy and quiet boy, gains confidence through his summertime friendship with an artist named Gregory.

5 ————. *Birthday Presents,* ill. by Sucie Stevenson. Orchard/Watts, 1987.

5 ————. *The Relatives Came,* ill. by Stephen Gammell. Bradbury, 1985. Exuberant color pencil drawings show the warmth shared when many relatives crowd together into a single house.

5 SCHICK, ELEANOR. *Neighborhood Knight,* ill. by author. Greenwillow, 1976.

SCHWARTZ, AMY. *Annabelle Swift, Kindergartner,* ill. by author. Orchard/Watts, 1988.

————. *Oma and Bobo,* ill. by author. Bradbury, 1987.

SCOTT, ANN. *On Mother's Lap,* ill. by Glo Coalson. McGraw, 1972.

5 SEGAL, LORE, *The Story of Mrs. Lovewright and Purrless Her Cat,* ill. by Paul O. Zelinsky. Knopf, 1985. Mrs. Lovewright learns that the cuddly kitten of her imaginings does not exist in the independent cat given to her by the grocery delivery man.

5 SENDAK, MAURICE. *In the Night Kitchen,* ill. by author. Harper, 1970.

5 ————. *The Nutshell Library,* ill. by author. Harper, 1962.

5 ————. *Outside Over There,* ill. by author. Harper, 1981.

5 ————. *Where the Wild Things Are,* ill. by author. Harper, 1963. Caldecott Medal.

SHARMAT, MARJORIE WEINMAN. *I'm Not Oscar's Friend Anymore,* ill. by Tony DeLuna. Dutton, 1975.

————. *Walter the Wolf,* ill. by Kelly Oechsli. Holiday, 1975.

————. *What Are We Going to Do About Andrew?* ill. by Ray Cruz. Macmillan, 1980. A blithe fantasy about a boy whose family adjusts to the fact that he can fly.

5 SHULEVITZ, URI. *Dawn,* ill. by author. Farrar, 1974.

5 ————. *One Monday Morning,* ill. by author. Scribner's, 1967.

5 ————. *Rain Rain Rivers,* ill. by author. Scribner's, 1967.

SIVULICH, SANDRA STRONER. *I'm Going on a Bear Hunt,* ill. by Glen Rounds. Dutton, 1973.

SKORPEN, LIESEL MOAK. *Mandy's Grandmother,* ill. by Martha Alexander. Dial, 1975.

5 SLEATOR, WILLIAM, ad. *The Angry Moon,* ill. by Blair Lent. Little, 1970.

SOBOL, HARRIET LANGSAM. *Jeff's Hospital Book,* photos by Patricia Agre. Walck, 1975.

☆ SONNEBORN, RUTH. *Friday Night Is Papa Night,* ill. by Emily McNully. Viking, 1970. A story that reflects the love and warmth in a Puerto Rican family.

STEIG, WILLIAM. *Brave Irene,* ill. by author. Farrar, 1986. As a blizzard rages, little Irene courageously sets out to deliver to the duchess a ball gown made by Irene's mother.

————. *Doctor DeSoto,* ill. by author. Farrar, 1982. A kindly mouse dentist responds to a miserable fox's plea for treatment, but cleverly foils the creature's attempt to devour his benefactor.

————. *Spinky Sulks,* ill. by author. Farrar, 1988.

————. *Sylvester and the Magic Pebble,* ill. by author. Windmill/Simon, 1969. Caldecott Medal.

————. *Yellow & Pink,* ill. by author. Farrar, 1984.

§ 5 STEPTOE, JOHN. *Mufaro's Beautiful Daughters,* ill. by author. Lothrop, 1987.

§ 5 ————. *Stevie,* ill. by author. Harper, 1969.

STEVENSON, JAMES. *The Great Big Especially Beautiful Easter Egg,* ill. by author. Greenwillow, 1983. Grandpa recounts his boyhood search for an exceptionally big Easter egg in this uproarious tall tale.

5 ————. *The Supreme Souvenir Factory,* ill. by author. Greenwillow, 1988. Chester, a modest dog, swells to superhero proportions as he overcomes the evil machinations of a factory manager.

————. *We Can't Sleep,* ill. by author. Greenwillow, 1982. A wildly improbable prebedtime adventure is the basis of another of Grandpa's outrageous yarns.

————. *What's Under My Bed?* ill. by author. Greenwillow, 1983.

5 ————. *The Worst Person in the World at Crab Beach,* ill. by author. Greenwillow, 1988. The elderly grouch-of-all-time goes to a seaside resort that has everything he likes: awful food, lots of mosquitoes and jellyfish, and cold fog.

————. *Yuck!* ill. by author. Greenwillow, 1984. An appealing little witch named Emma outwits two mean witches with the help of her animal friends.

§ STOLZ, MARY SLATTERY. *Storm in the Night,* ill. by Pat Cummings. Harper, 1988.

5 SWIFT, HILDEGARD. *The Little Red Lighthouse and the Great Gray Bridge,* ill. by Lynd Ward. Harcourt, 1942.

TAPIO, PAT DECKER. *The Lady Who Saw the Good Side of Everything,* ill. by Paul Galdone. Seabury, 1975.

TEJIMA, KEIZABURO. *Fox's Dream,* ill. by author. Philomel, 1987.

————. *Owl Lake,* ill. by author. Philomel, 1987.

————. *Swan Sky,* ill. by author. Philomel, 1988.

THIELE, COLIN. *Farmer Schultz's Ducks,* ill. by Mary Milton. Harper, 1988.

THOMPSON, PEGGY, ad. *The King has Horse's Ears,* ill. by David Small. Simon and Schuster, 1988. Betty, Horace the king's bride, wouldn't have him any other way after his horse ears are revealed at their wedding.

TITHERINGTON, JEANNE. *A Place for Ben,* ill. by author. Greenwillow, 1987.

TITUS, EVE. *Anatole in Italy,* ill. by Paul Galdone. McGraw, 1973.

TRESSELT, ALVIN. *The Dead Tree,* ill. by Charles Robinson, Parents' Magazine, 1972.

5 TURKLE, BRINTON. *Obadiah the Bold,* ill. by author. Viking, 1965

TURNER, GWENDA. *Playbook,* ill. by author. Viking, 1986.

○ UCHIDA, YOSHIKO. *The Birthday Visitor,* ill. by Charles Robinson, Scribner's, 1975.

5 UDRY, JANICE MAY. *The Moon Jumpers,* ill. by Maurice Sendak. Harper, 1959.

§ ————. *What Mary Jo Shared,* ill. by Eleanor Mill. Whitman, 1966.

UNGERER, TOMI. *Émile,* ill. by author. Harper, 1960.

5 VAN ALLSBURG, CHRIS. *The Polar Express,* ill. by author. Houghton, 1985. Caldecott Medal.

————. *The Garden of Abdul Gasazi,* ill. by author. Houghton, 1979.

5 ————. *Jumanji,* ill. by author. Houghton, 1981. Caldecott Medal.

5 ————. *The Mysteries of Harris Burdick,* ill. by author. Houghton, 1984.

VAN WOERKOM, DOROTHY. *The Queen Who Couldn't Bake Gingerbread,* ill. by Paul Galdone. Knopf, 1975.

VINCENT, GABRIELLE. *Ernest and Celestine,* ill. by author. Greenwillow, 1982. A bear, Ernest, consoles his mouse friend when she loses a favorite toy in this engaging story illustrated with delicate yet lively pastel-tinted scenes. Equally enjoyable sequels are *Bravo, Ernest and Celestine!* and *Merry Christmas, Ernest and Celestine.*

5 VIPONT, ELFRIDA. *The Elephant and the Bad Baby,* ill. by Raymond Briggs. Coward, 1970.

VOIGT, CYNTHIA. *Stories about Rosie,* ill. by Dennis Kendrick. Atheneum, 1986. Four stories about the adventures of Rosie the dog are told from her perspective.

WABER, BERNARD. *I Was All Thumbs,* ill. by author. Houghton, 1975.

5 ————. *Ira Says Goodbye,* ill. by author. Houghton, 1988.

————. *Ira Sleeps Over,* ill. by author. Houghton, 1972.

————. *Lyle Finds His Mother.* Houghton, 1974.

WADE, BARRIE. *Little Monster,* ill. by Katinka Kew. Lothrop, 1990. A conforming child tries to be as disruptive as her brother, in an attention-getting ploy.

WARD, LYND. *The Biggest Bear,* ill. by author. Houghton, 1952. Caldecott Medal.

WATANABE, SHIGEO. *How Do I Put It On?* ill. by Yasuo Ohtomo. Collins, 1979.

————. *What a Good Lunch!* ill. by Yasuo Ohtomo. Collins, 1980.

WELLS, ROSEMARY. *Benjamin and Tulip,* ill. by author. Dial, 1973.

5 ————. *Don't Spill It Again, James,* ill. by author. Dial, 1977.

————. *Hazel's Amazing Mother,* ill. by author. Dial, 1985.

5 ————. *Max's Chocolate Chicken,* ill. by Rosemary Wells. Dial, 1989. While big sister Ruby struggles to find all the hidden Easter eggs, Max finds and devours the prize of the hunt: the chocolate chicken.

5 ————. *Max's First Word,* ill. by author. Dial, 1979.

5 ————. *Morris' Disappearing Bag,* ill. by author. Dial, 1975.

————. *Shy Charles,* ill. by author. Dial, 1988.

5 WILDSMITH, BRIAN. *Brian Wildsmith's Circus,* ill. by author. Watts, 1970.

5 ————. *Brian Wildsmith's Puzzles,* ill. by author. Watts, 1971.

5 ————. *Daisy,* ill. by author. Pantheon, 1984.

5 ————. *The Little Wood Duck,* ill. by author. Watts, 1973.

5 ————. *Pelican,* ill. by author. Pantheon, 1983.

5 ————. *Professor Noah's Spaceship,* ill. by author. Oxford, 1980.

WILLIAMS, VERA B. *A Chair for My Mother,* ill. by author. Greenwillow, 1982. Bright, stylized paintings illustrate a warm story about a little girl, her mother, and grandmother who have lost their home in a fire and are saving coins in a jar to buy a comfortable armchair.

WOOD, AUDREY. *King Bidgood's in the Bathtub,* ill. by Don Wood. Harcourt, 1985.

5 _____. *The Napping House,* ill. by Don Wood. Harcourt, 1984. In cumulative folksong style, the bite of a flea starts a chain of events that awakens all the occupants of a sleepy house.

o 5 YASHIMA, TARO. *Umbrella,* ill. by author. Viking, 1958.

5 YOLEN, JANE. *Owl Moon,* ill. by John Schoenherr. Philomel, 1987. Double-page spreads of stark nighttime winter scenes show a child and father walking stealthily through a woods, hoping to glimpse an owl. Caldecott Medal.

5 YORINKS, ARTHUR. *Brave Minski,* ill. by Richard Egielski. Farrar, 1988.

5 _____. *Hey Al,* ill. by Richard Egielski. Farrar, 1986. Vibrantly colored paintings detail the travels of Al and his dog, Eddie, from the West Side to bird paradise, where the visitors are transformed into birds. Caldecott Medal.

5 ZEMACH, HARVE. *Duffy and the Devil,* ill. by Margot Zemach. Farrar, 1973. Caldecott Medal.

5 _____. *The Judge: An Untrue Tale,* ill. by Margot Zemach.

5 _____. *Small Boy Is Listening,* ill. by Margot Zemach. Houghton, 1959.

5 ZEMACH, MARGOT, ad. *It Could Always Be Worse: A Yiddish Folk Tale,* ill. by author. Farrar, 1976.

5 ZOLOTOW, CHARLOTTE. *May I Visit?* ill. by Erik Blegvad. Harper, 1976.

5 _____. *My Grandson Lew,* ill. by William Pène du Bois. Harper, 1974.

_____. *The Unfriendly Book,* ill. by William Pène du Bois. Harper, 1975.

_____. *When I Have a Little Girl,* ill. by Hilary Knight. Harper, 1965.

_____. *William's Doll,* ill. by William Pène du Bois. Harper, 1972.

Chapter Five

Artists and Children's Books

Browsing through the shelves of children's books in a bookstore or a library, one is always impressed by the beauty of design and the beauty and variety of illustration in old books and new. Although young children take pleasure in hearing a book read, it is the illustrations they look at, and when they look they are learning to appreciate line, color, pattern, humor, and to see the storytelling quality of a picture. While the visual appeal is especially important for young children, the way a book looks (illustration, layout, and typography) is of importance to readers of all ages.

To study or discuss children's literature and not to include an examination of children's book illustration would be to ignore a significant element in the value and the appeal of these books. Just as a body of writing for children developed slowly, with youngsters at first simply appropriating those adult books that had some interest for them, so has the illustration of children's books developed slowly, bursting finally into the wealth and variety of art we have in twentieth-century books.

What is the explanation for today's marvelous richness in children's book illustration? The answer derives in part from the fact that the first books published for children included illustrations either to instruct, as did the courtesy books and alphabet books, or to support and extend the author's text. From the beginning, then, illustrations have served these functions. Certainly the prevalence of illustration in books for children in the past and in the present reflects an adult decision that pictures will attract and hold children's interest or will help them to learn about a subject.

Then and now, artwork in children's books served several functions: to clarify or to add information to the text, in the case of nonfiction particularly; to enlarge or interpret the author's meaning; to evoke an appropriate mood, to establish setting or portray character in fiction; or simply to be decorative.

Art is communication, whether it is in a museum or in a book, and to judge the success of artwork in children's books we must evaluate it in terms of whether it speaks to the child. It must also be judged by how well it fits the story (or the informational text) and adapts to the confinements of page space and layout and color reproduction. And certainly we must evaluate the quality of the artwork itself, the artist's use of media and techniques.

Questions we can ask in judging the appropriateness of illustrations to text are:

Do the pictures reflect the mood of the story (as Uri Shulevitz's do in *Dawn*)? Or do they conflict with it?

Do the pictures have any details that conflict with a textual statement? If the story describes five children, or a boy carrying a book, or a flower that is blue, the illustrations should have the right number of children, the right object under the boy's arm, the right color in the flower.

Do the illustrations extend the text without distracting from it? If a page that shows musculature of the human body is so crowded with details that the printed information is obscured, the illustration is artistically inappropriate for the purpose of the text.

The question of whether the artwork speaks to the child is discussed under the heading "Children's Preferences" later in this chapter, but it should be kept in mind that children, especially young children, are not likely to have visual prejudices and preconceptions, and that they are a more eager audience for the artist's creative message than most adults. Certainly one way in which today's artists speak to children is to include in their illustrations youngsters of all ethnic backgrounds, drawn with no stereotypical details. Although books for younger children are usually more heavily illustrated, there are many profusely illustrated books that are most appropriate for older children because of their subjects, complexity, or sophistication. These are also, if one uses the term in a broader sense, picture books.

While there are no age barriers in the appreciation of art as art, illustrations must be considered with regard to the complexity of the concepts they contain and the relationship of those concepts to children's ability to understand at different ages. Most small children, for example, would find it difficult to understand the intricate details of David Macaulay's drawings in *The Way Things Work*, drawings that speak eloquently and appropriately to older children.

Finally, book illustration can be judged as art. Although individual reaction to an artist's work is subjective, all illustrations can be evaluated by artistic standards. Some of the questions we can ask in evaluating the elements in the illustration and its overall effect are:

How does the artist use color? If the colors are bold and brilliant, do they suit the text they accompany? Or have they simply been splashed about, as colors often are in mass market books, on the premise that the brighter the page, the more it will attract children? Is color an essential element in the layout of the page? Does the color obscure or complement the lines of the drawings? Is the color reproduction of good quality?

Does the artist use line effectively? A delicate line is appropriate for some stories, a bold one for others. Edward Ardizzone was a master of the economical line; Peter Parnall's line is spare and elegant; the light, broken line used by Robin Jacques is eminently suitable for the fairy tales he so often illustrates. Does the line express movement or is it static? Does the line give strength to the depiction of a person or object by being heavy or crosshatched? Is the line varied?

Is the artist successful in handling shape? Whether the shape is distinct or vaguely suggested, simple or ornamented, free-flowing or rigid, the shape must suit the mood and intent of the story. How do shapes relate to each other on the page? If the drawing is realistic, is the perspective correct? Do the shapes fill the page or do they clutter it? If they represent characters, do they suggest qualities with which the author has invested them?

Does the artist give texture to the illustrations? Arnold Lobel, in Cynthia Jameson's *The Clay Pot Boy*, gives the clay pot an unmistakable roundness and solidity; Bert Kitchen's animals have an almost tactile furriness. Many artists use collage, alone or in combination with another medium, to obtain a textural difference. Barbara Cooney achieves the texture of diaphanous fabric with a thin wash of color, a representational treatment, while other artists use stylized patterns and ornamentation. A vaporous look may suggest fog, while blobs of white out of which objects emerge may fail to do so.

How are the elements of each page or of facing pages arranged? Even when all other aspects of the illustration are effective, it may fail in its intent if the composition is awkward or if there is not enough space to set off the various parts of the picture or if the illustration does not balance well in relation to the type area. The parts should have balance and direction so that the illustration has both unity and focus. Peter Parnall uses white space to give his pictures a clean, bare look and to focus the eye on elements he wishes to stress. Composition can be used to accentuate a mood or setting; Tomie dePaola, in *Strega Nona*, fills each drawing with sturdy figures in harmony with the robust and humorous folk tale and frames the drawings to suggest an onstage performance.

In evaluating the visual impact of a book, the primary concern is the illustration, but one must also consider the effect and effectiveness of the book jacket, the endpapers, the typeface used, and the way print is used on the page, particularly when it is placed in such a way that print and illustration together make a pattern. Heavy block letters do not suit a delicate fairy tale while they may be both effective and appropriate for a book of modern poetry. A clear, clean type can be lost if it is printed on a dark background or is obscured by illustrative details.

It is clear, when one considers the many visual aspects of a book, that many people play a part in addition to the illustrator: the editor of the book, the department's art editor, and even the printer, whose expertise may be the decisive factor in producing good registration or color reproduction. Together they decide on layout and typography, aspects of the physical format that can enhance or mar the impact of the illustrations.

Training makes it easier to evaluate the artistic elements of a picture book or illustrated book, but it does not require formal training to achieve some proficiency in evaluation. Experience and awareness can help anyone judge the use of line, color, or mass, can train the eye in the use of perspective and effective composition, can confirm judgments about the ways in which the pictures do or do not clarify, interpret, and extend the text. Illustrations do not necessarily stand on their own but function in relation to each other and to the text to produce a unified whole.

Beautiful pictures can help sell a trivial book, and sometimes poor illustrations can cause a first-rate story to be overlooked. With today's offset printing and remarkable color reproduction, the eye appeal of books is of tremendous importance, and the artist therefore plays a significant role in books for children, whether they are picture books for younger children which have little or no text, picture story books in which the illustrations are an integral part of the whole, or illustrated books in which the pictures are few and play a comparatively minor role.

From what they see in comics and slick magazines as well as in books from supermarket shelves, children know many kinds of pictures. They "read" many parts of their environment, and often have great visual sophistication and experience before they become aware of printed matter, whether in books or on box tops. Due in large part to television, children today probably have a higher degree of visual experience than children of earlier generations. Building on such experience, we can begin to lead them into an awareness of finer examples of graphic art, old and new. For, as Bertha Mahony says in *Illustrators of Children's Books*, ". . . art in children's books is a part of all art, not an isolated special field. In every period the greatest artists have shared in it."[1] But in the evaluation of illustrations as in the evaluation of stories, the children themselves must be the starting point if we are to meet their needs and extend the range of art they appreciate.

[1]The Horn Book, Inc., 1947.

Children's Preferences

Children begin as stern literalists, demanding a truthful interpretation of the text. If a character is described as redheaded, no child is going to accept brown hair without protest. When Ludwig Bemelmans says that there are twelve little girls who go walking from Madeline's school, the child counts to see that the artist has included them all.

Even young children observe and enjoy all the cozy details of Randolph Caldecott's *Frog He Would A-Wooing Go* as readily as they follow the everyday drama of weather in Uri Shulevitz's *Rain Rain Rivers*. If the illustrations interpret the story, the child will accept such varied techniques as the splashy colors of Brian Wildsmith's *Daisy*, Robert Lawson's finely detailed pen-and-ink sketches of landscapes and small animals, and Leo and Diane Dillon's bold patterns for *Why Mosquitoes Buzz in People's Ears*.

Being literal, the young child also wants a picture synchronized precisely with the text. When *Make Way for Ducklings* has the mother duck leading her offspring across a busy Boston thoroughfare, the child is glad that Robert McCloskey placed his unforgettable picture with the description and not a page or two later. The older child as well is irked by illustrations that appear before or after the episode they are supposed to represent.

Children are as fond of action in pictures as in stories. They love Ernest Shepard's lively drawings of the skipping Christopher Robin and the droll, carefree abandon of Maurice Sendak's capering children. We know that young children also like bright colors, but not to the exclusion of black and white or the gentle colors in Adrienne Adams's illustrations for Alice Goudey's *Houses from the Sea* and the

From *Daisy*, written and illustrated by Brian Wildsmith.

Viewpoint

Evidence pointing to the aesthetic sensitivity of children can be gathered on all sides. They instinctively respond to balance, order, rhythm, originality—the artist's endless arrangements of color, line, shape, texture, and the writer's ingenious inventions and euphonies. But there are many exposures which can dwarf the natural growth of these responses. When the child is faced with a preponderance of inferior visual and literary impressions, a negative effect upon the development of taste and aesthetic enjoyment can be expected, as surely as a good effect can be predicted (all else remaining equal) when the child is surrounded by an artistic environment. He is not, after all, living in a vacuum.

Creating a beneficial environment for children is one of the most common objectives in education. Teachers and parents scrutinize the child and his surroundings with great care, trying to identify the activities which rouse curiosity and interest, which have strong and lasting effects and to which the child repeatedly returns. Yet they often overlook the arts or give them little emphasis, even when it is clear that few areas of experience involve children so completely and at such an instinctively high level.

Donnarae MacCann and Olga Richard, *The Child's First Books; A Critical Study of Pictures and Texts.* New York: H. W. Wilson Company, 1973, p. 7.

muted hues in Arnold Lobel's *Frog and Toad Together.*

On the whole, there is evidence that children do prefer color to black and white in book illustrations. Even more important to most children is that the illustrations have action, that they tell something. So young children delight also in Lynd Ward's powerful monochromes for *The Biggest Bear,* and older children are pleased with the fine, clear minutiae of William Pène du Bois's drawings for his *Twenty-One Balloons* or those of Edwin Tunis in *Shaw's Fortune.*

Adults often assume that small children do not see details in a picture, but they do. Children look for the small figures of the mice in Graham Oakley's *The Church Mice in Action.* But the same youngster who will gloat over small details in a picture may also enjoy the bold strength of a single object by Leonard Baskin, or the sharp, clear outlines of Trina Schart Hyman's illustrations for Myra Cohn Livingston's *Christmas Poems.*

Children, then, respond to a wide variety of book illustrations—even crude or saccharine drawings if they help tell the story. Their visual sensitivity can open their lives to positive early experience with books as well as enlarge their experience with art. The more they are exposed to authentic art of many styles, the greater the possibility that their tastes will diversify.

Reproducing the Work of the Artist

It's a long way from the drawing board to the finished book. We enjoy today a wealth of varied and beautiful books in part because of the technological advances in printing, in part because of the growing awareness of the importance of early childhood education, and in part because good artists, designers, and editors are dedicated to giving children the best. As Jean Karl, a children's book editor, has said:

It is the publisher's responsibility to choose the illustrator for a picture book, but most try to take the author's preferences into consideration, and all try to find the illustrator who will make the manuscript into a unified book. For this, the author's vision of the finished book is important, because it is part of the author's concept of what he has done.[2]

There are three basic methods of reproduction—relief, intaglio, and surface or plano-

[2]Jean Karl, *From Childhood to Childhood* (John Day, 1970).

graphic printing. Each of these may be direct (done largely by hand) or indirect (done by mechanical procedures).

There are many picture books in which the artist's conception of an author's characters and mood are enchanting in their perfection (for example, Garth Williams's illustrations for Natalie Carlson's *The Happy Orpheline* and Maurice Sendak's for Else Holmelund Minarik's *Little Bear* series). Some of the best picture books, however, are those written and illustrated by the same person. Rosemary Wells, Arnold Lobel, Martha Alexander, Maurice Sendak, Shirley Hughes, Helen Oxenbury, and Marcia Brown are among the contemporary author-artists in whose books the text and illustrations perfectly complement each other. This is true also of books done for older children by such author-illustrators as Leonard Everett Fisher and Edwin Tunis.

The editor and the book designer must, in collaboration with the illustrator, consider all the visual aspects that contribute both to the beauty of a book and to its appropriateness for its intended audience—the size and clarity of the type, the leading (space between lines), the layout of the page, the amount of print on each page, as well as the illustrations. Of course such picture books as John Goodall's *Paddy Under Water* and Iela and Enzo Mari's *The Apple and the Moth* (the first, a story; the second, the record of a moth's life cycle) have no words at all, but the pictures have been so carefully planned that what happens is crystal clear. In books for older children, too, the arrangement of all visual material (Anthony Ravielli's precise drawings for *Wonders of the Human Body* are fine examples) illuminates and expands the text.

As Edward Ardizzone stated, "drawing is of paramount importance."[3] The artist must be able to draw, to interpret the story, or, in informational books, interpret accurately the given facts, and to understand the printing processes by which original artwork is converted into illustrations for a book.

In *relief* the surface to be printed is raised. The most familiar examples of direct or manual techniques are probably the wood blocks or linoleum blocks on which a picture is drawn, the surrounding areas cut away, and the remaining portion inked to be impressed upon paper. The indirect or mechanical counterpart is the linecut (also called a line engraving or line block). In this process the illustration is photographed, being mechanically reduced to correct size, on a glass plate. When the film is hardened, it is transferred to a sensitized metal plate and is developed and washed. The lines of the drawing are brought into relief by bathing the plate in acid, which eats away the part that has no lines. The plate, nailed to a wooden block so that the drawing is type-high, will print the raised design on paper.

When a drawing has shadings, a halftone engraving is made. To obtain the shadings, tones between black and white, the drawing is photographed through a halftone screen, which is crosshatched at right angles with fine lines. This breaks the pictorial copy into tiny dots: the darker the gray, the larger the dots. The acid etching for the halftone requires much more care than that for the simple linecut and must be done in stages so that the deeper parts can be re-etched. If colors are used, only one color can be printed at a time. A four-color picture with varying strengths requires four half-tone blocks (black, yellow, magenta, and cyan blue can reproduce almost any color or shade of color) to reproduce the shading and intensity of the original.

The second method of reproduction is *intaglio.* In this process the part to be printed is below the surface rather than above the surface as in relief. Mezzotint, steel engraving, and etching are some of the direct or hand intaglio techniques. Photogravure is the indirect or mechanical technique. In this process the surface is broken into dots as for the halftone, but here each dot forms a pit—the variation is in depth rather than in size as in the halftone. The surface ink is scraped off with a knife and the remaining ink is picked out from the pits when paper is pressed on the cylinder. To print color photogravure, a separate plate must be made for each color.

The third method of reproduction is *surface* or *planographic* printing. Stencils and silk screens are examples of direct or hand techniques. Indirect or mechanical techniques in-

[3]Edward Ardizzone, "Creation of a Picture Book," *Top of the News,* December 1959.

clude collotype (very expensive and seldom used) and lithography. Lithography is based on the principle that water and grease do not mix. The process was discovered accidentally in 1796, when Aloys Senefelder used a crayon to write a list on a slab of limestone, and then wet and inked the stone. The water repelled ink except for the writing, which didn't hold water because of the crayon grease. In today's printing, the stone is replaced by a sheet of emulsion-coated zinc on which the images are printed photographically, much in the way that halftones are produced, except that the dots are on the emulsion and will accept ink. The

bare metal around the dots repels ink, and the dots are impressed in the printing process. Most lithographic work today is produced by offset process, using an extra roller to transfer the impression. The use of offset lithography for color work is one of today's most significant advances in the reproduction of illustrations.

Colors in illustrations may be mechanically separated as already mentioned, or the artist may pre-separate them; that is, make a separate drawing for each color, with transparent sheets perfectly aligned one over the other. If only two colors that do not touch each other are used, the artist can use red and black and instruct the printer to use them as keys for any other two colors.

Recognition of the importance of children's book illustration includes the establishment of the Caldecott Medal in the United States, the Greenaway Medal in England, the Howard-Gibbon Medal in Canada, and the international Hans Christian Andersen Medal for illustrators as well as authors. The American Institute of Graphic Arts now includes the names of children's book illustrators and designers in their annual "Fifty Books of the Year." The Children's Book Council's widely circulated posters by children's book illustrators call attention to Children's Book Week and also to the importance of the illustrations in books for young people.

Many of the artists who have contributed to children's books will be discussed here in chronological order, according to their birth dates. Author-artists like Maurice Sendak are discussed also in genre chapters and many creators of picture books are discussed in Chapter 4; in these other chapters, the focus is on their writing.

Viewpoint

Liberated by the capabilities of modern color printing, illustrators—despite the constraints of economics—seem to be limited only by their own talent, imagination, and judgment. Yet many contemporary picture books strike one as remarkably self-indulgent. Technically expert, pictures often lack illustrative cohesion and narrative energy; the artist seems to be carried away by his own work, using the book as a portfolio or an art gallery. Some illustrators create a complex graphic orchestration that overwhelms a simple text with a weight of irrelevant detail; over-sophisticated and pedantic artwork obscures what should be direct and comprehensible. Pseudo-Oriental, arty books—a recent rage—impose on children a purely adult nostalgia for ornate, decadent chinoiserie. And retellers, plundering the world's folklore, are irreverently adapting tales and sending forth a stream of picture books that lack individuality or that rely on elaborate, ornamental illustrations—lush productions whose texts are far too fragile to support the burden of the pictures.

Ethel L. Heins, "Storytelling Through Art: Pretense or Performance?" *The Horn Book Magazine*, February 1983, pp. 14–15. Copyright © 1983 by The Horn Book, Inc. Reprinted by permission.

Woodcuts and Engravings Before 1800

In 1484 William Caxton issued the first English edition of *Aesop's Fables*, illustrated with woodcuts by some unknown artist or artists. This was an adult book, but if children saw the pictures and heard the stories, they undoubtedly took the book as their own. Since Caxton's publication of the fables these little moralities have been continuously reprinted, usually illustrated by outstanding artists who were doubtless attracted by the dramatic situations the stories embody.

Between the Caxton edition of the fables and the epoch-making *Orbis Pictus,* there were hornbooks and battledores for children but with few or no pictures. There were also the popular chapbooks, enlivened with crude woodcuts, which were beloved by the story-hungry children of the sixteenth and seventeenth centuries.

The *Orbis Pictus* of Comenius is assumed to be the first picture book prepared for children. Today, we would say that it more nearly resem-

bles a primer. It was written in Latin in 1657 or 1658 by a Moravian bishop and translated into most European languages, including English in 1658. The pictures and text are stilted but not without charm. The word *Flores* appears above a small woodcut showing flowers in a vase and also in a field; the picture is followed by a pleasant commentary on spring flowers. Whatever the subject, there was a conscious effort to associate words and pictures and to use the latter to lead directly into the text. The *Orbis Pictus* seems tame and wooden today, but for English-speaking children it marked the beginning of picture books planned especially for them.

Even the Newbery publications, important as they are in the history of children's books, did little to advance the art of illustration. It is generally agreed that only for *Little Goody Two Shoes* (1765) did the artist (possibly Thomas Bewick) execute his woodcuts with unusual grace and synchronize them with the text so they are illustrations in the true sense of the word—interpreting or illuminating the story.

For the most part these earliest producers of crude woodcuts were minor artists, usually unknown. It was not until the advent of Thomas Bewick that children's books were adorned by a major artist.

Thomas Bewick's first book designed for children was *A Pretty Book of Pictures for Little Masters and Misses or Tommy Trip's History of Beasts and Birds* (1779). This book, exceedingly rare today, is an example of the artist's skill in the use of the woodcut. He developed better tools for this work, made effective use of the white line, and carried the woodcut to a new level of beauty. Most of Bewick's finest drawings seem to have been for books originally planned for adults as, for instance, his various editions of Aesop's fables, particularly those of 1784 and 1818. These pictures show the artist's knowledge and love of the whole outdoor world —plants, trees, birds, and beasts. Certainly Thomas Bewick, and to a somewhat lesser extent his brother John, raised the woodcut to a high level of artistic achievement.

An interesting by-product of Bewick's contribution is that artists of established reputations began to sign their pictures for children's books.

Flowers.   **XV.**   **Flores.**

Amongst the Flowers the most noted,	Inter flores notissimi,
In the beginning of the Spring are the *Violet,* 1. the *Crow-toes,* 2. the *Daffodil,* 3.	Primo vere, *Viola,* 1. *Hyacinthus,* 2. *Narcissus,* 3.
Then the *Lillies,* 4. white and yellow and blew, 5. and the *Rose,* 6. and the *Clove gilliflowers,* 7. &c.	Tum *Lilia,* 4. alba & lutea, & cœrulea, 5. tandem *Rosa,* 6. & *Caryophillum,* 7. &c.
Of these *Garlands,* 8. and *Nosegays,* 9. are tyed round with twigs.	Ex his *Serta,* 8. & *Servie,* 9. vientur.
There are added also *sweet herbs,* 10. as *Marjoram, Flower gentle, Rue, Lavender, Rosemary.*	Adduntur etiam *Herbœ odoratœ,* 10. ut *Amaracus, Amaranthus, Ruta, Lavendula, Rosmarinus,* (Libanotis).

From Comenius's *Orbus Pictus.*

The Nineteenth Century

William Blake had brought delicate colors into his book for children, *Songs of Innocence* (1789), not by color printing but by hand. Color printing, however, was widely used from about 1803 to 1835, though at the beginning of the nineteenth century the most notable illustrators were still working in black and white.

Examine in the color section the color illustrations by the famous nineteenth-century artists, Walter Crane (*King Luckie Boy's Party*); Randolph Caldecott (*Ride a Cock Horse*); and Kate Greenaway (*The Pied Piper of Hamelin*). They are interesting proof that publishers were beginning to recognize the lure of color in books for young children.

William Mulready

The century began propitiously, then, with some color printing for children's books, but it is the work of William Mulready that first brought distinction to those early years of the century.

This illustrator is remembered for his gay, fanciful drawings for *The Butterfly's Ball* (1807) by William Roscoe. This rhymed description of a fairy picnic enjoyed enormous popularity for

From *The Butterfly's Ball* by William Roscoe, illustrated by William Mulready. Published by J. Harris, 1807.

over fifty years, aided no doubt by Mulready's amusing pictures in black and white. Unfortunately, the texts of the children's books this gifted artist adorned do not stand the test of time as his drawings do. This is a fate that threatens the lasting fame of illustrators in each generation.

George Cruikshank

George Cruikshank, a great artist of this period, was a satirist and a cartoonist for England's famous *Punch*. In contrast to Mulready, Cruikshank had the good fortune to illustrate an English translation of the Grimms' *Collection of German Popular Stories* (1824 and 1826), a classic that is ageless in its appeal. In black and white, his humorous, lively, cleverly drawn pictures are the embodiment of the tales.

Sir John Tenniel

Inseparable from Lewis Carroll's *Alice's Adventures in Wonderland* (1865) and *Through the Looking Glass* (1871) are the illustrations by Sir John Tenniel, cartoonist for *Punch*. Other artists make pictures for this classic fantasy, but their illustrations usually seem inadequate when compared with Tenniel's beloved figures. Unforgettable are serious, pinafored, long-haired Alice, the smartly dressed, bustling White Rabbit, and all the other mad, topsy-turvy characters of the Wonderland and the Looking Glass worlds. Strong in line and composition, drawn with beautiful clarity and poker-faced drollery, these illustrations enhance the fantasy and give it convincing reality.

Arthur Hughes

The illustrations of Arthur Hughes are as strongly associated with George Macdonald's *At the Back of the North Wind* (1871) and *The Princess and the Goblin* (1872) as are Tenniel's illustrations with *Alice's Adventures in Wonderland*. Hughes worked in black and white and was an interpreter of fantasy, but his pictures are as different from Cruikshank's or Tenniel's as the Macdonald books are different from the Grimms' fairy tales or Carroll's *Alice*. For Macdonald's two fairy tales the never-never

From *German Popular Stories*, 1823. Figure by George Cruikshank, re-engraved by John Byfield, 1849.

land of the pictures is all mystery, gentleness, and lovely innocence. These qualities carry over to Hughes's more realistic pictures for Christina Rossetti's *Sing-Song* (1872), little masterpieces of tenderness and beauty.

Walter Crane

In *English Children's Books*, Percy Muir points out how much modern color printing owes to Edmund Evans, a publisher and an artist in his own right. A pioneer in color printing, Evans had long inveighed against the cheap, gaudy illustrations used in books for children. He firmly believed that even an inexpensive paperback book planned for the nursery child could be beautiful in design and color. In Walter Crane, Evans found an artist to carry out his theories.

Trained as a wood engraver, Walter Crane was greatly influenced by the work of the Pre-Raphaelites and also by his study of Japanese prints. Both of these influences are evident in his pictures—in the idealized figures of women and children and in the sparse, decorative landscapes. Between 1867 and 1876 Crane produced over thirty so-called "toy books,"[4] published chiefly by Routledge and generally undated. Crane took these books so seriously that he worked over every page, including the typography, so that it came out a well-com-

[4]The term "toy book" is used today to mean books with pop-ups or cut-outs that make them more toys than books. The Crane "toy books" were simply books intended for the nursery prereading child.

posed whole. His *Baby's Opera* and *Baby's Bouquet* were a series of English nursery songs with words, music, and pictures. Later he decorated, also in color, Hawthorne's *Wonder Book* (1892).

Kate Greenaway

Edmund Evans was greatly taken with the delicate colors and decorative borders of Kate Greenaway's pictures for her own rhymes. He printed her book *Under the Window* (1878) by a costly process that reproduced the pictures with remarkable fidelity. To her surprise, the artist found herself famous almost overnight, and she outsold all the other artists of her day, the initial sales of *Under the Window* running to some 70,000 copies. Her books still sell, and Evans's firm is still printing them.

Her style was unique—graceful but static figures in quaint old-fashioned clothes, at play, at tea, or otherwise decorously engaged. The pages are gay with garlands of fruits or flowers, mostly in delicate pastel colors. Her pictures often have a gentle humor, and their grace and charm still delight the eye (see color section).

Randolph Caldecott

Randolph Caldecott, for whom the Caldecott Medal is named, was the third of Edmund Evans's famous triumvirate and, like the others, owes much to that printer's bold experiments with color printing. Caldecott succeeded and far surpassed Walter Crane in the production of illustrated toy books.

Caldecott grew up in the Shropshire country, familiar with country fairs, the hunt, dogs, horses, and the lovely English landscape, all of which are evident in his pictures. Around 1878 he began to work on the nursery toy books with which we associate his name and fame. Probably his most famous illustrations (1878) are those for William Cowper's *The Diverting History of John Gilpin* (1785). Caldecott made Cowper's poem into a picture story, funny both to children and adults and a masterpiece of droll action. No one ever drew such humorous horses or such recklessly inept riders. His illustrated *Mother Goose* rhymes in papercovered book form are among his loveliest and most original creations. Caldecott did a number of these toy books, selling at one shilling, and they have seldom been surpassed by our best and most expensive modern picture books (see color section).

Arthur Frost

For that classic collection *Nights with Uncle Remus,* American Arthur Frost made pen-and-ink pictures as comic and irresistible as that gay rogue, Brer Rabbit himself. Whether he is "sashaying" down the road in his patched and droopy old pants or talking turkey to Tar Baby, he is a picture of rural shrewdness. Frost's whole gallery of animal folk provides characterizations as marvelous as any Caldecott ever made.

Howard Pyle

Howard Pyle was another American artist who worked in black and white. His heroic and romantic pictures for such books as *Robin Hood* (1883), *Otto of the Silver Hand* (1888), and *Men of Iron* (1890) are meticulous in their fidelity to

From *Uncle Remus and His Friends* By Joel Chandler Harris, illustrated by Arthur Frost. Published by Houghton Mifflin, 1892.

the historical costumes and weapons of the period. Yet his elaborations of robes, courtly trappings, and tournament details are always subordinated to the interpretation of character

Viewpoint

Picture books provide enjoyable opportunities for visual exploration, interpretation, and reflection. Unlike transitory electronic images, books are permanent, and children may reflect on them as long as they like and return to them as often as they like, questioning, accepting, or discarding what they see.

Artistic style is a matter of aesthetics and taste, and controversy over eternal values of beauty and truth has waged heatedly in criticism of children's books just as it has in the fine arts. Style in art reflects a society's standards or rebels against them, for art is a language that is constantly changed by and adapted to its speakers and its listeners. Artists have said they physically see things differently from others—pain and joy, loveliness and wretchedness, the tragic and the absurd. These opposing forces lie at the heart of their work and are sometimes thought of by them as curse as well as blessing. This different way of looking at things means artists move beyond facts into creation of personal perceptions that may become variously a celebration of people, a mood piece, a dance, an extension of oral tradition, an invitation to participation, or a spiritual awakening. As expression of perceptions, artistic style can be anything an artist chooses to make of it. The audience's role should not be as much an expression of personal liking or of social judgment as an evaluation of whether a particular work successfully communicates the artist's perception within the limits of its style and its conceptual intent.

Lyn Ellen Lacy, *Art and Design in Children's Picture Books: An Analysis of Caldecott Award-Winning Illustrations.* Chicago: American Library Association, 1986, pp. 2–3.

or mood. The poignancy of young Otto's tragedy moves anyone who looks at these pictures, and, in contrast, the high good humor of Robin Hood is equally evident. Here was an author-artist with a gift for telling stories in words and pictures.

Leslie Brooke

Although some of the work of the English Leslie Brooke was published as late as 1935, he is so much in the Caldecott tradition that he seems to belong to the nineteenth century. In delicate pastel colors he provides glimpses of the English countryside, pictures as charming as any Caldecott produced. His *Mother Goose* characters in *Ring o' Roses* (1922) are delightful, and his pigs are triumphs of whimsical characterization. The *Johnny Crow* books (1903, 1907, and 1935) are his own invention. Johnny Crow is the perfect host for two parties of birds and beasts so adroitly characterized both in verse and pictures that his books are classic examples of what picture books can be in the hands of a creative artist-writer.

The Twentieth Century

Beatrix Potter

Beatrix Potter's *The Tale of Peter Rabbit,* a milestone in children's literature, marks the beginning of the modern picture story—the book in which pictures are so integral a part of the story that the nonreading child can soon "read" the story from the pictures. In Beatrix Potter's books, her clear watercolors show small animals dressed up like human country folk pursuing their activities through fascinating English lanes and meadows or within cozy interiors. The pictures are as beautifully composed as the texts, and in her little books there is a perfect union of the two arts (see color section).

Arthur Rackham

Arthur Rackham, whose distinctive work is easily recognized, illustrated well over fifty books but seemed most at home in the field of folklore. His pictures for *The Fairy Tales of Grimm* made an immediate impression. There are no fluttering fairies to be found on his pages; instead, there are earthy old gnomes, ogres, and witches, eerie, mysterious, and sometimes menacing. In black and white or full color his pictures are alive with details that the casual observer may miss—small, furry faces or elfin figures peering out from leaves or half hidden in grasses. We are told that Rackham drew his pictures before painting them, a technique that seems to strengthen them, because whether the colors are dark and somber or clear and light they have body and vitality. For *The Wind in the Willows,* his characterizations of Mole, Ratty, Toad, and all the others are inimitable, and the details of picnics and cozy rooms enhance the warmth of that story. Here is an artist with unique gifts which he devoted almost entirely to the illustration of books for children (see color section).

Ernest H. Shepard

The deft pen of Ernest Shepard was drawing for *Punch* as early as 1907, but not until the publication of A. A. Milne's *When We Were Very Young* with the Shepard illustrations were his pen-and-ink sketches widely and affectionately known. Milne's *Winnie-the-Pooh, Now We Are Six,* and *The House at Pooh Corner* followed, all illustrated by Shepard. These pen-and-ink sketches of Christopher Robin, Pooh, and their companions show mood, character, and situation. Shepard's interpretative ability is shown again in illustrations for Kenneth Grahame's *The Reluctant Dragon* and *The Wind in the Willows.* Even Rackham's illustrations for this latter book cannot surpass some of Shepard's sketches. Mole "jumping off all four legs at once, in the joy of living," or Toad picnicking grandly or waddling off disguised as a washer-woman—these pictures and many others are sheer perfection. In 1957 Shepard made eight color plates for the *The World of Pooh* and followed, when he was eighty, with eight more for the Golden Anniversary Edition of *The Wind in the Willows.* His color plates are beautiful but add nothing to the virtuosity of his pen-and-ink sketches (see color section).

From *The House at Pooh Corner* by A. A. Milne, illustrated by Ernest H. Shepard.

To this group of artists, born in the nineteenth century but producing in the early or middle years of the twentieth century, more names could be added. Jessie Wilcox Smith used soft, dark colors in her illustrations for Stevenson's *A Child's Garden of Verses.* She was a pupil of Howard Pyle, as was N. C. Wyeth, whose illustrations for *Robin Hood* and *Robinson Crusoe* are powerful in composition and rich in color. Thomas Handforth won the Caldecott Medal for *Mei Li.* His black-and-white illustrations are vigorous and full of action, and they make the Chinese heroine seem real and understandable. *The Story About Ping,* another Chinese story, is by Marjorie Flack and is illustrated by the versatile Kurt Wiese, who used appropriately dignified sketches for the Newbery Award winner, Elizabeth Lewis's *Young Fu of the Upper Yangtze.* Another Caldecott winner is the picture book *The Big Snow* by Berta and Elmer Hader. It is typical of the Haders' work—a slight story, soft colors, and a warm feeling for birds, animals, and kindly people. *Nine Days to Christmas* by Marie Hall Ets won the Caldecott Medal but is, in spite of full, bright colors, less interesting than her *Gilberto and the Wind* and *Talking Without Words.*

No book of this size can hope to name and appraise half the talented people who are doing fine and original illustrations for children's books today. Of the sampling of these artists that follows, some were born in the nineteenth century, but most began their work in the thirties and some have continued producing in the years following. The exception was Wanda Gág, whose innovative book *Millions of Cats* appeared before the thirties.

Wanda Gág

In 1928, Wanda Gág's picture story *Millions of Cats* ushered in what came to be known as "The Golden Thirties" of picture books. It still outshines in strong story interest many of its successors. It is indeed about as close to perfection as a picture story can be. It is told with all the rhythm and cadence of the old European storytellers and is illustrated with striking black-and-white lithographs that repeat the flowing rhythm of the text. Wanda Gág was steeped in the European folk tales she heard told as a child, and so it is not surprising that her own completely fresh and original stories have a folk flavor. Her illustrations for *ABC Bunny* and for four small books of *Grimms' Fairy Tales* have the same flowing lines, dramatic black-and-white areas, and homey warmth that are characteristic of everything she did.

Marguerite de Angeli

Whether de Angeli gives us a rebellious young Quaker girl of long ago, kicking her bonnet down the stairs in *Thee Hannah!,* or whether she gives us some two hundred sixty illustrations for her *Mother Goose,* the people are always lovely to look at, the colors warm and soft, and the details of outdoor scenes or interiors are authentic and beautifully composed. Minority groups and historical subjects have held special interest for this artist. The Pennsylvania Dutch in *Henner's Lydia,* the Amish in *Yonie Wondernose,* the Polish children in *Up the Hill,* and the hero of her splendid historical story *Door in the Wall* (1949 Newbery Medal) are most appealing.

James Daugherty

Thomas Handforth's *Mei Li* was awarded the Caldecott Medal in 1939, but another picture story was also worthy of the award that year— *Andy and the Lion* by James Daugherty. Later, this author-artist received the Newbery Medal for his *Daniel Boone.* Both books are as distinguished for their illustrations as for the text. Warm earthiness and a tender appreciation of people mark his pictures. *Andy and the Lion* is entertaining, but the pictures are unforgettable. The rear view of young Andy reaching for a book on high library shelves, or Andy toppling over backward as he extracts the thorn—these have a great gusto. The heroic illustrations for *Daniel Boone* have vigor, and those for *Poor Richard* reveal his wonderful gift for characterization. James Daugherty's portraits are as distinctive as the heroes they record.

Robert Lawson

If pen-and-ink sketches can be described as witty, Robert Lawson's pictures certainly deserve the description. Who can ever forget the first glimpse of that mild young bull in *The Story of Ferdinand,* peacefully inhaling the fragrance of flowers instead of snorting around the bull ring, or Mr. Popper blandly coping with his penguins in *Mr. Popper's Penguins,* or the scene of the electric shock in *Ben and Me.* In contrasting mood are Lawson's gravely beautiful drawings for *Pilgrim's Progress* and for *Adam of the Road,* set in thirteenth-century England. Robert Lawson was a master draftsman, and every detail of scenes, costumes, and characterizations is meticulously executed. But not until he wrote as well as illustrated *Ben and Me* did his admirers realize the full scope of his talents and versatility. Text and pictures are equally amusing and full of the wry wisdom that appears again in his own *Mr. Revere and I, Rabbit Hill* (1945 Newbery Medal), and its sequel, *The Tough Winter.*

Edwin Tunis

Each book by Edwin Tunis is a product of intensive research and a model of clean draftsmanship and scrupulous accuracy. For his first six books, the line drawings were in pen and ink; to relieve strain on his arm muscles he adopted, on the advice of his physician, crayon-plus-wash both for his work in black and white and for the color drawings for *Chipmunks on the Doorstep.* His books are handsome and vastly informative; *Indians* has been used as a text in

Viewpoint

It is the world around the child that for better or for worse must provide the ingredients that will direct his imagination and ultimately shape the style of his literacy. One of the most important of these ingredients is the picture book. For it is here that the child will have his first encounter with a structured fantasy, mirrored in his own imagination and animated by his own feelings and imagery. It is here that, through the mediation of an adult reader, he will discover the relationship between visual and verbal language. Later, when he is alone and turns the pages over and over again, the illustrations will recall the remembered text. He will then utter his first conscious internal monologue. And with the memory of the reading voice that will color his silent words and pace their rhythm, he will have his first lesson in rhetoric. Unknowingly, he will learn about beginning and end, cause and effect, and sequence. And, most important of all, he will experience the discovery of a new kind of verbal world, so different in structure and style from the chaotic verbal traffic which has surrounded him until then. The picture book, in the midst of a complex, often repressive and incomprehensible environment, is for the child an imaginary island. Like the terrariums of my youth, it is an alternative world where, now that he can reenact the story, even his surprises are predictable.

Leo Lionni, "Before Images" from *Toward a New Understanding of Literacy* by Merald E. Wrolstad and Dennis Fisher. New York: Prager Publishers, 1984.

native American schools and *Weapons* as a text for the United States Air Force. *Frontier Living* was a Newbery Medal Honor Book; *The Young United States, Colonial Living,* and *Shaw's Fortune* are, like his other books, evidence that Edwin Tunis was a historian with a drawing board.

Edward Ardizzone

Only a first-rate artist like Edward Ardizzone could bless Tim with such splendid seascapes and glimpses of port towns. Whether the books come in the handsome, outsize edition of the first *Little Tim and the Brave Sea Captain* or in the small-size edition of *Tim All Alone,* the pictures are watercolors, beautifully reproduced, full of the power of the sea and the jaunty courage of seafaring folk. Master of the economical line, Ardizzone had a droll quality that made his figures memorable; his illustrations for Cecil Lewis's *The Otterbury Incident* and for Eleanor Estes's *Miranda the Great* are as beguiling as those for his own *The Wrong Side of the Bed.*

From *Little Tim and the Brave Sea Captain*, written and illustrated by Edward Ardizzone.

Roger Duvoisin

Roger Duvoisin used a variety of techniques and had an unfailing sense of strong composition and design. For Alvin Tresselt's books on weather and seasons, such as *White Snow, Bright Snow* (1947 Caldecott Medal), his colors are flat washes and the pictures simplified to a poster-like effect. For Louise Fatio's series of stories—*The Happy Lion* and its sequels—and for his own *Snowy and Woody,* Duvoisin's pictures are in soft colors with lively details. Gian-Carlo Menotti's *Amahl and the Night Visitors* is illustrated in dark, rich colors with a somber, dramatic quality that is at one with this story from the familiar opera. Duvoisin's own books about the hippopotamus Veronica, such as *Veronica and the Birthday Present* and *Veronica's Smile,* and the series of tales about the goose Petunia, such as *Petunia the Silly Goose Stories* and *Petunia's Treasure,* have rare humor. Here was a major artist giving his best to children's books.

Ingri and Edgar Parin d'Aulaire

Ingri and Edgar Parin d'Aulaire were the artists who brought the picture biography into its own. It is interesting that Norwegian-born Ingri and Swiss-born and French-educated Edgar should have turned to the heroes of America, their adopted land, for their subjects. After the d'Aulaires made their first sketches, they worked directly on the lithograph stone, which gave their pictures unusual strength and depth. These qualities were not so effective in their *George Washington,* in which the pictures have always seemed wooden. But by the time they wrote the text and made the pictures for *Abraham Lincoln,* they were using this difficult medium superbly. The colors in this book are deep and rich, and the pictures are full of authentic factual details. The lines and composition have a sort of primitive simplicity that suggests folk art. *Benjamin Franklin* is particularly rich in storytelling details; *Leif the Lucky* and *Columbus* are the most colorful; *Pocahontas* and *Buffalo Bill,* the most picturesque. Their large, handsome *The Book of Greek Myths, Norse Gods and Giants,* and *Trolls* are other examples of their versatility.

Lynd Ward

The Biggest Bear won the Caldecott Medal for Lynd Ward, who was already a well-known illustrator, and that book seems to have overshadowed the lovely pictures he made for Hildegarde Swift's *The Little Red Lighthouse and the Great Gray Bridge.* In spite of its long, awkward title, this is a significant picture story that is made doubly moving by Ward's illustrations. In both books—*The Biggest Bear,* in monochrome, and *The Little Red Lighthouse,* in dark blues and grays with touches of red—it is the artist's sure sense of dramatic contrast that tells the stories and grips and holds children's attention. In *The Silver Pony,* the pictures tell the story without a text. Ward used various artistic media, including oil, watercolor, mezzotint, and his favorite—lithography. He illustrated many books written by his wife, May McNeer, among them *America's Mark Twain* and *Stranger in the Pines;* he also illustrated Esther Forbes's Newbery Medal book, *Johnny Tremain.*

Adrienne Adams

Houses from the Sea by Alice Goudey includes some of the loveliest watercolor illustrations Adrienne Adams has made. Her colors are warm and delicate, her pictures full of fascinating details. A most happy collaboration is evident in her delightful pictures for Aileen Fisher's *Going Barefoot* and *Where Does Everyone Go?,* seasonal poems to which the pictures add lively charm. One of her most engaging conceptions has been the serried ranks of marching rabbits in her husband Lonzo Anderson's story *Two Hundred Rabbits.* In the Grimm brothers' *Hansel and Gretel,* the illustrations are particularly striking for their meticulous detail and dramatic use of color.

Evaline Ness

Evaline Ness used a variety of techniques ranging from hand-worked tapestry to woodcuts printed on tissue-thin paper, with separate blocks used for each color. Her constant experimentation brought freshness to her handsomely composed illustrations. She used collage with line-and-wash for *Sam, Bangs & Moonshine,* for which she received the Caldecott Medal in 1967. For the three preceding years, the books she illustrated were Honor Books: Sorche Nic Leodhas's *All in the Morning Early;* Rebecca Caudill's *A Pocketful of Cricket;* and her own version of *Tom Tit Tot.* Other books she illustrated were *Some of the Days of Everett Anderson* by Lucille Clifton; *The Truthful Harp* by Lloyd Alexander; and her own selection of poems about girls, *Amelia Mixed the Mustard.*

Garth Williams

Garth Williams has won a formidable number of awards and prizes, including the Prix de Rome for sculpture. His first venture into children's book illustration was for E. B. White's *Stuart Little* and he followed this with White's famous *Charlotte's Web.* For a new edition of Laura Ingalls Wilder's *Little House* books, Garth Williams spent ten years making the pictures, and as a result the pictures and stories are one. Equally successful are his illustrations for Natalie Carlson's books about the French Orphelines, Russell Hoban's *Bedtime for Frances* and George Selden's *Harry Cat's Pet Puppy.* The artist works both in black and white and full color, and his pictures are always characterized by authenticity of detail. The colors are fresh and soft, the composition vigorous. But whether the story he illustrates is realistic or pure fantasy, historical fiction or contemporary, his superb gift for characterization stands out. No pig could look more foolishly smug than Wilbur, no orphan could flee more desperately from the encircling bicyclists than Josine, no pioneers could look more cozy than the Little House dwellers.

Robert McCloskey

The first artist to be twice winner of the Caldecott Medal is Robert McCloskey, whose big, handsome picture stories are almost as popular with adults as with children. *Make Way for Ducklings* (1941 Caldecott Medal) vies with *Blueberries for Sal* in popularity. He has also illustrated Keith Robertson's *Henry Reed* stories with great humor. Only in *Time of Wonder* (1958 Caldecott Medal) and *Burt Dow, Deep*

Water Man has this artist used color, but in his powerful black and whites you do not miss the color, the pictures are so alive with realistic details and storytelling power.

William Pène du Bois

Few indeed are the children's book illustrators who can claim both a place in the New York Museum of Modern Art and a Newbery Medal. William Pène du Bois was awarded the Newbery Medal in 1948 for his *Twenty-One Balloons,* and he has written many distinguished books before and after that year, all with an illogical logic, all illustrated with paintings that are notable for their clean lines and clear colors, as evident, for example, in *Otto and the Magic Potatoes* and *Gentleman Bear.* His boyhood love for the circus is evident in *The Great Geppy* and *The Alligator Case.* Although he has illustrated the books of other writers—George Macdonald's *The Light Princess,* Rebecca Caudill's *Small Shepherd,* Charlotte Zolotow's *My Grandson Lew*—the books for which he is both author and illustrator have a felicitous harmony between text and pictures.

Ezra Jack Keats

In a tough section of Brooklyn, eight-year-old Ezra Jack Keats discovered the beneficial side effects of painting. Some neighborhood boys snatched a painting from him, but when they learned he was the artist, they treated him with respect. The first book he wrote and illustrated, *The Snowy Day,* earned him the Caldecott Medal and later was adapted into a prize-winning film. Keats worked as a choreographer does, hanging his illustrations in rows on the walls "to pace the text." Using oils and collage, he achieved a sunny simplicity. His books include *Whistle for Willie, Peter's Chair, Goggles!* (a Caldecott Honor Book), and *Louie.*

Leonard Weisgard

Leonard Weisgard is a major illustrator whose pictures have sold many a second-rate text. He is a great colorist and his paintings are full of exquisite details of small flowers and frolicking animals and decorative birds. His illustrations for Margaret Wise Brown's *Little Island,* painted on pressed wood in tempera and egg white, won him the Caldecott Medal. The seascapes are in deep blues and greens, with the island sometimes lost in mist. The landscapes are in lush yellow-greens and flashing blues. Some of the other books illustrated by this prolific artist are Phyllis McGinley's *A Wreath of Christmas Legends;* Charlotte Zolotow's *Wake Up and Good Night;* Rudyard Kipling's *How the Rhinoceros Got His Skin;* and his own *The Beginnings of Cities.*

Barbara Cooney

Children were delighted by Barbara Cooney's black-and-white pictures for a fine animal story —Rutherford Montgomery's *Kildee House,* but in color she did not come into her own until she made the pictures for Lee Kingman's *Peter's Long Walk.* They are in muted colors and interpret tenderly a child's sad homecoming which turns out cheerfully. She went on to win the Caldecott Medal for her scratchboard illustrations for *Chanticleer and the Fox,* adapted from Chaucer's "The Nun's Priest's Tale" in *The Canterbury Tales.* Every detail is historically accurate, but what the children love are those pages in bright clear reds, greens, and blues, alive with action. She prefers working in full color, using acrylic paints, but has also used pen and ink for *Cock Robin,* watercolor for *Island Boy,* and charcoal for her pictures in the Grimms' *Snow White and Rose Red.* Her illustrations for *Ox-Cart Man* by Donald Hall (1979 Caldecott Medal) and her own *Miss Rumphius*

From *Louie,* written and illustrated by Ezra Jack Keats.

From *Miss Rumphius*, written and illustrated by Barbara Cooney.

exemplify both her artistic diversity and the research that results in authentic detail.

Marcia Brown

No generalizations about the work of Marcia Brown are possible; she varies her style to suit the content of each story. Her illustrations for *Stone Soup* are colorful and earthy, like the rogues who taught the villagers a more generous way of life. Both *The Steadfast Tin Soldier* and *Cinderella* (1955 Caldecott Medal) are in misty pinks and blues grayed down to the gentle mood of the tales. The sturdy woodcuts in brown and black for *Dick Whittington and His Cat* are as substantial as the hero, and in the alphabet book, *All Butterflies,* the woodcuts are in muted colors. The book that won her second Caldecott Medal, *Once a Mouse,* differs completely from her earlier work. This fable of pride laid low is in jungle colors, and the stylized woodcut pictures have subtle details of expression or posture that tell the story and are worthy of study. Her third Caldecott Medal was awarded for *Shadow,* an African poem by Blaise Cendrars, a picture book with stunning collage silhouettes. Marcia Brown has written and illustrated some charming stories of her own, and has produced several concept books (see Chapter 4) with stunning photographs, but her major contributions to date are her brilliant interpretations of single folk tales.

Alice and Martin Provensen

Although they had both lived in Chicago and studied at the Art Institute there, the Provensens didn't meet until they worked in Hollywood on a training film for the Navy. They were married in 1944; the following year they came to New York and began working on the first of their many collaborations. Their first book was *The Animal Fair* and it was a harbinger of the many amusing animal books to come, books like the witty *The Year at Maple Hill Farm.* The Provensens' adaptability and versatility are demonstrated by the contrast between the humor and flamboyance of the paintings for that book, the sophisticated and stylized line drawings for *Shakespeare: Ten Great Plays* the sensitive interpretation of William Blake's genius in Nancy Willard's *A Visit to William Blake's Inn,* discussed in Chapter 9, and the quiet pastel decorum of *A Peaceable Kingdom: The Abecedarius.* Most of the Provensens' illustrations are in watercolor, and they show their command of that medium both in the technical aspects of palette, composition, and perspective, and also in the ease and often the humor with which they adapt to the subjects of their books. In 1984 they won the Caldecott Medal for their story of the daring flight of Louis Bleriot across the English Channel in 1909, *The Glorious Flight.* The book is an outstanding example of the wedding of text and illustrations, and the illustrations are among the Provensens' best, combining storytelling, humor, and some exquisite paintings of skies and clouds. *Shaker Lane,* another fine blend of text and illustrations, tells the story of the life and death of a small community with a quiet acceptance that is reflected in the calm paintings. Alice Provensen's book, *The Buck Stops Here: Presidents of the United States,* has a crisp rhyming text and uses the illustrations cleverly, to give historical facts and period details.

Mitsumasa Anno

An outstanding Japanese artist, Mitsumasa Anno has a sense of humor that pervades all of his distinctive books; his love of mathematics is also obvious, especially in *Topsy-Turvies*—an elegant compilation of mathematical impossi-

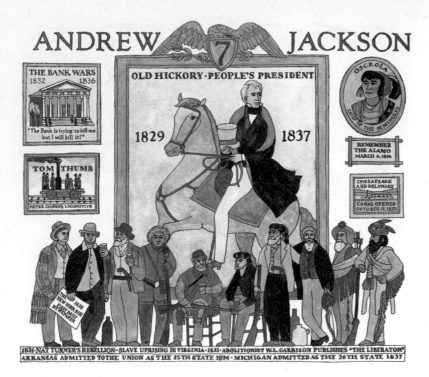

From *The Buck Stops Here: The Presidents of the United States*, written and illustrated by Alice Provensen.

bilities in space, with drawings that flout deliberately all known rules of perspective—and in *Anno's Math Games.* His line and watercolor paintings are beautiful in detail, and his experience as a book designer has contributed to the handsomeness of the page layouts. Few of Anno's books have much text, but their language is universal. In *Anno's Alphabet,* the woodgrain letters are beautifully framed by decorative black and white borders; in *Anno's Journey,* the artist records European art and architecture quite seriously but cannot resist a visual joke here and there (a gatehouse is engraved with "Anno 1976"); and in *Anno's U.S.A.,* he does the same sort of mixture of places and cultural jokes delightfully. In *Anno's Animals,* his love of humor and trompe l'oeil produce a forest full of hidden animals. Anno's draftsmanship is impeccable, his use of color restrained and sophisticated.

Erik Blegvad

The appeal of Erik Blegvad's illustrations is in the precise detail of his tidy, humorous drawings, the delicate tints of color, and the fidelity to the author's text. For Monica Stirling's *The Cat from Nowhere,* the black-and-white drawings were done in pen and india ink. When he works in full color, he uses a transparent watercolor wash, or a mixture of watercolor and poster colors. His tender feelings for animals and children are apparent in Lenore Blegvad's *The Great Hamster Hunt,* in her *Anna Banana and Me,* and in *Mr. Jensen & Cat,* which has enchanting illustrations of Copenhagen. In Ruth Craft's *The Winter Bear,* the full-color pictures capture the beauty of a snow scene, and in Charlotte Zolotow's *May I Visit?,* they reflect both the warmth and humor of the story. The full range of his versatility is most evident in *Self Portrait: Erik Blegvad.*

Charles Keeping

Charles Keeping won the Kate Greenaway Medal in 1967 for *Charley, Charlotte and the Golden Canary.* Keeping is noted for his bold approach, his use of vivid colors, and his highly individual style. For *Joseph's Yard* he used several layers of colored acetate, with drawings in colored ink, which were then shot together as one drawing.

Viewpoint

Today a sculptor can fashion clean rectangular boxes, or give an order to a cabinetmaker to fashion them, and announce that his work is signing the death warrant of all previous art. And the announcement is listened to and taken seriously. Critics write enthusiastically about shows of optical experiments that used to be part of a design student's art-school training. The latest fads from a fashionable art market are put forth for a child's consumption a few months after a brief foray in the advertising field. Many books seem to be put out for oversized children in adult skins. The huge and overwhelming single image on a page, when the object described is only an incidental detail in the story; the indiscriminate use of close and hot color harmonies derived from the fashion world; over-blown illustrations in overblown color in which the thread of a story or fable is lost in the extravagant garment given it—these are in the books that are not content to persuade but scream for attention and all too clearly proclaim their origin in a highly competitive market.

Speaking of a complex contemporary musical score of more visual than audible interest, Harold Schonberg, music critic of *The New York Times,* wrote of "Decibel Power versus Expressive Power." They are not the same. We could describe such books of decibel power as books for the eye (often of enormous visual interest as objects) instead of books for the eye and mind and heart, in which the whole book and each of its parts functions to express in just proportion the idea within. Many people have confounded the aims and methods of illustration with those of fine art, which has its origin in an entirely different level of the unconscious. They forget that a book starts with an idea, whether or not it has a text, and illustration is at its service. Successful illustration extends, embellishes, illuminates, but never obliterates the idea.

His remarkable range shows in the bold black-and-white india-ink drawings for Rosemary Sutcliff's *Heroes and History,* the unexpected perspectives in her *Knight's Fee,* and in the stunning use of line and texture in *The Golden Shadow* by Leon Garfield and Edward Blishen. Only in their swirling lines is there a resemblance between his black-and-white illustrations and the vibrant color illustrations he uses in his own picture books.

Maurice Sendak

Some of Maurice Sendak's first illustrations were for humorous books like Ruth Krauss's *A Hole Is to Dig* and Beatrice de Regniers's *What Can You Do with a Shoe?* They show the tender appeal of children even when they are most absurd—round-faced children grinning fiendishly or preternaturally solemn, dressed up in adult clothes or kicking up their heels and cavorting like young colts. This artist with his flair for comic exaggeration is tremendously popular, but in his illustrations for Meindert DeJong's books, *Wheel on the School,* for example, and for his own book, *Kenny's Window,* he shows a sensitive perception of the lonely, imaginative, struggling side of childhood, too. One book in full color is a superb example of his versatility. His pictures for Janice Udry's *Moon Jumpers* are in the green-blues of a moon-lit summer's night that suggest the poetry of childhood.

Sendak moved into further prominence with *Where the Wild Things Are,* which won the Caldecott Medal. Children rejoice over the ferocious, adoring creatures and over the small hero who, sated with adulation, goes home to

From *Dear Mili* by Wilhelm Grimm, translated by Ralph Manheim, illustrated by Maurice Sendak.

reality to find his dinner waiting, "still hot." Sendak's sensitivity to text and mood are evident in the contrast between his rakish, humorous illustrations in the Grimms' story *King Grisly-Beard*, his gravely beautiful and sophisticated pictures for a collection of Grimm tales, *The Juniper Tree*, and for Grimm's *Dear Mili*. The delicacy of the wash drawings for Else Minarik's *Little Bear*, the tenderness of the pictures in Randall Jarrell's *Animal Family*, the boldness of those in Sendak's own *In the Night Kitchen*, and the romantic vitality and richness of his *Outside Over There* show how completely Maurice Sendak adapts his illustrations to the story and make clear why he received the Hans Christian Andersen Medal in 1970, the first time an American artist was so honored. *Really Rosie* (1975), a paperback based on a television production, incorporates material from several Sendak books.

Shirley Hughes

For several years after she began illustrating books, Shirley Hughes worked only on stories written by others and she became known for her realistic, deceptively casual line drawings in black and white. It was, however, for her own story, *Dogger*, published in the United States under the title *David and Dog*, illustrated in full color that Hughes won the Greenaway Medal. This British artist proved to have the same warmth and ease as a writer as she did as an illustrator, particularly in books for younger children. *An Evening at Alfie's* is one of many stories about an engaging small boy, whose sister shares the stage in *The Big Alfie and Rose Storybook*. The writing, like the paintings, has children who are natural, even a bit scruffy, as in a humorous account of a plump, bespectacled *Angel Mae* who takes part in a very funny Christmas pageant. Hughes is a deft writer of concept books for very young children, having produced a series of small sturdy books like *All Shapes and Sizes*, with simple ideas, minimal text, bright and uncluttered pictures, and visually encouraging page layout.

Brian Wildsmith

Although he says he has "abstract tendencies," Brian Wildsmith's illustrations are brilliant and strongly representational. He sees the pictorial form as being at one with the text, yet each a thing unto itself—complementary—and each able to exist without the other. All of his work is in full color; a Wildsmith trademark is the use of bright contrasting colors in a harlequin pattern. In his technique, gouache is used, moving from impasto down to almost translucent watercolor effects. The subjects he treats lend themselves to strong visual impact: *The Little Wood Duck, Daisy,* and *Brian Wildsmith's ABC,* which won the Kate Greenaway Medal for 1962 and was published in the United States in 1963. One of the major British illustrators, Wildsmith has, in addition to his own books, created illustrations for several Jean de la Fontaine fables and for *The Oxford Book of Poetry for Children,* edited by Edward Blishen.

Margot Zemach

Margot Zemach worked in ink line and wash, using color to strengthen the drawing rather than obscure it. She used line in many ways, often boldly in central figures and sketchily in the background, or with careful detail to depict a piece of furniture, and with abandon to create frilly ruffles or a curly mop of hair. Most of her earlier books were written by her husband. Their first was *A Small Boy Is Listening,* and together they adapted and illustrated a Russian folk tale, *Salt,* an Ozark folk song, *Mommy, Buy Me a China Doll,* and a Russian nursery rhyme, *The Speckled Hen.* In her black-and-white pictures for Isaac Bashevis Singer's *When Shlemiel Went to Warsaw,* Margot Zemach demonstrated the essence of her economical use of line and adroitly echoed the peasant humor of the text. *The Judge: An Untrue Tale,* a Caldecott Honor Book, and *It Could Always Be Worse* have the same robust and earthy quality. In their *Duffy and the Devil,* the Zemachs adapted a Cornish variant of the Rumpelstiltskin story. It's told with verve, and the illustrations, soft in hues but bold in composition, are humorous and vigorous. In 1974 it was awarded the Caldecott Medal.

Ed Young

Although he uses a variety of techniques, Ed Young's interest in the art forms of the country of his birth is evident in many of his books. See, for example, *Chinese Mother Goose Rhymes,* com-piled by Robert Wyndham, which won the Caldecott Medal and which includes calligraphy in its illustration; and *Lon Po Po: A Red-Riding Hood Story from China,* which includes the incorporation of ancient Chinese panel art in Young's own retelling of a folk-tale variant. In *The Emperor and the Kite,* by Jane Yolen, he uses the colorful and intricate Oriental paper-cut style. Most of Young's illustrations, like the paintings in Margaret Hughes's adaptation of Lafcadio Hearn's story, *The Voice of the Great Bell,* are distinctive for the rich, misty, swirling abstractions out of which emerge representational forms that give hints, but leave much to the viewer's imagination. His versatility is further demonstrated in *The Other Bone,* a wordless book in which vigorous pencil drawings with fluid grace and antic humor tell the story.

Viewpoint

The modern illustrator—who is, as it were, the designing engineer of the book for children and adolescents—by no means merely repeats a literary depiction literally or mechanically. Although he takes his inspiration from the literary work, he makes his own comments on the text or paraphrases it. In a certain sense he is like a composer who transposes the musicality, the sound, of a text into graphic language. The modern approach to this graphic language is in part due to the tempestuous developments in picture technology. The far-reaching influence of broadcasted information, the suggestive images from film and television, the pictures we encounter in the various forms of advertising—on posters and in illustrated magazines—and, not least, the mechanization of our lives have brought about a much more rapid mental development in children than ever before, no matter if they live in rural or in urban communities.

From "Children's Book Illustration in Poland" by Zbigniew Rychlicki, *Bookbird*, Volume 27, Number 4, November, 1989. Reprinted by permission of the International Institute for Children's Literature and Reading Research.

Nonny Hogrogian

For the first children's book she illustrated, Nicolete Meredith's *King of the Kerry Fair*, Nonny Hogrogian used woodblocks, as she did for Robert Burns's *Hand in Hand We'll Go*. Her illustrations for the 1966 Caldecott Medal book, *Always Room for One More* by Sorche Nic Leodhas, were done in pen and ink, with gray wash and pastels to achieve the quality of mist and heather. Hogrogian's approach to illustration emphasizes the primacy of the manuscript; the pictures grow from it—the mood of the text dictates the artistic technique as much as possible. She used pastels to illustrate the story of the gentle, lovely *Vasilisa the Beautiful*, translated by Thomas Whitney; etchings for an edition of Grimms' tales; and oil paintings for her own *One Fine Day*, recipient of the 1972 Caldecott Medal, in which the illustrations have the full and vigorous quality of the story of a sharp-nosed fox who tries to retrieve his tail. Some of the other books she has illustrated are Isaac Bashevis Singer's *The Fearsome Inn;* and her own *The Contest* and *The Cat Who Loved to Sing*.

Nancy Ekholm Burkert

As might be expected from an artist who sees "absolute perfection" in the compositions of Arthur Rackham, Nancy Burkert's work is full of exquisite detail. In her imaginative treatment of Edward Lear's *The Scroobious Pip*, she is thoroughly at home with the infinite variety of nature, and both the line drawings and the full-color paintings have a firm delicacy. For Natalie Carlson's *Jean-Claude's Island*, she used conté pencil and crayon, and for Eva Le Gallienne's translation of Hans Christian Andersen's *The Nightingale*, she used brush and colored ink to achieve the wonderfully rich color; the authentic detail of her illustrations for this book she provided through her study of ancient Chinese scrolls. Among the other books she has illustrated are John Updike's *A Child's Calendar*, Roald Dahl's *James and the Giant Peach*, Andersen's *The Fir Tree*, the Grimms' *Snow-White and the Seven Dwarfs*, and her own verse adaptation of the medieval romance, *Valentine and Orson*.

From *The Tale of the Mandarin Ducks* by Katherine Paterson, illustrated by Leo and Diane Dillon.

Leo and Diane Dillon

Leo and Diane Dillon met while attending the Parsons School of Design and have been working together as one artist since 1957. Although they have distinctive, individual styles, they blend these when working on projects together, their work showing great variety of media and techniques. Their illustrations for *Why Mosquitoes Buzz in People's Ears*, a West African tale retold by Verna Aardema and awarded the 1976 Caldecott Medal, were done with watercolor and pastels in strong, soft colors and in bold, stylized compositions inspired by the designs of African fabrics. The following year, the Dillons again won the medal for their pictures in Margaret Musgrove's *Ashanti to Zulu*. The couple adapts the mood and medium of their work to the text it illustrates: for Virginia Hamilton's retellings of American black folk tales in *The People Could Fly*, the gray, black, and white pictures are soft but dramatic;

in the pictures for Erik Haugaard's *Hakon of Rogen's Saga,* a bleak Viking tale, they use strong black-and-white woodcuts; for Natalia Belting's *Whirlwind Is a Ghost Dancing,* acrylics and pastels are used for stylized, dignified pictures that reflect the grave beauty of native American poetry and incorporate tribal motifs. The tender story of a small child's love for a very old woman, *The Hundred Penny Box* by Sharon Bell Mathis, has pictures that are framed and slightly blurred in brown and white, giving the effect of an old photograph album. In Lorenz Graham's *Song of the Boat,* an African tale told with the poetic language and cadence of the oral tradition, the Dillons use woodcut style, but the pictures are quite unlike the starkly dramatic illustrations of the Viking tale; the solid masses are lightened by fine lines, patterns, and designs that give variety and movement to the figures. Watercolor and pastel paintings in the style of eighteenth-century Japanese woodcuts elegantly illuminate the folk tale retold by Katherine Paterson in *The Tale of the Mandarin Ducks.*

Arnold Lobel

Arnold Lobel believed that a good illustrator should have a wide repertory of styles at his or her command, his own work reflected this belief whether he used wash, pencil, or pen and ink, his favorite medium. His first book was *A Zoo for Mr. Muster,* but most of his work in the 1960s was illustrating books by other authors. For Millicent Selsam's *Benny's Animals and How He Put Them in Order,* he used a sketchy line appropriate for the lightness of the story; in Nathaniel Benchley's *Sam the Minuteman,* his style showed solid figures in framed drawings. In *Hildilid's Night* by Cheli Duran Ryan, a noodlehead tale, black-and-white pictures contain finely drawn parallel lines that give a soft solidity to the night scenes. This was a Caldecott Honor Book, as was *Frog and Toad Are Friends,* (discussed in Chapter 4) which was also a National Book Award finalist. An unusual book for Lobel was his *On the Day Peter Stuyvesant Sailed into Town,* historical fiction told in rhyme, in which the blue and yellow pictures are based on Dutch tiles. Lobel won the Caldecott Medal for *Fables,* a handsome and witty book of original fables. His illustrations for *The Random House Book of Mother Goose* are versatile and endlessly inventive; in the posthumous *The Turnaround Wind,* the text and pictures can be read right side up or upside down.

Anita Lobel

From the beginning of her career as a children's book illustrator and author, Anita Lobel has divided her time between illustrating her

Viewpoint

Proud I may be, but, in the matter of my work and of children's books in general, articulate I am not. There seems to be a loud clamor and demand for those of us who make picture books to haul our bodies up onto the podiums of America. We are asked to talk at length about what we do.

A good picture book should have a narrative that is simple. But this narrative must be composed skillfully. It must retain its interest with the repetition of many readings. Solid characterization, humor, drama, poetry . . . all these things contribute much.

A good picture book should have drawings that are neither too cartoony cute at one end of the scale, nor too sophisticated and adult at the other.

A good picture book should have artwork that is appropriate to the mood and subject matter of the story. In terms of pacing and selection of images, the artwork should be well integrated into the narrative.

A good picture book should be true. That is to say, it should rise out of the lives and passions of its creators. A book that is created as a commodity will remain just that, however successful that commodity may turn out to be.

From "A Good Picture Book Should . . ." by Arnold Lobel from *Celebrating Children's Books* edited by Betsy Hearne and Marilyn Kaye. Copyright © 1981 by Zena Sutherland Lectureship Fund. Reprinted by permission of Lothrop, Lee and Shepard, a division of William Morrow and Company.

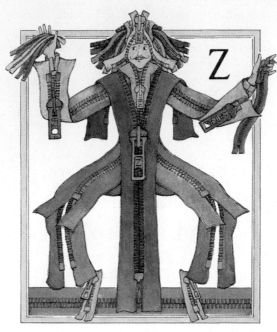

zippers.

From *On Market Street* by Arnold Lobel, illustrated by Anita Lobel.

own books and those of other writers: Her first book was self-written, *Sven's Bridge,* and in the next year she produced another self-written book, *The Troll Music,* but also illustrated Paul Kapp's *Cock-A-Doodle-Doo! Cock-A-Doodle-Dandy!* European-born, Lobel has always been interested in the decorative arts and in peasant or folk motifs in art. Almost all her work reflects this interest as well as her strong sense of design, and this is most noticeable in the details of interior scenes or of costumes. Lobel has shown this interest in the many folk-tale versions she has illustrated, like *The Pancake* or *The Straw Maid,* but her strong sense of design is most effective in the Caldecott Honor Book for which Arnold Lobel wrote the text, *On Market Street,* and for which she concocted a brilliant series of figures composed of such articles as musical instruments or vegetables or umbrellas, all marvelously detailed and notable for their use of color. Lobel also uses visual cumulation, a device children find appealing, in *The Rose in My Garden* with text by Arnold Lobel, a floral extravaganza.

Raymond Briggs

Raymond Briggs is best known for illustrations of *The Mother Goose Treasury,* which won him the Kate Greenaway Medal in 1967. To complete that collection of four hundred rhymes, which he selected and illustrated, he worked for two years. Sketching with pencil and working over with pen and ink for the black-and-white pictures and with gouache for those in color, he captured the exuberance and the humor of the rhymes. A prolific worker, Briggs wrote and illustrated *Jim and the Beanstalk* in 1970, and in the same year illustrated *The Elephant and the Bad Baby* by Elfrida Vipont, *The Christmas Book* compiled by James Reeves, and *The Book of Magical Beasts* edited by Ruth Manning-Sanders. His pictures are deft in composition and are gay with color and movement. For *Father Christmas* and *Father Christmas Goes on Holiday,* Briggs used a cartoon format as he did in a book about nuclear war for older readers, *When the Wind Blows.*

Uri Shulevitz

Uri Shulevitz, who was born in Poland and spent some of his childhood years in Israel and in France, shares, he says, the belief of the prophet Isaiah—"And a little child shall lead them." He works chiefly in ink, sometimes using it in combination with wash. For the illustrations in *Maximilian's World* by Mary Stolz, he used a Japanese reed pen. In Isaac Bashevis Singer's *The Fools of Chelm,* his line drawings have a grave yet comic quality that befits the folk-tale style. In illustrating Arthur Ransome's *The Fool of the World and the Flying Ship,* for which Shulevitz won the 1969 Caldecott Medal, his pictures in brilliant color are faithful to the art style of the Russian background of the book. In *Hanukah Money,* his scruffy, cheerful figures echo the humor of a classic story by Sholem Aleichem. Shulevitz has illustrated with sensitivity the stories of many writers, but has never surpassed the evocative mood and the harmony of pictures and text in his own *One Monday Morning, Rain Rain Rivers,* and *Dawn,* which was a Hans Christian Andersen Honor Book.

John Burningham

An English artist, John Burningham made a spectacular entrance into the world of children's books by winning the Kate Greenaway Medal in 1963 with his first book, *Borka, the Adventures of a Goose with No Feathers.* Like most of his work, it was done largely in full color. He uses a wide range of materials: pastels, ink, crayons, montage, charcoal, gouache, and photostats, giving textural variety to his pictures. He varies the style of his work to suit the subject of the book; in *John Burningham's ABC,* the composition on pages facing the letters is in bold poster style. Humor is a component of most of Burningham's work, even in the bland and dreamy pictures for *Mr. Gumpy's Outing* for which he also received the Greenaway Medal, the first time an artist had won it twice. A simply written book about a man who takes a crew of animals and children for a glorious boat ride and a high tea, it has flowery pastel pictures with a sunny, bucolic humor quite different from the bold vigor of the alphabet

From *The Daywatchers,* written and illustrated by Peter Parnall.

book illustrations. The blandly told story of *Avocado Baby* has a puny infant turn into a brawny hero on a diet of avocado. Four small books that have bright little crayon pictures—*The Baby, The Rabbit, The School,* and *The Snow*—are nicely done for very young children, as are a set of books with folding pages, like *Read One,* which stresses basic mathematical concepts.

Peter Parnall

Peter Parnall's drawings have a distinctive use of line and space. His work is always uncluttered, his line firm but delicate, often sinuous with movement achieved by parallels that break and flow into each other; and his drawings of flora and fauna are impeccably accurate. Many examples of Parnall's work have appeared in *Audubon Magazine* and *Scientific American.* Parnall has the ability to draw animals in a comic spirit, but in a book like *The Daywatchers,* his drawings of birds are meticulously realistic. In the picture books for which Parnall is both author and illustrator, he uses space beautifully, with print and picture placed on the page to the advantage of both. In 1979, Byrd Baylor's *The Way to Start a Day,* illustrated with reverence and dignity by Parnall, was selected as a Caldecott Honor Book. *Feet!* is an excellent informational book for the preschool child, integrating clear pictures and simple, minimal text.

Charles Mikolaycak

A book designer and illustrator, Charles Mikolaycak feels that children are capable of meeting a challenge, that they have instinctive understanding of art. His paintings are sophisticated and often sensuous, with soft modeling of the human figure combined with bold outlines and strong composition. Although he has illustrated such realistic stories as Vera Cumberlege's *Shipwreck,* he prefers to work with epics and folk tales. Earlier in his career, Mikolaycak tended to use one or two colors, always with modulations, as in the framed black and ash rose illustrations for Mirra Ginsburg's *How Wilka Went to Sea.* His full-color paintings for the Hawaiian legends compiled by Jay Wil-

From *A Child Is Born: The Christmas Story*, adapted from the New Testament by Elizabeth Winthrop, illustrated by Charles Mikolaycak.

liams, *The Surprising Things Maui Did,* and for Barbara Cohen's biblical adaptation, *I Am Joseph,* and for Carol Kismatic's adaption of a Ukranian folk tale, *The Rumor of Pavel and Paali,* are stunning in composition and in costume detail; they are serious, romantic, and almost voluptuous in use of color. Mikolaycak's sensitivity to the text he is illustrating is, however, equally evident in the sustaining of a dark mood for Alfred Noyes's *The Highwayman* and the reverence of *A Child Is Born,* Elizabeth Winthrop's version of the Nativity.

Trina Schart Hyman

Trina Hyman began her career as a prolific illustrator with a book for a Swedish publisher in 1961, and two years later did her first book for an American publisher; the first book that attracted wide attention to Hyman's work was Ruth Sawyer's *Joy to the World: Christmas Legends.* She uses a strong line and tempers a romantic mood with humorous details in such books as Grimms' *Rapunzel.* That sense of humor is most evident in the several books of

colonial biography Hyman illustrated for Jean Fritz, books like *Why don't you get a horse, SAM ADAMS?* and in the biographical information she provided for a reference book, listing her political stance as "Royalist" and her religion as "Druid." This quirky humor also appears in Hyman's profusely illustrated albeit brief biography, *Self-Portrait: Trina Hyman.* Her paintings are meticulously detailed, sometimes framed with geometric print borders, as in the lush compositions for Chaucer's *Canterbury Tales,* adapted by Barbara Cohen. In *A Christmas Carol,* by Charles Dickens, there are stunning paintings with accurate period details and a remarkable evocation of mood, as well as many small black and white drawings. She received the 1985 Caldecott Medal for her romantic, strong paintings in *Saint George and the Dragon,* retold by Margaret Hodges; their talents are pooled again in a retelling of *The Kitchen Knight: A Tale of King Arthur.*

From *Canterbury Tales* by Geoffrey Chaucer, selected, translated, and adapted by Barbara Cohen, illustrated by Trina Schart Hyman.

Susan Jeffers

Like most illustrators, Susan Jeffers began by illustrating another person's book, Victoria Lincoln's *Everyhow Remarkable*. While she has continued such work (Robert Frost's *Stopping by Woods on a Snowy Evening* and Andersen's *Thumbelina*), some of Jeffers's most successful books have been those she adapted and illustrated. Among these are *Three Jovial Huntsmen*, which was a Caldecott Honor Book and was awarded a Golden Apple at the Biennale of Illustrations Bratislava, and the edited version of Longfellow's *Hiawatha*, a beautifully illustrated book with meticulously detailed full-page paintings, some a riot of pastel verdancy, some in which crosshatching and parallel lines create a cold, threatening background. Other books Jeffers has illustrated with distinction are verses about horses from Mother Goose, *If Wishes Were Horses;* and from Charles Perrault, *Cinderella*, a version adapted by Amy Ehrlich, in which oversized pages have pictures that are impressive both for their page layout and their draftsmanship.

Rosemary Wells

Although she has written several stories for older children, Rosemary Wells is primarily known for the picture books she writes and illustrates. Picture story books like *Morris' Disappearing Bag* and *Don't Spill It Again, James* have a sense of wry comedy that pervades the illustrations as well as the text. The stumpy little animal children of her deft drawings appeal both because they capture the essence of children's behavior and because they have marvelously expressive faces. In *Benjamin and Tulip*, for example, much of the humor comes not from what the two do, but from how they look: Benjamin astounded and Tulip smugly victorious when she outwits him yet again. Text and pictures are smoothly complementary, and never more so than in the series of stories about Max; on heavy board pages Wells uses a minimal text, as Max—in *Max's First Word*—blandly comes out with a polysyllabic answer when his sister urges him to say a simple word. Breezy but touching, *Hazel's Amazing Mother* affirms a child's trust in parental omnipotence, while the

From *Hiawatha* by Henry Wadsworth Longfellow, illustrated by Susan Jeffers.

protagonist of *Shy Charles* proves a heroic deed can emanate from the least likely character. The amusing illustrations in these books are bright and colorful, and include appropriate detailing to capture and hold the attention of young children.

Barry Moser

Barry Moser has illustrated many books for his own Pennyroyal Press; his medium is wood engraving and his artistry such that a number of titles have been issued in new editions by academic presses. Among these books are such adult classics as Stephen Crane's *The Red Badge of Courage* and stories by Lewis Carroll, Washington Irving, and Mark Twain. With the publication of *Jump! The Adventures of Brer Rabbit*, text adapted by Van Dyke Parks and Malcolm Jones from the Joel Chandler Harris stories, Moser attracted the attention of the children's book world. His graceful, spacious watercolors for this and its sequels (*Jump Again* and *Jump on Over!*) both of which were adapted by Parks alone, are distinguished, whether in color or in black and white, for their humorous characterizations and their composition. In his illustrations for Mark Twain's *The Adventures of Tom Sawyer,* Moser shows his skill at portraying the human face and in establishing mood in landscape paintings. His range of style and mood is demonstrated effectively in dramatic paintings for Virginia Hamilton's *In the Beginning: Creation Stories from Around the World.*

From *The Adventures of Tom Sawyer* by Mark Twain, illustrated by Barry Moser.

David Macaulay

Born in England but now living in the United States, David Macaulay has made a distinctive contribution to children's literature. His first book, *Cathedral: The Story of Its Construction,* a Caldecott Honor Book, was the winner of the Deutscher Jugendbuchpreis for the best nonfiction picture book of 1975 when it was published in the German edition. A student of architecture, Macaulay has, in *Cathedral,* in *City: A Story of Roman Planning and Construction,* and in *Pyramid,* related significant architectural advances to the cultures from which they came. His humor is most evident in the bland spoof *Motel of the Mysteries,* a book that will appeal primarily to older readers, as will the ingenious four-tales-in-one *Black and White,* and *BAAA,* a satire on society that is anything but bland; humor is also the paramount appeal in a book for the read-aloud audience, *Why the Chicken Crossed the Road,* a spoof on cause-and-effect disasters. In *Unbuilding,* he shows the structure of the Empire State Building by dismantling it. His meticulously detailed drawings show, step by step, the construction procedures for the edifice. Whether the scene is a sweeping panorama of the city, a cutaway drawing that shows the architectural plan, or a small picture of one facet of ornamentation, the illustrations are impressive for the masterful handling of perspective and the consistency with which the artist combines informative drawing with visual beauty. His monumental *The Way Things Work* is a superb clarification of mechanical principles.

Chris Van Allsburg

It would not be a great exaggeration to say that Chris Van Allsburg was like a meteor erupting in the field of children's books; his first book, *The Garden of Abdul Gasazi* was cited as a Caldecott Honor Book; an ALA Notable Book, as one of the best books of the year on four standard lists; and as the winner of two awards. Van Allsburg's focus on sculpture in his academic studies was reflected in the bold carbon pencil drawings that achieve a stunning solidity and chiaroscuro virtuosity, solid in their mass and architectural forms. Although he used different techniques (conte pencil and conte

From *Black and White*, written and illustrated by David Macaulay.

dust) for his next book, the sense of mass and the play of light and shadow are also outstanding in *Jumanji*, which was awarded the Caldecott Medal. A second Caldecott Medal was awarded for *The Polar Express*. The sense of architectural form is evident in *Ben's Dream*, but there is more play with perspective in the drawings that make heavy use of parallel lines; in *The Wreck of the Zephyr* the artist moves to pastel paintings that are vastly different from his other work, yet have the same virtues of strong composition and bold use of mass. Van Allsburg's remarkable mastery of controlled, dramatic light is most evident in *The Mysteries of Harris Burdick;* and his sense of humor appears in *The Z Was Zapped,* in which there is a letter-by-letter destruction of the alphabet.

Other Notable Artists

There are so many creative twentieth-century illustrators of children's books that it is impossible to discuss them all—even briefly. Obviously this list should include Dorothy Lathrop, who won the first Caldecott Medal for the pen-and-ink sketches in *Animals of the Bible;* Helen Sewell, whose work is notable for its variation in style; Theodor Geisel, who, as "Dr. Seuss," uses cartoon art with great flair; Ludwig Bemelmans, whose Madeline stories are still popular; and Feodor Rojankovsky, whose amusing illustrations for John Langstaff's *Frog Went a-Courtin'* won the Caldecott Medal, and whose work is outstanding for its texture and draftsmanship.

Antonio Frasconi, one of the great woodcut artists of our time, published his first book in 1955, the multilingual *See and Say;* other Frasconi books are *The House That Jack Built* and *One Little Room, an Everywhere,* a collection of love poems edited by Myra Cohn Livingston. Virginia Burton's *Mike Mulligan and His Steam Shovel* and *The Little House* with their clear, bright colors, are still loved. Nicolas Mordvinoff won the Caldecott Medal for

From *Jumanji*, written and illustrated by Chris Van Allsburg.

Finders Keepers, in which he broke away from prettified art, creating strong, vigorous drawings for William Lipkind's text.

A notable artist, whose work as an author is considered in Chapter 13, is Leonard Everett Fisher. Known primarily for his dramatic scratchboard illustrations, Fisher, in the 1980s, added rich full-color paintings to his published book art. Leo Lionni's rice-paper collage for *Inch by Inch* is as effective as the collage and paint combination of *In the Rabbitgarden.* Gerald McDermott based his first book, *Anansi the Spider,* on an animated film version of an Ashanti tale. For *Arrow to the Sun,* he adapted a Pueblo Indian tale with stylized design and glowing colors; it won the 1975 Caldecott Medal. Brinton Turkle's realistic, simple pictures are effective in creating setting for the nineteenth-century town in *Obadiah the Bold.* John Steptoe used harsh, brilliant tones and a style reminiscent of Georges Rouault in *Stevie,* but in *Mufaro's Beautiful Daughters,* his paintings are just as dramatic but are representational.

The Caldecott Medal was awarded to Ed Emberley for *Drummer Hoff,* a folk verse adapted by Barbara Emberley and illustrated with bright colors over woodcut lines to achieve a leaded-glass effect. Woodcut illustrations were also used by Gail Haley in her Caldecott Medal book *A Story, A Story,* the retelling of an African folk tale. Blair Lent's pictures of grotesque,

impish Japanese spirits in Arlene Mosel's *The Funny Little Woman* were awarded the Caldecott Medal. The subtle shadings of Tom Feelings's pictures in Muriel Feelings's *Jambo Means Hello* have a gentleness that is also strength. The Coretta Scott King Award to a black illustrator has been won three times by Jerry Pinkney, whose pictures for Patricia McKissack's *Mirandy and Brother Wind* also earned it Caldecott Honor Book status.

Tomie dePaola's paintings are easily identifiable: the people are solid, even chunky; the colors are soft pastels; the arrangement of the composition is often in frieze form. Their endearing quality is nowhere more apparent than in the tender story of love between grandparent and child, *Nana Upstairs and Nana Downstairs,* or in the wistful story of the wordless *Sing, Pierrot, Sing.*

Two artists, one English and one American, have become noted from their gravely romantic paintings in the Rackham-Wyeth tradition. Michael Foreman, British artist and teacher, has illustrated many of his own books, but his most

From *Mirandy and Brother Wind* by Patricia C. McKissack, illustrated by Jerry Pinkney.

notable pictures have been created for such versions of classics as *The Brothers Grimm Popular Folk Tales* (the Brian Alderson translation) or for Charles Dickens's *A Christmas Carol*. Michael Hague, the American, has illustrated his own as well as other people's books; like Foreman, his best work has been done in illustrating folk material and other classics, including such contemporary classics as Kenneth Grahame's *The Wind in the Willows*.

Jean de Brunhoff delighted children with the adventures of that suave French elephant, Babar, and the Italian artist Bruno Munari provides children with such magnificent color use against white space that he could train the color blind to see and rejoice. The illustrations of Swiss Felix Hoffmann for *Sleeping Beauty* are in the grand style, romantic and grave. The first Hans Christian Andersen Award for illustrations went to Swiss Alois Carigiet, whose *Anton and Anne* is a good example of the vibrant delicacy of his work. The Danish artist Ib Spang Olsen, who received the Andersen Award in 1972, uses scribbly line and fresh, bright color in contrast to the gloomy smoke of a story about pollution in *Smoke*. Lisbeth Zwerger, another recipient of the Andersen Award, is an Austrian artist whose soft paintings in subdued colors are beautifully detailed in the romantic but humorous paintings for Hoffmann's *The Nutcracker and the Mouse King*.

The innovative humor of Pat Hutchins was evident in her first book, *Rosie's Walk*, and has continued to appeal with such sprightly picture books as *The Wind Blew*, which won the Greenaway Medal as the best picture book of 1974.

Paul Goble, British-born but long a resident in the United States, has made a significant contribution to our knowledge of native Americans with magnificently detailed and historically accurate pictures in books like *Lone Bull's Horse Raid;* in *The Girl Who Loved Wild Horses*, winner of the Caldecott Award; and in later books that added humor, like *Iktomi and the Berries*. Japanese-born Taro Yashima creates sensitive illustrations of children in Japan in *Crow Boy*, and of a Japanese child in America in *Umbrella*. Kazue Mizumura has portrayed lively pictures for the stories, set in Japan, of Yoshiko Uchida, as well as for her own *If I Built a Village*. . . .

From *Iktomi and the Berries: A Plains Indian Story*, retold and illustrated by Paul Goble.

This is indeed the day of the artist in children's books, and their pictures should afford some protection from the flood of meretricious art that is so readily available. Better one good book with distinguished illustrations than a dozen stereotypes with flashy, poorly executed pictures. Children must have a chance to look and look again at the illustrations in their books. Pictures can help them see the comic absurdities of life or its heroic struggles and tragedies. Pictures can give children a sudden breathtaking feeling for the beauty or the wonder of life. Such pictures deepen their perceptiveness and help them to grow.

Many of the children's books mentioned in this chapter appear in the Chapter 4 ("Books for Early Childhood") bibliography, where they are preceded by a "5" to indicate they are discussed here in Chapter 5.

Adult References and Book Selection Aids*

ALDERSON, BRIAN, *Looking at Picture Books 1973.*

BADER, BARBARA. *American Picturebooks from Noah's Ark to the Beast Within.*

BILLINGTON, ELIZABETH. *The Randolph Caldecott Treasury.*

BROOKE, HENRY. *Leslie Brooke and Johnny Crow.*

BROWN, MARCIA. *Lotus Seeds: Children, Pictures, and Books.*

CIANCIOLO, PATRICIA. *Illustrations in Children's Books.*

COMMIRE, ANNE. *Something About the Author: Facts and Pictures About Contemporary Authors and Illustrators of Books for Young People.*

DARLING, HAROLD, and PETER NEUMEYER, eds. *Image & Maker: An Annual Dedicated to the Consideration of Book Illustration.* (See Appendix A.)

EGOFF, SHEILA. *The Republic of Childhood: A Critical Guide to Canadian Children's Literature in English.* Chapter 7, "Illustration and Design."

EGOFF, SHEILA, G. T. STUBBS, and L. F. ASHLEY, eds. *Only Connect: Readings on Children's Literature.* Part 4 "Illustration."

ERNEST, EDWARD. comp., assisted by PATRICIA TRACY LOWE. *The Kate Greenaway Treasury.*

FEAVER, WILLIAM. *When We Were Young: Two Centuries of Children's Book Illustration.*

GOTTLIEB, GERALD R., and others. *Early Children's Books and Their Illustration.*

HOLTZE, SALLY HOLMES, ed. *Sixth Book of Junior Authors & Illustrators.*

HOPKINS, LEE BENNETT. *Books Are by People.*

HUDSON, DEREK. *Arthur Rackham: His Life and Work.*

HÜRLIMANN, BETTINA. *Picture-Book World.*

HUTCHINS, MICHAEL, ed. *Yours Pictorially: Illustrated Letters of Randolph Caldecott.*

JONES, DOLORES BLYTHE. *Children's Literature Awards and Winners: A Directory of Prizes, Authors and Illustrators.*

KINGMAN, LEE, ed. *The Illustrator's Notebook.*

————. *Newbery and Caldecott Medal Books; 1966–1975.*

KINGMAN, LEE, JOANNA FOSTER, and RUTH GILES LONTOFT, comps. *Illustrators of Children's Books, 1957–1966.*

KINGMAN, LEE, GRACE HOGARTH, and HARRIET QUIMBY, eds. and comps. *Illustrators of Children's Books, 1967–1976.*

KLEMIN, DIANA. *The Art of Art for Children's Books.*

————. *The Illustrated Book: Its Art and Craft.*

KNOX, RAWLE, ed. *The Work of E. H. Shepard.*

LACY, LYN ELLEN. *Art and Design in Children's Picture Books: An Analysis of Caldecott Award-Winning Illustrations.*

LANE, MARGARET. *The Magic Years of Beatrix Potter.*

————. *The Tale of Beatrix Potter: A Biography.*

LANES, SELMA G. *The Art of Maurice Sendak.*

LARKIN, DAVID, ed. *The Art of Nancy Ekholm Burkert.*

————. *Once Upon a Time: Some Contemporary Illustrators of Fantasy.*

LEAR, EDWARD. *Lear in the Original: 110 Drawings for Limericks and Other Nonsense.*

MacCANN, DONNARAE, and OLGA RICHARD. *The Child's First Books: A Critical Study of Pictures and Text.*

MAHONY, BERTHA E., LOUISE P. LATIMER, and BEULAH FOLMSBEE, comps. *Illustrators of Children's Books, 1744–1945.*

MAHONY, BERTHA, and ELINOR WHITNEY, comps. *Contemporary Illustrators of Children's Books.*

MARTIN, DOUGLAS. *The Telling Line: Essays on Fifteen Contemporary Book Illustrators.* Dell, 1990.

MEYER, SUSAN E. *A Treasury of the Great Children's Book Illustrators.*

MILLER, BERTHA MAHONY, and ELINOR WHITNEY FIELD, eds. *Caldecott Medal Books: 1938–1957.*

MUIR, PERCY. *English Children's Books, 1600 to 1900.*

NODELMAN, PERRY. *Words About Pictures: The Narrative Art of Children's Picture Books.*

NUDELMAN, EDWARD. *Jessie Wilcox Smith: American Illustrator.*

PETERSON, LINDA, and MARILYN SOLT, comps. *Newbery and Caldecott Medal and Honor Books: An Annotated Bibliography.*

PITZ, HENRY C. *Howard Pyle: Writer, Illustrator, Founder of the Brandywine School.*

————. *Illustrating Children's Books: History, Technique, Production.*

PREISS, BYRON, ed. *The Art of Leo and Diane Dillon.*

SCHWARCZ, JOSEPH H. *Ways of the Illustrator: Visual Communication in Children's Literature.*

SENDAK, MAURICE. *Caldecott & Co: Notes on Books and Pictures.*

TAYLOR, JUDY. *Beatrix Potter: Artist, Storyteller and Countrywoman.*

————. *That Naughty Rabbit: Beatrix Potter and Peter Rabbit.*

VIGUERS, RUTH HILL, MARCIA DALPHIN, and BERTHA MAHONY MILLER, comps. *Illustrators of Children's Books, 1946–1956.*

WARD, MARTHA E., and DOROTHY A. MARQUARDT. *Illustrators of Books for Young People.*

WHALLEY, JOYCE IRENE. *Cobwebs to Catch Flies: Illustrated Books for the Nursery and Schoolroom, 1700–1900.*

WHALLEY, JOYCE, and TESSA CHESTER. *The Bright Stream: A History of Children's Book Illustration.*

WHITE, GABRIEL. *Edward Ardizzone: Artist and Illustrator.*

*Complete bibliographic data are provided in Appendices A and B.

A Gallery of Children's Book Illustration

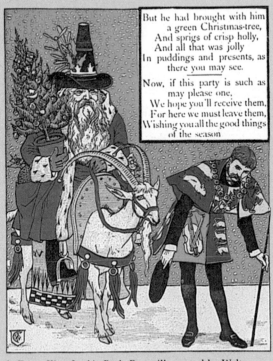

But he had brought with him
a green Christmas-tree,
And sprigs of crisp holly,
And all that was jolly
In puddings and presents, as
there you may see.

Now, if this party is such as
may please one,
We hope you'll receive them,
For here we must leave them,
Wishing you all the good things
of the season

1. From *King Luckie Boy's Party*, illustrated by Walter Crane (1871).

2. From *Sing a Song of Sixpence*, illustrated by Randolph Caldecott (1880).

A chronological look at the history of the illustration of children's books informs us about the improvements in art reproduction, as well as the distinctive accomplishments of some major illustrators. The pictures also indicate the variety of styles and techniques used, and reflect the artists' concept of what is appropriate for young viewers.

1 **Walter Crane** Flat color within stylized lines, characterizing much of Crane's work, is reminiscent of the Eastern art he admired; his formal, geometrically balanced designs evolved from an apprenticeship to a wood engraver.

2 **Randolph Caldecott** Although this meeting of three generations is sedate, Caldecott's painting has an innate vitality that gives his work a narrative quality. The pastel harmony of peach, white, and blue serves as a background for the darker dominating figure of the elderly visitor, whose posture and central position imply her authority.

3. From *The Pied Piper of Hamelin* by Robert Browning, illustrated by Kate Greenaway (1887).

4. From *The Tale of Two Bad Mice*, written and illustrated by Beatrix Potter (1904).

3 Kate Greenaway The strong central focus of the tree balances the Piper and anchors the numerous delicate shapes of children at play, a favorite subject that Greenaway always treated with decorous skill.

4 Beatrix Potter Keenly observant, Potter gave animals human characteristics without distortion. Her subtle watercolor miniatures have a precision strongly indicative of her frustrated ambition to be a botanical illustrator.

5. From *Peter Pan in Kensington Gardens* by James M. Barrie, illustrated by Arthur Rackham (1906).

5 **Arthur Rackham** Strong line, subdued shades, and elfish humor are trademarks of Rackham's drawing, which graced an astonishing range of stories and fairy tales at the beginning of the twentieth century.

6 **N.C. Wyeth** Although dark browns and greens predominate in the central figure and in the framing walls, it is the golden sunlight in the open doorway that captures the viewer's attention. Wyeth's reputation as one of the great illustrators rests in part on the sense of drama the painting projects, in part on his restrained romanticism, and in part on his controlled use of line, space, and light.

6. From *Rip Van Winkle* by Washington Irving, illustrated by N.C. Wyeth (1921).

7. From *Tanglewood Tales for Girls and Boys* by Nathaniel Hawthorne, illustrated by Edmund Dulac (1918).

7 Edmund Dulac Strongly influenced by the traditions of Eastern art, Dulac's preoccupation with color and pattern are evident in this watercolor painting. Brilliant tones, intricate design, and an attention to detail that is reminiscent of Persian miniatures are used in a picture that is appropriately opulent for mythic material.

8 Kay Nielsen Sharply elongated figures and contrasts of black with pale hues typify Nielsen's elegant pictures, most often associated with Nordic fairy tales and folklore.

8. From *In Powder and Crinoline*, illustrated by Kay Nielsen (1913).

9. From *In the Troll Wood*, translated by Olive Jones from the original text by Lennart Rudström, illustrated by John Bauer (c. 1910).

10. From *The Wind in the Willows* by Kenneth Grahame, illustrated by Ernest H. Shepard (1933).

9 John Bauer Simplicity of composition, restrained use of color, and romantic interpretation have made Bauer one of Sweden's foremost illustrators. In this quiet painting there are no harsh angles; all is soft and pliant and still, focusing on the boy's rapt glimpse of the fairy queen.

10 Ernest H. Shepard Although Shepard's signature work consisted of black-and-white pen drawings, this scene captures the earthy humor of Toad's travels by using verdant tones and rounded shapes, nicely spliced with the slanted line from the amphibian's mouth to the wooden rudder handle in a sturdy human hand.

11. From *The Story of Babar,* written and illustrated by Jean de Brunhoff (1933).

12. From *The Little Island* by Golden MacDonald (pseudonym for Margaret Wise Brown), illustrated by Leonard Weisgard (1946).

11 Jean de Brunhoff The naïveté of these mottled gray, toylike animals against bright greenery dotted with celebratory red marks a change in children's literature art to a more consciously childlike orientation.

12 Leonard Weisgard Sunshine touches the island and casts shadows on the sail, but it is a cool sunshine, an effect Weisgard captures by using black, blue, green, and white—all quiet colors. The blending of sea and sky and the contrast to that softness of the sharp lines of the sailboat make the craggy tilt of the island all the more effective.

13 Marc Simont Line and wash pictures reflect both the message and the simplicity of its style. With impressive economy of line and judicious use of color, Simont conveys the sturdiness and the bounty of an apple tree, as well as the manifest enjoyment of the children who are gathering its fruit.

14 Ezra Jack Keats His richly textured paper collage, lively urban environment, and appealing African-American characters made Keats a picturebook innovator.

13. From *A Tree Is Nice* by Janice May Udry, illustrated by Marc Simont (1956).

14. From *The Snowy Day*, written and illustrated by Ezra Jack Keats (1962).

15. From *Where the Wild Things Are,* written and illustrated by Maurice Sendak (1963).

16. From *Song and Dance Man*, written by Karen Ackerman, illustrated by Stephen Gammell.

17. From *Mr. Gumpy's Motorcar*, written and illustrated by John Burningham (1973).

15 Maurice Sendak The formal spacing of the branch-entwined trees is a clever device to set off, in theatrical fashion, the wonderful wild creatures of a modern classic and, happily joining them, Max in his wild suit and the crown that shows he is king of the wild things. Crosshatching and quiet colors soften the images and impact of the ebullient monsters who have become beloved creatures to Sendak's audience.

16 Stephen Gammell A rainbow of colors is the background for a former vaudeville performer as he dances for his grandchildren, and the ample white space provides the contrast needed to make this an effective composition. Shading is achieved by deft use of color in soft, almost smudged strokes, and the artist evokes the nostalgic pleasure Grandpa feels as he finds he can still tap dance.

17 John Burningham Color and exaggeration are used to heighten the comic effect in an illustration that uses variety in media and techniques.

18 Leo and Diane Dillon Richly decorative friezes and marginal symbols add to the beauty of every page, with full-page paintings marking the strong accents of a tragic story. The wistful loveliness of the enslaved Ethiopian Princess Aïda is symbolized in the free-flying birds, and the stylized plants at the bottom of the picture are a counterpoint to the slim, pliant figure of Aïda, as well as an interpretation of a motif heavily used in Egyptian art.

19 Nancy Ekholm Burkert Intricately detailed but never overcrowded, this illustration for a medieval romance is wonderfully patterned and placed. The colors are light and clear, the textural quality and sense of design strong in pictures that have a high narrative sense in addition to their beauty and humor.

18. From *Aïda*, adapted by Leontyne Price from the opera by Guiseppe Verdi, illustrated by Leo and Diane Dillon.

19. From *Valentine and Orson*, retold as a folk play in verse and illustrated by Nancy Ekholm Burkert.

20. From *The Way Things Work*, written and illustrated by David Macaulay.

21. From *Dogger* (also published as *David and Dog*), written and illustrated by Shirley Hughes (1978).

20 **David Macaulay** As part of an illustrated discussion of pressure power, Macaulay shows a cutaway picture of a pump, enlarged so that the parts and their relation to each other are clear. There are no bright colors to deflect a viewer's eye from the meticulously drawn machinery. Scale is maintained, but the exaggerated size permits the mild humor of tiny human figures within the pump.

21 **Shirley Hughes** Whether her paintings are in black and white or in color, there are several constants in this artist's work: one is her ability to draw the human figure; another, her deftness at portraying children; a third is her slightly scruffy, often cozy, realism. Here the warm colors help establish that coziness, as do the indicated proportions of David's room.

23. From *Carousel*, written and illustrated by Brian Wildsmith.

22. From *Flying*, written and illustrated by Donald Crews.

22 **Donald Crews** Books that are designed to give information or to introduce concepts to young children need not be handsomely illustrated but must have pictures that are comprehensible and informative. In this book, Crews achieves that goal, and his gouache painting is handsome as well. Clean geometric shapes and simple blocks of color do an admirable job of showing the perspective gained by an aerial view, and pictures the layout of a small airport.

23 **Brian Wildsmith** Since all of Wildsmith's work is distinctive for its use of brilliant colors and a strong sense of decorative design, it is satisfying to see both so appropriately used. Carousels are always bright and baroque, and in this painting the lavish ornamentation is set off by the clean white around it, and the elements of the picture are tied by the repeated use of circles.

24. From *Free Fall*, written and illustrated by David Wiesner.

25. From *Swan Lake*, written by Mark Helprin, illustrated by Chris Van Allsburg.

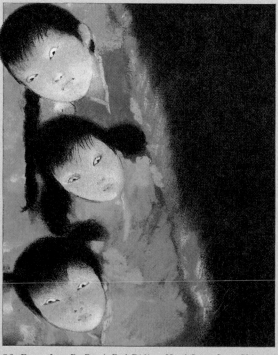

26. From *Lon Po Po: A Red-Riding Hood Story from China*, translated and illustrated by Ed Young.

174

24 David Wiesner A wordless picture book is effective both as the interpretation of a child's dream and as a sustained visual narrative. The tilted facades that belie the laws of perspective and the floating figures are bound by their fantastic quality and by the repetition of earth tones and the pure, clear blue in the figures and the sky.

25 Chris Van Allsburg There is a luminous quality to the painting, with rosy shafts of light and blue silhouettes of trees crossing above, while white swans fly free between the pillars of tall trees, violet and indigo. Van Allsburg, always a master at depicting the solidity of forms, here uses color and mist as effective contrast for the strong trees. Both are foils for the lovely curves of the swans' wings.

26 Ed Young Using watercolor and pastels as his media, the artist attains high dramatic effect by contrasting the solid, bright colors on the left with the dark shadow that cuts a diagonal on the page. The soft, impressionistic treatment is particularly appropriate for a tale adapted from oral narrative.

27 Mordicai Gerstein Mountains and sea indicate that the men and women in the framed circle are symbols for a world of people, and the unanimity of their gestures is a symbol of the universality of their desire for a child. In gouache and watercolor, Gerstein tells a story of reincarnation that was inspired by the Tibetan Book of the Dead.

28 Pauline Baynes In a full-page painting that reflects the logic-within-illogic that is the test of good fantasy, Baynes shows the meeting between Lucy and Mr. Tumnus circled by twisting branches. The green umbrella forms an inner circle; the lamplight on the snow is a third circle, while all the cool colors of night and snow are a contrasting background for the red scarf of the horned and hoofed Tumnus.

27. From *The Mountains of Tibet*, written and illustrated by Mordicai Gerstein.

28. From *The Land of Narnia*, an examination by Brian Sibley of the world of C. S. Lewis, illustrated by Pauline Baynes.

30. From *Mufaro's Beautiful Daughters: An African Tale,* written and illustrated by John Steptoe.

29. From *Oh, Brother,* written by Arthur Yorinks, illustrated by Richard Egielski.

29 **Richard Egielski** In a story that has farcical elements but is blandly told, the illustrations cleverly echo both qualities. The picture represents the book's theme of perpetual bickering, but it does so with restraint, using sober colors, an open format, and a humorous depiction of the apple-dotted air as an indication of the fact that the poker-faced twins are squabbling again.

30 **John Steptoe** The background details of the book's lush paintings are based on the Zimbabwe culture, but Mufaro and his two daughters have a beauty that is universal and timeless. Nuance is achieved through cross-hatching, and the combination of the swirled draping of clothing and the simple solidity of heads and arms has the visual appeal of poster art, although it is far more sophisticated.

31. From *In the Beginning: Creation Stories from Around the World,* told by Virginia Hamilton, illustrated by Barry Moser.

32. From *Heckedy Peg,* written by Audrey Wood, illustrated by Don Wood.

31 **Barry Moser** The oval, within a framing rectangle of swirling light-veined color, is filled by the strong, seamed face of the Old Man, the creator in a Blackfoot myth of the time before the earth was fully formed. The artist is adept at paintings that express personality; here, the quiet dignity of the Old Man contains a combination of resolve and compassion. Moser is many-faceted, and this is a fine example of his skill at portraiture.

32 **Don Wood** The dark earth tones of a representational painting are given contrast by an effective handling of light that focuses the eye on the merriment of children at play. The composition skillfully provides a centering of vigor and vitality, with shadowy figures of secondary interest above and below.

33. From *The Devil with the Three Golden Hairs,* illustrated by Nonny Hogrogian.

34. From *The Water of Life* by the Brothers Grimm, retold by Barbara Rogasky, illustrated by Trina Schart Hyman.

35. From *The Talking Eggs: A Folktale from the American South,* retold by Robert D. San Souci, illustrated by Jerry Pinkney.

33 Nonny Hogrogian The dark patterned snake above and dark hairy tail below, within the murky depths of his den, frame the devil's crimson cloak, while his horn punctures the illustration's border. The rat and its tail make an emphatic point of their own.

34 Trina Schart Hyman The final full-page picture in a new interpretation of a somber fairy tale has a happy-ending color and exuberance compared to the grave paintings that precede it. Medieval costume and Christian motifs are incorporated into a wedding scene that is the visual equivalent of the curtain call for a theatrical production.

35 Jerry Pinkney The moment of magic is caught in this painting, in which the obedient Blanche tosses the magical eggs over her shoulder and sees them change to golden coins and rich clothing. Pinkney captures both magic and movement in a tautly composed watercolor vignette.

36 Paul O. Zelinsky Oil paintings that are in the tradition of the Italian Renaissance show the artist's command of perspective as well as of architectural and costume detail. The queen soberly reads from her parchment scroll, and odd little Rumpelstiltskin poses in smug defiance. Zelinsky has composed this picture so that the glowing urn with its lavish design, the patterned floor, and the twilight vistas seen through casement windows are antiphonal rather than dominating notes.

37 Gennady Spirin In gold-toned paintings that are rich and soft, a distinguished Russian illustrator captures the romantic elegance of an old fairy tale. The details of architectural tracery are like filigree; costume details have the textural quality of medieval paintings; contrasts of scale lend dramatic interest.

36. From *Rumpelstiltskin* from the German of the Brothers Grimm, retold and illustrated by Paul O. Zelinsky.

37. From *The White Cat*, a retelling by Robert San Souci of ''La Chatte Blanche'' by Madame d'Aulnoy, illustrated by Gennady Spirin.

Part Two

Exploring the Types of Literature

Chapter Six

Folk Tales

Folklore is sometimes referred to as the "mirror of a people." It reveals their efforts to explain—and perhaps to propitiate—the phenomena of nature which they did not understand; it expresses their interpretation of the relationships among human beings and their fears and desires; it records the mores and the cultural patterns of the society from which it stems; and it gives expression to such deep, universal emotions as joy, grief, fear, jealousy, and awe. Folklore, in the broadest sense of the word, includes all of the great stream of anonymous creation that is the accumulated wisdom and art of everyday people: superstitions, games and songs, nursery rhymes and ballads, dance rituals, medicinal arts, old tales, verses and proverbs, fables, myths, legends, hero tales, and epics.

In early times, before universal education brought a widespread reading population, folk literature was meant for people of all ages; in today's more primitive societies where few people can read, this is still true, and the dependence on the oral tradition is still strong. What has changed, in more sophisticated societies, is the primary audience for the folk tale. Today most folk literature is read by children, or read or told to them, even though it was not created for them alone, for the most part. It is natural that children should be the primary audience for folk tales, since the qualities that are universally found in the tales are those to which children respond in any story: The folk tale starts briskly and continues to be filled with action; it often has humor; it appeals to children's sense of justice, since many tales reward good and punish evil; it has little nuance of characterization, so that characters are presented as entirely good, bad, obedient, lazy, and so on; it often includes rhyme or repetition; it is usually concise; it usually has a satisfying and definite conclusion. In other words, the folk tale has all the things that children, especially small children, like. And if it has magic—and most do—so much the better.

Of the many varieties of folklore, the folk tale is the most familiar and perhaps the most appealing. Scholarly interest in folk tales developed in the eighteenth century along with interest in old ballads, but in the nineteenth century a romantic interest in the old tales grew so strong that many thousands were collected all over the globe. Striking similarities were noticed among the folk tales found in different parts of the world, and many theories were advanced to explain these similarities.

Theories of Folk-Tale Origin

One of the earliest explanations for the similarities among folk tales of different peoples was the Aryan myth theory. The theory asserted that all folk tales came from the Teutonic myths of a single ancestral group. This is sometimes referred to as the theory of *monogenesis* or "single origin." Although the Aryan myth theory has been refuted, it is interesting today because it has been the springboard for some other theories of folk-tale origin.

One group of scholars believed in the theory of *polygenesis,* or "many origins." They asserted that human beings everywhere in the world are moved by much the same emotions—love and pity, fear and anguish, jealousy and hatred; that all people can observe the results of greed, selfish ambition, or quiet courage and kindliness; that all have seen the ways of cruel stepmothers (Were there no loving ones in the old days, one wonders?); and that all have seen neglected children come into their own. So Andrew Lang and other believers in polygenesis insisted that similar plots could develop in different parts of the world from similar situations common to all humanity. Lang used the widely disseminated story of Jason to prove his point. This theory would seem to account for the literally hundreds of variants of "Cinderella" found in Asia, Egypt, India, all parts of Europe, and among the North American Indians.

However, modern social anthropologists point out that people are *not* the same the world over. In some cultures, for instance, stepmothers may not be feared at all. The Andaman Islanders apparently are indifferent to whether the children they bring up are their own or other people's—no stepmother problem there! Another objection made to polygenesis is that the same story in all its peculiar details and chains of events could scarcely have grown up quite independently among entirely different groups isolated from each other. But whether there is any validity to the theory of polygenesis, one thing is certain: Almost all peoples have produced stories and there are striking similarities among tales of different groups. Students of psychoanalysis have proposed psychological bases for the origin of folk tales. From analyses of folk literature, folklorists have also suggested bases for the origin of tales.

Origins in Dreams and Unconscious Emotions

Psychoanalytic writers have studied those objects and ideas which appear frequently in fairy tales from all over the world and have asserted that they are *symbols of emotional fantasy* which all people experience. Among such supposedly universal feelings are unconscious sexual love for the parent, hatred of paternal or maternal authority, and love or jealousy among brothers and sisters. The ideas and objects representing these feelings are supposed to be the same in folk tales the world over and explain the similarities among these stories. But social anthropologists object to this theory, too. They main-

From *Yeh-Shen: A Cinderella Story from China,* retold by Ai-Ling Louie, illustrated by Ed Young.

tain that unconscious emotions vary among different people and so do the symbols which represent them. The unconscious emotions described, they say, may be the characteristic product of modern urban life rather than expressions that are universal among all peoples, places, and times.

Some authorities think that the stories originated in the *dreams or nightmares* of the storytellers. Stories about a poor girl sent out to find strawberries in the middle of winter (some versions clothe her in a paper dress) might well grow from the bad dreams we have when the night turns cold and we find ourselves with too few blankets. Or consider the story of the poor girl in "East o' the Sun," who kissed the prince and then found herself out on a lonely road— the prince gone, the castle vanished, the little bell that fulfilled her every wish lost forever, and she in rags once more. Is she the embodiment of our anxieties and our reluctance to return from our dreams to a workaday world? So the fatal questions, impossible tasks, and endless discomforts in the folk tales may suggest some of the anxieties that haunt us in our sleep now and then.

Another phase of the psychological interpretation of folk-tale origin is the idea that the people who created the tales found in fancy the *satisfaction of unconscious frustrations or drives.* These imaginative tales provide *wish fulfillment.* That is, the oppressed peasants who produced some of the tales were "motivated by naive dreams of the success of the despised," and so they told stories about cinder lads going from wretched hovels to fabulous castles, or about a goose girl marrying the prince. It is certain that fairy tales do satisfy deep human needs, particularly the needs for security and competence. In the folk tales, banquets, servants, glittering jewels, and rich clothes are concrete symbols of success. Granting that these tales are primarily for entertainment, there seems to be little doubt that they contain a deeper meaning and an inner significance which the child or adult feels without being conscious of the cause.

André Favat's study of children's interests in fairy tales indicated that fairy tales generally represent the world as children think of it. His findings also supported the notion that the predictable form and content of fairy tales appeals to children. On those bases, Favat makes a strong case for giving children considerable experience with folk tales.

In discussing Perrault's fairy tales, Jacques Barchilon and Henry Pettit say that:

the child, through the comparison between the fantastic and the real, gradually learns to test reality. When children realize that the fairy tale is

Viewpoint

Thus, more than most other literature, fairy stories provide the child with the "knowledge that he is born into a world of death, violence, wounds, adventure, heroism and cowardice, good and evil." Children will probably not yet know this to be true from their own experience, but this knowledge may still strike a chord within them, possibly even from memories of their own more violent fantasies and nightmares. It may also start providing them with some sort of mental preparation for those more violent aspects of adult society which they will soon also notice, for example by watching television news bulletins. In much children's literature, we often prefer to portray a world that is lacking in any serious problems or dangers; if this is overdone, however, there may then be a risk of presenting a picture which, however safe, may eventually seem a little dull. Fairy-tales, on the other hand, offer a universe of imaginative extremes, where the hero may and generally does get his heart's desire, but sometimes only after running fairly terrifying risks. As this may be put forward in quasi-magical terms, which reflect a type of wish-fulfillment, and may also keep close to a child's own intellectual formulations at this stage. In many senses, therefore, the fairy tale world is one of unique meaning to young readers, and as such something always to be treasured.

Nicholas Tucker, *The Child and the Book: A Psychological and Literary Exploration.* Cambridge University Press, 1981, pp. 95–96.

Viewpoint

There is nothing new about stating that the relationship between folklore and literature is as important as it is difficult to articulate and study. For some time now scholars in both disciplines have addressed the problems of folklore *in* literature, folklore *as* literature, and folklore *and* literature, even if with some discomfort and frustration, especially in the first two cases. On the one hand, the attempt to identify folk items within a literary text has often rested on the unspoken assumption that "Literature − Art = Folklore" and, as such, this approach has only confirmed long-standing prejudices. As Carl Lindahl remarks, folklorists have studied literature to establish "the existence of oral narratives at certain times and places in the past," while literary scholars have extended their interest to folklore merely to show how "the artist transforms the content of folklore and transcends the limits of tradition." On the other hand, the approach to folklore *as* literature has privileged in most instances its textual aspects (almost as if a folktale, for instance, were a medieval manuscript),

thereby ignoring its performative features and its distinctive social functions. In recent years, however, thanks to the lively interdisciplinary development of studies in the areas of semiotics, psychoanalysis, and performance, both folklorists and literary critics seem to have come to the valuable understanding that, as Richard Bauman writes: "all texts, oral or written, within a given field of expression and meaning, are part of a chain or network of texts in dialogue with each other." Stating that the study of folklore in literature "no longer is the outdated and outmoded search for cultural debris in literary documents," Steven Swann Jones writes that it has become "a current and vital exegesis of the way literary texts adapt and modify folkloric traditions in order to communicate to other audiences" and that, while retaining a specific focus (folklore's influence upon a literary text), it also productively "direct(s) our attention to the larger discipline," the study of folklore *and* literature.

Cristina Bacchilega, "Calvino's Journey: Modern Transformations of Folktales, Story, and Myth," *Journal of Folklore Research*, Volume 26, Number 2, 1989, pp. 82–83. Copyright © 1989 by the Folklore Institute, Indiana Univeristy. Reprinted by permission.

fictitious, they learn to enjoy it as fiction. This is one giant step not only in the process of rational maturation but in aesthetic development as well.[1]

Remnants of Myth and Ritual

Some students, convinced that the folk tales preserve the *remnants of nature myths*, continually interpret any traditional story as a nature allegory—whether it is about sleep or forgetfulness, about a hero battling with a dragon, or about a girl being carried off by a polar bear.

[1]Jacques Barchilon and Henry Pettit, *The Authentic Mother Goose Fairy Tales and Nursery Rhymes.* Swallow, 1960, p. 26.

"Little Red Riding Hood," for instance, has been interpreted as an allegory of sunset and sunrise. The wolf is supposed to symbolize night, and in many versions he succeeds in devouring the little girl, who in her red cape represents the setting sun. This symbolic interpretation is extended in the Grimm version of the story, in which the hunters cut open the wolf and release "Little Red-Cap," the sun, from her imprisonment in the wolf, or night. The Norse "East o' the Sun" with its polar bear and its disappearing Prince was, like the Balder myth (see Chapter 7), supposed to explain the disappearance of the sun.

Other folklorists, while not interpreting all the old stories as nature allegories, believed that many of these tales preserved *remnants of*

From *Little Red Cap* by the Brothers Grimm, illustrated by Lisbeth Zwerger.

other kinds of religious myth and ritual. For instance, Sir George Webbe Dasent thought that the Norse folk tales contained many of the elements of the Norse myths. He explained that after Christianity came to the Scandinavian countries, the old Norse gods lost their prestige and were gradually changed into the fabulous creatures of the folk tales. Odin became the Wild Huntsman riding through the sky with his grisly crew. And perhaps the nursery tale of "The Three Billy-Goats Gruff" preserves the memory of Thor's battle with the Frost Giants, for the billy goat was the ancient symbol of Thor, and the huge, stupid trolls could easily be the inglorious descendants of the Frost Giants.

Some scholars believe that cumulative tales like "The House That Jack Built" and "The Old Woman and Her Pig" have ritualistic origins. Other stories too, they think, preserve fragments of spells or incantations. In the Grimms' dramatic "The Goose-Girl," the heroine puts a spell on Conrad's hat:

Blow, blow, thou gentle wind, I say,
Blow Conrad's little hat away . . .

Ancient superstitions and customs surrounding christenings and marriage ceremonies may also be found in the folk tales. So may propitiations of spirits, witches, the devil, or certain powerful animals (like the bear in the Norse tales).

Cement of Society

In recent times the science of folklore has merged more and more into the science of social anthropology. To understand the why and wherefore of folk tales, anthropologists have lived intimately with many peoples, visiting their homes, markets, religious ceremonies, and festal celebrations. Their conclusion may be summed up in one sentence: Folk tales have been the *cement of society*. They not only expressed but codified and reinforced the way people thought, felt, believed, and behaved.

Folklorists now agree that the folk tale is created by most people at an early level of civilization. Historically, the tales may contain elements from past religions, rituals, superstitions, or past events. Psychologically, they may serve to satisfy in symbolic form some of humanity's basic emotional needs. Ethically, they may be "the cement of society"—reinforcing our faith in morality and the ultimate triumph of good over evil.

Diffusion of the Folk Tales

Students have found recognizable variants of such tales as "Jason and the Golden Fleece" and "Cinderella" in the manuscripts of ancient India, Egypt, and Greece and on the lips of storytellers in Zulu huts, Navaho hogans, and Samoan villages—from the Russian steppes to African jungles and the mountains of South America. The three tasks, the flight, the pursuit, the lost slipper or sandal, and the undoing of a spell are found in innumerable societies. If polygenesis and universal emotions do not explain these variations, then we must ask how the tales were carried.

First, of course, they were carried orally by the migrations of whole peoples. Later they traveled from one country to another with sailors and soldiers, women stolen from their tribes, slaves and captives of war, traders, minstrels and bards, monks and scholars, and young gentlemen on the grand tour. Some storytellers no doubt polished and improved the tales, while others debased them. If the folk tales traveled by land, they were passed on by many peoples and greatly changed in the retelling process; but if they traveled by sea, they stayed closer to the originals. Sometimes one story theme would combine with others, producing either a variant of the original tale or a relatively new one. So ancient storytellers preserved old stories, produced variants of others, and occasionally dreamed up new ones to pass on. This process is one that continues even today.

The literary (or written) sources of the popular tales did not begin to circulate in Europe until around the twelfth century. Then came the Indian and Irish manuscript collections, vivid and lively importations which were no doubt partly responsible for the flowering of folk art in the thirteenth century. Ballads and stories began to bubble up everywhere, often with the same plots or themes.

During the sixteenth century, popular literature in England made a dignified beginning in print with Caxton's fine English translations of Aesop's fables, the King Arthur stories, the Homeric epics. In England, too, the chapbooks

From *The Three Sillies*, retold and illustrated by Kathryn Hewitt.

Viewpoint

The student of fairy tales . . . is aware, of course, if he is experienced, that however ancient the stories may be he must not think of them as if they were archaeological remains, as if they were the actual objects that existed in the past; nor must he regard them (as folklorists used to do) as antiques that have been so scarred by time they have become almost unrecognizable, for this presupposes that they were once whole and perfect, and have ever since been in a state of decay. He knows instead that since they are living things, not fossils, they are subject to mutation. They are as likely to have grown as they became older, as to have shrunk. They are as likely to have acquired significance, or to have acquired fresh significance, as they have passed through sophisticated communities, as to have lost it.

Iona and Peter Opie, *The Classic Fairy Tales*. London: Oxford University Press, 1974, p. 17.

picked up fragments of tales from everywhere and kept them alive in garbled but recognizable versions, dearly beloved by the people.

Predominant Kinds of Folk Tales

No adult can read folk tales without being conscious of the varied groups into which they fall: cumulative tales, talking-beast tales, drolls or humorous tales, realistic tales, religious tales, romances, and, of course, tales of magic. Many classifications have been made, but those that follow seem to bring in most of the kinds and to emphasize their characteristics.

Cumulative Tales

Very young children enjoy the simplest of all stories, the cumulative or repetitional tale. Its charm lies in its minimum plot and maximum rhythm. Its episodes follow each other neatly and logically in a pattern of cadenced repetition. Sometimes, as in "The Old Woman and Her Pig," the action moves upward in a spiral and then retraces the spiral downward to the conclusion. Sometimes, as in the American-English "Johnny-Cake," the Norse "Pancake," and the American "Gingerbread Boy," the action takes the form of a race, and the story comes to an end with the capture of the runaway. Fortunately, the runaway in such stories has forfeited our sympathy by stupidity ("Henny Penny"), or by impudence ("The Pancake"), so that the capture becomes merely the downfall of the foolish or the proud.

Some cumulative stories, like "The House That Jack Built," are mere chants; others, like "The Three Little Pigs," "The Three Sillies," and "The Bremen Town-Musicians," are repetitional and sequential, but have well-rounded plots. Modern examples of the successful use of this pattern are Marjorie Flack's *Ask Mr. Bear,* Wanda Gág's *Millions of Cats,* and Maurice Sendak's *One Was Johnny.*

Talking-Beast Tales

Perhaps the best-loved folk tales by young audiences are the ones in which animals talk. Sometimes the animals talk with human beings as in "Puss in Boots," but more often with other animals as in "The Cat and the Mouse in Partnership." These creatures talk every bit as wisely as humans—or as foolishly. Possibly their charm lies in the opportunity they give the reader to identify with the cleverest of the three pigs or the most powerful and efficient of "The Three Billy-Goats Gruff." Perhaps the credulity of "Henny Penny" or of the two foolish pigs ministers to the listener's sense of superiority. Certainly children are amused by these old tales for the same reasons that modern children laugh at Snoopy in Charles Schulz's *Peanuts* cartoons. The animals in both the old and the modern creations are exaggerated characterizations of human beings, and in that exaggeration lie their humor and fascination.

These beast tales generally teach a lesson—the folly of credulity and the rewards of courage, ingenuity, and independence—though their didacticism does not stand out so much as in the fables. The stories are so lively and diverting that they are primarily good enter-tainment. Perhaps the most successful of the modern descendants of the ancient beast tales are Beatrix Potter's *The Tale of Peter Rabbit, The Tale of Benjamin Bunny,* and all her other *Tales.* These have joined the ranks of the immortals, along with "The Three Little Pigs."

The Drolls or Humorous Tales

A small body of the folk tales are obviously meant as fun and nonsense. These are the stories about sillies or numskulls, such as the Grimms' "Clever Elsie."

As you may remember, Elsie had a wooer who demanded a really clever bride. On one of his visits, Elsie's family sent her down to the cellar to draw some beer, and there, just over her head, she saw a pick-axe that had been left thrust into the masonry. Immediately she began to weep, thinking to herself:

If I get Hans, and we have a child, and he grows big, and we send him into the cellar here to draw beer, then the pick-axe will fall on his head and kill him.

She cried so hard and so long that first one member of the household and then another came down to the cellar, listened to her tale, and began to weep, too. Finally, Hans came and, hearing how things were, decided that Elsie was indeed a thoughtful, clever girl and married her. After the marriage, Hans, who had evidently taken his bride's measure at last, gave Elsie a task to do in the field and left her there alone. But Elsie, unable to decide whether to work first or sleep first, finally fell asleep in the field and slept until night. Returning home in a great fright, she asked:

"Hans, is Elsie within?" "Yes," answered Hans, "she is within." Hereupon she was terrified, and said: "Ah, heavens! Then it is not I."

And so she ran out of the village and was never seen again.

Like the cumulative tales, the drolls vary in the amount of plot they develop. Some have well-rounded plots; for instance, in "The Husband Who Was to Mind the House" (he does so with disastrous results) and in "Mr. Vinegar" (who trades off his cow as the start of a series of barters which brings him less and less until he has nothing left but a good cudgeling from his wife). The Norse story "Taper Tom" has not only all the droll antics to make the princess laugh but real adventure as well. Finally, the Norse "Squire's Bride" is not only a droll story but also a fine bit of adult satire on elderly wooers of young girls.

Realistic Tales

The people who created these old tales rarely used as story material their own "here and now," the stuff of everyday living. Even when they omit all elements of magic, they still tell a fabulous tale: The monster in "Blue Beard," for example, seems to have had some historic basis, but to young readers he is a kind of cross between an ogre and a giant. His English variant, "Mr. Fox," is even less realistic, though strictly speaking there is nothing in either story that could not have happened. Perhaps the most satisfying of all realistic stories in our folk-tale collections is the Norse "Gudbrand on the Hillside." This is "Mr. Vinegar," with a loving wife instead of a shrew. Gudbrand's old wife thinks her man can do no wrong; so, sure of his wife's love and understanding, Gudbrand makes a wager with a neighbor that his wife will not blame him no matter what he does. Just as Gudbrand expects, his wife's tender responses to his series of disastrous trades reaches a climax with her heartfelt exclamation:

"Heaven be thanked that I have got you safe back again; you do everything so well that I want neither cock nor goose; neither pigs nor kine."
   The Gudbrand opened the door and said, "Well, what do you say now? Have I won the hundred dollars?" and his neighbour was forced to allow that he had.

Religious Tales

Folk tales using elements of religious beliefs are rarely found in children's collections but are fairly frequent in the complete editions of almost any group. Coming down from the morality plays of the Middle Ages, the devil and St. Peter appear usually in comic roles. The story of the devil who begged to be taken back to hell in order to escape from a shrew of a wife is a popular plot throughout Europe.

The Virgin Mary is usually introduced respectfully and even tenderly. St. Joseph is also introduced as a figure of compassion and as the administrator of poetic justice. The religious folk tales are generally either broadly comic or didactic and are, on the whole, not well adapted to children.

Romances

Romance in the folk tales is usually remote and impersonal, and the characters are often stereotypes. Aucassin and Nicolette are less interesting than their adventures. Enchantments and impossible tasks separate folk-tale lovers, and magic brings them together, whether they are Beauty and the Beast, the Goose Girl and the King, or the girl who traveled east o' the sun and west o' the moon to find her love.

Tales of Magic

Tales of magic are at the heart of folk tales. These are the stories which justify the children's name for the whole group—"fairy tales." Fairy godmothers, giants, water nixies, a noble prince turned into a polar bear, the North Wind giving a poor boy magic gifts to make good the loss of his precious meal, three impossible tasks to be performed, a lad searching for the Water of Life—these are some of the motifs and some of the magical people that give folk tales a quality so unearthly and so beautiful that they come close to poetry. A large proportion of folk tales are based upon magic of many kinds—so it is worthwhile to study these motifs and the fairy folk who flit so mysteriously through the tales.

Fairies and Other Magic Makers

The Little People

The belief in fairies was once astonishingly widespread and persistent among Celtic peoples (particularly in Ireland and Scotland). Even when belief is gone, certain superstitions remain. From these countries comes the idea of trooping fairies, ruled over by a fairy queen, dwelling underground in halls of great richness and beauty. These fairy raths (or forts) are the old subterranean earthworks remaining today in Ireland and Scotland, with the gold and glitter of jewels added by the Celtic imagination. From these hiding places, according to tradition, the fairies emerge at night to carry off men, maidens, or children who have caught their fancy. They may put spells on the cattle or on the work of humans they dislike, or they may come to the assistance of those who win their gratitude. To eat fairy food or to fall asleep in a fairy ring (a ring of especially green grass) or under a thorn tree on May Eve or Halloween is to put yourself in the power of the fairies for a year and a day.

The name by which you refer to these blithe spirits is also a matter of importance in Celtic lore. If you want to play safe, you will never use the word f-a-i-r-y, which reminds them of the unhappy fact that they have no souls. So address them tactfully as "the good people," "the little people," or "the wee folk," if you would be well treated in return.

Other countries have these little creatures, too. In Cornwall, they are called pixies or piskeys, and they, like their Irish relatives, ride tiny steeds over the moors. In the Arabian tales you meet the jinns, who also live in deserted ruins, often underground, and are respectfully addressed as "the blessed ones." The German dwarfs are usually subterranean in their work and sometimes in their dwelling, too. Although they seem not to insist upon any special form of address, to treat them disrespectfully is to incur sure punishment.

The Norse hill folk live underground also, as do some of the small fairy folk of England and Scotland. There are other resemblances among these three groups. The Norse countries have house spirits, the Tomten, much like the English Lar or Lob-Lie-by-the-Fire and the Scotch Aikendrum. All these household spirits take up their abode in a house where they are well treated and make themselves useful in many ways. They may be propitiated by bowls of milk or offerings of parsley, chives, and garlic. But woe to the misguided soul who gives them clothes! Such a gift usually offends them and always drives them away, never to return. Oddly enough, the elves in the Grimms' "Shoemaker and the Elves" were in fact delighted by the tiny garments, but they did depart, forever.

Wise Women, Witches, and Wizards

A few of the fairy folk are consistently evil, but most of them fluctuate in their attitude toward human beings and may be either helpful or ruthless. The wise women, who come to christenings or serve as fairy godmothers, are, on the whole, a grave and serious group. They are not unlike the Fates, or Norns, who mark off the life span and foretell coming events. One of these wise women aided Cinderella, while a peevish one sent Beauty off to sleep for a hundred years.

Witches and wizards are usually wicked. They lure children into their huts to eat them, or they cast spells on noble youths and turn them into beasts. Russia has a unique witch, Baba Yaga, who lives in a house that walks around on chicken legs. When she wishes to fly, she soars off in a mortar and sweeps her way along with a besom (two objects which may have to be explained to children in advance, by the way). She has some other unique powers that make her quite as fascinating as she is gruesome.

The magicians and sorcerers cast spells but may sometimes be prevailed upon to do a kind deed and help out a worthy youth bent on the impossible. The Celtic "Merlin" is the most romantic of all the sorcerers, but he is seldom mentioned in the folk tales. The English "Childe Rowland," however, enlists Merlin's aid in rescuing Burd Ellen from Elfland.

Occasional imps, like the German "Rumpelstiltskin" and the English "Tom Tit Tot," are hard to classify. They seem to be a kind of hybrid elf and fiend, hoping to get hold of a lively laughing child to cheer their old age, or of the bride who has to guess their names.

Giants and Ogres

Ogres and ogresses are always bloodthirsty and cruel. Giants, however, are of two kinds: the children call them "bad" and "good." The "bad giants" are a powerful clan using brute force against opponents. They swallow their

From *Rumpelstiltskin* by the Brothers Grimm, illustrated by Donna Diamond.

pompous pretender, no mean soul ever secures this aid. It is freely given only to honest folk about whom shines the grace of goodness.

Fairy-Tale Animals

In the world of fairies, domestic animals are as kindly disposed toward human beings as they are in the world of reality. For example, there is that handsome cat of cats, "Puss in Boots"— surely a child given a magic choice of one handy assistant from all the gallery of fairy helpers would choose the witty and formidable Puss. The Norse "Dapplegrim" is a horse of parts and does fully as well for his master as the Russian Horse of Power in "The Firebird."

Occasionally wild animals take a hand in the magic events of the folk tales. In the Norse story, a gray wolf carries the king's son to the castle of "The Giant Who Had No Heart in His Body," and in the Czech story, old Lishka the fox gives "Budulinek" a ride on her tail, to his sorrow. Wild animals may be for or against human beings. Sometimes they serve merely as transportation, but often they are the real brains of an enterprise.

antagonists whole, as tremendous power seems always to do in any age. They are ruthless and unscrupulous and must be dealt with on their own terms—deceit and trickery. But fortunately they are often thickheaded and rely too much on force, so that clever boys and girls like Jack or "Molly Whuppie" can outwit them and leave them completely befuddled.

The other tribe of giants we meet is the helpful one. They aid the lad who shares his last crust of bread with them, and of course their aid is magnificent. They can drink up the sea and hold it comfortably until it is convenient to release it again. They feel cold in the midst of fire and suffer from heat in solid ice. They can step lightly from mountain to mountain, break trees like twigs, and shatter rocks with a glance. The lad who lines up these giants on his side is guaranteed to win the princess and half the kingdom into the bargain. But no sluggard, no

Magic Objects

In "Herding the King's Hares," Espen Cinderlad receives a remarkable whistle for his kindness to an old hag. With it he can bring order to every runaway bunny in the king's herd, and finally to the royal family as well:

Then the king and queen thought it best to give him the princess and half the kingdom; it just couldn't be helped.

"That certainly was some whistle," said Espen Cinderlad.

"Molly Whuppie," when pursued by the double-faced giant, runs lightly across the Bridge of One Hair, on which the giant dares take not so much as a single step. That is the kind of power every one of us needs to develop —the power to find a bridge, however slight, on which we can run lightly away from the ogres pursuing us. The folk tales are full of these "Fools of the World," who learn how to use magic tools as the pompous and pretentious

Viewpoint

I first became interested in folklore when most of us do, in childhood. But at that time I had no idea that the games, sayings, songs, rhymes, taunts, and jokes I knew; the things I wrote on walls; the superstitions I relied on; the tales I heard and learned; the customs we practiced at home; or the ways we had of doing things were all folklore. I also did not realize that much of this lore gave my life structure and continuity, that these games, songs, jokes, tales, and customs were often very old, that ordinary people like me had created them, and that all this had survived simply and remarkably because one person had told another. With each retelling the result—be it a tale or a taunt—often changed slightly to reflect the circumstances of the individual involved. In fact, when one considers the countless variants of any joke, saying, tale, ballad, or song, it is almost as if one were encountering the assembled impressions of a series of prints pulled from a stone—all are the same, yet each is different.

It also did not occur to me as a child that the folklore we create, pass on, and change says a good deal about us, about the times in which we live, and about the needs we have. Our jests provide pleasure, but they also provide emotional release. When they deal with racial and ethnic groups and with parents and siblings, they provide weaponry. The tall tales which so amuse us spring from the vastness of a frontier wilderness where life was brutal and the people diminished and fearful. They created incredible lies in which individuals were larger and taller than life and could not fail, no matter what. Our superstitions provide answers to things we do not understand and cannot explain. Even today, when we know so much, we turn for answers to astrology and to the occult; and like our ancestors, we continue to cross our fingers, wish on stars, and knock on wood.

Alvin Schwartz, "Children, Humor, and Folklore" from *Crosscurrents of Criticism: Horn Book Essays 1968–1977*, selected and edited by Paul Heins. Boston: The Horn Book, Inc., 1977, pp. 214–215.

never learn to do. Espen Cinderlad, with three impossible tasks to perform, hunts around until he finds the self-propelled axe, the spade, and the trickling water that only he could stop or let loose. Each of these magic objects told him it had been waiting a long, long time, just for him. The message would seem to be that magic is always waiting for those who know how to use it.

Enchanted People

Being put under a spell is just one of the many complications that besets the heroes and heroines of the fairy tales. Childe Rowland's sister unknowingly courted disaster by running around the church "widdershins"—counterclockwise—and so put herself under the power of the fairies. "Rapunzel," of the long, long hair, was locked up in a tower by a cruel enchantress who was so clever that only a superprince could worst her. And there are many variants of the folk tale about the royal brothers who are changed into birds, and who can be released from their enchantment only after their little sister has gone speechless for seven long years and spun each of them a shirt of thistledown. The Grimms' touching "The Frog-King" is one of many tales in which either the husband or the wife is a fairy creature or is in the power of some witch or sorcerer. Of these, the Grimms' "The Water-Nixie" is perhaps the most exciting and the Norse "East o' the Sun and West o' the Moon," the most beautiful. In all such stories only love, loyalty, and self-sacrifice can break the enchantment and restore the beloved.

On the whole, the good and evil supernatural forces in the folk tales act according to certain laws. If magic makes wishes come true and points the way to happiness, it does so only with struggles and hardships on the part of the hero or heroine. The true princess suffers pitifully before magic opens the king's eyes and he sees her for what she is—the rightful bride for his son and a gentle, loving girl. These stories are not didactic, but one after another show that courage and simple goodness work their own magic in this world, that evil must be conquered even if it carries us to the gates of death, and that grace and strength are bestowed upon those who strive mightily and keep honest, kindly hearts.

Distinctive Elements of Folk Tales

For generation after generation, folk tales have continued to be popular with children. Modern youngsters, surrounded by the mechanical gadgets and scientific wonders of our age, are still spellbound by their magic. A brief examination of their form, style, and character portrayal may help explain the charm of the old tales for children. First of all, the form or pattern of the folk tales is curiously satisfying both to children and adults.

The Introduction

The introduction to a folk tale does exactly what its name implies. It *introduces* the reader to the leading characters, the time and place of the story, and the problem to be solved, or the conflict which is the essence of the story.

The stories often involve the element of *contrast.* Sometimes there is the uneven conflict, which always makes a story more exciting: "Hansel and Gretel" and the wicked witch— two little children pitted against an evil power; Snow White and the cruel Queen. Sometimes the contrast lies within a like group; for example, in "The Three Little Pigs," there are not only pigs and a wolf but also a wise pig and foolish pigs. So in "Boots and His Brothers" the humble Boots shows the wisdom his older

From *Rapunzel* by the Brothers Grimm, retold by Barbara Rogasky, illustrated by Trina Schart Hyman.

brothers lack. Contrast heightens the conflict and rouses the reader's sympathy for the weaker or less fortunate or more kindly member of the group.

Folk tales are *objective* and *understandable,* never abstract. They have to do with winning security, earning a living or a place in the world,

Viewpoint

Fairy tales are survivors. Authorless, timeless, placeless, they are also flawless. . . .

And in their character how they vary! Some have morals, some laugh in the face of morals; some are savage, some merry; some are marvelously decked out, some plain. But they survive alike because they are all good stories.

Their plots have never been surpassed and are still in service. They have action—unflinching, unremitting, sometimes circular. They appeal to the senses, they charm the memory. Their formal structure pleases the sense of order and design; their conversation is suitable, intense, pragmatic, well-timed, and makes sense for its own story alone.

Children like fairy tales also because they are wonderfully severe and uncondescending. They like the kind of finality that really slams the door. "Then the Wolf pounced upon Red Riding Hood and ate her up." And fairy tales are not innocent; they have been to the end of experience and back.

From "And They All Lived Happily Ever After" by Eudora Welty, *The New York Times (Book Review)*, November 10, 1963. Copyright © 1963 by The New York Times Company. Reprinted by permission.

accomplishing impossible tasks, escaping from powerful enemies, outwitting wicked schemes and schemers, and succeeding with nonchalance. These plots are as vital today as ever and account for the vigor of these old tales.

Time is effectively accounted for by a conventional phrase such as "Once upon a time," "Long ago and far away," "In olden times when wishing still helped one," "A thousand years ago tomorrow," or "Once on a time, and a very good time too." Such folk-tale conventions do more than convey an idea of long age; they carry the reader at once to a dream world where anything is possible.

The *scene* is even more briefly sketched. It is a road, a bridge, a palace, a forest, or a poor man's hut—a place where something is going to happen and soon. No wonder these introductions catch the child's attention. They launch the conflict without distracting details.

Sometimes the folk tales, like the ballads, get off to such a brisk start that the introduction is almost imperceptible. This one for "The Three Billy-Goats Gruff" is a masterpiece of brevity:

Once on a time there were three Billy-goats, who were to go up to the hill-side to make themselves fat, and the name of all three was "Gruff."

On the way up was a bridge over a burn they had to cross; and under the bridge lived a great ugly Troll, with eyes as big as saucers, and a nose as long as a poker.

There you are! The scene is a bridge with a pleasant stretch of grassy hillside just beyond. The characters are three earnest billy goats of the Gruff family who are desirous of getting fat on the hillside. Obstacle, Conflict, and Problem live under the bridge in the person of an ugly Troll. In the fewest possible words, you have all the makings of a good plot. "The Sleeping Beauty," still a fairly uncomplicated story, must introduce the king, queen, courtiers, the grand christening for the baby princess in the palace, the good fairies for whom plates of gold have been prepared, and the evil fairy who is not invited and minus a gold plate and therefore thoroughly angry. What will happen? This is the mark of a good introduction: It whets the appetite for more; you "go on" eagerly. For children, brevity of introduction is an important part of the charm of these folk tales. The excitement gets under way with minimum description and delay.

The Development

The development carries forward the note of trouble sounded in the introduction. The quest begins, the tasks are initiated and performed, the flight gets under way, and obstacles of every kind appear, with the hero or heroine reduced to despair or helplessness or plunged into more and more perilous action. This is the heart of the story—action that mounts steadily until it reaches a climax, when the problem or conflict will be resolved one way or the other.

The vigorous plots of the folk tales, full of suspense and action, appeal strongly to young readers. The heroes and heroines *do* things— they ride up glass hills, slay giants, outwit wolves, get their rights from the North Wind, or pitch an old witch into an oven she intended for them. Here are no brooding introspectionists but doers of the vigorous sort.

If these tales are to carry conviction, development must be both logical (in terms of the story) and plausible. When in "The Three Little Pigs" one pig is so foolish as to build a house of straw and another to build a house of sticks, you know they are doomed. But when a pig has sufficient acumen to build his house stoutly of bricks, you know perfectly well he will also be smart enough to outwit his adversaries, for such a pig will survive in any society. Another example of a logical, plausible plot development is "Clever Manka," the witty Czech story that is a favorite with older children. Manka by her cleverness wins a fine husband, a judge and burgomaster; but he warns her that she will be banished from his house if she ever uses her cleverness to inter-

From *The Three Billy Goats Gruff*, retold and illustrated by Janet Stevens.

fere with his business. Knowing Manka and realizing that one cannot help using what wit the Lord gave one, you feel the conflict approaching. Of course Manka learns of a case where her husband has rendered a flagrantly unfair judgment, and in the interest of justice she interferes. She is found out and banished, but in the face of this ultimate catastrophe, she uses her wit and saves both herself and her husband from permanent unhappiness. Here is a realistic folk tale of clever mind against duller mind, with the clever one saving them both. The ending is surprising but completely logical.

Many of the tales we know preserve unity of interest. Every episode in "The Lad Who Went to the North Wind" concerns the boy's struggles to get his rights for the meal that the North Wind blew away. To achieve unity, a story must preserve a certain economy of incidents. Too many episodes, too long-drawn-out suspense, or too much magic destroys the unity of the tale. The development often contains three tasks or three riddles or three trials. Perhaps there is no particular significance in the "three" except that the old storyteller, always properly audience-conscious as a good storyteller should be, could see that suspense can be endured just so long before people get impatient. Molly Whuppie can use her bridge of one hair three times and after that she had better finish things off and get home. For it is on suspense that the successful development of folk-tale action depends. Suspense is built up and maintained until it reaches a peak in the climax, after which it declines and the action ends with a flourish.

The Conclusion

The conclusion usually comes swiftly and is as brief as the introduction. In "The Three Billy-Goats Gruff," the ringing challenge of the biggest billy goat announces the climax. The fight ensues, the biggest billy goat is the winner and the Gruff family is now free to eat grass for the rest of its days. In "The Sleeping Beauty," the kiss breaks the spell for the princess and the whole court, the royal wedding quickly takes place, and in most modern versions that is all, except for the conventional blessing "and they lived happily ever after."

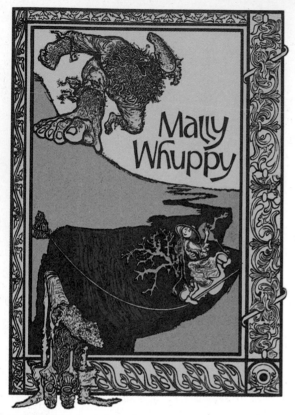

From *Alan Garner's Book of British Fairy Tales,* illustrated by Derek Collard.

The conclusion ends everything that was started in the introduction. Not only do the heroes and heroines achieve a happy solution for their troubles and a triumphant end to their struggles, but the villains are accounted for and satisfyingly punished. Such conclusions satisfy children's eye-for-an-eye code of ethics and apparently leave their imaginations untroubled —probably because they usually have no harrowing details and are so preposterous that they move cheerfully out of reality.

The folk tale has some conventional endings that are as picturesque as the openings. "The Three Billy-Goats Gruff" concludes:

Snip, snap, snout
This tale's told out.

Other endings are "if they haven't left off their merry-making yet, why, they're still at it"; "a mouse did run, the story's done"; "and no one need ask if they were happy"; "whosoever does

not believe this must pay a taler" (or as we should say, a dollar); "and the mouth of the person who last told this is still warm"; "and now the joy began in earnest. I wish you had been there too." For little children, the chance to vary the name in the last line of the following conclusion makes it one of their favorites:

My tale is done,
Away it has run
To little Augusta's house.

Style

One of the charms of the folk tale is the language and manner of telling the story. For these tales were never read silently; they were told until their form and language patterns were fixed. Consider "Go I know not whither, bring back I know not what," or:

"Little pig, little pig, let me come in."
"No, no, by the hair of my chinny chin chin."
"Then I'll huff and I'll puff and I'll blow your house in."

Or read that matchless ending, "As for the Prince and Princess, they . . . flitted away as far as they could from the castle that lay East o' the Sun and West o' the Moon." These are brief examples of folk-tale style—frequently cadenced, sometimes humorous, sometimes romantic—with the words suited to the mood and tempo of the tale.

The beginnings and endings of the stories, of course, are particularly good examples of the storyteller's skill in establishing the predominant mood of the story, or breaking off and sending the listeners back to their workaday world. But dialogue in these old stories is also a part of their style—it runs along so naturally that real people seem to be talking. Read aloud the conversation between the old man and his wife in "Gudbrand on the Hill-side." Never once does the swift interchange of news and comments falter for a descriptive phrase such as "said he *uneasily*," or "said she *reassuringly*." Here is just a rapid, natural give-and-take between two people:

"Nay, but I haven't got the goat either," said Gudbrand, "for a little farther on I swopped it away, and got a fine sheep instead."

"You don't say so!" cried his wife; "why, you do everything to please me, just as if I had been with you. What do we want with a goat! . . . Run out child, and put up the sheep."

"But I haven't got the sheep any more than the rest," said Gudbrand; "for when I had gone a bit farther I swopped it away for a goose."

"Thank you! thank you! with all my heart," cried his wife. . . .

So they proceed from disaster to disaster without a single literary interpolation. Notice, too, that the words suffice to establish unmistakably the attitude of each speaker. Words so perfectly chosen make long descriptions unnecessary.

Viewpoint

For centuries now theologians, educators, literary critics, psychologists, and librarians have debated the pros and cons of reading fairy tales to children. The basic question they continually ask is whether children should be exposed to the cruelty, violence, and superstition of make-believe worlds. This debate began practically the very moment the tales were written down and established a genre with children in mind—children as targets. From the late seventeenth century to the present, serious talk has centered on the moral aspect and related psychological effect of the *literary* tales. Yet, the pedantic posture of moralism has always been suspect, for its rigidity has prevented us from focusing on the real problem, if there is such a thing as the "real problem" *with* fairy tales. Instead of examining social relations and psychological behaviour first—the very stuff which constitutes the subject matter of the tales—*both* the proponents and opponents of fairy tales have based and continue to base their criticism on the harsh scenes and sexual connotations of the tales, supposedly suitable or unsuitable for children.

Jack Zipes, *Don't Bet on the Prince*. New York: Methuen, 1986, p. 1.

Another characteristic of folk-tale style is the use of rhymes. Indeed, the stories are sometimes part prose and part verse in the old sing-and-say pattern of "Aucassin and Nicolette." Such stories are called Cante-fables —that is, singing stories or verse stories. The frequency of rhymes in some of the old folk tales has caused some speculation about whether the folk tales came from the ballads or the ballads from the tales, since both often have the same subjects. This is a matter for the specialists to settle, but certainly the little rhymes add greatly to the interest of the tales.

"The Well of the World's End" ("The Frog-King") alternates prose and verse, with the frog singing over and over the same words except for the request in the first two lines in which he raises his demands each time:

"Give me some supper, my hinny, my heart,
Give me some supper, my darling;
Remember the words you and I spake,
In the meadow, by the Well of the World's End."

Some of the most striking verses in the folk tales are in the Grimms' "The Goose-Girl" and in the English "The Black Bull of Norroway." The former breaks into rhyme when the faithful horse, Falada, speaks to his mistress. And after he has been killed and his head nailed to the dark gateway, the Goose-Girl, who is really the princess, weeps beneath the gateway saying:

"Alas, Falada, hanging there!"

Then the head answers

"Alas, young Queen, how ill you fare!
If this your mother knew,
Her heart would break in two."

This piteous dialogue is followed by the song of the Goose-Girl, putting a spell on young Conrad, because he takes too much delight in her golden hair:

Blow, blow, thou gentle wind, I say,
Blow Conrad's little hat away,
And make him chase it here and there,
Until I have braided all my hair,
And bound it up again.

The Grimms' "Cinderella," "Hansel and Gretel," "The Fisherman and His Wife," "The

From *Hansel and Gretel* by the Brothers Grimm, illustrated by Anthony Browne.

her mind on parties and fine clothes. Red Riding Hood is good-hearted but irresponsible. The Lad who went to the North Wind to get his rights for the wasted meal is one of those dogged, stick-to-it boys who, with right on his side, is going to get his way in the world or know the reason why.

Sometimes the characters are passive, like the Sleeping Beauty, but still sufficiently individual so that each one arouses different reactions. Beauty's doom, hanging over her youth and loveliness like a black cloud, inspires only pity. But the silly, feckless girl in "Tom Tit Tot," with her big appetite and meager wit, is so absurd that you don't particularly mind the hard bargain "that" drives with her.

So while folk-tale people are strongly typed as "good" or "bad" with no subtle distinctions between, they may also be individualized. Sympathy or antagonism is aroused in different degrees by the brief characterizations. A whole portrait gallery of lads and lassies, goose-girls and princes, kings and queens remains in your memory, distinct and convincingly true to human nature.

Juniper Tree,'' ''Little Snow-White,'' and many others have memorable rhymes which some adults can still recite. The English tales are especially full of them. But many other folk tales are marked by the subtle art of the storyteller who has perfected a fine oral pattern in which rhymes frequently appear.

Character Portrayal

The interest of the modern short story frequently depends far more upon characters than upon plot or action. This is not true of folk tales. Plot is of first importance, and the characters are more or less typed. The good people in these stories are altogether good, and the wicked are so completely wicked that we waste no sympathy on them when, in the end, they are liquidated. So, too, the animals in the folk tales stand for simple traits like loyalty, cleverness, slyness, cruelty.

But look for brief flashes of characterization here and there. Cinderella is a teenage girl with

Why Use Folk Tales with Children Today?

When the poet W. H. Auden reviewed the Pantheon edition of *Grimms' Fairy Tales* for *The New York Times* (November 12, 1944), he made this rather startling statement:

For, among the few indispensable, common-property books upon which Western Culture can be founded—that is, excluding the national genius of specific peoples as exemplified by Shakespeare and Dante—it is hardly too much to say that these tales rank next to the Bible in importance.

Later in the review he added:

It will be a mistake, therefore, if this volume is merely bought as a Christmas present for a child; it should be, first and foremost, an educational "must" for adults, married or single, for the reader who has once come to know and love these tales will never be able again to endure the insipid rubbish of contemporary entertainment.

Ethical Truth

Some people raise a great hue and cry about the ethics of the fairy tales. Of course, the folk-tale ethics are not always acceptable to the modern moral code. These stories were told by adults to adults in an age when using wits against brute force was often the only means of survival, and therefore admirable.

But folk tales are predominantly constructive, not destructive, in their moral lessons. "The humble and good shall be exalted," say the stories of "Little Snow-White," "Cinderella," "The Bremen Town-Musicians," and dozens of others. "Love suffereth long and is kind" is the lesson of "East o' the Sun" and "One-Eye, Two-Eyes, and Three-Eyes." In "The Frog-King," the royal father of the princess enforces a noble code upon his thoughtless daughter. "That which you have promised must you perform," he says sternly, and again, "He who helped you when you were in trouble ought not afterwards to be despised by you." Indeed, so roundly and soundly do these old tales stand for morality that they leave an indelible impression of virtue invariably rewarded and evil unfailingly punished.

Satisfaction of Needs

Most adults rereading these stories begin to understand Auden's feeling that they are timeless in their appeal. Plumbing, kitchen gadgets, and modes of transportation may change, but human desires and human emotions continue strong and unchanging. These old fairy tales contain in their "picture language" the symbols of some of the deepest human feelings. They satisfy in fantasy many of the important human needs and desires discussed in Chapter 1, among them desire for well-being, knowledge, security, competence, and love.

Everyone longs for security, the simple physical security of a snug house, warmth, and good food. In the fairy tales, the little hut in the forest is cozy and warm, safe from ravening wolves, and full of the peace of the fireside, with a loaf of bread baking on the hearth and a flavorsome kettle of soup on the hob. And of course there are castles, too; they may be a bit cold and drafty, but Jack or Tattercoats or Espen Cinderlad always seems to settle down very comfortably in the new grandeur. Children identify themselves with either the elegance of the castle or the snug security of the house in the woods. Both are satisfying: the castle speaks of achievement, the little hut of peace and safety.

Human beings are always in search of love. There will never be a time when people do not need loving reinforcement against the hostile world and the thought of death. The old tales are full of loving compensations for fears and hardships. Hansel reassures his little sister and protects her as long as he is able, and Gretel comes to his rescue when he is helpless and in peril. Commoners and royalty alike pursue their lost loves and endure every kind of suffering to free them from enchantments. There is cruelty in these old tales and danger, too, but the real world, like the fairy world, can be cruel and perilous. In reassuring contrast are the symbols of love, lending strength to the weak, offering sanctuary to those in peril, and in the end rewarding their faithfulness or their struggles.

People long not only for love and security but for competence. They are eager to overcome difficulties, to right wrongs, and to stand fast in the face of danger—abilities essential for heroes of any generation. The fairy tales supply unforgettable stories of wicked powers defeated and of gallant souls who in their extremity are granted supernatural strength. Whether or not children are conscious of it, these stories may become sources of moral strength—a strength which is part faith, part courage, and wholly unshakable.

Collections and Collectors

The tales best known in this country come from the French, Norse, German, and English traditions. Although stories from other countries are becoming more available, the tales from these four cultures form the basis for much of the folk literature heard and read by children and adults. For that reason, the traditional tales from these cultures are discussed in more detail here than are some others.

French Fairy Tales

The history of Perrault's unique *Contes de ma Mère l'Oye*, published in 1697 and translated into English in 1729, has already been discussed. Perrault's eight stories have rather more polish and sophistication than is usual in the folk tales and they are available in editions of individual stories as well as in collections. The stories are lively with conversations and every necessary detail is logically provided for, or its omission underscored as a pivotal point in the plot.

Viewpoint

Nothing in the entire range of "children's literature"—with rare exceptions—can be as enriching and satisfying to child and adult alike as the folk fairy tale. True, fairy tales teach little overtly about the specific conditions of life in modern mass society; these tales were created long before modern society came into being. But from them a child can learn more about the inner problems of man, and about solutions to his own (and our) predicaments in any society, than he can from any other type of story within his comprehension. Since the child is exposed at every moment to the society in which he lives, he will learn to cope with its conditions—provided, that is, that his inner resources permit him to do so. The child must therefore be helped to bring order into the turmoil of his feelings. He needs—and the point hardly requires emphasis at this moment in our history—a moral education that subtly, by implication only, conveys to him the advantages of moral behavior, not through abstract ethical concepts but through that which seems tangibly right and therefore has meaning for him. The child can find meaning through fairy tales.

Bruno Bettelheim, "The Uses of Enchantment." *The New Yorker,* December 8, 1975, p. 50.

Barbara Leonie Picard's *French Legends, Tales and Fairy Stories* contains four hero tales, six courtly tales of the Middle Ages, and thirteen legends, or folk tales, with no repetition of Perrault's famous eight. There is more magic in these tales than in Perrault's; the epic tales are full of battles and various complexities, the courtly tales are highly romantic, and the folk tales, though they contain some variants of familiar themes, are more mature in style than the stories they resemble. Good readers will enjoy this collection, and the storyteller will find fresh and exciting material in such stories as "The Grey Palfrey," "The Mouse-Princess," "The Stones of Plouhinec," and "Ripopet-Barabas."

Geneviève Massignon's annotated, scholarly collection *Folktales of France* was published by the University of Chicago Press in the *Folktales of the World* series, a varied and representative selection. A collection long out of print has been made available again with the republication of the Comtesse d'Aulnoy's *The White Cat and Other Old French Fairy Tales,* edited and translated by Rachel Field.

German Folk Tales

The conscientious Grimm brothers (Jacob, 1785–1863; Wilhelm, 1786–1859) began collecting tales with a passionate concern for sources. They were university professors—philologists—and their interest in sagas, ballads, popular tales, and all forms of traditional literature was at first secondary to their interest in the roots and development of the German language. This interest in grammar remained paramount with Jacob, but Wilhelm gradually became more interested in the tales than in any other phase of their work. When they began their collection, it was not with children in mind. They undertook their research as a part of a vast and scholarly study of language origins.

When *Kinder- und Hausmärchen*[2] appeared in 1812 (the second volume in 1815), it caused no particular stir in literary circles. Some critics

[2]*Nursery and Household Tales* is the usual translation, but for the German *Märchen* we have no precise translation. *Märchen* is legend, fiction, a cock-and-bull story, romance—in short, a fairy tale.

From *Little Brother and Little Sister,* retold and illustrated by Barbara Cooney.

and tenderness, and so finding love. Here youth responds to the call of great tasks and accomplishes the impossible. These stories color readers' attitudes toward life, toward human relationships, and toward moral standards. They are both fantasy and reality, and they are supremely entertaining.

A number of both European and American artists have illustrated individual tales by the Grimm Brothers. A two-volume edition of the Grimms' tales, *The Juniper Tree and Other Tales from Grimm,* as translated by Randall Jarrell and Lore Segal in a forthright fashion, has been superbly illustrated by Maurice Sendak. Seldom have tales and illustrations been so perfectly matched. Sendak's work is imaginative, tender but terrible, a tour de force. Paul Zelinksy uses oil paintings in Renaissance style for *Rumpelstiltskin.* Barbara Cooney's attention to detail enhances her illustrations for *Little Brother and Little Sister.* Nancy Ekholm Burkert has individualized each dwarf in *Snow White and the Seven Dwarfs* with tenderness and delicacy. Trina Schart Hyman has given us another

considered the stories boorish; their publisher friend Brentano thought them slovenly; and yet somehow, in spite of the reviews, the stories were received with an unprecedented enthusiasm. Edition followed edition; translations began, first into Danish, Swedish, and French, then into Dutch, English, Italian, Spanish, Czech, and Polish—in all, some seventeen different languages.

The plots of these tales appeal to all ages— some to seven-year-olds and some to adults. The style has the peculiarly spellbinding quality of the great storytellers. The Grimms were fortunate in their sources. Besides the "story-wife," Frau Viehmann, there were Wilhelm Grimm's wife, Dortchen Wild, and her five sisters, who had been raised with these old tales and could tell them with effortless fluency. Other relatives, inlaws, and neighbors contributed to the collection.

To reread these stories is to find refreshment. Here are somber tales of children turned out to fend for themselves who find love and security after all their hardships. Here are fools, cheerful and irresponsible, and royal youths and maidens, dispossessed, reduced to misery and humiliation, but keeping their innate kindness

From *The Juniper Tree and Other Tales from Grimm,* illustrated by Maurice Sendak.

detailed interpretation of the same story as well as a romantic version of *The Sleeping Beauty*. An outstanding contemporary scholar of folklore, Kurt Ranke, has compiled a collection for the *Folktales of the World* series—*Folktales of Germany*, which includes stories from all German-speaking territories except Switzerland (those stories are in a separate volume). Like the other books in the series, this has a wealth of background information about the folklore of the country and a useful section of notes and indexes.

Norwegian Folk Tales

When people talk about Scandinavian folk tales, they usually mean a particular book, *East o' the Sun and West o' the Moon*, a collection most have known and loved, in one edition or another, all their lives. These stories probably rank with *Grimms' Fairy Tales* in their continuing popularity, and for similar reasons. They have the ring of complete sincerity and the oral charm of the storyteller's art at its best. They were recorded by Peter Christian Asbjörnsen (1812–1885) and Jörgen E. Moe (1813–1882), and turned into matchless English by a British scholar, Sir George Webbe Dasent (1817–1896), who was influenced by Jacob Grimm.

Asbjörnsen and Moe became interested in gathering the popular tales of their native Norway from the lips of old storytellers who were still relating them as they had been received from preceding generations. When Asbjörnsen, a zoologist, started out on a scientific expedition, he followed his folklore hobby in his spare time. Moe spent his holidays similarly employed, traveling to remote parts of the country and gathering the legends and stories of the district from the storytellers. Sir George Webbe Dasent became interested in the Norse folk tales and made his masterly translations of the Asbjörnsen-Moe collections, *Popular Tales from the Norse* and *Tales from the Fjeld*, the two sources for all subsequent English editions.

Folktales of Norway, edited by Reidar Christiansen, is another volume in the *Folktales of the World* series. In a fascinating foreword, the series editor, Richard Dorson, traces the historical development of the Norwegian tale. As in the other volumes, the provision of a glossary, an index of motifs, and a bibliography make this book of inestimable value to the scholar. *Great Swedish Fairy Tales*, compiled by Elsa Olenius and illustrated in romantic style by John Bauer, contains tales from other Scandinavian countries also. Other outstanding collections are *Scandinavian Legends and Folk-Tales*, by Gwyn Jones; *Norwegian Folk Tales*, translated by Pat Shaw Iversen and Carl Norman; *Scandinavian Folk and Fairy Tales* edited by Claire Booss, containing more than two hundred stories; two compilations by Mary Hatch, *Danish Tales* and *More Danish Tales;* and Sigrid Undset's adaptations from the Asbjörnsen and Moe collections, *True and Untrue, and Other Norse Tales.*

While the general mood of the Norwegian tales is serious, which is true of most folk tales, there is much more humor, or buoyancy, in the Norse collection than in the German. The people make the best of things with an amusing nonchalance.

There are no fairies in the gauzy-winged tradition, but there is a great deal of magic. Trolls, hill folk, giants, hags, and witch-wives are plentiful. A delightful combination of text and illustrations by Ingri and Edgar d'Aulaire,

From *Great Swedish Fairy Tales*, selected by Elsa Olenius, translated by Holger Lundbergh, illustrated by John Bauer.

Trolls is a definitive resource for details. There are magic objects in these tales—fiddles, axes, tablecloths, rams, and sticks. Winds talk and take a hand in the affairs of humans now and then. A polar bear (another symbol of the North) and a great dun bull are both men under enchantments, and there are the colossal horse Dapplegrim, the kindly wolf Gray-legs, and talking beasts of every variety.

For storytelling, "The Pancake" is probably the finest of all cumulative stories because of its humor and rollicking movement. "The Cock and Hen That Went to Dovrefell" has a witty surprise ending far more satisfying than its English equivalent, "Henny Penny." These tales, like the Grimms', run the whole gamut from sheer nonsense to the romantic and heroic. They are classics and matchless entertainment which all children should have a chance to hear.

British Folk Tales

When Joseph Jacobs (1854–1916) began compiling the English folk tales, his objective was different from that of the Grimms or of the men who had preceded him in the English field. He intended his collection not for the archives of the folklore society but for the immediate enjoyment of English children. So Jacobs omitted incidents that were unduly coarse or brutal, adapted the language somewhat, especially dialect, and even deleted or changed an occasional episode. He was scrupulous in recording these alterations. At the back of his books, in a section for adult readers called "Notes and References," he gives the sources for each tale and its parallels, and then notes the changes he made.

Jacobs obtained a few of his tales from oral storytellers—some from Australia and one from a gypsy are mentioned. But most of his tales he obtained from printed sources, which he acknowledged. Jacobs was editor of the British journal *Folk-Lore,* but his greatest contribution is probably in selection and adaptation. Had it not been for his collections, many of these tales might still be gathering dust in antiquarian volumes.

These English tales of Jacobs are remarkable for three things: the giant-killers, the humor, and the large number suitable for the youngest

children. From these collections of Jacobs come the favorites, "The Story of the Three Bears," "The Story of the Three Little Pigs," "Henny Penny," "Johnny-Cake," "The Old Woman and Her Pig," and many others.

"Tom Tit Tot," one of the stories which Jacobs rescued from the dusty oblivion of the journal *Folk-Lore,* is undoubtedly the most hilarious of all the variants of "Rumpelstiltskin." This is indeed an admirable example of the cheerfulness in the British stories. The superiority of this version lies in the full and consistent characterization of the silly girl, the impishness of "that," and the amusing hints as to the personality of the king.

The tales of giant-killers are another striking feature of the English collections, beginning with the old national hero story "St. George and the Dragon," and continuing through "Tom Hickathrift," "Jack the Giant Killer," and their only feminine rival, the resourceful "Molly Whuppie." These stout characters, who do away with monsters, were multiplied and perpetuated by the chapbooks, and their adventures have remained popular with British children ever since.

Jacobs remained the chief source of English folk tales until, beginning in 1954, volumes of English, Scottish, and Welsh folk tales were issued in the *Oxford Myths and Legends* series. Beautifully told, handsome in format and illustrations, these three books have greatly expanded the range of British folk tales.

In Alan Garner's *Book of British Fairy Tales,* sources are provided for retellings in the best sense of the oral tradition, with a nice mix of both familiar and less familiar tales. Flora Annie Steel's *English Fairy Tales* includes most of the well-known stories, smoothly retold and illustrated by Arthur Rackham. One of the tales, "Tattercoats," has been issued as a picture book, with delicate, romantic pictures by Diane Goode. *Folktales of England* edited by Katharine M. Briggs and Ruth L. Tongue (*Folktales of the World* series) is a collection derived almost exclusively from oral sources. Many of the tales are relics of pagan superstition; many are based on local folk history. The material is organized according to the type of tale: jocular tales, tall tales, modern legends, wonder tales, and so on.

From *Duffy and the Devil*, retold by Harve Zemach,
illustrated by Margot Zemach.

Welsh Legends and Folk Tales by Gwyn Jones
includes some of the hero tales of King Arthur
and his knights. There are such romances as
"Pwyll and Pryderi," "How Trystan Won
Esylit," and three about the fairy "Woman of
Llyn-Y-Fan." The folk tales are full of magic,
incantations, fairy folk, and difficult names.

In *Peter and the Piskies: Cornish Folk and Fairy
Tales*, Ruth Manning-Sanders has compiled a
lively selection of stories about the small supernatural creatures of Celtic lore. All of her
anthologies are excellent.

Harve and Margot Zemach's *Duffy and the
Devil* is a highly comic Cornish variant of
"Rumpelstiltskin."

The delightful books by Sorche Nic Leodhas
—*Claymore and Kilt*, *Gaelic Ghosts*, *Heather and
Broom*, and *Thistle and Thyme*—further enrich
the Scottish lore with both humor and romance. These stories have been written in such
perfect storytelling form that they may be read
or told without modification, and their charm
is irresistible.

African Folk Tales

The tradition of African folk tales includes
several forms of expression that enrich storytelling. Dancing and drumming are parts of the
tradition and song is often integrated into the
story. Collections and single-story editions of
these tales are an important contribution to the
field of folk literature available to children in
the United States. Although some books tapped
the wealth of African folk material before the
1960s, an outpouring of such material began in
that decade. Among the earlier collectors—
Harold Courlander, Wilfrid Hambly, Russell
Davis, Brent Ashabranner—the most prolific
has been Courlander, whose general and regional collections are a rich lode of cultural
information as well as a source of pleasure for
readers and storytellers. West African tales are
retold delightfully by Verna Aardema in *Tales
from the Story Hat* and *Tales for the Third Ear*.
East African tales are well represented in three
fine collections: Humphrey Harman's *Tales
Told Near a Crocodile*, Eleanor Heady's *When the
Stones Were Soft*, and W. Moses Serwadda's
Songs and Stories from Uganda. Folk tales from
South Africa are smoothly retold by Aardema
in *Behind the Back of the Mountain*. In addition
to the many collections of regional and tribal
tales, there are distinguished single-tale editions. John Steptoe's version of a Zimbabwe
tale, *Mufaro's Beautiful Daughters*, is based on
an animal-groom story and is illustrated with
lush, dramatic paintings. Some of the most
notable among the steadily growing number
of general collections are Joyce Cooper
Arkhurst's *The Adventures of Spider*, Frances
Carpenter's *African Wonder Tales*, and Edna
Mason Kaula's *African Village Folktales*. Illustrated editions of single tales, in picture book
versions, are listed in the bibliography for
Chapter 4 as well as in the bibliography for this
chapter. Aardema's retelling of *Half-a-Ball of
Kenki: An Ashanti Tale* captures the spirit of
rhythm and dance through the use of repeated
words to enhance the descriptions of sounds in
the story.

The stories reflect the fact that the oral
tradition is still very strong in Africa, with the
tales pertinent to contemporary life and the
written language echoing the cadence of
speech. Many of the tales are about animal
heroes like Anansi, the clever spider; many
explain natural phenomena as does the literature of any people who live close to nature;
many have a wry and sophisticated humor.

From *The Adventures of Spider*, retold by Joyce Cooper Arkhurst, illustrated by Jerry Pinkney.

Folk tales of the West Indies are interesting, too, because many tales derive from African folk tales. The early settlers of the islands came from South America. In 1496 the Spanish made the first permanent settlement and they were followed in the next two centuries by the English, French, and Dutch. As the islands began to flourish as centers for trade, the European colonies brought in large numbers of Africans to provide slave labor on the sugar cane plantations. With these people came a rich storytelling heritage from Congoland, Iboland, Ashantiland, and other areas of Africa. The Anansi stories are told with settings and creatures native to the islands rather than to Africa. *West Indian Folk Tales* retold by Philip Sherlock is a good collection to illustrate the African origin of the tales.

The Arabian Nights

The origin of *The Arabian Nights* is confused and lost in antiquity, partly because these stories belonged to the people and were not considered polite literature. In the Moslem world they circulated only in the coffee houses and the market place. The stories are very old, some of them seeming to stem from ancient India, others from North Africa, with an early collection from Persia. A Frenchman, Antoine Galland, made his translation of them in 1704 from a manuscript sent to him from Syria but written in Egypt. The stories were fortunate in that the translator was also a skillful storyteller. These tales of the Orient were given a Gallic touch, so they lack nothing of drama or color. Today, children have turned away from all but a few of these exceedingly long stories; one character remaining popular is Aladdin, who is drawn as a hero in the adaptation by Marianna Mayer in *Aladdin and the Enchanted Lamp*.

Russian Folk Tales

A. N. Afanasyev (1826–1871) collected the Russian folk tales as the Grimm brothers collected the German, and there is now an English

From *Arabian Nights*, edited by Andrew Lang, illustrated by Vera Bock. Copyright © 1898 by Longmans, Green and Co.

translation of the complete Afanasyev collection in the Pantheon edition, reissued in 1975. These stories are for adult students of folklore, not for children. They are bloody and horrible but full of excitement and color. Certain of these tales are rather generally familiar to American children—"The Snow Maiden" (sometimes called "Snegourka"), "The Firebird," and "Sadko." All lend themselves to dramatization and storytelling. These and other popular Russian stories are nicely told in Arthur Ransome's *Old Peter's Russian Tales*.

Miriam Morton's impressive anthology, *A Harvest of Russian Children's Literature,* has a sizable section of folk tales, and many tales have been published singly in illustrated editions. Two of Alexander Pushkin's poetic retellings of classic tales, *The Tale of the Czar Sultan* and *The Tale of the Golden Cockerel* have been opulently illustrated by I. Bilibin. Charles Mikolaycak's illustrations for *Peter and the Wolf,* translated by Maria Carlson, give children a good introduction to the story behind the music. Finally,

From *The Rumor of Pavel and Paali,* retold by Carole Kismaric, illustrated by Charles Mikolaycak.

Carole Kismaric recently adapted the Ukranian tale, "The Rumor of Pavel and Paali."

Spanish Folk Tales

One American storyteller, Ruth Sawyer, thought the Irish stories were matched only by the Spanish, and her collection seems to bear out her opinion. New and delightful stories for telling can be found in the collections of Spanish tales listed in the bibliography for this chapter. The stories for the youngest children are full of fun, those for the older ones full of grace. *Padre Porko,* for instance, is one of the most enchanting series of talking-beast tales to be found anywhere. The Padre, the gentlemanly pig, is both astute and benignant, and his canny solutions of neighborhood difficulties are made with great elegance. Adele Vernon adapted a clever tale from Catalonia, in which a poor charcoal maker solves *The Riddle*.

Collected Folk Tales

Excellent collections of folk tales have come to us in translation from many parts of the world. There are Dorothy Sharp Carter's *The Enchanted Orchard,* tales from diverse Central American cultures, and her delightful retellings of stories from the West Indies, *Greedy Mariani*.

Virginia Haviland selected thirty-two stories from around the world for *The Fairy Tale Treasury,* robustly illustrated by Raymond Briggs. *The Classic Fairy Tales,* selected and introduced by scholars Iona and Peter Opie, gives us twenty-four familiar fairy tales as they first appeared in English.

Two subject-oriented collections of note are Maria Leach's *Whistle in the Graveyard,* devoted to ghost stories, and Rosemary Minard's *Womenfolk and Fairy Tales,* a bringing together of folk tales with women as the main characters.

Many individual folk tales have been published in a picture-book format. Tomie dePaola's *Strega Nona* is a delightful noodle-head tale from Italy, and Harold Berson's *Kassim's Shoes* an amusing Moroccan story with graceful but comic pictures, while Arlene Mosel's *The Funny Little Woman,* with distinctive illustrations by Blair Lent, is from Japan.

From *Padre Porko* by Robert Davis, illustrated by Fritz Eichenberg.

It is likely that your librarian can provide native folk tales for practically any country you can name. Some of these have been better translated and adapted than others, but there is scarcely a collection not worth examining.

Although the country of origin may influence choice of material, the keys to selecting folk tales to share with children are, of course, the quality of the tales and the needs and interests of the children who will read or hear them.

Folk Tales in the United States

The United States is the fortunate recipient of folklore and folk tales from all over the world. This rich heritage includes stories from European collections such as the Grimm tales and British tales, stories that are essentially unchanged from the original versions except for minor changes stemming from translation. In addition, there are four categories of tales that can be considered typically American: (1) tales from African Americans, including the collections known as the Uncle Remus stories; (2) tales from the North American Indians; (3) variants of the European stories; and (4) tall tales. In the general discussion of folk tales few references are made to these American types, for definite reasons. In the first place, the European collections came into print long before American stories developed, and so they rather set the standard or pattern of such tales. Moreover, American collected tales differ in so many respects from those of the European groups that they often prove the exception to the very principles discussed as typical. They are, besides, far from a homogeneous group— no generalizations will cover all four varieties. An Uncle Remus tale differs from a North American Indian story quite as much as both of them differ from their European relatives or the tall tale differs from all three. In short, each of the four types of American folk tales needs to be considered separately.

African-American Folklore

Joel Chandler Harris (1848–1908) became interested in collecting the tales he heard the plantation slaves tell. Born in Georgia and raised on such stories as a child, he knew African-American dialect, humor, and picturesque turns of speech. Moreover, he had a deep love for the stories and for the people who told them.

The stories, told by Uncle Remus, a plantation slave, are mostly talking-beast tales and the hero is Brer Rabbit, the weakest and most harmless of animals, but far from helpless. Through his quick wit, his pranks, and his mischief, he triumphs over the bear, the wolf, the fox, and the lesser animals. Like the French "Reynard the Fox," he is a trickster, but unlike Reynard, he is never mean or cruel, only a practical joker now and then, a clever fellow who can turn a misfortune into a triumph.

These stories are, of course, reminiscent of the talking-beast tales of other countries. Some of them may have had their roots in India, but it is generally agreed that most of them originated in Africa or were created in this country. Variants of "The Tar Baby" are found in many countries, but there is a special flavor to the

From *The People Could Fly*, told by Virginia Hamilton, illustrated by Leo and Diane Dillon.

Uncle Remus stories. They show a homely philosophy of life, flashes of poetic imagination, a shrewd appraisal of human nature, a love of mischief, and a pattern and style unsurpassed by any other beast tales.

These stories do have their limitations, and in the original the dialect is one of them, but even when the stories are turned into standard English, they retain their witty folk flavor, just as tales translated from the Norwegian or East Indian or North American Indian do. Perhaps translation is the answer here, too. Ennis Rees, in *Brer Rabbit and His Tricks* and *More of Brer Rabbit's Tricks*, has provided such translations with great success, as have Julius Lester in his three volumes of retellings and Van Dyke Parks in his three. The simplest version for children is Margaret Wise Brown's edition of *Brer Rabbit*.

William Faulkner's *The Days When the Animals Talked* is another collection of tales from the African-American tradition that deserves mention. The stories are those of people in the guise of animals and Brer Rabbit is the central figure. There is much wit and wisdom in these stories and in the illustrations. The Foreword to the collection, written by Spencer Shaw, is valuable, too, for it provides information about the range of stories that belong to African-American folklore. Shaw points out that early tales of African-Americans in the United States involved a wide repertoire of oral retellings based on personal experiences as well as more traditional types of folk tales.

Virginia Hamilton in *The People Could Fly: American Black Folktales,* provides a rich source for storytellers; and in *The Adventures of High John the Conqueror,* Steve Sanfield presents a human trickster-supreme. The mighty deeds of John Henry, the African-American folk hero, are described in books by Harold Felton, Steve Sanfield, and Ezra Jack Keats, who has also provided bold, impressive illustrations. An excellent and varied collection of black Americana is Harold Courlander's *Terrapin's Pot of Sense.*

Ashley Bryan has collected and illustrated several volumes of songs from the African-American tradition in the United States in addition to his collections of African folk tales and some single-tale editions. His strikingly illustrated volumes of African-American spirituals are *Walk Together Children* and *I'm Glad to Sing.*

North American Indian Tales

The collecting of North American Indian tales began with the sporadic records of missionaries and explorers, but not until the 1830s was there any serious attempt to bring together the rich body of existing material. Henry Rowe Schoolcraft, a government agent for the Ojibwa Indians, zealously recorded their myths and legends, although not in pure form. Since his time, ethnologists and folklorists in the United States and Canada have collected a voluminous and varied storehouse of native American folklore. Most of the folklorists have collected tales of one tribe or people, such as Courlander's *People of the Short Blue Corn,* a Hopi anthology; Sleator's *The Angry Moon,* based on the lore of the Tlingit Indians of Alaska; or John Bierhorst's *The Naked Bear: Folktales of the Iroquois.* James Houston's two west coast Indian tales, *Eagle Mask* and *Ghost Paddle,* are good examples of single-tale editions.

While there are recurring themes and variants of specific tales, and even variants of European folk tales, the extant material provides a body of literature that differs distinctly according to region and tribe. Because the native American has a reverence for natural things, an affinity for the creatures of the earth and for the earth itself, much of the lore is concerned with nature as a part of religious beliefs and practices. Myths and legends that explain either the origins of natural phenomena, such as Paul Goble's retelling of a Cheyenne tale about the creation of the Big Dipper, *Her Seven Brothers,* or the attributes of wild creatures, are common to all the native American cultures, since all of them invested living things with magical powers.

There are five major types of North American Indian tales: creation myths; trickster tales, often humorous, in which the hero is either in human or in animal form, as in *Raven the Trickster: Legends of North American Indians,* retold by Gail Robinson, a collection of tales about the mischievous animal-god trickster; journeys to another world, a story type that often reflects mores and taboos of a tribe; hero tales, often including tests for maturity or courage, like Margaret Hodges's *The Fire Bringer,* in which a Paiute boy, with Coyote's help, seizes fire from the Fire Spirits to ease the winter suffering of his tribe; and marriages between human beings and animals. Each region usually had its own cycle of traditional tales, and as with folklore diffusion everywhere, there are themes and patterns that occur in different regions.

Native Variants of European Tales

The Southern "The Gingerbread Boy," printed in *St. Nicholas* in 1875, "Johnny-Cake" in Jacobs's *English Fairy Tales,* and Ruth Sawyer's story, "Journey Cake, Ho!" are all variants of the Scotch "The Wee Bannock" or the Norse "The Pancake." There are undoubtedly dozens of other European folk tales extant in this country in characteristically modified form, but so far the most amusing and significant collections are *The Jack Tales* and *Grandfather Tales* by Richard Chase, collected from American mountain people. Chase's account of these

light-hearted people makes you wish there were more of the stories. He has recorded them in the vernacular of the mountain people who have modified them to local speech and customs. The god Wotan or Woden appears, ancient, mysterious, but as helpful to Jack as he was to Sigurd or Siegfried. Jack is a country boy, unassuming but resourceful, and never nonplussed by the most fantastic adventures. The language is ungrammatical and sometimes rough, but it is humorously effective when handled by as gifted a storyteller as Richard Chase. The mood is decidedly comic, the setting rural. City children may not know "The Old Sow and the Three Little Shoats," but they'll recognize it as "The Three Little Pigs." Many of the tales have been found elsewhere in this country.

Tall Tales

The characteristic of the tall tale that distinguishes it from other humorous stories is its blatant exaggeration. Our older tall tales—with their swaggering heroes who do the impossible with nonchalance—embody delusions of power: dreams of riding a cyclone or mowing down forests, or, in short, blithely surmounting any and every obstacle. They are such flagrant lies that the lyingest yarn of all is the best one, provided it is told with a straight face and every appearance of truth. Babe, Paul Bunyan's blue ox, measures "forty-two axhandles between the eyes—and a tobacco box—you could easily fit in a Star tobacco box after the last axhandle." Pecos Bill, after riding the cyclone successfully, must figure a convenient way of getting down. In short, one characteristic of tall-tale humor is that there must be a great show of reasonableness and precise detail in the midst of the most hilarious lunacy.

There are no complete or satisfying answers to questions about the sources of all these tales. But regardless of their origins, they are almost invariably humorous. The New England coast produced Captain Stormalong. Paul Bunyan and his blue ox came from the lumber camps. The Western plains started Pecos Bill and his horse the Widow Maker on their careers, and are the setting for some improbably heroic deeds in the books by Glen Rounds. Mike Fink was a keelboatman on the Mississippi, while Davy Crockett, Tony Beaver, and John Henry all belong to the South. Walter Blair has contributed to the tall tale in *Tall Tale America* as has Adrien Stoutenburg in *American Tall Tales* and *American Tall-Tale Animals*. Moritz Jagendorf has compiled several volumes of regional material: *New England Bean Pot*, a book of tales from the middle Atlantic region, and *Folk Stories of the South*. Of the several collections by Maria Leach, an outstanding one is *The Rainbow Book of American Folk Tales and Legends*, which includes tall tales.

In our contemporary society, folk tales belong primarily to the young. Rarely do their elders read and enjoy these tales and so we lose sight of the fact that most folk tales were, in the beginning, story material for adults. Many of the tales are complex in motif and structure. Because of that, it is important to guard against the temptation to read or tell them to children at too early an age. It has been suggested that cumulative tales and talking animal stories have great appeal for young children. That is good advice and we can well save some other tales such as "Hansel and Gretel" for children of school age who can respond to them more fully than can the younger children.

There is a folk tale for every mood. There are drolls and romances, tales of horror and of beauty. They cover every range of feeling, and they can be used for storytelling, reading aloud, dramatizing, role-playing, and—without pedantry—learning by exposure such facts about literature as the way dialogue can establish character, or the importance of structure to narrative cohesion.

Undoubtedly, folk tales first appeal to children because of the *exciting action*. Things happen in these stories with just the hair-raising rapidity that children yearn for in real life, but rarely find.

Conversely, there is a strange quiet about these stories that attracts interest. The forest is so still you can hear one bird singing; a little lamb speaks softly to a fish in a brook; the enchanted castle is silent; and the prince falls asleep by the fountain from which gently flows the water of life. Reading some of these strange tales, the reader is soothed and relaxed. Here, there is time for everything.

Children are a natural audience for folk material as is shown in the ways they use rhymes in their play, from the two-year-old murmuring nursery-rhyme refrains to the older child engaging in intricate counting-out games. Most children show a predilection for the cadence and color that are a part of the oral tradition. Children's calm acceptance of magical events and talking beasts in folk tales is not far removed from their own invention of imaginary companions.

There is such variety of types of tales—of mood, subject, and setting—as to provide a folk tale for almost any circumstance. In the enjoyment of folk tales, children can assimilate a sense of their own cultural identity and an appreciation of others', and can share in the cultural literacy that should be the heritage of every child.

From *Paul Bunyan,* retold and illustrated by Steven Kellogg.

Adult References and Book Selection Aids*

AFANASYEV, ALEXANDER N., comp. *Russian Fairy Tales.*

ALGARIN, JOANNE. *Japanese Folk Literature: A Core Collection and Reference Guide.*

ASBJÖRNSEN, PETER C., and JÖRGEN MOE. *Norwegian Folk Tales.*

————. *Popular Tales from the Norse.*

BATOR, ROBERT, comp. *Signposts to Criticism of Children's Literature.* Chapter 5, "Fairy Tales."

BAUGHMAN, ERNEST. *A Type and Motif Index of the Folktales of England and North America.*

BETTELHEIM, BRUNO. *The Uses of Enchantment: Meaning and Importance of Fairy Tales.*

BIERHORST, JOHN, ed. *The Monkey's Haircut: And Other Stories Told by the Maya.*

BOOSS, CLAIRE, ed. *Scandinavian Folk & Fairy Tales: Tales from Norway, Sweden, Denmark, Finland, Iceland.*

BRIGGS, KATHARINE M. *A Dictionary of British Folk-Tales in the English Language.*

————. *An Encyclopedia of Fairies: Hobgoblins, Brownies, Bogies, and Other Supernatural Creatures.*

————. *The Personnel of Fairyland: A Short Account of the Fairy People of Great Britain for Those Who Tell Stories to Children.*

CLARKSON, ATELIA, and GILBERT CROSS, comps. *World Folktales: A Scribner Resource Collection.*

COLUM, PADRAIC, ed. *A Treasury of Irish Folklore.*

COOK, ELIZABETH. *The Ordinary and the Fabulous: An Introduction to Myths, Legends, and Fairy Tales for Teachers and Storytellers.*

COUGHLAN, MARGARET, comp. *Folklore from Africa to the United States.*

DORSON, RICHARD M. *American Folklore.*

————. *Buying the Wind: Regional Folklore in the United States.*

————, ed. *Folktales of the World* series.

————, ed. *Folktales Told Around the World.*

EASTMAN, MARY HUSE. *Index to Fairy Tales, Myths and Legends.*

ELLIS, JOHN M. *One Fairy Story Too Many: The Brothers Grimm and Their Tales.*

HEARNE, BETSY. *Beauty and the Beast: Visions and Revisions of an Old Tale.*

IRELAND, NORMA. *Index to Fairy Tales, 1949–1972: Including Folklore, Legends and Myths in Collections.*

JACOBS, JOSEPH, comp. *English Fairy Tales: Being the Two Collections English Fairy Tales and More English Fairy Tales.* These and other collections by Jacobs contain valuable information for serious students of folklore.

LEACH, MARIA, and JEROME FRIED, eds. *Funk and Wagnalls Standard Dictionary of Folklore, Mythology and Legend.*

LÜTHI, MAX. *Once Upon a Time: On the Nature of Fairy Tales.*

MACDONALD, MARGARET. *The Storyteller's Sourcebook: A Subject, Title and Motif Index to Folklore Collections for Children.*

MCGLATHERY, JAMES, ed. *The Brothers Grimm and Folktale.*

PELLOWSKI, ANNE. *The Story Vine: A Source Book of Unusual and Easy-To-Tell Stories from Around the World.*

SALE, ROGER. *Fairy Tales and After: From Snow White to E. B. White.*

SHANNON, GEORGE, comp. *Folk Literature and Children: An Annotated Bibliography of Secondary Materials.*

THOMPSON, STITH. *The Folktale.*

————. comp. *One Hundred Favorite Folktales.*

TRAVERS, PAMELA L. *About the Sleeping Beauty.*

ZIPES, JACK. *Breaking the Magic Spell: Radical Theories of Folk and Fairy Tales.*

————. *The Brothers Grimm: From Enchanted Forests to the Modern World.*

————. *Don't Bet on the Prince: Contemporary Feminist Fairy Tales in North America and England.*

ZIPES, JACK, trans. *Beauties, Beasts and Enchantment: Classic French Fairy Tales.*

————. *Fairy Tales and the Art of Subversion: The Classical Genre for Children and the Process of Civilization.*

*Complete bibliographic data are provided in Appendices A and B.

In the following bibliography these symbols have been used to identify books about a particular religious or ethnic group:

§ African American
★ Hispanic
☆ Native American
○ Asian American
● Religious minority

General Collections

BAKER, AUGUSTA, comp. *The Golden Lynx and Other Tales*, ill. by Johannes Troyer. Lippincott, 1960.
————. *The Talking Tree and Other Stories*, ill. by Johannes Troyer. Lippincott, 1955. Two fine selections by a noted storyteller.   8–11

CHILD STUDY ASSOCIATION OF AMERICA. *Castles and Dragons: Read-to-Yourself Fairytails for Boys and Girls*, ill. by William Pène du Bois. T. Crowell, 1958.   9–12

CLARKSON, ATELIA, and GILBERT CROSS, comp. *World Folktales*. Scribner's, 1980. Notes, comments, and lists of parallel stories follow each selection.   11 up

COLE, JOANNA, comp. *Best-Loved Folktales of the World*, ill. by Jill Karla Schwarz. Doubleday, 1982. A useful collection of 200 folk tales, divided by geographical regions and indexed by category of tale.   9–11

CROUCH, MARCUS. *The Whole World Storybook*, ill. by William Stobbs. Oxford, 1983. Twenty-six tales from around the world are retold in an animatedly casual style, with distinctive line-and-wash drawings.   9–11

DE LA MARE, WALTER. *Tales Told Again*, ill. by Alan Howard. Knopf. 1959. Graceful versions of familiar tales.   9–12

EHRLICH, AMY, ad. *Random House Book of Fairy Tales*, ill. by Diane Goode. Random House, 1985. Nineteen familiar folktales primarily from Grimm, Perrault, and Andersen are illustrated with soft pastels.   8–11

HAVILAND, VIRGINIA, ed. *The Fairy Tale Treasury*, ill. by Raymond Briggs. Coward, 1972.   9–11

JACOBS, JOSEPH. *The Pied Piper and Other Tales*, ill. by James Hill. Macmillan, 1963. An attractively illustrated edition.   10–12

LEACH, MARIA, *The Rainbow Book of American Folk Tales and Legends*, ill. by Marc Simont. World. 1958.   9–12

OPIE, IONA and PETER. *The Classic Fairy Tales*. Oxford, 1974.   9 up

OXENBURY, HELEN, comp. *The Helen Oxenbury Nursery Story Book*, ill. by comp. Knopf, 1985. The well-known tales selected for this humorous book are appropriate for preschoolers.   4–6

PROVENSEN, ALICE and MARTIN, comps. *The Provensen Book of Fairy Tales*, ill. by comps. Random, 1971. A dozen modern fairy stories illustrated with colorful pictures.   9–11

RACKHAM, ARTHUR, comp. *Arthur Rackham Fairy Book*, ill. by comp. Lippincott, 1950. A choice of Rackham's favorite tales.   8–10
————, ill. *Fairy Tales from Many Lands*. Viking, 1974. A reissue of 1916 title with beautiful, color plates.   10–11

ROSS, EULALIE, comp. *The Lost Half-Hour*, ill. by Enrico Arno. Harcourt, 1963. Good storytelling material.   9–11

WIGGIN, KATE DOUGLAS, and NORA A. SMITH, eds. *The Fairy Ring*, rev. by Ethna Sheehan, ill. by Warren Chappell. Doubleday, 1967. A good new edition of an old favorite.   9–11

WITHERS, CARL. *A World of Nonsense, Strange and Humorous Tales from Many Lands*, ill. by John E. Johnson. Holt, 1968. Fifty examples of the universal appeal of nonsense and exaggeration.   9–11

Subject Collections

BELTING, NATALIA. *The Earth Is on a Fish's Back: Tales of Beginnings*, ill. by Esta Nesbitt. Holt, 1965.   9–11
————. *Elves and Ellefolk: Tales of the Little People*, ill. by Gordon Laite. Holt, 1961.   8–12

GARNER, ALAN, ed. *A Cavalcade of Goblins*, ill. by Krystyna Turska. Walck, 1969. An excellent anthology of excerpts, poems, and stories from worldwide sources. A treasure for storytellers.   9–12

HARDENDORFF, JEANNE B., comp. *Tricky Peik and Other Picture Tales*, ill. by Tomie dePaola. Lippincott, 1967. A collection of trickster tales.   9–11

LEACH, MARIA, ed. *How the People Sang the Mountains Up: How and Why Stories*, ill. by Glen Rounds. Viking, 1967. Legends about natural phenomena from many lands.   10–12
————. *The Lion Sneezed: Folktales and Myths of the Cat*, ill. by Helen Siegl. T. Crowell, 1977. A varied collection of poems, tales, and sayings about cats including notes for adults, sources and information about each selection, and a bibliography.   9–11

LURIE, ALISON, ad. *Clever Gretchen and Other Forgotten Folktales,* ill. by Margot Tomes. Crowell, 1980. A selection of tales about women, told with grace and humor. 9–11

————, ad. *The Heavenly Zoo: Legends and Tales of the Stars,* ill. by Monika Beisner. Farrar, 1980. Handsome color paintings accompany these legends about animal constellations. 9–11

————. *Whistle in the Graveyard: Folktales to Chill Your Bones,* ill. by Ken Rinciari. Viking, 1974. 9–11

MANNING-SANDERS, RUTH. *A Book of Charms and Changelings,* ill. by Robin Jacques. Dutton, 1972.

————. *A Book of Devils and Demons,* ill. by Robin Jacques. Dutton, 1970.

————. *A Book of Magic Animals,* ill. by Robin Jacques. Dutton, 1975.

————. *A Book of Mermaids,* ill. by Robin Jacques. Dutton, 1968.

————. *The Red King and the Witch: Gypsy Folk and Fairy Tales,* ill. by Victor Ambrus. Roy, 1965. Each has a delightful style and well-chosen tales. 9–11

————. *Tortoise Tales,* ill. by Donald Chaffin. Nelson, 1974. 5–8

MINARD, ROSEMARY, ed. *Womenfolk and Fairy Tales,* ill. by Suzanna Klein. Houghton, 1975. 9–11

PHELPS, ETHEL. *The Maid of the North: Feminist Folk Tales from Around the World.* Holt, 1981. An unusual collection. 9–11

RIORDAN, JAMES, comp. *The Woman in the Moon and Other Tales of Forgotten Heroines,* ill. by Angela Barrett. Dial, 1985. Thirteen stories from as many countries feature strong and resourceful heroines. 9–11

SAWYER, RUTH. *Joy to the World: Christmas Legends,* ill. by Trina Schart Hyman. Little, 1966.

————. *The Long Christmas,* ill. by Valenti Angelo. Viking, 1941. Tales by a great storyteller. 8–12

SCHWARTZ, ALVIN, ad. *Fat Man in a Fur Coat and Other Bear Stories,* ill. by David Christina. Farrar, 1984. A conglomeration of recorded incidents, legends, tall tales, and anecdotes about bears is presented in a scholarly format. 9–11

SPICER, DOROTHY. *13 Dragons,* ill. by Sofia. Coward, 1974. Varied and sprightly. 9–11

Collections and Single Tales
African and Ethiopian

AARDEMA, VERNA. *Half-A-Ball-of-Kenki: An Ashanti Tale,* ill. by Diane Stanley Zuromskis. Warne, 1979.

————. *Tales from the Story Hat,* ill. by Elton Fax. Coward, 1960. 8–12

————, ad. *Behind the Back of the Mountain: Black Folktales from Southern Africa,* ill. by Leo and Diane Dillon. Dial, 1973. 9–11

————, ad. *Why Mosquitoes Buzz in People's Ears: A West African Folk Tale,* ill. by Leo and Diane Dillon. Dial, 1975. A "why" tale retold with verve; magnificently illustrated. Caldecott Medal. 5–8

ARKHURST, JOYCE COOPER. *The Adventures of Spider,* ill. by Jerry Pinkney. Little, 1964. 8–10

ARNOTT, KATHLEEN. *African Myths and Legends,* ill. by Joan Kiddell-Monroe. Walck, 1963. Tales from south of the Sahara tell of "animals, humans and superhumans." 11 up

————, ad. *The Adventures of Aku: Or How It Came About That We Shall Always See Okra the Cat Lying on a Velvet Cushion, While Okraman the Dog Sleeps Among the Ashes,* ill. by author. Atheneum, 1976. 9–11

BRYAN, ASHLEY, ad. *Lion and the Ostrich Chicks and Other African Folk Tales,* ill. by ad. Atheneum, 1986. Four stories from Masai, Bushman, Angola, and Hausa are retold in lilting rhyme and illustrated with folk design motifs. 9–11

BURTON, W.F.P. *Beat the Story-Drum, Pum-Pum,* ill. by author. Atheneum, 1980. Humorous tales and "why" stories, chiefly about animals. 9–11

CARPENTER, FRANCES. *African Wonder Tales,* Doubleday, 1963. 9–11

COURLANDER, HAROLD, and GEORGE HERZOG. *The Cow-Tail Switch, and Other West African Stories,* ill. by Madye Lee Chastain. Holt, 1947. Seventeen tales, told in lively style, reveal much about the customs of the people. 10–12

COURLANDER, HAROLD, and ALBERT PREMPEH. *The Hat-Shaking Dance, and Other Tales from the Gold Coast,* ill. by Enrico Arno. Harcourt, 1957. Humorous, droll, or wise are these twenty-one tales of Anansi. 9–12

DAYRELL, ELPHINSTONE. *Why the Sun and the Moon Live in the Sky: An African Folktale,* ill. by Blair Lent. Houghton, 1968. A story about the beginnings of times from the Efik-Ibibio peoples. Beautifully stylized artwork is based on African sources. 5–7

FUJA, ABAYOMI. *Fourteen Hundred Cowries and Other African Tales,* ill. by Ademola Olugebefola. Lothrop, 1971. Unusual stories recorded many years ago by a Yoruba scholar. 9–12

GILSTRAP, ROBERT, and IRENE ESTABROOK. *The Sultan's Fool and Other North African Tales,* ill. by Robert Greco. Holt, 1958. Eleven wise and witty tales, excellent for reading aloud and storytelling. 9–12

HALEY, GAIL E., ad. *A Story, A Story: An African Tale,* ill. by adapter. Atheneum, 1970. The story explains the origin of that favorite African folk material, the spider tale. Caldecott Medal.   5–7

HARMAN, HUMPHREY. *Tales Told Near a Crocodile: Stories from Nyanza,* ill. by George Ford. Viking, 1967.   10–11

HEADY, ELEANOR. *When the Stones Were Soft: East African Fireside Tales,* ill. by Tom Feelings. Funk, 1968.   9–11

HOLLADAY, VIRGINIA, comp. *Bantu Tales,* ed. by Louise Crane, ill. by Rocco Negri. Viking, 1970. Nineteen short, well-told tales.   9–11

KAULA, EDNA MASON. *African Village Folktales,* ill. by author. World, 1968.   9–11

KIMMEL, ERIC A. *Anansi and the Moss-Covered Rock,* ill. by Janet Stevens. Holiday House, 1988. Anansi, the African trickster spider, uses the power of a magic rock to steal the other animals' food, until the tables are turned on him.   4–7

MCKISSACK, PATRICIA. *Monkey-Monkey's Trick: Based on an African Folk Tale,* ill. by Paul Meisel. Random House, 1988. In an easy-reader format, the story of how Hyena helps Monkey-Monkey build his house makes for a satisfying trickster tale.   5–8

PITCHER, DIANNA, ad. *Tokoloshi: African Folk-Tales,* ill. by Meg Rutherford. Dawne-Leigh, 1981. Smoothly told tales based chiefly on Bantu sources make an excellent storytelling resource.   9–11

SERWADDA, W. MOSES. *Songs and Stories from Uganda,* transcribed and ed. by Hewitt Pantaleoni, ill. by Leo and Diane Dillon. T. Crowell, 1974.   8–10

STEPTOE, JOHN, ad. *Mufaro's Beautiful Daughters: An African Tale,* ill. by ad. Lothrop, 1987.   5–8

Arabian

COLUM, PADRAIC, *The Arabian Nights: Tales of Wonder and Magnificence,* ill. by Lynd Ward. Macmillan, 1964. Republished after thirty years, this outstanding collection will appeal to younger readers.   10–14

LANG, ANDREW, ad. *Aladdin and the Wonderful Lamp,* ill. by Errol Le Cain. Viking, 1981. Richly ornamented illustrations in the tradition of Persian painting tell the fabulous story of a poor boy whose life is changed when he meets a wish-giving genie.   8–10

————, ed. *Arabian Nights,* ill. by Vera Bock. McKay, 1946. Fine black-and-white drawings and large print make this a favorite edition for children's reading.   10–14

MAYER, MARIANNA, ad. *Aladdin and the Enchanted Lamp,* ill. by Gerald McDermott. Macmillan, 1985.   9–11

WIGGIN, KATE DOUGLAS, and NORA SMITH, eds. *Arabian Nights, Their Best Known Tales,* ill. by Maxfield Parrish. Scribner's, 1909. Here are the favorite stories—"Aladdin," "Ali Baba," "The Voyage of Sinbad the Sailor"—gorgeously illustrated in color and well told.   10–14

Canadian

BARBEAU, MARIUS. *The Golden Phoenix: And Other French-Canadian Fairy Tales,* retold by Michael Hornyansky, ill. by Arthur Price. Walck, 1958. Notes as to their origin give these eight tales a special interest. Told with humor and zest.   10–13

CARLSON, NATALIE SAVAGE. *The Talking Cat and Other Stories of French Canada,* ill. by Roger Duvoisin. Harper, 1952. Tales told with vitality and humor and excellent for reading aloud.   8–11

MARTIN, EVA, ad. *Tales of the Far North,* ill. by Lazslo Gal. Dial, 1986. Soft, romantic paintings illustrate twelve European fairy tales that have been altered in the New World.   9–11

Chinese

HEARNE, LAFCADIO. *The Voice of the Great Bell,* ad. by Margaret Hodges, ill. by Ed Young. Little, 1989.   5–8

KENDALL, CAROL, ad. *The Wedding of the Rat Family,* ill. by James Watts. McElderry, 1988. A pretentious rat couple's search for a powerful bridegroom for the youngest daughter ends in foolish selection of a cat.   5–8

LIYI, HE, tr. *The Spring of Butterflies and Other Folktales of China's Minority Peoples,* ed. by Neil Philip, ill. by Pan Aiqing and Li Zhao. Lothrop, 1986. Scholarly treatment of highly moralistic and very romantic tales from minority groups of China.   10–14

LOUIE, AI-LING. *Yeh-Shen: A Cinderella Story from China,* ill. by Ed Young. Philomel, 1982. An intriguing Chinese variant of the Cinderella story embellished with restrained, softly colored illustrations.   8–11

MOSEL, ARLENE, ed. *Tikki Tikki Tembo,* ill. by Blair Lent. Holt, 1968. An amusing picture book to read aloud. The wash illustrations have an appropriately Oriental beauty.   5–7

SADLER, CATHERINE EDWARDS, ad. *Treasure Mountain: Folktales from Southern China,* ill. by Cheng Mung Yun. Atheneum, 1982. Serene pencil drawings illustrate flowing retellings of six Chinese tales.   9–11

TIMPANELLI, GIOIA, ad. *Tales from the Roof of the World: Folktales of Tibet*, ill. by Elizabeth Kelly Lockwood. Viking, 1984. Four longish folk tales from Tibet give examples of virtuous behavior.   9–11

WOLKSTEIN, DIANE. *8,000 Stones: A Chinese Folktale*, ill. by Ed Young. Doubleday, 1972. A small boy ingeniously contrives a solution to his ruler's problem: how to weigh an elephant.   8–9

————. *White Wave: A Chinese Tale*, ill. by Ed Young. T. Crowell, 1979. A poor farm lad discovers that his cherished moon snail is the goddess White Wave.   8–11

YEP, LAURENCE. *The Rainbow People*, ill. by David Wiesner. Harper, 1989. Twenty stories are adapted from a 1930's WPA oral narrative project in Oakland's Chinatown.   10–14

YOUNG, ED, tr. *Lon Po Po: A Red Riding Hood Story from China*, ill. by tr. Philomel, 1989. Caldecott Medal.   7–9

Czechoslovakian

FILLMORE, PARKER. *Shepherd's Nosegay*, ed. by Katherine Love, ill. by Enrico Arno. Harcourt, 1958. Eighteen tales of Finland and Czechoslovakia compiled from Fillmore's out-of-print collections. Excellent for telling and reading aloud.   9–12

HAVILAND, VIRGINIA, ad. *Favorite Fairy Tales Told in Czechoslovakia*, ill. by Trina S. Hyman. Little, 1966.   8–10

Danish

BASON, LILLIAN. *Those Foolish Molboes!*, ill. by Margot Tomes. Coward, 1977. These simple, humorous tales are peopled by the Molboes, a blandly and cheerfully stupid bunch whose dilemmas will delight the young audience for whom they were written.   7–9

HATCH, MARY COTTAM. *13 Danish Tales, Retold*, ill. by Edgun (pseud.). Harcourt, 1947. These stories are excellent for reading or storytelling, and are carefully adapted from the Bay translation.   9–13

————. *More Danish Tales, Retold*, ill. by Edgun (pseud.). Harcourt, 1949.   9–13

JONES, GWYN. *Scandinavian Legends and Folk Tales* (see Norwegian tales).

English, Scottish, and Welsh

BRIGGS, KATHARINE, and RUTH TONGUE, eds. *Folktales of England*. Univ. of Chicago Pr., 1965. (*Folktales of the World* series).   10 up

BROWN, MARCIA. *Dick Whittington and His Cat*, ill. by author. Scribner's, 1950. A lively, readable adaptation of this classic hero tale with strong linoleum cuts in two colors.   4–8

CARRICK, MALCOLM, ad. *The Wise Men of Gotham*, ill. by adapter. Viking, 1975. Blithe and bouncy noodlehead tales.   9–11

COLWELL, EILEEN. *Round About and Long Ago: Tales from the English Counties*, ill. by Anthony Colbert. Houghton, 1974. Brisk, straightforward retellings of twenty-eight tales.   9–12

COOPER, SUSAN. *The Selkie Girl*, ill. by Warwick Hutton. McElderry, 1986. A lonely fisherman selfishly captures a beautiful selkie and keeps her as his wife until their youngest child helps her escape back to the sea.   5–7

CROSSLEY-HOLLAND, KEVIN. *British Folk Tales: New Version*. Orchard/Watts, 1987. Fifty-five unique versions of familiar stories.   9 up

GARNER, ALAN. *Alan Garner's Book of British Fairy Tales*, ill. by Derek Collard. Collins/Delacorte, 1985.   9–11

————. *A Bag of Moonshine*, ill. by Patrick James Lynch. Delacorte, 1986. Twenty-two stories from England and Wales offer entertaining variants of some well-known tales.   9–11

JACOBS, JOSEPH, ed. *English Fairy Tales*.

————. *More English Fairy Tales*, both ill. by John D. Batten. Putnam, n.d. These not only are reliable sources for the favorite English tales but also are appealing to children in format and illustrations.   9–12

JONES, GWYN. *Welsh Legends and Folk Tales*, ill. by Joan Kiddell-Monroe. Walck, 1955. Retellings of ancient sagas as well as folk and fairy tales are included. Illustrations in color are particularly outstanding.   11–14

MANNING-SANDERS, RUTH. *Peter and the Piskies: Cornish Folk and Fairy Tales*, ill. by Raymond Briggs. Roy, 1966.   10–12

NESS, EVALINE. *Tom Tit Tot*, ill. by author. Scribner's, 1965. A very attractive picture-book variation of the Rumpelstiltskin story, good for storytelling or for reading aloud.   5–8

NIC LEODHAS, SORCHE (pseud.). *Always Room for One More*, ill. by Nonny Hogrogian. Holt, 1965. A picture-book version of an old Scottish song. Handsome illustrations. Caldecott Medal.   5–8

————. *Claymore and Kilt*, ill. by Leo and Diane Dillon. Holt, 1967.   12–14

————. *Gaelic Ghosts,* ill. by Nonny Hogrogian. Holt, 1964.   10–12

————. *Heather and Broom,* ill. by Consuelo Joerns. Holt, 1960.   10–12

————. *Thistle and Thyme,* ill. by Evaline Ness. Holt, 1962.   10–12

STEELE, FLORA ANNIE. *English Fairy Tales,* ill. by Arthur Rackham. Macmillan, 1962.   8–12

————. *Tattercoats: An Old English Tale,* ill. by Diane Goode. Bradbury, 1976.   5–8

WILSON, BARBARA KER. *Scottish Folk Tales and Legends,* ill. by Joan Kiddell-Monroe. Walck, 1954. In addition to the folk tales, a section of stories on the legendary exploits of the Fians is included. Attractive format and illustrations.   11–14

ZEMACH, HARVE. *Duffy and the Devil: A Cornish Tale Retold,* ill. by Margot Zemach. Farrar, 1973. Caldecott Medal.   5–8

Finnish

BOWMAN, JAMES CLOYD, and MARGARET BIANCO. *Tales from a Finnish Tupa,* from a tr. by Aili Kolehmainen, ill. by Laura Bannon. Whitman, 1936. Here are the everyday folk tales of the Finnish people, not the epic stories. Beautifully told, with effective illustrations.   10–14

FILLMORE, PARKER. *Shepherd's Nosegay* (see Czecho-slovakian tales).

French

CARLSON, NATALIE SAVAGE. *King of the Cats and Other Tales,* ill. by David Frampton. Doubleday, 1980. Legendary creatures of Brittany figure in eight stories told to a small girl by her godmother.
8–10

D'AULNOY, MARIE C. *The White Cat and Other Old French Fairy Tales* by Mme. La Comtesse d'Aulnoy, tr. by Rachel Field, ill. by Elizabeth MacKinstry. Macmillan, 1967.   8–11

HUTTON, WARWICK, ad. *Beauty and the Beast,* ill. by ad. Atheneum, 1985. In a picture-book version of a classic tale, a horrible beast regains his true princely form when Beauty declares her love.
5–8

MASSIGNON, GENEVIEVE, ed. *Folktales of France,* tr. by Jacqueline Hyland. Univ. of Chicago Pr., 1968. (*Folktales of the World* series).   10 up

PERRAULT, CHARLES. *Cinderella: or The Little Glass Slipper,* ill. by Marcia Brown. Scribner's, 1954. Attractive pastel illustrations. Caldecott Medal.
5–9

————. *Cinderella,* ad. by Amy Ehrlich, ill. by Susan Jeffers. Dial, 1985. A simplified adaptation and oversize illustrations enlarge the well-known romantic tale.   5–7

————. *Puss in Boots,* ill. by Marcia Brown. Scribner's, 1952. Wonderful pictures enliven this story of the faithful cat who helps to make a lord of his poor young master.   6–9

PICARD, BARBARA LEONIE. *French Legends, Tales and Fairy Stories,* ill. by Joan Kiddell-Monroe. Walck, 1955. A rich and varied source of folklore ranging from epic literature to medieval tales; from legends to fairy tales.   10–14

German

GRIMM, JACOB and WILHELM. *About Wise Men and Simpletons: Twelve Tales from Grimm,* tr. by Elizabeth Shub, ill. by Nonny Hogrogian. Macmillan, 1971. Newly translated from the less familiar first edition, pithy versions of familiar tales.   9–11

————. *The Devil with the Three Golden Hairs,* ad. and ill. by Nonny Hogrogian. Knopf, 1983. 5–8

————. *The Fisherman and His Wife,* tr. by Randall Jarrell, ill. by Margot Zemach. Farrar, 1980. A story of greed and justice, illustrated by handsome pictures, delicate but comic.   5–8

————. *The Fox and the Cat: Kevin Crossley-Holland's Animal Tales from Grimm,* ad. by Kevin Crossley-Holland, ill. by Susan Varley. Lothrop, 1986. The eleven short and action-packed stories will appeal to young children.   8–10

————. *Grimm's Fairy Tales: Twenty Stories,* ill. by Arthur Rackham. Viking, 1973. Selections from an edition long out of print, illustrated with beauty and vigor.   9–11

————. *Grimm's Tales for Young and Old.* Doubleday, 1977. A good standard edition.   9–11

————. *Hansel and Gretel,* tr. by Elizabeth Crawford, ill. by Lisbeth Zwerger. Morrow, 1980. A new and excellent translation.   5–8

————. *The Juniper Tree and Other Tales from Grimm,* 2 vols., selected by Lore Segal and Maurice Sendak, tr. by Lore Segal with four tales tr. by Randall Jarrell, ill. by Maurice Sendak. Farrar, 1973.   9 up

————. *Little Brother and Little Sister,* ad. and ill. by Barbara Cooney. Doubleday, 1982.   5–8

————. *Little Red Riding Hood,* ad. and ill. by Trina Schart Hyman. Holiday, 1983. Lush, exquisitely detailed paintings complement the lovely edition of a favorite story.   7–9

————. *Rapunzel,* ad. by Barbara Rogasky, ill. by Trina Schart Hyman. Holiday, 1982. Romantic pictures framed by delicate borders suit this popular tale about the girl whose lover climbs her rope of golden hair.   8–10

————. *Red Riding Hood,* ad. and ill. by James Marshall. Dial, 1987. The humorous and cartoon-like illustrations flesh out the well-known moral tale.   4–8

————. *Rumplestiltskin,* ad. and ill. by Paul O. Zelinsky. Dutton, 1986.   4–8

————. *The Shoemaker and the Elves,* ill. by Adrienne Adams. Scribner's, 1960. Colorful illustrations add new beauty to one of the Grimms' best-loved tales for little children.   3–6

————. *The Twelve Dancing Princesses and Other Tales from Grimm,* ill. by Lidia Postma. Dial, 1986. A blend of familiar and less common Grimm tales, hauntingly illustrated in several styles by a single artist.   9–11

————. *The Sleeping Beauty, from the Brothers Grimm,* ill. by Trina Schart Hyman. Little, 1977.   9–11

————. *Snow White and the Seven Dwarfs: A Tale from the Brothers Grimm,* tr. by Randall Jarrell, ill. by Nancy Ekholm Burkert. Farrar, 1972.   9–11

————. *Tales from Grimm,* freely tr. and ill. by Wanda Gág. Coward, 1936.   9–11

————. *The Twelve Dancing Princesses,* ad. by Janet Lunn, ill. by Laszlo Gal. Methuen, 1980. Intricately detailed, romantic medieval scenes are the backdrop for this polished retelling.   5–8

GRIMM, WILHELM. *Dear Mili: An Old Tale,* tr. by Ralph Manheim, ill. by Maurice Sendak. Farrar, 1988. Rediscovered in 1983, the tale is a Gothic fragment that is sentimental, somber, and devout.   8–10

PICARD, BARBARA LEONIE. *German Hero-Sagas and Folk-Tales,* ill. by Joan Kiddell-Monroe. Walck, 1958. *Siegfried* and other sagas, as well as such folk tales as *Ratcatcher of Hamelin* give children a broader background of German lore than the more familiar Grimm tales.   11–14

RANKE, KURT, ed. *Folktales of Germany,* tr. by Lotte Baumann. Univ. of Chicago Pr., 1966 (*Folktales of the World* series).   10 up

ZEMACH, MARGOT, ad. *The Three Wishes: An Old Story,* ill. by ad. Farrar, 1986. A woodcutter and his wife accidently use up three magic wishes while they argue.   4–6

Indian and Pakistani

BROWN, MARCIA. *Once a Mouse,* ill. by author. Scribner's, 1961. The timid mouse was changed by a kindly hermit into a cat, a dog, and then a tiger who became so cruel he had to be punished. Caldecott Medal.   5–8

GRAY, JOHN E. B. *India's Tales and Legends,* ill. by Joan Kiddell-Monroe. Walck, 1961. Distinguished retellings of India's rich lore will appeal to older children.   11 up

HITCHCOCK, PATRICIA. *The King Who Rides a Tiger and Other Folk Tales from Nepal,* ill. by Lillian Sader. Parnassus, 1966. A dozen colorful, varied tales, retold in a light and graceful style.   9–11

JACOBS, JOSEPH, ed. *Indian Fairy Tales,* ill. by J. D. Batten. Putnam, 1969. Like Jacobs's other collections, these stories are selected from manuscript sources. They also throw light on fable and folktale origins.   9–12

Irish

COLUM, PADRAIC. *The King of Ireland's Son,* ill. by Willy Pogány. Macmillan, 1921, 1967. Seven Irish folk tales about a brave young royal lad.   10–12

DANAHER, KEVIN. *Folktales of the Irish Countryside,* ill. by Harold Berson. White, 1970. Fourteen tales heard by the author from six storytellers. Delightful to read alone or aloud, and a good source for storytellers.   10–12

JACOBS, JOSEPH. *Munachar and Manachar: An Irish Story,* ill. by Anne Rockwell. T. Crowell, 1970. The cumulation and the nonsense humor are appealing. Good for storytelling or reading aloud.   5–7

————, ed. *Celtic Fairy Tales,* ill. by John D. Batten. Putnam, 1892.

————, ed. *More Celtic Fairy Tales,* ill. by John D. Batten. Putnam, n.d. Jacobs includes Welsh, Scottish, Cornish, and Irish in his two Celtic collections. His copious notes are of great value.   9–12

MACMANUS, SEUMAS. *Hibernian Nights,* ill. by Paul Kennedy. Macmillan, 1963. The "last of the great Irish storytellers" compiled this rich collection of twenty-two of his favorite tales chosen from his earlier books.   11 up

O'FAOLAIN, EILEEN. *Irish Sagas and Folk-Tales,* ill. by Joan Kiddell-Monroe. Walck, 1954. This distinguished collection contains epic tales and folk tales to delight both reader and storyteller.   10–14

O'SHEA, PAT, ad. *Finn MacCool and the Small Men of Deeds,* ill. by Stephen Lavis. Holiday House, 1987. The Irish hero Finn MacCool gets involved with eight small magical men while rescuing the king's kidnapped children.   9–11

SHUTE, LINDA. *Clever Tom and the Leprechaun,* ill. by author. Lothrop, 1988. Tom Fitzpatrick catches a leprechaun and tries to wrangle a treasure out of him, but Tom loses the upper hand once he turns his back.   5–7

Italian

BASILE, GIAMBATTISTA. *Petrosinella: A Neopolitan Rapunzel,* ad. from the translation by John Edward Taylor, ill. by Diane Stanley. Warne, 1981. An interesting variant of "Rapunzel" with luxuriantly colored, sensitive paintings. 8–10

CALVINO, ITALO, comp. *Italian Folktales,* tr. by George Martin. Harcourt, 1980. 10 up

DE PAOLA, TOMIE, ad. *Strega Nona: An Old Tale Retold,* ill. by adapter. Prentice, 1975. 7–8

HAVILAND, VIRGINIA, ad. *Favorite Fairy Tales Told in Italy,* ill. by Evaline Ness. Little, 1965. 8–10

JAGENDORF, M.A. *The Priceless Cats and Other Italian Folk Stories,* ill. by Gioia Fiamenghi. Vanguard, 1956. An attractive and gay collection for the children's own reading. 10–13

Japanese

MCALPINE, HELEN and WILLIAM, comps. *Japanese Tales and Legends,* retold by the McAlpines, ill. by Joan Kiddell-Monroe. Walck, 1959. A choice selection of folklore, legends, and epic tales. 10–14

MOSEL, ARLENE, ad. *The Funny Little Woman,* ill. by Blair Lent. Dutton, 1972. Caldecott Medal. 5–8

SNYDER, DIANNE, ad. *The Boy of the Three-Year Nap,* ill. by Allen Say. Houghton, 1988. A lazy boy's plan to get rich is improved upon by his mother, who helps him win a beautiful bride and a job. 5–7

STAMM, CLAUS, ed. *Three Strong Women: A Tall Tale from Japan,* ill. by Kazue Mizumura. Viking, 1962. A sturdy girl, her mother, and her grandmother train a cocky young wrestler to new heights of strength for a court performance. 8–11

UCHIDA, YOSHIKO. *The Dancing Kettle and Other Japanese Folk Tales,* retold, ill. by Richard C. Jones. Harcourt, 1949. Fourteen folk tales, some of them familiar, many of them new, make this a welcome addition to folklore collections. 9–12

————. *The Magic Listening Cap: More Folk Tales from Japan,* ill. by author. Harcourt, 1955. This second collection is illustrated with the distinctive simplicity characteristic of Japanese art. 9–12

————. *The Two Foolish Cats,* ill. by Margot Zemach. McElderry, 1987. Two cats ask a monkey to judge which of their rice cakes is largest, and the trickster makes the cakes equal by eating them both. 5–7

WINTHROP, ELIZABETH. *Journey to the Bright Kingdom,* ill. by Charles Mikolaycak. Holiday, 1979. The blind wife of a ferryman is granted a visit to the legendary kingdom of Kakure-sato where she is able to gaze on her daughter for the first time. 8–10

YAGAWA, SUMIKO. *The Crane Wife,* tr. from the Japanese by Katherine Paterson, ill. by Suekichi Akaba. Morrow, 1981. Softly colored ink paintings bring a romantic aura to this smooth translation of a familiar folk tale. 8–10

Latin American

AARDEMA, VERNA, tr. *The Riddle of the Drum: A Tale from Tizapan, Mexico,* ill. by Tony Chen. Four Winds, 1979. A traditional Mexican folk tale, illustrated with bright paintings, about the quest of a prince. 5–8

BIERHORST, JOHN, ed. *The Hungry Woman: Myths and Legends of the Aztecs,* ill. by Aztec artists of the sixteenth century. Morrow, 1984. An important collection of creation myths and fierce legends about the founding and destruction of Mexico, all drawn from sixteenth-century Aztec narratives recorded shortly after the Spanish Conquest. 9 up

————. *The Monkey's Haircut and Other Stories Told by the Maya,* ill. by Robert Andrews Parker. Morrow, 1986. A fine collection of stories has notes that make it useful also for students of folklore. 11–14

CARTER, DOROTHY SHARP, ad. *The Enchanted Orchard: And Other Folktales of Central America,* ill. by W. T. Mars. Harcourt, 1973. 10–12

FINGER, CHARLES J. *Tales from Silver Lands.* Doubleday, 1924. The author gathered these outstanding folk tales from the Indians during his South American travels. Newbery Medal. 10–14

JAGENDORF, M. A., and R. S. BOGGS. *The King of the Mountains: A Treasury of Latin American Folk Stories,* ill. by Carybé. Vanguard, 1960. More than fifty tales, listed by country of origin. 10–14

Norwegian

ASBJÖRNSEN, PETER C., and JÖRGEN MOE. *East o' the Sun and West o' the Moon,* ill. by Hedvig Collin. Macmillan, 1953. An attractive edition of a title which first appeared twenty-five years earlier. Based on the Dasent translation. 10–14

————. *East o' the Sun and West o' the Moon,* ill. by Kay Nielsen. Doubleday, 1922. Fifteen favorite stories with highly imaginative illustrations. 10–14

————. *Norwegian Folk Tales* (see Adult References, this chapter). 10–13

————. *The Squire's Bride,* ill. by Marcia Sewall. Atheneum, 1975. A hilarious tale enhanced by comic black-and-white pencil drawings. 8–10

_____. *The Three Billy Goats Gruff*, ill. by Marcia Brown. Harcourt, 1957. A favorite folk tale appears in brightly colored picture-book format.   4–7

BOOSS, CLAIRE, ed. *Scandinavian Folk and Fairy Tales.* Crown, 1984.   9–11

CHRISTIANSEN, REIDAR T., ed. *Folktales of Norway*, tr. by Pat Shaw Iversen. Univ. of Chicago Pr., 1964. (*Folktales of the World* series)   10 up

D'AULAIRE, INGRI and EDGAR. *Trolls*, ill. by authors. Doubleday, 1972.   8–10

JONES, GWYN. *Scandinavian Legends and Folk Tales*, ill. by Joan Kiddell-Monroe. Walck, 1956. Another Oxford contribution to folk-tale collections, this contains several of the familiar stories. Others are hero tales and unusual examples of folklore told with humor and impressive art.   8–12

Polish

BORSKI, LUCIA M., and KATE B. MILLER. *The Jolly Tailor, and Other Fairy Tales*, ill. by Kazimir Klephacki. McKay, 1957. Reissued after many years, this collection translated from the Polish offers fine material for reading and storytelling.   9–12

DOMANSKA, JANINA. *King Krakus and the Dragon*, ill. by author. Greenwillow, 1979. A traditional tale about a humble shoemaker's apprentice who finds a way to slay a dragon is illustrated with stylized, geometric paintings in lavish colors.   5–8

HAVILAND, VIRGINIA, ad. *Favorite Fairy Tales Told in Poland*, ill. by Felix Hoffmann. Little, 1963. Six tales are retold and illustrated here. Large-print format appeals to younger readers.   8–10

PELLOWSKI, ANNE. *The Nine Crying Dolls*, ill. by Charles Mikolaycak. Philomel, 1980. Papercut collage pictures illustrate this brisk tale about an unusual remedy for a crying baby.   5–8

SINGER, ISAAC BASHEVIS. *When Shlemiel Went to Warsaw: And Other Stories*, tr. by author and Elizabeth Shub, ill. by Margot Zemach. Farrar, 1968. Eight stories, some based on traditional Jewish tales. The cadence of the writing is especially evident when read aloud. Good for storytelling.   10 up

_____. *Zlateh the Goat*, tr. by author and Elizabeth Shub, ill. by Maurice Sendak. Harper, 1966. Seven tales based on middle-European Jewish folk material, told and illustrated with distinction.   10–12

ZAJDLER, ZOE, comp. *Polish Fairy Tales*, ill. by Hazel Cook. Follett, 1968. A more extensive collection than the Borski or Haviland collections. Good for storytelling or independent reading.   9–11

Russian

AFANASYEV, ALEXANDER NIKOLAEVICH. *Russian Folk Tales*, ill. by Ivan Bilibin, tr. by Robert Chandler. Shambhala/Random, 1980. Reproductions of Bilibin's artwork, with its Slavic folk art motifs, decorate this delightful collection of seven classic Russian tales.   9–11

DANIELS, GUY, tr. *Foma the Terrible: A Russian Folktale*, ill. by Imero Gobbato. Delacorte, 1970. A funnier Russian noodlehead there never was. Adapted from the Afanasyev collection.   5–8

DOWNING, CHARLES. *Russian Tales and Legends*, ill. by Joan Kiddell-Monroe. Walck, 1957. Epic, folk, and fairy tales gathered from many areas of Russia.   11 up

GINSBURG, MIRRA, tr. *How Wilka Went to Sea*, ed. by the translator, ill. by Charles Mikolaycak. Crown, 1975. Finno-Ugric and Turkic tales abounding in witches, giants, and wizards.   9–11

_____, tr. *The Lazies: Tales of the Peoples of Russia*, ed. by translator, ill. by Marian Parry. Macmillan, 1973. Fifteen humorous tales.   8–10

HODGES, MARGARET, ad. *The Little Humpbacked Horse*, ill. by Chris Conover. Farrar, 1980. Ivan the Fool becomes Ivan the Tsar in this colloquial retelling of a Russian tale.   8–10

HOGROGIAN, NONNY. *The Cat Who Loved to Sing*, ill. by au. Knopf, 1988. A cumulative tale in which a cat starts trading a thorn in its foot for a needle and ends up with a mandolin to accompany its songs.   3–5

KISMARIC, CAROLE, ad. *The Rumor of Pavel and Paali: A Ukranian Folktale*, ill. by Charles Mikolaycak. Harper, 1988. Twin brothers, one good and one evil, wager to prove which of their characteristics is the more powerful.   8–10

LANGTON, JANE, ad. *The Hedgehog Boy: A Latvian Folktale*, ill. by Ilse Plume. Harper, 1985. A hedgehog boy, the magical son of a childless couple, uses his wit to marry the king's youngest daughter.   5–8

MIKOLAYCAK, CHARLES, ad. *Baboushka*, ill. by author. Holiday, 1984. Stunning paintings illustrate the Christmas legend about a woman who refused to follow the three kings.   5–8

MORTON, MIRIAM, ed. *A Harvest of Russian Children's Literature.* Univ. of Calif. Pr., 1967.   All ages

PEVEAR, RICHARD, ad. *Mister Cat-and-a-Half*, ill. by Robert Rayevsky. Macmillan, 1986. A stray cat makes his reputation among the fierce animals of the forest by relying on his fox bride's ability to tell an imposing tale.   5–7

PUSHKIN, ALEXANDER. *The Tale of the Czar Sultan*, tr. by Patricia Lowe, ill. by I. Bilibin. T. Crowell, 1975.   8–10

————. *The Tale of the Golden Cockerel*, tr. by Alessandra Pellizone, ill. by I. Bilibin. T. Crowell, 1975. 8–10

RANSOME, ARTHUR. *Old Peter's Russian Tales*, ill. by Dmitri Mitrokhim. Nelson, 1917, 1976. This is the teacher's most practical source for the Russian tales—in admirable style for telling, reading aloud, or dramatizing. 8–12

————, ad. *The Fool of the World and the Flying Ship: A Russian Tale*, ill. by Uri Shulevitz. Farrar, 1968. A retelling of a Russian tale is brought to life with these vigorous and colorful illustrations. Caldecott Medal. 5–8

RIORDAN, JAMES, ad. *Tales from Tartary*, ill. by Krystyna Turska. Viking, 1979. Warmth and humor distinguish these regional stories from the U.S.S.R. 9–11

ROBBINS, RUTH. *Baboushka and the Three Kings*, ill. by Nicolas Sidjakov. Parnassus, 1960. The familiar Russian folk tale of the selfish old woman and the Wise Men is enhanced by striking modern illustrations. Caldecott Medal. 5–10

WYNDHAM, LEE, comp. *Tales the People Tell in Russia*, ill. by Andrew Antal. Messner, 1970. Ten tales, told with gusto, for which sources are cited in an appended note. Also contains three fables and a short list of proverbs. 8–10

Spanish

BOGGS, RALPH STEELE, and MARY GOULD DAVIS. *The Three Golden Oranges and Other Spanish Folk Tales*, ill. by Emma Brock. McKay, 1936. Stories for older children, romantic and exciting. One remarkable ghost story. 10–12

DAVIS, ROBERT. *Padre Porko*, ill. by Fritz Eichenberg. Holiday, 1958. Padre Porko, the gentlemanly pig, has all the benignancy of the Buddha animals, and a certain mannerly elegance besides. Amusing tales, enhanced by good pen-and-ink sketches. 8–12

DUFF, MAGGIE, ad. *The Princess and the Pumpkin*, ill. by Catherine Stock. Macmillan, 1980. A frothy Majorcan tale-within-a-tale about a princess who is unable to laugh until an old woman relates a strange adventure. 5–8

HAVILAND, VIRGINIA, ad. *Favorite Fairy Tales Told in Spain*, ill. by Barbara Cooney. Little, 1963. Six delightful Spanish tales retold. 8–10

JIMENEZ-LANDI, ANTONIO. *The Treasure of the Muleteer and Other Spanish Tales*, tr. by Paul Blackburn, ill. by Floyd Sowell. Doubleday, 1974. Regional tales which reflect Moorish and Christian traditions. 10–13

VERNON, ADELE, ad. *The Riddle*, ill. by Robert Rayevsky and Vladimir Radunsky. Dodd, 1987. 5–8

Swiss

DUVOISIN, ROGER. *The Three Sneezes and Other Swiss Tales*, ill. by author. Knopf, 1941. Humorous tales, many of which are based on the theme of the stupid fellow who succeeds. 9–12

MÜLLER-GUGGENBÜHL, FRITZ. *Swiss-Alpine Folk-Tales*, tr. by Katharine Potts, ill. by Joan Kiddell-Monroe. Walck, 1958. These tales are a distinguished collection of national folklore in the Oxford series of Myths and Legends. 10–14

United States and Canada: Indian and Eskimo Tales

BAKER, BETTY. *And Me, Coyote!*, ill. by Maria Horvath. Macmillan, 1982. A shrewd coyote tries to take credit for the deeds of his brother, a World Maker, in this story based on California Indian creation myths. 5–8

BAYLOR, BYRD, comp. *And It Is Still That Way: Legends Told by Arizona Indian Children*. Scribner's, 1976. Stories from several native American tribes, some told with childlike directness, others with a true sense of the storyteller's cadence. 7–9

BIERHORST, JOHN. *The Naked Bear: Folktales of the Iroquois*. Morrow, 1987. 10–12

COURLANDER, HAROLD. *People of the Short Blue Corn: Tales and Legends of the Hopi Indians*, ill. by Enrico Arno. Harcourt, 1970. 9–11

CURTIS, EDWARD S., comp. *The Girl Who Married a Ghost and Other Tales from the North American Indian*, ill. with photos. Four Winds, 1978. Nine folk tales handsomely complemented by Curtis's posed, romantic photographs. 10 up

DEARMOND, DALE, ad. *The Seal Oil Lamp*, ill. by ad. Sierra Club/Little, 1988. Blind little Allugua, left to die by his own people, learns survival from Mouse Woman and gains acceptance back from his Eskimo tribe. 7–10

DE WIT, DOROTHY, ed. *The Talking Stone: An Anthology of Native American Tales and Legends*. Greenwillow, 1979. Tales arranged by region, with tribal sources given, form a varied selection. 10–12

ERDOES, RICHARD, ed. *The Sound of Flutes and Other Indian Legends*, ill. by Paul Goble. Pantheon, 1976. A fine collection of Plains Indian tales, the result of Erdoes's 25 years listening to native American storytellers. 10–12

ESBENSEN, BARBARA JUSTER, ad. *The Star Maiden: An Ojibway Tale*, ill. by Helen K. Davie. Little, 1988. A star maiden leaves the sky, follows a young brave, and finds fulfillment on earth by turning into a water lily.   4–7

FIELD, EDWARD, comp. *Eskimo Songs and Stories,* tr. by the compiler, collected by Knud Rasmussen, ill. by Kiakshuk and Pudlo. Delacorte, 1973. Rhythmic and vigorous, this collection reflects the cultural patterns of the tribes of the Hudson Bay area.   9–12

FRITZ, JEAN. *The Good Giants and the Bad Pukwudgies*, ill. by Tomie dePaola. Putnam, 1982. An entertaining *pourquoi* story based on legends of the Wampanoag Indians of Massachusetts explains how Nantucket and other islands off Cape Cod were formed.   5–8

GILLHAM, CHARLES EDWARD. *Beyond the Clapping Mountains: Eskimo Stories from Alaska*, ill. by Chanimum. Macmillan, 1943. Illustrated by an Eskimo girl, these are unusual and highly imaginative tales.   10–12

GOBLE, PAUL. *Buffalo Woman*, ill. by author. Bradbury, 1984. A handsomely illustrated legend about an Indian's brave quest to rejoin his buffalo wife and child.   9–11

————. *Her Seven Brothers*, ill. by author. Bradbury, 1988.   5–7

————. *Iktomi and the Berries*, ill. by author. Orchard, 1989.   5–8

————, ad. *Iktomi and the Boulder: A Plains Indian Story*, ill. by ad. Orchard/Watts, 1988. Another humorous Iktomi story.   5–8

GRINNELL, GEORGE BIRD, comp. *The Whistling Skeleton: American Indian Tales of the Supernatural*, ed. by John Bierhorst, ill. by Robert Andrew Parker. Four Winds, 1982. Nine supernatural stories from Plains Indian tribes come with an informative editorial preface.   10–12

HARRIS, CHRISTIE. *Mouse Woman and the Mischief-Makers*, ill. by Douglas Tait. Atheneum, 1977. A companion volume to *Mouse Woman and the Vanished Princesses*.   9–11

————. *Once Upon a Totem*, ill. by John Frazer Mills. Atheneum, 1963. Five superb tales of the Indians of the North Pacific.   9–12

————. *The Trouble with Princesses*, ill. by Douglas Tate. Atheneum, 1980. Each of seven tales is prefaced by a comparison between a New World princess and her Old World counterpart.   10–12

HODGES, MARGARET, ad. *The Fire Bringer: A Paiute Indian Legend*, ill. by Peter Parnall. Little, 1972.   8–10

HOUSTON, JAMES. *Kiviok's Magic Journey: An Eskimo Legend*, ill. by author. Atheneum, 1973. A vigorous and dramatic retelling of one of the most popular legends of the Eskimo folk hero.   8–10

MCDERMOTT, GERALD, ad. *Arrow to the Sun: A Pueblo Indian Tale*, ill. by adapter. Viking, 1974. Stylized designs and stunning color effectively complement the story of the Boy who brings the spirit of the Lord of the Sun to his pueblo. Caldecott Medal.   5–8

MACMILLAN, CYRUS. *Glooskap's Country, and Other Indian Tales*, ill. by John A. Hall. Walck, 1956. First published in 1918 as *Canadian Wonder Tales*, this is one of the finest collections of Indian stories available. They range from simple "how" stories to complex and mystical tales of magic, superbly told and illustrated.   8–12

MARTIN, FRAN. *Raven-Who-Sets-Things-Right: Indian Tales of the Northwest Coast*, ill. by Dorothy McEntee. Harper, 1975. Tales of a trickster-creator, smoothly told.   9–10

STEPTOE, JOHN, ad. *The Story of Jumping Mouse*, ill. by ad. Lothrop, 1984. After giving his eyes to a bison and sense of smell to a wolf, Jumping Mouse turns into an eagle in this myth.   5–8

TOYE, WILLIAM, ad. *The Fire Stealers*, ill. by Elizabeth Cleaver. Oxford, 1980. Bright collages by a Canadian artist make a Nanbosho story vivid.   5–7

United States: African-American Tales

BROWN, MARGARET WISE. *Brer Rabbit: Stories from Uncle Remus*, ill. by A. B. Frost. Harper, 1941.   8–10

CHESNUTT, CHARLES W. *Conjure Tales*, retold by Ray Anthony Shepard, ill. by John Ross and Clare Romano. Dutton, 1973. These stories by a black author, first published in 1899, are vigorous and humorous.   10–14

FAULKNER, WILLIAM J. *The Days When the Animals Talked: Black American Folktales and How They Came to Be*, ill. by Troy Howell. Follett, 1977. Dramatic and compellingly told animal tales (the chief character is Brer Rabbit) as well as a series of anecdotes about his days of slavery told by Simon Brown to Faulkner.   10 up

FELTON, HAROLD. *John Henry and His Hammer*, ill. by Aldren Watson. Knopf, 1950.   10–12

HAMILTON, VIRGINIA, ad. *The People Could Fly: American Black Folk Tales*, ill. by Leo and Diane Dillon. Knopf, 1985.   9–11

HARRIS, JOEL CHANDLER. *Brer Rabbit*, ill. by A. B. Frost. Harper, 1941.

————. *Complete Tales of Uncle Remus*, ed. by Richard Chase. Houghton, 1955.

————. *Further Tales of Uncle Remus: The Misadventures of Brer Rabbit, Brer Fox, Brer Wolf, the Doodang, and Other Creatures,* ad. by Julius Lester, ill. by Jerry Pinkney. Dial, 1990.

————. *Jump! The Adventures of Brer Rabbit,* ad. by Van Dyke Parks and Malcolm Jones, ill. by Barry Moser. Harcourt, 1986.   8–10

————. *Jump Again! More Adventures of Brer Rabbit,* ad. by Van Dyke Parks, ill. by Barry Moser. Harcourt, 1987.   8–10

————. *Jump On Over! The Adventures of Brer Rabbit and His Family,* ad. by Van Dyke Parks, ill. by Barry Moser. Harcourt, 1989.   8–10

————. *The Tales of Uncle Remus: The Adventures of Brer Rabbit,* ad. by Julius Lester, ill. by Jerry Pinkney. Dial, 1987.   10–12

————. *More Tales of Uncle Remus: Further Adventures of Brer Rabbit, His Friends, Enemies, and Others,* ad. by Julius Lester, ill. by Jerry Pinkney. Dial, 1988.   10–12

KEATS, EZRA JACK. *John Henry: An American Legend,* ill. by author. Pantheon, 1965.   5–8

REES, ENNIS. *Brer Rabbit and His Tricks,* ill. by Edward Gorey. W. R. Scott, 1967.   5–8

————. *More of Brer Rabbit's Tricks,* ill. by Edward Gorey. W. R. Scott, 1968.   5–8

SANFIELD, STEVE, ad. *The Adventures of High John the Conqueror,* ill. by John Ward. Orchard, 1989.   9–11

————, ad. *A Natural Man: The True Story of John Henry,* ill. by Peter Thorton. Godine, 1986.   9–11

United States: Variants of European Tales

CHASE, RICHARD, ed. *Grandfather Tales,* ill. by Berkeley Williams, Jr. Houghton, 1948.   9–12

————. *The Jack Tales,* ill. by Berkeley Williams, Jr. Houghton, 1943. American versions of old-world tales from the Cumberlands and the Smokies.   9–12

FRENCH, FIONA. *Snow White in New York,* ill. by author. Oxford, 1987. In this Art Deco spoof, the Snow White story is transplanted in modern day New York; the heroine's guardians are seven jazz musicians and her true love is a handsome society reporter.   9–10

JAGENDORF, MORITZ. *New England Bean Pot: American Folk Stories to Read and Tell,* ill. by Donald McKay. Vanguard, 1948. Folk tales of six New England states told with zest and humor. Other titles in this regional series are: *Sand in the Bag and Other Folk Stories of Ohio, Indiana and Illinois,* ill. by John Moment. Vanguard, 1952; *Upstate, Downstate: Folk Stories of the Middle Atlantic States,* ill. by Howard Simon. Vanguard, 1949; *Folk Stories of the South,* ill. by Michael Parks. Vanguard, 1973.   10–14

ROSS, TONY, ad. *Lazy Jack,* ill. by ad. Dial, 1986. The watercolor illustrations complement the folk tale of a boy who follows his mother's instructions literally—and always one day late.   4–6

SAWYER, RUTH. *Journey Cake, Ho!,* ill. by Robert McCloskey. Viking, 1953. Mountain folk-tale version of *The Pancake.* Lively illustrations make this an attractive picture book.   6–10

United States: Tall Tales

BLAIR, WALTER. *Tall Tale America: A Legendary History of Our Humorous Heroes,* ill. by Glen Rounds. Coward, 1944.   10–14

BOWMAN, JAMES CLOYD. *Mike Fink,* ill. by Leonard Everett Fisher. Little, 1957. Mike Fink was one of the greatest legendary riverboatmen, and his adventures are related in tall-tale tradition.   11 up

DEWEY, ARIANE. *Gib Morgan, Oilman,* ill. by author. Greenwillow, 1987. Elements of Paul Bunyan are transplanted to the south in the character of Gib Morgan, the oil-drilling superman.   7–9

FELTON, HAROLD W. *Bowleg Bill, Seagoing Cowpuncher,* ill. by William Moyers. Prentice, 1957. Tall-tale nonsense about a cowboy who solves his problems in his own cowboy way.   10 up

KELLOGG, STEVEN, ad. *Paul Bunyan,* ill. by ad. Morrow, 1984. The familiar Paul Bunyan story is given a fresh look with busy, detail-crowded illustrations.   5–8

————, ad. *Pecos Bill,* ill. by ad. Morrow, 1986. The legend of Pecos Bill is adapted into one story line and illustrated in Kellogg's distinctive style.   5–8

LENT, BLAIR. *John Tabor's Ride,* ill. by author. Atlantic, 1966. A tall tale based on a New England legend about a shipwrecked sailor. The appeal of the telling is in the exaggeration, the fantastic situations, and the abundance of salty marine terms.   5–8

MCCLOSKEY, ROBERT. *Burt Dow, Deep-Water Man: A Tale of the Sea in the Classic Tradition,* ill. by author. Viking, 1963. Jonah's story pales by comparison with this exuberant tall tale.   5–8

MALCOLMSON, ANNE. *Yankee Doodle's Cousins,* ill. by Robert McCloskey. Houghton, 1941. This is one of the finest collections of real and mythical heroes of the United States.   10–14

PURDY, CAROL. *Iva Dunnit and the Big Wind,* ill. by Steven Kellogg. Dial, 1985. Tough Iva Dunnit and her six children depend on each other while battling the West's legendary natural elements.   5–8

ROUNDS, GLEN. *Mr. Yowder and the Steamboat,* ill. by author. Holiday, 1977. A steamboat gets stuck under an elevated track in Manhattan.   8–11

————, ad. *The Morning the Sun Refused to Rise: An Original Paul Bunyan Tale,* ill. by ad. Holiday House, 1984. When a great blizzard freezes the earth's axis, the King of Sweden calls in Paul Bunyan.   9–11

SACHS, MARILYN. *Fleet-Footed Florence,* ill. by Charles Robinson. Doubleday, 1981. Two sports rivals marry and live happily ever after in this nonsexist baseball story strongly flavored with tall-tale humor.   5–7

SCHWARTZ, ALVIN, comp. *Kickle Snifters and Other Fearsome Critters Collected from American Folklore.* ill. by Glen Rounds. Lippincott, 1976. All of the "fearsome critters" are imaginary beasts of the tall-tale variety, and this is a list of illustrated definitions, with notes on sources included at the back of the book.   8–10

————, comp. *Unriddling: All Sorts of Riddles to Puzzle Your Guessery,* ill. by Sue Truesdell. Lippincott, 1983. A beguiling and substantive collection of riddles, many based on traditional American humor.   9 up

SHAPIRO, IRWIN. *Heroes in American Folklore,* ill. by Donald McKay and James Daugherty. Messner, 1962. Five tall-tale heroes include Casey Jones, Joe Magarac, John Henry, Steamboat Bill, and Old Stormalong.   9–12

SHEPHARD, ESTHER. *Paul Bunyan,* ill. by Rockwell Kent. Harcourt, 1941. The most complete edition of these tales, this book also has Rockwell Kent's superb pictures.   10–14

STOUTENBURG, ADRIEN. *American Tall Tales,* ill. by Richard M. Powers. Viking, 1966. Eight stories, each about a tall-tale hero.   9–11

Other Countries

AIKEN, JOAN. *The Kingdom Under the Sea and Other Stories,* ill. by Jan Pienkowski. Jonathan Cape, 1979. Eleven folk tales from eastern Europe retold with vigor and wit.   10–12

BATES, DAISY, comp. *Tales Told to Kabbarli,* retold by Barbara Ker Wilson, ill. by Harold Thomas. Crown, 1972. Daisy Bates devoted many years to recording aboriginal lore in Australia.   10 up

BELPRÉ, PURA. *Once in Puerto Rico,* ill. by Christine Price. Warne, 1973.

★ ————. *Perez and Martina,* ill. by Carlos Sanchez. Warne, 1961. Tales of Puerto Rico.   9–11

BERNDT, CATHERINE H., ad. and tr. *Land of the Rainbow Snake: Aboriginal Children's Stories and Songs from Western Arnhem Land,* ill. by Djoki Yunupingu. Collins, 1983. A valuable collection of tales and songs gathered by an anthropologist from women aborigines.   9–11

BERSON, HAROLD, ad. *Kassim's Shoes,* ill. by author. Crown, 1977.   5–8

BRYAN, ASHLEY, ad. *The Dancing Granny,* ill. by author. Atheneum, 1977. Based on a folk tale from the Antilles, this pits Granny Anika (who feels compelled to dance when she hears music) against Spider Ananse (who sings and steals her vegetables as she dances).   5–8

CARPENTER, FRANCES. *The Elephant's Bathtub: Wonder Tales from the Far East,* ill. by Hans Guggenheim. Doubleday, 1962. Burma, Cambodia, Malaya, Vietnam, and other lands of the Far East are represented here.   11–14

CARTER, DOROTHY SHARP, ad. *Greedy Mariani: And Other Folktales of the Antilles,* ill. by Trina Schart Hyman. Atheneum, 1974.   9–11

COURLANDER, HAROLD. *The Tiger's Whisker and Other Tales and Legends from Asia and the Pacific,* ill. by Enrico Arno. Harcourt, 1959. More humorous and philosophic tales gathered by a folklorist who has made a significant contribution to the lore of faraway lands.   9–13

CURCIJA-PRODANOVIC, NADA. *Yugoslav Folk-Tales,* ill. by Joan Kiddell-Monroe. Walck, 1957.   10–14

DEUTSCH, BABETTE, and AVRAHM YARMOLINSKY. *Tales of Faraway Folk,* ill. by Irena Lorentowicz. Harper, 1952. A unique collection of tales from Baltic, Russian, and Asiatic lands.   9–12

EL-SHAMY, HASAN, ed. and tr. *Folktales of Egypt.* Univ. of Chicago Pr., 1980. An erudite foreword is followed by a varied selection and extensive roles.   11 up

○ GINSBURG, MIRRA, ad. *The Chinese Mirror,* ill. by Margot Zemach. Harcourt, 1988. The soft colors and sly humor of the illustrations echo the quiet, amusing tone of a Korean tale in which a villager and his family mistake a mirror for a continually changing picture.   5–8

GRAHAM, GAIL B., ad. *The Beggar in the Blanket: And Other Vietnamese Tales,* ill. by Brigitte Bryan. Dial, 1970. Eight folk tales translated from French sources in Vietnam.   9–11

HELGADOTTIR, GUDRUN. *Flumbra: An Icelandic Folktale,* tr. by Christopher Sanders, ill. by Brian Pilkington. Carolrhoda, 1986. When an ugly giantess tries to take her eight revolting sons on a journey to meet their distant father, they all turn to stones in the morning sun.   5–8

● HIRSCH, MARILYN, ad. *Joseph Who Loved the Sabbath,* ill. by Devis Grebu. Viking, 1986. Honest Joseph's pious ways are sneered at by rich landowner Sorab, until, in a twist of fate, Joseph gains the wealth that Sorab loses.   4–7

KEELY, H. H., and CHRISTINE PRICE, ads. *The City of the Dagger: And Other Tales from Burma,* ill. by Christine Price. Warne, 1971. Folklore and legends are mingled in intricate tales, many of which concern hero-kings of the past.   10–12

KELSEY, ALICE GEER. *Once the Hodja,* ill. by Frank Dobias. McKay, 1943. Twenty-four tales from Turkey filled with humor and simple wisdom.

————. *Once the Mullah,* ill. by Kurt Werth. McKay, 1954. Stories told by Mullah give insight into Persian life and folklore.   9–12

OLENIUS, ELSA, comp. *Great Swedish Fairy Tales,* tr. by Holger Lundbergh, ill. by John Bauer. Delacorte, 1973.   9–11

PARKER, K. LANGLOH. *Australian Legendary Tales,* selected and ed. by H. Drake-Brockman, ill. by Elizabeth Durack. Viking, 1966. A selection of Australian aboriginal tales first published at the turn of the century.   11–14

• SCHWARTZ, HOWARD, ad. *Elijah's Violin & Other Jewish Fairy Tales,* ill. by Linda Heller. Harper, 1983. An impressive collection of tales that combine traditional fairy tale themes and motifs with legends and folklore of Jewish oral tradition.   11 up

SEROS, KATHLEEN, ad. *Sun and Moon: Fairy Tales from Korea,* ill. by Norman Sibley and Robert Krause. Hollym, 1982. Brightly colored paintings in stylized design accompany seven Korean folk tales, including some unusual variants of European tales.   8–10

SHERLOCK, PHILIP and HILARY. *Ears and Tails and Common Sense.* T. Crowell, 1974. Stories from the Caribbean told with verve and humor.   9–11

• SINGER, ISAAC BASHEVIS. *The Golem,* ill. by Uri Shulevitz. Farrar, 1982. A masterful, solemnly illustrated retelling of the legend of the golem, the huge clay man created by a rabbi that becomes a destructive monster in his quest to be human.   11 up

TASHJIAN, VIRGINIA A., ed. *Once There Was and Was Not,* based on stories by H. Toumanian, ill. by Nonny Hogrogian. Little, 1966. Seven Armenian folk tales, many with familiar elements, beautifully illustrated. A pleasure to read aloud and a good source for storytelling.   9–11

————, ed. *Three Apples Fell from Heaven: Armenian Tales Retold,* ill. by Nonny Hogrogian. Little, 1971.   9–11

TRAVERS, PAMELA L., ad. *Two Pairs of Shoes,* ill. by Leo and Diane Dillon. Viking, 1980. Two stories from the Middle East are coupled with ornately detailed pictures reminiscent of Persian miniatures.   9–11

VAN WOERKOM, DOROTHY O., ad. *Abu Ali: Three Tales of the Middle East,* ill. by Harold Berson. Macmillan, 1976. Three short tales for the primary grades reader; in two Abu Ali is outwitted; in a third, he outwits the friends who think they've outwitted him.   7–8

VO-DINH, ad. *The Toad Is the Emperor's Uncle: Animal Folktales from Viet-Nam,* ill. by ad. Doubleday, 1970. Stories that reflect humor as well as ethical principle.   9–11

WOLKSTEIN, DIANE, comp. *The Magic Orange Tree and Other Haitian Folktales,* ill. by Elsa Henriquez. Knopf, 1978. A collection distinguished for its humor and variety.   10 up

Chapter Seven

Fables, Myths, and Epics

Fables, Parables, Proverbs

Fables, myths, and epics, like the ballads and folk tales, are a part of the great stream of folklore. While they are not generally so popular with children as the folk tales, they have made an equally important contribution to our literary heritage. The fables have affected our attitudes toward moral and ethical problems. The myths and the epics have become a part of our everyday symbols in both writing and speech. Rarely, in today's literature, can one find heroes like Robin Hood or Finn MacCool or King Arthur to stir young people's imaginations. Fables, myths, and epics sustain children by helping them to meet some of the critical needs associated with childhood. The national epics and hero tales provide inspiration and vicarious satisfaction in the need to achieve competence. The language of well-told myths and epics satisfies the need for beauty and order. Fables, myths, and epics give children a sense of morality that may lead to a respect for the rules of social order. These three types of literature, while fundamentally different from each other, have in common their strong moral flavor.

Fables are brief narratives which take abstract ideas of behavior—good or bad, wise or foolish—and attempt to make them concrete and striking enough to be understood and remembered. The chief actor in most fables is an animal or inanimate object which behaves like a human being and has one dominant trait. Whether the characters are humans or beasts, they remain coldly impersonal and engage in a single significant act which teaches a moral lesson. These are the essential elements of the true fable.

Fables have a teasing likeness to proverbs and parables. All three embody universal truths in brief, striking form; and all three are highly intellectual exercises, as exact as an equation. Of the three, the *proverb* is the most highly condensed commentary on human folly or wisdom. It tells no story but presents a bit of wisdom succinctly:

A soft answer turneth away wrath: but grievous words stir up anger. (Proverbs 15:1)
Better is a dry morsel and quietness therewith, than a house full of feasting with strife.
(Proverbs 17:1)

It is interesting to find many examples in *Japanese Proverbs* by Rokuo Okada that are amazingly like Biblical proverbs in their implications:

He who wants to shoot the general must first shoot his horse.
A cornered mouse bites the cat.[1]

Perhaps the fable grew out of the proverb, to dramatize its pithy wisdom in story form.

The *parable* is like the fable in that it tells a brief story from which a moral or spiritual truth may be inferred. But its characters, unlike the personified animals or objects of most fables, are generally human beings, like the Wise and Foolish Virgins, or the Prodigal Son, or the Good Samaritan. If the story is told in terms of animals or objects, they are never personified but remain strictly themselves. That is, the seed that falls upon rocky ground has nothing to say for itself, and the house that was built upon sand goes down in the flood strictly a house. The parables use people or things as object lessons.

There are obvious differences among the stories discussed in the following pages under *Fable Collections*. Some are typical fables, some are parables, others resemble folk tales, and many contain maxims or proverbs. All of them, however, embody moral or spiritual wisdom.

From "The North Wind and the Sun" from *Aesop's Fables*, illustrated by Arthur Rackham.

Fable Collections

If you say "fables" to English-speaking children, they think at once of *Aesop's Fables*. To French children, La Fontaine and "fables" are inseparably associated, and so in the Orient it is *The Panchatantra, The Fables of Bidpai*, or the *Jatakas*. These major collections of fables, while resembling each other, also show striking differences.

Aesop's Fables

Some modern scholars doubt whether Aesop really existed. G. K. Chesterton suggests that he

may be as completely fictitious a character as that other slave, Uncle Remus, who also told beast tales. But his name and fame persist through one edition of the fables after another. Aesop is said to have lived in Greece between 620 and 560 B.C. and is thought to have been a Samian slave. Because free speech under the Tyrants was risky business, Aesop is supposed to have used the fables for political purposes, protecting himself and veiling his opinions behind the innuendos of these little stories. All we know is that the picturesque legends about Aesop have survived with his name.

Translated into Latin in the first and third centuries, the Aesop fables became the textbooks of the medieval schools. In Latin they found their way into England, France, and Germany, were translated into several languages, and were among the first books to be printed by Caxton when he started his famous press in England. Evidently there was infiltration from other sources. Joseph Jacobs said he could mention at least seven hundred fables ascribed to Aesop, although the first known

---

[1]From *Japanese Proverbs* by Rokuo Okada. Copyright by the Japan Travel Bureau. In *Japan Times Weekly*, December 1, 1962.

collection of them, made by Demetrius of Phalerum about 320 B.C., contained only about two hundred. Since India, like Greece, had long used the beast tale for teaching purposes, undoubtedly some of the Indian fables gravitated, in the course of time, to the Aesop collection. From whatever source they came, once included in Aesop they assumed the Aesop form, which is now regarded as the pure fable type. It is a brief story with inanimate objects or animals most frequently serving as the leading characters, and with the single action of the narrative pointing to an obvious moral lesson. James Reeves in his *Fables from Aesop* points out that the virtues which Aesop praises are not the heroic ones but rather "the peasant virtues of discretion, prudence, moderation and forethought. . . . That is why Aesop . . . has always had the affection and regard of ordinary people."

The Panchatantra

The Panchatantra, meaning "five books," was composed in Kashmir about 200 B.C.,[2] and is the oldest known collection of Indian fables. *The Hitopadesa,* or Book of Good Counsel, is considered only another version of *The Panchatantra,*[3] and still another is called *The Fables of Bidpai.* These collections were translated into Persian, Arabic, Latin, and many other languages. In the Latin version the tales became popular throughout medieval Europe.

After the extreme condensation of Aesop, the stories of *The Panchatantra* seem long and involved. They are a textbook on "the wise conduct of life," intricate stories-within-stories, and are interrupted with philosophical verses so numerous that the thread of the story is almost forgotten. Some of these poems are sixteen or twenty verses long, but the quatrain is the more usual type:

A friend in need is a friend indeed,
Although of different caste;
The whole world is your eager friend
So long as riches last.

[2]*The Panchatantra,* translated by Arthur W. Ryder. University of Chicago Press, 1925, p. 3.

[3]Joseph Gaer, *The Fables of India.* Little Brown, 1955, p. 53.

Make friends, make friends, however strong
Or weak they be;
Recall the captive elephants
That mice set free.[4]

These verses are summaries of the stories which seem more like folk tales than fables. On the whole, *The Panchatantra* is for adults rather than children.

The *Jatakas*

Another collection of ancient Indian fables is the group called the *Jatakas.* The time of their origin is not definitely known. They were in existence in the fifth century A.D., but carvings illustrating Jataka stories have been found which were made as early as the second or third centuries B.C.

Jatakas is a Buddhist name for stories concerning the rebirths of Gautama Buddha, who, according to tradition, was reincarnated many

[4]*The Panchatantra,* pp. 5, 273.

times in the forms of different animals until he became at last Buddha, the Enlightened One. These beast tales, then, are really about a man living briefly as an animal, consorting with other animals, and deriving from these experiences certain ethical lessons.

Joseph Gaer tells us that there are two or three thousand of these stories. Generally, the introduction and body of the tale are in prose, but the conclusions are often verses. Comparatively few of them are suitable for children and then only with considerable adaptation; one such is Nancy De Roin's *Jataka Tales,* a selective edition of simplified fables. Joseph Gaer's versions, in *The Fables of India,* keep close to the original form. Some Jatakas resemble parables from the Bible. Still others are like short folk tales with self-evident morals.

The Fables of La Fontaine

In the twelfth century, Marie de France introduced and popularized the fable in France.

From *The Fables of India* by Joseph Gaer, illustrated by Randy Monk.

Others followed her lead, but Jean de La Fontaine (1621–1695), a contemporary of Charles Perrault, made the fable so completely and gracefully his own that the French coined a word for him, *le fablier,* "the fable-teller." Adapted from an eighteenth century music book for children, *The Frogs Who Wanted a King and Other Songs from La Fontaine* contains Edward Smith's choices of fables; the songs are illustrated with brisk, humorous line drawings and handsome watercolors by Margot Zemach.

La Fontaine was a skilled poet and wrote his fables in graceful verses, which are delightful to read and easy to memorize. There are charming descriptions of birds and beasts and of the beautiful Champagne countryside where La Fontaine grew up. The courtier and the man of the world show themselves in the shrewd appraisals of character and the worldly philosophy that permeate the fables:

Now, as everyone knows, white paws do not grow on wolves.

My dear Mr. Crow, learn from this how every flatterer lives at the expense of anybody who will listen to him. This lesson is well worth the loss of a cheese to you.[5]

Although the fables were written in verse form, translations such as this one have generally emerged as prose, faithful to the message, if not the cadence.

La Fontaine used for his sources the Latin versions of Aesop and *The Fables of Bidpai,* and the versions of his predecessor, Marie de France. In spite of the verse form and the characteristic bits of philosophy, these fables of La Fontaine are closer to the Aesop pattern than to the tales from India. They maintain the brevity, the predominant use of animal characters, and, above all, the single striking episode which points to the moral.

Modern Editions of Fables

The fables are both didactic and universal; their universality makes their didacticism bearable, if not enjoyable. Children are made un-

[5]From *The Fables of La Fontaine,* translated by Margaret W. Brown. Harper, 1940, pp. 6, 8, and 19.

From *Chanticleer and the Fox* from *The Canterbury Tales* by Geoffrey Chaucer, illustrated by Barbara Cooney.

er, the Boy, and the Donkey. Wildsmith has retold and illustrated several other La Fontaine fables in addition to this favorite. There are also some attractive adaptations of fables from India for young children. Notable among them are Marcia Brown's Caldecott Medal book, *Once a Mouse*, an animal fable illustrated by color woodcuts; and Paul Galdone's *The Monkey and the Crocodile*, an adaptation of a Jataka tale.

A collection that has both fables and folk tales is Mirra Ginsburg's vivacious *Three Rolls and One Doughnut: Fables from Russia*. Another source of Russian fables is Ivan Krylov's *Fifteen Fables of Krylov*, in a colloquial translation by Guy Daniels. A delightful single-fable edition is Barbara Cooney's Caldecott Medal book *Chanticleer and the Fox*, based on Geoffrey Chaucer's "The Nun's Priest's Tale" from *The Canterbury Tales*. There are a number of fables in modern dress—a particularly good one is Jean Merrill's *The Black Sheep*, which is far longer than the usual compressed fable form but, in the true spirit of the fable, teaches a lesson about blind conformity.

Myths

comfortable by stories that preach directly, but if they see that the lessons of the fables apply to everyone, they can better appreciate the wisdom and humor of these tales.

There are excellent collections of fables available today. Among these are an illustrated edition of *The Fables of Aesop*, edited by Joseph Jacobs; John Bierhorst's *Doctor Coyote: A Native American Aesop's Fable* by Aztec Indians based on a Spanish edition of Aesop; and Anne Terry White's *Aesop's Fables*. White has retold the stories in an easy, simple style that is especially appropriate for younger children. Also noteworthy is Louis Untermeyer's *Aesop's Fables*, brightly illustrated by Alice and Martin Provensen, in an edition that is humorous and simple enough to read aloud to children as young as six or seven years of age.

The trend to present the fables in a form appropriate for younger children is most obvious in the publication of single-fable editions, such as Mary Calhoun's *Old Man Whickutt's Donkey*, Janet Stevens's *The Town Mouse and the Country Mouse*, and Brian Wildsmith's *The Mill-*

The fables are simple, highly condensed lessons in morality. The myth is far more complicated. It attempts to explain—in complex symbolism —the vital outlines of existence:

(1) cosmic phenomena (e.g., how the earth and sky came to be separated); (2) peculiarities of natural history (e.g., why rain follows the cries or activities of certain birds); (3) the origins of human civilization (e.g., through the beneficent action of a culture-hero like Prometheus); or (4) the origin of social or religious custom or the nature and history of objects of worship.[6]

It also attempts to make more acceptable the painful realities of existence—danger, disease, misfortune, and death—by explaining them as part of a sacred order in the universe.

The explanations may seem irrational and inconsistent to the science-minded modern. This is because they are not scientific hypothe-

[6]William Reginald Halliday, "Folklore," in an earlier edition of the *Encyclopaedia Britannica*.

ses but were created by and appeal to the imagination. The truth of the myth was unquestioned by primitive peoples because it was so closely associated with their sacred beliefs. For them, both nature and society were areas of reverent acceptance—not of objective study, as they are in this age of scientific inquiry.

Evolution of Myths

A number of writers have called attention to the various levels of myth development, their evolution from primitive to highly complex symbolic stories. These developmental stages are important to us because they throw light upon the various types of stories (for example, the creation myths of almost every culture and the *pourquoi* tales) included in myths and help to explain their suitability, or lack of it, as story material for children.

The early part of this evolution is, of course, shrouded in the darkness of prehistoric times. The evolution of myth and religion differs from people to people. Suffice it to say that the Greeks, like many other peoples, passed through a primary stage in which they worshiped an impersonal force believed to pervade all aspects of the universe: sun, moon, crops, rivers. Later these nature forces were personified in the myths.

Myths, then, did give body—both animal and human—to the mystic forces that early people felt in the universe. As these ideas developed, the tendency was to give complex human form to these impersonal forces. These bright skydwellers were created in humankind's own image but surpassed humanity in beauty, wisdom, and power.

Imagining these supernatural beings in their own likeness, the people interpreted a flood to mean that the river god was angry with them and intended to punish them. Droughts, earthquakes, good crops and bad crops were all dependent on how humanity stood in the graces of these nature gods. These primitive beginnings of myth were polytheistic; that is, they gave rise to many gods.

Presently these beings developed relationships among each other, assumed certain powers, and suffered limitations of power. Thus in the Greek mythology the first gods were all brothers and sisters—Hestia, Demeter, Hera, Poseidon, Hades, and Zeus. Because Zeus saved them from destruction, he was chosen as the supreme ruler, the sky god, while Poseidon ruled the waters and Hades, who dwelt below the earth, ruled the dominion of the dead. From their matings, their children, and the powers and limitations of each of these three powerful brothers arose endless squabbles that bear a melancholy resemblance to the earthly rows of humans.

Each god or goddess came to assume certain powers although every one except Zeus knew distinct limitations to power and was vulnerable to misfortunes in certain respects, even as humans are. Balder, the Norse sun god, whose mother, Frigga, made everything except the mistletoe promise not to harm him, was slain by the insignificant shrub which Frigga had thought too harmless to bother about. Balder the Beautiful died; he went out to sea in his fiery ship, burning like the autumn foliage; the earth wept for him, and cold and darkness followed—a picture of the coming of autumn and winter in the north country. So these deities developed relationships and powers but were subject to certain limitations from other powers.

The extension of a god's powers soon turned him or her into a symbolic figure, standing for certain abstract virtues. So Zeus, from being at first merely a sky god, became the symbol of power and law. Apollo began as the sun god, a beautiful young man with a fiery chariot to drive across the sky daily. Then he became also the god of health and healing, the patron god of physicians. Finally this idea of healing was expanded to include the related but less physical concept of purification, and Apollo then stood for the abstract idea of purity. In some such way as this, many of the gods evolved from mere nature personifications to become symbols of abstract moral attributes.

In some mythologies the deities have never signified anything more than spirits of earth, sky, sun, moon, or animals. In some American Indian cultures, "Old Man Coyote" is such a deity. On the other hand, the Navaho "Turquoise Woman" is not merely a sky goddess but seems to be also a symbol of beauty in the highest sense, meaning harmony and goodness.

Finally, when the gods had come to stand for moral attributes and powers, the next and last stage of mythmaking was the development of a priesthood, temples, and a ritual of worship. Then the myth was an organized religion. Apollo had a great temple at Delphi with priests, an oracle, vestal virgins, and elaborate ceremonies and rituals. The Apollo cult represents the last and most complex stage of mythmaking, which the mythologies of only highly civilized people attain.

Types of Myths

Among the simplest of myth stories are the why stories, or *pourquoi* tales. Why the woodpecker has a red head and how the arbutus came to be are from the North American Indians; in both Greek and Norse myths these *why* stories become more complex than in the woodpecker and arbutus examples. Take, for instance, the Greek explanation of summer and winter: Demeter (the earth mother) has been deprived of her beautiful child Persephone (the grain), who has been carried off by Hades to his realm below the ground; Demeter seeks her child, weeping, but Persephone must remain in Hades's underworld for six months of each year, leaving earth to darkness and cold. Such a story is neither simple nor fully explanatory for children. In much the same vein, the North American Indians of the Southwest have their desert seasonal story of little Burnt-Face, the scorched earth, who sees the invisible chief, the spring rains, and is made beautiful by him and becomes his bride. To children, these are just good fairy tales, as interesting as "Cinderella." However, if in the study of Greeks or Desert Indians you explain to the children the possible meaning of these stories for the people who created them, they are surprised and charmed with the secondary meaning.

Many of the myths are, on the whole, too adult in content and significance to be appropriate story material for children. But the simpler tales among them are accepted by the children exactly as they accept any folk tale. One of their favorites is "King Midas," who wished that everything he touched would turn into gold and soon found himself starving in the midst of plenty. Well-told versions of such

From *Persephone and the Springtime* by Margaret Hodges, illustrated by Arvis Stewart.

stories are suitable for children and may be used with or without the background of the people and their mythology.

The ways of the gods with humans are the subject of another group of stories which includes "King Midas." One of the most delightful is "Bellerophon and Pegasus." Bellerophon, a handsome youth, is sent by his host, Iobates, to kill the chimera, which is devastating Lycia. Although Iobates is sure the mission will mean the boy's death, the gods take pity upon Bellerophon and send him the winged Pegasus. That the name *Pegasus,* the winged horse of the gods, means "poetry" does not enter children's heads, but that Bellerophon could not kill the terrible chimera until he had first captured and tamed Pegasus makes a good adventure story of unusual beauty. Such stories are really hero tales with a background of myth and they comprise a particularly good group of stories for children. Some of them, like those in the *Odyssey,* later developed into national epics. Stories of the gods' amatory adventures among humans are legion and are not often adapted for children.

Some of the myths warn against particular sins. Pride seems to be especially offensive to the gods. Arachne was turned into a spider because she boasted of her weaving. Bellerophon, after he captured the winged horse, Pegasus, became so sure of himself that he attempted to ride into Zeus's dwelling and was promptly struck blind for his presumption. Some of these myths are almost like fables, and, like the fables, they could be summarized with a maxim or proverb.

Finally, the ways of the gods with other gods furnish us with another body of myth stories, often complex in their significance and adult in content. Here we encounter nature myths which even the folklorists interpret differently and which leave the reader baffled and a bit weary with all the things which aren't what they seem. Frazer's *Golden Bough* is a repository for these tales. Many myths, with their symbolism and inner meanings, are both complex and abstract, and some people feel that they have no place in children's literature.

Sources of Mythologies
Greek Myths

Most of the Greek myths came to us by the way of the poet Hesiod, who is supposed to have lived during the eighth century B.C. While he was guarding his father's flocks, so the story goes, the Muses themselves commissioned him to be their poet. So a poet he became, winning a contest and gratefully dedicating a tripod to the Muses, who had shown him the way.

His first famous poem, *Works and Days,* contains the earliest known fable in Greek, "The Hawk and the Nightingale."

Theogony, another poem attributed to Hesiod, contains the Greek myths of the creation and the history of Zeus and Cronus, including Zeus's great battle with the Titans. Hesiod's picture of the defeated Titans, confined and guarded by giants and by Day and Night, is a convincing one.

Hesiod is credited with bringing together in organized form the major portion of Greek mythology. The English translation, although in prose, is good reading.

Roman Myths

The Roman versions of the Greek myths are available to us in the more familiar *Metamor-*

phoses of the Latin poet Ovid. Born in 43 B.C., Ovid belonged to a wealthy and privileged family. He was educated under famous Roman teachers and became a poet against his father's wishes.

The *Metamorphoses* consists of fifteen books recounting tales of miraculous transformations, hence the title. It begins with the metamorphosis of Chaos to order, follows the Greek development of gods and humans, recounts innumerable *why* stories of flowers, rivers, rocks, and the like. It concludes, appropriately enough, with Julius Caesar turned into a star, and Ovid himself on his way to some form of immortality. These stories, even in our English prose translations, are amazingly dramatic. It is interesting to check modern versions with these stirring tales of Ovid, which are the source of most adaptations.

Norse Myths

Whether the Norse myths began in Norway, Greenland, Ireland, Iceland, or England, it was in Iceland that they were preserved orally and first written down. Iceland, remote from the rest of the world and settled largely by Norwegians, held to the old language, once the speech of all Northern peoples, and so kept the stories alive in their original form. The two collections are the *Elder* or *Poetic Edda,* and the *Younger* or *Prose Edda.*

The *Poetic* and the *Prose Eddas* follow the sing-and-say style, with the difference that the *Poetic Edda* is mostly verse with brief prose passages, while the *Prose Edda* is mostly prose with interspersed poetic passages. Both are difficult books, but there are several adaptations to use with children.

The word *Edda* was originally the Norse name or title for a great-grandmother. In time it came to stand for the Norwegian court-meter or the art of poetry. In both senses it seems to imply something traditional. The *Elder* or *Poetic Edda* (thirty-four poems) contains the Prophecy, which tells how the world was created, how the gods came to be, and how they fell. There is a book of proverbs, and finally there is the Norse epic, the saga of Sigurd the Volsung. These heroic lays were supposedly collected from oral tradition by Saemund the Learned and committed to writing about the eleventh or twelfth century. By then they must have been exposed to Christian ideas and to other cultures, but they remain, nevertheless, primitive and vigorous.

The *Younger* or *Prose Edda* was not collected until the thirteenth century. The first book, "The Beguiling of Gylfi," contains the bulk of the Norse myths. It was the work of Snorri Sturluson, an Icelander who combined a greedy and traitorous character with a real reverence for the traditional literature he recorded so faithfully.

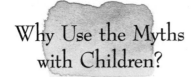

Why Use the Myths with Children?

It is the rare child who is not enchanted with the stories of mythology. The sky-dwellers of the Greeks and Romans not only left a mark on our language, but they continue to spellbind each succeeding generation of children. Bellerophon taming the winged horse, Icarus plummeting through the sky into the sea, Hermes stepping cloudward on his winged sandals— these somehow catch the imagination with their dramatic beauty. It is not an accident that most of the examples of myths in the preceding pages have been from the Greek. If children can sample only one mythology, it might well be the Greek or its Roman adaptation. Our language and our thinking are full of words and ideas derived from these sources.[7] For example, *titanic* comes from the powerful Titans; *erotic* from Eros, the god of love; *panic* from the god Pan; and *cereal* from Ceres, the grain goddess. Minerva with her owl gazes down on us in our libraries. Venus, rising from her sea shell, advertises bath salts or cosmetics. There is a dramatic quality about the myths which has so captured the imaginations of poets that poetry, and English poetry in particular, is filled with classical allusions. Not to know Greco-Roman mythology is to grope more or less blindly through the arts, particularly literature.

But the Norse myths too should be part of the experience of English-speaking children. The people who composed them were a vital source of our customs, laws, and speech. Yet the myths which are their finest expression and the clearest mirror of their life are not nearly so familiar to most of us as the myths of the ancient civilizations of Greece and Rome. The Norse gods do not have the beauty and grace of the classic deities, but they are cast in heroic mold, and there is a grandeur about the tales that is hard to match. Such stories as "How Thor Found His Hammer," "The Apples of Iduna," "Thor's Visit to the Giants," and "The Death of Balder" are fascinating with or without a study of the people.

Both Greek and Norse mythologies, moreover, furnish the background for the great national epics of those countries. Children must know Greek mythology in order to understand the *Iliad* or the *Odyssey,* and they must know Norse mythology in order to understand the ideals and motives of the heroic characters in the Norse epic *Sigurd the Volsung,* or in Wagner's opera cycle *The Ring of the Nibelungs,* the Teutonic form of the Sigurd epic.

[7]There is a book devoted to such sources: Isaac Asimov, *Words from the Myths.* Houghton, 1961.

From *Iduna and the Magic Apples* by Marianna Mayer, illustrated by Laszlo Gal.

These are a few of the reasons that myths should be used with older children, but the chief reasons are, after all, the beauty and the imaginative quality of the tales themselves.

What Versions of the Myths to Use

The chief difficulty in using mythology with children is to select satisfactory versions of the stories. Good versions of the myths for children have been made and new ones are still appearing. General standards should help us in selecting the best of these.

Although some adaptation may be necessary, myths should not be written down to children. When this is done, the author is usually trying to retell myths to children who are too young for them. Six- and seven-year-old children can take only the bare bones of these stories, but children from nine or ten years old to fourteen can enjoy rich versions of some of the originals. At home, some children may read myths earlier, but in the mixed groups of the average classroom, the appeal of myths is distinctly to older children.

Finally, adaptations should be simple enough to be thoroughly comprehensible to children without sacrificing either the spirit or the richness of the original versions. Simplification of some of the words is permissible and often even essential, but reject an adaptation that omits the rich, descriptive details of Ovid's tale. In the tale of Pegasus, for example, it would be a pity to miss the pictures of the palace, the chariot, and the horses of the Sun, the account of Apollo's love and anxiety for the reckless youth, the portrayal of the boy's terror of the lonely heavens, and the descriptions of the rushing speed, the earth aflame, and finally the Jovian bolt.

According to these standards, what versions of the myths are best to use with children? There has been a flood of adaptations of original versions, as well as some modern editions of old versions. Of the latter, one of the best is *The Heroes* by Charles Kingsley, Victorian scholar and poet. His stories of Perseus, Theseus, and Jason have a nobility that should prove a wholesome antidote to the banality of much of our mass media entertainment. Ellen Switzer connects and clarifies mythical stories in *Greek Myths: Gods, Heroes and Monsters: Their Sources, Their Stories and Their Meanings;* and Padraic Colum's *The Golden Fleece* and *The Children's Homer* are superb storytelling for good readers. The d'Aulaires' big, handsome *Book of Greek Myths* represents years of preparation: The stories are brief but have continuity; the copious and colorful illustrations are uneven in quality but imaginative. This is a splendid book for classroom use. It is also interesting to see how the myths appeal to poets, beginning with Kingsley and Colum. British poet Robert Graves brought out his version, *Greek Gods and Heroes,* in a lively text that makes clear what is often confusing in other versions. And Ian Serraillier, another poet, has told the stories of Perseus, in *The Gorgon's Head,* and Theseus, in *The Way of Danger,* with dramatic beauty. Both can be read by children or may serve as sources for storytelling. The illustrations in these editions suggest figures on Greek vases. Other tales by Serraillier include *Heracles the Strong,* which is illustrated with woodcuts that echo the vigor of the story; and *The Clashing Rocks,* the story of Jason.

Olivia Coolidge's twenty-seven tales in *Greek Myths* are mature in approach and are well told. Leon Garfield and Edward Blishen's *The God Beneath the Sea*, a flowing narrative version that clarifies the complexities of Olympian relationships, won the 1970 Carnegie Medal. *Strangers Dark and Gold* by Norma Johnston is a stirring synthesis of three early versions of Jason's quest for the Golden Fleece. Two very good source books are Edith Hamilton's *Mythology*, which gives excellent background, provides a sense of the sequence of the myths, and is written in polished prose; and Roger Lancelyn Green's *A Book of Myths*, which gives variants of myths from many of the ancient lands. The Greek pantheon is introduced and handsomely illustrated in Leonard Everett Fisher's *The Olympians: Great Gods and Goddesses of Ancient Greece*. Examine these editions and choose the one or two that best suit your needs as sources for story telling or references for the children to read themselves.

When you want to use Norse myths and hero tales, turn again to Padraic Colum, to his *Children of Odin*, a stirring and understandable version of those complex tales. Less difficult for younger readers are Catharine Sellew's *Adventures with the Giants* and *Adventures with the Heroes*, and Ingri and Edgar Parin d'Aulaire's *Norse Gods and Giants*. In this last book, the author-artists have illustrated with big, bold pictures and have retold Norse myths in a straightforward style with occasional passages in which the oral tradition is evident. *Axe-Age, Wolf-Age: A Selection from the Norse Myths*, by Kevin Crossley-Holland, has remarkable narrative flow. An early adaptation that still serves well is Abbie F. Brown's *In the Days of Giants*, while Dorothy Hosford's *Sons of the Volsungs* and *Thunder of the Gods* cover the myths and the hero cycles in superb style, either for storytelling or reading by the children themselves. These are, however, the most difficult of all stories to tell.

Epic and Hero Tales

In the source collections of myths, both Greek and Norse, there are (in addition to the stories of the gods) tales of human heroes buffeted

From *Norse Gods and Giants*, retold and illustrated by Ingri and Edgar Parin D'Aulaire.

violently by gods and humanity but daring greatly, suffering uncomplainingly, and enduring staunchly to the end. Such tales, having a human hero as the focus of the action and embodying the ideals of a culture, are called epics. The heroes of epics often emerge as legendary characters, humans who are said to have accomplished memorable and often impossible feats. Although many of these legendary characters never really existed, others did—like some of the characters in our American tall tales—and the legends telling of their deeds became part of the folk literature.

Characteristics of the Epic

Epics are sometimes written in verse, as in the *Iliad* or the *Sigurd Saga*, and sometimes in prose, as in Malory's *Morte d'Arthur*. The adventures of the legendary hero Robin Hood were preserved by the ballads. The term *epic* is often used quite flexibly to include such dissimilar materials as the great philosophical poem from the Hebrew, the Book of Job, the slight and romantic *Aucassin and Nicolette* from the medieval French, and the comparatively modern *Paradise Lost* by the English poet John Milton.

Most of us, however, think of epics as a cycle of tales, such as the *Odyssey* or the *Iliad*, gathered around one hero. These two heroic narratives have come to typify this particular field of literature. In them, legendary heroes pursue legendary adventures, aided or hindered by partisan gods who apparently leave Olympus for the express purpose of meddling in human affairs. In short, myth may still be with us in the epic, but the dramatic center of interest has shifted from the gods to a human hero. We have moved from Olympus to earth, transferring our sympathies from gods to humans, from divine adventures to human endeavors.

The epic is strongly national in its presentation of human character. Odysseus may never have lived, but he is the embodiment of the Greek ideals of manly courage, sagacity, beauty, and endurance; Sigurd is the personification of Norse heroism; King Arthur is the code of chivalry in the flesh; and Robin Hood is the mouthpiece for England's passionate love of freedom and justice, as he is the ideal of hardy, jovial English manhood. Study the epic hero of a nation and you discover the moral code of that nation and era—all its heroic ideals embodied in one character.

The *Iliad* and the *Odyssey*

The *Iliad* and the *Odyssey* are attributed to Homer, a legendary Greek poet. Songs about the siege of Troy are known to have been sung shortly after the events took place, although the first written forms of the epics did not appear until some six hundred years later. What Homer composed and what he compiled cannot be established, but the great epics known by his name were studied and recited by educated Greeks and there were apparently texts or arrangements of them from around 560 to 527 B.C. Authentic texts are established by 150 B.C. The date of Homer's birth has been variously estimated as from 1159 B.C. to 685 B.C., but by the time stories of Homer's life began to appear, nothing was authentically known about

Viewpoint

This oral art of taletelling is far older than history, and it is not bounded by one continent or one civilization. Stories may differ in subject from place to place, the conditions and purposes of taletelling may change as we move from land to land or from century to century, and yet everywhere it ministers to the same basic social and individual needs. The call for entertainment to fill in the hours of leisure has found most peoples very limited in their resources, and except where modern urban civilization has penetrated deeply they have found the telling of stories one of the most satisfying of pastimes. Curiosity about the past has always brought eager listeners to tales of the long ago which supply the simple man with all he knows of the history of his folk. Legends grow with the telling, and often a great heroic past evolves to gratify vanity and tribal pride. Religion also has played a mighty role everywhere in the encouragement of the narrative art, for the religious mind has tried to understand beginnings and for ages has told stories of ancient days and sacred beings. Often whole cosmologies have unfolded themselves in these legends, and hierarchies of gods and heroes.

Stith Thompson, *The Folktale*. Berkeley, California: University of California Press, 1977, pp. 5–6.

him. George Gilbert Aimé Murray sums up this disputable evidence in the following fashion:

The man "Homer" cannot have lived in six different centuries nor been born in seven different cities; but Homeric poetry may well have done so. The man cannot have spoken this strange composite epic language, but the poetry could and did.[8]

The *Iliad* is certainly complex and long, but the adventures in the *Odyssey*, or *Ulysses*, are exciting and understandable to children. A

[8]George Gilbert Aimé Murray, "Homer," in an earlier edition of the *Encyclopaedia Britannica*.

combined edition, *The Iliad and the Odyssey of Homer,* adapted by Alfred J. Church, has versions that are well suited to the nine- to eleven-year-old reader, as are the versions in the handsomely illustrated *The Iliad and the Odyssey* adapted by Jane Werner Watson. For a slightly older reader, Padraic Colum's *The Children's Homer* (previously cited) is a distinguished retelling. But for readers of twelve or older, Barbara Leonie Picard's *The Odyssey of Homer* gives more depth in its perceptive portrayal of character.

In this epic the Greek ideals of cool intelligence, patience, and resourcefulness are found in both Penelope and Odysseus. They exhibit these qualities and hold tenaciously to their goals even when humans and gods are arrayed against them. Over "the misty sea," "the wine-dark sea," Odysseus sailed for twenty years and none could stay him. This is a story of fortitude which every generation of children should know.

Sigurd the Volsung

The Norse epic *Sigurd the Volsung* is not so well known as it deserves to be. There is a rugged nobility about the saga stories which some children especially appreciate. Because these tales reflect a simpler social order, many people consider them better suited to children than the Greek epics. This is a debatable point, since anyone who has ever tried to tell the saga of Sigurd knows all too well its difficulties. Obscurities in the text, difficult names much alike, and unpalatable social relationships underlying the main action of the story require expert handling.

Certainly the saga has some elements of violence in common with those crime stories which the modern child may be reading in the newspapers or seeing in the movies or on television. But their differences are important. In the latter, the tales of blood and murder are often sordid, ignobly motivated, and horrifying. In the Sigmund-Sigurd stories, there is the nobility of great heroism, of keeping your word even though it costs you your life, of self-sacrifice for a great cause, of death rather than dishonor, of ideals of race and family, of intrepid courage and perseverance.

From *The Merry Adventures of Robin Hood,* retold and illustrated by Howard Pyle.

Robin Hood

Of all the hero cycles, *Robin Hood* is unquestionably the children's favorite. It may not be the loftiest epic, and Robin Hood may not be the noblest hero, but his mad escapades, his lusty fights, his unfailing good humor when beaten, his sense of fair play, and, above all, his roguish tricks and gaiety practically define "hero" for children. Children should read *Robin Hood,* see it in a movie or television version, and read it again. Indeed, no other hero lends himself so readily to dramatization on screen or in classroom as does this gallant outlaw leader.

Children enjoy hearing some of the ballads of Robin Hood read aloud, but the prose version by Howard Pyle, with his spirited illustrations, is the text they should know. It is hard reading for most children, and if they can't read it for themselves, they should hear it. For the lucky superior readers, it remains for generation after generation of children one of the most exciting narratives in all literature. Other rewarding versions of the story are Geoffrey Trease's *Bows Against the Baron* and Robin McKinley's *The Outlaws of Sherwood*, which uses a fresh viewpoint of events and deepens characterization.

King Arthur and the Knights of the Round Table

Opinions differ as to the appropriateness of the King Arthur stories for young children. Certainly they are more mature in content and significance than either the *Odyssey* or *Robin Hood*. The individual adventures of some of the knights are as understandable as those of the Sherwood Forest band, but the ideals of chivalry are far subtler than the moral code of Robin Hood and his men. Often brave deeds are performed for the love of a fair lady, and many feel the cycle is better for the adolescent period when romance is uppermost and codes of conduct are taken seriously.

From *The Boy's King Arthur* by Sidney Lanier, illustrated by N. C. Wyeth.

On the other hand, there are unusually good juvenile editions of the Arthur tales for children that, simplified though they are, satisfy the child's love of knights and knightly adventures. Two of the older editions of the stories of King Arthur and his court remain deservedly popular; Sidney Lanier's *The Boy's King Arthur* and Howard Pyle's *The Story of King Arthur and His Knights,* which Pyle both told and romantically illustrated. Barbara Leonie Picard's *Stories of King Arthur and His Knights* uses lucid language and evokes a feeling of the period. Several books tell separate episodes from the Arthurian legend: the collection of four Arthurian tales in T. H. White's *The Once and Future King* that begins with *The Sword in the Stone;* Margaret Hodges's retelling of *The Kitchen Knight;* Selina Hastings's *Sir Gawain and the Loathly Lady;* and—for older readers—Philip Neil's *The Tale of Sir Gawain* that tells the story of a valiant hero. For older children, Rosemary Sutcliff's trilogy of Arthurian retellings begins with *The Sword in the Circle,* continues with *The Light Beyond the Forest,* and concludes with *The Road to Camalann.* The enthusiasm of teachers who love the Arthur stories will positively influence the opinions of young listeners. Certainly an exposure to any of these hero cycles is an enriching experience.

It is the gentleness and beauty of these stories and the idealistic character of King Arthur and his knights which sometimes furnish children with their first idea of strength in gentleness, of the power that comes through disciplined restraint. Not that children can put these qualities into words, but the qualities are there, embodied in the strong, gentle men who are the heroes of these tales.

The *Ramayana* and the Mahabharata

There was no English version of the *Ramayana* for children until Joseph Gaer's *The Adventures of Rama* was published. This myth-epic of India tells how the god Vishnu came down to earth as Prince Rama, a mortal, to save humanity from the evil powers of Ravan. Once on earth, Rama behaves much like other epic heroes. He fights innumerable battles, marries the beautiful Sita, suffers banishment, gives way to suspicion and

From *Sir Gawain and the Loathly Lady,* retold by Selina Hastings, illustrated by Juan Wijngaard.

jealousy, and is put to shame by the gentle Sita's trial by fire. After that, all goes well, and throughout the ten thousand years of Rama's reign:

Unknown were want, disease and crime,
So calm, so happy was the time.

The individual stories resemble Greek myths more than the usual epic does. The illustrations suggest dance, a form in which the adventures of Rama are often shown in India. A splendid edition of the *Ramayana* has been adapted by Elizabeth Seeger, who has also retold one of India's great hero tales in *The Five Sons of King Pandu,* the story of the Mahabharata. Both books are beautifully illustrated in the Indian tradition, and both have the rolling prose that is so suitable to the intricacies of the stories and their lofty themes. *The Story of Prince Rama,* adapted by Brian Thompson, is a lively abridgement that clarifies a mass of material.

Other Epics and Hero Tales

The length and complexity of the epic form may seem a deterrent to young readers, but it allows time for real characterization and for a continual iteration of the moral code. Although the great national epics and hero tales are of particular interest to students of literature and to folklorists, they can be enjoyed by the adolescent reader; and many of the single episodes, especially those of the hero tales, can be appreciated by the pre-adolescent.

An excellent introduction to the genre is *Hero Tales from Many Lands,* edited by Alice Hazeltine. Her selection of retellings is discriminating, and the book includes sources, background notes, and a glossary. Barbara Leonie Picard's *Hero Tales of the British Isles* also has notes that provide historical information. The best four tales of the Welsh classic, the *Mabinogion,* are combined in *Tales from the Mabinogion,* translated by Gwyn Thomas and Kevin Crossley-Holland; the cycle consists of heroic legends, folklore, and mythology.

Beowulf, the oldest epic in English, has been retold in several editions for the young reader. A version that can be enjoyed by ten- to twelve-year-olds is Robert Nye's *Beowulf, A New Telling,* a quite simple prose interpretation of the epic poem. For older children, an outstanding prose version is Rosemary Sutcliff's *Beowulf* which has a poetic grandeur of style. Ian Serraillier's *Beowulf, the Warrior* is in sonorous and stately verse.

From *The Story of Prince Rama* by Brian Thompson, illustrated by Jeroo Roy.

The Babylonian story of Gilgamesh has been retold in several editions; the most notable both in style and illustration is that of Bernarda Bryson. However, a version that is easier to read is edited by Anita Feagles, *He Who Saw Everything, The Epic of Gilgamesh.*

The deeds of Cuchulain, the Irish warrior-hero who was the descendant of a god, are combined in a continuous story in Rosemary Sutcliff's *The Hound of Ulster.* Another Irish hero, Finn MacCool, leader of the Fenians, is described by Sutcliff in *The High Deeds of Finn MacCool,* a vigorous account of the Fenian legends. These legends are related in vivid style in *The Tangle-Coated Horse and Other Tales* by Ella Young; while Bernard Evslin provides a sophisticated, witty retelling in *The Green Hero.*

From continental Europe come other tales of heroes: stories of the legendary Spanish hero, the Cid; the story of Roland from France; the romantic tales from the Kiev cycle in *The Knights of the Golden Table* by E. M. Almedingen; and *The Nibelungenlied* from Germany.

Tales from other parts of the world, too, are available for children. Richard Lewis has adapted for younger readers a Hawaiian creation chant in *In the Night, Still Dark;* Marcia Brown, in *Backbone of the King,* retells the Hawaiian epic of the courtier Pakaa and his son Ku; and in *The Surprising Things Maui Did,* Jay Williams incorporates many of the deeds of a popular Polynesian deity. Dale Carlson's *Warlord of the Gengi* recounts the valorous deeds of a Japa-

nese folk hero. Jeanne Lee's retellings of Chinese legends explain mysteries of nature through the acts of legendary folk heroes. *Legend of the Li River: An Ancient Chinese Tale* deals with the origin of magical hills lining the river and *Legend of the Milky Way* presents an ancient Chinese explanation for that phenomenon. Roland Bertol's *Sundiata, The Epic of the Lion King* tells of the hero-king who founded the African empire of Mali.

Fable, myth, and epic are different from each other in many ways, yet all three are a part of the great stream of folk literature and are also embodiments of moral truths in story form.

The *fable* teaches briefly and frankly and provides children with their first excursion into the realm of abstract ideas and intellectual speculations about conduct.

The *myth* teaches through symbols which grow more and more complex. The symbolism soon ceases to have the simple, obvious moral of a fable and becomes as complicated as life, and it is then proportionately difficult for a

From *Tales from the Mabinogion* by Gwyn Thomas and Kevin Crossley-Holland, illustrated by Margaret Jones.

From *The Legend of the Milky Way*, retold and illustrated by Jeanne M. Lee.

leading to success. The canvas is larger here, and for many children the sweep and grandeur of mythology is even more appealing than the simpler folk tales. Children enjoy comparing versions of individual myths, or even editions of collected myths. The characters may be gods, but they provide insight into human behavior. Comparing stories from various cultures can foster the understanding that there is, despite differences in cultural patterns, a universality among people of all cultures. The myths, so dramatic for reading or telling, provide a good background for the heroic magnitude of the epic: The towering figures serve as role models and symbols of courage, altruism, loyalty, and leadership.

All of these literary forms—fables, myths, and epics—have emerged from the oral tradition, and have endured, stimulating and satisfying the imaginative powers of children.

child to understand. Fortunately, the myth stories possess a beauty that is satisfying in itself.

The *epics* demonstrate a triple value. They contribute to an appreciation of world literature, to an understanding of national ideals of behavior, and to a comprehension of the dimensions of the valor and nobility of heroism for all humanity.

Like the folk tales, the body of traditional literature that has been discussed in this chapter has an adaptability of use and a range of appeal that provide a firm basis for quick enjoyment and lasting appreciation.

Although some fabular themes are complex, young children respond to them as animal tales and may be captivated by their brevity, their pithy humor, and even by the moral—so much more palatable when it is directed to animals than to people. Because of their simple structure, fables are a good choice for dramatization.

Myths and legends, like folk tales, tend to embody some kind of cultural lore: explanations of creation, approved attitudes toward elders, and behavior that is socially condoned,

Viewpoint

The supernatural beings of legends sanction the norms of human society. Legends recount fears about the consequences of breaking social and religious taboos. In each case we must ask what suppressed potential lies behind the taboos the legends call upon us to uphold. In this context one can speak of the "cultural language of fear." Legends and belief stories are oral communications in which people try to verbalize anxieties and fears and, by explaining these away, to free themselves from the oppressive power of their fears. One could call this the "shock effect of supranormal experience." The telling of a legend can be compared to a therapeutic process and supranatural experiences constitute a kind of self-therapy.

James M. McGlathery, ed., *The Brothers Grimm and Folktale.* Urbana, Illinois: University of Illinois Press, 1988, p. 8.

Adult References and Book Selection Aids*

BARBER, RICHARD. *A Companion to World Mythology.*

BIERHORST, JOHN. *The Mythology of Mexico and Central America.*

————. *The Mythology of North America.*

————. *The Mythology of South America.*

BULFINCH, THOMAS. *Age of Fable: Or, Stories of Gods and Heroes.*

EASTMAN, MARY HUSE. *Index to Fairy Tales, Myths and Legends.*

FRAZER, SIR JAMES GEORGE. *The Golden Bough.*

IRELAND, NORMA. *Index to Fairy Tales, 1949–1972: Including Folklore, Legends and Myths in Collections.*

KIRK, GEOFFREY S. *Myth.*

LEACH, MARIA, and JEROME FRIED, eds. *Funk and Wagnalls Standard Dictionary of Folklore, Mythology and Legend.*

MOORMAN, CHARLES. *Kings and Captains: Variations on a Heroic Theme.*

MUNCH, PETER A. *Norse Mythology, Legends of Gods and Heroes.*

RANK, OTTO. *The Myth of the Birth of the Hero: A Psychological Interpretation of Mythology.*

SCHWAB, GUSTAV. *Gods and Heroes.*

SWITZER, ELLEN and COSTAS. *Gods, Heroes, and Monsters: Their Sources, Their Stories, and Their Meanings.*

*Complete bibliographic data are provided in Appendices A and B.

Aesop's Fables

In the following bibliography these symbols have been used to identify books about a particular religious or ethnic group:

§ African American
★ Hispanic
☆ Native American
○ Asian American
• Religious minority

Aesop's Fables, ill. by Heidi Holder. Viking, 1981. Nine familiar fables illustrated with gravely beautiful, intricately designed paintings.   9–12

Aesop's Fables, tr. by V. S. Vernon Jones, ill. by Arthur Rackham. Watts, 1967. This is one of the most satisfactory editions both for children and adults. Chesterton's introduction should not be missed. The illustrations appeal to older children. 10–14

ANNO, MITSUMASA, ad. *Anno's Aesop: A Book of Fables by Aesop and Mr. Fox,* ill. by ad. Orchard, 1989. Each fable has a counterpart, a story by Mr. Fox that provides a humorous matrix for Aesop's brief account and its moral.   8–10

BIERHORST, JOHN, ad. *Doctor Coyote: A Native American Aesop's Fable,* ill. by Wendy Watson. Macmillan, 1987.   7–9

The Hare and the Tortoise, ill. by Paul Galdone. McGraw, 1962. Action-filled color illustrations for this Aesop fable heighten suspense for the youngest.   4–7

JACOBS, JOSEPH, ed. *The Fables of Aesop,* ill. by David Levine. Macmillan, 1964.   9–11

KENT, JACK, reteller. *Fables of Aesop,* ill. by reteller. Parents' Magazine, 1972.   7–9

REEVES, JAMES, ad. *Fables from Aesop,* ill. by Maurice Wilson. Walck, 1962. In his selection of fifty fables, the narrator has introduced brief dialogue and descriptive phrases, while keeping to the spirit of the original. Illustrations, many in color, are exceptional in quality.   9–13

RICE, EVE, ad. *Once in a Wood: Ten Tales from Aesop,* ill. by author. Greenwillow, 1979. Nicely adapted for young readers, these Aesop stories are simple, direct, and pithy, concluding in most cases with a rhyming moral.   6–8

SPRIGGS, RUTH, ed. *The Fables of Aesop: 143 Moral Tales Retold,* ill. by Frank Baber. Rand, 1976. An oversize book, lavishly illustrated. The writing style is direct and colloquial, with a simply phrased moral in italics following the fables.   8–11

STEVENS, JANET, ad. *The Town Mouse and the Country Mouse,* ill. by ad. Holiday House, 1987.   4–6

UNTERMEYER, LOUIS, ed. *Aesop's Fables,* ill. by Alice and Martin Provensen. Golden Pr., 1965.   6–9

WHITE, ANNE TERRY, ed. *Aesop's Fables,* ill. by Helen Siegl. Random, 1964.   8–10

La Fontaine's Fables

CALHOUN, MARY. *Old Man Whickutt's Donkey,* ill. by Tomie dePaola. Parents' Magazine, 1975.

LA FONTAINE, JEAN DE. *The Fables of La Fontaine,* tr. by Marianne Moore. Viking, 1954. These fables retain their original verse form in this translation. A scholarly edition which includes La Fontaine's twelve books of fables and his own original preface. Chiefly an adult source.

————. *The Frogs Who Wanted a King,* ill. by Margot Zemach. Four Winds. 1977.   10–14

————. *The Hare and the Tortoise,* ill. by Brian Wildsmith. Watts, 1967.

————. *The Miller, the Boy and the Donkey,* ill. by Brian Wildsmith. Watts, 1969. Big pages, big print, and jeweltone colors make these and other single-title editions by Wildsmith attractive.   5–8

Other Fables

ANDERSEN, HANS CHRISTIAN. *The Ugly Duckling, The Emperor's New Clothes,* and others (see Bibliography, Chapter 8).

ATIL, ESIN. *Kalila wa Dimna: Fables from a Fourteenth-Century Arabic Manuscript.* Smithsonian, 1981. Although varied, all of the fables share the theme of a balanced universe.   10 up

BRENNER, ANITA. *A Hero by Mistake,* ill. by Jean Charlot. W. R. Scott, 1953. Afraid of his own shadow, this little man accidentally captures some bandits, is hailed as a hero, and learns to behave like one.   6–8

BROWN, MARCIA. *Once a Mouse* (see Bibliography, Chapter 6).

CHAUCER, GEOFFREY. *Chanticleer and the Fox,* ad. and ill. by Barbara Cooney. T. Crowell, 1958. Pictures of colorful beauty and design add delight to the old fable of the crafty fox and the vain cock. Caldecott Medal.   6–9

DAUGHERTY, JAMES. *Andy and the Lion* (see Bibliography, Chapter 4).

DE ROIN, NANCY, ed. *Jataka Tales;* ill. by Ellen Lanyon. Houghton, 1975.   8–9

DEMI. *A Chinese Zoo: Fables and Proverbs,* ill. by author. Harcourt, 1987. Illustrated with graceful paintings in an Oriental style, the selected fables feature animal characters.   5–8

GAER, JOSEPH. *The Fables of India,* ill. by Randy Monk. Little, 1955. Beast tales from three outstanding collections of Indian fables: The *Panchatantra,* the *Hitopadesa,* and the *Jatakas.* The stories are entertainingly presented, and there is excellent background material on the known history of fable literature for the student.   12–16

GALDONE, PAUL. *The Monkey and the Crocodile,* ill. by author. Seabury, 1969.   5–7

GINSBURG, MIRRA. *Three Rolls and One Doughnut: Fables from Russia,* ill. by Anita Lobel. Dial, 1970.   6–10

KRYLOV, IVAN. *Fifteen Fables of Krylov,* tr. by Guy Daniels, ill. by David Pascal. Macmillan, 1965.   12 up

LOBEL, ARNOLD. *Fables,* ill. by author. Harper, 1980. A pithy and often surprising moral is added, Aesop style, to single-paged fabular anecdotes that face handsome full-page paintings. Caldecott Medal.   8–10

MERRILL, JEAN. *The Black Sheep,* ill. by Ronni Solbert. Pantheon, 1969.   9–11

Greek and Roman Myths and Epics

ANDERSON, LONZO. *Arion and the Dolphins,* ill. by Adrienne Adams. Scribner's, 1978. In a graceful retelling of a Greek legend, young Arion is robbed of the gold he's won in a musical contest. He's rescued from harm by some dolphins while the king of Corinth deals with his assailants.   7–8

BARTH, EDNA, ad. *Cupid and Psyche: A Love Story,* ill. by Ati Forberg. Seabury, 1976. Beautifully illustrated with wash drawings, this is a moving version of the mythical tale of Cupid's love for the mortal, Psyche, and the vengeful jealousy of his mother Venus.   9–11

CHURCH, ALFRED JOHN, ad. *The Aeneid.* Macmillan, 1962. A simplified and dignified version.   10–14

————, ad. *The Iliad and the Odyssey of Homer,* ill. by Eugene Karlin, Macmillan, 1964.   10–14

————, ad. *The Odyssey of Homer,* ill. by John Flaxman. Macmillan, 1951. First published in 1906, this attractively done edition is an excellent source for children to read or adults to tell. Stories arranged in chronological order.   10–14

COLUM, PADRAIC. *The Children's Homer,* ill. by Willy Pogany. Macmillan, 1925, 1962. A distinguished version in cadenced prose, simple but in the spirit of the original. Vigorous illustrations.   10–14

————. *The Golden Fleece,* ill. by Willy Pogany. Macmillan, 1921, 1962. A companion edition to *The Children's Homer,* and equally fine.   10–14

COOLIDGE, OLIVIA E. *Greek Myths,* ill. by Edouard Sandoz. Houghton, 1949. Twenty-seven of the best known Greek myths. Here gods are not idealized, but the stories have authenticity.   10–16

D'AULAIRE, INGRI and EDGAR PARIN. *Ingri and Edgar Parin d'Aulaire's Book of Greek Myths,* ill. by authors. Doubleday, 1962.   8–11

EVSLIN, BERNARD. *Greeks Bearing Gifts; The Epics of Achilles and Ulysses,* ill. by Lucy Martin Bitzer. Four Winds, 1976. Evslin gives fresh life to old legends here; his versions of the *Iliad* and the *Odyssey* use a fluent, witty style that can be as delightfully irreverent as it is sonorous.   12 up

————. *Heraclea: A Legend of Warrior Women,* ill. by Lucy Bitzer. Four Winds, 1978.   12 up

————, ad. *Hercules,* ill. by Jos. A. Smith. Morrow, 1984. The dramatic, full-page drawings combine with a colloquial re-telling of the epic tale.   10–13

————, ad. *Jason and the Argonauts,* ill. by Bert Dodson. Morrow, 1986. Jason's classic adventures are chronicled in Evslin's contemporary style.   11–14

FISHER, LEONARD EVERETT. *The Olympians: Great Gods and Goddesses of Ancient Greece,* ill. by author. Holiday, 1984.   9–11

————, ad. *Theseus and the Minotaur,* ill. by ad. Holiday House, 1988. Theseus' search for the murderous Minotaur is depicted in somber, large-scale paintings.   5–8

GARFIELD, LEON, and EDWARD BLISHEN. *The God Beneath the Sea,* ill. by Zevi Blum. Pantheon, 1971.   11–14

GATES, DORIS. *The Golden God: Apollo,* ill. by Constantinos CoConis. Viking, 1973. The Apollo myths brought together into a coherent whole. Gates has done the same thing for the myths concerning Zeus in *Lord of the Sky: Zeus* (Viking, 1972); for the Athena myths in *The Warrior Goddess: Athena* (Viking, 1973); and for the Heracles myths in *Mightiest of Mortals: Heracles* (Viking, 1975).   10–11

GRAVES, ROBERT. *Greek Gods and Heroes,* ill. by Dimitris Davis. Doubleday, 1960.   12–15

GREEN, ROGER LANCELYN, ed. *A Book of Myths,* ill. by Joan Kiddell-Monroe. Dutton, 1965.   10–12

HAMILTON, EDITH. *Mythology,* ill. by Steele Savage. Little, 1942.   12 up

HAWTHORNE, NATHANIEL. *The Golden Touch,* ill. by Paul Galdone. McGraw, 1959. The old tale of King Midas is imaginatively illustrated with gold-toned pictures.   6–9

JOHNSTON, NORMA. *Strangers Dark and Gold.* Atheneum, 1975.   12–16

KINGSLEY, CHARLES. *The Heroes,* ill. by Vera Bock. Macmillan, 1954. Beautifully retold tales which make a fine cycle for the storyteller.   10–14

————. *The Heroes,* ill. by Joan Kiddell-Monroe. Dutton, 1963.   9–12

MCDERMOTT, GERALD. *Daughter of the Earth: A Roman Myth.* Delacorte, 1984.   7–11

MILLER, KATHERINE. *Apollo,* Houghton, 1970. 9–11

OLDFIELD, PAMELA, ad. *Tales from Ancient Greece,* ill. by Nick Harris. Doubleday, 1989. A re-telling of nine of the best-known myths.   9–11

PICARD, BARBARA LEONIE. *The Iliad of Homer,* ill. by Joan Kiddell-Monroe. Walck, 1960. A truly distinguished retelling of the *Iliad;* characters sympathetically portrayed. *The Odyssey of Homer* (1952) is an equally fine companion volume.   12–15

REEVES, JAMES. *The Trojan Horse,* ill. by Krystyna Turska. Watts, 1969. A Trojan boy describes the invasion of his city.   9–10

SELLEW, CATHARINE. *Adventures with the Gods,* ill. by George and Doris Hauman. Little, 1945. An introduction to the more familiar myths, simply written for younger children.   9–12

SERRAILLIER, IAN. *The Clashing Rocks: The Story of Jason,* ill. by William Stobbs. Walck, 1964.   10–13

————. *The Gorgon's Head: The Story of Perseus,* ill. by William Stobbs. Walck, 1962.   12–14

————. *Heracles the Strong,* ill. by Rocco Negri. Walck, 1970.   10–13

————. *The Way of Danger: The Story of Theseus,* ill. by William Stobbs. Walck, 1963.   12–14

SWITZER, ELLEN. *Greek Myths: Gods, Heroes and Monsters: Their Sources, Their Stories and Their Meanings,* ill. with photos by Costas. Atheneum, 1988.   12–17

TOMAINO, SARAH F., ad. *Persephone: Bringer of Spring,* ill. by Ati Forberg. T. Crowell, 1971. A graceful retelling of the Greek legend with delicate and dramatic illustrations.   8–10

VAUTIER, GHISLAINE. *The Shining Stars: Greek Legends of the Zodiac,* ad. by Kenneth McLeish, ill. by Jacqueline Bezencon. Includes star maps. Cambridge, 1981.   8–10

WATSON, JANE WERNER. *The Iliad and the Odyssey,* ill. by Alice and Martin Provensen. Golden Pr., 1964.   11–13

Norse Myths and Epics

BROWN, ABBIE FARWELL. *In the Days of Giants,* ill. by E. B. Smith. Houghton, 1902. This is a sterling adaptation of the Norse myths.   10–14

COLUM, PADRAIC. *Children of Odin,* ill. by Willy Pogany. Macmillan, 1920, 1962. Norse myths and hero tales retold in a continuous narrative ending with the death of Sigurd. Our best source for children. In fine modern format.   10–14

COOLIDGE, OLIVIA. *Legends of the North,* ill. by Edouard Sandoz. Houghton, 1951. A wide variety of stories includes tales of the northern gods and heroes, the Volsungs, and other sagas.   12–14

CROSSLEY-HOLLAND, KEVIN. *Axe-Age, Wolf-Age: A Selection from the Norse Myths,* ill. by Hannah Firmin. Andre Deutsch/Elsevier-Dutton, 1986.   12–15

D'AULAIRE, INGRI and EDGAR PARIN. *Norse Gods and Giants.* ill. by authors. Doubleday, 1967.   8–11

DE GEREZ, TONI, ad. *Louhi, Witch of North Farm,* ad. from the *Kalevala,* ill. by Barbara Cooney. Viking, 1986. In an adaptation of Finland's epic poem, the witch Louhi steals the sun and the moon, but her good counterparts force her to return them.   5–7

HOSFORD, DOROTHY G. *Sons of the Volsungs,* ill. by Frank Dobias. Holt, 1949. A splendid version of the Sigurd tales adapted from William Morris' *The Story of Sigurd the Volsung and the Fall of the Nibelungs.*   11–14

————. *Thunder of the Gods,* ill. by George and Claire Louden. Holt, 1952. Distinguished retellings of the Norse myths (Odin, Thor, etc.). Excellent for storytelling or reading aloud.   11–14

KOENIG, ALMA. *Gudrun,* tr. by Anthea Bell. Lothrop, 1979. A heroic romance based on the thirteenth-century poem, retold in prose smoothly translated from Middle High German.   11–13

SCHILLER, BARBARA, ad. *Hrafkel's Saga: An Icelandic Story,* ill. by Carol Iselin. Seabury, 1972. A family saga about one of the ancient Icelandic chieftains, told directly in heroic style.   11–13

SELLEW, CATHARINE. *Adventures with the Giants,* ill. by Steele Savage. Little, 1950.   8–11

————. *Adventures with the Heroes,* ill. by Steele Savage. Little, 1954. Retold in simple language are the stories of the Volsungs and Nibelungs.   9–12

English Epics and Hero Tales

HASTINGS, SELINA, ad. *Sir Gawain and the Loathly Lady,* ill. by Juan Wijngaard. Walker, 1985.   9–11

HIEATT, CONSTANCE. *The Castle of Ladies,* ill. by Norman Laliberte. T. Crowell, 1973. One of Gawain's romantic quests, adroitly retold. 10–12

————. *The Joy of the Court,* ill. by Pauline Baynes. T. Crowell, 1970.   9–11

HODGES, MARGARET, ad. *The Kitchen Knight: A Tale of King Arthur,* ill. by Trina Schart Hyman. Holiday House, 1990.   10–13

————. *Saint George and the Dragon,* ill. by Trina Schart Hyman. Little, 1984. Adapted from Edmund Spenser's *Faerie Queene.* Caldecott Medal.   9–11

MCKINLEY, ROBIN, ad. *The Outlaws of Sherwood.* Greenwillow, 1988.   11–15

MACLEOD, MARY. *Book of King Arthur and His Noble Knights,* ill. by Henry C. Pitz. Lippincott, 1949.   9–13

Mabinogion. Tales from the Mabinogion, tr. by Gwyn Thomas and Kevin Crossley-Holland, ill. by Margaret Jones. Overlook Press, 1985. Contemporary language mixes with ancient magic in a new translation of the Welsh medieval classic.   10–13

MALORY, SIR THOMAS. *Le Morte d'Arthur,* ill. by W. Russell Flint. London: Warner, publisher to the Medici Society [1921]. 2 vols. Children who are superior readers are fascinated with this source of the Arthur stories.   12–16

NYE, ROBERT. *Beowulf: A New Telling,* ill. by Allan E. Cober. Hill, 1968.   10–12

PHILIP, NEIL, ad. *The Tale of Sir Gawain,* ill. by Charles Keeping. Philomel, 1987.   11–14

PICARD, BARBARA L. *Hero Tales of the British Isles,* ill. by Eric Fraser. Criterion, 1963.   10–13

————. *Stories of King Arthur and His Knights,* ill. by Roy Morgan. Walck, 1955.   10–13

PYLE, HOWARD. *The Merry Adventures of Robin Hood of Great Renown in Nottinghamshire,* ill. by author. Scribner's, 1946. This is the great prose edition of the Robin Hood tales, the best source for reading and telling.   12–14

————. *The Story of King Arthur and His Knights,* ill. by author. Scribner's, 1933. Any Pyle edition is written with grace and distinction. This is no exception.   12–14

RIORDAN, JAMES. *Tales of King Arthur,* ill. by Victor Ambrus. Rand McNally, 1982. Richly colored, dramatic illustrations bedeck this flavorful retelling of traditional stories of Arthur and his knights.   9–11

SCHILLER, BARBARA. *Erec and Enid,* ill. by Ati Forberg. Dutton, 1970.   9–11

————. *The Kitchen Knight,* ill. by Nonny Hogrogian. Holt, 1965.   9–11

————, ad. *The Wandering Knight,* ill. by Herschel Levit. Dutton, 1971. A retelling of the deeds of the young Lancelot.   9–11

SERRAILLIER, IAN. *Beowulf, the Warrior,* ill. by Severin. Walck, 1961.   12 up

SUTCLIFF, ROSEMARY. *Beowulf,* ill. by Charles Keeping. Dutton, 1962.   11 up

————. *The Light Beyond the Forest.* Dutton, 1980.   11–15

————. *The Road to Camlann,* ill. by Shirley Felts. Dutton, 1982.   11–15

————. *The Sword and the Circle: King Arthur and the Knights of the Round Table.* Dutton, 1981. A trilogy.   11–15

————. *Tristan and Iseult.* Dutton, 1971. A tender retelling of a great love story.   11–14

TREASE, GEOFFREY. *Bows Against the Barons,* ill. by C. Walter Hodges. Hawthorne, 1967.   10–12

Other National Epics and Hero Tales

ALMEDINGEN, E. M. *The Knights of the Golden Table,* ill. by Charles Keeping. Lippincott, 1964.   12–15

BERTOL, ROLAND. *Sundiata: The Epic of the Lion King,* ill. by Gregorio Prestopino. T. Crowell, 1970.   9–12

☆ BIERHORST, JOHN, ed. *Black Rainbow: Legends of the Incas and Myths of Ancient Peru.* Farrar, 1976. Stories selected with discrimination are followed by notes on sources, a reading list, a glossary of terms, and a pronunciation guide.   13 up

☆ BIERHORST, JOHN, ed. *The Hungry Woman: Myths and Legends of the Aztecs,* ill. by Aztec artists of the sixteenth century. Morrow, 1984. A scholarly treatment of stories recorded from sixteenth-century Aztec narratives.

BOSLEY, KENNETH, reteller. *The Devil's Horse: Tales from the Kalevala.* Pantheon, 1971. Robust, colloquial retelling of the Finnish heroic ballads.
10 up

BROWN, MARCIA. *Backbone of the King,* ill. by author. Scribner's, 1966.   10–12

BRYSON, BERNARDA. *Gilgamesh,* ill. by author. Holt, 1967.   11–14

CARLSON, DALE. *Warlord of the Gengi,* ill. by John Gretzer. Atheneum, 1970.   11–14

☆ CURRY, JANE LOUISE, ad. *Back in the Beforetime: Tales of the California Indians,* ill. by James Watts. McElderry, 1987. Legends from a variety of tribes.   9–11

DEUTSCH, BABETTE. *Heroes of the Kalevala,* ill. by Fritz Eichenberg. Messner, 1940. This version has not only literary distinction but continuity. Text and illustrations bring out the lusty humor of the tales.   10–14

EVSLIN, BERNARD. *The Green Hero: Early Adventures of Finn McCool,* ill. by Barbara Bascove. Four Winds, 1975. A sophisticated, witty retelling in a sequential narrative.   11–14

FEAGLES, ANITA. *He Who Saw Everything: The Epic of Gilgamesh.* Scott/Addison, 1966.   9–11

GAER, JOSEPH. *The Adventures of Rama,* ill. by Randy Monk. Little, 1954. One of the best-loved epics of India is the story of Prince Rama and of his wife Sita, stolen from him by a demon king. The careful selection of incidents makes this an absorbing and unified tale.   12–14

GOLDSTON, ROBERT. *The Legend of the Cid,* ill. by Stephane. Bobbs, 1963. A simple version of the adventures of the Spanish hero.   10–13

HAMILTON, VIRGINIA, ad. *In the Beginning: Creation Stories from around the World,* ill. by Barry Moser. Harcourt, 1988. Twenty-five diverse creation myths are retold beautifully, can be used for comparative purposes, and are handsomely illustrated.   10–14

HAZELTINE, ALICE, ed. *Hero Tales from Many Lands,* ill. by Gordon Laite. Abingdon, 1961.   11–15

HODGES, ELIZABETH JAMISON. *A Song for Gilgamesh,* ill. by David Omar White. Atheneum, 1971. The story of a young potter of Sumer is woven around the journey of Gilgamesh to the Land of the Living.   11–13

HODGES, MARGARET. *Myths of the Celts,* ill. by Eros Keith. Farrar, 1973. Short tales, well told.   9–11

JAFFREY, MADHUR, ad. *Seasons of Splendour: Tales, Myths, and Legends of India,* ill. by Michael Foreman. Atheneum, 1985. The collection includes folktales and family stories in addition to accounts of Rama, Krishna, and other mythical characters.   10–13

LATTIMORE, DEBORAH NOURSE. *Why There Is No Arguing in Heaven: A Mayan Myth,* ill. by author. Harper, 1989. The Creator God challenges other gods in a complex myth.   7–10

LEE, JEANNE. *Legend of the Li River,* ill. by author. Holt, 1983.   7–9

————. *Legend of the Milky Way,* ill. by author. Holt, 1982.   7–9

LEWIS, RICHARD, ad. *In the Night, Still Dark,* ill. by Ed Young. Atheneum, 1988.   7–9

MARALNGURA, N. and others. *Tales from the Spirit Time,* rev. ed. Indiana Univ. Pr., 1976. A compilation of myths and legends, many of them "pourquoi" tales about animals, collected by Aborigine students in a teacher training program.   8–10

SEEGER, ELIZABETH. *The Five Sons of King Pandu,* ill. by Gordon Laite. Scott/Addison, 1969.   12 up

————. *The Ramayana,* ill. by Gordon Laite. Scott/Addison, 1969.   12 up

SEREDY, KATE. *The White Stag,* ill. by author. Viking, 1937. Based on the legend of the founding of Hungary, a tale of the hero Bendeguz and his son Attila. Newbery Medal.   10–14

SUTCLIFF, ROSEMARY. *The High Deeds of Finn MacCool,* ill. by Michael Charlton. Dutton, 1967.
11–14

————. *The Hound of Ulster,* ill. by Victor Ambrus. Dutton, 1964.   11–14

————. *The Light Beyond the Forest: The Quest for the Holy Grail.* Dutton, 1980. Tied by their quest, each of King Arthur's knights who sought the sacred cup is described in a separate chapter. A fine and fluent retelling.   10–12

TEHRANCHIAN, HASSAN, tr. and ad. *Kalilah and Dimnah: Fables from the Ancient East,* ill. by Anatole Ur. Harmony Books, 1985. Most of the fables are in the form of beast tales, with pointed commentary by the two jackal characters for whom the book is named.   8–10

THOMAS, GWYN, and KEVIN CROSSLEY-HOLLAND, tr. *Tales from the Mabinogion,* ill. by Margaret Jones. Overlook Press, 1985.   10–13

THOMPSON, BRIAN, ad. *The Story of Prince Rama,* ill. by Jeroo Roy and with original paintings. Viking, 1985.   9–12

UDEN, GRANT, ad. *Hero Tales from the Age of Chivalry; Retold from the Froissart Chronicles,* ill. by Doreen Roberts. World, 1969. Twelve tales by the great poet-historian of the fourteenth century. Historically interesting, romantic in approach.   11–13

WESTWOOD, JENNIFER. *Gilgamesh and Other Babylonian Tales.* Coward, 1970.   12 up

WILLIAMS, JAY. *The Surprising Things Maui Did,* ill. by Charles Mikolaycak. Four Winds, 1979.   5–8

YOUNG, ELLA. *The Tangle-Coated Horse and Other Tales: Episodes from the Fionn Saga,* ill. by Vera Bock. McKay, 1968.   12–14

Chapter Eight

Modern Fantasy

While folk literature is full of the truths that generations have deemed worthy of remembering and passing on to their children, and modern realistic fiction presents the facts of present-day life, fantasy is the art form that many modern writers have chosen to present another kind of truth, to lay out for children the realities of life—not in a physical or social sense, but in a psychological sense.

The folk tale often was a realistic story of daily events, but just as often a magical element was injected by means of supernatural beings such as fairies, elves, magicians, ogres, or dragons, or supernatural objects: a pot that skipped, a ship that flew. Folk tales with these magical elements were at times characterized as fairy tales, and we have continued to use this term for tales by modern writers which echo the folk-tale pattern.

Although the distinction between the old folk tale and the modern literary fairy tale is useful to adults, it is of no importance to children. Magic is magic to them whether they find it in Grimm, Andersen, or Dr. Seuss. Children do not think of their stories in the conventional categories of literature or of libraries but describe their favorites broadly as animal stories or funny stories or true stories or fairy tales, by which they mean any tale of magic, old or modern. Eleanor Cameron, in *The Green and Burning Tree*, says:

If we do not quibble over fineness of categories, we then avoid the danger of becoming one of that company of scholars (some of the folklorists among them) who seem to care less about experiencing the truth and beauty of a tale than in being "correct" in putting it into this compartment or that.[1]

The characteristics of the folk and fairy tales that make them particularly appealing to children are the same ones which make fantasy attractive. In fact, interesting story patterns, distinctive style, and memorable characterizations are essential to any good story for children. The special quality of fantasy is that it concerns things that cannot really happen or that it is about people or creatures who do not exist, yet within the framework of each story there is a self-contained logic, a wholeness of conception that has its own reality. If it does not, it fails. Some modern fantasies err

[1]Eleanor Cameron, *The Green and Burning Tree.* Atlantic/Little, Brown, 1969, p. 12.

because they are overly whimsical or unduly sophisticated or, worse still, because they talk down to children. As we select from the new fantasy being published each year, it is important to keep in mind (along with good story patterns, style, and characterizations) sincerity, directness, and imagination as essential characteristics.

From the single, short fairy tale modeled after the folk tale by such early writers as Perrault, writers of fantasy moved into the longer book-length tale, where they had more room to present the ambiguities and problems of humanity trying to live up to its best sense of self. J. R. R. Tolkien, Lloyd Alexander, Susan Cooper, Ursula Le Guin, and C. S. Lewis all found that more than one volume was needed to explore the implications of the basic struggle between good and evil. All but one of these writers, Susan Cooper, found it necessary to create different worlds for their characters.

Sometimes writers use only one element which is fantastic and tell an otherwise perfectly realistic story as Lucy M. Boston does in *The Children of Green Knowe*. Here the happenings are realistic, except that Tolly sees and plays with children who lived three hundred years before him.

Three primary elements of story—setting, characters, and time—are the elements most writers manipulate in order to create fantasy. Other worlds can be other planets, as in Robert Heinlein's stories of interspace travel or another world within this planet or one like it, as in Lloyd Alexander's *Prydain* series. In her trilogy beginning with *Below the Root,* Zilpha Keatley Snyder creates a world that is both like and unlike our world but essentially a world contained in the roots, trunks, and branches of trees.

The inclusion of supernatural characters is another device for achieving fantasy. Examples range from talking animals such as those in *Watership Down* and humanized animals like *Curious George* to the tiny people in Mary Norton's *The Borrowers,* a supergirl in *Pippi Longstocking,* and animated toys like Andersen's *The Steadfast Tin Soldier.*

The writer of fantasy has another powerful tool in the manipulation of time. John Christopher's *The White Mountains* trilogy takes readers 100 years into the future. Other books like Philippa Pearce's *Tom's Midnight Garden* and Lucy Boston's *The Green Knowe* series take readers centuries back in time.

Despite the obvious power of any single characteristic to produce fantasy, writers frequently combine created worlds with some form of character manipulation, as in Madeleine L'Engle's *A Wrinkle in Time* series, or movement over time with creation of another world, a common occurrence in science fiction.

While any work of imagination may be serious or humorous according to the intent of the author, playfulness and humor seem to have a particular place in fantasy. The exaggeration which is often found in this type of writing can be a rich source of humor, and children can also find humor in stories with one or two fantastic elements which contrast with ordinary, everyday events.

Exaggeration is often the basis for humor in fantasy. Children respond to the humor in amazing characters as different as Astrid Lindgren's *Pippi Longstocking* and Wilbur the pig in E. B. White's *Charlotte's Web.* They enjoy exaggerated incidents like those in Theodor Seuss Geisel's *The 500 Hats of Bartholomew Cubbins.* Surprise is another element of humor that appears frequently in fantasy. William Steig's *Doctor De Soto* provides a satisfying and genuinely funny ending because the fox is so surprised to find his teeth stuck tightly shut just when he was planning on a tasty meal of Doctor De Soto and his wife. First time readers may be just as surprised as the fox but their laughter continues beyond the first reading because it is the fox's surprise that generates the humor.

There is much that is serious, too, in fantasy and science fiction. In these books, religion often figures as people search out the underpinnings of their faith. Madeleine L'Engle's books have strong religious themes, as do those of C. S. Lewis. Related, though not so definitely religious, are the books dealing with supernatural beings. These stories often have their basis in folklore as, for example, Mollie Hunter's *The Kelpie's Pearls* and Rosemary Harris's *The Seal-Singing.* Another theme found in some fantasy is political or sociopolitical. Jean Merrill handles social/political issues humorously in *The*

Pushcart War. John Christopher treats political concerns seriously in *The White Mountains* trilogy and also in his more recent works.

Viewpoint

So fantasy and its archetypal patterns are not going to reach a mass audience very often today. Even amongst that limited part of the population which reads books—books, not newspapers or magazines or escapist thrillers or romances—even amongst them, it isn't going to reach everyone. Every teacher or librarian knows the sturdy child who is a dogged realist and thinks fantasy is for the birds. There are more children like that than there are fantasy readers, and from a practical point of view that's probably just as well. Back in the mists of time, as everyone sat around the campfire listening to the shaman telling the sacred stories, there was always the realist in the group. "I don't want to listen to those boring old myths," he said, and he went off on his own and invented the wheel.

"Your books seem to fit me just right," said the little girl. *Those* are the children we have to reach: to drop into the shadowy pool of their unconscious minds a few images that—perhaps, with luck—will echo through their lives and help them understand and even improve their world, our world. If America doesn't have what Aristotle and Mr. Campbell call an ethos, if instead there is a gap, we need to make sure that our children are given an early awareness of the timeless, placeless archetypes of myth. And since we have no one single myth, that has to mean all the different—and yet similar—mythic patterns we inherit, collectively, in this country from our very diverse beginnings. I am speaking not only of ancient myth but of the modern fantasy which is its descendant, its inheritor. Like poetry, these are the books which speak most directly to the imagination.

Susan Cooper, "Fantasy in the Real World," *The Horn Book Magazine,* May/June 1990, pp. 314–315.

Whatever the imaginative work the writer of fantasy produces, and whatever elements of magic and the supernatural enter into it, the whole must be acceptable to us as readers; it must have consistency and logic, so that we say to ourselves, "I never thought of it that way. But why not?"

The development of modern fantasy has been so astonishing and varied that it merits detailed examination. Because there are so many of these tales, this chapter can consider only a few—stories which have remained favorites over the years, recent ones which have attained great popularity, and certain ones which illustrate trends.

Early Writers— Lasting Influences

Many early writers of fantasy began by using their imaginations to embellish folk and fairy tales. Indeed, in the seventeenth century at the time of Louis XIV, much of the French court was engaged in this pastime. The cult continued for some fifty years and produced the memorable fairy tales of Perrault, Comtesse d'Aulnoy, and Madame Le Prince de Beaumont. These tales are adorned with fairy godmothers, fabulous footwear, and talking beasts. Both "The White Cat" by d'Aulnoy and "Beauty and the Beast" by Le Prince de Beaumont feature a human-turned-animal whose bewitchment is broken by the love and constancy of a human. An intriguing modern variant is Robin McKinley's *Beauty,* a tale written for older readers.

Hans Christian Andersen's first stories for children were likewise elaborations of folk and fairy tales already familiar to much of the population, but he soon began to allow his imagination full rein in the invention of plot, the shaping of character, and the illumination of the human condition. These later creations, solely from Andersen's fertile imagination, are called literary fairy tales, to distinguish them from the fairy tales of unknown origin, those created by common folk. Andersen's work has served as inspiration for many other writers.

John Ruskin, influential British literary critic, wrote "The King of the Golden River", in which the younger, kinder brother wins the inheritance. Howard Pyle, American illustrator par excellence of Robin Hood and King Arthur, wrote and illustrated his own fairy tales at the end of the last century. Oscar Wilde's allegories "The Happy Prince" and "The Selfish Giant" were sophisticated morality tales. Wilde's literary fairy tales, while having supernatural beings as characters, were concerned with good and evil rather than with magic for its own sake. The point of the tale was the human, not the marvelous, element.

The early writers of fantasy—Perrault, Ruskin, Pyle, Wilde, and especially Andersen—had a lasting influence on the form. They were all authors of highly regarded literature for adults; they had proven their ability to write well, and, in Pyle's case, to illustrate successfully. These men were not unknowns, seeking to carve out a career, but well-known writers, adding a new area to an already established reputation. Except for Oscar Wilde, most of what these writers produced for adults is not read so often today as their works for children. They set high standards for those who followed.

Hans Christian Andersen

Hans Christian Andersen (1805–1875) was born in Odense, Denmark, of a peasant family. His cobbler father owned a few books which his son also cherished. His mother worked hard to support her unusual, artistic son in the years between his father's death and Andersen's move to Copenhagen at age fourteen.

Andersen's first book, a travel diary of a walking trip, appeared in 1829, published by himself, and his first volume of *Fairy Tales, Told for Children* appeared in 1835. He was no supporter of organized religion, but he did have an abiding faith in God, often expressed in his tales. Andersen poured himself into his writing; it became the vehicle for expressing his emotions, flashes of humor, commentaries on life, and the follies of humankind. Some of his stories are retellings of folk tales: "Little Claus and Big Claus," "The Princess and the Pea," "The Emperor's New Clothes," "The Wild Swans," and "What Father Does Is Always

Right." In these, Andersen took the traditional story and added to it his own interpretation of character, providing motivation for the action in the tale. The heroes and heroines are not stereotypes; they live and breathe and become individuals, named or not. The princess who can feel a pea under twenty mattresses can never be confused in our thinking with any other princess, sensitive though she may be. Andersen imparted such life to these characters that we feel empathy for the emperor and his courtiers, none of whom naturally wish to admit they are stupid or unfit for office.

But it is in Andersen's own creations, his literary fairy tales, that his genius for characterization is shown. As we read "The Little Mermaid," we shudder at the pain the mermaid must feel as she puts foot to ground, and yet, so persuasive is Andersen's art that, in spite of the physical agony, we still agree with her that the prince is worth dying for.

"The Ugly Duckling" is, rightly or wrongly, seen as symbolic of Andersen's own life. The animosity of the neighbors to the "different" one seems so natural that we wonder if we

From *The Little Mermaid* by Hans Christian Andersen, illustrated by Katie Thamer Treherne.

They came to a pond.
"Mew, mew! We are thirsty!" cried the
            Hundreds of cats,
            Thousands of cats,
Millions and billions and trillions of cats.

From *Millions of Cats*, written and illustrated by Wanda Gág.

ourselves would have seen the promise implicit in the awkward creature. The conversations in the poultry-yard ring true both to human nature and the human ear. What mother would not say, "He is my own child and, when you look closely at him, he's quite handsome . . ."? Because of Andersen, every "ugly duckling" promises a swan.

Andersen's ability to draw character does not rest on extensive description. In a few carefully chosen words he establishes important qualities, leaving our imaginations so stimulated that we supply the rest of the picture. Of the hero of "The Steadfast Tin Soldier" Andersen says, ". . . he stood as firm and steadfast on his one leg as the others did on their two."[2] The only description that Andersen has given us of the soldier is that he has a red and blue uniform and a rifle. The outward description is not important; what Andersen is emphasizing is the constancy of this character.

Andersen's fantasies do not lack supernatural beings or things, and many of them have other-worldly settings, talking animals, and personifications of inanimate objects. But his main contribution was to make us look more sharply at daily life through the window of his imagination.

Andersen's superb use of language, his ability to write with the directness of colloquial speech, unfortunately suffers in the hands of

[2]From "The Steadfast Tin Soldier" in Hans Christian Andersen, *The Complete Fairy Tales*, translated by Erik Christian Haugaard, foreword by Virginia Haviland. New York: Doubleday & Company, 1974.

some translators. A good translation should maintain the tone and style of the original as nearly as possible. The passage cited above, from the translation by Erik Christian Haugaard, is well done in that respect, for it is clear that the translator has the necessary fluency in both languages and also has a strong sense of story.

Fantasy with Folk-Tale Elements

Writers of fantasy since the time of the French court writers have used folk-tale elements in their creations. Especially in the realm of the picture book, their works are often considered so authentic as to be classified as folk tales themselves. One such is *Millions of Cats* by Wanda Gág. The old man and the woman in the tale who want a cat find themselves forced to choose among "hundreds of cats, thousands of cats, millions and billions and trillions of cats." Told with the simplest of language; the barest of characterization, but with a consummate style which has omitted all but the essential words; illustrated with Gág's own flowing, childlike black-and-white drawings; this story truly seems to be a long-forgotten folk tale, the only fantasy being the number of cats and the method of reducing them to one.

Dragon of the Lost Sea by Laurence Yep is a longer and more complex story based on folk elements, specifically Chinese myths. Yep's tale is told by a centuries-old dragon possessing magical powers who is on a quest to find an evil creature and it is continued in *Dragon Steel*. Virginia Hamilton's *The Magical Adventures of Pretty Pearl* also blends fantasy and folklore, in this case African and American folklore.

James Thurber
The Great Quillow
Many Moons

The humor James Thurber showed as a cartoonist and as the author of delightfully satiric fables is evident in his fairy tales for children. *The Great Quillow* is about a toymaker, the only person in his village clever enough to think of a way to rid the town of a voracious giant who is depleting the communal larder. Quillow's attendance at meetings of the town council enables Thurber to poke sly fun at the prim requirements of parliamentary procedure.

In *Many Moons,* for which Louis Slobodkin's illustrations won the Caldecott Medal, the Little Princess Lenore lies ill, saying that she will recover only if she can have the moon. The King consults his assorted wise men, who are equally long-winded, opinionated, and useless. Only the jester has the wisdom to consult the Princess, making it clear that to her the moon is golden and small, since she can obscure it by holding up her thumb. She is delighted with the small golden globe the jester brings.

Thurber's light, seemingly effortless tales with their subtle wit have a surface simplicity that many children can enjoy, while those of wider experience can appreciate his perceptive delineation of human nature. Thurber's stories are certainly in Andersen's fairy-tale tradition.

J. R. R. Tolkien
The Hobbit
The Lord of the Rings

No other fantasy of our time has appealed to as broad an age range of readers as has *The Hobbit;* children are enthralled by it, and adults probe and discuss the inner meanings of the book and of its companion tale, *The Lord of the Rings,* a complex three-volume sequel. Professor Tolkien was an eminent philologist and an authority on myth and saga, and his knowledge provided so firm a base for the mood and style of his writing that there is no need for scholarly demonstration. Middle-earth *is.* Tolkien wrote of it as easily as one writes about one's own home, and the familiarity of approach lends credence to the world he created.

The hero of *The Hobbit* is Bilbo Baggins, a little creature who is neat and quiet, who loves his material comforts, and who has no desire to do great deeds. When he is tricked into going along on a quest, however, the little hobbit rises to the occasion, showing that even the common person (or hobbit) is capable of heroism.

There are several qualities that contribute to the stature of *The Hobbit.* The adventures are exciting, the characters are differentiated and

From *The Hobbit* by J. R. R. Tolkien, illustrated by Michael Hague.

distinctive, and the book bubbles with humor. One of the amusing qualities is the aptness of the invented personal and place names. Bilbo's mother's unmarried name was Belladonna Took, perfectly in accord with her reputation as a hobbit who had had a few adventures before she settled down as Mrs. Baggins. And what an admirable name for a dragon—Smaug, and what an equally appropriate name for his lair— the Desolation of Smaug. Perhaps a special appeal lies in the very fact that Bilbo Baggins is a quiet little creature whose achievements are due to a stout heart, tenacity, and loyalty to his friends rather than to great strength or brilliance. He puts heroism within the grasp of each reader. Many folk-tale elements are present—the human-beast, elves, the enchanted artifact—all woven naturally into the tale.

C. S. Lewis
The Chronicles of Narnia

Well known as a poet and author, C. S. Lewis created for children the strange new world of Narnia, which they first enter through an old wardrobe. *The Lion, the Witch, and the Wardrobe,* about the adventures of four children, is the first of a series of seven books. Narnia is no Utopia. In fact, once the children have become kings and queens of Narnia, they find themselves engaged in the endless conflict between good and evil, symbolized by the benignant Lion Aslan and the malicious Witch. After reigning for many years, the children return to their own world only to find that they have not even been missed, the time scheme in Narnia having differed so from that in their own world.

The Last Battle concludes the series, and brings the world of Narnia to an end. Lewis's stories are so clearly based on Christian theology and the Bible that we sometimes do not recognize the folkloric elements in the tales— the sacrifice of a king for the good of his people, the talking animals and trees, the healing apple.

While Lewis's style verges on the avuncular at times, it is perfectly suited to these Chronicles, where the children are definitely children and not expected to display qualities more appropriate for adults. The children are, on the whole, honest, steadfast, persevering, and able to resist temptation; the larger tasks are always accomplished with the aid of an adult, or a supernatural helper. It is taken for granted that the children do not have to *prove* their inherent goodness; rather there is sorrow that at times one or another of them may fall short of the best of which a child is known to be capable.

Patricia Wrightson
The Nargun and the Stars
An Older Kind of Magic
Balyet

Recipient of Australia's Children's Book Award for her first book, *The Crooked Snake,* which was not published in the United States, and again for *The Nargun and the Stars,* Patricia Wrightson has been a channel through which children of her own and other countries have learned the beauty and dignity of the legendary creatures of Aborigine mythology. In *An Older Kind of Magic* the theme is conservation, as some of the little people use their magic to foil a plan to destroy the botanical garden where they play. Here, and in *Balyet,* the lives of human children

and of ancient spirits are credibly intermeshed in a story that is structured with craft and affection for the mighty and mysterious spirits of an ancient world.

Some of the creatures of the earlier books appear in *The Ice Is Coming* as Wirrun, a young Aborigine, calls on the amoral spirits of rocks and water to help him find and stop the creeping ice. In a sequel, *The Dark Bright Water,* Wirrun again goes into the countryside on a mission; this time he gains love when a ceremonial fire changes a capricious waterspirit into a woman. Unlike *Down to Earth,* a humorous story of a visitor from Mars, these stories are serious in tone, cadenced and stately in style, yet filled with suspense and action.

Lloyd Alexander
The *Prydain* Books
The Marvelous Misadventures of Sebastian
The *Westmark* Trilogy

Lloyd Alexander had planned, in writing about Prydain, only to adapt the Welsh legends he loved, but he became so engrossed in the project that, as he said in his Newbery Medal acceptance speech, "it grew into something much more ambitious."

The first of the five-book Prydain cycle is *The Book of Three,* in which Taran, the hero, is introduced. Taran, Assistant Pig-Keeper, does not have great status, but of course few pig-keepers are responsible for such a pig as Hen Wen, who utters prophecies by using letter sticks. In this book, Taran goes forth with the great warrior Gwydion to fight against the evil Horned King, who has sworn allegiance to Arawn, Lord of the Land of Death. On the quest, Taran and Gwydion are joined by the capricious Princess Eilonwy, the Caliban-like creature Gurgi, and the boastful harpist, Fflewddur Fflam.

Each of the characters is strongly drawn. Unforgettable is the crafty, toadying, whimpering but loyal Gurgi, whose rhymed speech delights readers. The histrionics of Fflewddur have a touch of Mr. Micawber as he pontificates and prevaricates, but his harp, given him by Taliesin, is a rein on his fancy, for whenever he lies, a string breaks.

In the second book, *The Black Cauldron,* Taran again goes on a quest, this time to the Land of Death; in *The Castle of Llyr,* the Princess Eilonwy is kidnaped, and it is then that Taran first realizes his love for the saucy girl. In *Taran Wanderer* the hero goes forth to seek his true identity and learns that his worth, whatever it is, is dependent on his ability and his accomplishments rather than on his position. The final book in the Prydain cycle, *The High King,* was awarded the Newbery Medal. It tells of the last conflict between Taran and the Death Lord.

Alexander's fantasy is based firmly upon legend, with a multitude of natural and supernatural characters, and some halfway between. Indeed, we learn at the end that all of the major characters, except Taran himself, are from the Summer Land, where they live forever. Alexander creates distinctive characters, and he is a true master of the light, sophisticated style, preferring discussion to action, although there are great goings and comings in these books. There is much humor as well, but it is the wry shrug of the adult and not the slapstick antic of the child.

Alexander uses many elements of folk literature in his tales—the magic bauble or light that Eilonwy carries, the ability of the pig to prophesy, the magic cauldron and sword, the inexhaustible knapsack of food. Throughout the books runs the muted theme of the hero, the champion of good against the forces of evil—not just the external manifestations of it, but the evil within oneself—the hero who emerges triumphant at the end.

Another intricate tale by Alexander, *The Marvelous Misadventures of Sebastian,* received the National Book Award. The fantasy is slight here, being a matter of the exaggeration of reality rather than the creation of a new world or supernatural beings. Later books, *The Wizard in the Tree* and *The First Two Lives of Lukas-Kasha* have one or two magical characters or devices, but portray human nature quite realistically.

Alexander's trilogy, *Westmark, The Kestrel,* and *The Beggar Queen* are fine books of fantasy that focus on the characters and their plight. Mickle, a girl who lives by her wits, and Theo, a fugitive, find themselves in the palace of Augustine, King of Westmark. The story of conflict and treachery unfolds as the children take part in a war and survive it to a satisfying end in which Mickle discovers who her father is and assumes her place as Queen Augusta.

Ursula Le Guin
The *Earthsea* Books

Ursula Le Guin, like Tolkien, has created a world of her own, Earthsea. It is a place of wizards and mages, spells and charms. *A Wizard*

Viewpoint

Melancholy men, they say, are the most incisive humorists; by the same token, writers of fantasy must be, within their own frame of work, hardheaded realists. What appears gossamer is, underneath, solid as prestressed concrete.

Once committed to his imaginary kingdom, the writer is not a monarch but a subject. Characters must appear plausible in their own setting, and the writer must go along with their inner logic. Happenings should have logical implications. Details should be tested for consistency. Shall animals speak? If so, do *all* animals speak? If not, then which—and how? Above all, why? Is it essential to the story, or lamely cute? Are there enchantments? How powerful? If an enchanter can perform such-and-such, can he not also do so-and-so?

. . . And, as in all literature, characters are what ultimately count. . . . Fantasy . . . goes right to the core of a character, to extract the essence, the very taste of an individual personality. This may be one of the things that makes good fantasy so convincing.

Lloyd Alexander, "The Flat-heeled Muse," *The Horn Book Magazine,* April 1965, pp. 142, 143–144, 145.

of Earthsea introduces us to Ged, or Sparrowhawk, seventh son of a seventh son, and tells of his education as a wizard. At one point in his training, Ged cannot resist the temptation to show off his powers, and lets loose a nameless evil to roam the world. He struggles first to escape it, and finally realizes that he cannot avoid it and must meet it head on. *The Tombs of Atuan* introduces us to Arha, trained from early childhood to be the high priestess of the Kargad Lands, a part of Earthsea. Ged comes to the sacred precincts, searching for half of a magic amulet. He not only finds it, but frees Arha from her servitude to the dark gods. *The Farthest Shore* shows us Ged as the Archmage, setting out to discover the reason for the decline in potency of the wizards throughout Earthsea. With him goes Arren, destined to be the king of all the lands of Earthsea.

LeGuin is adept at creation of character, concentrating her efforts on her protagonists, defining minor characters in relationship to them. Ged's nature is built up gradually, through action and reaction, and because we learn to know him in this way, we accept him fully. There are marvels and mysteries aplenty —the ability to raise a favorable wind, to talk to dragons—but these are of minor importance to the tale of Ged as a person. Part of Le Guin's power as a storyteller lies in her style—serious, spare, precise. Not for her the earthy humor of Tolkien or the sophisticated wit of Alexander. The measured cadence of the language seems to be a retelling in a more modern idiom of an old, old tale. Le Guin's versatility is demonstrated in *Catwings* and *Catwings Return;* these books for younger readers are humorous and affectionate in tone, and are remarkably convincing in presenting kittens that fly.

Susan Cooper
The Dark Is Rising Books
Jethro and the Jumbie
The Selkie Girl

A British writer, now a resident of the United States, Susan Cooper has written a series of five books about the eternal battle between good and evil. In *Over Sea, Under Stone*, Simon, Jane, and Barnaby go to Cornwall on vacation with their parents and an old, white-haired professor friend of the family, Merriman Lyon. These characters provide a core on which other of Cooper's books are centered.

In *The Dark Is Rising,* we meet Will Stanton, who learns he is the youngest of the Old Ones, an ageless people whose destiny is to fight against evil until the end of time. His education about his heritage is undertaken in part by Merriman Lyon, another of the Old Ones.

Jane is the heroine of *Greenwitch,* while Will Stanton is the major character in *The Grey King,* a Newbery Medal book. Will is sent to Wales to recover from a severe illness. While there, he meets King Arthur's son, Bran, who was sent forward in time to protect Will from the forces of evil. In the last book, *Silver on the Tree,* Will, Bran, and other defenders of the Light triumph over evil.

Cooper has made increasing use of legend and folklore with each book in the series. Since we have accepted these elements in the stories previously, we are willing to immerse ourselves more deeply as the tale progresses. Setting is important in all of these stories, providing an atmosphere in which old tales naturally come true. Cooper's characterizations are vivid, especially of the three children and Will Stanton, with much action, described in rich, meaningful language.

Cooper moves into another level of fantasy in *Jethro and the Jumbie,* a humorous contemporary story for younger readers, in which an indomitable child on a Caribbean island outwits the local ghost. Also for younger readers is a retelling of the Selkie legend, *The Selkie Girl.*

Other Fantasy with Folk-Tale Elements

Alan Garner has drawn heavily on the legends of Cheshire to tell *The Weirdstone of Brisingamen* and its sequel, *The Moon of Gomrath.* Garner's earlier stories are filled with action at the expense of character development, but in *The Owl Service,* which won a Carnegie Medal, we come to know the young people well as they mysteriously reenact a Welsh legend, their actions inhibited and dictated by the English class structure which circumscribes their lives.

William Mayne has written a few stories

including folkloric elements, most notably *Earthfasts*, in which two boys are the means by which a soldier from the past comes alive. Mayne's *A Year and a Day* is about a fairy child who stays with two Cornish children; quiet and perceptive, the story is distinctive for its rich use of language. Leon Garfield's *The Wedding Ghost* is a sophisticated elaboration on the "Sleeping Beauty" theme.

Scottish folklore provides background and atmosphere in Mollie Hunter's *The Walking Stones, A Stranger Came Ashore,* and *The Mermaid Summer.* The rhythm of her writing lends credence to these tales of supernatural beings and happenings. Erik Haugaard, in *Prince Boghole,* tells a humorous story of medieval Ireland.

Rosemary Harris, a Carnegie Medal winner for *The Moon in the Cloud,* has used the ancient story of Noah and the flood to build a sophisticated, amusing tale.

Tales of Pure Imagination

While many writers of fantasy have chosen to use motifs from folklore in their work, others have created magical and unusual characters and happenings which seem unlike anything that has gone before.

Lewis Carroll, Charles Kingsley, George Macdonald, and Sir James Barrie all wrote fantasies in the late nineteenth and early twentieth centuries. Kingsley's *The Water-Babies* and Macdonald's *At the Back of the North Wind* and his Princess and Curdie stories are still enjoyed by a few children, but these tales seem overly long and very moralistic to modern readers. Lewis Carroll's tales, on the other hand, are full of pure nonsense and rare humor. Barrie's *Peter Pan* has been the most popular of his plays for almost a century. The book based on that play, *Peter and Wendy,* has perennial characters like the boy who won't grow up and the evil Captain Hook.

Lewis Carroll
Alice's Adventures in Wonderland
Through the Looking Glass

The "Alice" books cannot be accounted for on the basis of anything that had preceded them. Charles Lutwidge Dodgson was a sober, sedate cleric who lectured in mathematics at Christ Church, Oxford. Dr. Liddell, a colleague, had three little girls of whom Alice was evidently Dodgson's favorite. Picnicking on a riverbank on a summer afternoon, Dodgson entertained his young friends with the tale of "Alice's

From *Alice's Adventures in Wonderland* by Lewis Carroll, illustrated by John Tenniel.

Adventures Under Ground." Alice hoped there'd be nonsense in it, and no hopes ever materialized more gloriously. The next Christmas, Dodgson wrote his story as a gift for "a dear child in memory of a Summer day."

Three years after the famous picnic, the story appeared in book form, somewhat enlarged, with the new title *Alice's Adventures in Wonderland* and with Sir John Tenniel's matchless illustrations. That was 1865, and six years later the companion volume appeared, carrying Alice to further adventures when she walks into a mirror-world; both books were written under the pseudonym Lewis Carroll.

Does anyone who has read the *Adventures in Wonderland* ever forget those opening paragraphs, with the child's comment on books?

Alice was beginning to get very tired of sitting by her sister on the bank, and of having nothing to do: once or twice she had peeped into the book her sister was reading, but it had no pictures or conversations in it, "and what is the use of a book," thought Alice, "without pictures or conversations?"

Then plop! Right into the third short paragraph comes the White Rabbit, with waistcoat and watch. Down he goes into the rabbit hole, murmuring "Oh dear! Oh dear! I shall be too late!" And down the rabbit hole after him goes Alice, "never once considering how in the world she was to get out again." From then on madness takes over.

When do children enjoy *Alice*? Needless to say, it should never be required reading. Some children heartily dislike fantasy and to make them read *Alice* would be to turn reading into a penalty instead of a delight. When college students are asked what books they remember enjoying as children, there is often more disagreement over *Alice* than over any other book. Some disliked it heartily or were bored by it; some say *Alice* was one of their favorite books, not as children but at the high-school age. This is perhaps where it really belongs. Most of those who liked *Alice* as children, ten or under, had heard it read aloud by adults who enjoyed it. Those who had to read the book for themselves rarely found it funny until they were older.

Sir John Tenniel in his illustrations for *Alice* has fixed forever the face, figure, and dress of this beloved little girl, an appealing figure which no one ever forgets. The Tenniel White Rabbit is an equally unforgettable figure with his sporty tweed coat, his massive gold watch and chain, his swagger walking stick—just the kind of fellow who *would* keep the Duchess waiting. The drawings are so alive, so profoundly interpretative, so right, that it's almost impossible to think of these characters except as Tenniel pictured them.

William Pène du Bois
Bear Party
The Twenty-One Balloons

The fantasies of William Pène du Bois are as orderly and logical as mathematics, and his illustrations have the same graceful balance. His other lifelong interests are reflected in his books—his love of France, the circus, all forms of mechanized transportation, islands, Utopias, and explosions! Look at some of his most notable books: *Bear Party* is a reasonable fable about some quarrelsome bears who grow genuinely fond of each other when they have a fancy dress party. A bear Utopia results. In *Lazy Tommy Pumpkinhead* the author takes a healthy poke at the electronic age and what can happen when machines fail; and in *The Forbidden Forest* he burlesques the heroic war story by having a kangaroo named Lady Adelaide stop World War I.

And best of all there is his Newbery Medal book, *The Twenty-One Balloons*. When its hero, Professor Sherman, tires of teaching little boys arithmetic, he sets off in a balloon to see the world and be alone. He tells his story of landing on the island of Krakatoa and finding that its inhabitants are inventors of amazing supergadgets. These are described in great detail and drawn meticulously. Since the island is volcanic, the people have planned a fantastic machine for escape should the volcano erupt, and of course it does. And off they go in their airy-go-round. Related with the utmost simplicity, the story piles up suspense until the explosion is a relief.

Mary Norton
The Borrowers Books

As British as tea for breakfast, but with action, suspense, and characters of universal appeal, *The Borrowers* by Mary Norton was immediately popular in the United States as well as in Great Britain.

Borrowers are not fairies but small creatures who live in old houses and take their names from the places they inhabit—the Overmantels, for instance, the Harpsichords, and the Clocks, who live under a huge old grandfather clock in the hall. Homily, Pod, and their daughter Arrietty Clock are the only surviving family of Borrowers in the old house. When a Borrower is seen, there is nothing for him to do but emigrate. Only Pod, climbing curtains with the aid of his trusty hatpin,

borrowing a useful spoon now and then or a bit of tea or a portrait stamp of the Queen, has escaped detection. Arrietty is the problem now: Arrietty wants to see the world and she goes exploring, happily and trustingly even after the boy sees her. They become fast friends, but even the boy cannot prevent the disastrous ending, so catastrophic that young readers could not accept it as final. There had to be a sequel, and so we follow the fortunes of these fascinating characters in *The Borrowers Afield*, *The Borrowers Afloat*, *The Borrowers Aloft*, and *The Borrowers Avenged*.

No briefing of these stories can give any conception of their quality. Every character is unforgettably portrayed. There is poor Homily with her hair forever awry, loving but a chronic worrier, "taking on" first and then going capably to work. Pod is the sober realist, a philosopher and a brave one. Arrietty is youth and adventure, springtime and hope, too much in love with life to be afraid even of those mammoth "human beans." To read these books aloud is to taste their full richness.

From *The Borrowers* by Mary Norton, illustrated by Beth and Joe Krush.

Lucy M. Boston
The *Green Knowe* Books

Another distinguished English fantasy, beautifully written and completely absorbing, is *The Children of Green Knowe* by Lucy M. Boston. A lonely boy named Tolly is sent to live with his great-grandmother, Mrs. Oldknow, at the family's ancient manor house, Green Knowe. Tolly becomes aware of the presence of other children who come and go from the manor—he hears them but he cannot see them, although he knows his great-grandmother hears and sees them. Tolly learns that these children are his ancestors who died in the great plague during the seventeenth century. Eventually, Tolly is able to see the children also, but he can never touch them.

There are more books in this setting—*Treasure of Green Knowe* in which Tolly and his great-grandmother again appear; *An Enemy at Green Knowe*; and *The River at Green Knowe*. *A Stranger at Green Knowe*, one of the most moving boy and animal tales ever written, brings an escaped zoo gorilla to sanctuary at Green Knowe. Although published two decades after

From *The Stones of Green Knowe* by L. M. Boston, illustrated by Peter Boston.

the first book, *The Stones of Green Knowe* goes back to the twelfth century, when the house was built. In all of these stories, real life and fantasy are successfully mingled.

Boston's stories are never commonplace. They grow naturally out of the characters of Mrs. Oldknow and Tolly, interacting with the past which is still present in the old house, a subtle juxtaposition of present and past time.

A. Philippa Pearce
Tom's Midnight Garden

Philippa Pearce won the Carnegie Medal for *Tom's Midnight Garden,* an engrossing fantasy with time as a theme. Young Tom, much bored by life in his aunt and uncle's apartment, hears an ancient clock strike thirteen. Immediately he slips into an enchanting garden where he plays with Hatty, a child from the past. Their play is imaginative but made credible because of the logic of "Time no longer," the motto on the clock. These strange midnight adventures of Tom's are later explained somewhat by what adults might call thought-transference. However, they seem quite clear and uncomplicated to readers once they accept Tom's timeless midnight garden. Pearce's style is serene, unhurried, reflective—giving us time to absorb the experience as Tom lives it. Her skill is particularly evident in *Who's Afraid? And Other Strange Stories,* in which the same craft and composure are achieved in the less malleable short-story form.

As in all of these tales of pure imagination, it is the author's skill in character development that is most significant. We think at first that it is the action in the tale that delights us; but then we realize that any adventure would be exciting, providing that it happened to Carroll's Alice, or Norton's Arrietty, or Boston's Tolly, or Pearce's Tom.

Vivien Alcock
The Haunting of Cassie Palmer
The Monster Garden

English author Vivien Alcock emerged, with her first book, as a writer of rare ability, whose polished style, imaginative plots, and tart yet affectionate characterizations drew kudos on both sides of the Atlantic. In her first book, *The Haunting of Cassie Palmer,* Cassie, whose mother is a medium, is definitely not interested in testing her own psychic powers and is dismayed when, on a dare, she makes a ghost appear.

The dramatic quality of Alcock's work is attested to by the fact that many of her novels have been adapted for television in England. Whether in fantasy or in realistic stories, the structure is cohesive; to a high degree, in her fantasy, Alcock deftly meshes the fanciful elements and the realistic matrix that Lloyd Alexander refers to as "prestressed concrete." The blob that grows into a monstrous creature in *The Monster Garden* is pure fantasy, but the protective love a child feels for that creature is both believable and touching. Alcock adroitly creates suspense without sacrificing pace or credibility. The same craftsmanship permeates her ten short stories in *Ghostly Companions: A Feast of Chilly Tales.*

Diana Wynne Jones
Archer's Goon
Howl's Moving Castle
The Lives of Christopher Chant

Few writers of fantasy so consistently produce innovative plots as does Diana Wynne Jones. In *Archer's Goon,* seven wizard siblings have taken control of an English town. One of these children has gained power by using the words written by the father of two other children confronted by the Goon. The structure is intricate but so deftly developed that it is never confusing.

Howl's Moving Castle has the same inventiveness and yeasty humor as do Jones's earlier books; it pits the magic powers of Howl (whose castle rumbles its way across the moor) against that of a wicked witch whose spell turns the young heroine, for most of the story, into a ninety-year-old woman. This well-rounded fantasy is written in a polished, ebullient style. In *A Tale of Time City*, a child being evacuated from London at the time of the blitz is kidnapped by two boys from a place outside time. In *The Lives of Christopher Chant,* magic is treated as a humdrum chore, with education-for-witchcraft an accepted, if boring, part of the Chant children's training.

Penelope Farmer
Charlotte Sometimes
The Summer Birds

Charlotte Sometimes has the timeshift theme that is a familiar one in fantasy, but it has seldom been used more dramatically, perhaps because Charlotte alternates between two worlds. Somehow, while in boarding school, Charlotte finds that she is back in the days of World War I and that her name is Clare. Slowly she begins to realize that Clare is her double and that whenever she is in Clare's world, her own place is taken by her doppelgänger. The mystery and suspense are maintained to the end.

In *Emma in Winter* Charlotte's sister finds that she shares the same dreams as a boy she dislikes, a boy she and Charlotte met in *The Summer Birds,* the most moving of these books. In *The Summer Birds,* a strange boy teaches the sisters to fly, and then all the children in their school enjoy the soaring bliss and freedom of flight. When the summer ends, they learn the boy's identity and the magic is lost. They are again earthbound. The book has an almost palpable aura of magic and an ending with all the inevitability of Greek drama. In *Year King* the psychic sharing of twins is explored in a sophisticated book with deep psychological impllications.

Although Farmer's style is smooth, and her characterizations perceptive, we remember more the moods and settings of her stories rather than the people in them. We admire her ingenuity but at the same time we don't agonize over her characters' problems as we do over those of the Borrowers. The actual workings of the fantastic elements in Farmer's works are a little too obvious.

Viewpoint

With fantasy I believe that the author is required in the very beginning to establish a premise, an inner logic for his story, and to draw boundary lines outside which his fantasy may not wander. Without ever having to think about it, the reader must feel that the author is working consistently within a frame of reference. He is setting himself a certain discipline, and this will vary, of course, from tale to tale. Modern fantasy adds a certain delight: the element of contrast with the everyday world which provides a kind of reverberation arising from the fact that within his everyday world a little pool of magic exists possessing a strange, private, yet quite powerful and convincing reality of its own. And the pool of magic seems remorselessly to seep away if the first premise (or promise, you might call it) is not kept, if there is a kind of betrayal and the story is handled in opposition to the inner logic laid down in the beginning.

Eleanor Cameron, "The Inmost Secret," *The Horn Book Magazine,* February 1983, pp. 23–24.

Maurice Sendak
Where the Wild Things Are
Higglety Pigglety Pop!
In the Night Kitchen
Outside Over There

From *Outside Over There*, written and illustrated by Maurice Sendak.

Maurice Sendak's versatility and craftsmanship as an artist are discussed in Chapter 5. They are qualities that contribute both to the books he has illustrated for other authors and to those he has written himself. The integrity of his conception and the respect he has for children are nowhere more evident than in his own books of fantasy. Best known of his books is the 1964 Caldecott winner, *Where the Wild Things Are,* a picture book that was greeted with delight by many and apprehension by some. Max is a small boy whose noisy ebullience causes his mother to call him a Wild Thing. "I'll eat you up!" he retorts, and is sent to his room, where he consoles himself by imagining a kingdom of wild things, fanged and clawed, all bowing respectfully to their beloved ruler, Max, king of all the wild things. "Let the wild rumpus start," he proclaims, and a mammoth frolic takes place. When Max leaves, his creatures plead with him to stay because they love him so. But he goes back to his room, to real life, and to his supper waiting for him, "and it was still hot." The psychological implications are sound. Children see the reassurance in Max's return from his fantasy land when he "wanted to be where someone loved him best of all."

The subtitle of *Higglety Pigglety Pop!* is *There Must Be More to Life.* Although its heroine, Jenny, has everything a dog could want, she leaves home because she is not content. She wants something she does not have, and feels "there must be more to life" than having everything. Jenny was drawn from life, immortalizing a dearly loved household pet in soft and amusing black-and-white pictures that are quite different from the bold exaggeration and flamboyance of the wild things. The story ends with a poignant note from Jenny to her old master in which she says that she cannot tell him how to get to Castle Yonder, because she doesn't know where it is. "But if you ever come this way, look for me."

Maurice Sendak's childhood memories are the basis for much of the setting for *In the Night Kitchen.* The delicious smells of baking coming from the room below, the buildings, seen against a night sky, and the "Mickey Oven" label all contribute to the story of a small boy who, in his dream, falls down into the night kitchen where three identical bakers (all Oliver Hardy) try to stir him into the batter. Sendak's draftsmanship is particularly impressive in these illustrations, and both the pictures and the story are remarkable in their identification with a child's vision.

In *Outside Over There* Sendak moves into a different style in illustration and text. The tale is dreamlike with a haunting sense of urgency and is illustrated in an artistic style more romantic than his earlier, humorous book.

Natalie Babbitt
Tuck Everlasting
The Devil's Storybook

Natalie Babbitt shows a high sense of comedy in most of her writing, and a facility for combining ridiculous postures or plights with a bland, ingenuous writing style. Yet these are not the qualities that distinguish what is undoubtedly her most impressive book, *Tuck Everlasting.* It is a story about immortality and death, so smoothly crafted that the deeper implications permeate but do not obscure the action: a girl of ten is befriended by a family that has drunk at a spring that has given them eternal life—

Viewpoint

The thing to remember about fantasy, it seems to me, is that it's deeply rooted in reality. It didn't start out in story form. It's older than that. The fantasies came first, then the stories came along to embody them. When you're writing a fantasy story, you'd better understand that and keep it at the front of your mind, or the story won't work. For fantasy is primarily a symbolic language for dealing with three very real and fundamental human attributes: we fear, we hope, and, because life can be very dull sometimes, we need to be diverted. Of course, these three categories have a way of blurring into each other at the edges. Superstition, for instance, lies between fear and hope, and overlaps both. But in general, you can cover most of the territory by sticking to the big three.

Fear fantasies can be defined as what we don't want to believe. Hope fantasies are what we do want to believe. And diversion fantasies are what we half-believe because they make life more interesting.

All fantasy is rooted somewhere very deep in reality. It is the voice of our reachings-out for explanations of the riddles of our lives, and for enrichment of their texture. All can be set forth in stories told in many different ways: in dream stories like *Alice in Wonderland,* in stories where the fantasy world exists across some kind of threshold as with Oz and Narnia, in stories where some single element of fantasy appears in the hard, real world as with *Charlotte's Web,* or in stories where a rich fantasy world coexists on the same plane with reality, as Shakespeare presented it in such plays as *The Tempest* and *A Midsummer's Night Dream.*

From "The Roots of Fantasy" by Natalie Babbitt, *The Bulletin,* Spring 1986, Volume XII, Number 2. Reprinted by permission of the CLA Bulletin.

and eternal life proves a burden. The pace and drama of the family's attempt to escape observation end on a poignant note, as the protagonist helps their flight but weighs the possibility of drinking from the spring herself.

In *Knee-Knock Rise,* a whole village is terrified by the terrible Megrimum, a creature that doesn't exist. Babbitt's humor is strongest in *The Devil's Storybook* and *The Devil's Other Storybook,* in each of which an arrogant devil is outwitted in ten lively short stories. Babbitt's ingenious plots are often amusingly farfetched, and she delights in word play as much as Carl Sandburg does in his *Rootabaga Stories* with their garrulous humor.

Penelope Lively
The Ghost of Thomas Kempe
Uninvited Ghosts and Other Stories
The Voyage of QV 66

Penelope Lively has established herself as one of England's most interesting and versatile writers. She won the Carnegie Medal for *The Ghost of Thomas Kempe,* the story of a boy who moves into an old house and is plagued by the mischievous pranks of a dissatisfied ghost, a sorcerer for whose behavior the boy is blamed. The writing style is matter-of-fact, a good foil for the humorous concept of a Jacobean ghost puzzled by a saran-wrapped world.

Two books of short stories, *A House Inside Out* and *Uninvited Ghosts and Other Stories* also show Lively's effective combining of ludicrous situations and a bland style in graceful, witty cameo fantasies. In *The Voyage of QV 66,* a group of animals travels to London in a future, massively flooded England; this is Lively's most warm and amusing story, the animal characters used wittily to point out the foibles of humankind. There are suspense and momentum in *A Stitch in Time* as a shy and lonely child hears echoes of the past in a rented vacation home.

Helen Cresswell
The Winter of the Birds
A Game of Catch

Writing with equal facility and polish whether the stories are realistic or fantastic, Helen Cresswell is almost as well known in the United

From *The Devil's Other Storybook,* written and illustrated by Natalie Babbitt.

Other Tales of Pure Imagination

The field of fantasy has attracted a number of excellent writers. *Peter and Wendy*, the book based on Sir James Barrie's most popular play, *Peter Pan*, has perennial characters such as the boy who won't grow up and the evil Captain Hook. Anne McCaffrey has created a whole world in *Dragonsong* and *Dragonsinger*. Her writing style is fluent and vigorous, and her characterization vivid in recounting the adventures of a girl whose longing to become a harper is aided by her skill at training a band of flying fire-lizards to sing. The series continued with *Dragondrums*.

Jane Langton has taken the Concord, New Hampshire terrain as her own, and has constructed ingenious adventures for Eddy and Eleanor in *The Diamond in the Window* and *The Astonishing Stereoscope*. The window and the stereoscope project the children into magical times and places. In *The Fledgling*, Georgie's adventures with a Canada goose and her exhilaration as she learns to fly produce a fine story.

States as she is in England. In *The Winter of the Birds,* the concept of terrifying steel birds who come at night, borne by wires, to strike and slash, is deftly merged with a realistic story told from the viewpoints of two people and the author. She creates a true hero in the person of cheerful, generous Finn who helps the lonely old man frightened by the birds, and she vividly evokes the atmosphere of the shabby neighborhood in which they live.

In *A Game of Catch,* two children play ball with Kate—but they are children who have stepped from a museum painting. When Kate sees the picture a second time, the ball has changed from one hand to another. Nicely structured, convincingly meshing the real and the fanciful, the story is just the right length and complexity for readers in the middle grades. In *Moondial,* also a time-slip story, a firm friendship develops between lonely, time-separated children.

Among Cresswell's other stories of pure imagination are *The Piemakers,* in which there is a pride in craftsmanship that is a recurrent theme in her writing; and *The Bongleweed,* in which a mysterious plant goes on a rampaging spurt of growth and takes over a garden. In this book there is some of the humor that is so evident in Cresswell's realistic *Bagthorpe* series (see Chapter 10) and the structural craftsmanship that is seen in all her writing.

From *Peter Pan* by J. M. Barrie, illustrated by Greg Hildebrandt.

Viewpoint

Deeper meaning is essential in fantasy. For the characters involved, there is no need for very deep thought. They can enjoy the pleasure of realizing their dearest wishes, only occasionally speculating about their origin. Sometimes (as in E. Nesbit's stories) they can be changed a little, can learn a little from their adventures, as they miraculously travel the world, change their shape, or exploit the power of a button, a lamp-post or a pencil. But the reader who vicariously enjoys these delights should expect something more. The fantasy should exercise his imagination. For the characters in the story there is little time for Why and How. Questions are blown away as they rush from one adventure to another. But the reader can and should ask How and Why. He should be left with a sense of expansion, as if he himself had been flying on a magic carpet and breathing an air more rarefied than his accustomed oxygen.

Margery Fisher, *Intent Upon Reading.* New York: Watts, 1961, pp. 149–150.

Antoine de Saint-Exupéry's *The Little Prince* is a poetic, practically plotless fairy tale, whimsical and sophisticated in its concern with the inconsistencies of human behavior. The prince, who comes to earth from another planet, tells much of the story in dialogue form. The lack of action and the allusiveness of the dialogue limit the book's appeal to those readers who appreciate style and theme above all else.

The Animal Family by Randall Jarrell also has a poetic quality but is more cohesive in plot and is more smoothly written than *The Little Prince.* Alone in his home near the sea, a hunter falls in love with a mermaid, who comes to live with him. Their family is increased by a shipwrecked boy, a bear, and a lynx, and together they live in love and peace. The writing has a subtle simplicity and ingenuous humor that succeed both in making the element of fantasy believable and in avoiding any semblance of sentimentality.

Elizabeth Coatsworth's Newbery Medal book, *The Cat Who Went to Heaven,* which has a Japanese setting, is about a struggling young artist who is commissioned to paint a picture for the temple. The temple priest refuses to accept the picture because it shows a cat in the procession of animals approaching Buddha. The little household cat that had been a model for the picture dies, and a miracle occurs; the painted cat now appears at the head of the procession, under the hand of Buddha, which is stretched out in blessing. Coatsworth's tales are well written, whatever the genre.

Modern Stories of Talking Beasts

The talking beasts in the folk tales were, on the whole, a cheerful lot. Silly creatures were liquidated, but the wise pig survived; and smart billy goats gained the grassy hillside in spite of the troll. There was no brooding and no melancholy until Andersen's *Fairy Tales,* whose Ugly Duckling not only was mistreated by others but suffered spiritually. In the two English talking-beast masterpieces, *The Tale of Peter Rabbit* and *The Wind in the Willows,* there are animals with limitations who make mistakes and commit follies which they shake off with blithe determination. It is the tone and pattern of these lively tales rather than "The Ugly Duckling" which are dominant in animal fantasy. In many of these stories the only fantasy is the animal as near-human, living in human-type surroundings. The humor of these tales generally has the slapstick element that children enjoy.

Beatrix Potter
The Tale of Peter Rabbit

Beatrix Potter, English novelist of the nursery, has left her own account of how she happened to write her classic, *The Tale of Peter Rabbit.* In a letter to *The Horn Book,* May 1929, she said:

About 1893 I was interested in a little invalid child. . . . I used to write letters with pen and ink scribbles, and one of the letters was Peter Rabbit.

Noel has got them yet; he grew up and became a hardworking clergyman in a London poor parish. After a time there began to be a vogue for small books, and I thought "Peter" might do as well as some that were being published. But I did not find any publisher who agreed with me. The manuscript—nearly word for word the same, but with only outline illustrations—was returned with or without thanks by at least six firms. Then I drew my savings out of the post office savings bank, and got an edition of 450 copies printed. I think the engraving and printing cost me about £11. It caused a good deal of amusement amongst my relations and friends. I made about £12 or £14 by selling copies to obliging aunts. I showed this privately printed black and white book to Messers. F. Warne & Co., and the following year, 1901, they brought out the first coloured edition.[3]

Children quickly learn by heart these apparently simple little stories of Beatrix Potter's, and how they relish the names of her characters: Flopsy, Mopsy, and Cottontail, Jemima Puddle-Duck, Pigling Bland, Mrs. Tiggy-Winkle, Benjamin Bunny, Peter Rabbit.[4] The stories are plotted carefully, with plenty of suspense to bring sighs of relief when the conclusion is finally reached. Children chuckle over the funny characters, the absurd predicaments, and the narrow escapes. They pore over the clear watercolor illustrations, which are full of action, and absorb delightedly the lovely details of landscapes, old houses, and fine old furniture and china.

Children can soon "read" Peter's adventures for themselves, they know them so well; but the charms of that humorous and exciting plot never grow stale—disobedient Peter in Mr. MacGregor's cabbage patch, very complacent at first, then pursued and thoroughly frightened but still keeping his wits about him; next, Peter at home, properly repentant, chastened

by his mother, but snug in bed at last and secure. Here is a cheerful Prodigal Son, child-size.

Rudyard Kipling
Jungle Books
Just So Stories

Living in India for many years and thus familiar with the Indian *Jatakas* and the usual pattern of a "why" story, Rudyard Kipling wrote the *Just So Stories*, his own collection of explanatory tales, in amusing imitation of the old form. "How the Whale Got His Throat" and "How the Leopard Got His Spots" begin seriously and end with a logical kind of nonsense that reminds us of *Alice*.

A great favorite is "The Elephant's Child." This story explains how the elephant's "blackish, bulgy nose, as big as a boot" grew to the long trunk we see today. It was all because of the "'satiable curiosity" of the Elephant's

From "The Elephant's Child" from *Just So Stories* by Rudyard Kipling, illustrated by Safaya Salter.

[3]Beatrix Potter. From a letter to *The Horn Book Magazine*, May 1929. Copyright 1929 by The Horn Book, Inc.

[4]Among the companion volumes to *Peter Rabbit* are *The Tales of Benjamin Bunny, The Tailor of Gloucester, The Tale of Squirrel Nutkin, The Tale of Jemima Puddle-Duck, The Tale of Mrs. Tiggy-Winkle,* and *The Tale of Tom Kitten.*

Child who, after innumerable spankings, ran away to seek knowledge by the banks of "the great grey-green, greasy Limpopo River."

These are stories to be read aloud. They are cadenced, rhythmic, and full of handsome, high-sounding words which are both mouth-filling and ear-delighting. Children soon catch on to the grandiloquent style and absurd meanings. The mock-serious tone of these pseudo-folk tales adds to their humor.

In contrast to the *Just So Stories*, Kipling's animals in the *Jungle Books* may talk but they remain true to their natures. From these stories about the boy Mowgli and the animals who raise him, children receive an insight into that wild-animal nature, into the curious likeness of animals and humans, and into the still more curious lines of demarcation.

Kenneth Grahame
The Wind in the Willows

Kenneth Grahame was a lovable, literary, out-of-doorish sort of Englishman with a gift for storytelling. For his small son, nicknamed "Mouse," he used to spin continuous tales at bedtime. Once Mouse refused to go to the seaside because his trip would interrupt the adventures of "Toad" to which he was listening. In order to persuade the child to go, his father promised to send him a chapter in the mail daily, and this he did. Sensing their value, the nursery governess who read the chapters to Mouse mailed them back to his mother for safekeeping. From these letters and bedtime stories grew *The Wind in the Willows*.

Each chapter tells a complete adventure of the four friends—reflective Mole, kindly old Water Rat, shy Badger, and rich, conceited, troublesome Toad. The humor of *The Wind in the Willows*, particularly the humor of the conversations, is subtle, but Toad's antics, his bemused pursuit of his latest fad, his ridiculous conceit, the scrapes he gets into, and the efforts of his friends to reform him furnish enough broad comedy to satisfy everyone. The dialogue is that of the born storyteller, used to children's predilection for talk, improvising dialogue in his own fluent, individual vein. What talk it is—funniest when it is most grave, revealing more of the speaker than any explanatory paragraph. These conversations are as much a part of the style as the descriptions which make the book one of the masterpieces of English literature.

None of these things—humor, dialogue, or descriptions—accounts for the hold this book takes upon the heart and the imagination. As in Andersen's *Fairy Tales*, it is the inner significance of the story that counts. First of all, there is the warm friendliness of the animals. Each one makes mistakes, has his limitations, but no one ever rejects a friend. The four endure perils and pitfalls and come safely through only because they help each other. This continual kindliness, the overlooking of other people's mistakes, and the sympathetic understanding which pervade every page warm the reader's heart. There are no hidden meanings or didacticism here, just reassurance and comfort.

Robert Lawson
Ben and Me
Rabbit Hill

Robert Lawson, with his easy storytelling style and beautiful illustrations, added much to the glory of the talking-beast tale. Children consider *Ben and Me* one of the genuinely funny books. These biographical memoirs of Benjamin Franklin are supposedly written by Amos, a cheeky mouse who modestly admits that he supplied Ben with most of his ideas. Amos admits his disapproval of Ben's experiments with electricity; but having stuck by his friend in spite of many a shock, Amos helps Ben achieve some novel results. A series of these fantastic biographies followed.

Good as his humorous biographies are, Lawson really came into his own as a creative writer with *Rabbit Hill*, a Newbery Medal winner. This is the story of Father and Mother Rabbit, their high-leaping son, Little Georgie, aged Uncle Analdas, and a host of other animals. The story begins with the pleasant rumor that new folks are moving into the big house. The question is, what kind of folks will they turn out to be—mean and pinching, or folks with a thought for the small creatures who have always lived on the hill? The new folks begin well with a sign "Please Drive Carefully on Account of Small

Animals." Their crowning beneficence, however, is a beautiful pool and feeding station for the animals.

The Tough Winter, the sequel to *Rabbit Hill,* tells a moving story of what happens to small beasts when snow and ice last too long and there are no kindhearted humans to help.

These books may not have the superlative literary qualities of *The Wind in the Willows,* but they are exceedingly well written and marvelously illustrated. All of the animals, from suspicious Uncle Analdas to worrying Mother Rabbit, are delightfully individualized.

E. B. White
Charlotte's Web

E. B. White, essayist and editorial writer for *The New Yorker,* noted for his lucid, effortless prose, wrote *Stuart Little,* the story of a baby who resembled a mouse; "in fact he was a mouse." Some children liked Stuart's adventures, but many adults were disturbed by the biology of this mouse child of a human family. *The Trumpet of the Swan,* the story of a mute swan who learned to play an instrument so that he could woo his beloved, is a fascinating blend of fantasy and realistic details. But White's masterpiece is *Charlotte's Web.*

Fern, a farmer's child, persuades her father to give her the runt pig he is about to butcher. Fern names her pet "Wilbur," and raises him with a doll's nursing bottle for a feeder. When Wilbur gains girth, he is firmly banished to the barnyard, and here the fantasy begins. Fern spends long periods of time watching Wilbur daily and discovers that she understands what the animals are saying to each other. Wilbur has learned about the fall butchering and he doesn't want to die. Charlotte, the aloof, intelligent spider, feels sorry for the silly little pig and promises to save him. Her devices for doing this are unique and exceedingly funny. In the end, Wilbur is saved but Charlotte dies, true to her kind, leaving hundreds of eggs. Birth and death and life go on.

Charlotte's Web is a fantasy universally acclaimed by adults and universally loved by children. Wilbur is a true pig—he relishes slops and good soft muck. But he also is a child, lonesome, without a friend, turning to Char-

From *Charlotte's Web* by E. B. White, illustrated by Garth Williams.

lotte for understanding, reassurance, entertainment, love, and finally a solution to his most urgent problem. Wilbur is no hero: He weeps at the thought of death. But he is obedient and tries his best to live up to all the good things Charlotte weaves about him in her web.

White's writing style is confidential and intimate; he's telling a story just for you, and readers and listeners respond openly to the humor and pathos of these adventures.

Other Examples of Talking Beasts

People have observed and lived with animals for a long time, frequently identifying closely with them. It is no wonder that authors have chosen to make beasts talk and that their readers accept these tales so readily. Two books in this category have been awarded prizes: *Mrs. Frisby and the Rats of NIMH* by Robert O'Brien and *Watership Down* by Richard Adams. O'Brien's Newbery Medal tale has some science-fiction aspects, as he tells the story of the rats who have been used as experimental subjects, and who escape the National Institute of Mental Health and set up their own society. O'Brien's tale is rich in circumstantial detail, fact piled upon fact, yet compactly and reasonably told. The

From *Mrs. Frisby and the Rats of NIMH* by Robert O'Brien, illustrated by Zena Bernstein.

homily on the writing of poetry. His creatures speak and think, and the poetry written by the bat gives marvelously vivid pictures of the owl, the mockingbird, the chipmunk, and the bat.

Most of the fantasy tales about animals are humorous, as are Margery Sharp's *Miss Bianca* stories. Miss Bianca is the most genteel of mice, but her courage is unbounded. With her faithful (but quite ordinary) admirer, Bernard, she embarks on adventures as lurid and melodramatic as those of any detective story; always calm, she is completely in charge of all situations. Tucker, in George Selden's *The Cricket in Times Square,* is a Runyonesque mouse who welcomes Sylvester the Cricket to his home in a Times Square subway station. In an equally funny sequel, *Tucker's Countryside,* the mouse braves the terrors of a peaceful meadow.

Another popular talking animal is the enterprising young mouse, Ralph, who makes friends with a boy in Beverly Cleary's *The Mouse and the Motorcycle* and continues his adventures in *Runaway Ralph* and *Ralph S. Mouse.* The husband-and-wife team of Louise Fatio and Roger Duvoisin has produced the series of *Happy Lion* books. Not only are these stories well told with good plots, sly humor, and surprise endings, but the pictures are rich in details that children pore over. Several books by Dick King-Smith star ingenious animals: In *The Fox Busters* some flying chickens fend off raiding foxes by dropping hard-boiled eggs (laid in midair) on them; and in *Harry's Mad,* a parrot can talk as well as any person. A series of tales about *A Bear Called Paddington* by Michael Bond disarmingly describes life in a middle-class English family; the Browns adopt a small bear from Peru found wandering about in a railway station with a tag that pleads, "Please look after this bear."

William Steig, well known as a creator of adult cartoons, has given us droll, sophisticatedly simple animal characters in *Dominic* and in *The Amazing Bone.* For the younger child, an engaging young donkey is the central character in his Caldecott Medal book, *Sylvester and the Magic Pebble.* In *Doctor De Soto* the central characters are a mouse, who is a dentist, and a fox, whose tooth the mouse reluctantly agrees to extract. In *Abel's Island,* a mouse lives in cultured comfort until a flood maroons him on

rabbits in Richard Adams's Carnegie Medal book also seek a new home and, urged forward by a foreboding vision, find it on Watership Down. Adams creates not only a series of adventures, but a folklore for his migrating rabbits. Theirs is an epic struggle, serious and believable, although carried out by what we're accustomed to think of as small, rather helpless animals. Another small creature, Adam Mouse, is the hero of Lilian Moore's *I'll Meet You at the Cucumbers;* and in Nathaniel Benchley's *Kilroy and the Gull* a philosophical killer whale succeeds in his attempt to communicate with people.

In *The Bat-Poet,* Randall Jarrell wrote a story of grave sweetness, a quality echoed in the Maurice Sendak illustrations. This is a small

an island; the Robinson Crusoe appeal here is for readers in the middle grades who can appreciate the nuance of the writing.

Talking-beast stories are perhaps the first kind of fantasy that younger children encounter—and there has been an enormous number published, especially in the last several decades. All sorts of creatures, from pandas to goldfish, are talking and having adventures. Two venerable favorites are Margaret Wise Brown's *Goodnight Moon* and Marjorie Flack's *Ask Mr. Bear,* both of which have humor and warm, reassuring family relationships. Also over thirty years old but still appealing are the *Curious George* stories by H. A. Rey. Children easily identify with a monkey who can't help getting into trouble just because he wants to *know* about things.

Modern talking-beast tales should be chosen with discrimination. We can do no better than to reread Beatrix Potter and *The Wind in the Willows* when we are in doubt about the qualities that should distinguish the best new animal fantasies.

Personified Toys and Other Inanimate Objects

Although the fanciful story about the secret life of toys and other inanimate objects was Andersen's invention, it took the writers of the twentieth century to use this form at the child's level, with an inventiveness and charm that already have made some of these stories children's classics. Andersen's tales of the little china shepherdess and the chimney sweep or the steadfast tin soldier are faintly sad and decidedly adult. Later writers have avoided both of these pitfalls. Their dolls, trains, and airplanes are usually cheerful and lively.

Carlo Lorenzini
The Adventures of Pinocchio

The Italian classic *Pinocchio,* written in 1880 by a witty Tuscan, Carlo Lorenzini (pseudonym Collodi), was apparently first translated into English and published in the United States in

From *Abel's Island* written and illustrated by William Steig.

1892. From then on, it has held a place in the affections of American children and has undoubtedly influenced American writers.

The story concerns a rogue of a puppet which old Geppetto painstakingly carves out of wood. Hardly has the poor woodcarver finished when the saucy creature makes off in pursuit of his own sweet way. Although full of good resolutions, Pinocchio wastes his money, lies about it, plays hooky from school, and chooses bad companions. Every time he lies to his friend the Blue Fairy, his nose grows longer, until soon he can't turn around in a room without colliding with the walls. The climax is his journey to the Land of Toys, where he finds that he has grown a fine pair of donkey ears and a body to match. Saved again and again by the good Blue Fairy, he learns that she is ill and starving. He is roused at last, earns money to feed and care for both Geppetto and the Fairy, and wakes in the morning to find himself no longer a puppet but a real boy, living with Geppetto in a well-kept home.

This is the children's own epic, presenting young readers with themselves in wood, full of good resolutions, given to folly, sliding through somehow, but with one difference—Pinocchio always comes out on top and never quite loses face. But he does learn his lesson, and readers never doubt it. (Any classic that is in the public domain may have poorly translated or abbreviated editions. Of the many versions in print, only a few of the best have been included in the bibliography that follows this chapter.)

A. A. Milne
Winnie-the-Pooh
The House at Pooh Corner

A. A. Milne's *Winnie-the-Pooh* and *The House at Pooh Corner* are different from anything that preceded them. Having grown naturally out of poems about Milne's son, Christopher Robin, and Christopher's stuffed bear, Pooh, they also developed from his small son's demands to hear a story for Pooh. The accommodating Milne began to spin a series of tales about the bear: He calls on Rabbit and eats so much that he sticks in the door and can't get out; he flies up in a balloon to get some honey out of a tree, tries to imitate a cloud in order to distract the suspicious bees, and finally has to have the balloon shot in order to get down. *The House at Pooh Corner* introduces Tigger, a new and amusing character, and the tales go on in much the same vein.

Ernest Shepard's illustrations make it clear that most of the animals are really toys like Winnie-the-Pooh. The pictures are full of fascinating details both children and adults enjoy. For instance, Owl's house has two signs at the door. One, under the knocker says:

PLES RING
IF AN RNSER
IS REQIRD

The other, under the bell rope, reads:

PLEZ CNOKE
IF AN RNSR
IS NOT REQID

The stories are unusual in that Christopher Robin goes in and out of them on a familiar forest-dwelling level with the animals, but in the end he brings everything back to reality when he sets off up the stairs of his own house, headed for a bath, dragging his bear, Pooh, by one leg. The stories are finished, Christopher Robin is himself, and Pooh is Pooh.

Christopher Robin is omnipotent in these tales, surely a heady experience for children subject to the whims and demands of their elders. Milne's facility with words delights both children and adults, making this an excellent choice for parent-child sharing. His tone is childlike, innocent, uncondescending, allowing children to laugh at themselves without the necessity of looking to adults for cues.

Virginia Burton
Mike Mulligan and His Steam Shovel
The Little House

Virginia Burton used her brush and words in the happiest possible combination. *Mike Mulligan and His Steam Shovel* tells the story of Mike, who owns a fine steam shovel with which he does important jobs of excavation until his machine, Mary Anne, is outmoded by new and more powerful models. Then Mike reads about a town needing a cellar dug for its town hall. Mike and Mary Anne hasten to the scene, offering to dig it within the time constraints of one day—or no pay. Exactly on the hour, the excavation is finished, deep and well squared-off at the corners. The only trouble is that Mike, in his excitement, has dug himself in, and there is no way of getting Mary Anne out. So Mary Anne becomes the furnace of the new town hall with Mike as her attendant. Both live a warm, prosperous, and respected life ever after.

Burton's machine stories have certain marked characteristics which help to explain their popularity. The plot always involves a staggering task or action and has considerable suspense. The illustrations heighten the feeling of action by swirling, circular lines that rush across the page and stem from or center on the cause of it all.

But *The Little House*, the winner of the Caldecott Medal for 1943, is Virginia Burton's finest and most distinguished book. A house in the country presently finds itself in the center of a village, and then in the midst of a great city where it is an insignificant obstruction between skyscrapers, with elevated trains overhead, subways beneath, and swarms of people everywhere. Rescued by the descendants of its build-

From *The Little House*, written and illustrated by Virginia Lee Burton.

er, the little house is moved back to the country where it can once more watch the cycle of the four seasons revolving in ordered beauty.

There is a significance to this book that should make it permanently valuable as literature and art. The evolution of cities in all their complexity and the resultant loss of some of the sweetness of earth and sky are implied in text and picture. The pattern of every picture is the same—rhythmical curving lines which in the country are gracious and gentle but in the city become more and more violent and confused. The house has only a delicately suggested face, and the personification is subordinate to the pattern of these illustrations, something for children and adults to study with growing astonishment and delight.

Other Stories About Inanimate Objects

Two doll stories have won the Newbery Medal, *Hitty: Her First Hundred Years* by Rachel Field and *Miss Hickory* by Carolyn Sherwin Bailey. Hitty is carved from mountain ash and travels around the world; Miss Hickory is an apple tree twig with a hickory nut head who lives all her life on the same farm. Both dolls live bravely through adversity and boast definite, unique personalities, far above today's mass-produced dolls. Rumer Godden has written a series of doll stories in which the dolls are strongly characterized: *The Dolls' House, Candy Floss,* and *Miss Happiness and Miss Flower.*

In *The Dollhouse Caper,* Jean O'Connell has written a satisfying story about a family of dolls who come to life when people aren't about and who worry about being discarded by their owners, the three brothers who are out-growing them. This book has good characterization, sturdy plot, and smooth writing style. Another fine dollhouse story is Jane Gardam's *Through the Dolls' House Door.*

One of the most touching stories about a toy is Russell Hoban's *The Mouse and His Child.* They are a single unit, a wind-up tin toy that has been discarded. Repaired by a tramp, they go on a quest for love and security. The story has humor and tenderness, and an adventurous plot with general appeal. While the sophistication of its latent meaning and social comment and the difficulty of the vocabulary put special demands on readers, it is well worth the effort.

The Return of the Twelves (originally published as *The Twelve and the Genii*) by Pauline Clarke is an ingenious story about some wooden soldiers that had once belonged to the children of the famous Brontë family. Years after the Brontë times, eight-year-old Max Morley finds the Twelves and learns that they "freeze" when they are observed. He wins their confidence and they talk of the past. Max and his sister decide that the soldiers belong in their old home, Haworth, and let them march off rather than offend their dignity by carrying them. Winner of the Carnegie Medal, the book has a polished style, delightful individual characterizations of the soldiers, and enough literary references to intrigue adults as well as young readers. The story of a girl who turns into a doll, and back again, Richard Kennedy's *Amy's Eyes,* is long and complex, as the doll-girl loses her eyes while on a sea voyage, the ship's crew consisting of toys that have come to life.

Humorous Fantasy

While a number of the fantasies mentioned so far in this chapter, such as those by Thurber, Alexander, Carroll, Kipling, Lawson, White,

From *Amy's Eyes* by Richard Kennedy, illustrated by Richard Egielski.

blows *Mary Poppins* straight into the nursery of the Banks family, and a west wind carries her off. The children first see her coming up the walk, bag in hand, and the next thing she strikes the house with a bang. Once their mother has engaged her as a nurse, Mary slides lightly *up* the banisters as neatly as the children slide down. When she opens her bag, they see it is quite empty, but out of it she takes everything from a folding cot to a bottle of medicine from which she doses the children with incredibly delicious liquid, tasting of strawberry ice or lime-juice cordial or whatever you prefer.

The Poppins books are extremely British, with cooks, gardeners, maids, nannies, nurseries, and teas. The humor is sometimes adult and sometimes whimsical, but children who like this book and its sequels like them enormously and wear them to shreds with rereadings; others dislike them with hearty scorn. The character of Mary Poppins herself has a flavor all its own. Vain, stern, crotchety, continually overtaken by magic but never admitting it, she is adored by the children she disciplines and enchants.

and Milne, have a great deal of humor, it is the humor of word play or sly remarks on the foibles of animals or humans, a sophisticated humor, which demands a certain level of maturity for fullest enjoyment.

Other fantasies have an open, slapstick style of humor, the kind that is obvious at all levels of understanding and causes us to laugh aloud. Lucretia Hale's *The Peterkin Papers,* the stories of a family who cannot solve the most obvious problems without the advice of "the lady from Philadelphia," is a nineteenth-century example.

P. L. Travers
Mary Poppins

P. L. Travers grew up in Australia, where high, wild winds blow everyone into a dither and make almost anything possible. So an east wind

From "The Lady Who Put Salt in Her Coffee" from *The Peterkin Papers* by Lucretia Hale, adapted and illustrated by Amy Schwartz.

Theodor Seuss Geisel
And to Think That I Saw It on Mulberry Street
The 500 Hats of Bartholomew Cubbins

Theodor Seuss Geisel chose his middle name for a pen name and then added the "Dr." as a purely honorary touch. His first book for children was *And to Think That I Saw It on Mulberry Street*. A small boy sees only a horse and a wagon on Mulberry Street but begins working up a bigger and bigger yarn to tell his father. Each succeeding page pictures the next addition to his tale until, finally, two pages across are necessary to include everything. Then his father fixes him with a cold stare and his tale diminishes suddenly, leaving only the horse and wagon on Mulberry Street.

This rhymed narrative was only a sample of more and better nonsense to come. Of all the Seuss books, *The 500 Hats of Bartholomew Cubbins* is certainly one of the best. Bartholomew Cubbins takes off his hat to the King only to find the royal coach stopping, and the King commanding him to take off his hat. Puzzled, he puts his hand to his head and finds a hat there. He jerks it off hastily only to find another in its place—and another, and another, and another. He is seized and threatened with death, but still the hats continue to crown his bewildered head. Finally the King sees upon the boy's head the most gloriously regal hat he has ever beheld. In exchange for this elegant hat, he spares Bartholomew's life, and, as the befeathered hat goes on the King's head, Bartholomew finds his own head bare at last.

Dr. Seuss has the cartoonist's gift for expressing a great deal of humor in a single line or word, and he has maintained the ability to create in uncluttered pictures and text the kind of humor the younger child best enjoys—endless word play, incongruous situations, much action, sure punishment for the truly wicked. His heroes win out not because of brute strength but because the usual cycle of life, gamely lived through, comes round to their side once again.

Seuss has written numerous zany stories, nonsense with basic sense and, at times, basic vocabulary. Among them are *How the Grinch Stole Christmas*, and *The Cat in the Hat*. Children

From *The Cat in the Hat,* written and illustrated by Theodore Seuss Geisel.

enjoy them all, and will surely feel that Seuss deserves the Wilder Award, which he received in 1980.

Astrid Lindgren
Pippi Longstocking

A Swedish writer is responsible for creating a superchild, the heroine of *Pippi Longstocking*. Pippi is an outrageous and delightful child who lives competently with her monkey and horse and, in this book and its sequels, takes control of any situation in which she finds herself. She curbs some bullying boys, disrupts a school session, and outwrestles two policemen when they try to take her to an orphanage. Indeed, after carrying one in each hand, she sets them down so hard that it is some time before they can get up. Then they report she is not a fit child for the orphanage!

Pippi's antics are exceedingly funny to children. She is a child in charge of her own world, with a sea-captain father conveniently away on the high seas, a chest of gold for sundries, and the warmest of hearts, except for interfering adults. In a later book, Lindgren uses elements of folklore in *Ronia, the Robber's Daughter,* in which the humor is more subtle. In 1958, Lindgren was given the Hans Christian Andersen Award.

Other Humorous Fantasy

At the outset, *Mr. Popper's Penguins* by Richard and Florence Atwater gives every indication of being a simple, realistic story about a paperhanger with a passion for the Antarctic. The narration is grave and dignified, skidding suddenly into understated nonsense with the addition of a penguin, Captain Cook, to the family. *Imogene's Antlers* by David Small has humor based on incongruity, as little Imogene sprouts huge antlers overnight; her mother faints periodically but Imogene is undaunted.

Oliver Butterworth's *The Enormous Egg* blandly injects the hatching of a dinosaur into the modern scene; and Scott Corbett's *Ever Ride a Dinosaur?* tells of a brontosaurus (who can make himself invisible) sneaking in to have a look at a dinosaur exhibit. In contrast, the absurdity of an alien trapped in the body of a skunk has a realistic matrix for *Stinker from Space* by Pamela Service. In *Finzel the Farsighted,* Paul Fleischman creates a fool who, in true folk-tale style, mixes things up so that his behavior is hilarious.

Joan Aiken's humor tends toward sophistication and language play, but her ability to exaggerate gives her work the slapstick surprise that children appreciate. Her Gothic tale, *The Wolves of Willoughby Chase* drips with Victorian sentimentality and drama. In *Nightbirds on Nantucket,* Aiken displays a Dickensian relish for names that indicate character, and a sense of the ludicrous that results in such situations as a pink whale obligingly towing a transatlantic cannon. *Arabel and Mortimer* and its sequels are comic extravaganzas, and *The Whispering Mountain* is a broad burlesque of the fanciful adventure story. It has a rollicking plot and a spectrum of dialects overdone to the point of

From *Imogene's Antlers,* written and illustrated by David Small.

absurdity. Humorous treatment is a foil for the pervasive struggle of good against evil in Bill Brittain's story of the town of Coven Tree, in *Dr. Dredd's Wagon of Wonders.* Role reversal is the basis of the humor in Martin Waddell's *The Tough Princess,* since the doughty Princess slays dragons and valiantly rescues a prince.

Sid Fleischman's stories are also large-canvas affairs. In *The Ghost in the Noonday Sun,* a pirate kidnaps a boy who can, he thinks, lead him to the treasure of the man he murdered. A tropic isle, plank-walking, buried treasure, and mutinous pirates are just a few of the standard ploys at which the author pokes fun. In *Chancy and the Grand Rascal,* the young hero (so skinny he has to stand twice to cast a shadow) goes off to find his little sister Indiana, meets a rogue and shyster, Colonel Plugg, and then finds his uncle, whose ability to lie magnificently routs even the lying Plugg. *By the Great Horn Spoon* is a picaresque tale about the California Gold Rush, in which Young Jack and the family butler, Mr. Praiseworthy, go off to recoup their losses. In the McBroom stories, Fleischman has used the tall-tale style of humor to excellent advantage.

What's humorous in one culture is not necessarily funny in another, but Tove Jansson, whose work received the Hans Christian Andersen Award, is popular internationally. Her books about those engaging imaginary creatures the *Finn Family Moomintroll* have a daft logic all their own.

Science Fiction

Science fiction and fantasy are closely related genres, and they are sometimes difficult to distinguish clearly from one another. At one time science fiction was clearly an extrapolation from known scientific facts. That is, the events of a story were possible, given the advances promised by fact or theory, though perhaps many years in the future. Fantasy, on the other hand, was clearly unreality in the physical sense —talking animals, supernatural beings, a parallel world. Some novels of the future contain

From *Dr. Dredd's Wagon of Wonders* by Bill Brittain, illustrated by Andrew Glass.

unreal elements and may be called science fantasy, but contemporary science fiction often becomes a vehicle for commentary on what social scientists and physical scientists are telling us are facts. What kinds of new governments might we evolve? What stresses will crowding bring? How will we handle the social problems brought on by an ever-lengthening life span? Today's science fiction brings our judgment into play. We ask ourselves: What is right? what is wrong? and find ourselves not far from those fantasies that address the eternal battle between good and evil.

Children of today have seen the fulfillment of many prophecies of science fiction of the past. They seem readier at times than adults to welcome the future. Usually science fiction for children is less bleak than that written for adults, emphasizing the adventure of exploring the unknown, and the fascination of seeing another world and its inhabitants.

Robert Heinlein
Tunnel in the Sky
Podkayne of Mars

The fun and danger of *Tunnel in the Sky* and Robert Heinlein's many other books about interspace travel is that they seem completely reasonable and factual. No "airy-go-rounds" in these tales. Instead we have to pinch ourselves to remember that we are not pioneering on Mars, sending colonies to Ganymede, or commuting to Hespera. The stories are so well told they carry the reader along in a state of almost unbearable suspense. Although many science-fiction stories include girls, few of them have a girl as the central character. In *Podkayne of Mars*, a sixteen-year-old girl goes on her first trip to Earth and is kidnapped on a Venus stopover. Children just beginning to read science fiction enjoy Heinlein because he is technically accurate without being difficult.

Madeleine L'Engle
A Wrinkle in Time

Madeleine L'Engle's notable book *Meet the Austins* is a fine realistic family story. The opening of *A Wrinkle in Time* (1963 Newbery

Viewpoint

There are as many definitions of fantasy as there are of myth, or of religion, or of what it means to be a human being. There are also an equal number of misapprehensions. One definition I like—though perhaps it is *too* broad to be adequate—is those things that were true, are true, and will be true. Another, interesting, but less satisfactory is: those things that never were, but always are. The dictionary's definition leaves me cold: nonrealistic story, play, and so forth; train of thought or of mental images indulged in to gratify one's wishes; fancy, whim, illusion, hallucination. . . .

Fantasy is indeed a multifaceted word. Fantasy in literature, however, is not unreal. It is not something that is pleasant for little children but should be discarded for reality as soon as we come of age. It is not escapism. It is, rather, a search for a deeper reality, for the truth that will make us more free.

Stories of fantasy almost always start in the familiar world of the five senses, with what the reader can recognize; with kitchens, liverwurst sandwiches, stormy nights. Fantasy is rooted in and springs from the real. It is the real taken to that deeper reality that is beyond ordinary human perception.

From "Fantasy Is What Fantasy Does" by Madeleine L'Engle, *Children's Literature in the Classroom: Weaving Charlotte's Web*, edited by Janet Hickman and Bernice Cullinan. Christopher-Gordon Publishers, 1989, pp. 129–130.

Medal) suggests that it will be a similar kind of story. A storm is raging outside, but within the cozy kitchen Meg Murry and her brother, precocious five-year-old Charles Wallace Murry, are having hot cocoa with their mother. Into this family group comes a strange old woman, Mrs. Whatsit. She explains that she was "caught in a down draft and blown off course." But having finished her cocoa, she departs with one final word to the mother, ". . . there *is* such a thing as a tesseract." That is what the children's scientist father had been working on for the government when he disappeared. The children are warned that their father is in grave danger and that only they can save him and only if they are willing to tesser. This involves the "fact" that the shortest distance between two points is not a straight line, but a fold or wrinkle. The children prove to be only too willing to try it. There follows in the complex course of the rest of the book a battle between good and evil, love and hate. This space story is written in terms of the modern world in which children know about brainwashing and the insidious, creeping corruption of evil.

In a second story, *A Wind in the Door,* Charles Wallace seems near death. With the help of other-worldly teachers, Meg learns to extend her love even to those who do not seem to deserve it in order to save her brother. In a third title, *A Swiftly Tilting Planet,* Charles Wallace goes back in time to avert a looming tragedy.

L'Engle's books are complicated in their blend of science, philosophy, religion, satire, and allegory, but her ability to draw character and adventurous situations attracts readers.

John Christopher
The White Mountains trilogy
The Guardians

Christopher's stories of the future are written with a breadth of conception and a fidelity of detail that lend conviction. He succeeds admirably in *The White Mountains* in establishing the believability of his twenty-first-century world. In this world, machine creatures called Tripods control the earth and perpetuate their mastery over human beings by inserting steel caps in the skulls of all children when they reach the age of fourteen, an operation that renders them forever subservient. Three boys—Will, Henry, and Beanpole—have heard that there is a haven in a land the ancients called "Switzerland," and having learned from a Vagrant that free people live in the White Mountains, they decide to escape before they are capped. In the second volume, *The City of Gold and Lead,* Will takes part in an athletic contest, the winners of which are to have the privilege of serving the

Masters, the Tripods. The other boys go in a spirit of sacrifice; Will goes as a spy. In *The Pool of Fire* Will describes the intricate sabotage by which the Tripods are defeated, and the new freedom of humankind to set up its own government. As has happened before, there is quarreling and competition, so Will gives up his own plans to work with a small group of

people whose goals are world unity and peace. The ending is sober and realistic, a reminder that vigilance against tyranny must be constant. The whole concept of the trilogy is developed with pace and skill—the pitting of good against evil, in a world where few can see the evil, adding suspense to the well-structured action. A fourth volume, *When the Tripods Came,* is set earlier than the trilogy.

The Guardians is science fiction without a fantasy element. It is set in the year 2052, when England is divided into two societies: The megalopolis, huge and sprawling, is sharply divided by a frontier from the rest of England, a world occupied by the gentry and their servants.

In his later books for children, *The Lotus Caves* and its sequels and in the *Fireball* trilogy that ends with *Dragon Dance,* Christopher has used new settings and time periods, but has not succeeded in creating characters as credible as Will. All of Christopher's books are concerned with serious human problems and humanity's environment; his gift as a science-fiction writer is his ability to treat these problems seriously without making a tract out of an absorbing adventure story.

Viewpoint

First, viewed as a whole, SF shares several root assumptions with nonfiction attempts to anticipate the future: The future is, in some sense, knowable; pathways to the future, as far as we know, are flexible—that is, there are many possible futures that could conceivably result from the outcome of present trends; to some extent, the choices we make now, the decisions taken in the present, affect the possibilities of achieving particularly desirable, or avoiding particularly undesirable, futures. In SF, this concept of the importance of past and present decisions in making more probable one kind of future over others is an explicit theme in many stories dealing with precognition, time travel, and "parallel worlds". . . .

Second, it has been speculated that reading SF can serve as psychic preparation for a world of accelerating change, a kind of acculturation to future shock. While we may feel the effects of rapid social and technological change daily, it is difficult, precisely because of our immersion in a changeful environment, to gain perspective on what is happening. SF can provide the perspective insofar as it succeeds in gulling the reader to step for a while outside of his own time and place in order to witness vicariously the possible outcomes of present and future trends.

Dennis Livingston, "Science Fiction as an Educational Tool," *Learning for Tomorrow: The Role of the Future in Education,* edited by Alvin Toffler. Copyright © 1974 by Alvin Toffler. Reprinted by permission of Random House.

Peter Dickinson
The Weathermonger
Heartsease
The Devil's Children

An editor of the English humor magazine *Punch* and the author of adult mystery stories, Dickinson was immediately successful as a children's writer. His first book, *The Weathermonger,* is a vigorous fantasy about an England of the near future, a time in which the British Isles have become mysteriously subject to a state of feudalism in which any mechanical object is taboo, and in which the weather is controlled by magic. The plot is inventive, the characterization vivid, and the contemporary dialogue, often lightly humorous, a good contrast to the mystic elements of the story.

The second book in this trilogy about England in the time of the Changes is *Heartsease.* Two children find a "witch," buried beneath a pile of stones but still alive. He is an American, and he can hardly believe the hysteria and bigotry of the villagers who attacked him. The book is, as are its companion volumes, an indictment of prejudice. It is also the most dramatic of the three, with a taut suspense in the escape and chase sequences.

In *The Devil's Children,* a small girl who has been left alone in London joins a group of Sikhs, and is used by them to prevent their making innocent blunders. Despite the fact that they are reviled as the Devil's Children by the villagers, she comes to respect them for their intelligence and good will, as the village

Viewpoint

And why is science fiction particularly interesting to the young? Because it involves change. It involves changes in the level of science and technology; changes in society produced by those changes in science and technology; and changes in human life-style and human ways of thinking produced by those changes in society.

Change is a hard thing to accept. We grow used to things being the way they are. We have an emotional investment in our everyday lives and we don't *want* them changed. The older we are and the longer we've made that investment, the more we don't want things to change and the more strongly we resist the change.

But changes must take place, unless humanity falls back in complete stagnation—a condition which, to my way of thinking, would mean the end of our species. The changes that take place are accepted primarily by young people, whose investment in things as they are is still small, who are newly come to the world, and who are willing to try out new things.

That is why science fiction seems more exciting and less threatening to young people; why they greet it with enthusiasm. After all, it's *their* world of the future that is being described.

Isaac Asimov, *Why I Left Harry's All-Night Hamburgers.* New York: Bantam Doubleday Dell Publishing Group, 1990, p. viii.

people eventually do also. Logical plot development, strong characterization, and a sprightly writing style add to the appeal of a cracking good tale. These are superb examples of one facet that is common to many science-fiction stories: the expressed belief in brotherhood and love as necessary ingredients in a shrunken world.

Other Examples of Science Fiction

Andre Norton has made a specialty of the possibilities of communication between humans and animals in such tales as *The Zero Stone.* She creates interesting characters in *Wraiths of Time,* in which a young, black archeologist finds herself time-shifted to an ancient Nubian Kingdom. Another time-shift story is *Torch,* by Jill Paton Walsh, which knits history, legend, and quest in a story of the future in which the mysterious, magical torch is related to the Olympic games. Most of Alice M. Lightner's books have a medical theme, like that of *Doctor to the Galaxy,* in which a problem of medical research is pursued on a mythical planet; in her *The Galactic Troubadours,* however, the theme is the revival of musical performance in a society that frowns on young people who aren't satisfied with perfectly good taped music. Carefully structured, William Sleator's *The Duplicate* is a taut story of the complexities of living with two adolescent clones. Also realistic rather than fantastic are Sylvia Engdahl's *Journey Between Worlds,* which explores a theme of prejudice of Terrans against Martian colonists, and Paula Danziger's *This Place Has No Atmosphere,* which is set in a lunar colony.

Children enjoy stories about robots, such as Lester Del Rey's *The Runaway Robot* and Carol Ryrie Brink's *Andy Buckram's Tin Men. The Runaway Robot* is set in the future when robots are common, but it is an uncommon robot that becomes so close a friend of his human companion that the two run away together. Andy in *Andy Buckram's Tin Men* is a twelve-year-old who builds four robots out of tin cans, but not until they are struck by lightning during a storm do the four come alive and save Andy's life during the flood caused by the storm. Jack and his robot buddy Danny are the heroes of a mission to the planet Janus in Alfred Slote's *The Trouble on Janus.*

For younger children, anywhere from eight- to eleven-years of age, there are numerous fantasies. Among the amusing space stories are Ruthven Todd's *Space Cat,* Patricia Wrightson's *Down to Earth,* Jerome Beatty's *Matthew Looney* stories, Jay Williams and Raymond Abrashkin's *Danny Dunn* books, and Eleanor Cameron's *Wonderful Flight to the Mushroom Planet.* These books, together with their sequels, make absorbing reading and good introductions to this popular type of literature enjoyed by many young readers.

Books That Stir Controversy

Since we must be persuaded by writers of fantasy and science fiction to suspend the rules of the everyday world that we all have known from childhood, it is no wonder that books of this type may stir controversy.

It is hardly necessary to say that a book is not likely to excite discussion if it does not have some excellent qualities. Books that are patterned in plot and pedestrian in style fall by the wayside; books that have a few minor flaws outweighed by their strengths can be enjoyed by successive waves of young readers; and books that are the best of their kind live on to become classics.

Some of the controversial books of the past can be seen, in retrospect, to have been breakers of barriers and small classics of their time. Sometimes it is the content, sometimes the treatment, sometimes only a small facet of the story that causes disagreement about a book.

Certainly one perennial bone of contention has been the Oz books of L. Frank Baum. *The Wizard of Oz* and, to a lesser degree, its sequels have remained favorites of many children despite the fact that many authorities in the field of children's literature feel that the style is flat and dull, and that the inventiveness of the first book was followed by mediocrity and repetition in subsequent volumes. Another book that has been condemned for other reasons by some adults is Helen Bannerman's *The Story of Little Black Sambo,* which is set in India. It is offensive

From *The Trouble on Janus* by Alfred Slote, illustrated by James Watts.

because of the illustrations and because the names "Sambo," "Mumbo," and "Jumbo" have derogatory racial connotations.

Also attacked, with considerable justification it would seem, as casting aspersion on black people, are the *Dr. Dolittle* books by Hugh Lofting, one of which *(The Voyages of Dr. Dolittle)* won the Newbery Medal in 1923. Children have enjoyed the humorous reversal of roles in the series, with animals guiding and taking care of helpless human beings, and the gravity with which preposterous events are treated. Although the stories have action and humor, they also have disturbing racial epithets, illustrations, and incidents in the original series. A 1988 edition of the story of *Dr. Dolittle* is improved by the deletion of racial references.

Quite another sort of difference of opinion has been generated by the books of Julia Cunningham, some of which are fantasy (*Viollet*, in which a bird, a fox, and a man unite to save the life of a gentle old man) and others (like *Dorp Dead*) which can be taken as fantasy or as realism. Indeed, some of the controversy has been on this very point. Some adults dislike the books because they are sophisticated, complex, and heavy with symbolism and psychological import; others defend the books on the grounds that the symbolism and the author's concern with the struggle between good and evil in our society entitle the stories to be classed among the significant books of our time. Most agree that the writing style is polished and distinctive.

The characters and plots developed by Roald Dahl, primarily an adult author, have also generated sharp debate. In *Charlie and the Chocolate Factory,* five children win a contest to enter a wonderfully ingenious manufacturing plant invented by Willy Wonka and operated by pygmies—a device that has been criticized as being derogatory toward African Americans. Criticism has also been directed at Dahl's stereotyping of character as a means of discoursing on social behavior. Dahl's *The Magic Finger* is strong in its message: Shooting animals for sport is deplorable. An indignant eight-year-old girl points her magic finger at her neighbors who are hunters. The father and sons shrink to tiny winged creatures and the ducks grow enormous, sprout arms that can hold guns, and move into the family's house. Able to understand the animal point of view, the hunters make a pact with the ducks. Less humorous than *Charlie, The Magic Finger* has better construction and a light, easy style.

Edward Eager's stories (*Magic or Not? The Well Wishers, Half Magic, Seven-Day Magic,* and others) have intriguing plots and a good style, except for those books in which segments are purportedly but unconvincingly told by the child characters. The author has been criticized by those who feel his material is derivative and his children precocious.

The writing of Norton Juster in *The Phantom Tollbooth* delights many readers, young and old, who are intrigued by words and word play (a light meal consists of lights; a bee is a Spelling

From *The Wizard of Oz* by L. Frank Baum, illustrated by Michael Hague.

Bee) and by the Bunyan-like place names (for example, the Mountain of Ignorance and the Foothills of Confusion). To others, the dependence on latent meanings and on comprehension of allusions makes the book seem heavily burdened with references that will daunt many readers.

Under each category of modern fantasy many more authors and books could be listed. Most of the examples discussed in this chapter are outstanding because they pointed the way or were exceptions or became classics or seem likely to attain that distinction. Even with innumerable omissions, the list is a long one, and the numbers of these books are increasing yearly. Authors discussed here are generally outstanding in craftsmanship, inventiveness, and creation of character. They have something to say and they say it well.

Most children enjoy fantasy as a change from the here and now, as a breathing space in the serious process of growing up. Except for some children's poetry, fantasy can stir the reader's imagination more than books in any other genre. For those who have not yet learned to enjoy it, hearing a good fantasy read aloud, or trying titles that have been recommended because of their humor, interesting characters, or inventive plots may help broaden their reading tastes.

Humorous fantasy (King-Smith's *Harry's Mad* and Jean Merrill's *The Pushcart War*) is one of the best choices for reading aloud in installments to a group of children. Choose a story that extends, but does not tax, the comprehension with concepts or vocabulary that may present problems for the listening level of the intended audience. Use children's responses to make suggestions about other books that might be enjoyable, especially those that can wean a child from a reading rut.

Many of the facets of fantasy that appeal to young readers have been suggested in this chapter. It is obvious that the lure of magic itself is strong. Whether it is a magic word, a trip in time, or a change in shape—it is the meshing of the improbable or even impossible with the everyday that is provocative. Fantasy novels almost always have the sort of action and suspense that children enjoy. While some realistic fiction endures (*Little Women* and *The Secret Garden*), much of it is, inevitably, time-labeled. In fantasy, save for any specific details in those stories that have a realistic matrix, the stories seldom become dated.

In addition to the more evident attractions like magic and action, there are usually deeper qualities that children appreciate, although they may not as readily identify or express them. Fantasy often has a theme or message that deals with the eternal verities: the struggle between forces of good and forces of evil, the development of self-understanding (Lloyd Alexander's Taran), or the love that can cast out fear. It is not just the quest, but the meaning of the quest. In science fiction, there are often commentaries (implicit or explicit) on the ethics and problems of our society, particularly those that affect the peace, safety, or even survival of our world.

This type of literature stimulates lively discussions of literary quality. Most children enjoy talking about what it is that makes fanciful writing good or mediocre, especially as they increase in their understanding of inner logic within the illogical; of consistency in depicting an imagined world; or of the believability of the device that moves a story from realism to fantasy.

Fantasy helps children understand reality even as it provides them with a flight into other worlds that are incredible, exciting, and satisfying. This literature frees the imagination and helps the children face reality with more creativity and spontaneity of thought. Writers like Hans Christian Andersen, Kenneth Grahame, Beatrix Potter, E.B. White, Lucy Boston, Vivien Alcock, Lloyd Alexander, and others have shown children that much of the joy of life depends upon your willingness to take different points of view.

Adult References and Book Selection Aids*

ALDISS, BRIAN. *The True History of Science Fiction.*

BARRON, NEIL. *Anatomy of Wonder: A Critical Guide to Science Fiction*, 3rd. ed.

BATOR, ROBERT, comp. *Signposts to Criticism of Children's Literature.* Chapter 8, "Fantasy," and Chapter 10, "Science Fiction."

BAUM, L. FRANK. *The Wizard of Oz.*

BLOUNT, MARGARET. *Animal Land: The Creatures of Children's Fiction.*

BOVA, BEN. *Through Eyes of Wonder: Science Fiction and Science.*

CAMERON, ELEANOR. *The Green and Burning Tree: On the Writing and Enjoyment of Children's Books.* Part 1, "Fantasy."

CARROLL, LEWIS [pseud.]. *The Annotated Alice: Alice's Adventures in Wonderland & Through the Looking Glass.*

DEL REY, LESTER. *The World of Science Fiction 1926–1976: The History of a Subculture.*

EGOFF, SHEILA. *Worlds Within: Children's Fantasy from the Middle Ages to Today.*

EGOFF, SHEILA, G. T. STUBBS, and L. F. ASHLEY, eds. *Only Connect: Readings on Children's Literature.* Part 2, "Fairy Tales, Fantasy, Animals."

*Complete bibliographic data are provided in Appendices A and B.

FIELD, ELINOR WHITNEY, comp. *Horn Book Reflections.* Part 5, "Fantasy, Yesterday and Today."

FORD, PAUL F. *Companion to Narnia.*

GODDEN, RUMER. *Hans Christian Andersen: A Great Life in Brief.*

GREEN, PETER. *Kenneth Grahame.*

HAZARD, PAUL. *Books, Children and Men.*

HEARN, MICHAEL. *The Annotated Wizard of Oz.*

HELMS, RANDEL. *Tolkien's World.*

HIGGINS, JAMES E. *Beyond Words; Mystical Fancy in Children's Literature.*

LEWIS, C. S. *Of Other Worlds: Essays and Stories.*

PFLIEGER, PAT and HELEN M. HILL, eds. *A Reference Guide to Modern Fantasy for Children.*

SALE, ROGER. *Fairy Tales and After: From Snow White to E. B. White.*

SCHOLES, ROBERT, and ERIC S. RABKIN. *Science Fiction: History, Science, Vision.*

TOWNSEND, JOHN ROWE. *Written for Children.* Chapter 13, "Fantasy Between the Wars."

TYMN, MARSHALL B., KENNETH J. ZAHORSKI, and ROBERT H. BOYER. *Fantasy Literature: A Core Collection and Reference Guide.*

WAGGONER, DIANA. *The Hills of Faraway: A Guide to Fantasy.*

YOLEN, JANE. *Touch Magic: Fantasy, Faerie and Folklore in the Literature of Childhood.*

Children's Books

In the following bibliography these symbols have been used to identify books about a particular religious or ethnic group:

§ African American
★ Hispanic
☆ Native American
○ Asian American
• Religious minority

ADAMS, RICHARD. *Watership Down.* Macmillan, 1974. Carnegie Medal.   12 up

ADLER, C. S. *Eddie's Blue-Winged Dragon.* Putnam, 1988. Eddie's little brass dragon comes to life and vengefully protects Eddie, who has cerebral palsy, from the school bully.   9–11

AIKEN, JOAN. *Arabel and Mortimer,* ill. by Quentin Blake. Doubleday, 1981.   9–11

————. *Mortimer Says Nothing,* ill. by Quentin Blake. Harper, 1987.   10–12

————. *Mortimer's Cross,* ill. by Quentin Blake. Harper, 1984.   9–11

————. *Nightbirds on Nantucket,* ill. by Robin Jacques. Doubleday, 1966.   10–12

————. *Not What You Expected.* Doubleday, 1974. A collection of short stories.   10 up

————. *The Whispering Mountain,* ill. by Frank Bozzo. Doubleday, 1969.   10–14

————. *The Wolves of Willoughby Chase,* ill. by Pat Marriott. Doubleday, 1963.   11–13

ALCOCK, VIVIEN. *Ghostly Companions: A Feast of Chilling Tales.* Delacorte, 1987.   11–15

————. *The Haunting of Cassie Palmer.* Delacorte, 1982.   10–13

————. *The Monster Garden.* Delacorte, 1988.   10–14

————. *The Stonewalkers.* Delacorte, 1983. After bringing a statue to life with an ancient bracelet, Poppy and her friend are pursued across the moor by an army of "stonewalkers" in this chillingly suspenseful story with an involving, realistic backdrop.   10–13

ALEXANDER, LLOYD. *The Beggar Queen.* Dutton, 1984.   10–13

————. *The Black Cauldron.* Holt, 1965.   11–13

————. *The Book of Three.* Holt, 1964.   11–13

————. *The Castle of Llyr.* Holt, 1966.   10–13

————. *The First Two Lives of Lukas-Kasha.* Dutton, 1978.   10–12

————. *The High King.* Holt, 1968. Newbery Medal.   11–13

————. *The Kestrel.* Dutton, 1982.   10–13

————. *The Marvelous Misadventures of Sebastian.* Dutton, 1970. National Book Award.   9–11

————. *Taran Wanderer.* Holt, 1967.   11–13

————. *Westmark.* Dutton, 1981.   10–13

————. *The Wizard in the Tree,* ill. by Laszlo Kubinyi. Dutton, 1975.   9–11

ANDERSEN, HANS CHRISTIAN. *The Complete Fairy Tales and Stories,* tr. by Erik Christian Haugaard. Doubleday, 1974. Translated in a flowing style, in the cadence of the oral tradition.   9 up

————. *Fairytales,* ill. by Kay Nielsen. Viking/ Metropolitan Museum of Art, 1981. Delicately detailed paintings reproduced from a 1924 edition are the centerpiece of this collection.   9–11

Some single-story editions:

————. *The Fir Tree,* ill. by Nancy Burkert. Harper, 1970.   9–11

————. *The Little Match Girl,* ill. by Blair Lent. Houghton, 1968.   9–11

————. *The Nightingale,* tr. by Anthea Bell, ill. by Lisbeth Zwerger. Neugebauer/Alphabet, 1984.   9–11

————. *The Snow Queen,* ad. by Amy Ehrlich, ill. by Susan Jeffers. Dial, 1982.   8–10

————. *The Steadfast Tin Soldier,* tr. by M. R. James, ill. by Marcia Brown. Scribner's, 1953.   6–10

_____. *Thumbelina,* tr. by R. P. Keigwin, ill. by Adrienne Adams. Scribner's, 1961.   6–9

_____. *The Ugly Duckling,* tr. by R. P. Keigwin, ill. by Johannes Larsen. Macmillan, 1967.   6–9

ASIMOV, ISAAC and others, eds. *Young Mutants.* Harper, 1984. An intriguing anthology of theme-oriented science fiction. Other titles in the series deal with young extraterrestrials, witches, or star travelers.   11 up

ATWATER, RICHARD and FLORENCE. *Mr. Popper's Penguins,* ill. by Robert Lawson. Little, 1938.   8–12

BABBITT, NATALIE. *The Devil's Storybook,* ill. by author. Farrar, 1974.   9–11

_____. *The Devil's Other Storybook,* ill. by author. Farrar, 1987.   9–12

_____. *Knee-Knock Rise,* ill. by author. Farrar, 1970.   9–11

_____. *The Something,* ill. by author. Farrar, 1970. A pithy and funny story about Milo, a hairy little cave dweller, who is afraid of Something in the night. It turns out to be a modern girl. When they meet in dreams, both stoutly declare they are not afraid of each other.   4–6

_____. *Tuck Everlasting,* ill. by author. Farrar, 1975.   9–11

BAILEY, CAROLYN. *Miss Hickory,* ill. by Ruth Gannett. Viking, 1968. Newbery Medal.   10–13

BANNERMAN, HELEN. *The Story of Little Black Sambo,* ill. by author. Lippincott, 1923 (first pub. in 1900). Historically interesting but unacceptable.   4–7

BARBER, ANTONIA. *The Enchanter's Daughter,* ill. by Errol Le Cain. Farrar, 1988. An enchanter's daughter perseveres until she escapes from a land of magic where her false father has kept her a prisoner.   5–8

BARRIE, SIR JAMES. *Peter Pan,* ill. by Nora Unwin. Scribner's, 1950. Peter Pan and all his delightful companions are visualized for the children by Nora Unwin's illustrations for this edition.   9–12

BAUM, L. FRANK. *The Wizard of Oz,* ill. by W. W. Denslow. Reilly, 1956 (first pub. in 1900). This edition has many of the original illustrations.   8–11

_____. *The Wizard of Oz,* ill. by Michael Hague. Holt, 1982. A new edition of an old favorite is illustrated with handsome paintings whose nostalgic details are attuned to the original period of publication.   8–10

BELLAIRS, JOHN. *A Figure in the Shadows,* ill. by Mercer Mayer. Dial, 1975.   10–12

BENCHLEY, NATHANIEL. *Kilroy and the Gull,* ill. by John Schoenherr. Harper, 1977.   10–12

BIANCO, MARGERY WILLIAMS. *The Velveteen Rabbit,* ill. by William Nicholson. Doubleday, 1926, 1958. How a very old toy rabbit becomes real and goes off into the real world.   4–7

BISHOP, CLAIRE. *The Five Chinese Brothers,* ill. by Kurt Wiese. Coward, 1938.   5–10

BOND, MICHAEL. *A Bear Called Paddington,* ill. by Peggy Fortnum. Houghton, 1960.   8–10

_____. *Paddington on Top,* ill. by Peggy Fortnum. Houghton, 1975. One in a series of amusing sequels.   8–10

_____. *The Tales of Olga da Polga,* ill. by Hans Helweg. Macmillan, 1973. Episodic chapters about a complacent, mendacious guinea pig.   8–10

BOND, NANCY. *Another Shore.* McElderry, 1988. While spending the summer in Nova Scotia, seventeen-year-old Lyn accidently time-travels from the 1980s to colonial times and finds there is no way for her to return.   12 up

_____. *A String in the Harp.* Atheneum, 1976. The story of an American family moved to Wales for a year provides a successful setting for the fanciful element (based on Welsh legend) of a lost tuning key from the past that must be returned to its owner.   11–14

BONTEMPS, ARNA, and JACK CONROY. *The Fast Sooner Hound,* ill. by Virginia Lee Burton. Houghton, 1942. How this tall-tale hound could outrun any train, even the Cannon Ball, is gravely related and hilariously pictured.   8–12

BOSTON, LUCY M. *The Children of Green Knowe,* ill. by Peter Boston. Harcourt, 1955.

_____. *An Enemy at Green Knowe,* ill. by Peter Boston. Harcourt, 1964.

_____. *The Stones of Green Knowe,* ill. by Peter Boston. Atheneum, 1976.

_____. *A Stranger at Green Knowe,* ill. by Peter Boston. Harcourt, 1961. Carnegie Medal.

_____. *Treasure of Green Knowe,* ill. by Peter Boston. Harcourt, 1958.   9–11

BRINK, CAROL RYRIE. *Andy Buckram's Tin Men,* ill. by W. T. Mars. Viking, 1966.   10–11

BRITTAIN, BILL. *Dr. Dredd's Wagon of Wonders,* ill. by Andrew Glass. Harper, 1987.   10–12

BROOKS, WALTER. *Freddy and the Men from Mars.* Knopf, 1954.

_____. *Freddy Goes to Florida.* Knopf, 1949. Between these two books lies a long series of Freddy stories that have had great popularity.   9–12

BROWN, MARGARET WISE. *Goodnight Moon,* ill. by Clement Hurd. Harper, 1947.   4–6

BURTON, VIRGINIA LEE. *The Little House,* ill. by author. Houghton, 1942. Caldecott Medal.   5–8

_____. *Mike Mulligan and His Steam Shovel,* ill. by author. Houghton, 1939.   6–8

BUTTERWORTH, OLIVER. *The Enormous Egg,* ill. by Louis Darling. Little, 1956.   9–13

———. *The Trouble with Jenny's Ear,* ill. by Julian de Miskey. Little, 1960.   9–11

CAMERON, ELEANOR. *The Court of the Stone Children.* Dutton, 1973. Visiting a museum, Nina meets a ghost-girl from the Napoleonic period. National Book Award.   10–12

———. *Stowaway to the Mushroom Planet,* ill. by Robert Henneberger. Little, 1956.   9–11

———. *The Wonderful Flight to the Mushroom Planet,* ill. by Robert Henneberger. Little, 1954.   9–11

CARLSON, NATALIE SAVAGE. *The Ghost in the Lagoon,* ill. by Andrew Glass. Lothrop, 1984. Timmy and his father try to go fishing in a haunted swamp, but not until Timmy dons his Halloween costume can they scare the ghost away.   7–9

CARROLL, LEWIS [pseud. for Charles Lutwidge Dodgson]. *Alice's Adventures in Wonderland* and *Through the Looking Glass,* ill. by John Tenniel. Heritage, 1944 (first pub. in 1865 and 1871). One of the best-loved and most quoted fantasies for children.

Ill. by John Tenniel. Grosset, 1963.

Ill. by John Tenniel. Macmillan, 1963.

Ill. by John Tenniel. World, 1946.

Ill. by Arthur Rackham. Watts, 1966.   10 up

CHRISMAN, ARTHUR BOWIE. *Shen of the Sea: Chinese Stories for Children,* ill. by Else Hasselriis. Dutton, 1925; redesigned, 1968. Brisk and humorous fairy tales that were awarded the 1926 Newbery Medal.   10–12

CHRISTOPHER, JOHN. *Beyond the Burning Lands.* Macmillan, 1971. A sequel to *The Prince in Waiting.*

———. *The City of Gold and Lead.* Macmillan, 1967.

———. *Dragon Dance.* Dutton, 1986.   12–15

———. *The Guardians.* Macmillan, 1970.

———. *The Lotus Caves.* Macmillan, 1969.

———. *The Pool of Fire.* Macmillan, 1968.

———. *When the Tripods Came.* Dutton, 1988.   11–14

———. *The White Mountains.* Macmillan, 1967.   11–14

CLARKE, PAULINE. *The Return of the Twelves,* ill. by Bernarda Bryson. Coward, 1964. British title is *The Twelve and the Genii.* Carnegie Medal.   10–12

CLEARY, BEVERLY. *The Mouse and the Motorcycle,* ill. by Louis Darling. Morrow, 1965.   9–11

———. *Ralph S. Mouse,* ill. by Paul O. Zelinsky. Morrow, 1982. In a diverting sequel worthy of *The Mouse and the Motorcycle* and *Runaway Ralph,* the dauntless mouse goes to school.   9–11

———. *Runaway Ralph,* ill. by Louis Darling. Morrow, 1970.   8–10

COATSWORTH, ELIZABETH. *The Cat Who Went to Heaven,* ill. by Lynd Ward. Macmillan, 1930 and 1959. Newbery Medal.   10–14

COBALT, MARTIN [pseud. for William Mane]. *Pool of Swallows.* Nelson, 1974. Humor, mystery, and ghosts are combined in a sophisticated story from England.   11–15

COLLODI, CARLO [pseud. for Carlo Lorenzini]. *The Adventures of Pinocchio,* tr. by Carol Della Chiesa, ill. by Attilio Mussino. Macmillan, 1963.

———. *The Adventures of Pinocchio,* tr. by M. L. Rosenthal, ill. by Troy Howell. Lothrop, 1983. A childhood favorite, fluidly translated and illuminated with striking paintings and line drawings.   9–11

COOPER, MARGARET C. *Solution: Escape,* ill. by Rod Burke. Walker, 1980. A boy and his clone-twin thwart a power-hungry scientist in this ingenious novel set in an unnamed Slavic country in the twenty-first century.   11–13

COOPER, SUSAN. *The Dark Is Rising,* ill. by Alan E. Cober. Atheneum, 1973.

———. *Greenwitch.* Atheneum, 1974.

———. *The Grey King,* ill. by Michael Heslop. Atheneum. 1975 Newbery Medal.

———. *Jethro and the Jumbie,* ill. by Ashley Bryan. Atheneum, 1979.   8–9

———. *Over Sea, Under Stone,* ill. by Margery Gill. Harcourt, 1965.   10–12

———. *The Selkie Girl,* ill. by Warwick Hutton. McElderry, 1986.   5–8

———. *Silver on the Tree.* Atheneum, 1977.   10–12

CORBETT, SCOTT. *Ever Ride a Dinosaur?* ill. by Mircea Vasiliu. Holt, 1969.   9–11

CORRIN, SARA and STEPHEN, eds. *The Faber Book of Modern Fairy Tales,* ill. by Ann Strugnell. Faber, 1982. A distinctive collection of fifteen original stories in the fairy tale tradition written by prominent authors during the last century.   9–11

CRESSWELL, HELEN. *The Bongleweed.* Macmillan, 1973.   9–11

———. *A Game of Catch,* ill. by Ati Forberg. Macmillan, 1977.   8–10

———. *Moondial.* Macmillan, 1987.   10–13

———. *The Piemakers,* ill. by W. T. Mars. Lippincott, 1968.   9–11

———. *The Secret World of Polly Flint,* ill. by Shirley Felts. Macmillan, 1984.   9–11

———. *The Winter Birds.* Macmillan, 1976.   11 up

CROSS, GILLIAN. *The Dark Behind the Curtain.* Dell, 1988. The play *Sweeney Todd* parallels its performers' lives when a vandal disrupts the set daily. Jackus, the obvious culprit, must prove his innocence in this thriller.   12–15

CUNNINGHAM, JULIA. *Dorp Dead*, ill. by James Spanfeller. Pantheon, 1965.   12 up

_____. *Viollet*, ill. by Alan E. Cober. Pantheon, 1966.   10–11

CUYLER, MARGERY. *Sir William and the Pumpkin Monster*, ill. by Marsha Winborn. Holt, 1984. In a lightly amusing turnabout story, Sir William, the ghost, gets such a scare he never tries haunting again.   7–8

DAHL, ROALD. *Charlie and the Chocolate Factory*, ill. by Joseph Schindelman. Knopf, 1964.   10–11

_____. *The Magic Finger*, ill. by William Pène du Bois. Harper, 1966.   10–11

DALLAS-SMITH, PETER. *Trouble for Trumpets*, ill. by Peter Cross. Random House, 1984. Handsome, intricate paintings illustrate the story of the victory of an engaging race of little people, whose adventures are continued in *Trumpets in Grumpetland* (1985).   7–9

DANZIGER, PAULA. *This Place Has No Atmosphere*. Delacorte, 1986.   10–13

DE BRUNHOFF, JEAN. *The Story of Babar, the Little Elephant*, ill. by author. Random, 1933. A series of these books followed and have been continued since the author's death by his son Laurent.   5–8

DEL REY, LESTER. *The Runaway Robot*. Westminster, 1965.   11–14

DICKINSON, PETER. *A Box of Nothing*. Delacort, 1988. When a storekeeper gives James a box of pre-creation "original nothing," it proves to be a passport to a future world.   9–11

_____. *The Devil's Children*. Little, 1970.   10–14

_____. *Emma Tupper's Diary*, ill. by David Omar White. Atlantic/Little, 1971. A hoax involving sea monsters is at the center of this lively story set in the Scottish highlands.   10–13

_____. *The Gift*, Atlantic/Little, 1974. Davy's ability to read minds leads to a frightening adventure.   10–14

_____. *Healer*. Delacorte, 1985. An adolescent boy rescues a ten-year-old faith healer whose ability is being exploited.   11–14

_____. *Heartsease*. Little, 1969.   10–14

_____. *The Weathermonger*. Little, 1969.   10–14

DONOVAN, JOHN. *Family*. Harper, 1976. A touching story about a group of laboratory apes is told by one of their number.   11 up

DU BOIS, WILLIAM PÈNE. *Bear Party*, ill. by author. Viking, 1951 and 1963.   5–8

_____. *The Forbidden Forest*, ill. by author. Harper, 1978.   8–10

_____. *Lazy Tommy Pumpkinhead*, ill. by author. Harper, 1966.   7–9

_____. *The Twenty-One Balloons*, ill. by author. Viking, 1947. Newbery Medal.   10–12

DUNLOP, EILEEN. *Elizabeth Elizabeth*, ill. by Peter Farmer. Holt, 1977. In an excellent time-shift story set in Scotland, Elizabeth, twelve, finds a mirror that takes her into the eighteenth century.   10–12

_____. *The House on the Hill*. Holiday House, 1987. Philip and his cousin, Susan, meet reluctantly during a visit to their great-aunt Jane's, but soon both are working to uncover the supernatural mystery of Aunt Jane's old house.   10–12

EAGER, EDWARD M. *Half Magic*, ill. by N. M. Bodecker. Harcourt, 1954.

_____. *Magic or Not?* ill. by N. M. Bodecker. Harcourt, 1959.

_____. *Seven-Day Magic*, ill. by N. M. Bodecker. Harcourt, 1962.

_____. *The Well-Wishers*, ill. by N. M. Bodecker. Harcourt, 1960.   9–11

ENGDAHL, SYLVIA. *Beyond the Tomorrow Mountains*, ill. by Richard Cuffari. Atheneum, 1973. The story of a young man's maturing in a world that is rebuilding after earth is doomed.   11–14

_____. *Journey Between Worlds*, ill. by James and Ruth McCrea. Atheneum, 1970.   11–14

ENRIGHT, ELIZABETH. *Tatsinda*, ill. by Irene Haas. Harcourt, 1963. This original fairy tale offers children penetrating social comment, coupled with the suspense of a well-told story.   9–12

ESTES, ELEANOR. *The Witch Family*, ill. by Edward Ardizzone. Harcourt, 1960. Their pleasant game of drawing witches leads two small girls into incredible adventures when their witches come alive!   10–12

FARMER, PENELOPE. *Charlotte Sometimes*, ill. by Chris Connor. Harcourt, 1969.

_____. *Emma in Winter*, ill. by James J. Spanfeller. Harcourt, 1966.   10–12

_____. *The Summer Birds*, ill. by James J. Spanfeller. Harcourt, 1962.

_____. *Year King*. Atheneum, 1977.   13 up

FATIO, LOUISE. *The Happy Lion*, ill. by Roger Duvoisin. Whittlesey, 1954. The first in a consistently popular series.   5–7

FIELD, RACHEL. *Hitty: Her First Hundred Years*, ill. by Dorothy P. Lathrop. Macmillan, 1929. Newbery Medal.   11–14

FLACK, MARJORIE. *Ask Mr. Bear*, ill. by author. Macmillan, 1932, 1958.   3–7

• FLEISCHMAN, PAUL. *Finzel the Farsighted*, ill. by Marcia Sewall. Dutton, 1983. A jaunty noodlehead tale, comically illustrated.   8–10

FLEISCHMAN, SID. *By the Great Horn Spoon!* ill. by Eric von Schmidt. Little, 1963.   10–12

————. *Chancy and the Grand Rascal,* ill. by Eric von Schmidt. Little, 1966. 10–12

————. *The Ghost in the Noonday Sun,* ill. by Warren Chappell. Little, 1965. 10–12

————. *McBroom and the Beanstalk,* ill. by Walter Lorraine. Atlantic/Little, 1978. When McBroom's family urges him to enter a contest for liars (he's duly horrified of course) the result is another yeasty tall tale in true Fleischman style. 8–10

————. *McBroom Tells a Lie,* ill. by Walter Lorraine. Atlantic/Little, 1976. More whoppers. 8–10

————. *McBroom's Almanac,* ill. by Walter Lorraine. Little, 1984. Still more whoppers. 8–11

FLEMING, IAN. *Chitty-Chitty-Bang-Bang: The Magical Car,* ill. by John Burningham. Random, 1964. The car takes to the air. 10–11

FURLONG, MONICA. *Wise Child.* Knopf, 1987. Set in early Christian Britain, the story tells of Wise Child, who is taken in by the outcast sorceress Juniper after being abandoned by her parents. 11–13

GAG, WANDA. *Millions of Cats,* ill. by author. Coward, 1928. 5–8

GARDAM, JANE. *Through the Dolls' House Door.* Greenwillow, 1987. 10–12

GARFIELD, LEON. *The Empty Sleeve.* Delacorte, 1988. A spectre haunts one of a pair of twins in a picturesque story of the eighteenth century. 11–12

————. *The Restless Ghost: Three Stories,* ill. by Saul Lambert. Pantheon, 1969. Three splendid ghost stories, all set in the past and all with an authentic ring. 12–15

————. *The Wedding Ghost,* ill. by Charles Keeping. Oxford/Salem House, 1987. 12 up

GARNER, ALAN. *The Moon of Gomrath.* Walck, 1967. 10–12

————. *The Owl Service.* Walck, 1968. Carnegie Medal. 10–12

————. *The Weirdstone of Brisingamen.* Walck, 1969. 10–13

☆ GOBLE, PAUL. *The Girl Who Loved Wild Horses,* ill. by author. Bradbury, 1978. A story in folk tradition of a young Indian girl who becomes so close to the wild horses she loves that she finally becomes one of them. Caldecott Medal. 5–7

GODDEN, RUMER. *Candy Floss,* ill. by Adrienne Adams. Viking, 1960. 8–10

————. *The Dolls' House,* ill. by Tasha Tudor. Viking, 1962. 8–10

————. *The Dragon of Og,* ill. by Pauline Baynes. Viking, 1981. A dragon in peril is saved through friendship in this deft, whimsical tale; a happy union of a distinguished illustrator and an equally distinguished writer. 9–12

————. *Miss Happiness and Miss Flower,* ill. by Jean Primrose. Viking, 1961. 8–11

GRAHAME, KENNETH. *The Reluctant Dragon,* ill. by Ernest H. Shepard. Holiday, 1953. A subtly amusing tale about a boy who makes friends with a dragon and arranges to have him meet and fight St. George. 9–11

————. *The Wind in the Willows,* ill. by Ernest H. Shepard. Scribner's, 1953 (first pub. in 1908). 10–12

GRIPE, MARIA. *The Glassblower's Children,* ill. by Harald Gripe. Delacorte, 1973. Two children are kidnapped and held in a castle in this tale in a Gothic vein. 9–11

HAAS, DOROTHY. *The Secret Life of Dilly McBean.* Bradbury, 1986. Orphan Dilly McBean tries to keep his inherent magnetic powers a secret but he fails and is kidnapped by a mad scientist. 10–12

HALE, LUCRETIA P. *Peterkin Papers,* ill. by Harold Brett. Houghton, 1960 (first pub. in 1880). 10–12

HAMILTON, VIRGINIA. *Dustland.* Greenwillow, 1980. In a sequel to *Justice and Her Brothers,* the psychic quartet meets strange creatures on another planet. 11 up

————. *The Gathering.* Greenwillow, 1981. 12–15

————. *Justice and Her Brothers.* Greenwillow, 1978. Eleven-year-old Justice is aware of the strange telepathic communication which goes on between her twin brothers Thomas (whom she fears) and Levi (who protects her). Only when she unearths her own psychic powers does she learn how to combat Thomas' malevolence. 12 up

§ ————. *The Magical Adventures of Pretty Pearl.* Harper, 1983. This intricate story of a young god, Pretty Pearl, is a savory blending of fantasy, African and American folklore, history, and marvelous invention. 10–14

————. *Sweet Whispers, Brother Rush.* Philomel, 1982. In visions of Brother Rush, her mother's sibling, Tree pieces together a tragic family history in an evocative ghost story whose realistic dimensions are as potent as the fantasy element. 11–13

HARRIS, ROSEMARY. *The Moon in the Cloud.* Macmillan, 1970. Carnegie Medal. 10–13

————. *The Seal-Singing.* Macmillan, 1971. 11–14

————. *The Shadow on the Sun.* Macmillan, 1970. A sequel to *The Moon in the Cloud.* The vigorous characterization and dialogue make this as diverting as its predecessor. 10–13

HAUGAARD, ERIK CHRISTIAN. *Prince Boghole,* ill. by Julie Downing. Macmillan, 1987. 5–8

HEARNE, BETSY. *Eli's Ghost,* ill. by Ron Himler. McElderry, 1987. While nearly drowning in a swamp, Eli Wilson releases his ghost, who turns out to be the reverse side of Eli's serious nature. 9–12

HEIDE, FLORENCE PARRY. *Treehorn's Treasure,* ill. by Edward Gorey. Holiday, 1981. Treehorn tries to convince his parents that he has found a tree laden with dollar bills. A dryly witty commentary on the imperfections of human communications. 8–11

————. *Treehorn's Wish,* ill. by Edward Gorey. Holiday, 1984. A blandly funny tale about how the unflappable Treehorn uses three wishes to get a birthday cake. 8–10

HEINLEIN, ROBERT. *Podkayne of Mars: Her Life and Times.* Putnam, 1963. 12–15

————. *Tunnel in the Sky.* Scribner's, 1955.

HOBAN, LILLIAN and PHOEBE. *The Laziest Robot in Zone One,* ill. by Lillian Hoban. Harper, 1983. Sol-1, a tubby robot child, helps his robot friends and is in turn helped by them. 7–8

HOBAN, RUSSELL C. *The Mouse and His Child,* ill. by Lillian Hoban. Harper, 1967. 9–11

————. *A Near Thing for Captain Najork,* ill. by Quentin Blake. Atheneum, 1976. A wild spoof of adventure tales, hilariously larded with Victorian niceties. 8–10

HOWE, DEBORAH and JAMES. *Bunnicula: A Rabbit-Tale of Mystery,* ill. by Alan Daniel. Atheneum, 1979. The Monroe family's pet rabbit, Bunnicula, is suspected by their cat of being a vampire. 9–11

HUDDY, DELIA. *The Humboldt Effect.* Greenwillow, 1982. A sophisticated science fiction/time travel fantasy about the genesis of a biblical legend. 12–15

HUGHES, MONICA. *Devil on My Back.* Atheneum, 1985. *The Dream Catcher.* Atheneum, 1987. Two books about a domed city in a future time. 11–14

HUNTER, MOLLIE. *A Furl of Fairy Wind: Four Stories,* ill. by Stephen Gammell. Harper, 1977. A lonely orphan, a household Brownie, the Queen of the Fairies, and a suddenly greedy peddler are the central characters in these original tales told in felicitous adherence to the oral tradition. 8–10

————. *The Kelpie's Pearls,* ill. by Joseph Cellini. Funk, 1966. 10–13

————. *The Mermaid Summer.* Harper, 1988. 9–11

————. *A Stranger Came Ashore.* Harper, 1975. 11–13

————. *The Walking Stones,* ill. by Trina Schart Hyman. Harper, 1970. 10–12

JANSSON, TOVE. *Finn Family Moomintroll,* ill. by author. Walck, 1965. One of a successful series. 9–12

JARRELL, RANDALL. *The Animal Family,* ill. by Maurice Sendak. Pantheon, 1965. 10–12

————. *The Bat-Poet,* ill. by Maurice Sendak. Macmillan, 1967. 10 up

JONES, DIANA WYNNE. *Archer's Goon.* Greenwillow, 1983. 12–15

————. *Eight Days of Luke.* Greenwillow, 1988. Bored while living with his relatives during a school holiday, David helps his new friend Luke and finds they are embroiled in a battle of the Norse gods. 12–17

————. *Howl's Moving Castle.* Greenwillow, 1986. 11–14

————. *The Lives of Christopher Chant.* Greenwillow, 1988. 10–12

————. *The Magicians of Caprona.* Greenwillow, 1980. In an ingenious and polished tale, two families famous for their casting of spells end their feud when faced by a common enemy. 10–12

————. *A Tale of Time City.* Greenwillow, 1987. 11–13

————. *Warlock at the Wheel and Other Stories.* Greenwillow, 1985. The plots of Jones' short stories are as fresh and original as those of her novels. 10–13

JONES, TERRY. *Fairy Tales,* ill. by Michael Foreman. Schocken, 1983. Humorous original fairy stories carry strains of the romantic as well as the comic/grotesque that are reflected in imaginative paintings. 8–10

JUSTER, NORTON. *The Phantom Tollbooth,* ill. by Jules Feiffer. Random, 1961. 11–13

KÄSTNER, ERICH. *The Little Man,* tr. by James Kirkup, ill. by Rick Schreiter. Knopf. 1966. The diverting adventures of little Maxie, two inches high, who becomes a circus performer. Written in lively style by a distinguished German author. 10–11

KEMP, GENE. *Jason Bodger and the Priority Ghost.* Faber, 1986. Tough Jason, the despair of teachers, becomes cowed by and finally cooperates with a medieval ghost. 10–12

KENDALL, CAROL. *The Gammage Cup,* ill. by Erik Blegvad. Harcourt, 1959. Children who enjoy Tolkien's *The Hobbit* will appreciate this tale of mild revolt among the Minnipins, or little people, and its surprising outcome. A protest against conformity. 10–13

KENNEDY, RICHARD. *Amy's Eyes,* ill. by Richard Egielski. Harper, 1985. 9–11

————. *Inside My Feet: The Story of a Giant,* ill. by Ronald Himler. Harper, 1979. It is only after a dramatic and moving confrontation with an old, sad giant that a boy is able to find his lost parents. 9–11

KIDD, VIRGINIA, ed. *Millennial Women: Tales for Tomorrow.* Delacorte, 1978. In a science-fiction anthology, six women writers describe women of a future time. 12 up

KING-SMITH, DICK. *The Fox Busters,* ill. by Jon Miller. Delacorte, 1988. 10–12

———. *Harry's Mad,* ill. by Jill Bennett. Crown, 1987. 9–11

———. *Magnus Power-Mouse,* ill. by Mary Rayner. Harper, 1984. An appealing fantasy embellished with humorous wordplay about a giant, greedy mouse who finds love and security through the offices of an animal-loving human. 9–11

———. *The Queen's Nose,* ill. by Jill Bennett. Harper, 1985. By rubbing the Queen's nose on a magical coin, Harmony gets seven wishes in a story of change in a rebellious ten-year-old. 8–10

KINGSLEY, CHARLES. *The Water-Babies,* ill. by Harold Jones. Watts, 1961. 8–12

KIPLING, RUDYARD. *The Elephant's Child,* ill. by Leonard Weisgard. From the *Just So Stories,* 1902. Walker, 1970. 9–11

———. *The Jungle Book,* ill. by Philip Hays. Doubleday, 1964. Stories of India and the jungle life of the boy Mowgli, adopted by a wolf pack. 9–13

———. *Just So Stories,* ill. by author. Doubleday, 1902. Ill. by Nicolas (pseud. for Nicolas Mordvinoff). Doubleday, 1952. 8–12

KONIGSBURG, E. L. *Up From Jericho Tel.* Atheneum, 1986. Malcolm and Jeanmarie find that Jericho Tel, their secret place, is a doorway to another world and to the fascinating ghost named Tallulah. 9–11

KOOIKER, LEONIE. *The Magic Stone,* ill. by Carl Hollander. Morrow, 1978. The witch members of the Fine Thread Association are no match for a very ordinary boy who finds their most powerful magic object. 8–10

LANGTON, JANE. *The Astonishing Stereoscope,* ill. by Erik Blegvad. Harper, 1971. 10–12

———. *The Diamond in the Window,* ill. by Erik Blegvad. Harper, 1962. 11–14

———. *The Fragile Flag.* Harper, 1984. A flag with magical powers is carried in a modern children's crusade against war. 10–12

LAWSON, ROBERT. *Ben and Me,* ill. by author. Little, 1939. 9–12

———. *Mr. Revere and I,* ill. by author. Little, 1953. Revere's ride from his horse's point of view. 11–14

———. *Rabbit Hill,* ill. by author. Viking, 1944, 1968. Newbery Medal. 9–12

———. *The Tough Winter,* ill. by author. Viking, 1970. 9–12

LEGUIN, URSULA K. *Catwings,* ill. by S. D. Schindler. Orchard/Watts, 1988. 8–10

———. *Catwings Return,* ill. by S. D. Schindler. Orchard/Watts, 1989. 9–11

———. *The Farthest Shore,* ill. by Gail Garraty. Atheneum, 1972. National Book Award. 11–14

———. *The Tombs of Atuan,* ill. by Gail Garraty. Atheneum, 1971. 11–14

———. *A Wizard of Earthsea,* ill. by Ruth Robbins. Parnassus, 1968. 11–14

L'ENGLE, MADELEINE. *Many Waters.* Farrar, 1986. 11–14

———. *A Swiftly Tilting Planet.* Farrar, 1978. 11–14

———. *A Wind in the Door.* Farrar, 1973. 11–14

———. *A Wrinkle in Time.* Farrar, 1962. Newbery Medal. 11–14

LEWIS, CLIVE STAPLES. *The Lion, the Witch, and the Wardrobe,* ill. by Pauline Baynes. Macmillan, 1950. Other titles in the Narnia series, in order of appearance, are *Prince Caspian* (1951), *The Voyage of the Dawn Treader* (1952), *The Silver Chair* (1953), *The Horse and His Boy* (1954), *The Magician's Nephew* (1955), and *The Last Battle* (1956). 8–12

☆ LIFTON, BETTY. *Jaguar, My Twin,* ill. by Ann Leggett. Atheneum, 1976. This is the story of Shun, a Zinacantec Indian, who finds his jaguar, the twin animal spirit that comes to lucky ones in dreams. 9–11

LIGHTNER, ALICE. *Doctor to the Galaxy.* Norton, 1965. 11–14

———. *The Galactic Troubadours.* Norton, 1965. 12–14

LINDGREN, ASTRID. *Pippi Longstocking,* tr. by Florence Lamborn, ill. by Louis S. Glanzman. Viking, 1950. Followed by several hilarious sequels. 9–12

———. *Ronia, the Robber's Daughter,* tr. by Patricia Crampton. Viking, 1983. 9–11

———. *The Tomten,* adapted from a poem by Viktor Rydberg, ill. by Harald Wiberg. Coward, 1961. Unforgettably lovely pictures of the wintry Swedish countryside illustrate the story of a kindly little troll. Equally attractive is *The Tomten and the Fox* (Coward, 1966). 5–7

LIVELY, PENELOPE. *The Ghost of Thomas Kempe,* ill. by Antony Maitland. Dutton, 1973. Carnegie Medal. 9–11

———. *A House Inside Out,* ill. by David Parkins. Dutton, 1987. 9–11

————. *The Revenge of Samuel Stokes*. Dutton, 1981.   10–12

————. *A Stitch in Time*. Dutton, 1976.   9–11

————. *Uninvited Ghosts and Other Stories*, ill. by John Lawrence. Dutton, 1985.   9–11

————. *The Voyage of QV 66*, ill. by Harold Jones. Dutton, 1979.   9–11

LOFTING, HUGH. *The Story of Dr. Doolittle*, ill. by author. Lippincott, 1920.   9–12

————. *The Story of Dr. Doolittle*, ill. by author. Delacorte, 1988.   9–12

————. *The Voyages of Dr. Doolittle*, ill. by author. Lippincott, 1922. Newbery Medal.   9–12

MCCAFFREY, ANNE. *Dragondrums*. Atheneum, 1979. The third book in a science fantasy series, the protagonist here is masterharper Menolly's protégé Piemur, who must learn to adjust to two new assignments when his voice changes.   11–14

————. *Dragonsinger*. Atheneum, 1977.   11–13

————. *Dragonsong*. Atheneum, 1976.   11–13

MACDONALD, GEORGE. *At the Back of the North Wind*, ill. by George and Doris Hauman. Macmillan, 1950.

————. *The Light Princess*, ill. by William Pène du Bois. T. Crowell, 1962.

————. *The Princess and the Goblin*, ill. by Nora S. Unwin. Macmillan, 1964. Attractive editions of old favorites.   9–12

MCGINLEY, PHYLLIS. *The Plain Princess*, ill. by Helen Stone. Lippincott, 1945. In this parody of a fairy tale, the heroine's appearance improves as she becomes less selfish.   7–10

MCKILLIP, PATRICIA. *The Forgotten Beasts of Eld*. Atheneum, 1974. Sybel, who's called all the legendary beasts to her side, finds love is more important than power.   12–14

————. *Moon-Flash*. Atheneum, 1984. Two curious youngsters leave their primitive tribe and discover the technologically sophisticated world beyond.   12–15

MCKINLEY, ROBIN. *Beauty: A Retelling of the Story of Beauty and the Beast*. Harper, 1978.   11–14

————. *The Blue Sword*. Greenwillow, 1982.   12–15

————. *The Hero and the Crown*. Greenwillow, 1984. A stunning story of a princess who is a dragon-slayer. Newbery Medal.   12–15

§ MCKISSACK, PATRICIA C. *Mirandy and Brother Wind*, ill. by Jerry Pinkney. Knopf, 1988. Mirandy and clumsy Ezel win the neighborhood cakewalk when Brother Wind helps with their dance.   5–8

MACAULAY, DAVID. *BAAA*, ill. by author. Houghton, 1985. Sheep parody humans in a provocative fantasy about the end of the world.   10–12

MAHY, MARGARET. *The Changeover*. Atheneum, 1984. Laura becomes a witch in order to release her young brother from a wizard's spell.   11–14

————. *The Haunting*. Atheneum, 1982. A boy's inherited extrasensory perception leads him to an acquaintance with a similarly gifted great-uncle.   10–12

MARK, JAN. *Aquarius*. Atheneum, 1984. Viner is chosen to be king in a drought-ridden land where his talents as a dowser are valued.

MARTIN, C. L. G. *The Dragon Nanny*, ill. by Robert Rayevsky. Macmillan, 1988. After her forced retirement from the royal nursery, Nanny takes over the schooling of two baby dragons.   5–7

MAYNE, WILLIAM. *All the King's Men*. Delacorte, 1988. A collection of three long stories features fairies and Little People in medieval settings.   9–11

————. *The Blue Book of Hob Stories*, ill. by Patrick Benson. Philomel, 1984. One of a series of four short books about Hob, a goblin visible only to children.   5–8

————. *Earthfasts*. Dutton, 1967.   11–14

————. *The Mouldy*, ill. by Nicola Bayley. Knopf, 1983. A gracefully told fairy tale about a mole whose tunneling disrupts the lives of a king and his daffodil daughter.   7–9

————. *A Year and a Day*. Dutton, 1976.   8–10

MERRILL, JEAN. *The Pushcart War*, ill. by Ronni Solbert. Colorful dialogue and humor make this story of the revolt of pushcart peddlers against huge trucks a witty delight. Scott/Addison, 1964.   10–12

MILNE, A.A. *The House at Pooh Corner*, ill. by Ernest Shepard. Dutton, 1928.

————. *Winnie-the-Pooh*, ill. by Ernest Shepard. Dutton, 1926. These stories were reprinted in 1961, with larger type and more attractive format.

————. *The World of Pooh*, ill. by E. H. Shepard. Dutton, 1957. Distinctive color illustrations give a festive air to this new large-print volume, containing *Winnie-the-Pooh* and *The House at Pooh Corner*.   8–10

MOORE, LILLIAN. *I'll Meet You at the Cucumbers*, ill. by Sharon Wooding. Atheneum, 1988.   8–10

MYERS, BERNICE. *Sidney Rella and the Glass Sneaker*, ill. by author. Macmillan, 1985. After his fairy godfather gives Sidney his big chance on the football team, Sidney is recognized for his heroic teamwork when the glass sneaker fits his foot.   7–9

NORTON, ANDRE. *The Crystal Gryphon*. Atheneum, 1972. Kerovan, who has hoofs instead of feet, proves worthy of his betrothed.   12–14

§ ———. *Lavender-green Magic,* ill. by Judith Gwyn Brown. T. Crowell, 1974. A time-travel adventure with a black heroine.   12–14

§ ———. *Wraiths of Time,* Atheneum, 1976.   12–15

———. *The Zero Stone.* Viking, 1968.   12–14

NORTON, MARY. *The Borrowers,* ill. by Beth and Joe Krush. Harcourt, 1953. Carnegie Medal. This book was followed by *The Borrowers Afield* (1955), *The Borrowers Afloat* (1959), *The Borrowers Aloft* (1961), and *The Borrowers Avenged* (1982).   9–12

———. *Poor Stainless,* ill. by Beth and Joe Krush. Harcourt, 1971.   8–10

NÖSTLINGER, CHRISTINE. *Konrad,* ill. by Carol Nicklaus. Watts, 1977. The story of a factory-made child of seven who is delivered by mistake to a scatterbrained but delightful woman.   9–11

O'BRIEN, ROBERT C. *Mrs. Frisby and the Rats of NIMH,* ill. by Zena Bernstein. Atheneum, 1971. Newbery Medal.   9–11

———. *Z for Zachariah.* Atheneum, 1975. A taut science-fiction story of the last people left in the world.   11 up

O'CONNELL, JEAN S. *The Dollhouse Caper,* ill. by Erik Blegvad. T. Crowell, 1976.   8–10

ORMONDROYD, EDWARD. *Theodore,* ill. by John M. Larrecq. Parnassus, 1966. When he is caught in a laundromat load, Theodore, an aging toy bear, must arrange a few small capers to return him to his ordinary dirty state. A good read-aloud story.   3–6

———. *Time at the Top,* ill. by Peggie Bach. Parnassus, 1963. The elevator stops at an extra floor and Susan finds an 1890 family and home.   10–13

PARK, RUTH. *Playing Beatie Bow.* Atheneum, 1982.   10–13

PEARCE, A. PHILIPPA. *Tom's Midnight Garden,* ill. by Susan Einzig. Lippincott, 1959. Carnegie Medal.   10–13

———. *Who's Afraid? And Other Strange Stories.* Greenwillow, 1987.   10–14

PEARCE, MEREDITH ANN. *The Darkangel.* Little, 1982. The heroic Aeriel fights to free her husband and to rid the world of the White Witch. The trilogy continues with *A Gathering of Gargoyles* (Little, 1984) and *The Pearl of the Soul of the World* (Little, 1990).   11–14

PECK, RICHARD. *Blossom Culp and the Sleep of Death.* Delacorte, 1986. Fourth in the series.   10–14

———. *The Ghost Belonged to Me.* Viking, 1975. A boy of 1913 helps a restless ghost in her efforts to be reburied with her family, in a witty and nostalgic fantasy.   11–13

———. *Ghosts I Have Been.* Viking, 1977. A sequel to *The Ghost Belonged to Me.*   11–14

PEYTON, KATHLEEN. *A Pattern of Roses,* ill. by author. T. Crowell, 1973. The lives of a boy of the present and his counterpart in the past are strangely, convincingly linked.   11–14

PIERCE, TAMORA. *Alanna: The First Adventure.* Atheneum, 1983. A mettlesome girl masquerades as a boy at the king's court in a spirited tale of high magic and adventure. Has sequels.   10–13

POMERANTZ, CHARLOTTE. *The Downtown Fairy Godmother,* ill. by Susanna Natti. Addison, 1978.   8–10

POTTER, BEATRIX. *The Tale of Peter Rabbit,* ill. by author. Warne, 1903. Between 1903 and 1930, nineteen books were published in the series.   3–8

PREUSSLER, OTFRIED. *The Satanic Mill,* tr. by Anthea Bell. Macmillan, 1973. A prize-winning German book about an evil miller-magician whose apprentices are doomed to die.   11–14

PYLE, HOWARD. *Pepper and Salt,* ill. by author. Harper, 1923 (first pub. in 1885). Eight fairy tales, wittily retold and well illustrated.

———. *Wonder Clock,* ill. by author. Harper, 1943 (first pub. in 1887). Twenty-four delightful tales, a companion volume to the one above.   10–12

REY, HANS A. *Curious George,* ill. by author. Houghton, 1941. And its sequels.   4–8

RODGERS, MARY. *A Billion for Boris.* Harper, 1974. Annabel and her friend Boris find a television set that gives the news of the next day, including stock market prices!   9–11

———. *Freaky Friday.* Harper, 1972. What would a girl do if she woke one morning and found she'd turned into her mother? Annabel tells us what.   9–11

ROUNDS, GLEN. *Mr. Yowder and the Windwagon,* ill. by author. Holiday, 1983. An ingenious inventor attaches sails to a covered wagon and speeds across the prairie in this extravagant tall tale.   8–10

RUSKIN, JOHN. *The King of the Golden River,* ill. by Fritz Kredel. World, 1946.   10–14

SAINT-EXUPÉRY, ANTOINE DE. *The Little Prince,* tr. by Katherine Woods, ill. by author. Harcourt, 1943.   12 up

SANDBURG, CARL. *Rootabaga Stories,* ill. by Maud and Miska Petersham. Harcourt, 1922.   8–12

SARGENT, SARAH. *Weird Henry Berg.* Crown, 1980. In an adroit meshing of realism and fantasy, an elderly woman helps a boy find a solution to the problem of saving a pet dragon that appears in contemporary times.   9–11

SELDEN, GEORGE. *The Cricket in Times Square,* ill. by Garth Williams. Farrar, 1960. Sequels below.
8–10

_____. *Tucker's Countryside,* ill. by Garth Williams. Farrar, 1969.   8–10

_____. *The Old Meadow,* ill. by Garth Williams. Farrar, 1989.   8–10

SENDAK, MAURICE. *Higglety Pigglety Pop! Or There Must Be More to Life,* ill. by author. Harper, 1967.
8–10

_____. *In the Night Kitchen,* ill. by author. Harper, 1970.   5–7

_____. *Outside Over There,* ill. by author. Harper, 1981.   5–8

_____. *Where the Wild Things Are,* ill. by author. Harper, 1963. Caldecott Medal.   5–7

SERVICE, PAMELA F. *Stinker from Space.* Scribner's, 1988.   9–11

SEUSS, DR. (pseud. for Theodor Seuss Geisel). *And to Think That I Saw It on Mulberry Street,* ill. by author. Vanguard, 1937.   5–8

_____. *The Cat in the Hat,* ill. by author. Random, 1957. The Cat provides novel entertainment for two housebound children.   5–8

_____. *The 500 Hats of Bartholomew Cubbins,* ill. by author. Vanguard, 1938.   6–10

SHARP, MARGERY. *Bernard into Battle: A Miss Bianca Story,* ill. by Leslie Morrill. Little, 1979. Another mock romantic adventure centering around the beautiful white mouse Miss Bianca and her stalwart admirer Bernard.   11 up

_____. *The Rescuers,* ill. by Garth Williams. Little, 1959. Witty fantasy of three brave mice who rescue a Norwegian poet from imprisonment in a deep, dark dungeon. *Miss Bianca* (1962) relates another brave rescue.   10–13

• SINGER, ISAAC BASHEVIS. *The Fearsome Inn,* tr. by author and Elizabeth Shub, ill. by Nonny Hogrogian. Scribner's, 1967. A fanciful tale mingling the Polish-Jewish humor and gusto with the fairy tale genre most deftly. The illustrations have a graceful vitality.   10–12

SLEATOR, WILLIAM. *The Duplicate.* Dutton, 1988.
11–14

SLOTE, ALFRED. *C.O.L.A.R.: A Tale of Outer Space,* ill. by Anthony Kramer. Lippincott, 1981. Jack and his robot twin are attacked by hostile robots on a faraway planet.   8–10

_____. *The Trouble on Janus,* ill. by James Lippincott, 1985.   8–10

SMALL, DAVID. *Imogene's Antlers,* ill. by author. Crown, 1985.   5–7

SNYDER, ZILPHA KEATLEY. *And All Between,* ill. by Alton Raible. Atheneum, 1976. The two factions in *Below the Root* confront each other in a suspenseful story.   10–12

_____. *Below the Root,* ill. by Alton Raible. Atheneum, 1975. A science fantasy set in a community of tree-dwellers.   10–12

_____. *Squeak Saves the Day and Other Tooley Tales,* ill. by Leslie Morrill. Delacorte, 1988. Seven stories center on adventures of tiny folk called Tiddlers, who avoid human STOMPERS whenever they can.   9–11

STEELE, WILLIAM O. *Andy Jackson's Water Well,* ill. by Michael Ramus. Harcourt, 1959. Andy Jackson achieves the incredible by bringing back water to drought-ridden Nashville. A hilarious tall tale that is ideal for storytelling.   9–13

STEIG, WILLIAM. *Abel's Island.* Farrar, 1976.   9–11

_____. *The Amazing Bone.* Farrar, 1976.   5–7

_____. *Dominic,* ill. by author. Farrar, 1972.
9–11

_____. *Sylvester and the Magic Pebble,* ill. by author. Simon, 1969. Caldecott Medal.   5–7

STEWART, MARY. *A Walk in Wolf Wood,* ill. by Emanuel Schoengut. Morrow, 1980. Two children step back in time to help a medieval courtier escape the enchantment of a wicked wizard.   10–11

STOCKTON, FRANK RICHARD. *The Bee-Man of Orn,* ill. by Maurice Sendak. Holt, 1964. The Bee-Man is completely content until he is informed that he has been transformed from some other sort of thing. A charming story, republished with Sendak's delightful illustrations.   10–12

STOLZ, MARY S. *Belling the Tiger,* ill. by Beni Montresor. Harper, 1967. A pointed message in this humorous story.   7–10

_____. *Cat Walk,* ill. by Erik Blegvad. Harper, 1983. A barn kitten searches for a good home in a beguiling, yet wholly credible, animal fantasy.
8–11

_____. *The Cuckoo Clock,* ill. by Pamela Johnson. Godine, 1987. Young Erich learns about love and friendship from the old clockmaker, Ula, until he is brave enough to run away from his cruel foster parent.   9–11

THURBER, JAMES. *The Great Quillow,* ill. by Doris Lee. Harcourt, 1944.   8–11

_____. *Many Moons,* ill. by Louis Slobodkin. Harcourt, 1943. Caldecott Medal.   7–10

_____. *The Thirteen Clocks,* ill. by Marc Simont. Simon, 1950. The cold Duke's hold over Princess Saralinda is broken when Prince Zorn brings him 1000 jewels and the Princess's warmth restarts the clocks.   11–12

_____. *The Wonderful O,* ill. by Marc Simont. Simon, 1957. Life without "O" goes on, but love, even footnotes, are lost.   10 up

TILLSTROM, BURR. *The Dragon Who Lived Downstairs,* ill. by David Small. Morrow, 1984. An ebullient picture book tells how a friendly dragon releases a princess from enchantment and paves the way for her union with a commoner/knight. The knight and the dragon are pictured as puppet favorites Kukla and Ollie. 7–9

TITUS, EVE. *Basil in Mexico,* ill. by Paul Galdone. McGraw, 1976. Basil, the detecting mouse of Baker Street, is again called upon to deduce who has stolen an art treasure from a Mexican museum and replaced it with a clever forgery. 8–10

TOLKIEN, JOHN R. R. *The Hobbitt,* ill. by author. Houghton, 1938. 10–14

TOWNSEND, JOHN ROWE. *The Creatures.* Lippincott, 1980. In a future time, the elite are visitors from another planet. The lowly people of earth are the "creatures." 11–14

————. *The Persuading Stick.* Lothrop, 1987. Beth finds she has powers over others when she is in possession of a strange, silvery stick. 9–11

TRAVERS, P. L. *Mary Poppins,* ill. by Mary Shepard. Harcourt, 1934. Many sequels.

————. *Mary Poppins and the House Next Door,* ill. by Mary Shepard. Delacorte, 1989. Mary Poppins and the Man-in-the-Moon help a child from the South Sea Islands to get home from London. 8–10

VOIGT, CYNTHIA. *Building Blocks.* Atheneum, 1984. A boy of 12 travels back in time to experience his father's Depression Era upbringing. 9–11

WABER, BERNARD. *You're a Little Kid with a Big Heart,* ill. by author. Houghton, 1980. A girl of seven, given a magic wish, wants to be old enough to be independent; in a breezy story, she learns that being a child of thirty-nine is no fun. 5–8

WADDELL, MARTIN. *The Tough Princess,* ill. by Patrick Benson. Philomel, 1987. 7–9

WALLACE, BARBARA BROOKS. *Argyle,* ill. by John Sandford. Abingdon, 1987. In a modern myth about the origin of Argyle socks, Argyle, a sheep, is happiest when he blends with the rest of the flock until he has devoured a bunch of flowers and his wool turns to rainbow colors. 5–8

§ WALLIN, LUKE. *The Slavery Ghosts.* Bradbury, 1983. Two youngsters rescue a family of slaves from a fantastical netherworld that adheres to the slave-holding conventions of the Old South. 10–12

WALSH, JILL PATON. *Torch.* Farrar, 1988. 11–14

WELLS, ROSEMARY. *Through the Hidden Door,* ill. by author. Dial, 1987. Barney's morals are tested as he is persecuted by a gang of bullies at a posh private school and while he helps a younger student keep the secret of a miniature city found in a cave. 11–13

WESTALL, ROBERT. *The Devil on the Road.* Greenwillow, 1979. In a time-slip fantasy, John, a university student who thrives on taking chances, travels back to the seventeenth century. 12 up

————. *Futuretrack 5.* Greenwillow, 1984. In a science fiction novel of twenty-first-century Britain, Henry and Keri plot to escape, and then to destroy, the modern police state. 12 up

————. *Ghost Abbey.* Scholastic, 1989. When her father gets a job supervising the restoration of Foxwist Abbey, Maggi Adams is first intrigued by the medieval atmosphere and then horrified by the Abbey's supernatural powers. 10–14

WHITE, E. B. *Charlotte's Web,* ill. by Garth Williams. Harper, 1952. 10 up

————. *Stuart Little,* ill. by Garth Williams. Harper, 1945. 9–11

————. *The Trumpet of the Swan,* ill. by Edward Frascino. Harper, 1970. 9–11

WILDE, OSCAR. *The Happy Prince and Other Stories,* ill. by Peggy Fortnum. Dutton, 1968. 9–11

————. *The Selfish Giant,* ill. by Gertrude and Walter Reiner. Harvey, 1968. 9–11

————. *The Selfish Giant,* ill. by Lisbeth Zwerger. Neugebauer Press, 1984. Delicate, spacious paintings place Wilde's story of the giant who drives children and summer out of his garden in an Edwardian setting. 5–8

WILLIAMS, JAY. *The Practical Princess and Other Liberating Fairy Tales,* ill. by Rick Schreiter. Parents' Magazine, 1978. A collection of six previously published stories notable for their robust, sly humor, their doughty heroines, and their irreverent treatment of traditional fairy tale devices. 7–9

————, and RAYMOND ABRASHKIN. *Danny Dunn and the Antigravity Paint,* ill. by Ezra Jack Keats. McGraw, 1956. One of a popular series. 10–12

WILLIAMS, URSULA MORAY. *Bogwoppit.* Nelson, 1978. Orphaned Samantha has trouble adjusting to her wealthy Aunt Daisy who is eventually kept prisoner in a drain by the fantastical, furry bogwoppits. 10–11

WILLIS, VAL. *The Secret in the Matchbox,* ill. by John Shelley. Farrar, 1988. The idea of a dragon tiny enough to fit in a matchbox should appeal to the read-aloud audience. 5–8

§ WINTHER, BARBARA. *Plays from Folktales of Africa and Asia.* Plays, 1976. A collection of short one-act plays most of which are humorous. They're royalty-free, easy to stage and are provided with production notes. 8–10

WRIGHTSON, PATRICIA. *Balyet.* McElderry, 1989.
                                            10–13

————. *The Dark Bright Water.* Atheneum, 1979.
                                            12–14

————. *Down to Earth,* ill. by Margaret Horder.
Harcourt, 1965.   10–12

————. *The Ice Is Coming.* Atheneum, 1977.
                                            11–14

————. *A Little Fear.* Atheneum, 1983.   10–12

————. *Moon-Dark.* McElderry, 1988. Australian
animals start a war among themselves during a
food shortage, and the problem is resolved when
a young wallaby calls upon a mythical moon man.
                                            10–13

————. *The Nargun and the Stars.* Atheneum,
1974.   10–12

————. *An Older Kind of Magic,* ill. by Noela
Young. Harcourt, 1972.

YEP, LAURENCE. *Dragonwings.* Harper, 1975 and its
sequel, *Dragon Steel.* Harper, 1985.   11–14

YOLEN, JANE. *Dragon's Blood.* Delacorte, 1982. To
earn the price of his freedom, bond servant
Jakkin steals a dragon and trains it as a fighter.
Followed by *Heart's Blood* (Delacorte, 1984) and *A
Sending of Dragons* (Delacorte, 1987).   12–14

• YORINKS, ARTHUR. *It Happened in Pinsk,* ill. by Richard Egielski. Farrar, 1983. Life changes dramatically for chronically disgruntled Irv Irving when
he wakes up without a head.   7–9

Chapter Nine

Poetry

Poetry can bring warmth, reassurance, even laughter; it can stir and arouse or quiet and comfort. Above all it can give significance to everyday experience. To miss poetry would be as much of a deprivation as to miss music. For these reasons it is essential that we know poetry and that we know how to introduce it to children. The experience of poetry should come with so much pure pleasure that the taste for it will grow and become a permanent part of a child's emotional, intellectual, and aesthetic resources.

Not all of the qualities that distinguish poetry from prose are common to all its forms, but basic to the genre are the concentration or crystallization of mood, emotion, or experience; the use of words or sounds that are evocative; and the use of imagery, oblique or vividly clear. Most poetry provides the satisfaction and challenge of pattern and uses words in a way that is more musical or rhythmic than all but the most lyric prose. The alliteration and refrain that can be obtrusive or redundant in prose become, in a good poem, part of its appeal; in a mediocre poem, an abuse of these devices or a rigid adherence to rhyme, especially when it is forced, can result in doggerel. Rhyme and rhythm, particularly attractive to younger children, reinforce aural enjoyment, for poetry must be heard to be fully savored. The essence of poetry is revelation: By the way words are put together, by the richly imaginative use of those words, by the condensation of the poet's conviction, we see with sharpened understanding our own experiences or share with quickened empathy the experiences or dreams of others.

Definitions of poetry are seldom of interest to children, but they are valuable to adults since they throw light on the manner in which to present poetry. Robert Frost said that "a poem is a momentary stay against confusion. Each poem clarifies something . . . . A poem is an arrest of disorder."[1] Frost implied that our experiences come pell-mell, but a poem sorts them out, gives them order and meaning—not merely the essence of an experience but its significance. Others define poetry:

Absolute poetry is the concrete and artistic expression of the human mind in emotional and rhythmical language.

ENCYCLOPAEDIA BRITANNICA

[1]John Ciardi, "Robert Frost: Master Conversationalist at Work," *Saturday Review,* March 21, 1959.

The essence of poetry is invention; such invention as, by producing something unexpected, surprises and delights.

SAMUEL JOHNSON

If I read a book and it makes my whole body so cold no fire can ever warm me, I know that is poetry. If I feel physically as if the top of my head were taken off, I know that is poetry. These are the only ways I know it. Is there any other way?

EMILY DICKINSON

If you examine these definitions and others, you will discover certain ideas recurring: Poetry surprises and delights; it sings like music; it makes you feel intensely; poetry gives you an arresting thought often in rhythmic words, plus a shiver up your backbone. When poetry means these things to you, you have genuinely enjoyed it: It becomes a part of you. When it leaves you just where you were, neither aroused nor amused, neither enchanted nor solaced, then poetry has not happened to you; it has passed you by. So it is with children.

Elements of Good Poetry

But how about adults who enjoy doggerel, and children who accept anything that rhymes? Does enjoyment make poetry of these jingles they read? Perhaps for them it does temporarily, but doggerel need not remain their top level of appreciation. Good taste in any field— music, interior decoration, clothes, poetry—is largely a matter of experience. As we become familiar with the best in a particular field, we gain discrimination there, while in another field in which our experience is limited we may show very poor taste. Harry Behn said, "I believe that children's judgment of what books are best for them to expand into is better than *our* judgment if we make the best as easily available as television."[2] Children's taste will improve if they have repeated experiences with good poetry.

[2]Harry Behn, *Chrysalis.* Harcourt Brace Jovanovich, 1968, p. 16.

The Music of Poetry

One of the most important characteristics of good poetry is its singing quality, its melody and movement. In the nonsense jingles and humorous verse, for example, words and lines trip along with the lightness of children jumping rope. Clumsy doggerel—in contrast to the verses of Lear, Richards, and Milne—is heavy footed, and its words and lines have no sparkle. If, as Lillian Smith says in *The Unreluctant Years,* the verses of Milne and Lear are not true poetry, they are certainly as debonair and as skillfully written as light verse can be. If a poem is in a mysterious or meditative or wistful mood, the lines move slowly and the words fall subtly on the ear. These are clues to reading poetry aloud and emphasizing the musical pattern. On the whole, the poetry small children like is more lively and lilting than poetry for adults. The fact that children enjoy marked rhythms and crisp rhymes accounts for their ready acceptance of second-rate verse if it has these characteristics. But if their ears become attuned to the subtleties and varieties of rhythmic patterns found in poems like those by Stevenson, de la Mare, and McCord, they may detect the labored rhythms and forced rhymes that characterize most mediocre verse.

The Words of Poetry

Poetry uses strong, vigorous words or evocative, rich words or delicate, precise words that define with accuracy. Of course, prose may employ the same words, but poetry ordinarily uses them with greater condensation and in more melodious combinations so that their effect is more striking. Think of the amusing "sneezles and freezles" of Christopher Robin, of John Updike's "stripped and shapely Maple" grieving in November for "the ghosts of her departed leaves," or of Blake's "echoing green," which suggests the calls and shouts of children at their play. Read through these poems and notice both the exact, descriptive words and the sensory, connotative words and phrases which distinguish good poetry from the ordinary: "the still dark night," "skipping along alone," "rain in the city" falling "slant-wise where the buildings crowd," "soaked, sweet-

Viewpoint

I feel that poetry is the essence of living. Of course, as Brecht said, "First feed the face." One must have the basic essentials. But I feel that poetry—and the music of language—are so close to that.

I feel that poetry, the sounds of words, are directly related to the rhythms of one's body. I can't recite poetry and sit still. I have to be standing. I have to be able to move my whole body. I think that the body is so involved in poetry that one must just use it to develop the rhythm. So there, then, you can feel tensions in your body as you're breathing in, as you're breathing out, as you have a long flow of words or something staccato where you want to go "bick, bang, biff."

From "A Word or Two with Eve Merriam: Talking About Poetry", *The New Advocate*, by Susan Taylor Cox, Summer 1989. Reprinted by permission of the author.

smelling lane," "apple trees are snowing." Words that stir the imagination, that speak to the senses, that provoke laughter, that move us deeply and strongly—such words are part of the secret of good poetry.

The Content of Poetry

While poetry has strong emotional appeals, it is built around subjects or ideas, and appeals to the intellect as well as the emotions. Even a slight verse like "Little Miss Muffet" has a well-defined idea—security, fright, escape. Children's emotional response to poetry depends upon their grasp of the content. Of course poetry may have almost as varied subject matter as prose, but like any of the other arts, it must invest that content with arresting significance. A slippery baby in a bathtub is Carl Sandburg's "fish child," and Marianne Moore's jellyfish is "an amber-tinctured amethyst." John Ciardi's "thin grin-cat" stalking a bird is ominous in its suggestion of hunger and anticipated satisfaction. So poetry takes the

strange or everyday facts of life and gives them fresh meaning. We see colors that seem new because poetry has revealed them.

Selecting Poetry for Children

When we choose a poem for children, we may well test it with these questions: First, *does it sing*—with good rhythm, true, unforced rhymes, and a happy compatibility of sound and subject—whether it is nonsense verse or narrative or lyric poetry? Second, *is the diction distinguished*—with words that are rich in sensory and connotative meanings, words that are unhackneyed, precise, and memorable? Third, *does the subject matter of the poem invest the strange or the everyday experiences of life with new importance and richer meaning?* When a poem does these three things, it is good poetry.

People who do not like poetry usually have had unpleasant introductions to poems when they were children. Poetry should be chosen and presented to children with care if we wish to make it appealing to them. Following are some suggestions for do's and don'ts:

Do read poetry aloud often.
Do provide a variety of poems in records, books, and tapes.
Do make several anthologies available to children.
Do select contemporary poetry as well as older material.
Do help children avoid sing-song reading aloud.
Do choose poems with comprehensible subject matter.
Do encourage the writing of poetry.
Do choose poems that have action or humor.
Do try choral reading.

Don't introduce poetry by dissecting it.
Don't read poetry aloud without practicing enough to read it well.
Don't confuse poems that are *about* children with poems that are *for* children.
Don't present poems that are too long, or that have long descriptive passages.
Don't choose poems that have involved figures of speech or obsolete language.

Don't introduce poetry by having children read it silently.

Don't require children to memorize poetry.

Don't use poetry as a reading exercise.

Don't select poems that are pedantic or that are about a subject in which children probably have a minimal interest, such as reflections on growing old.

Don't select poems with obscure meanings or language too difficult for the child's comprehension.

These are general suggestions, and are not meant to imply that all figures of speech should be shunned, or that all subject matter in poetry should be wholly within the child's experience, but that aspects of poetry should be given careful consideration before poems are introduced to children. (See also the discussion on using poetry with children, at the end of this chapter.)

The Range of Poetry for Children

Although some children cling to one genre or subject in their reading, most like variety, and their preferences change with mood and age. Fortunately, there is such variety in poetry as to satisfy any taste: narrative, dramatic, or lyric; bound verse or free; poems about animals, people, nature, emotions, causes; poems that are thoughtful or stirring, tender or hilarious. Here we shall cross the lines of form and content in discussing both the wide variety of poetry for children and the poetry children are writing today. We shall consider poetry ranging from nonsense verse and the more serious poems about children's everyday experiences to the quiet probings of Langston Hughes's poetry and the patterned intricacies of poems by May Swenson and Myra Cohn Livingston.

A poem may be written in free verse, which has no requirements of rhyme and meter, or in bound verse, which does. It can be narrative, dramatic, or lyric. Dramatic poetry, a form seldom used in children's poems, reveals the personality of a character primarily through his or her speech or through the speech of other characters. Narrative poetry tells a story and is enjoyed by children for that reason, whether the poems are long and serious or brief and humorous. Lyric poems, which are usually short, express an emotion of some kind, often highly personal, and may range in content from the expression of a child's delight in "wiggly mud" to a sad farewell to departing summer.

Nonsense Verse

A good way to introduce children to poetry is with nonsense verse. For young children the gay tradition of nonsense verse was given a rousing start by *Mother Goose* rhymes (see Chapter 4). Children enjoy these amusing jingles, and most adults find a lifelong source of fun in humorous limericks and verse.

Not all people and not all ages are amused by the same jokes. Two-year-olds may chuckle over the hissing *s*'s of "sing a song of sixpence." The hilarity of older children is roused by other forms of nonsense. Just listen to seven-year-olds enjoying Laura Richards's "Eletelephony."

Nonsense verse, if it is skillfully composed, introduces the child to rhyme, rhythm, and meter and to various types of verse patterns. The neatly turned limerick and the patter of

From "Eletelephony" by Laura E. Richards in *Sing a Song of Popcorn*, selected by Beatrice Schenk de Regniers et al., illustrated by Richard Egielski.

humorous couplets or quatrains in exact meter train the ear to enjoy the sound of words and rhythms, a training that should carry over to catching similar sound patterns in poetry of a higher order.

From Nonsense to Humor

Although no hard and fast line divides humor from sheer nonsense, there is, nevertheless, a difference. Nonsense is more daft, more impossible, while humorous verse deals with the amusing things that befall real people, or might conceivably befall them. Edward Lear and Laura E. Richards sometimes wrote humorous verse, but for the most part their verse is hilarious nonsense. In contrast, A. A. Milne wrote occasional nonsense, but on the whole his poems involve people and situations that are amusingly possible, however improbable they may be.

Usually "The King's Breakfast" is the favorite with most Milne addicts. This starts reasonably with the king asking for a little butter on the "royal slice of bread," and it moves along smoothly until the sleepy Alderney upsets all royal regularity by suggesting "a little marmalade instead." From then on the dialogue becomes entirely daft, reaching a joyous climax when the king bounces out of bed and slides down the banister. This is, of course, the essence of the fun—the incongruity of a king who is so deeply concerned with marmalade that he whimpers, sulks, bounces, and finally slides down banister. The verse pattern of each episode reinforces the mood.

Other writers of humorous verse include the once popular James Whitcomb Riley and Eugene Field. Riley's verses have a mild humor, but they rarely bubble or sparkle. Field's "The Duel" is still enjoyed by children of five or six. This mock tragedy about the gingham dog and the calico cat who "ate each other up" has a pleasant swing and a delightful refrain. Another tragicomic verse is Vachel Lindsay's "The Potatoes' Dance," which tells of the blighted romance of a "tiny Irish lady" and a hapless sweet potato.

Eleanor Farjeon wrote skillful nonsense verse. Her lyrics are tender and beautiful, and her poetry reflects a sure knowledge of the child's world and wonderment. Her first book, for which she wrote her own music, was *Nursery Rhymes of London Town.* Her writing has zest and playfulness, enjoyment of words, and a variety of subjects and patterns with a seeming spontaneity and an unquestionable charm.

One of the most outstanding and prolific writers of humorous verse for children is David McCord, who wrote for adults before he began writing for children. McCord's poems are not all humorous, but the best of them have a captivating playfulness and ebullience that infectiously communicate an enjoyment of words and word play.

William Cole's *Oh, What Nonsense!* and *Oh, How Silly!* are anthologies of humorous poems, the first containing many counting rhymes and jump-rope chants; the second song lyrics and folk rhymes. X. J. Kennedy, in *One Winter Night in August, The Phantom Ice Cream Man,* and *Brats,* writes bouncy, comic poems with the appeal of nonsense. Dennis Lee's *Garbage Delight,* which won the 1978 award given by the Canadian Library Association as the best book of the year, depends on exaggeration, nonsense, and strong rhythm for its appeal.

In each of her collections of poetry, Eve Merriam provides some amusing gems. Like David McCord, she sometimes uses poetic

From *Brats* by X. J. Kennedy, illustrated by James Watts.

forms to explain the forms themselves, giving six examples of the couplet in "Couplet Countdown" and demonstrating in "Leaning on a Limerick" both the form and the playful use of words at which she excels.

Viewpoint

Although nonsense, like poetry, eludes definition, it seems important to me at a time when so much verse is being written in the name of nonsense that we seek to establish those elements that are the province of nonsense, and those that simply fall into the categories of humor, wit, word-play, parody, and wild imagination or illusion. Most critics would agree with G.K. Chesterton that nonsense is "lawless and innocent"; they would accept Phyllis Greenacre's contention that it is "not only the lack of reason or expected order, but it is the defiance of reason which men value most," and agree with Vivian Noakes that it "is a game played by a rational, methodical mind." But it is necessary, I believe, to go further and spell out the conditions under which we find the best in nonsense. Those who write nonsense verse must use the touchstones of reality—physical laws as well as objects and people—and transfer them, through carefully controlled imagination, to an *impossible* world, a world that poses no threat to us. It is essential that these conditions be carried out in order that we feel no sympathy, empathy, or compassion. The genius of the writer of true nonsense is such that we are able to enter his world with no physical or emotional threat to ourselves. Nonsense verse does not mirror back the frailties or weaknesses of humankind. Rather does it enable us, as well as those who inhabit its realm, to effect a complete escape.

Myra Cohn Livingston, *Celebrating Children's Books*, edited by Betsy Hearne and Marilyn Kaye. New York: Lothrop, Lee, & Shepard Books, 1981, pp. 123–124.

For older readers, Myra Cohn Livingston's *Speak Roughly to Your Little Boy* is both diverting and instructive. It is a collection of parodies and burlesques, each paired with the original material on which it was based. Some of the selections will also be enjoyed by younger children who can recognize little nuggets of burlesque like J. B. Morton's "Now We Are Sick."

Since anthologists have not found all the humorous verse that has been written, it is a rewarding activity for teachers to make a collection of favorites, or to encourage children to make such a collection. Clever, well-written verses that provoke a chuckle are worth having not only because they bring laughter into a world in need of laughter, but because their rollicking jingles cultivate the ear and lead naturally and painlessly to the enjoyment of lyric poetry.

Poetry of the Child's Everyday World

The world of fantastic nonsense and the child's everyday world of people, pets, and the outdoors may seem far apart. Yet many poets move easily from one to the other and, like the child, are at home in both worlds.

Actually, in the years before Edward Lear introduced his madcap world of nonsense, children had been given to understand that life was not only real but decidedly earnest. Poems were written and read to children for the purpose of improving their manners and uplifting their morals. Yet didactic as some of these early efforts seem today, they marked a dawning recognition of the child's everyday world of people and play, both real and imaginative. Slowly the idea took form and grew, the idea of a child not as a small adult but as an intensely active person, functioning in a world of his or her own.

The poems of Kate Greenaway marked the transition from verse written for children's instruction to verse written for their entertainment, verse that records the play world from the child's point of view. Even though her verses are often wooden and occasionally unchildlike, they reflect a new consciousness of real children and their everyday play. Other poets caught this point of view and began to write a new kind of verse for and about children. Their poems reflect both the child's everyday world of active play and the inner world of imaginative play.

Robert Louis Stevenson wrote only one book of poetry for children, *A Child's Garden of Verses,* but with that one book he became one of the great children's poets. His poems are truly childlike in their approach to play and in the manner in which they mirror the small adventures of a child's day. They are rhythmic and musical, and they see both the imagined and the real with a child's clear eye.

Elizabeth Madox Roberts had the ability to see, feel, and think in a childlike manner that strikes the adult as unerringly right and true. Her single book of poetry for children, *Under the Tree,* uses words and phrases that sound like a child speaking, but only an artist could have chosen words so brilliantly descriptive. Her narrative is as direct as prose, with no pretentiousness, no fanciness, no ethereal theme; but the imagery, the sensitivity, and the identification with the concerns of children bring her poems directly into the child's world of poetry.

Firefly

A little light is going by,
Is going up to see the sky,
A little light with wings.

I never could have thought of it,
To have a little bug all lit
And made to go on wings.

Elizabeth Madox Roberts

From "Firefly" by Elizabeth Madox Roberts in *Animals, Animals,* illustrated by Eric Carle.

Judith Viorst's *If I Were in Charge of the World and Other Worries: Poems for Children and Their Parents* involves children's concerns about themselves and their relationships with others, treating them in a humorous tone. An anthology that speaks to children of familiar things is *Once Upon a Rhyme,* compiled by Sara and Stephen Corrin with attention to popularity potential as well as poetic excellence.

Arnold Adoff, in *Make a Circle Keep Us In,* writes of the protective love and warmth in family life with fluent simplicity. In Cynthia Rylant's *Waiting to Waltz: A Childhood,* a cycle of thirty poems describes a girl's childhood in a small town.

John Updike, distinguished as a writer for adults and as the 1964 winner of the National Book Award for Fiction, has, in *A Child's Calendar,* written with fresh imagery about the familiar phenomena of the child's changing year.

In this chapter is just a sampling of the many poets who have brought their lyric gifts to interpret the everyday world the child sees and wonders about. Of all the poems available for children, however, those that tell a story have a special appeal for poetry lovers as well as for self-proclaimed detesters of poems.

Traditional Ballads

The ancient ballads are often, because of their dialect and archaic language, difficult for children to read or sing. Yet children are universally fond of poems that tell a story, and a more rousing collection of stories would be hard to find. Both the folk ballads and modern story poems have a common appeal: They tell a story in concentrated form, with a maximum of excitement and a minimum of words. Children may make little distinction between the types, for what they enjoy is the swift movement of verse or melody enhancing the dramatic appeal of a good story. The search for these story poems carries us back into folk rhymes and forward to present-day narrative poems, ranging from hilarious nonsense to romance and noble tragedy.

Traditional ballads were passed on by word of mouth long before they were printed, and they were so popular and so rapidly carried about by sailors and travelers that it is difficult today to determine whether a ballad is Danish, Scottish, English, or German in origin. The English and Scottish ballads flourished from the thirteenth to the middle of the sixteenth century. However, it was not until 1765, when Bishop Percy collected and published many of the ballads in his famous *Reliques,* that they became widely known and appreciated; the ballads that this collection contained had been found by chance in an ancient manuscript. They inspired Sir Walter Scott and others after him to search for and preserve other original ballad materials.

Characteristics of the Traditional Ballads.

The old ballad was a song story and its singing quality is still evident in the lilting verses and refrains and in the lively tunes that accompany the words. "Bonny Barbara Allan," for example, tells a tragic tale swiftly and movingly, but the opening verse suggests at once that here is a song:

> In Scarlet Town, where I was bound
>   There was a fair maid dwelling.
> Whom I had chosen to be my own,
>   And her name it was Barbara Allan.

In many ballads this songlike quality is enhanced by refrains that seem made for dancing. It is a good idea to help children respond to the musical character of the ballads by having them sing some or try to suit rhythmic movements to the words of others or even try lively dance steps to the lustier refrains.

Perhaps the most striking characteristic of the ballads is their dramatic and rapidly unfolding plots. In "Edward," for example, you sense immediately that something is wrong; then you learn that Edward has killed his own father, but not till the last stanza do you know that the mother herself planned the crime and persuaded her son to commit it.

There are of course some comic plots, too, but they are distinctly in the minority. "The Crafty Farmer" outwitting the thief is one of the children's favorites, and they like even better the broad slapstick farce of the stubborn old couple in "Get Up and Bar the Door." The folk-tale plot of trial by riddle with a bright

person substituting for a stupid one is amusingly used in "King John and the Abbot of Canterbury" ("King John and the Bishop").

On the whole, ballad plots are more likely to be tragic than humorous. They celebrate bloody and terrible battles, ghosts that return to haunt their true or their false loves, fairy husbands of human maids, infanticide, murder, faithless love punished, faithful love not always rewarded—sad, sad romance and tragedies in every possible combination.

Viewpoint

Ballads are widely considered to be plotted narratives, rising from relatively trained minds, taken over and fostered by the folk until they become the verses and masterpieces that our collectors uncover.

The word "plotted" is of particular significance. . . . Plotting is honored by the tradition in which the Anglo-American ballad is born, but there is little evidence to support a contention that the folk, in whose oral heritage the ballad lives, care very much at all for unified action. Their myths and their tales lack unified action, except as a vestige. Generally, the folk tend to discard plotting in favor of something one might call "impact" or "emotional core."

A ballad survives among our folk because it embodies a basic human reaction to a dramatic situation. This reaction is reinterpreted by each person who renders the ballad. As an emotional core it dominates the artistic act, and melody, setting, character, and plot are used only as means by which to get it across. This core is more important to the singer and the listeners than the details of the action themselves.

Tristram P. Coffin, "Mary Hamilton and the Anglo-American Ballad as an Art Form," in *The Critics and the Ballad,* readings selected and edited by MacEdward Leach and Tristram P. Coffin. Carbondale: Southern Illinois University Press, 1961, pp. 245, 246, 247.

Incremental repetition is an aid to storytelling. This is a ballad convention in which each verse repeats the form of the preceding verse but with a new turn that advances the story. Reading ballads that use incremental repetition, you will find it easy to imagine a leader starting the pattern by asking the question, a crowd of people singing the refrain, and the same leader, or perhaps the next person in the circle, answering the question.

The author always remains anonymous. Reference to the storyteller is comparatively rare, perhaps only in an opening line. The storyteller merely records the facts of the adventure as objectively as possible and remains completely anonymous.

The ballads, as we have observed, run the whole gamut of subjects and emotions. Here are some categories with a few examples:

Farce—"The Crafty Farmer"; "Get Up and Bar the Door"

Comedy—"King John and the Abbot of Canterbury" ("King John and the Bishop"); "A Gest of Robyn Hode" (with the exception of the account of Robin Hood's death)

Crime—"Edward"; "The Bonny Earl of Murray"; "Lord Randal"; "The Twa Sisters"

Noble tragedy—"Sir Patrick Spens"; "The Hunting of the Cheviot"; "The Battle of Harlaw"; "The Battle of Otterburn" (the ballads of the great battles are generally too involved for the elementary school)

Romance—"Lizie Lindsay"; "Bonny Barbara Allan"; "The Raggle, Taggle Gypsies" ("The Gypsy Laddie")

Fairylore—"The Wee Wee Man"; "Tam Lin"; "Hind Etin"

Ghost story—"The Wife of Usher's Well"

Melodrama—"The Daemon Lover" ("James Harris"); "Lord Randal"; "Bonny Barbara Allan"

Folk Ballads in the United States.

Early settlers brought the old Scottish and English ballads to this country, and children in states as remote from each other as Pennsylvania and Texas, or Wisconsin and the Carolinas,

From *Tam Lin*, retold by Jane Yolen, illustrated by Charles Mikolaycak.

heard their parents and grandparents singing the same ballads that *their* grandparents had sung in the mother country. "Bonny Barbara Allan," for example, was carried by the colonists and pioneer families from one end of the United States to the other.

The collection compiled by Francis Child (1825–1896) of Harvard stimulated such an interest in these old story songs that collectors began to search for and record their American variants. They found, as you might expect, a large number of ballads being sung or recited throughout the country, but especially in the Southern mountains. There the mountaineers, cut off from the mainstream of immigration and changing customs, had preserved the songs their ancestors brought with them. "Lord Randal" might be hailed democratically as "Johnny Randall," or even "Jimmy Randolph," but he was still begging his mother to make his bed soon for he was "sick to the heart and fain wad lie down." Sometimes the verses had been so altered and patched together that they were incoherent. Most of the ballads had, however, come through with less change than you might naturally expect from several hundred years of oral transmission.

Cecil J. Sharp (1859–1924), an English musician, made early and outstanding collections of these descendants of Scottish-English ballads in the Southern mountains of the United States. His books are valuable contributions to the ballad literature of America, and other collectors have followed his lead. Older children will enjoy the ballads in Sharp's first two volumes, while children as young as three and four are charmed with the *Nursery Songs*.

Once the collectors set to work gathering American variants of the old-world ballads, they began to encounter new ballads and folk songs that are as native to the United States as buckwheat cakes and hominy grits. Here was a rich treasure of ballad-making still in the process of creation. These songs achieve a wistful melancholy or a happy-go-lucky philosophy or a sheer braggadocio distinguishing certain groups of hardy settlers or certain workers such as the Western cowboys.

The native ballads of the United States tell, on the whole, fewer coherent and dramatic stories than do the Scottish-English ballads; but they sing with or without the music. The Negro spirituals reach heights of religious fervor never attained in any old-world ballad, but for their full beauty they need their music. The cowboys' ballads have sometimes a philosophic or a wistful air that is more in the mood of a song than of a story. The language is easier for us, even the dialect or vernacular, but some of it is rather rough.

With the increasing popularity of folk singing in the middle period of the twentieth century, there has been a renaissance of the ballad form. The outstanding performer-composers are the heroes of the young, the guitar the indispensable instrument, the ballad their own song. One of the most pleasant collections is *As I Walked Out One Evening: A Book of Ballads* compiled by Helen Plotz. And, for the younger children, there is an echoing trend in the publication of single songs in illustrated editions.

Once children realize that ballads are still remembered and treasured, they may turn collectors and discover some ballads in their own families or communities. Once they realize that ballads are still being made the children may wish to try group composition of a ballad. It is fun and less difficult than it sounds. Radio, newspapers, and television make constant use of current events for sketches and dramas. Why not try casting them into ballad form?

Narrative Poems

The story poem and the old ballad form have proved as attractive to poets as they have to readers. The rapid action, the refrains and repetition, and the rhythm all contribute to the interest and impetus of story poems.

For the youngest children, from five to eight or nine, there are two masterpieces—"A Visit from St. Nicholas" by Clement Clarke Moore and "The Pied Piper of Hamelin" by Robert Browning. It is interesting to recall that Browning wrote "The Pied Piper of Hamelin" for the amusement of a sick child, with the special intention of supplying him with subject matter

From *The Night Before Christmas* by Clement Moore, illustrated by Tomie dePaola.

he could illustrate. Perhaps this accounts, in part, for the visual quality of the poem, which has endeared it to illustrators. The story of "The Pied Piper" is too familiar to need reviewing, but particular qualities of the poem are worth noting. In the first place, the story moves rapidly. Words hurry and trip along, episodes follow each other swiftly, and lines have the racing tempo first of the scurrying rats and later of the skipping children. The dramatic conflict between greed and honor is sufficiently objective for children to understand, and they approve of the Piper's retributive revenge.

For broad comedy, Eugene Field's "The Duel" (the tale of "the gingham dog and the calico cat") and Laura Richards's "The Monkeys and the Crocodile" are perennial favorites. Two amusing ventures into history are Arnold Lobel's *On the Day Peter Stuyvesant Sailed into Town* and Maxine Kumin's *The Microscope,* with Lobel's pictures of Anton van Leeuwenhoek. In Natalie Babbitt's *Dick Foote and the Shark,* the poetic hero saves his own life and that of his terrified father by so doggedly spouting poetry from the bow that the befuddled shark swims away.

The story of Noah's Ark, more than slightly adapted, has several verse versions, including Countee Cullen's *The Lost Zoo,* a good choice for reading aloud to younger children; and *The Cruise of the Aardvark* in which Ogden Nash's pompous hero discovers belatedly that he is not on an ordinary pleasure cruise. A lasting favorite is "Custard the Dragon," also by Nash. Search your anthologies and books by single poets for more story poems, because even the fives and sevens enjoy the swiftness and suspense which the rhythmic flow of verse gives to a story. A bouncy, bald, plump little Knight is the hero of Roy Gerrard's *Sir Cedric* and *Sir Cedric Rides Again.* Also comic but with the addition of an eerie quality is *Tog the Ribber or Granny's Tale* by Paul Coltman.

Scott's "Young Lochinvar," a swashbuckling romance with a galloping tempo, is particularly enjoyed by older children; "The Highwayman" by Alfred Noyes is a favorite romance. May Sarton has written with sensitivity and grace "The Ballad of Ruby," based on an episode described in Robert Coles's *Children of Crisis.* It

From *The Microscope* by Maxine Kumin, illustrated by Arnold Lobel.

tells of a small black child's experience of discrimination when she goes to school. And not to be forgotten is that gem of Americana, Ernest L. Thayer's "Casey at the Bat."

For eleven- to fourteen-year-olds there are many story poems about great events in history. Certainly they should hear "The Landing of the Pilgrim Fathers" by Felicia Dorothea Hemans, with its unforgettable picture of that desolate arrival and its significance in our history. Children may also thrill to the galloping hoofbeats of Henry Wadsworth Longfellow's "Paul Revere's Ride" before they meet the more complex and workaday Revere of the biographies. Arthur Guiterman has written a number of fine historical ballads like "The Oregon Trail." These are significant both as poems and as history. In *Independent Voices,* Eve Merriam has written poems that tell, in a variety of rhyming verse patterns and with a vivid sense of the dramatic, the stories of many great American men and women. In Rosemary and Stephen Benét's *A Book of Americans,* there are many poems that have historical significance, but "Nancy Hanks" and "Abraham Lincoln" are the great favorites. Such poems can be introduced casually as the historical chronology unfolds, or children may become interested in the theme of heroism and start searching for hero poems.

Lyric Poetry

Lyric poetry developed from an ancient Greek form of poetry accompanied by a musical instrument, most often a lyre. A lyric poem is like a song. Lyric poems are frequently set to music and they generally express very clearly and directly one particular feeling or thought. In the Middle Ages, the form was evident in folk songs and hymns and evolved to the lyrical expression of emotion characteristic of romantic poets such as William Blake and lyric poets of the last two centuries, among them Emily Dickinson, Henry Wadsworth Longfellow, A. E. Housman, Edna St. Vincent Millay, and Dylan Thomas. This poetry is characterized by the mood that is evoked through well-chosen words and phrases.

Some children respond to the sounds while other children are caught by the charm of words and phrases, and without knowing why, they respond to the mood evoked by the words. In some such accidental way, children's taste for lyric poetry may begin. It is the responsibility of parents, librarians, and teachers to provide poetry experiences for children that will help them appreciate and enjoy lyric poems.

It is not that lyric poetry is characteristically obscure or that its sound is more important than its meaning. But authentic poetry not only conveys meaning but generally evokes an emotional response. Children who have the good fortune to hear a poem that gives them a shiver up their backbones or a swift upsurging flood of elation or a sense of quiet and peace are discovering some of the joys of poetry.

From the great body of English lyric verse, children will appropriate certain poems that suit them, and when they have spoken them repeatedly until they know them, the verses become truly their own. They may ask about them, too, and through discussions meaning will be enriched. If most children still prefer

the lightest of light verse, just remember that most adults do, too.

William Shakespeare is one of those poets who, although writing for adults, has songs that children enjoy. Children hearing the songs of Shakespeare without being forced to analyze or memorize them soon know the poems by heart. "Jog on, jog on," from *The Winter's Tale,* is a good march for any excursion of children. "Who is Sylvia?" from *The Two Gentlemen of Verona* and "Hark, hark! the lark," from *Cymbeline*—these poems have a singing quality and a simplicity of content that bring them within the enjoyment range of older children, especially if they hear the poems before they read them.

William Blake's *Songs of Innocence* is a landmark in English literature as well as in children's literature. The average child may not particularly enjoy some of the more difficult poems, but will enjoy many of them if they are read aloud by someone who likes their melodies—Blake's poems are songs, full of cadences and lovely sounds.

Christina Rossetti provides the young child with an ideal introduction to lyric poetry in the verses of *Sing Song,* published in 1872. Many of the verses have homely, familiar subjects, but they are written with lyric grace and with a subtle simplicity in the choice of words. What gentleness there is in "The Caterpillar":

Brown and furry
Caterpillar in a hurry

From *Sing Song* by Christina Rossetti, illustrated by Arthur Hughes (1872 edition).

Take your walk
To the shady leaf or stalk
Or what not,
Which may be the chosen spot.
No toad spy you,
Hovering birds of prey pass by you;
Spin and die,
To live again a butterfly.

Many poets of the twentieth century have written outstanding lyric poetry, including Walter de la Mare and Eleanor Farjeon, Sara Teasdale and Elizabeth Coatsworth. Eve Merriam, in *It Doesn't Always Have to Rhyme,* and Valerie Worth, in *Still More Small Poems,* or Langston Hughes, in "Snail" or "Dream Variations," have written lines as musical as any lyric poets of the past.

Poetry of Nature

Most of the poets discussed in this category are dissimilar in most respects, but they have one characteristic in common: They observe nature with sensitive interpretation and an imaginative turn that kindles a responsive spark in the reader.

The poems of Sara Teasdale are largely descriptive and often too subtle for the child under ten, but their lyric beauty and poignance captivate some children. Elizabeth Coatsworth's poems are less musical but rich with imagery, less complex but lucid and gay with a quick appeal.

Aileen Fisher, many of whose longer poems (*Once We Went on a Picnic* and *Listen, Rabbit*) have been published singly in picture-book form, has been a prolific writer of verses for children. Her writing is pleasant and patterned, and all of her nature poetry reflects both her awareness of the child's interests and her own deep love of the outdoors and of small, wild creatures. An example of her poetic vision is "Sun Prints":

Sun Prints

The lawn is full of footprints,
golden tracks that show
where the sun went walking
a day or two ago.

My father calls them dandelions.
I think they're sun prints, though.[3]

The Danish explorer Knud Rasmussen brought back from his fifth expedition to the Arctic a large collection of Eskimo poems. A selection from these has been made into a beautiful book for children, *Beyond the High Hills,* illustrated with breathtaking color photographs. The result is a dramatic re-creation of Eskimo thoughts and feelings of a way of life that is vanishing. These verses are in free form and have great strength and maturity. They will give children more of Eskimo life and thought than many factual books. *The Wind Has Wings,* a varied and handsomely illustrated collection of Canadian poetry compiled by Mary Downie and Barbara Robertson, includes Eskimo and French songs, and Jane Yolen's *Ring of Earth: A Child's Book of Seasons* has universal appeal.

The Trees Stand Shining, a selection of poetry of the North American Indians, has been compiled by Hettie Jones. The poems are, in fact, untitled songs, fragmentary and brief, often with the terse quality of haiku, that show the affinity the native American feels for the beauty and strength of nature. Humanity's close relationship to nature is also depicted in John Bierhorst's anthology *In the Trail of the Wind: American Indian Poems and Ritual Orations.* This volume includes poems of the Maya, the Aztec, and the Eskimo as well as those of North American Indian tribes. William Brandon's collection, *The Magical World: American Indian Songs and Poems,* is unusual for its inclusion of a large number of Nahuatl ceremonial songs.

In *A Few Flies and I,* some of the poems of the great Japanese poet Issa have been brought together by Jean Merrill and Ronni Solbert. Richard Lewis, in *Of This World,* also chose some of the Issa poems that show an infinite tenderness toward the small creatures of the world.

Of all the books that share this affection for animals, Carmen Bernos de Gasztold's *Prayers from the Ark* and *The Creatures' Choir,* translated from the French by Rumer Godden, are two of the most beguiling, each poem a percipient

---

[3]"Sun Prints" from *Out in the Dark and Daylight* by Aileen Fisher, Copyright © 1980 by Aileen Fisher. Reprinted by permission of HarperCollins Publishers.

From *Consider the Lemming* by Jeanne Steig, illustrated by William Steig.

picture of the animal that speaks. Another book that has the same gentle quality is Joanne Ryder's *Inside Turtle's Shell and Other Poems of the Field.*

Other books about animals are *Cats and Bats and Things with Wings* by Conrad Aiken, and *Brownjohn's Beasts* by the British poet Alan Brownjohn, whose animals, like those of Carmen Bernos de Gasztold, speak for themselves—and with great wit. Two books of light, rhythmic verse about animals are Jeanne Steig's *Consider the Lemming* and Patricia Hooper's *A Bundle of Beasts.*

Poetry from Around the World

Many books are bringing poetry of other lands to English-speaking children. Producing such books is a phenomenon not wholly new but noticeably burgeoning. Richard Lewis chose Japanese and Chinese poetry for *The Moment of Wonder* and selected haiku for younger readers in *In a Spring Garden.* In *The Luminous Landscape: Chinese Art and Poetry,* illustrated with reproductions of Chinese art, Lewis uses water and mountains as major sections of the book to show the important relationship between people and their environment. He selected poems of the haiku poet Issa in *Of This World.* Japanese poems are also found in Harry Behn's two collections of haiku, *Cricket Songs* and *More Cricket Songs.* Nursery rhymes of other lands are discussed in Chapter 4.

In William Jay Smith's *Poems from France,* each poem in French has the English translation on the facing page. Undoubtedly the French poetry best known to English-speaking children is that of de Gasztold, mentioned above.

Helen Plotz's *Poems from the German,* which provides the poems in the original and in English translation, is for older children. For younger readers there are several editions of Heinrich Hoffmann's *Slovenly Peter,* now a children's classic, one version of which was translated by Mark Twain.

The first section of Miriam Morton's anthology *A Harvest of Russian Children's Literature* has verses for young children, and there are a few other poems in the book, notably a long narrative poem, "The Little Humpbacked Horse," a fairy tale in verse that is also popular in Russia in dramatized form.

From India there is the poetry in Gwendolyn Reed's *The Talkative Beasts: Myths, Fables and Poems of India,* and in Rabindranath Tagore's slim volume *Moon, For What Do You Wait?* In *We, the Vietnamese: Voices from Vietnam,* edited by François Sully, there is a representative section of poetry, from a portion of "Kim Van Kieu," Vietnam's best-known epic poem, to the poetry of today's underground.

The indefatigable Richard Lewis has chosen poems and songs of primitive peoples of the world for *Out of the Earth I Sing,* most of the selections being from African and North American Indian tribes. *A Crocodile Has Me by the Leg,* compiled by Leonard Doob, has African poems that clearly stem from the oral tradition and have folk wisdom and humor.

In *If I Had a Paka: Poems in Eleven Languages,* and *The Tamarindo Puppy,* with lilting poems in English and Spanish, Charlotte Pomerantz has provided children with poems simple enough and clearly illustrated so that they are understandable even though there are non-English words and phrases.

From *If I Had a Paka: Poems in Eleven Languages* by
Charlotte Pomerantz, illustrated by Nancy Tafuri.

Poetry by Children

There have always been children who wrote
poetry, and there have been some—like Aliki
Barnstone—whose writing has been published
and extolled. Not every child is capable of
writing great poetry, and it is true that some of
the work being done with children is directed as
much toward therapeutic as esthetic goals, but
the amount of fine poetry that has been published is a testament to the emotional and
imaginative capacity of the young. The work of
one outstanding young black writer, Vanessa
Howard, has been included in several anthologies of poetry by children. The following untitled poem is an example of her depth and
vision:

> *I am frightened that*
> *the flame of hate*
> *will burn me*
> *will scorch my pride*
> *scar my heart*
> *it will burn and i*
> *cannot put it out,*
> *i cannot call the fire department*
> *and they cannot put out the flame*
>   *within my soul*

> *i am frightened that the flame*
> *of hate will burn me*
> *if it does*
> *I will die*[4]

The Voice of the Children, compiled by June
Jordan and Terri Bush, comprises some of the
best of the poetry written in a creative writing
workshop; Virginia Baron's anthology *Here I
Am!* contains poems written by young people
from diverse minority groups. "Inevitable
poets," Arnold Adoff calls the young people
whose poems poured in from all parts of the
country to be selected for *it is the poem singing
into your eyes.* Kenneth Koch's *Wishes, Lies, and
Dreams* contains both the author's description
of his work with children in a New York City
school and their poetry.

I Heard a Scream in the Streets, edited by
Nancy Larrick, is a collection of poems written
by young people in the city. Her other anthology of children's poetry, *Green Is Like a Meadow
of Grass,* shows the results of children's observation of nature, encouraged by teachers motivated in a poetry workshop.

Miriam Morton has gathered Russian children's poems in *The Moon Is Like a Silver Sickle,*
and Richard Lewis has gathered children's
poetry in a fine anthology: *Miracles,* a collection of poetry by children of the English-
speaking world. One of the most touching
collections of children's poetry is *I Never Saw
Another Butterfly,* poems written by Jewish children in a concentration camp. Many of the
poems are remarkable for their courage, vision,
and compassion.

Poetry for Now

In the increase of children's interest in reading
and writing poetry, there are several striking
trends. One is the subject matter with which
the young are concerned: They are reading and
some are writing poems about anything and
everything they see around them; and although
they are still aware of natural beauty and
intrigued by the intricacies and mystery of

[4]"I am frightened that" from *The Voice of the Children*
collected by June Jordan and Terri Bush. Copyright ©
1968, 1969, 1970 by The Voice of the Children, Inc.
Reprinted by permission of Henry Holt & Company.

themselves and other people, some of their poetry seethes with anger, sees beauty as well as despair in the urban scene, and faces with candor the afflictions of the world they inherit. In form, too, there is a new freedom: Most of the poetry they write and much of the poetry they read is free verse; some of it in shaped patterns, like that of May Swenson's "Redundant Journey," in which the print forms a sinuous pattern on the page; or it is the concrete poetry that moves from the oral tradition to appeal to the eye. Free verse, of course, is not new, but it has never been so enthusiastically employed.

Young people are reading avidly the contemporary multiethnic voices of protest. There is a marked increase in the numbers of African-American poets being heard and being represented in anthologies of modern poetry chosen especially for young readers. Contemporary poetry reflects a wide range of topics. Some of the urban poetry written for very young children is concerned with subjects and problems that were never mentioned in children's literature before, an acknowledgment of the sophistication of the young. Robert Froman plays with shapes in his intriguing book, *Street Poems,* manipulating print to accentuate the message in the words; the names of objects in a garbage heap are, for example, actually piled helter-skelter. Ian Hamilton Finlay's *Poems to Hear and See* are experiments in form by a poet who is a participant in the Concrete Poetry movement, which intends the word to stand for itself as does an ideogram.

In Nikki Giovanni's *Ego-Tripping and Other Poems for Young People,* some of the poems are tender, some angry; all are a celebration of being African American. May Swenson's poetry has enormous vitality and impact, and is filled with striking images, with patterns in print that she calls Shape Poems, and with the Riddle Poems that require the reader to make a personal contribution toward interpretation. June Jordan's *Who Look at Me* is a long poem that moves, as in a gallery, from one portrait to another of African-American people. The paintings are by distinguished artists, the poem a passionate statement about the dignity, the pain, the anger, and the pride of the African-American people:

> *Who see the block we face*
> *the thousand miles of alabaster space*
> *inscribed keep off keep out don't touch*
> *and Wait Some More for Half as Much?*[5]

Arnold Adoff, in *I Am the Darker Brother, Celebrations: A New Anthology of Black Poetry,* and *Black Out Loud* confines his selections to the work of modern African-American poets; such established writers as Langston Hughes, LeRoi Jones, Mari Evans, and Arna Bontemps are included, but there are many poems by writers less well known.

Among the best of the anthologies of modern poetry are *Lean Out of the Window* by Sara Hannum and Gwendolyn Reed; *The Music of What Happens: Poems That Tell Stories* by Paul Janeczko; *American Sports Poems* by R. R. Knudson and May Swenson; and *Reflections on a Gift of Watermelon Pickle* by Stephen Dunning, Edward Lueders, and Hugh L. Smith. Additional anthologies including other collections by these same compilers can be found in the bibliography following this chapter.

Young poetry lovers do read the poetry of the past, but for most of them the modern poets have a greater appeal, speaking as they do to the issues—and in the language—of the present. There has been no lessening of admiration for the poems of the past, but there are current poets whose names (in addition to those already mentioned in this chapter) crop up in almost every anthology index. Indeed, almost every contemporary poet is represented and has his or her faction of admirers.

One fact that emerges from a survey of poetry for children is that a poem, more than any other kind of literature, has no boundaries and that a suggestion for a reading level is only that—an indication that for many children the poem will probably be most appreciated at a certain age. For children often have a far greater comprehension in listening to a poem than in reading it for themselves, and the poem that awakens a response will produce more attention and understanding on the part of the reader or listener than the poem that can be accepted placidly.

---

[5]From *Who Look at Me* by June Jordan. Copyright © 1969 by June Jordan. Reprinted by permission of the author.

Not every poem is for every child, and some poetry needs intellectual as well as emotional participation. As Agnes Repplier said, in her introduction to a poetry anthology:

In the matter of poetry, a child's imagination outstrips his understanding; his emotions carry him far beyond the narrow reach of his intelligence. He has but one lesson to learn,—the lesson of enjoyment.[6]

The Range of Poets for Children

In contemplating the poetry that children enjoy, it is clear that the range is as varied as the children themselves. Some of the poets who are favorites did not write for children at all; some—like Theodore Roethke and Randall Jarrell—wrote occasionally for them; and others wrote only for them. Those contemporary poets who write in protest or who experiment with form are read as avidly as are the more conventional poets, past and present.

Early Writers — Lasting Influences

Many of the earliest writers of poetry for children wrote a few poems that are still read and loved, but they are revered more for the impetus they gave to writing for children than for the writing itself. Isaac Watts, a preacher who decided that "What is learnt in verse, is longer retained in the memory, and sooner recollected," put his homilies in *Divine and Moral Songs for Children* in 1715. The visionary artist and author William Blake in *Songs of Innocence* (1789) created mood and conveyed ideas through rhythmic verse that speaks to the emotions and to the imagination.

Two sisters, Ann and Jane Taylor, wrote poems as moralistic and didactic as those of Watts, but they wrote wholly for children, and among the *Original Poems for Infant Minds*

[6]From *An Anthology of Modern Verse*, ed. by A. Methuen. Methuen, 1921, p. xiii.

(1804) there were some that had suspense. They are best remembered for "Twinkle, twinkle, little star." Christina Rossetti's masterpiece is undoubtedly "Goblin Market," which appeared in 1862, a narrative poem that has suspense, vivid imagery, and colorful descriptions. Her *Sing Song* (1872) is a light-hearted nursery classic but it has more complexity than does *Mother Goose,* and it makes subtle and repeated use of vowel and consonant sounds to suggest the feeling or idea described by the words. Emily Dickinson's work has become increasingly beloved by the young. Her poems were revolutionary in their time: short, usually in four-line stanzas, sharply perceptive, often somber but at times playful or witty. (The bibliography includes several editions of her poetry that have been chosen for children.)

Lewis Carroll's poetry is much funnier in context, in *Alice's Adventures in Wonderland* (1865) and *Through the Looking-Glass* (1871), than it is when read separately, but his non-

Viewpoint

Poems signal in this way. They assume a voice that uses and goes beyond words as we define them. The sound is from the beginning, articulating the present, poised for the future. That is why hearing the poem is so important. Poetry, like music, is rooted in the oral traditions of a people. Still, most of our experience with poetry and, alas, that of most critics as well comes through seeing the poem on the page. Such an experience is limiting, just as it would be if one's knowledge of music were gained only through sight-reading, or one's conception of painting only through discussion. Hearing is so integral to poetry that it is as unlikely for one born deaf to become a poet as for one born blind to become a painter. The poem's sound must ultimately be experienced.

Ashley Bryan, "On Poetry and Black American Poets," *The Horn Book Magazine,* February 1979, p. 42.

From "Jabberwocky" in *Through the Looking Glass* by Lewis Carroll, illustrated by John Tenniel.

Edward Lear
The Book of Nonsense
Nonsense Songs and Stories
Whizz!

Edward Lear wrote some of the most famous nonsense in the English language, illustrating it with sketches so amusing that a Lear limerick without the Lear drawing is only half as funny as the two together.

The first collection of his limericks and sketches was published in 1846 as the first *Book of Nonsense.* Writing them must have been great fun for Lear. They were a rest from the painstakingly detailed scientific drawings of birds and animals that were his regular occupation; they were a safe release for his high spirits; and above all they must have been a blessed escape from the illness which pursued but never conquered him.

The second book, *Nonsense Songs and Stories,* published in 1871, includes a variety of humorous verses, among them the pseudoserious narrative poems that seem all the funnier because they are gravely told.

Lear's made-up words are one of the most obvious sources of amusement in these jingles. You find the Pobble who has no toes, the Quangle Wangle with the beaver hat, and the amorous Yonghy-Bonghy Bò. The words in Lear's five sets of alphabet rhymes are mostly of this tongue-twister variety. One begins:

> *A was once an apple-pie,*
> > *Pidy,*
> > *Widy,*
> > *Tidy,*
> > *Pidy,*
> > *Nice insidy,*
> > *Apple-Pie!*

Lear was an excellent craftsman. His meters are exact, his rhymes neat and musical, and his verse has a pleasant sound even at its wildest. Much of it is decidedly melodious. Children linger over the refrains; they also like the ridiculous and eccentric characters in these verses and are especially entertained by the mad troop that populates the limericks, six of which are used as a continuous text illustrated by Janina Domanska in *Whizz!*

sense verses can be enjoyed alone. Ebullient, daft, and rhythmic, poems like "Jabberwocky" have enchanted word-lovers for a century. Carroll's writing is discussed more fully in Chapter 8. In contrast, Kate Greenaway's verses were undistinguished, but they are simple, childlike, and mildly humorous; without the illustrations upon which her reputation rests, the poems in such books as *Under the Window* (1879) probably would not have survived.

In briefly examining the work of some of the major contributors to children's poetry, who will be discussed in chronological order by their dates of birth, it is possible to see both the diversity and the pattern—not only of what children read but—of what their society's changing ideas of a child's capabilities and preferences have been.

There was an Old Man on
  whose nose
Most birds of the
  air could repose;
But they all flew away at the closing of day,
Which relieved that Old Man and his nose.

From *The Complete Nonsense Book* by Edward Lear.

Laura E. Richards
Tirra Lirra: Rhymes Old and New

Laura E. Richards's father was Samuel Gridley Howe, who devoted himself to such diverse social causes as the Greek War for Independence, the education of the blind, and the founding of the first school for feebleminded children. Her mother, Julia Ward Howe, was the author of "The Battle Hymn of the Republic." It is not surprising that the children in this family in turn scribbled stories and poetry.

The poems of Laura Richards have a spontaneity and a freshness that are equaled only by their lyric quality. It was her husband who suggested that she send some of her verses to the new magazine for children, *St. Nicholas,* and she did. From then on, stories and poems came from her pen at an amazing rate. Between stories and biographies, the verses continued to "bubble up" with undiminished charm. But it wasn't until 1932 that a book of her verses called *Tirra Lirra: Rhymes Old and New* was published.

Laura Richards's verses abound in humorous, made-up words. Moreover, no one can play with words with more joyous confusion than she. Children from five to any age have always found much to chuckle over in "Eletelephony":

Eletelephony

Once there was an elephant,
Who tried to use the telephant—
No! no! I mean an elephone
Who tried to use the telephone—
(Dear me! I am not certain quite
That even now I've got it right.)

Howe'er it was, he got his trunk
Entangled in the telephunk;
The more he tried to get it free,
The louder buzzed the telephee—
(I fear I'd better drop the song
Of elephop and telephong!)[7]

Richards has caught in her verses some of the singing quality of words that children enjoy. This lyric quality not only gives distinction to her most extravagant nonsense but makes children more sensitive to the musical qualities of words. But this poet carries her fun beyond mere play with words. She has, in addition to the verse-maker's skill, the dramatic art of a first-rate storyteller.

Robert Louis Stevenson
A Child's Garden of Verses

The title "poet laureate of childhood" has often been bestowed upon Robert Louis Stevenson, who first captivated adult readers with his essays and fiction, then caught and held the affectionate regard of children with *A Child's Garden of Verses.* This collection appeared in 1885 as *Penny Whistles,* with sixty-three poems; a few of them are merely about children or are adult reminiscences of childhood and are to be avoided (for example, Stevenson's "Whole Duty of Children," or the rarely included "To Any Reader").

With these exceptions, no careful reading of the poems can fail to leave you impressed with the author's genuine understanding of children. The opening poem, "Bed in Summer," is every child's complaint:

[7]"Eletelephony" from *Tirra Lirra: Rhymes Old and New* by Laura E. Richards. Copyright © 1932 by Laura E. Richards, renewed 1960 by Hamilton Richards. Reprinted by permission of Little, Brown & Company.

And does it not seem hard to you,
When all the sky is clear and blue,
And I should like so much to play,
To have to go to bed by day?

His children get up shivering with cold on winter mornings; they yearn to travel; they discover the sea miraculously filling up their sand holes on the beach; they struggle with table manners; they wonder why they can't see the wind; and they enjoy a world of play and imagination as well. Here are real children, many-sided and with many interests. Especially true to child life are the poems involving dramatic play. In "A Good Play," the children explain:

We built a ship upon the stairs
All made of the back-bedroom chairs.

The poems bristle with the properties and imaginative transformations of that arch magician, the child of about four to seven years old.

Perhaps the largest group of poems under a single general classification is made up of those concerned with night. "Shadow March" is in perfect marching time, but it is an eerie, frightening march of bogies and shadows, not to be used before the children are old enough to stand it. Less scary and still finer is that pounding gallop called:

Windy Nights

Whenever the moon and stars are set,
Whenever the wind is high,
All night long in the dark and wet,
A man goes riding by.
Late in the night when the fires are out,
Why does he gallop and gallop about?

Whenever the trees are crying aloud,
And ships are tossed at sea,
By, on the highway, low and loud,
By at the gallop goes he,
By at the gallop he goes, and then
By he comes back at the gallop again.

Although teachers and parents who were raised on *A Child's Garden of Verses* may feel that the verses are overfamiliar, they must not forget that these poems are new to each generation of children. New poets of childhood may make their contributions, but Robert Louis Stevenson has left to young children a legacy of small lyrics.

MARCHING SONG

Bring the comb and play upon it!
  Marching, here we come!
Willie cocks his highland bonnet,
  Johnnie beats the drum.

Mary Jane commands the party,
  Peter leads the rear;
Feet in time, alert and hearty,
  Each a Grenadier!

All in the most martial manner
  Marching double-quick;
While the napkin like a banner
  Waves upon the stick!

Here's enough of fame and pillage,
  Great commander Jane!
Now that we've been round the village,
  Let's go home again.

From *A Child's Garden of Verses* by Robert Louis Stevenson, illustrated by Tasha Tudor.

Walter de la Mare
Rhymes and Verses
Peacock Pie

Adults and children of the English-speaking world lost a great lyric poet when Walter de la Mare died in 1956. For eighteen years he wrote stories and poems and published them under the pseudonym of Walter Ramal. The treasured *Songs of Childhood* was published in 1902 when he was working as a statistician.

All of his poems for young people are now collected in *Rhymes and Verses*. (There is also *Come Hither*, de la Mare's own selection of poems for children.) *The Voice* is a sequence of thirteen poems, and *Peacock Pie* has been reis-

From *The Voice*, poems by Walter de la Mare, selected and illustrated by Catherine Brighton.

sued. Many of his poems are difficult; nevertheless his work contains some poetry that should not be missed. Choose your favorite poems; try them with children; then try certain others that are beautiful but that are not so sure to be enjoyed at first hearing. Be adventurous and try a wide selection for the sake of that occasional child who may suddenly be carried away by the magic of poetry.

One characteristic of Walter de la Mare's poems is the use of the unanswered question which leaves the reader wondering. Many of his poems have this enigmatic quality. Of course, too much ambiguity may be discouraging to those children who are literal creatures and like things straight and plain. A little, however, stimulates children's imagination and provokes not only a healthy speculation but the ability to transcend the factual and go over into the world of dreams.

De la Mare could be direct and clear when he wished to, and his children are real flesh-and-blood children. The account of "Poor Henry" swallowing physic is as homely a bit of family life as you can find anywhere. Small children enjoy the matter-of-fact subject matter and the straight-forward treatment of such poems as "Chicken," and "The Barber's." Even these poems for the youngest children, however, are illumined with little touches that invariably lift them above the world of the commonplace.

Forrest Reid characterizes Walter de la Mare's poetry by saying that it is chiefly "poetry of imagination and *vision* with its hints of loveliness belonging to a world perhaps remembered, perhaps only dreamed, but which at least is not *this* world."[8] That de la Mare's work for children has the same beauty found in his books for adults is not surprising when he himself said in his introduction to *Bells and Grass*, "I know well that only the rarest kind of best in anything can be good enough for the young."

Robert Frost
You Come Too, Favorite Poems for Young Readers

Robert Frost was four times the recipient of the Pulitzer Prize for poetry. In 1950, the United States Senate adopted a "resolution of felicitation" on his seventy-fifth birthday, and in 1961, President-elect John F. Kennedy invited Frost to read one of his poems at the inauguration, the first time a poet had been so honored.

Which of Robert Frost's poems are simple enough for young children? Certainly, the picture book version of *Stopping by Woods on a Snowy Evening* is appropriate for them; and the poet answered this question with the title of his own selections—*You Come Too, Favorite Poems for Young Readers*. For the nines and tens and older, almost any poem in this collection will carry meaning, more meaning perhaps for the rural than for the urban child. The latter probably has never "out-walked the furthest city light," nor watched "A Hillside Thaw," nor tried "Mending Wall." But fortunately we can all learn by vicarious experiences, and in every poem, the pictures or episodes or ideas are sharply and clearly told with words that have a tonal beauty as captivating as music.

[8]*Walter de la Mare: A Critical Study*. Faber and Faber Ltd., 1929.

Frost once said, "Every poem is a new metaphor inside or it is nothing"[9]—which implies that the surface meaning of a poem is only the beginning. His poems grow in richness with thoughtful rereading. We may not wish to discuss the various levels of meaning in every poem, but it would be a pity to leave children with nothing more than the obvious scenes the verses report. "A Drumlin Woodchuck" is the amusing soliloquy of a canny old denizen of a hilltop (drumlin) telling how he has managed to evade the hunters. Here is the last verse:

It will be because, though small
As measured against the All,
I have been so instinctively thorough
About my crevice and burrow.[10]

Here is obviously more than meets the eye: rich, good-humored satire. It might be the poet speaking for himself or anyone who is trying to maintain a little privacy, to protect the right to be oneself, to live one's own life, to keep one's own secrets. Older boys and girls fighting for a place of their own can appreciate this.

Poems such as the ones in this small collection of Frost's poetry will help the children move gradually from the purely objective to deeper meanings. Slipped in among the lighter fare, these poems should be read and discussed, paralleled with personal experiences or the experiences of people we know or of people from history, and then they should be read still again for pure enjoyment and enriched meaning. Children should encounter some of Robert Frost's poems that will grow in significance as the children grow in years and experience.

Carl Sandburg
Early Moon
Wind Song

Carl Sandburg was almost forty years old before he began to be recognized as a writer. He became the author of what is certainly one of the greatest biographies of Abraham Lincoln, *The Prairie Years* and *The War Years,* and he occupies a secure position in American letters.

The publication of his *Chicago Poems* in 1915 created a sensation and brought down upon his head both praise and hostility. Critics seemed to feel either that poetry was going rapidly downhill or that here was another Walt Whitman, a prophet of a new day. His two books of poetry for children are *Early Moon* (1930) and *Wind Song* (1960), both included in *The Sandburg Treasury* along with *Rootabaga Stories, Prairie-Town Boy,* and *Abe Lincoln Grows Up.*

Sandburg's verse is free, the language sturdy and direct, the subjects often indicating his interest in all things American and his sympathy for its little people. Here is an example of his robust simplicity:

From "Stopping by Woods on a Snowy Evening" by Robert Frost in *Sing a Song of Popcorn,* illustrated by Marcia Brown.

[9]Charles R. Anderson, "Robert Frost," *Saturday Review,* February 23, 1963, p. 20.

[10]"A Drumlin Woodchuck" from *The Poetry of Robert Frost* edited by Edward Connery Lathem. Copyright © 1936 by Robert Frost. Copyright © 1964 by Lesley Frost Ballantine. Copyright © 1969 by Holt, Rinehart & Winston. Reprinted by permission of Henry Holt & Company.

Bubbles

Two bubbles found they had rainbows on their
curves.
They flickered out saying:
"It was worth being a bubble just to have held
that rainbow thirty seconds."[11]

Sandburg has given some good advice in "Primer Lesson." If you read this to children, let them talk it over:

Primer Lesson

Look out how you use proud words.
When you let proud words go, it is not easy to
call them back.
They wear long boots, hard boots; they walk off
proud; they can't hear you calling—
Look out how you use proud words.[12]

Eleanor Farjeon
Kings and Queens
Poems for Children
The Children's Bells

When Eleanor Farjeon began to write, she always took her manuscripts to her father's study, pushed them under the door, and then ran away. "I had a stomach-ache till he came and told me if he liked it," she wrote. "He never kept me waiting. Even if he was writing his own stories, he stopped at once to look at my last poem, and came straight to the Nursery to talk it over with me."

Her first book was the amusing *Nursery Rhymes of London Town,* for which she wrote her own music. This was followed by the lively historical nonsense, *Kings and Queens,* and from then on she wrote prolifically, both prose and poetry.

Kings and Queens, written with her brother Herbert, was republished in 1953 and will delight children wrestling with the solemnity of

English history. For instance, "Henry VIII" opens with:

Bluff King Hal was full of beans;
He married half a dozen queens;
For three called Kate they cried the banns,
And one called Jane, and a couple of Annes.[13]

And it continues with blithe irreverence to account for the six ladies and their much-marrying spouse.

At their best, Eleanor Farjeon's poems for children, whether nonsense or serious lyrics, are skillfully written. Her rhythms are often as lively as a dance; her meters and rhyme schemes are varied and interesting; and her subject matter has exceptional range. She is not adroit at describing the modern child's everyday activities, but the moment she turns imaginative, something wonderful happens, as in this poem from *Poems for Children:*

The Night Will Never Stay

The night will never stay,
The night will still go by,
Though with a million stars
You pin it to the sky.
Though you bind it with the blowing wind
And buckle it with the moon,
The night will slip away
Like sorrow or a tune.[14]

This curious and lovely poem might well give children their first sense of time, rushing irresistibly along in a pattern of starry nights that will not stand still. In *The Children's Bells,* her "What Is Time?" supplements this poem in a lighter mood. Children like the sound of her companion poems, "Boys' Names" and "Girls' Names," and the surprise endings amuse them.

Eleanor Farjeon was the first writer for children to receive the Hans Christian Andersen Award when it was established in 1956, and

[11]"Bubbles" from *Wind Song.* Copyright © 1960 by Carl Sandburg and renewed 1988 by Margaret Sandburg. Reprinted by permission of Harcourt Brace Jovanovich.

[12]"Primer Lesson" from *Slabs of the Sunburnt West.* Copyright © 1922 by Harcourt Brace Jovanovich, and renewed 1950 by Carl Sandburg. Reprinted by permission of the publisher.

[13]"Henry VIII" from *Kings and Queens* by Eleanor Farjeon. Copyright © 1933, 1961 by Eleanor Farjeon. Reprinted by permission of Harold Ober Associates Incorporated.

[14]"The Night Will Never Stay" from *Poems for Children* by Eleanor Farjeon (J. B. Lippincott). Copyright 1951 by Eleanor Farjeon. Reprinted by permission of HarperCollins Publishers.

each year in her memory the Children's Book Circle in England presents the Eleanor Farjeon Award for "distinguished services to children's books."

A. A. Milne
When We Were Very Young
Now We Are Six

At the time A. A. Milne was writing plays and other adult literature, he gave his wife a verse about their son Christopher Robin—"Vespers"—which she sent off to a magazine and which was accepted for publication. Then Rose Fyleman, who was publishing a magazine for children, asked Milne to contribute some children's verses. At first he refused but then changed his mind and sent the poems. When both the editor and the illustrator advised him to write a whole book of verses, he felt it was a foolish thing to do, but again he complied. The result was *When We Were Very Young*, published in 1924 and a major sensation in children's books both in England and America. It shares with the second book, *Now We Are Six*, an undiminishing popularity year after year. Milne's plays are amusing, but it is probable that his reputation as a writer will rest more securely upon his two books of verse for children and his two books of stories about Pooh than upon any of his adult stories and dramas.

The egocentricity of the young child's thought and language has never been recorded more accurately than it was by A. A. Milne. Christopher Robin goes to the market looking for a rabbit and is naively astonished that the market men should be selling mackerel and fresh lavender when *he*, Christopher Robin, wants rabbits. He catalogs his articles of clothing, fascinating because they are his. You can hear the smug emphasis on the personal pronoun. Changing the guard at Buckingham Palace may be very impressive, but the child's only concern is, "Do you think the King knows all about Me?" This is a typical four-year-old, thinking and speaking of everything in terms of himself.

We can analyze Milne's tripping trochees, his iambs and dactyls, but these academic labels do not seem to convey any idea of the fluid and flashing use he made of words, rhyme, and rhythm to convey character, mood, and action. When Christopher Robin hops through the jingle called "Hoppity," the lines go in exactly the pattern of a child's hop, ending with a big one and a rest, just as hopping always does. But best of all is that juvenile meditation "Halfway Down." Ernest Shepard's sketch, too, has caught the mood of suspended action that is always overtaking small children on stairs. (See the discussion of Shepard's work in Chapter 5.) Why they like to clutter up stairs with their belongings and their persons Milne has told us with arresting monosyllables that block the way as effectually as Christopher Robin's small person blocks the stairs. In the first stanza from "Halfway Down" notice "It" which sits as firmly in the middle of the verse as Christopher on the stair:

> Halfway down the stairs
> Is a stair
> Where I sit.
> There isn't any
> Other stair
> Quite like
> It.[15]

Over and over again, Milne makes a monosyllable or a single word equal three or four words in a preceding line by sheer intensity. It is a device that compels correct reading of the lines, regardless of scansion.

With all of these virtues, it is not surprising that some moderns have come to feel that Milne was the greatest poet for children, certainly their favorite poet. However, delightful as Milne's verses are, they do not cover the full range either of children's interests or of their capacity for enjoying poetry. Many poets achieve greater lyric beauty, more delicate imagery, and deeper feeling for the child's inner world, but certainly we shall never encounter a writer who understood more completely the curious composite of gravity and gaiety, of supreme egotism and occasional whimsy that is the young child.

[15]"Halfway Down" from *When We Were Very Young* by A.A. Milne. Copyright © 1924 by E.P. Dutton, renewed 1952 by A.A. Milne. Reprinted by permission of the publisher, Dutton Children's Books, a division of Penguin Books USA.

Elizabeth Coatsworth
Summer Green
Poems
The Sparrow Bush
Down Half the World

Elizabeth Coatsworth's *The Cat Who Went to Heaven* won the Newbery Medal for 1930 but is not as popular with children as her historical tales such as *Away Goes Sally* and *The Fair American.* Within the pages of these books are some of her best poems, and her poetry is collected in *Summer Green, Poems, The Sparrow Bush,* and *Down Half the World.*

A certain style in her poetry is well illustrated by the frequently quoted "Swift things are beautiful," from *Away Goes Sally:*

> *Swift things are beautiful:*
> *Swallows and deer,*
> *And lightning that falls*
> *Bright-veined and clear,*
> *River and meteors,*
> *Wind in the wheat,*
> *The strong-withered horse,*
> *The runner's sure feet.*
> *And slow things are beautiful:*
> *The closing of day,*
> *The pause of the wave*
> *That curves downward to spray,*
> *The ember that crumbles,*
> *The opening flower*
> *And the ox that moves on*
> *In the quiet of power.*[16]

Here are the comparisons that the author uses not incidentally but as the theme of the entire poem. You can find other examples of contrasts in all three books. Building a poem around a series of comparisons seems to be a favorite pattern for Elizabeth Coatsworth. It is an exceedingly provocative one for children to study and to try for themselves in their own writing.

Another aspect of her style is the smooth, flowing lines that fall so gently on the ear. Poem after poem has this quietness. The lyric text of *Under the Green Willow,* a picture book, has a subdued, rhythmic quality. Although the lines can frolic now and then, slow-moving calmness predominates. For this reason, it is best to read only one or two of her poems at a time.

Her nature poems seem to fall into two classes. Some are straight nature descriptions, and others are brief, lovely descriptions that lead toward, or climax in, a human mood or situation. These poems linking together nature and human concerns are notable but they may prove a bit subtle for children and may require discussion before the literal-minded children catch their implications. But the nature descriptions are understandable to all children.

The poetry of Elizabeth Coatsworth is more ideational than most juvenile verse. It belongs chiefly to older children and will stretch their minds and imaginations.

Rachel Field
Taxis and Toadstools
Poems

Rachel Field's first book of poems for children, *The Pointed People,* attracted favorable attention even though it appeared at the same time that A. A. Milne's *When We Were Very Young* was creating a sensation. Two years later Field's second book of poems, *Taxis and Toadstools,* was published.

From 1924 to 1942, in a period of only eighteen years, she published some thirty-six books, many of which she herself illustrated. Among her best-known books for children are *Calico Bush,* a historical novel; and the 1930 Newbery Medal book, *Hitty,* which is the story of a hundred-year-old doll.

Over and over, Rachel Field catches the curious wonderment of children. She shows a child turning back to look at the china dog with the "sad unblinking eye" and wishing for magic words to bring him to life; or wondering if skyscrapers ever want to lie down and never get up! These are authentic child-thoughts, and children respond to their integrity with spontaneous pleasure.

Field's unique contribution to children's verse is perhaps the three groups of city poems in her *Taxis and Toadstools* called "People," "Taxis and Thoroughfares," and "Stores and

---

[16]"Swift Things Are Beautiful" from *Away Goes Sally* by Elizabeth Coatsworth. Copyright © 1934 by Macmillan Publishing Company, renewed 1962 by Elizabeth Coatsworth Beston. Reprinted with permission of Macmillan Publishing Company.

Storekeepers,'' yet her evocation of the countryside is vivid in "Something Told the Wild Geese" from *Branches Green.*

Something Told the Wild Geese

Something told the wild geese
It was time to go.
Though the fields lay golden
Something whispered, "Snow."
Leaves were green and stirring,
Berries, luster-glossed,
But beneath warm feathers
Something cautioned, "Frost."
All the sagging orchards
Steamed with amber spice,
But each wild breast stiffened
At remembered ice.
Something told the wild geese
It was time to fly—
Summer sun was on their wings,
Winter in their cry.[17]

In the collection of her verses called *Poems*, children like "Good Green Bus," "At the Theater," "The Florist Shop," "The Animal Store," and the favorite "Skyscrapers." Rachel Field's poetry never attains the power and sureness of her best prose, but the complete absence of artificiality of juvenile cuteness in these poems commends them to both children and adults.

David McCord
Far and Few
Every Time I Climb a Tree
Take Sky
Away and Ago

Speaking at a conference on children's literature, David McCord gave as one of his rules for writing for children:

First, just be a child before you grow up and let nothing interfere with the process. Write it all out of yourself and for yourself. . . . Next, never take the phrase "writing verse for children" seriously.

If you write for them you are lost. Ask your brain's computer what you know about a child's mind. The answer is zero.[18]

In *Far and Few*, his first book for children, small beasts are presented—bats, grasshoppers, a snail, starfish, and an especially convincing crowd of crows "spilling from a tree." For sheer nonsense, "Five Chants," "Who Wants a Birthday?" and "Isabel Jones & Curabel Lee" are fun. It takes a perceptive older child to appreciate "The White Ships" and "The Star in the Pail." Children under six like the onomatopoeic refrains of "Song of the Train" and "The Pickety Fence" from *Every Time I Climb a Tree:*

[18]From David McCord's "Poetry for Children," in *A Critical Approach to Children's Literature* ed. by Sara Innis Fenwick. University of Chicago Press, 1967, p. 53.

From "Isabel Jones and Curabel Lee" in *Every Time I Climb a Tree* by David McCord, illustrated by Marc Simont.

[17]"Something Told the Wild Geese" from *Branches Green* by Rachel Field. Copyright © 1934 by Macmillan Publishing Company, renewed 1962 by Arthur S. Pederson. Reprinted with permission of Macmillan Publishing Company.

The Pickety Fence

The pickety fence
The pickety fence
Give it a lick it's
The pickety fence
A clickety fence
Give it a lick it's
A lickety fence
Give it a lick
Give it a lick
Give it a lick
With a rickety stick
Pickety
Pickety
Pickety
Pick[19]

Take Sky, McCord's second book of verse for children, is on the whole more completely humorous than *Far and Few.* His "Write Me a Verse" should appeal to youngsters wrestling with verse forms. In these poems couplets, quatrains, limericks, and triolets are amusingly defined and illustrated. However, there is also much entertainment in this book for the youngest children. In "Sing Song," "Three Signs of Spring," "Sally Lun Lundy," and many other verses, McCord has a wonderful time playing with the sounds of words. He also makes many clever uses of dialogue. The poems in *Away and Ago* are also light and sunny; in this collection he writes about parties, balloons, baseball, and holidays, and in "Like You As It" he plays with words. In 1978, his poems for children were published in a collection entitled *One at a Time.* The poet savors language, but he holds it—like the master craftsman he is—firmly in check.

Harry Behn
Cricket Songs
The Golden Hive
The Wizard in the Well

Harry Behn has written both prose and poetry for children, and has translated Japanese haiku with precise and delicate sensitivity in *Cricket Songs* and *More Cricket Songs,* both of which are illustrated by reproductions of paintings by Japanese artists.

In his book on poetry, *Chrysalis,* Behn pointed out that children see a world in every least little thing, and his poems explored with an ever-fresh awareness children's delight in little things about them. *The Golden Hive* is for older readers and includes some fine lyric poems, of which "The Painted Desert" and "Summer" are particularly evocative. His other small books of verse, decorated by the author, speak to young children, five to nine, with lyric charm and unusual variety. There are a few nonsense jingles like "Dr. Windikin," "Shopping Spree," and the lively "Tea Party."

There are many verses about the child's play world, both real and imaginative. "The New Little Boy" is refreshingly antisocial. "Picnic by the Sea" is a child's view of the queer grownups who sit sunning themselves when there are so many wonders to be explored. "Hallowe'en" is a particularly shivery celebration of that favorite holiday and is delightful for verse choirs to speak for their own pleasure or for an appreciative audience.

Behn's unique contribution is found in those poems where he is helping the child to look at everyday experiences with the eyes of the spirit. Notice the philosophy in "Others" from *The Wizard in the Well:*

Others

Even though it's raining
I don't wish it wouldn't.
That would be like saying
I think it shouldn't.
I'd rather be out playing
Than sitting hours and hours
Watching rain falling
In drips and drops and showers,
But what about the robins?
What about the flowers?[20]

[19]"The Pickety Fence" from *One at a Time* by David McCord. Copyright © 1974 by David McCord. Reprinted by permission of Little, Brown & Company.

[20]"Others" from *The Wizard in the Well; Poems and Pictures by Harry Behn.* Copyright © 1956 by Harry Behn. Copyright renewed 1984 by Alice Behn Goebel, Pamela Behn Adam, Peter Behn and Prescott Behn. Reprinted by permission of Marian Reiner.

Stephen Vincent Benét
Rosemary Carr Benét
John Brown's Body
A Book of Americans

Stephen Vincent Benét, a member of a famous family of writers, published his first book of verse while he was a student at Yale University. Twice winner of the Pulitzer Prize for poetry, Benét is probably best known for his epic poem about the Civil War, *John Brown's Body*. With his wife, Rosemary, he wrote *A Book of Americans*, in which popular figures in American history are described in moods ranging from the nonsensical to the deeply serious. "Pilgrims and Puritans," a humorous presentation of the two sides of these colonists, reads in part:

Pilgrims and Puritans

The Pilgrims and the Puritans
Were English to the bone
But didn't like the English Church
And wished to have their own
And so, at last, they sailed away
To settle Massachusetts Bay.

The stony fields, the cruel sea
They met with resolution
And so developed, finally,
An iron constitution
And, as a punishment for sinners,
Invented boiled New England dinners.[21]

Children like "Captain Kidd," "Peregrine White and Virginia Dare," and the larruping "Theodore Roosevelt." These are genuinely funny verses. The poem about the Wright brothers is particularly appreciated by nine- and ten-year-olds for its humorous account of a momentous event in human history.

This is not great poetry, but it gives the reader a series of vivid portraits of some great Americans, written with vigor and simplicity. It can be a delightful addition to the study of the lives of these Americans or of periods in American history.

[21]"Pilgrims and Puritans" by Stephen Vincent Benét from *A Book of Americans* by Rosemary and Stephen Vincent Benét. Copyright © 1933 by Rosemary and Stephen Vincent Benét. Copyright renewed 1961 by Rosemary Carr Benét. Reprinted by permission of Brandt & Brandt Literary Agents.

Langston Hughes
Selected Poems of Langston Hughes
Fields of Wonder

Langston Hughes began writing verse while he was in high school and later joined the New York group of black writers of the Harlem Renaissance movement. Much of his poetry is in a spirit of racial pride and protest, as in the following selection from *Selected Poems of Langston Hughes*:

I, Too, Sing America

I am the darker brother.
They send me to eat in the kitchen
When company comes,
But I laugh,
And eat well,
And grow strong.

From *Don't You Turn Back* by Langston Hughes, illustrated by Ann Grifaleoni.

Tomorrow,
I'll be at the table
When company comes.
Nobody'll dare
Say to me,
"Eat in the kitchen,"
Then.

Besides,
They'll see how beautiful I am
And be ashamed—

I, too, am America.[22]

Although many of his poems speak for and about black people, Hughes also wrote poetry that speaks for all humankind in *Fields of Wonder:*

Silence

I catch the pattern
Of your silence
Before you speak.

I do not need
To hear a word.

In your silence
Every tone I seek
Is heard.[23]

These are both serious poems, but there is an ironic humor in much of Hughes's writing, both poetry and prose. Although he wrote several books for children (on jazz, on Africa, on black heroes), his poetry was not created for them. They have, however, overruled him and claimed his poetry for their own. Children enjoy its candor, its humor, and the melodic style that is often reminiscent of ballads and the blues.

David Littlejohn says of Langston Hughes:

By moulding his verse always on the sounds of Negro talk, the rhythms of Negro music, by retaining his own keen honesty and directness, his poetic sense and ironic intelligence, he has maintained through four decades a readable newness distinctly his own.[24]

Aileen Fisher
Going Barefoot
Out in the Dark and the Daylight
Feathered Ones and Furry

Aileen Fisher sold her first verses to *Child Life Magazine* while working in Chicago. Yearning to return to the outdoors, she decided to buy a one-way ticket to Colorado, and there she has stayed, writing poetry about the wild creatures she loves. She has also written some excellent biographies and several collections of plays, and has published many books of poetry. Her topics cover the seasons, children's pets, and nature as the child encounters it.

With *Going Barefoot* Fisher attained a new freedom of verse patterns; a lighter, gayer touch; and a melodic line that makes this book a delight to read aloud either at one sitting or in parts day by day. It begins with the boy's question:

How soon
how soon
is a morning in June,
a sunny morning or afternoon
in the wonderful month
of the Barefoot Moon?

Then the young philosopher observes that rabbits go barefoot all year round, so do raccoons, bees, cats, deer, and other creatures, while he must suffer the handicap of socks, shoes, and even galoshes. At last comes the day when he and his mother consult the calendar and the narrative reaches a triumphant conclusion:

June!

The day is warm
and a breeze is blowing,
the sky is blue
and its eye is glowing,
and everything's new
and green and growing . . .
My shoes are off
and my socks are showing . . .

[22]"I, Too" from *Selected Poems of Langston Hughes.* Copyright © 1926 by Alfred A. Knopf, and renewed 1954 by Langston Hughes. Reprinted by permission of Alfred A. Knopf.

[23]"Silence" from *Fields of Wonder* by Langston Hughes. Copyright © 1947 by Langston Hughes. Reprinted by permission of Alfred A. Knopf.

[24]David Littlejohn, *Black on White; A Critical Survey of Writing by American Negroes.* Viking, 1969 (originally published in 1966 by Grossman).

My socks are off . . .

Do you know how I'm going?
    BAREFOOT![25]

This is free and melodic and as full of movement as the restless child waiting for the big day of emancipation from shoes. The poetry about the rabbits, the kangaroos, and other creatures may be read and enjoyed separately or enjoyed as part of the whole. Adrienne Adams's illustrations in full color, with authentic paw prints adorning the end pages, add enchantment to this delightful book.

Out in the Dark and the Daylight is a more varied collection than most of Fisher's books, permeated by imagery and insight. The autumnal *Where Does Everyone Go?* is not quite so exhilarating but exceedingly pleasant to hear and look at. *Up, Up the Mountain* and *In the Middle of the Night* are lyric comments on the beauties of nature; *Feathered Ones and Furry* and *But Ostriches . . .* communicate with humor an affection for animals and an appreciation of the beauty of nature.

Theodore Roethke
I Am! Says the Lamb
Dirty Dinky and Other Creatures

Theodore Roethke received many awards and honors for his poetry, including Guggenheim and Ford Foundation Fellowships, the Pulitzer Prize in 1954, and the National Book Award posthumously in 1965.

Some of his poems are included in anthologies for young people, but *I Am! Says the Lamb* and *Dirty Dinky and Other Creatures* are the only collections that can be enjoyed as a whole by children. The rhythm and the sharp imagery appeal to children, who enjoy the poet's wit and his occasional pithy bluntness. Roethke wrote with an ebullience and humor that are especially appealing in such nonsense poems as "The Kitty-Cat Bird." That some of his other poems can be enjoyed by children is obvious on reading "The Bat":

The Bat

By day the bat is cousin to the mouse.
He likes the attic of an aging house.

His fingers make a hat about his head.
His pulse beat is so slow we think him dead.

He loops in crazy figures half the night
Among the trees that face the corner light.

But when he brushes up against a screen
We are afraid of what our eyes have seen:

For something is amiss or out of place
When mice with wings can wear a human face.[26]

It is interesting to compare this poem with "Man and Bat" by D. H. Lawrence and with the poem that begins, "A bat is born . . ." in Randall Jarrell's *The Bat-Poet.*

Lilian Moore
Something New Begins
See My Lovely Poison Ivy

Lilian Moore decided, in her capacity as an editor, that writers often use too many words. This knowledge and her years of experience as a specialist in reading problems have influenced her poetry, which is simple and direct, yet fluent and witty in a way that younger children can comprehend and appreciate.

Moore has written several stories for children and compiled some poetry anthologies, but it is her own poetry that makes a unique contribution. Children respond to the cameo-clear small lyrics of the natural world in *Something New Begins;* and to the humor and incongruity of the lighthearted poems in *See My Lovely Poison Ivy,* especially those in which there is a surprising turn, as there is in the following poem:

Bedtime Stories

"Tell me a story,"
Says Witch's Child.

"About the Beast
So fierce and wild.

[25]"How Soon" and "June" from *Going Barefoot* by Aileen Fisher (Thomas Y. Crowell). Copyright © 1960 by Aileen Fisher. Reprinted by permission of HarperCollins Publishers.

[26]"The Bat" from *The Collected Poems of Theodore Roethke.* Copyright © 1938 by Theodore Roethke. Used by permission of Doubleday, a division of Bantam, Doubleday, Dell Publishing Group.

*"About a Ghost
That shrieks and groans.*

*"A Skeleton
That rattles bones.*

*"About a Monster
Crawly-creepy.*

*"Something nice
To make me sleepy."*[27]

John Ciardi
*The Man Who Sang the Sillies
You Read to Me, I'll Read to You
The King Who Saved Himself from
Being Saved*

John Ciardi was, for a number of years, active as a teacher, lecturer, critic, and writer. Much of his poetry for both adults and children has a brisk candor. In his poetry for children, though, the humor and nonsense soften a forthrightness that is sometimes tart. Many of his poems are satirical comments on the reprehensible behavior of children, a vein most appreciated by the sophisticated reader. However, the topics he develops are usually fresh and original, as, for example, "How to Tell the Top of a Hill." And when he chooses a familiar subject like "Halloween," he treats it freshly, so that it is unlike any other Halloween poem ever written—dramatic and weird, and a brain-tickler for the oldest and best readers.

The omission of words in "Summer Song," from *The Man Who Sang the Sillies*, makes a good language game:

Summer Song

*By the sand between my toes,
By the waves behind my ears,
By the sunburn on my nose,
By the little salty tears
That make rainbows in the sun
When I squeeze my eyes and run,
By the way the seagulls screech,
Guess where I am? At the . . . . !*

*By the way the children shout
Guess what happened? School is . . . !
By the way I sing this song
Guess if summer lasts too long?
You must answer Right or . . . . !*[28]

One of Ciardi's interesting experiments in verse for children is *I Met a Man* written with a controlled vocabulary of some four hundred words. It was planned as a first book for his own child to read and it moves from easy to more difficult in both words and content. "Poetry," the author says, "is especially well designed to

[28]"Summer Song" from *The Man Who Sang the Sillies* by John Ciardi (J. B. Lippincott). Copyright © 1961 by John Ciardi. Reprinted by permission of HarperCollins Publishers.

From *You Read to Me, I'll Read to You* by John Ciardi, illustrated by Edward Gorey.

[27]"Bedtime Stories" from *See My Lovely Poison Ivy* by Lilian Moore. Copyright © 1975 by Lilian Moore. Reprinted by permission of Marian Reiner for the author.

From *The Covered Bridge House and Other Poems* by Kaye Starbird, illustrated by Jim Arnosky.

lead the child to such recognition [of new words] for rhyme and pattern are always important clues."

Ciardi continues his experiment with a limited vocabulary in *You Read to Me, I'll Read to You* in which he alternates a poem the child is supposed to read with one for the adult to read, unrestricted by word lists. These, too, are clever verses. In *The King Who Saved Himself from Being Saved,* Ciardi tells an amusing and pointed story that spoofs the stereotypical hero who insists on improving a situation with which everyone else concerned is perfectly content. This narrative poem is illustrated by Edward Gorey, whose elegant grotesquerie is admirably suited to Ciardi's wit.

Kaye Starbird
A Snail's a Failure Socially
The Pheasant on Route Seven

Kaye Starbird wrote verses as a child and she had poems published in magazines while she was still in college. She has written both satirical verse and serious poetry for adults. In her writing for children she uses a conversational tone and sees everyday experiences from the child's point of view, as in *The Covered Bridge House and Other Poems.*

Her poems present a child voicing his or her honest opinions or questions about the bugs, beasts, people, and ideas he or she encounters. The poems about the kitten in the mailbox, the toad that needed a baby-sitter, the naughty imaginary sprite who takes over the body of a child who is misbehaving—these and many others are inventive and skillfully composed.

With each book, Kaye Starbird has grown as a poet: Her verse patterns are more deft, her moods more varied. Compare, for example, the humor of the first of the following poems, from the book by the same name, with the nostalgic thoughtfulness with which the second, "One Leaf," from *The Pheasant on Route Seven,* begins:

A Snail's a Failure Socially

A snail's a failure socially,
Which means you very seldom see
A crowd of happy, laughing snails
Collected all at once.
The reason's this: when asked to dine
A snail could answer "Yes" or "Fine,"
But if he lived a field away
The trip would take him months.

In short, the most excited snail,
Though pleased to hit the party trail,
Could promptly tidy up and take
A shortcut through the clover;
But asked to Easter luncheon—say—
And getting there Columbus Day,
There'd be at least an even chance
He'd find the party over.[29]

[29]"A Snail's a Failure Socially" from *A Snail's a Failure Socially* by Kaye Starbird. Copyright © 1966 by Kaye Starbird. Reprinted by permission of Ray Lincoln Literary Agency.

One Leaf

At least a month away from the autumn season
I saw a leaf from the maple break and fall,
Fluttering down for no apparent reason
One windless day when nothing else moved at
all.[30]

Eve Merriam
Finding a Poem
It Doesn't Always Have to Rhyme
A Poem for a Pickle

Eve Merriam is a teacher of creative writing as well as a writer of prose and poetry for adults and for children. Her first book of poetry for adults, *Family Circle,* won the Yale Series of Younger Poets prize.

Merriam's verse is varied in form, inventive, and often humorous. It usually speaks directly to the child's experience and is especially ap-pealing to the reader who enjoys word-play. Her essay on "Writing a Poem," in *Finding a Poem* describes the poet's search for the exact word or phrase to express and illuminate her meaning. Both this essay and the chapter entitled "'I,' Says the Poem" in Nancy Larrick's *Somebody Turned on a Tap in These Kids* are good reading for anyone working with children.

"Ping-pong" is a good example of the way she uses words like "chitchat" and "rickrack" for aural effect; bouncy and rhythmic, the poem evokes the patterned clicking of the game's sound. The same lilting appeal is in the blithe collection for young children, *Blackberry Ink.* In *It Doesn't Always Have to Rhyme,* Merriam—like David McCord—uses poems as illustrations of such literary devices as cliche, homonym, limerick, onomatopoeia, simile, and metaphor. In *A Poem for a Pickle,* a collection of humorous verses, the new words for a familiar tune amuse readers in "A New Song for Old Smoky."

A New Song for Old Smoky

On top of the teevee
all covered with rust,
I found a weird item
a-turning to dust.

I asked the computer
to please take a look
at whatever the thing was
and the printout read B*O*O*K.[31]

Gwendolyn Brooks
Bronzeville Boys and Girls

Gwendolyn Brooks's first poem was published when she was thirteen; in 1949 she won the annual prize given by *Poetry* magazine, and in 1950 she received the Pulitzer Prize for Poetry, never before awarded to an African American.

In all her poetry there is a concern for racial and personal identity. Dan Jaffe says:

From *Blackberry Ink* by Eve Merriam, illustrated by Hans Wilhelm.

[30]"One Leaf" from *The Pheasant on Route Seven* by Kaye Starbird. Copyright © 1968 by Kaye Starbird. Reprinted by permission of the author.

[31]"A New Song for Old Smoky" from *A Poem for A Pickle* by Eve Merriam. Copyright © 1989 by Eve Merriam. Reprinted by permission of Marian Reiner for the author.

The label "Black poetry" ignores Gwen Brooks' ability to speak as a hunchbacked girl, a male preacher, a white spokesman, in varying voices all clearly her own . . . it forgets that though Gwen Brooks learns from Langston Hughes, she also learns from T. S. Eliot; and that she must be more than a replica of either or both.[32]

Her poems for and about children, *Bronzeville Boys and Girls*, speak for any child of any race. Each of the poems is named for a boy or girl. They show a rare sensitivity to the child's inner life—the wonderments, hurts, and sense of make-believe and play. Here is one:

Cynthia in the Snow

It SUSHES.
It hushes
The loudness in the road.
It flitter-twitters,
And laughs away from me.
It laughs a lovely whiteness,
And whitely whirs away,
To be
Some otherwhere,
Still white as milk or shirts.
So beautiful it hurts.[33]

Myra Cohn Livingston
Whispers and Other Poems
Up in the Air
Sky Songs

Myra Cohn Livingston, interested in writing and music throughout all her school years, finally abandoned her music study to become a writer and teacher. As a teacher of creative writing, she feels very strongly about the paramount importance of free expression. As she has said in "What the Heart Knows Today":

Happily, we are no longer concerned with those who copy patterns or fill in blanks; the beginning

acceptance of blank verse, free verse, haiku has helped somewhat to break the rhyme barrier, but we have a long way to go before we can succeed in recognizing that the tools of poetry are not poetry.[34]

Nevertheless, her own mastery of rhyme and meter makes it clear that she herself is in command of the tools of poetry. Most of her books of verse deal with the sensory experiences, activities, and imaginings of young children, as in the following piece from *Whispers and Other Poems*:

Whispers

Whispers
  tickle through your ear
  telling things you like to hear.
Whispers
  are as soft as skin
  letting little words curl in.
Whispers
  come so they can blow
  secrets others never know.[35]

Any child who has flown in an airplane can recognize what is seen in *Up in the Air*, a continuing of triplets that begins:

Good-bye to the airport! Good-bye to the ground!
My seatbelt is buckled tightly around.
The airplane is full of a roaring sound.[36]

Nature is the focus of several books of poetry and art by Myra Cohn Livingston and Leonard Everett Fisher: *Sky Songs*, *A Circle of Seasons*, and *Earth Songs*. These books are beautifully written and illustrated for reading aloud or for an individual's enjoyment of the visual effect. Livingston has also edited an anthology for children, *Listen, Children, Listen*, and an excellent anthology for adolescent poetry lovers—*A*

---

[32]"Gwendolyn Brooks: An Appreciation from the White Suburbs," by Dan Jaffe. From *The Black American Writer*, v. 2, ed. by Christopher Bigsby (Everett/Edwards, 1969).

[33]"Cynthia in the Snow" from *Bronzeville Boys and Girls* by Gwendolyn Brooks. Copyright © 1956 by Gwendolyn Brooks Blakely. Reprinted by permission of HarperCollins Publishers.

[34]"What the Heart Knows Today" by Myra Cohn Livingston. From *Somebody Turned on a Tap in These Kids*, ed. by Nancy Larrick. Delacorte, 1971, p. 11.

[35]"Whispers" from *Whispers and Other Poems* by Myra Cohn Livingston. Copyright © 1958 by Myra Cohn Livingston. Reprinted by permission of Marian Reiner for the author.

[36]Excerpt from *Up in the Air* by Myra Cohn Livingston. Copyright © 1989 by Myra Cohn Livingston. Reprinted by permission of Marian Reiner for the author.

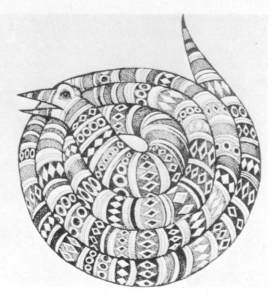

From *A Tune Beyond Us,* edited by Myra Cohn Livingston, illustrated by James J. Spanfeller.

Laughing Time has amused readers for several decades.

The first Newbery Award to a book of poetry was given in 1982 to Nancy Willard's *A Visit to William Blake's Inn: Poems for Innocent and Experienced Travelers.* The poems are inspired by images and characters from Blake's own poetry and succeed in creating a sense of recollection. Another Newbery Award was given for poetry in 1989, this to Paul Fleischman for *Joyful Noise: Poems for Two Voices;* those who enjoy choral reading should appreciate this and an earlier title, *I Am Phoenix: Poems for Two Voices.*

Most anthologies include one or more of the poems of James Tippett, E. V. Rieu, James Reeves, William Allingham, Frances Frost, Hilda Conkling, Vachel Lindsay, Sara Teasdale, and Elizabeth Madox Roberts. Elizabeth Madox Roberts's poems in *Under the Tree* and *Song in the Meadow* seem deceptively simple, but they display remarkable insight into children's feelings; they have nothing prettified or flowery but have a complete fidelity to child nature.

Tune Beyond Us—which includes many poems from other languages. In *Thanksgiving Poems* and other holiday anthologies, Livingston uses some traditional material but focuses on original selections by major contemporary children's poets. She is also the coeditor of *The Scott, Foresman Anthology of Children's Literature.*

Other Notable Poets

There are of course many other poets whose work is cherished by children, such as Dennis Lee or Karla Kushkin, whose simple verses appeal to younger children; or Arnold Adoff, who sees the humor of his own love of food in *Eats* and *Chocolate Dreams;* or Valerie Worth, in whose *Small Poems* and *More Small Poems* the free but disciplined verse has both vigor and delicacy. In *Hurry, Hurry, Mary Dear!* and other volumes, N. M. Bodecker gives children humorous verse through clear use of rhyme and, sometimes, an underlying but gentle irony. Jack Prelutsky's zany poetry derives humor from its characters, as in *The Sheriff of Rottenshot,* as well as on clever play on words. Shel Silverstein's poems in *Where the Sidewalk Ends* and *A Light in the Attic* entertain children with their emphasis on slapstick humor; and William Jay Smith's

From *Chocolate Dreams* by Arnold Adoff, illustrated by Turi MacCombie.

With the flourishing of new African-American poets, older boys and girls read with interest some of the earlier writers like Paul Laurence Dunbar and Countee Cullen. They enjoy the sharp imagery and the patterns that challenge readers in *Poems to Solve* and *More Poems to Solve*, by May Swenson. The bibliography at the end of this chapter reflects children's interest in modern poetry. It includes some excellent general anthologies and a selection of subject anthologies.

Using Poetry with Children

Know What Children Like About Poetry

To encourage the continuing enjoyment of poetry, we must know what children like about it. Research findings indicate the children in the upper elementary grades prefer everyday language to figurative language, that they dislike sentimental poetry and enjoy poems that are humorous, and that they have a strong liking for narrative poems.[37] Younger children share many of these preferences; and they enjoy limericks, rhymed verse, and story poems, particularly those that relate to childhood experiences or, on the other hand, deal with fantasy.[38]

Poetry's first and strongest appeal, however, lies in its *singing quality,* the *melody* and *movement* of the word patterns and lines. They are what make poetry an aural art like music, to be spoken and heard just as music is played and heard. Our business as adults is to savor this singing quality of verse and to learn how to maintain it in our reading. This aural quality can play a large part in hearing humorous verse read aloud, for children enjoy the sound of nonsense words, alliteration, and the repetition

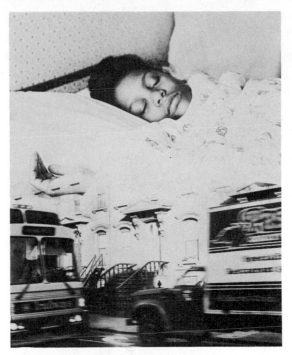

From *Song in Stone: City Poems,* selected by Lee Bennett Hopkins, photographs by Anna Held Audette.

of phrases in a refrain; they delight in identifying these elements in comic verse from Edward Lear to John Ciardi and X. J. Kennedy.

Poetry should be comprehensible to children, especially the sensory content that may be associated with their own experiences. Urban children may find it difficult to relate to images familiar to the rural child; anthologies intended particularly for these city children have made available poetry that reflects their lives: Nancy Larrick's *On City Streets,* Arnold Adoff's *City in All Directions,* and Lee Bennett Hopkins's *A Song of Stone: City Poems,* and such collections as Lilian Moore's *I Thought I Heard the City* and Ann Turner's *Street Talk.*

Provide Children with Rich Poetry Experiences

Children's encounters with poetry should include three types of response—*enjoyment, exploration,* and *deepening understanding.* These do not occur always as separate steps but simultaneously. Certainly, children must start

[37]Ann Terry, *Children's Poetry Preferences: A National Survey of Upper Elementary Grades.* National Council of Teachers of English, 1974.

[38]Carol J. Fisher and Margaret A. Natarella, "Young Children's Preferences for Poetry: A National Survey of First, Second, and Third Graders." *Research in the Teaching of English* 15 (1982): 339–354.

From *Out and About,* written and illustrated by Shirley Hughes.

with enjoyment or their interest in poetry dies. But if from the beginning they find delight in the poems they hear, they are ready and eager to explore further—more books and more poems of different sorts. Even the youngest children can learn to see implications beyond the obvious. To read for veiled meanings is to identify oneself with the poet, to ask the poet's questions. This is reading for deeper understanding, taking a thoughtful look at what lies beneath the surface. Enjoyment, exploration, and deeper understanding must all be part of children's experience with poetry if we are to help them to love it.

Read Poetry to Children

Poetry began as a spoken art; people listened to it and remembered it because rhyme and meter made it easier to recall than prose. So it should begin for children. Poetry should be heard because of its inherent lyric qualities. Adults should read or speak it aloud and encourage children to join in until, without even realizing it, they have memorized effortlessly dozens of poems which they can speak naturally and gaily.

By early adolescence most children have mastered the mechanics of reading and if their childhood experiences with poetry have been happy, they will go on reading it on their own.

Poetry should never be used as a reading exercise. When children have to struggle with a poem as a reading lesson, they are baffled and discouraged. John Erskine, writing for older students, says in *The Kinds of Poetry:* "The office of the teacher of poetry is easily defined; it is to afford a mediation between great poets and their audience." With children, effective oral reading is the surest mediation.

Nursery rhymes as traditional as *Mother Goose* or as contemporary as those in *Out and About* by Shirley Hughes are a natural starting point for very young children. They don't know that it is meter and rhyme to which they are responding when they march or sway or clap in time, but it is the poetry, the singing quality, to which they are responding.

The introduction to poetry for older children should begin as painlessly as it begins for the prereaders. That is, they should hear many poems vigorously read aloud for sheer pleasure, with no analysis during this exploratory stage. Some poetry should be slipped in and introduced with a comment like: "A new poem is like new music. Sometimes you have to hear it

From *Joyful Noise: Poems for Two Voices* by Paul Fleischman, illustrated by Eric Beddows.

several times before you know whether or not you like it.'' Read some of the poems for two voices, like those in Paul Fleischman's *I Am Phoenix* or *Joyful Noise*. Just the starting lines of ''Honeybees'' can win instant attention.

Honeybees

Being a bee *is a pain.*	Being a bee is a joy.
I'm a worker *I'll gladly explain.*	I'm a queen
I'm up at dawn, *guarding the hive's* *narrow entrance*[39]	I'll gladly explain. Upon rising, I'm fed by my royal attendants,

Explore Poetry Books with Children

In the process of enjoying poetry, children will encounter many books and different types of verse. Their explorations will include books by a single author and anthologies of poetry by many poets.

Anthologies are invaluable, and there is no reading experience more satisfying, either in a classroom, a library, or at home, than to settle down with your children to explore a new anthology. Needless to say, you will have explored it first to know its range and contents and to have chosen in advance a group of poems that you feel sure the children will understand and enjoy. Modern anthologies usually provide a high quality of poetry selections and convenient subject matter arrangements.

Here are a few criteria for selecting an anthology from among the many excellent ones available:

1. Examine the author index to discover the range and quality of writers represented. Does it lean heavily on poets of the past, Eugene Field, Riley, Stevenson, Longfellow, or are the best of these balanced by many good modern poets?

[39]Excerpt from ''Honeybees'' in *Joyful Noise: Poems for Two Voices* by Paul Fleischman. Copyright © 1988 by Paul Fleischman. Reprinted by permission of HarperCollins Publishers.

Viewpoint

I am certain we know that many of the children who come into our classrooms are not ''bathed in language'' from their earliest days; many do not even know Mother Goose, and I myself have discovered that as early as first grade I can instantly tell by a child's writing if he has been given good literature, or simply poor books which masquerade as literature at home. I know from the experience of having my poems reprinted in primers and textbooks over the years that any joy which the child might find in reading a poem which I, or any other poet, has written is quickly apt to be dispelled by questions such as: ''Why did the poet use a capital here?'' ''What word rhymes with ear?'' ''Where did the poet put a question mark and why?'' as well as asking questions about the poem which even I can't answer. Perhaps these teachers' aids and workbooks are necessary, for it is possible that I am some sort of idealist who has far more faith in teachers than many educators. I secretly hope that the teacher will simply skip the questions and allow children to just enjoy a poem. If he can only apprehend its meaning in the early grades, so much the better. There is plenty of time later to truly comprehend, for even at my age I find myself still searching to comprehend the meaning of many poems and simply wallow about delightedly in apprehension.

Myra Cohn Livingston, ''Beginnings,'' *Language Arts*, March 1978. Copyright © 1978 by the National Council of Teachers of English. Reprinted by permission of the publisher and the author.

2. How many poems does the book contain? Oddly enough, one anthology may contain over five hundred poems while another at approximately the same price includes only two to three hundred. If the quality of the two books is equally good, the first is obviously a better choice.
3. Look for indexes and classifications. The

indexes should include authors, titles, and, preferably, first lines. Teachers will find classifications by subjects equally important—such groupings as people, animals, nonsense, magic, our country, seasons, and the like. Organization by subjects is far more important than organization by grades. Indeed, grade levels for poems are impossible and undesirable, no matter how teachers yearn for them, because children's tastes and capacities vary as much as the poems themselves and depend on their varied experiences.

4. Format is important. A heavy volume may be useful in the school library as a reference book, but it will not be good for a child to use or an adult to handle with the child. Good paper, clear type, well-spaced pages, all add to the attractiveness of a book.

Some anthologies not only meet these basic criteria, but provide extra dividends in the form of attractive illustrations, brief introductions to or explanations of poems, and suggestions for reading aloud and choral speaking.

Teach children how to explore and use an anthology. A forthcoming holiday, for example, means a search for the best Halloween or Christmas poems. Undoubtedly the greatest value of a fine anthology is the feeling it gives children for the range and variety of poetry. They will look, browse further, and make discoveries.

In the same way, children should become acquainted with the books of single poets, not merely Stevenson's *A Child's Garden of Verses,* but David McCord's *Far and Few,* Marilyn Singer's *Turtle in July,* June Jordan's *Who Look at Me,* and others. This exploration of the works of individual poets guarantees that the child will encounter a range of poetry from the imaginative and subtle lyrics of Walter de la Mare to the robust nonsense of Dennis Lee. Such exploration will also help a discussion of reading poetry aloud. Speaking or reading poetry to children should continue all through their childhood.

Deepen Children's Understanding of Poems

A third phase of poetry experience involves a more intellectual response than either enjoyment or exploration. It is what John Ciardi has called "reading in depth" or reading for a more complete understanding of the poet's meaning. With the youngest children this begins with talking about word meanings and background

From *Turtle in July* by Marilyn Singer, illustrated by Jerry Pinkney.

experiences and with older children it progresses to a fuller consciousness of implications, double meanings, possible symbols, and even to some analysis of form.

To help younger children understand the meaning of a poem, we often need to evoke or supplement their background of experience. If they aren't familiar with the weasel, show them pictures before introducing Jeanne Steig's weasel poem in *Consider the Lemming,* or talk about the industrious beaver before reading in Marilyn Singer's *Turtle in July,* the poem in which a beaver speaks.

Sometimes the musical pattern of a poem affects its meaning in ways even very young children can sense. Five-year-olds know that the words in Stevenson's "The Swing" really swing and that the words of Milne's "Hoppity" do hop with Christopher Robin to the very last line which hops to a standstill. Hearing poetry read with an emphasis on its musical patterns, young children can be trained to the point where they are aware, consciously or unconsciously, of what the patterns are making them feel or understand.

Or take Elizabeth Coatsworth's beautiful study in contrasts—"Swift things are beautiful." Help the children to hear how the words and lines of the first stanza hurry along, with no long, sonorous vowels or words to delay the crisp, brisk movement. But in the second verse, the long vowels in such mouth-filling phrases as "The pause of the wave/That curves downward to spray" compel a slow, deliberate reading. You simply cannot dash off those last lines briskly.

These brief, simple examples of the way poets use the words and patterns of their verse to suggest action, mood, or meaning are obvious enough for children and are the beginnings of a deeper look at the poetry they enjoy. This deeper look will carry them into the below-the-surface meanings or implications or symbols the poet uses.

We would do well to remember how important it is that children still in the process of learning to read should hear most of their poetry before they are asked to cope with it on the printed page. The listening abilities of children exceed their reading abilities during the first few years of school; and so the effort of

reading poetry may, during those years, be greater than the pleasure of reading it. It is also important to keep in mind that contemporary poets are more understandable to today's children than are most of the poets of the past, whose work may be better understood and more easily introduced when children reach junior or senior high school.

The children who are reading and writing poetry today are searching and probing the issues and problems of our time. They want, in addition to poetry that is beautiful in grace and melody, poetry that is beautiful in strength and candor. They need to explore the new forms, to hear the voices of anger and concern about the happenings in their world. They should read Coatsworth, de la Mare, and Frost; but they should also read Nikki Giovanni, Vanessa Howard, Valerie Worth, Mari Evans, Karl Shapiro, and the many other poets who are most immediately concerned, as the children are, with the way things are today.

Adult References and Book Selection Aids*

AUSLANDER, JOSEPH, and FRANK ERNEST HILL. *The Winged Horse: The Story of Poets and Their Poetry.*

BATOR, ROBERT, comp. *Signposts to Criticism of Children's Literature.* Chapter 6, "Poetry."

BREWTON, JOHN E., and SARA W., comps. *Index to Children's Poetry.*

BREWTON, JOHN, and G. MEREDITH and LORRAINE BLACKBURN. *Index to Poetry for Children and Young People 1976–1981.*

EASTMAN, MAX. *The Enjoyment of Poetry.*

ESBENSEN, BARBARA JUSTER. *A Celebration of Bees: Helping Children Write Poetry.*

HEARNE, BETSY, and MARILYN KAYE, eds. *Celebrating Children's Books: Essays on Children's Literature in Honor of Zena Sutherland.* "Nonsense Verse: The Complete Escape" by Myra Cohn Livingston.

HOPKINS, LEE BENNETT. *Let Them Be Themselves.*

HUGHES, TED. *Poetry Is.*

KOCH, KENNETH. *Rose, Where Did You Get That Red?*

*Complete bibliographic data are provided in Appendices A and B.

————. *Wishes, Lies, and Dreams: Teaching Children to Write Poetry.*

LARRICK, NANCY, ed. *Somebody Turned on a Tap in These Kids.*

LIVINGSTON, MYRA COHN. *When You Are Alone/It Keeps You Capone: An Approach to Creative Writing with Children.*

MOORE, VARDINE. *The Pleasure of Poetry with and by Children.*

PAINTER, HELEN. *Poetry and Children.*

SHAPIRO, JON, ed. *Using Literature & Poetry Affectively.* Part 3, "Using Poetry."

SHAW, JOHN MACKAY. *Childhood in Poetry: A Catalogue.*

TERRY, ANN. *Children's Poetry Preferences: A National Survey of Upper Elementary Grades.*

WITUCKE, VIRGINIA. *Poetry in the Elementary School.*

Children's Books: Anthologies

There are so many good anthologies of poetry for children that it is not possible to list them all here. The following are especially useful for reasons the text or notes make clear.

In the following bibliography these symbols have been used to identify books about a particular religious or ethnic group:

§ African American
★ Hispanic
☆ Native American
○ Asian American
• Religious minority

§ ABDUL, RAOUL, ed. *The Magic of Black Poetry*, ill. by Dane Burr. Dodd, 1972. Includes poems from many countries.   11 up

§ ADOFF, ARNOLD, ed. *Black Out Loud*, ill. by Alvin Hollingsworth. Macmillan, 1970.   11–14

§ ————. ed. *Celebrations: A New Anthology of Black American Poetry.* Follett, 1977.   10 up

————. *City in All Directions*, ill. by Donald Carrick. Macmillan, 1969.   12 up

§ ————. *I Am the Darker Brother*, ill. by Benny Andrews. Macmillan, 1968.   11 up

————. *it is the poem singing into your eyes: anthology of new young poets.* Harper, 1971.   10 up

§ ————, ed. *My Black Me: A Beginning Book on Black Poetry.* Dutton, 1974.   8–11

§ ————, ed. *The Poetry of Black America: An Anthology of the 20th Century.* Harper, 1973.   12 up

§ ALLEN, SAMUEL, ed. *Poems from Africa*, ill. by Romare Bearden. T. Crowell, 1973. Broad in geographical and chronological scope.   12 up

ASSOCIATION FOR CHILDHOOD EDUCATION, LITERATURE COMMITTEE. *Sung Under the Silver Umbrella*, ill. by Dorothy Lathrop. Macmillan, 1935, 1962. A small collection of choice poetry, including selections from the Bible, modern poems, nonsense verse, and Japanese haiku.   4–9

★ • § BARON, VIRGINIA, ed. *Here I Am! An Anthology of Poems Written by Young People in Some of America's Minority Groups*, ill. by Emily Arnold McCully. Dutton, 1969.   8–11

BEHN, HARRY, tr. *Cricket Songs: Japanese Haiku*, with pictures selected from Sesshu and other Japanese masters. Harcourt, 1964.   10 up

☆ BELTING, NATALIA MAREE, comp. *Our Fathers Had Powerful Songs*, ill. by Laszlo Kubinyi. Dutton, 1974. Nine poems from American and Canadian Indian tribes.   9–12

☆ ————, comp. *Whirlwind Is a Ghost Dancing*, ill. by Leo and Diane Dillon. Dutton, 1974. Chiefly poems of creation or natural phenomena from North American Indian tribes.   9 up

BENNETT, JILL, comp. *Noisy Poems*, ill. by Nick Sharratt. Oxford/Merrimack, 1987. The twelve poems are each about a different noisy subject like trains or yaks.   5–8

☆ BIERHORST, JOHN, ed. *In the Trail of the Wind*, ill. Farrar, 1971.   12 up

☆ ————. *The Sacred Path: Spells, Prayers, and Power Songs of the American Indians.* Morrow, 1983. A discriminating compilation of American Indian poetry, arranged by stages of the life cycle and containing traditional as well as contemporary material.   10 up

BLISHEN, EDWARD, comp. *Oxford Book of Poetry for Children*, ill. by Brian Wildsmith. Watts, 1963. An excellent anthology covering a wide variety of subjects and styles with superb illustrations.   9–12

BOGAN, LOUISE, and WILLIAM JAY SMITH, eds. *The Golden Journey: Poems for Young People*, ill. by Fritz Kredel. Reilly, 1965.   10–14

☆ BRANDON, WILLIAM, ed. *The Magic World: American Indian Songs and Poems.* Morrow, 1971.   11 up

BREWTON, SARA and JOHN, comps. *Laughable Limericks*, ill. by Ingrid Feltz. T. Crowell, 1965.   9 up

————, comps. *Of Quarks, Quasars and Other Quirks: Quizzical Poems for the Supersonic Age*, ill. by Quentin Blake. T. Crowell, 1977. A diverse selection of poems of our time: pointed, funny, and containing much trenchant commentary.   10 up

☆ CLYMER, THEODORE, ed. *Four Corners of the Sky: Poems, Chants, and Oratory*, ill. by Marc Brown. Little, 1975. Poems of Native American cultures.   10 up

COLE, WILLIAM, ed. *Beastly Boys and Ghastly Girls*, ill. by Tomi Ungerer. World, 1964. Varied and humorous.   10–12

————, comp. *A Book of Animal Poems*, ill. by Robert Parker. Viking, 1973.   9 up

————, ed. *A Book of Nature Poems*, ill. by Robert Andrew Parker. Viking, 1969.   10–14

————, ed. *Humorous Poetry for Children*, ill. by Ervine Metzl. World, 1955.   8 up

————, ed. *Oh, What Nonsense!*, ill. by Tomi Ungerger. Viking, 1966.   9–11

COLUM, PADRAIC, ed. *Roofs of Gold: Poems to Read Aloud*. Macmillan, 1964. The editor's favorites from Shakespeare to Dylan Thomas.   11–15

CORRIN, SARA and STEPHEN, eds. *Once Upon a Rhyme*, ill. by Jill Bennett. Faber, 1982.   7–9

DE LA MARE, WALTER, ed. *Come Hither*, 3rd ed., ill. by Warren Chappell. Knopf, 1957.   12 up

————, ed. *Tom Tiddler's Ground*, ill. by Margery Gill. Knopf, 1962. First American edition of a choice compilation of verses for younger children. De la Mare's perceptive notes distinguish his anthologies.   9 up

DE REGNIERS, BEATRICE SCHENK, and others, comps. *Sing a Song of Popcorn: Every Child's Book of Poems*. Scholastic, 1988. In a new edition of *Poems Children Will Sit Still For* (1969), each section is illustrated by a different Caldecott Medalist.
                                                          5–10

§ DOOB, LEONARD, ed. *A Crocodile Has Me by the Leg: African Poems*, ill. by Solomon Irein Wangboje. Walker, 1967.   9–14

DOWNIE, MARY, and BARBARA ROBERTSON, comps. *The Wind Has Wings: Poems from Canada*, ill. by Elizabeth Cleaver. Walck, 1968, and its sequel, *The New Wind Has Wings*. Oxford/Merrimack, 1985.   9–12

DUNNING, STEPHEN, EDWARD LUEDERS, and HUGH SMITH, comps. *Reflections on a Gift of Watermelon Pickle*, Scott, Foresman, 1967.   11 up

————, comps. *Some Haystacks Don't Even Have Any Needle*, ill. Scott, Foresman, 1969. A splendid collection of poems complemented by reproductions of modern art in full color.   11 up

FLEMING, ALICE, comp. *America Is Not All Traffic Lights: Poems of the Midwest*, ill. with photos. Little, 1976.   10 up

————, comp. *Hosannah the Home Run! Poems about Sports*. Little, 1972.   10 up

FOWKE, EDITH, comp. *Ring Around the Moon*, ill. by Judith Gwyn Brown. Prentice, 1977. A compilation of riddles, rhymes, rounds, and songs.   8–10

GREGORY, HORACE, and MARYA ZATURENSKA, eds. *The Crystal Cabinet*, ill. by Diana Bloomfield. Holt,

1962. A refreshingly original anthology of lyric poetry, wide in range, from Chinese translations to poems by Edith Sitwell.   12 up

HALL, DONALD, ed. *The Oxford Book of Children's Verse in America*. Oxford, 1985. A scholarly work with child appeal, the collection consists of poetry indigenous to America, arranged chronologically from Puritan times to the present.   all ages

HANNUM, SARA, and JOHN TERRY CHASE, comps. *The Wind Is Round*, ill. by Ron Bowen. Atheneum, 1970.   10 up

HANNUM, SARA, and GWENDOLYN REED, comps. *Lean Out of the Window: An Anthology of Modern Poetry*, ill. by Ragna Tischler. Atheneum, 1965.   10–14

HARRISON, MICHAEL, and CHRISTOPHER STUART-CLARK, comps. *The Oxford Treasury of Children's Poems*. Oxford, 1988. An anthology of old and new favorites is illustrated with a variety of styles.
                                                          8–11

HOPKINS, LEE BENNETT, comp. *I Think I Saw a Snail: Young Poems for City Seasons*, ill. by Harold James. Crown, 1969. A selection of poems (four or five for each season) by accepted authors. A few are not particularly city poems.   5–8

————, comp. *More Surprises*, ill. by Megan Lloyd. Harper, 1987. This collection of poetry comes in a unique, easy-to-read format.   6–8

————, comp. *A Song in Stone: City Poems*, photos by Anna Audette. Crowell, 1983.   7–9

☆ HOUSTON, JAMES, ed. *Songs of the Dream People*, ill. by author. Atheneum, 1972. Chants and poems from North American Eskimo and Indian songs.
                                                           9 up

HOWARD, CORALIE, comp. *Lyric Poems*, ill. by Mel Fowler. Watts, 1968.   11–14

• ————. *I Never Saw Another Butterfly*. McGraw, 1964.   7–12

JANECZKO, PAUL B., ed. *Don't forget to fly: A cycle of modern poems*. Bradbury, 1981. A splendid compilation of modern poetry, chosen with discrimination and representing almost every major contemporary poet.   12 up

————. *The Music of What Happens: Poems That Tell Stories*. Orchard/Watts, 1988.   12 up

————. *Pocket Poems*. Bradbury, 1985.   11 up

————. *This Delicious Day: 65 Poems*. Orchard/Watts, 1987. A lively and brief assortment of free, unstructured verse fills this anthology for young readers.   10–12

☆ JONES, HETTIE, ed. *The Trees Stand Shining: Poetry of the North American Indians*, ill. by Robert Andrew Parker. Dial, 1971.   8–11

• § JORDAN, JUNE, and TERRY BUSH, comps. *The Voice of the Children*. Holt, 1970.   10 up

KNUDSON, R. R., and MAY SWENSON, comps. *American Sports Poems.* Orchard/Watts, 1988.   11–17

LARRICK, NANCY, comp. *Cats Are Cats,* ill. by Ed Young. Philomel, 1988. A solid collection is strikingly illustrated by pictures that capture feline moods and postures.   9–11

————, ed. *Green Is Like a Meadow of Grass,* ill. by Kelly Oechsli. Garrard, 1968.   5–9

§ ————, ed. *I Heard a Scream in the Streets: Poems by Young People in the City,* photos by students. Evans, 1970.   10 up

§ ————, ed. *On City Streets,* photos by David Sagarin. Evans, 1968.   10–14

————, comp. *Room for Me and a Mountain Lion: Poetry of Open Space.* Evans, 1974.   10 up

————, comp. *When the Dark Comes Dancing,* ill. by John Wallner. Philomel, 1983. A beautifully illustrated anthology of bedtime poems and lullabies.   2–5

LEWIS, RICHARD, ed. *I Breathe a New Song: Poems of the Eskimo,* ill. by Oonark. Simon, 1971. Poems that reflect the Eskimo's life and closeness to nature.   9 up

————, ed. *In a Spring Garden,* ill. by Ezra Jack Keats. Dial, 1965.   5–9

————. *The Luminous Landscape: Chinese Art and Poetry.* Publishing Center for Cultural Resources, 1981.   10–12

————, ed. *Miracles.* Simon, 1966.   all ages

————, ed. *The Moment of Wonder: A Collection of Chinese and Japanese Poetry,* ill. with paintings by Chinese and Japanese masters. Dial, 1964.   all ages

☆ ————, ed. *Out of the Earth I Sing: Poetry and Songs of Primitive Peoples of the World.* Norton, 1968.   8 up

————, ed. *The Wind and the Rain,* photos by Helen Buttfield. Simon, 1968.   8–10

LIVINGSTON, MYRA COHN, ed. *Calloph! Callay! Holiday Poems for Young Readers,* ill. by Janet Stevens. Atheneum, 1978. A fine holiday smorgasbord with a wide range of sources and a high standard in the included selections.   9–11

————, ed. *I Like You, If You Like Me: Poems of Friendship.* McElderry, 1987. Nearly one hundred poems are organized into nine sections on various aspects of friendship.   9–11

————, ed. *Listen, Children, Listen,* ill. by Trina Schart Hyman. Atheneum, 1972.   5–8

————. *My Head Is Red and Other Riddle Rhymes,* ill. by Tere LoPrete. Holiday, 1990.   7–9

————. *O Frabjous Day! Poems for Holidays and Special Occasions.* Atheneum, 1977.   11 up

————, ed. *Speak Roughly to Your Little Boy: A Collection of Parodies and Burlesques, Together with*

the Original Poems, Chosen and Annotated for Young People, ill. by Joseph Low. Harcourt, 1971.   11 up

————, ed. *Thanksgiving Poems,* ill. by Stephen Gammell. Holiday, 1985.   5–8

————, ed. *A Tune Beyond Us,* ill. by James J. Spanfeller. Harcourt, 1968.   12 up

————, ed. *What a Wonderful Bird the Frog Are: An Assortment of Humorous Poetry and Verse.* Harcourt, 1973.   9 up

MCDONALD, GERALD D., comp. *A Way of Knowing: A Collection of Poems for Boys,* ill. by Clare and John Ross. T. Crowell, 1959. A varied and popular collection, representative of modern and traditional poets. Appeals to girls as well as to boys.   10 up

MACKAY, DAVID, comp. *A Flock of Words,* ill. by Margery Gill. Harcourt, 1970.   11 up

MAYER, MERCER, ed. *A Poison Tree and Other Poems,* ill. by editor. Scribner's, 1977.   10 up

METCALF, JOHN, comp. *The Speaking Earth: Canadian Poetry.* Van Nostrand, 1973.   10 up

MOORE, LILIAN, comp. *Go with the Poem.* McGraw, 1979. These selections—most from contemporary poets—are grouped by such subjects as seasons, sports, or the city.   9 up

MOORE, LILIAN, and JUDITH THURMAN, comps. *To See the World Afresh.* Atheneum, 1974. An outstanding anthology.   10 up

MORRISON, LILLIAN, comp. *Best Wishes, Amen: A New Collection of Autograph Verses,* ill. by Loretta Lustig. T. Crowell, 1974.   9–13

————, comp. *Rhythm Road: Poems to Move To.* Lothrop, 1988. A volume of poetry comprises ten sections of poems related to movement, in all its forms.   10–15

————, comp. *Touch Blue: Signs and Spells, Love Charms and Chants, Auguries and Old Beliefs, in Rhyme,* ill. by Doris Lee. T. Crowell, 1958.   6–13

————, comp. *Yours till Niagara Falls,* ill. by Marjorie Bauernschmidt. T. Crowell, 1950.   9–13

MORTON, MIRIAM, ed. *A Harvest of Russian Children's Literature.* Univ. of Calif. Pr., 1967.   all ages

————, comp. *The Moon Is Like a Silver Sickle: A Celebration of Poetry by Russian Children,* ill. by Eros Keith. Simon, 1972.   9–13

NASH, OGDEN, comp. *I Couldn't Help Laughing.* Lippincott, 1957.   12–14

————, comp. *The Moon Is Shining Bright as Day,* ill. by Rose Shirvanian. Lippincott, 1953.   12–14

NESS, EVALINE, comp. *Amelia Mixed the Mustard and Other Poems,* ill. by comp. Scribner's, 1975. Twenty poems about girls.   8–10

OPIE, IONA and PETER, eds. *The Oxford Book of Children's Verse.* Oxford, 1973. A broad selection, chronologically arranged, also has adult reference use because of the Opies' notes.   5–13

PLOTZ, HELEN, comp. *As I Walked Out One Evening: A Book of Ballads.* Greenwillow, 1976.   11 up

————, comp. *Eye's Delight: Poems of Art and Architecture.* Greenwillow, 1983.   10 up

☆ ————, comp. *The Gift Outright: America to Her Poets.* Greenwillow, 1977. A judicious balance of traditional favorites and lesser known selections grouped by subject heading.   12 up

————, comp. *Gladly Learn and Gladly Teach: Poems of the School Experience.* Greenwillow, 1981. A nicely varied anthology of poetic commentaries on education and academia.   10 up

————, comp. *Imagination's Other Place: Poems of Science and Mathematics,* ill. by Clare Leighton. T. Crowell, 1955.   12 up

————, comp. *Poems from the German,* ill. by Ismar David. T. Crowell, 1967.   11 up

————, comp. *Saturday's Children: Poems of Work.* Greenwillow, 1982. A discriminating collection of poems about work: rural work, women's work, industrial labor, and unemployment.   10 up

★ POMERANTZ, CHARLOTTE. *If I Had a Paka: Poems in Eleven Languages,* ill. by Nancy Tafuri. Greenwillow, 1982.

PRELUTSKY, JACK, comp. *The Random House Book of Poetry for Children,* ill. by Arnold Lobel. Random House, 1983.   8–12

————, comp. *Read-Aloud Rhymes for the Very Young,* ill. by Marc Brown. Knopf, 1986. There is range and contrast among the two hundred poems based on child life.   1–4

READ, HERBERT. *This Way, Delight,* ill. by Juliet Kepes. Pantheon, 1956. Includes an excellent essay, "What is Poetry?"   8–12

REED, GWENDOLYN, comp. *Out of the Ark: An Anthology of Animal Verse,* ill. by Gabriele Margules. Atheneum, 1968. Old favorites and some lesser-known poems representing many centuries. Useful for independent reading or for reading aloud.   10–14

————, comp. *The Talkative Beasts: Myths, Fables and Poems of India,* ill. by Stella Snead. Lothrop, 1969.   8–12

SMITH, WILLIAM JAY, comp. *A Green Place: Modern Poems,* ill. by Jacques Hnizdovsky. Delacorte, 1982. A broad range of twentieth-century poets are represented in a topically arranged anthology.   10 up

————, ed. *Poems from France,* ill. by Roger Duvoisin. T. Crowell, 1967.   9 up

SULLY, FRANÇOIS, ed. *We, the Vietnamese: Voices from Vietnam.* Praeger, 1971. Includes poetry.   13 up

TRIPP, WALLACE, comp. *A Great Big Ugly Man Came Up and Tied His Horse to Me: A Book of Nonsense Verse,* ill. by comp. Little, 1973.   7–9

UNTERMEYER, LOUIS, ed. *Rainbow in the Sky,* ill. by Reginald Birch. Harcourt, 1935. Untermeyer was one of the first and most indefatigable anthologists for children. This is only one of his many books. They lean heavily on old and familiar poems.   7–12

WALLACE, DAISY, ed. *Fairy Poems,* ill. by Trina Schart Hyman. Holiday, 1980. Several old favorites are among the well-chosen selections in a handsomely illustrated book.   5–8

————. *Witch Poems,* ill. by Trina Schart Hyman. Holiday, 1976. Eighteen poems illustrated in black and white with a marvelous assortment of witches: comic, ominous, beautiful, and gruesome.   8–11

WOOD, NANCY, comp. *Prose and Poetry of the Pueblos,* ill. by Frank Howell. Doubleday, 1974. Thoughts of older members of the Taos.   10 up

————, comp. *War Cry on a Prayer Feather: Prose and Poetry of the Ute Indians,* ill. with photos. Doubleday, 1979. Poems included here provide an excellent background for understanding the tragic changes that have come to a once-strong people.   12 up

Children's Books: By Individual Poets

§ ADOFF, ARNOLD. *All the Colors of the Race,* ill. by John Steptoe. Lothrop, 1982. A fluid cycle of poems explores the feelings of a child who has one parent who is black and Protestant, one who is white and Jewish.   9–11

————. *Chocolate Dreams,* ill. by Turi MacCombe. Lothrop, 1989.   9–12

————. *Eats,* ill. by Susan Russo. Lothrop, 1979.   9–11

————. *Make a Circle Keep Us In,* ill. by Ronald Himler. Delacorte, 1975.   6–8

————. *Sports Pages,* ill. by Steve Kuzma. Lippincott, 1986. Soft, grayed pictures illustrate verse written in the hopeful or despairing voices of young athletes.   8–11

AIKEN, CONRAD. *Cats and Bats and Things with Wings,* ill. by Milton Glaser. Atheneum, 1965.   5–8

ALDIS, DOROTHY. *All Together: A Child's Treasury of Verse,* ill. by Helen D. Jameson. Putnam, 1952. Poems about everyday happenings.   5–9

ALLINGHAM, WILLIAM. *The Fairy Shoemaker and Other Fairy Poems,* ill. by Boris Artzybasheff. Macmillan,

1928. Poems by Allingham, Walter de la Mare, and Matthew Arnold. 9–12

ARMOUR, RICHARD. *All Sizes and Shapes of Monkeys and Apes,* ill. by Paul Galdone. McGraw, 1970. 5–8

————. *Odd Old Mammals: Animals after the Dinosaurs,* ill. by Paul Galdone. McGraw, 1968. In all his books, Armour's blithe verses give accurate information about animals.

BABBITT, NATALIE. *Dick Foote and the Shark,* ill. by author. Farrar, 1967. 9–11

————. *Phoebe's Revolt,* ill. by author. Farrar, 1968. 8–9

BEHN, HARRY. *The Golden Hive,* ill. by author. Harcourt, 1966. 9–12

————. *Windy Morning,* ill. by author. Harcourt, 1953.

————. *The Wizard in the Well,* ill. by author. Harcourt, 1956. 5–9

BELLOC, HILAIRE. *The Bad Child's Book of Beasts,* ill. by B. T. B. Knopf, 1965. Horrendous nonsense. 6–9

————. *Cautionary Verses,* ill. by B. T. B. and Nicolas Bentley. Knopf, 1959. 9–12

————. *Matilda, Who Told Lies and Was Burned to Death,* ill. by Steven Kellogg. Dial, 1970. A spoof of a Victorian morality tale. 9–12

BENÉT, ROSEMARY, and STEPHEN VINCENT. *A Book of Americans,* rev. ed., ill. by Charles Child. Holt, 1952. 8–14

BLAKE, WILLIAM. *Songs of Innocence,* ill. by Harold Jones. Barnes, 1961. A welcome edition which contains nineteen of Blake's more childlike poems. 6 up

BODECKER, N. M. *Hurry, Hurry, Mary Dear! And Other Nonsense Poems,* ill. by author. Atheneum, 1976. A few of these poems are sheer nonsense, some play with words, all are delightful to read aloud. 7–10

————. *Snowman Sniffles,* ill. by author. Atheneum, 1983. Small, animated line drawings illustrate a selection of brief, child-oriented poems, many about animals and winter. 7–9

BROOKE, L. LESLIE. *Johnny Crow's Garden.* Warne, 1903.

————. *Johnny Crow's New Garden.* Warne, 1935.

————. *Johnny Crow's Party.* Warne, 1907. 3–7

————. *Leslie Brooke's Children's Books,* 4 vols. Warne, n.d. 5–12

————. *Ring o' Roses* (see Bibliography, Chapter 3).

§ BROOKS, GWENDOLYN. *Bronzeville Boys and Girls,* ill. by Ronni Solbert. Harper, 1956. 7–11

BROWNJOHN, ALAN. *Brownjohn's Beasts,* ill. by Carol Lawson. Scribner's, 1970. 9–11

BURKERT, NANCY EKHOLM, ad. *Valentine and Orson,* ill. by author. Farrar, 1989. A folk-play version, in verse, of the classic medieval romance. 11–15

CARROLL, LEWIS. *Alice's Adventures in Wonderland* (see Bibliography, Chapter 8).

————. *The Annotated Snark,* with an introduction and notes by Martin Gardner. Simon, 1962. The full text of Lewis Carroll's great nonsense epic *The Hunting of the Snark* and the original illustrations by Henry Holiday.

————. *Poems of Lewis Carroll,* comp. by Myra Cohn Livingston, ill. by John Tenniel and others. T. Crowell, 1973. 5 up

CAUDILL, REBECCA. *Come Along!,* ill. by Ellen Raskin. Holt, 1969. Haiku poems about the year's cycle. 7–9

CAUSLEY, CHARLES. *Early in the Morning: A Collection of New Poems,* ill. by Michael Foreman, music by Anthony Castro. Viking, 1987. In a book of contemporary nursery rhymes, about half of the poems are set to music that is easy to play and sing. 4–7

CIARDI, JOHN. *The Reason for the Pelican,* ill. by Madeleine Gekiere. Lippincott, 1959. 5–9 Nonsense verses and imaginative poems in this collection launched John Ciardi's books for children. Others include:

————. *Doodle Soup,* ill. by Merle Nacht. Houghton, 1985. 7–9

————. *I Met a Man,* ill. by Robert Osborn. Houghton, 1961. 4–8

————. *The King Who Saved Himself from Being Saved,* ill. by Edward Gorey. Lippincott, 1965.

————. *You Read to Me, I'll Read to You,* ill. by Edward Gorey. Lippincott, 1962. 5–8

§ CLIFTON, LUCILLE. *Everett Anderson's Goodbye,* ill. by Ann Grifalconi. Holt, 1983. Poignant verses about a child's adjustment to his father's death. 5–8

§ ————. *Everett Anderson's Nine Month Long,* ill. by Ann Grifalconi. Holt, 1978. Another story poem about the small black boy who is about to be dethroned by a new sibling and is suffering the usual first-child doubts about his mother's love and attention. 5–7

§ ————. *Some of the Days of Everett Anderson,* ill. by Evaline Ness. Holt, 1970. 5–7

COATSWORTH, ELIZABETH. *Away Goes Sally* (see Bibliography, Chapter 11).

————. *Down Half the World,* ill. by Zena Bernstein. Macmillan, 1968. 12 up

————. *The Fair American* (see Bibliography, Chapter 11).

————. *The Sparrow Bush,* ill. by Stefan Martin. Norton, 1966. 9–12

————. *Summer Green,* ill. by Nora S. Unwin. Macmillan, 1948.   7 up

————. *Under the Green Willow,* ill. by Janina Domanska. Macmillan, 1971.   5–7

COLE, WILLIAM. *What's Good for a Four-Year-Old?,* ill. by Tomi Ungerer. Holt, 1967. One of a series.   3–4

COLTMAN, PAUL. *Tog the Ribber or Granny's Tale,* ill. by Gillian McClure. Farrar, 1985.   8–10

CULLEN, COUNTEE. *The Lost Zoo,* ill. by Joseph Low. Follett, 1969.   10 up

CUMMINGS, E. E. *Hist Whist and Other Poems for Children,* ed. by George James Firmage, ill. by David Calsada. Liveright, 1983. Wordplay and humor are among the chief charms of these selections.   8–11

DE GASZTOLD, CARMEN BERNOS. *The Creatures' Choir,* tr. by Rumer Godden, ill. by Jean Primrose. Viking, 1965.   11 up

————. *Prayers from the Ark,* tr. by Rumer Godden. Viking, 1962.   12 up

DE LA MARE, WALTER. *Peacock Pie,* ill. by Barbara Cooney. Knopf, 1961.   6 up

————. *Rhymes and Verses: Collected Poems for Children,* ill. by Elinore Blaisdell. Holt, 1947.   5 up

————. *The Voice,* ed. and ill. by Catherine Brighton. Delacorte, 1987.   7–10

DE REGNIERS, BEATRICE SCHENK. *May I Bring a Friend?,* ill. by Beni Montresor. Atheneum, 1964. A young child brings his (animal) friends with him when invited to visit the king and queen. Caldecott Medal.   5–7

————. *Something Special,* ill. by Irene Haas. Harcourt, 1958.   3–6

DICKINSON, EMILY. *Letter to the World,* ed. by Rumer Godden, ill. by Prudence Seward. Macmillan, 1969.

————. *Poems,* ed. by Helen Plotz, ill. by Robert Kipness. T. Crowell, 1964.

————. *Poems for Youth,* ed. by Alfred Hampson. Little, 1934.   11 up

FARJEON, ELEANOR. *The Children's Bells,* ill. by Peggy Fortnum. Walck, 1960.

————. *Eleanor Farjeon's Poems for Children.* Lippincott, 1951.   5–12

————. *Then There Were Three,* ill. by Isobel and John Morton-Sale. Lippincott, 1965.   4–7

FIELD, EUGENE. *Poems of Childhood,* ill. by Maxfield Parrish. Scribner's, 1904. First published in 1896.   8–12

FIELD, RACHEL. *Poems,* ill. by author. Macmillan, 1957.   6–12

————. *Taxis and Toadstools,* ill. by author. Doubleday, 1926.   7–12

§ FIELDS, JULIA. *The Green Lion of Zion Street,* ill. by Jerry Pinkney. McElderry, 1988. In verse and idiomatic speech, a group of children responds to a majestic sculpture of a lion.   5–8

FINLAY, IAN HAMILTON. *Poems to Hear and See.* Macmillan, 1971.   8–10

FISHER, AILEEN. *But Ostriches . . .,* ill. by Peter Parnall. T. Crowell, 1970.   8–10

————. *Feathered Ones and Furry,* ill. by Eric Carle. T. Crowell, 1971.   5–8

————. *Going Barefoot,* ill. by Adrienne Adams. T. Crowell, 1960.   4–8

————. *In the Middle of the Night,* ill. by Adrienne Adams. T. Crowell, 1965.   5–7

————. *Out in the Dark and the Daylight.* Harper, 1980.   5–10

————. *Up, Up the Mountain,* ill. by Gilbert Riswold. T. Crowell, 1968.   8–10

————. *Where Does Everyone Go?,* ill. by Adrienne Adams. T. Crowell, 1961.   4–8

FLEISCHMAN, PAUL. *I Am Phoenix: Poems for Two Voices,* ill. by Ken Nutt. Harper, 1985. Striking poetry to read aloud.   all ages

————. *Joyful Noise: Poems for Two Voices,* ill. by Eric Beddows. Harper, 1988. Newbery Medal.   9–11

FROST, FRANCES. *The Little Naturalist,* ill. by Kurt Werth. Whittlesey, 1959. Poems of nature. 8–12

————. *The Little Whistler,* ill. by Roger Duvoisin. Whittlesey, 1949. Poems of the seasons. 8–12

FROST, ROBERT. *Complete Poems of Robert Frost.* Holt, 1949.

————. *In the Clearing.* Holt, 1962.

————. *Stopping by Woods on a Snowy Evening,* ill. by Susan Jeffers. Dutton, 1978.   5–9

————. *You Come Too,* ill. by Thomas W. Nason. Holt, 1959.   11 up

GERRARD, ROY. *Sir Cedric.* Farrar, 1984. A brave little knight wins so decisive a battle that the war stops for tea.   5–8

————. *Sir Cedric Rides Again,* ill. by author. Farrar, 1986.   5–8

§ GIOVANNI, NIKKI. *Ego-Tripping and Other Poems for Young People,* ill. by George Ford. Lawrence Hill, 1974. Poems selected by the poet from her published works.   11 up

GREENAWAY, KATE. *Marigold Garden,* ill. by author. Warne, 1910.

————. *Under the Window,* ill. by author. Warne, 1910.   4–7

§ GREENFIELD, ELOISE. *Daydreamers,* ill. by Tom Feelings. Dial, 1981. A tender, poetic mood piece about the child who daydreams, profusely illustrated with portraits of African-American children.   8–10

§ ————. *Under the Sunday Tree,* ill. by Amos Ferguson. Harper, 1988. Rhythmic poetry is illustrated by artwork that is at times bold and at times contemplative.   7–10

HOBERMAN, MARY ANN. *Hello and Good-Bye,* ill. by Norman Hoberman. Little, 1959.   4–9

HOFFMAN, HEINRICH. *Slovenly Peter, or Pretty Stories and Funny Pictures for Little Children.* Tuttle, 1969.   5–8

HOLMAN, FELICE. *At the Top of My Voice: And Other Poems,* ill. by Edward Gorey. Norton, 1970. Wry, humorous poems.   8–10

————. *The Song in My Head,* ill. by Jim Spanfeller. Scribner's, 1985. Brief lyric poems.   8–10

HOOPER, PATRICIA. *A Bundle of Beasts,* ill. by Mark Steele. Houghton, 1987.   9–11

§ HUGHES, LANGSTON. *Black Misery,* ill. by Arouni. Eriksson, 1969.   10–14

§ ————. *Don't You Turn Back,* selected by Lee Bennett Hopkins, ill. by Ann Grifalconi. Knopf, 1969.   10 up

§ ————. *Fields of Wonder.* Knopf, 1947.   11 up

§ ————. *Selected Poems of Langston Hughes.* Knopf, 1959.   11 up

HUGHES, SHIRLEY. *Out and About,* ill. by author. Lothrop, 1988.   3–5

HUGHES, TED. *Moon-Whales and Other Moon Poems,* ill. by Leonard Baskin. Viking, 1976. The eminent British poet envisions a lunatic world; his eerie imagery is echoed by the adroit pen and ink drawings of Baskin.   11–14

————. *Season Songs,* ill. by Leonard Baskin. Viking, 1975. Poems and pictures about the seasons are equally beautiful. A stunning book.   11 up

ISSA. *A Few Flies and I: Haiku by Issa,* ed. by Jean Merrill and Ronni Solbert, from tr. by R. H. Blyth and Nobuyaki Yuasa, ill. by Ronni Solbert. Pantheon, 1969.   8–11

JANECZKO, PAUL. *Brickyard Summer.* Orchard, 1989. Poems about the people of a New England mill town.   13 up

JARRELL, RANDALL. *The Bat-Poet.* Macmillan, 1967.   9–11

§ JOHNSON, JAMES WELDON. *God's Trombones,* ill. by Aaron Douglas. Viking, 1927. Seven verse sermons. Introduction discusses dialect and vernacular.   11 up

§ JORDAN, JUNE. *Who Look at Me.* T. Crowell, 1969.   10 up

KENNEDY, X. J. *Brats,* ill. by James Watts. McElderry, 1986.   7–9

————. *One Winter Night in August and Other Nonsense Jingles,* ill. by David McPhail. Atheneum, 1975.   8–11

————. *The Phantom Ice Cream Man: More Nonsense Verse,* ill. by David McPhail. Atheneum, 1979.   8–11

KUMIN, MAXINE W. *The Microscope,* ill. by Arnold Lobel. Harper, 1984.   5–8

————. *No One Writes a Letter to the Snail,* ill. by Bean Allen. Putnam, 1962. Fresh, bouncy verses.   8–10

KUSKIN, KARLA. *Dogs & Dragons, Trees & Dreams: A Collection of Poems,* ill. by author. Harper, 1980.   7–9

————. *Near the Window Tree,* ill. by author. Harper, 1975. Each poem has a prefatory note, explaining how it came to be written.   7–9

————. *Something Sleeping in the Hall,* ill. by author. Harper, 1985.   3–7

• LEAR, EDWARD. *The Complete Nonsense Book,* ed. by Lady Strachey. Dodd, 1942. This volume includes both books referred to in the text: *The Book of Nonsense* and *Nonsense Songs and Stories.* These are available in the original attractive separate volumes from Warne.   8–14

————. *Incidents in the Life of My Uncle Arly,* ill. by Dale Maxey. Follett, 1969.

————. *The Jumblies,* ill. by Edward Gorey. W. R. Scott, 1968.

————. *The Owl and the Pussy Cat,* ill. by William Pène du Bois. Doubleday, 1962.

————. *The Quangle-Wangle's Hat,* ill. by Helen Oxenbury. Watts, 1969.   4–8

————. *The Scroobious Pip,* completed by Ogden Nash, ill. by Nancy Ekholm Burkert. Harper, 1968. Stunning, imaginative pictures.   9 up

• ————. *Whizz!,* ill. by Janina Domanska. Macmillan, 1973.   4–6

LEE, DENNIS. *Alligator Pie,* ill. by Frank Newfeld. Houghton, 1975. Bouncy, sunny verse by an eminent Canadian poet.   5–8

————. *Garbage Delight,* ill. by Frank Newfeld. Houghton, 1978. Canadian Book of the Year.   5–9

————. *Jelly Belly,* ill. by Juan Winjgaard. Bedrick/Blackie/Harper, 1985. A wide variety of poetry by one of Canada's leading poets is enhanced by softly colored paintings.   2–5

LENSKI, LOIS. *City Poems,* ill. by author. Walck, 1971. Most of the poems describe familiar urban sights and activities.   5–7

LEWIS, RICHARD, comp. *Of This World: A Poet's Life in Poetry,* ill. with photos by Helen Buttfield. Dial, 1968.   10 up

LINDSAY, VACHEL. *Johnny Appleseed, and Other Poems,* ill. by George Richards. Macmillan, 1928.   10 up

————. *Springfield Town Is Butterfly Town,* ed. by Pierre Dussert, ill. by Vachel Lindsay. Kent State Univ. Pr., 1969.   7–11

LIVINGSTON, MYRA COHN. *Birthday Poems*, ill. by Margot Tomes. Holiday House, 1989. Always child-oriented, a collection that has great appeal.   5–8

• ———. *A Circle of Seasons*, ill. by Leonard Everett Fisher. Holiday, 1982.   all ages

———. *Earth Songs*, ill. by Leonard Everett Fisher. Holiday House, 1986.   8–11

———. *Sky Songs*, ill. by Leonard Everett Fisher. Holiday, 1984.   all ages

———. *There Was a Place and Other Poems*. McElderry, 1988. Thirty-two poems expand on the theme of families faced with death, divorce, or remarriage.   9–11

———. *Up in the Air*, ill. by Leonard Everett Fisher. Holiday House, 1989.   5–8

———. *Whispers and Other Poems*, ill. by Jacqueline Chwast. Harcourt, 1958.   5–8

LOBEL, ARNOLD. *On the Day Peter Stuyvesant Sailed into Town*, ill. by author. Harper, 1971.   5–8

McCORD, DAVID. *Away and Ago*, ill. by Leslie Morrill. Little, 1975. Clever wordplay and a sense of fun prevail.   8–11

———. *Every Time I Climb a Tree*, ill. by Marc Simont. Little, 1967.   7–9

———. *Far and Few: Rhymes of the Never Was and Always Is*, ill. by Henry B. Kane. Little, 1952.   5–10

———. *One at a Time: His Collected Poems for the Young*, ill. by Henry B. Kane. Little, 1977. 8–13

———. *Take Sky: More Rhymes of the Never Was and Always Is*, ill. by Henry B. Kane. Little, 1962.   8 up

McGINLEY, PHYLLIS. *All Around the Town* (see Bibliography, Chapter 4)

———. *Mince Pie and Mistletoe*, ill. by Harold Berson. Lippincott, 1961.   6–12

———. *A Wreath of Christmas Legends*, ill. by Leonard Weisgard. Macmillan, 1967.   10–13

☆ MAHER, RAMONA. *Alice Yazzie's Year*, ill. by Stephen Gammell. Coward, 1977. Soft brown and white pictures illustrate a fluid, poetic text that highlights the events of a Navajo girl's eleventh year.   9–12

MARSHAK, SAMUEL. *The Pup Grew Up!*, tr. by Richard Pevear, ill. by Vladimir Radunsky. Holt, 1989. First published in Russia in 1926, this poem narrates the journey of a perplexed woman who boards a train with a tiny Pekingnese and departs with a Great Dane.   5–8

• MERRIAM, EVE. *Blackberry Ink*, ill. by Hans Wilhelm. Morrow, 1985.   3–6

• ———. *Finding a Poem*, ill. by Seymour Chwast. Atheneum, 1970.   11 up

———. *Fresh Paint*, ill. by David Frampton. Macmillan, 1986. Forty-five poems on a wide variety of subjects are constructed in simple, lyrical language.   9–12

———. *Halloween ABC*, ill. by Lane Smith. Macmillan, 1987. A sophisticated alphabet book describes each letter by creepy verse and surrealistic artwork.   8–10

• ———. *It Doesn't Always Have to Rhyme*, ill. by Malcolm Spooner. Atheneum, 1964.   10–14

———. *A Poem for a Pickle: Funnybone Verses*, ill. by Sheila Hamanaka. Morrow, 1989.   4–7

———. *You Be Good and I'll Be Night: Jump-on-the-Bed Poems*, ill. by Karen Lee Schmidt. Morrow, 1988. A collection of twenty-eight bouncy poems features jump-rope rhythms and chanting rhymes.   3–6

MILNE, A. A. *Now We Are Six*, ill. by Ernest Shepard. Dutton, 1927.

———. *When We Were Very Young*, ill. by Ernest Shepard. Dutton, 1924. These verses were reprinted in 1961, in larger type and more attractive format.

MIZUMURA, KAZUE. *I See the Winds*, ill. T. Crowell, 1966. The illustrations vary from attractive to lovely; the poetry ranges from adequate to good.   8–10

MOORE, LILIAN. *I Feel the Same Way*, ill. by Robert Quackenbush. Atheneum, 1967.   6–9

———. *See My Lovely Poison Ivy: And Other Verses about Witches, Ghosts and Things*, ill. by Diane Dawson. Atheneum, 1975.   8–10

———. *Something New Begins: New and Selected Poems*, ill. by Mary Jane Dunton. Atheneum, 1982.   8 up

NASH, OGDEN. *The Cruise of the Aardvark*, ill. by Wendy Watson. Evans, 1967.   7–9

———. *Custard and Company: Poems by Ogden Nash*, comp. and ill. by Quentin Blake. Little, 1980. Blake's breezy, comic drawings are perfectly appropriate for the inspired lunacy of Nash's wit.   8 up

OPPENHEIM, JOANNE. *You Can't Catch Me!*, ill. by Andrew Shachat. Houghton, 1986. A pesky fly who goes about chanting and otherwise annoying animals gets his comeuppance from a turtle who looks at first like a rock.   2–5

ORGEL, DORIS. *The Good-Byes of Magnus Marmalade*, ill. by Erik Blegvad, Putnam, 1966. Amusing, not-so-fond farewell remarks by a small boy. 8–9

PLATH, SYLVIA. *The Bed Book*, ill. by Emily Arnold McCully. Harper, 1976. No story here, but a happy romp of inventive fancy where beds behave in unexpected ways.   5–7

POMERANTZ, CHARLOTTE. *The Tamarindo Puppy: And Other Poems,* ill. by Byron Barton. Greenwillow, 1980.   5–8

PRELUTSKY, JACK. *The Baby Uggs Are Hatching,* ill. by James Stevenson. Greenwillow, 1982.   5–8

————. *It's Snowing! It's Snowing!,* ill. by Jeanne Titherington. Greenwillow, 1984.   5–8

————. *The New Kid on the Block,* ill. by James Stevenson. Greenwillow, 1984.   5–9

————. *Nightmares: Poems to Trouble Your Sleep,* ill. by Arnold Lobel. Greenwillow, 1976. This deliciously awful collection of poems is calculated to evoke simultaneous grins and shudders.   10–14

————. *Ride a Purple Pelican,* ill. by Garth Williams. Greenwillow, 1986. Each appealing rhyme refers to a city or region in America.   2–6

————. *Rolling Harvey Down the Hill,* ill. by Victoria Chess. Greenwillow, 1980.   5–7

————. *The Sheriff of Rottenshot: Poems,* ill. by Victoria Chess. Greenwillow, 1982.   5–8

RASMUSSEN, KNUD, comp. *Beyond the High Hills: A Book of Eskimo Poems,* ill. by Guy Mary-Rousselière. World, 1961.   7 up

RICHARDS, LAURA E. *Tirra Lirra: Rhymes Old and New,* ill. by Marguerite Davis, foreword by May Hill Arbuthnot. Little, 1955.   5–12

RILEY, JAMES WHITCOMB. *The Gobble-uns'll Git You Ef You Don't Watch Out!,* ad. from "Little Orphant Annie," ill. by Joel Schick. Lippincott, 1975. The illustrations give new humor to a once-popular poem.   8–9

ROBERTS, ELIZABETH MADOX. *Under the Tree,* ill. by F. D. Bedford. Viking, 1922.   6–10

ROETHKE, THEODORE. *Collected Poems,* Doubleday, 1966.   12 up

————. *Dirty Dinky and Other Creatures: Poems for Children,* selected by Beatrice Roethke and Stephen Lushington. Doubleday, 1973. Chiefly animal poems, most of them humorous.   8–11

————. *I Am! Says the Lamb,* ill. by Robert Leydenfrost. Doubleday, 1961.   10 up

ROSSETTI, CHRISTINA. *Goblin Market,* ill. by Arthur Rackham. Watts, 1970.   9 up

————. *Goblin Market,* ill. by Ellen Raskin. Dutton, 1970.   9 up

————. *Sing Song,* ill. by Marguerite Davis. Macmillan, 1952.   4–10

RYDER, JOANNE. *Inside Turtle's Shell and Other Poems of the Field,* ill. by Susan Bonners. Macmillan, 1985.   7–10

RYLANT, CYNTHIA. *Waiting to Waltz: A Childhood,* ill. by Stephen Gammell. Bradbury, 1984.   11–13

SANDBURG, CARL. *Early Moon,* ill. by James Daugherty. Harcourt, 1930.   10–14

————. *The Sandburg Treasury: Prose and Poetry for Young People,* ill. by Paul Bacon. Harcourt, 1970.   10–14

————. *Wind Song,* ill. by William A. Smith. Harcourt, 1960. Poems chosen for child appeal cover a wide range of subjects from prayers and people to nature and nonsense.   11–14

SEUSS, DR. *I Am Not Going to Get Up Today,* ill. by James Stevenson. Random House, 1987. A stubborn boy refuses to leave the warmth of his bed, even when threatened by the police.   6–8

SILVERSTEIN, SHEL. *A Light in the Attic,* ill. by author. Harper, 1981. More rollicking verses from the rhymer who produced the best-selling *Where the Sidewalk Ends.*   9–11

————. *Where the Sidewalk Ends: The Poems and Drawings of Shel Silverstein.* Harper, 1974. Fresh, breezy poetry; much of it has a pointed message for today.   8–11

SINGER, MARILYN. *Turtle in July,* ill. by Jerry Pinkney. Macmillan, 1989.   5–8

SMITH, WILLIAM JAY. *Laughing Time,* ill. by Juliet Kepes. Little, 1955.   4 up

STARBIRD, KAYE. *The Covered Bridge House,* ill. by Jim Arnosky. Four Winds, 1979. Poems about people, some lyric and some wittily narrative.   9–11

————. *Don't Ever Cross a Crocodile,* ill. by Kit Dalton. Lippincott, 1963.   5–10

————. *The Pheasant on Route Seven,* ill. by Victoria de Larrea. Lippincott, 1968.   10–13

————. *A Snail's a Failure Socially: And Other Poems, Mostly About People,* ill. by Kit Dalton. Lippincott, 1966.   9–11

————. *Speaking of Cows,* ill. by Rita Fava. Lippincott, 1960.   5–10

STEIG, JEANNE. *Consider the Lemming,* ill. by William Steig. Farrar, 1988.   9–12

STEVENSON, ROBERT LOUIS. *A Child's Garden of Verses.* There are many editions of this classic. These are representative: Ill. by Jessie Wilcox Smith. Scribner's, 1905, 1969. A large book with appealing pictures in soft colors. Ill. by Tasha Tudor. Walck, 1947. A full edition with pictures in soft pastels using the young Robert Louis himself as the child. Ill. by Brian Wildsmith. Watts, 1966. The loved and familiar poems are illustrated with the usual Wildsmith riot of color.   5–9

SWENSON, MAY. *More Poems to Solve.* Scribner's, 1971.   10 up

————. *Poems to Solve.* Scribner's, 1969.   12 up

TAGORE, RABINDRANATH. *Moon, For What Do You Wait?,* ed. by Richard Lewis, ill. by Ashley Bryan. Atheneum, 1967.   9 up

TEASDALE, SARA. *Stars To-night,* ill. by Dorothy Lathrop, Macmillan, 1930.   8–12

THOMAS, DYLAN. *A Child's Christmas in Wales,* ill. by Edward Ardizzone. Godine, 1980. Evocative drawings amplify these lyric remembrances of Christmas joys in a Welsh coastal town.   10 up

TIPPETT, JAMES S. *I Live in a City.* Harper, 1924.   5–7

TURNER, ANNE WARREN. *Street Talk,* ill. by Catherine Stock. Houghton, 1986.   7–9

UPDIKE, JOHN. *A Child's Calendar,* ill. by Nancy Ekholm Burkert. Knopf, 1965.   8–10

VIORST, JUDITH. *If I Were in Charge of the World and Other Worries: Poems for Children and Their Parents,* ill. by Lynne Cherry. Atheneum, 1982. A breezy, amusing collection of poems by a popular humorist.   8–11

WATSON, CLYDE. *Catch Me & Kiss Me & Say It Again: Rhymes,* ill. by Wendy Watson. World, 1978.   2–5

————. *Father Fox's Pennyrhymes,* ill. by Wendy Watson. T. Crowell, 1971.   3–6

WILBUR, RICHARD. *Opposites,* ill. by author. Harcourt, 1973. A series of verses deftly explains opposite terms.   10–12

WILLARD, NANCY. *East of the Sun and West of the Moon: A Play,* ill. by Barry Moser. Harcourt, 1989. Poetry alternates with colloquial modern prose in a fresh dramatization of the well-known tale.   9–12

————. *A Visit to William Blake's Inn: Poems for Innocent and Experienced Travelers,* ill. by Alice and Martin Provensen. Harcourt, 1981. Newbery Medal.   5–10

————. *The Voyage of the Ludgate Hill: Travels with Robert Louis Stevenson,* ill. by Alice and Martin Provensen. Harcourt, 1987. Stevenson's 1887 diary of a voyage to America is transformed into imaginative verse and brush-stroked paintings.   5–8

WORTH, VALERIE. *More Small Poems,* ill. by Natalie Babbitt. Farrar, 1976.   9 up

————. *Small Poems,* ill. by Natalie Babbitt. Farrar, 1972.   9 up

————. *Still More Small Poems,* ill. by Natalie Babbitt. Farrar, 1978. Evocative and laser-focused, bringing fresh insights into familiar things.   9 up

YOLEN, JANE. *Best Witches: Poems for Halloween,* ill. by Elise Primavera. Putnam, 1989. The macabre and the comic are nicely balanced, and both are reflected in lively illustrations.   8–10

————. *Ring of Earth: A Child's Book of Seasons,* ill. by John Wallner. Harcourt, 1986.   8–11

Chapter Ten

Modern Fiction

In the past several decades, realistic fiction has shown more change than any other kind of books for children. Chapter 1 touches on those changes and discusses some of the present-day trends: books by and about African Americans, Asian Americans, native Americans, and Spanish-speaking people; interest in the elderly and the disabled; reflections of the feminist movement and other social protest groups. There have been significant changes in the use of frank language and in the treatment of hitherto taboo subjects; and there has been an awareness of realistic fiction from other countries, an awareness reflected, to some extent, in the publication of translated books and, to a greater extent, of books published in other English-speaking countries. While some of these books, from our own country or others, cause concern to many adults because of their candid treatment of themes or subjects, many offer excellent writing.

Realistic stories may be just as exciting or humorous or romantic or imaginative as fantasy, but they are always plausible or possible. In a realistic story everything that happens *could* happen. Sometimes the adventures of the hero or heroine may seem rather improbable but still merit the classification of realistic because they are possible. A realistic story is a tale that is convincingly true to life.

Realistic fiction for children includes historical novels (Chapter 11), stories about people of other countries and stories about contemporary life in the United States; the last two categories are the major concern of this chapter, which includes books set after World War II. Such books help children better understand the problems and issues of their own lives, empathize with other people, and see the complexities of human relationships.

The books discussed in this chapter have been divided into three major groups: books for the youngest children (many of which are also discussed in Chapter 4), books for the middle group, and books for older children. These divisions are not hard and fast, since many children read above their usual reading level when they are interested or may go back to a childhood favorite of their past reading experience. And many adults have found that they can read aloud books intended for children older than those in their audience. The reading levels suggested in the bibliography of this chapter are equally flexible. Besides the three major categories, there are three minor categories: animal stories, sports stories, and mysteries—three of the favorite subject-matter interests of children.

The stories in this chapter are not divided by ethnic or regional groups or by countries. The chapter bibliography, however, is marked so that those who are interested, say, in finding books about African-American children can do so; the Subject Matter Index, too, will help readers find such stories.

Criteria for Realistic Stories

How can we evaluate this wealth of realistic fiction for children, when it ranges from picture stories for the youngest to mystery stories and romance for adolescents? First of all, it may be helpful to review the section in Chapter 2 entitled "Looking Closely at Books"; and to consider in these books just how effectively setting, point of view, characters, plot, theme, and style are handled. The primary consideration is the power of the story to captivate readers and keep them racing along from page to page, while having sufficient literary distinction to develop children's taste.

Most of this fiction, in addition to telling good stories, satisfies some of children's basic needs. From *One Morning in Maine* to *The Great Gilly Hopkins* there is continual emphasis on winning or holding security. The satisfaction of belonging is very important in *Journey Home* and *Are You There God? It's Me, Margaret*. Loving and being loved is a powerful motive in *The Pinballs* and *A Little Love*. Children's love of change and fun is a motivating force in *Henry Huggins* and *Little Eddie*. The need to know is important in *Tom Sawyer, Portrait of Ivan*, . . . *and now Miguel, Child of the Owl*, and in the mystery tales. The need for competence is a strong motivating force in *Ordinary Jack* and *My Side of the Mountain*, and in many other realistic stories of the past and present.

If these books center on children's basic needs; if they give them increased insight into their own personal problems and social relationships; if they show that people are more alike than different, more akin to each other than alien; if they convince young readers that

they can do something about their lives—have fun and adventures and get things done without any magic other than their own earnest efforts; then they are worthwhile books.

Stories about Minority Groups

No other country in the world has the variety of peoples to be found in the United States. There are such regional groups as the Southern mountain people, the Cajuns, and the migrant groups that follow the crops—picking cotton or beans or strawberries or oranges. Then there are the close-knit communities of immigrants and their descendants making a little Italy or Hungary or Sweden within a larger community. There are groups representing all the major and innumerable minor religious sects, and Americans of every racial background. Since all of these diverse people have contributed richly to the life of the nation, it is important that children should meet them vicariously in books in order that they may meet them in person sympathetically and with respect. Children see in books their own images, and if these are distorted or if there is stigma by omission, such self-images are damaged. And it is especially important that the minority group is pictured not as "them" but as "one of us," that the books about children of minority groups show the diversity within the group rather than a stereotype. When there is a need and a response, as there has been for books about African-American children, there are always the twin specters of the bandwagon book, tailored to fit the need, and of the tract, written with good intent but too burdened by its message to be a good story. Some of these books may be useful temporarily despite their mediocrity, but it is to be hoped that the day will come when there are so many good books for and about every kind of child that we can dismiss those that do not meet all the standards of good literature.

Stories about Children of Other Countries

In early stories about other countries there was a tendency to present the picturesque at the expense of the usual. Readers were given the China of bound feet, the Holland of wooden shoes and lace caps, South America by way of a primitive type of Indian tribe. Some of these

faults are still to be found in recently published books (both those written in the United States and those selected for importation from other countries), but such misconceptions are becoming far less common. We must check the information given in such stories against what we know to be true of the present everyday life of people. And we must question any implication that a way of life of people we don't know is queer or quaint rather than simply different. In many of these books the themes are universal, and the stories point up the fact that differences between children of one country and those of another are superficial—and that these differences based on cultural factors should be valued and preserved.

Books for Younger Children

Our youngest children, anywhere from two years old to seven, seem to have a special need for stories that are as factual and personal as their fingers and toes and the yards and neighborhoods they are beginning to explore.

Forerunners

In the 1920s, Lucy Sprague Mitchell called attention to the lack of realistic stories for the child under five, and supplied stories centering on the child's own activities, using the child's own language. In 1929, an example of realism for the youngest came from the Swedish. It was a translation of *Pelle's New Suit*, told and illustrated by Elsa Beskow. Pelle raises his own lamb and then, for each person who helps him with his suit, he performs some useful service. Finally, for his Sunday best he triumphantly wears his beautiful blue suit.

The most notable of the early followers of Lucy Sprague Mitchell was Margaret Wise Brown, who wrote also under the name of Golden MacDonald. Her *The City Noisy Book*, intended to stimulate the sensory perceptions of young children, was a pioneer and was followed by several more *Noisy* books. Then there was a series contrasting size: The hero of *The Little Fisherman* caught little fish and the big fisherman caught big fish, and so on.

Then he dyed his wool himself until it was all, all blue.

From *Pelle's New Suit*, written and illustrated by Elle Beskow.

Brown's contribution lay chiefly in her sensitive perception of the child's sensory responses to the big, booming confusion of the world.

The books by Margaret Wise Brown launched a torrent of awareness compositions for the young. There were books about night sounds, day smells, wetness, coldness, and colors. By the 1950s it began to look as if we were in for a kind of attrition of theme and plot, with language experiences in place of stories and pitter-patter in place of events. These books give children back themselves with little more —no rich entertainment, no additional insight, and no laughter.

These early examples of realism for the youngest have been followed by a continuing spate of books impressive in their variety, written and illustrated by authors and artists of distinction, and reflecting not only the needs and interests of young children but also the diversity and the changes within our society.

Alvin Tresselt
Hide and Seek Fog
White Snow, Bright Snow

Midway between the awareness and the theme-plot schools of writing for young children lie the picture stories of Alvin Tresselt. Tresselt constructs his stories about weather and nature in simple, rhythmic prose, and with Roger Duvoisin's pictures, they develop a real sense of drama. *Hide and Seek Fog*, for example, describes how the fog affects sea and seaside activities, and *What Did You Leave Behind?* encourages appreciative observation. These little everyday miracles of the weather are made exciting, something to be watched and enjoyed, never feared. Texts and pictures are full of reassurance and beauty. *White Snow, Bright Snow* won the 1948 Caldecott Medal for Duvoisin.

Edward Ardizzone
The *Little Tim* Stories

Even young children need a touch of wildness now and then, which is precisely what the English writer Ardizzone gave them in *Little Tim and the Brave Sea Captain*, his spirited account of Tim's adventures at sea. It all starts with Tim, who plays in and out of boats on the beach. How he becomes a stowaway, learns to be an efficient if reluctant deckhand, and experiences a shipwreck makes a thrilling story for the five- to eight-year-olds. Ardizzone's watercolors are as vigorous as his tale. Here is realism for the youngest at its most adventurous level. Tim's competence and achievements through a series of stories rouse the admiration of his young devotees. Ardizzone's books introduce other heroes, but Tim is the favorite.

Robert McCloskey
Make Way for Ducklings
Time of Wonder

Robert McCloskey was the first artist to win the Caldecott Medal twice, 1942 and 1958. If you look over his picture stories—*Make Way for Ducklings*, *One Morning in Maine*, and *Time of Wonder*—you discover that they are all built on a theme of reassurance. Children know the ducklings will come safely through their first perilous trip in city traffic because their mother has them in charge. And in that superb book in full color, *Time of Wonder*, the safe, secure world of woods and beach is threatened by the oncoming darkness of a hurricane. How the family prepares for and survives this menace is so convincingly told and pictured that children feel they too can meet and endure danger. The pictures in the first two books have humor and strength; some of the paintings in *Time of Wonder* have a breathtaking beauty. McCloskey's books for older children, *Homer Price* and *Centerburg Tales*, are written with a humor that has given them enduring popularity.

Carolyn Haywood
The *Betsy* Books
The *Little Eddie* Books

With the *Betsy* and the *Little Eddie* books of Carolyn Haywood, children progress from the picture story to the illustrated story, with the pictures ranking secondary in importance to the tale. Another mark of increasing maturity is that against a familiar background of family life, the young heroes and heroines move into an ever widening circle of neighborhood and school adventures, camps, and even travel.

"B" Is for Betsy launched the series of books about the everyday activities of a little girl in suburbia. While the characters in these books remained very close to stereotypes, it was the interpretation of their activities that held the attention of young readers. These gave the child greater self-knowledge, more understanding of other people and experiences, and a greater confidence in approaching their years of growing up. With *Little Eddie*, Carolyn Haywood developed the character of a real boy. Eddie is as earnest as Betsy, but much more alive. Also by Haywood, *The King's Monster* is both romantic and humorous, a tale in the folk tradition. These simply written stories have a warmth and a directness that win and hold young readers.

Taro Yashima
Crow Boy

Most of Taro Yashima's striking picture stories are set in his native Japan. *Plenty to Watch* by Taro and Mitsu Yashima tells of the shops and workers that Japanese children stop to watch as they walk home from school. The stores and the workers may differ from their American counterparts, but the story of children's insatiable curiosity is universal.

Crow Boy was a Caldecott Honor Book and also won the Child Study Award. It has unusual social values as well as pictorial beauty. Yashima's Crow Boy is a small, silent child who walks to school alone, sits alone, and does not talk. The children derisively call him "Chibi"— tiny boy. But a new schoolmaster discovers that the small outcast knows where wild potatoes and wild grapes grow, and he knows every call the crows make and can imitate them perfectly. When he does this for the children, they call him "Crow Boy" with respect, and he is one of them at last.

Joan Lexau
Olaf Reads
Benjie

Joan Lexau's stories have diversity of style, mood, and subject, but all of them have an understanding of the child's viewpoint, whether they are written for older readers or for children of kindergarten age. Her books for the youngest children are permeated with love and humor.

Olaf Reads is an amusing tale of a child so enthralled by his new prowess that he takes literally a sign that says "Pull," and finds the whole school responding with a fire drill. In *Benjie*, a very shy African-American child discovers, when he hunts for his grandmother's lost earring, that it isn't really so hard to talk to people; in *Benjie on His Own* he learns that he can call on his neighbors for help when his grandmother is ill.

Striped Ice Cream tells of a child in a working-class family who, tired of hand-me-down dresses from her sisters, is thrilled by a new dress *and* striped ice cream for her birthday. In *I'll Tell on You*, a girl feels she's not wanted by the coach of her Little League team.

Charlotte Zolotow
The Hating Book
A Father Like That
William's Doll

Few writers for small children so empathize with them as does Charlotte Zolotow, whose books—with some exceptions—are really explorations of relationships cast in story form and given vitality by perfected simplicity of style and by the humor and tenderness of the stories. *The Hating Book* describes the ups and downs of friendship. The mother of a fatherless child

From *The Hating Book* by Charlotte Zolotow, illustrated by Ben Shecter.

listens, in *A Father Like That*, to her son's catalog of virtues in his dream-father, who would *never* show off at parent-teacher meetings; *My Grandson Lew* is a tender story of remembrance. In *William's Doll*, Zolotow shows that little boys as well as little girls may want a doll with which to play. Zolotow's understanding of children's emotional needs and problems, and her ability to express them with candor, have made her one of the major contemporary writers of realistic books for small children.

Other Books for Younger Children

The profusion of picture-story books and books for the beginning reader makes it impossible to include every one of the many worthy books that have been published. Lois Lenski, whose regional stories are discussed later in this chapter, pioneered realism in books for the youngest children. The series that began with *The Little Auto*, followed by the later series about Debby and Davy, are direct and simple, with no wasted words. Johanna Hurwitz, in *Russell and Elisa*, takes a realistic look, affectionate and amused, at brother-sister relations. The engagingly homely children and deft humor of Harriet Pincus's illustrations add immeasurably to the bland text of Lore Segal's *Tell Me a Mitzi*, which has three stories of family life—as it really is. One tale is totally and amusingly improbable, but Mitzi and her little brother Jacob remain sturdily childlike.

Many authors have recognized the significance of grandparents for younger children. In *Now One Foot, Now the Other* by Tomie de Paola, a child whose grandfather had helped him learn to walk helps Grandpa relearn the skill after he's suffered a stroke. Max Lundgren, in *Matt's Grandfather*, a story set in Sweden, draws a realistic picture of a small child's acceptance of a senile grandparent. In Martha Alexander's *The Story Grandmother Told*, a bright-faced African-American child prompts Gramma to tell a favorite tale by telling it herself.

Death is shown as a part of life in an increasing number of books, even for younger children. In *The Two of Them* by Aliki, a grand-

From *Russell and Elisa* by Johanna Hurwitz, illustrated by Lillian Hoban.

father is remembered by his granddaughter. Tomie de Paola's *Nana Upstairs and Nana Downstairs* shows Tommy's adjustment to one death, and, much later, to another. The difficulty of adjusting to the death of a sibling, and particularly a twin, is honestly portrayed in *My Twin Sister Erika*, a story by Ilse-Margret Vogel, set in Germany.

Another part of life often overlooked by earlier writers was the disabled or mentally retarded child. In *He's My Brother* by Joe Lasker, a child who is simply slow is the center of interest. *Howie Helps Himself* by Joan Fassler describes Howie's final triumph of being able to manipulate his wheelchair by himself. Lucille Clifton's *My Friend Jacob* is a tender story of the friendship between a small African-American boy and a retarded white teenager.

Of the trends observable in contemporary publishing, the increased number of books about African-American children is a major one. Some of the books are simply affirmations of pride, like Ann McGovern's *Black Is Beautiful*; some reflect African-American history like Mary Sciosia's *Bicycle Rider*; and some are stories of African-American children showing competence, as in Janice Udry's *Mary Jo's*

From *The Two of Them*, written and illustrated by Aliki.

Grandmother or overcoming jealousy and learn-ing to love, as Robert does in John Steptoe's beautifully illustrated *Stevie*. Some books show adjustments to crowded living arrangements, as in June Jordan's *New Life: New Room* or a child seeking quiet in a crowded home, as in Elizabeth Hill's *Evan's Corner*. In some, the theme is one of problems raised by racial prejudice, such as Billy meets in *A New Home for Billy* by May Justus. In this story, an African-American family, anxious to move from a tene-ment to a house in the country, encounters barriers before they find a community that welcomes them.

Ruth Sonneborn's stories are about Puerto Rican children in the United States; they are stories of universal problems and joys, like the happiness of having the family all together in *Friday Night Is Papa Night*, rather than of difficulties faced because the children are Puerto Rican. *Magdalena* by Louisa Shotwell is the story of a lively Puerto Rican child and her beloved grandmother. Leo Politi's picture sto-ries focus on American children of various

ethnic backgrounds: Mexican-Americans in *Juanita*, Chinese in *Moy-Moy*, and Italian in *Little Leo*. In his Caldecott Medal book, *Song of the Swallows*, Politi describes the coming of spring to the mission of Capistrano. There is still a paucity of books about other minority groups for the youngest readers, but this may change.

Almost every trend in realistic fiction for older children seems to be followed by a similar trend in books for younger children. Topics that have been hitherto abjured have emerged, as does divorce in Beth Goff's *Where Is Daddy?*, or Judith Vigna's *Daddy's New Baby*.

Although children in the United States are enjoying more books from other countries than ever before, there are fewer picture stories being written about children of other lands. However, Ludwig Bemelmans's *Madeline*, set in France, is still read and loved. Marie Hall Ets is one of the few authors who writes about Mexican children; her books are discussed in Chapter 5.

Books for the Middle Group

Before examining present-day realistic stories for the middle and older children, we shall review some of the classic realistic stories that have been landmarks in the history of chil-dren's literature and that are popular still: *The Adventures of Tom Sawyer, Little Women, Hans Brinker, or the Silver Skates, Heidi,* and *The Secret Garden.*

Forerunners

A century ago, Samuel Clemens (Mark Twain) introduced children to the seamy side of village life. There, in *Tom Sawyer*, was the isolated country town Samuel Clemens himself had grown up in, with respectable churchgoers on one side and the village ne'er-do-wells on the other. Tom was the link between the two groups. By way of his friendship with Huck, the son of the town drunkard, he knew all the shady characters as well as his Aunt Polly's churchgoing friends. He saw a grave robbery and a murder and had other hair-raising adven-tures. This book gives children excitement, but it is not lurid or sensational. Along with the excitement and the humor, there is a steady emergence of Tom's code: He keeps his word to a friend; he may be scared to death, but he sees things through; in real peril, he protects a weaker person; and he uses his head, keeps cool, and keeps trying. This is as good a code today as it ever was.

Louisa May Alcott's *Little Women* deals with a family of four teenage girls, but it is to preteens that this book makes the greatest appeal— because of their interest in what lies just ahead, their first sense of romance, their dream of being grown up. Many young readers still enjoy *Little Women* as their great-great-grandmothers did. Here is the first great juvenile novel of family life—a warm, loving family group, struggling with poverty and with individual problems but sustained by an abiding affection for each other and an innocent kind of gaiety that could make its own fun. Not until the Laura Ingalls Wilder series do we again encounter such a picture of a family, and in no one of the Wilder series is each member of the group more distinctly drawn than are the unforgettable Beth, Jo, Meg, and Amy. Here is characterization that makes each girl a real human being—exasperating, lovable, heroic, absurd, delightful.

Hans Brinker, or the Silver Skates by Mary Mapes Dodge and *Heidi*, written in German by Johanna Spyri, a Swiss, and translated into English in 1884, introduced children in the United States and Canada to daily life in other countries through a strong and engaging story, a tradition that has continued. *Hans Brinker, or the Silver Skates* was immediately successful. It was translated into many languages, and the Dutch people accepted it as the best picture of childhood in Holland that had ever been written until that time.[1] Dodge had become deeply interested in the history of the Dutch republic and had a twofold purpose: to tell a story about the children of Holland and to weave into that story as much of the history and customs of the people as she could.

Heidi uses one of the most popular of themes—a variation of the Cinderella syndrome in which the unwanted, neglected child comes into her own. However, there is a convincing quality about *Heidi* which many modern Cinderellas lack. The child is full of the joy of living. She skips and leaps and she falls in love with an apparently grouchy old grandfather, the goats, and the mountains, all with equal vehemence and loyalty. No child who has read and loved *Heidi* will ever enter Switzerland without a feeling of familiarity. This is what books about other countries should do for children—leave them feeling forever a part of that country, forever well disposed toward the people. Such stories of other people create no sense of oddity, no feeling of irreconcilable differences, but a desire to know these people so like themselves.

For a long period after *Tom Sawyer*, *Little Women*, *Hans Brinker*, and *Heidi* appeared, there was as little substantial realism for older children as there was for the youngest. Frances Hodgson Burnett's *The Secret Garden* did in some measure span the gap between these early books and those realistic stories which are comparatively recent. It has maintained a following of devoted readers to this very day, telling a fairy tale of children misunderstood and suffering but conquering all. The heroine of *The Secret Garden*, Mary, is plain and bad tempered as well as orphaned and neglected. In the huge estate where she is sent to live, Mary discovers a secret garden, a master with a crooked back, and his ailing son, Colin. She also meets Martha and several members of her kind family. Among them, they get the wretched Colin into the secret garden with Mary; the children make the garden grow and bloom once more, without realizing that in the process they, too, will grow and bloom.

Eleanor Estes
The *Moffat* Stories
The Hundred Dresses
Ginger Pye

Within the United States one of the most captivating book families is unquestionably the Moffats, created by Eleanor Estes. There are four of these books—*The Moffats*, *The Middle Moffat*, *Rufus M.*, and *The Moffat Museum*.

[1]Bertha Mahony and Elinor Whitney, comps., *Realms of Gold in Children's Books*. Garden, 1929, p. 611.

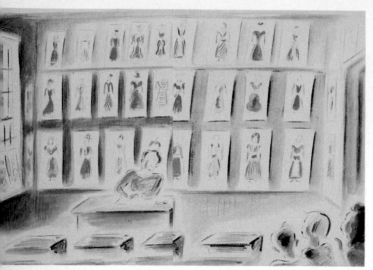

From *The Hundred Dresses* by Eleanor Estes, illustrated by Louis Slobodkin.

The stories are set in the 1910s, but the characters and their problems are so real and so universal they seem timeless. There is no general theme, no long suspense, and no exciting climax to these books. Each chapter is a complete episode in the life of one of the Moffats.

The ultimate humor in these situations, for all but the last in the series, is provided by the artist Louis Slobodkin. The Moffat tales and Slobodkin's illustrations represent the perfect union of story and pictures—Rufus M. leaping for a deadly catch in a baseball game; Janey viewing the world amiably from an upside-down angle, looking between her own stout legs, head almost on the ground.

Also illustrated by Slobodkin, Estes's *The Hundred Dresses* is one of the most effective indictments of prejudice in children's literature, and a poignant story told in an easy, natural style. Wanda Petronski is an outsider, poor and ill-clad, who says she has a hundred dresses at home. She does, and she's drawn them all. Her pictures, exhibited at school, win a medal, but Wanda isn't there to receive it. A note from her father says they have moved to a place where "No more holler Polack. No more ask why funny name. . . ." Eleanor Estes was awarded the Newbery Medal for *Ginger Pye*, a story about a family that loses its dog and finds

him through the kind offices of three-year-old Uncle Benny. In *The Lost Umbrella of Kim Chu*, a nine-year-old resident of New York's Chinatown solves a mystery. Estes creates real children wrapped up in their own concerns, playing, interacting, paying scant attention to mere adult problems.

Elizabeth Enright
The *Saturdays* Stories
The *Gone-Away Lake* Stories
Thimble Summer

Elizabeth Enright had a gift for realism. *The Saturdays* introduces the four Melendys, ranging in age from six to thirteen. They pool all their allowances and permit one child to use the whole amount for a Saturday, each in turn. The results are often startling and always amusing. *The Four Story Mistake* and *Then There Were Five* continue the family activities in the country and lead to the adoption of a country boy.

The Melendy family has been almost superseded by the popular cousins in *Gone-Away Lake*. In the first book, Portia and her cousin Julian discover an abandoned colony of summer cottages near a swamp that was once a lovely, sparkling lake. In the second book, *Return to Gone-Away*, the family makes the joyous decision to restore one of the old houses and live there the year round. Enright's style is so forthright and lively that this unusual setting becomes completely real and the reader shares the family's joy in that final decision.

The Newbery Medal was given to Enright's *Thimble Summer*, a family story set on a Midwestern farm in the midst of a burning drought. Just as the drought is broken by a drenching rain, Garnet finds a silver thimble, which she is convinced will bring her a lucky summer. Enright's children are, like those created by Estes, very real, although somewhat more venturesome.

Marguerite de Angeli
Bright April
Thee, Hannah!

Bright April was one of the earliest books to focus on the problems of an African-American child. The youngest in a prosperous, middle-class family, April finds a happy solution to her difficulties with a prejudiced member of her Brownie troop. There are many books for and about African-American children now, and books that show urban ghetto life, not just comfortable middle-class surroundings, but this was a rarity when it was published. Marguerite de Angeli was also a pioneer in relating stories about the minority groups around her home in Philadelphia. Her stories are slight, but the warm pictures she paints, both with colors and words, of Amish, Quaker, and Pennsylvania Dutch children are important. *Henner's Lydia*, *Yonie Wondernose*, and *Thee, Hannah!* are all pleasant stories about interesting people.

Of first importance are de Angeli's illustrations. These are beautiful in color with springtime freshness and innocence. To be sure, her children—whatever their sex, nationality, or disposition—always have the same little heart-shaped faces and wistful beauty, but they have also a skipping gaiety which is natural to childhood.

Lois Lenski
Strawberry Girl

In 1946, when the Newbery Medal was given to Lois Lenski's *Strawberry Girl*, attention was called to a unique series of books about regional groups from all over the United States.

Lois Lenski began her series with *Bayou Suzette*, a story about the French-speaking people in the bayou section of Louisiana. After *Strawberry Girl* of Florida came *Judy's Journey*, which followed the crop pickers from California to Florida and back to New Jersey. There are many more, including *High-Rise Secret,* which is set in a high-rise housing project.

Strawberry Girl is typical of these books at their best. It is the story of Birdie Boyer's family, newly moved to Florida's backwoods for the purpose of raising small crops of "sweet 'taters," strawberries, oranges, and the like.

The values of this series are to be found in its objective realism and compassion. Young members of disadvantaged families meet families like their own in these regional stories of Lois Lenski's. And they take heart, because always the ups and downs of these hardpressed, coura-

geous people yield a ray of hope. Things are, or give promise of becoming, better. And to the children of more affluent families, these books give a picture of a kind of family love and loyalty that may be new to them.

Beverly Cleary
The *Henry Huggins* Stories
The *Ramona* Stories
Mitch and Amy
Dear Mr. Henshaw

Beverly Cleary's *Henry Huggins* books are pure Americana, from supermarkets to backyard barbecues, delightfully humorous.

The Huggins family is an average group. The parents are sympathetic to Henry's enterprises but not overly indulgent. All the children in the stories are pursuing their own goals with the frustrations usual to children. The first book

From *Dear Mr. Henshaw* by Beverly Cleary, illustrated by Paul O. Zelinsky.

begins with Henry's determination to keep a stray dog he has acquired.

There are several other books about Henry; each book is built around a real struggle on Henry's part and involves some very funny situations before a hard-won success.

There are six delightful books about Henry's nemesis. Ramona is probably the first kindergarten dropout on record in *Ramona the Pest*, having become convinced that the teacher, whom she adores, doesn't love her any more. We follow *Ramona the Brave* to first grade, where she finds the basics boring, but life still worth living. In *Ramona Quimby, Age 8*, one of several sequels, Ramona battles her way through each day, adjusting to a new school and a new teacher; and in *Ramona Forever*, she faces the knowledge that changes lie ahead.

A serious problem for many children is presented in a realistic and encouraging way in *Mitch and Amy*. Mitch and Amy are fourth-grade twins, he a slow reader and she a proficient one. They are, except when under attack,

very competitive, yet it is Amy who finds the book that starts Mitch on the path to self-motivated reading. Cleary has continued to display versatility in her newer books. *Lucky Chuck* is a hilarious, deadpan story of an adolescent motorcycle rider. *Dear Mr. Henshaw*, for which the author was awarded the Newbery Medal, is an often poignant, often funny story of a child's correspondence with a writer whose books he enjoys. Through letters and journal entries, Cleary takes the protagonist from second grade to sixth, in a completely convincing picture of a child's maturation.

Cleary's characters are real boys and girls, convincingly alive, and the style of the books is correspondingly plain and everyday, but filled with the type of humor that appeals to her young audience. It is for the body of her work that she won the Wilder Award in 1975.

Meindert DeJong
The Wheel on the School
Journey from Peppermint Street
Far Out the Long Canal
The House of Sixty Fathers

The Wheel on the School, a tenderly told story which won the Newbery Medal, gives a remarkably detailed picture of life in a Dutch fishing village and also has unusual social values. The story begins in the tiny village school, when Lina, the only girl, asks, "Do you know about storks?" This leads to more questions and launches a series of activities that begins with the six children and the schoolmaster but presently draws into the circle every person in the village.

Although the book is long for its story, it reads aloud wonderfully and can promote many discussions about the people, the lonely land of sea and sky that is Holland, and the wonder of those great birds that fly home all the way from Africa.

Journey from Peppermint Street, which won the National Book Award for Children's Literature, is set in Holland in the early 1900s. Beautifully written, it is the story of a small boy who goes with his grandfather on a long night walk to visit an "inland aunt." The relationship between the old man and the child, the satisfac-

From *The House of Sixty Fathers* by Meindert DeJong, illustrated by Maurice Sendak.

tion at conquering his nervousness in a strange place, and the confidence gained by little Siebren as he meets new people, have a universality that transcends the setting.

Another story set in Holland is *Far Out the Long Canal*. Because the ice has been bad for several years, and he has had a long illness, nine-year-old Moonta is the only child in town who cannot skate. Any reader can sympathize with his embarrassment, his secret struggles, and the alternate teasing and comfort he gets from friends and family. *The House of Sixty Fathers* is a vividly realistic story, set in China, of a boy who searches for his lost family.

Although DeJong's style is often repetitious and occasionally ponderous, he has the gift of wonder and delight. Whatever the outward action of his tales, it is the inner grace of his children and animals that moves readers, young or old. It is not surprising that in 1962 he won the Hans Christian Andersen International Award for his contribution to the world of children's literature.

From *The Family Under the Bridge* by Natalie Savage Carlson, illustrated by Garth Williams.

Natalie Savage Carlson
The Family Under the Bridge
The *Orphelines* Books
The Empty Schoolhouse

Some of the liveliest stories about Paris are Natalie Carlson's *The Family Under the Bridge* and her series about the Orphelines. *The Family Under the Bridge* has to do with the post-World War II period in Paris when housing was difficult to find. The hero is an elderly, jaunty hobo who has found himself a snug corner under an old bridge. He returns there and finds it occupied by three children. This is the beginning of the end for carefree, soft-hearted Armand. His series of adventures are sometimes very funny and sometimes sad, but in the end he finds himself the adopted grandfather of a family. No pathos here, just a determined struggle for a stable, decent way of life.

The books about the Orphelines reverse the usual pattern of sad orphans hoping to be adopted. These French orphans love their home to the point where their one fear is adoption. When in *The Happy Orpheline* poor Brigitte is about to be adopted, she knows she must perform a very wicked deed of some kind to prove she isn't fit for adoption. What she does is hilarious and makes a fitting if confused climax to the adventures of the twenty Orphelines who are still twenty strong at the end.

Emma, who tells the story of *The Empty Schoolhouse*, has dropped out of school but is proud of her bright little sister Lullah. Lullah is African American, her friend Oralee white, and they are delighted that there is going to be an integrated school in their Louisiana parish. There is trouble, though, and parents keep their children away. When Lullah is hurt in a racial incident, the rift between her and Oralee grows—but it is healed, and the episode shocks some parents into a reversal of their decision.

Ann Aurelia and Dorothy is another book about an interracial friendship, and *Marchers for the Dream* tells about an eleven-year-old girl who goes with her grandmother to Washington to join the Poor People's March. Whatever their settings, Carlson's stories have realistic characters who often display a gentle humor.

Keith Robertson
The *Henry Reed* Stories
In Search of a Sandhill Crane

Children need books also which demonstrate that life is not always earnest, that it can in fact be highly entertaining. *Henry Reed, Inc.* is such a book. It is Henry's private journal. On a visit to his uncle and aunt who live in the country near Princeton, Henry hears all about the research at that university; so he decides to go into research. He takes over an old barn and paints an enormous sign: HENRY REED, RESEARCH. To the sign, a girl who finds her way into this intellectual domain adds: PURE AND APPLIED. She wants her name added too, but Henry is adamant—she must first prove her worth. Their research activities make this book hilarious reading. Other Henry Reed stories are direct narrative, equally amusing and often mirroring some new technological trend: Despite the cordless telephones and computers in *Henry Reed's Think Tank*, things haven't really changed much in Grover's Corner.

Robertson, a versatile author, writes another type of story in *In Search of a Sandhill Crane*. Fifteen-year-old Link spends the summer with an elderly aunt in the Michigan woods, and becomes passionately interested in sandhill cranes. The story is well structured, with a wealth of natural lore, and sympathetic, convincing characters.

Mary Stolz
By the Highway Home
The Noonday Friends
A Wonderful, Terrible Time
The *Barkham Street* Stories

Mary Stolz is a prolific author and one of the few who write with admirable perception for all ages. In *By the Highway Home*, the death of an older brother, the loss of the father's job, and a subsequent move to a new home create problems of adjustment for a girl of thirteen. A lost job also adds to the tensions in *The Noonday Friends*, in which Franny can see her friend only at lunchtime because Franny must take care of her little brother after school. The story is perceptive in reflecting the way emotions are affected by circumstances and in drawing the relationship between Franny and the small brother who depends on her.

The two friends in *A Wonderful, Terrible Time* are African-American girls who go to an interracial summer camp. Sue Ellen is apprehensive; Mady is thrilled and enjoys every moment. Sue Ellen never wants to talk about serious things; Mady—whose father had been killed in a voter registration drive—does. Integration is not the issue of the book but is one of several problems considered to show the differences in the reactions of the two girls.

The problems a close-knit family faces when one of them dies are honestly and perceptively described in *The Edge of Next Year*. In *A Dog on Barkham Street* and *The Bully of Barkham Street*, the same events are considered from different viewpoints. In *The Explorer of Barkham Street*, the ex-bully discovers that one of the frontiers of exploration is self-knowledge.

Stolz brings a special sense of reality to her characters; they are well developed, sympathetically presented, and worth knowing.

Jean Little
Mine for Keeps
Home from Far
Look Through My Window

Born blind, Canadian Jean Little understands the child who is different, and has the ability to spin a good story which makes such differences natural and comprehensible. In *Mine for Keeps*, Sally, who has cerebral palsy, comes home after five years at a school for disabled children, her apprehension about getting along mixed with self-pity. Through the help of her family and through her own interest in others, Sally gradually overcomes her fears and becomes more independent. The story treats the difficulties of a disabled child matter-of-factly, emphasizing that the family has to adjust to the situation and that each of them makes mistakes.

In *Home from Far*, soon after Jenny's twin brother Michael is killed, her parents bring two foster children into the home, one named Mike and the same age as Jenny. This is a sensitive study of the attitudes and emotions of children, particularly of Jenny, who at first bitterly resents Mike, and of Mike, who misses his real father. Another story of adjustment is Little's *Mama's Going to Buy You a Mockingbird*, dealing with the death of a parent.

In *Look Through My Window*, Emily's horizons are broadened by a new friend who has one Jewish parent. The discussions between Emily and Kate are candid; those between Emily and her mother tender and sensible; and those between Kate and her father perceptive and honest, as they talk about what it is to be Jewish. In the sequel, *Kate*, the girl moves further to explore her ambivalence and to discover why her father had severed connections with his family. Jean Little has a rare ability to see problems and their ramifications from the viewpoint of the child.

Yoshiko Uchida
The Birthday Visitor
Hisako's Mysteries
In-between Miya

Yoshiko Uchida's versatility is demonstrated by the fact that she has written books for all ages and in several literary styles, from the simplicity of picture story books through the several collections of Japanese folk tales cited in the bibliography for Chapter 6, to the historical fiction discussed in Chapter 11. American-born, Uchida was one of the many Nisei who were sent to a relocation center, an experience reflected in several of her books.

The Birthday Visitor (set in California) is colored by traditional quality: the respect due a guest in one's home. Emi, sulking because a minister from Japan is coming as a houseguest and will surely spoil her birthday dinner, is delighted when the guest proves to be both sympathetic and entertaining. Again, the quality of Japanese-American family life is reflected in the firm but gentle discipline Emi gets from her parents.

In such stories as *Hisako's Mysteries* and *In-between Miya*, both of which are about girls who visit relatives in Tokyo, Uchida explores some of the common problems of preadolescence: friendship values, self-image, conflicting goals, and one's relationships with parents.

Marilyn Sachs
The *Peter and Veronica* Stories
The Bears' House
Fran Ellen's House
The Fat Girl

In *Veronica Ganz* and *Peter and Veronica*, Marilyn Sachs introduces a perennial bully who becomes friends with the smallest boy in the class. Peter, in the second book, is first angry with his mother because she doesn't want his non-Jewish friend to come to his bar mitzvah then—after he has persuaded his mother—he is angry at Veronica because she doesn't attend. Both in the candor with which Peter and Veronica discuss their mothers' prejudices and in the new maturity with which they mend their quarrel, the story is honest and percipient.

A broken home and a mother unable to face reality create a burden impossible for Fletcher and Fran Ellen to shoulder in *The Bears' House*: Fantasies about the dollhouse in her classroom serve as a release for Fran Ellen's emotions; and finally, adults intervene in the situation. *Fran Ellen's House* brings the family's affairs to a touching conclusion. In *A Secret Friend*, an interracial friendship is established after a painful, jealous triangle situation is resolved.

For an audience slightly older than the one in the books just discussed, Sachs has written *The Fat Girl*, which has a Pygmalion theme. With great insight, Sachs develops a change in Jeff as fat Ellen, a girl whom he's disparaged and mocked, begins to respond to his program for improving her. In the end, Jeff's protégé becomes a "butterfly" who no longer needs him.

Sachs has done a fine job of writing for reluctant adolescent readers in *Bus Ride* and *Thunderbird*. She has a sympathetic understanding of children's concerns and problems, and handles conflicts between generations honestly and realistically. Her dialogue is fresh, breezy, and often very funny.

Louise Fitzhugh
Harriet the Spy
The Long Secret

The very funny and very touching story of *Harriet the Spy* aroused vigorous controversy for the portraits it drew of prying, quarrelsome

From *Harriet the Spy*, written and illustrated by Louise Fitzhugh.

Harriet and of her parents, too busy with their social life to pay much attention to their child until she was in real trouble. Eleven-year-old Harriet aspires to be a writer, and, encouraged by her nurse, Ole Golly, keeps notes about everything that happens to her and her friends and to the people she studies on her after-school spy route.

The sequel, *The Long Secret*, is less intense, more sophisticated, and equally funny at times. Harriet, curious as ever but now on very close terms with her parents, is at the beach for the summer. So is the shy Beth of *Harriet the Spy*, now terrified because her mother, a jet set butterfly, has come to disrupt the quiet life Beth and her grandmother lead. The inclusion of an evangelist family, several jaded characters of the jet set, and a wise old man make the book more cluttered and not as effective as *Harriet*, but it has two episodes that are particularly perceptive. In one, Harriet and her mother have a serious discussion of faith and religion, and in the other Harriet and her friends talk about menstruation, a long-standing taboo subject in children's books.

While Harriet has problems many children don't want, she also has a brash courage many children envy. Her honesty makes her an irresistible character.

Robert Burch
Queenie Peavy
The *Ida Early* Books

Queenie Peavy is a story of the Depression era, set in Georgia, where Queenie, thirteen, has a deserved reputation as a troublemaker and a hoyden. Fiercely loyal to her father, who is in jail, she faces a painful readjustment when he comes home, shows neither affection nor responsibility, breaks his parole, and is returned to jail. Queenie, a staunch little character, realizes that any change in her status must now come from her own changed attitude and behavior. Candid in treatment of the father, this is one of the books that lucidly exemplifies the end of the perfect-parent image in children's literature.

Joey's Cat, a pleasant story for younger children, is about a small African-American boy who is delighted when his mother changes her mind and lets him bring his cat and her kittens into the house. Burch introduced a new and beguiling character in *Ida Early Comes Over the Mountain* and *Christmas with Ida Early*. Ida is tall, rawboned, cheerful, and breezily competent, and she quickly wins the hearts of the children who have lost their mother. They have more than a housekeeper, they have a friend and protector, in stories that are both poignant and blithe.

Paula Fox
Maurice's Room
The Stone-Faced Boy
Portrait of Ivan
One-Eyed Cat
The Moonlight Man

With the publication of *Maurice's Room* in 1966, it became immediately clear that Paula Fox was one of the best new writers in the field of children's literature. Her style is quiet, her vision penetrating, her understanding of children deep and sympathetic. Maurice is an only child whose room is a haven for anything and everything he finds. His parents attempt subtle distractions, but there is no stopping a born collector: When the family moves to the country, Maurice is bored until he sees the barn, full of old things.

A Likely Place is a testament to the joy of competence. Lewis, tired of the adults who want to help or to improve him, takes great delight in his friendship with an elderly gentleman who treats him as an equal.

In *The Stone-Faced Boy*, a child who is shy and withdrawn in the midst of a boisterous family takes refuge in looking impassive. Only one elderly great-aunt sees what lies behind the stoic facade. This empathetic relationship between a child and someone outside his immediate family is used again in *Portrait of Ivan*, in which lonely Ivan's friendship with the artist who is painting his portrait helps Ivan gain confidence to approach his busy, remote father. The writing is skilled, and the characters are superbly drawn. *Blowfish Live in the Sea* exemplifies through a girl's acceptance of her brother's frailties, the bonds of family love. *How Many Miles to Babylon?* is the story of an African-American child persecuted by a gang of older boys.

One-Eyed Cat is remarkable for the nuance of the writing, the depth of its insight, the compassionate many-layered development of the protagonist and other characters. Told by his father that he's too young to use an air rifle, Ned sneaks out one night to try the rifle and thinks he has hit something. Later, seeing the one-eyed cat, Ned is racked by guilt and remorse. What is in Ned is in every child—most readers will recognize it. In *A Place Apart*, Fox explores the bittersweet experience of an adolescent girl who is at first captivated by, then disappointed in, a totally selfish charmer. In *The Moonlight Man*, Fox depicts the painful ambivalence of a child's love for an alcoholic father, and in *The Village by the Sea*, she shows how imaginative play can alleviate tension. With the historical novel *The Slave Dancer*, Fox won the Newbery Medal, and in 1978 she was given the Hans Christian Andersen Award.

Zilpha Keatley Snyder
The Egypt Game
The Headless Cupid and Other
Amanda Stories
A Fabulous Creature

One of the notable books of 1967 and a Newbery Honor Book, *The Egypt Game* is an absorbing story of sustained, imaginative group play and of interracial friendship. Surprisingly for a child's book, the characters include a murderer who almost captures one of the girls. The children are vividly real, their Egypt Game absorbing, their conversation and personalities distinctive.

The interest of the young in astrology and the supernatural is reflected in *The Headless Cupid*, in which an unhappy adolescent persuades her newly acquired stepbrothers and

From *Zeely* by Virginia Hamilton, illustrated by Symeon Shimin.

stepsisters to become her disciples in the occult. Only when there seems to be evidence of a poltergeist does Amanda lose her pose of superiority. In one sequel, *The Famous Stanley Kidnapping Case*, Amanda's brothers and sister insist—in a very funny story—on going along when she's kidnapped. In a second sequel, *Blair's Nightmare*, the youngest child is protected by his siblings.

Two Vietnamese children join Janie Stanley's "detective agency" in *Janie's Private Eyes*. In *A Fabulous Creature*, an adolescent boy is disillusioned when the girl on whom he has a crush breaks his trust and kills the beautiful stag he's told her about. Readers can decide for themselves whether it is the stag that is the fabulous creature or the young girl whose integrity and compassion stand in such stark contrast to the selfishness of the older girl who has shot the stag. *The Birds of Summer*, one of Snyder's most serious novels, is the story of a teenage girl who is determined to save her little sister from a shiftless, amoral mother. These stories are realistic but often involve some supernatural elements which give them an eeriness seldom found in children's books at this level.

Virginia Hamilton
Zeely
M. C. Higgins, the Great
The House of Dies Drear
Willie Bea and the Time the Martians Landed
A Little Love

A gifted African-American writer, Virginia Hamilton has shown versatility in the range of her books. In *Zeely*, a child visiting in the country is smitten by the beauty of a neighbor who looks like a Watusi queen. The book is impressive both as a picture of a girl's crush on an adult and as a record of a child's growing understanding of racial identity.

The danger posed by the Cumberland Mountains makes M. C., thirteen, long to have his family move. But M. C.'s experiences with a folklorist and a girl from "outside," as well as his father's attachment to his ancestral home, make his dreams seem impossible. *M. C. Higgins, the Great*, written in an intricate yet graceful style, won both the Newbery Award and the National Book Award in 1975.

In *The Time-Ago Tales of Jahdu* and *Time-Ago Lost: More Tales of Jahdu*, Lee Edward stays each day with Mama Luka until his mother is home from work, and each day he hears another story of the legendary Jahdu, crafty and powerful. The tales are beautifully told in the folk tradition, and the small boy learns the joy of being proud of his African-American heritage.

The House of Dies Drear is a dramatic story set in an old house that had been a station on the Underground Railroad; its sequel is *The Mystery of Drear House*. In *Arilla Sun Down*, Hamilton uses flashbacks to tell the story of a child who knows her African- and native-American roots, but seeks self-identity. *The Planet of Junior Brown*, a memorable book for older readers, is an imaginative and touching story of a friendship between two boys who are loners, each in a different way.

In an engrossing family story, *Willie Bea and the Time the Martians Landed*, Hamilton creates vividly the apprehension felt by many who listened to, and were duped by, the Orson Welles 1938 radio broadcast. In one of the most tender stories she has written for older children, the author creates a memorable heroine; Sheema is intellectually limited, short and fat—but in *A Little Love* she learns how deep and solid is the love her guardians and her lover have for her, and how important that love is.

Hamilton is a skilled writer, one of our great stylists, presenting the African-American experience with singular distinction of style and viewpoint, and with nuances of meaning for the more mature or culturally aware reader.

Vera and Bill Cleaver
The Ellen Grae Books
Where the Lilies Bloom

Although there had been other books about children of divorce before *Ellen Grae* was published, none had so firmly stated by implication the fact that a parent's love and responsibility are not changed by divorce. Ellen Grae tells her own story, and it becomes instantly apparent that she is an accomplished and artistic teller of tall tales and that she is a child with great sensitivity and loyalty. Despite the seriousness of the problem that faces Ellen Grae and despite its less than satisfactory resolution, the story is permeated with humor. Its sequel, *Lady Ellen Grae*, has less impact but is written with vivacity and sharp characterization.

The heroine of *Where the Lilies Bloom* is one of the strongest characters in children's fiction. Fourteen-year-old Mary Call Luther buries her father herself, and valiantly tries to hold together the family—which includes a mentally retarded older sister—so that the four children will not be sent to a county charity home. This is an excellent example of the need for security as well as of the need to achieve.

In *I Would Rather Be a Turnip* twelve-year-old Annie Jelks faces a problem that is seldom presented in children's books, the acceptance of an illegitimate child. The plight of an unwanted child is explored in *Moon Lake Angel*. *Sugar Blue* deals candidly with jealousy and resentment of a younger child. The Cleavers deal perceptively with the intricacies of serious problems yet lighten their stories with humor. These books are prime examples of the changes that have occurred in what has been considered appropriate in children's books.

Elaine Konigsburg
From the Mixed-Up Files of Mrs. Basil E. Frankweiler
Jennifer, Hecate, Macbeth, William McKinley, and Me, Elizabeth
(George)

In 1968, Elaine Konigsburg made history in children's books when her *From the Mixed-Up Files of Mrs. Basil E. Frankweiler* was awarded the Newbery Medal and her *Jennifer, Hecate, Macbeth, William McKinley, and Me, Elizabeth* was voted a Newbery Honor Book. They were her first two books. *From the Mixed-Up Files* is an engaging story of two children who leave home and take up residence in the Metropolitan Museum of Art, the details of the expedition capably planned by the older child, Claudia. The unlikely setting is made believable by the bland perfection of details.

Jennifer, Hecate, Macbeth, William McKinley, and Me, Elizabeth is a story of interracial friendship and sustained imaginative play in which Jennifer, a self-declared witch, permits Elizabeth (who tells the story) to become her apprentice. Both in the relationship between the two protagonists and in their relationships to others there is delightful warmth and humor.

(George) deals with a serious problem, the schizoid personality, yet the book has high humor, tenderness, and a lively plot. The distinctive achievement of *(George)* is that it enables the reader to see beyond the psychological problems of the boy: Ben is human, intelligent, loving.

About the B'nai Bagels is a cheerful story, less dramatic than the other Konigsburg books, but enjoyable for the felicity with which Mark describes the awfulness of having his mother manage his Little League team; the nervous pleasure of his first look at a girly magazine; and the indignation aroused by his first encounter with anti-Semitism. *Father's Arcane Daughter* is a deftly structured story in which the question is whether or not the woman who claims to have been kidnapped seventeen years earlier, is telling the truth. *Altogether, One at a Time* is a collection of four deftly written short stories, different in plot and mood, alike in their theme of compromise with circumstance. Eccentric but believable characters enliven the story of a boy who gets over being a snob in *Journey to an 800 Number*.

Whatever her theme, Konigsburg's stories are amusingly told, with solid substance underneath.

Betsy Byars
The Midnight Fox
The Summer of the Swans
The Night Swimmers
The Pinballs
The Bingo Brown Books

Although not all her books are humorous, there is in most of Betsy Byars's writing a quiet, understated sense of humor that children quickly recognize and enjoy. More evident, and just as much appreciated, are her compassion and her understanding of the deepest emotions of children. And, as in *The Midnight Fox*, there is an empathy with children's love of animals. Tom, an urban child visiting relatives, becomes

From *The Cybil War* by Betsy Byars, illustrated by Gail Owens.

In *The Night Swimmers*, Byars again explores a situation and a turning point in a child's life with insight, again writes with tenderness and grace, again creates a memorable character. Retta is the oldest of three children; motherless, she is a mother to her younger brothers; she is bereft when they develop other interests, confused by her own reactions of jealousy and resentment. The situation is resolved when a friend of their father's takes over; only when she realizes that she can be a child—that somebody else will assume the role of protector—does Retta accept the change in her role, in a story that is touching but never saccharine.

Byars has written some fantasy and some lightly humorous stories like *The Cybil War* and *The Not-Just-Anybody Family* (the Blossoms) and its sequels, but her strong forte is in depicting troubled children. In *The Pinballs,* she depicts the camaraderie of those who are joined in misfortune, in a vivid story about three foster children who gain security from each other and their affectionate foster parents; in *The TV Kid*, a hospitalized child gets over his addiction to television shows; in *Cracker Jackson*, a child reacts to the abuse of someone he loves. *The Burning Questions of Bingo Brown* and *Bingo Brown and the Language of Love* are sympathetic but very funny books about first love. In all her books, Byars affirms a respect for children's resiliency and strength.

Constance Greene
The *Al* Books
The *Isabelle* Books
The Unmaking of Rabbit

There is poignant sympathy for the girl in Constance Greene's *A Girl Called Al*. Plump and caustic, Al is a nonconformist who is won over by the understanding friendship of the building superintendent and then is catapulted into maturity by his death. *I Know You, Al* tells us more about Al as she faces the problems in her life: being the only girl in the class who hasn't yet begun to menstruate, not liking her mother's suitor, and meeting the father she hasn't seen for eight years. Both these stories are entertaining, warm, and perceptive, as are their sequels, *Your Old Pal Al, Al(exandra) the Great,* and *Just Plain Al.* Two stories about a

absorbed in watching a fox and her cub; when his uncle pens the cub as bait to trap the mother, Tom releases it, and is delighted when his aunt and uncle prove to be understanding about his deed.

The compassion depicted in Tom appears again in Byars's Newbery Medal book, *The Summer of the Swans*, one of the early books about a retarded child. Charlie's sister Sara is loving and protective, terrified when Charlie is lost, and glad of the help of a friend, Joe, in finding him. Sara, fourteen and shy, accepts a party invitation from Joe, and comes to a turning point. Like the swans she and Charlie have watched, she knows for the first time that she will move from a first, awkward flight to the confidence of being in her own element. The book has a tender quality and has enough action to balance the quiet unfolding of a situation.

fifth-grader who gravitates toward trouble are *Isabelle Shows Her Stuff* and *Isabelle and Little Orphan Frannie*.

Greene turns to boys and their problems in *The Unmaking of Rabbit*. Paul is shorter than the other boys in his class and has large ears that stick out. Paul gathers his courage, reads a paper in class about refusing to join a gang for break-ins, and is invited to join another group for sleep-outs. In *Ask Anybody*, an uneasy friendship ends when Ned's feckless family hastily leaves town. Both stories are realistic and written with ease and humor, with sympathetic characters who have believable problems.

Judy Blume
Are You There God? It's Me, Margaret
Then Again, Maybe I Won't
Tales of a Fourth Grade Nothing

Judy Blume has written a number of frank stories that discuss problems formerly referred to only in veiled terms in books for children. In *Are You There God? It's Me, Margaret*, Margaret and her friends are concerned with physical maturity: When will they begin to menstruate and when will their breasts develop? Margaret is also confused about religion; will she be Jewish like her father or Christian like her mother? Her problems are not completely resolved within the confines of the book, but Margaret does decide that her faith is strong, that she can worship in her own way, whatever her formal affiliation.

In *Then Again, Maybe I Won't*, Blume writes with sympathetic insight about an adolescent boy disturbed by his family's changed attitude when they become well-to-do, and by his first sexual stirrings. Two preadolescents admit a Vietnamese adoptee into their close friendship in *Just As Long As We're Together*. In both *Deenie* and *Blubber*, the protagonists are troubled by adjustment to physical disabilities.

Blume's books for younger children are sunny and humorous: *Tales of a Fourth Grade Nothing* and its sequel *Superfudge* explore the vicissitudes of life with a precocious little brother, and in *The Pain and the Great One*, a sister and her little brother express, in no uncertain terms, what each thinks of the other.

Blume is astute in her choices of contemporary themes; her dialogue is natural, her characters believable, and her style direct and unaffected. Her stories have a pervasive sense of humor as well as an affectionate understanding of children and young people.

Eleanor Cameron
The *Julia* Books
To the Green Mountains

Although Canadian-born Eleanor Cameron was first known as a writer of fantasy, and won the National Book Award in 1974 for the fantasy *The Court of the Stone Children*, it is in her realistic writing that her skill at perceptive characterization is most notable.

In *A Room Made of Windows*, the protagonist, Julia, wants to be a writer; self-centered and sensitive, she is distracted by the resentment she feels because her widowed mother plans to marry. The book has a deft meshing of minor plot threads and a smooth, logical development of change in Julia, as she grows more mature and more responsive to the needs of others. *Julia and the Hand of God* predates the first book, describing a younger Julia; it is more dramatic, including a fire that sweeps through the city; it is just as deftly written, and concludes with the family's move to a new home where Julia finds her many-windowed room. Set even further back are *That Julia Redfern* and *Julia's Magic*, while a book published after them, *The Private Worlds of Julia Redfern*, is a direct sequel to the first book.

In *To the Green Mountains*, there is more depth and maturity in Cameron's writing, and the same adroit integration of subplots. Kath, whose mother manages a small hotel, is devoted to an African-American man on the staff and disturbed because there is censure of her mother for helping him in his plans to become a lawyer. She's also upset when her mother decides she wants a divorce from her shiftless husband, but pleased by the prospect of returning to the mountains of the title, the green Vermont hills where her grandmother lives and which Kath has always thought of as her haven, and the book ends with Kath and her mother on their way to Vermont. Here, more than in any of her books, Cameron has shown the way in which people affect, and are inevitably affected by, each other.

Katherine Paterson
Bridge to Terabithia
The Great Gilly Hopkins
Jacob Have I Loved
Come Sing, Jimmy Jo

Katherine Paterson was already well known as the author of two fine historical novels set in feudal Japan, one of which, *The Master Puppeteer*, had won the National Book Award in 1977. It was a surprise and a delight to her readers when she chose another genre and wrote a realistic contemporary story, *Bridge to Terabithia*, which was given the Newbery Medal the following year. Her writing is polished and her characterization strong in describing the depth of friendship between a boy in a rural community and the daughter of a cultured,

intellectual pair who have just moved from the city. The two children are enthralled by their sustained imaginative play in a clearing, reached by a rope swing over a ravine, and Jess, the boy, gains security and insight from their relationship. He is desolate when he learns that Leslie, going to their haven alone, has been killed when the rope swing broke—but he realizes later that he has not completely lost

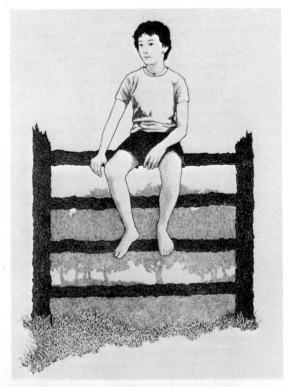

From *Bridge to Terabithia* by Katherine Paterson, illustrated by Donna Diamond.

Viewpoint

The National Book Award, the Newbery Medal, and the British equivalent of the latter, the Carnegie Medal, are what one might call the gifts of the children's literature "establishment"; the recipients on the whole—and there are certainly a few interesting and surprising exceptions—tend to write books that are conservative, fairly middle class . . . and above all, of high literary excellence. Let me say at once that I see nothing wrong with the criterion of high literary excellence. A novel for children should be judged, first and foremost, like any other novel—what merits does it have as a novel? How does it work as a piece of literature? Not: it is good because it has black kids in it, or because it deals with urban violence, or some aspect of life not dealt with elsewhere; no special pleading. It would be unlikely that Katherine Paterson, were she British, would receive The Other Award, for the kind of story she writes would not be of concern to the donors of that prize, the Children's Rights Workshop, who are particularly interested in books with an anti-sexist bias. There is nothing wrong with an institution like The Other Award; its intentions and the books it has honored are admirable, but it would be a sad day if the major establishment prizes were not given for works of high literary excellence.

David Rees, "Medals and Awards: Katherine Paterson" from *Painted Desert, Green Shade*. Boston: The Horn Book, 1984, pp. 89–90.

Leslie, but has gained from her the ability to share with his sister the warmth and joy he had received from his friend.

Paterson's compassion is again evident in *The Great Gilly Hopkins*, as eloquent a story as the first and as brilliant in characterization. The story of a tough foster child, illegitimate and rejected, is deftly constructed and touching, as Gilly learns to drop her façade of toughness when she meets love. The love comes from a slovenly, cheerful foster mother who teaches Gilly to accept love and to give it. Like *Bridge to Terabithia*, this is economically structured and is written with pace and momentum. *Gilly* won the National Book Award, and in 1981 Paterson again won the Newbery Award, this time for *Jacob Have I Loved*. *Come Sing, Jimmy Jo*, the story of a family of country music singers, is as perceptive and polished as its predecessors.

Lois Lowry
A Summer to Die
The *Anastasia Krupnik* Books
Rabble Starkey
Autumn Street

With her first children's book *A Summer to Die*, Lois Lowry won the award given annually by the International Reading Association to a new author whose work shows unusual promise. From the first, her stories have had a natural flow and polish achieved by few beginning authors. In this first bittersweet book, Meg is impatient with and jealous of Molly, two years older and prettier and more popular, and she is at first filled with guilt because she thinks her sister's illness is in some way her fault. Her parents make it clear that Molly's illness is irreversible, and the three comfort each other.

It is primarily for the series of books for the middle-grades reader that began with *Anastasia Krupnik* that Lowry has become well known. Already known as a skilled and sensitive writer, she added in the Anastasia stories, a sophisticated wit and humor that have captivated adult critics and child readers alike. Precocious, articulate, sophisticated for a ten-year-old, Anastasia adjusts, after some initial scorn, to the prospect of a new baby in her loving, tolerant, and entertaining home. Other books in the

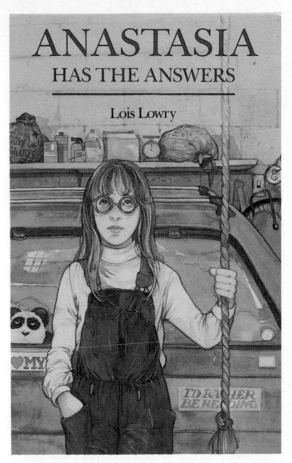

Cover illustration from *Anastasia Has the Answers* by Lois Lowry.

series include *Anastasia Has the Answers*, *Anastasia's Chosen Career*, *Anastasia at Your Service*, and *Anastasia on Her Own*.

Other outstanding stories are *Rabble Starkey*, a touching story of the power of love and love's fostering of sacrifice; also *Autumn Street*, a dignified and touching treatment of an interracial friendship and adjustment to death; and the semimystery, *The One Hundredth Thing About Caroline*, in which the protagonist plays detective when she finds a discarded letter that seems to threaten her life.

Lois Lowry has shown, in her first years as a writer for children, both a diversity in mood and theme, and a remarkable consistency in the integrity and craftsmanship in all her books. Her historical novel, *Number the Stars*, won the Newbery Award.

Viewpoint

There is another matter which some of us dragons wish St. George would ponder before he plunges in the sword. This has to do with the nature and uses of fiction. More often than not when a work of fiction for children is attacked, the fear is that it will set a bad example for children and therefore have a deleterious effect on their behavior.

In Kansas a few years ago parents protested the presence of *The Great Gilly Hopkins* in their school library because of its offensive language. Gilly, the angry foster child who lies, steals, fights, bullies the weak and handicapped, and displays a particularly tasteless variety of racial prejudice, is also caught with the occasional profanity upon her lips. It has always disturbed me that as often as the book has been challenged, not once has anyone objected to the rest of Gilly's rather awful behavior, only to her language.

A child, whether prompted by an adult or not, I do not know, asked me once why Gilly had to cuss. "Well," I said in an often repeated explanation, "a child who lies, steals, fights, bullies, and ferociously acts out her racial prejudice, is not usually a child

who says 'fiddlesticks' when frustrated.''

The child admitted that she knew a number of people rather like Gilly, and I was right. All of them had considerably fouler mouths than Gilly. "But," she said, "if you put it into a book, we might think it's okay of us kids to talk like that."

"Then, of course," I countered, "you would also think it's okay to lie, steal, fight, bully emotionally disturbed children, and make ugly racist remarks."

The child recoiled in shock. "Oh, no," she said, "of course not."

The whole point of the book is that Gilly's inappropriate behavior, including her language, is an angry defense against the world which has labeled her disposable. A novel, as the French philosopher Jacques Maritain reminds us, is different from all other forms of art in that it concerns itself directly with the conduct of life itself. A novel cannot, therefore, set examples, it must reflect life as it is. And if the writer tells her story truly, then readers may find in her novel something of value for their lives.

Katherine Paterson, *The New Advocate*, Volume 2, Number 1, Winter, 1989, pp. 5–6. Reprinted by permission.

Nina Bawden
Rebel on a Rock
The Robbers
The Outside Child

Nina Bawden is an English author who has steadily grown in popularity in other English-speaking countries; most of the books she has written for adults and children have been published in the United States. *Rebel on a Rock* is the story of one of Carrie's children, Carrie being the heroine of *Carrie's War*, discussed in the following chapter. Her daughter Jo is one of four children (two are black and adopted) who are vacationing in a small country ruled by a dictator; wanting to help the son of a banished

leader, Jo and her family find that they have unwittingly caused his arrest. Bawden creates vividly the atmosphere of the village and its rocky citadel; she writes with pace and momentum, eschewing the temptation of a heroic ending for the more probable and logical one. The book is a good adventure story, but it's also noteworthy for the delicacy with which the author depicts relationships within the family, especially the relationship between Jo and her stepfather.

In *The Robbers*, Bawden shows her understanding of children's loyalties and motivations, for nine-year-old Philip is the most honest and courteous of children, yet he is guilty of attempted robbery, a deed he and his friend

Darcy plan because Darcy's brother is in trouble. Philip, who has come to London to live with a cold, bullying father and a new stepmother, had been lonely until he met Darcy's warm and welcoming family. It is then, when Philip is in trouble himself and sees the difference between his father's icy anger and his grandmother's understanding of why sympathy had made him break his own code of behavior, that he decides he will go to live with his grandmother. The characterization is trenchant, the plot beautifully structured, and the writing style polished.

Among other books by Bawden are *A Handful of Thieves*, in which a group of children decides to steal back the money taken from the grandmother of one of them; *Kept in the Dark*, a masterful handling of suspense in a household terrorized by an adolescent bully; and *The Outside Child*, a sensitive but never melodramatic story of a girl who discovers her father has a second family. *Devil by the Sea* was published in England as an adult book. The story of a man who murders children, this book is perhaps indicative of the changing times in that it was considered appropriate to publish it as a book for children nine years after the original publication.

Jan Slepian
The Alfred Summer
The Night of the Bozos
The Broccoli Tapes

With a background in clinical psychology and speech therapy, it is not surprising that Jan Slepian writes authoritatively about children with handicaps. When *The Alfred Summer* appeared, however, it was clear that her previously published picture books had not given her the opportunity to show the polished writing style, the quiet humor, and the depth of characterization that appeared in that book and its sequel, *Lester's Turn*. Lester is fourteen; he has cerebral palsy and—because of that—an overprotective mother. Slepian writes about Lester and his new friend Alfred (younger, retarded) with understanding rather than with pity.

This ability to show people with problems as people first is a distinguishing feature of all Slepian's work. It is strong again in *The Night of the Bozos*, in which a reclusive boy of thirteen, a musical prodigy, is too shy to make friends. His one companion is his Uncle Hibbie, whose stuttering has made him another loner. It is through his role as a carnival Bozo (a human target to knock into the water) that Hibbie rises above his handicap and can speak without stuttering.

In *The Broccoli Tapes*, Slepian successfully uses a literary device: Sara's monologue is in the form of tapes sent from Hawaii to her teacher back in Boston. Many of the transcriptions have to do with Broccoli, the feral cat Sara has found while visiting the island. As in earlier books, this one expresses the pain of being different, the unhappiness of being displaced. Always, the message comes through that love is worth the price of pain.

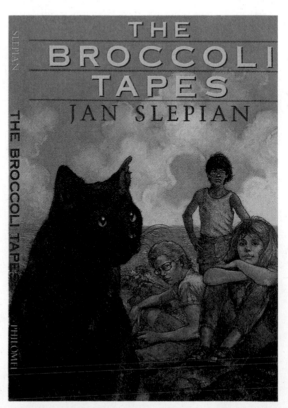

Cover illustration from *The Broccoli Tapes* by Jan Slepian.

Gillian Cross
Roscoe's Leap
A Map of Nowhere

Roscoe's Leap has all the suspense of a top-notch mystery, but Gillian Cross gives her readers much more: intricate relationships among the members of an English family, each depicted with depth and distinction; and a remarkable evocation of place. Roscoe's Leap is a house that is built in two parts over a turbulent stream: symbolically and literally a house divided. The exposure of a blocked memory of childhood terror is the key to solving the problem and reuniting the family.

A different kind of schism is the catalyst for action in *A Map of Nowhere*. An English schoolboy is torn between loyalty to a delinquent older brother whose gang is a threat to a poor shopkeeper's family, and the behavior that would help that family and that the boy knows is the ethical course of action. All of the intricacies of Nick's dilemma are tied to elements of the adventure game Nick plays. Cross writes with sharp insight, and she is particularly skilled at combining a dramatic, contemporary structure and an exploration of issues that transcend time.

From *Arthur, for the Very First Time* by Patricia MacLachlan, illustrated by Lloyd Bloom.

Patricia MacLachlan
Arthur, for the Very First Time
Unclaimed Treasures
The Facts and Fictions of Minna Pratt

Although she has written several excellent books for younger children (*Through Grandpa's Eyes, Seven Kisses in a Row*) and is best known for *Sarah, Plain and Tall*, which won the Newbery Medal and the Scott O'Dell Award for Historical Fiction, Patricia MacLachlan most often has written realistic stories for readers in the middle grades.

Arthur, for the Very First Time is a touching story about a shy child of ten who, while visiting elderly relatives, meets a lively, self-assured girl of his own age. She calls him "Mouse" until the end of the story, when he has gained enough security and self-confidence for her to use his name. The sense of family love, a strong element in many of the author's books, is a cohesive factor here, as well.

In *Unclaimed Treasures*, there is also a perceptive depiction of love in an extended family. While eleven-year-old Willa dreams of romantic love, she comes to realize that those close to her are all lovable, all "unclaimed treasures." In *The Facts and Fictions of Minna Pratt*, the protagonist is a young cellist, a passionate lover of Mozart, and an admirer of her friend Luke's conservative, organized parents. In a rite-of-passage story that has nuance, humor, and warmth, she gains confidence as a musician and learns to understand why Luke admires her nonconformist parents.

Other Books for the Middle Group

In books for children, realism today tends to mirror the contemporary scene, but there have been fine realistic stories written in the past and so vividly true to life that they, too, are enjoyed by today's children. One of these is Ruth Sawyer's Newbery Medal book, *Roller Skates*, in which ten-year-old Lucinda makes friends as she skates about New York. Another Newbery winner, Armstrong Sperry's *Call It Courage*, describes the conquest of fear when a Polynesian boy is marooned on a desert island. Other examples are Ursula Nordstrom's *The Secret Language*, in which a homesick child adjusts to the pattern of life at boarding school; and Virginia Sorenson's 1957 Newbery Medal book, *Miracles on Maple Hill*, the story of a family that moves to the country so that Father can regain his health. Louisa Shotwell's *Roosevelt Grady* concerns a migrant family's desire for a settled life and educational opportunities.

One of the notable developments in the books of the 1970s and 1980s was the increasing number of stories about lively, independent girls. Meg is an eleven-year-old who starts a consciousness-raising group in *The Manifesto and Me—Meg* by Bobbi Katz. Maggie, of Dorothy Crayder's *She, the Adventuress*, proves self-reliant when she travels alone on a ship bound for Italy. With brotherly and parental support, Barbara takes over her brother's newspaper route, overturning company rules in *The Real Me* by Betty Miles.

As is true of books for other age groups, books for the middle group show an increased awareness of children's concern with such situations as death, particularly the death of a family member; adjustment to living with grandparents; and the relationship between children and mentally retarded siblings. In Eth Clifford's *The Rocking Chair Rebellion*, a girl campaigns against discrimination toward old people, and in Sylvia Cassedy's *M.E. and Morton*, a girl of eleven has ambivalent feelings about a retarded brother. Another kind of acceptance is needed in Rose Blue's *Grandma Didn't Wave Back*, wherein a child reluctantly accepts the fact that only a nursing home will provide the appropriate constant care for Grandma. Doris Buchanan Smith explores the grief of a girl mourning the sudden death of her mother's lover, a gentle man she also loves, in *Return to Bitter Creek*.

Among the many books now available about African-American children in the United States, some have an interracial theme, while others are about only African-American children. Two good examples of the former are Eleanor Clymer's *Luke Was There*, the tender story of a child's dependence on an African-American social worker; and Barbara Cohen's *Thank You, Jackie Robinson*, the story of a fatherless white boy who finds a man-to-man relationship with Davey, the African-American chef, who likes baseball as much as Sam does. Some of the excellent stories in the latter group are *Sister* by Eloise Greenfield, in which a girl of thirteen is torn between finding her own path to maturity and following that of an older sister whom she's always adored but who now seems to be heading for trouble; and Bette Greene's *Philip Hall Likes Me, I Reckon Maybe*, and its sequel, *Get On Out of Here, Philip Hall*, stories about a loving family in rural Arkansas. In Carol Fenner's *The Skates of Uncle Richard*, a small African-American girl dreams of being a figure skater.

Eleanor Clymer also has written a sensitive story in *The Spider, the Cave, and the Pottery Bowl*

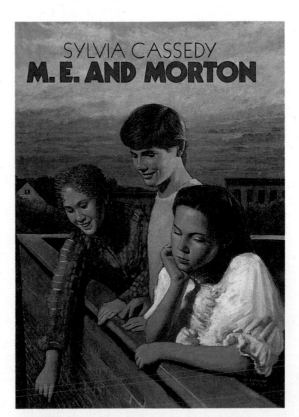

Cover illustration from *M.E. and Morton* by Sylvia Cassedy.

about a native-American child who learns pride in her heritage. A Korean orphan who has been adopted by an American couple speaks of adjustment and prejudice in Linda Girard's *We Adopted You, Benjamin Koo*. The story of two children who are misfits, cruelly treated by fellow campers, is a stunning first novel by Brock Cole, *The Goats*.

Children's problems are much alike everywhere in the world despite the fascinating differences of setting and idiomatic language. This is true of E. W. Hildick's *Louie's Snowstorm*, a funny, fast-paced, English Christmas story in which an American girl plays a lively role; it is a rollicking tale of a group of children that reflects basic needs. The hero of Patricia Windsor's *Mad Martin* is a lonely, uncommunicative orphan who learns how to love and laugh. In Helen Cresswell's *Dear Shrink*, a family is temporarily split up and then happily reunited.

The Australian stories of Reginald Ottley and Joan Phipson, too, demonstrate that children are much the same wherever they happen to live, but the most moving story from an Australian author is probably Patricia Wrightson's *A Racecourse for Andy*, its main character a retarded child whose mistaken belief that he owns a race track is treated with great sympathy and understanding by all his friends.

The universality of childhood experience is clear in Maria Gripe's stories of Swedish children—*The Night Daddy, Elvis and His Friends* and others—that won her the Hans Christian Andersen Medal in 1974. The mother who works while father studies is a familiar phenomenon in our country, but nobody has been more perceptive about the implications of this for children than Anne-Cath Vestly in her story of a Norwegian family, *Hello, Aurora*. Uganda is the setting for a quiet, serious story of the effects of education for *Mukasa* by John Nagenda. Through these books children may learn to feel more at home in their expanded world.

Books for Older Children

Although there have been many changes in realistic fiction for younger children and for children in the middle group, the most striking changes have been in realistic fiction for older children. In the most recent books, subjects which were once taboo or elided, such as premarital pregnancy or illegitimate children, are now common, and the image of the perfect parent appears in fewer and fewer stories. Problems that confront today's youth are treated with understanding: the generation gap, child abuse, the drug scene, the dissatisfaction with a materialistic society. And the language used reflects the speech of today, both in the admission of words that were once considered shocking and in the use of dialects. Some of the stories are didactic, but the best fiction can win young people because it shows their world and its relationships as they know them to be. Although such fiction is now a part of what is published for older readers, there are also many novels that do not deal with controversial issues or problems.

Ann Nolan Clark
Secret of the Andes
Santiago
Medicine Man's Daughter

Secret of the Andes represents something of Clark's range of experience with the people with whom she worked as an employee of the Bureau of Indian Affairs and of the Latin-American Bureau. Furthermore, she is able to interpret their ways of life so that modern children respect them, and her writing reflects her love for them. *Secret of the Andes*, a Newbery Medal winner, is the story of a dedicated Peruvian Indian boy, the last of a royal line, who has been brought up in the mountains and grows to understand his heritage and his responsibilities. *Santiago* is about a Guatemalan youth, raised in a Spanish home but determined to find his place in the world as an Indian. Both of these perceptive stories are beautifully written. *Medicine Man's Daughter* is the story of a girl who, at fifteen, is stunned when a white man heals a child she cannot help. Tall-Girl, in time, learns to appreciate the values of both cultures. The story moves slowly, but the information about Navaho life is interesting and the book sustains the mood of Tall-Girl's dedication.

For younger children Clark has written books that give authentic pictures of the life and ideals of the desert Indians. For older and younger children, she writes with a sense of the inner life and ideals of a people. Her cadenced prose is beautiful and unique.

Joseph Krumgold
. . . and now Miguel
Onion John

Joseph Krumgold has given the preadolescent two fine stories of growing up, both winners of the Newbery Medal.

The members of young Miguel's family in . . . and now Miguel have been sheepherders for generations, first in Spain, now in the Southwest country around Santa Fe, New Mexico. Twelve-year-old Miguel is struggling to prove to his father that he is as mature and competent a sheep man as his adored brother Gabriel, who is eighteen. His attempts to prove his maturity and responsibility supply the action of the story. This book, written in the first person, may have to be introduced to children, but it is well worth the time and effort.

Onion John was not so universally approved as Miguel but it too is concerned with problems in family relationships that are part of growing up. Andy is temporarily fascinated by a picturesque old hobo who lives in a shanty at the edge of town. This hero worship causes the first rift between Andy and his father. The story of the whole town trying to uplift and "do good" to the old tramp is an exceedingly funny and characteristic bit of Americana. But not until Onion John has fled from his do-gooders does Andy realize that he would rather be exactly like his father—the respected owner of the town hardware store—than anyone else.

William Mayne
A Swarm in May
A Grass Rope
The Jersey Shore
Gideon Ahoy!

William Mayne uses his own experiences as a member of the Canterbury Cathedral Choir School as background for A Swarm in May, a deft and humorous account of the ploys and problems of John Owen, ten years old and the youngest "singing boy" in the school. Mayne, in this early and still popular story, showed his ability to create vividly a distinctive atmosphere and to use dialogue in the establishment of character. Unlike many of his later books, this is a humorous story with an affectionate tone.

A Grass Rope, which received the Carnegie Medal, is one of many Mayne stories with a Yorkshire setting; while some of his books have a dark, somber note, this is a sunny tale in which some children investigate traces of an old legend, an interest Mayne explores more fully in some of his fantasy writing. Here one of the charms of the book is the delicacy with which the older children treat the conviction of the youngest that she will find the fairies of the legend; she even weaves a grass rope because she is sure that she will find a unicorn.

The Jersey Shore is set in the United States, but it is permeated with the English background of the New Jersey grandfather Arthur visits. While this is not Mayne's best writing, it is perhaps his most perceptive book, creating a deep sense of family continuity and the poignancy of an old man's memories. Mayne changed the ending for the American edition, eliminating the fact that Arthur's grandfather is black. Mayne's protagonist in Gideon Ahoy! is an adolescent, deaf and retarded, whose family's loving support helps him gain security.

Many of Mayne's books present stylistic difficulties, especially in his use of dialect and idiom; like other great stylists, he will probably never be one of the most popular children's writers—but he is one of the greatest contemporary writers.

Jean George
My Side of the Mountain
Julie of the Wolves

My Side of the Mountain is the record of a New York City boy who breaks away from his family to prove that he can maintain life completely on his own in a mountain wilderness for a year. How fourteen-year-old Sam perfects his house, makes a lamp from deer fat in a turtle's shell and clothes from deerskins, and creates a balanced diet from roots, wild onions, and livers of animals makes absorbing reading. Only the concluding reunion with his family seems mildly contrived.

In *Julie of the Wolves*, George not only tells the story of a girl caught between two cultures —Eskimo and white—but offers fascinating facts about the ways of the wolves. Julie learns to communicate with a small pack of wolves and thus gets food when she is starving on the Arctic tundra. The book won the Newbery Medal and is a good example of George at her best; she is as much a naturalist as a narrator, and excels in descriptions of wilderness flora and fauna. This quality is notable in *The Talking Earth*, the story of a Seminole girl's lonely adventure, and in *Water Sky*.

Emily Neville
It's Like This, Cat
Berries Goodman

There is no startling drama in *It's Like This, Cat*, a Newbery Medal book, but it is impressive both for its lightly humorous, easy style and the fidelity with which it portrays a fourteen-year-old boy, Dave, who tells the story. Dave has found the first girl with whom he really feels comfortable (her mother is delightfully sketched as an urban intellectual), and he learns, by seeing the relationship between his father and his friend, that his father really is a pretty good guy after all. The experience of seeing one's parents through a friend's eyes is a common one, usually revelatory and seldom touched on in books for young people.

Berries Goodman looks back on the two years in which his family lived in a suburb, years in which he had a friend who was Jewish and learned the subtle signs of adult prejudice: the nuances of tone and the light dismissal of subjects with painful implications. He also learns that Sidney's mother is just as biased. The book is an invitation to better understanding, and its serious import is not lessened by a light humor.

Neville understands children and their need to work out relationships and roles. Her style is matter-of-fact but quietly compelling.

From *Julie of the Wolves* by Jean Craighead George, illustrated by John Schoenherr.

Viewpoint

I do not know of a better way to show you the difference between scientific and nature writing than by quoting passages by a father and a son as they describe the same natural phenomenon. John Bartram was a botanist in eighteenth-century America. William, his son, a poet who inherited from his father a knowledge of nature, was to become America's first nature writer.

"The spring," wrote scientist John of a limestone bubbler in Florida, "smells like bilge," tastes "sweet and loathsome," and boils up from the bottom "like a pot."

"The spring," wrote nature writer William, "was an enchanting and amazing crystal fountain, which incessantly threw up, from dark rocky caverns below, tons of water every minute . . . the blue ether of another world."

To be a nature writer one must first study science, then feel the poetry, and finally "get bitten by the mosquitoes," as we call this part of our work today.

From "Writing for a Natural Audience" by Jean Craighead George, *The Five Owls*, January/February, 1987. Reprinted by permission of the author.

Ivan Southall
Ash Road
Let the Balloon Go
To the Wild Sky

One of Australia's most notable writers of children's books, Ivan Southall is particularly adept at placing his child characters in a situation of stress or danger, and showing in realistic and exciting fashion how the common sense and courage of the young can prevail over obstacles. In *Ash Road*, which won the Australian Children's Book of the Year Award, three boys who have been careless while camping start a bush fire. The suspense is built by Southall's use of fragmented incidents fitted together in jigsaw pattern.

Many of Southall's books concern a group, but in *Let the Balloon Go* the supreme effort of a spastic child, the great achievement of climbing a tree, is as tense and exciting as the fire of the earlier book. The theme of the story is that all young people want a chance to make their own decisions and take their own risks. *The Long Night Watch* is a provocative story of an adolescent's commitment to a moral rearmament group. All of Southall's books combine a faith in the abilities of the young and a dramatic setting in which they demonstrate their capability. *To the Wild Sky* also won the Book of the Year Award in Australia.

S. E. Hinton
The Outsiders
That Was Then, This Is Now
Rumble Fish
Tex

The Outsiders are the members of a tough, lower-class gang who have a running feud with a middle-class gang. Ponyboy is the outsider who tells the story, stark and vivid, of running off to a hideout with a pal who has committed murder. The two give themselves up, and Ponyboy's pal dies in the hospital. Ponyboy faces the fact that the advantage is with those on the inside of society's line, yet knows that if he cannot have help, he must and will help himself and end the vicious circle of hostility and reprisal. Honest and forthright, the story shows the desperation of the need to belong; it has also a bittersweet quality, especially in young Ponyboy's relationship with his older brothers.

The candor and insight that made the book so popular are evident also in *That Was Then, This Is Now*, which is basically a story of friendship and the choice that teenaged Byron must make when he finds that his best friend is pushing dope. Especially bitter because he has seen drugs ruin a younger boy of whom he is fond, Byron turns Mark in—and hates himself. The characters are vividly real, and no didactic tract on drug abuse could be more convincing than is the story seen from the viewpoint of an

Viewpoint

The official arrival of the new realism was acknowledged in 1964, when the American Library Association awarded the Newbery Medal to Emily Neville for her book, *It's Like This, Cat* (1963). Prior to this time, it was obvious to anyone who thought about it that there were areas of life that young readers could not confront through literature, for example, race relations, premarital sex, pregnancy, and abortion. Divorce and one-parent families, drugs and homosexuality, and the moral issues involved in the making of war were also missing from children's literature.

It is vitally important that young people have such confrontations through literature. It is important because literature can provide deeply involving, vicarious experiences. Literature can offer the reader the chance to know what it is like to become addicted to drugs; what it is like to live in abject and degrading poverty; what it is like to be a member of a different social or cultural group; what it is like to be an unwed and expectant mother.

Through the new realism the reader has the security of being involved without suffering the consequences of involvement. Young readers can test their beliefs and values against those revealed by the author. Within the exclusive privacy of a book, and without the ever-pressing impingement of peer and class values readers can rethink, reassess and, most importantly, refeel their own attitudes about themselves, about others, and about the world in which they live. The result of experience with the new realism can be readers who are more sensitive, more aware of their own humaness and the humaness of others, and more humane.

Shelton L. Root, Jr., "The New Realism—Some Personal Reflections." *Language Arts*, January 1977. Copyright © 1977 by the National Council of Teachers of English. Reprinted by permission of the publisher and the author.

adolescent who has himself been a fringe delinquent. *Rumble Fish* is the tragic story of two brothers—Motorcycle Boy, who has lost his will to live and is killed after committing a senseless robbery, and Rusty-James, the younger, who idolizes his brother and is almost destroyed by his death. The theme of love between brothers is paramount also in *Tex*.

Kristin Hunter
The Soul Brothers and Sister Lou
Guests in the Promised Land

Which side was she on? Lou, at fourteen, wasn't militant, but she didn't trust white policemen, and she warned the gang with whom she sang that a policeman was near and was acting provocative. She knew the gang carried weapons, but she also saw an unarmed boy shot by the police, and found it hard to believe that any white people had good motives. Yet the more she learned of her African-American heritage, the more proud and confident Lou became, until she made her decision: moderation, not militancy. *The Soul Brothers and Sister Lou* has too many episodes and a weak ending (sudden success as a vocal group), yet the book is valuable because it gives a vivid and honest picture of one segment of African-American society and of the dilemma of its young people. In *Guests in the Promised Land* Hunter's eleven short stories, varied and vigorous, examine facets of the problems of the African-American child in a white world.

John Rowe Townsend
Trouble in the Jungle
Good Night, Prof, Dear
Noah's Castle
Kate and the Revolution

John Rowe Townsend is one of the major writers of realistic fiction for young people in England. His *Trouble in the Jungle* tells of some slum children who show their mettle when they are temporarily abandoned by adults. To avoid being forced into an institution, the two older children take the younger ones to a refuge in a deserted warehouse and have a dangerous skirmish with criminals who also seek a hideout.

The story, which has good characterization and pace, ends on a realistic note: The shiftless father and his mistress return, and the children go back to their home. Although published earlier in the United States, *Good-Bye to the Jungle* is a sequel in which the family moves to a better home and a better life.

In *Good Night, Prof, Dear*, a shy and overprotected sixteen-year-old falls in love with a waitress he meets when his parents are away on a trip. Although the girl verges on a fallen-woman-with-heart-of-gold type, it is the contrast between her knowledgeable resilience and Graham's diffidence and insecurity that gives the story its real drama. *The Intruder*, another story about a sixteen-year-old, is discussed in Chapter 2.

Noah's Castle is a compelling, all-too-possible family story. Foreseeing food shortages, Father buys and barricades a huge house, stocks it, and prepares to survive. What his family thinks of all this precipitates more problems. Townsend is a versatile writer: *Kate and the Revolution* is a hilarious spoof of pseudo-political romantic adventure stories. In *Rob's Place*, an unhappy boy takes refuge in solitary imaginative play; *Downstream* is a forceful story of father-son jealousy; and *Cloudy-Bright* is a straightforward and perceptive love story.

Townsend has an ear for dialogue, as well as an understanding of adolescent psychology. His books are written with economy of structure and vitality of motive, the style utterly appropriate to the tale.

Theodore Taylor
The Cay

Although the German submarines that are attacking islands along the Venezuelan coast during World War II cause Phillip's departure, this novel by Theodore Taylor is in no sense a historical work, since all of the action takes place on a small Caribbean island, *The Cay*, with only two characters. The ship Phillip and his mother are on is torpedoed and the boy finds himself, some hours later, alone on a raft with Timothy, an old man. Infected by his mother's prejudice, Phillip feels only aversion for his black companion at first, but he becomes totally dependent on Timothy when he goes blind as a delayed result of the shipwreck injury. Slowly, patiently, stubbornly, Timothy teaches the boy to fend for himself, refusing to coddle him— and when old Timothy dies, Phillip knows how much he has come to love and respect the wise and charitable man. The bleakness of the setting is a dramatic foil for the action, and there is taut suspense within the economical framework of Taylor's plot.

John Donovan
I'll Get There. It Better Be Worth the Trip
Wild in the World

In a compassionate story of childhood's end, John Donovan draws a picture of thirteen-year-old Davy, caught and shaped by his environment in *I'll Get There. It Better Be Worth the Trip*. After the death of his grandmother, Davy comes to New York to live with his mother, a divorced, bitter alcoholic. All he clings to is his beloved dog, and the dog irritates his mother. Sent to a boys' school, Davy meets another pupil adjusting to bereavement, and the two have a brief homosexual relationship. It is handled with great dignity and compassion, not the core of the book but one of the scarring episodes that make Davy know his strength must come from within.

Donovan's *Wild in the World* is a quite different and an even stronger book, memorable for its stark setting and the dramatic impact of a solitary boy's deep need for love and companionship. John lives alone on a remote mountainside farm until a stray dog—or it may be a wolf, John is not sure—learns to trust him. For the first time, John plays and laughs with the creature he has named "Son." When John dies, still alone, and neighbors find him, his "Son" is chased off but steals back later to sleep and keep his vigil in John's house.

Richard Peck
Don't Look and It Won't Hurt
Representing Super Doll
Remembering the Good Times

The second of three daughters, Carol had to take care of her younger sister after their parents' divorce in *Don't Look and It Won't Hurt*. Mom, already bitter, didn't want Carol to have boyfriends and refused to have anything to do with her oldest daughter, Ellen, when she became pregnant. It was Carol who went to Chicago to see Ellen and beg her to come home. A gentle, loving girl, Carol had learned to look away from pain that cannot be alleviated; she has had heavy burdens, but they have made her understanding and mature rather than bitter like her mother.

In *Representing Super Doll* a beautiful but not very astute girl, Darlene, goes to New York for one round of a teenage beauty contest. Her ambitious mother convinces Verna, Darlene's classmate, to go along as companion. Verna, levelheaded and intelligent, scorns the contest proceedings and goes home—and Darlene does the same. To her mother's fury, she has quit just before the final round. The message is firmly feminist, but Peck does not let the message obscure the story; the plot is solid, the characters strong, and the treatment of adolescent concerns balanced. *Princess Ashley* is an astute story about a manipulative charmer, and *Remembering the Goods Times* a reminiscent look at a three-way friendship that leaves two of the friends sad and baffled by the suicide of the third. Dialogue is one of the strong aspects in all Peck's stories, and his books are notable for their fresh viewpoints and their vitality.

Norma Klein
Mom, the Wolf Man, and Me
It's Not What You Expect
Learning How to Fall

While Norma Klein has written for several age levels, her greatest impact has been in stories for younger adolescents. The "me" in *Mom, the Wolf Man, and Me* is Brett, an illegitimate child, who loves living alone with her mother and hopes that life will never change. Then the "wolf man," the owner of an Irish wolfhound, comes along, and the possibility of change looms. Brett's mother is candid and open, and the suitor is as concerned with Brett's feelings as with her mother's.

Many of Klein's stories are about single-parent homes, divorce, remarriage, and the adaptability required of children. In *It's Not What You Expect*, Carla, age fourteen, adjusts to her parents' separation; *Confessions of an Only Child* tells of eight-year-old Tonia's feelings before the birth and death of a premature baby brother, and her acceptance of the brother born a year later; and in *Learning How to Fall*, Klein examines the concept that what you want may not be best for you. A family's reaction to a grandmother with Alzheimer's disease creates the conflict in *Going Backwards*.

Klein, a thoughtful connoisseur of real people, set down her observations skillfully for us. Her children are not divorced from adult problems and relationships, and live closely, in their urban existences, with real and surrogate parents who are inevitably frank and open about their emotions. Only occasional older people —grandmothers, baby-sitters—suggest that different values might be held by other adults.

Cover illustration from *Going Backwards* by Norma Klein, photograph by Ken Robbins.

M. E. Kerr
Dinky Hocker Shoots Smack
Is That You, Miss Blue?
Little Little
The *Fell* Books

With *Dinky Hocker Shoots Smack*, a fresh, perceptive advocate for adolescents appeared in the person of M. E. Kerr. Dinky Hocker spends all her money for food and has no dates. When Dinky does establish a relationship with a boyfriend, her parents find the boy too reactionary and break up the romance. Dinky's revenge is to inscribe "Dinky Hocker shoots smack" on all the buildings and sidewalks in the neighborhood. Hilariously funny but touching at the same time, Kerr's book has an excellent style and convincing characterizations.

Flanders is sent to a private girls' boarding school in *Is That You, Miss Blue?* Angry with her mother for leaving home and with her father for apparently deserting her, Flan learns through her school experiences that everyone needs understanding love, even parents and teachers.

In *Little Little* the author laughs with—but never at—the midgets and dwarfs who are the main characters in a delightful social satire; *Him She Loves?* is a humorous love story. Kerr's fans should also enjoy her autobiographical reminiscences in *Me, Me, Me, Me, Me—Not a Novel*. In *Fell* and its sequel, *Fell Back*, Kerr adds a note of mystery to stories about a dominant clique in a private school for boys. Kerr never offers easy answers to the situations and experiences in which her characters are involved, but presents them sympathetically, honestly, and compassionately.

Sharon Bell Mathis
Listen for the Fig Tree
The Hundred Penny Box

An eloquent spokesperson for African-American culture, Sharon Bell Mathis has created a realistic and moving story of relationships between generations in *Listen for the Fig Tree*. Muffin, who is sixteen and blind, finds that coping with her grief-stricken Momma is a hard task, for Momma, mourning her husband's death, has taken to drink. Muffin's solace lies in her plans to attend her first celebration of the African Kwanza, and she makes a dress for the occasion, a dress in which she looks beautiful—too beautiful. A neighbor attempts rape; other neighbors rescue her, and one makes her a new dress. Muffin has a glorious time at Kwanza, and—although she comes home to find Momma still drinking, still insistent that Daddy's coming home—she faces her problems with new courage, courage gained from the feelings of solidarity and strength she had gained at Kwanza.

A story that is primarily for children in the middle grades, *The Hundred Penny Box* is so tender and delicate that it appeals to many older readers as well. A small boy becomes his great-great-aunt's confidant and protector when his mother wants to get rid of Aunt Dew's big box of pennies. Michael knows that without her pennies, one for each year of her life, something vital will leave Aunt Dew's life.

Mathis is very successful in delineating characters and establishing setting. Her writing is effectively restrained, her stories convincing and candid.

Robert Cormier
The Chocolate War Books
I am the cheese
The Bumblebee Flies Anyway

The controversy that arose with the publication of Robert Cormier's first novel, *The Chocolate War*, has abated but not stopped, and there is almost as much discussion of his other books. Even those who think that the stories are grim or shocking are in agreement, however, about the fact that the books are deftly crafted, exciting, and thought-provoking. Refusing to sell chocolates in the annual fundraising drive in a high school for Catholic boys, Jerry is abused and victimized both by a group of bullying classmates and by a sadistic teacher. Grim indeed, but unforgettable, as is the sequel, *Beyond the Chocolate War*.

Intricately structured and beautifully written, with three strands that are adroitly woven together, *I am the cheese* begins with a boy's bicycle trip and ends when it becomes clear that a pattern is being repeated in the memory of the boy who proves to be a political hostage. Cormier uses flashbacks and interviews brilliantly to create suspense. Different voices are used to tell the story of a man engaged in a secret government project threatened by the hijacking by terrorists of a bus full of children in *After the First Death*. In a story that is as trenchant as it is poignant, *The Bumblebee Flies Anyway*, Cormier depicts the courage and desperation of hospitalized adolescents who know that their deaths are imminent. Although tragic, it is a stunning book—it has, like other books by Robert Cormier, been popular with younger readers as well as those in the intended teenage audience, both because of its dramatic impact and candor.

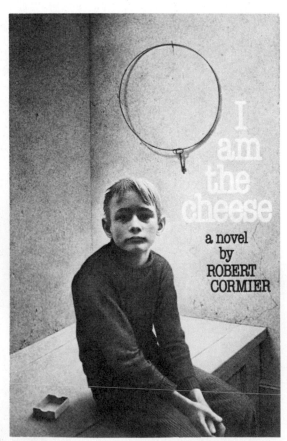

Cover illustration from *I am the cheese* by Robert Cormier.

Walter Dean Myers
The Young Landlords
Scorpions

Although some of his earlier nonfiction and stories for younger readers were well received, it is through his writing for and about adolescents that Walter Dean Myers is best known.

The Young Landlords is about a gang that acquires a slum building and determines to improve the property so that it will be on a sound financial basis. The book gives an attractive picture of an African-American urban neighborhood. *Scorpions*, on the other hand, has an antigang tone, showing the dilemma confronted by two boys of twelve (one African American, the other Puerto Rican) when they are pressed into joining a tough local gang.

Also good books about African-American adolescents are *Motown and Didi: A Love Story*, the tender romance that is gentle despite grim circumstances; and *Fast Sam, Cool Clyde, and Stuff*, which has more humor than most of Myers's stories of gangs, and as much warmth as any of them.

Other Books for Older Children

Mildred Lee's *The Rock and the Willow* was chosen a Notable Book, and deservedly. It is a powerful and incisive story set in rural Alabama during the Depression years, bleak in its honest portrayal of a hard life, with young Enie bearing the brunt of caring for the family after her mother's death and grudgingly accepting a stepmother. The characters are cameo clear, and Enie's dream of getting away from home and going to college is realistically achieved.

Another story of that period is Mildred Taylor's Newbery Medal book, *Roll of Thunder, Hear My Cry*. A black family encounters persecution and condescension as well as poverty, but is strong in their love for each other and for the land they own. William Armstrong's *Sounder*, a Newbery Medal book, is the grim and moving story of a black sharecropper's family whose father is jailed for stealing food for them.

Cover illustration from *Scorpions* by Walter Dean Myers.

Spanish Harlem is the setting for *Nilda* by Nicholasa Mohr, a sharp and candid picture of the life of a barrio child. A new arrival in Harlem, Phyl learns that although Edith is slovenly, her kindness is a bulwark in Rosa Guy's *The Friends*. Alice Childress tells a dramatic, moving story in *A HERO Ain't Nothin' But a Sandwich*: Thirteen-year-old Benjie insists that he can do without dope any time he wants, but his friends and relatives are more realistic. Maia Wojciechowska, winner of the Newbery Medal for *Shadow of a Bull*, dealt with deep insight into courage and fear; her *Tuned Out* is a stark story about drug addiction.

The consistent and distinctive first-person style of Scott O'Dell's *Child of Fire* brings vividly to life an adolescent Chicano boy, seen through the eyes of a parole officer.

Florence Crannell Means wrote with candor and insight about such problems as the adjust-ment of a Hopi girl who cannot accept her own or the white culture in *Our Cup Is Broken*. In *Us Maltbys*, Means explored the problems of adjustment within a white family that adds, among other foster children, an African-American baby boy.

Several authors deal candidly with serious problems. Norma Mazer, in *After the Rain*, writes movingly about the relationship of an adolescent and her gruff, dying grandfather. Virginia Wolff describes the frustrations of a slow learner in *Probably Still Nick Swansen*. In Lynn Hall's *The Giver*, a teacher treats a girl's crush with sensitivity.

Paula Danziger's *The Cat Ate My Gymsuit* shows how much an innovative teacher means to bored, self-hating Marcy. When the teacher is fired, Marcy and her friends lead a protest, in which Marcy's formerly timid mother joins.

The Pigman was what John and Lorraine called Mr. Pignati, whom they had met when pretending to collect for a charity. When he comes back from a hospital stay to find them having a wild party, Mr. Pignati is stunned. Remorseful, John and Lorraine try to make amends, but the old man has had too much excitement and dies of a stroke. Told alternately by John and Lorraine, this story by Paul Zindel shows more clearly than a reporter could the restless, pliant amorality that so often marks adolescent behavior, and the deep sensitivity beneath it. In *The Pigman's Legacy*, John and Lorraine atone for their guilt through their kindness to another elderly man. Cynthia Voigt's *Dicey's Song*, which won the Newbery Medal, is one of a series about the Tillerman family that includes among its sequels *A Solitary Blue*, *Sons from Afar*, and *Seventeen Against the Dealer*.

A dignified, perceptive story of a homosexual relationship, *Trying Hard to Hear You*, by Sandra Scoppettone, tells of a crucial summer in the lives of a group of adolescents. *Sex Education*, by Jenny Davis, is in fact about learning that it is love, not sex, that is important. In Harry Mazer's *When the Phone Rang*, three siblings find a way to stay together when their parents are killed in a plane crash.

The girl in Barbara Corcoran's *Sam* discovers for herself that there are all kinds of people, and that even those like Uncle Everett, a weakling and a gambler, have some redeeming qualities. In Corcoran's *A Dance to Still Music*, Margaret, deaf after an illness, rebels by running away when her mother plans to put her in a special school. In Corcoran's and Bradford Angier's *A Star to the North*, a brother and sister learn to accept each other's inadequacies on a trek through the Canadian wilderness. Paul Fleischman, winner of a Newbery Medal for his poetry, has produced excellent short stories and novels; in *Rear-View Mirrors*, flashbacks are used as a teenage girl confronts the father she had never before seen.

Winner of the 1976 Carnegie Medal, Jan Mark's *Thunder and Lightnings* is rich in Norfolk dialect and idiom; a quiet story, it is given warmth and depth by the strong family relationships and the altruistic friendship between Andrew and the newcomer, Victor, with his passion for Lightnings and any other kind of aircraft. Boys are not alone in such interests; it's motorcycles that fascinate Erica in *Handles*.

K. M. Peyton's *Pennington's Heir*, which follows *Pennington's Last Term* and *The Beethoven Medal*, about a brilliant young pianist with a rebellious temper, is also a story of an early, forced marriage. Pennington appears again in *Marion's Angels* when he helps save an old church that is slated for destruction. Peyton's ability to create vigorous, believable characters and situations is enhanced by her polished writing style.

A good story which may help readers to understand to some extent the bitterness rampant in Northern Ireland today is Joan Lingard's *The Twelfth Day of July*, the first of several stories about Protestant Sadie and Catholic Kevin.

It is interesting that two prize books from Holland are about children in other countries. Siny van Iterson's *Pulga* is the story of a Colombian waif who gets a job as a trucker's helper and gains self-confidence from his experience; and Jaap Ter Haar's *Boris* is a story of brotherhood set in Russia. One of the best of the translations from Russia is Vadim Frolov's *What It's All About*, in which a teenage boy copes with the bitter fact that his mother has left his father to be with another man. Sasha's

self-doubt, his budding love affair, and his relationships with classmates give the story balance and depth.

Hesba Fay Brinsmead's *Pastures of the Blue Crane* is set in Australia, its theme the intrinsic worth of all men. A girl of sixteen who has been living in boarding schools inherits property and finds, in her new home, that her most trustworthy friend is Perry, a quarter-caste. Indignant at the slurs cast on her friend, Amaryllis is not dismayed when she discovers that she herself is not, as she had always assumed, all white.

Miners in Australia's opal fields work in a harsh, uncompromising setting, which imposes unusual pressures on families. Both Colin Thiele's *Fire in the Stone* and Mavis Thorpe Clark's *Spark of Opal* tell of the effects of this life on children, white and aborigine, as they wait for that lucky strike. In Joan Phipson's *When the City Stopped* the setting is urban for a taut story in which two children cope when a strike paralyzes the city.

One of the best of the stories of conflict and resolution between the old ways and the new is *Sunrise Tomorrow* by Naomi Mitchison, a story of Botswana. Convincingly drawn characters show the different roles in which young people can contribute to a developing nation. Also indicative of cultural conflict is *Shabanu: Daughter of the Wind* by Suzanne Staples, the story of an adolescent desert dweller in contemporary Pakistan.

Animal Stories

Almost all children are interested in animals. Rhymes about "The Three Little Kittens" or the mouse that ran up the clock are early favorites, and *Mother Goose* is supplemented by the more realistic animal picture books. With these, children learn to name all the beasts under the sun from hippopotamuses to anteaters. The folk tales with animal heroes come next; "The Three Little Pigs," "The Little Red Hen," and all the other favorites are heard over and over with endless satisfaction. Children progress from these to the more complex, realistic stories about animals, and for many people the interest lasts a lifetime.

Animal stories can be divided into three groups: those in which animals behave like human beings, those in which they behave like animals save for the fact that they can talk, and those in which they behave like animals. Many of the books in the first two categories can be found in Chapter 4, Books for the Very Young, and in Chapter 8, Modern Fantasy; there are, of course, many animal stories in folk literature as well. The realistic tales range from lighthearted picture books like Nathan Zimelman's *The Lives of My Cat Alfred* to humorous stories like Phil Stong's *Honk: the Moose* or serious and touching stories like Theodore Taylor's *The Trouble with Tuck*, the story of a dog who goes blind.

A primary criterion for realistic fiction about animals is that the animals be objectively portrayed. The author should not interpret behavior or motives through giving the animal powers of speech or thought. Any conjecture about motives of animal protagonists should agree with the interpretation of animal behavior as reliable observers have recorded it. Since tragedy often occurs in the lives of animals, stories about them often are dramatic or melancholy. In evaluating such books, we need to be more than ordinarily alert to what is a true and consistent story, and to what is pure sentimentality or animal melodrama. A little melodrama or a few mediocre books are not going to hurt children, but they should not miss the great animal tales in a welter of second-rate ones.

Among the great stories is Sheila Burnford's *The Incredible Journey*, a detailed account of three heroic animals who travel through 250 miles of Canadian wilderness to the place and people that mean home and love to them. Attacked by wild creatures, delayed by well-meaning people, crossing hazardous terrain, a cat and two dogs struggle on to find their family. The animals are never humanized or sentimentalized, and they are described with dignity and restraint in a moving and beautiful story.

Many of the best books about animals are written by authors who specialize in this area. Marguerite Henry, for example, who is probably the most successful writer of horse stories

we have ever had, bases each book on thorough research; the stories are well told, the animal heroes are true to their species, and the people are often as memorable as the animals. For *King of the Wind*, which won the Newbery Medal, the author investigated the history of the great Godolphin Arabian, which sired a line of thoroughbreds and changed the physical conformation of racehorses. It is one of the most exciting horse stories ever written. Just as popular is *Misty of Chincoteague*, a history of the little wild horses on a Virginia Island. In *Gaudenzia* and *White Stallion of Lipizza*, Henry bases her stories on the annual horse race held in Siena and on the Lipizzaners, the precision drilled performing horses of the Spanish Riding School of Vienna.

Other authors who have written prolifically in the field of realistic animal fiction are Walt Morey, Jim Kjelgaard, and Jean George. All of Morey's books are set in the far North or Northwest, and are imbued with his love for that region and his affection for animals. In *Gentle Ben* and in *Gloomy Gus*, the protagonists are bears, animal personalities that are as vivid as the perceptively characterized human beings among whom they live. In *Year of the Black Pony*, a boy on an Oregon farm tames and trains a spirited pony, a plot that is deftly meshed with a tender family story. Kjelgaard specializes in dog stories, of which the best known is *Big Red*, which was followed by several books about the progeny of the lovable and courageous Irish setter. With John George, Jean George wrote many stories in a life-cycle pattern: *Vulpes, the Red Fox* and *Bubo, the Great Horned Owl*, for example, both make it clear that George is not only an animal lover, but a skilled naturalist. Among her finest books are *The Cry of the Crow* in which a girl must protect her trained crow from those who, like her father and brothers, will shoot any crow on sight; and *Gull Number 737*, the story of a boy who becomes so interested in his father's research on herring gulls that he develops his own project.

One of the most touching and trenchant animal stories is *The Yearling* by Marjorie Kinnan Rawlings. Although written for adults, it has been discovered by children as they discover certain adult books and make them their own in every generation. A lonely boy and his pet deer grow up together in the Florida wilderness, but when the growing animal begins to eat the family's scanty crops, the boy's father issues an order: the deer must be shot. Added to the boy's anguish over losing his pet are his own guilt feelings and his anger at his father. This is more tragic than most of the stories in which children give up wild pets, but there are many in which a child feels anguish because a wild creature grows from a baby to a size where it must be returned to live with its own kind.

Some animal stories are factual, based on an author's experience with wildlife. Perhaps the best known of these is Sterling North's *Rascal*, which was so popular that the author wrote a simplified version, *Little Rascal*, two years later—a better adaptation than most books rewritten for children. A description of the engaging ways of a pet raccoon, the first-person account is always objective in observations of animal behavior. Also based on observation is Emil Liers's *An Otter's Story*, a delightful book about one family of playful, affectionate freshwater otters in which the author makes clear their usefulness in the balance of nature both for farmers and for fishermen. While not based on personal experience, Patricia Beatty's *The Staffordshire Terror* is a well-researched story based on the illegal dogfights held throughout the United States. S. E. Hinton's *Taming the Star Runner* is a horse story that has depth and empathy.

The English naturalist Joyce Stranger has, in *Lakeland Vet*, so skillfully woven incidents about animals into the fictional account of a veterinarian's hard life that his love and compassion for all living things are more impressive than the story line. The same sense of compassion is strong in Meindert DeJong's *Along Came a Dog*, illustrated by Maurice Sendak. Gentle but never sentimental, DeJong's stories about animals have a quiet, poignant appeal; here the animals have strong personalities, as a stray dog establishes himself as the protector of a crippled, doughty little hen. A dozen short stories focus on the relationship between a person and an animal in Cynthia Rylant's *Every Living Thing*, and Jessie Haas, in *The Sixth Sense and Other Stories*, also examines such relationships.

Realistic animal stories for young children are on the whole a cheerful group, often containing excellent illustrations. Although many of Marjorie Flack's books were about dogs, the abiding favorite has been *The Story About Ping*, with Kurt Wiese's pictures catching the spirit of a brisk, homey tale about a rebellious little duck that lives on a boat on the Yangtze River. Lynd Ward's *The Biggest Bear* is a delectable comedy about a pet bear that grows from a cute baby into a large animal that causes so many problems that the only solution is sending it to a zoo.

In Beverly Cleary's *Socks*, the advent of a baby is told from a cat's viewpoint. Socks had been a pampered pet until the intruder came along, and he's resentfully jealous until the baby gets big enough to turn into a playmate. Socks always behaves and thinks like a cat, never a person, yet Cleary invests him with a definite personality in this delightful tale.

The animal stories by Miska Miles have in common a quiet tone, an absence of anthropomorphism, and, in most of them, a consistency in the way they reflect an animal's life from its own viewpoint. In *Nobody's Cat* a tough, self-sufficient alley cat awakens sympathy by being just what he is: lean, homely, and lonely—there is no sentimentality, no happy ending to his adventures. In Jean Little's *Lost and Found*, Lucy is unhappy when a stray dog's owners turn up, but she does choose another dog at an animal shelter.

It matters little where an animal story is set, since the interest and affection children feel for creatures, wild or tame, is universal. In *Just a Dog* by Helen Griffiths the story of a mongrel pup is set in Madrid, but the incidents could be duplicated in any city. Anne de Roo's *Cinnamon and Nutmeg* takes place in New Zealand, where a farm child, knowing her father won't let her keep the calf and kid she's found, hides them in an abandoned house and gives them loving care. Most of Lucy Boston's writing is fantasy, but she uses the same setting, an English country house, for *A Stranger at Green Knowe*, a powerful and original story about the understanding and mutual affection between a gorilla that has escaped from a zoo and a young refugee.

There is rarely any need to urge children to

read stories about animals. Pet stories bring out children's desire to nurture and protect and many of these books teach sex casually in the course of an absorbing story. For children who have little or no knowledge of breeding and the raising of young, these stories are especially valuable. From the stories that center on the proper training of dogs and horses, young readers gain a background for the training of their own pets. There is, of course, a great deal of overlap between such stories and informational books. Much of the fiction gives accurate information, and many informational books about animals have a narrative framework; indeed, it is at times difficult to decide in which class a book belongs.

Since the mere nature of the wild animal's life means chiefly pursuit or being pursued, escape or death; and since the drama of a pet's life turns upon the upsetting of its happy security with a tragic or triumphant outcome, there is bound to be a certain similarity in these tales. Too many of them in a row are monotonous or overly harrowing. Such stories should be read along with other books. But any child is the richer for having had his or her sympathies expanded and tenderness stirred by such great animal books as *Along Came a Dog*, *Gentle Ben*, and *The Yearling*. Any child is the poorer for having missed the drama of *King of the Wind*, *The Incredible Journey*, and *A Stranger at Green Knowe*.

Sports Stories

If there is one fault common to most sports stories, it is the formula plot; for example, the beginner, from school playground to professional team, who can't get along with another member of the team or the whole team or the coach because he or she is cocky or wants things his or her own way, eventually rising to heights of glory and acceptance by all by saving the final game in the final minute of play. Although game description is the most appealing element to some readers, another fault common to such stories is the thin plot wrapped around long and often tedious game sequences, some of which have unrealistic series of plays. Perhaps more than any other kind

From *The Incredible Journey* by Sheila Burnford, illustrated by Carl Burger.

of realistic fiction, the sports story needs good characterization and good style to give it depth, especially since there is usually little variation in setting and often little opportunity for a meaningful theme.

There are few realistic sports stories for the beginning reader, but Leonard Kessler's *Here Comes the Strikeout* has simplicity, humor, and an emphasis on perseverance and achievement. Bobby (white) cannot get a hit until he has been coached by his friend Willie (African American) and has worked hard to correct his faults. Beman Lord has written several books for this age group, one of which, *Shrimp's Soccer Goal*, reflects the increasing interest in that sport and is unusual in presenting a female teacher as the founder and coach of the team. Soccer is a new sport to the fourth-grade narrator of Mel Glenn's *Play-by-Play*. Another good soccer story from Sweden is Kerstin Thorvall's *Gunnar Scores a Goal*.

The popularity of each individual sport is echoed proportionately in children's books, with baseball and football stories far outnumbering all others. One of the most dependable writers for the nine-to-eleven group is Matt Christopher, whose productivity is impressive. *Johnny Long Legs* and *The Great Quarterback Switch* are examples of his style: simple, undistinguished plots; good game descriptions; and an emphasis on sportsmanship and team effort. *The Baseball Bargain* by Scott Corbett has more depth, since the protagonist is tempted to steal a mitt and strikes a bargain with the storekeeper whereby he earns it by working in the store—*if* he can first do three good deeds in a day. Corbett's light, easy style and humor make this a pleasant tale with serious overtones—and good baseball. Alfred Slote's *Stranger on the Ball Club* also is concerned with ethical values and has good sports writing and deeper characterization than is found in most books at this level; his *Matt Gargan's Boy* has good game sequences in a story about Danny, who resents having a girl on his team, especially a girl whose father is courting Danny's divorced mother. William Pène du Bois, in *Porko von Popbutton*, writes a merry tale of ice hockey at a boys' school.

The response by publishers to the demand for more books about African Americans and other minority groups has included sports fiction, but many of these stories seem obtrusive in their inclusion of such minorities. Indeed, one of the formulas has seemed to be the team in which each player represents a different ethnic background. Stories that approach the particular problems of the African-American player in sports with honesty and concern are rare, and therefore John Tunis's *All-American* was all the more exciting when it appeared in 1942. It tells the story of a boy who plays high-school football and learns to appreciate each player for his own worth and to fight discrimination. Two later books that deal incisively with the special problems of the African-American athlete are Robert Lipsyte's *The Contender*, in which a Harlem youth decides, after a successful start in a boxing career, to get an education instead; and *The Outside Shot*, by Walter Dean Myers, the story of a college basketball player who also wants an education.

In Donald Honig's *Way to Go, Teddy*, a young baseball player is in conflict with the father who wants him to become a lawyer. The details of a rookie's life are lively and authentic; the author

was a professional ball player. Another story with rare depth and characterization is *Stubborn Sam* by William Gault. Sam Bogosian goes to college as his father asks—but he still wants to play baseball, and does. In Robert Weaver's *Nice Guy, Go Home*, an Amish boy is drawn into a civil rights conflict in the town where his pro team plays; although he respects the Amish ideals, Johnny cannot remain neutral when he sees injustice.

As in other kinds of fiction, sports stories follow trends and issues. In the past, books about girls' sports have been undistinguished, but more are beginning to appear. *Not Bad for a Girl* by Isabella Taves is based on a real case of a girl who is put on a Little League team by a sympathetic coach. Sharon plays well, but there is such abuse and persecution by local residents that the coach and Sharon are expelled. The realistic ending gives more impact to the exposure of sexism than any formula happy ending could. Another good story for girls is Matt Christopher's *Red-Hot Hightops*. Good at all

From *Red-Hot Hightops* by Matt Christopher, illustrated by Paul D. Moek.

sports, Zan Hagen moves from football to basketball in R. R. Knudson's *Zanbanger* and participates in a marathon in the 1984 Olympics in *Zan Hagen's Marathon*. The popularity of running and jogging should provide a captive audience for the persevering heroine of Elizabeth Winthrop's *Marathon Miranda*. In Scott Corbett's *The Hockey Girls*, a group of high-school girls are horrified when they discover that an athletic program has been set up for girls, since not any of them are interested in sports. But the field hockey coach, an elderly English teacher, is competent and enthusiastic, and the girls find, once they have attained proficiency, that they enjoy the game.

The interest in the problem of drugs is reflected in William Heumann's *Fastbreak Rebel*, in which the white protagonist on a pro basketball team encourages his coach to sign on an African-American player who has given up drugs and is especially anxious to show the young people of his deprived neighborhood that there is a better way than the marijuana-to-heroin path. The ethical and biological problems raised by the use of steroids are considered in *Anything to Win*, by Gloria Miklowitz.

Although few American readers understand the fine points of cricket, nobody can miss the high-spirited humor of P. G. Wodehouse's *Mike and Psmith*, first published in 1909, but a timeless piece of school humor. Last, for really mature readers, *Today's Game*, by Martin Quigley, is valuable both because of the author's expert knowledge of baseball behind the scene and because of the brisk, professional approach to the problems of a manager, his moves and counter-moves in a crucial game. This is a side of baseball seldom described, and it paves the way for some of the adult baseball classics such as *Bang the Drum Slowly* by Mark Harris and *The Long Season* by Jim Brosnan.

Mystery and Adventure

A classification of children's books which cuts across all groups of realistic fiction in all countries and times is the mystery story. The mystery tale is certainly a striking example of the way in which children's books parallel predominant trends in adult reading interests. With many mothers, fathers, and grandparents all devoted to the "whodunit" school of writing, it is not surprising to find a seven-year-old marching into the children's room of a library and demanding a good mystery story.

The extreme popularity of the mystery tale at present may be a fad as far as children are concerned, artificially stimulated by adult emphasis. An element of mystery has always been a source of interest in a story and always will be. But when innumerable books are written merely for the sake of the mystery, the pattern and mood of such tales are liable to become tiresomely repetitious and the stories are likely to be trash. At their worst, such books are marked by preposterous plots, details left unaccounted for, too many episodes, violence piled upon violence, typed characters, and, finally, poor style.

The virtues of good adventure stories and mystery tales for children are numerous, but first among these is the atmosphere of excitement and suspense which serves as the most tempting of all baits for nonreaders. Comic-strip-addicted and television-fed children demand a highly spiced book fare if they are going to read at all, and these mystery tales are usually adventure stories with plenty of breathtaking action to keep young thrill-seekers absorbed. Another useful feature of such stories is that they help establish a much needed reading skill—rapid silent reading. Children unconsciously speed up their usual reading rate under the stimulus of an agreeable suspense. They will cover pages of a mystery tale at breakneck speed in their desire to find the answers and solve the mystery. This rapid rate of silent reading, together with a little skipping or skimming on the way, is a useful habit for fiction readers to establish—the younger the better. A carefully structured mystery story can help develop logical thinking.

Finally, if children can be supplied with adventure and mystery stories which are also well written and not too difficult for them to read, unbookish children can be persuaded to read a better type of literature than they might otherwise attempt.

The appeal of suspense often leads children to read above their usual level. Older children will plunge happily into adult mystery stories,

Viewpoint

Children's mysteries rely on action more than adult mysteries; there must be physical as well as cerebral adventure. Murder is not a necessary, if even desirable, ingredient.

Despite these differences, however, the appeal of mysteries for children and adults is fundamentally the same. First of all, mysteries are games. The more mysteries we read, the more adept at the game we become. A well-written mystery is a game we can't lose. If we succeed in solving the case before the sleuth does, we are impressed with our own cleverness.

While the appeal of writing mysteries is not unrelated to the appeal of reading them, there is another key factor at play and that has to do with the unique challenge of the craft. However one may wish to define it as a piece of literature, a mystery is always a puzzle. The challenge of writing the mystery is to construct the puzzle so that all the pieces fit; then take it apart, scramble the pieces, and know that when the reader gets to the final piece, everything will fit together again seamlessly.

While plot is crucial, a writer must always begin with character. Too many mysteries, especially for children, begin and end with plot. Character creates the solid foundation on which to build the story; and it is interesting, odd, fully human characters who prevent a story from evaporating the minute the reader has finished it. For me, beginning with character means writing character histories before I tackle the details of the plot. After all, my characters will ultimately dictate the nuances of the story. My characters will determine the "how" and "why" of the events.

In writing mysteries, as in any writing, one must make every effort to be specific. Stephen Sondheim once said in an interview that the telling detail is the essence of writing. I can think of no better words of advice for any writer.

James Howe, "Writing Mysteries for Children," *The Horn Book Magazine,* March/April 1990, p. 179.

---

and children in the middle grades may have favorite authors whose books are intended for older children. Even the youngest have mystery tales: short, easy to read, and wisely laced with humor. Some of these are Joan Lexau's *The Rooftop Mystery* and *The Homework Caper*, Elizabeth Levy's *Something Queer Is Going On*, and Crosby Bonsall's stories—*The Case of the Cat's Meow* and others with a lively interracial cast.

Popular with the eight-to-ten age group are the tales by Donald Sobol about a boy detective; in *Encyclopedia Brown Saves the Day* and others the astute ten-year-old solves a series of short mysteries, with answers at the back of the book. One of many in a series, David Adler's *The Fourth Floor Twins and the Skyscraper Parade* has two sets of twins who investigate a museum theft.

The series of adventure tales by Alan Coren that begins with *Arthur the Kid* has elements of mystery, but the author, editor of *Punch* magazine, uses outrageous and very funny exaggeration as ten-year-old Arthur solves all crimes and problems in this and other spoofs of the desperado tale.

It is for the ten- to twelve-year-olds that mystery stories begin to appear in large numbers, although any true fan will read any good mystery—and even some not so good. Although the plot of Frank Bonham's *Mystery in Little Tokyo* is somewhat contrived, Bonham draws a picture of the Japanese section of Los Angeles as a solid neighborhood community with rich tradition. Jane Curry's maturity as a writer is evident in *Ghost Lane*, with a tight plot and strong characterization giving substance to a mystery story about an art-theft ring in

England, and the American boy who becomes involved in it. Winner of the Newbery Medal, *The Westing Game*, by Ellen Raskin, posits a set of clues, presented by a wily millionaire to a chosen group of treasure hunters.

Philippa Pearce's *The Minnow Leads to Treasure* is a story notable for its distinctive style and well-paced plot. In *The Minnow*, two boys recover a family treasure that had been lost since the time of the Spanish Armada; to the lure of the subject and the suspense of the story are added superbly natural characters, humor, and an evocative atmosphere of long, golden summer days.

In Robert Newman's *The Case of the Murdered Players*, two young people help a Scotland Yard detective. Sid Fleischman's Newbery Medal book, *The Whipping Boy*, is a funny, robust adventure tale. A kidnapping is solved by a

From *The Whipping Boy* by Sid Fleischman, illustrated by Peter Sis.

doughty girl in Dorothy Crayder's *She and the Dubious Three*; and a heroine is herself kidnapped in Margaret Storey's *Ask Me No Questions*. Local legends permeate *Mystery at the Edge of Two Worlds* by Christie Harris, whose familiarity with Canada's northwest coast adds color to a fast-paced adventure story.

Lloyd Alexander, in a series of picaresque adventure stories set in the 1870s, features an intrepid teenage heroine who tackles anything fearlessly; Holly romps through *The Illyrian Adventure*, *The El Dorado Adventure*, *The Drackenburg Adventure*, *The Jedera Adventure*, and *The Philadelphia Adventure*. In Eva-Lis Wuorio's *Save Alice!* three children have an exciting journey through Spain, trying to discover why Alice (a bird) had been shoved into their car and what the dastardly villains who did it are up to. In addition to the fun, the story has delightful dialogue between the British and American contingents of the party.

When we come to the mystery and adventure tales for children of eleven and up, we face an avalanche. One of the great classic tales of adventure is Robert Louis Stevenson's *Treasure Island*, which has been published in many fine editions. The story of Long John Silver and his pirate crew has suspense, masterly characterization, a rousing plot, and an adroit contrast in moral codes.

One of the master storytellers of our time in the realm of high adventure is Leon Garfield. His stories are set in the eighteenth century, abound in picturesque language, period details, complicated plots, exaggerated characters (usually of very high or very low estate), and are written so deftly that the wildly implausible is made wholly convincing. In *Black Jack*, for example, a hanged man revives, captures an orphaned boy, and holds up a coach from which an insane girl escapes. The boy and girl join a caravan, she regains her sanity, her father is murdered, she goes to an asylum, the repentant highwayman rescues her, and the boy and girl sail off as stowaways in his uncle's ship, presumably to a much quieter life. Equally ebullient are *The Night of the Comet* and *The December Rose*. There is dramatic suspense in Amy Ehrlich's story of a girl whose mother moves from town to town in *Where It Stops, Nobody Knows*.

The books of Philip Turner are more boys-and-ploys than they are mysteries, though in *Colonel Sheperton's Clock* the boys, busily investigating an old mystery, find themselves involved with criminals. The first sequel, *The Grange at High Force*, was awarded the Carnegie Medal, and all of the books are distinguished by a vivid picture of an English town and by the sparkling dialogue, which is tossed back and forth from boy to boy like a ping-pong ball.

Felicity Bell tells her own story in Patricia Moyes's *Helter-Skelter*, an artfully plotted tale of a security leak at a British naval research base, during which the heroine confides in the culprit himself and thereby endangers her life. Also set in England are excellent suspense stories by authors of other kinds of books. Vivien Alcock's *The Mysterious Mr. Ross* has a Gothic element, and *On the Edge* by Gillian Cross is a story of a boy who has lost his memory.

Madeleine L'Engle's rather involved adventure story, *The Arm of the Starfish*, revolves around the kidnapping of Poly, the precocious twelve-year-old daughter of Calvin and Meg Murry O'Keefe (of L'Engle's science fiction trilogy). Calvin O'Keefe, now a marine biologist, is working on regeneration of body parts, and there are spies and agents prying about the Portuguese island that is the setting. Despite the complications of plot, the story is strong in appeal because of its theme of the triumph of good over evil, or at least of the humane over the inhumane. This is true also of the sequels, *Dragons in the Waters* and *A House Like a Lotus*.

A fledgling spy almost muffs his first assignment in Christopher Nicole's *Operation Destruct*, a story that has the mad pace of the adult spy stories it mocks, light humor, and refreshing variation in detail, such as the pretty girl reporter who is far more adept than the hero and who falls for a pop singer. William Mayne, writing under the name of Martin Cobalt, in *Pool of Swallows* produces a brilliant blend of ghostly happenings, humor, and suspense, as some mysterious pools that suddenly swirl and flood prove to have a logical explanation.

Frank Bonham's *Mystery of the Fat Cat* is set in a poor neighborhood, Dogtown, where the Boys' Club members suspect that the cat's caretaker has substituted another animal so that he will not lose his job (he is paid out of an estate which goes to the Boys' Club after the cat's death). The efforts of the boys to prove a fraud has been perpetrated are exciting and believable, and the inclusion of a mentally retarded child as a sympathetic character who contributes to the solution is a bonus. Gary Paulsen's *Hatchet* has a man-against-wilderness suspense, as a boy of thirteen is the sole survivor of a plane crash.

Of the many mystery anthologies, one that approaches the quality of the best compilations for adults is Joan Kahn's *Some Things Fierce and Fatal*. Other anthologies are included in the bibliography for this chapter.

The books discussed here should suffice to show how mystery cuts across most forms of fiction. Unlike adult "whodunits," the juvenile stories seldom involve murder. Rather, the element of mystery is introduced to heighten interest and suspense. Not all of these books have literary distinction, though many are competently written, and some are distinctive. Mystery tales for children are particularly valuable when, in the course of exciting action, they also emphasize desirable attitudes and social relationships.

The books mentioned in this chapter do not by any means exhaust the list of good realistic fiction for children and young people. To give only the best to children, the adult should be aware of the pedestrian books that are written as "bandwagon" books to satisfy a demand, and should evaluate new books with a critical appraisal of how well they meet the standards discussed in Chapter 2 and fulfill the needs discussed in Chapter 1. The best in this genre will always be those books that depict life honestly and accurately. They are the ones that are interesting in themselves, that present characters who evoke understanding or even self-identification, and that give children new insights into experiences both familiar and unknown.

Adult References and Book Selection Aids*

CLARK, ANN NOLAN. *Journey to the People.*

EGOFF, SHEILA. *The Republic of Childhood: A Critical Guide to Canadian Children's Literature in English.* Part 4, "The Realistic Animal Story."

————. *Thursday's Child: Trends and Patterns in Contemporary Children's Literature.*

EGOFF, SHEILA, G. T. STUBBS, and L. F. ASHLEY, eds. *Only Connect: Readings on Children's Literature.* Part 5, "The Modern Scene."

ELLIS, ANNE W. *The Family Story in the 1960's.*

FENWICK, SARA INNIS, ed. *A Critical Approach to Children's Literature.* "Literature for Children Without" by Marion Edman.

HILDICK, WALLACE. *Children and Fiction.*

HOPKINS, LEE BENNETT. *Books Are by People.*

LEPMAN, JELLA. *A Bridge of Children's Books.*

REES, DAVID. *The Marble in the Water.*

SIMS, RUDINE. *Shadow & Substance: Afro-American Experience in Contemporary Children's Fiction.*

TWAY, EILEEN, ed. *Reading Ladders for Human Relations.*

WHITE, DOROTHY. *Books Before Five.*

*Complete bibliographic data are provided in Appendices A and B.

For additional titles for the youngest children, see the Picture Story Books bibliography, Chapter 4.

For help in locating books with special purposes or about minorities, see Appendix A, "Book Selection Aids." In the following bibliography these symbols have been used to identify books about a particular religious or ethnic group:

§ African American
★ Hispanic
☆ Native American
○ Asian American
● Religious minority

Some Forerunners of Realistic Fiction

ALCOTT, LOUISA M. *Little Women,* ill. by Barbara Cooney. T. Crowell, 1955 (first pub. in 1868).

————. *Little Women,* ill. by Jessie W. Smith. Little, 1968.   10–13

BURNETT, FRANCES HODGSON. *The Secret Garden,* ill. by Tasha Tudor. Lippincott, 1962 (first pub. in 1909).   9–11

DODGE, MARY MAPES. *Hans Brinker: or the Silver Skates,* ill. by Hilda Van Stockum. World, 1948 (first pub. in 1865).   10–12

SPYRI, JOHANNA. *Heidi,* ill. by Greta Elgaard. Macmillan, 1962 (first pub. in 1884).   9–11

TWAIN, MARK (pseud. for Samuel Clemens). *The Adventures of Huckleberry Finn,* ill. by John Falter. Macmillan, 1962 (first pub. in 1885).   10 up

————. *The Adventures of Tom Sawyer,* ill. by John Falter. Macmillan, 1962 (first pub. in 1876).   10–14

————. *The Adventures of Tom Sawyer,* ill. by Barry Moser. Morrow, 1989.   10–14.

————. *The Adventures of Tom Sawyer* and *The Adventures of Huckleberry Finn,* ill. by Norman Rockwell, 2 vols. in 1. Heritage, 1952.   10–14

Realistic Fiction: The United States

§ ADOFF, ARNOLD, ed. *Brothers and Sisters: Modern Stories by Black Americans.* Macmillan, 1970. A discriminating selection of twenty short stories about African-American youth, varied in period, setting, style, and mood, chosen from a 40-year span.   12 up

§ AGLE, NAN HAYDEN. *Maple Street,* ill. by Leonora E. Prince. Seabury, 1970. An African-American Baltimore neighborhood is kind to a hostile white family in time of trouble.   8–10

ALEXANDER, MARTHA G. *Marty McGee's Space Lab, No Girls Allowed,* ill. by author. Dial, 1981. Somehow, it's the girls who triumph.   5–7

§ ————. *The Story Grandmother Told,* ill. by author. Dial, 1969.   3–6

ALIKI. *The Two of Them,* ill. by author. Greenwillow, 1979.   5–8

§ ARMSTRONG, WILLIAM. *Sounder,* ill. by James Barkley. Harper, 1969. Newbery Medal.   12–15

★ ☆ ● ASSOCIATION FOR CHILDHOOD EDUCATION. *Told Under the Stars and Stripes,* ill. by Nedda Walker. Macmillan, 1945. An interracial collection.   8–12

☆ BAKER, BETTY. *The Shaman's Last Raid,* ill. by Leonard Shortall. Harper, 1963. Two Apache children of today learn something of their tribal culture when great-grandfather visits them.   9–11

★ BARTH, EDNA. *The Day Luis Was Lost,* ill. by Lilian Obligado. Little, 1971. Newly arrived in the city, a Puerto Rican child has trouble finding his way to school.   8–10

BAUER, MARION DANE. *On My Honor.* Houghton/Clarion, 1986. Joel feels responsible for Tony's drowning after having challenged him to a swimming race.   10–13

§ BEIM, LORRAINE and JERROLD. *Two Is a Team,* ill. by Ernest Crichlow. Harcourt, 1945. An African American and a white child learn to cooperate.   5–8

★ BELPRE, PURA. *Santiago,* ill. by Symeon Shimin. Warne, 1969. Missing his pet, left behind in Puerto Rico, a child finds that his picture of her brings him a new friend.   8–9

§ BERENDS, POLLY BERRIEN. *The Case of the Elevator Duck,* ill. by James K. Washburn. Random, 1973. Gilbert, bright, African American, bespectacled, finds a duck in the housing project elevator, where no pets are allowed, and finally finds a home for it. A natural, funny story.   8–10

BLUE, ROSE. *Grandma Didn't Wave Back,* ill. by Ted Lewin. Watts, 1972.   8–10

• BLUME, JUDY. *Are You There God? It's Me, Margaret.* Bradbury, 1970.   10–12

————. *Blubber.* Bradbury, 1974.   9–11

————. *Deenie.* Bradbury, 1973.   10–13

∘ ————. *Just as Long as We're Together.* Orchard/Watts, 1987.   10–12

————. *The Pain and the Great One,* ill. by Irene Trivas. Bradbury, 1984.   5–8

————. *Superfudge.* Dutton, 1980.   8–10

————. *Tales of a Fourth Grade Nothing,* ill. by Roy Doty. Dutton, 1972.   8–9

————. *Then Again, Maybe I Won't.* Bradbury, 1971.   10–12

§ BONHAM, FRANK. *Durango Street.* Dutton, 1965. A story of a slum gang.   11–14

§ ————. *The Nitty Gritty,* ill. by Alvin Smith. Dutton, 1968. An African-American adolescent is torn between indolence and industry.   11–14

★ ————. *Viva Chicano.* Dutton, 1970. A Chicano youth on parole fights to escape from the burdens that have trapped him into delinquency.   13–16

BRIDGERS, SUE ELLEN. *All Together Now.* Knopf, 1979. Twelve-year-old Casey, spending a summer with her grandparents, befriends a retarded man of thirty.   10–12

BROOKS, JEROME. *Uncle Mike's Boy.* Harper, 1973. A boy adjusting to his parents' divorce and the death of a small sister finds his uncle a source of support and understanding. A warm, sensitive, at times touching, story.   10–12

BROWN, MARGARET WISE. *The City Noisy Book,* ill. by Leonard Weisgard. Harper, 1939.   4–6

————. *The Dead Bird,* ill. by Remy Charlip. W. R. Scott, 1958. A simple story of some children's burial of a bird.   5–7

————. *The Little Fisherman,* ill. by Dahlov Ipcar. W. R. Scott, 1945.   4–6

————. (Golden MacDonald, pseud.). *The Little Island,* ill. by Leonard Weisgard. Doubleday, 1946. Gentle descriptive prose. Caldecott Medal.   4–8

☆ BUFF, MARY and CONRAD. *Hah-Nee of the Cliff Dwellers,* ill. by Conrad Buff. Houghton, 1956. A story of the great pueblo cities of the Southwest.   10–12

BULLA, CLYDE ROBERT. *The Chalk Box Kid,* ill. by Thomas B. Allen. Random House, 1987. Everything in nine-year-old Gregory's life changes for the worse when his father loses his job, until Gregory is recognized for his artistic talent at his new school.   7–9

☆ ————. *Eagle Feather,* ill. by Tom Two Arrows. T. Crowell, 1953. Eagle Feather, a young Navaho, loved the outdoor life of a shepherd and had no wish to go to school until changed circumstances made school a longed-for goal.   7–10

☆ ————. *Indian Hill,* ill. by James Spanfeller. T. Crowell, 1963. Adjustment of a Navaho family moved to a city apartment.   8–10

BUNTING, EVE. *The Wednesday Surprise,* ill. by Donald Carrick. Clarion, 1989. Seven-year-old Anna teaches her grandma to read as a surprise for Dad's birthday.   5–8

BURCH, ROBERT. *Christmas with Ida Early.* Viking, 1983.   9–11

————. *Ida Early Comes over the Mountain.* Viking, 1980.   9–11

————. *Joey's Cat,* ill. by Don Freeman. Viking, 1969.

§ ————. *Queenie Peavy,* ill. by Jerry Lazare. Viking, 1966.   11–14

BYARS, BETSY C. *Bingo Brown and the Language of Love.* Viking, 1989.   10–13

————. *The Burning Questions of Bingo Brown.* Viking, 1988.   10–13

————. *Cracker Jackson.* Viking, 1985.   10–12

————. *The Cybil War,* ill. by Gail Owens. Viking, 1981.   8–10

————. *The Night Swimmers,* ill. by Troy Howell. Delacorte, 1980.   10–12

————. *The Not-Just-Anybody Family,* ill. by Jacqueline Rogers. Delacorte, 1986. And its sequels about the Blossom family.   10–12

————. *The Pinballs.* Harper, 1977.   10–12

————. *The Summer of the Swans,* ill. by Ted CoConis. Viking, 1970. Newbery Medal.   10–12

_____. *The TV Kid,* ill. by Richard Cuffari. Viking, 1976.   8–9

§ CAINES, JEANNETE FRANKLIN. *Abby,* ill. by Steven Kellogg. Harper, 1973. A small, African-American girl learns about her adoption.   3–6

§ CAMERON, ANN. *Julian's Glorious Summer,* ill. by Dora Leder. Random House, 1987. Julian unsuccessfully tries to conceal his fear of learning to ride a bicycle with a series of lies told to his family and best friend.   7–9

§ _____. *More Stories Julian Tells,* ill. by Ann Strugnell. Knopf, 1986. Short but carefully constructed anecdotes in a simple but lively style are narrated by Julian about his family.   7–9

CAMERON, ELEANOR. *Julia and the Hand of God,* ill. by Gail Owens. Dutton, 1977.   9–11

_____. *Julia's Magic,* ill. by Gail Owens. Dutton, 1984.   8–10

_____. *The Private Worlds of Julia Redfern.* Dutton, 1988.   11–14

_____. *A Room Made of Windows,* ill. by Trina Schart Hyman. Little, 1971.   10–13

_____. *That Julia Redfern.* Dutton, 1982.   8–10

§ _____. *To the Green Mountains.* Dutton, 1975.   10–13

§ CARLSON, NATALIE SAVAGE. *Ann Aurelia and Dorothy,* ill. by Dale Payson. Harper, 1968.   8–10

§ _____. *The Empty Schoolhouse,* ill. by John Kaufmann. Harper, 1965.   9–11

§ _____. *Marchers for the Dream,* ill. by Alvin Smith. Harper, 1969.   9–11

CASSEDY, SYLVIA. *M. E. and Morton.* T. Crowell, 1987.   10–13

§ CAUDILL, REBECCA. *A Certain Small Shepherd,* ill. by William Pène du Bois. Holt, 1965. An Appalachian Christmas story, movingly told.   9–11

_____. *Did You Carry the Flag Today, Charley?* ill. by Nancy Grossman. Holt, 1966.   5–7

§ ★ CHILD STUDY ASSOCIATION OF AMERICA. *Families Are Like That!* ill. by Richard Cuffari. T. Crowell, 1975. Ten stories of family life and relationships.   7–9

§ CHILDRESS, ALICE. *A Hero Ain't Nothin' But a Sandwich.* Coward, 1973.   11–14

☆ CLARK, ANN NOLAN. *Little Navajo Bluebird,* ill. by Paul Lantz. Viking, 1943.   8–12

☆ _____. *Medicine Man's Daughter,* ill. by Donald Bolognese. Farrar, 1963.   11–13

CLEARY, BEVERLY. *Dear Mr. Henshaw,* ill. by Paul O. Zelinsky. Morrow, 1983. Newbery Medal.   9–11

_____. *Ellen Tebbits,* ill. by Louis Darling. Morrow, 1951. The trials and tribulations of being in third grade.   8–12

_____. *Henry Huggins,* ill. by Louis Darling. Morrow, 1950. And other books in the series.   8–10

_____. *Lucky Chuck,* ill. by J. Winslow Higginbottom. Morrow, 1984.   5–8

_____. *Mitch and Amy,* ill. by George Porter. Morrow, 1967.   9–11

_____. *Ramona Forever!* ill. by Alan Tiegreen. Morrow, 1984.   8–10

_____. *Ramona Quimby, Age 8,* ill. by Alan Tiegreen. Morrow, 1981.   7–9

_____. *Ramona the Brave,* ill. by Alan Tiegreen. Morrow, 1975.   8–10

_____. *Ramona the Pest,* ill. by Louis Darling. Morrow, 1968.   8–10

CLEAVER, VERA. *Moon Lake Angel.* Lothrop, 1987.   10–12

_____. *Sugar Blue.* Lothrop, 1984.   9–11

CLEAVER, VERA and BILL. *Ellen Grae,* ill. by Ellen Raskin. Lippincott, 1967.   9–11

_____. *I Would Rather Be a Turnip.* Lippincott, 1971.   10–12

_____. *Lady Ellen Grae,* ill. by Ellen Raskin. Lippincott, 1968.   9–11

_____. *Where the Lilies Bloom,* ill. by Jim Spanfeller, 1969.   11–14

CLIFFORD, ETH. *The Rocking Chair Rebellion.* Houghton, 1978.   10–12

§ CLIFTON, LUCILLE. *Don't You Remember?* Ill. by Evaline Ness. Dutton, 1973. A charming African-American family story, with a four-year-old who remembers everything.   3–5

§ _____. *My Friend Jacob,* ill. by Thomas Digrazia. Dutton, 1980.   5–7

§ _____. *The Times They Used to Be,* ill. by Susan Jeschke. Holt, 1974.   10–11

CLYMER, ELEANOR. *The Get-Away Car.* Dutton, 1978. Maggie and her grandmother prove that grandma isn't ready for an old people's home.   9–11

§ _____. *Luke Was There,* ill. by Diane de Groat. Holt, 1973.   9–12

☆ _____. *The Spider, the Cave and the Pottery Bowl,* ill. by Ingrid Fetz. Atheneum, 1971.   8–10

• COHEN, BARBARA. *Molly's Pilgrim,* ill. by Michael J. Deraney. Lothrop, 1983. A Jewish immigrant to America helps her classmates understand the meaning of the Pilgrims.   7–8

§ • _____. *Thank You, Jackie Robinson,* ill. by Richard Cuffari. Lothrop, 1974.   9–11

COLE, BROCK. *Celine.* Farrar, 1989. A most perceptive and witty novel with a convincing first-person voice, a style that is outstanding for its flow, pace, and wit. More stress on relationships (varied) than plot.   12–15

_____. *The Goats,* ill. by author. Farrar, 1987.   10–13

COLLIER, JAMES LINCOLN. *Rich and Famous: The Further Adventures of George Stable.* Four Winds, 1975.   11–14

§ COLMAN, HILA. *Classmates by Request.* Morrow, 1964. A white girl requests a transfer to an all African-American school.   12–15

★ ———. *The Girl from Puerto Rico.* Morrow, 1961. A new arrival is shocked by the prejudice she encounters in the U.S.   12–15

CONFORD, ELLEN. *Felicia the Critic,* ill. by Arvis Stewart. Little, 1973. Why did people get so irritated when Felicia just used common sense and told the truth? Funny, completely natural dialogue.
                    10–12

CORCORAN, BARBARA. *A Dance to Still Music,* ill. by Charles Robinson. Atheneum, 1974.   11–13

CORMIER, ROBERT. *The Bumblebee Flies Anyway.* Pantheon, 1983.   12–15

• ———. *The Chocolate War.* Pantheon, 1974, and its sequel, *Beyond the Chocolate War.* Knopf, 1985.
                    12–16

CRAYDER, DOROTHY. *She, the Adventuress,* ill. by Velma Ilsley. Atheneum, 1973.   9–11

CRETAN, GLADYS YESSAYAN. *All Except Sammy,* ill. by Symeon Shimin. Little, 1966. The misfit in a musical Armenian-American family, Sammy finds status and satisfaction in art.   8–10

DANZIGER, PAULA. *The Cat Ate My Gymsuit.* Delacorte, 1974.   11–13

———. *There's a Bat in Bunk Five.* Delacorte, 1980. Marcy is a junior camp counselor in this entertaining sequel to *The Cat Ate My Gymsuit.*
                    11–13

DAVIS, JENNY. *Sex Education.* Orchard/Watts, 1988.
                    12–15

§ DE ANGELI, MARGUERITE. *Bright April,* ill. by author. Doubleday, 1946.   8–11

• ———. *Henner's Lydia,* ill. by author. Doubleday, 1936.   8–10

• ———. *Thee, Hannah!* ill. by author. Doubleday, 1940.   9–11

• ———. *Yonie Wondernose,* ill. by author. Doubleday, 1944.   6–9

DE PAOLA, TOMIE. *Nana Upstairs and Nana Downstairs,* ill. by author. Putnam, 1973.   5–8

———. *Now One Foot, Now the Other,* ill. by author. Putnam, 1981.   5–7

☆ DISTAD, ANDREE. *Dakota Sons,* ill. by Tony Chen. Harper, 1972. When Tad made friends with a native-American boy, he found out just how pervasive prejudice could be.   9–11

DONOVAN, JOHN. *I'll Get There. It Better Be Worth the Trip.* Harper, 1969.   11–14

———. *Wild in the World.* Harper, 1971.   11–14

☆ EMBRY, MARGARET. *Shadi.* Holiday, 1971. A story of cultural conflict for an adolescent Navaho girl.
                    11–14

ENRIGHT, ELIZABETH. *The Four-Story Mistake,* ill. by author. Holt, 1942.   9–11

———. *Gone-Away Lake,* ill. by Beth and Joe Krush. Harcourt, 1957.   8–10

———. *Return to Gone-Away,* ill. by Beth and Joe Krush. Harcourt, 1961.   8–10

———. *The Saturdays,* ill. by author. Holt, 1941.
                    9–12

———. *Then There Were Five,* ill. by author. Holt, 1944.   10–13

ESTES, ELEANOR. *Ginger Pye,* ill. by author. Harcourt, 1951. Newbery Medal.   9–11

———. *The Hundred Dresses,* ill. by Louis Slobodkin. Harcourt, 1944.   9–11

———. *The Lost Umbrella of Kim Chu,* ill. by Jacqueline Ayer. Atheneum, 1978.   8–9

———. *The Middle Moffat,* ill. by Louis Slobodkin. Harcourt, 1942.   9–11

———. *The Moffat Museum,* ill. by author. Harcourt, 1983.   8–10

———. *The Moffats,* ill. by Louis Slobodkin. Harcourt, 1941, 1968.   9–11

———. *Rufus M.,* ill. by Louis Slobodkin. Harcourt, 1943.   9–11

FASSLER, JOAN. *Howie Helps Himself,* ill. by Joe Lasker. Whitman, 1974.   6–8

§ FENNER, CAROL. *The Skates of Uncle Richard,* ill. by Ati Forberg. Random, 1978.   8–9

• FENTON, EDWARD. *Duffy's Rocks.* Dutton, 1974. Timothy, raised by his grandmother, can't rest until he sees his father for himself. An outstanding story of a Roman Catholic family in the Depression years.   11–13

• FITZGERALD, JOHN DENNIS. *The Great Brain Does It Again,* ill. by Mercer Mayer. Dial, 1975. One of a series about a Roman Catholic family living in a Mormon town. Lively and funny.   10–12

FITZHUGH, LOUISE. *Harriet the Spy,* ill. by author. Harper, 1964.   10–12

———. *The Long Secret,* ill. by author. Harper, 1965.   11–13

§ ———. *Nobody's Family Is Going to Change.* Farrar, 1974. An African-American father scoffs at the daughter who wants to be a lawyer like him, but Emma won't change her mind.   10–11

FLEISCHMAN, PAUL. *Coming-and-Going Men,* ill. by Randy Gaul. Harper, 1985. Set in the past, four linked stories of traveling men.   11–14

———. *Graven Images,* ill. by Andrew Glass. Harper, 1982. Three tales of human folly.   12–15

———. *Rear-View Mirrors.* Harper, 1986.
                    12–15

FOX, PAULA. *Blowfish Live in the Sea.* Bradbury, 1970.
                    11–14

§ ———. *How Many Miles to Babylon?* ill. by Paul Giovanopoulos. White, 1967.   9–10

————. *A Likely Place,* ill. by Edward Ardizzone. Macmillan, 1967.   9–11

————. *Maurice's Room.* ill. by Ingrid Fetz. Macmillan, 1966.   8–10

————. *The Moonlight Man.* Bradbury, 1986.   12–15

————. *One-Eyed Cat.* Bradbury, 1984.   10–12

————. *A Place Apart.* Farrar, 1980.   12 up

————. *Portrait of Ivan,* ill. by Saul Lambert. Bradbury, 1969.   10–12

————. *The Stone-Faced Boy,* ill. by Donald A. MacKay. Bradbury, 1968.   9–11

————. *The Village by the Sea.* Orchard/Watts, 1988.   10–13

★ GALBRAITH, CLARE K. *Victor,* ill. by Bill Comerford. Knopf, 1971. Victor has a hard time with a new language, and is delighted when Mamacita shows up at school on Parents' Night and airs her secretly learned English.   8–9

GATES, DORIS. *Blue Willow,* ill. by Paul Lantz. Viking, 1940. A story of migratory farm workers and ten-year-old Janey's longing for a permanent home.   10–12

GEORGE, JEAN C. *My Side of the Mountain,* ill. by author. Dutton, 1959.   11–14

☆ ————. *The Talking Earth.* Harper, 1983.   11–14

☆ ————. *Water Sky,* ill. by author. Harper, 1987.   11–14

★ ○ GIRARD, LINDA WALVOORD. *We Adopted You, Benjamin Koo,* ill. by Linda Shute. Whitman, 1989. 8–10

GOFF, BETH. *Where Is Daddy? The Story of a Divorce,* ill. by Susan Perl. Beacon, 1969.   3–5

GOFFSTEIN, M. B. *Two Piano Tuners,* ill. by author. Farrar, 1970. Orphaned Debbie lives with her grandfather, an expert piano tuner. He wants Debbie to be a concert pianist; she wants to be a piano tuner as good as Grandpa. The story has humor, affection, and charm.   8–9

§ GRAHAM, LORENZ. *North Town.* T. Crowell, 1965.

§ ————. *South Town.* Follett, 1958.

§ ————. *Whose Town?* T. Crowell, 1969. In these books the Williams family leaves the South because of discrimination, but finds much discrimination in the North as well. David, a teenager, wavers between militancy and moderation.   11–14

§ GREENE, BETTE. *Get on Out of Here, Philip Hall.* Dial, 1981.   9–11

§ ————. *Philip Hall Likes Me. I Reckon Maybe,* ill. by Charles Lilly. Dial, 1974.   9–11

• ————. *Summer of My German Soldier.* Dial, 1973. A mistreated Jewish girl living in a small Arkansas town in the 1940s befriends an escaped German prisoner.   11–14

GREENE, CONSTANCE C. *Al(exandra) the Great.* Viking, 1982.   10–12

————. *Ask Anybody.* Viking, 1983.   9–11

————. *A Girl Called Al,* ill. by Byron Barton. Viking, 1969.   9–11

————. *I Know You, Al,* ill. by Byron Barton. Viking, 1975.   8–11

————. *Isabelle and Little Orphan Frannie.* Viking, 1988.   8–10

————. *Isabelle Shows Her Stuff.* Viking, 1984.   8–10

————. *Just Plain Al.* Viking, 1986.   10–13

————. *The Unmasking of Rabbit.* Viking, 1972.   9–11

————. *Your Old Pal Al.* Viking, 1979.

§ GREENFIELD, ELOISE. *Sister,* ill. by Moneta Barnett. T. Crowell, 1974.   10–12

GREENWALD, SHEILA. *The Secret in Miranda's Closet,* ill. by author. Houghton, 1977. Should the daughter of a militant feminist play with dolls?   8–10

§ GUY, ROSA. *The Friends.* Holt, 1973.   12–15

§ ————. *The Ups and Downs of Carl Davis III.* Delacorte, 1989. In a series of letters, New Yorker Carl describes his difficulty adjusting to a life of exile with his grandma in South Carolina.   10–13

HALL, LYNN. *The Giver.* Scribner's, 1985.   12–15

§ ☆ HAMILTON, VIRGINIA. *Arilla Sun Down.* Greenwillow, 1976.   12–14

————. *The House of Dies Drear,* ill. by Eros Keith. Macmillan, 1968.   11–14

§ ————. *A Little Love.* Philomel, 1984.   12–15

§ ————. *M. C. Higgins, the Great.* Macmillan, 1974. Newbery Medal. National Book Award.   11–13

§ ————. *The Mystery of Drear House.* Greenwillow, 1987.   10–12

§ ————. *The Planet of Junior Brown.* Macmillan, 1971.   12–14

§ ————. *Time-Ago Lost: More Tales of Jahdu,* ill. by Ray Prather. Macmillan, 1973.   8–10

§ ————. *Time-Ago Tales of Jahdu,* ill. by Nonny Hogrogian. Macmillan, 1969.   8–10

§ ————. *Willie Bea and the Time the Martians Landed.* Greenwillow, 1983.   10–13

§ ————. *Zeely,* ill. by Symeon Shimin. Macmillan, 1967.   9–11

§ HANSEN, JOYCE. *Yellow Bird and Me.* Houghton/Clarion, 1986. In a sequel to *The Gift Giver,* sixth-grader Doris discovers her talented but irritating classmate, Yellow Bird, has a learning disability.   9–11

☆ HASELEY, DENNIS. *The Scared One,* ill. by Deborah Howland. Warne, 1983. A native-American boy better understands his own fears after rescuing a large injured bird.   9–11

HAUTZIG, DEBORAH. *Second Star to the Right.* Greenwillow, 1981. The complexities of a mother-daughter relationship are thrown into high relief in this compassionate story about a teenage victim of anorexia nervosa. 12–15

HAYWOOD, CAROLYN. *"B" Is for Betsy,* ill. by author. Harcourt, 1939, 1968. And other books in the series. 6–8

————. *The King's Monster,* ill. by Victor Ambrus. Morrow, 1980. 5–7

————. *Little Eddie,* ill. by author. Morrow, 1947. And other books in the series. 7–9

HEIDE, FLORENCE PARRY. *Growing Anyway Up.* Lippincott, 1976. The compulsive behavior patterns and self-denigration of a withdrawn, disturbed young girl are depicted with sharp perception. 10–12

————. *Tales for the Perfect Child,* ill. by Victoria Chess. Lothrop, 1985. Drawings of amicable monsters illustrate stories of how children outwit their parents in order to avoid chores. Told with dry humor. 8–10

————. *Time Flies,* ill. by Marylin Hafner. Holiday House, 1984. In a witty tale, Noah manages to survive daily life with his family, including his time-expert father and noisy new sibling. 9–11

§ HENTOFF, NAT. *Jazz Country.* Harper, 1965. A white jazz musician is accepted by an African-American group. 13 up

————. *This School Is Driving Me Crazy.* Delacorte, 1975. An interesting story of relationships between students and teachers. 10–13

HERMAN, CHARLOTTE. *Millie Cooper, Take a Chance,* ill. by Helen Cogancherry. Dutton, 1988. This sequel to *Millie Cooper, 3B* continues the story of Millie's trials and triumphs as a school-girl in 1947. 8–10

☆ HIGHWATER, JAMAKE. *Moonsong Lullaby,* photos by Marcia Keegan. Lothrop, 1981. 8–10

§ HILL, ELIZABETH. *Evan's Corner,* ill. by Nancy Grossman. Holt, 1967. 5–7

HINTON, S. E. *The Outsiders,* Viking, 1967. 13–15

————. *Rumble Fish.* Delacorte, 1975. 12–16

————. *Tex.* Delacorte, 1979. 12–15

————. *That Was Then, This Is Now.* Viking, 1971. 13–15

HOBAN, RUSSELL C. *The Sorely Trying Day,* ill. by Lillian Hoban. Harper, 1964. A family finds that hostile or friendly behavior can have a chain effect. 5–7

HOLLAND, ISABELLE. *The Man Without a Face.* Lippincott, 1972. A boy from an all-female household finds help in an older man's affection. A dignified treatment of a homosexual incident. 12–15

HOLMAN, FELICE. *Slake's Limbo.* Scribner's, 1974. Slake lives in a hideaway in the New York subway

for four months, existing like a Crusoe, through resourcefulness. A smooth, novel tale. 10–12

HUGHES, DEAN. *Family Pose.* Atheneum, 1989. A nightshift hotel crew becomes family for a runaway orphan. 10–15

HUNT, IRENE. *Up a Road Slowly.* Follett, 1967. Julie Trelling, left motherless at age seven, is sent to live with an aunt and uncle who provide her with insight into the qualities necessary to become a mature, happy individual. Newbery Medal. 11–14

§ HUNTER, KRISTIN. *Guests in the Promised Land.* Scribner's, 1973. 12–15

§ ————. *The Soul Brothers and Sister Lou.* Scribner's, 1968. 12–15

§ HURMENCE, BELINDA. *Tough Tiffany.* Doubleday, 1980. A finely developed account of the redoubtable youngest child in a large, African-American family. 10–12

HURWITZ, JOANNA. *Class Clown,* ill. by Sheila Hamanka. Morrow, 1987. Third-grade cut-up Lucas Cott finds that by learning to control his silliness and by accepting responsibility, he can make and keep friends. 8–10

• ————. *Hurray for Ali Baba Bernstein,* ill. by Gail Owens. Morrow, 1989. A sequel to *The Adventures of Ali Baba Bernstein* shows Ali Baba in a series of new adventures enhanced by his imagination. 8–10

————. *Russell and Elisa,* ill. by Lillian Hoban. Morrow, 1989. 5–8

§ JACKSON, JESSE. *Call Me Charley,* ill. by Doris Spiegel. Harper, 1945. 10–13

§ ————. *Charley Starts from Scratch.* Harper, 1958. Two sensitive stories of an African-American boy who lives in a white neighborhood. After high school, Charley finds many doors closed to him until he comes in first in Olympic trials. 12 up

§ ————. *Tessie,* ill. by Harold James. Harper, 1968. An African-American girl wins a scholarship to an all-white private school, and firmly insists on making the best of both worlds. 11–14

§ JORDAN, JUNE. *New Life: New Room,* ill. by Ray Cruz. T. Crowell, 1975. 5–8

• JORDAN, MILDRED. *Proud to Be Amish,* ill. by W. T. Mars. Crown, 1968. Katie has a hard time with guilt feelings when she envies the dress of a child who's not "plain." 10–11

JUKES, MAVIS. *Like Jake and Me,* ill. by Lloyd Bloom. Knopf, 1984. Alex discovers that his big ex-cowboy stepfather is afraid of spiders in a gentle story of a growing friendship, illustrated with soft pastels. 7–9

§ JUSTUS, MAY. *New Boy in School,* ill. by Joan Balfour Payne. Hastings, 1963. Lennie must adjust to being the only African-American boy in his class.   7–8

§ _____. *A New Home for Billy,* ill. by Joan Balfour Payne. Hastings, 1966.   5–8

KATZ, BOBBI. *The Manifesto and Me—Meg.* Watts, 1974.   9–12

KELLER, BEVERLY. *Desdemona—Twelve Going on Desperate.* Lothrop, 1986. While the landlord threatens to replace her family's house with a high-rise condo, Desdemona lives through the painful experiences of a pre-teen. Sequel to *No Beasts! No Children!*   10–13

KERR, M. E. *Dinky Hocker Shoots Smack.* Harper, 1972.   11–14

_____. *Fell.* Harper, 1987.   12–15

_____. *Fell Back.* Harper, 1989.   12–15

_____. *Gentlehands.* Harper, 1978. Buddy is impressed by Grandfather Trenker's culture and devotion to stray animals despite the rumors 'of his atrocious activities while in charge of a Nazi concentration camp.   12–14

• _____. *Him She Loves?* Harper, 1984.   12–15

_____. *Is That You, Miss Blue?* Harper, 1975.   12–16

_____. *Little Little.* Harper, 1981.   12–15

KLEIN, NORMA. *Confessions of an Only Child,* ill. by Richard Cuffari. Pantheon, 1974.   9–11

_____. *Going Backwards.* Scholastic, 1986.   12–15

_____. *It's Not What You Expect.* Pantheon, 1973.   11–14

_____. *Learning How to Fall.* Bantam, 1989.   11–14

_____. *Mom, the Wolf Man, and Me.* Pantheon, 1972.   10–13

§ KONIGSBURG, E. L. *Altogether, One at a Time,* ill. by Gail E. Haley and others. Atheneum, 1971.   9–11

_____. *The Dragon in the Ghetto Caper,* ill. by author. Atheneum, 1974.   10–12

_____. *Father's Arcane Daughter.* Atheneum, 1976.   10–14

_____. *From the Mixed-Up Files of Mrs. Basil E. Frankweiler,* ill. by author. Atheneum, 1967. Newbery Medal.   10–12

_____. *(George),* ill. by author. Atheneum, 1970.   11–14

§ _____. *Jennifer, Hecate, Macbeth, William McKinley, and Me, Elizabeth,* ill. by author. Atheneum, 1967.   9–11

_____. *Journey to an 800 Number.* Atheneum, 1982.   10–14

★ KRUMGOLD, JOSEPH. *. . . and now Miguel,* ill. by Jean Charlot. T. Crowell, 1953. Newbery Medal.   13–17

_____. *Onion John,* ill. by Symeon Shimin. T. Crowell, 1959. Newbery Medal.   11–14

LASKER, JOE. *He's My Brother,* ill. by author. Whitman, 1974.   7–9

_____. *Nick Joins In,* ill. by author. Whitman, 1980. In a story about the mainstreaming of exceptional children, Nick adjusts to attending public school.   7–8

☆ LAURITZEN, JONREED. *The Ordeal of the Young Hunter,* ill. by Hoke Denetsosie. Little, 1954. A distinguished story of a twelve-year-old Navaho boy who grows to appreciate what is good in the cultures of the white man and the native American.   11–14

§ LAWLOR, LAURIE. *How to Survive Third Grade,* ill. by Joyce Audy Zarins. Whitman, 1988. The class runt and outcast finds an ally in a new boy from Kenya.   7–9

LEE, MILDRED. *The Rock and the Willow.* Lothrop, 1963.   14–16

LE GUIN, URSULA. *Very Far Away from Anywhere Else.* Atheneum, 1976. A story of the problems of a seventeen-year-old intellectual, lacking in surface action but heavy on characterization and the complexity of human relationships.   12–15

L'ENGLE, MADELEINE. *Meet the Austins.* Vanguard, 1960. A fine family story.   10–13

_____. *The Moon by Night.* Ariel, 1963. The Austins go camping.   11–14

LENSKI, LOIS. *Bayou Suzette,* ill. by author. Stokes, 1943.   8–10

_____. *High-Rise Secret,* ill. by author. Lippincott, 1966.   8–9

_____. *Judy's Journey,* ill. by author. Lippincott, 1947.   8–10

_____. *Strawberry Girl,* ill. by author. Lippincott, 1945. Newbery Medal.   9–12

○ LEVINE, ELLEN. *I Hate English!* ill. by Steve Bjorkman. Scholastic, 1989. In a humorous and convincing story, a newcomer from Hong Kong resists speaking English until she finds an understanding teacher.   7–9

• LEVOY, MYRON. *Alan and Naomi.* Harper, 1977. Young Naomi, a refugee from Nazi oppression in France, finally begins to forget her fears when she's befriended by Alan only to have all progress negated by a bunch of prejudiced toughs at school.   11–13

★ LEWITON, MINA. *Candita's Choice,* ill. by Howard Simon. Harper, 1959. A warm and understanding story of an eleven-year-old who adjusts slowly to the move from Puerto Rico to New York.   9–11

§ LEXAU, JOAN. *Benjie,* ill. by Don Bolognese. Dial, 1964.   5–7

§ _____. *Benjie on His Own,* ill. by Don Bolognese. Dial, 1970.   5–8

§ _____. *I'll Tell on You*, ill. by Gail Owens. Dutton, 1976.   5–8

_____. *Olaf Reads*, ill. by Harvey Weiss. Dial, 1961.   6–7

§ _____. *Striped Ice Cream*, ill. by John Wilson. Lippincott, 1968.   7–9

○ LORD, BETTE BAO. *In the Year of the Boar and Jackie Robinson*, ill. by Marc Simont. Harper, 1984. In a story that has cultural dignity, young Chinese immigrant Shirley Temple Wong adjusts to life in Brooklyn and becomes a baseball fan.   8–10

LOWRY, LOIS. *All About Sam*, ill. by Diane de Groat. Houghton, 1988. Irrepressible Sam dominates new tales as well as legendary episodes from the Anastasia books.   9–12

_____. *Anastasia at Your Service*, ill. by Diane de Groat. Houghton, 1982.   9–11

_____. *Anastasia Has the Answers*. Houghton, 1986.   9–12

_____. *Anastasia Krupnik*. Houghton, 1979.
9–11

_____. *Anastasia on Her Own*. Houghton, 1985.
10–12

§ _____. *Anastasia's Chosen Career*. Houghton, 1987.   10–13

§ _____. *Autumn Street*. Houghton, 1980.   10–12

_____. *The One Hundredth Thing about Caroline*. Houghton, 1983.   10–12

_____. *Rabble Starkey*. Houghton, 1987.   10–13

MCCLOSKEY, ROBERT. *Blueberries for Sal*, ill. by author. Viking, 1948. Sal gets home safely after following a bear in the blueberry patch.   4–7

_____. *Centerburg Tales*, ill. by author. Viking, 1951. Humorous stories.   10–12

_____. *Homer Price*, ill. by author. Viking, 1943. Lively, funny stories about an irrepressible boy; one of the first books to spoof comic books.
9–12

_____. *Lentil*, ill. by author. Viking, 1940. A boy saves the day in a small town's welcome to a returning citizen by playing the harmonica.   7–9

_____. *Make Way for Ducklings*, ill. by author. Viking, 1941. Caldecott Medal.   6–8

_____. *One Morning in Maine*, ill. by author. Viking, 1952.   5–7

_____. *Time of Wonder*, ill. by author. Viking, 1957. Caldecott Medal.   8–10

§ MCGOVERN, ANN. *Black Is Beautiful*, ill. by Hope Wurmfeld. Four Winds, 1969.   5–8

○ MCHUGH, ELISABET. *Karen and Vicki*. Greenwillow, 1984. Stepsisters and opposites Karen and Vicki resent having to share a room after the new baby is born. Third in a series.   9–11

_____. *Raising a Mother Isn't Easy*. Greenwillow, 1983. Responsible Karen, an adopted Korean child, scouts out a new husband for her loving but disorganized mother.   10–12

MACLACHLAN, PATRICIA. *Arthur, for the Very First Time*. Harper, 1980.   9–11

_____. *Cassie Binegar*. Harper, 1982. Cassie comes to terms with her eccentric family, gets over a crush on a writer, and adjusts to her grandfather's death in this polished merging of colorful characters and shifting relationships.
9–11

_____. *The Facts and Fictions of Minna Pratt*. Harper, 1988.   9–12

_____. *Unclaimed Treasures*. Harper, 1984.
10–12

MAREK, MARGOT. *Different, Not Dumb*, ill. with photos by Barbara Kirk. Watts, 1985. During an emergency, Mike proves to himself and his classmates that he is smart even though he is learning disabled.   7–8

☆ MARTIN, BILL, and JOHN ARCHAMBAULT. *Knots on a Counting Rope*, ill. by Ted Rand. Holt, 1987. Rhythmic chants comprise a powerful dialogue between an old man and his blind grandson, Boy-Strength-of-Blue Horses.   5–8

§ MATHIS, SHARON BELL. *The Hundred Penny Box*, ill. by Leo and Diane Dillon. Viking, 1975.   8–11

_____. *Listen for the Fig Tree*. Viking, 1974.
12–16

MAYNE, WILLIAM. *The Jersey Shore,* Dutton, 1973.
11–12

MAZER, HARRY. *When the Phone Rang*. Scholastic, 1985.   11–14

MAZER, NORMA FOX. *After the Rain*. Morrow, 1987.
11–14

_____. *A Figure of Speech*. Delacorte, 1973. A moving, realistic story of a child's love for her grandfather.   11–14

☆ MEANS, FLORENCE CRANNELL. *Our Cup Is Broken*. Houghton, 1969.   12–15

§ ★ _____. *Us Maltbys*. Houghton, 1966.   11–14

MILES, BETTY. *Maudie and Me and the Dirty Book*. Knopf, 1980. A sixth-grade girl is aghast when parents attack her reading of an innocuous book to a first grade.   10–13

_____. *The Real Me*. Knopf, 1974.   9–11

★ MOHR, NICHOLASA. *El Bronx Remembered: A Novella and Stories*. Harper, 1975. A varied group of stories, atmospheric and told with simplicity of style.   12–14

★ _____. *Going Home*. Dial, 1986. Eleven-year-old Felita encounters friendship, romance, and prejudice on her first trip from New York to her native Puerto Rico.   9–11

★ _____. *Nilda*, ill. by author. Harper, 1973.
11–14

§ MURRAY, MICHELE. *Nellie Cameron,* ill. by Leonora E. Prince. Seabury, 1971.   9–11

§ MYERS, WALTER DEAN. *Fast Sam, Cool Clyde, and Stuff.* Viking, 1975.   11–14

§ _____. *Me, Mop, and the Moondance Kid,* ill. by Rodney Pate. Delacorte, 1988. A little league season brings success for two adopted brothers and adoption for their best friend.   10–12

§ _____. *Motown and Didi.* Viking, 1984.   12–15

§ ★ _____. *Scorpions.* Harper, 1988.   11–14

§ _____. *The Young Landlords.* Viking, 1979.   11–14

NATHANSON, LAURA. *The Trouble with Wednesdays.* Pacer/Putnam, 1986. As her orthodontist, Dr. Rolfman, becomes increasingly sexually aggressive, sixth-grader Becky begins to dread Wednesdays.   10–13

NAYLOR, PHYLLIS REYNOLDS. *The Keeper.* Atheneum, 1986. Nick's loyalty to his father is tested when Nick realizes he must reveal his father's paranoid delusions to those who can help.   12–15

NESS, EVALINE. *Sam, Bangs & Moonshine,* ill. by author. Holt, 1966. Sam is a small, mendacious girl and Bangs is her cat and moonshine is the word for all the lies she tells. Attractive illustrations. Caldecott Medal.   5–7

§ NEUFELD, JOHN. *Edgar Allan.* Phillips, 1968. A poignant story of a white family's adoption of an African-American child, and the pressure that forces them to give him up.   11–14

• NEVILLE, EMILY. *Berries Goodman.* Harper, 1965.   11–14

_____. *It's Like This, Cat,* ill. by Emil Weiss. Harper, 1963. Newbery Medal.   11–14

NEWTON, SUZANNE. *I Will Call It Georgie's Blues.* Viking, 1983. A Baptist minister's three children struggle to cope with their authoritarian, bullying father in a taut story of a troubled family.   12–15

NORDSTROM, URSULA. *The Secret Language,* ill. by Mary Chalmers. Harper, 1960.   7–9

☆ O'DELL, SCOTT. *Black Star, Bright Dawn.* Houghton, 1988. Bright Dawn courageously takes the place of her injured father in the Iditarod, the annual Alaskan dog sled race.   11–14

★ _____. *Child of Fire.* Houghton, 1974.   12–15

§ PANETTA, GEORGE. *The Shoeshine Boys,* ill. by Joe Servello. Grosset, 1971. Tony, an Italian-American, becomes a shoeshine boy to help out with the finances when his father loses his job. He joins forces with MacDougal Thompson, an African-American boy, and the Black and White Shoeshine Company is a great success.   8–10

PATERSON, KATHERINE. *Bridge to Terabithia,* ill. by Donna Diamond. T. Crowell, 1977. Newbery Medal.   10–12

_____. *Come Sing, Jimmy Jo.* Lodestar, 1985.   10–12

_____. *The Great Gilly Hopkins.* T. Crowell, 1978. National Book Award.   10–13

_____. *Jacob Have I Loved.* T. Crowell, 1980. Newbery Medal.   11–14

○ _____. *Park's Quest.* Lodestar, 1988. Park, eleven, convinces his overprotective mother to allow him to visit the family of his father, who was killed in Vietnam.   10–13

PECK, RICHARD. *Don't Look and It Won't Hurt.* Holt, 1972.   11–14

_____. *Princess Ashley.* Delacorte, 1987.   12–15

_____. *Remembering the Good Times.* Delacorte, 1985.   12–15

_____. *Representing Super Doll.* Viking, 1974.   11–15

• PECK, ROBERT NEWTON. *A Day No Pigs Would Die.* Knopf, 1972. Anecdotal story of a Shaker boy on a Vermont farm, where families have strong ties.   12–16

PEVSNER, STELLA. *And You Give Me a Pain, Elaine.* Seabury, 1978. Thirteen-year-old Andrea's older sister (sulky and rebellious) is the bane of her existence.   10–12

_____. *A Smart Kid Like You.* Seabury, 1975.   10–12

★ POLITI, LEO. *Juanita,* ill. by author. Scribner's, 1948.   5–7

_____. *Little Leo,* ill. by author. Scribner's, 1951.   5–8

_____. *Moy Moy,* ill. by author. Scribner's, 1960.   5–7

★ _____. *Song of the Swallows,* ill. by author. Scribner's, 1949. Caldecott Medal.   5–7

RASKIN, ELLEN. *Spectacles,* ill. by author. Atheneum, 1968. An amusing picture book about the trials and errors of a small girl who myopically sees strange creatures and finally is won over to wearing glasses.   5–7

ROBERTS, WILLO DAVIS. *Don't Hurt Laurie!* ill. by Ruth Sanderson. Atheneum, 1977. A trenchant story of child abuse ends on a note of hope.   9–11

ROBERTSON, KEITH. *Henry Reed, Inc.,* ill. by Robert McCloskey. Viking, 1958.   11–13

_____. *Henry Reed's Think Tank.* Viking, 1986.   9–12

_____. *In Search of a Sandhill Crane,* ill. by Richard Cuffari. Viking, 1973.   10–13

RODOWSKY, COLBY F. *H, My Name Is Henley.* Farrar, 1982. Henley endures a peripatetic life with a self-indulgent mother until finding security with an aunt.   10–12

§ ROSE, KAREN. *A Single Trail.* Follett, 1969. Ricky is white and entering a new sixth grade after nine moves. Earl is African American and antagonistic in school. Their friendship comes very slowly with help from an understanding mother. The story has a sturdy honesty. 10–11

• ———. *There Is a Season.* Follett, 1967. Katie Levin dates a new neighbor, a Roman Catholic boy, but finds that religious pressures interfere. 11–14

RYLANT, CYNTHIA. *A Blue-Eyed Daisy.* Bradbury, 1985. During the year Ellie is eleven, she and her father become closer when they get a special hunting dog. 10–12

• SACHS, MARILYN. *Amy Moves In,* ill. by Judith G. Brown. Doubleday, 1964. Amy moves to another section of the Bronx in this likable family story set in the 1930s. Followed by *Laura's Luck* (1965) and *Amy and Laura* (1966).

———. *The Bears' House,* ill. by Louis Glanzman. Doubleday, 1971. 9–12

———. *Bus Ride,* ill. by Amy Rowen. Dutton, 1980. 11–14

———. *The Fat Girl.* Dutton, 1983. 12–14

———. *Fran Ellen's House.* Dutton, 1987. 9–11

• ———. *Peter and Veronica,* ill. by Louis Glanzman. Doubleday, 1969. 9–12

§ ———. *A Secret Friend.* Doubleday, 1978. 9–11

———. *Thunderbird,* ill. by Jim Spence. Dutton, 1985. 11–14

• ———. *Veronica Ganz,* ill. by Louis Glanzman. Doubleday, 1968. 10–12

SAWYER, RUTH. *Roller Skates,* ill. by Valenti Angelo. Viking, 1936. Newbery Medal. 12–13

§ SCHOTTER, RONI. *Efan the Great,* ill. by Rodney Pate. Lothrop, 1986. When ten-year-old Efan's meager savings will not buy even the smallest Christmas tree, he works all day at a tree lot and decorates his block with the huge tree he receives as payment. 5–8

SCOPPETTONE, SANDRA. *Trying Hard to Hear You.* Harper, 1974. 13–18

§ SCOTT, ANN HERBERT. *Sam,* ill. by Symeon Shimin. McGraw, 1967. Although the story is more an expanded situation than a plot, it is a pleasant and realistic picture of Sam and his African-American, middle-class family. 3–6

• SEGAL, LORE. *Tell Me a Mitzi,* ill. by Harriet Pincus. Farrar, 1970. 5–7

SHARMAT, MARJORIE WEINMAN. *Goodnight Andrew Goodnight Craig,* ill. by Mary Chalmers. Harper, 1969. Two small boys, who have gone to bed, get noisier and noisier until their father comes in with an ultimatum. The illustrations echo the engaging tone of the story, which is all in dialogue. 4–6

———. *Maggie Marmelstein for President,* ill. by Ben Shecter. Harper, 1975. 9–11

§ ★ SHOTWELL, LOUISA R. *Adam Bookout,* ill. by W. T. Mars. Viking, 1967. An interracial story set in Brooklyn. Adam finds he can't avoid problems by moving from one relative's house to another. 9–11

★ ———. *Magdalena,* ill. by Lilian Obligado. Viking, 1971. 10–12

§ ———. *Roosevelt Grady,* ill. by Peter Burchard. World, 1963. 9–11

SHREVE, SUSAN. *The Flunking of Joshua T. Bates,* ill. by Diane de Groat. Knopf, 1984. A warm depiction of a teacher-pupil relationship features crisp dialogue and a sympathetic portrayal of a child repeating third grade. 7–9

———. *Lucy Forever and Miss Rosetree, Shrinks.* Holt, 1987. When playing as therapists, Lucy and Rosie become involved with a severely troubled five-year-old patient of Lucy's child-psychiatrist father. 9–10

SHURA, MARY FRANCES. *The Josie Gambit.* Dodd, 1986. As ruthlessly as she sacrifices her queen to try to win a chess game, Tory is willing to sacrifice Josie's friendship. 10–12

SHYER, MARLENE FANTA. *Welcome Home, Jellybean.* Scribner's, 1978. The painful, honest, convincing story of a retarded girl who comes home to live after years in an institution. 10–12

SLEPIAN, JAN. *The Alfred Summer.* Macmillan, 1980. 10–12

———. *The Broccoli Tapes.* Philomel, 1989. 10–12

———. *Lester's Turn.* Macmillan, 1981. 10–12

———. *The Night of the Bozos.* Dutton, 1983. 11–14

○ ———. *Something Beyond Paradise.* Philomel, 1987. Sixteen-year-old Franny is torn between loyalty to her mother and grandmother in Honolulu and a dance scholarship in New York City. 12–15

SLOTE, ALFRED. *Moving In.* Lippincott, 1988. *A Friend Like That.* Lippincott, 1988. In both books, eleven-year-old Robbie carries out elaborate plans to keep his widowed father from dating. 9–11

SMITH, DORIS BUCHANAN. *Kelly's Creek,* ill. by Alan Tiegreen. T. Crowell, 1975. An appealing story of a boy with a learning disability. 9–11

———. *Last Was Lloyd.* Viking, 1981. A poignant depiction of the blossoming of an insecure, overprotected child. 9–11

———. *Return to Bitter Creek.* Viking, 1986. 10–12

☆ SMUCKER, BARBARA. *Wigwam in the City,* ill. by Gil Miret. Dutton, 1966. One of the few stories about discrimination against native Americans in an urban setting. A Chippewa family in Chicago turns to the American Indian Center for help. 10–12

☆ SNEVE, VIRGINIA DRIVING HAWK. *High Elk's Treasure,* ill. by Oren Lyons. Holiday, 1972. A story of a Sioux Indian family that makes clear the attitudes of contemporary native Americans of different generations. 9–12

SNYDER, ZILPHA KEATLEY. *The Birds of Summer.* Atheneum, 1983. 12–15

————. *Blair's Nightmare.* Atheneum, 1984. 9–11

§ ————. *The Egypt Game,* ill. by Alton Raible. Atheneum, 1967. 9–12

————. *A Fabulous Creature.* Atheneum, 1981. 11–14

————. *The Headless Cupid,* ill. by Alton Raible. Atheneum, 1971. 9–11

○ ————. *Janie's Private Eyes.* Delacorte, 1989. 9–11

★ SONNEBORN, RUTH. *Friday Night Is Papa Night,* ill. by Emily A. McCully. Viking, 1970. 6–7

§ SORENSON, VIRGINIA. *Around the Corner,* ill. by Robert Weaver. Harcourt, 1971. An African-American family welcomes white neighbors. 10–12

————. *Miracles on Maple Hill,* ill. by Beth and Joe Krush. Harcourt, 1956. Newbery Medal. 10–12

● ————. *Plain Girl,* ill. by Charles Geer. Harcourt, 1955. An Amish girl adjusts to public school. 9–11

§ STEPTOE, JOHN. *Stevie,* ill. by author. Harper, 1969. 5–7

§ STERLING, DOROTHY. *Mary Jane,* ill. by Ernest Crichlow. Doubleday, 1959. A story of the beginning of school integration. 10–13

STOLZ, MARY. *The Bully of Barkham Street,* ill. by Leonard Shortall. Harper, 1963. 10–12

————. *By the Highway Home.* Harper, 1971. 11–13

★ ————. *Cider Days.* Harper, 1978. Fifth grader Polly helps a new friend, lonely for Mexico, adjust to Vermont. 9–10

————. *A Dog on Barkham Street,* ill. by Leonard Shortall. Harper, 1960. 10–12

————. *The Edge of Next Year.* Harper, 1974. 10–13

————. *The Explorer of Barkham Street,* ill. by Emily Arnold McCully. Harper, 1985. 10–12

★ ————. *The Noonday Friends,* ill. by Louis S. Glanzman. Harper, 1965. 9–11

§ ————. *A Wonderful, Terrible Time,* ill. by Louis S. Glanzman. Harper, 1967. 9–11

§ TATE, ELEANOR E. *The Secret of Gumbo Grove.* Watts, 1987. In first-person narrative, eleven-year-old Raisin creates community controversy with ques-

tions about the names on some tombstones in the local South Carolina graveyard. 10–12

§ TAYLOR, MILDRED. *Roll of Thunder, Hear My Cry,* ill. by Jerry Pinkney. Dial, 1976. 12–15

● TAYLOR, SYDNEY. *All-of-a-Kind Family,* ill. by Helen John. Follett, 1951. And its sequels. 9–11

§ TAYLOR, THEODORE. *The Cay.* Doubleday, 1969. 12–15

○ TERRIS, SUSAN. *The Latchkey Kids.* Farrar, 1986. Callie, eleven, is angry at her responsibilities as the oldest in a family of latchkey children, a situation brought about by her father's severe depression. 9–11

★ THOMAS, DAWN C. *Mira! Mira!* ill. by Harold L. James. Lippincott, 1970. A Puerto Rican child adjusts to a move to New York when he sees his first snowfall which he feels "fell from the sky to say 'Welcome'." 5–7

TRESSELT, ALVIN. *Hide and Seek Fog,* ill. by Roger Duvoisin. Lothrop, 1965. 5–8

————. *What Did You Leave Behind?* ill. by Roger Duvoisin. Lothrop, 1978. 5–8

————. *White Snow, Bright Snow,* ill. by Roger Duvoisin. Lothrop, 1947. Caldecott Medal. 5–7

UCHIDA, YOSHIKO. *The Birthday Visitor,* ill. by Charles Robinson. Scribner's, 1975. 7–9

○ ————. *The Promised Year,* ill. by William M. Hutchinson. Harcourt, 1959. A Japanese girl visits the U.S. 9–11

§ UDRY, JANICE MAY. *Mary Jo's Grandmother,* ill. by Eleanor Mill. Whitman, 1970. 5–7

————. *The Moon Jumpers,* ill. by Maurice Sendak. Harper, 1959. Beautiful color illustrations enhance this mood picture book which describes children frolicking in the moonlight until bedtime interrupts their imaginative play. 5–8

VIGNA, JUDITH. *Nobody Wants a Nuclear War,* ill. by author. Whitman, 1986. After two young children build a secret bomb shelter, their mother helps them face their fears of nuclear war. 5–7

VOIGT, CYNTHIA. *Dicey's Song.* Atheneum, 1982. Newbery Medal. 10–13

————. *Seventeen against the Dealer.* Atheneum, 1989. 11–14

————. *A Solitary Blue.* Atheneum, 1983. 11–14

————. *Sons from Afar.* Atheneum, 1987. 11–14

§ WALDRON, ANN. *The Integration of Mary-Larkin Thornhill.* Dutton, 1975. A white minister's daughter is assigned to a black junior high school in the South. 10–13

§ WEIK, MARY HAYS. *The Jazz Man,* ill. by Ann Grifalconi. Atheneum, 1966. A story that gives a poignant picture of a crippled child in Harlem.

This has had high praise for its tender treatment of the child and harsh criticism for the depiction of parental neglect. 9–11

§ WILKINSON, BRENDA. *Ludell.* Harper, 1975. Three years in the life of an African-American girl in a small Georgia town in the 1950s. 11–13

§ ————. *Ludell and Willie.* Harper, 1977. While this is a story about an African-American adolescent girl, it is also about problems all teenagers share. 11–14

WILL and NICOLAS. *Russet and the Two Reds.* Harcourt, 1962.

————. *The Two Reds.* Harcourt, 1950. Slight but lively stories with the realism of city streets. 5–8

WINTHROP, ELIZABETH. *Marathon Miranda.* Holiday, 1979. Miranda suffers from asthma but decides to join her new friend, Phoebe, in training for the Central Park marathon anyway. 9–11

WOJCIECHOWSKA, MAIA. *Tuned Out.* Harper, 1968. 14–16

WOLFF, VIRGINIA EUWER. *Probably Still Nick Swansen.* Holt, 1988. 11–15

○ YASHIMA, TARO. *Umbrella,* ill. by author. Viking, 1958. To small Momo it seemed that rain would never come so that she might use her new blue umbrella and bright red boots. New York background. 4–6

○ YEP, LAURENCE. *Child of the Owl.* Harper, 1977. The impressive story of a young girl who comes to San Francisco to live with a grandmother she hardly knows, her growing love for this new woman, and her adjustment to her Chinese heritage. 11–14

————. *Sea Glass.* Harper, 1979. Craig, an eighth grader who is short, plump, and awkward at sports, has problems when his family moves from San Francisco's Chinatown to the small coastal town where his father grew up and was a basketball star. 11–13

ZINDEL, PAUL. *The Pigman.* Harper, 1968. 11–14

————. *The Pigman's Legacy.* Harper, 1980. 11–14

ZOLOTOW, CHARLOTTE. *A Father Like That,* ill. by Ben Shecter. Harper, 1971. 5–7

————. *The Hating Book,* ill. by Ben Shecter. Harper, 1969. 5–7

————. *My Grandson Lew,* ill. by William Pène du Bois. Harper, 1974. 3–7

————. *William's Doll,* ill. by William Pène du Bois. Harper, 1972. 5–8

Realistic Fiction: Other Countries
Africa

§ BESS, CLAYTON. *Story for a Black Night.* Houghton, 1982. A Liberian father tells his children a tragic yet tender story from his childhood in a vividly distinctive novel narrated in cadenced prose. 10–13

§ BØDKER, CECILL. *The Leopard,* tr. by Gunnar Poulsen. Atheneum, 1975. When a leopard steals a calf, Tibeso sets out to see a wise man and becomes involved with a thief. Set in Ethiopia. 10–12

§ CLIFFORD, MARY LOUISE. *Salah of Sierra Leone,* ill. by Elzia Moon. T. Crowell, 1975. A boy is uncertain which side is right in the political maneuvering surrounding the 1967 elections. 11–13

§ DINNEEN, BETTY. *Lion Yellow.* Walck/McKay, 1975. A Kenyan game park is threatened with closing. 10–12

§ FEELINGS, MURIEL. *Zamani Goes to Market,* ill. by Tom Feelings. Seabury, 1970. Adventures of a small boy in Ghana. 5–8

§ ————. *Song of the Boat,* ill. by Leo and Diane Dillon. T. Crowell, 1975. 8–9

§ JONES, TOECKEY. *Go Well, Stay Well.* Harper, 1980. In a story of interracial friendship, two girls find that candor and patience are needed. 11–14

§ KAYE, GERALDINE. *Comfort Herself,* ill. by Jennifer Northway. Andre Deutsch, 1985. After her mother is killed in a street accident, Comfort is faced with the difficult decision of whether to live with her African grandmother in Ghana or her white grandmother in England. 10–12

§ • LEVITIN, SONIA. *The Return.* Atheneum, 1987. Desta and her younger sister, both Jewish Ethiopians, face bloodshed, starvation, and disease as they flee to Israel. 11–14

§ MITCHISON, NAOMI. *Sunrise Tomorrow: A Story of Botswana.* Farrar, 1973. 12–15

§ NAGENDA, JOHN. *Mukasa,* ill. by Charles Lilly. Macmillan, 1973. 9–11

§ STEVENSON, WILLIAM. *The Bushbabies,* ill. by Victor Ambrus. Houghton, 1965. A most unusual story, both in the setting and in the beautifully built-up relationship between two people different in age, sex, race, and station. The story moves across wild African country. 11–14

§ WELLMAN, ALICE. *Tatu and the Honey Bird,* ill. by Dale Payson. Putnam, 1972. A small boy helps his sister get an education too. Set in Angola. 8–10

Australia and New Zealand

§ BRINSMEAD, HESBA FAY. *Pastures of the Blue Crane.* Coward, 1966.   13–15

CLARK, MAVIS THORPE. *Spark of Opal.* Macmillan, 1973.   11–14

KLEIN, ROBIN. *Hating Alison Ashley.* Viking, 1987. Erica sulks when her position as academic star is preempted by the pretty new student, Alison Ashley.   9–11

MAHY, MARGARET. *The Catalogue of the Universe.* McElderry, 1986. After hearing all her life about the passionate love affair between her mother and her unknown father, Angela is devastated when she finally tracks down her cold, heartless father.   12–15

OTTLEY, REGINALD. *Boy Alone,* ill. by Clyde Pearson. Harcourt, 1966. The story of a young adolescent in the Australian outback. The atmosphere is wonderfully created; the writing is perceptive. Followed by *Roan Colt* (1967) and *Rain Comes to Yamboorah* (1968).   10–12

PHIPSON, JOAN. *Birkin,* ill. by Margaret Horder. Harcourt, 1966. An engaging story about several children in a small Australian town who care for a calf. Plenty of action and humor.   10–12

————. *Hit and Run.* Atheneum, 1985. Because of his father's wealth and influence, Roland Fleming has always gotten away with irresponsibility, but when he goes too far by stealing a car and knocking over a baby in a pram, he is relentlessly pursued by Constable Sutton.   12–15

————. *Polly's Tiger,* ill. by Erik Blegvad. Dutton, 1974. Polly has problems making friends in a new home.   8–9

————. *When the City Stopped.* Atheneum, 1978.   10–13

SOUTHALL, IVAN. *Ash Road,* ill. by Clem Seale. St. Martin's, 1966.   11–14

————. *Let the Balloon Go,* ill. by Ian Ribbons. St. Martin's, 1968.   11–13

————. *The Long Night Watch.* Farrar, 1984.   14 up

————. *To the Wild Sky,* ill. by Jennifer Tuckwell. St. Martin's, 1967.   12–14

SPENCE, ELEANOR. *The Devil Hole.* Lothrop, 1977. This depicts, with great dramatic impact, the effects on a family when the fourth child proves to be autistic.   11–14

THIELE, COLIN. *Blue Fin.* Harper, 1974. Snook's skipper father is firmly convinced that his son can't do anything right on a tuna boat, but Snook gets an opportunity to prove his worth in this exciting tale.   11–14

————. *Fire in the Stone.* Harper, 1974.   11–14

————. *The Hammerhead Light.* Harper, 1977. An old man and a young girl battle together to preserve a condemned lighthouse.   10–12

WRIGHTSON, PATRICIA. A Racecourse for Andy, ill. by Margaret Horder. Harcourt, 1968.   10–12

Canada

CORCORAN, BARBARA, and BRADFORD ANGIER. *A Star to the North.* Nelson, 1970.   11–14

HOUSTON, JAMES. *Frozen Fire,* ill. by author. Atheneum, 1977. Set in the far north, this is the suspenseful tale of two young boys who battle snow and cold to rescue a missing father.   9–11

☆ ————. *River Runners: A Tale of Hardship and Bravery,* ill. by author. Atheneum, 1979.   12–14

• KAPLAN, BESS. *The Empty Chair.* Harper, 1978. A cozy, realistic story about Jewish family life, this centers around eleven-year-old Becky, her adjustment to her mother's death, and her eventual acceptance of a stepmother.   11–13

☆ KLEITSCH, CHRISTEL, and PAUL STEPHENS. *A Time to Be Brave.* Annick Press/Firefly, 1985. Eleven-year-old Tafia, who lives with her grandmother, father, and brother in an Ojibway community in Ontario, proves her courage during a crisis.   9–11

LITTLE, JEAN. *Home from Far,* ill. by Jerry Lazare. Little, 1965.   10–13

• ————. *Kate.* Harper, 1971.   10–13

————. *Listen for the Singing.* Dutton, 1977.   10–12

• ————. *Look through My Window,* ill. by Joan Sandin. Harper, 1970.   9–11

————. *Mama's Going to Buy You a Mockingbird.* Viking, 1985.   10–13

————. *Mine for Keeps,* ill. by Lewis Parker. Little, 1962.   10–12

MAJOR, KEVIN. *Hold Fast.* Delacorte, 1980. Newly orphaned, a boy of fourteen misses his younger brother and his Newfoundland village; a sympathetic cousin joins him in running away and camping. Canadian Library Association, Best Book of the Year.   12–14

☆ PITSEOLAK, PETER. *Peter Pitseolak's Escape from Death,* ill. by author. Delacorte, 1978. The true account of an Eskimo caught in a swiftly moving ice field with his son.   8–10

Central and South America

★ BEHN, HARRY. *The Two Uncles of Pablo,* ill. by Mel Silverman. Harcourt, 1959. Small Pablo copes with two antagonistic uncles as well as his own problem of trying to gain an education in an appealing story of Mexico. 9–11

BONHAM, FRANK. *The Vagabundos.* Dutton, 1969. 12–15

★ BUFF, MARY and CONRAD. *Magic Maize,* ill. by authors. Houghton, 1953. Guatemalan Indians and their problems. 9–12

★ BULLA, CLYDE. *Benito,* ill. by Valenti Angelo. T. Crowell, 1961. The encouragement of a successful artist helps orphaned Benito assert his need for time from endless farm drudgery to develop his talent. 8–10

★ CLARK, ANN NOLAN, *Santiago,* ill. by Lynd Ward. Viking, 1955. 12–14

★ ⸺. *Secret of the Andes,* ill. by Jean Charlot. Viking, 1952. Newbery Medal. 12–14

★ COHEN, MIRIAM. *Born to Dance Samba,* ill. by Gioia Fiammenghi. Harper, 1984. A girl living in a shanty community outside Rio de Janeiro longs to be chosen as the solo dancer for a Carnival celebration. 9–11

★ ETS, MARIE HALL, and AURORA LABASTIDA. *Nine Days to Christmas,* ill. by Marie Hall Ets. Viking, 1959. Ceci, a little girl of Mexico, discovers the fun of Christmas with her first piñata. Caldecott Medal. 5–8

★ NESS, EVALINE. *Josefina February,* ill. by author. Scribner's, 1963. A warm, quiet read-aloud story set in Haiti. 5–7

★ O'DELL, SCOTT. *The Black Pearl,* ill. by Milton Johnson. Houghton, 1967. The stark simplicity of the story and the deeper significance it holds in the triumph of good over evil add importance to the book, but even without these elements it would be enjoyable as a rousing adventure tale with beautifully maintained tempo and suspense as Ramon searches for a giant black pearl in the waters of Baja California. 12–17

★ SOMMERFELT, AIMÉ. *My Name Is Pablo,* tr. by Patricia Crampton, ill. by Hans Norman Dah. Criterion, 1966. Reflects the problems of the poor in Mexico City. 11–14

★ STOLZ, MARY. *The Dragons of the Queen,* ill. by Edward Frascino. Harper, 1969. A simply written tale which contrasts new ways of life with the old in Mexico. 10–12

★ ⸺. *Juan,* ill. by Louis S. Glanzman. Harper, 1970. A story of an orphaned boy, this has fine characterization. 9–11

★ SURANY, ANICO. *Ride the Cold Wind,* ill. by Leonard Everett Fisher. Putnam, 1964. The story of a small Peruvian boy who wishes to go fishing with his father on Lake Titicaca. He and his sister go boating alone, and when a storm comes up, they must be rescued. An appealing theme and setting. 8–10

★ VAN ITERSON, S. R. *Pulga,* tr. from the Dutch by Alexander and Alison Gode, Morrow, 1971. 11–14

China and Japan

BUCK, PEARL. *The Big Wave,* ill. by Hiroshige and Hokusai. Day, 1948. Jiya leaves the coast after a tidal wave destroys his home and the entire fishing village. When he is grown, he courageously returns to his traditional occupation. There is a heroic quality in the telling which makes this Japanese story a memorable one. 9–13

○ DEJONG, MEINDERT. *The House of Sixty Fathers,* ill. by Maurice Sendak. Harper, 1956. 11–13

○ FRIEDMAN, INA R. *How My Parents Learned to Eat,* ill. by Allen Say. Houghton, 1984. In a simple and appealing story, a small girl describes her parents' courtship and how they learned to adjust to two styles of eating. 5–8

HANDFORTH, THOMAS. *Mei Li,* ill. by author. Doubleday, 1938. The pleasant adventures of a little Chinese girl at the Fair. Caldecott Medal. 5–8

MATSUNO, MASAKO. *A Pair of Red Clogs,* ill. by Kazue Mizumura. World, 1960. A little Japanese girl damages her new red clogs by playing a game with them. Beautifully illustrated in color, with a universal theme. 5–8

SAY, ALLEN. *The Inn-Keeper's Apprentice.* Harper, 1979. Kiyoi becomes an apprentice to Japan's greatest cartoonist at thirteen. 11–14

UCHIDA, YOSHIKO. *The Forever Christmas Tree,* ill. by Kazue Mizumura. Scribner's, 1963. 5–8

⸺. *In-between Miya,* ill. by Susan Bennett. Scribner's, 1967. 9–12

⸺. *Sumi and the Goat and the Tokyo Express,* ill. by Kazue Mizumura. Scribner's, 1969. Sumi has a brief but delicious moment in the limelight when she is the only one who can get old Mr. Oda's goat to move from the path of the new Tokyo express. A charming book. 7–9

VINING, ELIZABETH GRAY. *The Cheerful Heart,* ill. by Kazue Mizumura. Viking, 1959. Tomi and her family return to Tokyo after World War II and start life anew. 9–11

YASHIMA, MITSU and TARO. *Plenty to Watch,* ill. by Taro Yashima. Viking, 1954. 8–10

YASHIMA, TARO. *Crow Boy,* ill. by author. Viking, 1955. 8–10

England, Ireland, Scotland, Wales

ALCOCK, VIVIEN. *The Cuckoo Sister.* Delacorte, 1986. Kate makes the shocking discovery that she has an older sister who was kidnapped as a baby when a girl claiming to be that sister turns up on the doorstep.   11–15

ARDIZZONE, EDWARD. *Little Tim and the Brave Sea Captain,* ill. by author. Walck, 1955 (first pub. in 1936). First of several books about Tim's adventures at sea.   4–6

BAWDEN, NINA. *Devil by the Sea.* Lippincott, 1976.   10–11

————. *A Handful of Thieves.* Lippincott, 1967.   10–12

————. *Henry,* ill. by Joyce Powzyk. Lothrop, 1988. While waiting for the London Blitz to end and their father to return from the fighting, a family makes a pet of a squirrel and names him Henry.   9–11

————. *Kept in the Dark.* Lothrop, 1982.   10–12

————. *The Outside Child.* Lothrop, 1989.   10–13

§ ————. *The Robbers.* Lothrop, 1979.   9–11

BOND, NANCY. *Country of Broken Stone.* Atheneum, 1980. Polished writing distinguishes a story about local resentment against the team conducting an archaeological dig.   11–14

CRESSWELL, HELEN. *Dear Shrink.* Macmillan, 1982. A witty, vigorously appealing novel about three plucky children who weather a series of upheavals during their parents' extended trip to South America.   10–13

————. *Ordinary Jack.* Macmillan, 1977. The first in a series based on the Bagthorpe family, each member of which is nutty and endowed with assorted talents . . . except for ordinary Jack. Sequels are *Absolute Zero, Bagthorpes Unlimited, Bagthorpes V. the World, Bagthorpes Abroad, Bagthorpes Haunted,* and *Bagthorpes Liberated.*   10–12

————. *The Winter of the Birds.* Macmillan, 1976. A lonely, terrified recluse; a suicidal man; and a timid young boy are all convincingly rescued from their respective plights by Patrick Finn—loquacious, expansive, radiant, and a true hero.   11 up

CROSS, GILLIAN. *Chartbreaker.* Holiday House, 1987. After arguing with her mother, Janis runs away and works as a singer for a rock band whose tunes eventually become big hits.   13–15

————. *A Map of Nowhere.* Holiday House, 1989.   10–12

————. *Roscoe's Leap.* Holiday House, 1987.   10–13

DOUHERTY, BERLIE. *Grannie Was a Buffer Girl.* Orchard/Watts, 1988. In a beautifully crafted story, the matrix for memories of an extended English family is given by Jess, about to go to France for a university year abroad. Carnegie Medal.   11–14

DU BOIS, WILLIAM PÈNE. *Gentleman Bear,* ill. by author. Farrar, 1985. A story about several generations in a noble English family focuses on the young heir and the teddy bear who always accompanies him.   9–11

FINE, ANNE. *Alias Madame Doubtfire.* Little, 1988. In a funny story about the serious subject of divorce, an out-of-work actor and frustrated father of three dresses up in drag and tricks his ex-wife into hiring him as her housekeeper.   10 up

————. *My War with Goggle-Eyes.* Joy Street/Little, 1989. A lively story of adjustment and an objective look at the nuclear deterrent debate.   10–14

GARDAM, JANE. *Bilgewater.* Greenwillow, 1977. The story of an "ugly" girl's first brush with romance, friendship, and haute couture told in touching but humorous style.   12–15

————. *The Hollow Land,* ill. by Janet Rawlins. Greenwillow, 1981. A polished series of closely linked stories about the lifelong friendship between a rural lad and a London boy; apt selections for reading aloud.   10–12

GARNETT, EVE. *The Family from One End Street,* ill. by author. Vanguard, 1960. The story of the big, cheerful Ruggles family who live in a poor neighborhood. Carnegie Medal.   11–13

GODDEN, RUMER. *Mr. McFadden's Hallowe'en.* Viking, 1975.   8–12

————. *The Rocking-Horse Secret,* ill. by Juliet Stanwell Smith. Viking, 1978. Living alone with her mother, caretaker of old Miss Pomeroy's house, Tibby produces a will that will enable them to remain on the estate after their employer's death.   9–11

• HARRIS, ROSEMARY. *Zed.* Faber, 1984. Zed tells the story of being held hostage by Arab terrorists along with his father and uncle.   12–14

HILDICK, E. W. *Louie's Snowstorm,* ill. by Iris Schweitzer. Doubleday, 1974.   10–12

HOWKER, JANNI. *Badger on the Barge and Other Stories.* Greenwillow, 1985. In each of five long stories, there is a special relationship between a child and an elderly person who influences the child in a significant way.   11–15

§ HUGHES, SHIRLEY. *Angel Mae,* ill. by author. Lothrop, 1989. Among the multi-ethnic assortment of angels in a school Christmas play, Mae is the one who falls off her chair.   4–7

HUNTER, MOLLIE. *Cat, Herself.* Harper, 1986. Catriona, a child of a Scottish tinker family, has determined that when she marries, she will not be her husband's chattel, like the other wives in the close-knit traveling community.   11–14

————. *The Third Eye.* Harper, 1979. Set in contemporary Scotland, this story concerns an earl whose family is under a curse and whose death is being investigated and fourteen-year-old Janet who reluctantly becomes involved.   11–14

§ KEMP, GENE. *Gowie Corby Plays Chicken.* Faber, 1980. Set in the same school as *The Turbulent Term of Tyke Tiler,* this is the rollicking story of a rebellious student and an African-American friend.
9–11

————. *The Turbulent Term of Tyke Tiler,* ill. by Carolyn Dimas. Faber, 1980. The lively, funny tale of a girl who gets into scrapes protecting a mildly handicapped friend. Carnegie Medal.
9–11

KENNEMORE, TIM. *Wall of Words.* Faber, 1983. A yeasty story about a family of four sisters, one of whom believes herself to be retarded until she is diagnosed as a dyslexic.   10–12

KING, CLIVE. *Me and My Million.* T. Crowell, 1979. Ringo is a tough, street-wise London waif whose reading disability propels him into a series of wild and hilarious adventures.   9–11

• LINGARD, JOAN. *Across the Barricades.* Nelson, 1973. Catholic Kevin and Protestant Sadie fall in love in the beleaguered Belfast of today.   11–15

• ————. *Hostages to Fortune.* Nelson, 1977. The young Irish couple face continued threats to their Protestant-Catholic marriage both from within and without.   12–15

MACKELLAR, WILLIAM. *Wee Joseph,* ill. by Ezra Jack Keats. McGraw, 1957. Young Davie prayed hard, and a small miracle and a great scientific event combine to save Wee Joseph, his runt puppy, from being drowned. A heartwarming story of Scotland.   8–10

MCNEILL, JANET. *The Battle of St. George Without,* ill. by Mary Russon. Little, 1968. Urban children in a fight for turf.   10–12

————. *Goodbye, Dove Square,* ill. by Mary Russon. Little, 1969. In this sequel to the above title, all the Dove Square residents have left the area, cleared for renewal. A realistic picture of urban life.   10–13

MARK, JAN. *Handles.* Atheneum, 1985.   11–14

————. *Thunder and Lightenings.* T. Crowell, 1979. Carnegie Medal.   11–14

MAYNE, WILLIAM. *Gideon Ahoy!* Delacorte, 1989.
11–15

————. *A Grass Rope,* ill. by Lynton Lamb. Dutton, 1962.   10–12

————. *A Swarm in May,* ill. by C. Walter Hodges. Bobbs, 1957.   11–13

MORGAN, ALISON. *A Boy Called Fish,* ill. by Joan

Sandin. Harper, 1973. The story of a boy and his dog, set in rural Wales.   9–11

NESBIT, EDITH. *The Conscience Pudding,* ill. by Erik Blegvad. Coward, 1970. A Christmas story taken from *The New Treasure Seekers,* one of the books about the Bastable children that have become classics. When money is short, the children plan and produce an elaborate Christmas pudding. The period details are charmingly picked up in the illustrations.   9–11

PEARCE, PHILIPPA. *The Way to Sattin Shore,* ill. by Charlotte Voake. Greenwillow, 1983. Prompted by the arrival of a disturbing letter and the disappearance of her father's tombstone, Kate is determined to unravel the mystery of her father's drowning.   10–12

————. *What the Neighbors Did and Other Stories,* ill. by Faith Jacques. T. Crowell, 1973. Eight short stories.   9–12

PEYTON, K. M. *The Beethoven Medal,* ill. by author. T. Crowell, 1972.   12–15

————. *Marion's Angels.* Oxford, 1979.   12–15

————. *Pennington's Heir.* T. Crowell, 1974.
12–15

————. *Pennington's Last Term,* ill. by author. T. Crowell, 1971.   12–15

————. *"Who Sir? Me Sir?"* Oxford, 1983. An athletic competition between a private school team and their less privileged, plucky rivals produces hilarious results.   11–13

RANSOME, ARTHUR. *Swallows and Amazons,* ill. by Helene Carter. Lippincott, 1931. First of a series of stories about four children who live in the Lake District in England.   12–13

ROBINSON, VERONICA. *David in Silence,* ill. by Victor Ambrus. Lippincott, 1966. The story, set in a small English town, concerns a new boy, David, who has always been deaf. A poignant and interesting story about the isolation and hostility that often are the lot of the deaf.   10–12

STREATFIELD, NOEL. *The Children on the Top Floor,* ill. by Jillian Willett. Random, 1965. Life with a television celebrity.   10–12

————. *Thursday's Child,* ill. by Peggy Fortnum. Random, 1971. A foundling girl finds her place in life.   9–11

TATE, JOAN. *Wild Boy,* ill. by Susan Jeschke. Harper, 1973. The friendship between two boys, both solitary people. Set in Yorkshire.   10–12

§ THOMAS, RUTH. *The Runaways.* Lippincott, 1989. Two English children who are unpopular (black boy, white girl) and have little esteem for others or themselves are thrown together and learn trust and friendship.   10–12

TOWNSEND, JOHN ROWE. *Cloudy-Bright.* Lippincott, 1984.   12–15

––––––––. *Downstream.* Lippincott, 1987.   13–17

––––––––. *Good Night, Prof, Dear.* Lippincott, 1970.   12–14

––––––––. *Good-bye to the Jungle.* Lippincott, 1967.   12–14

––––––––. *The Intruder.* Lippincott, 1970.   11–14

––––––––. *Kate and the Revolution.* Lippincott, 1983.   12–14

––––––––. *Noah's Castle.* Lippincott, 1976.   10–14

––––––––. *Rob's Place.* Lothrop, 1988.   10–12

––––––––. *Trouble in the Jungle,* ill. by W. T. Mars. Lippincott, 1969.   10–12

TURNER, PHILLIP. *War on the Darnel,* ill. by W. T. Mars. World, 1969. Three lively English boys engage in a mighty battle with another set of boys who have set up a river barricade. Good characterization and even better dialogue.   10–14

§ URE, JEAN. *The Most Important Thing,* ill. by Ellen Eagle. Morrow, 1986. Nicola, a talented young dancer, infuriates her mother by giving up her scholarship to ballet school in order to pursue her studies in science.   10–12

––––––––. *You Two,* ill. by Ellen Eagle. Morrow, 1984. After her father loses his job, Elizabeth must leave her private school for a public one in which she is miserable until she meets Paddy.   9–11

VAN STOCKUM, HILDA. *The Cottage at Bantry Bay,* ill. by author. Viking, 1938.

––––––––. *Francie on the Run,* ill. by author. Viking, 1939.

––––––––. *Pegeen,* ill. by author. Viking, 1941.   10–12

WALSH, JILL PATON. *Gaffer Samson's Luck,* ill. by Brock Cole. Farrar, 1984. A boy's courage and compassion are notable in a beautifully crafted story of intergenerational friendship and village life.   9–11

––––––––. *Goldengrove.* Farrar, 1972. Madge makes a dramatic discovery about her family while visiting her grandmother in Cornwall.   11–13

––––––––. *Unleaving.* Farrar, 1976. A sequel to *Goldengrove.*   11–13

WINDSOR, PATRICIA. *Mad Martin.* Harper, 1976.   10–11

France

BEMELMANS, LUDWIG. *Madeline,* ill. by author. Viking, 1939. Other titles in the series include the Caldecott Medal book *Madeline's Rescue* (1953), *Madeline and the Bad Hat* (1957), *Madeline and the Gypsies* (1959).   5–7

BISHOP, CLAIRE HUCHET. *All Alone,* ill. by Feodor Rojankovsky. Viking, 1953. Villagers in the French Alps learn to work together when two children, herding in the mountains, are isolated by an avalanche.   9–11

––––––––. *Pancakes-Paris,* ill. by Georges Schreiber. Viking, 1947. A half-starved postwar French child receives a miraculous package of American pancake mix. How he meets two American soldiers and gets the recipe makes a heart-warming tale.   8–12

CARLSON, NATALIE SAVAGE. *The Family under the Bridge,* ill. by Garth Williams. Harper, 1958.

––––––––. *A Grandmother for the Orphelines,* ill. by David White. Harper, 1980. The story of the lively French orphans continues with this book about the children's determination to acquire a grandmother. Written with the same ingenuous sweetness and ebullience as the earlier books.   8–10

––––––––. *The Happy Orpheline,* ill. by Garth Williams. Harper, 1957.

Germany

BENARY-ISBERT, MARGOT. *The Ark,* tr. by Clara and Richard Winston. Harcourt, 1953. The Lechow family, a mother and four children, are trying to reestablish a somewhat normal life in a bombed-out city.   12–14

––––––––. *Rowan Farm,* tr. by Richard and Clara Winston. Harcourt, 1954. The family from *The Ark* welcomes home their father. Two superlative stories.   13–17

DONNELLY, ELFIE. *So Long, Grandpa,* tr. from the German by Anthea Bell. Crown, 1981. The absorbing story of a boy's first experience with the death of a beloved family member.   9–11

HÄRTLING, PETER. *Oma,* ill. by Jutta Ash. Harper, 1977. The story of an elderly German woman and her relationship with a small grandson who comes to live with her when his parents are killed.   8–10

PETRIDES, HEIDRUN. *Hans and Peter,* ill. by author. Harcourt, 1963. Two boys have the satisfaction of seeing a hut raised through their own efforts.   7–9

RETTICH, MARGARET. *The Silver Touch and Other Family Christmas Stories,* ill. by Rolf Rettich. Morrow, 1978. A collection of stories, some tender, some humorous, which celebrate the delights and the disasters of the Christmas season.   9–11

VOGEL, ILSE-MARGRET. *My Twin Sister Erika,* ill. by author. Harper, 1976.   6–9

VON GEBHARDT, HERTHA. *The Girl from Nowhere,* tr. by James Kirkup, ill. by Helen Brun. Criterion, 1959. No one believes her father will return, but a little German girl's faith surmounts mockery and pity and is happily rewarded.   10–13

Holland

DEJONG, MEINDERT. *Far Out the Long Canal,* ill. by Nancy Grossman. Harper, 1964.   10–13
————. *Journey from Peppermint Street,* ill. by Emily Arnold McCully. Harper, 1968. National Book Award.   9–11
————. *The Wheel on the School,* ill. by Maurice Sendak. Harper, 1954. Newbery Medal.   9–12
DODGE, MARY MAPES. *Hans Brinker: Or the Silver Skates* (see Forerunners).

India

ARORA, SHIRLEY. *The Left-Handed Chank.* Follett, 1966. A village in India accepts modern ideas.
11–14
BOTHWALL, JEAN. *The Little Flute Player,* ill. by Margaret Ayer. Morrow, 1949. Minor disasters stalk Teka, the little village flute player, and grow into tragedy when famine comes. The ten-year-old boy takes his father's place and saves his family from starvation.   9–12
GOBHAI, MEHILLI. *Lakshmi: The Water Buffalo Who Wouldn't,* ill. by author. Hawthorn, 1969. A simply written story about a family in India today. The tale has humor as well as an interesting setting, and the theme (mother and son amused at the come-down of father) a broad applicability.
7–9
RANKIN, LOUISE. *Daughter of the Mountains,* ill. by Kurt Wiese. Viking, 1948. Tells of the journey of a little Tibetan village girl to far-off Calcutta in search of her stolen puppy.   10–13
SOMMERFELT, AIMÉE. *The Road to Agra,* ill. by Ulf Aas. Criterion, 1961. Lalu walks the long road to Agra with his small sister, hoping the doctors there can save her eyesight.   10–11
————. *The White Bungalow,* ill. by Ulf Aas. Hale, 1963. A sequel to *The Road to Agra.*   10–12

Italy

BETTINA (pseud. for Bettina Ehrlich). *Pantaloni,* ill. by author. Harper, 1957. Colorfully illustrated, this is a warm story of Italian village life and of a little boy's search for his lost dog.   5–8
FLETCHER, DAVID. *Confetti for Cortorelli,* ill. by George Thompson. Pantheon, 1957. To be in the Children's Fancy Dress Parade, Angelo, an orphan of Sicily, needed a costume. How he earned it and gained a home as well makes an original and distinctive story.   6–8
REGGIANI, RENEE. *The Sun Train,* tr. from the Italian by Patrick Creagh. Coward, 1966. A mature story about a family that moves from an almost-feudal society in Sicily to find other problems just as serious in a contemporary Italian urban setting.
11–14
SNYDER, ZILPHA KEATLEY. *The Famous Stanley Kidnapping Case.* Atheneum, 1979.   9–12

Russia

• CORCORAN, BARBARA. *The Clown.* Atheneum, 1975. Liza, a diplomat's daughter who speaks Russian, helps to smuggle a Russian Jewish clown out of the country. Fast-paced adventure.   10–13
FROLOV, VADIM. *What It's All About,* tr. by Joseph Barnes. Doubleday, 1968.   13–15
KASSIL, LEV. *Once in a Lifetime,* tr. by Anne Terry White. Doubleday, 1970. The first-person story of a thirteen-year-old Russian girl's experience as a movie find. The story has a Moscow setting, with good balance of school and family life and excellent characterization.   11–14
KORINETZ, YURI. *There, Far beyond the River,* tr. by Anthea Bell, ill. by George Armstrong. O'Hara, 1973.   10–12
MAYAKOVSKY, VLADIMIR. *Timothy's Horse,* ad. by Guy Daniels, ill. by Flavio Constantini. Pantheon, 1970. A small boy's wish comes true when he and his father buy a hobby horse. Marvelous illustrations and a rhyming text.   5–7
TER HAAR, JAAP. *Boris,* tr. from the Dutch by Martha Mearns, ill. by Rien Poortvliet. Delacorte, 1970.
10–12

Scandinavia

ANCKARSVÄRD, KARIN. *Aunt Vinnie's Invasion,* tr. by Annabelle MacMillan, ill. by William M. Hutchinson. Harcourt, 1962. The six Hallsenius children live with Aunt Vinnie for a year. An amusing story of modern Sweden.   10–13
BESKOW, ELSA. *Pelle's New Suit,* ill. by author. Harper, 1929.   12–15
FREUCHEN, PETER. *Whaling Boy,* ill. by Leonard Everett Fisher. Putnam, 1958. Per List, not quite twelve, finds life aboard a Danish whaling ship a rugged and adventurous experience. A powerfully written and moving story.   10–13

FRIIS-BAASTAD, BABBIS, *Don't Take Teddy,* tr. from the Norwegian by Lise Sømme McKinnon. Scribner's, 1967. A moving story about a small boy who protects his older retarded brother.   10–13

GRIPE, MARIA. *Elvis and His Friends,* tr. from the Swedish by Sheila LaFarge, ill. by Harald Gripe. Delacorte, 1976.   9–11

————. *The Night Daddy,* tr. from the Swedish by Gerry Bothmer, ill. by Harald Gripe. Delacorte, 1971.   9–11

HAUGEN, TORMOD. *The Night Birds,* tr. from the Norwegian by Sheila LaFarge. Delacorte, 1982. Jake learns to handle his father's emotional crises along with some other problems.   8–10

LINDGREN, ASTRID. *The Children on Troublemaker Street,* tr. by Gerry Bothmer, ill. by Ilon Wiklund. Macmillan, 1964. Swedish children of today and their many activities.   7–9

————. *Rasmus and the Vagabond,* tr. by Gerry Bothmer, ill. by Eric Palmquist. Viking, 1960. Written in a more serious vein than the author's *Pippi Longstocking* series, this is an appealing story of a runaway orphan and the part-time tramp who befriended him.   9–12

LUNDGREN, MAX. *Matt's Grandfather,* tr. by Ann Pyk, ill. by Fibben Hald. Putnam, 1972.   5–7

SORENSON, VIRGINIA. *Lotte's Locket,* ill. by Fermin Rocker. Harcourt, 1964.   9–11

UNNERSTAD, EDITH. *The Saucepan Journey,* ill. by Louis Slobodkin. Macmillan, 1951. The Larsson children, all seven of them, spend a wonderful summer in the traveling caravan, helping father sell his saucepans through Sweden.   9–12

VESTLY, ANNE-CATH. *Aurora and Socrates,* ill. by Leonard Kessler. T. Crowell, 1977. In a sequel to *Hello, Aurora,* Vestly explores further the small problems of a child of a nuclear family in an urban setting.   8–10

————. *Hello, Aurora,* tr. from the Norwegian by Eileen Amos, adapted by Jane Fairfax, ill. by Leonard Kessler. T. Crowell, 1974.   8–10

Switzerland

CHÖNZ, SELINA. *A Bell for Ursli,* ill. by Alois Carigiet. Walck, 1953. One of the most beautiful picture stories to come out of Europe, this is also the exciting story of a small Swiss boy determined to have the largest bell to ring in the spring procession.   6–9

RUTGERS VAN DER LOEFF-BASENAU, ANNA. *Avalanche!* tr. by Dora Round, ill. by Gustav Schrotter. Morrow, 1958. Holland's prize-winning children's book for 1955 tells the dramatic story of an avalanche that struck the tiny Swiss village of Urteli and how it affected three young boys.   11–13

SPYRI, JOHANNA. *Heidi* (see Forerunners).

ULLMAN, JAMES RAMSEY. *Banner in the Sky.* Lippincott, 1954. A story of the self-discipline and stern code of ethics that governs the Alpine guides.   12–14

Other Countries

• ALEXANDER, SUE. *Nadia the Willful,* ill. by Lloyd Bloom. Pantheon, 1983. A Bedouin child finds that talking about her beloved brother, who disappeared in the desert, helps to assuage her grief.   7–9

AYER, JACQUELINE. *Nu Dang and His Kite,* ill. by author. Harcourt, 1959. A colorful introduction to Siamese life is provided by this story of a small boy's search along the river banks for his lost kite.   6–8

BALET, JAN B. *Joanjo: A Portugese Tale,* ill. by author. Delacorte, 1967. The story of Joanjo, a small Portuguese boy, and his acceptance of the independent life of the fisherman after dreams of glory.   5–7

★ CAMERON, ANN. *The Most Beautiful Place in the World,* ill. by Thomas B. Allen. Knopf, 1988. Set in Guatemala, Juan's story is of a young boy abandoned by first his father, then his mother, and of his gradual and tentative trust for his grandmother.   8–10

COWLEY, JOY. *The Silent One,* ill. by Hermann Griessle. Knopf, 1981. The plight of a deaf-mute boy in a primitive South Pacific island society is given haunting dimension.   9–11

FENTON, EDWARD. *The Morning of the Gods.* Delacorte, 1987. In the 1970s, when Greece was ruled by a tyrannical junta, Carla Lewis, twelve, comes to stay in a small village with relatives. Her courage saves the national poet from the military.   11–13

FOX, PAULA. *Lily and the Lost Boy.* Orchard/Watts, 1987. While summering on a Greek island, twelve-year-old Lily meets Jack, whose difficult life seems to have fated him for isolation and tragedy.   11–15

KING, CLIVE. *The Night the Water Came.* T. Crowell, 1982. Stranded in the aftermath of a cyclone, Apu braves pirates and a refugee camp to return to his beloved Indian-ocean island.   10–12

KRUMGOLD, JOSEPH. *The Most Terrible Turk: A Story of Turkey,* ill. by Michael Hampshire. T. Crowell, 1969. Uncle Mustafa and Ali are all that are left of a once-large family. Their relationship is warm and appealing, and the setting, Turkey today, is interesting.   8–10

MERRILL, JEAN. *Shan's Lucky Knife*, ill. by Ronni Solbert. W. R. Scott, 1960. Young Shan outwits the tricky boatman who has taken all his possessions. An excellent read-aloud tale with a Burmese background and folk-tale flavor.   7–10

NÖSTLINIGER, CHRISTINE. *Girl Missing*. Watts, 1976. Erika worships her older sister. Her loneliness when Ilse runs away from home turns to chagrin, when she learns she's been deceived about Ilse's whereabouts. Set in Vienna.   11–13

• OFEK, URIEL. *Smoke over Golan*, ill. by Lloyd Bloom. Harper, 1979. A young boy tells the story of his involvement in the battle on the Golan Heights.   11–13

SEREDY, KATE. *The Good Master*, ill. by author. Viking, 1935. A family who lives on a Hungarian ranch in the early 1900s teaches wild Kate gentler ways.   10–12

————. *The Singing Tree*, ill. by author. Viking, 1939. Another story of Kate, set during World War I.   10–14

SHANNON, MONICA. *Dobry*, ill. by Atanas Katchamakoff. Viking, 1934. Newbery Medal. Dobry, a Bulgarian peasant boy, finds himself longing both to stay at home and to go away to become a sculptor. A rich, multifaceted picture of a culture.   10–13

SPERRY, ARMSTRONG. *Call It Courage*, ill. by author. Macmillan, 1940. Newbery Medal. Published in England as *The Boy Who Was Afraid*.   10–13

• STAPLES, SUZANNE. *Shabanu: Daughter of the Wind*. Knopf, 1989.   12–15

• WATSON, SALLY. *To Build a Land*, ill. by Lili Cassel. Holt, 1957. War-orphaned Leo and his small sister, rescued from the streets of Naples, find a new life in a children's camp in Israel.   11–14

WOJCIECHOWSKA, MAIA. *Shadow of a Bull*, ill. by Alvin Smith. Atheneum, 1964. Newbery Medal.

12–15

WUORIO, EVA-LIS. *The Island of Fish in the Trees*, ill. by Edward Ardizzone. World, 1962. The day-long adventure of two little sisters who trail the doctor around the island to get him to mend their broken doll. The setting is the Balearic Islands, and both story and pictures are exceptionally appealing.

7–9

Animal Stories

ALCOCK, VIVIEN. *Travelers by Night*. Delacorte, 1985. Two circus children, Belle and Charlie, steal Tessie, an old elephant that is about to be put down, and all three travel by night in the effort to reach a safari park where Tessie can live, safe and undetected.   9–11

BAYLOR, BYRD. *Hawk, I'm Your Brother*, ill. by Peter Parnall. Scribner's, 1976. A boy who yearns to fly captures instead the joy of flight when he frees a young hawk he has caught and tamed.   8–10

BEATTY, PATRICIA. *The Staffordshire Terror*. Morrow, 1979.   10–12

BOSTON, LUCY M. *A Stranger at Green Knowe*, ill. by Peter Boston. Harcourt, 1961. Carnegie Medal.

11–14

BURNFORD, SHEILA. *The Incredible Journey*, ill. by Carl Burger. Little, 1961. Canadian Library Association Medal.   11 up

BYARS, BETSY. *The Midnight Fox*, ill. by Ann Grifalconi. Viking, 1968.   9–11

CALLEN, LARRY. *Sorrow's Song*, ill. by Marvin Friedman. Atlantic/Little, 1979. Pinch describes the tribulations he and his mute friend Sorrow have when they discover a small, disabled whooping crane.   10–12

CLEARY, BEVERLY. *Socks*, ill. by Beatrice Darwin. Morrow, 1973.   9–11

DEJONG, MEINDERT. *Along Came a Dog*, ill. by Maurice Sendak. Harper, 1958.   10–12

DE ROO, ANNE. *Cinnamon and Nutmeg*. Nelson, 1974.

9–11

DUNLOP, EILEEN. *Fox Farm*. Holt, 1979. Adam had come as a foster child to the Darke family but couldn't get along with their young son Richard until the two joined forces to save a wounded animal.   10–12

FLACK, MARJORIE. *Angus and the Ducks*, ill. by author. Doubleday, 1930, 1939. First of a series about a frisky, curious Scottish terrier.   4–7

————. *The Story About Ping*, ill. by Kurt Wiese. Viking, 1933.   5–8

§ GATES, DORIS. *Little Vic*, ill. by Kate Seredy. Viking, 1951. When Pony River, an African-American boy, sees Little Vic, he believes the colt will be as great as his sire, Man o' War. The boy endures every hardship willingly in his devotion to the colt.

9–12

————. *A Morgan for Melinda*. Viking, 1980. Gates reverses the usual horse story pattern, for it isn't until after her father has bought a horse that Melinda learns to love and ride it.   9–11

GEORGE, JEAN. *The Cry of the Crow*. Harper, 1980.

10–12

————. *Gull Number 737*. T. Crowell, 1964.

12–15

————. *Julie of the Wolves*, ill. by John Schoenherr. Harper, 1972. Newbery Medal.   10–13

GEORGE, JOHN and JEAN. *Bubo, the Great Horned Owl,* ill. by Jean George. Dutton, 1954.   11–14

———. *Vulpes, the Red Fox,* ill. by Jean George. Dutton, 1948.   10–14

GIPSON, FRED. *Old Yeller,* ill. by Carl Burger. Harper, 1956. Travis's mongrel dog, Old Yeller, is bitten by a rabid wolf while loyally defending his family. He becomes infected and has to be destroyed. This is a moving tale of a boy and his dog, set in pioneer Texas of the 1870s. In a sequel, *Savage Sam* (1962), Travis is aided by Old Yeller's equally gallant son in rescuing two children from Apaches.   11–14

GRIFFITHS, HELEN. *Just a Dog,* ill. by Victor Ambrus. Holiday, 1975.   10–12

HAAS, JESSIE. *The Sixth Sense: And Other Stories.* Greenwillow, 1988.   12–14

HALLARD, PETER. *Puppy Lost in Lapland,* ill. by Wallace Tripp. Watts, 1971. An injured puppy struggles for survival in the wilderness.   10–12

HENRY, MARGUERITE. *Gaudenzia: Pride of the Palio,* ill. by Lynd Ward. Rand, 1960.   11–14

———. *Justin Morgan Had a Horse,* ill. by Wesley Dennis. Rand, 1954. A story of the development of the Morgan breed of horses.   9–14

———. *King of the Wind,* ill. by Wesley Dennis. Rand, 1948. Newbery Medal.   9–14

———. *Misty of Chincoteague,* ill. by Wesley Dennis. Rand, 1947.   9–14

———. *White Stallion of Lipizza,* ill. by Wesley Dennis. Rand, 1964.   11–13

HINTON, S. E. *Taming the Star Runner.* Delacorte, 1988.   11–14

JAMES, WILL. *Smokey, the Cowhorse,* ill. by author. Scribner's, 1926. The adventures of a range horse. Newbery Medal.   11–16

KJELGAARD, JIM. *Big Red,* ill. by Bob Kuhn. Holiday, 1956.   12–16

LIERS, EMIL. *An Otter's Story,* ill. by Tony Palazzo. Viking, 1953.   10–13

LINDQUIST, WILLIS. *Burma Boy,* ill. by Nicolas Mordvinoff. Whittlesey, 1953. A thrilling tale of an elephant of the teakwood forests which goes wild, and of young Haji, the elephant boy, who wins his confidence and saves the villagers from disaster.   9–11

LITTLE, JEAN. *Lost and Found,* ill. by Leoung O'Young. Viking, 1986.   8–10

MCNEER, MAY. *My Friend Mac,* ill. by Lynd Ward. Houghton, 1960. An orphaned and fast-growing moose provides plenty of diversion for lonely little Baptiste of the Canadian woods.   7–9

MILES, MISKA. *Nobody's Cat,* ill. by John Schoenherr. Little, 1969.   8–9

MOREY, WALT. *Gentle Ben,* ill. by John Schoenherr. Dutton, 1965.   11–14

———. *Gloomy Gus.* Dutton, 1970.   10–12

———. *Year of the Black Pony.* Dutton, 1976.   10–12

MOWAT, FARLEY. *Owls in the Family,* ill. by Robert Frankenberg. Little, 1962. A funny and heart-warming story of two owls of northern Canada, told by their youthful rescuer.   9–12

MUKERJI, DHAN GOPAL. *Gay-Neck,* ill. by Boris Artzybasheff. Dutton, 1927, 1968. Gay-Neck's training as a carrier pigeon in India made him valuable as a messenger in France during World War I. Newbery Medal, 1928.   11–14

NORTH, STERLING. *Little Rascal,* ill. by Carl Burger, Dutton, 1965.   9–11

———. *Rascal: A Memoir of a Better Era,* ill. by John Schoenherr. Dutton, 1963.   12 up

O'HARA, MARY (pseud. for Mary Sture-Vasa). *My Friend Flicka.* Lippincott, 1941. Horsebreeding on a Western ranch.   12 up

PEARCE, ANN PHILIPPA. *The Battle of Bubble and Squeak,* ill. by Alan Baker. Dutton, 1979.   9–11

PHIPSON, JOAN. *Fly Free.* Atheneum, 1979. When Johnny, who loves to trap, is himself caught in an animal trap, he vows he'll give up the sport—if he lives.   12–14

RAWLINGS, MARJORIE KINNAN. *The Yearling,* ill. by N. C. Wyeth, Scribner's, 1938, 1962.   12 up

RYLANT, CYNTHIA. *Every Living Thing,* ill. by S. D. Schindler. Bradbury, 1985.   10–12

SETON, ERNEST T. *Lives of the Hunted,* ill. by author. Schocken, 1967. A favorite realistic saga.   10 up

SHARMAT, MARJORIE WEINMAN. *Morris Brookside, a Dog,* ill. by Ronald Himler. Holiday, 1973.   5–8

———. *Morris Brookside Is Missing,* ill. by Ronald Himler. Holiday, 1974.   5–8

STONG, PHIL. *Honk: the Moose,* ill. by Kurt Wiese. Dodd, 1935.   9–10

STRANGER, JOYCE. *Lakeland Vet.* Viking, 1972.   11 up

TAYLOR, THEODORE. *The Trouble with Tuck.* Doubleday, 1981.   10–12

WALKER, DAVID E. *Big Ben,* ill. by Victor Ambrus. Houghton, 1969. Fine writing style and characterization in this story about a St. Bernard who is unjustly suspected of being a sheep-killer.   9–11

WARD, LYND. *The Biggest Bear,* ill. by author. Houghton, 1952. Caldecott Medal.   5–8

ZIMELMAN, NATHAN. *The Lives of My Cat Alfred,* ill. by Evaline Ness. Dutton, 1976.   5–8

Sports Stories

BISHOP, CURTIS. *Little League Victory.* Lippincott, 1967. Ed's temper tantrums make it difficult for him to be accepted as a member of the team, but he succeeds in getting over this obstacle.   9–11

CHRISTOPHER, MATT. *Johnny Long Legs,* ill. by Harvey Kidder. Little, 1970.   9–11

————. *Quarterback Switch,* ill. by Eric Nones. Little, 1984.   9–11

————. *Red-Hot Hightops,* ill. by Paul Mock. Little, 1987.   9–11

CORBETT, SCOTT. *The Baseball Bàrgain,* ill. by Wallace Tripp. Little, 1970.   9–11

————. *The Hockey Girls.* Dutton, 1976. Published simultaneously in Canada by Clarke, Irwin.   9–11

DU BOIS, WILLIAM PÈNE. *Porko von Popbutton,* ill. by author. Harper, 1969.   9–11

GAULT, WILLIAM. *Stubborn Sam.* Dutton, 1969.   11–14

§ GEIBEL, JAMES. *The Blond Brother.* Putnam, 1979. When Rich Gaskins transfers to Marchmount High his life is complicated by being one of the few whites on a black team, a coach who picks him for a favorite, and his affection for an African-American girl.   12–15

GLENN, MEL. *Play-by-Play.* Houghton/Clarion, 1986.   8–10

§ HEUMANN, WILLIAM. *Fastbreak Rebel.* Dodd, 1971.   11–14

§ • HIGDON, HAL. *The Electronic Olympics.* Holt, 1971. A blithe tale of a computerized Olympics and an affable African track star.   11–14

§ HONIG, DONALD. *Way to Go, Teddy.* Watts, 1973.   11–14

HURWITZ, JOHANNA. *Baseball Fever,* ill. by Ray Cruz. Morrow, 1981. Friction between a baseball-loving son and his intellectual father is parlayed into a briskly enjoyable family story.   8–10

§ KESSLER, LEONARD. *Here Comes the Strikeout,* ill. by author. Harper, 1965.   7–8

KLASS, DAVID. *The Atami Dragons.* Scribner's, 1984. Jerry goes to Japan with his father and is surprised at how much he enjoys playing baseball with a local team.   10–13

KNUDSON, R. R. *Zan Hagen's Marathon.* Farrar, 1984.   11–14

————. *Zanbanger.* Harper, 1977.   11–14

• KONIGSBURG, E. L. *About the B'nai Bagels,* ill. by author. Atheneum, 1969.   10–12

§ LIPSYTE, ROBERT. *The Contender.* Harper, 1967.   12–15

LORD, BEMAN. *Shrimp's Soccer Goal,* ill. by Harold Berson. Walck, 1970. All of Lord's stories about several sports are sound and enjoyable for readers in the middle group.   8–10

MIKLOWITZ, GLORIA. *Anything to Win.* Delacorte, 1989.   12–15

§ MYERS, WALTER DEAN. *The Outside Shot.* Delacorte, 1984.   12–15

§ QUIGLEY, MARTIN. *Today's Game.* Viking, 1965.   13 up

RENICK, MARION. *Take a Long Jump,* ill. by Charles Robinson. Scribner's, 1971. A track story that also has good family relationships.   9–11

SLOTE, ALFRED. *Hang Tough, Paul Mather.* Lippincott, 1973. A poignant first-person story by a leukemia victim who tries to keep up with his greatest interest, playing Little League ball.   9–12

————. *The Hotshot,* photos by William LaCrosse. Watts, 1977. A hockey player learns about teamwork, in a story that's also suitable for slow older readers.   9–11

§ ————. *Jake.* Lippincott, 1971. A small boy's uncle gives up his free time to coach a baseball team.   9–11

————. *Matt Gargan's Boy.* Lippincott, 1975.   9–11

————. *Stranger on the Ball Club.* Lippincott, 1970.   9–11

TAVES, ISABELLA. *Not Bad for a Girl.* Evans/Lippincott, 1972.   9–11

THORVALL, KERSTIN. *Gunnar Scores a Goal,* tr. from the Swedish by Anne Parker, ill. by Serge Hollerbach. Harcourt, 1968.   8–10

TOWNE, MARY. *First Serve,* ill. by Ruth Sanderson. Atheneum, 1976. Thirteen-year-old Dulcie is torn between her desire to enter competitive tennis and her fear that her older sister, who also plays, will feel hurt.   11–14

§ TUNIS, JOHN. *All American,* ill. by Hans Walleen. Harcourt, 1942.   10–14

• ————. *Keystone Kids.* Harcourt, 1943. A fine sports story for the teenager—the happy resolution of anti-Semitic feeling is achieved by the students.   12–16

• WEAVER, ROBERT. *Nice Guy, Go Home.* Harper, 1968.   12–15

WINTHROP, ELIZABETH. *Marathon Miranda.* Holiday, 1979.   9–11

WODEHOUSE, P. G. *Mike and Psmith.* Meredith, 1969.   11 up

Mystery and Adventure

ADLER, DAVID. *The Fourth Floor Twins and the Skyscraper Parade,* ill. by Irene Trivas. Viking, 1987.   8–10

ALCOCK, VIVIEN. *The Mysterious Mr. Ross.* Delacorte, 1987.   10–13

ALEKSIN, ANATOLII GEORGIEVICH. *Alik the Detective.* Morrow, 1977. Six children visiting the cottage of a local author are trapped in the cellar by an inexplicably hostile caretaker.   10–12

ALEXANDER, LLOYD. *The Drackenberg Adventure.* Dutton, 1988.   10–13

☆ ———. *The El Dorado Adventure.* Dutton, 1987.   10–13

———. *The Illyrian Adventure.* Dutton, 1986.   10–13

———. *The Jedera Adventure.* Dutton, 1989.   10–13

———. *The Philadelphia Adventure.* Dutton, 1990.   10–13

§ BAWDEN, NINA. *Rebel on a Rock.* Lippincott, 1978.   10–13

§ • BETHANCOURT, T. ERNESTO. *Doris Fein: Legacy of Terror.* Holiday, 1984. An intrepid girl detective becomes involved in a mystery whose origins lie in the gangland terror of 1920s Chicago.   12–15

BONHAM, FRANK. *Mystery in Little Tokyo,* ill. by Kazue Mizumura. Dutton, 1966.   10–12

§ ★ ———. *Mystery of the Fat Cat,* ill. by Alvin Smith. Dutton, 1968.   10–14

§ BONSALL, CROSBY. *The Case of the Cat's Meow,* ill. by author. Harper, 1965. All of the Bonsall books are charming and useful.   7–8

COBALT, MARTIN. *Pool of Swallows.* Nelson, 1974.   11–15

★ COREN, ALAN. *Arthur the Kid,* ill. by John Astrop. Little, 1978.

———. *Klondike Arthur,* ill. by John Astrop. Little, 1979. The indomitable Arthur shows up again, this time to bring grace and culture to a rough Klondike enterprise, the Rotten Old Saloon. Others in the series are *Buffalo Arthur, The Lone Arthur,* and *Railroad Arthur.*   8–10

CORMIER, ROBERT. *After the First Death.* Pantheon, 1979.   12–15

———. *I am the cheese.* Pantheon, 1977.   12–17

CRAYDER, DOROTHY. *She and the Dubious Three,* ill. by Velma Iisley. Atheneum, 1974.   10–12

★ CROSS, GILLIAN. *Born of the Sun.* Holiday House, 1984. Paula is thrilled when her father, a famous explorer, asks her to go with him to find a lost city of the Incas, and she is dismayed when she discovers her father has a serious illness he hopes can be cured by an Indian healer.   12–15

———. *On the Edge.* Holiday House, 1985.   10–13

CURRY, JANE LOUISE. *The Bassumtyte Treasure.* Atheneum, 1978. A nicely rendered story turning on the familiar device of a long-lost treasure turning up to save a doomed estate from passing out of the hands of its owners.

———. *Ghost Lane.* Atheneum, 1979.   10–12

☆ DEKKERS, MIDAS. *Arctic Adventure.* Orchard/Watts, 1987. An exploratory expedition in the Arctic dramatically converts young Menno to the Greenpeace cause.   11–14

DILLON, EILIS. *The Singing Cave,* ill. by Stan Campbell. Funk, 1960. Suspense and mystery abound in this outstandingly written tale of the discovery and disappearance of Viking remains from a cave on the Irish isle.   12–15

EHRLICH, AMY. *Where It Stops, Nobody Knows.* Dial, 1988.   11–14

FLEISCHMAN, ALBERT SIDNEY. *The Whipping Boy,* ill. by Peter Sis. Greenwillow, 1986. Newbery Medal.   9–11

GARFIELD, LEON. *Black Jack,* ill. by Antony Maitland. Pantheon, 1968.   11–14

———. *The December Rose.* Viking, 1987.   11–14

———. *Footsteps.* Delacorte, 1980. A swashbuckling story of the hunt for a lost inheritance, set in eighteenth-century London.   10–13

GRIESE, ARNOLD. *The Wind Is Not a River,* ill. by Glo Coalson. T. Crowell, 1978. Two children living on an Aleutian island during World War II must decide whether to treat the wounded Japanese soldier they've found as an enemy or as a human being.   9–11

HALL, LYNN. *A Killing Freeze.* Morrow, 1988. The residents of a small Minnesota town are shocked when an elderly woman is killed during the local snowmobile dealer's winter carnival.   11–14

HARRIS, CHRISTIE. *Mystery at the Edge of Two Worlds,* ill. by Lou Crockett. Atheneum, 1978.   10–12

HIGHTOWER, FLORENCE. *Mrs. Wappinger's Secret,* ill. by Beth and Joe Krush. Houghton, 1956. Eccentric Mrs. Wappinger of a Maine resort island is quite sure she has ancestral buried treasure somewhere on her property.   11–14

HILDICK, E. W. *Louie's Ransom.* Knopf, 1978. In a fourth book centering around Louie, an English milkman, the protagonist comes to the United States, is kidnapped and held for ransom.   10–12

☆ HOUSTON, JAMES. *Long Claw: An Arctic Adventure,* ill. by author. Atheneum, 1981. A dramatic survival story about an Eskimo brother and sister who brave Arctic dangers to bring caribou meat to their starving family.   9–11

HUTCHINS, PAT. *The Mona Lisa Mystery,* ill. by Lawrence Hutchins. Greenwillow, 1981. A class of third-graders tracks down the missing *Mona Lisa* in Paris.   7–9

KAHN, JOAN, ed. *Some Things Fierce and Fatal.* Harper, 1971.   11–14

KIDD, RONALD. *Second Fiddle: A Sizzle and Splat Mystery.* Lodestar, 1988. A series of pranks that end in the burning of a Stradivarius violin gets trumpet-player Sizzle and tuba-player Splat busy investigating. 11–14

L'ENGLE, MADELEINE. *The Arm of the Starfish*. Farrar, 1965. 12–15

————. *Dragons in the Waters*. Farrar, 1976. 11–15

————. *A House Like a Lotus*. Farrar, 1984. 12–15

LEVY, ELIZABETH. *Something Queer Is Going On*, ill. by Mordicai Gerstein. Delacorte, 1973. 7–9

§ LEXAU, JOAN. *The Homework Caper*, ill. by Syd Hoff. Harper, 1966. 6–7

§ ————. *The Rooftop Mystery*, ill. by Syd Hoff. Harper, 1968. 6–8

LINDGREN, ASTRID. *Bill Bergson Lives Dangerously*, tr. by Herbert Antoine, ill. by Don Freeman. Viking, 1954.

————. *Bill Bergson, Master Detective*, tr. by Herbert Antoine, ill. by Louis Glanzman. Viking, 1952. These two stories from the Swedish are told with considerable humor in spite of their dramatic plots. 10–13

MOYES, PATRICIA. *Helter-Skelter*. Holt, 1968. 12–15

NEWMAN, ROBERT. *The Case of the Frightened Friend*. Atheneum, 1984. Two London children investigate a mystery surrounding a classmate's family; set in nineteenth-century England. 10–12

————. *The Case of the Murdered Players*. Atheneum, 1985. 10–12

NICOLE, CHRISTOPHER. *Operation Destruct*. Holt, 1969. 12–15

NIXON, JOAN LOWERY. *Secret, Silent Screams*. Delacorte, 1988. While attempting to prove the death of her friend, Barry, was not a suicide, Marti puts herself in a dangerous and vulnerable position. 12–15

PAULSEN, GARY. *Hatchet*. Bradbury, 1987. 11–14

PEARCE, PHILIPPA. *The Minnow Leads to Treasure*, ill. by Edward Ardizzone. World, 1958. 10–12

————. *The Way to Sattin Shore*, ill. by Charlotte Voake. Greenwillow, 1984. A sensitive child unravels a secret about her father, whom she has long believed dead. 10–12

PILLING, ANN. *Henry's Leg*, ill. by Rowan Clifford. Viking, 1985. Henry, a collector of junk, suspects the robbers of a local jewelry store when someone keeps trying to steal a mannequin's leg from his collection. 10–12

RASKIN, ELLEN. *The Westing Game*. Dutton, 1978. Newbery Medal. 10–13

ROBERTS, WILLO DAVIS. *The View from the Cherry Tree*. Atheneum, 1975. Preparing for a wedding, Rob's family is too busy to listen to his story of a neighbor's fall, which he's seen from a tree. Only the murderer pays attention. 10–13

ST. GEORGE, JUDITH. *Mystery of St. Martin's*. Putnam, 1979. Ruth, twelve, investigates the source of counterfeit bills that have been traced to her father's church. 10–12

SAMPSON, FAY. *The Watch on Patterick Fell*. Greenwillow, 1980. The anger of a mob causes Elspeth's father to send his family away from the English site where radioactive waste is stored, in a story with pace and suspense. 11–14

SHARMAT, MARJORIE WEINMAN. *Nate the Great and the Sticky Case*, ill. by Marc Simont. Coward, 1978. When his friend Claude announces that he's lost his stegosaurus stamp, Nate the great boy detective goes to work; there are others in this series. 7–8

SOBOL, DONALD. *Encyclopedia Brown Saves the Day*, ill. by Leonard Shortall. Nelson, 1970. 8–10

STEVENSON, ROBERT LOUIS. *Treasure Island*, ill. by N. C. Wyeth. Scribner's, 1945 (first pub. in 1883). 11–16

STOREY, MARGARET. *Ask Me No Questions*. Dutton, 1975. 10–12

TOWNSEND, JOHN ROWE. *The Fortunate Isles*. Lippincott, 1989. A feisty adolescent girl in an invented country sails to adventure, danger, and high honor. 11–14

TURNER, PHILIP. *Colonel Sheperton's Clock*, ill. by Phillip Gough. World, 1966.

————. *The Grange at High Force*, ill. by W. T. Mars. World, 1967. Carnegie Medal. 11–14

WELLS, ROSEMARY. *The Man in the Woods*. Dial, 1984. Helen stumbles into danger and more than one mystery when she witnesses a car accident caused by the "Punk Rock Thrower." 11–14

WUORIO, EVA-LIS. *Save Alice!* Holt, 1968. 10–12

Chapter Eleven

Historical Fiction

We require that modern fiction for children depict life honestly and accurately. This is also a major requisite for historical fiction. Children can check the experiences described in modern fiction against their own lives and those of their friends or can confirm them through the mass media. But children bring to historical fiction little knowledge of particular periods of history, either through study or reading, and must rely on the author's accuracy in this field.

Generally, the writer of historical fiction aims consciously to tell a story set in a past time about which the majority of the book's readers will have no direct knowledge. To tell a story which has the flavor of a chosen time, the author becomes as familiar as possible with the period through reading contemporary accounts in books, newspapers, and magazines, through historical studies, or through the use of interviews or oral history records. The writing of the book then becomes an expression of assimilated knowledge and vicarious experience. Characters may be actual historical personages, or they may be created by the author, people like

ourselves inside, although their clothing and habits may be very different. The author shows how these people are directly affected by their environment. Details of daily life—food, clothing, shelter—come naturally into the story as the characters deal with their problems. Emotions grow naturally out of the problems, and we see how these people were prepared physically and spiritually by their cultural background to meet their daily challenges.

Elizabeth George Speare's *The Witch of Blackbird Pond* is a good example for discussing historical fiction. Kit, raised in Barbados, comes to live with Puritan relatives in Connecticut in the 1600s and finds a serious, hard way of life, very different from the relaxed and carefree life she had known. Adaptation to her environment is not easy for Kit; her involvement in a witchcraft trial is a logical development in a plot set in New England in the 1600s.

A war story almost always involves battles; still the weapons used, the style of warfare, the support systems, all differ from war to war, from period to period. The Revolutionary War described in *George Midgett's War* by Sally Edwards or Avi's *The Fighting Ground* are very different from World War II, as seen through the eyes of a Russian teenager separated from his parents at the war's outbreak in Ephraim Sevela's *We Were Not Like Other People*.

From *The Fighting Ground* by Avi, frontispiece illustration by Ellen Thompson.

One of the most difficult tasks of the writer of historical fiction is to present natural conversations. If the words and sentence patterns are so archaic as to break the reader's concentration, the author is in difficulty. If the conversations are too contemporary in tone, the mood of the story may be destroyed. For children just mastering their own tongue, language—especially dialect—may be an overwhelming problem in reading historical fiction.

A time sense is also difficult for children to gain; they see their own parents' childhoods as being long ago and World Wars I and II as immeasurably distant in time. Names of historical characters may be difficult, and events taking place outside their own countries have a quality near fantasy for many children. Interest may lag if the author spends too much time building setting; conversely, bewilderment may result if not enough background is presented for full understanding of the plot.

As in any story for children, however, an exciting plot, realistic characters, judicious use of dialogue and dialect, a universal theme, and a strong sense of place and time will help a child over the difficulties created by lack of knowledge.

The successful writer of historical fiction is aware that historical points of view change with time and that treatment of character and fact is inevitably affected by the way these things are viewed in the period in which the author is writing. Thus the treatment of women, African Americans, and native Americans in historical fiction changed drastically in the 1970s and the writer should understand this change and see it in its historical perspective.

Occasionally a story is set in a historical period but it could just as well happen today: The social conditions of the times seem to have little impact on the characters' lives and seem to be of minor concern to the author. We can make this another test of historical fiction: Does the author intend to create a vivid picture of another historical period and is that picture vital to the telling of the story? If not, we may have an interesting story, but it is not historical fiction. Tales which were contemporary when written and which are still read by succeeding generations, such as Louisa May Alcott's *Little Women*, have become historical fiction in a sense, but they were not created as historical fiction and they, and others like them, have been considered in this book as realistic fiction.

Where do we draw the line between historical fiction and modern realistic fiction? For the purposes of this chapter we will discuss only those books whose backgrounds are no later than World War II. The books are divided into those for younger readers, the middle group, and older readers, and are arranged within each group by the period or year of the setting for the title discussed, or the first title if there are several titles. All of the books, in varying degrees, comply with the major requirements of good historical fiction for young readers. The research and the authoritative historical milieu are there, but they do not overpower the story. You will note that no single book ever presents all points of view. This need not be a problem if you choose books that present a balance.

What is the value of historical fiction for the children of today? The past is not simply a listing of dates and events, as important and momentous as these may be. The past is people and how people managed to live and love and find joy in accomplishment whatever the times. The historical novel clothes the bare historical facts with trappings of a thousand tiny details, bringing emotion and insight to scholarship. Children learn facts in social studies and history; it is the interpretation of the facts in historical fiction that makes them feel "we were there!"

Early Writers of Historical Fiction

Not all of the early historical fiction written for the children of the United States is still worth reading. A few writers, however, produced books which are as rewarding now as they were when first published.

Howard Pyle's work was steeped in the traditions and customs of the Middle Ages. He not only wrote fascinating stories, but provided powerful illustrations for his own books from a seemingly inexhaustible storehouse of detailed information. His running narrative is always clear, direct, and vigorous. Old speech forms add to the flavor of his tales without unduly impeding the reader.

Otto of the Silver Hand is a horrifying tale of the robber barons of Germany. One of these had plundered ruthlessly. For revenge, his enemies struck off the hand of his only son, the delicate Otto. Later, because of the silver substitute, the boy was known as Otto of the Silver Hand. The story presents two phases of the life of the period: the turbulent life within the castle strongholds of the robber barons and the peaceful, scholarly pursuits of the monks within their great monasteries. The mutilation of the boy is gently handled, underscoring the infinite pathos of a child in the power of cruel men.

In Pyle's *Men of Iron*, sixteen-year-old Myles Falworth is sent to be a squire to a powerful earl. There he learns that his own father is practically an outlaw, suspected of plotting to take the king's life. In the earl's great castle, Myles is trained in all the intricate feats of knighthood and in the code of chivalry and he is eventually knighted. He frees his father from suspicion and wins the earl's daughter for his wife. Myles has to battle with his own impulsiveness and his too-quick temper as well as with his enemies. This remains an outstanding book about medieval England.

Cornelia Meigs was interested not only in our historical past but also in the beginnings of ideas and their development. Her stories are always something more than historical fiction. Indeed, she manages frequently to illuminate certain problems of the present, as in *Master Simon's Garden*, which carries a striking theme. In the little Puritan New England settlement called Hopewell, where everything is done for utility and thrift, Master Simon develops his beautiful garden—a riot of colorful flowers and sweet herbs. It is an expression of his philosophy on tolerance and love in complete contrast to the intolerance and suspicion of some of his neighbors.

From *Otto of the Silver Hand*, written and illustrated by Howard Pyle.

Viewpoint

Try to imagine what daily life would be like if we knew no history. Without recollection, we would be adrift. For while history is not everything, it is an aspect of everything. It makes us aware of the character of our own time by helping us to see it in comparison and contrast with another. It won't tell us what to believe or how to act, it won't make us less bellicose or more peaceful, but as one scholar has put it, "it will add a new pleasure and breadth to our understanding of what it is we are. From it we can learn that we too are a part of our time, reflecting all the limitations, preconceptions, and special interests of our time." The sad truth is that "the past *is* the present. We live in the past and it does us good to know it. The present is the past, and not to experience that past imaginatively is to be dead to the real dimensions of the contemporary."

We are talking, really, about memory. An individual whose memory goes blank is in a dreadful state. It is no different for a society. A country out of touch with what happened in its past is disoriented, too. As for the child, when "it ceases to see people as static, frozen at a moment in time, but sees them instead as changing and developing creatures," we know it has taken a step toward maturity. "Such a perception," says the writer Penelope Lively, "is concerned with realizations about time and about aging, but also . . . with realizations about history. It is the perception, often startling, that places have a past, that they are now, but were also then, and that if peopled now, they were peopled then. It is a step aside from self, a step out of the child's self-preoccupation, and, therefore, a step toward maturity."

Milton Meltzer, "Beyond the Span of a Single Life," *Celebrating Children's Books,* edited by Betsy Hearne and Marilyn Kaye. New York: Lothrop, Lee, & Shepard Books, 1981, pp. 88–89.

Although Meigs was not a creator of memorable characters, her plots are absorbing and often exciting, stronger because of their genesis in a strong theme. It is the theme that makes the action of the storyline unified, and gives significance to the conclusion.

One of the finest books written by Rachel Field is *Calico Bush*, the story of Marguerite Ledoux, a French bound-out girl of thirteen, who travels to the state of Maine with a Massachusetts family in 1743. During the long sail from Marblehead to Mount Desert, Marguerite comes to know the Sargent family and proves to them that she is both gritty and resourceful. She remains, nevertheless, a servant and an alien in their midst. There are brief days of joy in the new settlement, but there are tragic and frightening days, too—the Sargent baby is burned to death, and an Indian raid is diverted only by Marguerite's courage and ingenuity. At the end of the story, the Sargents gratefully offer Marguerite her freedom, but she chooses not to leave them. The picture of the times and the people that Field paints is authentic and well balanced. The hardships, the monotony, and the perils of pioneer life are there, unvarnished and frightening. The compensatory rewards of this life-style may seem slight to modern readers, but there can be no doubt in their minds about the sturdy, undismayed character of these settlers.

Books for Younger Children

For young children who have little understanding of the past, historical fiction should be presented very simply, focusing on a person or just a few people, or on one problem or event. The story needs action and drama, and should avoid any references to events that demand knowledge not provided in the book. Historical fiction for young children is generally about exciting people in history to whom they have frequently been introduced by the mass media—knights, pirates, Vikings, soldiers, pioneers—whether these characters are real or invented.

Clyde Robert Bulla
John Billington, Friend of Squanto
Conquista!

Clyde Bulla's books for children are written in a simple style which does not condescend to young readers. He has the ability to concentrate on one aspect of character, and to describe events which enhance that aspect. In *Squanto* and *John Billington, Friend of Squanto*, Bulla gives a brief picture of the Pilgrims of Plymouth Colony. *The Sword in the Tree* tells of treachery punished when a young boy asks for King Arthur's help. Other books by Bulla take place during the Viking explorations of America; during the early colonial period as in *A Lion to Guard Us*; or—as in the story of Coronado's search for the city of gold in *Conquista!*—in the early days of the settlement of the Middle and Far West of the United States.

Alice Dalgliesh
The Courage of Sarah Noble
The Thanksgiving Story
Adam and the Golden Cock

Alice Dalgliesh had the ability to create realistic child characters and to make their concerns important to us without losing sight of the historical elements of her tales.

The Courage of Sarah Noble is richly historical and, according to Dalgliesh, a real episode of 1707. Eight-year-old Sarah is sent into the wilderness to cook and care for her father because her mother cannot leave or move a sick baby. Before Sarah and her father set off, her mother wraps the little girl in a cloak as warm as her love and says, "Keep up your courage, Sarah Noble." When wolves threaten them in the forest, or they sleep in strange cabins with unfriendly folk, or Sarah is left alone with an Indian family, she wraps her mother's cloak and words warmly about her and keeps up her courage.

Another tale of colonial times is *The Thanksgiving Story*, a fictional account of the voyage of the *Mayflower* and the first year at Plymouth, culminating in the Thanksgiving feast with the Indians. Centered on the experiences of the Hopkins family, especially the children, it is a

From *A Lion to Guard Us* by Clyde Robert Bulla, illustrated by Michele Chessare.

remarkably moving story, told with dignity and avoiding stereotyped episodes.

Adam and the Golden Cock is a Revolutionary War story in which a boy is caught in the conflict between friendship and loyalty, for Adam's friend Paul is from a Tory family. Children of today, aware of conflicting opinions about controversial issues, may see the timeless application of such conflict.

Brinton Turkle
The *Obadiah* Books

Set in the early nineteenth century, *Obadiah the Bold* is an engaging tale of the dreams of glory of a small Quaker boy who wants to become a pirate. He decides he will be a sailor like Grandfather after Father very cleverly talks about how brave a man Captain Obadiah

Starbuck had been. The text has minimal historical significance, but the illustrations show details of early Nantucket, and both this book and its sequels, *Thy Friend, Obadiah* and *Rachel and Obadiah* give children a sense of the period, the Quaker community, and the loving kindness of family life. The soft details of the illustrations are charming in themselves and they are accurately informative in showing costume, architecture, and artifacts of the period.

Ferdinand Monjo
The Drinking Gourd

A fine story about the Underground Railroad is told in *The Drinking Gourd*, in which young Tommy Fuller, sent home from church because of a prank, wanders into the barn and finds a runaway slave family. The explanation given Tommy of the Railroad clarifies it for readers as well as for Tommy, and he understands for the first time the degradation of slavery and the danger runaways face. When a search party comes along, Tommy quickly pretends that he himself is running away from home; the marshal laughs and decides not to search the hay wagon, and so Tommy helps the cause. That night Father explains that he is, he knows, breaking a law but that he must. The story has suspense and action, and in Tommy's participation there is both the joy of achievement and an appreciation of ethical issues.

In later books Monjo has woven stories around historical personages such as Thomas Jefferson (*Grand Papa and Ellen Aroon*), Abraham Lincoln (*Gettysburg*), and Nathan Hale (*A Namesake for Nathan*). Using a child of the family to tell the story, Monjo has effectively presented these men from a child's point of view. Whether these books are classified as historical fiction or biography, there is a sense of history and an emphasis on such qualities as courage, loyalty, and family love.

Other Books for Younger Children

Although it is set in the Middle Ages, Donald Carrick's *Harald and the Great Stag* is so simply written that it is comprehensible to younger children. Harald protests the treatment of a

From *Harald and the Great Stag*, written and illustrated by Donald Carrick.

wild animal, in a thoughtful blend of historical setting and contemporary concern.

Wilma Pitchford Hays has written a number of short, informational books with a historical setting. *May Day for Samoset* and *Yellow Fur and Little Hawk*, a story of the Dakota Sioux, are typical and show the author's knowledge and interest in historical details, which are somewhat purposefully inserted in the tales. An excellent story for beginning independent readers is Doreen Rappaport's *The Boston Coffee Party*.

One of the lightest books of historical fiction for young children is Arnold Lobel's *On the Day Peter Stuyvesant Sailed into Town*, delightfully illustrated by the author, a story in rhythmic verse that describes the irascible governor's successful efforts to clean up New Amsterdam. Lobel's book also is representative of the growing number of books of historical fiction written for beginning readers. Others are Nathaniel Benchley's *Sam the Minuteman*, a lively story of the American Revolution, and Betty Baker's *The Pig War*, based on a dispute between the United States and Great Britain in 1859 over possession of an island. Joan Sandin, in *The Long Way to a New Land* and its sequel, *The Long*

Way Westward, describes the journey of a Swedish immigrant family in the late 1860s.

Based on a true incident, Catherine Coblentz's *Martin and Abraham Lincoln* presents a dialogue between the president and a small boy that gives information about the American Civil War. The story not only characterizes Lincoln but poignantly shows how the duress of war affects a child.

Zekmet the Stone Carver by Mary Stolz is a story about the origins of the Sphinx. It is a good example of how to write simply for an audience not liable to be familiar with the period of setting.

From *Zekmet the Stone Carver* by Mary Stolz, illustrated by Deborah Nourse Lattimore.

Books for the Middle Group

By the time they reach the middle grades, children have acquired some sense of the past and some perspective on its relations to the present. Their lively curiosity leads to conjecture about people of other times. Historical fiction that tells a good story satisfies both their need to know and their appreciation of action. In the books for this group, most of the stories stress courage and problem solving, and the preponderance of historical fiction is set in the comparatively familiar bounds of our own country's past.

Marguerite de Angeli
The Door in the Wall

Marguerite de Angeli's Newbery Medal book, *The Door in the Wall*, is set in thirteenth-century England. Robin's noble father is off to the wars and his mother is with the queen when the plague strikes. Robin falls ill, unable to move his legs, and is deserted by the servants. Brother Luke finds the boy and cares for him. To the despairing Robin he says, "Always remember . . . thou hast only to follow the wall far enough and there will be a door in it." The monks teach the boy to use his hands and his head, "For reading is another door in the wall. . . ." Robin learns to swim and to get around swiftly on crutches, but his back never straightens. However, his spirit is strong, and he plays so heroic a part in saving a beleaguered city that the king

From *The Door in the Wall*, written and illustrated by Marguerite de Angeli.

Viewpoint

The study of history is about as close as children ever come in the classroom to a consideration of people, the formation of their personalities, their private and public tribulations, their conflicts, their foibles, and their strengths. This is the very *stuff* of life, yet, as every survey shows, history is not a popular subject with students. Indeed, history is often described as irrelevant. The trouble is that for political, economic, and various other indefensible reasons we are watering down history by either leaving people out of the story or by depicting them in only the simplest and most general terms. In ancient Greece, the opposite of the word for *truth* was not *falsehood* but *oblivion*. If it is not from oblivion that we need to rescue the characters of our past, it is from some place almost as indistinct.

Jean Fritz, "The Very Truth," *Celebrating Children's Books*, edited by Betsy Hearne and Marilyn Kaye. New York: Lothrop, Lee & Shepard Books, 1981, pp. 83–84.

honors him, and his parents are moved with joy and pride. This heart-warming story is beautifully illustrated in the author's most colorful style. The characters are less convincing than the situations, but the book is frequently of great interest to children.

Jean Fritz
The Cabin Faced West
Brady

In *The Cabin Faced West* there isn't much to console Ann. She misses her cousin in Gettysburg and there isn't another child in the pioneer country of Western Pennsylvania for her to play with until she finds a boy her own age. The high point of the story is a surprise visit from George Washington, an episode based on historical fact, but the most engaging incident is the one in which Ann's mother stops her work to play tea party with the lonely child.

Brady is a more mature story, set in the years just before the Civil War. Living in an area where people's feelings are divided, Brady is embarrassed by his father's strong antislavery feelings until events move him to take a position of responsibility. Both books are smoothly written and are convincing in their setting and in period details, but *Brady* also has a depth that stems from strong characterization and a vivid portrayal of the moral issues involved in the abolitionist position.

Fritz's *Early Thunder*, set in 1775 Salem, has strong characters and serious discussions. We appreciate the problems of the characters, but we don't feel close to them. On the other hand, the humor of which Jean Fritz is capable shines forth abundantly in her *Who's That Stepping on Plymouth Rock?* and *Can't You Make Them Behave, King George?* These are representative of the brief, factual tales for younger readers that are no less accurate than her more substantial stories.

From *Why Can't You Make Them Behave, King George?* by Jean Fritz, illustrated by Tomie dePaola.

Elizabeth Coatsworth
Away Goes Sally
Five Bushel Farm
The Fair American

Elizabeth Coatsworth was an experienced, interesting writer whose works encompass poetry, fantasy, and historical fiction for a range of ages. When writing for older children, she was a strong delineator of character rather than an inventor of exciting episode. *Away Goes Sally* introduces us to an early nineteenth-century family of three sisters and two brothers who are raising an orphaned niece. The interplay of family relationships is excellent, especially when Uncle Joseph finds a way to move to Maine even when Aunt Nanny has said she will not leave her home. He simply builds her a small house on a sledge and transports everyone in comfort during the snowy winter months. *Five Bushel Farm* introduces us to Andrew, who becomes a member of Sally's family in Maine. *The Fair American* takes the two children on a sea voyage where they help to save a French boy fleeing from the terrorists after the French Revolution.

All the small details of living are interestingly worked into the stories; the children are obedient but resourceful; family cooperation is the normal state of affairs.

Carol Ryrie Brink
Caddie Woodlawn

Caddie Woodlawn, which was awarded the Newbery Medal, belongs to the Civil War period, but the war plays no part in the story. Caddie and her family live in Wisconsin when Indians are considered a menace, but life on the whole is fairly comfortable. Redheaded Caddie and her two brothers extract every possible bit of fun and adventure the frontier settlement can yield. Caddie's long friendship with the Indians and her courageous personal appeal to them helps prevent a threatened uprising.

Laura Ingalls Wilder
The *Little House* Books

As has been noted, children's sense of the past is a confused one at best. Gaslights are more incredible to them than candlelight, and horse-and-buggy travel quite as odd as a trip by canal boat. Indeed, it may be easier for children to understand and enter into the colonial period of American history than into the more immediate past. The pioneering and settling of the Midwest have fewer picturesque details than has the dramatic first colonization. Frontier life has more humdrum struggle, with less romantic adventure. Until Laura Ingalls Wilder undertook the writing of her family's experiences in settling the Midwest, there were no books of this period which really held children's interest.

Children love all the "Little House" books and grow up with the Ingalls girls and the Wilder boys, from *Little House in the Big Woods* to the romantic *These Happy Golden Years* when Laura Ingalls and Almanzo Wilder are married. The first book appeals to children of eight or nine; the latter is written for the older reader, who by this time may feel that Laura is an old and dear friend. Few other books give children this sense of continuity and progress.

The saga begins with the Ingalls family in their log cabin in the Wisconsin forest, in *Little House in the Big Woods*. The children are all girls. The oldest is Mary (who later goes blind), then the active Laura, and baby Carrie. Grace eventually displaces Carrie as the baby. Next, the family moves out to the wild Kansas country and begins the adventures described in the *Little House on the Prairie*. *On the Banks of Plum Creek* finds the Ingalls family in Minnesota; *By the Shores of Silver Lake* carries them to the Dakota Territory, where they remain either on their lake or in town.

The Long Winter finds the Ingalls family living in town. Of the whole series, this book is one no modern child should miss. One blizzard follows another until the railroads cease to run and the little town is cut off from supplies for months. Finally the wheat begins to give out, and the whole community faces starvation. Then it is Almanzo Wilder, not Pa Ingalls, who rides out into the snow-driven prairie to buy wheat from a farmer who has it. Later books carry Laura into teaching and then into marriage with Almanzo. *The First Four Years*, a posthumously published book, tells of Laura and Almanzo's first years as struggling farmers. In *These Happy Golden Years*, a title which speaks for the whole series, Laura Ingalls Wilder wrote in her daughter's copy:

And so farewell to childhood days,
Their joys, and hopes and fears.
But Father's voice and his fiddle's song
Go echoing down the years.[1]

Other Books for the Middle Group

Patricia MacLachlan, in *Sarah, Plain and Tall*, drew a touching picture of a mail-order bride of pioneer times, whose stepchildren adore her; the book won the Newbery Medal and the Scott O'Dell award. Another fine pioneer story is Brett Harvey's *My Prairie Year: Based on the Diary of Elenore Plaisted*.

Carolina's Courage by Elizabeth Yates is one of many tales of the wagon trains that crossed the Great Plains. Lonzo Anderson's *Zeb* is a taut story of a boy who survives a winter alone in the wilderness when his father and older brothers are accidentally killed. In *Trouble River* by Betsy Byars, Dewey escapes the Indians by rafting himself and his querulous grandmother downriver.

A good Civil War story for the middle group is F. N. Monjo's *The Vicksburg Veteran*. In the story, General Grant's son participates in the Union victory that gains control of the Mississippi. In Anna Gertrude Hall's *Cyrus Holt and the Civil War*, a boy of nine initially finds the war exciting, but as time goes by, becomes increasingly aware of the men wounded and dead, and of the growing burden of deprivation and unwanted responsibilities. Although it is set in the period before the Civil War, *A Gathering of Days: A New England Girl's Journal, 1830–32*, for which Joan Blos was awarded the Newbery Medal, is concerned with the issue of whether Catherine (the writer of the journal) is justified in helping a runaway slave despite the New Hampshire laws. A trenchant post-Civil War book is *Little John and Plutie* by Pat Edwards, the story of an interracial friendship in the South in 1897.

[1]Irene Smith, "Laura Ingalls Wilder and the Little House Books," *The Horn Book*, September/October 1943, p. 306. Delightful account of the author, with family photographs of Ma, Pa, the four girls, and Almanzo.

From *My Prairie Year: Based on the Diary of Elenore Plaisted* by Brett Harvey, illustrated by Deborah Kogan Ray.

The story of the Battle of Little Big Horn is told by fifteen-year-old Red Hawk in *Red Hawk's Account of Custer's Last Battle* by Paul and Dorothy Goble. Red Hawk, the only fictional character, says sadly, "Once all the earth was ours; now there is only a small piece left which the White Men did not want." He knows that the cause is lost despite the victory won by the native Americans. The list of sources provided indicates the research that gives the book its authenticity of historical detail.

Yoshiko Uchida, whose realistic fiction was discussed in the previous chapter, also has written three excellent books about the Depression Era. In the first, *A Jar of Dreams*, eleven-year-old Rinko describes the double burden of financial pressure and the increasing prejudice against Japanese-Americans. The sequels, *The Best Bad Thing* and *The Happiest Ending* are more personal but also create vividly the atmosphere of the period. Prejudice becomes persecution in *Journey to Topaz*, a story of evacuation and internment, and its sequel, at the end of the war, *Journey Home*. *The Bombers' Moon* by Betty Vander Els is set in China during the Japanese invasion of 1942, as is its sequel, *Leaving Point*.

The Peppermint Pig by Nina Bawden shows an English family temporarily forced to live with relatives as their fortunes fail around the turn of the century, while *Carrie's War* describes the lives of World War II evacuees in the English countryside. Bawden is skilled in creating credible characters and evoking sympathy for them.

For children who have never experienced the horror of war, books that tell of the plight of children in wartime can evoke some understanding. Alki Zei's *Wildcat Under Glass* is a story of life under the oppression of dictatorship as experienced by a child, Melia, who lives on a Greek island during the time of prewar German occupation. The story, which begins in August 1936, has drama and momentum, and is particularly effective in showing the reactions of the very young to a rigid regime. In *Petros' War*, Zei describes, from the point of view of a ten-year-old boy, the Italian occupation of Athens during World War II, and in *The Sound of the Dragon's Feet* she portrays a child's awareness of inequity in prerevolutionary Russia.

In Susan Cooper's *Dawn of Fear*, a small group of boys, busy with their games and school, are shocked into awareness and fear when one of their number is killed in an air raid.

The effect of the Germans on the lives of European Jews is graphically portrayed in Johanna Reiss's *The Upstairs Room*, where Annie lives hidden away in a farmhouse in wartime Holland; and in its sequel, *The Journey Back*, when Annie goes back to find the poignant, tragic aftermath of war and occupation. Austria is the setting for Peter Härtling's *Crutches*, winner of the Batchelder Award, in which two victims of World War II, a boy and a crippled man, help each other find security. In *A Pocket Full of Seeds* by Marilyn Sachs, French Nicole arrives home for lunch one day to find her family completely gone.

Judith Kerr, in *When Hitler Stole Pink Rabbit*, follows a family as they flee from Germany to Switzerland to France to escape extinction. They come finally to wartime England in *The Other Way Round*, a sequel for older readers. A family of Russian Jews adjusts to the United States in *Call Me Ruth* by Marilyn Sachs.

With *The Stone Book* Alan Garner, whose books for older readers are stylistically intricate, begins a quartet of linked stories, each a cameo, set in the Cheshire countryside, following four generations of a family. Each is distinctly an entity; each is written with clarity and depth. The others are *Granny Reardun*, *Tom Fobble's Day*, and *The Aimer Gate*.

From *Granny Reardun* by Alan Garner, illustrated by Michael Foreman.

Books for Older Children

Older readers can range through many time periods, and in their historical fiction there is no need to avoid the complexities of social movements and relationships that existed in the past as they do today. Erik Haugaard's Hakon can move from one cultural pattern to another, Rosemary Sutcliff's Aquila can have a divided allegiance that young people understand. They can enjoy the rich tapestry of a story that has intricate patterns of action in an unfamiliar setting and appreciate the implications that past events have for the present.

Eloise Jarvis McGraw
Mara, Daughter of the Nile

A novel set in ancient Egypt is *Mara*, a hair-raising tale of royal intrigue, spies, and true love, in the days when a female Pharaoh, Hat-shepsut, has usurped the throne from the rightful king. Mara is a slave who vaguely remembers better days and is determined to escape. She is bought by a mysterious man who offers her luxury if she will serve at court as a spy for the queen. She accepts, but also sells her services as a spy for the king to a young nobleman, Lord Sheftu. Eventually, her love for Sheftu and a deep pity for the wronged king change her from a liar and a cheat to a selfless heroine who endures torture rather than betray her new loyalties. Detailed pictures emerge of the daily life of different classes—shopkeepers, rivermen, soldiers, slaves, and royalty.

A second book about ancient Egypt by this writer is *The Golden Goblet*. While it is not quite so powerful a tale as *Mara*, it, too, affords a detailed picture of the times, with a vigorous plot and convincing characters.

Olivia E. Coolidge
Egyptian Adventures

Olivia E. Coolidge is a scholar, and in the course of her entertaining *Egyptian Adventures* she gives children lively pictures of the Egyptians' superstitions and magic, harvests and hunts, festivals and funerals. The characters emerge fully drawn and colorfully alive. These twelve well-written stories will do much to develop children's feeling for the people and adventures of a far-distant past.

Men of Athens, *Roman People*, and *People in Palestine* are in the same format, each tale complete in itself and the whole giving a remarkably vivid picture of the diversity of the culture in a historical period. *The King of Men* is a complex and absorbing novel based on the Agamemnon legend, and *The Maid of Artemis* tells of a year in the life of an Athenian girl and her choice for the future. In all these books, the combination of scholarly research and a fine writing style re-creates the period so convincingly that the reader has no sense of a disparate culture; each detail of rites and customs, of mores and superstitions, is an integral part of the story.

Henry Treece
Viking's Dawn

An English poet, critic, and teacher, Henry Treece was distinguished both for the sonorous quality of his prose and for his ability to create convincingly the mood and language of the distant past. *Viking's Dawn* is the first of a trilogy about Harald Sigurdson who, in the eighth century, was the only man on his crew to return from a voyage filled with disasters. In *The Road to Miklagard* Sigurdson becomes a Moorish slave and travels to Constantinople and then to Russia; and in *Viking's Sunset* the Vikings come to a new land and live with Eskimos and other native Americans.

Treece used ancient Britain as a setting for lively tales like *The Centurion*, a story of a Roman legionnaire. His last book, *The Dream Time*, takes us back to Stone Age Britain. Like Rosemary Sutcliff, Treece was so steeped in history that his stories have a remarkable unity:

Viewpoint

Why write about the past when all our concerns are with the present? In fact, why bother with history at all? After all it is only, as Ambrose Bierce said, "an account mostly false, of events mostly unimportant, which are brought about by rulers mostly knaves, and by soldiers mostly fools." Yet I think Bierce's definition itself to be sufficient reason to study history. If the young discover that in the past they have been governed, led, abused, and slaughtered by fools and knaves, then perhaps they will look about them and see that matters have not greatly changed, and possibly they will do so before they vote.

But are not such matters dealt with better by the conscientious historian than by the fiction writer? Not altogether. The historian, if honest, gives us a photograph of the past; the storyteller gives us a painting. Imagine, if you can, a photograph of Rembrandt. What would you see? A fat Dutch merchant, down on his luck, and none too tidy or clean. A man of little account. It would be a likeness of value only to a policeman. But look at a painting of the same man, and you would see one of the greatest spirits that ever lived. You might not have recognized him in the street, but you would have recognized him in your heart. So which is the more important: the outward appearance or the spirit within? The spirit within, we all say, as if amazed that such a question could be seriously put. Yet there isn't the smallest doubt that we all spend a good deal more on clothes than we do on books.

From "Historical Fiction for Our Global Times" by Leon Garfield in *The Horn Book Magazine*, November/December 1988, pp. 736–742. Reprinted by permission of The Horn Book, 14 Beacon St., Boston, Mass. 02108.

Details of dress and architecture, language, and references to other events have a consistency that makes his books convincing and alive.

Erik Christian Haugaard
Hakon of Rogen's Saga
A Messenger for Parliament

Hakon of Rogen's Saga is not a traditional saga but a realistic story taking place in the last days of the Vikings. To Hakon, Rogen Island and his powerful father seem indestructible—but there is a bloody family feud that reads much like an old Norse saga. The author, a Dane familiar with Icelandic sagas, says at the beginning:

"Your dog, your horse, your friend, and you yourself: all shall die. Eternally live only your deeds and man's judgment over them," this was the credo of the Vikings.

In this book the Vikings are of heroic stature and the author clothes their story with nobility.

Its sequel, *A Slave's Tale*, is told by the small slave girl Helga, to whom Hakon is like a beloved brother. Their affection ripens into love, but this is a minor facet of the story, which is primarily a tale of a voyage to Frankland in a longboat. The writing, in explication and dia-logue as well as in the period details, vividly creates the historical milieu and has the sweep and cadence of a Norse epic.

A testament of hope and an indictment of war, *The Little Fishes* is a moving story of an Italian waif during World War II. *The Rider and His Horse* is set in ancient Israel at the final battle between the Jews and Romans at Masada, while *The Untold Tale* gives an all-too-clear picture of life for the poor in Denmark in the 1600s. Haugaard's heroes always face horror realistically and unflinchingly, and tragedy is as often the outcome as is triumph. In *A Messenger for Parliament* a young man named for Oliver Cromwell tells his life story as a camp follower of the Parliamentary Army, in a story that vividly depicts the fierce allegiances of a divided country.

In *Leif the Unlucky* Haugaard writes commandingly of the last remnants of the Greenland colony in the early fifteenth century. In *The Samurai's Tale* Haugaard shows depth and sweep in his story of the power struggles of the feudal warlords of sixteenth-century Japan.

From *Hakon of Rogen's Saga* by Erik Christian Haugaard, illustrated by Leo and Diane Dillon.

Rosemary Sutcliff
The Lantern Bearers
Dawn Wind
Song for a Dark Queen
Bonnie Dundee
Warrior Scarlet
Flame-Colored Taffeta
Blood Feud

Most critics would say that at the present time the greatest writer of historical fiction for children and young people is unquestionably Rosemary Sutcliff. Her stories are superior because they are authentic records of history and also because every one of her memorable books is built around a great theme. Her characters live and die for principles they value and that people today still value.

The theme of all her stories, as Margaret Meek[2] points out, is:

[2]*Rosemary Sutcliff.* A Walck Monograph, Walck, 1962. p. 250.

the light and the dark. The light is what is valued, what is to be saved beyond one's own lifetime. The dark is the threatening destruction that works against it.

In *The Lantern Bearers*, the blackness of despair is concentrated in the heart of Aquila, a Roman officer who, when a Saxon raid sweeps down on his father's farm, sees his father slain, and his sister Flavia carried off by the raiders. He himself is left tied to a tree for the wolves and later made a slave by another band. Years later, after he has escaped his thralldom, an old friend says to him:

Viewpoint

The true historians, the men and women whose profession is to delve into the past, know that at best all they can achieve is a partial resurrection of the events which make up history. This fact might be frustrating to minds so orderly that they like to pigeonhole everything, but it is also what makes studying the past so interesting. History is not an exact science and never will be; it deals with material which is often suspect, if not actually false. Yet false information can inadvertently contain the truth, for lies are told in order to hide something. Not only must the historian suspect his material, but he must be aware that he is not unprejudiced, that he is viewing the past from a certain position. And just as the past casts its shadow into the future, so does the present bear upon the historian's study of the past. History is what we choose to recall. If this were not true, all history books would be alike, and the only difference among them would be the latest discovery of some ancient facts. But the study of history, like everything else, changes with fashion; and what one generation thinks is important is considered insignificant by the next.

Erik Christian Haugaard, "Before I Was Born, History and the Child," Part II, *The Horn Book Magazine*, December 1979, p. 700.

It may be that the night will close over us in the end, but I believe that morning will come again. . . . We are the Lantern Bearers, my friend; for us to keep something burning, to carry what light we can forward into the darkness and the wind.[3]

No briefing of these stories can give any conception of their scope and power. They may be difficult, not because of vocabulary, but because of the complexities of the plots in which many peoples are fighting for dominance.

Fortunately, *Dawn Wind*, one of the finest of the books, is also the least complex. Chronologically it follows *The Lantern Bearers*, but it is complete in itself and will undoubtedly send many readers to the trilogy. The fourteen-year-old hero, Owain, finds himself the sole survivor of a bloody battle between the Saxons and the Britains in which his people, the Britains, are destroyed. In the gutted remains of the city from which he had come, the only life the boy finds is Regina, a pitiable waif of a girl, who is lost and half-starved. Owain carries her to a Saxon settlement where the girl will receive proper care, even though he knows he will be sold into slavery. After eleven years, he is freed and sets out at once to find his people and Regina, to start all over again with those basic qualities that have always made for survival.

In *Song for a Dark Queen*, Boadicea's story is told by an old harpist, who remembers her as an imperious little girl and as the tragic warrior-queen. Historical details are integrated into the narrative fabric of the smoothly written story. Sutcliff is at her engrossing best in *Bonnie Dundee*, a vivid story of the battle to keep the house of Stuart on the Scottish throne. Whether it is her great trilogy or the story of eighteenth-century smuggling, *Flame-Colored Taffeta*; or *Warrior Scarlet*; or *Blood Feud*, a Viking story, Rosemary Sutcliff gives children and young people historical fiction that builds courage and faith that life will go on and is well worth the struggle.

[3]*The Lantern Bearers* is the third book in a trilogy which also includes *The Eagle of the Ninth* and *The Silver Branch*.

Cynthia Harnett
Nicholas and the Wool-Pack
Caxton's Challenge

Cynthia Harnett's sketches add to the wealth of informative detail about fifteenth-century England in *Nicholas and the Wool-Pack*, winner of the Carnegie Medal in 1951 under its British title, *The Wool-Pack*. It is not only an exciting story with an element of mystery, but also a colorful picture of the weaving industry and of the everyday life of the period. Nicholas, an apprentice to his father, a wool merchant, foils the two Lombardians who are secretly attempting to ruin his father.

Another smoothly written story of the same period is *Caxton's Challenge* (*The Load of Unicorn* in the British edition), which gives a vivid picture of London at that time, both the text and the maps indicating the careful research that lends authenticity to historical fiction. Again an apprentice is a leading character; Bendy is entranced by the printing machines of his master, William Caxton, and becomes involved in the struggles Caxton has against the resentful scriveners.

The Writing on the Hearth embroils would-be Oxford scholar Stephen in fifteenth-century English politics. Harnett's stories are solid and sedate, well researched and meticulous in their detail.

Elizabeth Janet Gray Vining
Adam of the Road
I Will Adventure

Elizabeth Gray Vining is a born storyteller, although paradoxically her stories are weak in plot construction. Her books develop little excitement; the conflicts are mild, with no breath-taking suspense leading to a climax. Yet she is a careful historian, and her tales have all the authentic minutiae of everyday life long ago which make history convincing. But chiefly she is concerned with people.

In *Adam of the Road*, for which the author won the Newbery Medal, the protagonist lives in the thirteenth century. Adam's two loves are his golden cocker spaniel and his minstrel father, but he loses them both for a time. How he seeks the two of them up and down the roads of old England gives children a glimpse into every variety of medieval life—that of jugglers, minstrels, plowmen, and nobles, as real as the people today.

The hero of *I Will Adventure* is Andrew Talbot, a most beguiling young imp, who takes to himself a line from Shakespeare's *Romeo and Juliet*, "I will adventure." Andrew is journeying to London to be a page to his uncle Sir John Talbot when he has the good luck to hear this play and, by way of a fight with one of the boy players, meets Master Burbage and Shakespeare himself. Through Andrew's eyes the reader comes to know intimately many facets of London life in 1596, especially the theater, the plays, and the audiences. Andrew's problems are happily solved, thanks to Shakespeare and a sympathetic uncle.

Vining's *The Taken Girl* moves us from England to Philadelphia during pre-Civil War days, when Veer, an orphaned servant girl, works with John Greenleaf Whittier in the abolitionist movement.

Marchette Chute
The Wonderful Winter
The Innocent Wayfaring

Marchette Chute, the author of *Shakespeare of London* and similar studies of Chaucer and Ben Jonson for adult readers, has also written some delightful stories for young people. *The Wonderful Winter* carries young readers straight into Shakespeare's theater with young Robin, Sir Robert Wakefield, who has escaped from an intolerable home situation. London seems to spell starvation for him until he is befriended by some actors and is taken into the home of the famous John Heminges. Through the warmth and affection of this crowded household, Robin learns to give and accept love and gaiety. Meanwhile he works and plays small parts in the Burbage Theater, knows the great Shakespeare, and falls in love with *Romeo and Juliet*. Robin returns home happy and confident as a result of his wonderful winter.

The Innocent Wayfaring is fourteenth-century England brought vividly and authentically to life. Anne, averse to learning the arts of housewifery, runs away from her convent school with the prioress's pet monkey for company. Her adventures provide a view of fourteenth-century life, from seamy inns to manor houses.

Both books are beautifully written by a scholar who can paint a glowing background for her stories.

Barbara Willard
The Lark and the Laurel

While several American writers, notably Laura Ingalls Wilder and Leonard Wibberley, have followed a family through the years, Barbara Willard has spanned more than a hundred years of English history, from the early sixteenth century to the mid-seventeenth century, through a family living in Ashdown Forest, in and around a house called Mantlemass. The first of the series, *The Lark and the Laurel*, tells of a child marriage for political ends. The cycle continues with *The Sprig of Broom*, which introduces Richard Plashet, or Plantagenet, unacknowledged son of Richard III, and his son, Medley, who marries into the Mantlemass Manor family. *A Cold Wind Blowing* shows how the family weathers the Reformation, while in *The Iron Lily* an unacknowledged Medley woman takes over as the iron-willed mistress of her husband's forge at his death. Mantlemass is destroyed in the last tale, *Harrow and Harvest*, when civil war erupts. Willard has a strong feeling for place, and it is the locale we remember as much as the events and people.

Patricia Clapp
Constance
I'm Deborah Sampson

With the exception of one character, all of the people described by *Constance* in her journal existed, and the events are based on the real life of an ancestress of Patricia Clapp's husband. The historical details are smoothly woven into the story, and the description of the early days of the Plymouth Colony is unusually vivid. As she tells of her growing understanding of the native Americans, her relationship with her stepmother, her doubts about herself, and her friendship with the young man she will marry, Constance is always a convincing character. The book, which concludes with her marriage in 1626, is particularly valuable because of the graphic depiction of the hardships of the first grim winter and the struggles of the colonists with their English backers.

In writing a novel about the Revolutionary War period, Clapp uses a real person but invents the details of the story told by Deborah in *I'm Deborah Sampson: A Soldier in the War of the Revolution*. The real Deborah did indeed enlist in Washington's army and successfully masquerade as a man. The writing is vividly detailed, and the language and concepts consistent with the period. Colonial New England is also the setting for *Witches' Children: A Story of Salem*, while the perspective of a newly arrived English girl gives objectivity to *The Tamarack Tree: A Novel of the Siege of Vicksburg*.

Hester Burton
Beyond the Weir Bridge
Time of Trial

Beyond the Weir Bridge is a vivid piece of historical writing, consistent in language and viewpoint, informative about the period in which it

From *Beyond the Weir Bridge* by Hester Burton, illustrated by Victor G. Ambrus.

is set, and a truly dramatic story. Richard and Richenda, whose fathers had been killed in 1644 in Cromwell's service, are both fond of shy, bookish Thomas although he is a Royalist. Richenda, indeed, comes to love him when they are grown and with him joins the Quakers, a denomination then reviled. It is only when Richard, who has become a doctor, sees Thomas's faith bring him to plague-ridden London to help as best he can, that he understands the true humility of the Quaker credo.

Time of Trial, winner of the 1963 Carnegie Medal, also is concerned with the courage of the nonconformist. Seventeen-year-old Margaret Pargeter is the daughter of a London bookseller who is sent to prison for advocating social reform and for printing a book judged inflammatory. *Kate Ryder* is a compelling tale of England's Civil War, with another strong heroine. Burton's characters always reflect the mores and customs in a time of change, yet are developed as distinctive individuals, and her stories are all the more convincing because her characters' goals are realistically modest.

Mollie Hunter
The Ghosts of Glencoe
The Stronghold

Ensign Robert Stewart, the protagonist of Mollie Hunter's *The Ghosts of Glencoe*, is an officer of the king's army, dedicated to keeping peace in the Highlands. Like many other Scottish officers, Ensign Stewart finds that he is torn between loyalty to his king and sympathy for his own people. Shaken by the vengefulness of those who do not share that sympathy, Stewart finally warns the rebels when an attack is planned. The dialogue rings true, and the period details are as meticulously correct as is the historical material.

This careful treatment of fact is a firm base in all of Mollie Hunter's books, although most of them are more highly fictionalized than is *The Ghosts of Glencoe*. *The Spanish Letters* is a cloak-and-dagger adventure story, set in Edinburgh in the late sixteenth century, in which two Spanish agents are allied with Scottish traitors planning to abduct King James. *The Lothian Run* is a tale of spies and smugglers which, like *The Spanish Letters*, is full of plot and counterplot, romantic and sinister. Hunter's *A Sound of Chariots* and its sequel, *Hold on to Love*, deal with an adolescent girl who struggles for education and independence in 1930s' Scotland.

The Thirteenth Member deals with a coven of witches and part of a plot to kill James I of Scotland. In *The Stronghold*, winner of a Carnegie Medal, Hunter's ability to construct a convincing tale from historical fragments is very evident. In this book Coll discovers a way to build the multistoried tower within which his small Scottish tribe can withstand Roman raids during the first century A.D. Hunter smoothly combines fact and fiction in *You Never Knew Her As I Did*, a story about Mary, Queen of Scots.

Elizabeth George Speare
The Witch of Blackbird Pond
The Bronze Bow
The Sign of the Beaver

The Witch of Blackbird Pond was the winner of the 1959 Newbery Medal. Orphaned Kit, luxuriously raised in tropical Barbados, comes to live with her Puritan relatives in Connecticut. These cousins try to be kind but they disagree with Kit about almost everything. Her silk dresses and befeathered bonnets scandalize the whole community, and Kit willfully flouts local customs in many ways, most seriously by making friends with an old Quaker woman, Hannah Tupper, the suspected witch of Blackbird Pond. Kit's recklessness climaxes in her arrest, imprisonment, and trial for witchcraft. This terrifying experience brings Kit to realize that none of us can live without family or friends. Her stern old uncle defends her even at considerable danger to himself and his family. A forlorn waif Kit had befriended stands by her, and her disapproving, seafaring beau Nat finally manages to extricate Kit. The strength of this book lies in its theme and its well-drawn characters. They are neither wholly good nor wholly bad but a very human mixture of heroism and bigotry, frailty and courage, rebellious recklessness and generous loyalty.

The 1962 Newbery Medal winner, *The Bronze Bow*, is set in Israel during the time Jesus lived. The title comes from II Samuel 22:35—

"He trains my hands for war, so that my arms can bend a bow of bronze." This verse fascinates young Daniel, who, along with many Israelites, is looking for the Deliverer to drive the cruel Romans out of their land. Daniel had seen his mother and father wantonly slain by these conquerors. Blinded by his hatred, Daniel kills his sister's hope of love, thereby driving her into mental darkness. Not until he has seen his mute but devoted follower killed and has almost lost his love, Thacia, does Daniel come face to face with the healing love of Jesus. Then at last he understands that it is not hatred and violence, but only love that is strong enough to bend the bow of bronze.

The Sign of the Beaver not only was a Newbery Honor Book but also won the Scott O'Dell Award for Historical Fiction, the first book to attain that honor. Set in the Maine wilderness in the eighteenth century, the tautly structured story describes the friendship between a lonely, young white settler and a slowly acquired native American friend. Like other Speare titles, this has fine narrative flow over an unobtrusive base of research. In 1989, Elizabeth Speare won the Laura Ingalls Wilder Award for the body of her work.

John and Patricia Beatty
At the Seven Stars
Who Comes to King's Mountain?

John and Patricia Beatty's historical novels are based on sound research; their aim was to entertain rather than to instruct their readers. As Patricia Beatty says, "We hope that our books are more than escape fiction, but we are aware that all fiction offers escape."[4] In *At the Seven Stars*, a fifteen-year-old boy from Philadelphia comes to London in 1752 and meets some of the very real people of that turbulent period. Richard becomes involved in the struggle between the Hanoverian and Stuart supporters, takes refuge in William Hogarth's home, is imprisoned, escapes, enlists the aid of the actor David Garrick, and gets back to America with the help of the Duke of Newcastle.

[4]Patricia Beatty, "The Two-headed Monster," *The Horn Book*, February 1967, p. 100.

Who Comes to King's Mountain? shows the difficulties a Scottish South Carolina boy has in serving with the rebels rather than the British during the last years of the Revolution. There is never a dearth of action in books by the Beattys or in the books that Patricia Beatty writes alone. In *Hail Columbia*, for example, a suffragette in Oregon in 1893 stirs up the town of Astoria by her vigorous dedication to causes. Since John Beatty's death, Patricia Beatty has focused on the American past in such frontier-heroine stories as *That's One Ornery Orphan*, set in 1889, or *Turn Homeward, Hannalee* which is about Southern mill workers in the Civil War. It gives—as do most of Beatty's books—an appended note on sources; in its sequel, *Be Ever Hopeful, Hannalee*, Beatty explores the problems of war's aftermath. *Charley Skedaddle*, also a Civil War story, won the Scott O'Dell Award.

Esther Forbes
Johnny Tremain

Esther Forbes received the 1942 Pulitzer Prize for her adult biography *Paul Revere and the World He Lived In*. Her *Johnny Tremain*, which was an outgrowth of the research expended on *Paul Revere*, received the 1944 Newbery Medal. In her Newbery acceptance speech, Forbes explained that while she was working on the adult biography she had to stifle any tendency toward fiction. But she was continually teased by the story possibilities of Boston's apprentices, who were always getting into scrapes of one kind or another. So Forbes promised herself that as soon as possible she would write some fiction about the apprentices. The resulting book, *Johnny Tremain*, represents a high point in American historical fiction for children and young people.

Johnny Tremain tells the story of a silversmith's apprentice who lived in the exciting days that marked the beginning of the American Revolution. Johnny is cocky, overbearing with his fellow apprentices, and ambitious for himself, and the apprentices decide to play a joke on him, with tragic results. Johnny is left with a burned hand, maimed for life. His career as a silversmith is over.

This is the beginning of a story that carries Johnny and his friend Rab into the thick of Boston's pre-Revolutionary activities. In the first little skirmish of the Revolution, men and boys lined up in the square—some to die. But they knew what they were dying for, Forbes assures us, and they believed it "was worth more than their own lives."

Johnny Tremain has so many values they are difficult to summarize. This book is not limiting or biased in its account of pre-Revolutionary days but makes the colonists and redcoats come alive as histories never seem to. The British, especially, are amazingly human in their forbearance, while the confusion and uncertainty of the colonists are frighteningly real; the details of the everyday life of the period are expertly woven into the story.

Rebecca Caudill
Tree of Freedom
The Far-Off Land

Tree of Freedom, a story about the Revolutionary War period, is sound historical fiction because of its vivid characterizations and homely details of everyday living, which make the past understandable and natural. Each child of a family moving to Kentucky may take one prized possession. Stephanie chooses an apple seed, which is what her grandmother brought from France. When eldest son Noel wants to take his dulcimer, it starts anew the feud between father and son. But the mother intervenes:

Twon't hurt him any. An' a little music won't hurt Kentucky, either. . . . He's got his rifle, ain't he, as well as his dulcimore? He'll use it like a man. See if he don't.

And he does, but the quarrel is not resolved until the end of the war.

Another fine story is Caudill's *The Far-Off Land* in which a young girl is taken by flatboat in 1780 from the Moravian settlement in Salem to French Lick. Although she becomes accustomed to the rough ways of the settlers, Ketty cannot accept their hostile behavior toward native Americans, since she has been brought up to practice brotherly love. The characterization is strong, the period details convincing and smoothly incorporated into the story.

From *Johnny Tremain* by Esther Forbes, illustrated by Lynd Ward.

Leonard Wibberley
The *Treegate* Series

Leonard Wibberley paints his stories of Peter Treegate's adventures during the Revolutionary War on a broad canvas. In the first book, *John Treegate's Musket*, John Treegate is a solid, respectable Boston citizen who is loyal to his king, but his son Peter becomes increasingly convinced of the rectitude of the patriot cause and fights against the British at Bunker Hill. In *Peter Treegate's War*, Peter becomes a war prisoner, escapes, and crosses the Delaware with Washington. *Sea Captain from Salem* tells the story of Peace of God Manly, who saved Peter's life in the first book, and who is sent on a mission by Benjamin Franklin, in an effort to win French support for the cause. The move to France gives the series variety, and the plot provides some rousing sea battles. *Treegate's Raiders* ends with the defeat of Cornwallis. All the books give realistic pictures not only of the Revolutionary War but of the significance of that war to the ordinary citizen of the time and to history.

William O. Steele
Wayah of the Real People
The Perilous Road
The Far Frontier

Few writers re-create wilderness life more vividly and movingly than William O. Steele. His stories are well written in the vernacular of the

From *Wayah of the Real People* by William O. Steele, illustrated by Isa Barnett.

Viewpoint

I have a mistrust of the historical novel, with one or two shining exceptions. Nevertheless, I think the children's writer has a role to play in generating awareness of the past; what I am wary of is the danger of didacticism—the awful shadow that looms over us all, the legacy of the nineteenth century. It dies hard, and it survives best not only in the novel of social relevance but in the fatal note of instruction that creeps into so many stories dealing with the past, even an immediate past. And at that point the life goes out of them. The child is being told what is what—or rather what was what; he is not being offered that far more exciting and stimulating liberation of finding out for himself. To stimulate historical curiosity you have first to persuade people—of any age—of the reality of the past, which is far more difficult or subtle than telling them how things were done then. Or how you think they were done. Because that is the other truth I would want to get across to children—the notion that history itself is fluid, that it is not received opinion but a matter of debate and discussion and interpretation. Plenty of educational systems never suggest this.

Penelope Lively, "Bones in the Sand," *The Horn Book Magazine,* December 1981, p. 648.

times, with good dialogue, plenty of suspense and action, and flesh-and-blood characters—grownups who struggle and survive in a tough pioneer world and expect their children to do the same.

Wayah of the Real People is an unusual story about a Cherokee boy's year of schooling at Brafferton Hall in mid-eighteenth-century Williamsburg. Wayah suffers all the problems of any child placed in an environment culturally different from his own. Afraid that he has changed, Wayah finds when he has returned to the Real People, that his year away has helped him mature.

In *The Perilous Road*, young Chris Brabson, who hates the Yankees, cannot understand how his parents can accept the fact that his older brother has joined the Union Army. After Union soldiers have raided the Brabson livestock, Chris tries a bit of revenge and is surprised, when he gets to know some of the soldiers, that they are people like himself.

The Far Frontier shows another strong-willed boy who is outraged when he finds himself bound out to an absentminded scientist from Philadelphia. But before their long, danger-beset journey through the Tennessee wilderness is over, Tobe has acquired a deep respect for his brave, eccentric companion. Best of all, the boy survives with a lasting hunger for learning and is well on his way with both reading and figuring. Tobe and the naturalist, Mr. Twistletree, are a memorable pair.

Scott O'Dell

Island of the Blue Dolphins
The King's Fifth
Carlota
The Captive
Sarah Bishop

Of the good realistic stories about the American Indian set in the past, one of the most powerful is *Island of the Blue Dolphins* (1961 Newbery Medal).

In the early 1800s off the coast of California, a twelve-year-old Indian girl boards a ship that is to carry the tribe away from their island home where they are being harried and destroyed by Aleutian seal hunters. But when Karana sees that her little brother has accidentally been left behind, she jumps off the moving ship and swims back to him and their island home; the two are left stranded. A pack of wild dogs kills her brother and begins to stalk the solitary girl. This is the beautifully told story of her survival on the island for eighteen years. Shining through her struggles and hardships are her quiet resignation, her endurance, her genuine love for her island home, and the great fortitude and serenity she develops. The story of Karana is historically true. Her incredible battles with a bull sea elephant, a devilfish, ferocious dogs, and, above all, her years of solitude command the reader's humble admiration for human courage. The sequel, *Zia*, is a poignant story of Zia's efforts to find her aunt, Karana.

Also based on history is the story told by Esteban in *The King's Fifth*, his reminiscences of the journey made as a fifteen-year-old car-

tographer to Coronado. Put ashore to find Coronado's camp, his small group has a dangerous journey searching for the fabled gold of Cibola, and Esteban is later imprisoned on the charge that he has withheld the king's share of the treasure. The transitions between past and present are smoothly bridged, and the historical details are used to enhance rather than obscure an adventurous tale.

In *Carlota*, O'Dell records the efforts of Spanish Californians to maintain their independence after the Mexican-American War. With *The Captive*, O'Dell moves to the sixteenth century and a young Spanish seminarian who is horrified by the slavery he finds in the New World. This powerful story of greed, conquest, and corruption is extended in *The Feathered Serpent* and *The Amethyst Ring*. O'Dell explores aspects of American history in *Sarah Bishop*;

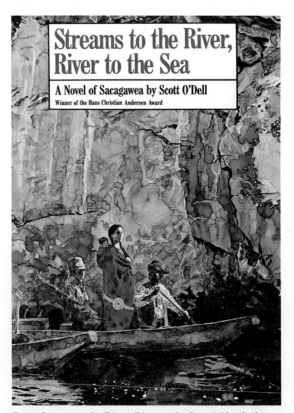

From *Streams to the River, River to the Sea: A Novel of Sacagawea* by Scott O'Dell, cover illustration by Ted Lewin.

Viewpoint

Our youth comes into this world, as Wordsworth has said, "trailing clouds of glory." They also come straight from the forehead of Jove, or so they do believe. And if I may judge from my own youth, my talks with thousands of the young, they're allowed to remain unaware of what has gone on before they appeared.

This ignorance is disastrous. As George Santayana has said, "those who cannot remember the past are condemned to repeat it." What he did not say was that those who don't know the past are condemned to live unfulfilled and narrow lives.

I strongly believe that cooperation between parents and librarians, teachers and writers of historical novels, can eliminate the ignorance so rampant in today's schools, where a majority of high school students has never heard of Joseph Stalin or Winston Churchill and one third of our seventeen-year-olds do not know that Columbus appeared on these shores before 1750.

The advantage of good historical novels over the history that emerges from history books, usually dull, can be dramatic. They're mined from history yet they are alive. Their characters speak human words, think human thoughts, humanly respond to the problems and the place in which they live. To this end, the writer must embrace history in an act of identification.

Scott O'Dell, "History and Fiction," *The Five Owls*, Volume III, Number 3, January/February 1990.

Streams to the River, River to the Sea: A Novel of Sacagawea; and *The Serpent Never Sleeps: A Novel of Jamestown and Pocahontas*. In all his work, O'Dell exemplified that combination of adherence to literary standards and that dramatic flair of the natural storyteller who creates books that are as popular with readers as they are with critics. In 1972, Scott O'Dell received the Hans Christian Andersen Award.

Christie Harris
Raven's Cry
West with the White Chiefs

Raven's Cry was given the Canadian Library Association's award as the best children's book of the year in English. The dramatic and impressive story describes the dreadful consequences for the Haida people when white men came in 1775 to hunt sea otter, cheating the people and destroying their way of life until only a handful remained. The story is told from the Indian viewpoint, in a vigorous narrative that is complemented by the strong illustrations of Bill Reid, a descendant of the last Haida chief, who duplicates the form of Haida art.

West with the White Chiefs is based on the journal written by two Englishmen, a story of high adventure in which a small party crosses the Rockies in 1863. The characterization of the whites and native Americans, who become friends on the journey, is excellent, and there is some comedy in the pedantic, quarrelsome schoolmaster who foists himself on the party of explorers.

Betty Baker
The Dunderhead War
Walk the World's Rim
And One Was a Wooden Indian

The Dunderhead War is one of the few good books for young people about the Mexican War, which serves as a background for Betty Baker's story of seventeen-year-old Quincy, who is too young to enlist, but travels with his Uncle Fritz and shares some of the adventures of the volunteers. Uncle Fritz has just come to the United States, and his complacent superiority and criticism of that "army of dunderheads" give an outsider's viewpoint and add humor to a lively story.

Many of Baker's books, from stories for beginning readers to serious fiction for adolescents, are about native Americans. Two of the best are *Walk the World's Rim*, the story of the African-American slave, Esteban, who wandered across the country with Cabeza de Vaca and became the hero of the native-American boy, Chakoh; and *And One Was a Wooden Indian*, a sensitive novel about a young Apache of the nineteenth century and his first encounter with white people. One of her lighter stories, *The Great Desert Race* has two teenage girls who enter a steam-powered automobile in a 1908 contest.

Harold Keith
Rifles for Watie

Rifles for Watie, winner of the 1958 Newbery Medal, is substantial historical fiction. The hero of the book is young Jefferson Davis Bussey, who despite his name is a Kansas farm boy and a rabid Unionist. Once in the army, Jeff's name and his stubborn forthrightness get him into trouble with a brutal officer, who persecutes him endlessly. Finally, Jeff is sent as a spy behind the Rebel lines to try to discover where Confederate Stand Watie, a full-blooded Cherokee Indian, is getting the new rifles issued for the Union armies. Jeff is captured by the Rebels, but his name, together with a plausible story, allays suspicions. Jeff lives, works, and fights with this native-American regiment for fourteen months. When he finally gets his information and escapes to the Northern side, he leaves his Confederate friends with real regret. He leaves them also with the disturbing realization that heroic, well-intentioned men are fighting and dying on both sides in this horrifying struggle.

Keith has created unforgettable characters and has given us all the hunger, dirt, and weariness of war to balance the heroism of men and boys on both sides.

Peter Burchard
Bimby
Jed

Peter Burchard's approach to the writing of historical fiction is to pinpoint his theme by using a compressed, concise account of an incident or a single day and creating thereby a dramatic impact. In *Bimby*, the author follows a young slave through one crucial day in which the boy sees an old friend killed and also learns that his father had died of the punishment received when he tried to escape. Knowing that she will never see her son again, Bimby's mother gives him information that will enable him to escape, both of them aware that life without freedom is empty. The writing is subdued, so that the poignancy and tension of the story emerge from the events themselves.

In *Jed*, Burchard again avoids didacticism and lets the ethical implications of a boy's conduct make their own impact on the reader. Although he is only sixteen, Jed has already fought at Shiloh. He is disturbed by the behavior of some of the Yankee soldiers who are his companions at arms: Foraging is stealing, and war is no excuse; war, in fact, is not glamorous. When he finds a small boy who has been hurt, Jed takes the child back to his Confederate family and befriends him. *The Deserter* is a Civil War spy story, and *Chinwe*, set in 1838, is a story of a brave Ibo woman who is taken by slave traders.

K. M. Peyton
The *Flambards* Trilogy

Before K. M. Peyton's *Flambards* trilogy, she produced a series of excellent adventure stories, many of which are set in the past but have little sense of history. With the publication of *Flambards*, Peyton made the Edwardian period an integral part of the book. Flambards is the Russell estate to which Christina Parsons, a young orphan, comes to live with her uncle and his two sons, Mark and Will. World War I is looming, and quiet Will is enthralled by flying. The emphasis on the first frail, experimental planes is a major part of the story, although the plot focuses on Christina's rejection of the powerful bully Mark and her love for Will. One of the ways in which Peyton reflects the changing mores of the period is in Christina's ambivalence about servants: She resents her uncle's treatment of them, yet cannot quite feel that the groom, Dick, is an equal.

The book was a runner-up for the Carnegie Medal, which was awarded to Peyton for the second book of the three, *The Edge of the Cloud*. In this book Will and Christina take refuge with an aunt in Battersea, since Mark and his father are irate over Christina's choice. The story ends with their marriage, but it is less a love story than an account of the early days of flying, with its stunt men, and the camaraderie of the still-small group of flyers.

In *Flambards in Summer*, the time is 1916, and Christina is a widow. She finds that Mark has an illegitimate son and brings the boy to Flambards, the neglected estate that she now manages. Eventually she falls in love again. It is significant of the changes in Christina and of the changes in the times that it is Dick, the former groom, that she plans to wed. In an addition to the trilogy, *Flambards Divided*, Christina plans to wed a third time. The characterization is strong and the heroine's development into maturity is both convincing and an accurate microcosmic picture of the new social structure that came out of World War I.

Elizabeth Foreman Lewis
Young Fu of the Upper Yangtze
To Beat a Tiger

Elizabeth Lewis, who lived in China for many years, wrote *Young Fu of the Upper Yangtze*, winner of the 1933 Newbery Medal. It is the exciting story of a thirteen-year-old Chinese country boy who is brought to the rich city of Chungking in the 1930s and apprenticed to a skillful coppersmith. In time, Young Fu becomes a fine craftsman, but neither easily nor quickly. Meanwhile, he explores the great city and finds everywhere the conflict of old and new ideas. Fu is no idealized hero but exhibits the usual contradictory human traits; he is brave and honest, yet he wastes his master's time and gets into trouble; he works hard, grows skillful, and then gets unbearably cocky; he is frugal one moment and wasteful the next.

Lewis wrote a later book, *To Beat a Tiger*, for preteens and young adults. It is the grim story of sixteen Chinese boys living by their wits on the outskirts of Shanghai. They all know the proverb, "To beat a tiger, one needs a brother's help." Their tiger is starvation and death, and so they lie, steal, and cheat, but share their wretched scraps of food, their hut, filthy rags, and scanty heat. It is a complex story, but once the large gallery of characters is identified, the plot gains momentum and suspense is high.

While Lewis creates many unusual happenings and adventures for her characters, it is in the presentation of the people that she excels. Even minor characters have individuality and presence, and linger in the reader's memory.

James Lincoln Collier and Christopher Collier
My Brother Sam Is Dead
Jump Ship to Freedom

Although James Lincoln Collier, a freelance writer, had produced many books for children, and his brother Christopher, a history professor, had published in a scholarly vein, it was not until they collaborated on *My Brother Sam Is Dead* that the Colliers entered, with notable success, the field of historical fiction.

Viewpoint

I have been highly critical of most—I really think I can safely say nearly all—historical fiction. On what basis do I level such criticism? In the first place I approach the genre from the position of both a historian and a teacher. My criteria reflect that position. I am judging works of historical fiction by their social and pedagogical usefulness—that is, their ability to teach history. Given those assumptions, my criteria are five. The books must:

1. focus on an important historical theme, an understanding of which helps us to deal with the present
2. center on an episode in which the theme inheres in fact
3. attend to the historiographic elements
4. include characters that interact meaningfully (in terms of the theme) and interestingly with historical characters
5. present detail accurately

From "Historical Novels in the Classroom: What They Can Do and How They Should Do It," by Christopher Collier, *The Bulletin*, Spring 1982. Reprinted by permission of the CLA Bulletin.

Based in large part on actual events, the book is a first-person account of a Connecticut family during the Revolutionary War. Tim, the adolescent narrator, is disturbed because his father is trading with the British and worried about his brother Sam, serving in the Patriot cause. With Sam's death, Tim is even more convinced of the folly of war. Strong characterization gives substance to this story, and the vivid depiction of bitter suffering is an effective indictment of war, as it is in *The Bloody Country* and *The Winter Hero*, a novel based on Shays' Rebellion.

The authors explore the plight of African-American people during the Revolutionary War in *Jump Ship to Freedom*, a solidly constructed adventure story about a youngster whose father had been a free man although he himself was still a slave. The book focuses on the enactment by the Constitutional Convention of the fugitive slave law; appended notes draw a careful distinction between fact and fiction. The story was followed by two sequels, *War Comes to Willy Freeman* and *Who Is Carrie?*

Jill (Gillian) Paton Walsh
Fireweed
Children of the Fox
The Emperor's Winding Sheet

Like Rosemary Sutcliff, the English writer Jill Paton Walsh has so deep a knowledge of the details of historical periods that facts about clothing, or food, or mores of the period are never obtrusive but blend smoothly into the background. This quality is not as evident in *Fireweed* as it is in some of her later books, not because the details of wartime London are not there or not vivid, but because the focus of this book is on a personal relationship. Two adolescents, both of whom are supposed to have been evacuated from London during the blitz, meet and decide to stay together in an abandoned building; only when it is bombed does Bill realize he has come to love Julie. When he finds her, he knows they will never be together, for her wealthy family has traced her whereabouts. Sharply etched, the ending is sad, moving, and wholly believable.

In books like *Children of the Fox*, Walsh combines her knowledge of the past and her

From *Children of the Fox* by Jill Paton Walsh, illustrated by Robin Eaton.

strong sense of narrative: Three young people who lived during the time of the Persian Wars each tell a story of an adventure, and the adventures are linked by the fact that each of them has met the Athenian hero, Themistokles. The stories are given vitality by the enthusiasm of their narrators; each is stirring, and all are based on careful research.

Among other books by Walsh, *The Emperor's Winding Sheet* is distinctive for the sweep of events in the siege and fall of Constantinople as seen from the viewpoint of a young British seaman who is first the captive of the Emperor Constantine and later his willing servant and devoted admirer. *The Huffler* (published in England under the title *The Butty Boy*) tells the story of a girl who runs away from her very proper Victorian family and poses as a servant in order to fit into the life of a canal-boat family. Here the lore of canal life is an added appeal, but it is always as a storyteller that Jill Paton Walsh gives most delight; and that quality is evident in her story of the plague years in England, *A Parcel of Patterns*.

Other Books for Older Children

A story of ancient times is Madeleine Polland's *To Tell My People*. A British girl, taken by Roman invaders, is sent to Rome as a slave. When she escapes and returns to her people, she hopes to share the knowledge she has gained, but they are ignorant and only sneer. She had hoped to bring them peace; they will do nothing but fight. Polland has set several books in this era, telling believable stories with strong characters.

Hans Baumann's stories are always exciting, even though sometimes slowed down by details. In *I Marched with Hannibal*, an old man tells two children about his boyhood experiences, a narrative device that gives the book a sense of immediacy and scope for vivid personal accounts of the marches and battle scenes. Baumann's historical personages are never stock characters but are vividly depicted to add depth to stories with authentic background.

The Namesake and *The Marsh King* by Cyril Walter Hodges are sequential tales of King Alfred's struggle against the Danish invaders, stories full of action and fascinating historical details. Another English writer, Geoffrey Trease, moves his hero in *The Red Towers of Granada* from England in the time of Edward I to Spain. Cast out of his village as a leper, young Robin learns from a Jewish doctor that he has only a minor skin disease. When the doctor leaves England for Spain, Robin goes with him.

Fifteenth-century Poland is the setting for Eric Kelly's 1929 Newbery Medal book, *The Trumpeter of Krakow*, a story based on the oath of the Krakow trumpeters to sound their defiant song every hour. The setting is colorful, the story intriguing both because it has dramatic adventure and because it gives an absorbing picture of the problems of the Polish people.

I, Juan de Pareja, for which Elizabeth Borton de Treviño was awarded the Newbery Medal, is the story of the black slave of the painter Velazquez. Written in autobiographical form, it comes close to biography, but is told as a story. An aspiring artist himself, de Pareja painted secretly until his master realized his talent as an artist—and freed him. In de Pareja's descriptions of court affairs and of Velazquez as a person, there is appeal for the reader interested in history and in art, and the story itself moves with pace and dignity.

Another story with a black protagonist is Ann Petry's *Tituba of Salem Village*, a dramatic fictionalization of the inexorable hysteria of the Salem witch-hunt and trials. In Alice Marriott's *Indian Annie: Kiowa Captive*, Annie comes to love her foster parents and marries into the tribe. The story is set in the antebellum years, and Annie is struck by the fact that a freed slave cannot identify, as she does, with another minority group. Weyman Jones writes evocatively of the half-white Cherokee, Sequoyah, in *The Talking Leaf* and *The Edge of Two Worlds*. Evelyn Lampman's sympathetic identification with native Americans is evident in *Squaw Man's Son*, the story of a Modoc-white boy, and in *White Captives*. In *The Tilted Sombrero*, she gives a vivid picture of the stratification of Mexican society in 1810 when their War of Independence began. A Blackfoot girl is the heroine in Jan Hudson's story, *Sweetgrass*, set in Canada in the nineteenth century.

E. M. Almedingen has written many charming historical novels set in Russia, most of them based on family records. *Katia* is an adaptation of a great-aunt's memoirs, published in Russia in 1874. *Young Mark* is the true and romantic story of Almedingen's great-great-grandfather, who became a court favorite because of his beautiful singing, grew wealthy, and established the family fortune. The writing is intricate and mature, but the style and the fidelity of the historical background are very appealing.

No group of stories within the genre of historical fiction demonstrates so clearly that literature is an international heritage as do the books about World War II. From Denmark comes Anne Holm's *North to Freedom*, the story of a boy of twelve who escapes from a prison camp in eastern Europe and makes his way to his mother in Copenhagen. Irina Korschunow's *A Night in Distant Motion* and Hans Peter Richter's *Friedrich*, both translated from the

German, are alike in being told by children who are at first loyal to Hitler but who change their allegiance. Both stories are all the more effective for their portrayal of ordinary people. This is also true of the Dutch story, *War Without Friends* by Evert Hartman; and of a book from France, Colette Vivier's *House of the Four Winds*, for the people who live in the house (an apartment building) are a cross-section of middle-class Parisians, and their valor (or cowardice) during the German occupation has a homeliness that makes the historical period come alive.

Printing a Danish underground paper brings death to Peter's father in *A Kind of Secret Weapon* by Elliott Arnold. Nathaniel Benchley's *Bright Candles* shows other facets of the Danish resistance to the Nazi occupation, from sabotage to nationwide support of the Jews. Suspense and vigorous action are hallmarks of books by this versatile writer. Other well-written stories of the relocation-by-rescue of Danish Jews are Lois Lowry's *Number the Stars*, which won the Newbery Award; and *Lisa's War* by Carol Matas. Els Pelgrom's *The Winter When Time Was Frozen* is a moving story of a compassionate farm family in the Netherlands.

The ravages of war are a recurrent theme in James Forman's books. *Horses of Anger* concerns a Nazi soldier who begins to doubt the propaganda he has heard and to understand his own prejudice. In Forman's *The Traitors*, a Bavarian pastor suffers because his congregation and his only child espouse the Nazi cause, and he joins the underground rebellion. Forman's books are mature and sophisticated, often profound and provocative, demanding the most of a young reader.

Few books have been written with a South American setting. Of these, *The Honorable Prison* by Lyll Becerra de Jenkins is a powerful story, winner of the Scott O'Dell Award, about the abuses of a dictatorial regime.

We have seen a number of books for children on the Jewish experience before, during, and after World War II—many of them written out of personal knowledge and with objectivity. With the pervasiveness of the mass media, we are less inclined today to shelter children from the misdeeds of adults, and more willing to present life whole, the bad—although not

dwelt upon at length—with the good. We are also awaking to the fact that children do not come equipped with a value system, that good citizenship and character must be taught.

Historical novels are often used to supplement the curriculum, especially in the area of the social studies. Adults who encourage such use should be aware that, in addition to any social implications, much historical fiction has as strong a plot, as dramatic a development, and as percipient an establishment of character as any adventure story. The establishment of the Scott O'Dell Award for Historical Fiction has spurred interest in the genre. If it is true that understanding events of the past makes people better able to cope with problems of the present, the best historical fiction is making a singular contribution toward the development of today's children, who will be tomorrow's adults.

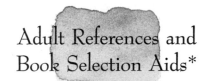

Adult References and Book Selection Aids*

BATOR, ROBERT, comp. *Signposts to Criticism of Children's Literature.* Chapter 9, "Historical Fiction."

EGOFF, SHEILA. *The Republic of Childhood: A Critical Guide to Canadian Children's Literature in English.* Part 3, "Historical Fiction."

FIELD, ELINOR WHITNEY, comp. *Horn Book Reflections.* Part III, "Recreating Other Times."

HOTCHKISS, JEANETTE, comp. *American Historical Fiction and Biography for Children and Young People.*

————, comp. *European Historical Fiction and Biography for Children and Young People.*

HOWARD, ELIZABETH. *America as Story: Historical Fiction for Secondary Schools.* (See Appendix A.)

HUNTER, MOLLIE. *Talent Is Not Enough.* "Shoulder in the Sky."

SUTCLIFF, ROSEMARY. *Blue Remembered Hills.*

*Complete bibliographic data are provided in Appendices A and B.

Some historical fiction titles may be found in the bibliography for Chapter 10. In the following bibliography these symbols have been used to identify books about a religious or a particular ethnic group:

§ African American
★ Hispanic
☆ Native American
∘ Asian American
• Religious minority

Historical Fiction: The Ancient World

BAUMANN, HANS. *I Marched with Hannibal,* tr. by Katherine Potts, ill. by Ulrik Schramm. Walck, 1962.   12–15

BEHN, HARRY. *The Faraway Lurs.* World, 1963. Tribes of differing cultures meet in early Denmark, with tragic consequences for two young people.   12–15

BULLA, CLYDE ROBERT. *Viking Adventure,* ill. by Douglas Gorsline. T. Crowell, 1963. A Viking's son grows into a man on the long voyage to Wineland and home again.   8–10

CARTER, DOROTHY S. *Queen Hatshepsut,* ill. by Michele Chessare. Lippincott, 1987. Queen Hatshepsut is thirteen in a realistic tale of ancient Egyptian life, complete with historical notes and a bibliography.   11–14

CLARKE, PAULINE. *Torolv the Fatherless,* ill. by Cecil Leslie. Faber, 1978. A Viking waif is accidentally stranded when his ship sails without him and is adopted by an elderly earl who later dies fighting Vikings at the Battle of Maldon.   11–14

COOLIDGE, OLIVIA. *Egyptian Adventures,* ill. by Joseph Low. Houghton, 1954.   12–16

————. *King of Men,* ill. by Ellen Raskin. Houghton, 1966.   12 up

————. *The Maid of Artemis,* ill. by Bea Holmes. Houghton, 1969.   10–14

————. *Men of Athens.* Houghton, 1962.   12–15

• ————. *People in Palestine.* Houghton, 1965.
                                                            12 up

————. *Roman People,* ill. by Lino Lipinsky. Houghton, 1959.   12–15

FYSON, J. G. *The Three Brothers of Ur,* ill. by Victor G. Ambrus. Coward, 1966. Lively tale of a trader's household in the ancient city.   10–14

GARD, JOYCE. *The Mermaid's Daughter.* Holt, 1969. An intricate novel, set in Britain at the time of the Roman occupation, based on the mermaid-goddess cult.   11–14

HAUGAARD, ERIK CHRISTIAN. *The Rider and His Horse,* ill. by Leo and Diane Dillon. Houghton, 1968.
                                                           12–17

HODGES, MARGARET. *The Avenger.* Scribner's, 1982. Set in Greece, a lively story begins in 492 B.C.
                                                           11–14

LILLINGTON, KENNETH. *Young Man of Morning.* Faber, 1980. A young Greek sculptor witnesses the battles of Thermopylae and Salamis.   12–14

LINEVSKI, A. *An Old Tale Carved Out of Stone,* tr. by Maria Polushkin. Crown, 1973. The trials of a young, insecure shaman as he tries to lead his tribe wisely in early Siberia.   11–15

MCGRAW, ELOISE JARVIS. *The Golden Goblet.* Coward, 1961.   11–15

————. *Mara, Daughter of the Nile.* Coward, 1953.
                                                           11–15

MADDOCK, REGINALD. *The Great Bow,* ill. by Victor Ambrus. Rand, 1968. A tightly constructed and convincing story about prehistoric people. Atta is a thoughtful fourteen-year-old who fails his test of manhood because he does not want to kill.
                                                           10–12

POLLAND, MADELEINE. *To Tell My People,* ill. by Richard M. Powers. Holt, 1968.   11–13

☆ SCHWEITZER, BYRD BAYLOR. *One Small Blue Bead,* ill. by Symeon Shimin. Macmillan, 1965. Beautifully illustrated, a rhyming text tells a story of primitive people in Arizona.   7–9

SPEARE, ELIZABETH G. *The Bronze Bow.* Houghton, 1961. Newbery Medal.   12 up

STOLZ, MARY. *Zekmet the Stone Carver: A Tale of Ancient Egypt,* ill. by Deborah Nourse Lattimore. Harcourt, 1988.   7–9

SUTCLIFF, ROSEMARY. *Blood Feud.* Dutton, 1977.
                                                           12–14

————. *Song for a Dark Queen.* T. Crowell, 1979.
                                                           12–15

————. *Warrior Scarlet,* ill. by Charles Keeping. Walck, 1958.   12–16

TREECE, HENRY. *The Centurion,* ill. by Mary Russon. Meredith, 1967.   11–15

WALSH, JILL PATON. *Children of the Fox,* ill. by Robin Eaton. Farrar. 1978.   10–13

European Historical Fiction

AIKEN, JOAN. *The Teeth of the Gale.* Harper, 1988. The last of a trilogy set in a turbulent period of Spanish history, this is romantic and dramatic.
                                                           12–15

ALMEDINGEN, E. M. *Katia*, ill. by Victor G. Ambrus. Farrar, 1967.   11–14

————. *Young Mark: The Story of a Venture*, ill. by Victor G. Ambrus. Farrar, 1968.   12–15

ARNOLD, ELLIOTT. *A Kind of Secret Weapon*. Scribner's, 1969.   10–13

BALDERSON, MARGARET. *When Jays Fly to Barbmo*, ill. by Victor G. Ambrus. World, 1969. Residents of a Norwegian island cope with Nazi invaders.

11–14

BAWDEN, NINA. *Carrie's War*. Lippincott, 1973.

10–14

————. *The Peppermint Pig*. Lippincott, 1975.

10–14

BEATTY, JOHN and PATRICIA. *At the Seven Stars,* with Hogarth prints and line drawings of Douglas Gorsline. Macmillan, 1963.   12–14

————. *Master Rosalind*. Morrow, 1974. A fascinating and lively picture of Elizabethan theatrical life and the court and criminal circles of the time.

12–14

• BENCHLEY, NATHANIEL. *Bright Candles*. Harper, 1974.   12–15

BENTLEY, PHYLLIS. *The Adventures of Tom Leigh*, ill. by Burt Silverman. Doubleday, 1964.   10–14

————. *Forgery*. Doubleday, 1968.   10–14

BØDKER, CECIL. *Silas and Ben-Godik*. Delacorte, 1978. A sequel to *Silas and the Black Mare*.

10–12

————. *Silas and the Black Mare*. Delacorte, 1978. A series of adventures centering around young Silas and the mare he has bargained for culminates in a long and stirring episode involving all the characters from previous incidents.   10–12

————. *Silas and the Runaway Coach*. Delacorte, 1978. A third book in the "Silas" series finds the doughty adolescent again on his own and this time temporarily settled in the home of a wealthy family grateful for his rescue of their runaway coach.   10–12

BULLA, CLYDE. *The Sword in the Tree,* ill. by Paul Galdone. T. Crowell, 1956.   8–10

• BURSTEIN, CHAYA. *Rifka Grows Up*, ill. by author. Hebrew Pub. Co., 1976. A sequel to *Rifka Bangs the Teakettle* set in a small Russian village finds Rifka, now twelve, determined to pass the exam that will permit her to go to high school despite being warned that there is a quota for Jews.

10–12

• BURTON, HESTER. *Beyond the Weir Bridge*, ill. by Victor G. Ambrus. T. Crowell, 1970.   12–15

————. *Castors Away!* ill. by Victor G. Ambrus. World, 1962. A story centering on the great naval battle at Trafalgar.   12–15

————. *Kate Ryder,* ill. by Victor G. Ambrus. T. Crowell, 1975.   12–15

————. *Time of Trial,* ill. by Victor G. Ambrus. World, 1964. Carnegie Medal.   12–15

CARRICK, DONALD. *Harald and the Great Stag*, ill. by author. Clarion, 1988.   5–8

CHUTE, MARCHETTE. *The Innocent Wayfaring*, ill. by author. Dutton, 1955.   11–14

————. *The Wonderful Winter*, ill. by Grace Golden. Dutton, 1954.   11–14

CLARKE, JOAN. *Early Rising*. Lippincott, 1976. A lovely period piece, this is set in an English vicarage in the 1880s, where Erica and her brothers and sisters are being brought up by a widowed father and a loving staff.   10–13

COOPER, GORDON. *An Hour in the Morning,* ill. by Philip Gough. Dutton, 1974.   10–11

COOPER, SUSAN. *Dawn of Fear,* ill. by Margery Gill. Harcourt, 1970.   10–11

DARKE, MARJORIE. *A Question of Courage*. T. Crowell, 1975. A fine story about women's suffrage is set in Birmingham and London before the first world war.   12–14

DE ANGELI, MARGUERITE. *The Door in the Wall,* ill. by author. Doubleday, 1949. Newbery Medal.

8–11

§ DE TREVINO, ELIZABETH B. *I, Juan de Pareja*. Farrar, 1965. Newbery Medal.   12–15

DEGENS, T. *Transport 7-41-R*. Viking, 1974. A grim tale of the aftermath of war as evacuees return to Cologne in 1946.   11–14

FENTON, EDWARD. *The Refugee Summer*. Delacorte, 1982. Five children, including two Americans, living in a suburb of Athens in 1922 form a patriotic secret society. Their game turns to reality when refugees from Greece's war with Turkish Anatolia begin to enter their community.   11–14

FOREMAN, JAMES. *Horses of Anger*. Farrar, 1967.

13 up

• ————. *The Traitors*. Farrar, 1968.   13 up

FRANK, RUDOLF. *No Hero for the Kaiser,* tr. by Patricia Crampton, ill. by Klaus Steffens. Lothrop, 1986. Jan, a young Polish boy, loses his whole family during World War I and is adopted by an invading German artillery unit. This controversial book was burned in 1933 by Nazi officials. Batchelder Award.   12–15

GARFIELD, LEON. *The Night of the Comet: A Comedy of Courtship Featuring Bostock and Harris*. Delacorte, 1979. The path of true love, or even of reasonable facsimiles thereof, runs far from smoothly in the romping, ridiculous tale of three tangled love affairs.   11–13

GARNER, ALAN. *The Stone Book; Granny Reardun*, ill. by Michael Foreman. World, 1978. *The Aimer Gate; Tom Fobble's Day,* ill. by Michael Foreman. World, 1979.   8–10

GARRIGUE, SHEILA. *All the Children Were Sent Away.* Bradbury, 1976. Along with hundreds of other 1940 English evacuees, eight-year-old Sara boarded the H.M.S. Duke of Perth under the stern, dictatorial care of Lady Drume.

GRUND, JOSEF CARL. *Never to Be Free,* tr. by Lucile Harrington. Little, 1970.   12–15

HARNETT, CYNTHIA. *Caxton's Challenge,* ill. by author. World, 1960. Carnegie Medal.   12–16

————. *Nicholas and the Wool-Pack,* ill. by author. Putnam, 1953.   11–15

————. *The Writing on the Hearth.* Viking, 1973.   12–15

HARTLING, PETER. *Crutches.* Lothrop, 1988. Batchelder Award.   10–13

HARTMAN, EVERT. *War Without Friends,* tr. from the Dutch by Patricia Compton. Crown, 1982.
                                11–14

• HAUGAARD, ERIK CHRISTIAN. *Chase Me, Catch Nobody!* Houghton, 1980. Set in 1937, the story of a Danish boy who rescues a Jewish girl while on a visit to Germany.   11–14

————. *Hakon of Rogen's Saga,* ill. by Leo and Diane Dillon. Houghton, 1963.   11–14

————. *The Little Fishes,* ill. by Milton Johnson. Houghton, 1967.   12 up

————. *A Messenger for Parliament.* Houghton, 1976.   12–14

————. *A Slave's Tale,* ill. by Leo and Diane Dillon. Houghton, 1965.   11–14

————. *The Untold Tale,* ill. by Leo and Diane Dillon. Houghton, 1971.   12–15

• HEUCK, SIGRID. *The Hideout,* tr. by Rika Lesser. Dutton, 1988. Two Jewish children, Rebecca and Sami, create a fantasy world that allows them to escape the fact they have been separated from their parents in World War II Germany.   11–13

HODGES, C. WALTER. *The Marsh King,* ill. by author. Coward, 1967.   12–15

————. *The Namesake,* ill. by author. Coward, 1964.   12–14

HOLM, ANNE. *North to Freedom,* tr. from the Danish by L. W. Kingsland. Harcourt, 1965.   11–13

HUNTER, MOLLIE. *The Ghosts of Glencoe.* Funk, 1969.
                                11–14

————. *Hold on to Love.* Harper, 1984.   12–15

————. *The Lothian Run.* Funk, 1970.   12–15

————. *The Sound of Chariots.* Harper, 1972.
                                12–15

————. *The Spanish Letters.* Funk, 1967.   12–15

————. *The Stronghold.* Harper, 1974. Carnegie Medal.   10–14

————. *The Thirteenth Member.* Harper, 1971.
                                12–15

————. *You Never Knew Her As I Did.* Harper, 1981.   12–15

KELLY, ERIC. *The Trumpeter of Krakow,* rev. ed. Macmillan, 1966. Newbery Medal.   12–14

• KERR, JUDITH. *The Other Way Round.* Coward, 1975.
                                12–15

• ————. *When Hitler Stole Pink Rabbit.* Coward, 1972.   10–12

KING, CLIVE. *Ninny's Boat,* map by Ian Newsham. Macmillan, 1981. Ninny, a little-valued slave in fifth-century Britain, learns more about his origins and grows in self-confidence.   10–13

• KOEHN, ILSE. *Mischling, Second Degree: My Childhood in Nazi Germany.* Greenwillow, 1977. The author tells how her family, liberals and intellectuals, coped with a government and a philosophy they detested.   12 up

KORSCHUNOW, IRINA. *A Night in Distant Motion,* tr. by Leigh Hafrey. Godine, 1983.   11–14

KULLMAN, HARRY. *The Battle Horse,* tr. from the Swedish by George Blecher and Lone Thygesen-Blecher. Bradbury, 1981. A provocative exploration of social strata in Stockholm fifty years ago in the form of a cruel caste system inflicted by private school boys on their public school peers. Batchelder Award.   11–13

• LEVITIN, SONIA. *Journey to America,* ill. by Charles Robinson. Atheneum, 1970. The first-person story of a young Jewish girl and her family from Germany in the late 1930s. Dramatic and well written.   10–12

LIVELY, PENELOPE. *Fanny's Sister,* ill. by Anita Lobel. Dutton, 1980. In a tender, amusing story, a Victorian child rebels.   9–11

LOVETT, MARGARET. *Jonathan.* Dutton, 1972. The grinding poverty of 1815 England as seen in the struggles of a boy caring for orphaned children.
                                11–14

• LOWRY, LOIS. *Number the Stars.* Houghton, 1989. Newbery Medal.   10–12

MCCAUGHREAN, GERALDINE. *A Little Lower Than the Angels.* Oxford, 1987. Set in medieval England, the story concerns an apprentice, Gabriel, who is so cruelly treated that he runs away to join a band of traveling players and becomes the focus of a belief in miracle healing.   11–13

MAGORIAN, MICHELLE. *Good Night, Mr. Tom.* Harper, 1982. A London child evacuated to a village for safety during World War II and his crusty caretaker learn to love and need each other. International Reading Association Award.   11–14

• MATAS, CAROL. *Lisa's War.* Scribner's, 1989.   10–13

MATTINGLEY, CHRISTOBEL. *The Angel with a Mouth Organ,* ill. by Astra Lacis. Holiday House, 1986. Told from a child's perspective, the story describes a World War II refugee family through several moves and the agonizing wait for father's return.   8–10

MINARD, ROSEMARY. *Long Meg,* ill. by Philip Smith. Pantheon, 1982. A brisk tale about a legendary character who posed as a man in order to join the army of Henry VIII in its invasion of France.
9–11

MONJO, FERDINAND N. *The Sea Beggar's Son,* ill. by C. Walter Hodges. Coward, 1975. A stirring tale of a Dutch hero of the seventeenth century. 9–12

NÖSTLINGER, CHRISTINE. *Fly Away Home,* tr. by Anthea Bell. Watts, 1975. A gripping survival story set in World War II Vienna. 11–14

OLIVER, JANE [pseud.]. *Faraway Princess,* ill. by Jane Paton. St. Martin's, 1962. Princess Margaret, in flight from England after the Norman Conquest, finds sanctuary in Scotland and later a throne. Excellent historical fiction. 10–13

• ORGEL, DORIS. *The Devil in Vienna.* Dial, 1978. The story of a Jewish girl and her best friend (the daughter of a Nazi officer) who suffer through the tension and agony of the Nazi occupation of Austria. 11–13

• ORLEV, URI. *The Island on Bird Street,* tr. from the Hebrew by Hillel Halkin. Houghton, 1984. A gripping Holocaust survival story describes a boy's lonely wait in a ghetto hideout for his father's return. Batchelder Award. 10–12

• PELGROM, ELS. *The Winter When Time Was Frozen,* tr. from the Dutch by Maryka and Rafael Rudnik. Morrow, 1980. Batchelder Award. 9–11

PEYTON, K. M. *The Edge of the Cloud,* ill. by Victor G. Ambrus. World, 1970. Carnegie Medal.

————. *Flambards,* ill. by Victor G. Ambrus. World, 1968.

————. *Flambards Divided.* Philomel, 1982.
12–15

————. *Flambards in Summer,* ill. by Victor G. Ambrus. World, 1970. 12–15

POLLAND, MADELEINE. *Children of the Red King,* ill. by Annette Macarthur-Onslow. Holt, 1961. Grania and Fergus, children of Ireland's embattled king, are sent as captives to their father's enemy in a vivid story of the Norman Conquest. 11–13

PYLE, HOWARD. *Men of Iron,* ill. by author. Harper, 1891.

————. *Otto of the Silver Hand,* ill. by author. Scribner's, 1888. 10–14

• REISS, JOHANNA. *The Journey Back.* T. Crowell, 1976.
10–13

————. *The Upstairs Room.* T. Crowell, 1972.
9–12

RETTICH, MARGRET. *Suleiman the Elephant,* tr. by Elizabeth D. Crawford, ill. by author. Lothrop, 1986. Prince Maximilian from Austria woos Princess Maria of Spain with the gift of an elephant, in this sophisticated picture book. 7–9

• RICHTER, HANS PETER. *Friedrich,* tr. from the German by Edite Kroll. Holt, 1970. Batchelder Award.
11–14

ROSEN, BILLI. *Andi's War.* Dutton, 1989. In a post-World War II story, eleven-year-old Andi and her younger brother Paul live with their grandmother while their parents, Communist guerrillas in the Greek Civil War, battle the Monarchists for control of the country. 11–14

• SACHS, MARILYN. *A Pocket Full of Seeds,* ill. by Ben Stahl. Doubleday, 1973. 9–12

SERRAILLIER, IAN. *The Silver Sword,* ill. by C. Walter Hodges. Criterion, 1959. Unforgettable journey of four children who make their way from Warsaw to Switzerland in World War II. 11–14

• SEVELA, EPHRAIM. *We Were Not Like Other People,* tr. by Antonina Bouis. Harper, 1989. 11–15

SKURZYNSKI, GLORIA. *The Minstrel in the Tower,* ill. by Julek Heller. Random House, 1988. Set in 1192, this story for young readers describes Alice and Roger's lives, as they wait for their father to return from the Crusades. 8–11

————. *What Happened in Hamelin.* Four Winds, 1979. A story told by a poor orphan boy which offers a plausible explanation of what happened to children of Hamelin. 10–12

• SLOBODKIN, FLORENCE. *Sarah Somebody,* ill. by Louis Slobodkin. Vanguard, 1970. The warm and sympathetic story of a nine-year-old girl in a Polish village in 1893 who gets a chance to learn to read and write—and to become somebody. 8–10

STREATFEILD, NOEL. *When the Sirens Wailed,* ill. by Judith Gwyn Brown. Random, 1976. A Cockney family is separated during the London blitz.
9–11

• SUHL, YURI. *The Merrymaker,* ill. by Thomas di Grazia. Four Winds, 1975. Turn-of-the-century Eastern Europe is the setting for a story of a poor Jewish family. 9–12

• ————. *On the Other Side of the Gate.* Watts, 1975. A young Jewish couple in World War II Poland smuggle their baby to safety in a suspenseful tale.
12–16

SUTCLIFF, ROSEMARY. *Bonnie Dundee.* Dutton, 1984.
12–15

————. *Dawn Wind,* ill. by Charles Keeping. Walck, 1962; Walck, 1973. 12–15

————. *Flame-Colored Tafetta.* Farrar, 1986.
11–13

————. *The Lantern Bearers,* ill. by Charles Keeping. Walck, 1959. Carnegie Medal. 12–15

• TREASE, GEOFFREY. *The Red Towers of Granada,* ill. by Charles Keeping. Vanguard, 1967. 11–14

TREECE, HENRY. *The Dream Time,* ill. by Charles Keeping. Meredith, 1968. 11–14

_____. *The Road to Miklagard,* ill. by Christine Price. Criterion, 1957.   11–14

_____. *Viking's Dawn,* ill. by Christine Price. Criterion, 1956. First in an absorbing trilogy of eighth-century Viking life, in which youthful Harald Sigurdson accompanies his father on his first dangerous sea journey. In *The Road to Miklagard* (1957) his voyages are interrupted when he becomes a Moorish slave. In *Viking's Sunset* (1961) Harald, now a chieftain, sails his longboat to the shores of Lake Superior, and death intervenes on this last voyage. Harald's life saga conveys the vast scope of early Viking travels.   11–14

_____. *Viking's Sunset,* ill. by Christine Price. Criterion, 1961.   11–14

VAN STOCKUM, HILDA. *The Winged Watchman,* ill. by author. Farrar, 1962. The Verhagen family, in constant danger from an informer, conceals a British pilot during the occupation.   10–12

VINING, ELIZABETH GRAY. *Adam of the Road,* ill. by Robert Lawson. Viking 1942. Newbery Medal.   12–14

_____. *I Will Adventure,* ill. by Corydon Bell. Viking, 1962.   11–14

• VIVIER, COLLETTE. *The House of the Four Winds,* tr. and ed. by Miriam Morton. Doubleday, 1969.   11–14

VOIGT, CYNTHIA. *Jackaroo.* Atheneum, 1985. Gwyn assumes the role of Jackaroo, a medieval vigilante, when she discovers the legendary costume in her father's inn.   11–14

VON CANON, CLAUDIA. *The Inheritance.* Houghton, 1983. Set in Europe against the backdrop of the Spanish Inquisition.   12–15

WALSH, JILL PATON. *The Huffler,* ill. by Juliette Palmer. Farrar, 1975.   10–12

_____. *A Parcel of Patterns.* Farrar, 1983.   12–15

WELCH, RONALD. *Tank Commander.* Nelson, 1974. A compelling story of an officer's experiences in World War I.   12–15

WESTALL, ROBERT. *The Machine Gunners.* Greenwillow, 1976. Set in England during World War II, this is the story of a group of youngsters who find a machine gun and hide it in an underground shelter which they equip and man. Carnegie Medal. In *Fathom Five* (1980), the friends expose a spy who is sending radio signals to a German submarine.   10–14

WILLARD, BARBARA. *A Cold Wind Blowing.* Dutton, 1973.   11–15

_____. *Harrow and Harvest.* Dutton, 1975.   11–15

_____. *The Iron Lilly.* Dutton, 1974.   11–15

_____. *The Lark and the Laurel.* Dutton, 1970.   11–15

_____. *The Sound of the Dragon's Feet.* Dutton, 1979.   9–11

_____. *The Sprig of Broom.* Dutton, 1972.   10–14

ZEI, ALKI. *Petros' War,* tr. by Edward Fenton. Dutton, 1972. Batchelder Award.   10–14

_____. *Wildcat Under Glass,* tr. from the Greek by Edward Fenton. Holt, 1968. Batchelder Award.   10–12

United States Historical Fiction

☆ ARMER, LAURA ADAMS. *Waterless Mountain,* ill. by Sidney Armer and Laura Adams Armer. McKay, 1931. An early Newbery Award book, the story of Dawn Boy, a Navajo boy destined to be a medicine man.   11–15

AVI. *Encounter at Easton.* Pantheon, 1980. Fast-paced, this is a smoothly written account of the escape of two indentured servants, set in 1768.   10–12

_____. *The Fighting Ground.* Lippincott, 1984. Scott O'Dell Award.   10–12

§ BACON, MARTHA. *Sophia Scrooby Preserved,* ill. by David Omar White. Atlantic, 1968. A romantic tale of a cultured black girl whose lively adventures are described in the mannered style of early English novelists.   11–13

☆ BAKER, BETTY. *And One Was a Wooden Indian.* Macmillan, 1970.   11–15

_____. *The Dunderhead War.* Harper, 1967.   11–14

_____. *The Great Desert Race.* Macmillan, 1980.   10–13

_____. *The Pig War,* ill. by Robert Lopshire. Harper, 1969.   7–8

§ ☆ _____. *Walk the World's Rim.* Harper, 1965.   11–14

BAUER, MARION DANE. *Rain of Fire.* Houghton/Clarion, 1983. Steve is puzzled by his older brother's brooding silences following his return from post-World War II Hiroshima. A trenchant probing of ideas about war and heroism.   10–12

BEATTY, JOHN and PATRICIA. *Who Comes to King's Mountain?* Morrow, 1975.   11–15

§ BEATTY, PATRICIA. *Be Ever Hopeful, Hannalee.* Morrow, 1988.   10–13

_____. *Charley Skedaddle.* Morrow, 1987. Scott O'Dell Award.   10–12

_____. *Hail Columbia,* ill. by Liz Dauber. Morrow, 1970.   10–12

_____. *That's One Ornery Orphan.* Morrow, 1980.   10–12

_____. *Turn Homeward, Hannalee.* Morrow, 1984.   10–13

BENCHLEY, NATHANIEL. *Sam the Minuteman*, ill. by Arnold Lobel. Harper, 1969.   7–9

BLOS, JOAN. *A Gathering of Days: A New England Girl's Journal*, 1830–32. Scribner's, 1979. Newbery Medal.   10–12

BOLTON, CAROLE. *Never Jam Today*. Atheneum, 1971. Young Maddy becomes involved, through her Aunt Augusta, in the cause of women's suffrage. Maddy passes up two love interests for the time being in favor of college and a career.   11–14

BRENNER, BARBARA. *On the Frontier with Mr. Audubon*. Coward, 1977. Thirteen-year-old Joseph Mason describes his travels as Audubon's pupil-assistant. The journal is a fictional device but the documented facts it records present a memorable picture of the artist and his work.   10–13

§ ☆ _____. *Wagon Wheels*, ill. by Don Bolognese. Harper, 1978. A fine frontier story for beginning independent readers describes the experiences of a black family which comes from Kentucky to Kansas in the 1870s.   6–8

☆ BRINK, CAROL RYRIE. *Caddie Woodlawn*, ill. by Kate Seredy. Macmillan, 1935. Newbery Medal.
          9–12

• BROOKS, JEROME. *Make Me a Hero*. Dutton, 1980. With three brothers in service, a boy tries, through getting a job and studying for his Bar Mitzvah, to gain status. Set in Chicago during World War II.   10–13

☆ BULLA, CLYDE. *John Billington, Friend of Squanto*, ill. by Peter Burchard. T. Crowell, 1956.   7–9

_____. *A Lion to Guard Us*, ill. by Michele Chessare. T. Crowell, 1981.   8–10

BULLA, CLYDE, and MICHAEL SYSON. *Conquista!* ill. by Ronald Himler. Crowell, 1978.   9–11

§ BURCHARD, PETER. *Bimby*, ill. by author. Coward, 1968.   9–11

_____. *Chinwe*. Putnam, 1979.   11–13

_____. *The Deserter*. Coward, 1974.   10–12

_____. *Jed*, ill. by author. Coward, 1960.   10–13

_____. *North by Night*, ill. by author. Coward, 1962. Swift-moving escape tale of two Yankee soldiers from a South Carolina Confederate prison.   12 up

BYARS, BETSY. *Trouble River*, ill. by Rocco Negri. Viking, 1969.   9–12

• CAUDILL, REBECCA. *The Far-Off Land*, ill. by Brinton Turkle. Viking, 1964.   12–14

_____. *Tree of Freedom*, ill. by Dorothy Bayley Morse. Viking, 1949.   12–14

☆ CLAPP, PATRICIA. *Constance: A Story of Early Plymouth*. Lothrop, 1968.   12–15

_____. *I'm Deborah Sampson: A Soldier in the War of the Revolution*. Lothrop, 1977.   10–13

_____. *The Tamarack Tree: A Novel of the Siege of Vicksburg*. Lothrop, 1986.   12–14

_____. *Witches' Children: A Story of Salem*. Lothrop, 1982.   11–14

CLARK, ANN NOLAN. *Year Walk*. Viking, 1975. A sixteen-year-old Basque sheepherder comes to Idaho in the early 1900s.   8–11

COATSWORTH, ELIZABETH. *Away Goes Sally*, ill. by Helen Sewell. Macmillan, 1934.

_____. *The Fair American*, ill. by Helen Sewell. Macmillan, 1940.

_____. *Five Bushel Farm*, ill. by Helen Sewell. Macmillan, 1939.   10–12

COBLENTZ, CATHERINE. *Martin and Abraham Lincoln*, ill. by Trientja. Childrens Pr., 1967.   7–10

☆ § COLLIER, JAMES and CHRISTOPHER. *The Bloody Country*. Four Winds, 1976.   11–14

§ _____. *Jump Ship to Freedom*. Delacorte, 1981.
          11–15

_____. *My Brother Sam Is Dead*. Four Winds, 1974.   11–14

§ _____. *War Comes to Willy Freeman*. Delacorte, 1983.   12–14

§ _____. *Who Is Carrie?* Delacorte, 1984.   11–14

_____. *The Winter Hero*. Four Winds, 1978.
          11–14

DALGLIESH, ALICE. *Adam and the Golden Cock*, ill. by Leonard Weisgard. Scribner's, 1959.   8–9

☆ _____. *The Courage of Sarah Noble*, ill. by Leonard Weisgard. Scribner's, 1954.

☆ _____. *The Thanksgiving Story*, ill. by Helen Sewell. Scribner's, 1954.   7–10

☆ EDMONDS, WALTER D. *The Matchlock Gun*, ill. by Paul Lantz. Dodd, 1941. Newbery Medal. Describes an Indian attack on colonial settlers. A book that gives only the settlers' perspective.   10–12

§ EDWARDS, PAT. *Little John and Plutie*. Houghton, 1988.   9–11

EDWARDS, SALLY. *George Midgett's War*. Scribner's, 1985.   11–13

§ FALL, THOMAS. *Canalboat to Freedom*, ill. by Joseph Cellini. Dial, 1966. Orphaned Benja is indentured as a canalboat worker. There he meets Lundius, a freed slave who becomes his friend and teacher. When Lundius is killed working for the Underground Railroad, Ben grieves. The emphasis in the story is on their developing friendship and on Ben's gradual realization of the horrors of slavery.   11–14

☆ FARBER, NORMA. *Mercy Short*. Dutton, 1982. Ransomed from her Indian captors, Mercy wrestles with demonic visions and ambivalence about the Indian way of life under the guidance of Cotton Mather. A riveting depiction of the late seventeenth-century Massachusetts Colony.   12–15

☆ FIELD, RACHEL. *Calico Bush*, ill. by Allen Lewis. Macmillan, 1931.   10–14

FINLAYSON, ANN. *Rebecca's War,* ill. by Sherry Streeter. Warne, 1972. A lively tale of the British occupation of Philadelphia.   11–14

FLEISCHMAN, PAUL. *Coming-and-Going Men,* ill. by Randy Gaul. Harper, 1985. In four linked stories, a procession of salesmen or showmen visits a small town in Vermont and in some way affects the residents there.   11–14

FLEISCHMAN, SID. *Mr. Mysterious & Company,* ill. by Eric von Schmidt. Little, 1962. Traveling under their intriguing stage name, the delightful Hackett family give magic shows in small pioneer towns as they work their way west from Texas to a San Diego ranch. A very different and appealing story of the early West.   10–12

FORBES, ESTHER. *Johnny Tremain,* ill. by Lynd Ward. Houghton, 1943. Newbery Medal.   12–14

☆ FORMAN, JAMES. *The Life and Death of Yellow Bird.* Farrar, 1973. The story of some of the Indians who did not come to government reservations after the battle at Little Bighorn in 1867.   12–16

§ FOX, PAULA. *The Slave Dancer,* ill. by Eros Keith. Bradbury, 1973. A white boy of 1840 is impressed into work on a slave ship. Newbery Medal.   11–14

§ FRITZ, JEAN. *Brady,* ill. by Lynd Ward. Coward, 1960.   10–13

————. *The Cabin Faced West,* ill. by Feodor Rojankovsky. Coward, 1958.   8–10

————. *Can't You Make Them Behave, King George?* ill. by Tomie dePaola. Coward, 1977.   8–10

————. *Early Thunder,* ill. by Lynd Ward. Coward, 1967. Set in Salem in 1775, the story of a boy whose loyalty moves from the King to the Patriot cause.   10–14

GAUCH, PATRICIA LEE. *This Time, Tempe Wick?* ill. by Margot Tomes. Coward, 1974. Tempe prevents colonial soldiers from requisitioning her horse.   8–10

☆ GOBLE, PAUL and DOROTHY. *Red Hawk's Account of Custer's Last Battle,* ill. by authors. Pantheon, 1970.   10–12

☆ GREGORY, KRISTIANA. *Jenny of the Tetons.* Gulliver/Harcourt, 1989. The story of Jenny, a Shoshone woman married to a British trapper, is narrated by fifteen-year-old Carrie, whose family was killed in an Indian raid.   10–12

☆ HAIG-BROWN, RODERICK. *The Whale People,* ill. by Mary Weiler. Morrow, 1963. A dignified picture of the great whale hunters and the training of a young Indian chief.   10–12

HALL, ANNA GERTRUDE. *Cyrus Holt and the Civil War,* ill. by Dorothy Bayley Morse. Viking, 1964.   9–11

§ HAMILTON, VIRGINIA. *The Bells of Christmas,* ill. by Lambert Davis. Harcourt, 1989. A black family welcomes its kin at an 1890 Christmas celebration.   9–11

§ HANSEN, JOYCE. *Out from This Place.* Walker, 1988. *Which Way Freedom?* Walker, 1986. In *Which Way Freedom?* slave Obi obtains his freedom, and in the sequel, he is followed by Easter, whose search for Obi takes her north.   11–14

HARVEY, BRETT. *Cassie's Journey: Going West in the 1860s;* ill. by Deborah Kogan Ray. Holiday House, 1988. Based on actual accounts, Cassie's diary narrates the story of a mid-nineteenth-century wagon-train journey.   7–9

————. *My Prairie Year: Based on the Diary of Elenore Plaisted,* ill. by Deborah Kogan Ray. Holiday House, 1986.   8–10

HAUGAARD, ERIK CHRISTIAN. *Orphans of the Wind,* ill. by Milton Johnson. Houghton, 1966. A sea story set during the Civil War.   10–12

☆ HAYS, WILMA PITCHFORD. *May Day for Samoset,* ill. by Marilyn Miller. Coward, 1968.   7–9

☆ ————. *Pilgrim Thanksgiving,* ill. by Leonard Weisgard. Coward, 1955. The story of the first Thanksgiving.   7–9

☆ ————. *Yellow Fur and Little Hawk,* ill. by Anthony Rao. Coward, 1980.   7–9

HILTS, LEN. *Timmy O'Dowd and the Big Ditch: A Story of the Glory Days on the Old Erie Canal.* Gulliver/Harcourt, 1988. In 1845, Dennis comes to stay with his cousin Timmy at his house near the new, bustling Erie Canal.   8–10

☆ HOTZE, SOLLACE. *A Circle Unbroken.* Clarion, 1988. Rachel Porter, seventeen, is unhappy to have been rescued from the Sioux community where she has lived for eight years, and she finds it hard to adjust to life with her father.   11–14

HUNT, IRENE. *Across Five Aprils.* Follett, 1964. An impressive book both as a historically authenticated Civil War novel and as a beautifully written family story. The realistic treatment of the involved emotional conflicts within a border-state family is superb.   12 up

§ HURMENCE, BELINDA. *Tancy.* Houghton/Clarion, 1984. Emancipation takes a young slave away from her North Carolina plantation home and into the wider world where she finds work, love, and independence.   13–15

☆ JONES, WEYMAN. *The Edge of Two Worlds,* ill. by J. C. Kocsis. Dial, 1968.   10–13

☆ ————. *The Talking Leaf,* ill. by Harper Johnson. Dial, 1965.   10–12

☆ KEITH, HAROLD. *Rifles for Watie.* T. Crowell, 1957. Newbery Medal.   12–16

☆ LAMPMAN, EVELYN. *Cayuse Courage.* Harcourt, 1970. A story of the Whitman Massacre told from the viewpoint of a young Indian boy.   10–12

☆ ————. *White Captives.* Atheneum, 1975.   11–13

• LASKY, KATHRYN. *Beyond the Divide*. Macmillan, 1983. The wrenching saga of an Amish girl's covered wagon journey is imbued with a gritty realism.   12–15

☆ LATHAM, JEAN. *This Dear-Bought Land*, ill. by Jacob Landau. Harper, 1957. An outstanding story of Captain John Smith and the settlement of Jamestown.   11–14

☆ LEECH, JAY, and ZANE SPENCER. *Bright Fawn and Me*, ill. by Glo Coalson. T. Crowell, 1979. Set a century ago, this story is told by a Cheyenne child whose family is participating in an inter-tribal fair, and whose pleasure is dimmed by the fact that she is in charge of her small sister.   5–7

LEVINSON, NANCY SMILER. *Clara and the Bookwagon*, ill. by Carolyn Croll. Harper, 1988. Despite her father's objections, pioneer-child Clara gets a chance to learn to read due to the persuasiveness of a traveling librarian.   6–8

§ LEVY, MIMI COOPER. *Corrie and the Yankee*, ill. by Ernest Crichlow. Viking, 1959. Corrie, a little black girl on a South Carolina plantation, rescues a wounded Yankee soldier and helps him to safety.   10–13

LOBEL, ARNOLD. *On the Day Peter Stuyvesant Sailed into Town*, ill. by author. Harper, 1971.   5–8

LORD, ATHENA V. *A Spirit to Ride the Whirlwind*. Macmillan, 1981. Women mill workers in Lowell, Massachusetts, attempt to organize a union in 1836.   11–14

LOWREY, JANETTE. *Six Silver Spoons*, ill. by Robert Quackenbush. Harper, 1971. A British soldier helps two children carry safely the silver spoons made by Paul Revere during the Revolutionary War.   6–8

☆ MCGRAW, ELOISE JARVIS. *Moccasin Trail*. Coward, 1952. A white boy attacked by a grizzly is rescued and raised by the Crow Indians. When he meets his family, his conflicts are convincingly portrayed.   11–14

MACLACHLAN, PATRICIA. *Sara, Plain and Tall*. Harper, 1985. Newbery Medal; Scott O'Dell Award.
                    8–10

☆ MARRIOTT, ALICE. *Indian Annie: Kiowa Captive*.
                    11–14

MEIGS, CORNELIA. *Master Simon's Garden*, ill. by John Rae. Macmillan, 1929.   11–14

MOERI, LOUISE. *Save Queen of Sheba*. Dutton, 1981. Lone survivors of a Sioux attack, King David and his six-year-old sister struggle to rejoin the advance party of their wagon train.   9–11

§ MONJO, FERDINAND. *The Drinking Gourd*, ill. by Fred Brenner. Harper, 1970.   7–8

———. *Gettysburg: Tad Lincoln's Story*, ill. by Douglas Gorsline. Windmill/Dutton, 1976.
                    8–11

☆ ———. *Indian Summer*, ill. by Anita Lobel. Harper, 1968. A Kentucky family defends itself against Indian attack while their father is away fighting with George Washington.   7–8

———. *Poor Richard in France*, ill. by Brinton Turkle. Holt, 1973. Franklin's grandson reports on his exploits in France.   7–9

———. *The Vicksburg Veteran*, ill. by Douglas Gorsline. Simon, 1971.   7–10

MOORE, S. E. *Secret Island*, ill. by Judith Gwyn Brown. Four Winds, 1977. Set in 1865, Johnny (who has come from New York City to stay at his aunt's farm) becomes involved with his cousin in spying on Southern sympathizers who are hunting the buried gold from a robbed train.   10–13

★ O'DELL, SCOTT. *Carlota*. Houghton, 1977.   11–14

☆ ———. *Island of the Blue Dolphins*. Houghton, 1960. Newbery Medal.   11–14

★ ———. *The King's Fifth*, ill. by Samuel Bryant. Houghton, 1966.   12–15

———. *Sarah Bishop*. Houghton, 1980.   11–14

☆ ———. *The Serpent Never Sleeps: A Novel of Jamestown and Pocahontas*, ill. by Ted Lewin. Houghton, 1987.   11–14

☆ ———. *Sing Down the Moon*. Houghton, 1970. Bright Morning is a young Navaho girl whose tribe is forced from their homes by white people and driven to Fort Sumner. She persuades her husband to escape and they start their peaceful life anew. The simple, almost terse, style makes more vivid the tragedy and danger.   11–14

☆ ———. *Streams to the River, River to the Sea: A Novel of Sacagawea*. Houghton, 1986. Scott O'Dell Award.   12–15

☆ ———. *Zia*. Houghton, 1976.   10–13

OLSON, ARIELLE NORTH. *The Lighthouse Keeper's Daughter*, ill. by Elaine Wentworth. Little, 1987. During her father's unexpected absence from the lighthouse island because of a winter storm, Miranda keeps the lights burning for several weeks.
                    5–7

§ PETRY, ANN. *Tituba of Salem Village*. T. Crowell, 1964.
                    12–15

RAPPAPORT, DOREEN. *The Boston Coffee Party*, ill. by Emily Arnold McCully. Harper, 1988.   6–8

§ RINALDI, ANN. *The Last Silk Dress*. Holiday House, 1988. The issues of the Civil War become confusing to fourteen-year-old Susan, an ardent Confederate who discovers she is the illegitimate daughter of a Yankee.   12–15

☆ ROCKWOOD, JOYCE. *Groundhog's Horse*, ill. by Victor Kalin. Holt, 1978. Eleven-year-old Groundhog, a mid-eighteenth-century Cherokee, goes on a solitary quest to rescue his stolen horse.   9–11

☆ ———. *To Spoil the Sun*. Holt, 1976. Rain Dove describes her family, her marriages, and the terrible scourges of illness and persecution that came with pale-skinned strangers who are so inexplicably hostile.   11–14

• ROSTKOWSKI, MARGARET I. *After the Dancing Days.* Harper, 1986. A warm story set in a small midwestern town after World War I tells of thirteen-year-old Annie, who disobeys her mother and befriends a disfigured veteran.   10–13

• SACHS, MARILYN. *Call Me Ruth.* Doubleday, 1982.   9–11

SANDIN, JOAN. *The Long Way to a New Land,* ill. by author. Harper, 1981, and its 1989 sequel, *The Long Way Westward.* Simple and clear, two stories about a Swedish emigrant family.   6–9

☆ SANDOZ, MARI. *The Story Catcher,* ill. by Elsie J. McCorkell. Westminster, 1963. The dramatic and moving story of Lance, a young Sioux brave who longs to achieve status with his people. The blending of style and subject is impressive.
                    11–14

§ SEBESTYEN, OUIDA. *Words by Heart.* Atlantic/Little, 1979. Set in the Reconstruction Era, this is an impressive novel about race relationships and nonviolence centering around a black family strong in their love and pride.   10–12

☆ SHARP, EDITH LAMBERT. *Nkwala,* ill. by William Winter. Little, 1958. Stirringly written historical tale of a young Spokane Indian who at last wins his adult name.   11–13

SHUB, ELIZABETH. *Cutlass in the Snow,* ill. by Rachel Isadora. Greenwillow, 1986. In 1797, Sam and his grandpa are forced by a snowstorm to spend the night on an island, and a cutlass starts them on the trail to buried treasure.   8–10

SKURZYNSKI, GLORIA. *The Tempering.* Houghton/ Clarion, 1983. A 1912 Pennsylvania steel town is the backdrop for this involving story about a young steelworker on the brink of manhood.
                    12–15

SMITH, DORIS BUCHANAN. *Salted Lemons.* Four Winds, 1980. Darby, newly arrived from Washington, D.C., and Japanese-American Yoko are both labeled outsiders in World War II Atlanta.   9–11

SNOW, RICHARD. *Freelon Starbird: Being a Narrative of the Extraordinary Hardships Suffered by an Accidental Soldier in a Beaten Army During the Autumn and Winter of 1776,* ill. by Ben F. Stahl. Houghton, 1976. Enlisting in the Continental Army on a lark, Snow's protagonist Freelon presents a tart, funny, vivid picture of life in Washington's army and the surprise attack on Trenton.   12–14

○ SNYDER, ZILPHA KEATLEY. *And Condors Danced.* Delacorte, 1987. On a California ranch in 1907, eleven-year-old Carly must adjust to the death of

her mother, which she does with the help of her great-aunt Mehitabel and her servant, Woo Ying.
                    9–12

☆ SPEARE, ELIZABETH GEORGE. *Calico Captive,* ill. by W. T. Mars. Houghton, 1957. Stirring junior novel of Miriam Willard, a young Indian captive taken to Canada during the French and Indian Wars.
                    11–15

☆ ————. *The Sign of the Beaver.* Houghton, 1983. Scott O'Dell Award.   11–14

• ————. *The Witch of Blackbird Pond.* Houghton, 1958. Newbery Medal.   12–16

STEELE, WILLIAM O. *The Buffalo Knife,* ill. by Paul Galdone. Harcourt, 1952. A thousand-mile flatboat trip is an exciting adventure for a boy of nine.   9–12

————. *The Far Frontier,* ill. by Paul Galdone. Harcourt, 1959.   10–14

————. *The Perilous Road,* ill. by Paul Galdone. Harcourt, 1958.   11–13

☆ ————. *Wayah of the Real People,* ill. by Isa Barnett. Holt, 1964.   11–13

§ TAYLOR, MILDRED. *The Friendship,* ill. by Max Ginsburg. Dial, 1987. A short story about race relations in rural Mississippi during the Depression focuses on an incident between an old black man, Tom Bee, and a white storekeeper, John Wallace.   9–12

§ ————. *Roll of Thunder, Hear My Cry,* ill. by Jerry Pinkney. Dial, 1976. Newbery Medal.   12–14

TAYLOR, THEODORE. *The Odyssey of Ben O'Neal,* ill. by Richard Cuffari. Doubleday, 1977. A sequel to *Teetoncey* and *Teetoncey and Ben O'Neal* is set aboard ship at the turn of the century.   11–13

————. *Teetoncey,* ill. by Richard Cuffari. Doubleday, 1974.   10–13

————. *Teetoncey and Ben O'Neal,* ill. by Richard Cuffari. Doubleday, 1975. Teetoncey is the one female survivor of a shipwreck off Cape Hateras in 1898. The first book tells of her rescue, while the second recounts the struggle to recover valuable cargo aboard the sunken ship.   10–13

THRASHER, CRYSTAL. *The Dark Didn't Catch Me.* Atheneum, 1975. First of a series of five books about an indigent family in the Depression Era. Others are *Between Dark and Daylight* (1979), *Julie's Summer* (1981), *End of a Dark Road* (1982), and *A Taste of Daylight* (1984).   11–13

• TURKLE, BRINTON. *Obadiah the Bold,* ill. by author. Viking, 1965.   8–9

————. *Rachel and Obadiah,* ill. by author. Dutton, 1978.   8–9

• ————. *Thy Friend, Obadiah,* ill. by author. Viking, 1969.   7–9

TURNER, ANN. *Grasshopper Summer.* Macmillan, 1989. In 1874, narrator Sam White goes west with his family from Kentucky into Dakota Territory, where they are plagued by grasshoppers.   9–11

○ UCHIDA, YOSHIKO. *A Jar of Dreams.* Atheneum, 1981. Rinko's embarrassment over her Japanese heritage is diminished with the aid of a self-confident aunt in this Depression Era story. Followed by *The Best Bad Thing* (1983) and *The Happiest Ending* (1985)   8–10

○ ————. *Journey Home,* ill. by Charles Robinson. Atheneum, 1978. In a sequel to the title below, the family adjusts to its return home.   10–12

○ ————. *Journey to Topaz,* ill. by Donald Carrick. Scribner's, 1971. A story of the Japanese-American relocation.   11–12

○ ————. *Samurai of Gold Hill,* ill. by Ati Forberg. Scribner's, 1972. A well-paced story of a group of Japanese immigrants who come to California in 1869.   10–12

VINING, ELIZABETH GRAY. *The Taken Girl.* Viking, 1972.   11–14

☆ WHELAN, GLORIA. *Next Spring an Oriole,* ill. by Pamela Johnson. Random House, 1987. Ten-year-old Libby Mitchell and her family suffer the discomforts of wagon-train travel in 1837.   7–9

WIBBERLEY, LEONARD. *John Treegate's Musket.* Farrar, 1959. First in an outstanding series. Other titles are: *Peter Treegate's War* (1960), *Sea Captain from Salem* (1961), *Treegate's Raiders* (1962).   12–15

WILDER, LAURA INGALLS. *The First Four Years,* ill. by Garth Williams. Harper, 1971. Found among the author's papers after her death, and published without revision, this is the story of her first years as a farmer's wife on a South Dakota homestead. The same charm and virtues as the Little House books.   10–14

————. *Little House in the Big Woods,* ill. by Garth Williams. Harper, 1953. Other titles in the series are: *Little House on the Prairie, On the Banks of Plum Creek, By the Shores of Silver Lake, Farmer Boy, The Long Winter, Little Town on the Prairie, These Happy Golden Years.*   9–14

☆ WILSON, HAZEL. *His Indian Brother,* ill. by Robert Henneberger. Abingdon, 1955. Based on a true incident of the 1800s is this story of Brad Porter, left alone in a Maine pioneer cabin and rescued from starvation by an Indian chief and his son.   10–14

☆ WOJCIECHOWSKA, MAIA. *Odyssey of Courage: The Story of Alvar Nuñez Cabeza de Vaca,* ill. by Alvin Smith. Atheneum, 1965. Cabeza de Vaca's journey, stressing his affection for the Indians and their regard for him.   12–14

§ ☆ WORMSER, RICHARD. *The Black Mustanger,* ill. by Don Bolognese, Morrow, 1971. Set in Texas in the period after the Civil War, the story of a white boy whose mentor is a cowboy, half black and half Apache.   10–14

§ WRISTON, HILDRETH. *Susan's Secret,* ill. by W. T. Mars. Farrar, 1957. Suspense-filled story of a little Vermont girl who undertook her absent family's task of guiding fugitive slaves to the next Underground station.   9–12

YATES, ELIZABETH. *Carolina's Courage,* ill. by Nora S. Unwin. Dutton, 1964.   8–10

○ YEP, LAURENCE. *Dragonwings.* Harper, 1975. A fascinating view of life in the Chinese community of San Francisco in the first years of the twentieth century, including a description of the earthquake.   10–14

Historical Fiction: Other Countries

BAUMANN, HANS. *Sons of the Steppe.* Walck, 1958. Authentic background adds to the story of two of Genghis Khan's grandsons.   12–16

CHAUNCY, NAN. *Hunted in Their Own Land,* ill. by Victor G. Ambrus. Seabury, 1973. The tragic story of the gradual annihilation of the aborigines in Tasmania by the whites.   12–15

DICKINSON, PETER. *Dancing Bear,* ill. by David Smee. Little, 1973. In Byzantium in 558, Silvester, a slave, accompanied by a bear and a holy man, searches for his mistress who was kidnapped by the Huns.   10–14

★ DE JENKINS, LYLL BECERRA. *The Honorable Prison.* Lodestar, 1988. Scott O'Dell Award.   13 up

○ GARRIGUE, SHEILA. *The Eternal Spring of Mr. Ito.* Bradbury, 1985. While staying in Canada for the duration of World War II, Sara helps change her family's wartime prejudice against their Japanese gardner, Mr. Ito.   9–11

☆ HARRIS, CHRISTIE. *Raven's Cry,* ill. by Bill Reid. Atheneum, 1966.   10–15

☆ ————. *West with the White Chiefs,* ill. by Walter Ferro. Atheneum, 1965.   11–15

HAUGAARD, ERIK CHRISTIAN. *Leif the Unlucky.* Houghton, 1982.   11–13

————. *The Samurai's Tale.* Houghton, 1984.   11–14

HOLMAN, FELICE. *The Wild Children.* Scribner's, 1983. A gripping survival tale follows the fortunes of a band of homeless children who roam the streets of Russian cities in the 1920s.   11–14

☆ HOUSTON, JAMES. *The White Archer: An Eskimo Legend,* ill. by author. Harcourt, 1967. Kungo is a young Eskimo who vows revenge when his parents are killed and his sister is taken captive by a band of Indians. The description of his years of cold, patient planning is in low key.   10–12

☆ HUDSON, JAN. *Sweetgrass.* Philomel, 1989.   11–14

★ LAMPMAN, EVELYN. *The Tilted Sombrero,* ill. by Ray Cruz. Doubleday, 1966.   11–14

LEWIS, ELIZABETH FOREMAN. *To Beat a Tiger: One Needs a Brother's Help,* ill. by John Heuhnergarth. Holt, 1956.   14–17

————. *Young Fu of the Upper Yangtze,* ill. by Kurt Wiese. Holt, 1932. Newbery Medal. The 1973 edition of this book contains illustrations by Ed Young.   13–15

LITTLE, JEAN. *From Anna,* ill. by Jean Sandin. Harper, 1972. Anna adjusts to Canadian life after her family emigrates from Germany during the Nazi regime.   9–11

————. *Listen for the Singing.* Dutton, 1977. Anna's family encounters prejudice when World War II starts.   10–12

MARUKI, TOSHI. *Hiroshima No Pika,* ill. by author. Lothrop, 1982. An unforgettable picturebook story about the day the atom bomb was dropped on Hiroshima, illustrated with boldly colored, impressionistic paintings. Batchelder Award.   7–9

☆ MAYNE, WILLIAM. *Drift.* Delacorte, 1986. Tawena, an Indian girl, takes Rafe into the wilderness, steals his knife, and deserts him in an exciting survival story.   10–14

MUHLENWEG, FRITZ. *Big Tiger and Christian,* ill. by Rafaello Busoni. Pantheon, 1952. Long but well-sustained story of the journey of two boys across China and the Gobi Desert in the 1920s.   11–13

NAMIOKA, LENSEY. *Island of Ogres.* Harper, 1989. An adventure story of medieval Japan features three ronin (retired samurai) as they struggle for power on an island.   11–14

————. *The Samurai and the Long-Nosed Devils.* McKay, 1976. Two sixteenth-century Japanese ronin take on the job of protecting a Portuguese missionary and his soldier-companion.   12–14

————. *Village of the Vampire Cat.* Delacorte, 1981. Two young samurai of medieval Japan determine to capture a murderous creature known as the vampire cat.   12–15

★ O'DELL, SCOTT. *The Captive.* Houghton, 1979. A sixteenth-century story of an idealistic missionary who comes from Spain to the New World, is shipwrecked, and is helped by a Mayan girl. Followed by *The Feathered Serpent* (1981) and *The Amethyst Ring* (1983).   12–14

§ ————. *My Name Is Not Angelica.* Houghton, 1989. In a story of the slaves' revolt on St. John Island, Raisha rejects the name given to her by the Danish family who bought her.   11–14

PATERSON, KATHERINE. *The Master Puppeteer,* ill. by Haru Wells. T. Crowell, 1976.   11–15

————. *Of Nightingales That Weep,* ill. by Haru Wells. T. Crowell, 1974.   11–15

————. *The Sign of the Chrysanthemum,* ill. by Peter Landa. T. Crowell, 1973.   8–11

Three novels of feudal Japan.

————. *Rebels of the Heavenly Kingdom,* Lodestar, 1983. A riveting novel set in mid-nineteenth-century China follows two young peasants who are caught up in a patriotic religious movement dedicated to overthrowing the Manchu overlords.   12–14

RITCHIE, RITA. *The Golden Hawks of Genghis Khan,* ill. by Lorence F. Bjorklund. Dutton, 1958.

————. *Secret Beyond the Mountains.* Dutton, 1960.

————. *The Year of the Horse,* ill. by Lorence F. Bjorklund. Dutton, 1957. These are outstanding tales of the years of Mongol supremacy.   12–15

○ VANDER ELS, BETTY. *The Bombers' Moon.* Farrar, 1985.   9–11

○ ————. *Leaving Point.* Farrar, 1987.   10–12

● VINEBERG, ETHEL. *Grandmother Came from Dworitz: A Jewish Story,* ill. by Rita Briansky. Tundra, 1969. One of a series of books on the origins of Canadians, this has a text that is sedate but the material is fascinating, giving a vivid picture of the restrictions upon nineteenth-century Russian Jews, their communal life, and their emigration.   9–12

WALSH, JILL PATON. *The Emperor's Winding Sheet.* Farrar, 1974.   11–14

§ WATSON, SALLY. *Jade.* Holt, 1968. A lively tale of an eighteenth-century girl who becomes a pirate.   11–14

YEP, LAURENCE. *The Serpent's Children.* Harper, 1984. A peasant family is deeply embroiled in the political upheaval of nineteenth-century China. The sequel, *Mountain Light,* appeared the following year, 1985.   11–14

Chapter Twelve

Biography

B iography may be defined as that branch of literature that deals with the history of individual men's and women's lives. Thus the three essential ingredients of good biography are history, the person, and literary artistry. Facts should be authentic and verifiable; the subject should be considered as an individual rather than as a paragon or type; and the writing should be a conscious work of art. This description—with some amplification—not only defines the genre, but suggests the standards by which it can be judged.

Biography As History

Authenticity

If a biography is the history of a person's life, it should be as accurate and authentic as research can make it. That statement is true for all biographies, but its application varies, depending on the nature of the subject's contributions, whether or not the subject lived in a time when records were kept, and the life the person led.

Even today, we know very little about Emily Dickinson's life, and authors wishing to write books about Dickinson are forced to do a great amount of internal analysis of her poems for insights into the kind of person who might have written them. For literary figures, internal analysis of their writings is essential regardless of how much we know about their public and private lives. When they leave detailed diaries or journals, as the writer André Gide did, the biographer is faced with a different problem: The mass of information must be checked against the recorded impressions of the people named by Gide. If these seem contradictory, the biographer must discover what the attitude of Gide's contemporary was—friendly, worshipful, or definitely antagonistic. This may involve consulting the available writings of still other contemporaries who knew both individuals and who in turn left records of their relationships.

When the subject of a biography is a famous public figure, such as George Washington, the search for authenticity takes the biographer to government archives for official papers relating to Washington's life as president. But that is only the beginning, for the same checking and cross-checking with contemporaries' opinions must be pursued. The mass of documents is overwhelming, but rarely definitive, and a good biographer informs the reader that what is being written is based on known available evidence. A good biographer resembles a good detective: following clues, interviewing people, hearing what the subject has to say, and then—and only then—reaching a tentative conclusion that is presented to readers, the "jury."

Accuracy and authenticity are easier to achieve when writing about people of the past. They are very difficult to achieve when writing of the living or the recently dead, for whom records may not be available and about whom long perspective doesn't exist. In biography for children, much of what we know is true may have been deleted because it is contrary to the image children's authors and publishers wish to convey to young readers. The problem of accuracy can be demonstrated by looking at three biographies of Martin Luther King, Jr., written for children of elementary school age. The easiest of these books, *The Picture Life of Martin Luther King, Jr.*, by Margaret B. Young, covers the tumultuous year of the Montgomery, Alabama bus boycott in one sentence: "After a year the laws were changed." Ed Clayton's *Martin Luther King: The Peaceful Warrior* and James T. De Kay's *Meet Martin Luther King, Jr.* contain more detail about the violence of that year but raise questions about authenticity: Is Clayton right when he says that the bomb attempt on King's house found Mrs. King and their daughter in danger ("Coretta grabbed their infant daughter and ran to the rear of the house")? Or is De Kay more accurate in telling us that Coretta King was talking to a friend while Yoki (the daughter) slept in a back room? This particular example of discrepancy may seem minor, but it alerts us to the fact that very few biographies for children can be considered accurate or authentic because the authors are simplifying information for young readers, and seldom engage in primary source research.

Objectivity

All data are filtered through human minds. The best biographers are aware of their own biases and take special care to be sure they do not interfere with the search for whatever degree of truth can be found. Good biographers know they are not free to offer personal opinions as fact or to present an interpretation for which there is no evidence. They let deeds speak for themselves. If the behavior of the subject seems ambiguous, the author may speculate about the contradictory evidence, but may not take sides to tell the reader what to think. Was Sam Houston completely honest and disinterested in his dealings with the native Americans and with his Cherokee foster father? Marquis James in *The Raven*, a biography of Sam Houston, never tells us how he regards Houston's actions. He presents the evidence and lets us draw our own conclusions. And readers of *The Raven* may differ in their judgment of Sam, just as Sam's contemporaries themselves differed.

It also follows that the biographer may report only those words and thoughts which were recorded, either by the subject or by those contemporary observers in a position to know. Some biographers have got around this strict limitation by saying, "Perhaps he thought . . ." or "Perhaps he meant what he said, who knows?" Lytton Strachey uses this device for maintaining objectivity repeatedly in his *Queen Victoria*. When the gouty old king whom she was to succeed asked the young Victoria for her favorite tune, she replied without a moment's hesitation, "God Save the King." This, Strachey tells us, "has been praised as an early example of a tact which was afterwards famous." Then he adds cryptically, "But she was a very truthful child, and perhaps it was her genuine opinion." He closes his book with a dramatic use of objectivity. Describing the dying queen, old, blind, and silent, he suggests that she *may perhaps* have recalled her past. Then, as if Victoria were thinking aloud, he briefly and tenderly reviews her life, going back to the little girl in "sprigged muslin, and the trees and the grass at Kensington." Jeanette Eaton uses a similar technique in her account of the dying Washington in *Leader by Destiny*. It is a legitimate device but, if overused, may become a not too subtle method of influencing the reader's opinions.

Documentation

For many people, two of the most important tests of a good biography are the accuracy and thoroughness of its documentation. In the past, few juvenile biographies were documented by footnotes, although most authors did supply sources in a separate section, a bibliography, or an afterword. Some juvenile biographies, such as *Anthony Burns: The Defeat and Triumph of a Fugitive Slave* by Virginia Hamilton, do contain footnotes as well as extensive bibliographies. Others, such as *Fanny Kemble's America* by John Anthony Scott, are written by people whose authority has been established by their adult writings on the subject. Whether children read the footnotes or are impressed by the author's qualifications is not important. What matters is that these changes reflect an increased concern on the part of authors and publishers to give young readers the best biographies possible within the restrictions imposed by age.

Biography As the Individual

All of us are familiar with older biographies which presented Washington the ever truthful, Lincoln the sad, and Benjamin Franklin the thrifty. Franklin seems to have been cast in the role of the thrifty merely because he wrote a number of wise saws on the desirability of this virtue. As a matter of fact, he sent home from England a continual stream of handsome and extravagant presents, such as silver-handled knives, fine china, carpets, and even a harpsichord for his daughter, Sally. Later, in France, his bills for his wine cellar were lavish, and he finally remarked plaintively that frugality was "a virtue I never could acquire in myself."[1] So "perhaps," as the biographers say, his adages on thrift were reminders for his unthrifty self, as well as for the rest of the world.

Franklin is indeed a good example of a figure almost spoiled for young people in the past because he had been typed as a paragon. In later biographies, such as Thomas Fleming's *Benjamin Franklin* or Milton Meltzer's *Benjamin Franklin: The New American*, young people and even children may catch a glimpse of the real Franklin—witty, worldly, urbane, adored by the ladies and adoring them in turn, equally at home in the wilderness and in the court, a scientist, a man of letters, a diplomat, an amateur musician, lazy and prodigiously industrious—in short, a composite of strength and weakness on a grand scale, with a tremendous brain directing the whole. To have made Franklin, of all men, into the image of a stuffy prig was a crime. To rediscover the whole Franklin and reveal him to this generation, as Carl Van Doren has done, is a crowning achievement of modern biography.

Another achievement of current biography for both adults and children is the growing recognition that white males were not the only members of the human race to lead exciting lives and to contribute to civilization, but that women and members of racial and ethnic minorities also have a rich heritage, and have made significant contributions.

The Whole Person

James Boswell's *Life of Samuel Johnson* is considered one of the greatest biographies in the English language; it is a fully developed portrait. But, despite Boswell's early demonstration of what a good biography should be, the majority of biographies for both adults and children have treated their subjects as paragons rather than as fallible human beings.

From *Anthony Burns: The Defeat and Triumph of a Fugitive Slave* by Virginia Hamilton, cover illustration by Leo and Diane Dillon.

[1]Carl Van Doren, *Benjamin Franklin,* p. 637.

Why this idealization took place is a complex story, but basically biography was treated less as a literary genre than as a political and social tool. In the United States, following the publication in 1880 of *The Life and Memorable Acts of George Washington* by the Reverend Mason Weems, the pattern was set for American biographers to depict the country's leaders as paragons. Part of this impetus came from the religious leaders of the nation; part of it came from the historians who were depicting the new nation as fulfilling its "Manifest Destiny." In England, the rise of what we now term Victorian morality dictated that the more human side of people be suppressed, and political factors here, too, influenced whom biographers saw as worthy subjects.

In scholarly biographies, read only by people deeply interested in the person being written about, it has been customary throughout most of the past two centuries to depict the subject as a whole person. Popular biographies, on the other hand, written for the general adult public, have traditionally ignored the personal life if the subject had what were termed "vices." When writing for children the cleansing process was taken a step further and personal tragedies and failures were passed over. In many cases, juvenile biographies did not even depict the person's death.

As society's values have changed and new areas of research have developed, the content acceptable in juvenile biographies has also changed. Divorce is not now seen as a vice, to be suppressed, but as an event to be described. Incidents of failure, rather than lessening a person's worth, show readers that all people face setbacks at some point in their lives. And we are coming to understand that death is a part of life and cannot be ignored.

By broadening the parameters of what constitutes acceptable content in juvenile biographies, we have also broadened the range of people about whom these accounts can be written. When the older, rigid standards were in effect, many significant people were excluded. It was impossible for an author to think of writing a juvenile biography about Margaret Sanger, the great birth-control pioneer, or about African Americans like Malcolm X who had led horrendous childhoods.

This new openness does not mean that anything and everything is acceptable in juvenile biography. While the definition of what constitutes good taste has changed, the concept itself remains. Authors must always be sure that they are not sensationalizing any events of a person's life. They must be able to point out if a particular fact in their subject's life was very important to that individual, or if it was an idiosyncrasy. Boswell tells us that Samuel Johnson would sneak out after dark to buy oysters for his cat and that he did not want the servants to know. That was an idiosyncrasy. Had he been sneaking out to visit a mistress, that information would be more important to an understanding of Johnson.

Vivid Details

One of the best methods of assuring that the whole person is presented in a biography is to include rich and arresting details. An adolescent or an adult reading about how Samuel Johnson always had to go through a door on one particular foot finds that information interesting. The reader may already know that certain baseball players always touch third base on their way to the outfield. Few of us, whether children or adults, can easily identify with people who have changed history—whether through politics or breaking Babe Ruth's home run record—and these human details help us know that great feats in life are accomplished by human beings and not by paragons.

In the past, biographies written for young people failed at precisely this point. They told children about the large affairs in which their subjects played a part but neglected to give any account of the individuals' amusing idiosyncrasies, peculiar bents, and special talents which made them uniquely human. Children delight in Franklin's account of himself as a boy floating in a pond on his back propelled by a kite; or of Lincoln holding a child upside down to make tracks on the ceiling as a joke on the stepmother he dearly loved, a joke he righted with a fresh coat of whitewash.

To be told that Penn dressed in sober clothes is dull enough. To learn that even after he turned Quaker he still loved good apparel and went to meet the velvet-clad Lord Baltimore in sober brown but cut by the best London tailor from the finest materials—ah, that is more human. To read that Penn was tried for holding a meeting with other Quakers is dreary, but young people warm immediately to the picture of Penn on trial, shut up in a cage at the back of the courtroom, shouting out his own defense so effectively that he won the jury to his side and later won the right of the jury to have its decisions upheld in the English courts. Little incidents and big ones which reveal spirited human beings who will not be downed and who travel their own unique way bring the individual to life for the reader. Revealing details are the very essence of good biography.

Biography As Literature

If biography is a branch of literature, then it, like any other work of art, should be a consciously planned composition. It has a subject, a theme, unity attained through that theme, style, a pattern of the whole, and a pattern of the parts. These may not be evident to the casual reader, but if the account is written with any skill, they are there.

Theme and Unity

Biography, like history, is based on documented facts. No liberties may be taken with these facts; no flights of fancy are permissible. The biographer begins by assembling all the documents and examining all the evidence. But good biographers feel that they should not give all their accumulated research to the reader in its endless and often trivial details. They recognize that there is a difference between the rich and arresting details discussed earlier and endless presentation of trivia. Each biographer must choose those details which will most truly reveal the subject as the author has come to know him or her. It is in this matter of selection and organization that the biography ceases to be purely history and becomes a work of art. For the author, in reading all the sources and weighing all the evidence, gradually develops a theme. The theme of a biography makes a fundamental statement about the person's life as seen by the biographer. This theme is not, and never can be, the total truth about the

From *Susette La Flesche: The Voice of the Omaha Indians* by Margaret Crary, photograph from the Nebraska State Historical Society.

person's life, but if it has emerged from the research, it provides readers with a unified view of the man or woman about whom the author has written. Biographers fail to write good biography if they approach the research process with a theme in mind, for then, despite all good intentions, they will make the data fit their preconceptions.

Turning to children's or young people's biographies, we often find the theme in the title—*Matthew Henson: Explorer, Invincible Louisa* (Louisa May Alcott), and *Susette La Flesche: The Voice of the Omaha Indians*.

In *Leader by Destiny*, the life of George Washington, Jeanette Eaton shows how circumstances and the times repeatedly interfered with Washington's life and called him to other ways of living. He might have been a homespun frontiersman, playing a gallant part no doubt, but his brother's death gave him Mount Vernon and turned him into a country gentleman. This role was forwarded by his neighbor's wife, the lovely Sally Fairfax (destiny again), who taught him the manners and ways of gentlemen. Then the country squire was called upon for soldiery and more soldiery, and finally he was made the head of the Continental Army. Seven long years of campaigning followed, with his whole heart yearning for the gracious life of Mount Vernon. Then came peace and a chance to realize his desires, but destiny called him once more, this time to the presidency, the gravest responsibility an American had ever faced. Washington played a great part in every role he undertook, but it would seem that these roles were not of his own choosing. He would have been a leader in any situation, but destiny called him to national greatness.

Similar in theme is James Haskins's *Ralph Bunche: A Most Reluctant Hero*. Bunche's life was filled with "firsts": the first African American to earn a Ph.D. in political science; the first African American to have a desk in the State Department; and the first African American to win the Nobel Peace Prize. He was a man who seemed always to be in the right place at the right time and his skills were recognized and appreciated by the world's leaders. He would have been content to teach, write, and spend time with his family, but world events called him, like Washington, to greatness.

Not all biographies adhere so closely and obviously to theme and unity as those just cited, certainly not the early examples of biography. But modern biographies, including those for young people, seem to follow this pattern and are organized around themes which give dramatic unity to these books.

Style and Pattern

If biography is to be judged as literature, it must also have a pleasing style. As one authority has said, style is "the auditory effect of prose." The prose must be good to read and it must be appropriate to the subject matter and to the mood of the story. A fine example of style and pattern in biography is Carl Sandburg's *Abe Lincoln Grows Up*, adapted from his book for adults, *The Prairie Years*, which reads aloud so easily and naturally you just keep reading. Of Tom Lincoln, the father, Sandburg writes:

He wasn't exactly lazy, he was sort of independent, and liked to be where he wasn't interfered with. . . . He was a wild buck at fighting, when men didn't let him alone. A man talked about a woman once in a way Tom Lincoln didn't like.

And in the fight that came, Tom bit a piece of the man's nose off. . . . Though he was short spoken, he knew yarns, could crack jokes, and had a reputation as a story-teller when he got started.

A different use of pattern is well illustrated by the opening chapter of Elizabeth Gray Vining's *Penn*, written under her maiden name, Elizabeth Janet Gray. She describes Penn's father, young Captain Penn, already rising in the English navy, in which eventually he becomes admiral; his wife with her Irish estates; the king with two sons, James and Charles; a shoemaker named George Fox; an eight-month-old heiress, Gulielma Springett; and the lusty baby, William Penn.

And all these scattered lives were to play their part in the life of the baby who slept and cried and ate and slept again in sight of the steep walls of the old, grim Tower, into which had gone, down the centuries, many prisoners, young and old, frightened and defiant; and from which fewer had come out. The Tower too had its part.

Here, we are told, are all the threads of the story, all the important elements in the life of the baby, who grew to be the man of whom it was said later, "the world has not yet caught up with William Penn." There in that first chapter are the small patterns which will make up the large pattern.

These examples show how biography, although as scrupulously documented as history, may become in the act of composition a branch of literature. Yet good adult biographies are as sound sources for facts as histories. This may also be true of biographies for children and young people but with certain differences.

Biography for Children

Historically, juvenile biographies have differed greatly from adult biographies, but the gap between the two has narrowed as children have become more knowledgeable and adults have become more respectful of children's abilities. While not all current biographies are documented, more and more of them contain footnotes and bibliographic references since the authors know they may be reviewed by people who know the subject as well as by people who are engrossed by the story.

No longer do authors systematically and automatically suppress the human weaknesses of their subjects or avoid relating personal tragedies. As was indicated earlier in the discussion of "The Whole Person," a new level of integrity has been achieved in the writing of juvenile biography.

However, differences remain. Biographies for children will probably never approach the level of documentation that is found in the scholarly adult biographies. Children who can cope with that kind of writing should be introduced to the adult biographies and allowed to find their own levels of understanding.

But if we compare juvenile biography with the popularized adult biographies, we find very few differences, and those that do exist are in favor of the juvenile authors. No biography for children exploits the person being written about to the degree that popularizations for adults do. If personal scandal is introduced into a juvenile biography, it is because it is absolutely vital for understanding the life of the woman or man about whom the author has written. In adult biographies, such scenes are often present to titillate the reader rather than to shed light on the subject.

Biographers for young readers usually feel that it is legitimate to cast known facts about an episode into actual dialogue and to interpret the thoughts of their characters; that is, they put words into their subjects' mouths and thoughts into their heads for which there is no documentary evidence. Popularized adult biographies do the same. The authors' excuse, and it is a legitimate one, is that this technique produces a more dramatic narrative.

Undocumented dialogue produces one of two hybrids of genuine biography: first, there is *fictionalized biography*, in which the facts are documented and only a few liberties are taken, such as occasional dialogue for which there is no record; and, second, there is *biographical fiction*, which takes a historical character as a basis for a story semihistorical in nature.

Fictionalized Biography

Most biographies for children are fictionalized. That is, they are based on careful research, but known facts are often presented in dramatic episodes complete with conversation. For instance, Elizabeth Vining, in relating the moving quarrel between Admiral Penn and his young son lately turned Quaker, begins the account with the old Admiral exploding wrathfully, ". . . three people you may *not* thee and thou —the King, the Duke of York, and myself." This is much more exciting than the plain statement, "The Admiral objected to his son's Quaker use of thee and thou." The quarrel continues the next day, climaxing in the Admiral's terrible threat:

"I am going to kneel down and pray to God that you may not be a Quaker, nor go ever again to any more of their meetings."

And in William's frenzied reply:

"Before I will hear thee pray after any such manner," he cried, "I'll leap out of the window."

It was a high window, too, and, according to Vining, William was saved only by the interruption of one of his father's most elegant friends come to call. Since Vining is a scrupulous research scholar, she probably had some documentary evidence for this quarrel. She does, for instance, provide the Admiral's actual letters to William summoning him home for this grim conference. Assuming then that there is a historical basis for the scene, we accept the dialogue, which certainly heightens the drama, the words fairly crackling with suppressed emotion.

Perhaps fictionalized biography is the best pattern of biography for young people. There is no doubt that dialogue based on facts, written by a scholar and an artist, brings history to life and re-creates living, breathing people, who make a deep impression on children.

Biographical Fiction

Jean Lee Latham's Newbery Medal book, *Carry On, Mr. Bowditch* is sometimes catalogued as fiction, but the reason is not clear. In her acceptance speech the author describes her book as fictionalized biography. She probably makes no more use of imaginary dialogue than does Vining in *Penn*, which is listed as biography, but there are more authorial liberties taken, especially in the inclusion of half-a-dozen imaginary characters.

Viewpoint

As to the question about the moral obligation of the author to distinguish between fact and fiction in juvenile biography—the author should not pretend to be writing one hundred percent fact if he is introducing invented scenes and dialogue. What I imagine is always based on facts that make the scenes possible and usually even likely. I make the dialogue as plausible as I can, and I always use historical dialogue whenever history obliges me by preserving the words I happen to need.

So much for the line between fact and fiction. Even more important are the needs of the present times. We need to inspire our gifted young people to make an attempt at greatness. We need to make them want to reach out after that splendid, elusive, brass ring known as achievement and make it theirs. Our age is more tawdry than we wish it to be, and we yearn for some heroes and heroines for ourselves and for the future. I have not yet utterly abandoned the Western world. It has produced many men and women who still make my skin prickle. I have not yet abandoned the American experiment, for it has produced large numbers of people whom I wish I might have emulated. That is why I would like my books to arouse young people. To make them understand that all great human beings were once uncertain children, unaware of their powers. I want my books to incite children to dare to do something marvelous. For, if they dare, perhaps they will succeed.

F. N. Monjo. "Great Men, Melodies, Experiments, Plots, Predictability, and Surprises," *The Horn Book Magazine,* October 1975. Copyright © 1975 by The Horn Book. Reprinted by permission.

These distinctions among different types of historical literature are not greatly important to the children's use of the books. When young people read biographical fiction, they might be warned, "This is the way it *may* have happened, but history does not tell us for sure." And when they read biography or even fictionalized biography, they might be told, "Insofar as the author can find historical records, this is the way it *did* happen."

Briefly, the chief distinctions between biographies for adults and those for children are that, in the latter, sources are less often stated, there is more emphasis on childhood; unsavory episodes are more likely to be omitted, and recorded events are more likely to be enlivened with imaginary dialogue. On the whole, however, modern biographies for children represent scholarly research and conscientious retelling of events in a dramatic style. Such characteristics make these books some of the finest modern contributions to children's literature.

Work Methods of Biographers

From bookjackets, authors' notes, lists of suggested readings, prefatory remarks, articles by authors on their research methods, and even from those pages in which writers express thanks to those who have helped them, it is clear that the research for biographies for children is taken very seriously indeed. Evidence of careful documentation is found in more and more books for younger and younger children.

Dorothy Sterling, for example, when working on *Captain of the Planter*, a biography of Robert Smalls, went to Beaufort and Charleston, where she talked to people who had known Smalls, and had two visits with his son. She pored over old newspapers and photographs, ransacked library collections and archives, and picked up every lead by correspondence.

Aileen Fisher and Olive Rabe, in "Writing About the Alcotts,"[2] explain how they used the source material collected and published by others and the biographies of men and women who had played a part in the Alcotts' lives, reading whatever could be found about the family and the period. Each worked on the same chapter separately; one welded the two versions and the other edited and revised the resulting chapter. The authors decided to write

[2]Aileen Fisher and Olive Rabe, "Writing About the Alcotts," *The Horn Book Magazine,* October 1968.

the story from the viewpoint of a family member so that the book would have an intimate feeling, although they knew it restricted the action to what could be observed.

There are small variations in the ways in which authors patiently dig, sift, compare, record, and revise, but one thing is paramount: a respect for the truth. Marchette Chute says it beautifully:

To put the whole thing into a single sentence: you will never succeed in getting at the truth if you think you know, ahead of time, what the truth ought to be.[3]

The Series

The Bobbs-Merrill Childhood books seem to have launched, in 1932, the biography fever with both children and publishers. As a result, not only is the numerical impact of these books staggering, but the duplication of biographies has reached the point where it is a major feat of memory to recall which George Washington is whose and whose Abraham Lincoln is which.

It would be convenient to be able to make a judgment of each series as a whole, but this is impossible, because within one set of books some are thin or pedestrian and others are of major importance. Although it is difficult to select from a list, it is wasteful for schools or homes or libraries to order every one of any series. It is best to judge each book individually and to watch for authoritative reviews of individual books. Many of the books discussed in this chapter are from one or another of the series. However, since each series is designed to perform a definite function in the child's reading program, several should be familiar to adults working with children.

Two outstanding series for the beginning reader are the Harper & Row I Can Read history books and the Young Crowell Biographies. The former includes several life stories told from the child's viewpoint; the latter emphasizes minority group members, although it does not focus on them exclusively. The Bobbs-

Merrill Childhood of Famous Americans series has high-interest, low-vocabulary books, rigidly patterned and quite often determinedly merry. The Random House Step-Up Books, the Carolrhoda Creative Minds Books, the Putnam See-and-Read Books, and the Watts Picture Life series are all simply written and variable in quality.

In 1950, Random House launched the Landmark Books, presenting people, movements, and moments in history that have been landmarks in our national life. Some of the contributors are notable, and some of the books are of superior literary quality, but in a series as extensive as this one, it is not surprising that high standards are not always maintained.

The Crowell biographies of women and of poets are outstanding series books for older readers, as are the Harper & Row Breakthrough Books, which emphasize, as the title indicates, breakthroughs in achievements or in human relations. Putnam publishes both a Sports Hero series and an American Hero series, which, like the Houghton Mifflin North Star series, contain lives of heroes in American history. The Horizon Caravel Books and the American Heritage Junior Library were both distinguished for their profuse and beautiful illustrations as well as for their accuracy.

Collective Biographies

Because of the brevity of treatment of each subject in collective biographies, they will not be discussed singly in this chapter. However, many are included in the bibliography, since this form of the genre serves two purposes admirably. The collective biography is an excellent choice for the child whose span of attention is limited, and for the reader who is particularly interested in the career, race, sex, period, or country that is the common denominator for the collection. This is an especially popular form for sports biographies—or biographical sketches—but it is also used widely to catch the interest of those children who are infatuated, say, with ballet or medicine (*anything* about ballet or medicine) or with women who have broken into new professional fields or with African-American scientists. Not that col-

[3]Marchette Chute, "Getting at the Truth," *Saturday Review*, September 19, 1953.

lective biographies are catchalls: Such books as Isaac Asimov's *Breakthroughs in Science* or Russell Freedman's *Indian Chiefs* are exciting books and make a distinctive contribution to children's literature.

The following discussions of biographies are grouped under three main divisions: Books for Younger Children, Books for the Middle Group, and Books for Older Children. Within each of these main groups, the discussions are arranged according to the birth date of the subjects of the biographies, so that there is a chronological progression within each section.

The main emphasis throughout is on the authors who are outstanding biographers. However, most of the author-title subsections not only highlight one biography of the author and give some indication of the range of his or her work, but also mention parallel biographies of the principal subject by other authors.

From *Indian Chiefs* by Russell Freedman.

Books for Younger Children

Young children do not have the sense of time necessary to appreciate biography as history. Nor do they have the ability to empathize that makes biography a source of heroes and heroines for older readers. But young children do enjoy a good story and those biographies designed to be read aloud serve that purpose. Young children are also exposed to much more information these days and biographies for them familiarize them with the people behind the names they hear in their everyday lives, such as Washington, Lincoln, and Columbus, who have holidays named after them; and people who have airports, schools, and highways named after them, such as Martin Luther King, Jr., John Kennedy, and others.

There have been some good biographies for young children in the past; they are still valuable, especially for reading aloud. What is flourishing now is the simply written life story or partial biography for the beginning independent reader. The best of this kind are just as accurate as books for older readers, but the person's life is often seen from a child's viewpoint—as in Ferdinand Monjo's *The One Bad Thing About Father*, which gives a son's-eye view of Theodore Roosevelt. For the young child whose time sense cannot fully encompass the past, this is one good way to give a biography immediacy and reality.

Alice Dalgliesh
The Columbus Story

Although the text of the picture biography *The Columbus Story* is less than thirty pages long, it is vividly alive and re-creates with simple dignity, in a direct writing style, the boyhood of Columbus and the struggles he had in getting support for his first successful voyage. The book carries Columbus through that journey, with none of the tragedy of the later years, and can be read aloud to children as young as five or six. Some second-graders and most third-graders can read it for themselves. Leo Politi's brilliantly colored illustrations complement the dignified tone of the story.

From *The One Bad Thing About Father* by F.N. Monjo,
illustrated by Rocco Negri.

With Dalgliesh's gift for making the past
come alive for children (see Chapter 11), it is
logical that she should also succeed in writing
enjoyable biographies for young children. In
her picture biography for readers in the middle
grades, *Ride on the Wind*, she describes the
dramatic solo flight of Charles Lindbergh
across the ocean in "The Spirit of St. Louis."

Other authors have written notable biographies about Christopher Columbus for younger
readers. An appendix in Ann McGovern's *The
Story of Christopher Columbus* gives information
about the way facts were obtained from source
materials. In *Where Do You Think You're Going,
Christopher Columbus?* Jean Fritz supplies her
extensive notes at the conclusion.

Patricia Miles Martin
Pocahontas

Patricia Miles Martin begins her story of *Pocahontas* when the native-American girl is eleven
years old and sees an English ship arrive. She
learns English, becomes friendly with the
Jamestown colonists, marries John Rolfe when
she is grown, and dies in England, homesick
and ready to return to America. Written for
beginning independent readers, the book is
hampered stylistically by the demands of a
limited vocabulary, but it is not dull and not
unduly fictionalized. The story of Pocahontas
has all the requisites of romantic drama, although there is some question about whether
the familiar scene in which she saves the life of
John Smith did occur, since Smith did not
include it in the first edition of his own book.

Jan Wahl's *Pocahontas in London* focuses on
the native-American girl's experiences in Lon-

From *The Double Life of Pocahontas* by Jean Fritz,
illustrated by Ed Young.

don. However, the writing is stiff and the book notable only for the brilliant color and striking composition of John Alcorn's illustrations. A good choice for reading aloud to young children is *Pocahontas* by Ingri and Edgar Parin d'Aulaire, with its direct approach, large and colorful pictures, and emphasis on action. *The Double Life of Pocahontas* by Jean Fritz, for the middle grades and also appropriate for reading aloud to younger children, is unusual in the amount of background information given about the Jamestown colony.

Daniel Boone is a good example of the many other biographies that Patricia Martin has written for young readers, most of them about famous persons in America's history. *Daniel Boone* tends to be somewhat over-simplified in style, with short sentences and large print, but it gives the major facts about Boone's life at a level comprehensible to the beginning reader. These books are useful but not outstanding, giving young children information rather than an understanding of the subject's role in history.

Clyde Robert Bulla
Squanto, Friend of the Pilgrims

Children are usually enthralled by the amazing story of Squanto's life. He was taken to England in 1605 and lived there for eight years. Then he returned to this country with John Smith only to be captured and sold to Spain by slave hunters. In Spain he was rescued by the friars and returned once more to his native land. The story is beautifully told by Clyde Bulla, who has a gift for writing easy-to-read books that are never commonplace. His historical tales have a pleasant lilt and swing and substantial content. *Squanto* was published in 1954 with the subtitle *Friend of the White Men*, and in 1969 the title was changed to *Squanto, Friend of the Pilgrims*. The book has the same virtues as Bulla's historical fiction, the genre used in *John Billington, Friend of Squanto*. The other biographies of Squanto written for this age group appear dull and stilted when compared to Bulla's story.

Bulla's *Pocahontas and the Strangers* is written for eight- to ten-year-olds, but the suspense of the story and the simplicity of style make it appropriate for reading aloud to younger children, especially if read in installments. Other good biographies by Bulla for the beginning independent reader are *Song of St. Francis* and *Washington's Birthday*.

Aliki Brandenburg
A Weed Is a Flower

Aliki Brandenburg, who writes as "Aliki," illustrates her own books. In *A Weed Is a Flower*, a biography of George Washington Carver, her pictures show a realistic range of skin tones. The story of the great African-American naturalist is told in a dry, quiet style and a simple vocabulary. The title is based on a comment attributed to Dr. Carver: "A weed is a flower growing in the wrong place." Born of slave parents, Carver worked his way through school, leaving the college where he had been a student and then a faculty member to join the staff of Tuskegee Institute at the invitation of Booker T. Washington. His distinguished career in agricultural research brought him many honors, and he is probably, along with Martin Luther King, Jr., the most popular African American of note as a subject of biographies for children. Another biography for this group is *George Washington Carver* by Samuel and Beryl Epstein, a stolid and factual account.

Aliki also has written and illustrated other attractive picture biographies: *The Story of Johnny Appleseed* and *The Story of William Penn*.

Ingri and Edgar Parin d'Aulaire
Abraham Lincoln

The picture-book biographies of Ingri and Edgar Parin d'Aulaire are a real contribution to young children. They are large books, copiously illustrated with full-page lithographs in deep, glowing colors on alternate pages, and with black-and-white and innumerable small pictures in between. These small pictures fulfill a definite purpose in each book, sometimes adding droll touches to the interpretation of the hero's character, sometimes showing something of his work or progress. In *Benjamin Franklin*, for instance, the decorative borders throughout the book carry a series of Franklin's wise sayings. These are fun for children to discover and read, and they make *Poor Richard's Almanac* more real. Throughout the series, the illustrations are somewhat stylized and occasionally stiff. But this is a minor criticism of pictures that are usually alive with action and full of humor.

Study the details of the pictures in *Abraham Lincoln*. No need to talk about the doorless dwellings—in one picture a horse has stuck his head into the single room of the cabin and seems to be taking a neighborly interest in the new baby. Notice the little boys' single galluses upon which hang all the responsibility for holding up their scanty pants. No need to say that Mary Todd was somewhat domineering, nor that she had a few problems to contend with in Abe. That picture of the wildly disordered parlor, with Abe on the floor in stocking feet, and with Mary, arms akimbo, reflected in the elegant mirror, is a demonstration of their fundamental unlikeness. The book is full of the sort of sly humor that characterized Abe.

In the early d'Aulaire books, the texts were

From *Abraham Lincoln*, written and illustrated by Ingri and Edgar Parin d'Aulaire.

simple and the life stories were incomplete. But with *Benjamin Franklin*, *Pocahontas*, *Buffalo Bill*, and *Columbus*, the content grew richer, with more details. In the case of *Columbus*, the man's whole life is related, even those tragic last voyages.

A weakness in the d'Aulaires' writing is their propensity for using "never" and "always." They tell children in their *George Washington* that "he learned to be good and honest and never tell a lie." After recounting a delightful incident in which young Ben Franklin spent too much money for a whistle, they say "That was the only time Benjamin ever spent a penny unwisely." Children are apt to take these overstatements of virtue too seriously and should remember the more human aspects of the people being written about.

Of the many biographies of Abraham Lincoln, one of the best is Clyde Bulla's *Lincoln's Birthday*. Wilma Hays's *Abe Lincoln's Birthday*, despite the similar title, is fiction, based on the events of Lincoln's twelfth birthday. Clara Ingram Judson's *Abraham Lincoln* has a rather flat style, but is useful because it is easy to read, factually accurate, and balanced in coverage; her other Lincoln biography is for older readers.

Tobi Tobias
Maria Tallchief

Tobi Tobias has had a lifetime interest in the dance and she writes of Maria Tallchief, world renowned ballerina, with clarity and admiration. She conveys to young readers the dedication and hard work that go into making a person a superstar. Tobias handles tastefully Tallchief's divorce from choreographer George Balanchine and, without belaboring the point, informs readers that family life is very difficult to combine with a ballet career.

Another dance biography by Tobias is *Arthur Mitchell*, a book about the man whose determination to dance overcame the bias against African-American ballet dancers. In *Marian Anderson*, Tobias recounts the story of the woman who made musical history with one of the great voices of the twentieth century. Tobias's interest in the arts goes beyond music and dance and is reflected in her biography *Isamu Noguchi: The Life of a Sculptor*.

Other Books for Younger Children

There have been increasing numbers of very simply written biographies to satisfy the curiosity of children in the primary grades. While the majority of them are about famous men and women in American history, there are also numerous biographies of famous sports figures, people in the news, and little known people who have careers of interest to children.

Maggi Scarf's *Meet Benjamin Franklin* touches on the most familiar events and achievements in Franklin's life. In *The Story of Ben Franklin*, Eve Merriam gives a brief but balanced treatment of Franklin as a family man. Ormonde De Kay's *Meet Andrew Jackson* is one of the better books in the Random House Step-Up Series. Many of the books in Chapter 11 that deal with important figures, such as those by Jean Fritz, have biographical interest. A compelling story of human endeavor is Barbara Mitchell's *Shoes for Everyone: A Story About Jan Matzeliger*.

Martin Luther King, Jr., is a favorite subject, and a favorite book with young readers is Margaret B. Young's *The Picture Life of Martin Luther King, Jr.* Other figures in the news who have been written about in an easy-to-read style include *Gordon Parks* by Midge Turk, the story of a versatile and creative African-American photographer and writer; Ruth Franchere's *Cesar Chavez*, a good picture of the plight of the migrant worker and of the Chicano labor leader; and *Rosa Parks* by Eloise Greenfield, the story of the woman who precipitated the Montgomery bus strike by refusing to move to the back of the bus.

Marshall and Sue Burchard have developed a satisfactory style and format for their sports hero biographies and have offered young readers the opportunity to read about hockey star Wayne Gretzky, tennis great Billie Jean King, baseball's Henry Aaron, and football's Terry Bradshaw. Like all biographies of living athletes, such books are, alas, soon outdated.

While young children may not be familiar with the writings of Langston Hughes and James Weldon Johnson, they can, nevertheless, find much to interest them in Alice Walker's *Langston Hughes, American Poet* and Ophelia

From *Shoes for Everyone: A Story About Jan Matzeliger* by Barbara Mitchell, illustrated by Hetty Mitchell.

Egypt's *James Weldon Johnson*, both of which reflect the consistently high quality of the Crowell Biography Series. This series is one of the most balanced, containing biographies of women, African Americans, native Americans, and other minorities; as well as biographies about such people as *Eleanor Roosevelt* by Jane Goodsell and *The Ringling Brothers* by Molly Cone, which tells of a circus-smitten family who achieved the dream of so many children. Two unusual subjects for picture-book biographies were chosen and successfully presented by Diane Stanley in *Peter the Great* and, with Peter Vennema, in *Shaka: King of the Zulus*.

Books for the Middle Group

Children in the middle grades want to know everything there is to know about their special heroes and heroines, the doers—from explor-

From *Peter the Great*, written and illustrated by Diane Stanley.

ers and scouts of the Old West to today's astronauts and baseball stars. Children are not usually ready for career stories unless they are stories of action, nor are they overly concerned with character development. Least of all are most children able to appreciate an account of the pursuit of an abstract idea. Penn, with his deep concern for Quakerism and social ideals, is a hero for older children, as is Jefferson, who was so predominantly a man of ideas.

However, through their reading of fairy tales and realistic fiction, children arrive gradually at some broad standards of right and wrong. They may not understand self-abnegation or altruism, but they know all about fair play, kindness, bravery, and justice. These actions they respect, and they admire the heroes and heroines who embody these virtues.

The increasing awareness on the part of authors and editors that young readers like their biographies to be tales of action and achievement rather than stories of the child-hood pranks of a great man or woman, straightforward and accurate rather than adulatory, has brought a decided improvement in most of the books for this age group.

Aileen Fisher
Jeanne d'Arc

Aileen Fisher's *Jeanne d'Arc* is beautifully illustrated with Ati Forberg's quiet, reverent pictures. The story begins with Jeanne at the age of eleven, listening to her father's angry complaints about the English invaders and to his expressed hope that the Dauphin somehow could ascend the throne left vacant by his father's death. When first Jeanne sees a dazzling light and hears a voice tell her that she will be guided by the saints, she is happy and trustful but not, in her piety, surprised. The faith she has in her power to defeat the English and to see the Dauphin crowned, and the tragedy of her imprisonment and death are described with grave simplicity. Aileen Fisher writes in a direct and unembellished prose appropriate to Jeanne's modesty and conviction and she successfully portrays her as a heroine by describing her acts rather than by commenting on them.

Fisher, in collaboration with Olive Rabe, has also written *We Alcotts* for older readers. The biography is told by Mrs. Alcott—in language delightfully stately and appropriate for the period—and focuses on the family's participation in the intellectual ferment of their circle, the abolitionist movement, and new educational theories.

In *Joan of Arc: Her Life as Told by Winston Churchill*, reprinted from Churchill's *A History of the English-Speaking Peoples*, comments by the author such as these are frequent: "Unconquerable courage, infinite compassion, the virtue of the simple, the wisdom of the just, shone forth in her." For older readers, Albert Paine's *The Girl in White Armor* (abridged from an earlier version) is well written, historically accurate and detailed, and broad in scope.

Ronald Syme
Columbus, Finder of the New World

Ronald Syme's series of biographies of explorers began as easy-to-read books for the middle and upper grades—Columbus, Cortes, Champlain, Balboa, Magellan, and others—and broadened to include more detailed biographies of La Salle, John Smith, and Henry Hudson. *Columbus, Finder of the New World* is typical of the style and approach of all the books. Christopher Columbus is a difficult character to present in a full biography, since the drama of his life rises grandly to the successful conclusion of his first voyage. After that, failure takes over. It is greatly to Syme's credit that he presents the gloom as well as the glory. In this brief, well-written biography, the Admiral of the Ocean Sea goes down to his death apparently defeated, but his name and his achievements live after him.

In addition to his books about explorers, Syme has written several biographies of heroes of Latin American countries. For older children, *Bolivar the Liberator* is a good example of the dramatic pattern of events, set off by a restrained style, that makes Ronald Syme's books as exciting as they are informative. Simon Bolivar became president of the Republic of Great Colombia, which included Venezuela, Colombia, Peru, Ecuador, and Bolivia. Although his fortune and his power were lost, and he died in poverty and isolation, Bolivar's reputation as the most important political figure in South American history has grown with the passing of time. As always, Syme is candid in appraisal and lucid in explaining the complexities of political upheaval. These are characteristics also of *Garibaldi: The Man Who Made a Nation*; of *Toussaint: The Black Liberator*; and of *Zapata, Mexican Rebel*, the latter for readers of nine to twelve, simply written, not as smooth in style as the books for older readers but just as objective.

Readers of nine to twelve may enjoy Armstrong Sperry's *Voyages of Christopher Columbus*. For another slant on Columbus, children can read Nina Brown Baker's *Amerigo Vespucci*, which, in discussing why America was named for Amerigo rather than for Columbus and in describing the relationship between the two explorers, gives a picture of Columbus that helps explain his downfall.

Harold W. Felton
Mumbet: The Story of Elizabeth Freeman

In our era of consciousness of the exclusion, for many years, of the African-American contributors to American history, such heroes as Benjamin Banneker and Matthew Henson and such heroines as Sojourner Truth and Mary McLeod Bethune have been described many times. Elizabeth Freeman, though, is one heroine whose true story, dramatic and courageous, is seldom heard. Harold Felton's *Mumbet* tells how Elizabeth had become "Mumbet" to the Ashleys, the Massachusetts family whose slave she was. When Elizabeth heard of the new Massachusetts constitution which stated that all men were created equal, she called on a lawyer who had visited the Ashley home. He argued her case and in 1781 the black slave won her freedom in the courts of Massachusetts. Uneducated but intelligent, firm in her resolve, Elizabeth Freeman is a fascinating heroine, her

From *Jeanne d'Arc* by Aileen Fisher, illustrated by Ati Forberg.

triumph given suspense by the obstacles put in her way by the Ashleys, and her later years graced by the indomitable way in which she drove Shays' raiders from the lawyer's home.

Adroitly fictionalized, *Mumbet* is written in a vigorous style, the lengthy introduction making evident the research (with many sources quoted) that provided a firm base for the biography. Felton's careful balance between fact and fiction is again evident in his biography of the woman who donned men's clothing to serve in Washington's army, *Deborah Sampson: Soldier of the Revolution*.

Harold Felton's other books are primarily about the heroes of America's tall tales or about such African-American heroes of the West as *Jim Beckwourth* and *Edward Rose*, all action-filled stories.

Genevieve Foster
The *An Initial Biography* Series

The books in this series of biographies by Genevieve Foster are brief and add little to our knowledge of the American heroes they describe, but they are written in restrained literary style and provide children with a summary of each person's childhood, youthful struggles, and mature contributions. *George Washington* has the same accuracy that distinguishes Foster's *George Washington's World*, but is more simplified, yet not patronizing. Many of the legendary exploits are omitted. In *Abraham Lincoln*, the legends are included and explained—especially the Ann Rutledge affair. Her *Theodore Roosevelt* makes lively reading as she captures the exuberance of the man.

In *The World of William Penn*, Foster looks at what happened during Penn's lifetime in England, the Continent, the Far East, and colonial America. While not a full biography, it is engrossing reading.

Doris Faber
I Will Be Heard: The Life of William Lloyd Garrison

The subject of Doris Faber's *I Will Be Heard: The Life of William Lloyd Garrison* is not an idealized figure: opinionated, irascible, with a high estimate of his own ability, he was a man whose greatest virtues were a belief in the equality of man and an unwillingness to compromise in any way in the pursuit of that belief. It was a meeting with Benjamin Lundy, whose experiences in the South had caused him to devote his life to speaking against slavery, that started Garrison on the long fight for abolition of that evil. Reviled for many years for the stridency of his views, Garrison did not catch up with the times—the times caught up with him. By the time the Civil War was over, he—who had been threatened, mobbed, and jailed—was lauded and cheered, welcomed by the President, and carried through the streets of Charleston by freed slaves. Through Garrison's biography, the whole pattern of the fight against slavery can be seen. Describing her sources in an afterword, Faber notes that much of the material about abolition is not readily available but was gathered from the files of contemporary journals and from the four-volume biography published by Garrison's sons. Older readers may prefer Jules Archer's *Angry Abolitionist: William Lloyd Garrison*.

Other Faber biographies for the middle group include *Horace Greeley: The People's Editor* and *Franklin D. Roosevelt*. For older children, Faber has written *Oh, Lizzie: The Life of Elizabeth Cady Stanton*, the famous nineteenth-century feminist.

Clara Ingram Judson
Abraham Lincoln, Friend of the People

Clara Ingram Judson began writing biography in 1939. In 1950, when her *Abraham Lincoln, Friend of the People* appeared, it was evident that this writer, competent in so many fields, had attained new stature as a biographer. It was also evident that Judson's research into source materials was to yield a fresh slant on the man. Her careful studies convinced her, for example, that Abe's childhood was no more "poverty stricken" than that of most of the neighbors. She also brought out the warm family love and loyalty of the Lincoln clan, and Abe himself emerges as a real person. The contrast between this book and Judson's Lincoln biography for younger readers shows how much better a stylist she was when she wrote for older readers. Many think *Abraham Lincoln, Friend of the People* is the finest book in Judson's biography series. Certainly it can take its place with the Sandburg and Daugherty Lincolns. The illustrations are unique also. In addition to the pen-and-ink drawings, there are colored photographs of the Lincoln dioramas from the Chicago Historical Society. These pictures are eye-catching and vivid.

Clearly, Judson believed the only justification for new biographies of such well-known national figures as George Washington, Thomas Jefferson, Andrew Jackson, and Theodore Roosevelt is that they throw fresh light on, and give children new facts or a new point of view about, the man. Before she wrote a biography, she read the letters, journals, or papers of her hero, searched contemporary magazines and newspapers, and studied the life of the times. As a result, she rescued Washington from the stereotypes that had nearly obliterated him. She even made Jefferson, the man of ideas, intelligible to children. Judson's writing is sometimes stilted, but somehow her deep love of family, her respect for all kinds of people, and her sense of the struggles through which these men came to greatness communicate themselves to children.

Other Books for the Middle Group

Many biographies for the middle grades seem to have been published with more thought for their usefulness as supplementary curricular material than for their literary merit, but they should be used for that purpose and for giving information only if better books are not available. Fortunately, there are now so many good biographies that a reader who enjoys the genre and is not just seeking information about a particular individual has a wide choice.

Famous women, known for their talents and for the strength of their convictions, have been the subject of biographies for children in the middle grades. *Nothing Is Impossible: The Story of Beatrix Potter* by Dorothy Aldis is simply written and uses extracts from Potter's letters and journal to give added color and establish atmosphere. Another sensible biography is Elizabeth Buchan's *Beatrix Potter.* Margaret Davidson's *The Story of Eleanor Roosevelt* is a good biography of that indomitable woman for this age group. Arnold Dobrin tells the story of another strong woman in *A Life for Israel: The Story of Golda Meir*; and in *Belva Lockwood Wins*

From *Bill Peet: An Autobiography*, written and illustrated by Bill Peet.

Her Case, Drollene Brown describes the first woman who earned the right to practice law before the Supreme Court.

Television, despite its encroachment on reading time, has brought a wider acquaintance with public figures and, for most children, an increased awareness of the fact that there are interesting people behind the public images. Larry Kettelkamp, for example, writes with admiration but not effusiveness in *Bill Cosby, Family Funny Man*, and a major figure of early film days, Lillian Gish, describes her life as a child and as an adult star in *An Actor's Life for Me*. Gloria Kamen ties personal background with themes that appear in Rudyard Kipling's work in *Kipling: Storyteller of East and West*; a lively autobiography of a popular contemporary illustrator includes Bill Peet's years at the Disney Studios in *Bill Peet: An Autobiography*. Subjects range from limelight personalities like *Princess Diana* in a candid and well-balanced biography by Mary Virginia Fox, or the Russian leader objectively depicted in *The Picture Life of Mikhail Gorbachev* by Janet Caulkins, to such giants of the past as Henry David Thoreau, which clarifies for the middle-grades reader the thoughts of a philosopher, in Robert Burleigh's *A Man Named Thoreau*. In an especially successful use of paper engineering combined with handsome collage, Alice and Martin Provensen integrate illustration with a lively text to describe the amazing diversity of da Vinci in *Leonardo da Vinci: The Artist, Inventor, Scientist, in Three-Dimensional Movable Pictures*.

Jean Fritz brings skills and spirit to her biographies; some of the most enjoyable for this age group are *Where Was Patrick Henry on the 29th of May?; Why Don't You Get a Horse, Sam Adams?;* and *What's the Big Idea, Ben Franklin?* Ferdinand Monjo added to Lincolniana in *Me and Willie and Pa*, the story of the Lincoln years in the White House as told by Tad. Aliki, in *The King's Day: Louis XIV of France*, vividly depicts the Sun King and his court. An excellent biography of an explorer is Jean Latham's *Far Voyager: The Story of Captain Cook*; a new kind of explorer is described in *Space Challenger: The Story of Guion Bluford* by James Haskins and Kathleen Benson.

Arnold Adoff's *Malcolm X* is very simply written; *The Life of Malcolm X* by Richard Curtis, for the more mature reader, is candid and comprehensive; and *The Picture Life of Malcolm X* by James Haskins is simply written and straightforward.

With as many biographies as are published today, it is impossible to mention them all. Additional titles are listed in the chapter bibliography, and more are available through sources cited in Appendices A and B, "Adult References" and "Book Selection Aids."

Books for Older Children

Children in the middle grades usually demand action, but adolescent readers are also interested in men and women of ideas and ideals. While they enjoy a biography that is dramatic and well told, they may also read biographies for their historical background, their association with causes and movements, or their association with a field in which the reader has a

So glorious was Louis that he was called the "Sun King," and the sun became his symbol.

From *The King's Day: Louis XIV of France*, written and illustrated by Aliki.

special interest. One reader may consume avidly any biography with a Civil War background; another, any book about a musician; others, books about people whose lives as dancers, chemists, doctors, or teachers satisfy an orientation toward the profession.

Throughout this chapter, parallel biographies have been mentioned, and they exist in profusion for older readers. Adults working with children will want to know such books so that they may help children explore various presentations. Comparing Catherine Owens Peare's *Mahatma Gandhi: Father of Nonviolence* and Olivia Coolidge's *Gandhi*, the reader can see that Peare's book with its fictionalized, rather informal narrative style is easier to read and more dramatic, but that Coolidge's is more detailed, dignified, and analytical. Jeanette Eaton's *Gandhi: Fighter Without a Sword* is notable for the perceptive picture it gives of Gandhi as a man and a spiritual leader. Comparing biographies gives children an opportunity to see how emphasis, style, and viewpoint, the amount of fictionalization or of documentation, and the amount of historical detail can shape a book.

Sidney Rosen
Galileo and the Magic Numbers

From the moment Master Jacopo Borghini introduced the young Galileo to the Pythagorean magic numbers, Galileo's life as a physicist and astronomer was determined. Although money was a problem, Galileo acquired an education and, eventually, a teaching position. His annoying habit of asking "Why?" and "How do you know?" made him unpopular with his teachers and colleagues as well as with Roman Catholic authorities. In *Galileo and the Magic Numbers*, Rosen shows clearly the heroism of the man who defied the theological beliefs of his time to make important contributions to human knowledge.

Wizard of the Dome is an appealing biography for the general reader, since Rosen portrays Buckminster Fuller as a lively, tenacious inventor whose patterns of success and failure as a designer-inventor have a cliff-hanger appeal; to the scientifically oriented girl or boy, it has the added attraction of presenting with unusual

Viewpoint

Perhaps one of the reasons we all find stories so satisfying is that stories, both invented and true ones, are like a thin layer torn from part of the globe—rounded, incomplete circles evolving into spirals (the mystic, magic symbol common to ancient cultures) and always open-ended. For how can you wrap up life or even a single life and say, *"This is it"*? Trying to write authentic history or an authentic biography requires not only research but a coming to terms with that open end. I often wish I could begin biographies the way Russians begin their fairy stories, "There once was and there was not." There once was a very brave man named Benedict Arnold, who was also not very brave at all. There once was a man named Christopher Columbus, who was right when everyone else was wrong and wrong when everyone else was right. And on it would go. Recently I heard a group of biographers, writers of adult books, speak at a symposium. All agreed that they had to *like* the characters they wrote about. I was surprised. *Like* seems a mild word to suggest the struggle one goes through with one's subject: the strengths one discovers which can twist into weaknesses; the motives—above ground and underground; indeed, the human predicament stamped into every childhood, clinging in some shape or other throughout life. I don't have to *like* the people I write about, but I do need to understand them. And however we end up—my subject and I—I expect to share with my readers a compassion that springs from looking at the world through someone else's eyes.

Jean Fritz, "The Once Was," *The Horn Book Magazine*, July/August 1986, pp. 432–433.

clarity the theories for which Fuller became famous, especially the application of geodesic structure and his now-famous geodesic dome construction. The book makes clear the importance and the innovatory nature of his work. In

Doctor Paracelsus, Rosen tells the story of Theophrastus Bombastus von Hohenheim, a Swiss doctor who rebelled against superstitions of medical belief and practices of the early sixteenth century.

Elizabeth Yates
Amos Fortune, Free Man

Born an African prince, sold in Boston, well treated by a series of masters, Amos Fortune learned the tanner's trade and eventually bought his freedom. After that, this humble, mighty soul devoted everything he earned to buying freedom for other slaves. Freedom and education were the greatest things in his life. He died a respected member of the little New Hampshire town of Jaffrey, where he had lived so long. When Elizabeth Yates saw the tombstone of Amos, she tells us, she knew she must write his biography. *Amos Fortune, Free Man* (1951 Newbery Medal winner) is written with warmth and compassion. Since most books about slavery deal with the South, it is important to have this picture of slaverunning and sales in the North. The details are grim, but Amos Fortune carried suffering lightly because his eyes were on the freedom of the future. It is this characteristic of Fortune's, so clearly depicted by Yates, that causes some modern critics to disparage the book. They disapprove of the quiet way Amos Fortune bore his enslavement with courage and dignity, forgetting the circumstances under which he achieved his own personal integrity and offered the chance to live free to other African Americans.

In *Prudence Crandall: Woman of Courage*, Yates writes of the Quaker schoolmistress who engendered bitter hostility in 1833 when she opened a school for black girls in a Connecticut town.

James Daugherty
Poor Richard

For superior readers with mature interests, this book has unusual distinction. It covers Franklin's whole life and activities, plus his amazing talent for friendship among people of all varieties and ages. The chapter "An American in Paris" opens in this way:

One man alone captured a city. An American had taken Paris single-handed.

All the king's horses and all the king's men could not do what the friendly seventy-year-old journeyman printer was doing in spite of himself. He was surprised and pleased to find himself a hero. He was ready to act the part, knowing all that it might mean for America.[4]

The chapter includes the scandalized Abigail Adams's report of a dinner where Mme. Helvétius sat with one arm around Franklin's shoulder and the other on the chair of Abigail's own John. "After dinner," wrote the outraged Mrs. Adams, "she threw herself on a settee where she showed more than her feet." Here, obviously, is a somewhat mature interpretation of the times, written and illustrated with Daugherty's usual gusto and swing.

Daugherty's *Abraham Lincoln* covers Lincoln's whole life. This book avoids the usual anecdotes found in most of the other juveniles, and with remarkable clarity and power tells the story of Lincoln in relation to the stormy war years. A reviewer summarizing Daugherty's contribution in his three biographies wrote:

"Daniel Boone," "Poor Richard," and now "Abraham Lincoln"—are linked together in unity of spirit, an appreciation, in the true sense, of the restless, surging, visionary America which, with all its faults, has borne Titans.[5]

There is something in the spirit animating Daugherty's pen and brush that seems particularly adapted to the interpretation of titans. His *Abraham Lincoln* illustrations show all the rowdy vigor of his earlier drawings, but predominant in the book is the brooding melancholy of the strangest and perhaps loneliest of our great presidents. *Abraham Lincoln* is the most serious of Daugherty's three biographies, as we should expect, and is a magnificently clear if tragic picture of this great man.

Daugherty's *Daniel Boone*, for which he won the Newbery Medal, is a spirited biography that has been attacked for bigotry in recent years by some critics. It is true that this book reflects the

[4]James Daugherty, *Poor Richard*, p. 125.
[5]Ellen Lewis Buell, "The Story of Honest Abe," a review of Daugherty's *Abraham Lincoln* in *the New York Times Book Review*, December 19, 1943.

"Manifest Destiny" theory of the westward movement in American history. It is true that both native Americans and African Americans are treated in an offhand manner by Daugherty. But that is how Boone would have perceived them, and to criticize Daugherty for not making Boone a twentieth-century liberal is overstepping the boundaries of critical analysis. Another good Boone biography is Laurie Lawlor's *Daniel Boone*, which is objective, candid, and carefully researched.

Jeanette Eaton
Leader by Destiny

Washington is undoubtedly one of the most difficult figures to bring alive for children, both because he has been belittled by the trivial anecdotes told about him and because he has the subtle, intangible qualities of a highly civilized human being. Self-discipline and restraint are not easy for children to understand or to appreciate, and for this reason in particular Washington is a better character for adolescents than for children.

The best juvenile biography of Washington, Jeanette Eaton's *Leader by Destiny* is for teenagers, but it is such an extraordinary book that adults could also profit by reading it. You catch in it, for instance, Washington's life-long regret for his inadequate education. You also find in this book Washington's single indiscretion, in his relations to his friend's wife, the beautiful Sally Fairfax. He wrote her one letter declaring his love. This letter Sally kept secret until the day of her death, and it remained secret for a hundred years after. In this book you see Washington's affectionate relations with his wife's children, and you see Martha herself as a charming and devoted wife to Washington, who came to appreciate her more and more. This book will help young people and adults know Washington as a very human, often bewildered man with a remarkable gift for inspiring confidence in others.

Jean Lee Latham
Carry On, Mr. Bowditch

Between the great leaders in the American Revolution and the sturdy frontier people of the push westward is the unique figure of Nathaniel Bowditch. Born in Salem, Massachusetts, in 1773, he never had a day's schooling after he was ten years old. Yet he became an outstanding astronomer, mathematician, and author of *The New American Practical Navigator*, published in 1802 and still a basic text of modern navigation.

In *Carry On, Mr. Bowditch*, we learn how, when Nathaniel was twelve, his father bound him out for nine years to a ship's chandler. The boy was near despair, when an old fellow told him, "Only a weakling gives up when he is becalmed! A strong man sails by ash breeze!" That is, he "sails" his boat with ash oars. So Nat sailed. His story is one of continuous toil in the chandlery by day and with books at night. Then came the end of his indenture, and a knowledgeable young man set off on the first of his five adventurous voyages. There is romance in Nat's story, and some tragic as well as some extremely humorous episodes. The climax came when Harvard, a university which he had yearned to attend, bestowed upon this unschooled but brilliant scientist an honorary degree. It is a thrilling story of New England fortitude and love of learning. Jean Latham has told it splendidly, and strong illustrations add to the distinction of this 1956 Newbery Medal book.

Elisabeth Kyle
Girl with a Pen: Charlotte Brontë

Elisabeth Kyle's *Girl with a Pen* is a story about Charlotte Brontë's life from her seventeenth year to her thirty-first. Competently fictionalized, the biography evokes vividly the bleak parsonage and the beloved moorland country, the affection among the Brontë children and the growing development of their literary interests.

Particularly engaging is the section that describes the reception at the London publishing house of Smith and Elder of a book titled *Jane Eyre* by a writer who called herself Currer Bell. The subsequent acclaim of the book is followed by Charlotte's timid report to her father that she had had a book published and his announcement to her sisters: "Girls, do you know that Charlotte has been writing a book, and it is much better than likely?"

From *Carry On, Mr. Bowditch* by
Jean Lee Latham, illustrated by
John O'Hara Cosgrave II.

The portraits of Charlotte and her sisters are candid, and the impression of their restricted horizons is so strong that the reader is always conscious of the courage it must have taken the three Brontë sisters as women—and particularly as women from a modest parsonage—to submit their manuscripts.

In her afterword, Kyle refers to this book as a story rather than a biography, but it succeeds in the task of a good biography: It reveals the character of its subject and her achievements, and in stimulating interest in its subject, this captivating biography—or story, as Kyle describes it—is exceptionally successful.

Another of Kyle's lively biographies of writers is *Great Ambitions: A Story of the Early Years of Charles Dickens*, covering in great detail Dickens's life between the ages of twelve and twenty-seven.

James Playsted Wood
Spunkwater, Spunkwater! A Life of Mark Twain

"The United States has always paid its entertainers extravagantly," says James Wood in *Spunkwater, Spunkwater!* "Whatever his other excellences, and he had many—and whatever deep, dark mystique ingenious critics have read into his life and work—Mark Twain was first and last an entertainer. It was his celebrity as an entertainer that led to his being enthroned as the American sage. He was the articulate and even voluble symbol of the kind of practical wisdom Americans most admired. He was about as tragic as anyone else, applauded and honored everywhere he went, who was having a wonderful time. . . ." Such candid comment is typical of the fresh and thoughtful approach of James Wood, whose sophisticated style pays readers the compliment of assuming that they will appreciate the nuance of humor and oblique reference.

Mark Twain's life as river pilot, newspaperman, author, lecturer, caustic world traveler, and deeply devoted husband and father is familiar material, included in most of the biographies of Twain. Wood gives an added dimension by his perceptively analytical discussion of Twain's volatile and ebullient personality and by his criticism of Twain's writing. A list of important dates and a bibliography add to the book's general usefulness, and some delightful photographs add to its appeal.

The mature wit and percipience of Wood's analysis of Twain are also evident in his other biographies of writers. In *The Lantern Bearer: A Life of Robert Louis Stevenson*, he is candid in appraisal of Stevenson as a romantic, often illogical man and a superb craftsman. Wood's

The Admirable Cotton Mather is particularly interesting because he disputes Mather's reputation as vindictive and bigoted.

Polly Longsworth
I, Charlotte Forten, Black and Free

Polly Longsworth's *I, Charlotte Forten* is based on Ray Allen Billington's edition of Charlotte's diary, and, according to the author's acknowledgments, is "as close a re-creation of Miss Forten's life and experiences as I am capable of achieving." This explains why the biography begins with Charlotte's sixteenth year, when she came to Salem, Massachusetts, so that she might attend an unsegregated school.

Having become a teacher, she volunteered to join the Port Royal Commission that was going to the South Carolina Sea Islands to teach the neglected African Americans of Saint Helena. In 1864, she came North to attend her father's funeral, and there the biography ends, although a final chapter describes the Grimké family and her marriage to Francis Grimké, and speaks briefly of their joint years of dedication to helping the African-American cause through the hard days of postwar disillusionment.

The book is written in first person, in a heavy and rather ornate style appropriate for a nineteenth-century woman of good family. It is nevertheless an exciting book, in part because the pages read like a roll call of all the early crusaders against slavery; in part because the events are intrinsically dramatic; and in part because the picture of a frail and gentle girl so unselfishly devoted to a cause is romantic in the best sense.

Esther Douty's *Charlotte Forten: Free Black Teacher*, a biography for the middle grades, is based on the diary also, but written in third person. More fictionalized than the Longsworth book, this has a few childhood episodes and includes some quotations from the diary. Otherwise the books cover most of the same incidents and major events, though there is much more detail and more background in Longsworth's account.

Another outstanding biography by Longsworth is *Emily Dickinson: Her Letter to the World*, written in a quiet style that is a good foil for the romantic subject, and with a balanced attention to the poet's writing and to her personal life.

Dorothy Sterling
Captain of the Planter: The Story of Robert Smalls

Robert Smalls's owner was Henry McKee. Because he could earn more money for McKee by being hired out, Smalls was sent to Charleston, where he worked in a sailing loft and watched the pilots carefully until he became adept at handling boats himself. In 1861, Smalls shipped on the *Planter* as a deckhand. The ship was in the service of the Confederate Navy, and it was the resemblance between its captain and himself that gave Smalls his great idea: an idea that would bring him freedom and put the ship into Union hands. At three A.M. on the morning of May 13, 1862, the African-American crew quietly maneuvered the ship out of the harbor, stopping to take on some of their wives and children; they were given freedom to pass by the sentinel at Fort Sumter, and the crew proudly hailed a Union ship and turned the *Planter* over.

Disappointed by the fact that the Union Army included no African-American troops, Smalls visited President Lincoln and persuaded him to change his policy. Dedicated to the causes of freedom and equality, he became a public speaker and a member of Congress.

Dorothy Sterling's story of Robert Smalls, well documented by a list of sources and an extensive bibliography, is dramatic because of its subject matter: Smalls's personal achievement and the events of the years of the Civil War and the Reconstruction. What Sterling has added to the inherent drama of the *Captain of the Planter* is a powerful picture of the tragedy of the postwar years and a personal portrait of a man whose true greatness lay not in one single courageous act but in the fact that he never compromised his principles for the sake of expediency.

Other biographies by Sterling are *Freedom Train: The Story of Harriet Tubman* and *The Making of an Afro-American: Martin Robison Delaney 1812–1855*, an extensively documented account of an early exponent of African-American nationalism. While Dorothy Sterling has written stories, informational books on such diverse topics as caves and caterpillars, and series books, her strongest commitment is clearly to the cause of African-American equality. Young readers who enjoy her biographies may also want to read her study of events related to the Emancipation Proclamation in *Forever Free*, her history of the American civil rights movement in *Tear Down the Walls!* and *Speak Out in Thunder Tones* and *The Trouble They Seen*, both compilations of statements by African Americans, covering the years 1787–1877.

Shannon Garst
Crazy Horse

Toward the end of the period of westward expansion came the terrible struggles between the advancing hordes of whites and the defending native Americans. Several fine biographies of native-American leaders of this period give children the story of these events from the native-American point of view. *Crazy Horse* is one of the best of these. It begins with Crazy Horse's training as a boy, shows his bitter experiences with the bad faith and cruelties of the whites and his growing determination to stop their invasion at all costs. The end is sheer tragedy. Crazy Horse is defeated, his people scattered or herded into a reservation, and Crazy Horse, rather than submitting, fights to his death. No child who reads this moving record will ever believe the cruelties were all one-sided.

Shannon Garst also writes sympathetically of the Sioux way of life in *Sitting Bull, Champion of His People* and of Sitting Bull's tenacious and courageous fight in a losing battle against white encroachment. Garst's *Kit Carson, Trailblazer and Scout* is a lively book of frontier life, full of action and the romance of the Old West.

Shirley Graham
Booker T. Washington

Although Graham's husband, William E. B. DuBois, had major philosophical differences with Booker T. Washington, she writes objectively in *Booker T. Washington*.

Born a slave, Booker was nine when the Emancipation Proclamation brought him freedom and an opportunity to go to West Virginia, where he worked in a salt mine and a coal mine. He took the name "Washington," in fact, from the name of the salt mine and the "Taliaferro" from the name of his father. Bent on getting an education, young Washington worked doggedly to pay his way through Hampton Institute, his academic prowess earning him an appointment as principal of Tuskegee, the new normal school that became Tuskegee Institute.

Although Booker T. Washington became famous for his development of Tuskegee, for bringing George Washington Carver to the faculty, for dining with presidents, and for being the first African-American man to get an honorary degree from Harvard University, he has always stirred some controversy because of the stand he took on race relations in the famous speech often referred to as the "Atlanta Compromise." In her biography, Shirley Graham has submerged any difference in viewpoint she might have with Washington. Her story is told with an understanding of how Washington's life and experience shaped his ideas. The biography is adroitly fictionalized, many of the incidents based on Washington's autobiography *Up from Slavery*, with anecdotes and dialogue woven smoothly into the narrative. A bibliography gives sources, and a lengthy index makes textual material accessible.

Shirley Graham has also written *The Story of Phillis Wheatley*, which is well researched but more fictionalized; *Your Most Humble Servant*, the story of Benjamin Banneker; and *His Day Is Marching On*, memoirs of her husband, W. E. B. DuBois.

Mature readers will want to read Booker T. Washington's autobiography *Up from Slavery* and *The Souls of Black Folks* by W. E. B. DuBois.

Catherine Owens Peare
The Louis D. Brandeis Story

Catherine Owens Peare is never adulatory in her attitude toward the men and women whose biographies she writes, but her affection and respect for her subjects are usually clear, as they are in *The Louis D. Brandeis Story*. Coming from a close-knit Austrian-Jewish family that had migrated to Louisville, Brandeis grew up in a circle in which it was taken for granted that cultural, academic, and political interests would be shared and discussed. An ardent student, Louis Brandeis made a distinguished record at Harvard Law School.

With a passion for justice and a concern for the underprivileged, Brandeis became a respected figure in the legal hierarchy of Boston, and grew wealthy enough to espouse reform measures and to take cases without a fee to protect the public interest against the depredations of big business monoliths. In his years as an associate justice of the Supreme Court, he won distinction for his idealism, his concern for humanity, and his farseeing understanding of ethical and social implications of the issues involved in cases heard. An ample bibliography of sources is included with Peare's story of his life.

Many of Peare's biographies are concerned with public figures: *The Herbert Hoover Story* stresses Hoover's role in humanitarian projects, and *The Woodrow Wilson Story*, Wilson's idealism and his influence on world events. In *Mary McLeod Bethune*, she draws an exciting picture of the remarkably energetic African-American educator.

Iris Noble
Emmeline and Her Daughters: The Pankhurst Suffragettes

Emmeline and Her Daughters, like many of Iris Noble's other biographies, describes with enthusiastic sympathy a pioneer in a reform movement, a champion of a cause. The book's bibliography includes works by Emmeline Pankhurst and by each of her three daughters, clearly the source of many of the intimate details that give the account vitality and authenticity. The tumultuous record of the Pankhursts is seen both as a personal narrative and as the opening salvo in the long battle for equality for women.

Emmeline Pankhurst had been a demure, cultured Victorian wife and mother until her husband, who had long fought for feminine liberation, challenged her to take an active part in the struggle. He began her education as a militant participant by taking her to hear de-

bates in Parliament, helping her organize the Women's Franchise League, and encouraging her to run for a minor political office. She was forty when he died, and without his backing her role was even more difficult. It was her daughter Christabel who conceived the idea of a new organization, "*of* women *for* women, one that will lead all the women of Britain into militant action." So the Women's Social and Political Union was born, the group that was a vigorous spearhead for feminine equality. The actions taken against this dedicated army of women led them to mass demonstrations and acts of violence, but their courage in the face of brutal reprisals eventually won them public admiration, the support of much of the press, and, in 1928, at long last, full suffrage.

Iris Noble deals objectively with dramatic and important events and shows the long struggle as not only a dominating motive in the lives of the four Pankhurst women but the cause of a bitter rupture between Christabel and Sylvia Pankhurst.

Objectivity in reporting and sympathetic understanding of a crusader's ardor are also evident in Noble's *Susan B. Anthony*, the story of the persistent crusader for women's rights.

The obstacles that faced women during the nineteenth century are made clear in Patricia Clapp's biography of Elizabeth Blackwell, *Dr. Elizabeth: The Story of the First Woman Doctor*. Written in the first person, this biography is never guilty of over-dramatization.

That the fight begun by the Pankhursts and Anthony is not over can be seen in two very fine biographies of Shirley Chisholm, the first African-American woman to serve in the United States Congress. Susan Brownmiller's *Shirley Chisholm* is for slightly younger readers than James Haskins's *Fighting Shirley Chisholm*. Haskins writes here, as in all his books, with a frankness still rare in children's books, a trait also evident in his *Barbara Jordan*.

Howard Greenfeld
Gertrude Stein: A Biography

Of the several biographies of Gertrude Stein that were written for young people in honor of the hundredth anniversary of her birth, Howard Greenfeld's *Gertrude Stein* is the most sensitive in depicting her personality and the most thorough in analyzing her writing and her role in the turbulent artistic and literary circles of Paris. Greenfeld provides evidence of painstaking research with a lengthy bibliography of sources, and he uses many quotations from Stein's writing or from current articles to corroborate his statements.

The balanced treatment of personal and artistic facets that Greenfeld uses in the Stein biography is also a strong feature of his *Pablo Picasso* and *Marc Chagall*. In *F. Scott Fitzgerald*, Greenfeld describes the tragedy of Fitzgerald's life with a compassion that never lapses into sentimentality or melodrama. He achieves, in all his biographies, a polished, dignified writing style, and he succeeds in presenting knowledgeable, candid, and vivid pictures of individuals while making clear their roles in artistic or literary history.

Miriam Gurko
Restless Spirit: The Life of Edna St. Vincent Millay

Miriam Gurko's *Restless Spirit* is a mature and thoughtful biography for adolescent readers. Her sources include published and unpublished material, letters, and interviews. "Curiously, as the mass of notes grew, the more elusive the subject seemed to become," Gurko states in her foreword. And she goes on:

From this assortment of fact and characterization I have had to select those elements which appeared the most credible, and which seemed to have undergone the least alteration as a result of the passage of time or the presence of certain personal factors.

Brought up by her mother after her parents had separated, "Vincent" and her sisters had a childhood in which they early became self-reliant. Vincent wrote poetry at the age of five, and many of her childhood poems were published in *The St. Nicholas Magazine*. She had already published "Renascence" and become modestly famous when she entered Vassar at the age of twenty-one. After her graduation, Edna, who no longer used Vincent as her name, went to New York to join in the intellectual ferment of Greenwich Village life and in the activities of the newly formed Provincetown Players. After several abortive love affairs, she married Eugen Boissevin, a marriage that was ideal for a poet, since Eugen felt it his role to protect Edna and encourage her work.

The biography includes quotations from Edna St. Vincent Millay's poetry only when they are relevant to the text, and Gurko has integrated smoothly the personal material, the background of the artistic and literary circles in which Edna moved, and the discerning discussion of the poet's work and its place in modern poetry.

Other biographies by Miriam Gurko include *Clarence Darrow*, interesting both as an account of the famous Scopes trial and as a study of the nonconformist lawyer who was a defender of unpopular causes; and *The Lives and Times of Peter Cooper*, which is concerned with other figures as well as with that of the protagonist, for the inventor and industrialist Cooper was constantly involved in industrial, political, and educational movements.

Theodora Kroeber
Ishi: Last of His Tribe

At the end of the nineteenth century a small band of Yahi Indians lived in solitude and secrecy at the foot of Mount Lassen, their way of life threatened by the white settlers and seekers of gold. *Ishi* and his people knew that they could survive only if they remained hidden, their ancient villages having been destroyed by the ruthless invaders. As long as they could, the people clung to the sacred ways, the quiet and peaceful pattern of Yahi life. One by one, the others died, and Ishi was alone. "There is nothing to wait for in this empty land, nothing—I am free to go." And so he left, and took the trail to the west, lost his way, and met the saldu, the whites.

To his surprise, they did not kill him; a Stranger was brought, a museum-saldu, who spoke in the tongue of the People, and took Ishi on a train. And so Ishi came to live with the whites in peace, an adviser to the museum people on the ways and the crafts of the Yahi. One of the most striking aspects of *Ishi* is the consistency with which Theodora Kroeber maintains Ishi's viewpoint; even after he comes to live and work with the museum staff, the relationships are seen through Ishi's eyes, and the writing continues to have the beautiful cadence and dignity of Yahi. At the end:

Death came to him as he wished—with his friends in the museum-watgurwa. Majapa and the museum men released his spirit in the old Yahi way. And they saw to it that Ishi had with him those things that a Yahi hunter must take from the World of the Living, for the journey to the west.

The names used are always the Yahi names that Ishi had given.

Alfred Kroeber was Curator of the Museum of Anthropology and Ethnology at the University of California when Ishi was brought there, and his wife had the benefit of his professional knowledge as well as first-hand information from Ishi. Such familiarity permits a biographer to incorporate cultural details so that they are as intrinsic a part of a life story as they are in *Ishi*, and in Theodora Kroeber's anthropological study for adult readers, *Ishi in Two Worlds*.

Milton Meltzer
Langston Hughes

Perhaps because *Langston Hughes: A Biography* is about a colleague and friend, it has an immediacy and warmth that Meltzer's other biographies do not have. Perhaps it is that the poet himself sheds light and grace. "Within a few years of his first book," Meltzer says, "he was the poet laureate of his people." Hughes's life and work were a testament to his belief that it was a proud thing to be African American, his poetry more bittersweet than bitter.

In Topeka, Kansas, he was the only African-American child in school; he spent some time on his father's Mexican ranch; he washed dishes in a Paris cafe and worked on a Staten Island truck farm. While working as a waiter in a Washington hotel, he put three of his poems on Vachel Lindsay's table, and that night Lindsay read the poems aloud in public. He went to Spain as a reporter during the Civil War there, and he traveled in Asia and in Russia—in short, he had an exciting and colorful life.

But his travels, his involvement in causes, and his amazingly varied and prolific outpouring of magnificent prose and poetry are almost overshadowed by his passion for truth and justice. That is what Milton Meltzer has succeeded in conveying to the readers of *Langston Hughes*.

In an article on the distortions in children's history books, Milton Meltzer says:

Biography is another way to re-create the past. The life of a Tom Paine, a Benjamin Banneker, a Sojourner Truth . . . lets the reader see history from inside, from the mind and heart of an individual struggling to reshape his own time. In history books, Wendell Philips and William Lloyd Garrison are only a paragraph or a line, too often dismissed as irresponsible fanatics. Or there is a glancing reference to that other "fanatic," Thaddeus Stevens, painted darkly in the sky of Washington like some vulture hovering over the capital to pick the bones of Southern heroes ennobled in defeat.[6]

Meltzer's *Thaddeus Stevens* destroys this picture and presents a mature and thoughtful biography of the Pennsylvania lawyer whose tenure in the national Congress was marked by bitter opposition from the South, particularly because of his battle against the fugitive slave laws. Thaddeus Stevens was a champion of public education and racial equality, his efforts on behalf of African-Americans' civil rights continuing after the Civil War and through the years of Reconstruction. Meltzer's description of those years and of Stevens's leadership in the move to impeach President Andrew Johnson is direct and vigorous, one of the most valuable aspects of fine biography that does, indeed, see history from the viewpoint of an individual struggling to reshape his own time.

Tongue of Flame: The Life of Lydia Maria Child and *A Light in the Dark: The Life of Samuel Gridley Howe* are, like the Stevens biography, imbued with enthusiasm for the causes to which the subjects were dedicated, yet they are not eulogistic in tone. Lydia Child founded the first

[6]Milton Meltzer, "The Fractured Image," *Library Journal*, Oct. 15, 1968, p. 3923.

Viewpoint

When you write history, it is people you try to place in the real world, people who love and hate, work and play, invent fantasies and tell lies. When you write biography, you present history through the prism of a single life, a life that is, of course, connected to other lives. Is that life worth writing about? *Every* life is worth recording, worth getting down truthfully. And isn't the truth about human character desirable, no matter that the character is? The biographer investigates that life, eager to find and tell the truth about it, no matter what the outcome of his search. What could be more fascinating, and more useful, than to explain a human life in all its strength and frailty? Even when we are reading about a life long gone, a life lived a hundred, five hundred, a thousand years ago. For the life we live today is enlarged and enriched by what we learn about past lives.

Writing biography, like writing history, is taking part in the creation of the collective memory. All too often, the historian Peter Gay points out, the writer gives in to the demands of his culture by remembering events that did not happen, and in forgetting events that did. The culture—or its dominant powers—want a past that they can use. But there are times when society calls not for reassuring tales but the harsh facts about the past. We should not forget that for many decades following the defeat of Reconstruction, historians created a damning indictment of that brief time when blacks and whites tried to build freedom, equality and democracy in the postwar south just as other historians before them created a myth about the beneficence of slavery. Memory, Peter Gay warns us, can be "the supple minister of self-interest."

Such historians were "creative" but in the harmful sense of building false legends about the past. In the practice of history and biography the word "creative" does not mean to invent. It means to give the past, to give those many lives or the single life, an artistic form. Teachers of English in search of literary values they can illuminate for young readers can surely seek and find evidence of literary art in biographical history.

From "The Reader and the Writer" by Milton Meltzer *The Bulletin,* Spring 1982. Reprinted by permission of the CLA Bulletin.

---

children's magazine in this country, ran a newspaper, and was a pioneer in the fight against slavery. Howe was a pioneer in work for the blind and for prison reform, in programs to aid the mentally retarded, and provided help to fugitive slaves. Meltzer has let their amazing records speak for them, serving their reputations simply by recording their lives. Perhaps because he is a social historian, Meltzer's interests are broad; he gives new insights in *Benjamin Franklin: The New American*, and candor to *George Washington and the Birth of Our Nation*, but he is also concerned with the more contemporary scene in *Betty Friedan: A Voice for Women's Rights* and in *Winnie Mandela: The Soul of South Africa*.

Other Books for Older Children

By far the greatest number of biographies are written for readers in the upper grades and high school. Many are, of course, read by younger children. It is not possible to include discussion of all the fine books that are available; fortunately reference books in the field of biography make the material easily accessible to readers seeking information about individuals' lives. Here will be added just a few more outstanding biographies to indicate further the scope of the genre.

Margaret Leighton's *Cleopatra: Sister of the Moon* gives a good picture of the complicated pattern of Mediterranean countries and depicts

Cleopatra not as a siren but as an intelligent woman aware of the transitory nature of her power. In Alice Curtis Desmond's *Cleopatra's Children* the picture of shifting alliances, feuds, and mounting intrigue is even stronger.

Cornelia Spencer writes objectively and authoritatively of one of China's most important figures in *Sun Yat-sen, Founder of the Chinese Republic*. For insight into the China of the twentieth century, an excellent title is Jules Archer's *Chou En-lai*.

Among the notable biographies of American historical figures are Esther Forbes's *America's Paul Revere*; Nardi Campion's *Patrick Henry*; *Andrew Jackson, Soldier and Statesman* by Ralph K. Andrist, which is profusely illustrated with material from the time, as is the pattern with other American Heritage books; and *Traitor, the Case of Benedict Arnold* by Jean Fritz. Russell Freedman, in *Lincoln: A Photobiography*, award-ed the Newbery Medal, has done a masterful job of selecting and organizing illustrations for a fluent text. There are also excellent and objective biographies of major figures in recent history, such as Mary Benson's *Nelson Mandela*, Judith Bentley's *Archbishop Tutu of South Africa*, and *John F. Kennedy* by Judie Mills.

Ann Petry has told a well-documented story of another famous American in *Harriet Tubman: Conductor on the Underground Railroad*. The dramatic story of this courageous woman is also told in Hildegarde Swift's *Railroad to Freedom*. One slave who did not escape was Peter Still, who worked all his life to save enough money to buy his freedom. Still's story is told by Peggy Mann in *The Man Who Bought Himself: The Story of Peter Still*.

Fanny Kemble, the great nineteenth-century Shakespearean actress, cared enough about freeing the slaves that it cost her her marriage to Pierce Butler, Jr., the loss of her children, and divorce at a time when it was not condoned. Her story is told with vigor by John Anthony Scott in *Fanny Kemble's America*. Another unusual artist is Zibby O'Neal's *Grandma Moses: Painter of Rural America*.

Invincible Louisa: The Story of the Author of Little Women by Cornelia Meigs was first published in 1933 and won the Newbery Medal. It gives a remarkably broad view of the period and of the people in Louis May Alcott's life as well as a perceptive study of Alcott herself.

The 1969 National Book Award went to Isaac Bashevis Singer for *A Day of Pleasure: Stories of a Boy Growing Up in Warsaw*. Illustrated with photographs of the Singer family and of scenes of Warsaw, the nineteen autobiographical stories, told in delightful style, provide a lively picture of the ghetto community and of the author as a child. An excellent companion volume is *Isaac Bashevis Singer* by Paul Kresh; two candid accounts by writers of their own lives are Beverly Cleary's *A Girl from Yamhill* and Jean Little's *Little by Little: A Writer's Education*.

Biography, like many other literary forms, reflects contemporary interests, and so there have been increasing numbers of books about minority group representatives in the United States and about women. One such is James Terzian and Kathryn Cramer's *Mighty Hard*

From *Archbishop Tutu of South Africa* by Judith Bentley.

From *A Girl from Yamhill: A Memoir* by Beverly Cleary.

Until recently almost all books about native Americans focused on tribal chiefs, but in recent years authors have begun to give us the stories of lesser known figures. Among the best of these are Margaret Crary's *Susette La Flesche: Voice of the Omaha Indians*, which tells the story of a courageous woman who fought against nineteenth-century injustices perpetrated against the Poncas, and Patrick Des Jarlait's autobiography, *Patrick Des Jarlait: The Story of an American Indian Artist*, which is enhanced by examples of Des Jarlait's brilliant watercolors.

Road: The Story of Cesar Chavez, which is liberally fictionalized but a good study both of Chavez and of the migrant workers' struggle against exploitation. Another is James Haskins's *Adam Clayton Powell: Portrait of a Marching Black* which presents a very human picture of the flamboyant African-American leader. In *The Life and Death of Martin Luther King* Haskins probes thoughtfully into King's philosophy and his convictions, and in several books, he has explored the problems of African-American women in the performing arts: *I'm Gonna Make You Love Me: The Story of Diana Ross*; a biography of a great dancer, *Katherine Dunham*; and the incomparable *Lena Horne*. As is true of most biographies of entertainers and sports figures, these books have a much wider audience than the adolescent readers for whom they were written.

Virginia Hamilton's *Paul Robeson: The Life and Times of a Free Black Man* is a moving biography of the great African-American artist whose political views caused him so much trouble. One of the better biographies of a great jazz musician is James Lincoln Collier's *Louis Armstrong: An American Success Story*.

At every level of writing for children, but most particularly for those of junior high school age and up, biographers have made great strides in presenting human portraits of the people about whom they have written. Authors, publishers, librarians, teachers, and parents have come to understand that protecting children from knowledge of the human foibles of a person is giving them less than the truth. Children have a right to the truth, the whole truth, in order that they may understand more clearly the men and women about whose lives they are reading.

Adult References and Book Selection Aids*

ALTICK, RICHARD D. *Lives and Letters: A History of Literary Biography in England and America.*

BERRY, THOMAS ELLIOTT, ed. *The Biographer's Craft.*

BOWEN, CATHERINE DRINKER. *Biography: The Craft and the Calling.*

BREEN, KAREN. *Collective Biographies for Young People,* 4th ed. (See Appendix A.)

FISHER, MARGERY. *Matters of Fact.* Chapter 4, "Biography."

HOTCHKISS, JEANETTE, comp. *American Historical Fiction and Biography for Children and Young People.* (See Appendix A.)

————, comp. *European Historical Fiction and Biography for Children and Young People.* (See Appendix A.)

KULKIN, MARY-ELLEN. *Her Way: Biographies of Women for Young People.*

NICHOLSEN, MARGARET. *People in Books: A Selective Guide to Biographical Literature Arranged by Vocations and Other Fields of Reader Interest.*

SILVERMAN, JUDITH. *An Index to Young Readers' Collective Biographies.*

STANIUS, ELLEN, comp. *Index to Short Biographies: For Elementary and Junior High Grades.*

*Complete bibliographic data are provided in Appendices A and B.

In the following bibliography these symbols have been used to identify books about a religious or a particular ethnic group:

§ African American
★ Hispanic
☆ Native American
○ Asian American
● Religious minority

Collective Biographies

§ ALEXANDER, RAE PACE, comp. *Young and Black in America.* Random, 1970. Well-known African-American men and women describe the problems they encountered in their youth.   11 up

§ ● ASIMOV, ISAAC. *Breakthroughs in Science,* ill. by Karoly and Szanto. Houghton, 1960.   11 up

BAKELESS, KATHERINE. *Story-Lives of American Composers,* rev. ed. Lippincott, 1962.

————. *Story-Lives of Great Composers,* rev. ed. Lippincott, 1962. For each collection nineteen composers have been selected.   12–15

● BEARD, ANNIE E. S. *Our Foreign-Born Citizens,* 6th ed. T. Crowell, 1968. Short biographies of Americans of foreign birth or parentage.   10–14

BENÉT, LAURA. *Famous American Poets,* ill. with photos. Dodd, 1950. Over twenty poets both recent and past are introduced in brief biographies.
                                                11–14

§ BONTEMPS, ARNA. *Famous Negro Athletes.* Dodd, 1964. Short sketches include personal and career information.   10–12

BOWMAN, KATHLEEN. *New Women in Medicine.* Childrens Pr., 1976. Seven brief biographies, admiring but not adulatory in tone, describe career preparation with emphasis on the problems these medical people faced as women.   10–12

§ ● BUCKMASTER, HENRIETTA. *Women Who Shaped History.* Macmillan, 1966. A fine collective biography of Dorothea Dix, Prudence Crandall, Elizabeth Stanton, Harriet Tubman, and Mary Baker Eddy.
                                                12–15

§ ● COHEN, TOM. *Three Who Dared.* Doubleday, 1969. Three young men who risked their safety to help bring civil rights to southern African-American people.   11–14

COY, HAROLD. *The First Book of Presidents,* rev. ed., ill. by Manning Lee. Watts, 1973. A useful ready reference source.   8–10

CRAWFORD, DEBORAH. *Four Women in a Violent Time.* Crown, 1970. Mary Dyer, Anne Hutchinson, Penelope Van Princes, and Deborah Moody fought for personal liberty in colonial times.
                                                11–14

DAUGHERTY, SONIA. *Ten Brave Men,* ill. by James Daugherty. Lippincott, 1951. Good accounts of such national heroes as Roger Williams, Patrick Henry, Thomas Jefferson, and Andrew Jackson.
————. *Ten Brave Women,* ill. by James Daugherty. Lippincott, 1953.   11–15

§ DOBLER, LAVINIA, and WILLIAM A. BROWN. *Great Rulers of the African Past,* ill. by Yvonne Johnson. Doubleday, 1965. Five brief biographies of rulers of African kingdoms during the years 1312–1617.   10–13

DUNSHEATH, PERCY. *Giants of Electricity.* T. Crowell, 1967. Useful both for its biographical and its scientific information.   12 up

FANNING, LEONARD M. *Fathers of Industries.* Lippincott, 1962. Emphasis is on men who from industrial revolution days to the present have contributed significantly to inventions having social and economic significance.   12 up

FISHER, AILEEN, and OLIVE RABE. *We Alcotts,* ill. by Ellen Raskin. Atheneum, 1968.   11–14

FOX, MARY VIRGINIA. *Women Astronauts: Aboard the Shuttle.* Messner, 1984. Describes the lives and training of eight women astronauts.   11–14

FREEDMAN, RUSSELL. *Indian Chiefs,* ill. with photos. Holiday House, 1987.   12–17
————. *Teenagers Who Made History.* Holiday, 1961. Stories of eight famous people of the past and present who became eminent in their careers before the age of twenty.   12–14

GUTMAN, BILL. *Modern Women Superstars.* Dodd, 1977. Designed to appeal to the slow reader but not condescending in style, this includes short biographies of Nadia Comaneci, Chris Evert, Dorothy Hamill, Kathy Kusner, Cindy Nelson, and Judy Rankin.   9–12

§ HASKINS, JAMES. *A Piece of the Power: Four Black Mayors.* Dial, 1972. Getting elected is not a guarantee of power or support, as these African-American leaders discovered.   12–15

HIRSHBERG, AL. *The Greatest American Leaguers.* Putnam, 1970. Typical of many such sports biographies, this is breezy and anecdotal.   10–14

JOHNSTON, JOHANNA. *Women Themselves,* ill. by Deanne Hollinger. Dodd, 1973. Brief biographical descriptions of fourteen women.   9–12

§ JONES, HETTIE. *Big Star Fallin' Mama: Five Women in Black Music.* Viking, 1974. Good view of popular music through the lives of Ma Rainey, Bessie Smith, Mahalia Jackson, Billie Holiday, and Aretha Franklin.   12 up

KENNEDY, JOHN. *Profiles in Courage.* Young Readers Memorial ed. abr. Harper, 1964. The Pulitzer Prize was awarded this compilation of stories of men who took courageous stands in some decisive moments in our history.   10–12

LEVY, ELIZABETH. *Lawyers for the People: A New Breed of Defenders and Their Work.* Knopf, 1974. An exciting overview of the lawyers working to defend the public.   11–15

§ MCNEER, MAY, and LYND WARD. *Armed with Courage,* ill. by Lynd Ward. Abingdon, 1957. Brief, entertaining biographies of seven dedicated men and women: Florence Nightingale, Father Damien, George W. Carver, Jane Addams, Wilfred Grenfell, Gandhi, and Albert Schweitzer.   9–12

§ MITCHISON, NAOMI. *African Heroes,* ill. by William Stobbs. Farrar, 1969. Eleven tales of great Africans from the sub-Sahara, told in the fluent prose of a storyteller. Much history is included, but the books' impact lies in the richness and dignity of the people and their complex traditions.   12 up

ORR, FRANK. *Hockey's Greatest Stars.* Putnam, 1970. A Canadian sportswriter gives a lively and informative account of twenty-odd outstanding players.   10–13

§ RICHARDSON, BEN. *Great American Negroes,* rev. by William A. Fahey, ill. by Robert Hallock. T. Crowell, 1956. Vivid accounts of twenty African-American people who have overcome obstacles and who have contributed to American culture in many fields.   12–16

§ ROLLINS, CHARLEMAE HILL. *They Showed the Way: American Negro Leaders.* T. Crowell, 1964. Each life story is very brief, but the book is valuable for information about African-American leaders not available elsewhere. Other Rollins biographies are about black poets and black entertainers.   11–14

★ ROSENBLUM, MORRIS. *Heroes of Mexico.* Fleet, 1970. A survey of emperors, revolutionaries, artists, statesmen, and others who influenced the country's development.   12 up

SABIN, FRANCENE. *Women Who Win,* ill. with photos. Random, 1975. Both amateur and professional athletes are included.   11–14

§ SHOEMAKER, ROBERT H. *The Best in Baseball,* rev. ed. T. Crowell, 1974. From Ty Cobb and Babe Ruth to Cincinnati's Johnny Bench.   10 up

SILLS, LESLIE. *Inspirations: Stories about Women Artists,* ill. with photos. Whitman, 1989. Generous, full-color art reproductions illustrate smoothly written, brief biographies of four women artists.   12–17

SMITH, ROBERT. *Pioneers of Baseball,* ill. with photos. Little, 1978. A series of brief sketches of some of the men who were baseball "firsts" includes some unexpected names along with the old familiar heroes.   6–9

§ STEVENSON, JANET. *Pioneers in Freedom: Adventures in Courage.* Reilly, 1969. Life histories of men and women, slave and free, who had the courage to fight for the truths stated in the Declaration of Independence.   9–11

STODDARD, HOPE. *Famous American Women*. T. Crowell, 1970. An unusually good collective biography, distinguished by a sprightly style, a variety of fields of endeavor, and the evidence of careful research that makes the book a reference source as well as entertaining reading.   11–15

§ TERKEL, LOUIS. *Giants of Jazz*, ill. with photos. T. Crowell, 1975. A fine overview of jazz musicians and the music they make.   12–16

§ WALKER, GRETA. *Women Today: Ten Profiles*. Hawthorn, 1975. Modern women working in a variety of interesting occupations.   11–14

• § WEBB, ROBERT. *Heroes of Our Time*. Series 1. Watts, 1964. Followed by companion volumes; Series 4, for example (Watts, 1969), describes influential leaders of their countries and includes Brandt, Dayan, Indira Gandhi, Ho Chi Minh, and others.   11–13

WEINBERG, ARTHUR and LILA. *Some Dissenting Voices: The Story of Six American Dissenters*. World, 1970. Life stories of Steffens, Debs, Darrow, Altgeld, Addams, and Ingersoll, with emphasis on their ideas.   11–15

★ YOUNG, BOB and JAN. *Liberators of Latin America*. Lothrop, 1970. Eleven biographical sketches are preceded by a chapter giving historical background and a concluding section on the rise of the new republics.   11–14

§ YOUNG, MARGARET B. *Black American Leaders*. Watts, 1969.   10–14

§ ————. *The First Book of American Negroes*, ill. with photos. Watts, 1966.   10–14

Individual Biographies

§ AARON, HENRY LOUIS (1934–   )
Burchard, Marshall and Sue. *Henry Aaron: Sports Hero*, rev. ed., ill. with photos. Putnam, 1974.   8–11
Gutman, Bill. *Hank Aaron*. Grosset, 1973. This book about baseball's superstar is useful for slow older readers as well as young readers.   8–10

ADAMS, SAMUEL (1722–1803)
Chidsey, Donald Barr. *The World of Samuel Adams*. Nelson, 1974. An affectionate but not laudatory biography of the querulous patriot.   12–15
Fritz, Jean. *Why Don't You Get a Horse, Sam Adams?* ill. by Trina Schart Hyman. Coward, 1974.   8–10

ADDAMS, JANE (1860–1935)
Meigs, Cornelia Lynde. *Jane Addams: Pioneer for Social Justice*. Little, 1970. The writing has warmth and cohesion and gives a vivid picture of

an era in this excellent biography of an important social reformer.   11–15

ALCOTT, LOUISA MAY (1832–1888)
Meigs, Cornelia. *Invincible Louisa*. Little, 1968 (first pub. in 1933). Newbery Medal.   12–14

ALLEN, ETHAN (1738–1789)
Holbrook, Stewart. *America's Ethan Allen*, ill. by Lynd Ward. Houghton, 1949. Spirited illustrations in color add to the dramatic story of the "Green Mountain Boys" and their fighting leader.   11–15

§ ANDERSON, MARIAN (1902–   )
Tobias, Tobi. *Marian Anderson*, ill. by Symeon Shimin. T. Crowell, 1972.   7–9

ANTHONY, SUSAN B. (1820–1906)
Noble, Iris. *Susan B. Anthony*. Messner, 1975.   11–14

§ ARMSTRONG, LOUIS (1900–1971)
Collier, James Lincoln. *Louis Armstrong: An American Success Story*. Macmillan, 1985.   11–15
Eaton, Jeanette. *Trumpeter's Tale: The Story of Young Louis Armstrong*, ill. by Elton Fax. Morrow, 1955. Good biographical writing, and a good history of the development of jazz.   12–14

ARNOLD, BENEDICT (1741–1801)
Fritz, Jean. *Traitor: The Case of Benedict Arnold*. Putnam, 1981.   11–14

BACH, JOHANN SEBASTIAN (1685–1750)
Wheeler, Opal, and Sybil Deucher. *Sebastian Bach, the Boy from Thuringia*, ill. by Mary Greenwalt. Dutton, 1937. An easy, popular introduction to this composer.   9–10

★ BALBOA, VASCO NÚÑEZ DE (1475–1517)
Syme, Ronald. *Balboa, Finder of the Pacific*, ill. by William Stobbs. Morrow, 1956. Other explorer biographies include *Champlain of the St. Lawrence* (1952), *Henry Hudson* (1955), *Magellan, First Around the World* (1953).   10–12

§ BANNEKER, BENJAMIN (1731–1806)
Graham, Shirley. *Your Most Humble Servant: Story of Benjamin Banneker*. Messner, 1949.   14 up

BARTON, CLARA (1821–1912)
Boylston, Helen Dore. *Clara Barton, Founder of the American Red Cross*, ill. by Paula Hutchison. Random, 1955. Emphasizes Barton's work as a Civil War nurse rather than as the founder of the American Red Cross.   9–12

§ BECKWOURTH, JAMES PIERSON (1798–1867)
Felton, Harold. *Jim Beckwourth: Negro Mountain Man*, ill. with photos and prints of the period and maps. Dodd, 1966.   11–14

BEETHOVEN, LUDWIG VAN (1770–1827)
Wheeler, Opal. *Ludwig Beethoven and the Chiming Tower Bells*, ill. by Mary Greenwalt. Dutton, 1942. Not a fully candid biography, but appealing to younger children.   9–10

• BERNSTEIN, LEONARD (1918–1990)

Ewen, David. *Leonard Bernstein: A Biography for Young People.* Chilton, 1960. Story of the notable American composer and conductor. 13 up

§ BETHUNE, MARY McLEOD (1875–1955)

Greenfield, Eloise. *Mary McLeod Bethune,* ill. by Jerry Pinkney. T. Crowell, 1977. This biography for younger readers does not have all the fascinating details of the life of the great educator, but it gives salient facts and is nicely balanced in treatment. 7–9

Meltzer, Milton. *Mary McLeod Bethune: Voice of Black Hope,* ill. by Stephen Marchesi. Viking Kestrel, 1987. Bethune's social, educational, and political work are the focus of a narrative describing the life of the pioneer African-American educator. 9–11

Peare, Catherine Owens. *Mary McLeod Bethune.* Vanguard, 1951. 13–15

BLACKWELL, ELIZABETH (1821–1910)

Clapp, Patricia. *Dr. Elizabeth: The Story of the First Woman Doctor.* Lothrop, 1974. 11–15

BLEGVAD, ERIK (1923–)

Blegvad, Erik. *Self-Portrait: Erik Blegvad,* ill. by author. Addison, 1979. A brief autobiography marked by the same quirky sense of humor that has contributed to the popularity of Blegvad's children's book illustrations. 10 up

§ BLUFORD, GUION (1942–)

Haskins, James, and Kathleen Benson. *Space Challenger: The Story of Guion Bluford.* Carolrhoda, 1984. 8–11

★ BOLIVAR, SIMON (1783–1830)

Syme, Ronald. *Bolivar the Liberator,* ill. by William Stobbs. Morrow, 1968. 9–12

BOONE, DANIEL

Daugherty, James. *Daniel Boone,* ill. by author. Viking, 1939. Newbery Medal. 12–15

Martin, Patricia Miles. *Daniel Boone,* ill. by Glen Dines. Putnam, 1965. 7–9

Lawler, Laurie. *Daniel Boone,* ill. by Bert Dodson and with photos. Whitman, 1989. 10–14

BOWDITCH, NATHANIEL (1773–1838)

Latham, Jean Lee. *Carry On, Mr. Bowditch,* ill. by John O'Hara Cosgrave II. Houghton, 1955. Newbery Medal. 11–15

BRAILLE, LOUIS (1809–1852)

Keeler, Stephen. *Louis Braille,* ill. by Richard Hook and with photos. Bookwright/Watts, 1986. A nicely balanced biography of Braille, whose blindness caused by an accident at age five led to his invention of a system of raised dots for text conversion. 8–10

• BRANDEIS, LOUIS (1856–1941)

Peare, Catherine Owens. *The Louis Brandeis Story.* T. Crowell, 1970. 11–13

BRONTË, CHARLOTTE (1816–1855)

Kyle, Elisabeth. *Girl with a Pen: Charlotte Brontë.* Holt, 1964. 12 up

BUCK, PEARL (1892–1973)

Block, Irving. *The Lives of Pearl Buck: A Tale of China and America.* T. Crowell, 1973. Smoothly written and balanced biography of an amazing woman who was both a talented writer and a compassionate human being. 12 up

§ BUNCHE, RALPH (1904–1971)

Haskins, James. *Ralph Bunche: A Most Reluctant Hero,* ill. with photos. Hawthorn, 1974. 12–16

BUONARROTI, MICHELANGELO (1475–1564)

Ripley, Elizabeth. *Michelangelo.* Walck, 1953. A discussion of the artist's life as it related to his major works. 12–15

§ BURNS, ANTHONY

Hamilton, Virginia. *Anthony Burns: The Defeat and Triumph of a Fugitive Slave.* Knopf, 1988. 12–17

CABOT, JOHN (1450–1498)

Hill, Kay. *And Tomorrow the Stars: The Story of John Cabot,* ill. by Laszlo Kubinyi. Dodd, 1968. An excellent biography, convincingly fictionalized and carefully researched, giving vivid pictures of the dream-driven mariner Cabot and of Venice at the zenith of her power. Canadian Library Association Award. 12 up

§ CAMPANELLA, ROY

Schoor, Gene. *Roy Campanella: Man of Courage.* Putnam, 1959. A warm life story of the Dodger catcher who fought against crippling injuries. 9–11

CARSON, CHRISTOPHER (1809–1868)

Bell, Margaret E. *Kit Carson, Mountain Man,* ill. by Harry Daugherty. Morrow, 1952. A short dramatic biography with large print and many illustrations. 8–11

Garst, Shannon. *Kit Carson, Trail Blazer and Scout,* ill. by Harry Daugherty. Messner, 1942. 11 up

CARSON, RACHEL (1907–1964)

Kudlinski, Kathleen V. *Rachel Carson: Pioneer of Ecology,* ill. by Ted Lewin. Viking Kestrel, 1988. The balance between Carson's personal and professional life is nicely maintained, and the writing is clear, direct, and informative. 10–12

Sterling, Philip. *Sea and Earth: The Life of Rachel Carson.* T. Crowell, 1970. A beautifully balanced biography, written with skill and restraint. 12 up

§ CARVER, GEORGE WASHINGTON (1864?–1943)

Aliki. *A Weed Is a Flower: The Life of George Washington Carver,* ill. by author. Prentice, 1965. 5–8

CASSATT, MARY (1845–1926)

Wilson, Ellen. *American Painter in Paris: A Life of Mary Cassatt.* Farrar, 1971. Photographs and reproductions of paintings enliven the story of a distinguished artist.   11 up

CATHER, WILLA SIBERT (1873–1947)

Franchere, Ruth. *Willa,* ill. by Leonard Weisgard. T. Crowell, 1958. Willa Cather's pioneer childhood in Nebraska is vividly portrayed, and younger readers unfamiliar with her novels will enjoy the biography as a good story.   11–14

• CHAGALL, MARC (1887–1985)

Greenfeld, Howard. *Marc Chagall.* Follett, 1967.
                                                        12–15

§ CHAMBERLAIN, WILT (1936–   )

Rudeen, Kenneth. *Wilt Chamberlain,* ill. by Frank Mullins. T. Crowell, 1970. The basketball star is described in a simply written and balanced book.
                                                        7–9

CHAPLIN, CHARLES (1889–1977)

Jacobs, David. *Chaplin, the Movies, and Charlie,* ill. with photos. Harper, 1975. A total picture of the man who gave pleasure to millions as a comic/commentator on our human frailties.   12 up

CHAPMAN, JOHN (1774–1845)

Aliki. *The Story of Johnny Appleseed,* ill. by author. Prentice, 1963.   7–8

★ CHAVEZ, CESAR (1928–   )

Franchere, Ruth. *Cesar Chavez,* ill. by Earl Thollander. T. Crowell, 1970.   7–9
Terzian, James, and Kathryn Cramer. *Mighty Hard Road: The Story of Cesar Chavez.* Doubleday, 1970.   11–14

CHILD, LYDIA MARIA (1802–1880)

Meltzer, Milton. *Tongue of Flame: The Life of Lydia Maria Child.* T. Crowell, 1965.   13–15

§ CHISHOLM, SHIRLEY (1924–   )

Brownmiller, Susan. *Shirley Chisholm,* ill. Doubleday, 1970.   10–14
Haskins, James. *Fighting Shirley Chisholm,* ill. with photos. Dial, 1975.   12–16

CHOU EN-LAI (1898–1976)

Archer, Jules. *Chou En-lai.* Hawthorn, 1973.
                                                        12–15

CHUKOVSKY, KORNEI (1882–1969)

Chukovsky, Kornei. *The Silver Crest: My Russian Boyhood,* tr. by Beatrice Stillman. Holt, 1976. A delightful reminiscence by a major Russian writer for children.   11 up

CHURCHILL, SIR WINSTON LEONARD SPENCER (1874–1965)

Coolidge, Olivia. *Winston Churchill and the Story of Two World Wars,* ill. with photos. Houghton, 1960. The twentieth century becomes vividly alive and significant in this story of the great British statesman.   13–16

CLEARY, BEVERLY (1916–   )

Cleary, Beverly. *A Girl from Yamhill: A Memoir,* ill.

with photos. Morrow, 1988.   11 up

CLEMENS, SAMUEL LANGHORNE (1835–1910)

McNeer, May. *America's Mark Twain,* ill. by Lynd Ward Houghton, 1962. Colorful illustrations and a lively text make this biography attractive to a wide range of readers.   10–14
Meltzer, Milton. *Mark Twain: A Writer's Life,* ill. with photos. Watts, 1985. Historical photographs, cartoons, and manuscript pages illustrate a good biography of the controversial writer.
                                                        11–15
Wood, James Playsted. *Spunkwater, Spunkwater! A Life of Mark Twain,* ill. with photos. Pantheon, 1968.   11–15

CLEOPATRA, QUEEN OF EGYPT (69–30 B.C.)

Desmond, Alice Curtis. *Cleopatra's Children,* ill. with maps, charts, and photos. Dodd, 1971.
                                                        11–14
Leighton, Margaret. *Cleopatra: Sister of the Moon.* Farrar, 1969.   12–15

CODY, WILLIAM (BUFFALO BILL) (1846–1917)

d'Aulaire, Ingri and Edgar Parin. *Buffalo Bill,* ill. by authors. Doubleday, 1952.   7–9

COLUMBUS, CHRISTOPHER (1451–1506)

Dalgliesh, Alice. *The Columbus Story,* ill. by Leo Polti. Scribner's, 1955.   8–10
d'Aulaire, Ingri and Edgar Parin. *Columbus,* ill. by authors. Doubleday, 1955.   7–9
Fritz, Jean. *Where Do You Think You're Going, Christopher Columbus?* ill. by Margot Tomes. Putnam, 1980. A lively, informally written biography evokes some interesting facts about Columbus' personality and ideas.   8–10
McGovern, Ann. *The Story of Christopher Columbus.* Random, 1963.   7–10
Sperry, Armstrong. *Voyages of Christopher Columbus,* ill. by author. Random, 1950.   8–10
Syme, Ronald. *Columbus, Finder of the New World,* ill. by William Stobbs. Morrow, 1952.   10–13

COOK, JAMES (1728–1779)

Latham, Jean. *Far Voyager: The Story of James Cook,* maps by Karl W. Stuecklen. Harper, 1970.
                                                        10–13
Syme, Ronald. *Captain Cook: Pacific Explorer,* ill. by William Stobbs. Morrow, 1960. The English navigator's eighteenth-century explorations of the South Pacific climax a fast-paced, fully illustrated biography.   10–13

§ COSBY, BILL (1937–   )

Kettelkamp, Larry. *Bill Cosby: Family Funny Man.* Messner, 1987.   8–10

CRANDALL, PRUDENCE (1803–1889)

Yates, Elizabeth. *Prudence Crandall: Woman of Courage,* ill. by Nora S. Unwin. Aladdin, 1955.
                                                        12–15

☆ CRAZY HORSE, OGLALA CHIEF (1842?–1877)

Garst, Doris Shannon. *Crazy Horse, Great Warrior of the Sioux,* ill. by William Moyers. Houghton, 1950. 12–15

Meadowcroft, Enid. *The Story of Crazy Horse,* ill. by William Reusswig. Grosset, 1954. Biography of the Oglala chief who opposed Custer and who died escaping imprisonment. 9–12

CURIE, MARIE (1867–1934)

Veglahn, Nancy. *The Mysterious Rays: Marie Curie's World,* ill. by Victor Juhasz. Coward, 1977. A quietly dramatic picture of the long years of patient research that led Marie Curie to the tracing and isolation of radium. 8–10

DARROW, CLARENCE (1857–1938)

Faber, Doris. *Clarence Darrow: Defender of the People,* ill. by Paul Frame. Prentice, 1965. A balanced and objective book. 10–12

Gurko, Miriam. *Clarence Darrow.* T. Crowell, 1965. 13 up

• DAVID, KING OF ISRAEL (c. 1000 B.C.)

Bolliger, Max. *David,* ill. by Edith Schindler. Delacorte, 1967. The life of David up to the point of his becoming King of Israel. 9–12

DA VINCI, LEONARDO (1452–1519)

Noble, Iris. *Leonardo da Vinci: The Universal Genius,* ill. Norton, 1965. Despite a considerable amount of fictionalization, the painter comes alive as a distinctive personality. 11–14

Provensen, Alice and Martin. *Leonardo da Vinci: The Artist, Inventor, Scientist in Three-Dimensional Movable Pictures,* ill. by author. Viking, 1984. 9–13

§ DELANY, MARTIN ROBISON (1812–1885)

Sterling, Dorothy. *The Making of an Afro-American: Martin Robison Delany 1812–1885.* Doubleday, 1971. 11 up

☆ DES JARLAIT, PATRICK (1921–1972)

Des Jarlait, Patrick. *Patrick Des Jarlait: The Story of an American Indian Artist,* as told to Neva Williams. Lerner, 1975. 11–14

DIANA, PRINCESS OF WALES (1961–   )

Fox, Mary Virginia. *Princess Diana,* ill. with photos. Enslow, 1986. 9–11

DICKENS, CHARLES (1812–1870)

Kyle, Elisabeth. *Great Ambitions: A Story of the Early Years of Charles Dickens.* Holt, 1968. 12–15

DICKINSON, EMILY (1830–1886)

Acts of Light, introduction by Jane Langton, ill. by Nancy Ekholm Burkert. Little/New York Graphic, 1980. A biographical and critical essay introduces an evocatively illustrated selection of Dickinson's poems.

Fisher, Aileen, and Olive Rabe. *We Dickinsons: The Life of Emily Dickinson as Seen Through the Eyes of Her Brother Austin,* ill. by Ellen Raskin. Atheneum, 1965. 12–15

Longsworth, Polly. *Emily Dickinson: Her Letter to the World.* T. Crowell, 1965. 13 up

§ DOUGLASS, FREDERICK (1817?–1895)

Douglass, Frederick. *Life and Times of Frederick Douglass,* ad. by Barbara Ritchie. T. Crowell, 1966. First published in 1842 and last revised by the author in 1892. This is a very good adaptation with no deletion of important material. 11–15

Graham, Shirley. *There Was Once a Slave: The Heroic Story of Frederick Douglass.* Messner, 1947. 12 up

§ DREW, CHARLES RICHARD (1904–1950)

Bertol, Roland. *Charles Drew,* ill. by Jo Polseno. T. Crowell, 1970. First director of the Red Cross Blood Bank, the distinguished black doctor fought prejudice throughout his life. 7–9

§ DUBOIS, W. E. B. (1868–1963)

Hamilton, Virginia. *W. E. B. DuBois: A Biography,* ill. with photos. T. Crowell, 1972. An eminent scholar becomes a political activist. 12–16

§ DUNBAR, PAUL LAURENCE (1872–1906)

Gayle, Addison. *Oak and Ivy: A Biography of Paul Laurence Dunbar.* Doubleday, 1971. A candid account of the African-American writer. 11–14

§ DUNHAM, KATHERINE (1909–   )

Haskins, James. *Katherine Dunham.* Coward, 1982. 11 up

EDISON, THOMAS ALVA (1847–1931)

North, Sterling. *Young Thomas Edison,* ill. by William Brass. Houghton, 1958. Outstanding biography of Edison both as a man and as an inventive genius. 11–15

ELEANOR OF AQUITAINE (1122?–1204)

Brooks, Polly Schoyer. *Queen Eleanor: Independent Spirit of the Medieval World.* Lippincott, 1983. This vivacious biography offers an engrossing depiction of the twelfth century, particularly the royal courts of France and England. 12 up

Konigsburg, Elaine. *A Proud Taste for Scarlet and Miniver,* ill. by author. Atheneum, 1973. Not quite biography, yet more than historical fiction, this is a delightful look at Eleanor, Henry II, and the people around them. 12–16

ELIZABETH I, QUEEN OF ENGLAND (1533–1603)

Hanff, Helene. *Queen of England, The Story of Elizabeth I,* ill. by Ronald Dorgman. Doubleday, 1969. 10–13

ELIZABETH II, QUEEN OF ENGLAND (1926–   )

Hamilton, Alan. *Queen Elizabeth II,* ill. by Karen Heywood. Hamish Hamilton, 1983. A candid yet respectful life story provides good background on the Queen's reign and duties. 8–10

§ ELLINGTON, DUKE (1899–1974)

Gutman, Bill. *Duke: The Musical Life of Duke Ellington.* Random, 1977. A musical rather than a

personal biography, this is useful as a contribution to musical history in the United States.
12–15

ERICSSON, JOHN (1803–1889)

Burnett, Constance Buel. *Captain John Ericsson: Father of the "Monitor."* Vanguard, 1961. Failure as well as success marked the life of the Swedish-born genius.   12–16

ERIKSSON, LEIF (b. tenth century)

Shippen, Katherine. *Leif Eriksson: First Voyager to America.* Harper, 1951. Well-written, exciting biography of the explorer of Vinland.   11–13

FITZGERALD, F. SCOTT (1896–1940)

Greenfeld, Howard. *F. Scott Fitzgerald.* Crown, 1974.   12–15

§ FORTEN, CHARLOTTE (1838–1914)

Douty, Esther M. *Charlotte Forten: Free Black Teacher.* Garrard, 1971.   9–11

Longsworth, Polly. *I, Charlotte Forten, Black and Free.* T. Crowell, 1970.   11–14

§ FORTEN, JAMES (1766–1842)

Douty, Esther M. *Forten the Sailmaker: Pioneer Champion of Negro Rights,* ill. with photos. Rand, 1968. A carefully researched study of the life of a distinguished Philadelphian.   12–15

§ FORTUNE, AMOS (1709?–1801)

Yates, Elizabeth. *Amos Fortune, Free Man,* ill. by Nora S. Unwin. Dutton, 1950. Newbery Medal.
10–13

FRANCIS OF ASSISI, SAINT (1182–1226)

Bulla, Clyde. *Songs of St. Francis,* ill. by Valenti Angelo. T. Crowell, 1952. The appealing story of St. Francis of Assisi presented in simple fashion for younger readers.   8–10

FRANKLIN, BENJAMIN (1706–1790)

Daugherty, Charles Michael. *Benjamin Franklin: Scientist-Diplomat,* ill. by John Falter. Macmillan, 1965. This very simple biography gives a quite adequate biographical outline. Barely fictionalized and not condescending.   8–10

Daugherty, James. *Poor Richard,* ill. by author. Viking, 1941.   12–15

d'Aulaire, Ingri and Edgar Parin. *Benjamin Franklin,* ill. by authors. Doubleday, 1950.   7–9

Fleming, Thomas J. *Benjamin Franklin.* Four Winds, 1973. Insightful and witty with information not found in most other juvenile biographies.
11–14

Fritz, Jean. *What's the Big Idea, Ben Franklin?* ill. by Margot Tomes. Coward, 1976.   8–10

Meltzer, Milton. *Benjamin Franklin: The New American.* Watts, 1988.   11 up

Merriam, Eve. *The Story of Ben Franklin,* ill. by Brinton Turkle. Four Winds, 1965.   7–9

Scarf, Maggi. *Meet Benjamin Franklin,* ill. by Harry Beckhoff. Random, 1968.   7–11

§ FREEMAN, ELIZABETH (1744?–1829)

Felton, Harold W. *Mumbet: The Story of Elizabeth Freeman,* ill. by Donn Albright. Dodd, 1970.
9–11

FRIEDAN, BETTY (1921–   )

Meltzer, Milton. *Betty Friedan: A Voice for Women's Rights,* ill. by Stephen Marchesi. Viking, 1985.
10–12

FRITZ, JEAN (1915–   )

Fritz, Jean. *Homesick: My Own Story,* ill. by Margot Tomes. Putnam, 1982. In a partial autobiography, Fritz describes the last years of her childhood in China and in *China Homecoming* (1985), her return.   11 up

FULLER, RICHARD BUCKMINSTER (1895–1983)

Rosen, Sidney. *Wizard of the Dome: R. Buckminster Fuller, Designer for the Future.* Little, 1969.   12 up

GALILEI, GALILEO (1564–1642)

Cobb, Vicki. *Truth on Trial: The Story of Galileo Galilei,* ill. by George Ulrich. Coward, 1979. Focusing on Galileo's ideas rather than his personal life, this has as its center the conflicting Ptolemaic and Copernican theories of the structure of the universe.   9–10

Rosen, Sidney. *Galileo and the Magic Numbers,* ill. by Harve Stein. Little, 1958.   12 up

GALLAUDET, THOMAS (1787–1851)

Neimark, Anne E. *A Deaf Child Listened: Thomas Gallaudet, Pioneer in American Education.* Morrow, 1983. A slightly fictionalized story is both a biography of Gallaudet and a historical record of the status of treatment and education of the deaf.
11–14

GANDHI, MOHANDAS K. (1869–1948)

Coolidge, Olivia. *Gandhi.* Houghton, 1971.
11–14

Eaton, Jeanette. *Gandhi: Fighter Without a Sword,* ill. by Ralph Ray. Morrow, 1950.   13–15

Peare, Catherine Owens. *Mahatma Gandhi: Father of Nonviolence.* Hawthorn, 1969.   12 up

GANNETT, DEBORAH (SAMPSON) (1760–1827)

Felton, Harold. *Deborah Sampson: Soldier of the Revolution.* Dodd, 1976.   10–12

McGovern, Ann. *The Secret Soldier: The Story of Deborah Sampson,* ill. by Ann Grifalconi. Four Winds, 1975. A simply written account of the woman who donned men's clothing to serve in the Continental Army.   8–10

GARIBALDI, GIUSEPPE (1807–1882)

Syme, Ronald. *Garibaldi: The Man Who Made a Nation,* ill. by William Stobbs. Morrow, 1967.
11–14

§ GARRISON, WILLIAM LLOYD (1805–1879)

Archer, Jules. *Angry Abolitionist: William Lloyd Garrison.* Messner, 1969.   12 up

Faber, Doris. *I Will Be Heard: The Life of William Lloyd Garrison.* Lothrop, 1970. 9–12

★ GAUTIER, FELISA RINCON DE (1897–)

Gruber, Ruth. *Felisa Rincon de Gautier: The Mayor of San Juan,* ill. with photos. T. Crowell, 1972. A biography that combines Puerto Rican history with the life of an amazing woman. 11–14

☆ GERONIMO, APACHE CHIEF (1829–1909)

Wyatt, Edgar. *Geronimo, the Last Apache War Chief,* ill. by Allan Houser. Whittlesey, 1952. The story of a great native-American hero. 11–14

• GERSHWIN, GEORGE (1898–1937)

The Story of George Gershwin, ill. by Graham Bernbach. Holt, 1943. Memories of an American composer of popular music by a personal friend. 12–16

GISH, LILLIAN (1910–)

Gish, Lillian, and Selma Lanes. *An Actor's Life for Me,* ill. by Patricia Henderson Lincoln. Viking Kestrel, 1987. 9–11

GORBACHEV, MIKHAIL (1931–)

Caulkins, Janet. *The Picture Life of Mikhail Gorbachev.* Watts, 1985. 8–10

GRAHAM, MARTHA (1894–)

Terry, Walter. *Frontiers of Dance: The Life of Martha Graham,* ill. with photos. T. Crowell, 1975. A nice combination of objectivity and affection makes the great dancer real as both artist and person. 11 up

GRANDMA MOSES (1860–1961)

Oneal, Zibby. *Grandma Moses: Painter of Rural America,* ill. by Grandma Moses and Donna Ruff. Viking, 1986. 10–13

GREELEY, HORACE (1811–1872)

Faber, Doris. *Horace Greeley: The People's Editor,* ill. by Paul Frame. Prentice, 1964. 9–12

GRIEG, EDVARD (1843–1907)

Kyle, Elisabeth. *Song of the Waterfall: The Story of Edvard and Nina Grieg.* Holt, 1970. Also gives a good picture of life in nineteenth-century Norway. 10–12

HAMILTON, ALICE (1869–1970)

Grant, Madeleine P. *Alice Hamilton: Pioneer Doctor in Industrial Medicine.* Abelard, 1968. The inspiring story of a woman whose career encompassed both science and social reform. 12–14

HANCOCK, JOHN (1737–1793)

Fritz, Jean. *Will You Sign Here, John Hancock?* ill. by Trina Schart Hyman. Coward, 1976. An amusing but accurate biography of a signer of the Declaration of Independence, and president of the Continental Congress. 8–10

• HAUTZIG, ESTHER (1930–)

Hautzig, Esther. *The Endless Steppe: Growing Up in Siberia.* T. Crowell, 1968. The true and harrowing story of five arduous years spent by Esther and her family in forced labor in Siberia, all the more effective because it is told with direct simplicity and no bitterness. 11–15

HAWTHORNE, NATHANIEL (1804–1864)

Gaeddert, Louise. *A New England Love Story.* Dial, 1980. As rich in its depiction of New England intellectualism as it is in describing the lively, devoted Nathaniel and his Sophia. 12–14

HENRY, PATRICK (1736–1799)

Campion, Nardi Reeder. *Patrick Henry: Firebrand of the Revolution,* ill. by Victor Mays. Little, 1961. 12 up

Fritz, Jean. *Where Was Patrick Henry on the 29th of May?* ill. by Margot Tomes. Coward, 1975. 8–10

§ HENSON, MATTHEW (1867–1955)

Gilman, Michael. *Matthew Henson: Explorer,* ill. with photos. Chelsea House, 1988. 10–14

HITLER, ADOLF (1889–1945)

Shirer, William L. *The Rise and Fall of Adolf Hitler,* ill. with photos. Random, 1961. In this biography of the Nazi dictator, emphasis is on political events, stirringly recorded for younger readers. 11–14

• HOOVER, HERBERT CLARK (1874–1964)

Peare, Catherine Owens. *The Herbert Hoover Story.* T. Crowell, 1965. 11–14

§ HORNE, LENA (1917–)

Haskins, James. *Lena Horne.* Coward, 1983. 12 up

HOUSTON, SAMUEL (1793–1863)

Fritz, Jean. *Make Way for Sam Houston,* ill. by Elise Primavera. Putnam, 1986. Houston's aggressive personality is presented objectively, through accounts of his devotion to fair treatment for Indians, the prevention of civil war, and the founding of Texas. 11–14

HOWE, SAMUEL GRIDLEY (1801–1876)

Meltzer, Milton. *A Light in the Dark: The Life of Samuel Gridley Howe.* T. Crowell, 1964. 12–15

§ HUGHES, JAMES LANGSTON (1902–1967)

Meltzer, Milton. *Langston Hughes: A Biography.* T. Crowell, 1968. 12 up

Walker, Alice. *Langston Hughes, American Poet,* ill. by Don Miller. T. Crowell, 1974. 7–9

○ INOUYE, DANIEL (1924–)

Goodsell, Jane. *Daniel Inouye,* ill. by Haru Wells. T. Crowell, 1977. This is just short of adulatory in describing Inouye's determination, industry, courage, and altruism. 8–9

☆ ISHI (d. 1916)

Kroeber, Theodora. *Ishi: Last of His Tribe,* ill. by Ruth Robbins. Parnassus, 1964. 12 up

JACKSON, ANDREW (1767–1845)

De Kay, Ormonde. *Meet Andrew Jackson,* ill. by Isa Barnett. Random, 1967. 7–9

Fritz, Jean. *Stonewall,* ill. by Stephen Gammell.

Putnam, 1979. Fritz focuses on Jackson's prowess as a military leader, and skillfully establishes Jackson's probity, eccentricity, and toughness.   11–14

§ JACKSON, MAHALIA (1911–1972)

Jackson, Jesse. *Make a Joyful Noise unto the Lord! The Life of Mahalia Jackson, Queen of Gospel Singers,* ill. with photos. T. Crowell, 1974. Excellent biography of a woman of courage, vitality, and integrity.   11–14

JEFFERSON, THOMAS (1743–1826)

Fleming, Thomas J. *Thomas Jefferson.* Grosset, 1971.   11–14

Lisitzky, Gene. *Thomas Jefferson,* ill. by Harrie Wood. Viking, 1933. A well-balanced picture of the many facets of this complex man.   12–16

• JOAN OF ARC, SAINT (1412–1431)

Churchill, Winston. *Joan of Arc: Her Life as Told by Winston Churchill,* ill. by Lauren Ford. Dodd, 1969.   8 up

Fisher, Aileen. *Jeanne d'Arc,* ill. by Ati Forberg. T. Crowell, 1970.   8–10

Paine, Albert. *The Girl in White Armor,* ill. by Joe Isom. Macmillan, 1967 (first pub. in 1927).   11–14

§ JOHNSON, JAMES WELDON (1871–1938)

Egypt, Ophelia Settle. *James Weldon Johnson,* ill. by Moneta Barnett. T. Crowell, 1974.   8–10

JONES, JOHN PAUL (1747–1792)

Sperry, Armstrong. *John Paul Jones: Fighting Sailor,* ill. by author. Random, 1953. The life of the naval hero who suffered injustice throughout his career.   10–13

JONES, MARY (1830–1930)

Atkinson, Linda. *Mother Jones: The Most Dangerous Woman in America.* Crown, 1978. A serious, forthright record of Mary Jones, the woman who devoted her life to the labor movement.   12 up

§ JORDAN, BARBARA (1936–   )

Haskins, James. *Barbara Jordan,* ill. with photos. Dial, 1977.   12 up

☆ JOSEPH, NEZ PERCÉ CHIEF (1840–1904)

Davis, Russell, and Brent Ashabranner. *Chief Joseph, War Chief of the Nez Percé.* McGraw, 1962. The tragic story of a peace-loving chief forced into war as his people opposed the westward movement.   12–16

KEMBLE, FRANCES ANN (1809–1893)

Scott, John Anthony. *Fanny Kemble's America.* T. Crowell, 1973.   12–16

KENNEDY, JOHN FITZGERALD (1917–1963)

Mills, Judie. *John F. Kennedy.* Watts, 1988. 12 up.

KING, BILLIE JEAN (1943–   )

Burchard, Marshall and Sue. *Sports Hero: Billie Jean King,* rev. ed., ill. with photos. Putnam, 1975.   8–11

§ KING, MARTIN LUTHER, JR. (1929–1968)

Clayton, Ed. *Martin Luther King: The Peaceful Warrior,* ill. by David Hodges. Prentice, 1964.   9–11

De Kay, James T. *Meet Martin Luther King, Jr.,* ill. with photos and drawings by Ted Burwell. Random, 1969.   7–9

Haskins, James. *The Life and Death of Martin Luther King, Jr.,* ill. with photos. Lothrop, 1977.   12 up

Patterson, Lillie. *Martin Luther King, Jr.: Man of Peace,* ill. by Victor Mays. Garrard, 1969.   8–9

Young, Margaret B. *The Picture Life of Martin Luther King, Jr.,* ill. with photos. Watts, 1968.   7–8

KIPLING, RUDYARD (1865–1936)

Kamen, Gloria. *Kipling: Storyteller of East and West,* ill. by author. Atheneum, 1985.   9–11

LAFAYETTE, MARIE JOSEPH PAUL YVES ROCH GILBERT DU MOTIER, MARQUIS DE (1757–1834)

Eaton, Jeanette. *Young Lafayette,* ill. by David Hendrickson. Houghton, 1932.   12–16

☆ LA FLESCHE, SUSETTE (1854–1903)

Crary, Margaret. *Susette La Flesche: The Voice of the Omaha Indians.* Hawthorn, 1973.   11–14

LA GUARDIA, FIORELLO (1882–1947)

Kamen, Gloria. *Fiorello: His Honor, the Little Flower,* ill. by author. Atheneum, 1981. An admiring chronicle of the man who became New York's beloved mayor and a national figure.   8–10

LAVOISIER, ANTOINE LAURENT (1743–1794)

Grey, Vivian. *The Chemist Who Lost His Head: The Story of Antoine Laurent Lavoisier.* Coward, 1982. The capably written story of a gifted scientist who was guillotined during the French Revolution.   11–14

LAWRENCE, THOMAS EDWARD (1888–1935)

MacLean, Alistair. *Lawrence of Arabia.* Random, 1962. The absorbingly told life story of the great military leader in the Arab-Turkish revolt.   11–14

LAWSON, ROBERT (1892–1957)

Jones, Helen L., ed. *Robert Lawson, Illustrator,* ill. Little, 1972. Lawson's illustrations and his editor's commentary should interest students of children's literature as well as young readers who have enjoyed his books.   10 up

• LEE, ANN (1736–1784)

Campion, Nardi Reeder. *Ann the Word: The Life of Mother Ann Lee, Founder of the Shakers.* Little, 1976. Based on extensive research, Campion's narrative brings a remarkable woman vividly to life.   12 up

LEE, ROBERT EDWARD (1807–1870)

Commager, Henry Steele. *America's Robert E. Lee,* ill. by Lynd Ward. Houghton, 1951. Lee is a hero all America should be proud of, and this biography shows why.   11–15

LINCOLN, ABRAHAM (1809–1865)

Daugherty, James. *Abraham Lincoln*, ill. by author. Viking, 1943.   12–15

d'Aulaire, Ingri and Edgar Parin. *Abraham Lincoln*, ill. by authors. Doubleday, 1939. Caldecott Medal.   12–14

Foster, Genevieve. *Abraham Lincoln: An Initial Biography*, ill. by author. Scribner's, 1950.

Freedman, Russell. *Lincoln: A Photobiography*, ill. with photos. Houghton/Clarion, 1987. Newbery Medal.   10–14

Hays, Wilma P. *Abe Lincoln's Birthday*, ill. by Peter Burchard. Coward, 1961.   7–10

Judson, Clara Ingram. *Abraham Lincoln*, ill. by Polly Jackson. Follett, 1961.   7–9

————. *Abraham Lincoln, Friend of the People*, ill. by Robert Frankenberg and with photos. Follett, 1950.   11–15

Monjo, Ferdinand N. *Me and Willie and Pa*, ill. by Douglas Gorsline. Simon, 1973.   8–10

Sandburg, Carl. *Abe Lincoln Grows Up*, ill. by James Daugherty. Harcourt, 1928.   11–16

LINCOLN, MARY TODD (1818–1882)

Randall, Ruth Painter. *I Mary*, ill. with photos. Little, 1959. A sincere and honest biography of Mary Todd Lincoln which helps to dispel some of the unhappy legends associated with her life.   12–16

LINDBERGH, CHARLES (1902–1974)

Dalgliesh, Alice. *Ride on the Wind*, ill. by Georges Schreiber. Scribner's, 1956.   7–9

LITTLE, JEAN. (1932–   )

Little, Jean. *Little by Little: A Writer's Education*, ill. with photos. Viking, 1988.   10–14

LOCKWOOD, BELVA (1830–1917)

Brown, Drollene P. *Belva Lockwood Wins Her Case*, ill. by James Watling. Whitman, 1987.   9–11

☆ LONESOME STAR (c. 1815)

Sobol, Rose. *Woman Chief*. Dial, 1976. A sound biography of Lonesome Star, who lived as husband and wife with another woman and won the name Woman Chief, this also gives a sympathetic and detailed picture of the Plains Indians.   11–13

LOUIS XIV, KING OF FRANCE (1638–1715)

Aliki. *The King's Day: Louis XIV of France*, ill. by author. Crowell, 1989.   8–10

§ LOVE, NAT (1854?–1921?)

Felton, Harold W. *Nat Love, Negro Cowboy*, ill. by David Hodges. Dodd, 1969. Gives a lively picture of the Old West.   9–10

LUTHER, MARTIN (1483–1546)

McNeer, May. *Martin Luther*, ill. by Lynd Ward. Abingdon, 1953. The fighting spirit of Martin Luther makes his life story both difficult and thrilling. Superb illustrations add distinction to this book.   12–14

§ MALCOLM X (1925–1965)

Adoff, Arnold. *Malcolm X*, ill. by John Wilson. T. Crowell, 1970.   8–10

Curtis, Richard. *The Life of Malcolm X*. Macrae, 1971.   11–15

Haskins, James. *The Picture Life of Malcolm X*, ill. Watts, 1975.   8–10

§ MANDELA, WINNIE (1936–   )

Haskins, Jim. *Winnie Mandela: Life of Struggle*. Putnam, 1988. Mandela's character and achievements show through in a smoothly written, well-researched text.

Meltzer, Milton. *Winnie Mandela: The Soul of South Africa*, ill. by Stephen Marchesi. Viking, 1986.   10–13

§ MARSHALL, THURGOOD (1908–   )

Young, Margaret B. *The Picture Life of Thurgood Marshall*. Watts, 1971.   8–10

MATHER, COTTON (1663–1728)

Wood, James Playsted. *The Admirable Cotton Mather*. Seabury, 1971.   13 up

§ MATZELIGER, JAN (1852–1889)

Mitchell, Barbara. *Shoes for Everyone: A Story about Jan Matzeliger*, ill. by Hetty Mitchell. Carolrhoda, 1986.   7–9

MAURY, MATTHEW FONTAINE (1806–1873)

Latham, Jean Lee. *Trail Blazer of the Seas*, ill. by Victor Mays. Houghton, 1956. Absorbing story of the scientific U.S. Naval Lieutenant Matthew Fontaine Maury, who studied winds and currents to reduce ships' sailing time.   11–15

MEAD, MARGARET (1901–1978)

Epstein, Samuel and Beryl. *She Never Looked Back: Margaret Mead in Samoa*, ill. by Victor Juhasz. Coward, 1980. This focuses on one period, but covers all of the anthropologist's life.   9–11

● MEIR, GOLDA (1898–1978)

Dobrin, Arnold. *A Life for Israel: The Story of Golda Meir*. Dial, 1974.   9–12

MICHELANGELO. See BUONARROTI, MICHELANGELO.

MILLAY, EDNA ST. VINCENT (1892–1950)

Gurko, Miriam. *Restless Spirit: The Life of Edna St. Vincent Millay*. T. Crowell, 1962.   13 up

Shafter, Toby. *Edna St. Vincent Millay: America's Best-Loved Poet*. Messner, 1957.   12 up

§ MITCHELL, ARTHUR (1934–   )

Tobias, Tobi. *Arthur Mitchell*, ill. by Carole Byard. T. Crowell, 1975.   8–10

MOZART, JOHANN CHRYSOSTOM WOLFGANG AMADEUS (1756–1791)

Komroff, Manuel. *Mozart*, ill. by Warren Chappell and with photos. Knopf, 1956. Written to commemorate the two-hundredth anniversary of Mozart's birth, this is an outstanding biography.   11–15

Monjo, Ferdinand N. *Letters to Horseface: Being the Story of Wolfgang Amadeus Mozart's Journey to Italy 1769–1770 When He Was a Boy of Fourteen,* ill. by Don Bolognese and Elaine Raphael. Viking, 1975.   10–12

MUSIAL, STANLEY FRANK (1920–   )

Robinson, Ray. *Stan Musial: Baseball's Durable "Man."* Putnam, 1963. Comments from Musial's colleagues attest to the popularity of "Stan the Man."   10–12

MUSSOLINI, BENITO (1883–1945)

Lyttle, Richard B. *Il Duce: The Rise and Fall of Benito Mussolini.* Atheneum, 1987. The drama of Mussolini's life comes through in this detailed look at a complex character.   12 up

NAVRATILOVA, MARTINA (1956–   )

Knudson, R. Rozanne. *Martina Navratilova: Tennis Power,* ill. by George Angelini. Viking, 1986. The career of the Czechoslovakian champion tennis player is described in terms of her moody personality and struggle with laziness.   9–12

NIGHTINGALE, FLORENCE (1820–1910)

Nolan, Jeannette Covert. *Florence Nightingale,* ill. by George Avison. Messner, 1946. Florence Nightingale's life story stresses her work rather than her personal life.   11–14

NOGUCHI, ISAMU (1904–1988)

Tobias, Tobi. *Isamu Noguchi: The Life of a Sculptor,* ill. T. Crowell, 1974.   8–10

PAINE, THOMAS (1737–1809)

Coolidge, Olivia E. *Tom Paine, Revolutionary.* Scribner's, 1969. An infinitely detailed and vivid picture of affairs in France, England, and the colonies during Paine's career, and an objective picture of the man. Sophisticated biographical writing.   12 up

PANKHURST, EMMELINE (1858–1928)

Noble, Iris. *Emmeline and Her Daughters: The Pankhurst Suffragettes.* Messner, 1971.   11–14

PARACELSUS, PHILIPPUS (1493–1541)

Rosen, Sidney. *Doctor Paracelsus,* ill. by Rafaello Busoni. Little, 1959.   12–16

§ PARKS, GORDON

Turk, Midge. *Gordon Parks,* ill. by Herbert Danska. T. Crowell, 1971.   7–8

§ PARKS, ROSA (1913–   )

Greenfield, Eloise. *Rosa Parks,* ill. by Eric Marlow. T. Crowell, 1973.   7–9

Meriwether, Louise. *Don't Ride the Bus on Monday,* ill. by David Scott Brown. Prentice, 1973. A more detailed portrait than the Greenfield title, this

conveys the quiet courage and determination Rosa Parks demonstrated when she set off the Montgomery bus boycott.   8–10

PEET, BILL (1915–   )

Peet, Bill. *Bill Peet: An Autobiography,* ill. by author. Houghton, 1989.   9–11

• PENN, WILLIAM (1644–1718)

Aliki. *The Story of William Penn,* ill. by author. Prentice, 1964.   8–9

Foster, Genevieve. *The World of William Penn,* ill. by author. Scribner's, 1973.   9–12

Vining, Elizabeth Gray. *Penn,* ill. by George Gillett Whitney. Viking, 1938.   12–16

PETER THE GREAT, KING OF RUSSIA (1672–1725)

Stanley, Diane. *Peter the Great,* ill. by author. Four Winds, 1986.   7–9

PICASSO, PABLO (1881–1973)

Greenfeld, Howard. *Pablo Picasso: An Introduction.* Follett, 1971.   12–15

☆ POCAHONTAS (1595?–1617)

Bulla, Clyde. *Pocahontas and the Strangers.* T. Crowell, 1971.   8–10

d'Aulaire, Ingri and Edgar Parin. *Pocahontas,* ill. by authors. Doubleday, 1949.   7–9

Fritz, Jean. *The Double Life of Pocahontas,* ill. by Ed Young. Putnam, 1983.   9–11

Martin, Patricia Miles. *Pocahontas,* ill. by Portia Takakjian. Putnam, 1964.   7–8

Wahl, Jan. *Pocahontas in London,* ill. by John Alcorn. Delacorte, 1967.   8–9

POTTER, BEATRIX (1866–1943)

Aldis, Dorothy. *Nothing Is Impossible: The Story of Beatrix Potter,* ill. by Richard Cuffari. Atheneum, 1969.   9–11

Buchan, Elizabeth. *Beatrix Potter,* ill. by Beatrix Potter and Mike Dodd. Hamish Hamilton, 1987.   8–10

§ POWELL, ADAM CLAYTON, JR. (1908–1972)

Haskins, James. *Adam Clayton Powell: Portrait of a Marching Black,* ill. with photos. Dial, 1974.   12 up

REVERE, PAUL (1735–1818)

Forbes, Esther. *America's Paul Revere,* ill. by Lynd Ward. Houghton, 1946. Vigorous prose and superb illustrations do much to illumine the history of the Revolutionary period.   11–15

RINGLING BROTHERS

Cone, Molly. *The Ringling Brothers,* ill. by James and Ruth McCrea. T. Crowell, 1971.   7–9

★ RIZAL, JOSÉ (1861–1896)

Reines, Bernard. *A People's Hero: Rizal of the Philippines.* Praeger, 1971. A foresighted leader who fought against Spanish tyranny. Rizal was ahead of his time in the battle for equality and civil rights.   7–11

§ ROBESON, PAUL (1898–1976)

Hamilton, Virginia. *Paul Robeson: The Life and Times of a Free Man,* ill. with photos. Harper, 1974.   12 up

§ ROBINSON, JOHN (1919–1972)

Robinson, Jackie, and Alfred Duckett. *Breakthrough to the Big Leagues.* Harper, 1965. Candid about Robinson's problems as the first black player in the major leagues, and very well written.   11–14

Rudeen, Kenneth. *Jackie Robinson,* ill. by Richard Cuffari. T. Crowell, 1971.   7–9

ROOSEVELT, ELEANOR (1884–1862)

Davidson, Margaret. *The Story of Eleanor Roosevelt.* Four Winds, 1969. One of the better biographies of an indomitable woman.   9–11

Goodsell, Jane. *Eleanor Roosevelt,* ill. by Wendell Minor. T. Crowell, 1970.   8–10

ROOSEVELT, FRANKLIN DELANO (1882–1945)

Faber, Doris. *Franklin D. Roosevelt,* ill. Abelard, 1974.   8–11

Peare, Catherine Owens. *The FDR Story,* ill. T. Crowell, 1962. A remarkably perceptive biography of Roosevelt as an individual and as a political figure.   12–15

ROOSEVELT, THEODORE (1858–1919)

Foster, Genevieve. *Theodore Roosevelt,* ill. by author. Scribner's, 1954.   9–12

Monjo, Ferdinand N. *The One Bad Thing about Father,* ill. by Rocco Negri. Harper, 1970.   7–8

§ ROSE, EDWARD (1811–1834)

Felton, Harold W. *Edward Rose, Negro Trail Blazer,* ill. with photos and prints of the period, and maps. Dodd, 1967.   10–14

§ ROSS, DIANA (1944–   )

Haskins, James. *I'm Gonna Make You Love Me: The Story of Diana Ross.* Dial, 1980.   12–15

☆ ROSS, JOHN (1790–1866)

Clark, Electa. *Cherokee Chief: The Life of John Ross,* ill. by John Wagner. Crowell-Collier, 1970. John Ross was a man whose Scottish ancestors had married into the Cherokee Nation and whose integrity earned him the respect of white statesmen as well as the leadership of his tribe. A dramatic and tragic story of the persecution of the Cherokee people.   10–14

• ROTH-HAND, RENEE

Roth-Hand, Renee. *Touch Wood: A Girlhood in Occupied France.* Four Winds, 1988. In diary format, this long book is an account of the experiences of a preadolescent Jewish girl in occupied France, 1940–1943.   10–14

§ RUSSWURM, JOHN BROWN (1799–1851)

Sagarin, Mary. *John Brown Russwurm: The Story of Freedom's Journal, Freedom's Journey.* Lothrop,

1970. The subject is interesting both as a little-known figure in antebellum black history in the United States and as an important one in the turbulent early days of Liberian history.   12–15

☆ SACAJAWEA (1786–1884)

Farnsworth, Frances Joyce. *Winged Moccasins: The Story of Sacajawea,* ill. by Lorence Bjorklund. Messner, 1954. An interesting and authentic account of the life of Lewis and Clark's Indian guide.   12–15

• SADAT, ANWAR EL- (1918–1981)

Sullivan, George. *Sadat: The Man Who Changed Mid-East History.* Walker, 1981. Published just prior to the Egyptian president's assassination, this well-balanced treatment does not shy away from controversial periods of Sadat's life.   10–13

SAMPSON, DEBORAH. See GANNETT, DEBORAH (SAMPSON).

SCHLIEMANN, HEINRICH (1822–1890)

Braymer, Marjorie. *The Walls of Windy Troy.* Harcourt, 1960. Distinguished biography of Heinrich Schliemann, who achieved his dream of archeological research on the site of ancient Troy.   12–16

§ SHAKA, KING OF THE ZULUS (1787–1828)

Stanley, Diane, and Peter Vennema. *Shaka: King of the Zulus,* ill. by Diane Stanley. Morrow, 1988.   7–9

• SINGER, ISAAC BASHEVIS (1904–   )

Kresh, Paul. *Isaac Bashevis Singer: The Story of a Storyteller,* ill. by Penrod Scofield. Lodestar, 1984.   11–14

Singer, Isaac Bashevis. *A Day of Pleasure: Stories of a Boy Growing up in Warsaw,* photos by Roman Vishniac. Farrar, 1969. National Book Award.   11 up

☆ SITTING BULL, SIOUX CHIEF (1831–1890)

Garst, Shannon. *Sitting Bull, Champion of His People,* ill. by Elton C. Fax. Messner, 1946.   11 up

§ SMALLS, ROBERT (1839–1915)

Meriwether, Louise. *The Freedom Ship of Robert Smalls,* ill. by Lee Jack Morton. Prentice, 1971. Simply told, the story of the captain of *The Planter.*   8–10

Sterling, Dorothy. *Captain of the Planter: The Story of Robert Smalls,* ill. by Ernest Crichlow. Doubleday, 1958.   12–15

§ SMITH, BESSIE (1894–1937)

Moore, Carman. *Somebody's Angel Child: The Story of Bessie Smith.* T. Crowell, 1970. The dramatic and sad story of the greatest blues singer of them all.   11–14

☆ SQUANTO, PAWTUXET INDIAN (d. 1622)

Bulla, Clyde. *Squanto: Friend of the Pilgrims,* ill. by Peter Burchard. T. Crowell, 1954.   7–9

STANTON, ELIZABETH CADY (1815–1902)
Faber, Doris. *Oh, Lizzie: The Life of Elizabeth Cady Stanton.* Lothrop, 1972.   12–16

• STEIN, GERTRUDE (1874–1946)
Greenfeld, Howard. *Gertrude Stein: A Biography.* Crown, 1973.   12 up

§ STEVENS, THADDEUS (1792–1868)
Meltzer, Milton. *Thaddeus Stevens and the Fight for Negro Rights.* T. Crowell, 1967.   13 up

STEVENSON, ROBERT LOUIS (1850–1894)
Wood, James Playsted. *The Lantern Bearer: A Life of Robert Louis Stevenson,* ill. by Saul Lambert. Pantheon, 1965.   12 up

§ STILL, PETER (1800–?)
Mann, Peggy. *The Man Who Bought Himself.* Macmillan, 1975.   12–15

STOWE, HARRIET BEECHER (1811–1896)
Johnston, Johanna. *Harriet and the Runaway Book: The Story of Harriet Beecher Stowe and Uncle Tom's Cabin,* ill. by Ronald Himler. Harper, 1977. A smoothly fictionalized biography emphasizing the writing of *Uncle Tom's Cabin* but giving balanced treatment to other aspects of Stowe's life.   8–10

STRATTON, CHARLES (1838–1883)
Cross, Helen Reeder. *The Real Tom Thumb,* ill. by Stephen Gammell. Four Winds, 1980. The intriguing story of the midget who was given the stage name of "Tom Thumb" by his mentor and friend, Phineas Barnum.   9–11

○ SUN YAT-SEN (1866–1925)
Spencer, Cornelia. *Sun Yat-sen: Founder of the Chinese Republic.* Day, 1967.   12–15

☆ TALLCHIEF, MARIA (1925–   )
Tobias, Tobi. *Maria Tallchief,* ill. by Michael Hampshire. T. Crowell, 1970.   7–9

§ TAYLOR, MARSHALL (1878–?)
Scioscia, Mary. *Bicycle Rider,* ill. by Ed Young. Harper, 1983. A pleasant family story about the incident that prompted a great black bicycle racer to enter his first competition.   7–9

TERESHKOVA, VALENTINA VLADIMIROVA (1937–   )
Sharpe, Mitchell R. *"It Is I, Sea Gull," Valentina Tereshkova, First Woman in Space,* ill. with photos. T. Crowell, 1975. Excellent view of the woman who made space flight history.   11–15

THOREAU, HENRY DAVID (1817–1862)
Burleigh, Robert. *A Man Named Thoreau,* ill. by Lloyd Bloom. Atheneum, 1985.   7–10

§ TOUSSAINT L'OUVERTURE, PIERRE DOMINIQUE (1746?–1803)
Syme, Ronald. *Toussaint: The Black Liberator,* ill. by William Stobbs. Morrow, 1971.   10–13

§ TUBMAN, HARRIET (1820–1913)
Lawrence, Jacob. *Harriet and the Promised Land,* ill. by author. Windmill, 1968. In this story of Harriet Tubman, the writing is simple, rhythmic, and effective and the pictures are dramatic and vigorous.   7–9
Sterling, Dorothy. *Freedom Train: The Story of Harriet Tubman,* ill. by Ernest Crichlow. Doubleday, 1954.   10–12
Swift, Hildegarde. *Railroad to Freedom: A Story of the Civil War,* ill. by James Daugherty. Harcourt, 1932.   12–14

§ TUTU, DESMOND, ARCHBISHOP
Bentley, Judith. *Archbishop Tutu of South Africa.* Enslow, 1988.   11–14

VAN GOGH, VINCENT (1853–1890)
Dobrin, Arnold. *I Am a Stranger on the Earth: The Story of Vincent Van Gogh,* ill. with reproductions. Warne, 1975. Effectively conveys the essence of Van Gogh's personality and the reproductions convey the essence of his work.   10–12

VERRAZANO, GIOVANNI DA (c. 1480–1527?)
Syme, Ronald. *Verrazano: Explorer of the Atlantic Coast,* ill. by William Stobbs. Morrow, 1973. Direct, brisk account of the explorer, written with Syme's usual concern for accuracy.   9–11

VESPUCCI, AMERIGO (1451–1512)
Baker, Nina Brown. *Amerigo Vespucci,* ill. by Paul Valentino. Knopf, 1956.   9–12

§ WASHINGTON, BOOKER TALIAFERRO (1859?–1915)
Graham, Shirley. *Booker T. Washington: Educator of Hand, Head and Heart.* Messner, 1955.   10–12
Washington, Booker T. *Up from Slavery.* Houghton, 1917.   12 up
Wise, William. *Booker T. Washington,* ill. by Paul Frame. Putnam, 1968.   7–9

WASHINGTON, GEORGE (1732–1799)
Bulla, Clyde. *Washington's Birthday,* ill. by Don Bolognese. T. Crowell, 1967.   6–8
d'Aulaire, Ingri and Edgar Parin. *George Washington,* ill. by authors. Doubleday, 1936.   7–9
Eaton, Jeanette. *Leader by Destiny,* ill. by Jack Manley Rosé. Harcourt, 1938.   12–15
Foster, Genevieve. *George Washington.* Scribner's, 1949.   9–11
Judson, Clara Ingram. *George Washington, Leader of the People,* ill. by Robert Frankenberg. Follett, 1951.   11–15
McNeer, May. *The Story of George Washington,* ill. by Lynd Ward. Abingdon, 1973. Handsome pictures and simple text.   7–9
Meltzer, Milton. *George Washington and the Birth of Our Nation.* Watts, 1986.   10–12

WASHINGTON, MARTHA (1731–1802)
Vance, Marguerite. *Martha, Daughter of Virginia: The Story of Martha Washington,* ill. by Nedda Walker. Dutton, 1947.   9–11

• WEST, BENJAMIN (1738–1820)

Henry, Marguerite, and Wesley Dennis. *Benjamin West and His Cat Grimalkin,* ill. by Wesley Dennis. Bobbs, 1947. An enchanting biography of one of America's first artists. 9–12

§ WHEATLEY, PHILLIS (1753?–1784)

Graham, Shirley. *The Story of Phillis Wheatley,* ill. by Robert Burns. Messner, 1949. 12–14

WHITMAN, NARCISSA (PRENTISS) (1808–1847)

Eaton, Jeanette. *Narcissa Whitman: Pioneer of Oregon,* ill. by Woodi Ishmael. Harcourt, 1941. This inspiring life of a great pioneer woman is based on early letters and memoirs. 12–16

WHITMAN, WALT (1819–1892)

Deutsch, Babette. *Walt Whitman: Builder for America,* ill. by Rafaello Busoni. Messner, 1941. A sensitive study of the man, illustrated with copious selections from his poems. 14–16

WILDER, LAURA INGALLS (1867–1957)

Blair, Gwenda. *Laura Ingalls Wilder,* ill. by Thomas B. Allen. Putnam, 1981. A biography based largely on events narrated in the "Little House" books, plus some material on Wilder's career as an author. 7–9

Wilder, Laura Ingalls. *West from Home: Letters of Laura Ingalls Wilder, San Francisco, 1915,* ed. by Roger Lea MacBride: historical setting by Margot Patterson Doss. Harper, 1974. For all those who have loved the Wilder "Little House" books.

WILLIAMS, ROGER (1603?–1683)

Jacobs, William Jay. *Roger Williams,* ill. with authentic prints and documents. Watts, 1975. Authoritative introduction to a genuine free spirit of Puritan times. 10–12

WILSON, WOODROW (1856–1924)

Peare, Catherine Owens. *The Woodrow Wilson Story: An Idealist in Politics.* T. Crowell, 1963. 12–15

§ WONDER, STEVIE (1950–   )

Haskins, James. *The Story of Stevie Wonder,* ill. with photos. Lothrop, 1976. An objective and astute biography of the blind musician. 11–14

§ YOUNG, ANDREW (1932–   )

Haskins, James. *Andrew Young: Man with a Mission.* Lothrop, 1979. 10 up

★ ZAPATA, EMILIANO (1869?–1919)

Syme, Ronald. *Zapata, Mexican Rebel,* ill. by William Stobbs. Morrow, 1971. 9–11

Chapter Thirteen

Informational Books

Evaluating Informational Books

If there is one trait that is common to children of all ages, of all backgrounds, of all ethnic groups, it is curiosity. Children read informational books to satisfy that curiosity, whether their books have been chosen to answer questions on a particular subject or to fulfill a desire for broader knowledge. While the criteria (discussed on the following pages) by which all informational books can be judged should serve as a basis for evaluating the thousands of factual children's books in print, additional qualities invest some of them with such distinction that they can be called fine literature. Originality of presentation or concept can contribute to this distinction, but it rests primarily with that least tangible of literary virtues, distinguished style. It is apparent in the clarity and vigor of Isaac Asimov's writing, in the scholarship and wit of Alfred Duggan, in the lyric simplicity of Jean George's *Spring Comes to the Ocean*. Each author uses prose in a way that is individual, each uses phrase and cadence appropriate to the subject, and each achieves distinctive style without sacrificing the basic qualifications for good informational writing.

The variety of informational books is vast, ranging from the simplest concept books (which, along with alphabet and counting books, are discussed in Chapter 4, Books for the Very Young) to books for older readers on a variety of complex subjects. The best informational books are written by authors who know their subjects well, and who write about them imaginatively, with an understanding of the needs and limitations of their audience. An expert on a subject may tend toward verbosity or a heavy use of jargon or unnecessarily technical terminology. A practiced writer, on the other hand, may lack the subject knowledge to write with depth. Each book must be judged on its own merits, and those who evaluate books should consider the author's purpose in writing a book and judge not only whether the book meets all criteria for factual writing but also whether the author has written the book so as to fulfill its purpose.

Accuracy

What are the basic criteria by which nonfiction may be judged? Probably the first tenet that would occur to anyone is accuracy. While, clearly, we seek only correct information about a subject all we can ask of authors is that they be accurate within the boundaries of knowledge at the time a book is written. There is no reason for a book about prehistory to be inaccurate, unless startling new facts have come to light since the book's publication; on the other hand, the author of a survey of the American political system as it functions today must be very guarded about statements on congressional control of election procedures, for example, since this is a fluid situation. To avoid inaccuracy, an author must specify that a piece of legislation or a procedure was functioning in a certain way at a certain time.

In writing for young children, who are limited in experience, vocabulary, and knowledge of concepts, authors often find it necessary to omit material; in such cases, their obligation is to omit nothing that is of major importance; that is, the book need not be comprehensive but it must cover major points or it will have the same effect as inaccuracy. We should not substitute simplified terminology if the correct word is not too difficult for young children; that, too, is a form of inaccuracy. A first book on human anatomy need not, for example, use "clavicle" rather than the more familiar "collarbone," but there is no reason not to use "lymph" even if it is an unfamiliar word, since there is no acceptable substitute.

If we supply children with factual information which is out of date or superficial, we only add to their confusion. Suppose, for instance, we give children purportedly modern books about the Africa of picturesque costumes and villages or about the old China of rickshaws and queues. Meanwhile, newspapers, magazines, and television newscasts show them pictures of progressive Africa today and of China's program of industrialization. Discerning children can only conclude that books are less reliable references than other sources.

Obviously, accuracy is one of the most important criteria for judging any informational book. There has never been a greater need for accurate information than there is today to help counteract the widely disseminated misinformation to which children are subjected. Adults should encourage them to check so-called facts in reliable sources. This is one way of arming children against credulity and teaching them to weigh arguments, question sources, and search for facts.

Timeliness

Timeliness is closely related to accuracy. In many informational books, the date of copyright is especially important. For some subjects, this is of minor importance—David Macaulay's books on architectural landmarks of the past, for example, have been for many years, and are likely to be for many more, some of the best of their type—but even in history or archeology there are new discoveries or new theories. Informational books should represent not only the heritage and the knowledge of the past, but the latest research and contemporary experience as well.

Timeliness is usually a preeminent factor in choosing the best science books. Since complete bibliographic data are given for all books listed at the end of this chapter, readers can use dates of publication to judge the currency of each entry. Even in subjects where new facts are important, however, some older books are valuable because of breadth of coverage, the quality of illustrations, the usefulness of charts or maps, or other special qualities. A good example of the appropriateness of both kinds of books is the inclusion of Helen Sattler's *The Illustrated Dinosaur Dictionary*, remarkable for its extensive coverage and its logical organization of a mass of material. It is, therefore, useful despite the fact that there is some newer information in a book like Patricia Lauber's subsequently published *The News About Dinosaurs*, which includes material based on recent scientific discoveries.

In many science experiment books, great changes have taken place, and any evaluation of these books would need to consider their timeliness. Formerly, directions might be given something like this: "Take a teaspoon of this, a teaspoon of that, mix, and . . . will happen." This kind of instruction reflected traditional teaching methods: The teacher demonstrated an experiment, the students tried to duplicate it, and results were expected to be identical. With the discovery method, which emphasizes why things happen, new books give children options as they experiment, and stress observation of scientific method, keeping records, and drawing inferences from conclusions. Changes

Viewpoint

Notice that it is not the child—the inner light of the child, the spirit of the child, the beauty of the child—that has changed through the ages. It is instead the attitudes of adults toward the child which have changed. It is, of course, we adults who serve to shape the child—who fashion his clothes and nourish his body and mind. Adults who have created reading material for children through the ages reveal varied purposes through their works. Some authors have merely wanted to instruct a child in manners, morals or religion; some have wanted to help the child come to know basic facts about his world. The earliest writers reveal these purposes. But later writers have tried to enlarge the child's world, to make him laugh and cry, to allow him to use his imagination, to urge him to exercise his capacity to sympathize. In today's literature for children, traces of the past remain. I think it will be clear to you which books or types of books or themes from the past are still present in literature for today's children. . . .

I often wonder how many of the thousands of books published for children today will be in print for children in 2030. I wonder if we're doing as well for our children today as the authors and publishers of the early 1900s did for their children and for subsequent generations of children. I wonder in this International Year of the Child how many authors, publishers and teachers truly believe as did Walter de la Mare that "only the rarest kind of best" is good enough for children, humanity's hope.

Jane Bingham, "Focus: Other Places, Other Times," Newsletter of Children's Literature Assembly, Fall/Winter 1980, pp. 11–12.

in educational practices in any area, then, should be reflected in changes in the literature; methods as well as content should be up-to-date.

Organization and Scope

In considering the accuracy and timeliness—and therefore the effectiveness—of any informational book, we must decide how successfully the author has simplified material and limited the scope of the subject for the intended audience. One reason the Crowell science books for beginning readers have been successful is that the authors and editors, in limiting the scope of their material, have been careful to select the important facts about a subject and to present them in logical sequence. Too much information, or information that is supplementary, may confuse and mislead a child even though there are no inaccurate statements in the text.

The presentation of material in logical sequence is particularly important. Only in very short books is a continuous text appropriate; in books of substantial length, the text should be broken up with heads and subheads that clarify the relations of the separate parts. A table of contents can also help make clear the organization of the text and the contents of each chapter. Though few books for very young children have an index, even here such aids are found more frequently than before. For most informational books for children in the middle grades and up, an index is a necessity, and the best indexes have cross-references.

Generally, the text material should move from the familiar to the unfamiliar, or progress from the simple to the complex, or be in chronological order; arrangement will vary with the nature of the subject. Historical material lends itself to chronological treatment, project books to a simple-to-complex arrangement, and explanation of an aspect of human physiology, for example, to the familiar-to-unfamiliar sequence.

The Author's Responsibility

Any book that teaches a child how to make something, as in experiment books, should include safety rules and should present complete, accurate lists of materials needed and sources for acquiring them if they are not available in the home. Science experiment books and cookbooks should also make clear when adult supervision or adult participation in a stage of a procedure is needed. Too, all activities suggested should conform with scientific method.

It is also the author's responsibility to ensure the absence of stereotyping by sex, race, age, or religion either in the text or in the illustrations. There are women chemists and business executives; an African-American doctor may have a white nurse and both may be of either sex; children of all ethnic backgrounds may be interested in a physics experiment and should be so represented in illustrations.

The writing should reflect a scientific attitude, not only in *what* is said, but in *how* it is said: no "Mother Nature" in books about plants and animals, no anthropomorphism in animal characters, although for the very young child some personification of animals is permissible. The facts must not only be current and accurate, but they should be presented so that they build toward concepts and principles. And it is incumbent on the author to keep the intended audience in mind so that the vocabulary, scope, and concepts are close to the child's ability to comprehend.

Authors should carefully distinguish between fact and theory or opinion. To signal an opinion or a theory, they should use such phrases as "in my opinion," "it may be that," or "one group of scientists believes." They should avoid the unsupported generalization and the untenable, all-inclusive generalization, which lets readers assume that the part they have been reading about is the whole. It just isn't true that if you've seen one, you've seen them all, and to imply this is particularly reprehensible in a book about people. Professional men and women often have a bias about theories in their field, and the dependable author informs the reader that he or she holds one idea, but that there are others, or that the text covers only some aspects of a subject. Some of these facts can be learned from the author's background; both the limitation of coverage and the adherence to a theory should be clear.

The Author's Competence

One of the clues to the author's competence is the material considered, that is, the material he or she chooses to include and to omit. John Navarra, for example, includes a chapter on pollution and politics in *The World You Inherit*, presumably because, as an expert in the field, he is aware of the urgency of getting enabling legislation for corrective measures. One reason that *China's Long March* by Jean Fritz compares favorably with adult books on the topic is that, having lived in China until she was thirteen, Fritz could understand the comments of survivors of the 1934 trek.

Authors who have scientific backgrounds should be aware of, and should make explicit, the social implications of their subjects: the effects on people and institutions. An author who is an authority on a subject can write with more originality than the writer who can only reassemble facts provided by others. A true scientist, for example, is not hesitant about showing that—at certain stages—answers must be inconclusive.

Evaluation of the writer's competence is made easier if his or her credentials are given. The book's accuracy may be further confirmed by a list of readers whose specialties qualify them to vouch for the book's information. A list of sources, a bibliography, a glossary, or a chronology add to the value of a book and usually attest to the authoritative knowledge or research involved.

Format

Format should be examined in evaluating an informational book. The child in fifth grade will scorn the book that, because of its size or shape or style of illustration, looks like second-grade fare. The type size and page layout are of more importance in informational books than in other types of books, since confusion may lead to misinterpretation. The reader can be confused by paragraphs irregularly arranged on a page with insufficient blank space to make sequence apparent. The chapter heads and subheads should be explicit indicators of content. A photograph or map can lose its value if it is located too far from the discussion to which it pertains. The illustration should always be accurate and should complement and clarify the printed text; it can give too little information or too much. Inadequate labels or captions can lessen or obviate the value of maps, pictures, and diagrams. Photographs that are posed or that are decorative rather than informative can be an irritant. There are some books for which photographs are the best illustrative medium, as they are in *A Life of Their Own* by Aylette Jenness and Lisa Kroeber, and here even the posed pictures of a Guatemalan family *are* informative. The best illustrations reflect some quality of the text, as Leonard Everett Fisher's black-and-white scratchboard drawings reflect the sturdy individuality of the colonial craftsmen in books like *The Tanners*, or as Edwin Tunis's meticulous drawings enhance the reference use of *Frontier Living*.

Style

Finally, informational books must be clearly and interestingly written. Nonfiction can be abysmally dull. The wrong way to combat dullness is to dress it up. Information can and should be written in a straightforward fashion; young readers need no palliative with books on science or geography or nature study. No "Mother Nature knew it was springtime" is admissible in children's nonfiction books, nor does a squirrel need to be referred to as "Little Nutsy." Children don't like books that condescend. They can take information straight, although they can be bored stiff if the writing is too dry or too heavy. A book may be useful—and there are many that are mediocre in style but useful—but a child will not cherish it unless it is also interesting.

The vocabulary should be geared to the reading ability of the child. Books that are used by young children for identification or concept books should present ideas simply but with a grouping or repetition that will encourage observation, classification, and deduction. A controlled vocabulary may be helpful for the beginning reader, but most children enjoy writing that has some unfamiliar words. Older children appreciate the challenge of some new terms that expand their vocabulary and widen their horizons.

Viewpoint

In all media, the reviewer of nonfiction most of the time limits himself to asking how much information the book contains. And how accurate or up-to-date it is. Infrequently a reviewer will compare the book with others on the same subject, but only as to factual content. Rarely will he ask what more there is to the book than the mere facts. I would want to ask how well it is organized. What principle of selection animated the writer; what is the writer's point of view; does the writer acknowledge other opinions of value? And then, beyond all this, what literary distinction, if any, does the book have? And here I do not mean the striking choice of word or image but the personal style revealed. I ask whether the writer's personal voice is heard in the book. In the writer who cares, there is a pressure of feeling which emerges in the rhythm of the sentences, in the choice of details, in the color of the language. Style in this sense is not a trick of rhetoric or a decorative daub; it is quality of vision. It cannot be separated from the author's character because the tone of voice in which the book is written expresses how a human being thinks and feels. If the writer is indifferent, bored, stupid, or mechanical, it will show in the work. The kind of man or woman the writer is—this is what counts. Style in any art is both form and content; they are woven together.

Milton Meltzer. "Where Do All the Prizes Go? The Case for Nonfiction," *The Horn Book Magazine*, February 1976. Copyright © 1976 by The Horn Book. Reprinted by permission.

With the increasing use of trade books to supplement texts and other curricular materials, the criteria for evaluation seem even more important today than in the past. Even in those books for young children in which a fictional framework is used, the purpose of an informational book is to inform. The best of such books expose a child to differences and lead to ques-

Viewpoint

Over the past decade there has been a dramatic shift in the way juvenile nonfiction books are conceived, written, and published. Take, for instance, a book Clarion published in 1974, *Juvenile Justice* by Willard A. Heaps. The book was typical of many nonfiction titles of its time. Aimed at readers of junior-high age and up, it offered a broad overview of the entire juvenile justice system from the time a young person commits a crime until his or her case is decided and punishment is determined. The book had a standard trim size of 5½″ by 8¼″ and was 224 pages long. Fourteen actual case histories were woven into the text, and the book included a list of sources and readings and an index. But it had no illustrations. *Juvenile Justice* received excellent reviews in the library media and was named a "Notable Children's Trade Book in the Field of Social Studies." It went through four printings and was counted a solid success. But we wouldn't publish the book in the same style and manner today.

Why not? Because times have changed, and with them the way in which authors and publishers approach juvenile nonfiction topics. If Willard Heaps were planning a similar book now, he'd probably team up with a photographer, and they might decide to focus on one day's activities in a typical juvenile court. Or they might decide to follow a single juvenile offender through the whole process from apprehension to disposal of the case. Whichever course they chose, the basic facts about the juvenile justice system would emerge at appropriate points in the text. But the manuscript would be tight; instead of over two hundred pages, the new project would probably run to no more than fifty pages. There would be at least one photograph on every spread and sometimes two or three. The finished book would have a larger-than-usual trim size and be sixty-four or ninety-six pages long.

These hypothetical concepts point up four features that seem to me to be characteristic of the new approach to juvenile nonfiction. They apply to books for all age groups, from preschool picture books to titles aimed at young adults. The four key features include a close focus on one significant aspect of a topic that will serve to reveal other aspects; a concise, tightly written text that will catch and hold the interest of young readers; a built-in emphasis on illustrations, whether they are photographs or drawings or a combination of the two; careful attention to the overall design of the book to make sure it is visually inviting. The visual look of nonfiction is especially important today, when books have to compete with so many other media for a young person's attention.

From "A Publisher's Perspective" by James Cross Giblin in *The Horn Book Magazine,* January/February 1987, pp. 104–107. Reprinted by permission of The Horn Book, 14 Beacon St., Boston, Mass. 02108.

tioning and comparing books, to evaluating conflicting theories. The best nonfiction goes beyond the presentation of facts to presentation of principles, concepts, theories, interpretation, and evaluation.

Accuracy, timeliness careful organization and presentation, a scientific attitude, responsibility in dealing with fact and opinion, format, and interesting style are some of the criteria for judging informational books. In the rest of this chapter, these criteria will be further examined as they pertain to particular books. The first section presents twenty-six outstanding authors of informational books for children and some of the books they have written. The second section discusses briefly a number of other important authors and significant books organized by subject matter (the biological sciences, the physical sciences, the social sciences, religion and the arts, activities and experiments, and reference books). This discussion gives a glimpse of the variety and the riches available in today's informational books.

Major Authors
Irving Adler
The Wonders of Physics

Irving Adler, who has been a teacher of mathematics at the high-school and college levels, is the author of more than fifty books on scientific subjects. His work is notable for the skill and lucidity with which he makes complicated material comprehensible. In *The Wonders of Physics*, for example, written for older children, the clarity of his prose is such that the book can be given even to a seven-year-old child to explain the difference between the Centigrade and Fahrenheit temperature scales.

The Wonders of Physics bears out Jerome Bruner's assertion that ". . . the foundations of any subject may be taught to anybody at any age in some form."[1] Adler defines the four states of matter (solid, liquid, gaseous, and plasma) succinctly, then discusses them, using subheadings and drawings to make the material easier to understand. The index includes "see also" references. Page numbers in boldface type refer to a page where there is an illustration of the subject. Throughout the text, cross-references are excellent.

Tools in Your Life is an account of the development of tools from the primitive ax to atomic energy, tracing the sociological effects of the adoption of new tools or of the clinging to old ones. *Magic House of Numbers* describes number systems built on bases other than ten, and includes many intriguing puzzles. Two books for children in the middle grades are *Evolution* and *Sets*, and for those even younger, *Sets and Numbers for the Very Young*.

Brent Ashabranner
Children of the Maya

Brent Ashabranner's first books were retellings of Ethiopian folk tales, all written in collaboration with Russell Davis when the two worked together for the Ministry of Education in that country. The range of subjects in his more recent books indicate the breadth of Ashabranner's concern for people everywhere, and for the relationships between cultures.

In *Children of the Maya*, he follows the stories of those who were the survivors of Guatemalan army violence, who took refuge in Mexico, and who eventually settled in Indiantown, Florida, a population center for African-American, Hispanic, and native-American migrant workers.

Always to Remember: The Story of the Vietnam Veterans Memorial is a model of nonfiction writing. It is thoughtful and objective; it touches the emotions without indulging in sentimentality; it is accurate in the facts it presents and pertinent in the anecdotes it includes. All of Ashabranner's books are coherent and cohesive, incorporating facts unobtrusively in a smoothly written narrative. In *Dark Harvest: Migrant Workers in America* and *The Vanishing*

From *Children of the Maya* by Brent Ashabranner, photographs by Paul Conklin.

---

[1]Jerome S. Bruner, *The Process of Education*. Cambridge: Harvard Univ. Press, 1966, p. 12.

Border: A Photographic Journey Along Our Frontier with Mexico, both the author and the photographer, Paul Conklin, have a humanitarian interest that imbues text and pictures with sympathetic concern.

Isaac Asimov
Words from History
The *How Did We Find Out About* Series

Biochemist Isaac Asimov has written his own reference book, *Asimov's Biographical Encyclopedia of Science and Technology*, and his writing covers a wide range of subjects, from authoritative discussions of astronomy in books like *Mars, the Red Planet* and distinctive science fiction to a story for the preschool child, *The Best Thing*.

Words from History is a good example of Asimov's work in a field outside his own. Like all of his other books, it is distinguished for a witty, informal style and smoothly carries authoritative information. Using one page of text for each word, he gives its etymology and sets it in historical perspective. His other *Word* books follow the same format as *Words from History*, that is, one word and its explanation on each page. *Words from the Exodus* and *Words in Genesis* show how much of our everyday speech comes from the Bible.

The Shaping of North America and its sequel, *The Birth of the United States 1763–1816*, are two of several Asimov books about the formative years of a country; his fresh viewpoint and easy, informal style make history interesting even when he covers familiar information. All of Asimov's history books, despite his tendency to crowd the pages with names and dates, have a breadth and sweep that give readers perspective on events, personalities, and factions.

How Did We Find Out About Robots? gives information on the topic and also shows how individuals contribute to a body of scientific or technological knowledge. A useful series of books on astronomy includes *How Did We Find Out About Atoms?* and *How Did We Find Out About Black Holes?* This format was also used for *How Did We Find Out About the Beginning of Life?* and *How Did We Find Out About Genes?* One of

the most successful of Asimov's many books about space is *ABC's of Space*, which is illustrated with photographs and drawings from the space program, with short paragraphs for each item. This may be used with very young children, despite the fact that the terminology is sometimes complex.

Franklyn M. Branley
The Milky Way: Galaxy Number One

Franklyn Branley was, before retirement, an astronomer on the staff of the American Museum Hayden Planetarium, and Director of Educational Services. Both his professional knowledge and his familiarity with presenting facts to the lay person are reflected in his many books on astronomy and other scientific subjects. He collaborated with Eleanor K. Vaughan on two interesting books for the very young, *Mickey's Magnet* and *Timmy and the Tin-Can Telephone*, which present scientific facts in attractive formats.

The Milky Way is one of his books for older readers, using scientific terminology and a scholarly approach. It begins with a history of astronomy, describing early telescopes, the beliefs of early scientists and the ordinary people, and the conflict between Ptolemaic and Copernican theories. The book includes an appendix for finding stellar magnitudes and distances—intended for those who understand logarithms—and a bibliography. *Mysteries of the Planet Earth* and *Mysteries of the Universe* probe many questions that scientists have, some answered and some still unsolved.

Branley has also written many books for younger children. *Shooting Stars* is a simple explanation in picture-book format, and *A Book of Mars for You* speculates about an unmanned landing. These books are in the Crowell Let's-Read-and-Find-Out-Science Books series. In the same series an intriguing title is *Journey into a Black Hole*. Branley is particularly skilled at selecting salient facts and omitting minor ones, so that his books for readers in lower and middle grades are succinct as well as accurate. In *Pieces of Another World*, he discusses the collection and analysis of moon rocks, carefully distinguishing between fact and theory, and

I think I found one.

From *Journey into a Black Hole* by Franklyn M. Branley, illustrated by Marc Simont.

making clear the interdisciplinary effort of scientists; and in *Color: From Rainbows to Lasers* he discusses color in relation to light.

Branley's versatility is demonstrated in the authority with which he writes on such diverse subjects as *Shivers and Goose Bumps: How We Keep Warm* and *Tornado Alert.*

None of Franklyn Branley's books has been more popular than *The Christmas Sky*, which is based on the Christmas lecture at the Hayden Planetarium. It discusses the biblical, historical, and astronomical clues as to the true date of the birth of Jesus, and deftly combines scientific facts with a reverent approach.

Joanna Cole
The Human Body: How We Evolved
The Magic School Bus Inside the
Human Body

Her years as a children's book editor have stood Joanna Cole in good stead, inculcating high standards of stylistic and organizational performance. Although she has also written juvenile fiction, it is her science books that have won award after award; all of these books have been chosen for the annual list, "Outstanding Science Trade Books for Children."

The Human Body: How We Evolved, a continuous text, is sequential in its development and is lucidly written. Cole describes the evolution of human beings, showing how adaptations of form made possible such distinctively human characteristics as upright posture, the opposable thumb, and the ability to communicate through words rather than through just sounds and gestures. Her versatility is evident in the very different treatment of information in *The Magic School Bus Inside the Human Body*, in which a class takes a field trip (as they have, in an earlier book, visited the inside of the earth) through the amazing and wonderful components of the human body. This book has a humorous approach whereas the first one is serious, but each in its way is capably designed to give facts clearly, simply, and accurately, and to stimulate interest in further exploration of the subject.

Other books about the structure and functioning of species (*A Bird's Body* and *A Dog's Body*) have the same clarity and vivid phrasing as those books just discussed, which makes them suitable for reading aloud to younger children. In the companion volumes *Large as Life Daytime Animals* and *Large as Life Nighttime Animals*, oversize pages are illustrated by Kenneth Lilly's lifesize paintings of small animals; the pictures are as meticulously detailed as the text.

Leonard Everett Fisher
The Tanners

The Tanners is one of a series of books by Leonard Everett Fisher on colonial Americans and colonial American craftsmen. The books are well designed, with a full-page picture on the right facing three-quarters of a page of text on the left, with an occasional double-spread picture. The scratchboard illustrations, drawn with vigor, depict costume details and customs, and there are many small, accurate drawings of the tools of each trade, carefully labeled and described. The first third of *The Tanners* is devoted to history, the last two-thirds to technique, an arrangement used for all books in the series. The author includes a glossary of terms and an index, but provides no bibliography or acknowledgments of any kind. The text is replete, however, with references which are evidence of research. Fisher explains how the tanner played an important part in the economy of the American colonies. The tanner prepared the skins for the parchment-maker, who in turn made vellum, a superior writing surface —on which were written both the Declaration of Independence and the Constitution.

Among his books on colonial Americans are *The Homemakers* and *The Blacksmiths*. In a series of books about America in the nineteenth century, Fisher comments on the societal changes as well as the institutions he describes in *The Factories* and *The Unions*. For younger children he wrote a book about fire engines entitled *Pumpers, Boilers, Hooks and Ladders*. *Two If by Sea* is a dramatic description of the actions of Paul Revere and three others during two hours of an eventful evening: April 18, 1775. Evidence of Fisher's broad interests are *The Great Wall of China* and *Pyramid of the Sun, Pyramid of the Moon*, a history of Teotihuacán pyramids in the Valley of Mexico.

Genevieve Foster
George Washington's World

Because the subject of history confused her as a schoolgirl, Genevieve Foster decided to write history books for children in terms of concurrent events and the people who lived at the same time. By quoting from primary sources,

From *The Blacksmiths*, written and illustrated by Leonard Everett Fisher.

she imparts a sense of nearness to the happenings of long ago.

George Washington's World is divided into six parts, beginning when Washington was a boy and ending with his presidency. The book does an admirable job of presenting a horizontal look at history, a slice of life crosswise instead of strung out chronologically. When George Washington was a farmer, for instance, James Watt invented the steam engine, James Cook discovered Australia on the other side of the world, and Pompeii was uncovered. California was settled; Japan was a feudal state closed to the world; Marie Antoinette was married in France.

This book, like its counterparts in the series, is a large volume with interesting illustrations, a full index, and separate indexes of places, nations, and events. Although these books are rather formidable, and graded for eleven-to-fourteen-year-olds, the style is so lively and understandable that they are excellent sources for reading aloud to younger children. Two other books in the series are *The World of Columbus and Sons* and *The World of William Penn*.

The Year of the Pilgrims—1620, for a younger audience, is more simply written and introduces color in a small volume of sixty-two pages. In this and in *The Year of the Horseless Carriage—1801*, also for younger children, the text extends beyond the date given in the title.

Russell Freedman
Buffalo Hunt
Children of the Wild West

Russell Freedman's work has crossed genre boundaries to include biography as well as books on biological topics and in the social sciences. He is skilled at choosing, from the facts collected in careful research, those that are most pertinent and in using those incidents or facts that lend his work color and credence by their authenticity.

In *Buffalo Hunt*, Freedman gives excellent background information on the role of the buffalo in the life and the legends of the native American before describing a Plains Indian hunt. The book concludes with a discussion of the factors that contributed to the decimation

From *Buffalo Hunt* by Russell Freedman.

others, but because of the unusual and explicit way in which it presents ecology to young children.

In *All Upon a Sidewalk*, which also reflects the unity of a microcosm, a yellow ant explores her small world. George brings into the text, simply written as it is, such aspects as chemical messages and mutually profitable relationships between species. Again in this book the whole world of the sidewalk is pictured only at the end of the book. Another sort of intense scrutiny— in time rather than space—is evident in *One Day in the Desert* and *One Day in the Prairie*.

Most of George's books for older readers are fictional, but all of them are concerned with some facet of the natural sciences: wolf behavior in *Julie of the Wolves*, the effects of pollution on wild creatures in *Who Really Killed Cock Robin?* and the remarkable intelligence of crows in *Cry of the Crow*. None of her fiction for older readers, however, surpasses in writing style *Spring Comes to the Ocean*, in which each chapter describes one form of marine life, beginning with the stirring of the reproductive instinct in

of the herd. The illustrations (paintings and drawings of the period) speak eloquently of a way of life long gone.

Children of the Wild West provides a great deal of information about frontier and pioneer life, as well as about the experiences of children during the nineteenth century in the West. The material is varied, including some primary source citations, some anecdotes, and lucid exposition. In this book and in *Cowboys of the Wild West*, the texts make it clear that while most of the pioneer children were white or African American, some were Mexican or native American, as were the cowboys. These books explain the romantic attraction in the colorful history of the Wild West for many readers, but the author also points out the dangers and hardships.

Jean Craighead George
All Upon a Stone
Spring Comes to the Ocean

All of Jean Craighead George's books are distinguished for her authoritative treatment of biological subjects and minute knowledge of the habits and the habitat of wild creatures. *All Upon a Stone* has been singled out not because it is more profound or perceptive than the

From *One Day in the Prairie* by Jean Craighead George, illustrated by Bob Marshall.

the spring. Authoritative, accurate, logically organized, the book is imbued with a sense of wonder and pleasure in the marvelous intricacies of ocean life.

Shirley Glubok
The Art of Ancient Greece

Shirley Glubok majored in art and archeology and received her master's degree in early childhood education. She is well prepared, then, to explain and introduce the arts and crafts of ancient cultures, and her books are impressive because of the combination of authoritative knowledge, simple presentation, dignified format, and a recurrent emphasis on the relationships between an art form and the culture in which it was created.

The Art of Ancient Greece has clear photographs of sculpture, architecture, pottery, and reliefs in a survey of Greek art. Presented for the middle grades, it is a guided tour in print of art objects gathered from museums all over the world. The book begins with a paragraph describing Greece, and then discusses ancient Greek vases, their beauty, and their various uses. Greek sculpture is discussed, with reproductions of Aphrodite and Apollo and of the Parthenon and its sculpture. Enlarged photographs of the heads are shown so that readers can see the details in the carving. The pages on armor are particularly well designed, with the figures facing each other from opposite pages, both backed by squares of brilliant pink to set off the black-and-white photographs. Glubok has expanded this theme into an entire book, *Knights in Armor*, which is based mostly on the collection of armor in the Metropolitan Museum of Art.

In all of Glubok's books the page layout and the quality of the reproductions are good; the correlation between the text and the pictures has been careful, and locations in museums are given for all objects pictured.

The Art of Ancient Mexico is simply written and includes some materials children would be interested in for their familiarity: a pottery figure which appears to be a child in a swing, and a series of pieces on an ancient ball game. *The Art of Egypt Under the Pharaohs* gives a good look at the customs and beliefs of the ancient Egyptian culture through its art, particularly the sculpture and painting in tombs and temples.

While most of the books in the series are about ancient cultures, Glubok has also written many books about art in the United States, including *The Art of Colonial America* and *The Art of the Plains Indians*. This series is unique in its field. It does not give a comprehensive art history of a culture, but it is unexcelled as an introduction for the beginner.

James Haskins
The Consumer Movement
Street Gangs, Yesterday and Today

As a teacher at every level from elementary school to university, James Haskins has become familiar with the interests of young readers as well as with their problems, some of which he describes in *Diary of a Harlem Schoolteacher*. He has written many biographies about African-American men and women as well as nonfiction in the social sciences; his writing is notable for its forthright tone, its casual but dignified style, its objectivity, and the research that is evident in the glossaries, bibliographies, and carefully compiled and cross-referenced indexes.

The Consumer Movement is, like most of Haskins's books, written for older readers but has minor reference use for children in the middle grades. It is organized by such topics as "The Consumer Movement and the Drug Industry" and "The Consumer Movement and the Toy Industry." Within each section, there is some background material, followed by a history of problems, dangers, consumer action, and legislation; each chapter concludes with a summary statement on ways the consumer may encourage solutions to problems. The subject chapters are preceded by discussions on the consumer movement and consumer needs, and the final chapter emphasizes consumer awareness and the importance of joining the consumer movement.

Street Gangs, Yesterday and Today is a serious investigation based on newspaper accounts, sociological studies, and interviews. It covers the subject from colonial times to the present, pointing out the fact that there have always been ties of political and criminal elements, and that there are no easy solutions for a social phenomenon that has as some of its causes poverty, loneliness, low status, and class distinctions. Haskins's concern with societal problems is clearly conveyed in *Who Are the Handicapped?* He has also written on such diverse topics as *Witchcraft, Mysticism and Magic in the Black World*; *The Creoles of Color of New Orleans*; *The Child Abuse Help Book*; and *Black Music in America: A History Through Its People.*

Holling Clancy Holling
Paddle-to-the-Sea

In a book as imaginative as its title, Holling C. Holling set down the travels of a little wooden native American sitting in a canoe carved of wood. Launched in the water in Nipigon country in Canada, the carving floats down through all of the Great Lakes, and finally reaches the sea. During this odyssey of *Paddle-to-the-Sea*, he becomes frozen into the lake water, caught in a forest fire, and picked up by strangers, but always they heed the carving on the bottom of the canoe: "Please put me back in the water. I am Paddle-to-the-Sea," and he is put back in the water to continue his journey.

Fictionalized, this is also a geographical tour de force and a description of the ecology of the land through which Paddle floats. While *Paddle-to-the-Sea* is in truth a demonstration that water from north of Lake Superior makes its way to the Atlantic Ocean, it is also a picture of the wildlife that surrounds Lake Superior and a unique work of art. *Paddle-to-the-Sea* was a Caldecott Honor Book in 1942.

Each chapter consists of one page of print alternating with full-page illustrations in full color, so that the story unfolds quickly as Paddle makes his way from the north, through the locks at Sault Ste. Marie, and on down to the ocean. The author shapes each chapter or page around a momentous happening, such as the breaking up of the ice on the river, or going over Niagara Falls. His easy, descriptive style, interspersed with lively conversation, makes the book attractive to children. Just as attractive are the pencil drawings which decorate the margins of the text, intricate accurate diagrams of the locks at the Soo, of a sawmill, or a lake freight-

From *Paddle-to-the-Sea*, written and illustrated by Holling C. Holling.

er. Labeled well, they describe material which is not covered in the text. Coupled with the full-color paintings, these drawings both complement and enlarge the text, and they show as well as the text does the extensive research that Holling did for his book.

Aylette Jenness
Along the Niger River: An African Way of Life
Dwellers of the Tundra

Living in different parts of the world while on anthropological projects, Aylette Jenness became interested in the lives of the people she met, and she recorded them in several excellent photo-documentary volumes. She does not write as an uninvolved observer, but as a sympathetic visitor who hopes to be accepted by those she visits. She writes of peoples who lead lives that are, in varying degrees, primitive, but she does not write with an attitude of superiority nor does she assume that customs, foods, or clothing are odd or quaint—a weakness in many books about people of other countries.

Along the Niger River is based on observations made during the three years that Jenness lived in Nigeria. The photographs are excellent, some informative and others merely decorative. The text discusses tribes of the savanna lands that border the Niger in northern Nigeria, and it gives historical background that is a firm base for understanding how modern technology is impinging on traditional living patterns. Comments on customs, mores, and cultural integration are perceptive, and the writing has both objectivity and the warmth that comes only from personal observations and relationships.

Jenness writes, in fact, only about things she has observed. While her first book, *Gussuk Boy*, is fiction, it is based on a year of life in a village on the Bering seacoast. It incorporates many details of Alaskan-Eskimo life, but there is far more of interest in *Dwellers of the Tundra* and its companion volume, *In Two Worlds: A Yupik Eskimo Family*, written on a subsequent visit, in which she examines, in collaboration with an Eskimo friend, the changes in the community and the impact of white culture on its residents. The writing style is casual and conversational but the tone is serious; Jenness writes with candor and sympathy. Despite cultural or political changes that may have taken place since they were written, these books have value because of the combination of scientific objectivity and personal involvement.

The same qualities are in *A Life of Their Own: An Indian Family in Latin America*, written with Lisa Kroeber. The authors spent much time with one family, but also explored the school, the health clinic, the market, and the government of a Guatemalan town, so that the text and photographs together give a well-rounded picture of a community.

Patricia Lauber
Who Discovered America?

In a sharp departure from her earlier works, Patricia Lauber, in *Who Discovered America?* has written a speculative view of early explorers of America beginning with the people who may have crossed the land bridge between Siberia and Alaska; the Paleo-Indians, who may have inhabited the state of California 17,000 years ago; people who may have come from Southeast Asia to Middle America; the ones who named Vinland; and on through the voyages of Columbus. Lauber has done an excellent job of gathering and synthesizing the often controversial material about this important subject.

Two chapters are particularly interesting: "Visitors from Distant Lands" and "Vinland the Good." In the first, the author presents photographs and documentation of inventions, designs, and motifs that are common to Asia as well as Latin America and asks the question, "Borrowed from the old world or invented in the new?"

This story is not easy to believe. It seems almost impossible that the fishermen could have drifted 8,000 miles and landed in Ecuador, where they taught the Indians to make pottery. Yet archeologists cannot find another way to explain the sudden appearance of this particular pottery in a region where there are no traces of earlier pottery. (p. 64)

In the chapter on Vinland she presents the evidence for the discovery of Vinland as it is outlined in *The Saga of Eric the Red* and *The Greenlander's Saga* and tends to agree with scholars who think that the basic events of these sagas are true. The format of the book is

From *Get Ready for Robots* by Patricia Lauber, illustrated by True Kelley.

attractive, and the reproductions of photographs, prints, and maps are excellent. The book's nine chapters are well organized and well indexed.

Lauber has written widely in the fields of the sciences and social studies. In *Tales Mummies Tell*, she discusses mummification, as well as contemporary methods of scientific investigation. *Voyagers from Space: Meteors and Meteorites* deals lucidly with a complex subject. *Tapping Earth's Heat* clearly examines volcanic action and the uses of geothermal energy. Two easy-to-read volumes for younger readers are *What's Hatching Out of That Egg?* and *Get Ready for Robots!* Lauber's interest in ecology and conservation is evident in *Everglades Country: A Question of Life or Death*. A quality that makes Lauber's books stimulating is their sense of lively curiosity—a provocative relish that can be shared by readers and may entice them to seek additional information.

Robert M. McClung
Thor: Last of the Sperm Whales

In a book with overtones of *Moby Dick*, Robert McClung begins with the story of a sperm whale that destroyed the ships of whalers hunting him 150 years ago. *Thor* goes on to describe a sperm whale of today that bears the same marking as his ghostly forebear, ramming into the stern of a modern-day catcher boat carrying harpooners. In between there is a detailed description of the birth, feeding, growth, mating, and death of the great sperm whale as it travels the oceans, a great monster of the deep, fifty feet in length and "forty tons of bone and muscle, overlaid by an insulating blanket of blubber nearly a foot thick on his breast." While this is a scientific description of the life of the sperm whale, it is also a story of the relentless slaughter of whales in our century, destruction so great that three species, the great blue whales, the finbacks, and the sei whales, are in danger of extinction.

McClung, a prolific author in his field, has written sympathetically but without sentimentality of all kinds of wildlife. He manages to be thorough, but not dry, and weaves a story without anthropomorphism into his factual approach. Threaded through all of his work,

From *Lili: A Giant Panda of Sichuan* by Robert M. McClung, illustrated by Irene Brady.

including *Honker: The Story of a Wild Goose* and *Hunted Mammals of the Sea*, is the persistent theme of good conservation practices. His clear, simple writing never descends to oversimplification.

McClung's ability to write for different age levels is evident in comparing *Lili: A Giant Panda of Sichuan*, which is written in concise prose, with *Gypsy Moth*, which is detailed enough for adult readers; at both levels the writing is lucid and the information accurate. An excellent book on animal camouflage, *How Animals Hide*, uses color photographs, showing examples of protective adaptation far better than any drawing could.

Milton Meltzer
In Their Own Words

The first of the three-volume survey of African-American history in America, *In Their Own Words* contains material not previously known to many readers—drawn from letters, diaries, journals, autobiographies, speeches, resolutions, newspapers, and pamphlets of African-Americans in slavery. It traces life on the plantation and conditions in the North in letters from escaped slaves in the free states, and tells of the day of Emancipation. In these excerpts, one can see Milton Meltzer's selectivity in showing the wide range of activity and writings of slaves and freed slaves. The three books are an excellent source of information on what living conditions have been for African-American people through American history. Each excerpt is short, some only two pages; occasionally a document is quoted in full. Each has an introduction by Meltzer and the source is identified at the close. The volumes cover three periods: 1619–1865, 1865–1916, and 1916–1966. Reissued as a single volume with some new material, the 1984 edition is entitled *The Black Americans: A History in Their Own Words*. The same format is used in *The American Revolutionaries: A History in Their Own Words, 1750–1800* and in *Voices from the Civil War*.

Meltzer's books show his interest in social reform and its effects on the American people. *Time of Trial, Time of Hope*, written with August Meier, describes the many problems and few victories of African-Americans in the United States between the First and Second World Wars. The authors write with authority and from a broad viewpoint that includes political, economic, educational, and cultural problems as well as the role of labor. As is true in all his books, the sources cited in *Bound for the Rio Grande: The Mexican Struggle, 1845–1850* give evidence of the author's meticulous research.

Meltzer's concern for any group that has suffered from prejudice is evident in his range of subjects: *All Times, All Peoples: A World History of Slavery; The Chinese Americans;* and *The Hispanic Americans*. Several of Meltzer's books concern the Jewish people: *Never to Forget: The Jews of the Holocaust* discusses the mistreatment of Jews in Nazi Germany; in contrast, another, more admirable aspect of this historic period is presented in Meltzer's descriptions of the heroic efforts of many in *The Story of How Gentiles Saved Jews in the Holocaust*. In *Remember the Days*, Meltzer writes a brief history of American Jewry.

Dorothy Hinshaw Patent
Evolution Goes On Every Day
Butterflies and Moths: How They Function

A zoologist, Dorothy Hinshaw Patent has become established as an author whose books are distinguished for their combination of authoritative knowledge, detached and objective attitude, and an ability to write for the lay person with fluency and clarity. Like Millicent Selsam, she communicates a sense of wonder at the complexity and beauty of animal life by her zest for her subject rather than by comments on the marvelous intricacy of the natural order. In *Evolution Goes On Every Day*, she explains some of the evolutionary changes in progress in contemporary species of flora and fauna, analyzing the various factors that effect change or that encourage the emergence of a new species.

Butterflies and Moths: How They Function is a text that is a model of broad coverage, good organization of material, and clarity in writing style. The book examines almost every aspect of lepidopterans, and discusses the ways in which moths and butterflies, in their various stages, are considered pests or benefactors by people. Patent is a prolific writer; among her other books are *How Insects Communicate*; *Bacteria: How They Affect Other Living Things*; *The Whooping Crane: A Comeback Story*; *Buffalo: The American Bison Today; Germs!* and *Where the Bald Eagles Gather*. In all her books, Patent carefully distinguishes between fact and conjecture but makes it clear that conjecture and theory, even when erroneous, are part of the scientific method and can be built on to reach truth.

Laurence Pringle
Follow a Fisher
Nuclear Power: From Physics to Politics

A former science teacher and, for many years, editor of *Nature and Science*, the magazine published by the American Museum of Natural History, Laurence Pringle combines in his books the ability to explain logical relationships and the succinct marshalling of facts that clarify such relationships, especially when they are intricate. In one of his earlier books, *Follow a*

From *Follow a Fisher* by Laurence Pringle, illustrated by Tony Chen.

Fisher, Pringle demonstrates his understanding of writing for younger children as he describes in crisp, straightforward style the habits and habitat of a member of the weasel family. His concern for conservation of species and for preservation of ecological balance is smoothly incorporated into the simply written, continuous text.

Nuclear Power: From Physics to Politics is for older readers, an objective approach to the complex dilemma of the nuclear power plant. Although he states that he is "not neutral," Pringle is in fact quite objective in discussing the safety hazards, the violations, the problems of nuclear waste, and the role of the Atomic Energy Commission. The text is as lucid in descriptions of processes as it is in evaluation of moral and ethical questions involved in the provision of energy through nuclear power. His position is restated in *Nuclear War: From Hiroshima to Nuclear Winter* in which he shows the devastation that would follow a nuclear war.

Pringle's interest in ecological balance is manifest in *What Shall We Do with the Land?* In *The Economic Growth Debate: Are There Limits to Growth?* he considers the impact on the planet and its resources of such aspects of economic growth as dwindling food supplies, pollution, and depletion of natural resources. He considers both plight and danger in *Feral: Tame Animals Gone Wild* and the conflicting viewpoints within our society in *The Animal Rights Controversy*. The breadth of Pringle's interests is indicated by the fact that, although he trained

as a wildlife biologist, his books often consider the total environment, sociological factors, and legal or ethical implications of biological problems.

Millicent E. Selsam
Benny's Animals

Millicent E. Selsam, one of the most dependably competent authors of science books, writes for all age levels, but she is undoubtedly best known for her books for young readers. Her style is simple and clear, with no extraneous material and no trace of popularization. She defines good science books as:

those that show the methods of science at work, that elucidate basic principles of science and are not a mere assembly of facts, that convey something of the beauty and excitement of science, and that interest young people in thinking up good questions for new young scientists to test by experiment.[2]

Benny's Animals is a particularly good example of the inclusion of methodology and basic principles in a science book for the beginning reader. It is a clear lesson in how animals are classified, with a fictional framework that facilitates the explanation. Benny was a child who wanted to organize his collection of material from the seashore, and this led to questions about the differences between animals. Finally Benny went to the museum to talk with Professor Wood, who suggested that he put the specimens in two piles according to whether or not they had a backbone; then his next step was to divide the animals with backbones into fish, amphibians, reptiles, birds, and mammals. The book ends on just the right note, having explained the basic steps in classification and having made the point that there is a rational way of dividing living things. The format is excellent, with continuous text, large print, and plenty of space between the lines. Arnold Lobel's illustrations are appropriate in their

[2]"Writing About Science for Children," by Millicent E. Selsam. From *A Critical Approach to Children's Literature*, edited by Sara Innis Fenwick. Chicago and London: The University of Chicago Press, 1967.

earth colors, casually realistic when he portrays the boy and the family, and close enough to reality to be recognizable when he draws the

Viewpoint

At a recent conference on children's books, an editor declared that accuracy is the single most important characteristic of science books. Well, sure, accuracy ranks right up there with apple pie, but I wonder, "accuracy of what?" Minor details, major ideas, values, attitudes? Which would you rather read: a book marred by some factual errors that is also sprightly, inspiring, and memorable, or one that is perfect in every factual detail but dull as a hoe? We should not have to make such a choice, since most publishers routinely pay experts to check manuscripts of nonfiction books. (Of course, experts can be careless, make or miss mistakes, and also may disagree among themselves.) The perfect book has yet to be published, but the best science books are accurate in details and especially in concepts. Respect for the truth, to the extent it is known, is part of the appealing integrity of doing science.

A special problem of children's science books is their brevity. Writers cannot afford to dawdle or be encyclopedic. They must first have a firm grasp of the overall subject, then select and convey the key ideas. Done well, this produces a highly accessible introduction to a subject—just right for adults, it is often remarked.

In some fields of science the knowledge is more secure than in others. Whatever the subject, however, the reader should not be given the idea that everything is known, and that he or she just absorbed it all in sixty-four pages. Almost invariably it is safe to say that there's more to learn, and more to discover.

Laurence Pringle, "Science Done Here," *Celebrating Children's Books,* edited by Betsy Hearne and Marilyn Kaye. New York: Lothrop, Lee, & Shepard Books, 1981, pp. 14–15.

animals, often giving them a little personality. *Greg's Microscope* and *Let's Get Turtles* are other titles in this Science I Can Read series.

Bulbs, Corms, and Such and *Tree Flowers* are for independent readers in lower and middle grades, illustrated with large handsome photographs, some in color, by Jerome Wexler. Examples of a group of books which are illustrated by several different artists are *See Through the Jungle* and *See Along the Shore*, a colorful volume that deals with tides and animals and plants of the seashore.

For still older children are *Land of the Giant Tortoise: The Story of the Galapagos* and *The Language of Animals*, the latter a fascinating story of communication between animals including sounds, smells, facial expressions, and tail positions. Introductory texts that stress observation are *A First Look at Caterpillars*, written with Joyce Hunt, and *A First Look at Spiders*. One of Selsam's most interesting books for older readers was written with Jacob Bronowski—*Biography of an Atom*, which traces the history of one carbon atom from its birth in a young star, through the millennia, to a conjectural fate today.

Paul Showers
Before You Were a Baby

Before You Were a Baby, the only book by Paul Showers for which he has a coauthor (his former wife, Kay Showers), is an excellently paced book for readers in the second and third grades, and it is clear enough to be read aloud to younger children. There are repetition and rhythm in sentences like "This new cell grew and grew and grew. And at last it became you." Particularly dramatic are the pictures which show, in color, the increasing size of the baby inside the uterus. On these pages the text is almost nonexistent, and the reader's eye is carried forward by the power of the graphic drawings as they progress from the hunchback figure at six weeks to the completely formed baby of eight months. Using all of the correct terms, such as *testes, sperm,* and *penis,* the book gives an accurate explanation of conception without being either coy or evasive. The simple style and use of large print, with a minimum of labeled diagrams, is typical of the Let's-Read-

and-Find-Out science books which include *Be-fore You Were a Baby*. Showers gives accurate information in the very simplest language, chooses important facts, and tells them in logical sequence, so that the child can read the books alone or the adult can use them as a springboard for discussion.

Showers's other books include *Your Skin and Mine* and *Look at Your Eyes*. The first gives some of the basic facts about skin: sensation, temperature adjustment, hair follicles, and color differences, explaining the latter so that the message about skin color is casual, while the illustrations show children of various colors in connection with the text rather than as an ethnic spectrum for its own sake. In the second, an African-American child's daily activities are used to show how eyes adjust to light, that eyes are different colors, how the parts of the eye work. *Me and My Family Tree* and *You Can't Make a Move Without Your Muscles* are other concise, informative science books by Paul Showers.

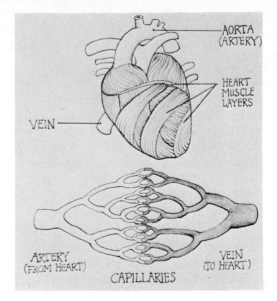

From *Heartbeats: Your Body, Your Heart* by Alvin and Virginia Silverstein, illustrated by Stella Ormai.

Alvin and Virginia Silverstein
The *All About Them* Series
The *Systems of the Body* Series

Alvin Silverstein is a biology professor and Virginia Silverstein a translator of Russian scientific literature; they have collaborated on over thirty books for young people, from books that deal with a narrow area, such as *Apples: All About Them* to books on such complex topics as *Sleep and Dreams*. Their work is carefully organized and written in a clear, direct style, and is dependably accurate. The more complicated subjects are not always covered in depth, but they are given balanced treatment, and the Silversteins' writing usually shows their attention to current research and always maintains a scientific attitude.

Hamsters is one of a series of books for the middle elementary school grades, all subtitled *All About Them*. It is illustrated with photographs that are well placed in relation to textual references, although not all the pictures are informative. Following a brief discussion of the way in which hamsters were introduced into the United States as research animals and became popular as pets, the text gives detailed advice

on the care of hamsters, including information on housing and breeding. A concluding chapter describes the importance of the hamster in laboratory studies. Pervading the book is an attitude of respect for the rights and well-being of pets, and there is no trace of fictionalization or anthropomorphism.

The Silversteins have written many books in a series called Systems of the Body, with books such as *The Skeletal System* and *Heartbeats* that have accurate texts, include facts on recent research, and give concise explanations of intricate physiological functions. Their emphasis on current research is evident in these books and in *World of the Brain*. It is stressed particularly in *The Code of Life*, which explores genetic engineering as well as genetic inheritance and how it functions; and in *AIDS: Deadly Threat*. The Silversteins are consistently concerned with the effects of biological research and health-related crises on society; citizen support of pollution control and of supervisory legislation; and sociological implications of biological problems, as in *Aging*.

Hilda Simon
Living Lanterns: Luminescence in Animals

As a student of art and biology, Hilda Simon is well qualified both as author and artist for the books she has written and illustrated in the field of biology. Her drawings are beautifully detailed and accurate, and the same accuracy is evident in her writing, which is informal and lucid. While there are scientific terms used, the writing is not laden with jargon but can be understood by readers with little background. However, since Simon uses neither anthropomorphism nor condescension and since she treats her subjects in some depth, her books are also appropriate for readers who do have background in biology.

In *Living Lanterns* Simon begins with a brief survey of what has been known about the phenomenon of luminescence in the past, then describes luminescent creatures according to their habitats (land, air, or sea), and concludes with a discussion of the anatomy of luminescence. Observations are validated by citing research, and the text is explicit in stating the fact that not all the questions about bioluminescence have been answered. Simon's books exemplify the best kind of science writing, authoritative and accurate, illustrated with pictures that are carefully placed and informative, and supplied with indexes, bibliographies, and —in some books—maps that show the ranges of species.

Most of her books are for older readers, but Simon's *The Amazing Book of Birds* is for the middle grades. Written in a light, informal style, it gives many facts about birds, but the random arrangement makes it less cohesive and therefore less useful than her later work. A study of imitative patterns or adaptations in the insect world, *Insect Masquerades*, is a typical example of Simon's writing: logically organized, and leading from the discussions of individual creatures to conclusions about the survival potential of insects which have such advantages.

Seymour Simon
The Rock-Hound's Book
The Long View into Space

Seymour Simon's many years as a public school science teacher are reflected in his books both by the knowledgeable ease with which he adapts his style to the comprehension level of the intended audience and by the fact that in many of his books he includes experiments that are clearly explained and that illustrate the principles he is discussing. He moves from the familiar to the less familiar, from the simple to the more complex, in the best tradition of teaching, but his writing has a natural, informal flow that has no didactic tone.

In *The Rock-Hound's Book*, Simon encourages the novice collector, pointing out that rocks are everywhere, that they are composed of minerals, and that rock-collecting is a safe, pleasant, endlessly interesting hobby. He describes qualities that identify mineral components, and supplies advice on where and how to collect with effective zeal. In *The Long View into Space*, he

From *Storms* by Seymour Simon, photographs by the National Center for Atmospheric Research.

creates a photographic essay that is handsome, accurate, lucid, and serious: an excellent introduction to astronomical bodies and the phenomena peculiar to each. It is typical of Simon's writing that he carefully explains, in this book, such subjects as novae or spiral galaxies without telling middle-grade readers so much that they are confused—or so little that the subjects are not comprehensible. Other astronomy books that share this lucidity are *The Long Journey from Space*, *Galaxies*, and *Stars*.

Among the over fifty other books by Simon are *Computer Sense*; *Computer Nonsense*; *Your First Home Computer*; *Animal Fact, Animal Fable*; *Shadow Magic*; *Storms*; *Volcanoes*; *Strange Mysteries*, a potpourri of odd phenomena reported or documented; and the beautifully illustrated *Hidden Worlds*, which has magnified photographs, some in color.

Edwin Tunis
Frontier Living

The immense amount of detail produced in *Frontier Living* reflects painstaking research; the text contains little conjecture, but only fact upon fact about all aspects of frontier living. Organized generally in an east-to-west pattern, the book, by the author's admission, concentrates mostly east of the Mississippi because, as he said:

Nearly every phase of the far West has been dealt with . . . while the forest frontier, with a few notable exceptions, has been bypassed since James Fenimore Cooper stopped romancing about it.

And so the book progresses from sections dealing with the Piedmont, in which native Americans, forts, and medicine and witchcraft are described; on through the old Northwest Territory; passing then out to Kansas, Colorado, and California. "The Old Northwest" has much excellent material on day-to-day living, and the section on housekeeping is an example of both the author's style and the meticulousness of his research.

The black-and-white line drawings are of uniform excellence and accuracy, whether of a panoramic view of moving half of a canal boat over a mountain, or detailing the intricate works of a small arsenal of early western arms. The author's captions are revealing, too, and often humorous. Of the Bowie knife, he wrote:

The mild and quiet Colonel Bowie didn't design this toadsticker; he gave it his name by way of the mayhem he did with it.

Frontier Living was a Newbery Honor Book, and *Colonial Living*, with a similar format, won the Thomas Alva Edison Foundation's Children's Book Award for special excellence in portraying America's past. *Wheels: A Pictorial History* and *Indians* are so comprehensive and profusely illustrated with authoritatively detailed drawings that they have reference use. Although, like any such books, they cover material only up to the time of publication, they are always as useful as they are accurate and comprehensive. In *The Tavern at the Ferry*, Tunis follows the changes that occur in the life of a Quaker family and in the building they own; through this, he gives an immediacy to the colonial way of life and to events of the Revolutionary War. Tunis's wit had been evident in his other books, but with the publication of *Chipmunks on the Doorstep*, his first book in the field of natural science, he added a wry humor to the appeals of perceptive observation and beautiful pictures.

Harvey Weiss
Pencil, Pen and Brush: Drawing for Beginners

A major criterion for an activity book is that the instructions tell exactly how to perform the activity. Harvey Weiss's arts and crafts books are clear in explaining procedures, and they encourage readers to use their own initiative.

Pencil, Pen and Brush has a sophisticated approach for a how-to-do-it book. Using the work of major artists, from Leonardo da Vinci to Maurice Sendak, as well as photographs for models, Weiss presents his instructions in easy steps, never talking down to his readers. Practical advice is given for each step, and readers are given suggestions for striking out on their own; the discussion ends on an encouraging note, with questions and suggestions.

Other books by Weiss deal with three-dimensional materials: *Ceramics from Clay to Kiln* and *Carving*. Weiss is always clear and explicit, moving from simple projects to more complicated ones; in *Model Cars and Trucks and How to Build Them*, for example, the first model is a solid, one-piece racing car, and the last a large, intricate car that can be ridden. The same careful progression from the familiar and simple to the less familiar and intricate is evident in *How to Run a Railroad*, a book on model trains; *Machines and How They Work*; and *Shelters: From Tepee to Igloo*.

Herbert Zim
Life and Death

Herbert Zim taught for over thirty years in the fields of science and science education. With Sonia Bleeker, he wrote *Life and Death*, one of the best books on this subject for children of elementary school age. The book discusses life expectancy, aging, the clinical definition of death, and the rituals and legal procedures that are followed after death occurs. It concludes with a brief description of death rituals as they are practiced throughout the world.

Zim's lifelong interest in collecting nature specimens is reflected in a series of small volumes with large print that have proved most attractive to young children. In them, as in *The New Moon*, a text that gives information obtained from lunar probes, the continuous texts are comprehensive. His books on geology, such as *Quartz*, and on the human body, *Our Senses and How They Work* and *Your Heart and How It Works*, are for the slightly older child. A professor of science education, Zim exemplifies the objectivity of the scientist's attitude.

It is obviously impossible to include, in the discussion and the bibliography that follow, all the good informational books or indeed books on every subject. The chapter and the reading lists are meant to give the reader a broad picture of the kinds of material that are available to provide children with pleasure and to satisfy their need for information.

Whenever books are classified as in the following discussion, problems arise, because some of them simply refuse to fit neatly into preordained slots. For example, the early con-

From *Shelters: From Tepee to Igloo*, written and illustrated by Harvey Weiss.

cept books (discussed in Chapter 4) for young children could be in a separate group here, also: books that present ideas of big and small, books that simply introduce familiar objects, books that familiarize a child with colors. There are books that bridge the physical and biological sciences, books that are about religious holidays but are also activity books, books that describe musical instruments and also tell the reader how to make simple instruments. Books on pollution, for instance, involve weather, natural resources, and chemical change; they involve living things; and they illustrate the problems created by our careless destruction of our environment, problems that have sociological repercussions. Since pollution is a tragedy created by humanity, such books have been placed in the social science list.

The books have been arranged in five broad categories: biological sciences, physical sciences, social sciences, religion and the arts, and activities and experiments. The bibliography for this chapter follows the same pattern.

The Biological Sciences

Partly because of the nationwide concern for more science in the schools, the list of science books has grown phenomenally each year. The list has also grown in breadth of subject. No longer are books in the biological sciences confined to those about familiar plants and animals—today they cover almost every topic from a hen's egg to cryogenics and space medicine. Children's books have abandoned, for the most part, the pseudo-scientific stories

Viewpoint

It is not clear who said: "A child is not a vase to be filled, but a fire to be lit." The author, unfortunately, has remained elusive. But the statement is nonetheless true and applies to children as they read, especially to children reading nonfiction. You can almost divide the nonfiction they read into two categories: nonfiction that stuffs in facts, as if children were vases to be filled, and nonfiction that ignites the imagination, as if children were indeed fires to be lit.

A great many nonfiction books are well done. They cover a subject, often an important subject, with clarity and authority. Reviewers praise them; librarians buy them, grateful for the reliable information between the covers. But, alas, these same books may seem long and dull and difficult to children who are not dedicated readers. As a matter of fact, the books may seem long and dull and difficult to the rest of us, too. We would all prefer books that are readable and exciting. Isn't it reasonable to expect that nonfiction be as exciting as fiction?

From "Filling Vases, Lighting Fires" by Jo Carr in *The Horn Book Magazine*, November/December 1987, pp. 710–713. Reprinted by permission of The Horn Book, 14 Beacon St., Boston, Mass. 02108.

and watered-down information of the past and have adopted instead a seriousness and a straightforward approach that children and adults alike can appreciate.

Reports from teachers and librarians show that science rates high both in the types of questions children ask and in the types of books they request. Properly presented, almost any area of scientific knowledge can be made both fascinating and comprehensible to children.

The criteria for informational books discussed earlier in this chapter of course are applicable in evaluating science books. It is important that the author keeps in mind the child's point of view.

Authors should begin within the framework of the child's limited world. They must expand that world *step by step* at a pace which the child can follow—if they leap, they may leave the child behind. Leading, though, is not enough, for the child will choose to stay behind if the journey becomes uninteresting. What, therefore, is necessary to maintain interest?

Naturally clarity and good organization are of primary importance. Yet no matter how carefully and logically an author develops material, if it sounds like an article for an encyclopedia, the child will often lose interest. Unfortunately many adults look upon science as a cold collection of facts. To them it is devoid of emotion, entirely unrelated to imaginative writing. To the child, however, finding out about science is full of excitement, fascination, joy, and reassurance. What are some more of the books that not only present information clearly and understandably but maintain the reader's interest?

Books like Sarah Riedman's *Naming Living Things* discuss seriously the classification of plants and animals. There is a wide spread between the sophistication of this book and the simple approach of *Benny's Animals* by Millicent Selsam, described earlier, but in terms of accuracy each fulfills its purpose.

With the current stress on ecological balance, many books explore both the plants and the animals of a living community. *The Living Community* by Carl Hirsch is an introduction to interrelationships among plants and animals; Berniece Freschet's *Year on Muskrat Marsh* and Alvin Tresselt's *The Beaver Pond* give a similar

From *From Flower to Fruit*, written and illustrated by Anne Ophelia Dowden.

picture of an ecosystem for younger children.

Lucy Kavaler's *Wonders of Fungi* discusses the myriad uses of some of the 100,000 known species of fungi that are disease producers or that are used as food or medicine. Among the most beautifully illustrated books about plants are Carol Lerner's *Plant Families* and Anne Ophelia Dowden's *This Noble Harvest: A Chronicle of Herbs* and *From Flower to Fruit*—all of which can be used for identifying plants. The latter can be used as an introduction to botany; it also stresses the importance of plants in the ecology.

Both plants and animals are discussed in Glenn Blough's *Soon After September*, the story of what happens in winter to plants, hibernating animals, and migrating birds; and *Who Lives in This House?* is about animal families. Both of these books are illustrated by Jeanne Bendick and are appealing to younger children; the typeface is large and clear, and the language is simple.

Probably the greatest number of books about the animal kingdom are accounts of a single animal. Alice Goudey's stories are authoritative and simply written, giving the life cycle, habits, and habitat in such books as *Here Come the*

Dolphins. Another author whose books are dependably accurate and have a direct and dignified style is Dorothy Shuttlesworth, who writes chiefly about insects, although her works include *The Story of Rodents* and *To Find a Dinosaur*. The evidence here of thorough research is seen also in Shuttlesworth's similar books on ants and on spiders. Jane Werner Watson's *Whales: Friendly Dolphins and Mighty Giants of the Sea* is a well-rounded book for the middle grades. Certainly the most beautifully written book on the subject is Victor Scheffer's *Little Calf*, which is for older readers. Russell Freedman covers all aspects of a subject that fascinates many children in *Sharks*.

Of all the books about dinosaurs, Roy Chapman Andrews's *All About Dinosaurs* adds another dimension to information, for a large part of the book is devoted to his own experiences, and he conveys with relish the excitement of locating the first dinosaur eggs found in our time. *Dinosaur Bones* by Aliki introduces young children to the ways in which dinosaurs are classified. A most impressive reference source is Helen Sattler's *The Illustrated Dinosaur Dictionary*; *Tyrannosaurus Rex and Its Kin: The Mesozoic Monsters* is one of her many other books on dinosaurs.

Louis Darling's most impressive book is *The Gull's Way*. Here, there is excellent correlation between Darling's text and his pictures. On a remote coastal island, he observed closely the behavior of two herring gulls as they courted, mated, brooded their eggs, and then departed when their offspring became independent. Darling's style changed, in this book, from his competent but conventional description of a bird in *Greenhead*, the study of a mallard duck, to a philosophical, almost tender, outlook on wildlife.

A good book for identifying seashells is Elizabeth Clemons's *Shells Are Where You Find Them*, which gives advice on collecting and on a separate page describes each shell listed. Appropriate for use with very young children is Alice Goudey's *Houses from the Sea*. The slow, easy pace and the delicate illustrations by Adrienne Adams make it a good choice for reading aloud; the fact that two children, wandering along the beach, find fifteen kinds of shells means that there is not too much information for small children to assimilate. The book is prefaced by a note on collecting and closes with a brief account of how shells are formed. *Houses from the Sea* was a Caldecott Honor Book.

In addition to books on animal species, there are excellent ones that explore some special aspect of animal life. Dorothy Shuttlesworth, for example, in *Animal Camouflage*, explains countershading, disruptive coloration, and mimicry. Jack Scott discusses characteristics that have enabled some species to flourish in *The Survivors*; in *Alligator* and *Island of Wild Horses* he describes two species that have done so. Fascinating accounts of animal training are Anna Michel's *The Story of Nim: The Chimp Who Learned Languages* and *Koko's Kitten*, Francine Patterson's story of a pet gorilla.

All kinds of vertebrate life are considered in Margaret Cosgrove's *Bone for Bone*, a study of comparative anatomy by a medical artist. Cosgrove discusses, in graceful prose, the relation-

ships between parts of the body, the graduation from simple to complex vertebrates, and the adaptive process by which each animal fits into a way of life.

Cosgrove's *Eggs—and What Happens Inside Them*, for a slightly younger audience, deals with eggs that develop in water or on land, and eggs without shells, concluding with a discussion of the parts of the egg that develop into different parts of the body. A book with remarkable photographs is *Window into an Egg: Seeing Life Begin* by Geraldine Lux Flanagan. Through a glass window sealed into an eggshell, we see an embryo develop into a chick.

The miracle of reproduction is described in books for every age, from Paul and Kay Showers's *Before You Were a Baby*, discussed earlier in this chapter, and Sheila Kitzinger's *Being Born*, both of which are clear explanations that use correct terminology yet have a reverent approach toward the miracle of birth, to Eric Johnson's *Love and Sex in Plain Language*, which discusses sexual intercourse and sex mores with frankness and dignity. Photographs are used to illustrate the candid, clear text for the child of eight to ten in a book translated from the Swedish, Lennart Nilsson's *How Was I Born?*

The Physical Sciences

Many of today's children know more about science than do some adults. Parents can sympathize with the mother and father who hadn't the remotest idea of the answer when their fourth-grader asked them whether the ionosphere or the troposphere was nearer the earth. Teachers can report numerous situations similar to the one in which a fifth-grader was able to give the class an impromptu lecture in answer to another child's question on how a rocket works. Where are the children getting this knowledge?

Some of it may come from television programs, but science books for children are certainly one of the most important sources of information. In both the extent of subjects covered and in the vocabulary used, children's science books show that there is a new respect for the reader's intelligence and interest.

From *Koko's Kitten* by Dr. Francine Patterson, photographs by Dr. Ronald H. Cohn.

Many of the concept books for young children, like Eric Carle's *My Very First Book of Shapes,* can stimulate curiosity.

Isaac Asimov's story about gravity, *The Best New Thing* or *How Big Is Big? From Stars to Atoms* by Herman and Nina Schneider lead young children to curiosity about the world in which they live and about why things happen the way they do. Jeanne Berdick deals with the interdependence of human, plant, and animal life in *A Place to Live.* When children begin to ask "how" and "why," then we know that they are ready to explore further in the world of science. It is the primary purpose of all of these books to encourage this desire to know more.

One of the first things a child becomes aware of is the weather. Alvin Tresselt's *Hide and Seek Fog* is an excellent introduction to aspects of weather for very young children. Benjamin Bova's *Man Changes the Weather* describes the ways in which man has affected the atmosphere, including pollution and a discussion of control agencies, and in John Navarra's *Wide World Weather*, older readers can investigate the scientific, social, and governmental aspects of getting and sharing information, and of weather control and weather satellites.

Melvin Berger's *The New Water Book* explains the water cycle and the variation in rainfall in different parts of the earth, the uses of water, water resources, and water pollution. A good first book about the earth is *Your Changing Earth* by Hy Ruchlis, which describes the beginnings of the earth and the solar system; the development of land, sea, and air; and the ways in which natural forces change the earth's surface.

Oceanography is another rapidly expanding frontier; like many other areas of science, it is a subject in which many books bridge the scientific disciplines. Although newer books report some of the more recent knowledge about the sea floor, no book on the subject is more exciting than Rachel Carson's *The Sea Around Us,* which describes the formation of the oceans, tides and currents, marine flora and fauna, and the ocean floor with its volcanic activity. Younger children can get facts from Rhoda Blumberg's *The First Travel Guide to the Bottom of the Sea.*

Books about the earth and volcanic activity may stimulate a child's interest in the past ages in which the earth as we know it was shaped. *First Days of the World* by Gerald Ames and Rose Wyler explains the formation of the solar system, the beginnings of oceans, atmosphere, and living things, and goes on to describe the geological changes through the ages. Seymour Simon, in *Volcanoes*, explains very clearly and simply how volcanoes are formed and how they erupt.

People have always been fascinated by stars, but never before the space age has there been such general interest and such immediate concern with the far reaches of our universe. Many of Franklyn Branley's books were discussed earlier in the chapter; no writer in the field of astronomy is more adept at writing simply for young children. Another clever approach, designed for beginners, can be found in *You, Among the Stars* by Herman and Nina Schnei-

From *The First Travel Guide to the Bottom of the Sea* by Rhoda Blumberg, illustrated by Gen Shimada.

der. As in other books by these same authors, the emphasis is on orienting the young child. Through the theme of an envelope address, the child moves from the family home outward into space step by step until the familiar street address becomes greatly elaborated.

Ask children today what area of science they want to study, and more often than not they will answer "space." In the minds of today's children, studying space often means studying rockets and satellites, not the sun and moon. Rhoda Blumberg, in *The First Travel Guide to the Moon*, gives information in a straight-faced spoof. Bernice Kohn, in *Communications Satellites*, describes the principles by which satellites function, and Ben Bova's *Workshops in Space* discusses knowledge garnered from satellites. Two books that have the immediacy of experience are Sally Ride's *To Space and Back* and James McCarter's *The Space Shuttle Disaster*.

To understand the mechanics of the space program, so much of which is based on intricate mathematics, readers must be aware of the mathematical computations on which scientists rely. Lancelot Hogben's *The Wonderful World of Mathematics* relates the growth of mathematics as a science to changing human needs. With the modern curriculum, in which children are learning new concepts at earlier stages, there have been many books published that use the process approach or deal with one aspect of mathematical concepts. An excellent series, the Crowell Young Math Books, examines one aspect in each volume. Typical of the series are *Long, Short, High, Low, Thin, Wide* by James Fey, which discusses measurement and encourages the reader to observe and compare, and Jane Srivastava's *Averages*. These books teach something about scientific methods as well as the immediate subject with which they are concerned. Mitsumasa Anno, in *Math Games* and *Math Games II*, adds the appeals of humor and riddles to books that present challenges in mathematical logic. In *What Do You Mean by "Average"?* Elizabeth James and Carol Barkin's discussion of such concepts as mean, median, and mode is for older readers. The basic principles of computer mathematics are explained in *The New World of Computers* by Alfred Lewis, and the simplest kind of computer programming is introduced to younger children in

Viewpoint

I like books of knowledge; not those that want to encroach upon recreation, upon leisure, pretending to be able to teach anything without drudgery. There is no truth in that. There are things which cannot be learned without great pains; we must be resigned to it. I like books of knowledge when they are not just grammar or geometry poorly disguised; when they have tact and moderation; when, instead of pouring out so much material on a child's soul that it is crushed, they plant in it a seed that will develop from the inside. I like them when they do not deceive themselves about the quality of knowledge, and do not claim that knowledge can take the place of everything else. I like them especially when they distill from all the different kinds of knowledge the most difficult and the most necessary—that of the human heart.

Paul Hazard, *Books, Children and Men*, translated by Marguerite Mitchell. Boston: The Horn Book, 1944, p. 43.

Seymour Simon's *How to Talk to Your Computer*.

To prepare children for possible conversion from our traditional system of measurement to the metric system, many authors have discussed its advantages. June Behrens, in *The True Book of Metric Measurement*, gives a clear explanation for readers in the primary grades. For slightly older readers, Miriam Schlein's *Metric—The Modern Way to Measure* discusses both the way in which the metric system works and the reasons some think it preferable to the old system of measuring. Books for readers in the upper elementary grades and in high school describe historical development and discuss opposition to the change as well as explaining the need for conversion and the functioning of the metric system.

When we come to physics and chemistry we are entering realms of science which have increasingly enabled humanity to reorder natural existence to suit particular desires or needs.

· 5 ·

Counting Water

From *Anno's Math Games II*, written and illustrated by Mitsumasa Anno.

While we want our children to appreciate fully these achievements of applied science, they must also be helped to recognize its limitations if they are to gain a realistic picture of the world in which they live. In this nuclear age, it is perhaps more apparent than ever before that science can bring great good or harm, depending on how we put it to use.

The science of chemistry can be traced back to early times. Roy A. Gallant's *Exploring Chemistry*, for example, begins with the discovery of fire and thereafter tells the absorbing history of efforts to understand and change matter. Isaac Asimov, in *Building Blocks of the Universe*, makes clear, in his usual witty and informal style, the chemical elements that are the foundation of all matter. While the complexities of chemistry are seldom explored as a whole for younger children, aspects of the subject are discussed in such books as *Millions and Millions of Crystals*

and *Oil: The Buried Treasure*, both by Roma Gans, who makes complicated topics very clear in both books by wise selection of facts.

In the purest sense, chemistry is the study of matter only—its composition, its nature, and the changes it constantly undergoes—while physics is the study of matter and energy and the relationship between them. Even at the elementary school level, more and more books are appearing that cross boundary lines and reveal the strong interrelationship between these sciences. For example, there are now several books which borrow knowledge from chemistry regarding atoms and molecular structure and then go on to apply this knowledge to the recent developments in physics regarding atomic energy and its many uses. Jeanne Bendick's *Solids, Liquids, and Gases* suggests basic criteria for comparison and testing.

An excellent example for younger children is John Lewellen's *The Mighty Atom*, which very simply, with the aid of familiar analogies and Ida Scheib's clever illustrations, moves from a discussion of the atom with its neutrons, protons, and electrons, to molecular structure and the basic elements and finally to atomic power, the construction and operation of atomic furnaces and engines, and the uses of atomic energy in both war and peace. Neil Ardley's *Atoms and Energy* describes the production and uses of atomic energy, and David Woodbury's *The New World of the Atom* stresses the uses of atomic energy in medicine, in carbon-14 testing, and in nuclear power plants for space exploration.

Mechanics, an area of great interest to children, paves the way for a study of transportation, and is one of the areas in which children can observe and experiment from the first time they are fascinated by the moving parts in their toys. An interesting book for young children is *The True Book of Toys at Work*, in which John Lewellen describes the mechanical principles involved in such things as whistles, electric trains, and balloons. For the reader in the middle grades, *The Simple Facts of Simple Machines* by Elizabeth James and Carol Barkin is an excellent book that discusses principles of physics. Also for the middle grades is *The Macmillan Book of How Things Work* by Michael and Marcia Folsom; and for older readers there is David Macaulay's *The Way Things Work*, a comprehensive book that is witty, ingenious, handsome, and authoritative.

Naturally the machines which people have built on the principles of mechanics would have limited use indeed without the harnessing of some type of energy other than human power to run them. One of the most comprehensive books on this subject, excitingly illustrated in color by John Teppich, is Lancelot Hogben's *Wonderful World of Energy*. This book constantly reminds the child that, of all the many sources of energy, the greatest is the one which has mastered the others—humanity's own will and drive to go forward. We learn how people have gradually harnessed and put to work energy from wind, water, steam, fire, electricity, and now the atom and the sun. The problems of diminishing sources of energy and the social implications for the future are described in Daniel Halacy's *The Energy Trap*, which discusses possible solutions through new developments and action by individuals and authoritative bodies.

Of all the forms of energy, however, the one with which the child has had the most direct experience is usually electricity. This is not an easy subject for children, and yet it plays such an important role in their everyday lives that we should help them gain at least an appreciation of its great value and some understanding of how it operates. One of the clearest and simplest explanations of this complex subject can be found in *The First Book of Electricity* by Sam and Beryl Epstein. Since this book is designed for the beginner with no previous knowledge of electricity, new concepts have been fully explained. For older children who already have a basic knowledge of this subject, the greater complexities of electricity are explained in Ira M. Freeman's *All About Electricity*, which introduces a good deal of the history of the development of electrical power and contains whole chapters on various uses of electricity. An electro-optical engineer, Jack White, describes the infrared range and the instruments that put it to use in *The Invisible World of the Infrared*.

Many of the topics we have mentioned are included in *Understanding Science* by William Crouse. It is a panoramic view in which no subject is treated in depth, but it gives the reader a broad picture of the worlds of pure and applied science. Also for such background, books like Corinne Jacker's *Window on the Unknown: A History of the Microscope* and Aaron Klein's *The Electron Microscope* are most useful.

The Social Sciences

Under the rubric of the social sciences are those subjects that have to do with people in their association with other groups of people: history, political science, anthropology, economics, geography, law, and many others, often—as is true of other sciences—overlapping each other or other disciplines. With so broad a scope, this chapter can only mention some of the good books in areas so extensive yet so finely divided.

Since an understanding of many of these areas is partially dependent on seeing a relationship between past and present, perhaps the best background book for a young child is one that clarifies time concepts. Three such are *The True Book of Time* by Feenie Ziner and Elizabeth Thompson, which teaches children that there are other ways, in addition to clocks, for measuring time; Miriam Schlein's *It's About Time*, which helps clarify the puzzling relationships implied in "long time, short time"; and Melvin

From *The Invisible World of the Infrared* by Jack R. White, illustrated by Valerie Temple.

Berger's *Time After Time*, which discusses days, seasons, time measurement, and the inner time-sense of living things in a clear, open-ended text.

Often small children are fascinated by dinosaurs before they understand the earth's time scale, and books about dinosaurs can be used to introduce the beginnings of human prehistory. Julian May's *The First Men*, for the early grades, may be followed in the middle grades by *The First People in the World* by Gerald Ames and Rose Wyler. For older readers, two reliable books about prehistoric people in North America are William Scheele's *The Earliest Americans*, which investigates the puzzle of when humans first migrated to this continent, and Anne Terry White's *Prehistoric America*, which describes modern discoveries that have led to a better understanding of prehistoric times.

Sonia Bleeker examined cultural patterns in *The Ibo of Biafra*; *The Maya: Indians of Central America*; and *The Eskimo: Arctic Hunters and Trappers*. An anthropologist, Bleeker wrote vivid accounts based on visits, and was exemplary in her objective approach.

To understand how information about prehistory and early civilizations is acquired, children may turn to a book about archeology as a science. W. John Hackwell's *Digging to the Past* and Leonard Cottrell's *Digs and Diggers: A Book of World Archeology* give information about the development of the science, its methodology, and some of the great discoveries of the past. Dora Hamblin's *Pots and Robbers* tells true stories about the dramatic aspects of archeology, including many incidents involving thefts and forgeries.

There is a wealth of material on ancient civilizations, for many facets of which the art books by Shirley Glubok are good supplementary reading. Both Lila Perl's *Mummies, Tombs, and Treasures: Secrets of Ancient Egypt* and Jeanne Bendick's *Egyptian Tombs* give a great deal of cultural and historical information. Ruth Karen's *Kingdom of the Sun* describes the Inca empire with a combination of vigorous style and scholarly research. Katharine Savage, in *The Story of Africa: South of the Sahara*, gives a history of the exploration and exploitation of this region.

Many of the Columbian biographies include conjecture about the first "discoverers" of America, with honors usually divided between Columbus and the Vikings. Ellen Pugh, in *Brave His Soul*, presents convincing evidence for the theory that a Welsh prince exiled him-

From *Digging to the Past: Excavations in Ancient Lands*, written and illustrated by W. John Hackwell.

self and came to North America in 1170. A stunning book that uses source material and binds the excerpts smoothly with the compiler's comments is *The New Land* by Phillip Viereck.

Often books that are not written as historical accounts can illuminate a period. Among such books are Joe Lasker's *A Tournament of Knights* and *Merry Ever After: The Story of Two Medieval Weddings*; another is Grant Uden's *A Dictionary of Chivalry*, which won the Greenaway Medal for Pauline Baynes's exquisite illustrations and was a runner-up for the Carnegie Medal, a book as useful as it is handsome. David Macaulay's description of some nineteenth-century cotton mills in *Mill* serves admirably as social history. A book about quests in the Southwest, Sheila Cowing's *Searches in the American Desert*, gives vivid anecdotes about events and movements of historical importance.

Books which give children a factual account of the early history of America, its discovery and settlement, include Alice Dalgliesh's *America Begins* and Louise Rich's *The First Book of New World Explorers*. Jean Fritz's *Who's That Stepping on Plymouth Rock?* (see Chapter 11) is as lively as her brief stories of colonial leaders.

The American Revolution and the Declaration of Independence are events of special significance for children, and there are many good books about this period of revolution and confederation. *The First Book of the American Revolution* by Richard B. Morris will help younger readers understand the meaning of these events for the people of that time and for those of today. Betsy Maestro's *A More Perfect Union* presents a clear discussion of the Constitutional Convention for younger readers; and *Shh! We're Writing the Constitution* by Jean Fritz, which is for the middle grades, makes this landmark event an exciting story. The crucial role of women during this period in our history is described in Linda De Pauw's *Founding Mothers*. An unusual viewpoint is given by Clorinda Clarke in *The American Revolution 1775–83: A British View*, a book that has a judicious, long-range outlook and a lively style.

Charles Flato's *The Golden Book of the Civil War* is adapted from an American Heritage picture history. Profusely illustrated, it gives a broad and vivid picture of the war years. G.

From *A Tournament of Knights*, written and illustrated by Joe Lasker.

Allen Foster's *Sunday in Centerville* is as interesting for the discussion of the complex causes of the war, and the preparations for it, as it is for the detailed account of the first Battle of Bull Run.

Daniel J. Boorstin's *The Landmark History of the American People* deviates from the usual compilation of facts and dates to discuss the people who influenced patterns of change; its emphasis is on movements and on regional and national patterns. The approach is stimulating, the style informal, and the analyses acutely perceptive, as might be expected from an eminent historian.

Of the many books on African-American history in the United States, some of the best are Robert Goldston's *The Negro Revolution*; Dorothy Sterling's *Tear Down the Walls!* and *The Trouble They Seen: Black People Tell the Story of Reconstruction* (both discussed in Chapter 12); and Johanna Johnston's *Together in America*— all comprehensive and as objective as is consistent with a history of slavery and oppression. Marilyn Miller's *The Bridge at Selma* tells the tragic-heroic story of a major event in the civil rights struggle; a good companion book is Elaine Pascoe's history of discrimination in the United States, *Racial Prejudice*.

Unfortunately, no comparable body of material exists for other minority groups in the United States. Books about native Americans, however, are growing in number and scope. Richard Erdoes, in *The Native Americans: Navajos* discusses traditional and modern life styles. Ann Nolan Clark's *Circle of Seasons* is a dignified and reverent description of the rites and observances of the Pueblo year. *Red Hawk's Account of Custer's Last Battle*, by Paul and Dorothy Goble, is the historically accurate account told dramatically from the viewpoint of a boy who realizes after the battle at Little Big Horn, that while the Indian victory was definitive, the Indian's fight against white invasion was hopeless. Franklin Folsom's *Red Power on the Rio Grande* gives the native-American point of view on the Pueblo Revolution of 1680, and Dee Brown has ably adapted *Wounded Knee* from the moving and powerful *Bury My Heart at Wounded Knee*. Robert Hofsinde, adopted by the Chippewas, compiled *Indian Sign Language*, a glossary of over 500 universal signs of North American tribes. One of the best books available is *The American Indian* by Oliver La Farge, which contains both historical and contemporary material.

In addition to Milton Meltzer's history of American Jews discussed earlier, other books about minority groups include Harold Coy's *Chicano Roots Go Deep* and Alberta Eiseman's *The Spanish-Speaking in the United States*, which are candid and sympathetic evaluations of discriminations suffered by Hispanic peoples in the years they have lived in the United States. Edwin Hoyt, in *Asians in the West*, examines with equal candor the record of Caucasian discrimination.

Several books provide information about Canada. Adam Bryant, in *Canada: Good Neighbor to the World*, describes the history and geography of the country as well as its ethnic diversity and its economic and social patterns today. Lithographs by Lynd Ward help to make May McNeer's *Canadian Story* an exciting account of the history of Canada from the time of the Vikings to the opening of the St. Lawrence Seaway.

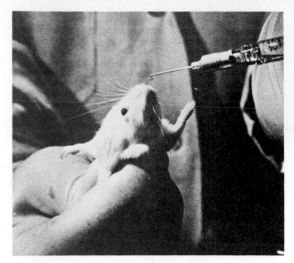

From *Lives at Stake: The Science and Politics of Environmental Health* by Laurence Pringle, photographs by the National Food and Drug Administration.

Among the books that give information about other parts of the world are *The First Book of South America* by William Carter, which gives an account of the folklore, religions, and history of the continent; John Gunther's books about Africa and Don Lawson's *South Africa*. Others of note are Aliki's *The King's Day: Louis XIV of France*, Rhoda Blumberg's *Commodore Perry in the Land of the Shogun*, and Lois Hobert's *Mexican Mural*. In fact, there are so many books about other parts of the world that it would be impossible to present a representative list in one chapter on informational titles.

Because of the spread of urbanization, the interest in cities is greater today than it has ever been, both from the standpoint of allure and, alas, from the standpoint of the complex problems in urban life. Few are more urgent than pollution. In *Dangerous Air*, Lucy Kavaler cites the causes of air pollution throughout the world and discusses what government, industry, and individual citizens must do to eliminate this danger. John Navarra considers the same problem in *The World You Inherit: A Story of Pollution* and adds, in a cogent chapter, the legislation and litigation that are involved; in *Our Noisy World*, he discusses the problem of noise pollution. Many of the same issues are discussed by Laurence Pringle in *Lives at Stake: The Science and Politics of Environmental Health*; in *Rain of*

Troubles: The Science and Politics of Acid Rain, he also considers a broad range of problems and issues. James and Lynn Hahn look to solutions in *Recycling*; and in *The Population Puzzle* by A. H. Drummond, the associated problems of increasing population density and decreasing resources are examined.

Children are indefatigably curious about the way other people live and where they live—and why they live there if it's hot (or cold, or rainy, or mountainous . . .). They are curious about differences, open-minded rather than insular. Books can help foster their awareness of the superficiality of differences and the similarity of people everywhere. *Why We Live Where We Live* by Eva Knox Evans helps them understand the interdependence of people and the geographic limitations upon the choice of homes.

Many of the recent books for children have been written with the objective of making the story of our past and present a "real experience" rather than a superficial one. The story of changes that come to a small community are described and beautifully illustrated in Alice and Martin Provensen's *Shaker Lane*. A stimulating volume to which older children can be guided is *People and Places* by Margaret Mead. The book is richly informative, springing out of Mead's expert knowledge of people and countries. She begins by stating that human beings are curious about each other and that even the most primitive peoples in the world today wonder about those unlike themselves, and she concludes with discussions about similarities and differences among peoples of the world. She also offers suggestions as to what steps must be taken to solve humanity's problems so that all may live in a more orderly world. All in all, Mead's book challenges its readers to a deeper understanding not only of themselves but also of other people and places.

Religion and the Arts

Books of religious instruction and prayers are used by devout families in the home, and biographies of religious leaders or stories that present religious diversity can help children understand and respect the beliefs or the non-belief of others. Books on comparative religion, however, belong in any collection to which children turn for information. There continues to be fine picture books and books for younger independent readers that give fresh interpretations to familiar Bible stories—from the exuberantly illustrated version of *The Nativity* as pictured by Julie Vivas or *Noah and the Ark*, with richly detailed paintings by Greenaway Medalist Pauline Baynes, to the adaptation for the older group of the first five books of the Old Testament, *The Book of Adam to Moses*, as eloquently retold by Lore Segal and illustrated by Leonard Baskin. An unusual variant, *Spirit Child: A Story of the Nativity*, is illustrated by Caldecott Medalist Barbara Cooney and translated by John Bierhorst from an Aztec-language version that was influenced by late Middle Ages tradition.

Ruth Smith's *The Tree of Life* is an anthology consisting of selections from the world's great religions, and is an excellent companion volume to Katharine Savage's *The Story of World*

From *Jerusalem, Shining Still* by Karla Kuskin, illustrated by David Frampton.

Religions. In Betsy Smith's *Breakthrough: Women in Religion,* the text examines the experiences and philosophies of five contemporary female religious leaders. Edward Rice's *The Five Great Religions* gives more background than other books that examine major faiths, since Rice believes that the mystical aspects of each are rooted in its beginnings. Karla Kuskin's *Jerusalem, Shining Still* is an evocative history of the city that is holy to many religions.

The series of books about religious denominations by Kathleen Elgin, of which *The Unitarians* is an example, describes the history and the beliefs of each denomination; lists some of its famous members, past and present; and gives a lengthy biography of a leader or prominent member. In *The Vatican,* John Deedy describes that community's members and its art and history. Howard Greenfeld, in *Passover* and *Rosh Hashanah and Yom Kippur,* describes the origins and the celebration of major Jewish holidays. Elizabeth Seeger describes Buddhism, Confucianism, Hinduism, Shintoism, and Taoism in *Eastern Religions.* John Snelling's *Buddhism* describes the philosophy of Siddhartha Gautama, its leader, and the spread of Buddhism from India to other parts of Eastern Asia.

Books that encourage the child's interest in music range from such narrow treatments as Larry Kettelkamp's *Flutes, Whistles and Reeds,* which introduces woodwinds and explains how they produce sounds, to the comprehensive treatment in *The Wonderful World of Music* by Benjamin Britten and Imogen Holst, a history of music, musicians, and instruments that is mature in concept. Much of the book can be appreciated by the reader with no musical background, but the discussions of theory and harmony may present difficulties for the general reader. David Ewen is one of the most prolific and authoritative authors of books about music, writing on musical forms: *Opera, Orchestral Music, Vocal Music,* and others. Roy Hemming, in *Discovering Music,* gives suggestions for the collector of tapes and records.

There is comparatively little material available about the music of other countries. Betty Warner Deitz and Michael Babatunde Olatunji have written an outstanding book about the way music is used in African cultures south of the Sahara in *Musical Instruments of Africa*; and in *Folk Songs of China, Japan, and Korea,* Dietz collaborated with Thomas Choonbai Park. These books have been compiled with scholarly care, and can help children understand other cultures through their music.

Langston Hughes wrote several books about music: *The First Book of Rhythms, Famous Negro Music Makers,* and *The First Book of Jazz.* The latter presents a concise history of the development of jazz in the United States and of its spread to other countries. Hughes discusses the diverse elements that contributed to the complex rhythms of jazz: African, French, and Spanish elements in New Orleans; worksongs and blues; and spirituals, ragtime, and minstrel music. Only the melodic line is provided in Ashley Bryan's *Walk Together Children: Black American Spirituals.* Arnold Shaw's *The Rock Revolution* includes discussions of performers and comments of critics. In *Gold Guitars* Irwin Stambler and Grelun Landon tell the story of country-and-western music.

Books about opera; libretti of individual operas; collections of songs, like Ann Durell's *The Diane Goode Book of American Folk Tales and Songs* and Jane Yolen's *The Lullaby Songbook*; and books that describe the composition and arrangement of orchestras are listed in the bibliography, as are some of the many songbooks published for children. One knowledgeable but humorous approach is Roger Englander's *What's All the Screaming About?* There is also a considerable amount of information about music and musicians in the biographies cited in Chapter 12.

A book that bridges the worlds of music and dance is *American Indians Sing* by Charles Hofmann, in which the information about music, dances, and song-poems includes melodic and dance notation. The relationship of dance to religious observance is emphasized in Lee Warren's *The Dance of Africa,* which discusses also the impact of cultural changes on traditional forms. Perhaps the most comprehensive book on the dance is Arnold Haskell's *The Wonderful World of Dance.* In an impressively authoritative volume, Haskell describes the evolution of the dance and dance forms, with biographical material about famous dancers and choreographers, and with many diagrams of dance notation.

From *Michelangelo's World*, written and illustrated by
Piero Ventura.

There is an especially good section on ritual
dances of the Orient; and, throughout the
book, dance forms are related to the cultural
context in which they evolved. Narrower in
scope, *Ballet: A Pictorial History* by Walter Terry
is a good introduction for the reader who is not
a balletomane, but it has enough material about
outstanding dancers of each historical period
to appeal to the lover of ballet. Noel
Streatfeild's *A Young Person's Guide to Ballet*
gives a wealth of interesting detail about techniques and ballet history.

Olga Maynard's *American Modern Dancers:
The Pioneers* is an excellent survey of the evolution of modern dance through discussions of
the work of great dancers, giving authoritative
analyses of techniques, theories, trends, influences, and comparative schools. Maynard gives,
in *The Ballet Companion*, a detailed guide to
four ballets, and a glossary of ballet terms and

techniques. Stunning photographs illustrate
Jill Krementz's *A Very Young Dancer*, a photographic essay about a real child who is a ballet
student.

When we turn to books about art there is a
positive cornucopia of fine books. One of the
best general surveys is Janet Moore's *The Many
Ways of Seeing*, which discusses the relationship
between art and nature, and the relationship
between the artist and the world. It analyzes the
ways an artist perceives in terms of light, color,
composition, and line; it also describes media,
materials, and techniques, and suggests ways in
which the reader can try some of the ideas
discussed and learn to see the elements of an
art form. A similar book with examples ranging
from ancient treasures to contemporary works
is *Looking at Sculpture* by Roberta Paine.

Marion Downer's *The Story of Design* uses a
variety of art objects, shown in photographs, to
illustrate the appreciation of design the world
over, from primitive times to today. M. J.
Gladstone's *A Carrot for a Nose* and Elinor
Horwitz's *Contemporary American Folk Artists*
discuss folk art. In *Looking at Art*, Alice
Elizabeth Chase, an art historian, describes the
ways in which artists have interpreted their
worlds, and the author's explicit and clearly
presented views on the nature of art make the
book an excellent choice for the reader who is
on unfamiliar terrain. Howard Greenfeld
writes with authority and zeal in *The Impressionist Revolution* and *They Came to Paris*; and
Michaelangelo's World by Piero Ventura has
value for its relevance to art history as well as
for its discussion of the artist's own work.

The Pantheon Story of Art for Young People by
Ariane Ruskin Batterberry is competently written but slights contemporary work; it has, however, an unusually large number of full-page,
full-color illustrations. Some of the series are
by Ariane Ruskin under that name; some are by
Michael Batterberry; and some are written
jointly by the two, as is *Primitive Art*. Ruskin's
Art of the High Renaissance emphasizes painters
and painting but the comprehensive text covers
all art forms. All of the books in this series are
profusely and handsomely illustrated.

There are few art books written for adults
that cannot be enjoyed by children, if the books
are illustrated. Books on color for the pre-

school and primary-age child can encourage aesthetic appreciation as well as teach colors, and some of the first concept books, like Tana Hoban's *Shapes and Things*, can stimulate an awareness of form as well as encourage observation. An effective way to stimulate interest before a visit to an art collection is to introduce *Visiting the Art Museum* by Laurene Krasny Brown and Marc Brown. In other words, information about art can come from many sources other than books about art.

Friedrich von Schlegel called architecture "frozen music," and in Mary Louise King's *A History of Western Architecture*, the illustrations show the patterned precision of Greek temples and the soaring lift of Gothic cathedrals that make this phrase so apt. King emphasizes the new developments of each period, and discusses the factors that influence style. A simpler, more succinct book on architectural history is *Understanding Architecture* by George Sullivan, which explains styles and construction techniques from the rudimentary post-and-lintel

buildings to today's skyscrapers and the plans for ecologically oriented homes of tomorrow.

Anne Rockwell's *Glass, Stones and Crown: The Abbe Suger and the Building of St. Denis* is as interesting for its historical background as it is for the story of Suger, the boyhood friend of Louis Capet, whose life as abbot was devoted to rebuilding St. Denis and incorporating those features that became popular throughout Europe: stained glass windows, flying buttresses and piers, and ribbed vaulting.

The construction of a modern building is described in Ely Jacques Kahn's *A Building Goes Up*, in which the erection of an office building is detailed from planning to completion. Although David Macaulay's books are discussed in Chapter 5, they also belong here as outstanding books on architecture; his *Underground, City,* and *Mill* have particular application for the social studies.

Activities and Experiments

One of the most popular kinds of activity books is the puzzle book. Martin Gardner's *Perplexing Puzzles and Tantalizing Teasers* contains riddles, scrambled words, mazes, and puzzles that require logic for achieving solution. It has a sufficient number of difficult puzzles to tempt the child who is adept, but not so many as to discourage the child who is a beginner. Another kind of brain teaser is Gardner's *Codes, Ciphers, and Secret Writing*, which describes codes used in history, explains how to concoct or decipher messages, and explains the difference between codes and ciphers. Paul Janeczko, in *Loads of Codes and Secret Ciphers*, also describes creating your own codes and breaking those of others. *Egyptian Hieroglyphs for Everyone* by Joseph and Lenore Scott gives an explanation of how the language developed and makes it easier for the reader to understand hieroglyphic writing. Stephanie Calmenson introduces turn-of-the-page suspense in *What Am I?* a riddle book for very young children. William Steig challenges independent readers in *CDB!* and *CDC?* Once children decipher "RUOK?" as "Are You O.K.?", for example, they enjoy this type of word play tremendously.

From *City*, written and illustrated by David Macaulay.

At the other end of the spectrum are the books that give instruction for physical activities, usually sports. Few of them can teach a child all he or she needs to know in order to play; most of them, however, can help. One such is S. H. Freeman's *Basic Baseball Strategy*, which is packed with so much information that it can be used by players older than the middle-grades audience to whom it is addressed, or by coaches for the clear explanations of such fine arts as base stealing, the squeeze play, and when to use the hit-and-run. *Better Softball for Boys and Girls* by George Sullivan gives advice on play and explains the game clearly. *Bicycling* by Charles Coombs tells the reader how to choose, use, and take care of a bicycle. In Jim Moore's *Football Techniques Illustrated*, there are discussions of offensive and defensive play; advice on running, kicking, passing, and tackling; and the rules of play. Other how-to-do-it sports books can easily be found listed under the names of the sports in such guides as *Children's Catalog* or *Subject Guide to Children's Books in Print*. Any book that includes a physical action that can be injurious, whether it be sports, crafts, or cooking, should include safety precautions.

A useful group of activity books are those in the fields of arts and crafts: Jan Adkins, in *Toolchest*, gives succinct advice to the amateur carpenter; in *Collage*, Mickey Klar Marks gives instructions for seven different kinds of collage; Don Bolognese and Elaine Raphael, in *Pencil, Pen and Ink* and *Printmaking*, explain techniques and materials for each medium. *Mask-Making with Pantomime and Stories from American History* by Laura Ross provides good background history as well as clear instructions. Among the many books on puppetry, two of the best are Eleanor Boylan's *How to Be a Puppeteer*, which presents directions for making and costuming puppets, manipulating them, making sets and scenery, and so on; and David Currell's *The Complete Book of Puppetry*, which is comprehensive enough to have reference use. An unusual book in this field is *The Rooster's Horns: A Chinese Puppet Plan to Make and Perform* by Ed Young and Hilary Beckett.

There are general craft books like Susan Purdy's *Festivals for You to Celebrate*, in which the projects are grouped by seasons and sug-

From *The Fun of Cooking* by Jill Krementz, photographs by Jill Krementz.

gestions are given for group activities, or James Baker's *Birthday Magic*, one of a holiday series that focuses on magic tricks appropriate for the occasion. Camille Sokol's *The Lucky Sew-It-Yourself Book* is a hand-sewing book with very simple projects for the seven to nine-year-old child. An example of a specialized book is Carolyn Meyer's *Rock Tumbling*. Older children can use almost any cookbook, but *Kids Cooking* by Aileen Paul and Arthur Hawkins makes cooking easy by listing ingredients and implements on one page, and giving the instructions on the facing page. *The Natural Cook's First Book* by Carole Getzoff stresses wholesome recipes; children share recipes in *The Fun of Cooking* by Jill Krementz.

Both Joan Harvath's *Filmmaking for Beginners* and Robert Ferguson's *How to Make Movies* give detailed and practical advice on every aspect of the art. Yvonne Andersen gives both the techniques of preparation and the intricacies of filming in *Make Your Own Animated Movies*. Terry Staples, in *Film and Video*, includes advice on making both in a text that gives information about historical development and technological advances.

One of the most sensible books on pets is Dorothy Broderick's *Training a Companion Dog*, which is explicit and detailed and gives advice on equipment. In *Look What I Found!* Marshal Case explains how to capture small wild creatures, with suggestions for duplicating the animal's natural habitat and an emphasis on showing kindness and respect for all life forms; and Roger Caras, in *A Zoo in Your Room*, gives sensible advice on pet care. William Weber's *Wild Animal Babies* does the same for the care of abandoned or injured small creatures.

In addition to the books that describe specific activities and crafts, there is the comprehensive "doing" book, which presents information about a variety of scientific topics through suggested experiments and activities. And there are books in very specialized areas, like Remy Charlip's *Handtalk: An ABC of Finger Spelling and Sign Language* and *Handtalk Zoo*, by George Ancona and Mary Beth, a photographic record of a visit to the zoo by a group of children who sign or finger spell to communicate.

The experiment book has a definite value in that it guides the child toward direct participation in the discovery of knowledge, and, since so many experiences must be gained vicariously, first-hand discovery should be encouraged whenever possible. But experiment books also have a more subtle value. We realize today that education must do more than impart knowledge—it must also teach the child how to use that knowledge in the solution of problems. Glenn Blough once stated:

If pupils are to grow in ability to solve problems they must grow in ability to think of appropriate things to do to discover solutions.[3]

Teaching children how to set up sound experiments and how to interpret the results of these experiments is one way of training them to "think of appropriate things to do."

Good experiment books, for obvious reasons, will suggest only those activities which are safe and those which can be performed with readily available and inexpensive materials; and there are such books today for every age level.

[3]Glenn O. Blough, "Quality Is What Counts!" *Instructor*, September 1958, p. 6.

Whatever the interest, a child who likes to experiment can benefit from Thomas Moorman's *How to Make Your Science Project Scientific*, which exemplifies the scientific attitudes and methods it describes.

Prove It! by Rose Wyler and Gerald Ames is for the beginning reader and presents simple experiments performed with ordinary objects. Harlow Rockwell's *I Did It* has varied, simple experiments and projects for beginning readers to try. Rose Wyler's *What Happens If . . . ?* has safe, easy experiments designed by a teacher of science and science education. Vicki Cobb's activity books are varied, with subjects like *Chemically Alive! Experiments You Can Do at Home* for older readers; *The Trip of a Drip*, a book about the water cycle that has clear examples for the middle grades; and *Gobs of Goo* for the primary grades. Franklyn Branley's *Timmy and the Tin-Can Telephone*, briefly mentioned earlier in this chapter, is written as a story in which two children learn about the transmission of sound by making a "telephone" out of tin cans, string, and buttons. Harry Milgrom's *Adventures with a Paper Cup* has an assortment of easy experiments in which a cone-shaped cup is used to demonstrate such phenomena as air resistance and sound amplification. This and similar books by Milgrom—or Nancy Larrick's *See for Yourself*, which has

From *Gobs of Goo* by Vicki Cobb, illustrated by Brian Schatell.

simple experiments with air, water, and heat—can stir or encourage an interest in scientific exploration and discovery in young children. A. Harris Stone's *The Chemistry of a Lemon* was one of the first, and is still one of the best, open-ended experiment books in simple chemistry, a fine example of the scientific method. For the child with a short attention span, Herman Schneider's *Science Fun for You in a Minute or Two* offers experiments that are brief and require little equipment or preparation.

One of the most varied books of experiments, containing material in many of the sciences, is *700 Science Experiments for Everyone*, compiled by UNESCO in 1956. William Moore's *Your Science Fair Project* has projects grouped by levels from grades three to eight, and is particularly useful for the average student who is required to participate. Salt and water are the primary ingredients for Seymour Simon's home demonstrations in *How to Be an Ocean Scientist in Your Own Home*.

Elizabeth Cooper's *Science in Your Own Back Yard* suggests ways of observing, collecting, and experimenting in the field of nature study in a book that can stimulate the interest of the individual reader or a group. There is an emphasis on conservation in Ted Pettit's *A Guide to Nature Projects*. Each section of the book deals with a single aspect of the subject and provides background information before discussing experiments.

In Molly McLaughlin's *Earthworms, Dirt and Rotten Leaves: An Exploration in Ecology*, all experiments include precautions about respecting the worms being studied, and the graceful writing adheres to principles of scientific inquiry. Christina Björk, in *Linnea's Almanac* and in *Linnea's Windowsill Garden*, gives accurate information in a crisp, informal style for a variety of natural science projects and for every aspect of indoor gardening. Another longer book that is also for the middle grades is *The Victory Garden Kid's Book: A Beginner's Guide to Growing Vegetables, Fruits, and Flowers* by Marjorie Waters; it is simply written and so broad in coverage as to have reference use.

For the child who has a specific interest, there are such books as Harry Sootin's *Experiments with Magnetism* or his mineralogy book, *The Young Experimenter's Workbook*, written in

From *Linnea's Windowsill Garden* by Christina Björk, illustrated by Lena Anderson.

collaboration with Laura Sootin. Paul Czaja's *Writing with Light* shows how one can make pictures without a camera. Both books require only materials that are available in the home or are inexpensive, and the experiments are practical and clearly explained. Bernie Zubrowski's *Wheels at Work: Building and Experimenting with Models of Machines* is an exemplary how-to-book: instructions are clear, sequential, and explicit, and most of the required materials are inexpensive or are available in most homes. Rocco Feravolo's *Easy Physics Projects: Air, Water and Heat* and A. Harris Stone's books are for children of the same age, but they are quite different in approach. Rather than using the open-ended process approach of the Stone experiment books, Feravolo answers the questions raised; little is left to the student's imagination, but the concepts are lucidly presented and the book can be useful to children hesitant about taking initiative.

Reference Books

Although encyclopedias and dictionaries, fact books and almanacs, and indexes and bibliographies are the kinds of books usually meant when reference books are mentioned, it should be remembered that many other kinds of books have reference use.

Children's rooms in public libraries often have books that reflect the particular interests of their community, such as foreign language source books, reference materials that give information about local industries, or books about indigenous flora and fauna. School library collections may stress books that fit into curricular units. Both types of libraries will gather as much as they can about local history, and both will include in their collections some books intended for adult reference use.

There are so many dictionaries and encyclopedias that are valuable, that guides to them are reference books in themselves. Most professional journals include reviews of reference books; *Booklist* and *Wilson Library Bulletin* have special sections devoted to them. Carolyn Sue Peterson's *Reference Books for Elementary and Junior High School Libraries* is a useful annotated bibliography that suggests in its introduction methods of evaluation, most of which require examination of the volumes being considered. Another good reference is *General Encyclopedias in Print.* Almost every dictionary and encyclopedia has a coterie of devoted users who feel that their favorite is the best. Each differs, and libraries that can afford to buy all the reference books which meet critical standards usually do so.

In assembling a home reference library, parents would do well to examine carefully the different reference books they are considering. If possible, a home collection for children should include one of the major children's encyclopedias, a reliable dictionary appropriate for the ages of the children in the family, and an atlas. Parents of children with limited vision may want an atlas printed in large type, which is also useful for younger children because the maps are easy to read. In making decisions, parents will want to examine the way material is arranged and to make sure that the type is uncrowded and is large enough to read without strain; they will look for the quality and placement of illustrations and the adequacy of captions or labels, and they will consider aids to pronunciation, glossaries, indexes, and other auxiliary material provided on prefatory or appended pages, including an explanation of symbols used, or other features of the book.

Most adults feel that children should have their own dictionaries, but they are not so sure that children need their own encyclopedias. In homes where books must be carefully budgeted, many families feel that an adult encyclopedia is the better investment. When children are young, parents can help them use the books, and the older children can use them themselves. The best adult encyclopedias last for a lifetime; they may become dated in some respects, but the bulk of the material will carry a child through high school, college, and adult life. If a choice must be made, then decidedly the adult set should be purchased because of its greater richness and long-range value. But when a family can afford both, the children should have their own set.

Many informational series books have reference use, from such erudite books as the American Heritage historical series, to Leonard Everett Fisher's books on colonial crafts. But each book in a series must be evaluated on its own merits. As is true in library collections, a home reference collection will include such books when they are appropriate for the family's particular interests. And if a member of the family is a bird-watcher or a stamp collector, Roger Tory Peterson's *Field Guide to the Birds* or *Scott's Standard Postage Stamp Catalogue* may seem an absolute necessity.

Some families may feel that reference books that reflect their interests are a better investment than an encyclopedia, since it is possible to keep such a subject collection current with less financial outlay than the purchase of an encyclopedia would require. Library-owned encyclopedias are apt to be more current than home sets and are therefore more useful for school assignments.

The library reference collection should include the Bible and other sacred writings and books on comparative religion, whether they are discussions of denominations like Kathleen

Elgin's separate treatments or a compendium like Katharine Savage's *The Story of World Religions*. Also useful for information about religion are biographies of religious leaders and such books as Susan Purdy's *Jewish Holidays: Fact, Activities and Crafts*.

Despite the abundance and variety of informational books, they are often given short shrift in discussion of literary quality. To be sure, some are distinguished more for their usefulness than for their style, but many of these books, such as *Chipmunks on the Doorstep* by Edwin Tunis, are as graceful in their prose as are some of the works of fiction that have won awards. And remember that the first Newbery Medal was given to Hendrik Willem Van Loon for *The Story of Mankind*, a history of humanity's origin and evolution that is witty and authoritative, the sort of informational book that amuses, informs, and stimulates readers to further inquiry. What more could one ask?

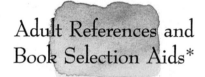

Adult References and Book Selection Aids*

CARR, JO, ed. *Beyond Fact: Nonfiction for Children and Young People.*

CZARRA, FRED R., comp. *A Guide to Historical Reading: Non-Fiction.*

FISHER, MARGERY. *Matters of Fact: Aspects of Non-Fiction for Children.*

FRIEDBERG, JOAN and others. *Accept Me As I Am: Best Books of Juvenile Nonfiction on Impairments and Disabilities.* (See Appendix A.)

HEARNE, BETSY, and MARILYN KAYE, eds. *Celebrating Children's Books: Essays on Children's Literature in Honor of Zena Sutherland.* Essays by David Macaulay, Milton Meltzer, and Laurence Pringle.

KOBRIN, BEVERLY. *Eyeopeners! How to Choose and Use Children's Books About Real People, Places, and Things.* (See Appendix A.)

PETERSON, CAROLYN SUE. *Reference Books for Elementary and Junior High School Libraries.*

SADER, MARION, ed. *Reference Books for Young Readers: Authoritative Evaluations of Encyclopedias, Atlases, and Dictionaries.* (See Appendix A.)

*Complete bibliographic data are provided in Appendices A and B.

SMITH, RUTH, ed. *The Tree of Life.*

VANCE, LUCILLE, and ESTHER TRACEY. *Illustration Index.*

In the following bibliography these symbols have been used to identify books about a religious or a particular ethnic group:

§ African American
★ Hispanic
☆ Native American
○ Asian American
● Religious minority

The Biological Sciences

ADLER, IRVING and RUTH. *Evolution,* ill. by Ruth Adler. Day, 1965.   8–10

ALIKI. *Digging Up Dinosaurs,* ill. by author. T. Crowell, 1981. Explains how dinosaur fossils are excavated and mounted as museum exhibits.   7–9

————. *Dinosaur Bones,* ill. by author. T. Crowell, 1988.   5–8

ANDREWS, ROY CHAPMAN. *All About Dinosaurs,* ill. by Thomas W. Voter. Random, 1953.   9–12

ARNOLD, CAROLINE. *Trapped in Tar: Fossils from the Ice Age,* ill. with photos by Richard Hewett. Houghton/Clarion, 1987. Photographs of fossils and children at a museum illustrate a book that describes paleontologic research at the California tar pits.   9–11

ASIMOV, ISAAC. *ABC's of Ecology.* Walker, 1972.   8–11

————. *How Did We Find Out About Genes?* Walker, 1983.   9–11

————. *How Did We Find Out About the Beginning of Life?* ill. by David Wool. Walker, 1982.   10–12

BENDER, LIONEL. *Lizards and Dragons,* ill. with photos. Gloucester/Watts, 1988. Simple text and large color photographs introduce the types of snakes and lizards that can be kept for research or pets.   7–9

BENDICK, JEANNE. *How Heredity Works: Why Living Things Are As They Are.* Parents Magazine, 1975. A good introduction to genetics.   7–9

————. *A Place to Live,* ill. by author. Parents Magazine, 1970.   5–8

BIRKHEAD, MIKE. *The Falcon over the Town,* ill. with photos by author. Gareth Stevens, 1988. Excellent color photographs accompany a text that describes the habits and habitats of kestrels.
                                                         9–11

BLOUGH, GLENN O. *Soon after September: The Story of Living Things in Winter,* ill. by Jeanne Bendick. McGraw, 1959.   7–9

————. *Who Lives in This House? A Story of Animal Families,* ill. by Jeanne Bendick. McGraw, 1957.
7–9

BRANLEY, FRANKLYN M. *Shivers and Goose Bumps: How We Keep Warm,* ill. by True Kelley. T. Crowell, 1984.   10–12

CLEMONS, ELIZABETH. *Shells Are Where You Find Them,* ill. by Joe Gault. Knopf, 1960.   8–10

COBB, VICKI. *For Your Own Protection: Stories Science Photos Tell.* Lothrop, 1989. Describes the use of specialized photographic techniques for detecting function and malfunction in the human body. Striking color pictures.   8–11

COLDREY, JENNIFER, and KAREN GOLDIE-MORRISON, eds. *Hide and Seek.* Putnam, 1986. Many well-organized examples instruct on the subject of protective coloration, imitative shape, and other types of camouflage used by wildlife.   7–9

COLE, JOANNA. *Asking About Sex and Growing Up,* ill. by Alan Tiegreen. Morrow, 1988. In a question-and-answer format, straightforward and reassuring information on many aspects of sex.   9–11

————. *A Bird's Body,* photos by Jerome Wexler. Morrow, 1982. Sharply focused photographs and diagrams help to explain the unique anatomical features of a bird.   8–10

————. *A Dog's Body,* ill. with photos by Jim and Ann Monteith. Morrow, 1986.   5–8

————. *Evolution,* ill. by Aliki. T. Crowell, 1987. A lucid and sequential text moves from the introduction of fossil remains to an explanation of the evolutionary process to the emergence of humans.   6–8

————. *The Human Body: How We Evolved,* ill. by Walter Gaffney-Kessell and Juan Carlos Barberis. Morrow, 1987.   7–9

————. *Large as Life Daytime Animals,* ill. by Kenneth Lilly. Knopf, 1985.   5–8

————. *Large as Life Nightime Animals,* ill. by Kenneth Lily. Knopf, 1985.   5–8

————. *The Magic School Bus Inside the Human Body,* ill. by Bruce Degen. Scholastic, 1989. 7–9

COSGROVE, MARGARET. *Bone for Bone,* ill. by author. Dodd, 1968.   11–15

————. *Eggs—And What Happens Inside Them,* ill. by author. Dodd, 1966.   8–12

CURTIS, ROBERT. *Medical Talk for Beginners,* ill. by William Jaber. Messner, 1976. A dictionary of medical terms with many cross-references, phonetic spellings where the author deems necessary, and adequately labeled illustrations.   9–11

DARLING, LOUIS. *Greenhead.* Morrow, 1954. 10–14

————. *The Gull's Way,* photos and ill. by author. Morrow, 1965.   11–15

DOWDEN, ANNE OPHELIA. *From Flower to Fruit,* ill. by author. T. Crowell, 1984.   11 up

————. *This Noble Harvest: A Chronicle of Herbs,* ill. by author. Collins, 1980.   10 up

DUNBAR, ROBERT. *Mental Retardation,* ill. with photos. Watts, 1978. This is valuable both as a vehicle for general information and as a platform for the author's purpose of encouraging the acceptance of the mentally handicapped.   9–12

FENNER, CAROL. *Gorilla Gorilla,* ill. by Symeon Shimin. Random, 1973. A narrative framework for a lifecycle book.   8–10

FLANAGAN, GERALDINE LUX. *Window into an Egg: Seeing Life Begin,* ill. with photos. Scott/Addison, 1969.   9–11

FRADIN, DENNIS. *Heredity,* ill. with photos. Childrens Press, 1987. Simple writing in large print discusses genetic structure and function, multiple births, dominant and recessive genes, and genetic engineering.   7–9

FRANK, JULIA. *Alzheimer's Disease: The Silent Epidemic.* Lerner, 1985. A psychiatrist and member of a medical school faculty describes a typical case of Alzheimer's disease as it progresses, giving a candid picture of the misery of the victim and the emotional, practical, and financial problems for the family.   11–15

FREEDMAN, RUSSELL. *Sharks,* ill. with photos. Holiday House, 1985.   8–11

FRESCHET, BERNIECE. *The Flight of the Snow Goose,* ill. by Jo Polseno. Crown, 1970.   7–9

————. *The Web in the Grass,* ill. by Roger Duvoisin. Scribner's, 1972. Handsome illustrations show the spider's world.   4–7

————. *Year on Muskrat Marsh,* ill. by Peter Parnall. Scribner's, 1974.   8–10

GANS, ROMA. *When Birds Change Their Feathers,* ill. by Felicia Bond. T. Crowell, 1980. Gans moves from the general to the specific, describing how different birds molt, in a lucidly written book.   7–8

GEORGE, JEAN CRAIGHEAD. *All upon a Sidewalk,* ill. by Don Bolognese. Dutton, 1974.   7–8

————. *All upon a Stone,* ill. by Don Bolognese. T. Crowell, 1971.   7–8

————. *One Day in the Desert,* ill. by Fred Brenner. T. Crowell, 1983.   9–11

————. *One Day in the Prairie,* ill. by Bob Marshall. T. Crowell, 1986.   9–11

————. *Spring Comes to the Ocean,* ill. by John Wilson. T. Crowell, 1965.   9–11

GORDON, SOL. *Girls Are Girls and Boys Are Boys: So What's the Difference?* ill. by Frank C. Smith. Day, 1974.   8–9

GOUDEY, ALICE E. *Graywings,* ill. by Marie Nonnast.

Scribner's, 1964. Life cycle of herring gull.
6–10

_____. *Here Come the Dolphins,* ill. by Garry MacKenzie. Scribner's, 1961. 7–9

_____. *Houses from the Sea,* ill. by Adrienne Adams. Scribner's, 1959. 5–7

HALMI, ROBERT. *Zoos of the World.* Four Winds, 1975. Focuses on the increasing attention paid to the comfort and security of zoo animals. 10–12

HERZIG, ALLISON CRAGIN, and JANE LAWRENCE MALI. *Oh Boy, Babies!* photos by Katrina Thomas. Little, 1980. A useful, amusing photodocumentary profiles an elective course in a boys' school that instructs in the care and handling of babies. 9–11

HIRSCH, S. CARL. *The Living Community: A Venture into Ecology,* ill. by William Steinel. Viking, 1966.
12–14

HOBAN, TANA. *Big Ones, Little Ones,* photos by author. Greenwillow, 1976. 2–5

HUTCHINS, ROSS E. *The Travels of Monarch X,* ill. by Jerome P. Connolly. Rand, 1966. The description of a southward migration of a tagged Monarch butterfly from Toronto to Mexico. 8–10

HYDE, MARGARET OLDROYD and LAWRENCE E. *Cancer in the Young: A Sense of Hope.* Westminster, 1985. An accurate text explains types of cancers, treatments, statistics for remission and cure, the known and theoretical causes of cancer, and some of the ways in which young cancer patients are helped to adjust to their illness. 11 up

HYDE, MARGARET OLDROYD, and ELIZABETH H. FORSYTH. *Know About AIDS,* ill. by Debora Weber. Walker, 1990. A factual and compassionate text with careful distinctions made between the facts and myths surrounding AIDS. 9–13

JOHNSON, ERIC W. *Love and Sex in Plain Language,* rev. ed., ill. by Russ Hoover. Lippincott, 1974.
12–17

KAMIEN, JANET. *What If You Couldn't? A Book About Special Needs,* ill. by Signe Hanson. Scribner's, 1979. Particular kinds of handicaps are dealt with in separate chapters and some of the causes explained. 10–12

KAVALER, LUCY. *Life Battles Cold,* ill. by Leslie Morrill. Day, 1973. A discussion of the many ways living things adapt to extreme cold. 11–15

_____. *The Wonders of Fungi,* ill. with photos and with drawings by Richard Ott. Day, 1974. 11–14

KITZINGER, SHEILA. *Being Born,* ill. with photos by Lennart Nilsson. Grosset, 1986. 7–9

KLINGSHEIM, TRYGVE B. *Julius,* photos by A. Jakobsen. Delacorte, 1987. Lively color photographs document the story of Julius, a baby chimpanzee rejected by his mother and raised by officials of Norway's Kristiansand Zoo. 5–7

KUKLIN, SUSAN. *Fighting Back: What Some People Are Doing about AIDS,* ill. with photos by author.

Putnam, 1989. The author's nine months' of research at the Gay Men's Health Crisis organization in New York provided her with case histories of what life is like for people with AIDS. 12 up

_____. *Thinking Big: The Story of a Young Dwarf,* ill. by author. Lothrop, 1986. A candid photodocumentary/essay focuses on eight-year-old Jaime Osborn and her family, who belong to the Little People of America because Jaime is a dwarf. 7–9

LAUBER, PATRICIA. *Everglades Country,* photos by Patricia Caulfield. Viking, 1973. 11–14

_____. *The News About Dinosaurs,* ill. Bradbury, 1989. 8–10

_____. *Seeds: Pop, Stick, Glide,* photos by Jerome Wexler. Crown, 1980. 7–9

_____. *What's Hatching Out of That Egg?* ill. with photos. Crown, 1979. 7–9

_____. *Your Body and How It Works,* ill. by Stephen Rogers Peck, photos by Florence Burns. Random, 1962. 8–10

LERNER, CAROL. *Moonseed and Mistletoe: A Book of Poisonous Wild Plants,* ill. by author. Morrow, 1988. A handsomely formatted book that describes and illustrates various types of poisonous plants. 9–11

_____. *Plant Families,* ill. by Carol Lerner. Morrow, 1989. 10–13

_____. *Seasons of the Tallgrass Prairie,* ill. by author. Morrow, 1980. Seasonal changes on the tallgrass prairie are charted in a thoughtful narrative and meticulous fine-line drawings. 10 up

LEVINE, EDNA S. *Lisa and Her Soundless World,* ill. by Gloria Kamen. Behavioral Publications, 1974. A discussion of the abilities and limitations of a deaf child. 8–10

MCCLUNG, ROBERT M. *Gypsy Moth,* ill. by author. Morrow, 1974. 10–14

_____. *Honker,* ill. by Bob Hines. Morrow, 1965.
8–10

_____. *How Animals Hide.* National Geographic, 1973. 7–10

_____. *Hunted Mammals of the Sea,* ill. by William Downey. Morrow, 1978. 10–13

_____. *Lili: A Giant Panda of Sichuan,* ill. by Irene Brady. Morrow, 1988. 8–10

_____. *Thor: Last of the Sperm Whales,* ill. by Bob Hines. Morrow, 1971. 8–10

MCNULTY, FAITH. *Peeping in the Shell: A Whooping Crane Is Hatched,* ill. by Irene Brady. Harper, 1986. The plight of the endangered whooping crane is personalized through the narrative of a relationship between an ornithologist and a whooping crane named Tex. 7–10

MARI, IELA and ENZO, ills. *The Apple and the Moth and the Chicken and the Egg.* Pantheon, 1970. First published in Italy, two charming books that tell stories clearly without text. 3–5

MICHEL, ANNA. *The Story of Nim: The Chimp Who Learned Language*, ill. with photographs, Knopf, 1980. An account of an experiment in which a baby chimpanzee learned to communicate in sign language. 9–11

NEWTON, JAMES R. *A Forest Is Reborn*, ill. by Susan Bonners. T. Crowell, 1982. A forest devastated by fire gradually comes back to life in this beautifully illustrated science book. 7–9

NILSSON, LENNART. *How Was I Born? A Photographic Story of Reproduction and Birth for Children.* Delacorte/Seymour Lawrence, 1975. 8–11

NOURSE, ALAN E. *The Body,* by Alan E. Nourse and the Editors of *Life.* Time-Life, 1964. Illustrated with superb photographs. 13 up

OXFORD SCIENTIFIC FILMS. *Bees and Honey,* ill. with photos. Putnam, 1977. A six-page text, divided into brief topics and crisply written, is followed by captioned full-page color photographs, most of which are greatly enlarged.

————. *Jellyfish and Other Sea Creatures,* photos by Peter Parks. Putnam, 1982. First-rate color photographs illuminate this interesting discussion of the anatomy of the jellyfish. 9–11

PAIGE, DAVID. *Behind the Scenes at the Aquarium,* ill. with photos. Whitman, 1979. Profusely illustrated, this gives readers a fine introduction both to the beauty and interest of aquarium exhibits and to the responsibilities of the staff. 9–11

PATENT, DOROTHY HINSHAW. *Babies!* ill. with photos. Holiday House, 1988. An easy-to-read guide for younger children about the stages of infant development. 4–7

————. *Bacteria: How They Affect Other Living Things.* Holiday, 1980. 11 up

————. *Buffalo: The American Bison Today,* ill. with photos by William Monoz. Houghton/Clarion, 1986. 9–11

————. *Butterflies and Moths: How They Function.* Holiday, 1979. 12 up

————. *Evolution Goes on Every Day,* ill. by Matthew Kalmenoff. Holiday, 1977. 13 up

————. *Germs!* ill. with photos. Holiday, 1983. 8–10

————. *How Insects Communicate.* Holiday, 1975. 9–12

————. *Where the Bald Eagles Gather,* photos by William Munoz. Houghton/Clarion, 1984. 8–10

————. *The Whooping Crane: A Comeback Story,* ill. with photos by William Munoz. Houghton/Clarion, 1988. 9–11

PATTERSON, FRANCINE. *Koko's Kitten,* ill. with photos by Ronald H. Cohn. Scholastic, 1985. 9–11

POWZYK, JOYCE. *Tracking Wild Chimpanzees,* ill. by author. Lothrop, 1988. Watercolors illustrate a diary describing author's journey through the Kibira Park forest in Burundi, Central Africa. 9–12

PRINGLE, LAURENCE. *The Animal Rights Controversy.* Harcourt, 1989. 11–14

————. *Feral: Tame Animals Gone Wild.* Macmillan, 1983. 10–14

————. *Follow a Fisher,* ill. by Tony Chen. T. Crowell, 1973. 7–9

————. *Here Come the Killer Bees,* ill. with photos. Morrow, 1986. A careful piece of research, this describes the devastating effects the northern migration of Africanized honeybees will have on the products of the bee and pollination industries. 10–13

————. *Home: How Animals Find Comfort and Safety.* Scribner's, 1987. With uncompromised commitment to scientific reporting, this describes some of the homes that animals build or borrow. 9–11

————. *What Shall We Do with the Land? Choices for America,* ill. with photos. T. Crowell, 1981. 12–15

RIEDMAN, SARA R. *Naming Living Things: The Grouping of Plants and Animals,* ill. by Jerome P. Connolly. Rand, 1963. 10–12

RUSSELL, SOLVEIG PAULSON. *Like and Unlike: A First Look at Classification,* ill. by Lawrence Di Fiori. Walck, 1973. Authoritative introduction to classification of plants and animals. 8–10

SATTLER, HELEN RONEY. *The Book of Eagles,* ill. by Jean Day Zallinger. Lothrop, 1989. General information about classification and species is followed by an excellent illustrated glossary. 10–14

————. *Dinosaurs of North America,* ill. by Anthony Rao. Lothrop, 1981. A comprehensive volume provides extensive coverage of North American dinosaurs, including descriptions of each type of dinosaur and a list of fossil sites. 10–14

————. *Giraffes, the Sentinels of the Savannas,* ill. by Christopher Santoro. Lothrop, 1990. Accurate, informative, and meticulously illustrated. 10–14

————. *Pterosaurs, the Flying Reptiles,* ill. by Christopher Santoro. Lothrop, 1985. An oversized book allows for sweeping views of the many varieties of "flying reptiles" that are described in a well-organized, continuous text. 9–11

————. *Tyrannosaurus Rex and Its Kin: The Mesozoic Monsters,* ill. by Joyce Powzyk. Lothrop, 1989. 9–11

SCHEFFER, VICTOR B. *The Amazing Sea Otter,* ill. by Gretchen Daiber. Scribner's, 1981. An eminently readable text traces the development of a newborn sea otter in the wild and in captivity. 12 up

————. *Little Calf,* ill. by Leonard Everett Fisher. Scribner's, 1970. 12 up

SCOTT, JACK DENTON. *Alligator,* ill. with photos by Ozzie Sweet. Putnam, 1984. 10 up

————. *The Book of the Pig,* photos by Ozzie Sweet. Putnam, 1981. Information about pigs; a testament to the intelligence of the species.   8–10

————. *Island of Wild Horses,* ill. with photos. Putnam, 1978.   10 up

————. *The Survivors: Enduring Animals of North America,* ill. by Daphne Gillen. Harcourt, 1975.   10–14

————. *Swans,* ill. with photos by Ozzie Sweet. Putnam, 1988. Facts about anatomical structure and flight, habitats, migrations, and mating are paired with beautiful and informative color photographs.   10–13

SELSAM, MILLICENT ELLIS. *Animals of the Sea,* ill. by John Hamberger. Four Winds, 1976. Simply written, illustrated in full color, and authoritative, this introduction to marine life may also be used for reading aloud to preschool children.   7–8

————. *Benny's Animals, and How He Put Them in Order,* ill. by Arnold Lobel. Harper, 1966.   6–8

————. *Bulbs, Corms, and Such,* photos by Jerome Wexler. Morrow, 1974.   8–10

————. *Greg's Microscope,* ill. by Arnold Lobel. Harper, 1963.   6–8

————. *Land of the Giant Tortoise: The Story of the Galapagos,* ill. with photos. Four Winds, 1977.   9–12

————. *The Language of Animals,* ill. by Kathleen Elgin. Morrow, 1962.   10–14

————. *Let's Get Turtles,* ill. by Arnold Lobel. Harper, 1965.   7–8

————. *See Along the Shore,* ill. by Leonard Weisgard. Harper, 1961.   7–9

————. *See Through the Jungle,* ill. by Winifred Lubell. Harper, 1957.   7–9

————. *Strange Creatures That Really Lived,* ill. by Jennifer Dewey. Scholastic, 1987. Softly drawn detailed illustrations in colored pencil show creatures that have lived on earth and become extinct.   5–7

————. *Tree Flowers,* ill. by Carol Lerner. Morrow, 1984.   9 up

————. *Tyrannosaurus Rex,* ill. with photos. Harper, 1978. Gives as much information about the scientific method as it does about dinosaurs.   8–10

SELSAM, MILLICENT ELLIS, and JOYCE HUNT. *A First Look at Caterpillars,* ill. by Harriett Springer. Walker, 1987.   6–8

————. *A First Look at Seals, Sea Lions, and Walruses,* ill. by Harriett Springer. Walker, 1988. An attractive science book, this serves to teach readers to recognize different types of seals and sea lions and to distinguish them from walruses.   6–8

————. *A First Look at Spiders,* ill. by Harriett Springer. Walker, 1983.   6–8

SHEFFIELD, MARGARET. *Where Do Babies Come From?* ill. by Sheila Bewley. Knopf, 1973.   5–7

SHEPHERD, ELIZABETH. *No Bones: A Key to Bugs and Slugs, Worms and Ticks, Spiders and Centipedes, and Other Creepy Crawlies,* ill. by Ippy Paterson. Macmillan, 1988. An informative text on invertebrates is presented in a choose-your-own-adventure type of format.   8–11

SHOWERS, PAUL. *Look at Your Eyes,* ill. by Paul Galdone. T. Crowell, 1962.   6–7

————. *Me and My Family Tree,* ill. by Don Madden. T. Crowell, 1978.   7–8

————. *You Can't Make a Move Without Your Muscles,* ill. by Harriett Bart. T. Crowell, 1982.   7–8

§ ————. *Your Skin and Mine,* ill. by Paul Galdone. T. Crowell, 1965.   6–8

SHOWERS, PAUL and KAY. *Before You Were a Baby,* ill. by Ingrid Fetz. T. Crowell, 1968.   7–8

SHUTTLESWORTH, DOROTHY. *Animal Camouflage,* ill. by Matthew Kalmenoff. Natural History Pr., 1966.   11–14

————. *The Story of Rodents,* ill. by Lydia Rosier. Doubleday, 1971.   9–12

————. *To Find a Dinosaur.* Doubleday, 1973.   9–12

SILVERSTEIN, ALVIN and VIRGINIA B. *AIDS: Deadly Threat.* Enslow, 1986.   11–14

————. *Apples: All About Them,* ill. by Shirley Chan. Prentice, 1976.   9–12

————. *The Code of Life,* ill. by Kenneth Gosner. Atheneum, 1972.   12 up

————. *Hamsters: All About Them,* photos by Frederick Breda. Lothrop, 1974.   9–12

————. *Heartbeats: Your Body, Your Heart,* ill. by Stella Ormai. Lippincott, 1983.   9–11

————. *The Mystery of Sleep,* ill. by Nelle Davis. Little, 1987. A simple and precise text presents scientific information on the study of sleep patterns.   9–11

————. *The Skeletal System: Framework for Life,* ill. by Lee J. Ames. Prentice, 1972.   9–11

————. *Sleep and Dreams.* Lippincott, 1974.   12–15

————. *So You're Getting Braces: A Guide to Orthodontics,* ill. by Barbara Remington. Lippincott, 1978. Useful facts and sensible advice about orthodontic care.   10–14

————. *Wonders of Speech.* Morrow, 1988. Using a well-organized, clear narrative, the authors discuss the ways in which sound is produced in the human body.   12 up

————. *World of the Brain.* Morrow, 1986.   12 up

SIMON, HILDA. *The Amazing Book of Birds.* Hart, 1958.   9–11

————. *Exploring the World of Social Insects,* ill. by author. Vanguard, 1963. A study of group behavior.   9–13

————. *Insect Masquerades.* Viking, 1968.   11–14

————. *Living Lanterns: Luminescence in Animals,* ill. by author. Viking, 1971.   11 up

————. *Animal Fact/Animal Fable,* ill. by Diane de Groat. Crown, 1978. Debunks some popular misconceptions.   7–8

————. *The Dinosaur Is the Biggest Animal that Ever Lived: And Other Wrong Ideas You Thought Were True,* ill. by Giulio Maestro. Lippincott, 1984. Two pages are devoted to each popular fallacy in a book well-suited to the middle grades audience.   8–10

SIMON, SEYMOUR. *101 Questions and Answers About Dangerous Animals,* ill. by Ellen Friedman. Macmillan, 1985. The question-and-answer format, organized by types of animals, provides facts and refutes commonly held misconceptions about animals.   8–11

————. *Strange Mysteries.* Four Winds, 1980.   9–12

STOUTENBURG, ADRIEN. *A Vanishing Thunder: Extinct and Threatened American Birds,* ill. by John Schoenherr. Natural History Pr., 1967. A sobering reminder of human carelessness.   10–12

SUSSMAN, SUSAN, and ROBERT JAMES. *Lies (People Believe) About Animals,* ill. with photos by Fred Leavitt. Whitman, 1987. Framed black-and-white photographs illustrate information about animals, alphabetically arranged, with each section labeled "Lie" or "Truth."   8–10

THOMSON, PEGGY. *Keeper and Creatures at the National Zoo,* ill. with photos by Paul S. Conklin. T. Crowell, 1988. The work of the National Zoo keepers is described with informal, detailed anecdotes.   10–14

TRESSELT, ALVIN. *The Beaver Pond,* ill. by Roger Duvoisin. Lothrop, 1970.   5–7

TUNIS, EDWIN. *Chipmunks on the Doorstep,* ill. by author. T. Crowell, 1971.   10 up

WATSON, JANE (WERNER). *Whales: Friendly Dolphins and Mighty Giants of the Sea,* ill. by Richard Amundsen. Western, 1975.   9–12

WEISS, MALCOLM. *What's Happening to Our Climate?* ill. by Paul Plumer. Messner, 1978. A clear and well-organized text discusses the long-range changes in the world's climate and all the factors that have contributed to them and will affect the climate of the future.   10–12

ZIM, HERBERT S. *Our Senses and How They Work,* ill. by Herschel Wartik. Morrow, 1956.   9–11

————. *Your Heart and How It Works,* ill. by Gustav Schrotter. Morrow, 1959.   9–11

ZIM, HERBERT S., and SONIA BLEEKER. *Life and Death,* ill. by René Martin. Morrow, 1970.   9–12

ZIM, HERBERT S., and LUCRETIA KRANZ. *Crabs,* ill. by René Martin. Morrow, 1974.   8–10

————. *Snails,* ill. by René Martin. Morrow, 1975.   8–10

The Physical Sciences

ADLER, IRVING. *The Changing Tools of Science: From Yardstick to Cyclotron.* ill. by Ruth Adler. Day, 1958; 1973.   12–14

————. *Magic House of Numbers,* ill. by Ruth Adler. Day, 1957; 1974.   10–14

————. *Petroleum: Gas, Oil and Asphalt,* ill. by Peggy Adler. Day, 1975.   9–11

————. *Stars: Decoding Their Messages,* rev. ed. Crowell, 1980.   11–14

————. *The Sun and Its Family,* ill. by Ruth Adler. Day, 1958.   12–14

————. *Tools in Your Life,* ill. by Ruth Adler. Day, 1956.   10–14

————. *The Wonders of Physics: An Introduction to the Physical World,* ill. by Cornelius DeWitt. Golden Pr., 1966.   12 up

ADLER, IRVING and RUTH. *Sets,* ill. by Ruth Adler. Day, 1967.   9–11

————. *Sets and Numbers for the Very Young,* ill. by Peggy Adler. Day, 1969.   6–8

AMES, GERALD, and ROSE WYLER. *First Days of the World,* ill. by Leonard Weisgard. Harper, 1958.   8–10

ANNO, MITSUMASA. *Anno's Math Games,* ill. by author. Philomel, 1987.   7–9

————. *Anno's Math Games II,* ill. by author. Philomel, 1989.   7–9

APFEL, NECIA H. *Nebulae: The Birth and Death of Stars,* ill. with photos. Lothrop, 1988. A clear and authoritative text describes how nebulae are formed and their appearance and consistency at different times during their life cycle.   8–10

ARDLEY, NEIL. *Atoms and Energy.* Warwick Press, 1982.   10–14

————. *Computers.* Warwick/Watts, 1983. This generously illustrated volume is a good introduction to many aspects of computer science, from programming techniques to computer applications.   10–13

ASIMOV, ISAAC. *ABC's of Space,* ill. Walker. 1969.   8–10

————. *The Best New Thing,* ill. by Symeon Shimin. World, 1971.   5–7

————. *How Did We Find Out About Atoms?* ill. by David Wool. Walker, 1976.   10–12

————. *How Did We Find Out About Black Holes?* ill. by David Wool. Walker, 1978.   10–12

————. *How Did We Find Out About Oil?* ill. by David Wool. Walker, 1980.   10–12

————. *How Did We Find Out About Robots?* ill. by David Wool. Walker, 1985.   10–12

————. *Mars, the Red Planet,* ill. with photos. Lothrop, 1977.   12 up

_____. *Words of Science: and the History Behind Them,* ill. by William Barss. Houghton, 1959. 12–15

BEHRENS, JUNE. *The True Book of Metric Measurement.* Childrens Pr., 1975. 7–9

BENDICK, JEANNE. *Solids, Liquids and Gases,* ill. by author. Watts, 1974. 8–10

BERGER, MELVIN. *The New Water Book,* ill. by Leonard Kessler. T. Crowell, 1973. 9–11

BILLINGS, CHARLENE W. *Fiber Optics: Bright New Way to Communicate,* ill. with photos. Dodd, 1986. 8–11

BLUMBERG, RHODA. *The First Travel Guide to the Bottom of the Sea,* ill. by Gen Shimada. Lothrop, 1983. 9–11

_____. *The First Travel Guide to the Moon: What to Pack, How to Go, and What to See When You Get There,* ill. by Roy Doty. Four Winds, 1980. 9–13

BOURNE, MIRIAM. *What Is Papa Up To Now?* ill. by Dick Gackenbach. Coward, 1977. Sally, Benjamin Franklin's small daughter, describes Papa's excitement and pleasure at each discovery he makes while experimenting with electricity. 7–8

BOVA, BENJAMIN. *Man Changes the Weather.* Addison, 1973. 10–13

_____. *Workshops in Space.* Dutton, 1974. 11–14

BRANLEY, FRANKLYN M. *A Book of Flying Saucers for You,* ill. by Leonard Kessler. T. Crowell, 1973. A discussion of the phenomena that have been reported as flying saucers. 8–9

_____. *A Book of Mars for You,* ill. by Leonard Kessler. T. Crowell, 1968. 6–10

_____. *The Christmas Sky,* ill. by Blair Lent. T. Crowell, 1966. 9–11

_____. *Color: From Rainbows to Lasers,* ill. by Henry Roth. T. Crowell, 1978. 11–15

_____. *Journey into a Black Hole,* ill. by Marc Simont. T. Crowell, 1986. 7–8

_____. *The Milky Way: Galaxy Number One,* ill. by Helmut K. Wimmer. T. Crowell, 1969. 12 up

_____. *Mysteries of the Planet Earth,* ill. with diagrams by Sally Bensusen. Lodestar/Dutton, 1989. 10–13

_____. *Pieces of Another World: The Story of Moon Rocks,* ill. by Herbert Danska. T. Crowell, 1973. 10–13

_____. *Shooting Stars,* ill. by Holly Keller. T. Crowell, 1989. 6–8

_____. *Tornado Alert,* ill. by Giulio Maestro. T. Crowell, 1988. 6–8

BRANLEY, FRANKLYN M., and ELEANOR K. VAUGHAN. *Mickey's Magnet,* ill. by Crockett Johnson. T. Crowell, 1956. 5–7

BRONOWSKI, JACOB, and MILLICENT E. SELSAM. *Biography of an Atom,* ill. by Weimar Pursell and with photos. Harper, 1965. 10–14

CARLE, ERIC. *My Very First Book of Shapes.* T. Crowell, 1974. 2–4

CARSON, RACHEL. *The Sea Around Us,* ad. by Anne Terry White, ill. with photos, maps, and drawings. Golden Pr., 1958. 11–14

COBB, VICKI. *Why Doesn't the Earth Fall Up? and Other Not So Dumb Questions About Motion,* ill. by Ted Enik. Lodestar, 1989. Cartoon-style drawings illustrate a series of questions and answers concerning the laws of motion. 8–10

COLE, JOANNA. *The Magic School Bus Inside the Earth,* ill. by Bruce Degen. Scholastic, 1987. In an energetic geology book, a fictional class of young students goes on a journey to the center of the earth with their unconventional science teacher. 7–9

COOMBS, CHARLES. *Lift-Off: The Story of Rocket Power,* ill. by R. H. Foor. Morrow, 1963. A clear explanation of rocket engines and guidance systems. 9–11

CROUSE, WILLIAM H. *Understanding Science,* rev. ed., ill. by Jeanne Bendick and D. Mahanes. McGraw, 1956. 10–14

DEMING, RICHARD. *Metric Power: Why and How We Are Going Metric.* Nelson, 1974. 11–15

EPSTEIN, SAM and BERYL. *The First Book of Electricity,* ill. by Robin King. Watts, 1953. 9–12

§ FEELINGS, MURIEL. *Moja Means One,* ill. by Tom Feelings. Dial, 1971. Soft illustrations add appeal to a counting book that gives numbers 1–10 in Swahili. 5–8

FEY, JAMES T. *Long, Short, High, Low, Thin, Wide,* ill. by Janie Russell. T. Crowell, 1971. 7–9

FOLSOM, MICHAEL and MARCIA. *The Macmillan Book of How Things Work,* ill. by Brad Hamann. Macmillan, 1987. 9–12

FREEMAN, IRA M. *All About Electricity,* ill. by Evelyn Urbanowich. Random, 1957. 10–13

GALLANT, ROY A. *Exploring Chemistry,* ill. by Lee Ames. Garden City, 1958. 9–13

GANS, ROMA. *Millions and Millions of Crystals,* ill. by Giulio Maestro. T. Crowell, 1973. 7–8

_____. *Oil: The Buried Treasure,* ill. by Giulio Maestro. T. Crowell, 1975. 7–8

GOUDEY, ALICE E. *The Day We Saw the Sun Come Up,* ill. by Adrienne Adams. Scribner's, 1961. Two children rise before dawn, and Mother explains night and day, shadows, and the turning earth. 5–7

HALACY, DANIEL S. *The Energy Trap.* Four Winds, 1975. 12–15

HIRSCH, S. CARL. *Meter Means Measure: The Story of the Metric System.* Viking, 1973. 11–15

HOGBEN, LANCELOT. *The Wonderful World of Energy,* ill. by Eileen Aplin and others. Garden City, 1957. 11–14

_____. *The Wonderful World of Mathematics,* ill. by

Andre. Charles Keeping, Kenneth Symonds. Garden City, 1955; rev. ed., 1968. 10–14

JACKER, CORINNE. *Window on the Unknown: A History of the Microscope,* ill. by Mary Linn and with photos. Scribner's, 1966. 13 up

JAMES, ELIZABETH, and CAROL BARKIN. *The Simple Facts of Simple Machines,* photos by Daniel Dorn, diagrams by Susan Stan. Lothrop, 1975. 9–11

————. *What Do You Mean by "Average"?* ill. by Joel Schick. Lothrop, 1978. 10–12

JESPERSON, JAMES, and JANE FITZ-RANDOLPH. *Rams, Roms, and Robots,* ill. with diagrams by Bruce Hiscock and with photos. Atheneum, 1984. The many facets of computer functions are explained by precise writing in a clear book on a complicated subject. 11–15

KLEIN, AARON E. *The Electron Microscope: A Tool of Discovery.* McGraw, 1974. 13 up

KNIGHT, DAVID C. *Robotics: Past, Present, and Future,* ill. with photos. Morrow, 1983. A logically organized survey of robotics: past history, present applications, and likely future uses. 11–14

KOHN, BERNICE. *Communications Satellites: Message Centers in Space,* ill. by Jerome Kuhl. Four Winds, 1975. 9–11

————. *Echoes,* ill. by Dan Connor. Dandelion, 1979. In a direct and simple explanation of a phenomenon that intrigues most children, Kohn explains how sound waves travel to create echoes. 7–9

LAUBER, PATRICIA. *Get Ready for Robots!* ill. by True Kelly. T. Crowell, 1987. 7–8

————. *Tapping Earth's Heat,* ill. by Edward Malsberg. Garrard, 1978. 8–10

————. *Voyagers from Space: Meteors and Meteorites,* ill. by Mike Eagle and with photos. T. Crowell, 1989. 9–12

LEWELLEN, JOHN. *The Mighty Atom,* ill. by Ida Scheib. Knopf, 1955. 8–10

————. *The True Book of Toys at Work,* ill. by Karl Murray. Childrens Pr., 1953. 6–8

LEWIS, ALFRED. *The New World of Computers,* ill. with photos. Dodd, 1965. 9–12

MCCARTER, JAMES. *The Space Shuttle Disaster.* Bookwright/Watts, 1988. 9–11

MACAULAY, DAVID. *The Way Things Work,* ill. by author. Houghton, 1988. 11 up

NAVARRA, JOHN. *Earthquake.* Chicago Museum of Science and Industry/Doubleday, 1980. A professor of geoscience describes the causes, effects, and measuring of earthquakes. 10–13

————. *Wide World Weather.* Doubleday, 1968. 11 up

PRINGLE, LAURENCE. *Energy: Power for People.* Macmillan, 1975. 11–13

————. *Rain of Troubles: The Science and Politics of Acid Rain.* Macmillan, 1988. 10–14

RIDE, SALLY, and SUSAN OKIE. *To Space and Back,* ill. with photos. Lothrop, 1986. 8–11

RUCHLIS, HY. *Orbit: A Picture Story of Force and Motion,* ill. by Alice Hirsch. Harper, 1958. 10 up

————. *Your Changing Earth,* ill. by Janet and Alex d'Amato. Harvey, 1963. 7–9

SCHLEIN, MIRIAM. *Metric—the Modern Way to Measure.* Harcourt, 1975. 8–10

SCHNEIDER, HERMAN and NINA. *How Big Is Big: From Stars to Atoms,* ill. by Symeon Shimin. W. R. Scott, 1950. 8–11

————. *You, Among the Stars,* ill. by Symeon Shimin. W. R. Scott, 1951. 8–10

SCHWARTZ, DAVID M. *How Much Is a Million?* ill. by Steven Kellogg. Lothrop, 1985. Humorous, bouncy pictures of small children help in the conceptualization of very large numbers. 5–8

————. *If You Made a Million,* ill. by Steven Kellogg. Lothrop, 1989. Extends the concepts and is more sophisticated than the first book. 7–9

SELSAM, MILLICENT E. *Birth of an Island,* ill. by Winifred Lubell. Harper, 1959. The evolution of a volcanic island. 8–10

SILVERSTEIN, ALVIN and VIRGINIA. *The Chemicals We Eat and Drink.* Follett, 1973. 10–13

SIMON, SEYMOUR. *Computer Sense, Computer Nonsense,* ill. by Steven Lindblom. Lippincott, 1984. 8–11

————. *Galaxies,* ill. with photos. Morrow, 1988. 7–9

————. *Hidden Worlds.* Morrow, 1983. 9 up

————. *How to Talk to Your Computer,* ill. by Barbara and Ed Emberley. T. Crowell, 1985. 5–9

————. *The Long Journey from Space,* ill. with photos. Crown, 1982. 8–10

————. *The Long View into Space,* ill. with photos. Crown, 1979. 8–10

————. *Shadow Magic,* ill. by Stella Ormai. Lothrop, 1985. 5–7

————. *Stars.* Morrow, 1986. 7–9

————. *Storms,* ill. with photos. Morrow, 1989. 9–11

————. *The Sun.* Morrow, 1986. 7–9

————. *Volcanoes,* ill. with photos. Morrow, 1988. 6–8

————. *Your First Home Computer,* ill. by Roy Doty. Crown, 1985. 9–12

SRIVASTAVA, JANE JONAS. *Averages,* ill. by Aliki. T. Crowell, 1975. 7–9

————. *Statistics,* ill. by John J. Reiss. T. Crowell, 1973. An excellent introduction explains both the ways statistics are compiled and the ways compilation can affect results. 7–8

TRESSELT, ALVIN R. *Hide and Seek Fog,* ill. by Roger

_____. Duvoisin. Lothrop, 1965.   5–8

_____. *It's Time Now,* ill. by Roger Duvoisin. Lothrop, 1969.   5–8

_____. *Sun Up,* ill. by Roger Duvoisin. Lothrop, 1949.   5–8

_____. *White Snow, Bright Snow,* ill. by Roger Duvoisin. Lothrop, 1947. Caldecott Medal.   5–7

TUNIS, EDWIN. *Wheels: A Pictorial History,* ill. by author. World, 1955.   11 up

WATSON, CLYDE. *Binary Numbers,* ill. by Wendy Watson. T. Crowell, 1977. One of the simplest descriptions of the binary system yet published for beginners, nicely integrated with helpful illustrations.   7–9

WEISS, HARVEY. *Machines and How They Work,* ill. by author. T. Crowell, 1983.   10–12

WHITE, JACK R. *The Invisible World of the Infrared,* ill. with photos and drawings. Dodd, 1984. An accessible text describes the use of infrared instruments in research, crime prevention, laser surgery, and other areas.   10–13

WOODBURY, DAVID O. *The New World of the Atom.* Dodd, 1965.   9–11

ZIM, HERBERT S. *The New Moon.* Morrow, 1980.   9–11

_____. *Quartz,* ill. with photos and diagrams. Morrow, 1981.   8–10

The Social Sciences

★ ADAMS, FAITH. *El Salvador: Beauty Among the Ashes,* ill. with photos. Dillon, 1986. The effects of civil war and poverty on daily life in El Salvador are combined with information on history, culture, religion, and economics.   9–12

ADAMSON, WENDY WRISTON. *Saving Lake Superior: A Story of Environmental Action.* Dillon, 1974. A citizens' group fights pollution.   11–14

ADLER, DAVID. *Prices Go Up, Prices Go Down: The Laws of Supply and Demand,* ill. by Tom Huffman. Watts, 1984. A simply written text clearly explains a basic economic principle.   7–9

§ ADOFF, ARNOLD, ed. *Black on Black: Commentaries by Negro Americans.* Macmillan, 1968. A collection of material spanning the thinking of African Americans from Frederick Douglass to Dick Gregory. Their viewpoints may differ but they unite in speaking of the problems of a fragmented society.   13 up

ALIKI. *How a Book Is Made,* ill. by author. T. Crowell, 1986. Comic-strip and step-by-step illustrations are an appealing format to younger readers in showing every aspect of book production.   6–8

_____. *The King's Day: Louis XIV of France,* ill. by author. T. Crowell, 1989.   8–11

_____. *A Medieval Feast,* ill. by author. T. Crowell, 1983. Preparations for a royal feast, handsomely pictured, impart information about medieval society.   7–9

AMES, GERALD, and ROSE WYLER. *The First People in the World,* ill. by Leonard Weisgard. Harper, 1958.   8–10

ASHABRANNER, BRENT. *Always to Remember: The Story of the Vietnam Veterans Memorial,* ill. with photos by Jennifer Ashabranner. Dodd/Putnam, 1988.   10–13

☆ _____. *Children of the Maya: A Guatemalan Indian Odyssey,* ill. with photos by Paul Conklin. Dodd, 1986.   10–14

§ ★ _____. *Dark Harvest: Migrant Workers in America,* ill. with photos by Paul Conklin. Dodd, 1985.   12–17

★ _____. *The Vanishing Border: A Photographic Journey along Our Frontier with Mexico,* ill. with photos by Paul Conklin. Dodd, 1987.   11–15

○ ASHABRANNER, BRENT and MELISSA. *Into a Strange Land,* ill. with photos. Dodd, 1987. Young Indo-Chinese refugees are interviewed about why they left their native country, their sometimes dangerous escapes and journeys, and their adjustment to life in the United States.   10 up

ASIMOV, ISAAC. *The Birth of the United States 1763–1816.* Houghton, 1974. A sequel to *The Shaping of North America.*   11–15

_____. *The Dark Ages,* ill. Houghton, 1968. From the year 1000 to the advent of chivalry.   12–17

_____. *Our Federal Union.* Houghton, 1975. Third in the series on the United States.   13 up

_____. *The Shaping of North America: from Earliest Times to 1763.* Houghton, 1973.   13 up

_____. *Words from the Exodus,* ill. by William Barss. Houghton, 1963.   11 up

_____. *Words from History,* ill. by William Barss. Houghton, 1968.   11 up

_____. *Words in Genesis,* ill. by William Barss. Houghton, 1962.   11 up

☆ BAKER, BETTY. *Settlers and Strangers: Native Americans of the Desert Southwest and History As They Saw It.* Macmillan. 1977. A top-notch historical survey told in narrative style.   9–14

○ BALES, CAROL ANN. *Chinatown Sunday: The Story of Lilliann Der.* Reilly and Lee, 1973. A photodocumentary examines the life of a Chinese-American family in Chicago.   8–10

☆ _____. *Kevin Cloud: Chippewa Boy in the City.* Reilly, 1972. A photodocumentary that is both candid and dignified.   8–10

☆ BAYLOR, BYRD. *Before You Came This Way,* ill. by Tom Bahti. Dutton, 1969. Walking in the quiet of a canyon in the southwest, you wonder if you are the first to pass this way and then you see the wall paintings of the past. A handsome, thought-provoking book.   7–9

☆ ──────. *The Way to Start a Day,* ill. by Peter Parnall. Scribner's, 1978. A poetic text in picture book format presents some of the ways the sun has been greeted in various times and places.   8–10

BENDICK, JEANNE. *Egyptian Tombs,* ill. and with photos. Watts, 1989.   8–10

§ BERGER, MELVIN. *In Africa.* Atheneum, 1973. A survey of life styles in a coastal village, a city, a savannah, a forest, and a nomad community.

5–8

──────. *Time After Time,* ill. by Richard Cuffari. Coward, 1975.   7–9

BERNSTEIN, JOANNE, and STEPHEN GULLO. *When People Die,* ill. with photos. Dutton, 1977. A discussion of death that is sensible, fairly comprehensive, and tender without being somber or mawkish.   5–8

BLEEKER, SONIA. *The Eskimo: Arctic Hunters and Trappers,* ill. by Patricia Boodell. Morrow, 1959.

9–12

§ ──────. *The Ibo of Biafra,* ill. by Edith G. Singer. Morrow, 1969.   10–12

☆ ──────. *The Maya, Indians of Central America,* ill. by Kisa N. Sasaki. Morrow, 1961.   9–12

○ BLUMBERG, RHODA. *Commodore Perry in the Land of the Shogun.* Lothrop, 1985.   11 up

☆ ──────. *The Incredible Journey of Lewis and Clark,* ill. and with photos. Lothrop, 1987. Profusely illustrated with photographs of artifacts and prints from museums and institutional archives, this dignified but exciting narrative describes the three-year journey of exploration led by Meriwether Lewis and William Clark.   11 up

§ BONTEMPS, ARNA. *Story of the Negro,* 3rd ed., ill. by Raymond Lufkin. Knopf, 1958. An authoritative and perceptive black history.   11–14

BOORSTIN, DANIEL J. *The Landmark History of the American People,* 2 vols., ill. Random, 1968; 1970.

10–14

☆ BROWN, DEE. *Wounded Knee.* Holt, 1974. Adapted by Amy Ehrlich from the adult title, *Bury My Heart at Wounded Knee.*   11–14

BRYANT, ADAM. *Canada: Good Neighbor to the World.* Dillon, 1987.   9–12

BUSHEY, JERRY. *Farming the Land: Modern Farmers and Their Machines,* ill. with photos. Carolrhoda, 1987. Well-composed color photographs and a glossary supplement an explanation of both the organic and technological aspects of modern farming.   8–10

CARLSON, DALE BICK. *Girls Are Equal Too: The Women's Movement for Teenagers,* ill. by Carol Nicklaus. Atheneum, 1973. A discussion of the causes and solutions in contemporary sexism.   11–14

★ CARTER, WILLIAM E. *The First Book of South America.* Watts, 1961.   9–12

● CHAIKIN, MIRIAM. *A Nightmare in History: The Holocaust 1933–1945,* ill. and with photos. Clarion, 1987. Clear and blunt, this describes all the stages of Hitler's systematic destruction of European Jews during World War II.   11–13

CLARK, ANN NOLAN. *Circle of Seasons,* ill. by W. T. Mars. Farrar, 1961.   10–14

CLARKE, CLORINDA. *The American Revolution 1775–83: A British View,* ill. McGraw, 1967.   10–14

§ ☆ COHEN, ROBERT. *The Color of Man,* photos by Ken Heyman. Random, 1968. A fine book on the physical differences among people, and on the nature and dangers of prejudice.   10–13

COLE, JOANNA. *Cars and How They Go,* ill. by Gail Gibbons. T. Crowell, 1983.   7–9

COLE, SHEILA. *The Great Declaration: A Book for Young Americans,* ill. by Donald Bolognese. Bobbs, 1958.

12–14

──────. *Working Kids on Working.* Lothrop, 1980. Interviews with a wide variety of children, some as young as nine, show the size and diversity of the juvenile labor market.   10–14

COOMBS, CHARLES. *Cleared for Takeoff: Behind the Scenes at an Airport.* Morrow, 1969. An interesting backstage view.   11–15

COTTRELL, LEONARD. *Digs and Diggers: A Book of World Archaeology,* ill. with photos. World, 1964.

13 up

§★☆● COWING, SHEILA. *Searches in the American Desert.* McElderry, 1989.   11–14

★ COY, HAROLD. *Chicano Roots Go Deep.* Dodd, 1975.

11 up

DALGLIESH, ALICE. *America Begins: The Story of the Finding of the New World,* rev. ed., ill. by Lois Maloy. Scribner's 1958.   8–11

DEAN, ANABEL. *Up, Up, and Away! The Story of Ballooning.* Westminster, 1980. This lively history of ballooning is profusely illustrated with photographs, drawings, and explanatory diagrams.

11–13

DE PAUW, LINDA. *Founding Mothers: Women of America in the Revolutionary Era.* Houghton, 1975.   12 up

★ DOBRIN, ARNOLD. *The New Life—La Vida Nueva: The Mexican-Americans Today.* Dodd, 1971. A survey of attitudes, problems, and factors that influence the Chicano, using interviews.   10–12

DRUMMOND, A. H. *The Population Puzzle: Overcrowding and Stress Among Animals and Men.* Addison, 1973.   12–15

§ DURHAM, PHILIP, and EVERETT L. JONES. *The Negro Cowboys,* ill. with photos. Dodd, 1965. A great deal of information about African Americans who participated in the westward expansion.   13 up

★ EISMAN, ALBERTA. *Mañana Is Now: The Spanish-Speaking in the United States.* Atheneum, 1973.   12 up

ELLIOT, SARAH. *Our Dirty Air,* ill. with photos. Messner, 1971. Suggests ways that children can help. 8–10

☆ ERDOES, RICHARD. *The Native Americans: Navajos,* ill. with photos. Sterling, 1979. 9–11

EVANS, EVA KNOX. *Why We Live Where We Live,* ill. by Ursula Koering. Little, 1953. 9–12

§ EVANS, MICHAEL. *South Africa,* ill. and with photos. Gloucester/Watts, 1988. The author discusses concisely the complexities and issues surrounding controversial South Africa. 11–14

§ EVITTS, WILLIAM J. *Captive Bodies, Free Spirits: The Story of Southern Slavery.* Messner, 1985. A history of African-American slavery in the United States strikes a good balance between personal stories and historical accounts of laws and living conditions. 11–14

★ FISHER, LEONARD EVERETT. *The Alamo,* ill. and with photos. Holiday House, 1987. A detailed, well-researched history of the Alamo is illustrated by large-scale maps, reproductions of old prints and photographs and original drawings. 10–12

———. *The Blacksmiths,* ill. by author. Watts, 1976. 10–12

———. *The Factories,* ill. by author. Holiday, 1979. 10–12

○ ———. *The Great Wall of China,* ill. by author. Macmillan, 1986. 8–10

———. *The Homemakers,* ill. by author. Watts, 1973. 10–12

———. *The Hospitals,* ill. by author. Holiday, 1980. 10–12

———. *The Peddlers,* ill. by author. Watts, 1968. 10–12

———. *Pumpers, Boilers, Hooks and Ladders,* ill. by author. Dial, 1961. 5–8

☆ ———. *Pyramid of the Sun, Pyramid of the Moon,* ill. by author. Macmillan, 1988. 9–11

☆ ———. *The Railroads,* ill. by author. Holiday, 1979. 10–12

———. *The Silversmiths,* ill. by author. Watts, 1964. 10–12

———. *The Tanners,* ill. by author. Watts, 1966. 10–12

———. *The Tower of London,* ill. by author. Macmillan, 1987. Illustrated with dramatic black, white, and gray double-page spreads is a concise history of the changes in and uses of the Tower of London. 8–11

———. *Two If by Sea,* ill. by author. Random, 1970. 10–11

———. *The Unions,* ill. by author. Holiday, 1982. 10–12

§ FLATO, CHARLES. *The Golden Book of the Civil War,* ad. from *The American Heritage Picture History of the Civil War,* Golden Pr., 1961. 10–12

☆ FOLSOM, FRANKLIN. *Red Power on the Rio Grande: The Native American Revolution of 1680,* ill. by J. D. Roybal. Follett, 1973. 12–15

FOSTER, GENEVIEVE. *George Washington's World,* ill. by author. Scribner's, 1941. 11–14

———. *The World of Columbus and Sons,* ill. by author. Scribner's, 1965. 11–14

———. *The World of William Penn,* ill. by author. Scribner's, 1973. 9–12

———. *The Year of the Horseless Carriage—1801,* ill. by author. Scribner's, 1975. 10–11

———. *The Year of the Pilgrims—1620,* ill. by author. Scribner's, 1969. 8–10

☆ FREEDMAN, RUSSELL. *Buffalo Hunt,* ill. with photos. Holiday House, 1988. 10–13

———. *Children of the West,* ill. with photos. Houghton/Clarion, 1983. 9–12

———. *Cowboys of the Wild West,* ill. with photos. Houghton/Clarion, 1985. 10–14

———. *Immigrant Kids,* ill. with photos. Dutton, 1980. Vintage photographs illustrate this historical account of experiences of immigrant children in an urban environment. 9–12

○ FRITZ, JEAN. *China's Long March: 6,000 Miles of Danger.* Putnam, 1988. 12 up

———. *Shh! We're Writing the Constitution,* ill. by Tomie DePaola. Putnam, 1987. 9–12

———. *Who's That Stepping on Plymouth Rock?* ill. by J. B. Handelsman. Coward, 1975. 8–10

GIBLIN, JAMES CROSS. *Walls: Defenses Throughout History,* ill. by Anthony Kramer and with photos. Little, Brown, 1984. Well-placed and labeled drawings and photographs complement the text of a carefully organized book about famous walls. 9–14

☆ GOBLE, PAUL. *Death of the Iron Horse,* ill. by author. Bradbury, 1987. A picture book recounts the one time in United States history that native Americans derailed a train. 5–8

☆ GOBLE, PAUL and DOROTHY. *Brave Eagle's Account of the Fetterman Fight: 21 December 1866,* ill. by Paul Goble. Pantheon, 1972. An Oglala Sioux chief describes native American resistance to white encroachment. 10–12

☆ ———. *Red Hawk's Account of Custer's Last Battle,* ill. by authors. Pantheon, 1970. 10–12

§ GOLDSTON, ROBERT C. *The Negro Revolution,* ill. Macmillan, 1968. 13 up

GURNEY, GENE and CLARE. *The Launching of Sputnik, October 4, 1957: The Space Age Begins.* Watts, 1975. 10–13

HABENSTREIT, BARBARA. *Men Against War.* Doubleday, 1973. A survey of pacific protest from colonial times to today. 12–15

HACKWELL, W. JOHN. *Digging to the Past: Excavation in Ancient Lands,* ill. by author. Scribner's 1986. 10–14

HAHN, JAMES, and LYNN. *Recycling: Re-Using Our*

World's Solid Wastes. Watts, 1973.   9–12

HAMBLIN, DORA JANE. *Pots and Robbers.* Simon, 1970.   12 up

★ HARLAN, JUDITH. *Hispanic Voters: A Voice in American Politics,* ill. with photos. Watts, 1988. The political impact in the U.S. of various Hispanic communities is explained in a discussion of their institutional, cultural, and demographic forces.   12–17

HASKINS, JAMES *The Child Abuse Help Book.* Addison-Wesley, 1982.   11–14

———. *The Consumer Movement.* Watts, 1975.   12 up

§ ———. *The Creoles of Color of New Orleans,* ill. by Don Miller. T. Crowell, 1975.   11–14

———. *Street Gangs, Yesterday and Today.* Hastings, 1974.   13 up

———. *Who Are the Handicapped?* Doubleday, 1978.   12 up

———. *Witchcraft, Mysticism and Magic in the Black World.* Doubleday, 1974.   11–14

☆ HIRSCHFELDER, ARLENE. *Happily May I Walk: American Indians and Alaska Natives Today,* ill. with photos. Scribner's, 1986. A comprehensive research tool includes detailed chapters on tribal governments, reservations, languages, religion, education, history, and culture.   10–14

★ HOBART, LOIS. *Mexican Mural: The Story of Mexico, Past and Present.* Harcourt, 1963.   15 up

HODGES, C. WALTER. *Magna Carta,* ill. by author. Coward, 1966. An excellent survey of the conditions leading to the signing of the Magna Carta.   10–14

———. *The Norman Conquest,* ill. by author. Coward, 1966. A companion volume to the above title. Text is crisply informational; illustrations are unusually beautiful and informative.   10–14

☆ HOFSINDE, ROBERT (GRAY-WOLF). *Indian Sign Language,* ill. by author. Morrow, 1956.   9–13

☆ ———. *Indians at Home,* ill. by author. Morrow, 1964. A discussion of six major types of Indian homes. One of the best of the author's books on the cultures of North American Indians.   9–12

HOLLING, HOLLING C. *Paddle-to-the-Sea,* ill. by author. Houghton, 1941.   9–11

HOWE, JAMES. *The Hospital Book,* photos by Mal Warshaw. Crown, 1981. This excellent introduction to hospital procedures is both candid and comprehensive.   7–9

HOYT, EDWIN P. *Asians in the West.* Nelson, 1975.   12 up

———. *Whirlybirds: The Story of Helicopters,* ill. by George J. Zaffo. Doubleday, 1961. Attractive color illustrations.   10–13

§ HUGHES, LANGSTON. *The First Book of Africa,* rev. and rewritten, ill. with photos. Watts, 1964. Explorers, missionaries, the history of ancient Africa, and an evaluation of Africa today are included in this fine introductory book.   10–12

§ ———. *The First Book of Negroes,* ill. by Ursula Koering. Watts, 1952. Not comprehensive, but a competent introduction to African-American history.   9–11

HYDE, MARGARET. *Hotline!* 2nd ed. McGraw, 1976. Although substantially revised and augmented, this contains as before a general discussion of hotlines followed by separate chapters on hotlines for different needs.   12 up

ISAACSON, PHILIP M. *Round Buildings, Square Buildings, and Buildings that Wiggle Like a Fish,* ill. with photos by author. Knopf, 1988. Ninety-three international buildings are presented by beautifully composed and reproduced color photographs in a lesson on contrasting architectural styles.   11–17

JANEWAY, ELIZABETH. *The Vikings,* ill. by Henry C. Pitz. Random, 1951. Includes a chapter on Vineland.   9–11

§ JENNESS, AYLETTE. *Along the Niger River: An African Way of Life,* photos by author. T. Crowell, 1974.   10 up

———. *Dwellers of the Tundra: Life in an Alaskan Eskimo Village,* photos by Jonathan Jenness. Crowell-Collier, 1970.   11–14

☆ JENNESS, AYLETTE, and LISA W. KROEBER. *A Life of Their Own: An Indian Family in Latin America,* photos by authors, drawings by Susan Votaw. T. Crowell, 1975.   10–13

☆ JENNESS, AYLETTE, and ALICE RIVERS. *In Two Worlds: A Yupik Eskimo Family,* ill. with photos. Houghton, 1989.   9–13

JOHNSON, GERALD W. *America Grows Up: A History for Peter,* ill. by Leonard E. Fisher. Morrow, 1960. One of a series of lively and lucid books on the history and government of the United States.   10–13

§ JOHNSTON, JOHANNA. *Together in America: The Story of Two Races and One Nation,* ill. by Mort Künstler. Dodd, 1965.   11–14

§ JOSEPH, JOAN. *Black African Empires.* Watts, 1974.   10–12

JUSTER, NORTON. *As: A Surfeit of Similes,* ill. by David Small. Morrow, 1989. Line drawings, often hatched, add humor to a clever rhyming text that explains and illustrates the use of the comparative words *like* and *as.*   8–11

☆ KAREN, RUTH. *Kingdom of the Sun: The Inca, Empire Builders of the Americas,* ill. with photos. Four Winds, 1975.   12 up

☆ ———. *Song of the Quail: The Wondrous World of the Maya.* Four Winds, 1973. A vivid account of the impressive achievements of the Mayan civilization.   11 up

KAVALER, LUCY. *Dangerous Air,* ill. by Carl Smith. Day, 1967.   12 up

☆ KIRK, RUTH. *David, Young Chief of the Quileutes: An American Indian Today,* ill. with photos by author. Harcourt, 1967. The true story of a Pacific coast tribe that has moved gracefully into modern life while keeping its respect for Quileute tradition.

KREMENTZ, JILL. *How It Feels to be Adopted,* ill. with photos. Knopf, 1982. Interviews with children ages eight to sixteen explore feelings about being adopted; illustrated with warm photographs of the children and their families.   9–12

KURELEK, WILLIAM. *Lumberjack,* ill. by author. Houghton, 1974. A depiction of life in a Canadian lumber camp.   10 up

————. *A Prairie Boy's Summer,* ill. by author. Houghton, 1975. This and the title below recreate in text and pictures the quality of life on a Manitoba farm.   8–10

————. *A Prairie Boy's Winter,* ill. by author. Houghton, 1973.   8–10

KURELEK, WILLIAM, and MARGARET S. ENGELHART. *They Sought a New World: The Story of European Immigration to North America,* ill. by William Kurelek. Tundra, 1985. Vivid and varied paintings show large-scale outdoor scenes and details of working people.   10 up

★ KURTIS, ARLENE HARRIS. *Puerto Ricans: From Island to Mainland.* Watts, 1965. A simply written survey, with historical background provided.   9–12

☆ LA FARGE, OLIVER. *The American Indian.* Golden Pr., 1960.   10–12

LASKER, JOE. *Merry Ever After: The Story of Two Medieval Weddings,* ill. by author. Viking, 1976.
                                                                  8–10

————. *A Tournament of Knights,* ill. by author. T. Crowell, 1986.

LAUBER, PATRICIA. *Tales Mummies Tell.* T. Crowell, 1985.   9–12

§ LAWSON, DON. *South Africa.* Watts, 1986.   10–13

LESHAN, EDA. *What's Going to Happen to Me? When Parents Separate or Divorce,* ill. by Richard Cuffari. Four Winds, 1978. The message that feelings of fear, anger, and loss are natural and should not be repressed is presented in a clear, candid style.
                                                                  9–12

§ LESTER, JULIUS. *To Be a Slave,* ill. by Tom Feelings. Dial, 1968. Excerpts from source material, chronologically arranged, give a moving and explicit picture of slavery.   11–14

LIFTON, BETTY JEAN. *Return to Hiroshima,* ill. with photos by Eikoh Hosoe. Atheneum, 1970. A matter-of-fact, serious, objective assessment of the enduring ramifications of the bombing of Hiroshima. Excellent photos.   10–17

LISTON, ROBERT A. *Who Really Runs America?* Doubleday, 1974. An analysis of the power structure in the United States.   12–15

§ LOBSENZ, NORMAN M. *The First Book of Ghana,* ill. with photos. Watts, 1960. A competent historical and cultural overview.   9–11

MACAULAY, DAVID. *Mill,* ill. by author. Houghton, 1983. Precise, carefully labeled drawings amplify this narrative about the building and operation of nineteenth-century Rhode Island mills and corollary sociopolitical issues.   12 up

————. *Underground,* ill. by author. Houghton, 1976.   10 up

MAESTRO, BETSY. *A More Perfect Union: The Story of Our Constitution,* ill. by Guilio Maestro. Lothrop, 1987.   7–9

MANNICHE, LISE, tr. *How Djadja-Em-Ankh Saved the Day: A Tale from Ancient Egypt,* ill. by author. T. Crowell, 1977. Available in scroll form or folded accordion style, this ancient Egyptian fantasy reads from right to left and is also told in hieroglyphs.   9–11

☆ MARRIN, ALBERT. *Aztecs and Spaniards: Cortes and the Conquest of Mexico.* Atheneum, 1986. Dramatic and action-packed, this includes colorful cultural background on the Aztecs and conquistadors and fine portraits of Montezuma and Cortes.   12 up

————. *The War for Independence: The Story of the American Revolution.* Atheneum, 1988. A spirited and thoughtful account of the American Revolution is profusely illustrated with prints, paintings and maps.   12 up

MAY, JULIAN. *The First Men,* ill. by Lorence F. Bjorklund. Holiday, 1968.   7–9

MEAD, MARGARET. *Anthropologists and What They Do.* Watts, 1965. The interview is used to introduce some of the specialized fields and techniques of anthropology. A lively and informative career guidance book.   12 up

————. *People and Places,* ill. by W. T. Mars and Jan Fairservis and with photos. World, 1959.
                                                                  12–14

MELTZER, MILTON. *Ain't Gonna Study War No More: The Story of America's Peace Seekers.* Harper, 1985. Individuals, organizations, movements, and religious groups that have opposed war are discussed in a comprehensive, forceful treatise based on careful research.   12 up

§ ————. *All Times, All Peoples: A World History of Slavery,* ill. by Leonard Everett Fisher. Harper, 1980.   10–12

§ ☆ ————. *The American Revolutionaries: A History in Their Own Words, 1750–1800,* ill. with photos. T. Crowell, 1987.   11 up

§ ————, ed. *The Black Americans: A History in Their Own Words.* T. Crowell, 1984. See also listing below for the compiler's three-volume series, *In Their Own Words*.   12–15

★ _____. *Bound for the Rio Grande: The Mexican Struggle 1845–1850*, ill. with prints and photos. Knopf, 1974.   12 up

○ _____. *The Chinese Americans*, ill. with photos. T. Crowell, 1980.   12 up

★ _____. *The Hispanic Americans*, photos by Morrie Camhi and Catherine Noren. T. Crowell, 1982.
                    12 up

§ _____, ed. *In Their Own Words: A History of the American Negro;* Vol. 1, 1619–1865. T. Crowell, 1964.

§ _____, ed. *In Their Own Words: A History of the American Negro;* Vol. 2, 1865–1916. T. Crowell, 1965.

§ _____, ed. *In Their Own Words: A History of the American Negro;* Vol. 3, 1916–1966. T. Crowell, 1967.   12–15

● _____, ed. *Never to Forget: The Jews of the Holocaust*. Harper, 1976.   12 up

● _____. *Remember the Days: A Short History of the Jewish American*, ill. by Harvey Dinnerstein. Doubleday, 1974.   12 up

● _____. *Rescue: The Story of How Gentiles Saved Jews in the Holocaust*, ill. with photos. Harper, 1988.   10–14

§ MELTZER, MILTON, and AUGUST MEIER. *Time of Trial, Time of Hope: The Negro in America, 1919–1941*, ill. by Moneta Barnett. Doubleday, 1966.   11–14

● MEYER, CAROLYN. *Amish People: Plain Living in a Complex World*, ill. with photos. Atheneum, 1976. Meyer creates an imaginary but very convincing family to illustrate the roles and problems of various positions in an Amish family and to describe various everyday events.   12 up

☆ _____. *Eskimos: Growing up in a Changing Culture*, ill. with photos. Atheneum, 1977. Meyer postulates a year with an imaginary family; gives a vivid, perceptive picture of the cultural patterns of Eskimos living near the Bering Sea.   12–14

§ MILLER, MARILYN. *The Bridge at Selma*, ill. with photos. Silver Burdett, 1985.   11–14

MORRIS, RICHARD B. *The First Book of the American Revolution*, ill. by Leonard E. Fisher. Watts, 1956.
                    9–13

☆ MORRISON, MARION. *Atahuallpa and the Incas*. Bookwright/Watts, 1986. Profusely illustrated, the text describes the establishment of the Inca empire, the ways it grew and functioned, and its conquest by Spanish soldiers.   10–12

MORRISON, VELMA FORD. *Going on a Dig*, ill. with photos. Dodd, 1981. An enlightening survey of archeology looks closely at ongoing excavations in the United States.   10–12

§ MUSGROVE, MARGARET. *Ashanti to Zulu: African Traditions*, ill. by Leo and Diane Dillon. Dial, 1976. A paragraph of text on each page of an oversize book describes some aspect of the cultures of twenty-six African tribes. Caldecott Medal.
                    8–10

☆ NABOKOV, PETER, ed. *Native American Testimony: An Anthology of Indian and White Relations*. T. Crowell, 1978. A tragic record, eloquently expressed, comprise statements by native Americans of many tribes over four centuries.   12 up

NAVARRA, JOHN. *Our Noisy World: The Problem of Noise Pollution*. Doubleday, 1969.   11–14

_____. *The World You Inherit: A Story of Pollution*. Natural History Pr., 1970.   12–14

● NAYLOR, PHYLLIS REYNOLDS. *An Amish Family*, ill. by George Armstrong. O'Hara, 1975. A competent survey of Amish society is based on a study of a three-generation family.   11 up

NICKMAN, STEVEN L. *When Mom and Dad Divorce*, ill. by Diane de Groat. Messner, 1986. A pediatrician and psychiatrist, the author uses a series of anecdotes as bases for discussions of different aspects of children's coping with divorce and of different kinds of separation situations.   9–12

☆ OSINSKI, ALICE. *The Chippewa*, ill. and with photos. Childrens Press, 1987. This easy reader, one in a series on native-American tribes, focuses on the environment, background, and traditional and current lifestyles of the Chippewa people.   7–9

PACE, MILDRED (MASTIN). *Wrapped for Eternity: The Story of the Egyptian Mummy*, ill. by Tom Huffman. McGraw, 1974. A description of Egyptian death practices includes many facts about the culture of ancient Egypt.   10–14

PARKER, NANCY WINSLOW. *The United Nations from A to Z*, ill. by author. Dodd, 1985. This collection of one-page descriptive reports is a mini-encyclopedia of U.N. history, activities, and trivia.   9–11

_____. *Voices from the Civil War*, ill. with photos. T. Crowell, 1989.   12–15

PARNALL, PETER. *The Mountain*, ill. by author. Doubleday, 1971. Pollution ruins the peace and beauty of a mountainside.   5–7

§★☆○ PASCOE, ELAINE. *Racial Prejudice*, ill. with photos. Watts, 1985.   11–14

§ PERKINS, CAROL MORSE, and MARLIN PERKINS. *"I Saw You from Afar": A Visit to the Bushmen of the Kalahari Desert*, ill. with photos. Atheneum, 1965. The daily life of the bushmen in photographs and simple text. The treatment is sympathetic and dignified.   9–11

PERL, LISA. *Mummies, Tombs, and Treasure: Secrets of Ancient Egypt*, ill. by Erika Weihs. Houghton/Clarion, 1987.   10–13

POWELL, ANTON. *The Rise of Islam*. Warwick, 1980. A detailed account of Islamic culture until the sixteenth century.   10–13

PRINGLE, LAURENCE P. *The Economic Growth Debate: Are There Limits to Growth?* Watts, 1978.   12 up

————. *Nuclear Power: From Physics to Politics,* ill. with photos. Macmillan, 1970.   12 up

————. *Nuclear War: From Hiroshima to Nuclear Winter.* Enslow, 1985.   12–15

PROVENSEN, ALICE and MARTIN. *Shaker Lane,* ill. by authors. Viking, 1987.   5–8

PUGH, ELLEN, with the assistance of DAVID B. PUGH. *Brave His Soul,* ill. Dodd, 1970.   12–15

RAU, MARGARET. *The People of New China,* ill. with photos. Messner, 1978. The focus here is on such aspects of modern life as education, industry, familial relationships, and the arts.   10–12

————. *The People's Republic of China.* Messner, 1974. Gives both historical background and a full discussion of China today.   10–12

RICH, LOUISE DICKINSON. *The First Book of New World Explorers,* ill. by Cary Dickinson. Watts, 1960.   9–11

• ROGASKY, BARBARA. *Smoke and Ashes: The Story of the Holocaust,* ill. with photos. Holiday House, 1988. The author provides details of the Nazi plan to eliminate European Jews through slave labor and death camps.   12–17

ROSENBERG, MAXINE B. *Finding a Way: Living with Exceptional Brothers and Sisters,* ill. with photos by George Ancona. Lothrop, 1988. The experiences of siblings of children with special physical problems are discussed in a calm, clear tone.   7–9

§○• ————. *Living in Two Worlds,* ill. with photos by George Ancona. Lothrop, 1986. Candid photographs and text document the lives of children of biracial parents.   7–9

ROSENBLUM, RICHARD. *The Golden Age of Aviation,* ill. by author. Atheneum, 1984. An inviting chronicle of aircraft and their pilots from the time of Lindbergh's solo flight across the Atlantic to the outset of World War II.   7–11

SANCHA, SHEILA. *The Luttrell Village: Country Life in the Middle Ages.* T. Crowell, 1983. An interestingly detailed description of life in an English village in the year 1328, based in part on rare contemporary drawings.   10–14

SANDERLIN, GEORGE. *A Hoop to the Barrel.* Coward, 1974.   11–15

§ SAVAGE, KATHARINE. *The Story of Africa: South of the Sahara,* ill. with photos and maps. Walck, 1961.   12 up

☆ SCHEELE, WILLIAM E. *The Earliest Americans,* ill. by author. World, 1963.   10–14

SCHLEIN, MIRIAM. *I, Tut: The Boy Who Became Pharoah,* ill. by Erik Hilgerdt. Four Winds, 1978. The six-year-old prince begins his story; his friend Hekenefer takes up the tale after Tutankhamun's mysterious death at age eighteen.   8–10

————. *It's About Time,* ill. by Leonard Kessler. W. R. Scott, 1955.   6–8

SCOTT, ELAINE. *Ramona: Behind the Scenes of a Television Show,* ill. with photos by Margaret Miller. Morrow, 1988. Shows the backstage production of a television show based on the popular Beverly Cleary character, Ramona.   9–11

SCHWARTZ, ALVIN. *The City and Its People: The Story of One City's Government,* photos by Sy Katzoff. Dutton, 1967. An excellent description of a city of 300,000 people, its administrative structure, problems, and planning.   9–12

————. *The Night Workers,* photos by Ullie Steltzer. Dutton, 1966. Interesting chronological treatment.   7–10

————. *Old Cities and New Towns,* ill. with photos. Dutton, 1968.   11–14

SHIPPEN, KATHERINE B. *The Pool of Knowledge: How the United Nations Share Their Skills,* rev. ed., ill. with photos. Harper, 1965. A good explanation of some of the work of the U.N.   11 up

SILVERSTEIN, ALVIN, VIRGINIA, and GLENN. *Aging.* Watts, 1979.   6 up

★ SINGER, JULIA. *We All Come from Puerto Rico, Too,* ill. with photos. Atheneum, 1977. In commentary mostly by children, this gives a rich and varied picture of Puerto Rican life, achieving an antidote to the "poor emigrant" stereotype presented in most children's stories set in Puerto Rico.   8–10

SPIER, PETER. *The Legend of New Amsterdam,* ill. by author. Doubleday, 1979. Wonderfully detailed paintings support a text that is mostly descriptive with a bit of narrative interest.   7–9

§ STERLING, DOROTHY. *Tear Down the Walls! A History of the American Civil Rights Movement,* ill. Doubleday, 1968.   12 up

§ ————, ed. *The Trouble They Seen: Black People Tell the Story of Reconstruction.* Doubleday, 1976.   12 up

STEVENS, LEONARD A. *The Town That Launders Its Water,* ill. with photos. Coward, 1971. A California town has eight man-made lakes for recreation, the water reclaimed from sewage.   11 up

§ STEVENSON, JANET. *The School Segregation Cases: (Brown v. Board of Education of Topeka and others): The United States Supreme Court Rules on Racially Separate Public Education.* Watts, 1973. A comprehensive examination of protest, dissent, and legislation about school integration.   10–14

SULLIVAN, GEORGE. *All About Football,* ill. and with photos. Dodd, 1987. Facts about football history, game play, rules, and penalties are explained in a text with good organization and sequential flow.   9–12

TOYE, WILLIAM. *Cartier Discovers the St. Lawrence,* ill. by Laszlo Gal. Toronto: Oxford, 1959. An authoritative account of Cartier's three exploratory voyages. 10–12

TUNIS, EDWIN. *Colonial Craftsmen and the Beginnings of American Industry,* ill. by author. World, 1965. Well-organized and superbly illustrated, the text is comprehensive, lucid, and detailed. 11–14

————. *Colonial Living,* ill. by author. World, 1957. 10–12

————. *Frontier Living,* ill. by author. World, 1961. 10 up

☆ ————. *Indians,* ill. by author. World, 1959. 11 up

• ————. *The Tavern at the Ferry,* ill. by author. T. Crowell, 1973. 9–12

UDEN, GRANT. *A Dictionary of Chivalry,* ill. by Pauline Baynes. T. Crowell, 1968. 11 up

UNSTEAD, R. J. *Living in a Medieval Village,* ill. by Ron Stenberg. Addison, 1973. One of a series of informative books about medieval times stresses the occupations of villagers. 9–11

VAN LOON, HENDRIK WILLEM. *The Story of Mankind,* ill. by author. Liveright, 1921, rev. ed., 1951. Newbery Medal. 12–14

VENTURA, PIERO. *Man and the Horse,* ill. by author. Putnam, 1982. Handsome small-scale paintings and a topical text detail the ways humans have used horses from prehistoric times to the present. 9 up

VIERECK, PHILLIP, comp. *The New Land: Discovery, Exploration, and Early Settlement of Northeastern United States, from Earliest Voyages to 1621, Told in the Words of the Explorers Themselves,* ill. by Ellen Viereck. Day, 1967. 14 up

☆ VON HAGEN, VICTOR W. *Maya, Land of the Turkey and the Deer,* ill. by Alberto Beltran. World, 1960. 11–14

VON TSCHARNER, RENATA. *New Providence: A Changing Cityscape,* ill. by Denis Orloff. Gulliver/Harcourt, 1987. An interesting visual history presents a small, fictitious and typical American city as it goes through several decades of change. 9–11

WALSH, GILLIAN PATON. *Lost and Found,* ill. by Mary Raynor. Andre Deutsch/Elsevier/Dutton, 1985. The complexity of history is demonstrated in the simplicity of a picture book, as each child loses an item that is found by a child in a subsequent time period. 7–9

WARREN, RUTH. *Pictorial History of Women in America.* Crown, 1985. A survey of women's contributions from colonial times on. 12 up

WEISS, HARVEY. *Shelters: From Teepee to Igloo,* ill. by author. T. Crowell, 1988. 9–11

WHITE, ANNE TERRY. *Prehistoric America,* ill. by Aldren Watson. Random, 1951. 9–11

WHITNEY, SHARON and TOM RAYNOR. *Women in Politics,* ill. with photos. Watts, 1986. Concerned with the process that has gotten women into political office, the authors discuss where women politicians get support and what inequity remains in representation. 12–15

WINN, MARIE. *The Fisherman Who Needed a Knife: A Story About Why People Use Money,* ill. by John E. Johnson. Simon, 1970. This introduces the concept of money as a common medium of exchange. 4–7

————. *The Man Who Made Fine Tops: A Story About Why People Do Different Kinds of Work,* ill. by John E. Johnson. Simon, 1970. A light fictional framework describing the father who made his son a top is used to explain the division of labor. The ideas are perfectly clear and the author wisely stopped when her point was made. 5–7

★ WOLF, BERNARD. *In This Proud Land: The Story of a Mexican American Family,* ill. with photos. Lippincott, 1978. A photo-documentary, straight-forward, objective, and candid, describing a family of Mexican-Americans living in Texas. 11–14

☆ ————. *Tinker and the Medicine Man: The Story of a Navajo Boy of Monument Valley,* photos by author. Random, 1973. A small boy learns the arts practiced by his father, a medicine man. 9–11

ZINER, FEENIE, and ELIZABETH THOMPSON. *The True Book of Time,* ill. by Katherine Evans. Childrens Pr., 1956. 6–8

Religion and the Arts

• ADLER, DAVID. *A Picture Book of Hanukkah,* ill. by Linda Heller. Holiday, 1982. A simply narrated telling of the events that led to the Miracle of Light, the historical basis for the celebration of Hanukkah. 5–8

• ASHABRANNER, BRENT. *Gavriel and Jemal: Two Boys of Jerusalem,* ill. with photos by Paul Conklin. Dodd, 1984. The lives of two boys from Jerusalem are juxtaposed to demonstrate the problems, similarities, and differences between the Arabs and the Jews in the Middle East. 9–11

BASKIN, TOBIAS, and others. *Hosie's Zoo,* ill. by Leonard Baskin. Viking, 1981. Stunning ink-and-wash paintings capture the individual qualities of animals in this remarkable "zoo." 9 up

BATTERBERRY, ARIANE (RUSKIN). *The Pantheon Story of Art for Young People,* rev. ed. Pantheon, 1975. 10 up

☆ BATTERBERRY, ARIANE and MICHAEL. *The Pantheon Story of American Art for Young People.* Pantheon,

1976. An impressive work which proceeds chronologically from native Americans to white settlers and on through to the twentieth century. 11 up

BATTERBERRY, MICHAEL. *Art of the Middle Ages.* McGraw, 1972. Well organized and cohesive, a beautifully illustrated book. 12 up

BATTERBERRY, MICHAEL, and ARIANE RUSKIN, ads. *Primitive Art.* McGraw, 1973. 12 up

BAYNES, PAULINE, ill. *Noah and the Ark.* Holt, 1988. 4-8

BEIRNE, BARBARA. *Under the Lights: A Young Model at Work,* ill. with photos. Carolrhoda, 1988. An eleven-year-old professional model describes her work, including both the glamour and the drudgery.

BELLVILLE, CHERYL WALSH. *Theater Magic: Behind the Scenes at a Children's Theater,* ill. with photos by author. Carolrhoda, 1986. An attractive and informative photo-essay shows the behind the scenes activities necessary for producing a play. 8-11

☆ BIERHORST, JOHN. *A Cry from the Earth: Music of the North American Indians.* Four Winds, 1979. A description of native-American songs and, to a lesser extent, of the instruments used to accompany singers. 11 up

☆ _____, ad. *Songs of the Chippewa;* ad. from the collections of Frances Densmore and Henry Rowe Schoolcraft, and arranged for piano and guitar by John Bierhorst; ill. by Joe Servello. Farrar, 1974. Simple musical notation is provided; lyrics are in English. 9 up

☆ • _____, tr. *Spirit Child: A Story of the Nativity,* ill. by Barbara Cooney. Morrow, 1984. 8-9

BONI, MARGARET BRADFORD, ed. *The Fireside Book of Favorite American Songs,* arr. for piano by Norman Lloyd, ill. by Aurelius Battaglia. Simon, 1952. From songs of the Pilgrims to ballads of the Nineties. 8 up

BORTEN, HELEN. *A Picture Has a Special Look.* Abelard, 1961. Describes and illustrates some of the media used by artists. 9-11

BRITTEN, BENJAMIN, and IMOGEN HOLST. *The Wonderful World of Music,* rev. ed. Doubleday, 1968. 8-12

BROWN, LAURENE KRASNEY and MARC. *Visiting the Art Museum,* ill. by author. Dutton, 1986. 5-8

§ BRYAN, ASHLEY. *Walk Together Children: Black American Spirituals,* selected and ill. by Ashley Bryan. Atheneum, 1974. 8-10

BULLA, CLYDE ROBERT. *Stories of Favorite Operas,* ill. by Robert Galster. T. Crowell, 1959. Twenty-three libretti of popular operas. 10-14

CESERANI, GIAN PAOLO. *Grand Constructions,* ill. by Piero Ventura. Putnam, 1983. Architectural landmarks and famous sites are depicted in impressively detailed, spacious paintings. 11 up

• CHAIKIN, MIRIAM. *Make Noise, Make Merry: The Story and Meaning of Purim,* ill. by Demi. Clarion, 1983. Historical background on Purim plus a discussion of why the holiday grew in importance and how it is celebrated. 9-11

CHASE, ALICE ELIZABETH. *Looking at Art,* ill. T. Crowell, 1966. 11 up

CUMMING, ROBERT. *Just Look . . . A Book About Paintings.* Scribner's, 1980. Designed to help children understand components of paintings such as perspective, composition, color, and light. 9-11

DEEDY, JOHN. *The Vatican,* ill. with photos. Watts, 1970. 10-12

DE MILLE, AGNES. *The Book of the Dance,* ill. by N. M. Bodecker. Golden Pr., 1963. Social, ritual, and theatrical dance history in full, with many color photographs. 11 up

★ DE PAOLA, TOMIE. *The Lady of Guadalupe,* ill. by author. Holiday, 1980. A warmly pictured retelling of the legend of the patron saint of Mexico, Our Lady Mary of Guadalupe. Available in both English- and Spanish-language editions. 5-8

§ DIETZ, BETTY WARNER, and MICHAEL BABATUNDE OLATUNJI. *Musical Instruments of Africa,* ill. by Richard M. Powers and with photos. Day, 1965. 11-12

DIETZ, BETTY WARNER, and THOMAS CHOONBAI PARK. *Folk Songs of China, Japan, and Korea,* ill. by Mamoru Funai. Day, 1964. 9 up

DOWNER, MARION. *Discovering Design.* Lothrop, 1947. An analysis of the elements of design in nature. 11 up

_____. *The Story of Design,* ill. with photos. Lothrop, 1964. 11 up

DURELL, ANN, comp. *The Diane Goode Book of American Folk Tales and Songs,* ill. by Diane Goode. Dutton, 1989. 5-8

• ELGIN, KATHLEEN. *The Unitarians,* ill. by author. McKay, 1971. And others in the series. 9-11

ENGLANDER, ROGER. *Opera: What's All the Screaming About?* Walker, 1983. 12 up

ENGLISH, BETTY LOU. *You Can't Be Timid with a Trumpet: Notes from the Orchestra,* photos by author, drawings by Stan Skardinski. Lothrop, 1980. Interviews with musicians in several major orchestras introduce instrumental groupings and characteristics of music careers. 10-12

EWEN, DAVID. *Opera: Its Story Told Through the Lives and Works of Its Foremost Composers.* Watts, 1972. 12 up

_____. *Orchestral Music: Its Story Told Through the Lives and Works of Its Foremost Composers.* Watts, 1973. 12 up

_____. *Vocal Music: Its Story Told Through the*

Lives and Works of Its Foremost Composers. Watts, 1975.   12 up

• FAHS, SOPHIA BLANCHE LYON, and ALICE COBB. *Old Tales for a New Day: Early Answers to Life's Eternal Questions,* ill. by Gobin Stair. Prometheus, 1981. An anthology intended primarily for religious education collections organizes stories by issue-oriented themes.   9–11

FAULKNER, MARGARET. *I Skate!* ill. with photos. Little, 1979. Profusely illustrated, the text centers around young skaters and is substantial in both extent and coverage.   10–13

FISHER, LEONARD EVERETT. *Number Art: Thirteen 1 2 3s from Around the World,* ill. by author. Four Winds, 1982. Numerical notation systems from several regions of the world are explained and illustrated with distinctive scratchboard illustrations.   10 up

————, ad. *The Seven Days of Creation,* ill. by adapter. Holiday, 1981. Splendidly evocative paintings help tell the Biblical story of creation.   all ages

GIBLIN, JAMES CROSS. *The Skyscraper Book,* ill. by Anthony Kramer, photos by David Anderson. T. Crowell, 1981. A smoothly informative account of the development and proliferation of skyscrapers.   10–14

GLADSTONE, J. J. *A Carrot for a Nose: The Form of Folk Sculpture on America's City Streets and Country Roads.* Scribner's, 1974.   10–13

GLAZER, TOM. *Eye Winker, Tom Tinker, Chin Chopper: Fifty Musical Fingerplays,* ill. by Ron Himler. Doubleday, 1973. Fifty songs are included, as are directions for hand movements.   5–11

————. *Music for Ones and Twos: Songs and Games for the Very Young Child,* ill. by Karen Ann Weinhaus. Doubleday, 1983. Brisk little line drawings illustrate an excellent collection of songs, many of which serve also as games, finger plays, or learning devices.   1–5

GLUBOK, SHIRLEY. *The Art of America in the Early Twentieth Century,* ill. with photos. Macmillan, 1974. Reflects more than do most of Glubok's books, the breadth and variety of art forms within a given period.   10–13

————. *The Art of Ancient Greece,* ill. with photos. Atheneum, 1963. And other books in this series.   10–13

————. *The Art of Colonial America,* ill. with photos. Macmillan, 1970.   9–12

————. *The Art of the Comic Strip.* Macmillan, 1979. Focuses on artistic style.   9–12

————. *The Art of Egypt under the Pharaohs.* Macmillan, 1980.   10–12

☆ ————. *The Art of the Plains Indians,* ill. with photos. Macmillan, 1975.   9–12

★ ————. *The Art of the Spanish in the United States and Puerto Rico,* ill. with photos. Macmillan, 1972. Includes architecture, room interiors, crafts, and religious art objects.   8–10

GREENFELD, HOWARD. *Books: From Writer to Reader.* Crown, 1976. Greenfeld discusses the roles of each participant in the book-making process and of the steps in production, literary and physical.   12 up

• ————. *Chanukah.* Holt, 1976. A dignified retelling of the episode in Jewish history that is commemorated by Chanukah.   11 up

————. *The Impressionist Revolution.* Doubleday, 1972.   12 up

• ————. *Passover,* ill. by Elaine Grove. Holt, 1978.   10–12

• ————. *Rosh Hashanah and Yom Kippur,* ill. by Elaine Grove. Holt, 1979.   10–12

————. *They Came to Paris.* Crown, 1975.   13 up

GRIGSON, GEOFFREY. *Shapes and Stories: A Book About Pictures.* Vanguard, 1965. Perceptive comments about a selected group of pictures.   10–12

HASKELL, ARNOLD LIONEL. *The Wonderful World of Dance.* Doubleday, 1969.   11–14

§ HASKINS, JAMES. *Black Music in America: A History Through Its People,* ill. with photos. T. Crowell, 1987.   12–15

HEMMING, ROY. *Discovering Music: Where to Start on Records and Tapes, the Great Composers and Their Works, Today's Major Recording Artists.* Four Winds, 1974.   12 up

☆ HOFMANN, CHARLES. *American Indians Sing,* ill. by Nicholas Amorosi. Day, 1967.   10–13

☆ HOFSINDE, ROBERT (GRAY-WOLF). *Indian Arts,* ill. by author. Morrow, 1971. An intriguing and decorative book on aspects of North American Indian cultures.   8–11

☆ ————. *Indian Music Makers,* ill. by author. Morrow, 1967.   9–12

• HOGROGIAN, NONNY, ad. *Noah's Ark,* ill. by adaptor. Knopf, 1986. The simple and brief adaptation and gentle illustrations make this edition of the Bible story ideal for young children.   3–5

HORWITZ, ELINOR. *Contemporary American Folk Artists.* Lippincott, 1975.   11 up

§ HUGHES, LANGSTON. *Famous Negro Music Makers.* Dodd, 1955.   11–14

§ ————. *The First Book of Jazz,* ill. by Cliff Roberts, music selected by David Martin. Watts, 1955.   11 up

————. *The First Book of Rhythms,* ill. by Robin King. Watts, 1954.   11–14

HURD, MICHAEL. *The Oxford Junior Companion to Music,* 2d. ed. Oxford, 1980. Comprehensive and informative.   11 up

• HUTTON, WARWICK, ad. *Adam and Eve: The Bible Story,*

ill. by adaptor. McElderry, 1987. The biblical version of the creation and the fall of man is illustrated in a vertical perspective, with a blue and green wash.   5–7

JESSEL, CAMILLA. *Life at the Royal Ballet School,* ill. with photos. Methuen, 1979. A most successful effort to show the slow, arduous, dedicated work that goes into becoming a ballet dancer.   11 up

§ JOHNSON, JAMES WELDON, and J. ROSAMOND JOHNSON. *Lift Every Voice and Sing: Words and Music.* Hawthorn, 1970. Simply arranged for piano and guitar chords, a song that has endured as a hymn of African-American hope since it was written in 1900.   9–11

KAHN, ELY JACQUES. *A Building Goes Up,* ill. by Cal Sacks. Simon, 1969.   10–14

KETTELKAMP, LARRY. *Flutes, Whistles, and Reeds,* ill. by author. Morrow, 1962.   9–11

KING, MARY LOUISE. *A History of Western Architecture,* ill. with photos and diagrams. Walck, 1967.

12–16

KREMENTZ, JILL. *A Very Young Dancer.* Knopf, 1976.

9 up

————. *A Very Young Gymnast,* ill. with photos. Knopf, 1978. Excellent photographs and a text which has the casual intimacy of a child's conversation portray the lifestyle of a dedicated young gymnast.   9 up

• KUSKIN, KARLA. *Jerusalem, Shining Still,* ill. by David Frampton. Harper, 1987.   8–10

§ • LAIRD, ELIZABETH. *The Road to Bethlehem: An Ethiopian Nativity.* Holt, 1987. Illustrated with paintings from eighteenth-century illuminated manuscripts, the text combines New Testament motifs with popular Ethiopian legends and miracles.

7–9

§ ☆ LANGSTAFF, JOHN M., comp. *The Season for Singing: American Christmas Songs and Carols,* musical settings by Seymour Barab. Doubleday, 1974. Some songs are of European origin; native American and African-American music are included.

all ages

§ LANGSTAFF, JOHN, and JOHN ANDREW ROSS, comp. *What a Morning! The Christmas Story in Black Spirituals,* ill. by Ashley Bryan. McElderry, 1987. The nativity story is told by alternating illustrated Bible verses and music for five African-American spirituals.   4–8

LARRICK, NANCY, comp. *The Wheels of the Bus Go Round and Round: School Bus Songs and Chants,* ill. by Gene Holtan. Golden Gate, 1972. Songs—many of which are old favorites—for singing while riding.   8–10

LUTTRELL, GUY. *The Instruments of Music.* Nelson, 1977. Luttrell describes standard orchestral instruments, American folk instruments, the human voice, and electronic instruments, including in his discussion historical background and how each operates.   11–14

MACGREGOR, ANNE and SCOTT. *Domes: A Project Book,* ill. by authors. Lothrop, 1982. Meticulously drafted diagrams and drawings illustrate this analysis of domes in architecture.   10 up

MACAULAY, DAVID. *Castle,* ill. by author. Houghton, 1977. Described here is the planning and building of an imaginary but typical Welsh castle and town of the late thirteenth century.   10 up

————. *Cathedral: The Story of Its Construction.* Houghton, 1973.   10 up

————. *City: A Story of Roman Planning and Construction.* Houghton, 1974.   10 up

————. *Pyramid.* Houghton, 1975. All of Macaulay's books give almost as much information about the culture as they do about the architectural details of the construction of great edifices. The illustrations are profuse and meticulously detailed.   10 up

————. *Unbuilding,* ill. by author. Houghton, 1980.   10 up

MANCHEL, FRANK. *When Pictures Began to Move,* ill. by James Caraway. Prentice, 1969. One of the best histories of the motion picture industry for young people, ending with the death of the silent film. Good bibliography.   11–14

MAYNARD, OLGA. *American Modern Dancers: The Pioneers,* Atlantic/Little, 1965.   11 up

————. *The Ballet Companion.* Macrae, 1957.

11–15

○ • MILLER, LUREE. *The Black Hat Dances: Two Buddhist Boys in the Himalayas,* ill. with photos by Marilyn Silverstone. Dodd, 1987. Portrayals of the lives of two boys in Sikkim, India, show how an entire Buddhist community is involved in supporting its monastery.   10–11

MOORE, JANET GAYLORD. *The Many Ways of Seeing: An Introduction to the Pleasures of Art,* ill. World, 1968.

13 up

§ NAYLOR, PENELOPE. *Black Images: The Art of West Africa,* photos by Lisa Little. Doubleday, 1973. Relates art objects to the cultural beliefs and traditions they reflect.   12 up

PAINE, ROBERTA M. *Looking at Sculpture,* ill. Lothrop, 1968.   9 up

PEARSON, TRACEY CAMPBELL, ad. *Old McDonald Had a Farm,* ill. by adaptor. Dial, 1986. Active, witty drawings illustrate a lap-sized picture book of the popular children's song. Music provided.   3–6

POSTON, ELIZABETH, comp. *The Baby's Song Book,* ill. by William Stobbs. T. Crowell, 1972. Includes songs from other languages as well as English in a collection for young children.   2–5

• POWELL, ANTON. *The Rise of Islam.* Warwick, 1980. An information-packed survey of Islamic culture from the seventh to sixteenth centuries.   10–13

POWERS, BILL. *Behind the Scenes of a Broadway Musical,* ill. with photos. Crown, 1982. A generously illustrated narrative tells how a Broadway musical, Maurice Sendak's *Really Rosie,* is put together from the planning stages to opening night.   9–11

§ PRICE, CHRISTINE. *Made in West Africa,* ill. with photos. Dutton, 1975. Descriptions of art objects are arranged by techniques and media.   11 up

§ _____. *Talking Drums of Africa.* Scribner's, 1973. Discusses the drums, the drumming, and the songs and dances of the Ashanti and Yaruba peoples.   8–10

PROVENSEN, ALICE and MARTIN. *Leonardo da Vinci: The Artist, Inventor, Scientist in Three-Dimensional Movable Pictures,* ill. by authors. Viking, 1984. Paper engineering, used to full advantage, adds to the lovely paintings to create a stunning book.   9–13

• PURDY, SUSAN GOLD. *Jewish Holidays: Facts, Activities, and Crafts,* ill. Lippincott, 1969.   10–12

• RADFORD, RUBY L. *Many Paths to God.* Theosophical, 1970. The basic ideas of twelve living religions and many of their parallel teachings. Each chapter has a list of suggested readings.   10–14

REISS, JOHN. *Colors,* ill. by author. Bradbury, 1969. Not only useful for color identification, but for awakening aesthetic appreciation.   2–5

• RICE, EDWARD. *The Five Great Religions,* photos by author. Four Winds, 1973.   12–15

ROBBINS, KEN. *Building a House,* photos by author. Four Winds, 1984. Expertly organized, this volume traces the steps in house construction with the aid of well-composed photographs.   8–11

ROCKWELL, ANNE. *Glass, Stones, and Crown: The Abbe Suger and the Building of St. Denis.* Atheneum, 1968.   11–13

ROUNDS, GLEN, ad. *Old McDonald Had a Farm,* ill. by adaptor Holiday House, 1989. The illustrator appeals to a child's fondness for repetition as he adds more and more animals to the familiar song, ending with a comical skunk.   1–6

RUBIN, MARK. *The Orchestra,* ill. by Alan Daniel. Douglas & McIntyre, 1984. The roles of conductor and composer, the makeup of the orchestra, and the families of musical instruments are explained and illustrated with lively line-and-wash drawings.   7–9

RUSKIN, ARIANE. *Art of the High Renaissance,* ill. McGraw, 1970.   12 up

_____. *Nineteenth Century Art.* McGraw, 1968.   13 up

_____. *The Pantheon Story of Art for Young People,* ill. Pantheon, 1964.   11–14

_____. *17th and 18th Century Art,* ill. McGraw, 1969. Lucid and informative, a book that serves

as an excellent introduction to the art history of two centuries, but is comprehensive and authoritative enough for the knowledgeable reader.   12 up

SAMACHSON, DOROTHY and JOSEPH. *The First Artists,* Doubleday, 1970. A competent survey, with good photographs of cave paintings and engravings, more extensive than the usual treatment of the subject.   10–14

• SAVAGE, KATHARINE. *The Story of World Religions,* ill. with photos and maps. Walck, 1967.   13 up

• SEEGER, ELIZABETH. *Eastern Religions.* T. Crowell, 1973.   12–15

SEGAL, LORE, ad. *The Book of Adam to Moses,* ill. by Leonard Baskin. Knopf, 1987.   9–12

SEGOVIA, ANDRES, and GEORGE MENDOZA. *Segovia: My Book of the Guitar; Guidance for the Beginner,* ill. with photographs by Harold Gscheidle. Collins, 1979. Although this gives instruction and might be included as an activities book, it is also in part autobiographical and describes many of Segovia's ideas about music.   10 up

SHAW, ARNOLD. *The Rock Revolution,* ill. Crowell-Collier, 1969.   12 up

SMITH, BETSY. *Breakthrough: Women in Religion,* ill. with photos. Walker, 1978.   10–12

☆ • SMITH, RUTH, ed. *The Tree of Life,* ill. by Boris Artzybasheff. Macmillan, 1942, 1946.   13 up

○ • SNELLING, JOHN. *Buddhism.* Bookwright/Watts, 1986.   9–11

• SPIER, PETER, ill. *Noah's Ark.* Doubleday, 1977. Save for a poem, this has no text. The pictures are delightful, showing in precise detail the venerable old story. Caldecott Medal.   5–8

_____. ill. *The Star-Spangled Banner.* Doubleday, 1973. Pictures are filled with historic details; text includes a discussion of the War of 1812 and a chart of official flags.   8–11

SPRUYT, E. LEE. *Behind the Gold Curtain: Hansel and Gretel at the Great Opera House,* ill. by author. Four Winds, 1987. The author, a scenic designer, gives a full picture of the many services and effects created by the staff as well as of the work of creative artists at the Metropolitan Opera House.   8–10

STAMBLER, IRWIN, and GRELUN LANDON. *Golden Guitars, the Story of Country Music,* ill. with photos. Four Winds, 1971.   12–16

STREATFEILD, NOEL. *A Young Person's Guide to Ballet,* ill. by Georgette Bordier. Warne, 1975.   9–12

SULLIVAN, GEORGE. *Understanding Architecture.* Warne, 1971.   10–14

TERRY, WALTER. *Ballet: A Pictorial History,* ill. Van Nostrand, 1970.   10–12

VENTURA, PIERO. *Great Painters,* ill. by author. Putnam, 1984. Ventura uses his own excellent paintings to tie together material about the history of painting. Fine reproductions are included.

10 up

————. *Michelangelo's World,* ill. by author. Putnam, 1989.   12–15

————. *Venice: Birth of a City,* ill. by author. Putnam, 1988. Diverse and detailed paintings are used in effective combination with brief blocks of text to tell a cohesive and chronological history of Venice.   10–12

VIVAS, JULIE, ill. *The Nativity.* Gulliver/Harcourt, 1988.   4–6

§ WARREN, FRED and LEE. *The Music of Africa: An Introduction,* ill. with photos and line drawings by Penelope Naylor. Prentice, 1970. Includes lists of books and recordings.   11–14

§ WARREN, LEE. *The Dance of Africa: An Introduction,* ill. by Haris Petie, photos by Vyvian D'Estienne and others. Prentice, 1972.   11 up

§ ————. *The Theater of Africa: An Introduction.* Prentice, 1976. Varied and comprehensive.

11 up

WILDER, ALEC, music by. *Lullabies and Night Songs,* ed. by William Engvick, ill. by Maurice Sendak. Harper, 1965. The choice of songs is very good, the arrangements are simple, the lyrics smooth; the illustrations are delectable.   all ages

WINN, MARIE, ed. *The Fireside Book of Fun and Game Songs,* musical arrangements by Allan Miller, ill. by Whitney Darrow. Simon, 1974. Amusing pictures, a wide variety of songs.   all ages

WINTHROP, ELIZABETH, ad. *A Child Is Born: The Christmas Story,* ill. by Charles Mikolaycak. Holiday, 1983. Retold from the King James Bible, with boldly colored, dignified paintings.   6–9

YOLEN, JANE, ed. *The Lullaby Songbook,* musical arrangements by Adam Stemple; ill. by Charles Mikolaycak. Harcourt, 1986.   1–5

————, ed. *Rounds About Rounds,* ill. by Gail Gibbons. Watts, 1977. A very nice collection, from the simple to the more intricate.   9–12

Activities and Experiments

ADKINS, JAN. *The Craft of Sail,* designed and ill. by author. Walker, 1973. The text moves from physical principles and facts about sailboats to techniques of sailing.   11 up

————. *Toolchest,* ill. by author. Walker, 1973.

10 up

§ ○ ANCONA, GEORGE, and MARY BETH. *Handtalk Zoo.* Four Winds, 1989.   8 up

ANDERSEN, YVONNE. *Make Your Own Animated Movies: Yellow Ball Workshop Film Techniques.* Little, 1970.

10–13

APFEL, NECIA H. *It's All Relative: Einstein's Theory of Relativity,* diagrams by Yukio Kondo, ill. with photos. Lothrop, 1981. Concepts inherent to an understanding of Einstein's theory of relativity are illuminated with experiments that can be performed at home.   11 up

§ ARCHER, ELSIE. *Let's Face It: The Guide to Good Grooming for Girls of Color,* rev. ed. Lippincott, 1968. Hair, complexion, makeup, clothes, speech, manners are all covered in this guide.

11–14

ASHE, ARTHUR, and LOUIE ROBINSON. *Getting Started in Tennis,* ill. with photos. Atheneum, 1977. Ashe gives a great deal of sensible advice clearly and sequentially.   10–14

BAKER, JAMES W. *Birthday Magic,* ill. by George Overlie. Lerner, 1988.   8–11

————. *Christmas Magic,* ill. by George Overlie. Lerner, 1988.   8–11

————. *Halloween Magic,* ill. by George Overlie. Lerner, 1988.   8–11

————. *Valentine Magic,* ill. by George Overlie. Lerner, 1988.   8–11

BJORK, CHRISTINA. *Linnea's Almanac,* tr. by Joan Sandin, ill. by Lena Anderson. Farrar, 1989.

9–11

————. *Linnea's Windowsill Garden,* tr. by Joan Sandin, ill. by Lena Anderson. Farrar, 1988.

9–11

BOLOGNESE, DON, and ELAINE RAPHAEL. *Pen and Ink,* ill. by authors. Watts, 1986.   10 up

————. *Pencil,* ill. by authors. Watts, 1986.   10 up

————. *Printmaking,* ill. by authors. Watts, 1987.

10 up

BORGHESE, ANITA. *The Down to Earth Cookbook,* rev. ed., ill. by Ray Cruz. Scribner, 1980. A well-organized cookbook, with background information on American dietary habits and culinary techniques.   10–12

BOYLAN, ELEANOR. *How to Be a Puppeteer,* ill. by Tomie dePaola. McCall, 1970. Gives directions for making and costuming puppets, manipulating them, making sets and scenery, etc. Plays for a single puppeteer and a group are included.

8–10

BRANLEY, FRANKLYN M., and ELEANOR K. VAUGHAN. *Timmy and the Tin-Can Telephone,* ill. by Paul Galdone. T. Crowell, 1959.   5–7

BRODERICK, DOROTHY. *Training a Companion Dog,* ill. by Harris Petie. Prentice, 1965.   9–12

BUNTING, GLENN and EVE. *Skateboards: How to Make Them, How to Ride Them.* Harvey, 1977. The first section is devoted to making wooden skateboards, the rest to photographs and descriptions of basic and advanced figures.   10–14

CALMENSON, STEPHANIE. *What Am I? Very First Rid-*

dles, ill. by Karen Gundersheimer. Harper, 1989. 3–6

CARAS, ROGER. *A Zoo in Your Room,* ill. by Pamela Johnson. Harcourt, 1975. 10–13

CASE, MARSHAL T. *Look What I Found! The Young Conservationist's Guide to the Care and Feeding of Small Wildlife,* with photos by author. Chatham/Viking, 1971. 9–11

CHARLIP, REMY, MARY BETH and GEORGE ANCONA. *Handtalk: An ABC of Finger Spelling & Sign Language.* Parents' Magazine, 1974. 8 up

CHEKI HANEY, ERENE and RUTH RICHARDS. *Yoga for Children,* ill. by Betty Schilling. Bobbs, 1973. Simple instructions and adequate warnings about not overdoing. 8–10

COBB, VICKI. *Chemically Alive! Experiments You Can Do at Home,* ill. by Theo Cobb. Lippincott, 1985. 10–14

————. *Gobs of Goo,* ill. by Brian Schatell. § ☆ ○ Lippincott, 1983.

————. *The Secret Life of School Supplies,* ill. by Bill Morrison. Lippincott, 1981. Readers learn about the history and manufacture of everyday school supplies (ink, writing tools, rubber, and the like) through activities that demonstrate their physical properties. 9–12

————. *The Trip of a Drip,* ill. by Elliot Kreloff. Little, 1986. 8–10

COCHRANE, LOUISE. *Tabletop Theatres,* ill. by Kate Simunek. Plays, 1974. Directions for making stages, puppets, and costumes plus scripts for plays. 10–13

COOMBS, CHARLES IRA. *Bicycling,* ill. with photos and diagrams. Morrow, 1972. 10–13

COOPER, ELIZABETH K. *Science in Your Own Back Yard,* ill. by author. Harcourt, 1958. 10–13

CURRELL, DAVID. *The Complete Book of Puppetry.* Plays, 1975. 11 up

CZAJA, PAUL CLEMENT. *Writing with Light: A Simple Workshop in Basic Photography.* Chatham/Viking, 1973. 11 up

FENTEN, D. X. *Indoor Gardening,* ill. by Howard Berelson. Watts, 1974. Brisk, sensible advice about caring for a wide variety of plants. 9–12

FERAVALO, ROCCO V. *Easy Physics Projects: Air, Water and Heat,* ill. by Lewis Zacks, Prentice, 1966. 8–10

FERGUSON, ROBERT. *How to Make Movies: A Practical Guide to Group Filming.* Viking, 1969. 13 up

FREEMAN, S. H. *Basic Baseball Strategy,* ill. by Leonard Kessler. Doubleday, 1965. 10–14

GARDNER, MARTIN. *Codes, Ciphers and Secret Writing.* Simon, 1972. 11 up

————. *Perplexing Puzzles and Tantalizing Teasers,* ill. by Laszlo Kubinyi. Simon, 1969. 8–11

GEORGE, JEAN CRAIGHEAD. *The Wild, Wild Cookbook,* ill. by Walter Kessell. Coward, 1982. A useful wildfood cookbook, organized by seasons. 11 up

GETZOFF, CAROLE. *The Natural Cook's First Book: A Natural Foods Cookbook for Beginners,* ill. by Jill Pinkwater. Dodd, 1973. 9–11

GILMORE, SUSAN. *What Goes On at a Radio Station?* photos by author. Carolrhoda, 1984. A view of the work flow, staff responsibilities, and practical business matters that characterize a radio station's activities. 8–10

GRYSKI, CAMILLA. *Super String Games,* ill. by Tom Sankey. Morrow, 1988. Step-by-step instructions are given in text and diagrams. 10–12

HADDAD, HELEN R. *Potato Printing,* ill. by author. T. Crowell, 1981. An exemplary how-to book on the homespun art of potato printing, with crisp explanations, logical organization, and room for creativity. 8–11

HALDANE, SUZANNE. *Painting Faces,* ill. with photos. Dutton, 1988. Full-page color photographs depict face painting as it is done by many cultures for ritual and drama, and step-by-step instructions show the reader how to imitate the authentic models. 9–11

HAUTZIG, ESTHER. *Make It Special: Cards, Decorations, and Party Favors for Holidays and Other Celebrations,* ill. by Martha Weston. Macmillan, 1986. The materials for the projects in this how-to book are either free or inexpensive, and the reader is invited to follow or adapt the instructions. 9–11

HAWKINSON, JOHN. *Pastels Are Great:* Whitman, 1968. The author explains the basic skills of the technique with enticing examples and explicit instructions. 8–10

HELFMAN, HARRY. *Making Your Own Movies.* Morrow, 1970. Lucid instructions on preparation, equipment, and filming. 10–14

HODGSON, MARY ANNE, and JOSEPHINE RUTH PAINE. *Fast and Easy Needlepoint.* Doubleday, 1978. Instructions for seven simple projects as well as tips on making designs, coping with mistakes, and adding finishing touches. 9–12

HOLZ, LORETTA. *Mobiles You Can Make,* photos by George and Loretta Holz. Lothrop, 1975. Clear, step-by-step instructions for making three kinds of mobiles. 10–14

HORVATH, JOAN. *Filmmaking for Beginners.* Nelson, 1974. 11–15

HUDLOW, JEAN. *Eric Plants a Garden,* ill. by author. Whitman, 1971. Clear photographs show a beaming young gardener planning, planting, tending, and harvesting his crop. 7–9

HUSSEY, LOIS J., and CATHERINE PESSINO. *Collecting for the City Naturalist,* ill. by Barbara Neill. T. Crowell, 1975. 9–11

JACKSON, CAARY PAUL. *How to Play Better Soccer,* ill. by Don Madden. T. Crowell, 1978. Simply and clearly written, this includes a history of the game, rules, and techniques.   10–14

JANECZKO, PAUL B. *Loads of Codes and Secret Ciphers.* Macmillan, 1984.   10 up

KALB, JONAH. *The Easy Hockey Book,* ill. by Bill Morrison. Houghton, 1977. Not a book intended to teach readers to play hockey but a compilation of advice on individual aspects of the game.
                    8–10

KIDDER, HARVEY. *Illustrated Chess for Children,* ill. by author. Doubleday, 1970. A really fine book for the beginning chess player. The clear diagrams are very helpful as is the proceeding from basic moves to increasingly complicated ones.   10–13

KRAMER, ALAN. *How to Make a Chemical Volcano and Other Mysterious Experiments.* Watts, 1989. Twenty-nine home demonstrations clearly explain the solutions in a chatty cookbook-approach to chemical posers.   9–12

KREMENTZ, JILL. *The Fun of Cooking,* ill. with photos by author. Knopf, 1985.   10–14

KUJOTH, JEAN. *The Boys' and Girls' Book of Clubs and Organizations.* Prentice, 1975. Gives sources of information for activities and projects described in the text.   9–12

KUKLIN, SUSAN. *Mine for a Year,* photos by author. Coward, 1984. A boy takes charge of a puppy destined to become a guide dog for the blind in a one-year training program.   9–11

LARRICK, NANCY. *See for Yourself,* ill. by Frank Jupo. American Bk., 1952.   6–8

LASSON, ROBERT. *If I Had a Hammer: Woodworking with Seven Basic Tools,* photos by Jeff Murphy. Dutton, 1974. Shows incorrect as well as correct procedures in completing simple projects.
                    10–13

LIPSON, SHELLEY. *It's BASIC: The ABCs of Computer Programming,* ill. by Jancie Stapleton. Holt, 1982. Logically formulated explanations of five core commands in the BASIC programming language.
                    9–11

LOPSHIRE, ROBERT. *A Beginner's Guide to Building and Flying Model Airplanes.* Harper, 1967. Step-by-step instructions for assembling planes, and many small tips to ensure good workmanship.   10–12

————. *It's Magic?* ill. by author. Macmillan, 1969. Simple tricks are described within the framework of a humorous story.   7–9

LORD, HARVEY G. *Car Care for Kids and Former Kids,* photos by Kathryn J. Lord. Atheneum, 1983. A practical guide demonstrating how to perform routine car repairs and upkeep comes with ample safety warnings and illustrative photographs.
                    11 up

MCLAUGHLIN, MOLLY. *Earthworms, Dirt and Rotten Leaves: An Exploration in Ecology,* ill. by Robert Shetterly. Atheneum, 1986.   9–11

MARA, THALIA, and LEE WYNDHAM. *First Steps in Ballet: Basic Exercises for Home Practice,* ill. by George Bobrizky. Garden City, 1955. Twelve basic barre exercises meant to be used in conjunction with formal training.   8–14

MARKS, MICKEY KLAR. *Collage,* ill. by Edith Alberts and with photos by David Rosenfeld. Dials, 1968.
                    8 up

MEYER, CAROLYN. *Saw, Hammer and Paint: Woodworking and Finishing for Beginners,* ill. by Tony Martignoni. Morrow, 1973. Materials and techniques are described; projects range from simple to difficult.   11 up

MEYER, CAROLYN, and JEROME WEXLER. *Rock Tumbling,* photos by Jerome Wexler. Morrow, 1975.
                    10–14

MILGROM, HARRY. *Adventures with a Paper Cup,* ill. by Leonard Kessler. Dutton, 1968.

————. *Adventures with a Straw,* ill. by Leonard Kessler. Dutton, 1967.   4–7

————. *First Experiments with Gravity,* ill. by Lewis Zacks. Dutton, 1966. A series of home demonstrations, each prefaced by an explanation of the principle involved.   8–10

MOORE, JIM. *Football Techniques Illustrated,* rev. ed., ill. by Tyler Micoleau. Ronald, 1962.   10–14

MOORE, WILLIAM. *Your Science Fair Project.* Putnam, 1964.   8–13

MOORMAN, THOMAS. *How to Make Your Science Project Scientific.* Atheneum, 1974.   10–14

MOTT, CAROLYN, and LEO B. BAISDEN. *The Children's Book on How to Use Books and Libraries,* ill. Scribner's, 1961. Meets a wide variety of elementary grade needs ranging from writing a book review to using reference books and the library catalog.
                    9–11

NEUMANN, BILL. *Model Car Building,* ill. with photos. Putnam, 1971. Full instructions on building, painting tools, materials, and adhesives. Big, clear photographs of equipment and procedures.
                    10–14

OLNEY, ROSS. *Gymnastics,* ill. by Mary Ann Duganne. Watts, 1976. Olney describes equipment, training, clothing, safety measures, differences between men's and women's events, and judging.
                    9–11

PARISH, PEGGY. *Beginning Mobiles,* ill. by Lynn Sweat. Macmillan, 1979. A simple, explicit, nicely illustrated project book in a step-by-step format.
                    7–9

PAUL, AILEEN. *Kids Outdoor Gardening,* ill. by John DeLulio. Doubleday, 1978. A logically organized book for the beginning young gardener.   9–11

PAUL, AILEEN, and ARTHUR HAWKINS. *Kids Cooking*. Doubleday, 1970.   9–11

PETERSON, JOHN. *How to Write Codes and Secret Messages,* ill. by Bernice Myers. Four Winds, 1966. Lucid explanations of an alluring subject.   9–11

PETTIT, TED S. *A Guide to Nature Projects,* ill. by Walt Wenzel. Norton/Grosset, 1966.   9–12

PURDY, SUSAN. *Festivals for You to Celebrate: Facts, Activities, and Crafts.* Lippincott, 1969.   9–12

RITTER, LAWRENCE S. *The Story of Baseball,* ill. with photos. Morrow, 1983. A fine historical overview of the United States' favorite sport, plus chapters on special aspects of the game, such as pitching and strategy.   10–14

ROCKWELL, HARLOW. *I Did It.* Macmillan, 1974.
                                     6–7

———. *Look at This,* ill. by author. Macmillan, 1978. Three very simple projects with instructions written for the beginning independent reader.   6–7

ROSS, FRANK XAVIER. *The Tin Lizzie: A Model-Making Book.* Lothrop, 1980. For model buffs in search of a challenge, these vintage car models are assembled from construction paper, matchsticks, and other inexpensive materials.   10–14

ROSS, LAURA. *Hand Puppets: How to Make and Use Them,* ill. by author. Lothrop, 1969. Includes suggestions for a puppet play.   9–12

———. *Mask-Making with Pantomime and Stories from American History,* ill. by Frank Ross. Lothrop, 1975.   9–11

———. *Puppet Shows Using Poems and Stories,* ill. by Frank Ross, Jr. Lothrop, 1970. Each poem, story, or excerpt is provided with production notes. Simple enough for children to use alone, yet good source material for adults.   9–11

ROTH, ARNOLD. *Pick a Peck of Puzzles,* ill. by author. Norton, 1966. Varied selections: riddles, rebuses, tongue-twisters, pictures with hidden clues, etc.
                                     8–10

SARNOFF, JANE, and REYNOLD RUFFINS. *The Code and Cipher Book.* Scribner's, 1975. Includes such variant puzzlers as pig Latin and cockney slang as well as the usual kinds of codes and ciphers.   9–12

SCHNEIDER, HERMAN and NINA. *Science Fun for You in a Minute or Two: Quick Science Experiments You Can Do,* ill. by Leonard Kessler. McGraw, 1975.
                                     7–10

SCOTT, JOSEPH, and LENORE. *Egyptian Hieroglyphs for Everyone: An Introduction to the Writing of Ancient Egypt.* Funk, 1968.   11 up

SEGOVIA, ANDRES, and GEORGE MENDOZA. *Segovia: My Book of the Guitar: Guidance for the Beginner,* ill. with photos. World, 1979. Rudimentary informa-

tion, a series of short musical studies, and a glossary of musical terms.   10 up

SIMON, SEYMOUR. *How to Be an Ocean Scientist in Your Own Home,* ill. by David A. Carter. Lippincott, 1988.   9–12

———. *The Rock-Hound's Book,* ill. by Tony Chen. Viking, 1973.   9–11

SOKOL, CAMILLE. *The Lucky Sew-It-Yourself Book,* ill. by Bill Sokol. Four Winds, 1966.   7–9

SOOTIN, HARRY. *Experiments with Magnetism,* ill. by Julio Granda. Norton/Grosset, 1968.   9–12

SOOTIN, HARRY and LAURA. *The Young Experimenter's Workbook: Treasures of the Earth,* ill. by Frank Aloise. Norton/Grosset, 1965.   8–11

STAPLES, TERRY. *Film and Video.* Warwick Press, 1986.
                                     11 up

STEIG, WILLIAM. *CDB!,* ill. by author. Farrar, 1984.
                                     9 up

———. *CDC?,* ill. by author. Farrar, 1984.   9 up

STONE, A. HARRIS. *The Chemistry of a Lemon,* ill. by Peter P. Plasencia. Prentice, 1966.   8–11

SULLIVAN, GEORGE. *Better Gymnastics for Girls.* Dodd, 1977. The bulk of the text is devoted to step-by-step directions for each movement; also included are a brief history of the sport and an explanation of the four events and the evaluation system.
                                     10–14

———. *Better Soccer for Boys and Girls.* Dodd, 1978. Clear diagrams and photographs complement a comprehensive text that describes the way the game is played, explains the rules, and gives detailed advice on each aspect of play.   9–12

———. *Better Softball for Boys and Girls.* Dodd, 1975.   9–14

———. *Screen Play: The Story of Video Games,* ill. with photos. Warne, 1983. Information on the invention of video games, descriptions of individual games, and a discussion of controversy over the games' popularity.   11–14

———. *This Is Pro Hockey,* ill. with photos. Dodd, 1976. A brief history of the game precedes a description of how it is played.   10 up

SWENINGSON, SALLY. *Indoor Gardening.* Lerner, 1975. Simple, explicit, adequately illustrated.   8–10

TISON, ANNETTE, and TALUS TAYLOR. *The Adventures of the Three Colors.* World, 1971. Shows color mix by use of transparencies.   5–8

UNESCO. *UNESCO Source Book for Science Teaching: 700 Science Experiments for Everyone,* 2nd ed. UNESCO, 1962.   10–14

UNKELBACH, KURT. *You're a Good Dog, Joe: Knowing and Training Your Puppy,* ill. by Paul Frame. Prentice, 1971. Includes warnings on safety of the puppy and very sensible training procedures.
                                     7–9

WATERS, MARJORIE. *The Victory Garden Kid's Book: A Beginner's Guide to Growing Vegetables, Fruits, and Flowers,* ill. by George Ulrich and with photos by Gary Mottau. Houghton, 1988.   8–12

WEBER, WILLIAM. *Wild Orphan Babies: Mammals and Birds.* Holt, 1975.   10 up

WEISS, HARVEY. *Carving: How to Carve Wood and Stone.* Addison, 1976.   11–14

————. *Ceramics from Clay to Kiln.* W. R. Scott, 1964.   10–14

————. *Collage and Construction,* ill. W. R. Scott, 1970. A good do-it-yourself book in art, simple enough for the younger reader, dignified enough for the older. Discusses not only the materials (easy-to-get) and techniques, but artistic conception.   9–12

————. *How to Run a Railroad: Everything You Need to Know About Model Trains.* T. Crowell, 1977.   10 up

————. *Model Cars and Trucks and How to Build Them,* ill. with photos, plans, and drawings. T. Crowell, 1974.   9–12

WYLER, ROSE. *What Happens If . . . ? Science Experiments You Can Do by Yourself,* ill. by Daniel Nevins. Walker, 1974.   7–9

WYLER, ROSE, and GERALD AMES. *Prove It!* ill. by Talivaldis Stubis. Harper, 1963.   5–8

YOUNG, ED, and HILARY BECKETT. *The Rooster's Horns: A Chinese Puppet Play to Make and Perform,* ill. by Ed Young. World, 1978.   8–9

ZUBROWSKI, BERNIE. *Wheels at Work: Building and Experimenting with Models of Machines,* ill. by Roy Doty. Morrow, 1986.   9–11

Part Three

Bringing Children and Books Together

Chapter Fourteen

Literature Throughout the Curriculum

Children who are read to, who later discover books that they love to read, and who are able to respond to what they read should grow into adults who love books. They should, and yet too often the interest in reading fades as children mature. That does not have to happen. Adults who are readers and can show their own excitement about books are the key. A teacher or librarian who perceives literature as a part of the elementary curriculum is most important, for it is through continuing and rewarding experiences with literature that children mature into adults who love to read. Those experiences can—and should—include much good oral reading by adults, opportunity for children to talk about what they read and hear, opportunity at times to participate in activities that can enhance response to and understanding of literature. Experiences with literature may be a separate part of the curriculum or a part of the school library program. They may also be consciously woven into other parts of the curriculum so that they permeate language arts and reading and are present, too, in social studies, science,

art, and music. We believe that a literature program deserves a place in every classroom so that children are introduced to well-chosen books of all genres. At the same time, we recognize that children's books, rather than basal readers, are now the material used for reading instruction in many classrooms. We will describe two classrooms where literature-based reading programs integrate the learning of literacy skills and will discuss ways to make literature an integral part of writing and social studies, as well. The focus, in any event, should be on the many ways of responding to literature.

Patterns of Response to Literature

From the earliest times, people have waited with anticipation for the wandering storyteller, bard, or minstrel. The old tales such as "The Bremen Town-Musicians" must have brought laughter and a muttered agreement that the poor old animals did, indeed, deserve the comforts they won by their own wits. Other tales, such as "Rumpelstiltskin" or "Tom Tit Tot," may have brought a sense of relief that the imp who would strike such a hard bargain was outwitted at the end of the story. "Cinderella" was a wonderful fantasy for poor people as they entered into the role of the poor cinder girl, seeing the ball through her eyes and experiencing her rise from rags to riches.

A good storyteller saw, in the faces of listeners, response to the story, and shared the audience's reactions to the plight of the characters, feeling their suspenseful interaction with a good plot. Sometimes there was response to the style of the telling. People listening to "The Three Billy-Goats Gruff" came to expect and to repeat, with the storyteller, "Who's that walking over my bridge?" and the favorite ending, "Snip, snap, snout. This tale's told out." This variety of response still is heard and seen when children hear a story well told.

The old tales inspire not only the obvious reactions of laughter or tears, but also the deeper sense of a story linking us to human lives over the ages, a story that has been told time and again in many parts of the world. As Paul Hazard wrote, "Once upon a time . . . at a period so far removed from us that we are unable to visualize it to ourselves, there was the very same story."[1]

New tales may bring the same quality of response from readers and listeners. A nine-year-old tells of reading and rereading Laura Ingalls Wilder's *The Long Winter* because the descriptions of the blizzards sent chills up her spine and made her wish that she could be with Laura and Mary beside a roaring fire. A five-year-old nods wisely as Peter, in Ezra Jack Keats's *The Snowy Day*, discovers that the snowball he put in his pocket yesterday has melted.

This chapter and the two chapters that follow are concerned with children's response to literature—the different forms it can take and some ways of encouraging it.

Literature is a part of the curriculum in most elementary schools. In traditional literature programs, children are read to on a regular basis and are encouraged to read independently books obtained at the library and from book clubs and bookstores. In many schools, teachers and librarians also involve children in story-telling sessions, book discussions, choral speaking, and dramatic activities, such as story theater and Readers Theatre. Examples of those activities and suggested materials are included in Chapter 15. Our first concern is that children be encouraged to enjoy literature in the classroom, the library, and at home. Enjoyment can be enhanced by a literature program that introduces children to books they might not find on their own. A well-planned literature program should establish regular times for oral reading by teachers and librarians and opportunities for children to share books with one another.

It is becoming common for literature to be included in many aspects of the school day. The change in treatment of literature may present some problems as well as new possibilities for those who are concerned with the experiences children may have with books. If literature is associated with many curricular areas, it can become an important part of every school day for children. On the other hand, if it is treated primarily as informational text or as a means of teaching reading skills, there is a danger that children will miss out on the aesthetic experience of literature. In describing the aesthetic stance toward reading, Louise Rosenblatt says:

the reader's primary purpose is fulfilled during the reading event, as he fixes his attention on the actual experience he is living through. This permits the whole range of responses generated by the text to enter into the center of awareness, and out of these materials he selects and weaves what he sees as the literary work of art.[2]

In a classroom where reading literature is treated as an aesthetic experience, there is likely to be much emphasis on reading for enjoyment. That reading can take the form of oral reading by the teacher, independent reading by students, or students reading in pairs or small groups. Much of the responsibility for selecting books belongs to the children.

We believe that response to books is an essential part of any literature-based program, whether it involves reading instruction, chil-

[1]Paul Hazard, *Books, Children and Men*, translated by Marguerite Mitchell. Boston: The Horn Book, 1944, p. 158.

[2]Louise Rosenblatt, *The Reader, the Text, the Poem*. Carbondale, Ill.: Southern Illinois University Press, 1978, pp. 27–28.

dren's writing, or social studies learning. We start with the assumption that responding to literature is a positive, enriching experience, one we would like to share with children. Very young children react with instinctual pleasure to stories and rhymes. Yet, too often that joy is lost as they grow older. Our concern is to help children retain their spontaneous love for literature. We hope that by giving children books that meet their needs at different ages, we can encourage a range of appropriate responses and, in the end, see them become adults who read with pleasure and true engagement. But activities to encourage response should never be simply busy work. They should be rooted in the material and should serve the needs and interests of the children. This point bears repeating: Activities to encourage response to literature must grow naturally out of the reading, and different responses—both in variety and quality—must be respected and nurtured.

A giggle over some amusing passage and a tear shed in sympathy for a story character's misfortunes are signs that the reader is interacting with the story. Such interaction is the substance of response. Response to literature need not be overt, as with giggles or tears, but we hope it occurs whenever children become involved with books which have stimulating content and are well written. Reading becomes enjoyable when children experience adventure right along with a story character, find answers to their questions in a book of nonfiction, or remember and repeat favorite poems. Literature becomes enlightening when children be-

Children involved in reading in an informal setting. Each is developing a response—emotional, interpretive, or critical—to literature.

Viewpoint

In great fiction, the dream engages us heart and soul; we not only respond to imaginary things— sights, sounds, smells—as though they were real, we respond to fictional problems as though they were real: We sympathize, think, and judge. We act out, vicariously, the trials of the characters and learn from the failures and successes of particular modes of action, particular attitudes, opinions, assertions, and beliefs exactly as we learn from life. Thus the value of great fiction, we begin to suspect, is not just that it entertains or distracts us from our troubles, not just that it broadens our knowledge of people and places, but also that it helps us to know what we believe, reinforces those qualities that are noblest in us, leads us to feel uneasy about our faults and limitations.

John Gardner, *The Art of Fiction: Notes on Craft for Young Writers* New York: Vintage Books, 1985, p. 31. (Taken from "Readers and Library Texts" by Robert Probst in *Literature in the Classroom: Readers, Texts and Contexts,* edited by Ben F. Nilms, NCTE, 1988.

gin to interpret incidents and conversations which take place in a story, when they begin to tie fictional events to circumstances in their own lives. Books become intriguing as children gain the sophistication needed to understand the themes that run through them, become aware of the techniques an author has used to develop interesting characters, or begin to appreciate a certain style of writing. Literature can be challenging if children are encouraged to evaluate content in terms of general quality, interesting ideas, or accuracy of information. All of these experiences involve the response of a reader to a book.

Forms of Response

Response can take many forms. It can be overt and immediate. Then again, it may not be distinguishable at once and, perhaps, not ever.

Many responses to literature do not surface until long after the book has been put down. Even then, the response may be a composite of responses to many literary works which have influenced the reader. A composite literary response can emerge, for instance, when we try to deal with a minor misfortune by stating our belief in humanity's ability to succeed through perseverance, an idea we may have encountered in many works of literature, popular as well as classic. A response may surface in an unexpected way, as when children respond to a cartoon character with giggles because the character reminds them of Henry Huggins. More clearly defined is the response of children saying, simply, that the story character has the same problems that they themselves have.

Many responses of children and adolescents involve an emotional interaction with the story or with a story character. Other responses are more complex, sometimes involving the emotional response along with an awareness of the meaning of the story or an evaluation of its quality. Occasionally, a response shows the child's ability to note the author's style or means of developing plot or characterization. It is not likely or even desirable that all of these kinds of responses appear at the same time. If we set a priority, very likely the most important form of response is involvement with a story. Without emotional interaction, young people are not likely to go on to develop a broad range of responses.

Literary response can stem from the experience of an individual child with an individual book; from group experience with literature through storytelling, choral speaking, story theater, or some other dramatic activity; or from literature presented and accompanied by discussion.[3] A response need not be active. It does not increase in value because it is overt. It is enough that a child has read or heard a literary selection that inspired interaction with the characters or ideas in the work.

We should not insist or even hope that all response to literature be observable. Neverthe-less, response frequently can be seen and it can also be encouraged. As teachers or librarians, we can become aware of the occasions which draw a response, the selections that inspire interaction of readers with books, and the signs of response in faces of readers, listeners, or players. Increasing our awareness, we are better able to nurture response and to make it an important part of a child's reading experience. The key is to watch for and acknowledge response without interfering with it. A response is a very personal thing for a child, and if it is made public by an unthinking adult, the youngster's attitude toward reading may be severely affected. It goes without saying that any response should be treated with the utmost respect and that it should be recognized by adults as a sign that the experience with a story or poem has been strong enough to evoke a reaction.

As you note responses children make to literature, you may also absorb information about the kinds of literary selections particular children enjoy. They may be especially alert to aspects of characterization, plot, or an author's way of creating humor or suspense, or empathic with the predicaments of a story character. Use your observation as a guide to recommending books for the child and offering active involvement with books.

This emphasis on literary response is not new. Writing in 1938, Louise Rosenblatt suggested that the point at which a student meets and interacts with a piece of literature is crucial to response.[4] Her interest was in the way that response may bring a recognition of a value structure in the literature. Response may include an awareness of a universal truth that is passed on from one generation to the next through the literary tradition. Such awareness may help a young reader to cope more easily with life's problems.

More recently, the 1966 Dartmouth Conference papers showed a clear focus on the importance of response to the literary experience. Scholars from Great Britain and the United States met to consider the relationship of response to literary experiences at all age levels.

[3]D. W. Hardy, "Response to Literature: The Report of the Study Group," *Response to Literature*, ed. J. Squire. Urbana, Ill: National Council of Teachers of English, 1968.

[4]Louise Rosenblatt, *Literature as Exploration*. East Norwalk, Conn.: Appleton, 1968; 1938.

Strong recommendations were made for an elementary English curriculum which allows students to respond to aspects of literature which affect them personally—to make an emotional response as well as a response to literary form and style.

A number of researchers in recent years have investigated the nature and form of literary response. Two of them, James Squire and Alan Purves, have made important contributions to our knowledge about responses of older students, and the information has triggered interest in the responses of younger students, as well. The work of those two men will be used here to provide a framework for the discussion of literary response.

The Emotional Reaction

When we become engaged with a story we are reading so that we interact with it, one of the consequences is an emotional response to the work. Test this out by thinking of a piece of fiction you have read and with which you have become involved. Emotional response is shown when a child comments that she could almost feel the cold on the frozen tundra as she read about Julie's experiences with survival (Jean Craighead George's *Julie of the Wolves*). When children remark that the bully, Martin, in Mary Stolz's *The Bully of Barkham Street* is like a school bully who terrifies many of them, they are making personal responses to the story. Similarly, children who remark that the house in Elizabeth Hill's *Evan's Corner* looks much like their own are reacting in a personal way. You can also observe nonverbal emotional responses. Emotional reaction can show in children's body movements and in facial expressions when they read or listen to stories. Nonverbal response is evident, too, in dramatization and in pantomime. Information from theories about children's needs represented by the work of Maslow and Erikson and described in Chapter 1 can help us to anticipate some emotional reactions and to understand why children react to some story characters and situations as they do.

Far from being a low-level response to literature, as some English specialists in the past suggested, the emotional response is probably the most important base upon which to build other responses, those involving evaluations of the literary qualities of a work or interpretation of the selection. In fact, Squire, studying the responses of ninth- and tenth-grade students to short stories, found that students who were personally involved with the stories also responded by evaluating the literary qualities of those works. We do not know just how the two forms of response complement each other, but the evidence does at least show the importance of involvement.[5]

In a study of the elements of response present when students write about a work of literature, Alan Purves and Victoria Rippere identified a number of responses termed "engagement-involvement."[6] They range from personal reaction to the work or the author to involvement with characters and relating incidents in the story to the reader's own life. As you begin to bring children actively together with books you will find that many such responses result. The child who expresses pleasure on hearing another story by Robert McCloskey is showing engagement with the work of a particular author. Another youngster who laughs at old Sneep in McCloskey's *Lentil* and comments that he'd like to see the school principal in the same position is making an emotional response to the work. A student responding to Farley Mowat's *Owls in the Family* by describing his own hilarity when his dog chased its tail so hard it tripped and rolled over and over, is showing emotional reaction to the story.

Children who can respond through pantomime may show emotional involvement in their evident relish of a character part or a particularly interesting scene. One child was so engrossed in her characterization of Goldilocks that she forgot to be frightened when Little Bear woke her up. Instead, she greeted him joyfully and took him on home with her to meet her parents! Dramatization opens many doors to active involvement with a story, as does oral

[5]James R. Squire, *The Responses of Adolescents While Reading Four Short Stories.* Urbana, Ill.: National Council of Teachers of English, 1964.

[6]Alan C. Purves with Victoria Rippere, *Elements of Writing About a Literary Work; A Study of Response to Literature.* Urbana, Ill: National Council of Teachers of English, 1968.

interpretation of literature. Emotional response is present, too, when children read or speak character parts with evident enjoyment and good interpretation. Such emotional responses should be valued and encouraged.

The Interpretive Reaction

Teachers and librarians responsible for recommending books to children hope that their recommendations will be books to which readers can relate and interpret. Teachers of reading are (or should be) very concerned about developing interpretation skills. Therefore, it is important to look for and recognize interpretive responses that children are capable of making and to provide opportunities for them to gain experience in interpreting literature.

Several types of interpretive response have been identified. Responses made by readers generally have to do with interpretation of stylistic devices such as metaphor, allusion, irony, and symbols; inferences about happenings prior to and following the action of the story, based on information given in the text; and inferences about the nature of a character, about the setting, or about the author's motive.

A child makes an inference or an interpretation when she decides that Russell Hoban's *A Bargain for Frances* was probably written because the writer wanted to show that it is not good to trick your friends. Another inferential response is saying that Sara, in Betsy Byars's *Summer of the Swans*, was really a great person but she was kind of hard to get along with because she didn't have much self-confidence. A student may be so inspired by the clear descriptions in Sheila Burnford's *The Incredible Journey* that he asks to illustrate several of the most memorable scenes. His explanation, that he wants to re-create an atmosphere that goes beyond the bare description, suggests that he is making inferences about the setting and is reconstructing scenes from the story. Response that is interpretive can also inspire a child to extend the interpretation to his or her own experience, perhaps writing a descriptive piece involving the child's own pet.

We cannot emphasize strongly enough that much of what seems essentially interpretation of a story has with it a solid element of personal involvement. If the personal reaction triggers enough interest in a character, setting, bit of action, or underlying idea, the reader will be willing to enter into the spirit of the work and try to interpret it. The obvious need is for us as adults to provide material for response that intrigues, excites, or simply compels the reader to become immersed in the story.

The Critical Reaction

James Squire, in his study of adolescents' responses, defines a category of responses in which the reader judges the general literary quality of the story or reacts specifically to language, style, or characterization. In the Purves classification scheme, some responses to literary elements are included which can be seen in reactions of even young children. They are those responses that show attention to the language and the content of a work. Responses dealing with language include comments a reader makes about writing style, use of rhetorical devices such as personification, use of metaphor and simile, and of imagery. The reaction to language also includes response to the author's use of dialogue and description. The response to content includes reactions to the subject matter or topic, to action in the work, to character description, character relationships, and setting. Other responses identified by Purves as literary perception responses and of interest here are reactions to plot, mood, point of view assumed by the author, and attempts to define the genre of the work.

An example of a child's reaction to literary qualities is a statement that a book was boring because there was not enough action. A child who smiles over a poem because it is a limerick, and proceeds to write one, is responding to a literary element. So is a child who expresses pleasure over the perfect little people Mary Norton creates in *The Borrowers*. A reader may laugh at Astrid Lindgren's *Pippi Longstocking* because the author always lets Pippi get the better of adults who try to take advantage of her. Recognizing the author's way of developing humor is a response to a literary element.

Children's responses to literary characteristics may be as specific as: "I didn't get interested in any of the characters because there wasn't enough information about how they looked and felt." Literary judgment may also reflect the specific interest in language, as when a child repeats over and over the line, "I think mice are nice," and pronounces it a favorite line because of the good sound of *mice* and *nice*. On a more general level, children have been known to respond to a book by wondering aloud why the author bothered to write it or by excitedly asking whether there are any other books in the library that are like that one.

Responses that reflect some degree of literary judgment often reflect a strong emotional response as well, as is shown by the above examples. We may encourage the literary dimension of a response, if it seems appropriate, by taking a few minutes to talk with the child about the way an author is developing humor, or what an author might do to make a story character really interesting by use of dialogue as well as description.

The Evaluative Reaction

Although Squire includes judgments about the story in the same category as comments about the literary qualities of the work, he defines another kind of judgment which he calls a "prescriptive judgment." Responses in this category are those in which a reader tells what he or she thinks a character ought to do, based on some absolute standard. Such responses occurred infrequently in the patterns of ninth- and tenth-graders he studied and may not be very common among responses made by young children, either.

Purves, in his scheme for classifying responses, identifies a whole group of responses he terms "elements of evaluation." Among them are responses in which the reader evaluates the emotional appeal of the story. In addition, there are responses which evaluate an author's method: for instance, whether a work is a good or bad example of its genre (as a good or bad poem), or whether the author has used a fresh and interesting approach. Another kind of evaluative response deals with the moral significance of the work and the moral acceptability of lessons taught through the work.

Children are likely to make some kinds of evaluative responses more frequently than others. You should be alert to them so that they can be acknowledged and perhaps discussed further. The prescriptive judgment is easily recognized and can be expanded through discussion. For example, if a reader says emphatically that Harriet, in Louise Fitzhugh's *Harriet the Spy*, ought to throw away her notebook, it would be interesting to ask the child why Harriet might need to keep her notebook about people. What good is it doing her? By helping a reader to explore a response, some reaction to the literary characteristics may also emerge. At the elementary level, however, we are not as interested in instruction as we are in releasing response in children.

We hear fairly often evaluative responses which represent some of the types included in the Purves scheme. Children who say a book is one of the funniest they have ever read are responding with an affective evaluation. A reader who likes a mystery because the plot is different from most is evaluating the author's method of writing as well as evaluating the selection as a good example of its genre. The following response to Robert Lipsyte's *The Contender* shows an evaluation of the moral significance of the book: "It's worth reading because it shows that if you work hard you can get ahead."

Literature and the Reading Program

The purpose of this chapter is not to present a literature-based reading program but to describe some ways that literature is used within that context. Children's books have become the focal point in many reading/language arts programs that might be described as "integrated instruction." Such programs can vary greatly as to the way in which learning occurs, but one main feature of this kind of teaching is an attempt to integrate the closely related aspects of literacy, rather than teaching them as separate skills as reading has traditionally been taught. Thus, an integrated program might focus attention on story sequence, and at the same time provide activities such as drama and creative writing. In the process, children have an opportunity to examine story organization through oral language and pantomime; and they can practice the mechanical skills of handwriting, spelling, and punctuation.

Here is an example of integrated instruction from Mrs. Lee's first grade. The lesson begins with her students reading from paperback copies of the classic story, *Millions of Cats*. When they have finished reading, Mrs. Lee asks the children to retell the story collaboratively. The structure of the story is circular and can be displayed clearly in a visual manner: Using a large circle she has drawn on chart paper, Mrs. Lee draws small pictures, or rebus figures, along the circle to show the movement of the story action. (In traditional reading programs, these are called the "sequence of events.") At the top of her large circle is a house with stick figures, representing a man and a woman, standing beside it; this symbolizes the story introduction which tells us that an old man and an old woman live all alone in their little house. Clockwise around the circle are pictures representing the settings, the characters, and the events that transpire as the old man tries to select just the right cat to take home to his lonely wife. But, as the repetition reminds us, he finds "millions and billions and trillions of cats"; and because they are all so pretty, he finally takes all the cats home with him. Horrified to see all those cats, the wife says they can keep only the prettiest one. Each cat claims to be the most beautiful and a fight ensues. In the end, only one scraggly little cat remains; she hid because she didn't think she was pretty. The old couple gladly takes her into their home; with care, she becomes a pretty, fluffy cat.

When the children finish retelling the story with the aid of the circle chart, Mrs. Lee gives each child a large sheet of drawing paper so the children can structure their own stories in a visual manner. Matt first makes a large circle, and then he opens his writing folder to examine the topics he has listed for future stories about which he might write. Matt decides on "Rascal's Trip to the Store," based on funny things his dog does. At the top of his circle he outlines and then colors a picture of Rascal. Then, going clockwise as the teacher did, he draws pictures to show the events on the day Rascal ran away to the store and came back several hours later. The first picture shows Rascal

After reading and retelling a story, students display their drawings of the story sequence. Art activities are an excellent means of encouraging response to literature.

meeting Jerry, the dog from across the street; the following picture shows the two dogs walking side by side. Next, Matt draws a picture of a big cat chasing the dogs. Subsequent pictures show the dogs entering the meat market; then leaving with a string of frankfurters hanging from each dog's mouth; the angry shop keeper standing in the door shaking his fist; and finally, Rascal sitting in front of his own dog house with a smile on his face.

For many children in the first years of school, drawing is an important facet of written expression, as well as a means of visualizing and thinking about story sequence. Because Matt is adept at writing with "invented spelling," he progresses from the circle chart to recording his story in writing:

> *DOGS EAT DOGS*
> *MY DOGS NAM IS RSCL ONE DAY HE RAN*
> *AWAY FROM HOM. HE FIST WENT TO SE*
> *JAIR. THEN THA RAN DON THE STRET*
> *TO THE MET MARCT. THA SAW A **BIG** CAT*
> *AND IT SHAST AFTER RSCL AND JAIR.*
> *WEN THA GOT TO THE STOR THA GRABD*
> *SUM HOT DOGS AND RAN HOM. MR*
> *GREN YELD AT THEM BUT THA ATE THE*
> *HOT DOGS ANIHO. THE DOGS ATE THE*
> *DOGS. HA HA.*

Matt proudly pastes his written story beneath the circle picture and displays it on the bulletin board at the writing center, where Kelly is telling her story to Mrs. Lee. Katie records her story onto a tape which she labels "I SKATE by Katie." The children in this room are at many stages in developing literacy skills, yet all are able to plan a sequenced story and tell or write it in some form for others to enjoy.

Because the children enjoy the story so much, a subsequent lesson involves story theater dramatization. (See Chapter 15 for more information on this type of activity.) Two children are chosen to play the parts of the old man and the old woman and the rest are cats. Various parts of the classroom are designated with labels as House, Hill, and Lake. As Mrs. Lee rereads the story, the children listen carefully and pantomime the appropriate actions, adding appropriate noises. They enjoy the activity so much that they decide to repeat it for a Parents' Day performance.

Through their enjoyment of one story, Mrs. Lee's class has many opportunities to read and use language skills: speaking, listening, writing, spelling, and acting. During the days that follow, Mrs. Lee reads other stories with similar plots to the children and displays books at the reading center which the children can read independently or in pairs. Among the books are *Peace at Last! Rosie's Walk*, and *Bears in the Night*.

What is the key to successful integrated-language activities? Most important is choosing the appropriate book and planning activities that draw from the characters, plot, and setting of the story. Planning a skills lesson that misuses the book is a mistake. For example, a worksheet that requires children to circle all of the "n's" in "hundreds of cats, thousands of cats, millions and billions and trillions of cats" does nothing to encourage understanding and enjoyment of the story. However, encouraging children to repeat the refrain as it occurs in the story is a good way to develop sense of rhythm; suggesting children say or write their own refrain about different animals might lead to:

> *"Brown dogs,*
> *Black dogs,*
> *Red and white and spotted dogs."*

The children in Mrs. Lee's room love stories and poetry; they are confident in their growing abilities as readers and writers. Their responses to books suggest emotional involvement and enjoyment as well as understanding of form and content.

In another wing of Jefferson School, a group of Mr. Parker's fifth graders are involved with a reading/language arts unit based on Farley Mowat's *Owls in the Family*. Finishing Chapter 5, in which Billy describes the appearance and actions of his two pet owls, the students prepare for a response group discussion. This chapter is a good resource for discussion, as Mowat describes situations that underscore the contrast between the two owls (Wol and Weeps) and their tame and wild behavior. Mr. Parker divides his students into two groups of five each. They function independently of the teacher, but each group has a leader who is responsible for maintaining the discussion. The first discussion item has to do with the children's feelings as they learn about owls, focusing on emotional/personal responses to the story and to critical/evaluative responses.

Mr. Parker appoints a recorder for each group. One group is asked to make a chart showing the different appearances and actions of the two owls. With help from the others, the recorder sets up the following chart:

	Wol	Weeps
color		
size		
food eaten		
flying experience		
playing		

The other group creates a chart comparing the owls' actions that demonstrate tame or wild behavior:

	Tame	Wild
foods eaten		
play behavior		
treatment of other animals		

The charts are housed at the reading corner for additions as the children read further in the book. To summarize the chapter, all ten students briefly discuss their assessment of whether the owls tend to be more tame or wild. The discussion grows heated as some students defend Wol's wild behavior in killing a cat and chewing a dog's ears. Others, disturbed by this behavior, feel that no one should keep pets that are so dangerous to other animals. The discussion groups clearly engage children in an emotional response, as they use critical thinking to evaluate the actions of the two owls.

As a follow-up to the reading session, Mr. Parker encourages students to write about their own pets. This activity is a natural extension of the content and structure of the episode from *Owls in the Family.* Independent reading of related books is encouraged, too, and Mr. Parker supplies the reading table with titles such as Mowat's *Never Cry Wolf,* Patterson's *Koko's Story,* Burnford's *The Incredible Journey,* George's *Julie of the Wolves,* and North's *Rascal.*

Response and Reading Comprehension

The relationship of literary response to reading comprehension is an important idea for teachers and librarians who work with children of elementary school age, for a good literary experience can help to develop the higher-level comprehension skills necessary for effective reading. A good reading program that aims to develop a child's ability to make inferences about, evaluate, and appreciate literature can also enhance literary response. In either event, the experiences children bring to reading can greatly influence comprehension and response to literature and should be considered in selecting reading material.

Writing about the development of reading comprehension abilities, Robert Ruddell describes comprehension as occurring on three levels—*factual, interpretive,* and *applicative.*[7] He

notes that the *factual* level involves mostly the information and ideas the reader finds. A child comprehending at the *interpretive* level, however, analyzes the information and infers such relationships as cause and effect, infers main ideas, and predicts the outcome of an event in the story. Also at this level, readers begin to deal with their own values by inferring or interpreting character traits or identifying the author's motive. They bring personal judgment and their own experiences to bear on their interpretations.

At another comprehension level, which Ruddell terms *applicative,* readers apply the knowledge from the story to new situations, make and substantiate value judgments, and engage in problem solving. The comprehension skills at the interpretive and applicative levels can be related to the literary response abilities we have been discussing. At the interpretive level, the ability to infer is closely related to the interpretive response to literature. A child who identifies traits of a key story character by

[7]Robert B. Ruddell, *Reading-Language Instruction; Innovative Practices.* Englewood Cliffs, N.J.: Prentice-Hall, 1974.

Viewpoint

I am hoping for characters, perhaps I am *searching* for characters, that children can identify as human, characters they can understand, with whom they can sympathize, or with whom they can themselves identify. Out of this type of shared experience a boy or a girl might catch on to the idea that trying to know your friend is better than judging him. They might come around to the idea that all kinds of people have all kinds of problems, grown-up people even, and other kids, and his or her personal load of guilt or doubt or anxiety might begin to weigh a little less. Yet this is not the primary aim; perhaps it is pompous to have an aim at all; if it is possible to express a *hope* in words, it is simply to continue a shared journey of discovery into the wonderland of human experience.

Ivan Southall, *A Journey of Discovery: On Writing for Children.* New York: Macmillan Publishing Company, 1975, p. 36.

inferring from that character's actions, speech, and unspoken thoughts, is engaging in character trait analysis and also noting, though perhaps not intentionally, the techniques an author uses to develop a character. Thus, a child may describe the protagonist in Beverly Cleary's *Henry Huggins* as a boy who is not especially brave or confident and may judge Henry's actions as inappropriate by suggesting a better way to deal with a problem. In response to the follow-up question, "Why doesn't Henry seem to have much self-confidence?" a child may reply that Henry was not sure he could convince his mother to let him keep the stray dog. The reader may also note that Henry sounds fearful when he calls his mother and that his lack of confidence is also clear when he tries to get on the bus with his dog. Such responses do indicate that the reader is aware of some ways an author can give depth to characterization. Many children would make an emotional as well as literary response to a question about Henry Huggins. Some would admit that they sometimes act the way Henry does or that they would be embarrassed—or would laugh—if they had the same predicament on the bus as Henry had when the dog got loose. Children may also suggest that Henry did not use good sense in handling the problem but should have tried some other scheme or given up entirely on the new dog. Value judgments call for a knowledge about the character and the situation. They also require the reader to infer and predict on the basis of what is known. Furthermore, an emotional response gives reason to believe that the child is responding to the story as a piece of literature and that the author has succeeded in drawing captivating characters and situations. The evidence of literary response is even more clear at the applicative level where readers are expected to make value judgments and to substantiate those judgments by referring to the story.

Mature readers understand the material and are able to relate it to their own experiences or to other information that they have. Reading comprehension is the key to literacy. Although literary responses and reading comprehension skills are not specifically the same abilities, there are relationships which can be identified and used so that development of reading skills grows naturally into a mature response to literature. These relationships can be seen in the table on page 575, which juxtaposes the Barrett Taxonomy of Reading Comprehension and the literary responses we have been discussing.

The Barrett Taxonomy includes affective as well as cognitive reading skills. The addition of affective responses to reading, shown in the category termed "Appreciation," draws the classification toward the concerns we have about response to literature—emotional involvement with the story or poem *plus* an attempt to interpret it, evaluate it, and, perhaps, discuss aspects of its literary structure.

When we look at the reading comprehension and response to literature schemes together, the interrelationships are clear. A response to a story or poem which is simply a retelling appears to be similar to and rest upon the comprehension skills identified as literal recall. This retelling relies mainly on the ability to recall details in sequence.

The details might be important if the reader uses them to infer cause and effect, to figure out the solution to a mystery, to interpret the behavior of a story character, or to form a response to the beautiful setting described by an author. Unless the information that is recalled is extended to other modes of response, the factual retelling is of no great importance when we talk of literary response. Recalling information about character traits can be useful if a child goes on to see how an author develops characterization. Similarly, recall of sequence may be important when a child points out similar plots in two stories. Recognizing character traits and plot structure in these two instances constitutes a response to literary qualities. A number of inferential comprehension skills are important when children respond to literature by trying to interpret it.

Children who have developed skills of inference have background for comparing the clothing of Laura and Mary (the *Little House* books) with current clothing styles (inferring comparisons), talking about why an author included certain characters in the story (inferring cause and effect), or suggesting events that could occur after the story has ended (inferring sequence).

A child who says of *Owls in the Family*, "Wol's bad experience when he first flew came because he didn't have a mother owl to teach him how to fly," shows comprehension of cause and effect. If you look at the statement in terms of literary response, it shows an *interpretation* of a story character's problem.

The difficulties of Ramona (*Ramona the Pest* by Beverly Cleary) were explained by one child as caused by the fact that Ramona wants to do the right thing but usually doesn't succeed. That child cited several instances when Ramona's obedience actually got her into trouble (as when she sat in her seat all morning "for the present"). The character interpretation is built on character trait inference. By asking open-ended questions ("why" rather than "what, who, and where"), you give children experience with inference. Those "why" questions can enrich reading instruction as well as discussion of literature.

Evaluative reading is an important skill which is related directly to evaluation of literature as was shown in the chart.

This classification of reading skills which includes affective as well as cognitive abilities also shows the close relationship between reading comprehension and emotional involvement with literature—in this case, appreciation.

Children who are encouraged to respond to characters, content, plot, and theme and to react to the author's use of language are being given experiences that can open the door to a satisfying emotional response to literature. Children who have begun to show involvement with literature may respond with comments like

Viewpoint

Prolonged contact with literature may result in increased social sensitivity. Through poems and stories and plays, the child becomes aware of the personalities of different kinds of people. He learns to imaginatively "put himself into the place of the other fellow." He becomes better able to foresee the possible repercussions of his own actions in the life of others.

Louise M. Rosenblatt, *Literature as Exploration*, Revised Edition. New York: Noble & Noble, 1976, p. 184.

Reading Comprehension Skills and Literary Response

Reading Comprehension* ⟷ **Literary Response**

Literal Recall ⟷ **Narration**

Recall of details, main idea, sequence, comparisons, cause and effect, character traits

Squire's term for a factual retelling of the story**

Inference ⟷ **Interpretation**

Inferring supporting details, main idea, sequence, comparisons, cause and effect, and character traits; predicting outcomes; inferring literal meanings from figurative language

Making sense of the story; relating the work to what the reader knows about life

Evaluation ⟷ **Evaluation**

Judgments of reality/fantasy; fact/opinion; adequacy/appropriateness; worth, desirability, or acceptability

Literary judgment—judgments of the worth of a story or of the quality of writing, depth of characterization, or effectiveness of plot; comments about the appropriateness of a character's behavior

Appreciation ⟷ **Emotional Involvement**

Emotional response to content, plot or theme; reaction to author's use of language

Comments showing interaction with a story or poem which may reflect joy, excitement, dislike or a range of other emotions

*Adapted from Barrett, Thomas C., "A Taxonomy of Reading Comprehension," *Reading 360 Monograph* (1972). Lexington, Massachusetts: Ginn & Company (Xerox Corporation). Reprinted by permission.

**See James Squire, *The Responses of Adolescents While Reading Four Short Stories*. National Council of Teachers of English, 1964.

these: "I just hated Martin (*The Bully of Barkham Street*) until he stopped beating up on little kids," "That description of the doughnuts (*Homer Price* by Robert McCloskey) falling all over the floor was really funny," or "If I had been Ramona, I would have pulled that girl's curls, too."

In Barrett's taxonomy, the appreciation skills are based on inference and evaluation. The appreciation level represents ability to react emotionally in addition to grasping the meaning of the story. The emotional reaction can be consciously fostered through the reading program. Emotional response is a base for other responses which occur at the same time or even at later stages of development and therefore the emotional response must be encouraged and emphasized whenever possible.

When you are aware of the important ties between reading instruction and a literature program, you can strengthen them by building experience with literature into the reading program. You can also extend reading experiences by encouraging children's response to books during library and free-reading periods.

Interpreting Pictures

Young children are often taught, as a part of the beginning reading program, to get information from pictures and to interpret them. When they are asked for factual information, they are then often asked to use that information to predict what will happen to characters in the pictures or to interpret what is taking place in the scene.

Picture reading is very likely an important readiness activity for literary response as well as for reading comprehension. A child who is asked to "tell the story" in a book that is completely or almost entirely without text is being asked to respond to the illustrations. John Goodall's *The Ballooning Adventures of Paddy Pork* and Mercer Mayer's *The Great Cat Chase* are examples of wordless books that give children a chance to infer a story from illustrations. Young children of kindergarten age and below may, as often as not, respond with a factual account of what they see in the pictures. Older or more mature "picture readers" are more likely to respond by combining factual observations with their own inferences about what goes on in the story.[8] The younger children are giving a narrational response, the older or more mature ones a response that usually combines emotional involvement with inferences about the pictorial information. Such a story "told" by more mature children may include a considerable number of inferences about the characters and about the plot, including predictions of what may occur as the story progresses. The response, therefore, is a literary response at the same time that it is an exercise in picture comprehension. By providing good experiences with picture books and asking appropriate questions, we can help young children to develop inference skills.

The need for a strong library reading program to complement the skill instruction that goes on in reading class should be evident. Through planned library activities, children can be brought into contact with—and, we hope, interaction with—fine and interesting books. They can have time and opportunity to respond emotionally to the books, to whet their curiosity through reading experiences, and to begin to reorganize some perceptions of the world in which they live. They can use vicarious literary experiences as guides to the interpretation of some of life's events.

Literature and Children's Writing

Experiences with literature can have a profound effect on what and how children write. Writing often stems from personal experiences or from special interests that lead to some form of research in order to gather information. Beyond the origin of ideas comes the need to organize writing in a coherent and effective manner. There is no doubt that most children, either consciously or unconsciously, make use of literary models when they write. An opening

[8]Mary Jett Simpson, *Children's Inferential Responses to a Wordless Picture Book; Development and Use of a Classification System for Verbalized Inference.* Unpublished doctoral dissertation. University of Washington, 1976.

By responding to the illustration in a book read aloud to them, children are soon able to make their own interpretations and predictions as to the outcome of a story.

statement, "Once there was a girl who lived in a tree in the forest," sounds suspiciously like a folk-tale beginning. A story development in which a character tries unsuccessfully twice to solve a problem and succeeds on the third try is also reminiscent of folk literature, with the pattern of three. The language of literature is also often reflected in children's writing. "They wandered hither and yon in their search," is certainly a more literary than childlike description of the behavior of story characters, and so is the phrase, "great, gray, and beautiful" to describe a cat. Yet young writers are capable of producing both.

Experiences in responding to literature can give children background for dealing with most rhetorical situations. Fantasy is especially rich in description. *Peter Rabbit* and *Watership Down*, greatly different in level of sophistication, are nevertheless both excellent examples of descriptive writing and of fantasy. Realistic fiction and fantasy give experience with the sense of story, the knowledge of how to begin and end a story and how to keep it going. Historical fiction, too, can serve this purpose. Well constructed nonfiction gives children a glimpse into some of the ways they can organize text and illustrations to impart information clearly and artistically. They need to hear expository

material read to them, too, so that they can become familiar with style appropriate for that form of writing.

Prewriting is an important concept in the teaching of writing, for it has to do with experiences that give children background for writing. Good books children hear and read can give ideas for structure and style as well as content of their own writing. Wordless picture books like Mayer's *Frog Goes to Dinner* provide good storytelling experience when children tell the story they see in pictures. This leads children naturally to drawing their own pictures and telling or writing the story that goes with them. Vibrant use of language in books like Bryan's *The Cat's Purr* and Rylant's *Night in the Country* encourages children to appreciate the sound of language and to use interesting words in their stories, words that describe so clearly as to arouse the reader's emotions. A book like Viorst's *The Tenth Good Thing about Barney* sets children to thinking about their own pets and what they love about them. The story structure creates a framework for story writing.

Even though children have many ideas for writing, they can find models for developing those ideas in well-written stories and poems. Creative use of language in poems, like Esbensen's *Words with Wrinkled Knees*, encourages children to experiment with interesting descriptions. Development of a story problem through repeated attempts at resolution enhances a story greatly yet this is not usually characteristic of children's writing. Hearing or reading about Henry Huggins's attempts to get his new dog, Ribsy, onto a bus in order to bring him home helps children to appreciate why that scene is so enjoyable. If Henry had succeeded the first time, the story would fall flat. Instead, Cleary chooses to have him fail not once, but twice; each new attempt is described with such detail that the episode becomes a classic in humorous writing. This is not to say that children are expected to write with the sophistication of an adult author. It does suggest, however, that providing them with models of well-structured stories is an important part of fostering writing development.

Children's writing takes many forms from letters to diaries, stories, poems, and informational writing. The letters in MacLachlan's

Sarah, Plain and Tall and Cleary's *Dear Mr. Henshaw* are fine examples of the use of letters to communicate important information about ourselves to interested readers; *Dear Mr. Henshaw* goes one step further by showing diary entries, as well. The sense of story in Yolen's *Owl Moon* immerses the reader in one short-lived event and shows clearly the power of a storyteller who can build anticipation for the sighting of an owl. In George's *Water Sky*, the story includes a number of important incidents centered around a boy's coming to understand himself amidst the clash of two cultures. Both books may encourage children to experiment with their own storytelling, perhaps drawing from experiences they have had.

Poetry, too, can serve as an inspiration as children work with that form of writing. Viorst's *If I Were in Charge of the World* is a collection of poems to which most children can

Literary models for developing written response to literature can be used by students in first reading or listening to a well-known story, and then interpreting its structure and style when composing their own stories.

relate. The feelings described focus on friendships and on problems, real and imagined. Such models can suggest topics, as well as forms, for children's poems. Children engage in a good deal of informational writing as part of the school day. They may draw inspiration for developing a personal style from books such as George's *One Day in the Prairie* or Sewall's *The Pilgrims of Plymouth*. Both transmit useful and interesting information but do so in forms that enhance the reader's appreciation of the facts. Children should be encouraged to experiment as they write so that they can find their own style.

Literature and the Social Studies Program

An important part of the social studies program is acquainting children with the lives of people who lived in other times and other places, and with the lives of people from a variety of cultures living in our world today. Although textbooks may provide useful facts about history and geography, children's books have the potential to allow readers to experience other lives and, consequently, other places and times. Fiction is an important genre for it evokes the reader's emotions and encourage personal response to the universal feelings of story characters. Feelings such as joy, fear, love, and hope unite people everywhere.

Indeed, children have a natural curiosity about the lives of children in other places. For example, fifth and sixth graders were asked what they would most like to know about the life of an Australian child. Their responses reflected a wide range of physical and psychological human needs. These were the most often asked questions:

What kinds of foods do you eat?
What kinds of clothes do you wear?
What are your houses like?
What kinds of pets or animals do you have?
What are your schools like?
What is your weather like?
Do you have any brothers or sisters?
Do you have many friends?
Do you ever get lonesome?

Social studies instruction can be augmented by the use of literature. For example, the genres of biography and historical fiction introduce students to the human aspect of history or to other cultures in today's world.

Although the answers to some of these questions might appear in textbooks, the children's queries could also be satisfied by books such as Klein's *Penny Pollard in Print*, Park's *Playing Beatie Bow*, Southall's *Josh*, Wrightson's *I Own the Racecourse*, or Thiele's *Shadow Shark*.

A library corner featuring these and other good books with Australian settings would add an important dimension to the study of that country and its people. Readers would find that Australian children eat many foods typical of an American diet, including eggs, bacon, toast, and cornflakes for breakfast and fried chicken for dinner. They would also read about foods that are unfamiliar to most U.S. families, asparagus sandwiches, pancakes with tomato sauce, and an Irish Stew sandwich, among them.

Children have many of the same questions about their counterparts who grew up during earlier periods in their own country. A literature supplement for a social studies unit on pioneers might include these books:

Caddie Woodlawn by Carol Ryrie Brink
Cassie's Journey: Going West in the 1860's by Brett Harvey
Dakota Dugout by Ann Turner
Little House in the Big Woods by Laura Ingalls Wilder
My Prairie Year: Based on the Diary of Elenore Plaisted by Brett Harvey
A Prairie Boy's Winter by William Kurelek
Prairie Songs by Pam Conrad

In order to encourage critical reading and thinking about lives in other times and places, offer students pairs of fiction and nonfiction books on related topics:

• *The Slave Dancer* by Paula Fox
 To Be a Slave by Julius Lester
• *My Brother Sam Is Dead* by James and Christopher Collier
 America's Paul Revere by Esther Forbes
• *Dragonwings* by Laurence Yep
 The Wright Brothers at Kitty Hawk by Donald J. Sobol
• *Homesick: My Own Story* by Jean Fritz
 Two Chinese Families by Catherine Sadler
• *On the Banks of Plum Creek* by Laura Ingalls Wilder
 Cassie's Journey: Going West in the 1860's by Brett Harvey

In teaching social studies, teachers and librarians are wise to consider the human aspect in the history of the past as well as in history in the making. Bunting's *How Many Days to America?* is a compelling account of the desperate search of boat people seeking a new home. As children experience other lives through literature, they can develop empathy for people whose needs and feelings may be similar to theirs, even though their lives are very different. Through emotional interaction with stories, readers frequently become involved with characters. The child who reads Mildred Taylor's *Roll of Thunder, Hear My Cry*, learns about poverty and discrimination and may be experiencing the problems of ill-treated people for the first time. A youngster, listening to a story of a barrio child, wonders at the problems of daily existence. A child reading Yep's *Child of the Owl* can come to know the sometimes wonderful, sometimes confusing experience of living within two cultures. Examining the characters' conflicts through discussing and role-playing brings children into closer relationship with the characters and helps them develop a sense of empathy.

Evaluating Children's Response

Evaluation of children's learning about literature is seldom done formally. Nevertheless, there are literary behaviors which can be identified and observed throughout a school year. Formal and informal observation can also help you to look at the success of your literature program. Evaluation, carried out throughout the course of a program, can give information about these behaviors:

1. knowledge about literature
2. ability to apply that knowledge in comparing stories or poems or tracing their cultural roots
3. expressed response—either through oral, dramatic, or artistic form; or through talking or writing about response
4. willingness to participate in literary experiences or to respond to literature.[9]

Behaviors (3) and (4) above are closely related to experiences described in the two chapters that follow. You might, for example, evaluate whether oral reading and discussion develops more positive attitudes in your students than role-playing, as shown by children's comments that indicate greater emotional involvement with a story or poem. The best means of assessing response to literature at the elementary level seems to be through adult observation of children's behavior and reactions to literature heard and read.

Willingness to participate in literary experiences and to respond to literature can be assessed by observing children's reading habits, either informally or with a questionnaire, and by noting reactions to literature presented in class. A questionnaire asking children to rank reading according to its importance in their lives might include such other choices as television viewing, participating in sports, or spending time with hobbies. By using such a questionnaire at the beginning and end of a year, it is possible to get some idea of the success of a literature program. Informally noting whether individuals or a group can better interpret literature at the end of the year can add to this evaluation. So, too, can the use of tests of knowledge about literature.

Judgment of the success of an entire program serves its purpose when we make plans for future programs. Evaluation carried out during a program can help us to make changes while the program is still in use. If creative dramatics is not an effective way of involving a certain group of children with literature, frequent observations should make that clear. Another approach, such as discussion, can be substituted and a check made of changes in attitude and/or knowledge as a result of the new strategy. The evaluations need not be more formal than observations of children's reading behavior. However, conscious evaluation can help to keep a literature program interesting and develop mature responses.

As adults who are involved in bringing children and books together, we would like to make that experience a rewarding one. In this chapter we have discussed a wide range of current theory and research on children's response to literature. Our purpose in this discussion has been to provide a basis for thinking about children's experiences with literature and for organizing activities—the subject of the two chapters that follow.

Adult References and Book Selection Aids*

APPLEBEE, ARTHUR N. *The Child's Concept of Story: Ages Two to Seventeen.*

AQUINO, JOHN. *Fantasy in Literature.*

CRAGO, MAUREEN and HUGH. *Prelude to Literacy: A Pre-school Child's Encounter with Picture and Story.*

HAZARD, PAUL. *Books, Children, and Men.*

HOPKINS, LEE BENNETT. *The Best of Book Bonanza.*

PURVES, ALAN C., with VICTORIA RIPPERE. *Elements of Writing About a Literary Work: A Study of Response to Literature.*

——— and others. *Reading and Literature: American Achievement in International Perspective.*

ROSENBLATT, LOUISE M. *Literature as Exploration.*

RUDDELL, ROBERT B. *Reading-Language Instruction: Innovative Practices.*

SQUIRE, JAMES, ed. *Response to Literature.*

TUCKER, NICHOLAS. *The Child and the Book: A Psychological and Literary Exploration.*

VANDERGRIFT, KAY E. *Child and Story: The Literary Connection.*

*Complete bibliographic data are provided in Appendices A and B.

[9]Alan C. Purves, "Evaluation of Learning in Literature," in *Handbook of Formative and Summative Evaluation of Student Learning.* Benjamin S. Bloom, J. Thomas Hastings, and George Madaus, eds. New York: McGraw-Hill, 1971, pp. 703–710.

Children's Books Mentioned in This Chapter

BERENSTAIN, STAN AND JAN. *Bears in the Night,* ill. by authors. Random House, 1971.

BRINK, CAROL RYRIE. *Caddie Woodlawn.* Macmillan, 1935, 1963.

BRYAN, ASHLEY. *The Cat's Purr,* ill. by author. Atheneum, 1985.

BUNTING, EVE. *How Many Days to America?* Clarion, 1988.

BURNFORD, SHEILA. *The Incredible Journey.* Little, 1961.

BYARS, BETSY. *The Summer of the Swans.* Viking, 1970.

CLEARY, BEVERLY. *Dear Mr. Henshaw,* ill. by Paul Zelinsky. Morrow, 1983.

———. *Henry Huggins,* ill. by Louis Darling. Morrow, 1950.

———. *Ramona the Pest,* ill. by Louis Darling. Morrow, 1968.

COLLIER, JAMES AND CHRISTOPHER. *My Brother Sam Is Dead.* Four Winds, 1974.

CONRAD, PAM. *Prairie Songs.* Harper, 1988.

ESBENSEN, BARBARA. *Words with Wrinkled Knees,* ill. by John Stadler. Crowell, 1986.

FORBES, ESTHER. *America's Paul Revere,* ill. by Lynd Ward. Houghton, 1946.

FOX, PAULA. *The Slave Dancer,* ill. by Keith Eros. Bradbury, 1973.

FRITZ, JEAN. *Homesick: My Own Story,* ill. by Marget Tomes. Dell, 1982.

GÁG, WANDA. *Millions of Cats,* ill. by author. Coward, 1928.

GEORGE, JEAN. *Julie of the Wolves,* ill. by John Schoenherr. Harper, 1972.

———. *One Day in the Prairie,* ill. by Bob Marshall. Crowell, 1986.

———. *Water Sky.* Harper, 1987.

GOODALL, JOHN. *The Ballooning Adventures of Paddy Pork.* Atheneum, 1969.

HARVEY, BRETT. *Cassie's Journey: Going West in the 1860's,* ill. by Deborah K. Ray. Holiday House, 1988.

———. *My Prairie Year: Based on the Diary of Elenore Plaisted,* ill. by Deborah K. Ray. Holiday House, 1986.

HOBAN, RUSSELL. *A Bargain for Frances,* ill. by Lillian Hoban. Harper, 1970.

HUTCHINS, PAT. *Rosie's Walk,* ill. by author. Macmillan, 1968.

KEATS, EZRA JACK. *The Snowy Day,* ill. by author. Viking, 1962.

KLEIN, ROBIN. *Penny Pollard in Print.* Oxford Press, 1986.

KURELEK, WILLIAM. *A Prairie Boy's Winter,* ill. by author. Houghton, 1973.

LESTER, JULIUS. *To Be a Slave,* ill. by Tom Feelings. Dial, 1968.

LINDGREN, ASTRID. *Pippi Longstocking,* ill. by Louis Glanzman. Viking, 1950.

McCLOSKEY, ROBERT. *Homer Price,* ill. by author. Viking, 1943.

———. *Lentil,* ill. by author. Viking, 1940.

McLACHLAN, PATRICIA. *Sarah, Plain and Tall.* Harper, 1985.

MEYER, MERCER. *Frog Goes to Dinner,* ill. by author. Dial, 1974.

———. *The Great Cat Chase,* ill. by author. Four Winds, 1975.

MOWAT, FARLEY. *Never Cry Wolf.* Little, 1963.

———. *Owls in the Family,* ill. by Robert Frankenberg. Little, 1961.

MURPHY, JILL. *Peace at Last!* ill by author. Dial, 1980.

NORTH, STERLING. *Rascal.* Dutton, 1963.

NORTON, MARY. *The Borrowers,* ill. by Beth and Joe Krush. Harcourt, 1953.

PARK, RUTH. *Playing Beattie Bow.* Atheneum, 1982.

PATTERSON, FRANCINE. *Koko's Story,* photos by Ronald H. Cohn. Scholastic, 1987.

RYLANT, CYNTHIA. *Night in the Country,* ill. by Mary Szilagyi. Bradbury, 1986.

SADLER, CATHERINE. *Two Chinese Families.* Atheneum, 1981.

SEWELL, MARCIA. *The Pilgrims of Plimoth,* ill. by author. Atheneum, 1986.

SOUTHALL, IVAN. *Josh.* Macmillan, 1972.

TAYLOR, MILDRED. *Roll of Thunder, Hear My Cry,* ill. by Jerry Pinkney. Dial, 1976.

THIELE, COLIN. *Shadow Shark.* Harper, 1985.

TURNER, ANN. *Dakota Dugout,* ill. by Ronald Himler. Macmillan, 1985.

VIORST, JUDITH. *If I Were in Charge of the World and Other Worries,* ill by Lynn Cherry. Atheneum, 1981.

———. *The Tenth Good Thing About Barney,* ill by Eric Blegvad. Atheneum, 1971.

WILDER, LAURA INGALLS. *Little House in the Big Woods,* ill by Garth Williams. Harper, 1953.

———. *The Long Winter,* ill. by Garth Williams. Harper, 1940.

———. *On the Banks of Plum Creek,* ill. by Garth Williams. Harper, 1937.

WRIGHTSON, PATRICIA. *I Own the Racecourse.* Penguin, 1971.

YEP, LAURENCE. *Child of the Owl.* Harper, 1977.

———. *Dragonwings.* Harper, 1975.

YOLEN, JANE. *Owl Moon,* ill. by John Schoenherr. Philomel, 1987.

Chapter Fifteen

Encouraging Response to Literature

To become mature readers children need opportunities to respond to a variety of reading material. Some children will respond easily to selections that interest them, showing response in their comments as well as in their facial expressions as they read, hear, or recall a story or poem. Other children will need more encouragement and may respond more freely if they are allowed to use physical as well as verbal response, as in a puppet production of a story. Your role is to encourage but never force response, to offer activities that will allow children to actively respond to a selection, to observe and help to extend responses to literature so that they include interpretation and evaluation. At the same time, you should realize that some of the most deeply reflective responses are not observable and that those responses must be honored and not destroyed by too much emphasis on activity. Remind yourself that your goal is not a polished dramatic production but a group of children enjoying an experience with a fine story.

Response-centered activities discussed in this chapter begin with those designed for listening enjoyment—reading aloud to children and storytelling. A third activity, discussion, adds active verbal interchange to listening, and leads to interpretation and evaluation of a selection. The chapter then moves to dramatic activities —role-playing, story theater, oral interpretation, creative dramatics, and puppetry—activities which encourage physical/motor response as an aid to involvement with a story. Writing activities are described last. The act of writing about a literary work requires a certain amount of skill in written expression. Children who have only minimal writing skill will be inhibited in developing response to literature if made to write about what they have read. For that reason, written responses may be fine for some children and some situations but should be used selectively.

Reading Aloud to Children

Parents, teachers, librarians, baby-sitters, all of us who work with children, can enrich our lives as well as those of children when we provide and encourage delight in hearing a good story read aloud well. Pleasurable experiences in listening can create interest in books that carries on through years of adolescence and adulthood. Listening can also provide natural opportunities for development of a listening vocabulary and acquaintance with English syntax. When you read to children, you give them a chance to hear an author's style, to identify with well-developed characters, and sometimes to try to predict the direction the plot will take in tomorrow's installment. Most important of all, you help them to know good books and poems in a relaxed, warm atmosphere.

Oral reading will be most successful when you give the listeners time to get ready to hear a story. For most groups, that readiness involves a few minutes of quiet and a chance to get as comfortable as possible. If the illustrations are important to the story, it also means settling the children close enough to you so that all can see. When you read from a picture book, it is important that you either hold the book so that they can see as you read or pause at the end of a page, taking time to show the illustrations.

Selecting Material to Read Aloud

For many people, and certainly for inexperienced readers, the two basic guidelines for selecting materials to read aloud are (1) that you like the selection and (2) that it is well written. As to the first guideline, you are more likely to draw an emotional reaction from listeners if you are involved with the story yourself. You will probably also do a better job of interpreting the characters and developing a sense of mood. However, unless you have chosen a well-written story, you may fail on both counts even though you like the book. A poorly written selection can cause you to feel awkward, to stumble over words, and to fail to make sense of the syntax because the writing lacks grace and polish.

Vivid characterization and a fairly fast-paced story line (a compact, factual account that concentrates more on action and less on description) are also important factors to keep in mind when you select a book to read aloud. Choose characters who will interest listeners and whose dialogue will be interesting and comfortable for you to read. Choose a plot or an organizational scheme that moves at a pace fast enough to keep reader attention, exercising your judgment about what may appeal to the group and keeping in mind age, past experiences, and interests.

The amount of time you can devote to an oral reading session will also influence the way you select material. Never try to read a long selection when you know the attention span of the children is likely to be no more than twenty minutes. You can usually find good stopping points if you have skimmed the material in advance. Sometimes an intriguing question can give the children a chance to wonder about what will happen next. If the story must be continued for several days, let the children, rather than you, review the story before continuing on with the next reading. Longer selections require special treatment but they are often very appealing to children because they allow fuller appreciation of a good plot and a chance to get well acquainted with the characters. Reading full-length books also gives some children a chance to know certain books they would never read on their own. If you cannot continue a story with the same group of children, consider the many fine poems that they may like. Think, too, of books like Beverly Cleary's *Henry Huggins* and Robert McCloskey's *Homer Price* that have episodic plots, each chapter usually a self-contained reading experience.

Reading aloud should not be limited to young children. Older children also enjoy being read to and often will read books they have heard previously. Additionally, the oral reading provides a group experience with literature in contrast to the more frequent silent reading activities in which older children engage. Another bonus for children of any age is the opportunity to enjoy the style of a piece. The *Just So Stories*, for example, are far more enjoyable to hear than to read silently. Sensitivity to style is subtle but may be enhanced through good oral reading.

Oral Reading Techniques

When you have chosen a story that is right for you and your children, you are ready to begin preparing to read aloud. Even experienced readers often use some pre-presentation techniques to make a reading more effective. They focus on the literary aspects of a story, qualities such as characterization and author's style, which must be conveyed when you read aloud. That can be done only if you have read, or at least skimmed, the selection to note high points in the plot. The same is true for noting crucial points to be emphasized when you are reading biography or informational material.

Previewing, or studying a selection in advance, will call your attention to the general tone the author uses. Is it serious, cynical, humorous, matter-of-fact? How should the narrator's parts be handled to provide contrast with character parts? Previewing should also show you the personality traits of the story characters so that you can use that information in your interpretation of dialogue. Skimming combined with a more complete reading of some sections of a story can give you an idea of the author's style: Are there long descriptive phrases? Does the author use short, action-packed sentences to instill excitement? Does the writer use unusual words? Are there words or word clusters that must be emphasized as you read? Skimming can help you to prepare quickly to make the most of a character part, a well-written line, or a build-up of conflict within the plot.

If you are a beginner at oral reading, you may want to practice a story aloud several times before reading it to the group. If you are reading from your own copy of a book, you may even want to mark it, underlining words needing emphasis and key punctuation marks so that you will make the most of a phrase or a sentence. If you have trouble keeping a wide enough eye-voice span to read ahead a sentence at a time, try at least to read for phrases so that your oral reading is smooth. The smoothness is the mechanical part of the reading. Beyond that, you must try to give listeners the mood of a selection. Creating mood requires you to bring together all of your knowledge about a work—understanding of theme, plot structure, characterization, and style. Using your voice, you can create a mood that helps listeners into their own interpretation of a story and brings them far enough into a work so that they are able to react intellectually as well as emotionally. Your level of pitch, tone of voice, and the pace of your reading all contribute to mood—a quiet, hushed reading for parts of Robert McCloskey's *Time of Wonder* and a brisk, rapid one for his *Homer Price*.

When you work on characterization, you should consider what you know about the character's personality. How would the person talk? Should you interpret the character as good-natured? domineering and aggressive? frightened or unsure? angry? Would the character generally speak slowly? fast? softly? Would the rate and volume of speech vary, depending on what was being said? You may find it easier

Viewpoint

Reading aloud to children stimulates their interest, their emotional development, and their imagination. There is also a fourth area which is stimulated by reading aloud and it is a particularly vital area in today's world. It is the child's language. We have seen children's spongelike reaction to television commercials. They continue this imitative behavior with words until their language development peaks around age 13. They will speak the language primarily as they have heard it spoken.

When you take time to read to your class you are not neglecting the curriculum. Reading *is* the curriculum. The principal ingredient of all learning and teaching is language. Not only is it the tool with which we communicate the lesson, it is also the product the student hands back to us—whether it is the language of math or science or history.

In that light, the classroom teacher who reads aloud helps the class to become better listeners and develop greater verbal skills. The more they hear other people's words, the greater becomes their desire to share their own through conversation and writing. Each read-aloud, then, is a language arts lesson, bolstering the four language arts: the art of reading, the art of listening, the art of writing, and the art of speaking.

Jim Trelease, *The Read-Aloud Handbook.* Middlesex, England: Penguin Books, Ltd., 1982, pp. 28, 37.

and more rewarding to try to think as the story character thinks and to really put yourself into the role, reading each bit of dialogue as though you were in the shoes of that character. Regardless of the technique you use, you should achieve enough of the spirit of the story so that characters are distinguishable from one another and so that they evoke some emotional response from children who are listening to the story. Needless to say, oral reading should never be overly dramatic or the desired effect will be lost.

Poetry is one of the literary forms most often read aloud, as it surely deserves to be. Poetry must be read to children who are not fluent enough readers to appreciate their own poetry reading. Poetry presents a visual barrier to many children reading it—a barrier that doesn't exist when the poetry is heard read aloud.

The question is often asked, "How can a person with little knowledge of poetry and less knowledge of oral interpretation learn to read poetry acceptably?" The answer is to read a poem aloud repeatedly until its tune and its meaning grow. Fortunately, the nonsense ditties of *Mother Goose*, Edward Lear, and Laura Richards, with their crisp or explosive consonants and brisk rhythms, practically force the reader into vigorous, precise speech and give one a sense of tempo and variety. The subtle lyrics of writers such as William Blake, Christina Rossetti, and Walter de la Mare, and the thought-provoking poetry of Robert Frost, however, require something more than vigor and swing. The works of such poets demand a delicate, precise interpretation that doesn't evolve with just one reading. So read a poem aloud to yourself first to get the general mood or feeling.

You make many discoveries when you read poetry aloud, because skilled poets write for the ear, and they employ melody and movement consciously for specific ends: (1) sometimes melody and movement are used to suggest the action described in the poem; (2) sometimes they help to establish the mood of the poem; or (3) they may furnish clues to its meaning. When you read a poem aloud, therefore, you catch elements you miss when you read it silently. The second time you try it orally

you will interpret it even better because you understand it better.

Observing Response

Responses to the oral reading of a story or poem are usually spontaneous. Watch for the grin as you show an illustration that captures the humor of a *Homer Price* episode or the sober expressions as listeners enter into the boy's problems in Louisa Shotwell's *Roosevelt Grady*. Many of the responses are likely to reflect emotional involvement with the selection as it is being read.

A pause at the end of the story or poem can give children time to wonder about the selection and try to make some interpretations. A child who comments that he knows how the boy in the story feels because he lost his bike once, too, is making a sort of interpretation by showing empathy for a story character. He is also responding emotionally to the story. Another child may remark that she doesn't like a story character because he often hurts other children and makes them afraid to play outside. She further reflects that this would be a terrible place to live if there were many bullies like that. Value judgment shows up in her response. At the same time, the judgment might reflect interpretation of the theme of a story and an evaluation of a story character's behavior.

Reading aloud may generate many kinds of responses. They should be accepted and encouraged, extended by questions when the occasion is right. Above all, remember that a good book, well read, brings responses from children who could not enjoy and respond to the book on their own because their reading ability would not permit it or from children who can read but too often, don't.

Storytelling

The storyteller's concerns are much like those of the oral reader, with the most apparent difference being that the storyteller does not use a book in presenting material to children. If you want to be a storyteller who re-creates a story so that it captivates your listeners, you might keep these three ideas in mind:

1. Choose a story that you like. If you enjoy the story, you will be able to infuse it with your special insight.
2. Know the story well enough to be comfortable with it and to avoid worry about a lapse of memory.
3. When you tell a story, it is important to establish a relationship with the audience so that they will share the mood of the story with you.

A person with a head full of stories to tell never needs to carry books. When a class goes on a field trip, the bus is often late; a good storyteller can gather the class around and make the time pass quickly. Many a situation which can alarm children unnecessarily or require restless waiting has been soothed with a story.

The successful storyteller learns how to capture the attention of the audience and hold it. You learn to observe those subtle signs of interest: staring eyes, still hands. You also learn the signs of flagging interest: wiggling, head-turning. By interpreting these signs correctly, the storyteller uses the tricks of the trade to revive interest, to retrieve the child who is on the verge of distraction. With knowledge of your audience, you emphasize those elements of a story that you know will be relished.

Selecting a Story to Tell

The easiest stories to begin with are folk tales. They are easy because they were created orally by storytellers and have perfect form for narration. The form is invariable: a clear, brief introduction that launches the conflict or problem; the development or body of the story with a rising action, increasing suspense, and an exciting climax that marks the turning point in the story and the fortunes of the hero; and, finally, a satisfying conclusion that settles everything—problems, conflicts, and villains all suitably resolved. From the simplest cumulative "Pancake" type of story, through "The Bremen Town-Musicians" and "Snow White," to the more subtle "Clever Manka" for the oldest children—these folk tales tell themselves with ease and will help you fall into the storytelling habit and develop your own unique style.

The skillful storyteller treats his or her material freely, but within traditional limits. Certain events, background, and word order in folk tales, for instance, are so traditional that they are an indispensable part of a storyteller's presentation.

Another good source of stories to tell are the myths. Many of the myths are long and may take two or three story periods to tell; for example, the stories of Perseus and of Theseus. Fortunately, these two tales have been well told by Ian Serraillier in *The Gorgon's Head* and *The Way of Danger*. Reading these books will show you why even the simplest myths demand more imagination in the telling and a more choice vocabulary than the folk tales.

Most stories written these days are for reading, not for telling, but here and there you will find little stories that are as perfect for telling as any folk tale. "Paddy's Three Pets" by Mary Phillips is a good example, also *Torten's Christmas Secret* by Maurice Dolbier, "Peter the Goldfish" by Julian Street, and *The Bears on Hemlock Mountain* by Alice Dalgliesh.

If you begin with your favorite folk tales and tell enough of them to get the feel and fun of storytelling in your very bones, then you will be better able to spot a likely candidate for your repertoire, whether it is old or new.

Learning and Telling a Story

Probably no two people learn and re-create stories in quite the same way, but visualizing characters and scenes often helps. In "The Pancake," you might see a snug kitchen with a mother standing close to the stove, her seven hungry children crowding much too near her to watch that fat, sizzling pancake. An old grandfather is sitting over in the corner smoking his pipe. Through the open door—it must be open because the pancake rolls through it—you might see a road winding over the hills and across the country and clear out of sight. You must see the characters, too, some in more detail than others, depending upon how dramatic their words or their roles are in the tale. Visualizing them undoubtedly helps in characterizing them; so if you see the sneering faces of Cinderella's sisters, something of the sneer gets into your interpretation of their words and behavior. Not that you do actually sneer, of course—that is stage business, not storytelling—but still a derisive suggestion creeps in. And if you are telling a hero tale, something noble and serious comes into your voice, face, and manner.

Choice of words is important in storytelling. As a storyteller, you cannot go far with a meager vocabulary; moreover, you must develop a sensitivity to language, so that you cannot possibly tell an Irish tale with the same vocabulary and cadence you use for a Norwegian story. Read the story aloud first until you get the feel and flavor of its special vocabulary and word patterns. While exact memorizing is usually the wrong approach to the folk tale, the other extreme is much worse—a slipshod telling, a careless use of words.

Such modern colloquialisms as "Boots got real mad," or "The princess looked really great," or "'OK,' said the lad," can ruin the mood and magic of a tale. Words must be chosen with a sensitive perception of the individual style of each tale. The dreamlike romance of "Sadko" calls for a very different choice of words from the rural dialect of the old man and his good wife in "Gudbrand on the Hillside." Voice, diction, and vocabulary demand the training of your ear. Listen to yourself—to your voice, your speech, and above all, to the appropriate word choice for your story.

Obviously, if you are going to tell a story you must know it thoroughly. This involves over-learning to such a degree that you cannot possibly forget the tale, but can stand aside and play with the interpretation of the story because you have no worries about the mechanics of recall. Some people feel that memorizing is the only solution. Others consider memorizing the wrong approach to the folk tale for two reasons: First, these naive tales do not have the formal perfection of the literary story; they were always kept fluid and personal by the old tellers. If they are memorized, they are likely to sound stilted and impersonal. Ruth Sawyer, in *The Way of the Storyteller*, pays a tribute to the storytelling of her Irish nurse, who was proud of her art and used it with great dignity. She would close a story with the saying, "Take it, and may the next one who tells it better it." This is exactly what can happen. Second, exact memorizing is not recommended because forgetting a single phrase or a connecting sentence may throw you off completely, so that you have to stop or start over or pause awkwardly while you rack your brain for the lost word. Such a pause, of course, spoils a story. On the other hand, if the story is thoroughly learned but not memorized it will remain in your memory for years.

The beginnings and endings of your stories, particularly, should be polished until they are smooth and sure. Some storytellers recommend memorizing the beginning and ending of a story and simply writing on a card the key phrases that will help you to recall each section of the story so that you do not omit an important part. The beginning requires special care because it establishes the mood of your tale. You may announce your story informally in any of a dozen ways: "Today we are going to hear about our old friends, 'The Three Billy-Goats Gruff.'" Or, "I've a new story for you today, and it's called 'The Fox and His Travels.'" Or, "You have all heard stories about 'Jack the Giant Killer,' but do you know there was a woman who got the best of a powerful giant? Our story is about her, and her name is 'Molly Whuppie.'"

Then, having announced your story, pause a moment—not too long, not long enough to let the children start squirming again, just long enough for a deep, quiet breath—and then begin.

Observing Response

A storyteller who has established rapport with the group and is able to maintain eye contact with the audience is in a unique position to notice the children's response to the story. The response in a listener's eyes or facial expression that indicates interest, enjoyment, or sadness is the kind of emotional response that is basic to other responses that may follow. That signal, subtle though it may be, indicates a grasp of the story and an ability to interact with characters, with the story line, or with a particular word choice which the listener finds appealing. In a sense, then, a good storyteller monitors the listener's reactions to a story by noticing physical responses and, primarily, facial expressions. You might ask yourself these questions when you have finished telling a story to a group of children:

1. Which children showed response during the story period?
2. What parts of the story evoked the most response?
3. How did the children show their reactions?
4. Did the reactions influence, in any way, your telling of the story?
5. Did any child comment about the story at some time after the story hour? If so, did the comment indicate emotional response? interpretation of the story? attention to literary characteristics such as style?
6. Do their reactions give you ideas for future story choices for this group?

Book Discussions

Book discussions can range from a highly structured classroom situation to a simple exchange of opinions between a librarian and a child after a storytelling session has concluded. Discussions can serve many purposes. They give children opportunity to vent their feelings about a story or poem. The give-and-take of discussion may help children interpret the meaning of a selection. Under adult guidance, book discussions can give children insight into an author's purpose and a character's motives and can help them to make reasoned evaluations of the general quality of a book. Discussions can also open children's minds to the many life experiences they meet vicariously through books—the problems of the aged, poor, orphaned, or disabled, or the way a story character forms values and changes behavior accordingly. Talking about incidents from a story can help children to develop empathy for people they might never know personally. There is a great need to prepare all children to accept and respect the disabled children who are being mainstreamed in many school districts. Reading and discussing books with disabled characters who are presented honestly and sensitively may be an important key. Discussions can also point out ways that books help us to know ourselves better.

Book discussions can help you to gain insight into children's values and can permit you to observe children's responses. The material on values-clarification discussion in Chapter 1 suggests some of the ways we might expect children to respond. Sometimes putting problems in terms of book characters makes them easier for children to discuss. For example, a classroom group discussed Kate's outrageous behavior in the first chapter of *The Good Master*. Of course they thoroughly enjoyed her antics, but they came to the conclusion that she behaved that way because she was "mad" at her father for sending her away, and so she took it out on her uncle's family. It was further agreed that most of us are likely to behave foolishly when we think we have received unjust treatment.

Selecting Material for Discussion

Book discussions may be based on selections children have read or on stories to which they have listened. A natural opportunity for discussion is following a storytelling or reading aloud session. Stories that are worthy of discussion have clearly developed themes of enough depth to raise questions that will encourage children to draw on their own experiences, interests, and concerns. Select material that allows children to discuss the humorous as well as the serious incidents in literature. Through the humor of Rosemary Wells's *Noisy Nora*, children see a view of life that makes it easier to accept misfortunes and disappointments. Humorous incidents as well as serious ones can lead children to examine their own values.

Fiction, poetry, nonfiction, picture books—all can be effective for stimulating discussion. Children's interests and reading and listening abilities should, of course, be taken into account when selecting material for discussion. The length of time available for the session, too, will influence your decision of how many aspects of a selection, or how complex a work, you will be able to explore. A third guideline should be your own knowledge of the literature you plan to use. In order to conduct a good discussion, you should have a thorough grasp of the themes and literary structure of the work, including an understanding of each character and of the techniques the author has used for character development. Your preassessment of a selection influences the depth and quality of a guided discussion; you draw on that as you plan your sequence of questions.

Discussion of wordless picture books is a fine vehicle for encouraging young children to respond to illustrations and to develop a sense of plot structure at the same time. The best wordless picture books interest children enough to evoke emotional involvement with the story told through the pictures. They also have enough plot so that the action carries a child along from one page to the next. Perhaps most important, however, the pictures supply some details necessary to create a good story but they leave enough to the child's imagination to encourage inference about details of characterization and plot. Those inferences are the heart of response to wordless picture books. They can be encouraged by repeated experiences in telling the story from the pictures, especially in a one-to-one situation between an adult and a child. An adult guiding the retelling of a wordless picture-book story can encourage inferences by asking questions such as: What do you think will happen next? Why is she doing that? Where do you think he is going? and others specific to the story.

Formulating Questions

As you prepare for a book discussion, you will need to keep in mind both the qualities of the selection and the abilities of the children. In order to make a pre-assessment of the material, you might ask yourself these questions:

1. What are the important ideas to be gained from the selection?
2. What aspects of the story will require exploration if children are to understand and interpret them?
3. With which story characters are children most likely to identify?
4. Will they need help in understanding a character's motives?
5. Are there aspects of style or figurative language that should be discussed in order to aid in interpretation?
6. How can this selection be related to children's experiences, interests, and concerns?

Using these questions as steppingstones, you can formulate specific questions that will guide children to interpret and evaluate literature, to note devices an author or poet has used, and, above all, to interact emotionally with the story.

Studies of teachers' questions during reading instruction have indicated that teachers rely too much on factual questions that have only one right answer. Such questions do not lead to a discussion of a work, they simply result in a sort of tennis game between adult and children. (What was the name of the dog? Where did the pirate bury the treasure? and the like.) Aside from a few factual questions which may be necessary in order to produce information to serve as a basis for later discussion, most of your questions should ask children to infer, to interpret, to evaluate, and to identify with characters. Their answers of course may vary because each child comes to a literary experience with a different background.

Examples of some open-ended questions based on one chapter of Farley Mowat's *Owls in the Family* follow, with types of possible responses shown in parentheses:

In what ways are the owls, Wol and Weeps, different? (comparing characters and identifying characterization)

Why do you think the author made the two owls so different? (literary judgment, interpretation)

What questions would you like to ask Billy about his owls? (involvement, interpretation)

What was the funniest part of the story? (involvement, evaluation)

What is so funny about the scene where two owls try to learn to fly? (literary judgment, involvement)

How did Wol feel when he fell to the ground the first time he flew? Have you ever felt that way? How did you behave? (involvement, empathy)

Were the owls tame or wild? What information did you get from the story to back your answer? (interpretation, literary judgment regarding character traits)

Many other questions could, of course, also be used. A discussion should be fluid and kept personal in terms of the story and the group, following up on answers so that students can pursue a question to greater depth. As a follow-up to the last question in the previous list, you might want to ask: What can happen to a wild animal after it has been tamed? What is the author telling you in this story that might apply to any wild animal? (evaluation, interpretation of main idea, literary understanding of theme)

In general, then, discussion questions focus on characters, on favorite parts of the plot, on the relationship between episodes, on the author's message, and on evaluation of a selection. Some basic question types which can be adapted to many books include:

Which story character did you like best? Why? (evaluation, involvement)

If you had been a character in this story, how would you have acted if _____? (involvement, empathy, interpretation)

Do you think _____ did the right thing when he/she _____? (evaluation, valuing)

How else could _____ have handled the problem about the _____? What would you have done? (involvement, evaluation, valuing, interpretation)

What do you think this author is trying to tell us about the way people learn to have respect for themselves? (interpretation, literary understanding of theme)

What important idea (or theme) did you find throughout this story? (interpretation of main idea, literary understanding of theme)

What was the most interesting or exciting part of the story? (evaluation, involvement)

Did you learn anything from the story that will help you get along better with people and perhaps understand yourself better? (valuing, empathy)

How is this story like _____ (another story they know)? (literary judgment, interpretation)

How did the author manage to make this so funny that you laughed out loud? What techniques did he/she use? (literary judgment of style, involvement)

What does _____ (figure of speech) mean in this poem? (literary knowledge, interpretation)

In general, the questions beginning with *why*, *what*, and *which* lead to a more open discussion than the sorts of questions beginning with *when* and *where*.

A questioning technique which can be very effective in helping children to become involved with a story character or situation requires that you preface a question by asking the child to take the point of view of a story character. This technique works not only to create involvement with human characters, but also with animal characters in some stories. In *Owls in the Family*, for instance, some children become so involved with the owls that they are easily able to respond to a question like: "You are Mutt [the family dog]. Why do you defend Weeps from other dogs even though you don't seem to like owls yourself?" Answers may show that children recognize that quality in a family dog that demonstrates a responsible feeling to protect all who live under that roof and perhaps senses that the weaknesses of some family members require greater care. Using the character-point-of-view question as a beginning, you can help children to sense the author's point of view by asking questions such as: "How would the story be told if the author were telling it through Wol's eyes?" "Who is the author using as the storyteller here?" "Is it one of the story characters or is the author reporting everything that all characters experience and think?"

Pacing a Discussion

An adult guiding a book discussion has the responsibility of keeping it going by interjecting appropriate questions. Since children are responding to one another's questions as well as to the adults' questions, skill is required to keep the discussion from rambling and to maintain a pace that holds interest. The ability to know *when* to ask another question or to probe an answer more deeply is one of the keys to an effective discussion. Linked to that ability is the sense of how long and when to pause so that students can reflect on the question and synthesize their thoughts to formulate a good answer.

Some work has been reported in science education which relates to pace of questioning.[1] Essentially, the work has involved monitoring the amount of time between questions to see whether the length of time allowed influences the kinds of responses given. Findings suggest that a greater amount of "wait-time" leads to responses showing higher levels of thinking about the problem (above factual reporting, for example). These findings in turn have led to some work in training teachers to increase the amount of time they allow students before going on to another question or giving the answer themselves.

The increase in interpretation and other higher-level responses in science activities may be a guideline to adults who lead book discussions. A factual question, as "Who were the characters in this story?" may not require a very long wait for answers. It simply requires recalling information. A question that requires interpretation or evaluation, however, requires children to relate their own experiences to the story and, in the case of evaluation, to make judgments based on that synthesis. If you ask, "Do you think that Max acted wisely in the way he treated the wild things? Why or why not?" children will need a longer time. Questions of this sort require an interaction with the story to formulate an answer and will usually require some reflection. The combination of open-ended questions and enough time for reflective answers should encourage literary responses that show involvement with a story but also some attempt to interpret the story or to make judgments about it.

Viewpoint

No longer is it enough to discuss literature as though one were on a treasure hunt, a hunt for an author's or teacher's intended meaning. Now teachers must consider the text, and the readers, and the context in which a text is read and discussed. If students don't connect with what they're reading, we need to ask why, not simply to assume that they weren't trying. If students differ in their interpretations of a text, both among themselves and with us, we need to explore the roots of these differences and try to understand how they arose, what they mean, and how they can make our discussions richer. We need to consider what students can teach each other about literature, and what they can teach us. We need to be readers ourselves, as well as teachers, ready to explore the possibilities that every encounter with a literary text holds. When we do that we model fruitful behavior, allow our students to be real readers, and allow literature to take its rightful place in our lives. Reading a good book should encourage rather than discourage, should enrich rather than impoverish. Knowing the complexity that surrounds any act of aesthetic reading can sensitize us, as teachers and readers, to the needs of our students, both as learners and as human beings.

From, "Readers, Texts, and Contexts: A Response-Based View of Literature in the Classroom" by Lee Galda, *The New Advocate,* Spring, 1988, Volume 1, Number 2. Reprinted by permission of the author.

[1]Mary Budd Rowe, "Reflections on Wait-time: Some Methodological Questions." *Journal of Research in Science Teaching* 11 (1974): 263–279.

Organizing for Discussion

Many book discussions are adult-led because they follow the reading or telling of a story to a group. The adult may be a parent, librarian, or a teacher. A large-group discussion requires a leader who is able to maintain a good pace, to encourage many children to participate, and to keep the discussion pertinent. Obviously, the open-ended question, especially one which asks for a personal involvement with some aspect of the story or an interpretation based on personal experiences, can permit almost every child to respond if there is time. A leader must be able to accept all responses but keep children focused on the question. Furthermore, the leader should try to maintain a neutral attitude in conducting discussions and not interject his or her own opinions. If children know that you censure the behavior of a certain story character, they are less likely to give you open, candid answers. On the other hand, you can build on their naive responses in some cases to lead them to a better understanding of a character's behavior and why certain kinds of behavior are not highly valued in our society.

An adult-led small-group discussion is often more enjoyable for children than a large-group discussion. They need to be at ease with the other participants and to feel free to ask as well as answer questions. Small-group discussions can follow oral reading or storytelling by an adult. They can also work well when the children have all read the same story on their own. In working with gifted children, a seminar version of the small-group discussion is effective. In this arrangement, each student either reads the same book or reads a book that represents a particular genre. For example, all may choose one book of modern fantasy. Your questions during the discussion guide the students to see how all of their books are similar in terms of fantasy. Have characters been manipulated so that they are talking animals, small people, superhuman beings? Is the setting on another planet, inside our earth, or in a mythical country? Has the time been manipulated so that the story takes place far in the future? Such a discussion can help children to note literary devices used by an author. It can also lead to evaluation of the books and to interpretation of events in the stories.

Another kind of small-group discussion is that in which one child acts as leader. Though a child must be relatively mature to keep a discussion going, the group's responses can be much freer than when an adult is in the group. Because student leaders will not be adept at keeping a discussion going at a good pace, the amount of time allotted should be fairly short, probably not more than fifteen minutes.

Viewpoint

Although children long for laughter, too often the child's point of view is considered suspect by many adults who feel that the purpose of any book written for children is to teach; and they ask authors the earnest question, What are you trying to teach in your books?

Many children, pressured into believing that the books they read should teach them a lesson, write sad little remarks in letters from school, such as "I like *Runaway Ralph* because it taught me to be satisfied with what I have." I cannot believe that a fantasy about a mouse who runs away on a miniature motorcycle to a children's camp in search of peanut butter-and-jelly sandwiches does any such thing; and I feel sorry for the boy who asks, "Is the moral of *Henry Huggins* if you find a dog without a collar, you get to keep it?" The fourth-grade child who writes a desperate-sounding letter from school saying, "I read *The Mouse and the Motorcycle* and couldn't find a single thing wrong with it," is meeting a different kind of pressure; he is expected to be a critic instead of being allowed to enjoy reading. Children would learn so much more if they were allowed to relax, enjoy a story, and discover what it is they want or need from books. They might even learn to enjoy reading, especially if they find in the early grades humorous books that make them laugh.

From "The Laughter of Children" by Beverly Cleary in *The Horn Book Magazine*, October, 1982. Copyright © 1982 by Beverly Cleary. Reprinted by permission of the author.

Book discussions can occur in many situations, among them a one-to-one discussion of child and adult or child and child. In these informal discussions, the child can use an adult as a sounding board as was the case when a child asked, "Were you disappointed when Sam (Jean Craighead George's *My Side of the Mountain*) had people as visitors?" Children need time to sit quietly and chat with one another about books, too. When you overhear some of those conversations, notice the kinds of information discussed. (Needless to say, you do not intrude.) Some of the most persuasive "book-selling" goes on in those meetings and some good ideas about favorite passages are also exchanged. To facilitate discussions, you can set up a classroom or library corner where children and adults feel free to talk about books in their spare time. By providing the right atmosphere, you can inspire a natural response to literature and a love for many kinds of books.

Dramatic Activities

Dramatic activities provide marvelous opportunities for children to interact with literature. They are especially good for young children who are able to respond physically even though they may not be able to respond verbally with much ease. The activities we will discuss which work well as vehicles for literary response are role-playing, story theater, oral interpretation (including Readers Theatre), creative dramatics, and puppetry. Story theater and puppetry are activities that children who are slow learners can enjoy.

Role-Playing

Role-playing is an educational strategy. It sets up a problem situation for children to come to grips with and allows them to "play through" the problem in order to discover alternate solutions and the results of those solutions. The emphases are on decision making and its consequences, and the goal is to promote social values. In the process, personal values may be influenced rather significantly.

Experiences with literature can be enhanced by role-playing. When children are involved with a character and are confronted with that character's problem as they are in role-playing, the way is open to a satisfying literary response. By sharing the challenges and frustrations of a literary character, children may learn to appreciate an author's way of handling plot and characterization and at the same time develop personal and social values.

The material best suited to role-playing is the problem story, so-called because it develops a problem students can become involved in, and try to cope. Some stories written especially for the role-playing situation are included in *Role-Playing for Social Values* by Fannie and George Shaftel. A well-written piece of realistic fiction can also provide thought-provoking problem situations. In choosing episodes from literature, be certain that the characters are well developed and the problem situation is clearly defined. Beyond these points, the plot should have a logical stopping place so that students can play out their endings. Books with episodic plot structure, in which each chapter is an almost self-contained story, work well because the length of the selection is easier to handle than a full-length book.

What kinds of problems provide good material for role-playing? First of all, they should be problems with which students can identify. That means well-stated universal fears, concerns, or temptations—difficulties common to people in all kinds of environments. If the setting and story characters are familiar to your students, the problem situation may also be easier for them to manage. A second basis for judging material is whether the problem it raises will help students to develop a personal value system.

The problem stories included by the Shaftels involve situations dealing with integrity, responsibility for others, being fair, accepting others, and wishing you were bigger or better. Some books with sections that develop these problems include these:

Responsibility for Others—*Don't Take Teddy* by Babbis Friis-Baastad
Being Fair—*A Bargain for Frances* by Russell Hoban
Accepting Others—*After the Goat Man* by Betsy Byars, *Take Wing* and *From Anna* by Jean Little, "Inviting Jason" from *Altogether, One at a Time* by Elaine Konigsburg

Accepting Others, Surmounting Prejudice
—*The Other Side of the Fence* by Molly
Cone, *Berries Goodman* by Emily Neville,
and *The Borrowed House* by Hilda Van
Stockum

Wishing You Were Bigger or Better—*Wait
for William* by Marjorie Flack, *The Ears of
Louis* by Constance Greene

The general procedure for conducting a
role-playing session includes these nine steps
recommended by Shaftels:[2]

1. Warming-up (teacher introduction and
   reading of the problem story)
2. Selecting role-players
3. Preparing the audience to observe
4. Setting the stage
5. Enactmenting
6. Discussing and evaluating
7. Further enactmenting
8. Further discussing
9. Generalizing

In Step 1, the adult encourages children to
think about how the story might end. This
alerts them and helps them to identify with
literary characters. A typical question would
be, "What do you think will happen now?" In
Step 2, the adult can ask students to describe
characters and then ask a student who seems to
identify with a character to play that role. Step
3 requires that the audience members be prepared for their part. They may be asked to
watch carefully to decide whether the solution
is a realistic one. In Step 4, the players decide
what they are going to do but do not practice
dialogue. The adult can help them get into the
roles by encouraging them to describe the
staging they are using. Step 5 focuses on the
role-playing itself with each actor playing the
part of the character he or she represents.
Acting ability should not be criticized, since the
focus is on the problem solution. Step 6 includes the follow-up discussion and evaluation.
During that period the observers discuss their
opinions of the character portrayals and of the
consequences of their actions. Adults should

encourage children to think in terms of consequences and alternative behaviors. In Steps 7,
8, and 9, the role-players try new interpretations based on ideas that came from the discussion in Step 6. The final step is important
because it encourages students to make some
assessment of the outcomes of each portrayal
and to determine what they think is the best
way to deal with the problem.

Although the approach to role-playing developed by Fannie Shaftel uses an unfinished
problem story with which children must work,
this procedure can be adapted so that after
reading an entire book, as a sort of post-
reading or listening experience, children are
asked to explore different possible solutions to
a problem situation by playing the roles of story
characters as they might deal with that problem. For example, this situation might be set up
for Vera and Bill Cleaver's book *Where the Lilies
Bloom:* You are Mary Call Luther and her
family. You have been offered a lot of money to
let a motion picture company film your home
and tell the story of your lives. How are you
going to handle this? What will you decide? In
this technique, as with point-of-view questioning, broach the first question as "You are
_____" to help children get into their roles
and see the problem through their characters'
eyes.

During Steps 5–9 of the Shaftel strategy for
conducting role-playing, children's responses
should be obvious to the adult observer. Questions such as the following will help you to
evaluate the kinds and degrees of responses
made:

1. Do students seem able to interpret a
   character's feeling about the problem?
2. Do students show emotional involvement
   with characters and with the problems
   posed? Are they able to put themselves
   into a character role?
3. In discussion and enactment, do students
   show empathy for characters?
4. Does the question of values enter into the
   discussion, either explicitly or implicitly?

In role-playing, response is, of course, the key
to success. And as in other activities, some
responses show greater depth of interpretation
than others. Certainly, a child who is able to

[2]From *Role-Playing for Social Values* by Fannie R. and
George Shaftel. Englewood Cliffs, N.J.: Prentice-Hall,
1967, p. 84.

speak convincingly in the role of a story character is making an attempt to interpret that character's approach to the problem. If a child is also able to assume some of the emotions of a character, so much the better. In many children, a strong interaction with a character shows in the content of what is spoken, in the tone of voice used, and in nonverbal signals such as facial expression and body movements.

As important as response to characters is, however, the crucial reaction in role-playing is a reasoned response to the problem situation. Children's responses often show them grappling with their own values in order to seek out a solution to the problem. Sometimes a response is complete enough to include reasons for the solution or to show the mental steps the child went through before arriving at the solution. Children who are able to carry out dialogue effectively while staying within the roles of their story characters can arrive at a problem solution through the conversation. This shows a high level of response in terms of interpretation, emotional involvement, and evaluation of a situation. Whether their problem solution achieves a high moral value should be looked at separately.

Story Theater

Story theater is a kind of dramatization in which a narrator reads or tells the story while the actors pantomime the action. In story theater, inanimate objects—a rock, for example—as well as animal or human characters may be represented by players in the pantomime.

Directing story theater is not difficult. The emphasis on pantomime rather than more formal acting with dialogue removes some of the demands and complexity of creative dramatics. The important steps in directing are these:

1. Read aloud or tell the story to be dramatized.
2. Help children to identify characters (animate and inanimate).
3. Guide the group pantomiming of each character part and make sure some child will be responsible for that part in the dramatization.
4. Review the story plot with the group so that children will be ready to participate.
5. Allow time for individuals to practice the actions they plan to use for their pantomimes.
6. Arrange the area where the dramatization will take place. As with creative dramatics, no props are needed. Instead, in story theater, children can portray inanimate objects referred to in the story.
7. Read or tell the story as the actors pantomime it. (Note: a child may also serve as narrator, especially if the story is read.)

A description of the preparation for a story theater production of *Anansi the Spider*, illustrated by Gerald McDermott, will illustrate the steps outlined above. With the children sitting comfortably around her, the leader read aloud the story of Anansi, showing McDermott's brilliantly colored illustrations. At the close of the reading, she asked students to think back through the story to identify the characters they would need if they were to dramatize it. She wrote the names of characters on the board as they were mentioned and again showed the illustration of the globe of light to remind the children that they might also need to include it, as well as the forest in which it was seen. The character list complete, the leader called attention to one character at a time, asking children how they would pantomime that character and giving them a few minutes to try out the characterization. When all the characters had been discussed and dramatized, the leader asked for volunteers to take the character parts in the story theater production. She then reviewed the plot briefly with the group. They arranged themselves in the proper locations for the beginning of the story (some outside of the "stage" area, waiting for entrance) and the leader began reading the story, pacing it so that children had time to carry out their actions, and to make entrances. When the story was over, several children expressed a desire to try it again because they weren't quite satisfied with their performances. After a short discussion of the problems they encountered, they practiced for a few minutes and the leader again read the entire story. What evaluation there is must be done by the actors, since

Wearing self-made costumes, these first graders are taking part in story theater activities—pantomiming the action while a narrator reads or tells the story. Stories and picture books with a strong sense of rhythm and movement are excellent sources of material.

everyone is a participant. (If you have a large group, expand the numbers and kinds of inanimate objects portrayed such as trees, doors, flowers, and the like.) However, the focus is not on evaluation so much as on freedom to participate and a genuine enjoyment of the experience. That freedom is enhanced because there is no audience. The experience is really one of group cooperation toward a common goal.

When you select material for story theater, bear in mind that the best material for work with children is a folk tale or a myth with distinctive characters and a relatively uncomplicated plot. Since children will interpret the characters through pantomime only, the best selections will provide clear distinctions among characters that can be shown easily through large body movements. In *Anansi the Spider*, for example, the six sons have such names as Roadbuilder, River Drinker, Stone Thrower, Game Skinner, See Trouble, and Cushion. Children find it easy to devise movements that will indicate the character.

The cumulative plot commonly found in folk tales works well for story theater, especially with young children who need a fairly simple plot structure. Stories such as "The Three Billy-Goats Gruff" or "The Three Little Pigs" are fun for preschool and primary age children. In "The Three Little Pigs," the cast of characters can be augmented by allowing some children to play the roles of the pigs' houses. A more elaborate folk-tale plot, such as "The Bremen Town-Musicians," is great fun for older children. In addition to the four animals, you can have as large a band of robbers as the stage area can accommodate.

As you read folk literature, try to pick out tales and myths that would lend themselves well to pantomime. Keep your own file of good story theater selections. Remember that children (even intermediate-grade children) enjoy playing animal roles as much as they do human roles. Don't overlook tales such as "Gudbrand on the Hillside" where the husband sets off to sell his cow but trades it stupidly for a whole succession of animals and comes home with only a shilling. That story has enough animal roles and interesting human characters to make it a good choice. *Why Mosquitoes Buzz in People's Ears*, told by Verna Aardema and illustrated by Leo and Diane Dillon, is a fine choice for younger children.

Story theater material need not be limited to folk literature. Picture books such as *Drummer Hoff* by Ed and Barbara Emberley, *Rosie's Walk* by Pat Hutchins, or *Mr. Gumpy's Outing* by John Burningham are good sources for dramatization. So are poems like "Days That The Wind Takes Over" from Karla Kuskin's *Near the Window Tree*, "The Monkeys and the Crocodile" from Laura Richards's *Tirra Lirra*, and any number of *Mother Goose* rhymes like "Hey! diddle, diddle."

Material for use with older students should

include some of the more complex folk tales and myths. Many of Aesop's fables are effective in story theater, among them "The Lion and the Mouse" or "Belling the Cat." Good folk tales are "Momotaro: Boy-of-the-Peach," "The Tiger, the Brahman and the Jackal," and "Anansi's Hat-shaking Dance." Myths and epics that make effective productions are "Atalanta's Race," "Cupid and Psyche," and "The Curse of Polyphemus." Selected episodes from *Robin Hood* also provide good material for pantomime as do episodes from *Pippi Longstocking*, *Homer Price* (especially the dough-nut-machine scene with students representing the machine), *The Pushcart War*, and other contemporary books. Once you begin to work with story theater, you will find many poems, tales, and episodes from full-length books which work well.

Response to literature is seen in story theater in creative character portrayal which shows appreciation for the story character in relation to the complete story. Response is also revealed through the smoothness with which a child fits a character interpretation into the ongoing dramatization. When this happens, a child has grasped the plot structure and, in some cases, shows an appreciation for the style of the story by attempting to suit the style and pace of the action to the style of the selection. A young child responding to the rhythm of "Ride a cock horse" by playing the character role in perfect rhythm with the *Mother Goose* rhyme is acknowledging the style of a piece. As you observe children engaged in story theater, you will notice many other examples of emotional response, interpretation, and response to the literary qualities of a piece.

Oral Interpretation

Another response activity for children to try is to orally interpret a story. By oral interpretation we mean a degree of dramatization with the voice to re-create a story vividly for listeners and to give a sense of the kinds of people that story characters might be. Notice that we said "dramatization with the voice." Oral interpretation does not include physical acting out except for an occasional gesture. Oral interpre-

tation techniques are, of course, necessary for any successful oral reading, and are frequently used by adults who read to children and by children who read aloud, either voluntarily or as part of a classroom assignment. People who read aloud effectively, whether adults or children, have mastered the art of using the voice expressively. Because children need guidance and practice in that skill, oral interpretation work should be part of every classroom literature and reading program. Suggestions given here may be useful for adults, too, who wish to improve their oral reading.

Oral interpretation enriches the literary experience for reader and listener. At its best it grows out of interaction with a story and its characters. It is a re-creation of the original story, not a transformation of it as in creative drama, but a reading in which the reader interprets underlying themes, characters, and plot, and projects the combined image for listeners. The child who reads obviously must understand and appreciate the story. It is also important that the story characters take shape and become almost real for the reader. As to plot, the reader must recognize major scenes and transition passages so that the reading carries on at a pace that highlights important events and contrasts one character with another. Because oral interpretation does not demand the more physical interpretation involved in role-playing, creative drama, and story theater, children who are hesitant about performing may find it a more rewarding and less threatening response activity.

As with all the activities we have been discussing, the first and most important consideration in selecting material is that it should be interesting to the children who will read it. In many cases, that means it should be about experiences they have shared. A fast-paced mystery or action story is another good choice to interest readers and listeners.

In choosing stories for oral interpretation, look for selections that have a number of characters, preferably characters that differ in ages and/or personality so that the readers will be challenged to use their voices expressively to differentiate one character from another. The quality of the dialogue is, therefore, of prime importance.

Material for use with younger readers might include Else Minarik's *A Kiss for Little Bear* or any of the other *Little Bear* books. They are easy reading books, yet are well written with dialogue that makes sense and is not stilted. The cumulative folk tales like "Henny Penny" or "The Gingerbread Boy" provide enough dialogue and repetition to keep young readers interested. Pat Hutchins's *The Surprise Party* works well, too. Another book which does not have dialogue but can work for oral interpretation is *Drummer Hoff* by Barbara and Ed Emberley. Stories that are superior in characterization and style of writing and that give children a chance to use their voices to interpret joy, anger, fear—a range of emotions—can be used for a good oral interpretation experience. A book that is weak in style or its characterization will not work. You can easily get a sense of an author's style by reading aloud a page or two. A book written by a good stylist practically reads itself and you find yourself naturally making the most of every nuance. Identify and keep a file of books you feel have these qualities.

It is easier to find oral interpretation material for children above third grade. Some authors seem to write dialogue more naturally than others. E. L. Konigsburg, Madeleine L'Engle, and Beverly Cleary are three authors who write character parts that children enjoy interpreting and dialogue that seems natural. *The Wind in the Willows* and *The Hobbit* have chapters which make excellent material for oral interpretation, too. As you find other authors you enjoy reading aloud, add their books to your list of recommended materials. Remember, though, that a book should be scanned for those passages which may be too difficult or less interesting for young readers.

Poetry is a rich source of material for practice of oral interpretation skills. The second stanza of "The Pied Piper of Hamelin" by Robert Browning is a good one to use; so are Carl Sandburg's "Buffalo Dusk" (*Smoke and Steel*), and "Seal" by William Jay Smith (*Boy Blue's Book of Beasts*). "Warblers" by Paul Fleischman is a poem that invites oral reading because it is for two voices. The effect can be achieved by individuals or by groups reading in unison.

Warblers

Warblers warbling	*Warblers warbling*
Nashville warblers	*Nashville warblers*
Townsend's Myrtle Mourning Wilson's warblers	*Townsend's Myrtle Mourning Wilson's warblers*
Yellow-throated	*Yellow-throated*
Chestnut-sided	*Chestnut-sided*
Dozens of them	*Dozens of them*
Each one different.	*Each one different.*
	Hooded warblers
Hooded warblers	
	Hermit warblers
Hermit warblers	
	Bachman's Brewster's
Bachman's Brewster's	
Blue-winged warblers warbling.	*Blue-winged warblers warbling.*[3]

This poem, like some others suitable for oral interpretation, is written in a form that immediately gives a young reader some clues about how it should be read. Lines are repeated in a two-part arrangement that is suitable for oral interpretation.

Another poem that is great fun to read aloud is David McCord's "Every Time I Climb a Tree." Children understand the joy of tree climbing and can use their voices effectively to relate the excitement of finding a nest high in a tree and looking down over all the nearby countryside.

[3]"Warblers" from *I Am Phoenix: Poems for Two Voices* by Paul Fleischman. Copyright © 1985 by Paul Fleischman. Reprinted by permission of HarperCollins Publishers.

Every Time I Climb a Tree

Every time I climb a tree
Every time I climb a tree
Every time I climb a tree
I scrape a leg
Or skin a knee
And every time I climb a tree
I find some ants
Or dodge a bee
And get the ants
All over me

And every time I climb a tree
Where have you been?
They say to me
But don't they know that I am free
Every time I climb a tree?
I like it best
To spot a nest
That has an egg
Or maybe three

And then I skin
The other leg
But every time I climb a tree
I see a lot of things to see
Swallows, rooftops and TV
And all the fields and farms there be
Every time I climb a tree
Though climbing may be good for ants
It isn't awfully good for pants
But still it's pretty good for me
Every time I climb a tree[4]

These poems not only read aloud exceptionally well, but they sharpen children's sensitivity to the use of language and the creation of mood.

When you guide students in preparation for the oral interpretation of a story or poem, you first need to encourage them to read the passage through carefully in order to note: (1) the characters—who they are, what kinds of people they are, and how each might talk; (2) the plot—how it develops, what the climax is, and where it occurs; (3) high points of the plot which should be emphasized in the reading; and (4) specific words or phrases which should be emphasized. In reading poetry, this last point is the crucial one. Obviously such close analysis will require several close readings of the selection. You may want to encourage students to underline (mentally or with a soft pencil) the crucial words, to show where the voice would be raised or lowered, or to mark critical punctuation marks so that important pauses will be observed.

Viewpoint

These teachers continually helped children make connections between poets and between poems with similar themes or styles. The emphasis of these activities was on heightening enjoyment and building a shared context of common experiences with poetry. Additionally, they hoped children would begin developing an awareness of the body of poetic literature.

Both teachers helped children build functional knowledge of poets' names as well as an ability to discern the unique voices of different poets like Carl Sandburg, Robert Frost, David McCord and Myra Cohn Livingston through reading poetry by a wide variety of poets, always mentioning the poet's name as they did this. Gradually, as the children acquired a repertoire of experiences with professionally written poetry, the teachers would challenge them to make connections through questions like the following:

"Does anybody know anything else by this poet?"

"What kinds of poems does this person write?"

"What did we think about when we read those other poems by this person?"

Eventually, the children became so skilled at this that the teachers would often introduce a poem without stating the poet's name, then challenge the children to guess who wrote the poem by listening to its "voice."

From "Sharing Poetry with Children" by Amy McClure, The Bulletin, Spring 1987, Volume 8, Number 7, p. 7. Reprinted by permission of the CLA Bulletin.

[4]"Every Time I Climb a Tree" from *One at a Time* by David McCord. Copyright © 1952 by David McCord. Reprinted by permission of Little, Brown.

Once this kind of analysis has been completed, children should turn to the vocal interpretation of what is on the page. And this involves an interpretation of character roles which draws on the reader's ability to interact with the feelings and ideas of those characters. Vocal interpretation also involves manipulation of the voice to produce tone, inflection, and pauses that will create the desired effect and convey the emotional tone of the passage.

If the oral interpretation involves poetry, children should practice the oral reading until the flow of words is appropriate to the rhythm pattern of the poem. Children working with free verse may need even more guidance in suiting the pace of reading to the mood of the poem. When they have had time to perfect the reading of poem or story, the finished performance should be taped or presented to an audience.

Choral Speaking

You may want to introduce your class to choral speaking to give an added dimension to their enjoyment of poetry. Choral speaking is an oral interpretation activity which gives children opportunity to enjoy and experiment with the sound of literature. Although some prose, especially folk literature, adapts well to choral speaking, poetry is the easiest form to use and usually the most effective, since a poet is generally concerned with effects of sound. The rhyme and meter of poetry appeal to children, and rhymes that are pleasant to hear can also be fun to say. The pleasure of interpreting a favorite poem orally is one of the rewards of choral speaking. Another is the sense of group participation toward an artistic effect. When children are accustomed to hearing poetry; when they have discovered how much like music it is in its variety of rhythms, moods, and melodies; and when they like it well enough to explore further, you may tell them something about choral speaking or speaking choirs.

Effective choral speaking requires the same attention to key words and pauses as effective oral interpretation of any kind. Children should probably hear a poem several times in order to sense the mood they will want to convey, whether rollicking, funny, sad, mysterious, or wondering. The next step is to help them identify key words in a line that should be emphasized. That helps to develop a natural flow to the speaking, one that clarifies the sense, and can help to eliminate some of the sing-song quality that often goes with poetry reading. In that regard, you may want to call attention to the punctuation marks which are signals to pause—periods, commas, and dashes. Attention to them can help to keep a group together as well as to increase the effectiveness of the presentation.

Mood is important in choral speaking and can be enhanced by building contrast between parts of the selection. Grouping voices for effect is a good technique. A mysterious or scary part can be taken by a group of children with lower voices. By contrast, children with high voices can be grouped to speak lines that have a lilt and a happy swing. Another way of achieving contrast in sound is to have the whole group speak most of the lines and assign lines requiring special effects to a single voice. Remind children to keep their voices light and natural. Increase in volume can be achieved by adding more voices rather than forcing the tone.

Choral speaking is much like singing. Careful breath control and attention to rhythm are important. Sometimes, with formal verse choirs, one person acts as a director, using hand movements similar to those used with a singing chorus, but this is rare. For most informal situations, you need not direct the children but just get them started together, letting the rhythm of the piece carry them through.

Familiar lines and phrases in poetry and prose can be a good introduction to choral speaking. If you are reading aloud a folk tale such as "The Three Billy-Goats Gruff," encourage children to join you in "Trip, trap! Trip, trap! Trip, trap! went the bridge," increasing in volume when the middle-sized goat crosses and becoming very loud for the big billy goat's crossing.

For older children, "Overheard on a Saltmarsh" by Harold Monro is a good introduction to choral speaking through unison speaking of lines. This poem is essentially a dialogue between a goblin and a nymph. After several unison readings, you might want to read the goblin part (marked with a *G*) and let the whole group of children read the nymph part (*N*).

Later, you can divide the children into two groups so that one group takes each part. This same procedure can be useful in introducing other poems, too.

(G) *Nymph, nymph, what are your beads?*
(N) *Green glass, goblin. Why do you stare at them?*
(G) *Give them me.*
(N)   *No.*
(G) *Give them me. Give them me.*
(N)   *No.*
(G) *Then I will howl all night in the reeds,*
    Lie in the mud and howl for them.
(N) *Goblin, why do you love them so?*
(G) *They are better than stars or water,*
    Better than voices of winds that sing,
    Better than any man's fair daughter,
    Your green glass beads on a silver ring.
(N) *Hush, I stole them out of the moon.*
(G) *Give me your beads, I desire them.*
(N)   *No.*
(G) *I will howl in a deep lagoon*
    For your green glass beads, I love them so.
    Give them me. Give them.
(N)   *No.*[5]

A good choral-speaking file of poetry and prose is useful. Anthologies of children's literature, such as *The Scott, Foresman Anthology*,[6] contain many poems and folk tales suitable for choral speaking. Try to find a number of poems you would like to use plus several folk tales or other short prose pieces. Keep them in a looseleaf notebook or card file and add new selections as you find them.

Readers Theatre

In addition to choral speaking, the form known as Readers Theatre has become popular as a means of staging oral interpretation presentations. Readers Theatre requires not one reader, but a narrator and as many readers as are needed to cover all the character parts. This more formal technique is especially effective for children who are secure enough readers that they can direct their attention to the interpretation of character parts, following the written story only as a sort of script.

When you look for Readers Theatre material, look for good characterization and a style that reads aloud comfortably. You can judge the effectiveness of the style by reading a section aloud and listening for a natural flow of language. Selections for Readers Theatre should have enough characters to make the reading interesting but probably not more than five or six for a smooth production. The narrator provides the description that cannot be handled through dialogue and serves as a bridge between dialogue sections so that the plot moves along clearly. If the narrator's part includes lengthy discussions or descriptions and if the selection is otherwise effective, you might want to consider cutting the length of such passages. Some books that provide good excerpts for Readers Theatre are Robert O'Brien's *Mrs. Frisby and the Rats of NIMH*, Elaine Konigsburg's *From the Mixed-Up Files of Mrs. Basil E. Frankweiler* and *About the B'nai Bagels*, and Else Minarik's *A Kiss for Little Bear*. Although this last book may be read completely, short sections of the other books may be selected on the basis of the criteria we have been discussing.

Guiding Readers Theatre requires a somewhat more elaborate sequence of steps than other forms of interpretation. First, the children who are going to interpret the story must choose the character parts they will play. Generally, the narrator should be a strong reader. In fact, when Readers Theatre is adapted for use with young children, an adult can read the narrator's part, cuing the children if they have trouble following the format.

When character parts have been decided on, the readers should be encouraged to become familiar with the whole selection so that they identify the themes to be emphasized and are aware of unique qualities of the author's style. Each reader turns next to an in-depth analysis of his or her part, getting to know the character (in the case of the narrator, getting acquainted with all characters) and trying to decide how that character looks, acts, and talks. Allow time

---

[5]"Overheard on a Saltmarsh" from *Collected Poems* by Harold Monro. Reprinted by permission of Gerald Duckworth & Co., Ltd.

[6]See *The Scott, Foresman Anthology of Children's Literature*, Parts One and Two.

for the children to practice their parts, providing a tape recorder for them to use, if possible. And remind them not to read the "he said's" and "she said's." The production will sound smoother without them.

When individual parts have been rehearsed, it is time to put the production together. This involves, at first, rather informal practice sessions with the readers standing or sitting facing the narrator. Enough time should be allowed for these rehearsals so that students are able to read expressively and coordinate the reading with other parts. The help of an adult at this point can be valuable. If you notice that a reader is having trouble coming in at the right time, help the child to circle the key words that the previous reader will say and to listen for cues.

The final step is to stage the production. Because no props or costumes are used, this is really quite simple. You should try to find enough folders alike so that the readers can use them to hold their copies of the story. If high stools are available, they can be used also. If not, readers may sit on low chairs and rise to read or they can remain standing throughout the reading. Whichever arrangement is used, it is effective to have the readers of character roles facing the narrator and placed in a semicircle so that they can see one another. In that way, both audience and readers have a feeling of interaction among the characters and a recognition that the narrator is keeping the thread of the plot running smoothly.

The Readers Theatre production is now ready for an audience. Younger children often enjoy watching and listening to this kind of presentation. If the readers have done a good job preparing, they can serve as good models to the younger children, too. An alternative to presentation before an audience is to prepare a videotape or a regular tape recording. If this is done, you can add background music or other sound effects which enhance the performance. A videotape is especially interesting to children later on, as they can notice how well they complemented the vocal interpretation with facial gestures and other bodily motions, limited though they are by staying in one place and holding a script.

The readers' responses to the story are most evident in tone of voice and facial expressions used to convey character interpretation. A lively interpretation or one which is especially moving indicates a high degree of emotional response by the reader. A reader who is able to show a character's feelings clearly has also been successful in interpreting the motives of the character and has probably recognized some fine points of the author's talent for characterization. The reader may also have sensed the author's purpose in including that character in the story. A narrator who successfully keeps the production moving shows awareness of the progression of incidents in the plot, of the importance of each incident, and, often, recognition of the relationships among story characters. Though Readers Theatre is not a discussion technique or a form that utilizes dramatization, it does, nevertheless, give opportunity for in-depth response to literature.

Occasionally, a reader may fail to interpret a role effectively or a narrator may show, by halting voice and stilted presentation, that he or she does not sense where the plot is going. You can seize those opportunities to engage the readers in interpretation of the story by such questions as: In *The Mixed-Up Files of Mrs. Basil E. Frankweiler*, how does Jamie feel toward Claudia? How would he show it? What will

"The Three Little Pigs" provides good material for creative dramatics activities in this classroom. The big bad wolf is always great fun to portray; there is enough action to make this story a favorite to dramatize.

happen as a result of the conversation? Working from questions that guide the readers in understanding the story more clearly, you can move to questions that require them to rethink their interpretations of character and narrator parts, questions such as: What tone of voice would Jamie use to show that he is a little afraid of Claudia even though he does admire her? How can the narrator effectively lead up to the next happening in the story by changing his or her reading? How can you show, by your voice and face, what Claudia is thinking? By working from story interpretation to character interpretation, you may help the readers to an increased emotional response to the characters and to the story itself.

Creative Dramatics

While role-playing develops responses that show interpretation of a story problem and Readers Theatre develops involvement with characters, creative dramatics develops responses that indicate a child's involvement with characterization and plot structure. In role-playing, you ask children to deal with a "what if" proposition, to extend a plot in order to create their own conclusions. In creative dramatics, you ask children to interpret a story which is structurally complete, using suitable voice and actions. The dramatization centers on interpreting character and plot to draw out the major themes. Dialogue is improvised but is true to the sense of characters and theme.

Children who participate in creative dramatics need certain technical skills, to be sure. They must be able to recall the sequence of episodes in the plot, to interpret an author's characterization so as to create real characters, to use vocal ability and body gestures to produce a dramatization that is believable. With guidance, children grow in ability to handle these literary and dramatic interpretation skills. They become skilled in interpreting a story, learning to infer missing details they need for their recreation of a character, dialogue, or plot. Children also gain personally from experiences with creative dramatics. In addition to the value of the experience itself, they learn to work together and to express themselves unaffectedly and fluently as the dramatization provides an avenue for release of tension and for enjoyment of a story. Development of personal values and appreciation for good literature can also grow from participation in creative dramatization.

Selecting Material for Dramatization

A well-written story, one interesting to children, with some kind of conflict and a fair amount of action, provides good material for dramatization. Characters should be well enough developed so that children can distinguish different character types in the story. Good dialogue is important for children who are not very adept at improvising dialogue.

Some stories successful with primary-age children are: single chapters from Beverly Cleary's *Ramona* books or *Henry Huggins*; Marjorie Flack's *Ask Mr. Bear*; Pat Hutchins's *Rosie's Walk* and *The Surprise Party*; and folk tales such as "The Three Billy-Goats Gruff," "The Three Little Pigs," or "The Pancake." The repetitious plot structure of folk tales makes them easy for young children to handle and the characters, though not highly developed, contrast well enough so that children can portray them effectively.

Material for older students might include: "The Bremen Town-Musicians" and other more complex folk tales like "Urashima Taro and the Princess of the Sea" and "The Tiger, the Brahman, and the Jackal"; Dr Seuss's *The King's Stilts*; episodes from Mark Twain's *Tom Sawyer* or Kenneth Grahame's *The Wind in the Willows*; or scenes from contemporary stories such as Jean Craighead George's *Julie of the Wolves* or Elaine Konigsburg's *From the Mixed-Up Files of Mrs. Basil E. Frankweiler*.

Preparing a Dramatization

The adult who guides a creative dramatization has many things to keep in mind. The adult leader has the responsibility to set the mood for a dramatization and to plan warm-up activities that will prepare children to move freely and speak easily. Creative drama can be initiated with children of any age but the leader must be sure to base the activities on the children's past experiences with drama. A simple warm-up activity is pantomiming favorite animals while classmates try to guess their identity. A similar activity for older students involves pantomiming an awkward or embarrassing experience so that other members of the group can tell what it is. Once a mood for drama has been set, it is time to tell or read the story or poem you have chosen. This presentation should be made vivid by your use of description and emphasis on important parts of the plot. Above all, the story line must be clear so that the plot is easy for children to grasp.

Following the telling of the story, help children to identify the scenes they will need to dramatize and write them on the board. This requires you to think through the story in advance in order to give help in working through the scenes. Taking one scene at a time, help the children break it down into a sequence of smaller actions, thinking of characters who will be needed and the action that is involved. At this point you may analyze each of the major scenes until all have been discussed, or you may begin by having students dramatize just the first scene before they analyze the others.

The first step of dramatization should include discussion of characters—how they look, how they act, even what they think. You may want to let all the students pantomime the characters before proceeding to the dramatization of the scene. At that point, children should be given a chance to volunteer for the parts they wish to play. Remember that in creative dramatics the cast and audience both have a part to play. To prepare the cast, after characters have been discussed and progression of the plot has been reviewed, give them some time in a private place to rehearse and work out their dramatization. Encourage them to create dialogue they think is natural for those characters. Prepare the audience so that they are ready to look for good things in the performance, and also for some things that they think could be changed in order to create a better production.

The first playing of a scene should be carefully set up so that the area where the production will be given is cleared except for any necessary furniture. (Most costumes and props can be left to the viewer's imagination.) A signal should be given by the adult leader to show the students when to begin and bring to a close

their dramatization, since it is sometimes necessary to limit the amount of time allowed or to stop so that action can be discussed. You may simply hold up your hand, or you may prefer to dim the lights or to use a soft bell so that you can be heard even though the players are not looking at you.

When children have played a scene (or sequence of scenes), engage the audience in discussion of the performance to help them evaluate the effectiveness of characterization and dialogue. Try to get them also to judge the faithfulness to the plot structure of the original story. Following the discussion, the scene may be replayed by the same group of children or by another group selected from the audience. This procedure of playing, discussing, and replaying continues until the entire story has been enacted. If students have done one scene at a time, they then put together the entire sequence in one performance with the audience watching to see how smoothly they can connect the scenes.

In summary, the steps in guiding a creative dramatics production are as follows:

1. Choose a good story or poem.
2. Tell or read it to the children.
3. Involve them in identifying the characters and the scenes needed for dramatization.
4. Carry out in-depth discussion of character traits and allow time for pantomiming of characters.
5. Let children decide who will play each character part.
6. Give the players a short time to analyze the first scene and to plan and practice their performances, creating their own dialogue.
7. Prepare the audience to critique the performance.
8. Have the scene played before the audience.
9. Guide audience discussion of the scene.
10. Allow for a replaying of the scene, either with the same cast or with a new group.
11. Work on each scene in the same way, then play through the entire story.
12. Guide audience discussion of the complete enactment.
13. Replay, if there is time.

Observing Response

Creative dramatics allows for many forms of response to a selection. Children are challenged to identify and interpret an author's development of characterization and plot. During the dramatization itself and also during the discussion that follows, notice responses related to recognition of literary characteristics of the story and interpretation of the work. Some children are able to talk of plot structure, for example, as the child who said it was important for the big billy goat to walk over the bridge, too, before he butted the troll to pieces because the story should show the same thing happening to all three of the goats. Children respond to characterization by pointing out words an author uses to describe a character, by conveying through facial expression something of the character's personality, or by using dialogue which shows a character's feelings. Such responses show a grasp of the literary qualities of a piece. Response to characterization can also emerge as an emotional response when a student shows vividly, through actions, an involvement with a character.

A spirited dramatization is usually evidence of emotional response to the story. So is a thoughtful discussion after the playing, a discussion that reveals interest of the audience in the story as well as in the quality of the dramatization. When the emotional response is added to an intelligent interpretation of the ideas in the story, a very good dramatization usually is given.

Puppetry

Puppetry allows children to plan a dramatization, create dialogue, and work for effective use of the voice. In those respects it is similar to creative dramatics. However, since the puppeteer is not in view of the audience, the voice becomes extremely important as the means of creating a story interpretation. Puppetry is less threatening than other forms of dramatic activity for children who do not feel comfortable physically performing before an audience. Creating a puppet that will suit the character part unites puppetry with art in much the same way that drama relies on the artistic sense of set and costume designers. In puppetry, as in other forms of drama, the goal is to produce a unified visual and auditory effect that will effectively show the plot and the characters but, above all, will capture the spirit of the story. If the mood of the story is humorous, the puppet production should reflect that accurately. That is why so much literary response is involved in the planning of any successful dramatic presentation.

Action is an important ingredient in a good story for puppetry. Conflict is also a desired, though not a necessary, attribute. The number of characters is limited by the size of a puppet stage (not more than five or six characters, as a rule) and those characters should contrast enough to make the production interesting. Subtle character differences will be lost. The popular Punch and Judy shows are good examples of the effectiveness of action, conflict, and strong characterization.

In creative dramatics and other theater productions, the actors are able to create three-dimensional characters with a range of emotions. The use of puppets tends to make the characters flat, often limiting them to such strong emotions as anger, fear, or joy but rarely showing much depth of feeling. Again, subtle emotions will be lost. For that reason, folk tales with their relatively flat characters are a good choice for puppet presentation.

Although puppet shows can involve a fairly elaborate plot, including several acts and scenes, beginners should choose stories with simple plots. The repetitive plot structure of

Puppetry is a creative activity uniting drama with art to effectively convey the plot and characters of a story to an audience.

many folk tales is another good reason for selecting them. If you produce "The Three Billy-Goats Gruff," for example, you have action consisting of three similar conflicts between the goats and the troll. The progression is easy to follow because of the order in which the goats enter the story—small to large—and the ending is easy to remember. The plot structure and the small number of characters make it a good choice.

Bear in mind the kind of setting you might need for a story and think about ways that the characters could be made into puppets. In "The Three Billy-Goats Gruff" the only necessary additions to a bare puppet stage would be the bridge and a hill with green grass. The characters can easily be constructed as paper-bag puppets, or hand puppets with papier-mâché heads. They can be made distinctive because of the contrasting sizes of the three goats and because the troll is evil and menacing in contrast to the goats. Remember that the puppet production will highlight the plot and the contrast between characters.

"Gudbrand on the Hill-side" is suitable for puppetry because it has a repetitive plot and the cast of characters can be whittled down by having only the animals and their owners appear on stage. "The Pancake" works well because of its repetitive language. Children's voices offstage can be used for several parts. "The Bremen Town-Musicians" can be easily adapted for puppetry by using an open box at one end of the stage for the robber's house. Some other tales which can be adapted for puppetry are "Tom Tit Tot," "Snow White," "Henny Penny," "The Three Little Pigs," and "The Three Bears."

A puppet production can take several forms, depending upon the kind of puppets used and whether a script is read or the dialogue is created by the puppeteers. Those decisions are made on the basis of the story you choose and the age level of children who will participate. Marionettes (puppets moved by strings from overhead) require a good deal of skill to handle but finger puppets, hand puppets, stick puppets, paper-bag puppets, balloon puppets, and adaptations of these are easy for preschool and elementary school children, and even for many disabled children, to make and handle. With

these options in mind, you can easily help children find or create puppets to go with a story.

When you have chosen a story for the production—and you may wish to do this on your own or with the help of the children—read it to the group, asking them to listen first for the characters they will need to represent by puppets. At the close of the reading, involve the children in a discussion so that they identify the characters and talk about the personality of each, whether that character's actions are predictably good or bad, whether the character is happy, sad, angry, funny, and so forth.

When the characters have been listed and discussed, children are ready to begin planning the puppets they will want to use. At this point, you may want to have several different types of puppets to show if you want the children to help with the decision of what kind to make. In preparation, you should think through the story to determine the most suitable kind of puppet for the characters, also keeping in mind the amount of time available to produce the puppets and the abilities of the children.

Although we will not give specific instructions here for making puppets, some possible means of preparing them may be helpful. Hand puppets may be purchased. They may be made from old socks with eyes, ears, noses, and mouths made of felt or some other material. Papier-mâché heads can also be fitted with mittens or socks for use as hand puppets. Finger puppets can be made from toilet-paper rolls or from mittens, in which case each finger can represent a different character. Stick puppets usually have heads made of papier-mâché set onto a dowel rod. A dress or clothing of some sort can be attached to the head, covering the stick and allowing the puppeteer to simulate arm movements of the puppet. Paper-bag puppets, among the simplest to make, require only decoration with eyes, ears, hair, and so forth. The balloon puppets are decorated with cut paper features and arms and limbs. They can be manipulated by a length of small dowel rod attached to the balloon opening.

When children design the facial features of the puppets, they should keep in mind the most important personality traits of the characters. If a puppet must appear happy and sad in the show, what kind of features will be best? Mood change can be made by manipulating the face of a sock puppet. Can it also be shown by the way the puppet moves on the stage? How should the villain of a play look? the hero? How can a puppet's looks show kindness or helplessness? Such problems must be dealt with by puppeteers, and children will learn about character traits as they work with puppets. Encourage them to refer to the story from time to time to refresh memories about the characters.

When the puppets have been produced, guide the children in a review of the story in preparation for the show. The review should focus on identification of key episodes (later translated to scenes) which can be portrayed by the puppets and sections of the story which can be told by the narrator. You might want to help children make a simple chart showing a breakdown of the story line as this example for "The Three Billy-Goats Gruff" shows:

Narrator
Scene 1: Smallest goat walks over bridge
Narrator
Scene 2: Middle-sized goat walks over bridge
Narrator
Scene 3: Biggest goat walks over bridge and
        fights with troll
Narrator

When the simple outline has been made, the puppeteers may rehearse their dialogue for each of the scenes. When dialogue is created by the children, only one child is needed to operate the puppet and supply the voice. If you have students read dialogue from a story, they will probably have to work in pairs, one child reading and the other operating the puppet. An option is to have the dialogue recorded in advance of performance. That gives children more freedom to concentrate on maneuvering the puppets. If students with special needs are mainstreamed in a regular classroom, they can participate as puppeteers more easily if they do not have to memorize or read dialogue. Background music can also be recorded over the dialogue and at scene changes to fill the pauses.

The puppet show should be rehearsed so that children learn to use a puppet stage to the best effect, especially to show the conflicts between characters clearly. If a puppet stage is not available, a table may be used as a stage by turning it on its side or by leaving it upright and covering it with a sheet, the children crouching out of sight behind it. Children should have opportunities to present their puppet shows to audiences so that they see the effect the characters and voices have on spectators. A videotape of the performance can also let them see the results of their work.

Response to the puppet show should reveal enjoyment as well as some understanding of the literary components of the story. Children who are eager to give their show to another class or to watch a show again reveal emotional involvement. A young child who comments that he likes the witch because she sounds as scary as she looks is responding to the characterization. Children often respond to plot by working hard to get just the right build-up of suspense or by highlighting an ending.

Written Response

If writing about literature is to be truly response, the students should be good enough writers that the act of writing does not interfere with expression of their feelings and ideas about a selection. The writing assignment should be structured for less mature writers so that they are not required to produce lengthy reports or essays about books. Whatever the format, you should keep in mind the purpose of written response—to encourage children to think about the meaning of a story or poem and to react to its value.

Writing activities can develop awareness of the literary characteristics of prose and poetry. Sometimes a written response will carry a child beyond a response to that single book and inspire a creative effort to write an original story or poem. Through written response, children can experiment with form and style, trying to develop their own stories or poems based on plot structure or poetic form they have enjoyed. They may respond to point of view and characterization by trying to rewrite a story or episode as it might have been seen through the eyes of one of the characters. They can become more aware of the interaction of characters by trying to write a script for a favorite story.

For some children, the written response may be the fullest expression of their responses to literature. These may be children who are somewhat shy about entering into a discussion or into dramatic activities. They most certainly are children who have well-developed writing skills. They may also be children who delight in mulling over a selection, thinking it through and pondering its meaning. That takes time and, for some children, it also takes solitude.

Keeping a diary record of books read, including a reaction to each book, is one kind of written assignment that older children can handle. The writing need not be lengthy, but children should be encouraged to record every book they begin even though the reaction may be, "I didn't finish it because it wasn't interesting." You may also want to encourage them to comment about ideas they gained from the book. Children may evaluate the books according to whether they are good enough to recommend to other students. If you sit down with a child after the diary has been kept for a period of time you both will find it interesting to identify favorite types of books and to look at the kinds of reactions to each book. If a diary has been kept for an entire year, children will find changes in their reading interests over that period of time, moving perhaps from an exclusive interest in animal stories to some interest in fantasy, and you will often find an increase in ability to show several different kinds of responses, including interpretation, evaluation, or literary judgment as well as emotional involvement.

Keeping a diary may lead students to illustrate a story in order to express their response to it. Children who are not adept at writing should be encouraged to illustrate key episodes and write a caption of one or two sentences for each. To do this the reader must determine which episodes are important and which can also be illustrated. The written caption should describe what is happening in the picture and should tell how it relates to the rest of the story. The exercise calls for close attention to character description and ability to interpret the descriptions artistically. The illustrations may be kept by a child as a diary of books read or may be used as part of a bulletin board display about books.

The traditional written book report is generally not the best way to encourage response to a story. It usually becomes an exercise to be read only by the teacher, especially when the writing process is a burden to the child who is required to write the report. A slight change in approach can make these reports useful to other students and give some purpose to the project. A card file of book reviews written by the children can be set up and can become an important part of the reference section of a classroom or library. A recommended format for the cards includes title and author, a short plot summary, and some comments indicating what the student felt was good or not good about the book. This written work should encourage an evaluation response and often some reaction to literary qualities as well.

Another variation on the traditional book review is the point-of-view book report. To introduce this format, you might ask a child who has just finished a book to name his or her favorite character from the story. Follow by saying, "You are _____ (*name of story character*). Tell the story the way you saw it." Once children become accustomed to the idea, you can simply instruct them to choose one story character and retell the story as they think that character would tell it. This approach leads to many opportunities for identifying with story characters, to emotional involvement with the story, and to interpretation of events.

Reports are not the only kinds of useful written responses to books. Creating a script from a favorite book can allow children a good deal of creative interpretation. The script can be designed for a puppet show or for a dramatization of the story. This activity requires that the child select an episode and decide which ideas can be conveyed by means of the dialogue already in the story and what information will have to be supplied by a narrator. Some of the narration can be drawn from the story, but the child will have to write an introduction to the episode, to be read by the narrator. The finished script can be performed before an audience. Seeing his or her script produced, however simply, should encourage the writer.

Children not only write about literature. They also learn about writing by reading literature. Creative writing often is inspired by books and poems children read. They may experiment with the plot structures and poetic forms they have enjoyed in their recreational reading. Many stories for young children— Pat Hutchins's *Rosie's Walk* and John Burningham's *Mr. Gumpy's Outing*, for example—follow a simple plot in which the principal character sets out on a journey and returns home at the end of the story. Stories with that structure can be shown on a flannelboard or chalkboard as circle stories, with the beginning and ending scenes at the top of the circle and the others proceeding around clockwise. After reading or hearing several such stories, children can make their own circle stories, drawing the illustrations, placing them on a large piece of chart paper, and writing a caption or short sentence under each picture so that the story can be told by words or by pictures. At all stages of the writing process, from prewriting experiences that give ideas for stories through revision of early drafts, the books children have heard and read can be important influences on their writing.

Older children may enjoy working with a more elaborate plot structure, perhaps developing a problem/solution situation in which a story character must take steps to solve a problem or escape from a frightening circumstance. These writers can be encouraged to notice how their favorite authors build a story, often allowing a character to try several means of dealing with the problem before actually succeeding. Thinking through a plot may take place at the prewriting stage, using ideas from remembered books. It often occurs again at the revision stage when children are encouraged to expand the story line.

Just as experiences with good literature can help young writers with plotting, they can also give ideas for the use of descriptive language to develop setting and characterization. Natalie Babbitt's *Tuck Everlasting* and Katherine Paterson's *Rebels of the Heavenly Kingdom* have many descriptive sections that help to create a sense of place.

When a story has been written, revised, and edited so that it is in a form to be read by others, it deserves an audience. The sense of audience should be impressed on children so that they begin to recognize the responsibility a

Viewpoint

A reader's experience of a book is influenced by both the book-object itself, and by the patterns of meaning created quite intangibly in the reader's head. What we must recognize is that this "text," this construct of object and meaning-pattern, lives only within the reader's imagination and is a constantly changing *gestalt*. We cannot take it out and look at it, or show it to someone else. Even as we try to describe it, it changes. Each time we talk about a book we discover that our sense of it, our ideas about it, our understanding of what it is and means, even the details we remember, have changed and shifted and come to us in different arrangements, different patterns. During our reading our idea of the book, its *gestalt*, changes because new information is added—new scenes, more details about the characters, and so on. After a reading, the patterns go on shifting according to our memory, our recall of the information, and whatever personal needs we have at that time and which particular features of the book "speak to."

. . . So talk that concentrates on the text as Text—on the patterns created in our imaginations by our reading—is an attempt to discover the work of literature itself. This kind of talk is made up of all the other kinds discussed so far, but goes beyond them. And paradoxically the deeper we search for the Text, the more we discover about ourselves. In the same way that people who climb Everest or sail alone around the world tell us that in the very act of concentration on a work so difficult and dangerous they discover far more than ever before about themselves.

Aidan Chambers, *Introducing Books to Children*, 2nd edition, The Horn Book, 1983, pp. 167–168.

writer has toward potential readers and to think about the kinds of responses they hope to get from readers. Who do they see as most likely to want to read the stories they write?

They should have opportunity to consider and to experiment with a variety of audiences ranging from peers and teachers to parents and younger children. The finished draft may be read to younger children or placed on a "writing corner" table to be read by others in the classroom or library.

The activities described in this chapter are suggested as ways of providing active participation in literature for those children who respond well to an activity-centered literature program. The ideas should also provide means of tempting and drawing out the child who is less enthusiastic about books and reading. Regardless of the approach you use, be ever alert to the hint of a response, whether it is a look of pleasure or concern over a book, poem, or passage; awareness of literary structure, style, or characterization; or interpretation of some aspect of a selection or judgment of the merit of a piece. By fostering that early response, you may lead a child to a depth of response that can produce an avid and sensitive reader.

Adult References and Book Selection Aids*

AUSTIN, MARY, and ESTHER JENKINS. *Promoting World Understanding through Literature, K–8.*

BAUER, CAROLINE FELLER. *This Way to Books.*

CHAMBERS, DEWEY W. *Literature for Children: Storytelling and Creative Drama.*

COGER, LESLIE IRENE, and MELVIN R. WHITE. *Readers Theatre Handbook: A Dramatic Approach to Literature.*

COLWELL, EILEEN. *Storytelling.*

CURRELL, DAVID. *The Complete Book of Puppetry.*

FORDYCE, RACHEL. *Children's Theatre and Creative Dramatics: An Annotated Bibliography of Critical Works.*

GILLIES, EMILY. *Creative Dramatics for All Children.*

KIMMEL, MARGARET MARY, and ELIZABETH SEGEL. *For Reading Out Loud! A Guide to Sharing Books with Children.*

LAMME, LINDA LEONARD, and others. *Raising Readers: A Guide to Sharing Literature with Young Children.*

LEONARD, CHARLOTTE. *Tied Together: Topics and Thoughts for Introducing Children's Books.*

MONSON, DIANNE, and DAYANN MCCLENATHAN, eds. *Developing Active Readers: Ideas for Parents, Teachers, and Librarians.*

MOORE, VARDINE. *The Pre-School Story Hour.*

POLKINGHARN, ANNE T., and CATHERINE TOOHEY. *Creative Encounters: Activities to Expand Children's Responses to Literature.*

SHEDLOCK, MARIE L. *The Art of the Storyteller.*

STEWIG, JOHN WARREN, and SAM L. SEBESTA, eds. *Using Literature in the Elementary Classroom.*

THOMAS, JAMES, and RUTH LORING, eds. *Motivating Children and Young Adults to Read.*

TOOZE, RUTH. *Storytelling.*

TRELEASE, JIM. *The New Read-Aloud Handbook.*

WAGNER, JOSEPH A. *Children's Literature Through Storytelling.*

WARD, WINIFRED. *Playmaking with Children from Kindergarten Through Junior High School.*

*Complete bibliographic data are provided in Appendices A and B.

Chapter Sixteen

Introducing Literature to Children

In Chapters 4 through 13 we discussed the various types of writing for children—poetry, fantasy, and biography, for example. Suggestions for introducing children to these specific kinds of books are developed in this chapter. In a sense, this material represents a synthesis and application of ideas discussed in the preceding two chapters, where we considered the patterns of response to literature and methods of encouraging that response. The suggested activities here are based on the question: How can I best present this book to encourage children's responses? These responses may show involvement, interpretation, awareness of literary qualities, and/or evaluation of the story.

The goal of a literature program is to develop reading habits that will stay with children through adulthood. As children grow older, more and more of their reading should be independent reading from books of their own selection. The activities discussed here are designed to open doors to literature and to encourage reaction to books.

Formal study of literature is not usually a part of the elementary school curriculum. Experiences with literature most often come through the library program, the reading program, or the language arts program. A review of Chapter 15 will show the close ties of many of the activities there with what is typically included in language arts. A review of Chapter 14 will suggest relationships between what is considered literary response and the comprehension skill development included in a good reading program. Librarians will recognize that ideas from both chapters are related to sound objectives of a library program. A strong literature program can contribute substantially to the general educational experience and, above all, help children to enjoy reading.

Two questions underlie any recommendations for literature-related activities: What abilities can children develop at this level? What materials and activities are appropriate for developing those abilities? As we saw in Chapter 1, the answers to such questions are closely tied to developmental characteristics of children. Communication skills continue to grow from infancy but require guidance and practice for fullest development. Skill in speaking, listening, dramatization, and writing can help children respond to and enjoy literature. At the same time, those skills are enhanced when children discuss books, respond to one another's ideas about a story, re-create a story through role-playing, oral interpretation, or creative dramatics, or respond to a literary selection by engaging in some creative writing. Foremost is the importance placed on literature and the enjoyment that comes from hearing and reading good selections.

Selecting appropriate materials for developing these abilities requires great care. Making a story or poem serve the activity by changing or manipulating a character or plot is generally not a good idea, as it shows a certain lack of respect for literature and for an author's purposes. Sensitive selection of material, on the other hand, can enhance the appeal of literature by showing how it helps us to understand and deal with our uncertainties and fears, how it provides release from tension through laughter, and how it gives us appreciation for the beauty of the language.

The use of media such as films, cassettes, and television productions based on literature can be an interesting addition to the curriculum. Comparison of a book with a film or television production is also a means of creating good discussions about literary characteristics.

Careful matching of activities with books is critical if those activities are to enhance rather than detract from the literary work. The activity should focus on a significant quality of the literature and not distort a poem or story simply for the sake of providing some activity for children. For instance, a story should not be used for puppetry if the literary qualities of plot, characterization, or style would be trivialized by such an adaptation. The same caution holds true for such activities as creative dramatics, story theater, role-playing, and oral interpretation. When activities are carefully selected and developed around appropriate material to generate responses, the combination can take a child into a book so that a memorable experience results. That is the goal of the abbreviated plans in this chapter.

The chart on pages 614–615 suggests how a teacher or librarian could introduce children to a wide variety of books and encourage various kinds of responses. The chart lists recommended book activities discussed later in the chapter.

Included are books for young children (preschool to age six), for primary-age children (ages six to eight or nine), and for children in the intermediate grades (ages nine to twelve). Books for the first group are coded with a (Pre); for the second group with a (Pri); and for the third group with an (Int). If a book is usable with a broad range of ages, this is indicated by more than one designation. Some blocks on the chart are blank because activities do not seem appropriate for certain types of literature as, for example, storytelling with informational books; others are open so that you can use ideas from previous chapters in combination with books you select to create your own additions to the chart.

The starred books on the chart are those for which detailed activity plans are included in this chapter. You may also find that many books can be used successfully with more than one activity, and suggested alternatives are listed with each title.

You should not, by any means, look upon the books and activities described here as guidelines to be followed to the letter. Rather, they are simply included as models with the hope that you will try them and then use the ideas to create your own activities for the books and poems you choose. If you follow through with the presentation of stories and poetry suggested here (or with alternate selections of your own choice), a fairly well-balanced, response-centered literature program can result. The program would not be complete, of course, unless children also were involved in a great deal of independent reading of library materials.

Picture Books

Since picture books appeal to primary-age children as well as preschoolers, some of the activities have been developed for primary-grade and could even be used with intermediate-grade children. This is especially true of the story theater presentation. Some of the activities require little time. Others are best done over a period of several days.

Reading Aloud

May I Bring a Friend? by Beatrice Schenk de Regniers, illustrated by Beni Montresor.

This is a fine book to read aloud to pre-schoolers who are delighted by the imaginative quality of the colorful illustrations. The "reading" of the pictures shares importance with listening to the lively text, so children should be seated where they can see the illustrations as the story is read.

Emotional response to the fun of the story can be developed as well as literary response to the amusing illustrations, to the rhythm and rhyme of the verse, and to a recognition of the problems and solutions that make up each episode of the plot.

You can use the cover illustration effectively to introduce the story by asking children who they see on the cover and who the little boy's friend is. Encourage them to listen and watch the illustrations to see what happens in this story about a queen, a king, and a little boy. As you read, be sure to emphasize the rhythm and rhyme of the lines, as young children generally respond well to these effects.

To encourage greater interaction with the events of the plot, you might want to pause after reading "So I brought my friend . . . ," inviting children to guess the identity of the friend, or to say whom they would take if they were having tea at the palace. The words spoken by the king and queen provide opportunity for use of good oral interpretation techniques and you will probably find children joining you on "Hello" each time the king greets a new guest. Children may also enjoy anticipating the problems that may arise with the arrival of each subsequent guest (for example, the hippopotamus). They might like to suggest where the elephant can sit and will be amused at the solution.

Throughout the reading, allow ample time for viewing the illustrations. You might want to take time following the story to show all of them again, inviting the children's attention to the detailing in the pictures, such as the king and queen hanging their feet over the dock while they fish and the dismayed look on the king's face when the hippopotamus tries to sit next to

him. Children will want to hear the story many times; encourage them to join you on familiar verses so that they learn to use their voices to interpret rhythm and rhyme. The choral speaking and role-playing may encourage a greater response to the story.

Discussion

Ox-Cart Man by Donald Hall, illustrated by Barbara Cooney.

These illustrations will very likely evoke an emotional response without the aid of discussion. However, if children are given a chance to talk about the text and illustrations, the importance of the illustrative technique may become more clear. Discussion will be most effective with a small group of children who are seated so that they can see the illustrations clearly because the illustrations form an important part of the historical perspective.

The discussion ought to arouse curiosity about everyday life more than 150 years ago. Some of the information is in the text, but the details are in the illustrations. The focus of this book is on self-sufficiency. It is important, too, for children to recognize that the story and illustrations show activities of the ox-cart man's family across seasons—in fall, winter, and spring.

The cover illustration provides a good discussion introduction. Let the children study the representation of the ox-cart man, his ox, and his cart. Also of interest are details of the barn with wood stored neatly and the fallen golden leaves that suggest autumn. With that introduction, read the story, emphasizing the poetic quality of language and showing the illustrations. Ideally, children should also have a chance to study the illustrations at close range.

To initiate discussion, you might ask the children to describe some of the things the family made and grew: Where did they get their yarn, linen, wood, sugar, apples, potatoes, and other things? How is that different from our lives? Why did the ox-cart man have to make such a long trip in order to sell the things his family had made? At this point, you might want to direct the children's attention to the pictures

Genres	Suggested Activities			
	Reading Aloud	**Storytelling**	**Discussion**	**Role-Playing**
Picture Books and Wordless Picture Books	*May I Bring a Friend? (Pre) **Millions of Cats (Pre, Pri)	The Tale of Peter Rabbit (Pre)	Nothing Ever Happens on My Block (Pre, Pri) *Ox-Cart Man (Pri)	Crow Boy (Pri, Int)
Folk Literature	*Tikki Tikki Tembo (Pre, Pri)	*"The Fisherman and His Wife" (Pri, Int)	*The True Story of the 3 Little Pigs! (Pri)	The Cat's Purr (Pri)
Poetry	Far and Few (Pri, Int) *Where the Sidewalk Ends (Pri, Int)		*"Low Tide" (Int)	
Fantasy	Mr. Rabbit and the Lovely Present (Pre)	"The Emperor's New Clothes" (Pri)	*The Borrowers (Pri) The White Mountains (Int)	The Pushcart War (Int)
Animal Stories	Nobody's Cat (Pre, Pri) The Incredible Journey (Int)		*Owls in the Family (Pri, Int)	*The Biggest Bear (Pre) A Bargain for Frances (Pre, Pri)
Realistic Fiction	*My Brother Louis Measures Worms (Pri, Int)		The Hundred Penny Box (Int)	The Bully of Barkham Street (Pri, Int) *Child of the Owl (Int)
Historical Fiction/ Biography	*Ragtime Tumpie (Int)	*The Story of Johnny Appleseed (Pre)	Journey to Topaz (Int)	Cesar Chavez (Pri, Int) *The Sign of the Beaver (Int)
Informational Books	*Jambo Means Hello (Pri, Int)		*How to Turn Lemons into Money (Int)	*Handtalk Birthday (Pri, Int)

*Book is discussed in this chapter
**Pre = Preschool; Pri = Primary; Int = Intermediate

Suggested Activities

Creative Dramatics	Story Theater	Oral Interpretation	Puppetry	Writing Activities
*Where the Wild Things Are (Pre, Pri) Night in the Country (Pre)	*Why Mosquitoes Buzz in People's Ears (Pri, Int) Drummer Hoff (Pre, Pri)	A Kiss for Little Bear (Pre, Pri)	"The Three Billy-Goats Gruff" (Pre)	*Doctor De Soto (Pri, Int) Miss Nelson Is Missing (Pri)
*"The Four Musicians" (Pri)	"The Hare and the Tortoise" (Pre) "The King's Drum" (Pri)	*The Legend of the Bluebonnet (Pre, Int)	*"The Pancake" (Pre, Pri)	
	"Little Miss Muffet" (Pre)	"Mice" (Pri) Prayers from the Ark (Int)		Hailstones and Halibut Bones (Pri, Int)
Caps for Sale (Pre, Pri)	*In the Forest (Pre) The King's Stilts (Int)			Paul Bunyan (Pri, Int)
Rabbit Hill (Pri, Int)	Sylvester and the Magic Pebble (Pri)	Runaway Ralph (Pri, Int)		*The Bat-Poet (Int)
The Adventures of Tom Sawyer (Int)	The Time-Ago Tales of Jahdu (Pri, Int)	*Ramona the Pest (Pri, Int)		My Side of the Mountain (Int) The Great Gilly Hopkins (Int)
The Witch of Blackbird Pond (Int)		The Little House Books (Pri, Int)		North to Freedom (Int) *Number the Stars (Int)
Push-Pull, Empty-Full (Pre)			How to Be a Puppeteer (Pri) Puppet Shows Using Poems and Stories (Int)	Castle (Int) Zoo City (Pre, Pri)

of the ox-cart man's journey: What did he see along the way? What scenes do they like best?

Call attention to the other illustrations in the book, encouraging children to decide which of the activities on the farm they would most enjoy. Which illustrations do they like the best? What feeling does the illustration give them? Why is it so interesting? Finally, show all the illustrations again, asking children to look carefully at the trees. How do they show clearly the time of year in which each scene takes place? What other details has the illustrator included to give us a real sense of how time passes? Through discussion, children may become aware of how illustrations shape our understanding of life in other times.

Creative Dramatics

Where the Wild Things Are by Maurice Sendak.

This picture book is well known to many children. Attracted to the vivid illustrations, they enter gladly into the wild rumpus, enjoying the humor of the situation and reveling in the rhythm of the ungainly dance. And, at the close of the festivities, they understand Max's desire to go home to where "someone loved him best of all," emphasizing the need for close relationships with those who play important roles in their lives rather than the adulation of a large number of strangers.

Dramatization encourages emotional response through enjoyment of story and pictures, resulting in empathy for Max's situation. Some children will also recognize and interpret the theme: the importance of being with people who love you. Children may also respond to the literary style and artistic qualities of the book. The plot structure reveals a story within a story and this can be clearly shown through the dramatization. The marvelous illustrations add to the enjoyment of Max's characterization: Children will note Max's changes of mood, shown by his posture and facial expressions, and use that information to develop their own pantomimes.

Introduce this splendid picture book so that all the children in the group can enjoy the pictures. For example, show the cover picture as you read the title and ask the children whether they would like to go to a land inhabited by creatures resembling the one in this illustration. What kinds of adventures might they have? Turn, next, to the first-page illustration of Max in his wolf suit and tell children to listen to the story and watch the pictures to find out what happens to Max. Each picture has a wealth of detail that children will enjoy, so pace your reading to allow time for them to examine each one. Allow time, too, for the spontaneous expressions of delight that the story is likely to elicit. When the story has been read completely, you can decide whether to continue with the dramatization or to save it for a second session: A good picture book is enjoyed even more at a second reading.

Whenever possible, provide an opportunity for children to enjoy the pictures on their own between the two readings. Prior to the second reading, you may want to show the pictures to the group and give them time to tell what they especially enjoy in each. You can call attention to Max's various facial expressions, asking children to show their own expressions of wickedness, shrewdness, delight, and sadness. This is good preparation for dramatization. In fact, with young children, a "dramatization" may consist of rereading the story while all children mime the part of Max, or participate in the wild rumpus scene in a story theater format.

During the second reading, encourage older children to notice the order in which the events occur. Ask them also to listen for story lines that are repeated several times during the story. When you have finished reading, you might ask the children to identify where the story begins and ends (in Max's house) and where the rest of it takes place (the ocean and the kingdom of the wild things). To further establish the setting for older children, you might help them identify the sequence of scenes: Max's house, Max's room, the ocean, the land of the wild things, the ocean, and Max's room.

With those scenes in mind, ask children to decide what characters they will need for dramatizing each scene. They may include Max's dog and inanimate objects, such as the vines and the boat, which are important for the action of the story. There can be any number of wild things, so that all children in the group can be involved in the dramatization. The next steps are to determine who will play each part and to give them time to practice pantomiming their roles, improvising dialogue where it is needed. Be sure to make the illustrations available again for attention to the movement in each picture.

Prior to the dramatization, the staging should be planned so the children know the areas of the room that represent Max's room, the ocean, and the land of the wild things. You will want to remind the children to listen well so that they come in at the right time. If the children are very inexperienced, you might provide the narration by reading from the text and pausing at the speaking parts, letting children supply the dialogue. A word of caution: Since Max has a very active part, it might be wise to choose a child who is quite independent and able to remember the story line to play the part.

As a follow-up to the dramatization, you can talk with the children about their performances. What did they especially enjoy about the story? Why did Max go on his journey and why did he return home? Was his behavior similar to anything they have done? If you want to emphasize the literary structure, you might reread the first and last sections that take place in Max's room and ask children whether these parts could be a story in themselves. Then read the "journey" section, beginning and ending with the boat trips so that children can identify the story-within-a-story.

This book has many possibilities for extending enjoyment of literature and, indeed, the arts. If an appropriate record is available, you might play it during the wild rumpus scene to create the spirit of the sort of dance that is shown in the illustrations.

Story Theater

Why Mosquitoes Buzz in People's Ears by Verna Aardema, illustrated by Leo and Diane Dillon.

Picture books that have illustrations with a strong sense of rhythm and movement are good sources of material for story theater productions. Story theater is closely related to dance. Like dance, it requires an interaction with mood and a depiction of that mood through movement. In a fine picture book, the mood is conveyed directly through the illustrations and also, usually, through the words of the story.

In *Anansi the Spider*, Gerald McDermott's graphics are beautifully designed. The book is a fine vehicle for story theater because the actions of story theater do not have to "use" the book; they develop spontaneously from interaction with it. The same is true of *Why Mosquitoes Buzz in People's Ears*, in which the Dillons' illustrations show strong, flowing movement. Indeed, every curve of an animal functions as part of the overall design. The rhythmic prose and stylistic touches of onomatopoeia emphasize the movements of the animals. In reading the text and looking at the illustrations, you are struck with the strong sense of physical movement; children who have listened to the story and studied the pictures may interact with them to give a meaningful interpretation. The story theater experience encourages emotional response to the characters and their common problem; literary response, showing appreciation for style of illustrations and style of writing, especially the onomatopoeia; and interpretation of the theme, telling how the tribal people arrived at the mythical explanation of the mosquito as a nuisance.

When the reading is completed, you might let children review the story, identifying the key characters in the order of their appearance. Children will want to talk about the sequence of events that lead to the mosquito's banishment from the council of the animals. You might explain that this is a folk tale and ask how such a story might have started. In the discussion, you may introduce the myth as one way the people of long ago tried to explain happenings they could not understand, such as earthquakes and volcanic eruptions.

Since the pictures tell the story so beautifully, you would be wise to display them again, encouraging children to notice how the animals look and how they seem to move. Some children may enjoy recreating the story through storytelling, using the illustrations to guide the retelling.

For story theater dramatization, plan for a second day, beginning that day with a repeated reading of the story. Ask children to listen for sounds used to describe each animal and for the sequence of events. When the reading is completed, ask children to repeat the onomatopoetic sounds ("mek, mek," and the like) used in the story to describe each animal. Allow the children to develop their own interpretations of these animals, basing them on illustrations and on the verbal descriptions. They might enjoy trying to show how an iguana might move so as to make a sound like "mek, mek, mek, mek." At this time, children might also decide who will play the part of each animal during the story theater production. After allowing time for practice and determining how to allocate space for a stage, you are ready for the reading. Read with the best oral interpretation techniques, pacing the story so that children have time to pantomime the character parts and emphasizing the onomatopoetic words so that your reading inspires the actors.

For follow-up discussion to the story theater production, you might focus on such questions as:

What events in nature are being explained in this story?
How did the storyteller and the illustrators let us know what the characters were like?
Which illustrations do you like best? Why?

The format of this plan can be adapted for use with other folk tales, including many of the Anansi stories.

Writing Activity

Doctor De Soto written and illustrated by William Steig.

This humorous tale is about Doctor De Soto, a mouse-dentist, and his successful encounter with a fox who turns out to be a wily patient. The author-illustrator, through words and pictures, shows the thinking that leads the fox to determine he will eat the dentist and his wife once they have installed his new tooth; he wonders if it would be "shabby" of him but decides that they are too delectable to overlook. Dr. De Soto's way of dealing with this problem surprises the fox—and delights the reader—with a clever solution. The illustrations are every bit as important to the story and the humor as are the words.

Responses to the story are likely to be emotional. Children will respond to the humor; they may also respond with some degree of

From *Doctor De Soto*, written and illustrated by William Steig.

empathy to the doctor when they realize the fox sees him as a potential meal; they may even empathize with the fox at the end of the story when he finds himself unable to consume the tasty morsel so near at hand. With some guidance, children may also recognize how cleverly the artist has used the illustrations to reinforce the incongruity of a very small but wise animal working as a dentist for a very large animal who is overconfident. They may also enjoy role-playing the two characters in several scenes, putting the characters' thoughts into words.

Children who enjoy the relationship of illustration to text may be encouraged to write and illustrate their own stories based on the wise beast/foolish beast pattern where one animal sets out to harm another but is foiled by clever action of the wiser character. Prewriting time may be used to let students discuss situations and character pairs that would work well for such a story.

You might introduce the activity by asking children to think about "The Hare and the Tortoise" or another fable with which they are familiar. Who is the wise beast? Who is the foolish beast? Why does the contrast between the two make the fable funny? Following this, each child might list a few "wise beast" characters about whom he or she would like to write. Next to each "wise beast," the child can describe a "foolish beast" who could be in the same story. Then, selecting one animal pair, have the child describe a problem with which the two creatures contend. This conflict can be used as a basis for a story in which the wise beast fools the foolish one.

Folk Literature

Reading Aloud

Tikki Tikki Tembo retold by Arlene Mosel, illustrated by Blair Lent.

This retelling of a Chinese folk tale has enough suspense to involve children with the problems and misfortunes of Chang and his brother, Tikki tikki tembo. The illustrations capture the rather easygoing mood of the village but they also depict quite explicitly the dangerous position of being in the bottom of a well!

Responses that may be generated through a reading of the story include emotional involvement as children feel concern for the safety of first one boy and then the other. Children may also respond to literary qualities of the story, particularly the cumulative plot structure and the use of rhythm and rhyme in the long name; the children will love to repeat: "Tikki, tikki, tembo-no sa rembo-chari bari ruchi-pip peri pembo."

You might preface the story by asking children to think of the longest name they have ever heard. Then read the title of the story and tell them that this is just part of the long name of one of the brothers about whom they will hear. Explain that they will discover the problem created by the boy's name.

As you read, use your voice and hand gestures to emphasize the development of plot and the movement of action from one place to another (from the well to the stream to the old man and again to the well) and try to pause during the second episode, when Tikki tikki tembo falls into the well, so that children have a chance to anticipate the action based on their knowledge of Chang's escapade. Let children

join you each time Chang struggles to pronounce Tikki tikki tembo's long name. They will want to hear the story again and again and will enjoy retelling it themselves. In fact, you can show the illustration at the end of the story and let children use it to prompt their retelling of the tale. Children will also enjoy responding to the story through story theater.

Storytelling

"The Fisherman and His Wife" from *Grimm's Household Tales*, translated by Margaret Hunt.

As part of the oral tradition folk tales are the single richest source for storytelling. "The Fisherman and His Wife" has a moral children cannot miss. It is a good choice for storytelling because the incidents are repetitious, yet they build in such a way that it is quite easy to remember plot sequence. The rhyme that is repeated each time the fisherman goes to seek the flounder also provides a structure for the story; children will enjoy repeating it with you as they become familiar with it.

Responses that develop naturally to this story are emotional reactions to the woman's greed and her undoing as well as interpretation of the theme and literary response through appreciation for the repeated rhyme. Responses may reflect that children are examining their own values.

The story is easy to follow because of its organization. A fisherman catches a flounder that is really an enchanted prince. The fisherman gladly releases the fish, but his wife is furious that he has not asked the flounder to grant a wish. The poor fisherman returns to the sea, calls the flounder, tells his wife's wish, and the flounder grants it. This process is repeated six times until finally the flounder sends the couple back to their original living quarters, a hovel. The secret in learning the story is to think of the sequence of the wishes: (1) that the couple live in a cottage, (2) that they live in a castle, (3) that the wife should be King, (4) that she should be Emperor, (5) that she should be Pope, and (6) that she should be like God. The last request is too much for the flounder and he returns the couple to their condition at the start of the story.

From *The True Story of the Three Little Pigs* by Jon Scieszka, illustrated by Lane Smith.

There is certainly a lesson in the story, and the children should reflect on the outcome of the wife's greedy ways. If children respond spontaneously or with a little encouragement to "think about what that story tells us," the way is open to a discussion in which they may share their own experiences that bear on the same lesson. If children do not share their ideas spontaneously, do not force a discussion. That would put the focus on the "lesson" and perhaps on self-righteous moralizing and not on enjoyment of the story itself.

Children may notice that the same episode is repeated over and over with just a little change each time. If they do, encourage them to think about other stories like "The Three Billy-Goats Gruff" that have similar repetitive story patterns. For young children, the repetitive pattern and small cast of characters make the story effective material for puppetry.

Discussion

The True Story of the 3 Little Pigs! by Jon Scieszka, illustrated by Lane Smith.

This story can be read aloud, providing time afterward for a discussion, or it can be paired with a traditional version of "The Three Little Pigs" to show children the change in a story when it is told from the viewpoint of the characters instead of a narrator. Responses to this version of the story may include laughter at the wolf's attempt to convince the reader that he did the most reasonable thing by eating the pigs; after all, should he let a perfectly good ham go to waste? Children may respond to the similarity between this version and the traditional one and the fact that each episode involves all three of the pigs. They may recognize the common repetition of three as it relates to other folk tales such as "The Three Bears" or "The Three Billy-Goats Gruff."

When you have read the story, pause for the children's spontaneous responses. You may want to encourage children to talk about the language that makes this story seem like a folk tale and the personalities of the characters that fit the folk tale mode (the contrast between good and evil, smart and stupid, and so on). A good activity to include in the discussion involves asking children to retell the story from the viewpoint of the first, second, or third little pig, instead of the wolf. How would each pig describe his own behavior compared to that of the wolf?

Creative Dramatics

"The Four Musicians" from *The Oak Tree Fairy Book*, ed. by Clifton Johnson.

This tale has enough action and enough surprises to provide good material for creative dramatics. Children will respond with empathy to the plight of the animals and express pleasure at the good turn their lives take. Emotional response may also be evident in laughter as children realize that the robber has misunderstood the rooster's crowing for the cries of a man on the roof shouting, "Chuck him up to me." Children are sure to enjoy the dramatic experience. In addition, they may react to literary structure by recognizing the common folk-tale theme of the poor-but-good person overcoming the villain.

When the tale has been told or read, ask the children to think about the story characters. Who were the musicians, and what talents did they use to make their journey a success? Before proceeding further with the plot review, you might want to let the children pantomime each character, adding sound effects if your walls are thick enough! Be certain to remind them that these are old, unwanted animals, poor in spirit at the beginning, but gaining courage when they are together. They may also want to pantomime the robbers as they are surprised with their meal. With that background, ask children to recall the sequence of events for producing a dramatization based on this tale. Essentially, there are three major scenes: the first when the four animals meet along the road; the second when they come upon the house, see the robbers inside, frighten them away, and finish the feast; and the third when the robbers return and are frightened away again by the animals. Once characters have been chosen, each scene can be rehearsed —first pantomimed and then spoken with dialogue created by the children. Finally, all three scenes are played in a continuous dramatization. Younger or less experienced children may be more comfortable with the pantomime of story theater.

Oral Interpretation

The Legend of the Bluebonnet retold and illustrated by Tomie dePaola.

Children will need to study the illustrations to notice how the use of color and composition give strength to the telling of this story. Listening to the story read well, children will be aware of the strong phrasing and understated rhythm of the text, which offer considerable potential for oral interpretation. The story begins with a chant and the narration that follows is broken by statements made by the runner, the shaman, She-Who-Is-Alone, a warrior, and a woman. Because of the arrangement of parts, the story is well suited to a Readers Theatre format.

When children have heard or read the story several times, they can decide who will read each part, giving special thought to the emo-

From *The Legend of the Bluebonnet*, retold and illustrated by Tomie dePaola.

tions of that character and the manner in which the lines should be delivered. In the Readers-Theatre style, children can present the reading to an audience of peers or younger students. Offering the audience opportunity to study the illustrations, either during the reading or independently later, will give added enjoyment. The informational aspect of the story may encourage children to do research on their state flower and use information gained as a basis for writing fantasy or factual pieces.

Puppetry

"The Pancake" from *Tales from the Fjeld* by Peter Asbjörnsen and Jörgen Moe, translated by Sir George Webbe Dasent.

"The Pancake" is one of several versions of this tale. Another well-known one is *Journey Cake, Ho!* by Ruth Sawyer. "The Pancake" can be adapted quite easily for puppetry, using paper bag puppets, finger puppets, or balloon puppets. A balloon puppet attached to a stick is especially effective in creating a sense of movement, for the pancake is, of course, always moving. This idea is adapted from a production of "Henny Penny" by Aurora Valentinetti.[1]

[1]Alvina Burrows et al., *New Horizons in the Language Arts.* New York: Harper & Row, 1972, p. 163.

Responses will include emotional reaction as children enjoy the escapades of the pancake and foresee its demise. In terms of literary response, children may notice the use of rhyming names and repeat them along with the storyteller. They will notice the cumulative plot structure, with the pancake repeating the names of all the animals it has outwitted each time a new character appears. You may provide a literary comparison by reading *Journey Cake, Ho!* after children have completed the puppet production of "The Pancake." Ask them to decide which version they most enjoyed.

A number of words and sayings are repeated throughout the story, so the telling of the story should be true to the original to keep the flavor of the language. Unless you can memorize it, a reading will probably be more effective than a telling. When the story has been presented and perhaps repeated, with the children joining in on the familiar parts, they will be ready to assemble the cast of characters needed for a puppet show.

During the show, one child is responsible for each character. Using a table turned on its side as a stage, the action takes place with the pancake crossing in front of the stage over and over, each time meeting one of the hungry creatures, beginning with Manny Panny and ending with Piggy Wiggy. As Piggy Wiggy swallows the pancake, the puppeteer behind the table can pop the balloon, creating an ending that especially satisfies young audiences. In order to keep the story line moving, the adult reader should pay careful attention to pacing.

Poetry

Reading Aloud

Where the Sidewalk Ends written and illustrated by Shel Silverstein.

The poems in this collection are most notable for their humor. Reading aloud enhances the humor, so that play on words is heightened and the pacing of each poem suits the treatment of theme. Before you read, decide what is funny about each poem. How does the author create

the humor? Is it through alliteration, play on words, pacing? How should the poem be read so as to get the best effect?

Children will want to hear the poems more than once. In the case of those such as "Boa Constrictor," encourage them to join in on the second or third reading, adding pantomime as they begin to memorize the poem.

A bit of discussion following some of the poems will help children to recognize why a poem is funny. They will realize that the children in these poems are much like themselves; you might explain that it is often fun to laugh at ourselves. These poems may motivate children to do their own reading aloud and writing of poetry.

Discussion

"Low Tide" from *The Malibu and Other Poems* by Myra Cohn Livingston.

> *Found. One red starfish*
> *at low tide. One*
> *plump, prickly starfish wrested by arm,*
> *by leg, squirming among*
> *purple, bubbling sea urchins.*
>
> *Plop him in a pail? Scoop up the*
> *salt water? His color will fade.*
> *He will miss his bubbling urchins.*
>
> *Grab him by the arm. Return him*
> *to his rock, his pink anemone.*
> *One red starfish. Lost.*[2]

If a poem is to be discussed, it should have form and content that will inspire discussion. That is essential because a forced discussion will become simply a question-answer period and will very likely lead to a dislike for poetry. "Low Tide" is a poet's description of an experience similar to that of many children; they may never have seen a live starfish or an anemone, but they have probably captured tadpoles or even small water bugs in puddles.

Response may be an emotional reaction, centering on the joy of finding something as fascinating as a starfish. Children may relate to the speaker in the poem, explaining what they would have done if they had found the starfish, perhaps thinking of their values concerning ecology. There may also be a reaction to the literary qualities of the poem, responses that show a listener's attention to description or to form.

The title is a good introduction to the poem. Read it and ask children what they would expect to see on a beach at low tide. If your children are not acquainted with ocean and tidal changes, it may be necessary to explain briefly the way a beach looks when the water sweeps out to sea, leaving hundreds of yards of exposed sand. Read the poem once, not too quickly, emphasizing the first and last words so that children get a sense of the form of this free verse. Let them discuss it informally if they offer comments. Then read it again.

After the second reading, you may want to open up a discussion by asking children whether they have ever had an experience like this poet is describing. Why did the speaker in the poem decide not to keep the starfish? Is the last part of the poem as fast-moving and happy as the first? Why not? How does the pace of the poem reflect the speaker's mood?

To help children think about the use of descriptive words and phrases, ask if they could draw a picture of what they heard. If necessary, reread, asking them to listen for all the ways this poet paints a word picture. How is the starfish described? the sea urchins? Children may also become aware of form if you show the poem so that they can see the one-word beginning and ending. Ask children how "Found" and "Lost" shape the poem, even though it does not have a regular rhyme scheme.

Fantasy

Discussion

The Borrowers by Mary Norton.

This book can give children some ideas about the characteristics of fantasy. Most important, it can generate strong emotional response. Children are intrigued with the lives of the tiny

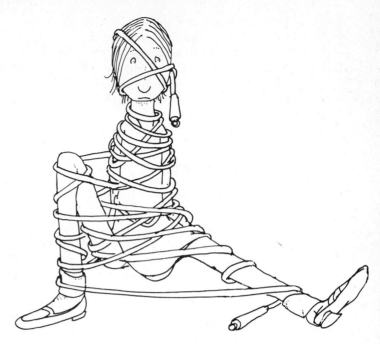

From "Jumping Rope" from *Where the Sidewalk Ends*, written and illustrated by Shel Silverstein.

people; they share the Borrowers' fear of discovery and they enjoy the clever uses the Borrowers have for items we "lose." The stories are so intriguing that more than one child has remarked that it almost seems possible there could be little people behind the walls. Children can also respond to literary aspects of the story. They begin to appreciate the use of point of view to create an effect and it is rather a surprise when they realize that the "human beans" described by the tiny Borrowers in this story are very much like themselves. With some guidance, children can also see that the author has used manipulation of characters in a clever way to create this fantasy: In this story it is the characters who make it a fantasy. They are not talking animals as in Russell Hoban's *A Bargain for Frances*, nor are they people from another planet. They are tiny people who look and talk and feel just like us. The setting is realistic; only the characters have been manipulated to produce the fantasy.

There is enough suspense in the episodes to hold attention as you read them aloud. Take advantage of the places where good oral interpretation skills will pay off. At the end of the first chapter, pause and give children a few minutes to react spontaneously to the story. Some children will enter into the spirit of the story if you ask them what they have lost lately and how the Borrowers might be able to put the item to use. Give them a chance to think about how the Borrowers must feel when they hear the heavy tramp of footsteps entering a room near them. You might try some point-of-view questions such as: You are Pod. Where were you when you first realized the boy had seen you? What were your first thoughts? That information is quite clearly given in the book. To switch point of view, you might then say: You are the boy. What did you think when you saw the tiny creature halfway up the curtain in the nursery?

When the book has been completed, you should give children a chance to think back over the story. Did it seem real to them? What could have happened? What could not be possible? How did the author change the characters so that she made the story a fantasy rather than a realistic story? Interpretation may come into play, too, when children discuss the reasons that some things terrified the Borrowers but seem completely harmless to us. Writing is a natural follow-up as children try to describe what the Borrowers might experience in their classrooms and homes.

Story Theater

In the Forest by Marie Hall Ets.

This enjoyable story is simple enough so that young children can dramatize it. There are twelve animal characters in addition to a boy and his father, so it is possible to involve a large group. Response to the story will surely be at the emotional level as children interact with the joyousness of the walk. Some children will show involvement with the characters through good pantomime.

Because the pictures are not large, you may want to gather children closely around you for the reading. Following that, let them think over the characters to decide which they enjoyed most. A second look at the pictures may aid them in remembering the cast of characters. As a story character is identified, you might want

to let children imitate the character, encouraging them to use bodily motion and good facial expressions to develop the pantomime. When all characters have been identified and mimed, let children choose their parts and designate the various settings as locations in the room. Read the story, pausing so children can play the character roles, adding appropriate noises when they can.

Animal Stories

Discussion

Owls in the Family by Farley Mowat.

Farley Mowat, a Canadian naturalist, wrote this highly entertaining story about a boy and his two pet owls. Oral reading of part or all of the story followed by discussion gives children a chance to share their enjoyment and to appreciate the information about wild creatures. Emotional response should emerge in the form of laughter at amusing incidents and descriptions and, for some children, in an understanding of Billy's friendship with his owls. Feelings of empathy for one or another of the characters may also be expressed. Through discussion, children may become aware of a literary quality of the story as they see how frequently the author injects humor involving a story character's mishaps. Evaluation can be a part of the response pattern if children are asked how the author has succeeded in giving the owls qualities that are both human and animal-like.

The entire book is suitable for reading aloud and is written with an episodic plot structure so that each chapter stands alone. Too much discussion of any book can interfere with enjoyment of the story. Nevertheless, there are times when discussion is important so that children can share their thoughts about a story and, with your guidance, begin to understand why they appreciate the writing. Discussion can be reserved for the end of the story or, as we suggest here, initiated at the end of a chapter or of several chapters.

To set a situation for discussion of the Mowat book, you might want to read the first five chapters aloud, pausing after Chapter 5 to give the children a chance to react. You can begin the discussion by noting parts of the story that brought laughter from the group as you read. Ask why they laughed. What had the author done to create a funny scene? Why did they laugh when Wol falls with a thud as he is learning to fly? Why did they laugh when Weeps refuses to even try to open his wings and falls like a rock instead? Perhaps they will recognize the ridiculousness of each situation and also the fact that we often laugh at another person's misfortune. (They may recall laughing when a friend got his shoe caught in a bicycle wheel and tumbled off.) Why does that make us feel good?

Children may be interested in talking about the relationship Bill has with his owls. Why does he seem to know what they are thinking? Some children may be able to compare their relationships with pets to the example in the story. A natural extension of this questioning tack leads to student evaluation of the way these animals are presented. You can pursue this by asking children in what ways the owls in the story appear human and in what ways they appear like wild animals. If students are able to make these comparisons, you might ask whether they think the author should have included the wild animal episodes (such as the killing of the cat) as well as the accounts of the owls' almost human behavior. What is he telling us? Children who have pets will enjoy writing descriptions of their pets' behavior and appearance.

Role-Playing

The Biggest Bear by Lynd Ward.

The fact that this animal story is based on an underlying set of values makes it possible for readers to relate to the situations in which Johnny finds himself. Children should be encouraged to respond emotionally to the story —to enjoy the pictures as well as the story line and to identify with Johnny's feelings about his bear. They may also evaluate the story ending first by role-playing and then by discussing the author's solution to Johnny's problem.

Successful role-playing depends on the degree to which children can interact with a problem and work out their own solutions. The story must set up a problem children understand and care about. *The Biggest Bear* can draw a strong emotional response from children and can also encourage interpretation of the story and sometimes evaluation of the story ending. Responses may also indicate that the story involves children in value formation.

It is a good idea to read the story aloud to the group, showing the pictures so that all the children can enjoy them. There are several good places to stop for role-playing of a story problem situation. The first is on page 47 when Johnny is told that the bear must go. When the children have looked at that picture, you might pose this point-of-view situation: You are Johnny. Talk the situation over with your father. What will you do? Ask two children to volunteer to play the roles of Johnny and his father and let them carry on a conversation to help Johnny decide what to do about the bear. Several other pairs of children may also want to participate when the first group is finished.

Continue reading the story. You may want to stop again on pages 52, 56, and 60 so that Johnny and his father can try to solve the problem of the bear each time he returns. Or you may prefer an uninterrupted reading of the story, stopping at page 76 where the bear is captured for a zoo. Children will enjoy giving opinions of that problem solution. You may want to invite them to be Johnny and his friends. Ask: Was this a good solution to the problem for Johnny *and* for the bear? What other ending can you think of? Which do you prefer?

Writing Activity

The Bat-Poet by Randall Jarrell.

This story, with prose interwoven with poetry, is unusual and beautifully written. Because of its quality, it deserves to be read aloud by an experienced reader. The approach suggested here is a combination of oral reading, discussion, and follow-up writing activities.

Responses to be encouraged are an emotional response to the bat's need to share his experiences with others. Many children will empathize with the bat's frustration at not being able to interest the other bats in the wonderful things he sees during his daytime excursions. Children will also respond to the

From *The Bat-Poet* by Randall Jarrell, illustrated by Maurice Sendak.

content of the poems as well as to such literary characteristics as the author's choice of words. Certainly they should hear the poems several times so that they are aware of the musical quality combined with superb description.

You might present the book to children by asking whether they have ever thought what the world might look like to an animal, such as a squirrel or a bird. What would they notice? What could be important to such creatures? In this book, they will view life through the eyes of a bat. The story is too long to be read at one sitting, so you may read only certain parts or find good stopping points. It would be a good idea to pause occasionally to let children repeat and enjoy some of the poetry and other especially fine descriptive passages. In order to prepare for later writing activities, you may want to begin a chart titled "Good Descriptions," writing a few phrases from the opening of the story and encouraging children to help you decide what to add to the chart as you go along. Some ideas for the beginning are: "the color of coffee with cream in it," "a fur wave went over them," and "squirrels chattered . . . like two rocks being knocked together." At this point, the children may want to discuss their interpretations of the story and the author's use of language.

The follow-up writing activity can be based

on children's appreciation of descriptions used in the story. You might simply ask them to choose some animal with which they are quite familiar and perhaps can observe frequently. Several options are available for a writing activity based on this story. Some children may want to write a prose and poetry description of the creature, as was done in *The Bat-Poet*. Others may prefer to describe the world as it might be seen by the creature, getting experience in writing from a different point of view. In either case, emphasis should be on producing fresh, descriptive phrases, emphasizing some of the techniques used by the writer of this fine book.

Modern Fiction

Reading Aloud

My Brother Louis Measures Worms by Barbara Robinson.

The author of *The Best Christmas Pageant Ever* has produced another wonderfully humorous book for children. Louis is an unusual boy, to be sure, but then his entire extended family appears to teeter on the brink of madness. In addition to measuring worms, Louis seems bound to turn each day into an adventure. He even manages to drive his mother's car, quite successfully for a seven-year-old boy, and does so until he absentmindedly gives himself away. Each chapter in this book involves a new episode in the lives of Louis and his family and so this book works well to read aloud when time is limited. The style of writing is smooth and the humorous passages are particularly well written and easy to read. In discussion that follows, children may want to share amusing things that have happened to their own family members. Such episodes make good material for creative writing, too.

Role-Playing

Child of the Owl by Laurence Yep.

In order to participate fully in role-playing, children must recognize and relate to the story characters' problems. They must be able to experience situations in the story from the characters' points of view. *Child of the Owl* presents a clear-cut situation for role-playing because the story focuses on Casey's difficult adjustment to life in San Francisco's Chinatown. Caught between two cultures—her grandmother's Chinese way of life and her father's westernized life—Casey is constantly faced with situations that are puzzling to her. To enter into the story completely, children must also be able to understand how Casey's grandmother, Paw-Paw, feels about her life in Chinatown.

To lead children into the role-playing, you might wait until the entire book has been read and then pose situations such as these: You are Casey and it is just after your arrival in Chinatown. Describe Paw-Paw as you saw her then. What does she mean to you? When students have had time to recapture that effect, ask them to shift to a later part of the story. Now Paw-Paw is in the hospital. Describe the thoughts that you have about her. What does she mean to you now? Why have your thoughts about her changed?

For a somewhat more difficult challenge, set up this situation. Read aloud or have children read pages 28–29, where Casey first meets Paw-Paw. Then say: You are Paw-Paw. Your grandchild is coming to stay with you. You don't really know her but you know that her way of life is different from yours. What thoughts are going through your mind as you see her arrive? You might ask them to take Paw-Paw's point of view after she and Casey have come to know each other, say after the two of them have been to Chinese movies (pp. 83–93). Now, as Paw-Paw, how would you describe Casey? Have your feelings about her changed? How?

Whatever the questions used to motivate role-taking, they should help children to understand more fully the concerns that motivate story characters. The questions may be used to motivate writing, as an alternative to role-playing.

Oral Interpretation

Ramona the Pest by Beverly Cleary.

This is a delightful book to read aloud to children. Listeners are amused by Ramona's antics, but they also realize that she is a little

person with fears and needs quite like their own. They can respond emotionally by laughing at her but also by feeling compassion and empathy for her. Building on the emotional response, children can begin to interpret the story by inferring that Ramona seems to be a little girl who doesn't mean to be naughty but who sometimes gets into trouble because she thinks she has been badly treated by someone. They may also infer that the author is trying to show us the things that can happen to make kindergarten (or any school experience) difficult for children.

Oral reading of the story should take advantage of the many dialogue parts that help to build Ramona as a character. Numerous sections of the story are appropriate for Readers Theatre work. It is preferable, of course, that children read or hear the entire story before singling out one section for oral interpretation. An effective section is near the beginning, where Ramona goes to school for the first time (pp. 10–17, ending with the amusing "present" misunderstanding). Another good section is the scene where Ramona is stuck in the mud and must be pulled out by Henry Huggins (pp. 114–125). A third choice is the "dawnzer" episode (pp. 171–173). Third- and fourth-graders are far enough advanced to read these sections and they are also enough older than Ramona that they can feel a sort of security in having passed through the difficult kindergarten period. They may enjoy recreating the episode through creative drama, as well as Readers Theatre.

Historical Fiction and Biography

Reading Aloud

Ragtime Tumpie by Alan Schroeder.

This fictionalized biography is based on the early life of entertainer Josephine Baker. The text is elaborated in the paintings by Bernie Fuchs. "Tumpie," as she was called, loved to dance from the time she was a small girl living in St. Louis in 1915, surrounded by the catchy rhythm of ragtime. This is a joyous story, told in

From *Ragtime Tumpie* by Alan Schroeder, illustrated by
Bernie Fuchs.

fine orchards. Children respond emotionally to
the character of Johnny Appleseed, especially
when the story is told convincingly. The picture
book by Aliki provides a basic story line that
storytellers can use or adapt. You may want to
show the illustrations from the book as you tell
the story of Johnny Appleseed's life.

Role-Playing

The Sign of the Beaver by Elizabeth George
Speare.

Set in the Maine wilderness in the 1700s, this is
the story of a white boy who owes his survival to
the friendship and help of an Indian family.
Left alone while his father travels back to find
the rest of the family, Matt is faced with adult
responsibilities in a desolate setting. The reader
is allowed to experience the emotions of Matt,
the young settler, and also Attean, his young
Indian friend. Through the eyes of the two
boys, we come to see how the white settlers' way
of life causes the original inhabitants to adapt
their ways to accommodate to the new frontier.
The story stirs curiosity, too, as frontier survival is detailed in the means of obtaining food
that Matt learns from his Indian friends.

The story is well written and there are numerous passages suited for reading aloud so
that children experience a situation through
the eyes of the characters. After such a reading,
it is effective to ask children to speak in the
voice of a character. For example, in the situation at the end of Chapter 3, when Ben awakens
to find the stranger and his father's rifle missing, you might say to a child, "You are Ben. If
your father came home right now, how would
you describe the previous days to him? Tell him
what you are feeling as well as what happened."
To another child you might say, "You are Ben's
father. What would you say to your son about
his experiences? What advice would you give
him?"

Engaging students in role-playing through
conversation can lead to greater recognition of
characterization and of the techniques an author uses to develop a character. Writing
through the eyes and the mind of a character is
another means to help children explore
characterization.

a style that has rhythm of its own. It is a fine
book to read aloud so that children can savor
the sounds and scenes of that magical time.

You may want to introduce the story with a
tape of some ragtime music so that children can
visualize Tumpie dancing to it. As an additional
activity, children may want to create their own
paintings that reflect the rhythm of ragtime
music.

Storytelling

The Story of Johnny Appleseed by Aliki.

Young children are interested in living things;
they enjoy planting seeds and watching them
sprout. Though they may not be able to imagine a country without carefully tended orchards and fields, they will be interested in this
story about a man who cared enough about
trees and people to spend part of his life
planting seeds that could eventually produce

Writing Activity

Number the Stars by Lois Lowry.

The story is set in Denmark during World War II, when German soldiers occupied the country. It involves the lives of two families, the Johansens and the Rosens, but more specifically, their girls, Annemarie and Ellen. The tension between the Danes and the German soldiers who patrol the streets is clear from the outset of the book. As the Germans impose more and more restrictions on the Danish Jews, the Danes and their King Christian X pull together in defense of their Jewish neighbors. When it is learned that the Germans intend to arrest all Jews, the Rosen family goes into hiding and Ellen becomes temporarily part of Annemarie's family. The tension in the story is heightened when German soldiers come to the Johansen home in the middle of the night, looking for the Rosen family. As they open the door to the room where Ellen and Annemarie

are huddled, Annemarie quickly breaks a gold chain from Ellen's neck and hides the Star of David necklace in her own hand. The soldiers leave, but the Johansens know they must help their friends escape to neutral Sweden. The incidents that lead to the escape include numerous other tense moments.

An activity that follows naturally from the story is construction of a diary that might have been kept by either Ellen or Annemarie, keeping a record of the events that lead up to the escape. You might provide as examples other books that include diaries, such as *Ann Frank: The Diary of a Young Girl* or *Dear Mr. Henshaw*.

This story also provides a good vehicle for dramatization. You might read the entire story over a period of several days and then encourage students to recreate episodes that work well for pantomime, creative drama, or Readers Theatre. Intermediate grade students can work in groups to plan their presentations.

Cover illustration from *Number the Stars* by Lois Lowry.

Informational Books
Reading Aloud

Jambo Means Hello by Tom and Muriel Feelings.

This beautifully illustrated picture book is an alphabet book that will interest older children as well as those in the primary grades. Information in the book ranges from an introduction with a map showing countries where Swahili is spoken to definition and pronunciation of twenty-four Swahili words, one for each letter of the Swahili alphabet. Word concepts are elaborated in the double-page illustrations.

Do not neglect the introduction when you read the book aloud, for it presents important information about the people who speak Swahili. Use it to acquaint children with the fact that an introduction is an important part of many nonfiction books. As you read the book, show the pictures so that children can see how the pictures help to develop word concepts. You may want to let children speak some of the words together, pantomiming the concepts as they say the new words. That is an effective procedure for words like *heshima* (respect), *jambo* (hello), *rafiki* (friend), and *Karibu* (welcome).

Responses to be sought and encouraged are, of course, enjoyment of the language and curiosity about word meanings, responses that touch on emotional reaction, interpretation, and attention to literary qualities. Children may show interest in similarities between Swahili and English, evident in words for father, mother, and school. Discussion may lead children to seek other information about how words enter a language.

Discussion

How to Turn Lemons into Money by Louise Armstrong.

This guide to economics, described in terms children can understand, is likely to promote lively discussion. A lemonade stand is used as the model for a business; as the business of running the stand is described, the vocabulary of economics is introduced. Discussion could focus on interpretation of the text and illustrations and on application of the ideas to new situations. Appropriate questions to generate discussion might be: If *you* were to go into business, what would you make and sell? How would you decide on the market value of your product? Where might you get a *capital loan* if you needed one? What would you call another person who was selling the same product? Suppose you were ready to liquidate your assets. What would they be? What other kind of business would you like to open next? Write a set of guidelines for someone else who is thinking of starting a business.

Role-Playing

Handtalk Birthday by Remy Charlip, Mary Beth, and George Ancona.

Handtalk Birthday is a book that builds children's curiosity about ways of communicating without speech. You may want to introduce children to *Handtalk* first, acquainting them with the rudiments of signing and finger spelling. Experience with these books should help children to develop empathy with hearing-impaired people and admiration for the way they are able to communicate.

You may want to introduce this informational

THANK YOU.

From *Handtalk Birthday* by Remy Charlip and Mary Beth, photographs by George Ancona.

book by having children talk about what they would like as birthday presents and how they could show those objects through pantomime. Then go through the book, spending extra time on pages that show the signing for the presents about which Mary Beth thinks. Children will enjoy learning how to sign the happy birthday song as they sing it.

When children have had a chance to study the book, they will be ready for a role-playing situation in which you ask a question, perhaps inquiring about their favorite food, and ask them to answer it by signing. Other opportunities for practice are numerous and may depend on the students' curiosity about what it is like to be hearing-impaired. They may want to get acquainted with some children with hearing problems so that they can practice their new skill and learn, firsthand, how these children cope with tasks that hearing youngsters take for granted. Children may also want to practice signing informally when they want to send messages to one another or dramatize an idea or a scene from a story they are reading.

Summary

In all the books recommended and activities suggested in this chapter and in all the books and activities you find work well in your own experiences, the key to your success will be building on children's enjoyment. Response to literature can take place only when children have enjoyed a story or poem. This idea may seem obvious on the surface, and yet it can be lost sight of so easily when choosing books and activities for a particular group of children with particular needs and tastes. If you take pleasure or enjoyment as the starting point and as the goal of a literature program, you are likely to have most success measured in terms of enthusiastic readers. Through the enjoyment, a sense of literary structure may develop and children may be encouraged to try to interpret aspects of the work. Occasionally, they will look at the story or poem critically, evaluating it in some fashion. Most important, however, we hope children will enjoy these experiences with literature so much that they will want to read and reread books independently, to take time alone with favorite picture books, and to investigate the books of other authors.

A second hope is that you, the adult, will seek out other books and poems that you would enjoy sharing with children, adapting some of the activities in this chapter to your own material. A further hope is that you can provide plenty of books and a pleasant reading environment. An activity-centered program in combination with a strong program of independent library reading can provide the basis for ever-increasing enjoyment of and reliance on reading as a leisure-time pursuit.

Children's Books Mentioned in This Chapter

AARDEMA, VERNA. *Why Mosquitoes Buzz in People's Ears,* ill. by Leo and Diane Dillon. Dial, 1975.

ALIKI. *The Story of Johnny Appleseed,* ill. by author. Prentice, 1963.

ALLARD, HARRY. *Miss Nelson Is Missing,* ill. by James Marshall. Houghton, 1977.

ANDERSEN, HANS CHRISTIAN. *The Emperor's New Clothes,* ill. by Virginia Lee Burton. Houghton, 1962.

ARMSTRONG, LOUISE. *How to Turn Lemons into Money,* ill. by Bill Basso. Harcourt, 1976.

ASBJÖRNSEN, PETER, and JÖRGEN MOE. *Tales from the Fjeld,* tr. by Sir George Webbe Dasent. (See "The Pancake.")

————. *The Three Billy-Goats Gruff,* tr. by Sir George Webbe Dasent, ill. by Marcia Brown. Harcourt, 1957.

BOYLAN, ELEANOR. *How to Be a Puppeteer.* McCall, 1970.

BRYAN, ASHLEY. *The Cat's Purr,* ill. by author. Atheneum, 1985.

CHARLIP, REMY, MARY BETH, and GEORGE ANCONA. *Handtalk,* ill. with photos. Parents, 1974.

————. *Handtalk Birthday,* ill. with photos. Four Winds, 1987.

CHRISTOPHER, JOHN. *The White Mountains.* Macmillan, 1967.

CLEARY, BEVERLY. *Ramona the Pest,* ill. by Louis Darling. Morrow, 1968.

————. *Runaway Ralph,* ill. by Louis Darling. Morrow, 1970.

COURLANDER, HAROLD. *The King's Drum,* ill. by Enrico Arno. Harcourt, 1962.

DE GASZTOLD, CARMEN BERNOS. *Prayers from the Ark,* tr. by Rumer Godden. Viking, 1962.

DEPAOLA, TOMIE. *The Legend of the Bluebonnet,* Putnam's, 1983.

DE REGNIERS, BEATRICE SCHENK. *May I Bring a Friend?* ill. by Beni Montresor. Atheneum, 1964.

EMBERLEY, BARBARA. *Drummer Hoff,* ill. by Ed Emberley. Prentice, 1967.

ETS, MARIE HALL. *In the Forest,* ill. by author. Viking, 1944.

FEELINGS, MURIEL. *Jambo Means Hello,* ill. by Tom Feelings. Dial, 1974.

FRANCHERE, RUTH. *Cesar Chavez,* ill. by Earl Thollander. Crowell, 1970.

FYLEMAN, ROSE. *Sun under the Silver Umbrella.* Macmillan, 1962. (See "Mice.")

GÁG, WANDA. *Millions of Cats,* ill. by author. McCann, 1928.

GEORGE, JEAN CRAIGHEAD. *My Side of the Mountain,* ill. by author. Dutton, 1959.

HALL, DONALD. *Ox-Cart Man,* ill. by Barbara Cooney. Viking, 1979.

HAMILTON, VIRGINIA. *The Time-Ago Tales of Jahdu,* ill. by Nonny Hogrogian. Macmillan, 1969.

HOBAN, RUSSELL. *A Bargain for Frances,* ill. by Lillian Hoban. Harper, 1970.

HOBAN, TANA. *Push-Pull, Empty-Full.* Macmillan, 1972.

HOLM, ANNE. *North to Freedom,* tr. from the Danish by L. W. Kingsland. Harcourt, 1965.

HUNT, MARGARET, tr. *Grimm's Household Tales.* Penguin, 1983. (See "The Fisherman and His Wife.")

JARRELL, RANDALL. *The Bat-Poet,* ill. by Maurice Sendak. Macmillan, 1967.

JOHNSON, CLIFTON, ed. *The Oak Tree Fairy Book.* Dover Publications, 1968 (1905). (See "The Four Musicians.")

LAWSON, ROBERT. *Rabbit Hill,* ill. by author. Viking, 1944.

LEWIS, STEPHEN. *Zoo City.* Greenwillow, 1976.

LIVINGSTON, MYRA COHN. *The Malibu and Other Poems.* Atheneum, 1972.

LOWRY, LOIS. *Number the Stars.* Houghton, 1989.

MCCORD, DAVID. *Far and Few,* ill. by Henry B. Kane. Little, 1952.

MACAULAY, DAVID. *Castle.* Houghton, 1977.

MATHIS, SHARON BELL. *The Hundred Penny Box,* ill. by Leo and Diane Dillon. Viking, 1975.

MERRILL, JEAN. *The Pushcart War,* ill. by Ronni Solbert. Scott/Addison, 1964.

MILES, MISKA. *Nobody's Cat,* ill. by John Schoenherr. Little, 1969.

MINARIK, ELSE. *A Kiss for Little Bear,* ill. by Maurice Sendak. Harper, 1968.

MOSEL, ARLENE. *Tikki Tikki Tembo,* ill. by Blair Lent. Holt, 1968.

MOWAT, FARLEY. *Owls in the Family,* ill. by Robert Frankenberg. Little, 1962.

NORTON, MARY. *The Borrowers,* ill. by Beth and Joe Krush. Harcourt, 1953.

O'NEILL, MARY. *Hailstones and Halibut Bones,* ill. by Leonard Weisgard. Doubleday, 1953.

PATERSON, KATHERINE. *The Great Gilly Hopkins.* T. Crowell, 1978.

POTTER, BEATRIX. *The Tale of Peter Rabbit,* ill. by author. Warne, 1903.

RASKIN, ELLEN. *Nothing Ever Happens on My Block,* ill. by author. Atheneum, 1966.

ROBINSON, BARBARA. *My Brother Louis Measures Worms.* Harper & Row, 1988.

ROSS, LAURA. *Puppet Shows Using Poems and Stories.* Lothrop, Lee, & Shepard, 1970.

RYLANT, CYNTHIA. *Night in the Country,* ill. by Mary Szilagyi. Bradbury, 1986.

SAWYER, RUTH. *Journey Cake, Ho!* ill. by Robert McCloskey. Viking, 1953.

SCHROEDER, ALAN. *Ragtime Tumpie,* ill. by Bernie Fuchs. Little, Brown, 1989.

SCIESZKA, JON. *The True Story of the 3 Little Pigs!* ill. by Lane Smith. Viking, 1989.

SENDAK, MAURICE. *Where the Wild Things Are,* ill. by author. Harper, 1963.

SEUSS, DR. *The King's Stilts.* Random House, 1939.

SHEPHARD, ESTHER. *Paul Bunyan,* ill. by Rockwell Kent. Harcourt, 1941.

SILVERSTEIN, SHEL. *Where the Sidewalk Ends,* ill. by author. Harper, 1974.

SLOBODKINA, ESPHYR. *Caps for Sale,* ill. by author. W. R. Scott, 1947.

SPEARE, ELIZABETH GEORGE. *The Sign of the Beaver.* Houghton, 1983.

————. *The Witch of Blackbird Pond.* Houghton, 1958.

STEIG, WILLIAM. *Doctor De Soto,* ill. by author. Farrar, 1982.

————. *Sylvester and the Magic Pebble,* ill. by author. Windmill, 1969.

STOLZ, MARY. *The Bully of Barkham Street,* ill. by Leonard Shortall. Harper, 1963.

SUTHERLAND, ZENA, and MYRA COHN LIVINGSTON. *The Scott, Foresman Anthology of Children's Literature.* Scott, Foresman, 1984. (See "The Bremen Town-Musicians," "The Hare and the Tortoise," and "The Pancake.")

TWAIN, MARK. *The Adventures of Tom Sawyer.* Grosset & Dunlap, 1946.

UCHIDA, YOSHIKO. *Journey to Topaz.* Scribner's, 1971.

WARD, LYND. *The Biggest Bear,* ill. by author. Houghton, 1952.

WILDER, LAURA INGALLS. *The Little House in the Big Woods,* ill. by Garth Williams. Harper, 1953. (See others in the series also.)

YASHIMA, TARO. *Crow Boy,* ill. by author. Viking, 1955.

YEP, LAURENCE. *Child of the Owl.* Harper, 1977.

ZOLOTOW, CHARLOTTE. *Mr. Rabbit and the Lovely Present,* ill. by Maurice Sendak. Harper, 1962.

Part Four

Areas and Issues

Areas and Issues
Children and Books

Introduction

Peggy Sullivan

Many of the figures of speech that are applied to children refer to them as part of a political entity. We speak of the *republic of childhood,* the *world of children,* the *land of youth,* the *world of children's literature.* In a book which explores so thoughtfully many of the aspects of children, their books, and reading, it makes sense to deal with some of the broad aspects of that world which includes children and books. Like any nation or world, the world of children's literature includes problems and opportunities, rules and needs, pleasures and principles. It is important to understand something about these aspects if one is to understand the citizens of that world and their relationship to books and reading.

In the essays that follow, the areas and issues that relate to children and books are explored. Ann Carlson calls attention to the fact that children, from their first days, are living in a world of changes, and that they are participating in those changes themselves. She notes how their awareness of themselves and of the people and events around them helps to form them as individuals, and how their social development affects the kinds of books and reading they will enjoy. As an expert in children's literature, Ms. Carlson knows what kinds of books will appeal to different ages; just as she knows, as a parent, when a child may be at just the right stage for a particular concept. While each child is an individual, it is possible to trace similarities that occur at different stages in their young lives. For the preschool child, about whom she writes here, it may be the parent who will have the best information about where a child is in terms of development, and it is certainly the parent who will want to use that information to provide the most appropriate reading experiences for the young child.

The child's developing independence eventually leads to his or her own discovery of the pleasures of reading. Almost all children will learn to read in the setting of an elementary school, and their reactions to the experience will be affected by the way reading is taught and modeled for them. Marie Sorensen explores some of the current thinking about and various approaches to reading. The concept of *whole language* is much discussed among experts in reading, as she notes. Children deserve to have access to the best that is written for them or available to them from the broader base of literature which they have often selected for themselves. They need to experience the integration of their reading with other activities, for this, too, is a part of development and growth.

Access to a wide variety of reading materials is important for children if they are to acquire the skills that make them literate, but access to ideas is an important need as well. Alice Naylor has championed many of the causes related to broader access to materials for children; and in her essay she shares her view of the significance of the freedom to select reading material as the First Amendment of the U.S. Constitution has guaranteed. In any country, there are likely to be censors, those who would limit the access of others to ideas that may be controversial, but they are especially likely to thrive in a republic as open as the United States of America. Their rights as censors are often protected by the same rights that they would deny to others. Issues in this area can become quite complicated, and Ms. Naylor explores briefly some of the court issues that need to be known and understood by adults if they are to defend the rights of access for children. She also provides a list of sources which can help any individual or group that may be a target of a censorship attack, and she suggests ways both to avoid and to deal with such attacks.

Just as freedom of access is intended to make a broad range of materials available for children's reading, knowledge of materials that are less easily available is needed if children are to have the rich experiences they deserve. Children in English-speaking countries are fortunate to have access to many different kinds of books from other countries, at least in the sense that their language provides such access. In actuality, however, unless publishers seek out and bring to this country books that are published elsewhere, children may miss knowing about them. In some instances, this will mean having them translated from other languages as well. Based on her familiarity with organizations that recognize significant literary contributions from around the world, Amy Kellman touches on some of the problems that inhibit international access to children's books.

Always, when one is concerned with literature for children, there is the tension between the need to provide great numbers of books and the need to select from among them, to ensure that children and those who select books for them get correct information about new materials that are of high quality. One of the activities that provides that kind of information is the giving of awards for children's books. In my own essay on this topic, I have focused on the major children's book awards in the United States and on the growing number of awards which are based on children's own preferences. While authors and illustrators receive the recognition that such awards provide, everyone in the world of children's books benefits from knowing what titles have been selected as outstanding in a given year, although it is also important to keep in mind that selectors of awards are not infallible, and that excellence, which is honored with awards, is not the only criterion to be followed in developing a program of individual reading and enjoyment.

The world of children's literature is not an isolated microcosm. It is, in fact, of increasing interest to many kinds of scholars. Kay Vandergrift, herself a scholar, reviews the research that has developed around children's literature. She notes that books that have been around a long time can be studied in such a way as to produce new discoveries and insights; and

she recognizes the value of placing children's literature in a context that makes such insights possible. Many students using this book will probably have the experience of writing a paper or preparing some kind of research report about children's literature. Vandergrift suggests the range of kinds of research that might be considered and conducted.

Time and events have the power to alter the significance of issues and areas. The six issues cited in this introduction have been identified as significant as the 1990s begin. One also needs to recognize that other points of view or topics might be considered more important than some of those about to be explored. What follows are just some of the important ideas being discussed in regard to children and books today. If the result of this discussion is to bring to light other issues of equal importance that might in time be included in a similar group of essays, that is all to the good. It would be ironic, indeed, if a book so devoted to opening up possibilities for children in their reading did not also open up the possibilities of further thought and exploration for the adults who work with them.

Peggy Sullivan, dean of the College of Professional Studies at Northern Illinois University, is a librarian who has written extensively about children, books, and libraries.

Young Children and Literature-Centered Activities

Ann D. Carlson

An important reason for bringing young children and books together is to instill in the children a love of books and reading early in life. Parents, nursery school teachers, caregivers, children's librarians, and library media specialists all play vital roles in helping children develop this love for books and reading.

Even though development of skills in language, listening, and looking, and the reinforcement of concepts are important immediate objectives of book activities for young children, they should never be emphasized to such an extent that the child's enjoyment of books is jeopardized. A caring adult who shares books with a young child provides that child with a feeling of security and a time for enjoyment. These experiences may not only make it easier for the child to learn to read when she is older, but may also help develop a lifetime reading habit.

Parents, teachers, caregivers, and librarians need to be aware that activities meant to foster the enjoyment of books and reading, if they are to fulfill their purpose, must be developmentally appropriate for the children. The rest of this essay presents a compilation of important developmental characteristics of children from birth to four years of age as well as suggestions for developmentally appropriate literature-centered activities by six age groups.

Arranging developmental characteristics according to the age of the child, while convenient, is arbitrary. Human development is continuous and only partially correlated with chronological age. Thus, the listed characteristics are those of an "average" child; they will fit any particular child only approximately.

The Newborn to Six-Month-Old
Developmental Characteristics

From the moment the child is born, she experiences her world through her senses, and her curiosity begins to control much of her behavior. She is busy exploring her world visually, aurally, tactilely, and orally. She shows visual recognition of familiar objects, stares at her surroundings including large or moving objects, and enjoys looking at people's faces. By four months of age, she is seeing in color and her vision approximates that of the adult.

Sound is an important part of her life. She has been hearing language from birth, and by one month she may recognize a parent's voice. By three months, she may move her mouth and body rhythmically to adult speech that is directed to her, and coo and hum using mostly vowel sounds. By six months, she may coo or stop crying on hearing music and react to a change in volume.

The mastery of hands as tools is a major development of this period. By three months she begins to swipe at objects and to explore her face, eyes, and mouth with her hands. She wants to touch, grasp, turn and shake objects, and she reaches for and tries to put in her mouth seemingly everything within her grasp.

Suggestions for Activities

Some adults begin showing picture books to the infant soon after birth, but she probably does not benefit from looking at the pictures until her visual abilities mature (usually around four months of age). Therefore, books for the young infant should be selected for their language and not their visuals. A nursery rhyme collection is an ideal choice for a first book.

Toward the end of this period the infant should be provided with visual variety in her environment. She enjoys looking at large, clear pictures, especially those with faces or high contrast, and mobiles. Pictures should be at her eye level.

Around four months, she begins to show interest in looking at pictures in books. Since she is likely to try to put them in her mouth, durable books with heavy cardboard or plastic coated pages are preferred. The books should show large, clear pictures in bright but real-life colors. Pictures should be of whole objects, usually one to a page, and should realistically depict the things in the infant's environment.

Adults are encouraged to talk to the infant in a pleasant tone, positioning their faces close to her face. When she coos, the adult can repeat the sounds that she has made. Throughout this period, singing songs or saying rhymes or jingles is more important than the act of looking at a book. These experiences should be shared when both the baby and the adult are relaxed with the adult holding the baby; they should not extend beyond her interest and enjoyment.

The Seven- to Fourteen-Month-Old
Developmental Characteristics

The child is busy listening to and experimenting with language. By seven months, he has a vocabulary of clearly enunciated simple syllables, like ma, di, or ba, which he repeats and combines. He enjoys listening to his own vocalizations and those of others, especially his parents'. By nine months, he may be expressing a thought with a single word, developing increasing awareness that words are symbols for familiar objects. For example, if someone says the word *airplane,* he may point to the sky, or if he hears the word *dog,* he may growl.

The child at this stage babbles with a great variety of sounds and inflections. It is fun to watch him as he begins to attempt new words and to mimic the mouth and jaw movements of others. By one year of age, he may be saying sentences of gibberish in which meaningful words are sometimes embedded.

He delights in turn-taking with an adult, which is very important, and enjoys "conversations." He will identify simple objects in his environment that he has heard adults name, such as *cup, ball, book, duck;* and, by fourteen months, he is able to identify people and some parts of his body.

As his memory grows—and depending on his previous social experiences, he may experience anxiety when separated from his parents. He has and will continue to exhibit great emotional attachment to his parents and caregivers; when he becomes mobile he may crawl (usually around eight months) and later walk (usually around twelve months) after them.

The abilities to crawl and walk aid him in his exploration. At first, he will use one hand as a support, and the other to explore. As he investigates his surroundings, which are a source of fascination to him, he remains within the eye-range of his parent or caregiver; gradually he may venture further out to explore, coming back to his parent or caregiver for reassurance, and then moving out again.

Suggestions for Activities

During this period adults are encouraged to respond in conversation using real words to the child's babbling. Conversation helps him put new sounds together. The sound of language continues to be of great importance, and nursery rhymes and songs are ideal.

The infant takes a greater interest than before in looking at books. The pictures should continue to be of whole objects, ideally one or a few to a page, realistically depicting familiar items, such as food, toys, pets, objects, or clothing.

When presenting picture books to the child, the adult should point to and name the object in the picture and help the child recall any experiences he may have had with the real object. The child should then be asked to repeat the name of the pictured object—a turn-taking technique. Adults can show the child a real object along with a picture of the object and talk about the object and its use or qualities. This exposes the child to the relationship between pictures and reality—the pictures becoming more meaningful. In time, he will realize that a two-dimensional picture represents a three-dimensional, real object.

At this age, the child may have one or more favorite books. He enjoys repetition and familiarity and may bring the same book to an adult over and over again. However, adults should not yet expect the child to show interest in books with plots. He will be able to do that soon.

Since the child is eager to practice his hand-eye coordinating abilities and is fascinated with hinged objects, small durable books are good for him to handle on his own. Not yet able to control his movements, he will often inadvertently rip regular paper pages out of books. Parents, teachers, and caregivers can make simple books or individual pages by gluing pictures of familiar objects to heavy cardboard. The use of textured materials for homemade books adds a further dimension since they provide tactile as well as visual experiences for the child. He also enjoys looking at photograph albums that include snapshots of himself, other family members, and pets. Simple finger plays provide fun and challenge for him.

The Fifteen- to Twenty-Three-Month-Old
Developmental Characteristics

Few periods in development are as fascinating to watch as this one. The child's language is growing rapidly. At the beginning of the period she is still interspersing babbling with real words, but by the end she has discarded most babbling and actively imitates words. She understands much of what is said to her, and enjoys question-and-answer games. She continues to be engrossed by sounds and repetition, and she may imitate simple sounds on request. By the end of this period, she has discovered that everything has a name and repeatedly asks, "What's that?"

Mastery of gross-motor skills, such as climbing, walking, marching, running, and the increased smoothness of hand-eye coordination allows her to do more. She enjoys manipulative play with experimentation, and likes to turn on faucets, fit things together, and zip and unzip zippers. She gets engrossed in toys that can be pushed and pulled and taken apart. She delights in exploring cabinets and drawers.

Personality development is one of the most dramatic themes of this period as she tries out her newfound sense of power. Increasingly, she becomes more demanding and self-assertive, establishing herself as a member of the family. She explores the effect she has on others and learns that people react in different ways. Her desire for autonomy brings on negativism. She may, for example, deliberately touch an object in full view of the adult who told her not to touch it. She is testing limits as well as her abilities and the right to have her own way.

Suggestions for Activities

Since the child is learning to master motor skills, adults are encouraged to provide colorful catalogs and magazines with which she can practice turning pages. Imbued with a growing sense of autonomy, she will want to turn the pages without adult assistance. Simple puzzles, either homemade out of a few pieces of poster board or manufactured out of wood, allow her to manipulate shapes. Singing action songs, such as "The Eensy, Weensy Spider," and doing simple finger plays together should also be continued.

Adults should respond to the child's babbling in a conversational manner. She enjoys hearing simple explanations and learning the names of more objects around her, such as foods, clothing, or furniture. She also continues to be fascinated by the sound of language in chants, nursery rhymes, and songs. Picture books with poems, nursery rhymes, and songs that can be sung, such as "Hush Little Baby" or "Skip to My Lou" are favorites.

Adults should continue to provide visual variety in the environment. The child enjoys looking at large, clear pictures that show some type of action or multiple objects. When looking at pictures in books, she should be encouraged to identify the objects and talk about them.

Pictures in books that refer to and reinforce experiences she has had, such as going to the zoo, are especially enjoyable for the child. When adults are sharing books with her, they can look at the pictures of the animals that were at the zoo and talk about them.

The child enjoys looking at picture books with people in them whom she can associate with family members. She continues to enjoy looking at photograph albums that contain family photographs that include her. Adults should talk about the people in the photographs, where they were taken, and the action in the photos.

The Two-Year-Old
Developmental Characteristics

All of the learning of the first two years begins to come together during the child's third year of life. His skills at using language, knowledge, and imagination develop rapidly.

He is intellectually curious about his animate and inanimate environment: people, small animals, familiar objects, places. He shows evidence of a budding sense of humor and he laughs at harmless accidents, animal actions, tricks, and mistakes. Along with this, he delights in simple guessing games and loves to anticipate "what comes next?" His interest in change is evident as he enjoys observing, for example, growing flowers, day and night, and weather.

Imitation of others and symbolic imitation of objects are important aspects of development during this period. While playing, he will assume the role of an adult by putting on adult clothing in "dress-up" activities, and will transform one object into another, such as taking a block and pushing it, saying "car." He also enjoys imitating adults around him. If adults have read to him, it will seem very natural to him to tell stories to his stuffed animal or doll.

Socially, even though he has a growing interest in play with other children, parallel play still predominates. He may play contentedly next to another child in the same sandbox, but he has difficulty with cooperative activities. Emotionally, his growing autonomy and pride in accomplishments make "do it myself" a common refrain as he is assuming an increasingly more self-sufficient attitude.

Suggestions for Activities

During this period, the child is ready for books with very simple plots. He enjoys picture story books with one picture per page and limited text with short sentences and repetition. The story characters should appear in several of the pages in the story so that he becomes aware of the story sequence. In addition, the books should be short enough to be completed in one reading session.

He likes it best when stories are read clearly at a naturally slow pace to allow him time to assimilate the meaning of the words and to translate the pictures into the words that he is hearing. Adults should show enthusiasm with voice inflection when they read to him, but not to the point that it distracts from the story.

He continues to enjoy books of nursery rhymes, picture books, and homemade books and photo albums. He is fond of having adults reread the stories he enjoys, such as those that are short and funny; stories that include change, such as growing things, weather, and the like; and stories that include guessing or finding objects or characters.

Since he likes "to do it myself," he will want to "read" books independently after hearing them. He may also want to select the books he wants the adult to read. Adults should continue to ask questions about the pictures in books, encouraging the child to talk about his own experiences and feelings as they relate to the story. They should also remember that they need to be patient when he repeatedly asks for the same story or activity, such as a finger play.

Children of this age enjoy the familiarity of repetition.

Many stories of interest to the two-year-old lend themselves to the use of a flannel board. A flannel board made from heavy cardboard covered with flannel is easy to construct. (It can be made from the side of a sturdy cardboard box.) Story characters and objects may be drawn on and cut out of felt or other materials, or pictures from magazines may be used by securing strips of sandpaper to the back of the pictures so that they adhere to the flannel. As a character or object appears in the story, the child can place the figure on the flannel board. Since the child must listen carefully to know when the characters and objects appear in the story, this activity also develops listening skills.

Finally, role models play an important part in the child's development. Adults should let him see them reading. They should reinforce the idea that he is becoming a reader; that this is something exciting and wonderful to be.

The Three-Year-Old
Developmental Characteristics

This period of development is characterized by the child's great enthusiasm. She delights in talking, although this does not necessarily mean that she wants to talk with others. She talks for the fun of it and enjoys language play, not requiring that every word carry meaning. Her vocabulary expands as she learns new concepts and words denoting them. (The average vocabulary sizes for three- and three-and-a-half-year-olds are 1,000 and 1,200 words, respectively.) However, in spite of her growing language ability, much of her communication with others remains nonverbal.

Her ability to recite the alphabet or numbers does not reflect real understanding of the underlying concepts. Instead, the recitation is a series of verbalizations and may be associated with an activity, such as when she counts to ten in preparation for racing or running up to kick a ball.

Intellectually, she continues to view the world egocentrically, she has difficulty thinking from another's point of view. She also has fixed perceptions so that she believes what she sees and can focus usually on only one attribute of an object at a time, most likely the predominant feature. When classifying objects, she finds it easiest to work with gross categories such as big and small or tall and short, with little or no middle ranges within categories. As in the case of objects, when classifying sex roles, she finds it easiest to do so based on gross differences. Therefore, she may initially imitate behavior that is clearly male or clearly female.

She continues to be extremely curious about the people, events, and things in her environment, such as her neighborhood. She has a keen interest in living and growing things, especially animals. She enjoys matching and naming activities, simple games of guessing and pretend games, and "what comes next?" activities. These games and activities relate to reading, at a time when sequencing events, recognizing individual characters, and being able to believe in the creative worlds of others are important for full enjoyment.

As she grows, she is gaining a more concrete sense of time and is interested in her own past, her infancy. She is also able to participate in more imaginative play. At the same time, her growing imagination may cause her to experience fantastic fears of such things as dogs, water, going down drains, loud noises, or the dark.

As for motor development, she has gained more coordination and enjoys galloping, jumping, climbing, marching to music, running with vigor, and riding a tricycle. Circle and simple movement games in groups, such as "London Bridge," "Farmer in the Dell," and "Ring around the Rosie" allow her to combine her motor skills with singing. She becomes interested in projects that require finer motor manipulation, such as drawing with crayons or pencils, playing with small blocks and cubes, or possibly using scissors to cut paper.

She thrives in a structured environment with plenty of time for play, and she may be made uncomfortable by changes in her daily routine. In her own way she is attempting to develop self-restraint and she needs the structure to aid her. Socially, parallel play is gradually displaced as she is able to play cooperatively with other children. She may experience a close relationship with her grandparents and usually enjoys being with them. However, if a sibling is born, she may feel jealous and demand more attention from those close to her.

Suggestions for Activities

The child now enjoys stories and activities that have straightforward plots, clear illustrations, and brief text. She usually prefers those that have, at most, a few main characters and pictures that are realistic in their general outlines and free from confusing detail.

Her favorite stories, poems, and songs include those with repeated language phrases, rhymes, silly words, and those that are about her; the clothing she wears, the emotions she feels, her family, her pets, and so on. In addition, simple, factually correct informational books that will answer some of her questions fascinate her, such as those about animals, neighborhood and community workers, babies, machines, and the like. She is learning that books hold answers.

She is more interested than before in books about basic concepts such as color, size and shape, and the alphabet. Early exposure to letters and numbers will come to have meaning for her later. Adults are often misled by her large vocabulary: In spite of her verbal powers, she is only at the threshold of abstraction. She must first build a base of experiences and see relationships among them before she is able to form abstractions.

When adults are sharing books with her, they can make her aware of the reading process by occasionally following the text with a finger. This lets her see that letters and words form written language. They can also help her understand the mechanics of using books, for example, by showing how to hold and correctly turn the pages of the book, how words are ordered from left to right and from the top to the bottom of the page, and how to select a book and return it to the shelf or book box.

The child likes to select the books she wants to read and enjoys being involved in the story activity, such as participating in the telling or talking about her own experiences and feelings as they relate to the story. She may also enjoy retelling the story in her own words and/or actions. When she dramatizes or retells stories or poems to which she has listened, the vocabulary and storyline are reinforced in her memory.

Adults should be prepared to reread stories or repeat activities, such as finger plays or songs, that are the child's favorites. Not only does she express preferences, but she enjoys repetition. In a world that is changing so quickly for her, a favorite, familiar story or poem provides security and comfort.

Having an adult transcribe stories that the child dictates makes her feel that what she has to say is important because an adult is interested enough to write it down. Her self-confidence expands, and so does her interest in words. Adults should seek out opportunities that encourage the child to see herself as a writer.

She continues to enjoy creating books out of inexpensive photo albums, placing in them favorite pictures from gift catalogs, labels from cans of food she likes, photographs of special people or places, leaves from a tree in her neighborhood, postcards from friends, and her drawings. She experiences a sense of pride in creating books—her affection for them may be transferable to books in general.

Adults need to establish a routine time and place for reading with the child, in addition to impromptu reading times. The child should also be encouraged to "read" on her own, with her books accessible to her for casual and frequent use. Adults must continue to let her see them read. Adults who look at books, comment about pictures or words in books, and use books as reference sources serve as models. The child will come to see that books are read both for fun and to find out information.

Since many three-year-olds attend preschools, nursery schools, and library storytimes, teachers, caregivers, and librarians may find the following list of suggestions helpful when planning storytimes:

Since three-year-olds are active and may be more interested in starting than in finishing activities, intersperse the storytime with activities that involve the children, such as finger plays, creative dramatics, sing-alongs, and so forth. The pace should be brisk but calm.

Help children understand how to interpret pictures. Ask them to discuss what is happening in the picture. Children may view pictures literally, without adding insights of their own. For instance, a child may assume that a character has lost a part of his arm if it is not shown in the picture.

Allow children to engage in word play by repeating refrains in stories or poems as they are read. This practice can also build listening skills since children must listen and be ready for the appropriate time to repeat the refrain. Some adults find it helpful to use a hand signal which the children recognize as the cue.

The Four-Year-Old
Developmental Characteristics

In many ways this is an "out-of-bounds," risk-taking period for the four-year-old. At the same time, it is also a period when he is gaining control over his body and his emotions. He tends to be more motivated and is able to work longer at tasks in which he is interested.

His language is developing at a fast pace. By and large, his articulation is no longer infantile, and even though he has not yet completely mastered language, he has little trouble describing situations and his thoughts. (The average four-year-old has as many as 1,550 words at his command; by four-and-a-half years, this increases to approximately 1,900 words.)

Talking may still be more important than listening, but to a less extent than when he was three. The child delights even more in the sound and patterns of language, such as the alliteration or onomatopoeia of chants, nonsense words, riddles, simple tongue twisters, and cumulative tales. He enjoys playing with words he knows: whispering, shouting, and even inventing new words.

He continues to question in earnest and to accompany his every action with running commentary, which is especially noticeable in play and drawing activities. He also grasps the power of words, and boasts, brags, exaggerates, prevaricates, and swears. He may often use over and over any word which he finds gets a strong response from adults.

He truly enjoys music now, and with his ability to remember more words, he sings alone or in a group. He makes music with his own voice or with his hands and feet, or by playing percussion instruments. He continues to enjoy moving his body to music; this may help him understand the meaning of position words such as *high, low, behind, under, slow,* and *fast.*

Intellectually, he remains prelogical or "pre-operational" throughout the preschool period. The fact that his language is sophisticated does not mean he is logical. Listening carefully to his language or asking him questions often reveals the gaps between his speaking and thinking.

However, he is becoming slightly more flexible or "decentered" in his thinking so that his perceptions are becoming a bit less fixed. He is able to understand the difference between what is real and what is imagined when it is carefully explained by an adult.

He continues to be extremely curious about people, events, and things around him. He is especially curious about his natural and material environment. In addition, he develops an interest in kinds of families and communities other than his own.

He begins to be able to classify, compare, and order objects according to some common property. As his curiosity grows, he wants to know more about his own body and how it works. He is curious about how the body digests food, eliminates waste, breathes air, circulates blood, and experiences sensations. He may also be interested in knowing about reproduction and death.

He is developing a better sense of time and begins to use correctly words and phrases like days, months, minutes, and "time to go home." He also begins to realize that time is a continuum, and that people existed and events took place before *now* and will do so after *now.* He is curious about the childhoods of grandparents or parents.

He enjoys his new abilities and likes to try out physical stunts by combining running, climbing, and jumping. His fine motor coordination has improved so that he enjoys painting, coloring, drawing, and cutting on a line with scissors. He can make designs and experiments with shape, line, color, and pattern. His interest in written language and increased skills may enable him to print his first name and some letters and numerals.

This is a time when he seems to be emotionally secure and comfortable, sometimes to the point where he boasts and brags about how superior he and his family are. Although he also experiences emotional extremes, laughing and crying loudly even on mild provocation, he has self-confidence not found in previous periods and loves adventures so that he is willing to try new tasks. However, he still considers it more important to get things started than to finish them.

It is interesting to note that in spite of the frustration he exhibits when adults do not acquiesce to his desires, he appears to appreciate boundaries set by adults. He continues to thrive in a structured environment with daily routine.

Since he is more able to play cooperatively with other children, at preschool he strongly identifies with the group, loves parties and celebrations, and enjoys eating with others. However, he still has limited ability to play games with rules since he has difficulty understanding game rules. He is happiest when he is the winner and does not find it at all illogical for all the participants to be winners. Races in which all who cross the finish line or searches in which all who locate something in a picture are rewarded are much enjoyed.

The four-year-old becomes increasingly aware of roles, such as his role as an individual family member, or an adult's career role. He will try on these roles in play. As he enters into dramatic play, he "decenters" or sees things from points of view other than his own. He may also do this with simple hand puppets. His play may include imaginary playmates. Although incomprehensible to adults, they are ideal companions who are always around when wanted, never fight, and agree to every suggestion the four-year-old makes.

Suggestions for Activities

The list offered previously for the three-year-old continues to be useful for the adult selecting stories and activities for the four-year-old. Stories and activities listed there will also interest him, albeit for a shorter period of time. Since he has more breadth of experience and is able to assimilate ideas more rapidly, he is ready for somewhat longer, more complicated materials.

His favorite stories and activities include those with more sophisticated language play and language patterns, such as alliteration and onomatopoeia. He enjoys hearing longer, more complex Mother Goose verses, such as the entire "Old Mother Hubbard," and some of the less well-known verses.

He continues to like stories that are about him and his environment but is ready to hear others which depict different ages, cultures, and kinds of families in a positive way. He also enjoys simple, factually correct informational books that will answer his increasingly numerous questions.

For example, with his growing interest in his body, he needs informational books that introduce simple concepts of biological processes such as digestion, excretion, respiration, circulation, reproduction, and death. Helping him form correct concepts early can allay anxieties and fears that may arise when he picks up misconceptions from friends or from half-heard conversations. Encouraging his questions and responding to them honestly and accurately strengthen his confidence in the adult, and may ensure his checking information obtained elsewhere with this trusted source.

The four-year-old enjoys both realism and fantasy, but may need help in sorting them out. Since he may have difficulty separating real from pretend, he likes simple, straightforward imaginary stories and activities which do not abruptly jump from one realm to another but provide a slow transition into fantasy.

Since play is an important part of his life, he may be ready to dramatize stories and activities which are well-known to him. For those four-year-olds who are not ready for creative drama, the use of puppets is suggested since the child can take on a number of roles without feeling shy or embarrassed. He may like playing with his friends using a simple puppet stage made from a large appliance carton with a rectangular opening cut out of it. He also enjoys simple games like simon says, which are a good way of practicing motor skills and fitting actions with verbal instructions.

Books play an important role in his environment. For example, an adult can help him become a better observer of nature by showing him the importance of observing before acting. Books such as Marie Hall Ets's *Play with Me* help him learn the important concept of being a quiet observer, not a possessor or a destroyer.

His environment should be such that he is given ample opportunities to color, draw, "write," and cut. He enjoys activities such as cutting a picture into parts and then putting it together again, puzzle fashion. Adults should respect his "writing" and scribbling since those marks may represent more than random squiggles. Talking or asking about them gives the adult insight into his interests and ideas, and may reveal a consistency or creativity not immediately apparent.

Adults should recognize that activities designed solely to teach the alphabet or numbers or writing skills are much less appropriate than providing a print-rich environment that stimulates language. The four-year-old is acquiring many skills, but he needs to get the sense of why and how these skills will enrich his life and extend his world.

Since many four-year-olds attend preschools, nursery schools, and library storytimes, teachers, caregivers, and librarians may find the following list of suggestions helpful when planning programs:

With their longer attention spans and greater physical control, children of this age can sit for longer periods before becoming fidgety. However, the pace should be quick, and activities that encourage the children to move, such as finger plays, marching to music, creative dramatics, and singing, should be included.

The environment should be inviting for preschoolers. It should be furnished with child-sized furniture and displays and decorated at children's eye level with realistic pictures.

Depending on prior social and storytime experiences, children may be able to sit through and enjoy hearing stories without the use of visuals. Tell the stories slowly and clearly, and be certain to give each child eye contact at some time during the story. When telling stories without visuals, select those that are short, contain repetition, and have few characters. Stories with short introductions, lots of action, and quick endings are popular.

For the child, talking may be more important than listening, so continue to be patient but firm when he interrupts. When several children in a group are eager to talk, help them remember that they must take turns in speaking so that each can be heard.

Inasmuch as the four-year-old's ability to distinguish the real from the unreal is still developing, imaginative stories should be introduced with careful consideration given to helping the children realize the distinction between what is *real* and what is *pretend*.

Ann D. Carlson is an assistant professor in the Graduate School of Library and Information Science at Rosary College in River Forest, Illinois. She is the author of *Early Childhood Literature Sharing Programs in Libraries* (Shoe String Press, 1985) and *The Preschooler and the Library* (Scarecrow Press, forthcoming) which discuss this topic in more detail.

Developments in Reading Related to Children's Literature

Marie Louise Sorenson

Children who learn to read early and without difficulty are often the same children whose parents began reading to them regularly when they were quite young. Some of these children are already reading when they begin school, and many others learn to read when they start school no matter what reading method their teachers use. It has been suggested that those children who learn to read easily do so because their early exposure to children's literature makes them care about learning to read. British critic and author John Rowe Townsend is credited with saying that a reading child can often be identified before conception,[1] meaning that being born into a literate family greatly influences whether or not a child becomes a reader.

A personal example of the importance of giving books to even very young children occurred when my grandniece, at the age of eighteen months, greeted the arrival of her new brother by placing one of her beloved board books on top of him as he sat in his infant carrier moments after his parents carried him into the house from the hospital. There is no doubt in the mind of anyone who knows Julianna that she is already a reader. When Julianna was twenty-months-old, her mother wrote me a note in which she said, "Julianna is *reading!* She can read two titles of books, *Peek-a-Boo!*[2] and *Runaway Bunny!*"[3] In asking for books by title, Julianna at this age is not actually reading; the important point here is that if her mother acts as though her daughter is reading, Julianna will believe she is reading. She already knows which is the front of the book, how to hold it, and how to turn the pages of the book as she reads. She is behaving like a reader, and the adults who know her know better than to tell her that she is not "really" reading. As she follows along in the book while her parents or other interested adults read to her, she will begin to repeat familiar parts of the story, and soon she *will* be reading.

Children can learn to read naturally, much in the same way they learn to talk. Most people do not worry about whether their children will learn to talk; they assume they will. Parents have been known to do some interesting things indicating their excitement when they hear their child speak his or her first word. Regardless of whether or not that first utterance sounds exactly like the word the child is trying to say, parents seldom try to correct the child's pronunciation. Instead, the usual reaction of

[1]Betsy Hearne, *Choosing Books for Children: A Commonsense Guide.* (Delacorte, 1981), p. 52.

[2]Janet and Allan Ahlberg, *Peek-a-Boo!* (Viking, 1981).

[3]Margaret Wise Brown, *Runaway Bunny.* (Harper, 1972/1942).

parents to the child's initial effort to communicate encourages that child to make additional attempts at using language. In school, we want to create the same kind of literate climate that encourages children willing to experiment with and learn about language, including learning to read and to write. We also want children to learn to care about reading. We have come to realize it is not enough to help children learn *how* to read—our goal should be to create readers who *want* to read. It has been estimated that 40 percent of Americans are aliterate; they know how to read but do not or will not spend their time reading because they have not experienced the joy and personal satisfaction that can come from good literature.

In the foreword to *Children's Literature in the Reading Program*, edited by Bernice Cullinan, noted illustrator and author Tomie dePaola writes of how eager he was to learn to read when he started school. When his kindergarten teacher told him on the first day that he would learn to read in first grade, not that year, he left school and went home, announcing he would be back the next year. DePaola then describes something many children have discovered. Confronted with his first reader when he finally got to first grade, he immediately noticed the difference between the stilted language used in that beginning reader and the language of "real" books, the kind he wanted to be able to check out of the library.

Many children today are expected to learn to read the same way Tomie was taught, using publishers' basal reading programs. These systems are still in place in most schools in the United States. Planned to encompass every aspect of teaching children to read, these programs include grade-leveled texts of reading selections, a teacher's manual that tells the teacher exactly what to do in each step of the lesson, and workbooks and other options which a school district may decide to purchase. These programs are based on the premise that there is a hierarchical list of skills which must be learned for a reader to be able to decode words; however, since consultants devising these lists do not agree on the hierarchy, the sequenced order of the lists of skills varies with the publisher. In addition, the way in which publishers' reading programs develop vocabulary is based on the premise that children can only read words that have been introduced to them in the series, or that they have been taught to decode, so each program has its own basic vocabulary, which varies among programs. The publishers who plan and market these programs do so with good intentions, based on certain beliefs about how we learn to read, but current research challenges many of those beliefs. (Read Kenneth Goodman's 1988 article in *The New Advocate* on the "basalization" of children's literature for an expanded explanation of the differences between many basal reader systems and literature.)

There is evidence that older children also recognize the difference between reading for pleasure outside of school and the kind of reading instruction that often takes place in schools. Many adults will remember encountering a list on the chalkboard of "work" to be completed during reading time when they were in elementary school. As Jane Hansen points out in her book, *When Writers Read*, the assigned work frequently included workbook pages or duplicated sheets of skills drills. Often the last item on the list was something like, "when you have finished your work, read a library book." Implied was the idea that reading children's literature was a luxury only afforded to those who had finished their "important" school work. Unfortunately, that usually meant that those children who did not finish their assignments early had limited opportunity to read for pleasure.

Although research suggests that time spent reading independently influences how well children read, other studies reported in the late 1970s showed that the amount of time elementary school children spent reading from books during the school day often averaged less than seven minutes, and usually the books read were basal readers.[4] Similar studies conducted by Donald Graves concerning writing concluded that one likely reason high school students were graduating without having become proficient writers was that they had been asked to spend

---

[4]Richard C. Anderson, Elfrieda H. Hiebert, Judith A. Scott, and Ian A. G. Wilkinson, *Becoming a Nation of Readers: The Report of the Commission on Reading.* (U.S. Department of Education, 1985), p. 76.

very little time writing during their entire school careers. Instead, teachers had been breaking the elements of reading and writing into separate subjects such as penmanship, grammar, punctuation, spelling, listening skills, speech, and vocabulary development.[5]

In a skills-based approach, children were taught to recognize many little words before they could begin reading anything. The vocabulary was controlled with words being carefully chosen so that reading would be manageable. Some of the reading material created in the effort to make reading easier for children also succeeded in making it boring for them. Often, the simplified text actually made reading more difficult because what the children were given to read no longer sounded like real language.

Similarly, there was a standard way to teach writing. Children were not permitted to write until they had learned to print the letters of the alphabet and copy sentences which the teacher had written on the board. In short, all kinds of "readiness" activities were considered necessary before children suddenly reached that magical developmental level at which they were ready to learn to read or write: We thought that if we taught children *about* reading and writing we were preparing them for learning *how* to read and write. Many teachers in training were told—as I was, thirty years ago—that children first "learn to read" and then "read to learn." We now realize that children learn to read by reading and learn to write by writing, in the same way that children learn to speak by speaking.

In the 1980s, children's literature gained widespread recognition as the most appropriate and effective kind of reading material for children when they are learning to read. There have always been many teachers who supplemented their reading programs with children's literature, and there have always been some teachers who believed that children could learn to read by reading children's books rather than the texts featured in publishers' basal reading programs. But now, as we enter the decade of the 1990s, there is substantial evidence from research supporting the idea that a whole language, literature-based, process approach to teaching reading is the state of the art in reading instruction.[6]

Whole language refers to the idea of leaving language whole or natural, of treating language as something that one does not break apart into little pieces. Goodman captures the essence of whole language in a simple yet thorough explanation in his 1986 book, *What's Whole in Whole Language?* In classrooms where whole language is used, the emphasis is on learning language by using language, so activities in such classrooms encourage children to write, read, talk, and listen for a variety of real, functional purposes. In such a classroom, children listen to and read from "real" books, which is where the term *literature-based* originates.

Process approach refers to learning to write and read by engaging in the experience of writing and reading, rather than by emphasizing the end product of these skills, just as children learn to talk by engaging in the process of talking.[7] The terms *whole language, literature-based,* and *process approach* are often used as synonyms for what occurs in classrooms where teachers are influenced by what they have come to believe about how children learn.

Many educators have moved toward this whole language, literature-based, process approach to teaching after observing and reflecting upon how children in their classrooms learn. As teachers have learned more about this process and have looked for ways to share their ideas with others, TAWL (Teachers Applying Whole Language) support groups have been formed all over the country. Richard C. Owen Publishers' quarterly, *Teachers Networking: The Whole Language Newsletter,* is devoted to reporting on the concerns of such teachers. When

---

[5]Donald Graves, "Balance the Basics: Let Them Write" (Ford Report), *A Researcher Learns to Write,* (Heinemann, 1984).

[6]Jerome C. Harste, *New Policy Guidelines for Reading: Connecting Research and Practice* (NCTE, 1989); and Michael O. Tunnell and James S. Jacobs, "Using 'Real' Books: Research Findings on Literature Based Reading Instruction," *The Reading Teacher,* March 1989.

[7]For more on process teaching see Donald Graves, *Writing: Teachers and Children at Work.* Heinemann, 1983; and Nancie Atwell, *In the Middle: Writing, Reading, and Learning with Adolescents.* Boynton/Cook, 1987.

professional organizations such as the National Council of Teachers of English (NCTE) and the International Reading Association (IRA) hold their annual conventions, the titles of the scheduled sessions also reflect this current interest in whole language. In this grass roots movement, many teachers have learned about this from one another, so it is not surprising that there is some similarity from one classroom to the next when teachers describe their version of a whole language, literature-based, process approach. A number of effective practices can be found in such classrooms, based on the principles which good teachers hold in common.

Children start becoming aware of the print they see around them long before they go to school. They recognize the names of commonly used products from their packages, and children also learn to associate the names of supermarkets, department stores, and gas stations with the signs and logos that represent them. Making sense of this environmental print is an important step in becoming literate, so a classroom that uses natural or whole language as its base will encourage young children to find and bring to school examples of this kind of print.

From the very first day children start school, they should be given the opportunity to use a variety of paper, pencils, markers, and crayons. Many children will already have started writing their names and some will be attempting to write other words as well. Children should be encouraged to use all of the information they have previously learned about language. Teachers may write letters to each child and encourage them to write replies and send notes to other children. They also may be asked to sign up for various activities by writing their names. These examples of surrounding the children with print are what we mean by writing and reading for real, functional purposes.

Children develop a love for reading when they have the opportunity to experience children's literature and when they are surrounded with print media. A classroom collection should be available so that children in preschool and the primary grades have frequent opportunities to explore a variety of children's books on their own. They should also have access to a school or public library where they are encouraged to borrow books. Regular reading aloud to children and telling them stories are other important activities.

Daily instruction in reading in a whole language primary classroom often begins with a group of children gathered together sharing a "big book," sometimes one that has been heard before. Each child in the group can readily see these large-format children's books, which have usually been selected because of their predictability. Predictable books have story lines with repeated sequences or cumulative patterns that allow children to use the knowledge they learned about the world prior to coming to school to predict what the author is going to say.[8] As children hear familiar stories repeated, they are encouraged to join in when they can and soon they begin to learn to recognize some of the words. Even difficult words can be learned when children see or hear them in a meaningful context. After the shared reading of several books, children might be paired for "friend-to-friend" reading which usually involves the pairing of a more successful reader with a less successful one. During this time, two children sit together and take turns reading to each other, collaborating on decoding words they might not immediately recognize.

Children of all ages are encouraged to decide which of several strategies to try when they come to a word that is not immediately recognizable. Although sounding out a word may sometimes work, children need to learn that there are other options. Trying a word that makes sense in the sentence is one strategy that quite often works, even for adults. Masha Rudman, in *Children's Literature: Resource for the Classroom*, suggests that children be encouraged to ask themselves, "What makes sense here?" or "How does the word I tried match with the way the word looks?" The emphasis is on making meaning from what is on the printed page. When readers know what a story is about, they can often predict what idea or word to expect as they read. Children can learn that if

[8]For a list of predictable books see Lynn K. Rhodes and Curt Dudley-Marlin, *Readers and Writers with a Difference: A Holistic Approach to Teaching Learning Disabled and Remedial Students.* Heinemann, 1988.

what they read does not make sense, they should go back and try to figure out what would make sense.

Several principles apply at all grade levels when reading and language arts programs are based on literature. Children should be given a regularly scheduled period of time during which they can read without interruption. They should be allowed to choose many of their own reading materials from a classroom collection of books and other print representing a wide range of difficulty and interest levels, and they should be offered help in determining how to make appropriate choices of what to read. Children at all grade levels enter school having had different experiences; therefore, they should be invited to choose how they will respond to what they have read from a variety of options, which might include writing, drama, and art activities. Harste refers to these curricular choices as open-ended because each child can enter and leave these activities at his/her own respective developmental level.[9] Class assignments where all of the products look the same are thus discouraged.

Conferences in which teachers meet with each child on a regular basis, often weekly, to discuss what that individual is reading are an important aspect of classrooms where whole language is used. (For additional information about conducting conferences see Atwell, 1987; Graves, 1983; Hansen, 1987; Rhodes & Dudley-Marling, 1988; Routman, 1988; Rudman, 1984 & 1988.) When books children have read are discussed, teachers ask open-ended questions that encourage critical thinking and different answers from different children. Teachers avoid questions which invite "yes" or "no" answers and which might discourage children's elaborated responses. Rudman notes that teachers should avoid "guess the answer that's in my head" kinds of questions.

The same considerations should apply to writing; children can be invited to choose their own topics and be given regular periods of uninterrupted time for writing. Children in primary grades are often encouraged to write their own stories, sometimes using language patterns similar to the ones in the stories they have read. As children gain experience with this, they are often given the opportunity to "publish" some of the stories they have written. Publishing may consist of choosing and perhaps investigating a topic about which to write, writing a first draft, conferring with the teacher or other children about possible changes, and then eventually writing a final draft. Parents sometimes help by using a primary typewriter to type finished stories, which may be illustrated by the author and then bound into a hand-made book which then becomes available to all of the children in the classroom as additional reading material.[10]

Children, beginning in the primary grades, can learn how to confer about their writing as well as their reading. As Jane Hansen points out in *When Writers Read*, children should often be asked such questions as, "How do you think you will figure that out?" or "How did you figure that out?" and "What will you do next?" These kinds of questions help children develop strategies about writing and reading, encouraging them to take responsibility for and retain ownership of their own learning.

As these concepts are carried into the middle and upper grades, children are able to handle longer periods of uninterrupted time for reading and writing. When children know that they can count on a definite period of time for reading each day or several times each week, they may be encouraged to attempt to read longer books because they are confident of being able to continue reading the following day. Nancie Atwell, in her 1987 book, *In the Middle*, describes how she tried to replicate in her eighth-grade classroom the kinds of discussions that occurred in her home when she, her husband, and their friends sat around their dining-room table and discussed the books they had read. This kind of literate community can be created in classrooms when there are regular opportunities for children to reflect on and discuss ideas that come out of what they have

[9]Harste, *New Policy Guidelines for Reading: Connecting Research and Practice*, p. 49.

[10]For information on writing and publishing see Graves, *Writing*, 1983.

read and what they have written.

These examples of the kinds of activities that take place in whole language, literature-based, process approach classrooms demonstrate that whole language is a philosophy and that teachers' beliefs about how children learn greatly influence the instructional decisions that are made in classrooms. The bibliography at the end of this essay includes some of the best writing on three aspects of recent developments in the field of reading: accounts that chronicle and explain the reasons teachers change the way they help children learn to read; reports on how research supports this changed way of teaching; and information for current or prospective teachers on how to institute these recommendations.

In his 1983 book, *Writing: Teachers and Children at Work*, Donald Graves explains how teachers can help children learn to support each other as they write and learn through writing. Although Graves is widely regarded as being one of the first people to help teachers learn about the process approach to the teaching of writing, in Chapter 7 of that book he credits Jane Hansen with helping him transfer what he knew about writing to the reading process when they collaborated on research with teachers and children in a school. In her book, *When Writers Read*, Hansen tells how she completely changed her thinking about reading after working with Donald Graves. She repeatedly compares the way she did things as a classroom teacher in the mid-sixties and seventies with the way she now encourages teachers to do things differently as a result of current knowledge about theory and experience in classrooms where theory is put into practice. The idea of thoughtfully considering how we might change and improve the way we teach is an important aspect of empowering teachers to make informed decisions about what occurs in their classrooms.

In her 1988 book, *Transitions*, Regie Routman describes how she changed the way she teaches; she also offers examples of many classroom procedures. Routman's book contains an extensive bibliography of additional resources to help those interested in learning more about implementing this changed way of teaching. The use of this approach is even being extended to children who have difficulty learning to read, as evidenced by the title of the 1988 book by Lynn Rhodes and Curt Dudley-Marling: *Readers and Writers with a Difference: A Holistic Approach to Teaching Learning Disabled and Remedial Students*. The authors of the four books mentioned here and in the preceding paragraphs all reflect upon the influence their changed thinking has had upon their teaching. (These books all come from Heinemann Educational Books, one of the leading publishers of books on the whole language approach to the teaching of reading and writing.)

In the article, "Using 'Real' Books: Research Findings on Literature Based Reading Instruction," Professors Michael O. Tunnell and James S. Jacobs review a number of studies which looked into various aspects of how reading children's literature influenced reading scores and children's opinions about reading. Tunnell and Jacobs discuss the basic elements of such programs and then conclude that children can learn to read when teachers use literature and other reading materials beyond those provided by publishers of basal reading programs.

In *New Policy Guidelines for Reading: Connecting Research and Practice*, a monograph jointly commissioned by NCTE and the Educational Resources Information Center (ERIC), Professor Jerome C. Harste makes recommendations for reading instruction based on two federally funded studies which thoroughly reviewed recent research on *reading comprehension* and *instructional practice* regarding effective teaching of reading. It is particularly interesting that Harste set out to examine how *reading comprehension* could most effectively be taught; in other words he did not begin his study with a bias toward using literature. Based on his review of the research, Harste lists twenty guidelines for improving the ways in which we help children learn to read. Those recommendations include the kinds of things mentioned in this essay, activities already being used by teachers who espouse a whole language, literature-based, process approach to teaching. Harste's book should be especially useful because he explains the theory behind each guideline and also provides examples of appropriate classroom activities.

Suggestions for Adding Literature to Your Classroom

Learn as much as you can about children's literature. This may be done by taking a course; reading this and other textbooks; reading articles about children's literature; and attending lectures, institutes, or workshops, to name a few ways. Dates and locations of such conferences are often listed in current issues of *School Library Journal* and *The Horn Book*.

Begin to consider how you will add literature to your classroom. Remember that there are good ideas for "Bringing Children and Books Together" in Part Three of this textbook. Although it may seem overwhelming to think of running the kind of literature-based reading program discussed in this essay, it is not necessary to do everything at once. You may add elements of literature to your reading program one step at a time.

Read aloud to your students on a daily basis. Even if you are teaching in a school that encourages the use of a publisher's reading program, reading aloud is one of the simplest but best ways to begin adding literature to your classroom. Reading aloud gives value to reading and listening, and people—of any age—learn to appreciate literature by being in the company of others who value literature. Reading part of a book aloud is a good way to introduce books that children might hesitate to start reading on their own.

Initiate silent sustained reading (SSR) in your classroom. This is a daily period of time when everyone in the classroom reads without interruption, including the teacher. One teacher told me that after starting with ten minutes of SSR, she gradually increased the amount of time until her second graders were reading for half an hour each day. She even asks anyone who comes to her classroom door with a message during that time to sit down and read. Many schools observe a fifteen-minute period of SSR at the same time each day in all classrooms in the building, with all of the people who work in the school participating, including the principal, the custodian, and the secretary. This gives students the message that *reading is important*. Students are expected to be prepared for SSR by having a book or magazine on hand to read. It is important to allow students to choose the material they will read during this period.

Build a classroom collection of reading materials. Children can be encouraged to contribute books and magazines from home, either by lending them or by donating items they no longer care to keep. Sometimes previously owned children's books can be purchased inexpensively at garage sales or at the annual book sales many schools and public libraries hold to raise money. Teachers can also offer students the opportunity to buy paperback books through one of the book clubs. In addition to being an inexpensive way for children to buy books, book clubs usually offer bonus points which can be used to acquire additional books for the classroom collection. Having books available in the primary classroom is especially important so that children may choose additional reading materials whenever they are ready to do so.

Take your students to the library. Regular trips to the school and public library are important because that is where children are more likely to be able to find books and audiovisual materials on a specific topic. Help your students understand how knowledgeable and helpful their school librarian or media center director can be. Get to know the children's librarian at your local public library, too. When librarians know that a teacher and his or her students are interested in finding out about particular categories of books, they are more than happy to share information about new books as soon as they have received them. Often it will be possible to borrow a quantity of books from the school library and/or the public library that can be used in the classroom for a period of time and then exchanged for other books.

Read some of the books in the bibliography which accompanies this essay. The books about teacher change and information about research confirming the advantages of a whole language, literature-based, process approach to the teaching of reading have already been discussed briefly. The paperback book, *Ideas and Insights*, edited by Dorothy Watson for NCTE, includes ideas for activities contributed by classroom teachers from schools representing all elementary grade levels and also conveys insights about the thinking behind these ideas. Another inexpensive source, Cullinan's *Children's Literature in the Reading Program*, contains articles by many people involved in the world of reading and children's literature who contribute further suggestions on how to get started using children's books as major sources in the reading program. The journals, *Language Arts* and *The Reading Teacher*, sponsored respectively by NCTE and IRA, often contain articles about using literature in the classroom. *The New Advocate*, a quarterly designed to help teachers implement literature-based reading programs, has been published by Christopher-Gordon Publishers since 1988 when they began concentrating on whole language publications. They also publish books on this subject. *Children's Literature: Resource for the Classroom*, for example, includes a chapter in which Masha Rudman, who also edited the book, describes such a reading through literature program and then answers commonly asked questions concerning this approach. Another useful Christopher-Gordon book, *Children's Literature in the Classroom: Weaving Charlotte's Web* edited by Janet Hickman and Bernice Cullinan, also includes articles on many additional aspects of this subject.

Investigate using literature across the curriculum. This refers to learning about a specific or broad topic by using literature to explore all subjects studied. Children's literature can be a valuable source of information for all fields of study, as demonstrated in the section of this text that discusses historical fiction, informational books, and biographies. One school I visited in Massachusetts has not purchased social studies or science textbooks for the last eight years; instead, the librarian in that school uses available funds to select a broad range of informational books so that pupils and teachers can find material in the library media center on any subject they might be studying. Harste recommends that schools purchase a few copies of several different textbooks on the same subject instead of sets for whole class use.

Encourage a variety of perspectives by having each student choose a different book on a related topic. Using literature in this way is explained by Brozo and Tomlinson in a 1986 article in *The Reading Teacher*. Rudman's 1984 book, *Children's Literature: An Issues Approach*,

groups and discusses titles of recommended books by a variety of topics such as divorce, stepfamilies, sex, aging, death, war, and multicultural issues; she then makes suggestions about how books on these subjects may be evaluated and used in the reading program. Rudman believes that instead of avoiding controversial issues, children are better served if they confront such subjects and become aware of various points of view.

Join a Teachers Applying Whole Language (TAWL) group. (See *Teachers Networking* for the location of a nearby group.) Or start a support group locally where you may talk to other teachers and share ideas about implementing a literature-based reading program. Sharing literature with children will make you aware of additional titles of children's books; in much the same way, you will become familiar with additional ways of extending the use of literature in the classroom.

This brief essay has presented an overview of recent developments in the field of reading. Because these are complex ideas that are not always understood when one is first exposed to them, it is hoped that the reader may begin to seek answers to questions by consulting the sources of information mentioned here. Many of the educators who speak or write about how they help children learn to read suggest that although they are happy to share what they do in their classrooms with others, listeners or readers will most likely want to try some of these ideas in their classrooms, and then modify and further adapt them until they have made them their own.

Marie Louise Sorensen holds an M.A. in Library Science from Northern Illinois University, where she has taught classes in children's literature. Her doctoral research at the University of Massachusetts studies teachers who help children learn to read with children's literature.

Bibliography

AHLBERG, JANET and ALAN. *Peek-a-Boo!* Viking, 1981.

ANDERSON, RICHARD C., ELFRIEDA H. HIEBERT, JUDITH A. SCOTT, and IAN A. G. WILKINSON. *Becoming a Nation of Readers: The Report of the Commission on Reading.* U.S. Department of Education, 1985.

ATWELL, NANCIE. *In the Middle: Writing, Reading, and*

Learning with Adolescents. Boynton/Cook, 1987.

BROWN, MARGARET WISE. *Runaway Bunny.* Harper, 1972.

BROZO, WILLIAM G., and CARL M. TOMLINSON. "Literature: The Key to Lively Content Courses." *The Reading Teacher,* Volume 40, pp. 288–293. December, 1986.

CULLINAN, BERNICE E., ed. *Children's Literature in the Reading Program.* IRA, 1987.

GOODMAN, KEN. *What's Whole in Whole Language? A Parent/Teacher Guide to Children's Learning.* Heinemann, 1986.

GOODMAN, KENNETH S. "Look What They've Done to Judy Blume!: The 'Basalization' of Children's Literature." *The New Advocate,* Volume 1, pp. 29–41, 1988.

GRAVES, DONALD H. "Balancing the Basics: Let Them Write" (Ford Report), *A Researcher Learns to Write.* Heinemann, 1984.

————. *Writing: Teachers and Children at Work.* Heinemann, 1983.

HANSEN, JANE. *When Writers Read.* Heinemann, 1987.

HARSTE, JEROME C. *New Policy Guidelines for Reading: Connecting Research and Practice.* NCTE, 1989.

HEARNE, BETSY. *Choosing Books for Children: A Commonsense Guide.* Delacorte, 1981.

HICKMAN, JANET, and BERNICE E. CULLINAN, eds. *Children's Literature in the Classroom: Weaving Charlotte's Web.* Christopher-Gordon Publishers, 1989.

The New Advocate: For Those Involved with Young People and Their Literature. Published quarterly by Christopher-Gordon Publishers.

RHODES, LYNN K., and CURT DUDLEY-MARLING. *Readers and Writers with a Difference: A Holistic Approach to Teaching Learning Disabled and Remedial Students.* Heinemann, 1988.

ROUTMAN, REGIE. *Transitions: From Literature to Literacy.* Heinemann, 1988.

RUDMAN, MASHA KABAKOW. *Children's Literature: An Issues Approach,* 2nd ed. Longman, 1984.

————, ed. *Children's Literature: Resource for the Classroom.* Christopher-Gordon Publishers, 1989.

Teachers Networking: The Whole Language Newsletter. Published quarterly by Richard C. Owen Publishers.

TUNNELL, MICHAEL O., and JAMES S. JACOBS. "Using 'Real' Books: Research Findings on Literature Based Reading Instruction." *The Reading Teacher,* Volume 42, pp. 470–477, March, 1989.

WATSON, DOROTHY J., ed. *Ideas and Insights: Language Arts in the Elementary School.* NCTE, 1987.

Perspectives on Censorship

Alice Phoebe Naylor

Censorship of children's books is part of current news as well as part of history. It occurs in many ways, and, as this essay will point out, can be caused by different motives. No one censors books without a reason, so we will explore those: psychological, social, political. Just as literature can be very powerful in our lives, the efforts to suppress it can also be very powerful. Those who resist censorship must also exert power; strong convictions increase the efforts and the strength of both sides of censorship issues. Legal decisions about censorship have helped to shape current attitudes and actions. But issues and cases based on censorship are still developing and will continue to inform and change people's views and actions.

Censorship must be viewed in the context of society. As power shifts among different parts of society, censorship may shift in different directions. Anyone who believes that children should have access to books that stimulate, delight, inform, and satisfy has a role to play in resisting censorship. Resistance is a part of the professional responsibility of teachers and librarians, indeed of all the adults whose concerns include children and books and free access to them and the ideas they contain. This essay touches on all of these points, but it is intended to encourage more reading on this many-faceted topic of censorship as well.

Censorship Defined

The term *censorship* applies to several different forms of action taken to prevent others from having access to a book or to information. Actions of censors range from an author's deliberate exclusion of material to politically motivated organizations which support legal, and sometimes illegal, action against libraries and schools with the ultimate purpose of reshaping and controlling the political nature of the community or nation.

The American Family Association, led by Robert Simonds, sponsors a Committee for

Effective Education which states as its purpose, "to bring public education back under the control of Christians." On the surface it may seem that the conflict here is between that organizational goal and the constitutional principle of separation of church and state. However, the activities of this organization and others similar to it, seem also to be directed toward censoring ideas and beliefs on a national level.

Judy Blume, the most censored author of children's books and ardent defender of children's right-to-know, has admitted succumbing to a publisher's request to delete a passage from *Deenie* about masturbation. (Blume has said she will not succumb to that kind of pressure again.)

In this country, references to "censored books" usually mean that a single school, library, or classroom has been pressured by community individuals or groups to withdraw a book from use. The final decision on whether to withdraw items is usually made by the governing boards of schools and libraries. Sometimes the censor and the defender of the freedom of speech end up in court to debate definitions. Censorship is also engaged in by professionals: teachers, librarians, or administrators who occasionally do not make materials available because they are afraid of the censor, or because they personally do not approve of the item.

To say that a book has been censored does not mean that the book is unavailable nationwide or that it is a crime to possess the material, although these circumstances were true at one time in our country and are true in other countries at the present time. A recent extreme example is that of Salman Rushdie's *Satanic Verses*, for which the author has been condemned to die by the Iranian government. (At the time of this writing, Rushdie is being protected and held incognito by the English government.) In earlier times it was not unusual for governments, including ours, to put people to death for opinions which were conveniently labeled either heresy or sedition.

A censor is a person or an organization that publicly objects to words, subjects, and/or information in books, films, and other media and seeks to deprive others from seeing or viewing the same items. The means used to deprive others of information or books are sometimes legal but more often are to rouse public sentiment in favor of removing an item from public access. Often the censor reasons that the material is unsuitable for children. Children are assumed to be climbing up the developmental ladder of a well-regulated childhood and in need of protection from matters belonging strictly to adulthood.

Censors act on the belief that values and behaviors of children should be prescribed and inculcated by controlling the information as well as the models available to them, and that parents and schools have the right to do this. Some frequently censored books include Maurice Sendak's *In the Night Kitchen*, which has an illustration of a naked boy and explores a child's nighttime fantasies; Mark Twain's *The Adventures of Huckleberry Finn*, which uses the colloquial language of 1885, when the book was published, including the pejorative word, *nigger;* and Judy Blume's *Are You There, God? It's Me, Margaret*, in which the protagonist discusses puberty and is allowed to choose her own religion.

Opposed to censorship are those deeply concerned with the principle of intellectual freedom. They defend the rights of children to have good quality literature in spite of profane words, unsavory topics, or information on the so-called controversial subjects such as sex, race, politics, and religion. ("Controversial" usually means there are differing viewpoints on a subject or that unpleasant, but truthful, aspects about human life are acknowledged and discussed.) Those who nurture intellectual freedom believe children should be encouraged to explore authentic experiences and a variety of beliefs. They learn to think, to weigh, and to choose values by reading about other people and viewpoints and by interacting with literary models. A champion of intellectual freedom for children needs to be well-versed in assisting readers to explore themes, to recognize the contexts in which media are produced, and to evaluate the artist's craft.

Why Censor Books for Children?

The fact is that everyone, even defenders of the First Amendment, censors for several reasons: some psychological, others sociological, and some political. Freud defines censorship as "the psychological force which represses ideas, impulses, and feelings and prevents them from entering consciousness in their original form." People have the capacity to repress unconsciously that which makes them uncomfortable. Readers often exhibit this kind of censoring when they read. This impulse can alter the meaning of text for each reader. The meaning of any text is determined by an interaction between the reader and the text. Louise Rosenblatt, in *The Reader, The Text, The Poem*, suggests that the meaning of text is 50 percent in the text and 50 percent determined by the individual reader's background. A text may have one meaning to one reader and a totally different meaning to another, depending on their individual experiences. Shel Silverstein's *The Giving Tree*, for example, has on the one hand been the target of censorship attempts by feminists as a text condoning sexist stereotypes, while on the other hand, it is perceived by thousands of Sunday School teachers as having a valuable message about the virtue of giving.

Persons who live in the same community and share the same cultural paradigms or social values may still have widely disparate perceptions of *The Giving Tree*. The milieu in which we grow up and live shapes our construct of the world and severely limits our ability to see other constructs. For example, Margaret Steig, in "The Nazi Public Library and the Young Adult," writes of youth librarians in Nazi Germany who made great strides in the development of library service, never stopping, however, to assess or recognize the immorality of the information they were disseminating. More recently, a Romanian journalist on the television program, *Sixty Minutes*, expressed dismay at her own lack of conscience about writing lies to protect the now deposed president, Ceaușescu. One way to break through the barrier of our own cultural boundaries is to read good literature at all ages.

Literature has the power to shock and to challenge dearly held ideas and feelings. Literature for children is no exception. Some readers prefer neither to be disturbed by what they read nor to entertain ideas different from their own, and they choose their reading accordingly. This is a matter of personal choice.

However, literature, in one way or another, is selected for children by adults. Children do not have complete freedom of choice in what is available for them to read. Adults write the books; other adults as editors select the manuscripts to be published; adults review the titles for periodicals; and adults, whether librarians, teachers, or parents, do the vast majority of buying of children's books. Thus, adults have the power to determine the very nature of children's literature, and with that power comes an awesome responsibility.

Adults must understand the characteristics of juvenile literature; and they must be aware of their own values and prejudices. Ultimately, adults working with children's literature must be willing to grapple with the complex concept of a child's right to information, whether that right be legal, moral, or simply developmentally sound. Only when armed with such knowledge and a willingness to accept such responsibility can adults appropriately select materials for children. The underlying philosophy that helps define "appropriate" considers literature and information and the development of critical reading and viewing skills as essential to the process of learning. *Informed adults will recognize that the process of applying critical criteria in reading is what ultimately educates children.*

Schools and libraries face the dilemma of meeting their charge to encourage reading and at the same time pacify pressure groups wanting to censor what is read. How do professionals maintain their obligation to educate children to want to read while under pressure from censorship organizations to remove what is to be read? How do professionals and parents create happy reading experiences for children when others in the community are expressing such hatred of books that dissension and legal battles between citizens and institutions result? We are living in a period of history when these conflicts are widespread.

The choice is either to censor or to educate. To censor reflects a lack of confidence in how children learn. To censor is the antithesis of education. The fortunate reader approaches a fork on the reading road when the story or information in a book overpowers previously held thoughts and feelings. Some readers continue in the direction established by the author. Others rebel, become angry, and, in the extreme, initiate a frenzy of activity to punish the author and those tolerant of her/his literary work. The road on which the author wants readers to journey is a vicarious one. We are led to imagine we are somewhere else, doing things we may never have done, and thinking thoughts other than our own.

What is not vicarious are the reactions we have to those journeys. W. H. Auden has said that first-rate literature prompts the reader to say, "I never thought about that before, and now that I have I never will be the same again." Literature has the power to elevate and to inspire but also to antagonize readers of all ages. We know this from our own experience, but also from listening to the furor of the censors and by reviewing the long history of book banning around the world.

The Legal Battleground

In the United States, the Supreme Court is charged with defending the First Amendment of the constitution which reads:

Congress shall make no law respecting an establishment of religion, or prohibiting the free exercise thereof; or abridging the freedom of speech, or of the press . . . .

The United States Supreme Court has been asked many times to interpret the First Amendment as it applies to specific disagreements on these issues. By 1990, the Court had rendered only three decisions under the First Amendment affecting youth rights. In 1943, *Barnette* v. *West Virginia* established the right of children not to be forced to salute the flag if, as in this case, their religion (Jehovah's Witnesses) forbade them to do so. *Tinker* v. *Des Moines Independent School District* in 1969 declared that students have the right to express political opinions in school. The case involved the wearing of black armbands to protest the Vietnam War; one of the youths involved was ten years of

age. A third case in 1988, *Hazelwood School District* v. *Kuhlmeier,* gave school administrators the power to control content of a school newspaper if the paper is administered as part of the curriculum. However, in 1989 a U.S. District Court decision in New York in *Romano* v. *Harrington* did not apply that decision to extracurricular activity for which students did not receive credit.

A number of other Federal District Courts have ruled on the question of the right of Boards of Education to remove materials from school libraries. Decisions in *Minarcini* v. *Strongsville City School District* (1976), *Chelsea Right to Read Committee* v. *Chelsea School Governing Committee* (1978), and *Slavail* v. *Nashua Board of Education* (1979), have denied school boards the right to remove materials from school shelves simply because a majority of the board members find the materials personally offensive. On the other hand, decisions in *Bicknell* v. *Vergennes Union High School* (1979) and *Pico* v. *Board of Education, Island Trees* (1979) have ruled that school boards have the right to remove any materials—for whatever reason—the board members wish removed.

Obviously the rulings are in conflict, indicating that the Supreme Court will undoubtedly continue to rule and reiterate the meaning of "the law of the land" regarding First Amendment rights for children. All of the above cases involved senior high schools and it is unclear whether the judges in the Strongsville, Chelsea, and Nashua cases would write the same decisions if the conflict involved children in elementary schools. While young children's right of free speech has not been argued before the courts yet, the censorship of books for younger children is, nevertheless, an everyday occurrence.

Other countries have or are adopting similar legal protection for citizens to say what they think regardless of prevailing opinion. The number of such countries is increasing, especially since qualitative changes are taking place in the Eastern Bloc countries of Europe. Confusion remains, however, about the difference between the democratic process of voting so that a majority decision determines the law, and the purpose of the First Amendment, which is to assure freedom of expression by any one individual and to assure that person is not subject to any government regulation or community vote.

The Social Context of Censorship

The character of censorship attempts during the last decade has given proponents of intellectual freedom reason to be concerned about preserving the rights provided by the First Amendment. A decade ago the Moral Majority was a financially and politically powerful organization leading censorship attacks on schools and libraries across the country. Today, however, that organization and many others like it no longer exist partly because, they say, their mission has been achieved.

It is true that censorship is tolerated in our culture more than ever before. The fear generated by the work of the Moral Majority and others during the 1980s has made those responsible for children's books more cautious. In her unpublished dissertation studying the attitudes of school library media specialists toward intellectual freedom and censorship, Elizabeth Norris White found that the state in which the media specialists were employed was a statistically significant factor in determining their selection practices. Presumably, in states where censors are more active, media specialists feel less free in selection and circulation of materials. For example, in a Virginia community a school board voted to remove the original version of Kipling's *How the Leopard Got Its Spots* from library shelves for its racist content. A school board in North Carolina, however, voted to retain the same book after a similar complaint. The latter board also passed a unanimous resolution that pejorative name-calling be treated the same as if someone has "hit one's neighbor." The First Amendment protects the right to "name-call," but educational institutions have an obligation to teach how language is used to wield and maintain power. (Audrey and Don Wood's *Elbert's Bad Word* is a children's book which can stimulate discussion and thought among children in primary grades,

making them aware of the power of "name-calling.")

The proponents of censorship have not gone away; rather, many have entered official community and government positions of power. In an era when less than 50 percent of the electorate vote, it is not difficult to get elected to school boards, county commissions, and city councils—or even the presidency—if one only has a large enough financial backing and organization.

Censors have managed to gain control of such bodies in communities across the country and have forced changes in the policies and operation of schools and libraries. In Arizona, for example, a school district nationally known for its integrated, literature-based curriculum has now returned to basal readers at the direction of the newly elected, procensor, radical-right membership of the Board of Education.

Censoring organizations in the 1980s targeted textbooks as the prime offenders of their sensibilities. Since then, the movement to use literature instead of basal readers in the schools has gained widespread acceptance. The textbook critics had great success in controlling textbook content and the same furor has carried over to the textbook anthologies of literature. Many of the new texts start the publishing process with the selection of good literature but end with edited and expurgated versions of the original stories. The reasons vary but textbook publishers will generally use any method to deter attacks by the censor which may interfere with state adoptions of their texts.

Zena Sutherland reiterates on every page of *Children and Books* the great influence that literature can have in the life and education of children. Never has the need to protect the child's right to read been more crucial—for the survival of childhood and democracy. Joshua Meyrowitz in *No Sense of Place* states that today children "have gained access to social information in no particular pattern or sequence . . . . In the shared environment of television, children and adults know a great deal about one another's behavior and social knowledge—too much, in fact for them to play out the traditional complementary roles of innocence versus omniscience."

The culture of American children is overwhelmingly determined by the electronic media. By watching television and movie videos, children are exposed to every aspect of matters once considered strictly for adults. Worse is the destruction of childhood innocence among the 20 percent of children living in poverty, without homes, as victims of racism and sexual abuse, or without adequate medical care. In this century, and the next, our concern should be to assist children in coping with what must seem to many of them an unfriendly, bizarre, and unfathomable world. More important than ever before is the quality of the literature that is available to children. The very materials that the censor attacks are often the ones that could help children identify the incongruities of our culture, as well as to survive them.

Katherine Paterson's *Jacob Have I Loved* is currently facing censorship because it portrays a young girl's infatuation with an older man. Censoring this powerful story about growing up will not eradicate adolescent infatuation. This story will, however, help adolescents to understand themselves. Shel Silverstein's *Where the Sidewalk Ends* has a poem beginning, "Someone ate the baby . . ." and a school board member objected because everyone knows no one would do that. The poem, of course, is a humorous expression of feelings of jealousy and sibling rivalry which makes children laugh. The result is catharsis, not emulation.

Often people who have been deprived of extensive knowledge of literature interpret metaphor in concrete terms. The importance of metaphor to human understanding cannot be overestimated. Childhood should be a time for "bathing" in story in order to gain understanding of oneself and the world through example and metaphor. The censor often does not appreciate either metaphor or the facts. Brock Cole's *The Goats* is a sensitive story of children's cruelty to peers. The book is not objected to because it portrays cruelty but because the children are left without clothes and discuss the menstrual period. Banning the book will not erase cruelty or menstrual periods. The book does present an understanding perspective on both. Many adults hesitate to show Toshi Maruki's *Hiroshima No Pika* to children. The devastating effects of the atomic bomb on the Japanese city leave the reader with feelings that war is far from a glorious human achievement. Children, who are developing their own views of the world, need to see the effects of war if they are to value the concept of peace.

Professional Responsibilities

The previous sections explain *why* controversies arise over books and information for children. How these controversies are resolved depends a great deal on professional participation in support of children's access to quality literature. What follows are some suggestions for involvement at many levels.

Provide children with opportunities to discuss their reactions to controversial books. These discussions might take place in schools, libraries, or other meeting places. An adult leader can help to focus discussion on the meaning of the First Amendment and its defense of free expression.

Serve as role models for free expression. It is a travesty for adults to resist external censorship, and then to restrain free expression of opinions different from their own in their homes, classrooms, or communities.

Be sure that schools and libraries have board-approved policies and procedures concerning the selection and maintenance of materials in their collections. The National Council of Teachers of English (see "Useful Sources" at the end of this essay) has guidelines for the preparation of such documents.

Beware of excluding media that may be of interest to a limited number of students or that may contain possible controversial elements. This is especially important in schools serving a limited number of grades, such as middle or primary schools.

Administrators should be cautioned not to use their authority to remove materials simply because they *fear* that a parent or influential member of the community may be offended.

Maintain a distinction between issues of free speech and educational policy, and the importance of each.

Resist censorship on as broad a front as the censors may attack. If the controversy is made public by the censors, be informed through the many articles in the library and general press on how censorship attempts have been successfully handled elsewhere.

In dealing with the press or other news media, keep in mind that freedom of the press is related to issues of censorship, and that representatives of the media can often be good allies.

Question candidates running for school boards and other community offices about their positions on issues of freedom, and inform voters accordingly.

Join organizations which are working to protect rights guaranteed by the First Amendment. A number of these are listed in the following section of Useful Sources, and often they are noted for their willingness to assist when individual professionals are faced with problems related to censorship.

This essay could be endlessly revised. The targets and sources of censorship, like the reasons for censorship, change. Thomas Jefferson emphasized our task when he said, "Eternal vigilance is the price of liberty." Consistent concern for providing children with access to reading may bring one into conflict with a variety of agencies and people, but the conflict can be diminished when good practices and policies are in place in schools and libraries, and when children and adults have a firm grasp on the principles that guide their own reading.

Alice Phoebe Naylor, professor in the Reich College of Education, Appalachian State University, is a leader and articulate spokesperson for the rights of children.

Works Cited in the Text

BLUME, JUDY. *Are You There, God? It's Me, Margaret.* Bradbury, 1970.

_____. *Deenie.* Bradbury, 1973.

BURRESS, LEE. *Battle of the Books: Literary Censorship in the Public Schools, 1950–1985.* Scarecrow, 1989.

COLE, BROCK. *The Goats.* Farrar, Straus, Giroux, 1988.

MARUKI, TOSHI. *Hiroshima, No Pika.* Lothrop, Lee & Shepard, 1982.

MEYROWITZ, JOSHUA. *No Sense of Place: The Impact of Electronic Media on Social Behavior.* Oxford, 1985.

PATERSON, KATHERINE. *Jacob Have I Loved.* Harper & Row, 1980.

ROSENBLATT, LOUISE. *The Reader, The Text, The Poem: The Transactional Theory of the Literary Work.* Southern Illinois University Press, 1978.

RUSHDIE, SALMAN. *Satanic Verses.* Viking, 1988.

SENDAK, MAURICE. *In the Night Kitchen.* Harper, 1970.

SILVERSTEIN, SHEL. *The Giving Tree.* Harper, 1964.

_____. *Where the Sidewalk Ends.* Harper, 1974.

STIEG, MARGARET. "The Nazi Public Library and the Young Adult," *Top of the News,* Volume 43, pp. 45–57, Fall, 1986.

WHITE, ELIZABETH NORRIS. "A Heuristic Study of the Attitudes of School Library Media Specialists toward Intellectual Freedom and Censorship." Unpublished dissertation, Georgia State University, 1988.

WOOD, AUDREY and DON. *Elbert's Bad Word.* Harcourt Brace & Jovanovich, 1988.

Organizations

The American Civil Liberties Union. 22 E. 40th Street, New York, NY 10016. (Membership in this organization is one way of supporting freedom of speech. The organization also provides legal support for people involved in litigation.)

The American Library Association (ALA). Office for Intellectual Freedom. 50 E. Huron Street, Chicago, IL 60611. (This office maintains an 800 telephone number (800-545-2433) to accept calls from people facing censorship problems and provides packets of information and materials. It publishes the *Newsletter on Intellectual Freedom.*)

Freedom to Read Foundation. 50 E. Huron Street, Chicago, IL 60611. (The Foundation provides financial and legal advice to people in need.)

The National Coalition Against Censorship. 132 W. 43rd Street, New York, NY 10036. (This is an activist organization willing to make contacts and give advice on censorship cases. It publishes the *Censorship News.*)

The National Council of Teachers of English (NCTE). 1111 Kenyon Road, Urbana, IL 61801. (NCTE has many helpful publications, especially the guidelines for handling complaints about materials used in the classroom.)

People for the American Way. 1015 18th Street, NW, Washington, DC 20036. (This is a very active organization in publicizing and researching the status of intellectual freedom at the state and national levels.)

Internationalism and Children's Books

Amy Kellman

Children's books keep alive a sense of nationality, but they also keep alive a sense of humanity. They describe their native land lovingly, but they also describe faraway lands where unknown brothers live. They understand the essential quality of their own race; but each of them is a messenger that goes beyond mountains and rivers, beyond the seas, to the very ends of the world in search of new friendships. Every country gives and every country receives—innumerable are the exchanges—and so it comes about that in our first impressionable years the universal republic of childhood is born.[1]

One need only look at the world around us to understand the importance of sharing with children books set in all parts of the globe. Even a cursory glance at the daily newspaper suggests that events which happen in another part of the world, however remote, reverberate in the United States. It is also clear that the key issues, such as the health of our environment, economy, and political stability, cross national boundaries. Providing children with books that give insights about other cultures and other people enriches their world and enhances their abilities to work with other countries as they assume the leadership positions of the very

near future. As the world changes, the need increases for a vital body of children's books that mirrors these changes.

In October, 1945, Jella Lepman, a remarkable woman who believed international understanding could be accomplished by the exchange of children's books, was sent from London to Frankfurt to serve as an advisor for women and youth affairs for the Information Control Division of the U.S. Army of Occupation. She tells her story with dynamism and commitment in *A Bridge of Children's Books* (trans. Edith McCormick). The results of her work exist today as the International Youth Library, established in 1949 and housed in Munich, and as the International Board on Books for Young People (IBBY), founded on November 18, 1951.

The International Youth Library is a mecca for scholars, publishers, librarians, educators, those interested in researching children's books from around the world, and, most importantly, for children. Books sent by publishers to this library from all over the world are shared through programs, exhibitions (many of which travel), and publications. Housed in a medieval castle on the outskirts of Munich, the International Youth Library celebrated its fortieth anniversary in 1988 with a conference on "the future of internationalism in children's literature research and, as an integral part of this meeting, the library's own future in a rapidly changing world."[2]

IBBY, which has its secretariat in Basel, Switzerland, boasted fifty national sections in 1990 representing countries from every part of the world. The activities of the sections described in *Bookbird*, a joint publication of IBBY and the International Institute for Children's Literature and Reading Research, speak to the vitality of the organization.

An IBBY Congress is held every two years and is attended by publishers, educators, librarians, writers, and illustrators from all over the world. In 1990 the first Congress in the United States was organized by the United States Board on Books for Young People (USBBY) and

[1]Paul Hazard, *Books, Children & Men* (Horn Book, 1947), p. 146.

[2]Jeffrey Garrett, "The International Youth Library," (*The Horn Book Magazine*, September/October 1988), p. 682.

held in Williamsburg, Virginia. Proceedings of each Congress reflect the diversity of interests and speakers. What is not conveyed by the formal papers is the excitement of interacting with people from all over who are drawn together by a commitment to children's books.

The IBBY Honor List, which has been presented and published at each Congress since 1956, consists of three books selected by each National Section that represent excellence in text, illustration, and, beginning in 1978, translation from the past two years. It is a major resource for publishers looking for important books to translate and publish in their country and for anyone else interested in knowing what is being added to the literature for children from around the world.

In the United States, USBBY continues the momentum through its newsletter; and through programs at the conferences and meetings of its patron members—the American Library Association, the Children's Book Council, the International Reading Association, and the National Council of Teachers of English—and by committee work done by USBBY members on bibliographies, awards, and other projects which are part of IBBY's program or in response to the needs in this country.

IBBY also sponsors one of the most prestigious children's book awards, the Hans Christian Andersen award, given since 1956 to an author, and since 1966 also to an illustrator, "who have made a lasting contribution to literature for children and young people."[3] United States winners include authors Meindert DeJong (1962), Scott O'Dell (1972), and Paula Fox (1978), and illustrator Maurice Sendak (1970).

Zena Sutherland's assessment of the impact of international awards goes to the heart of this activity:

There are peripheral benefits to those who participate in all international award giving; each of us gains a measure of understanding which can help in the work we do with or for children. Each of us acquires knowledge we share with our colleagues at home. We are further armored in the constant battle against the "kiddie-lit" deprecators by the increased status given children's literature by the awards and even by the publicity attendant on the meetings at which the awards are decided or bestowed, or even by the publicity for meetings such as this one.

But most important, the awards benefit children. Each international prize means that some children who would otherwise never see the work of an individual author or artist will have that opportunity, that children's aesthetic experiences will be that much more enriched.[4]

In addition to the Andersen Medals, four other awards spotlight children's books on an international scale. Two of them are chosen from submissions from all over the world in any language, and two are for English-language books originating in any country.

The Biennale of Illustrations Bratislava (BIB), an international exhibition of children's book illustrations, takes place every other year in Bratislava, Czechoslovakia. An international jury awards a Grand Prix, five Golden Apples, ten Golden Plaques, and four Honorable Mentions. Other citations may be made. In 1989, for example, additional Honorable Mentions were given to John Steptoe in memoriam and to publishers from Sri Lanka, France, and Finland.

The United States has not always participated in BIB because of the difficulties involved in sending the required original art and the philosophical objections by U.S. jurors to judging the art outside the context of the finished book. Recently the ties between the art and the book have been strengthened but the emphasis is unquestionably on the art and the artist. In 1989, 352 illustrators from 48 countries participated. For the first time, Malta, Senegal, and South Korea were among the nations represented at the BIB.[5]

The International Reading Association Children's Book Award, first given in 1975, is for

---

[3]*Bookbird* (September, 1988), p. 3.

[4]Zena Sutherland, "Golden Apples and Blue Ribbons: The Meaning of International Awards," *Proceedings Children's Books International 3* (Boston Public Library, 1978), p. 55.

[5]*USBBY Newsletter* (Spring 1990), p. 12.

the first or second book by an author who shows unusual promise in the field of children's books. Books originating in any language are eligible, but for a book not written in English, the IRA requires an abstract and a translation into English of one representative chapter or section. Since 1987 the award has been extended to two books—one for younger and one for older children.

The Mildred L. Batchelder Award was established in 1966 by the American Library Association in honor of the woman who personally and professionally promoted internationalism and encouraged translations of books from other countries in her capacity as the Executive Secretary of the American Library Association's Children's Services Division, now the Association for Library Service to Children (ALSC). First given in 1968 to Knopf for Erich Kästner's *The Little Man*, which was translated by James Kirkus, the award is given annually for a distinguished book first published in a foreign language in a foreign country, translated, and then published in the United States.

The Batchelder Award spotlights translations from one language to another. Edward Fenton, who has translated three Batchelder winners, articulates the joys and hazards of this necessary and difficult task. Necessary because:

in our secure fortress of English, it does not behoove us to remain complacent. The problem of translation is fully as important for us as it is for the less-privileged languages. We too require to be nourished by other cultures and by other ages. Without our bridges to them we would become isolated, insular, falsely arrogant—not to say inbred. Without this exchange we would suffer a kind of cultural anemia.[6]

The difficulty is that of

"Translator: traitor," as the Italian proverb has it. On the other hand, the translator can also provide a bridge between nations as well as across centuries. He can fire the passion which compels people in war time to risk their lives for another country because they had read and loved, say,

Dickens and Lewis Carroll. The translator can, as the Italians claim, sink us all. But at best he can link us all.[7]

In the past ten years it has been difficult finding enough worthy candidates from which to choose. Happily, this trend seems to be reversing since the late 1980s because of the continued commitment of editors like Dorothy Briley and Margaret K. McElderry, who have served on the board of IBBY, and the increased interaction of publishers from around the globe. Awards, such as these described, do encourage editors to seek out and publish the best from many countries. The adults responsible for introducing children to books must, in turn, buy and use these books not because the publisher needs to be subsidized, but because they are good books that will not find an instant audience without some assistance.

This increased activity in global publishing is exemplified by the dramatic growth of the Bologna International Children's Book Fair, an annual spring event during which books are bought and sold by publishers from all over the world. Herbert R. Lottman describes it as:

the world's biggest and most useful specialized book event, centering on the international market for children's and young adult books, with comics and (especially on the Italian side) textbooks and educational software thrown in. Bologna's original raison d'etre was to allow producers of picture books and packaged series to introduce their lines to partners in the major trading nations; more recently the fair has become as significant in its sector for translation rights as the autumn Frankfurt fair is for adult books.[8]

The Fair, which began in 1964 with fourteen European publishers and one United States imprint, has grown so that in 1990 over 1,000 exhibitors from fifty-plus nations were transacting business at Bologna. For American publishers, the most valuable aspects of the Bologna Book Fair are the opportunities to meet with their counterparts from other countries,

[6]Edward Fenton, "Blind Idiot, or, The Problems of Translation," *Proceedings and Book Catalog, Children's Books International 2* (Boston Public Library, 1977), p. 54.

[7]Fenton, "Blind Idiot, or, The Problems of Translation," p. 54.

[8]*Publishers Weekly* (March 16, 1990), p. 26.

to view completed picture books, and to participate in open discussion about novels, translations, and other rights issues. Both Dorothy Briley and Margaret McElderry noted in telephone interviews that getting to know people from countries one did not usually visit enabled them to develop relationships that allowed for follow up on projects of mutual interest and benefit.

Publishing books from other English-speaking countries, especially Great Britain, is not a new trend in the U.S. Even these books need some "translation" of words for the American edition, such as from "bonnet" for the hood of a car and from "lift" for elevator. Editorial decisions are constantly being made that balance degrees of comprehension with the need to retain the flavor, spirit, and sense of place of the original text. At an ALSC preconference on international children's books in 1988, much discussion was heard about whether and how much these kinds of "translations," sometimes made over the objections of the authors, are needed.

When asked about the increased number of books being published by authors from Australia and New Zealand, Margaret McElderry observed that an "enormous surge of creativity" that began with films, especially *Breaker Morant*, is responsible for this trend. McElderry has published what might be described as the "first wave" of Australian writers, Joan Phipson and Patricia Wrightson, in the late 1960s and 1970s. Dorothy Briley and Margaret McElderry agreed that American readers seem to understand Australian and New Zealand humor and style, perhaps because they are young countries like the United States. The books travel well and we are the richer for them.

Programmatic opportunities abound to focus attention on children's books from other countries or set in other countries and cultures. The United Nations declared 1979 the Year of the Child; 1990 is International Literacy Year. Posters, a special logo, and statements by public figures are all grist for the educator's mill to promote reading internationally.

April 2 is the birthday of Hans Christian Andersen, that well-loved storyteller. It is also International Children's Book Day, a celebra-

tion sponsored by IBBY. Every year a different "National Section" picks a theme, prepares a poster, and issues a "Message" to children all over the world. For 1990 the Canadian National Section of IBBY chose the theme "Books: Paths to Many Worlds."

Why bother to promote and encourage participation in Hazard's "universal republic of childhood?" Why become familiar with books from other parts of the world? Do not do it just because they are "worthy" books. Do not do it to reward the publishers who make them available, or even because these books have a role in preparing children to understand one another as adults. Read them and share them with children because they are rewarding and life-enhancing. Let Paul Hazard have the last word:

Fasten to every book that goes far off into the distant parts of the world one of those invisible threads; they multiply and cross each other in every direction, so that throughout the universe continuously, endlessly, currents of human sympathy flow.[9]

Amy Kellman is District Children's Coordinator, The Carnegie Library of Pittsburgh, and 1990–1991 President of the U.S. Board on Books for Young People.

Bibliography
Works Cited in the Text

Bookbird. September, 1988.

Children's Books International. Boston Public Library. Volume 1, 1976; Volume 2, 1977; Volume 3, 1978; Volume 4, 1979.

DUNHOUSE, MARY BETH, comp. *International Directory of Children's Literature.* Facts on File, 1986.

FENTON, EDWARD. "Blind Idiot, or, The Problems of Translation," *Proceedings and Book Catalog. Children's Books International 2.* Boston Public Library, 1977.

GARRETT, JEFFREY. "The International Youth Library," *The Horn Book Magazine.* September/October 1988.

HAZARD, PAUL. *Books Children & Men.* Horn Book, 1947.

HÜRLIMANN, BETTINA. *Three Centuries of Children's Books in Europe.* tr. and ed. Brian W. Alderson. Oxford University Press, 1967; World, 1968.

[9]Hazard, *Books Children & Men*, p. 152.

JONES, DOLORES BLYTHE. *Children's Literature: Awards and Winners; a Directory of Prizes, Authors, and Illustrators,* 2nd ed. Gale, 1988. Updated with supplements.

KELLMAN, AMY, ed. *Guide to Children's Libraries and Literature Outside the United States.* ALA, 1982.

LEPMAN, JELLA. *A Bridge of Children's Books,* tr. Edith McCormick. ALA, 1969.

MAISSEN, LEENA, ed. *International Board on Books for Young People International Directory of Children's Literature Specialists.* K. G. Saur, 1986.

PELLOWSKI, ANNE. *The World of Storytelling.* Bowker, 1977.

Publishers Weekly. Bowker, March 16, 1990.

SUTHERLAND, ZENA. "Golden Apples and Blue Ribbons: The Meaning of International Awards," *Proceedings Children's Books International 3.* Boston Public Library, 1978.

USBBY Newsletter. Spring 1990.

Periodicals

Bookbird: Institute for Children's and Reading Research. Lusia Binder, ed. A joint publication of the International Board on Books for Young People and the International Institute for Children's Literature and Reading Research.

Booklist. American Library Association. Regularly publishes bibliographies of books from other countries.

CBC Features. Children's Book Council. Spotlights international events, publishers, and prizes.

Children's Literature in Education: An International Quarterly. Human Sciences Press.

The Horn Book Magazine. Horn Book. Articles by and about authors from around the world.

Phaedrus: An International Journal of Children's Literature Research. Fairleigh Dickinson University.

Publishers Weekly. Bowker. Profiles publishers from abroad and international book events.

The United States Board on Books for Young People Newsletter. International Reading Association. Free to members of USBBY.

Organizations

Children's Literature Center. Library of Congress, Washington, DC 20540.

Information Center on Children's Cultures. U.S. Committee for UNICEF, 331 East 38th Street, New York, NY 10016. Provides lists of children's books sources from other countries; lists of books about individual countries.

International Association of School Librarianship. P.O. Box 1486, Kalamazoo, Mich. 49005.

International Board on Books for Young People. IBBY Secretariat, Leonhardsgraben 38A, Postfach, CH-4003 Basel, Switzerland.

International Institute for Children's Literature and Reading Research. Mayerhofgasse 6, A-1040, Vienna, Austria.

International Reading Association. 800 Barksdale Road, Newark, Del. 19711.

International Research Society for Children's Literature. LASIC, Maison des Sciences de l'homme, Domaine Universitaire, 33405 Talence, France.

The International Youth Library. Schloss Blutenberg, D-8000 Munich 60, Federal Republic of Germany.

The United States Board on Books for Young People (USBBY). Secretariat: International Reading Association, P. O. Box 8139, Newark, Del. 19714-8139.

Awards for Children's Books

Peggy Sullivan

Award-winning children's books appear with medallions featured on their covers; lists of children's books include notations for "award-winning" books. What do these awards mean? There are several answers to this question.

Nature of Children's Book Awards

Each award that is established and maintained for a period of time has a purpose. It may be to encourage the publication of more and better children's books, to call good books to the attention of a wider audience, or to show appreciation for the contributions that authors and illustrators have made to a particular cause. Sometimes, single awards may have several purposes.

The person, group, or institution that gives an award has a mission, usually reflected in the criteria for the award. For example, the Jane Addams Children's Book Award, established in 1953, is given to the author of a book with literary merit and constructive themes. International peace, and concern and respect for different kinds of people are themes that characterized Jane Addams's life, so it is not surprising that many of the books that have won this award have been based on those themes.

Similarly, the Coretta Scott King Awards were established in 1969, the year after Martin Luther King Jr.'s death, and they are named to commemorate him and to honor his widow. Recipients are black authors and illustrators selected for having made outstanding inspirational and educational contributions to children's literature. The awards are presented annually at the American Library Association (ALA) conference.

Sometimes, awards are given to manuscripts. Usually, this happens when a publisher is searching for new authors or wishes to encourage the writing of certain kinds of books. The company will offer an award, often in dollars paid in advance as part of the author's royalties. These awards usually bear the name of the publishing company.

There are some awards in the large field of children's books with which this essay is not concerned. Amy Kellman's essay, "Internationalism and Children's Books," has dealt with the major international awards, so they are not included here. Other awards, such as the one named for Laura Ingalls Wilder, which are given for the many contributions of an author, illustrator, or publisher over a period of years, are also beyond the scope of this essay. So are awards which go to editors or librarians or other participants in the world of children's books. Here, we are concerned with those given for individual books—and there are quite a few of them.

Different awards have various levels of prestige. Like respect, prestige is earned over a long period of time. Observers see that awards are made according to established criteria and accomplish the goals intended for them; recipients and would-be recipients are aware of the award and are proud when their books are recognized. To sum it up: when awards make a difference, they merit prestige.

Major National Awards for Overall Excellence

When Frederic Melcher suggested the idea of the Newbery Medal to the American Library Association in 1921, he wanted to encourage the publication of more books of high quality for children. As the award was administered by the ALA committees of children's and school librarians over the years, it increased in prestige and it also achieved Melcher's goal. Publishers supported new children's departments and children's book editors encouraged authors to write for children. All of this occurred in the marketplace of the literary world, but the dream of recognition surely provided some of the motivation. Annual announcements of the awards have become media events that help to boost the sales of the award books and of the honor books, recognized for their excellence although not award winners.

Sixteen years after establishing the Newbery Medal, Melcher provided support for the Caldecott Medal, to be given annually to the most distinguished picture book published in the preceding year. He was acknowledging what many judges and committees have also experienced: the difficulty comparing the best of picture books with the best of books where text is more dominant. Illustrators are the recipients of the Caldecott Medal, which has also grown in prestige and newsworthiness over the years of its existence.

It is interesting to note that both of these American awards are named for Englishmen: John Newbery, an early printer, and Randolph Caldecott, a nineteenth-century illustrator. Two comparable awards in Great Britain are administered by The Library Association. The Carnegie Medal has been awarded annually since 1937 to the most distinguished children's book of the preceding year. It is named for Andrew Carnegie, the steelmaker-philanthropist who supported libraries so effectively. The Kate Greenaway Medal, another Library Association award, was first given in 1957 for the most distinguished illustrations in a book for children published during the preceding year. Note that the book receiving the Greenaway Medal need not be a picture book, although the author-illustrator for whom it is named produced many such books.

Other countries have established similar awards, including the Canadian Library Association's Book of the Year for Children, first awarded in 1947. The establishment of the Hans Christian Andersen Award has probably helped to stimulate interest in national awards, since the national groups that nominate authors and illustrators for this international award benefit from knowing who has been recognized for excellence within their own countries.

Children's books in the U.S. achieved additional status when they were included as a category in the National Book Awards. They maintained that status in the American Book Awards, administered by the Association of American Publishers from 1980 to 1983, as successors to the National Book Awards. There are values in having children's books recognized as a genre of the literary world, just as there are values in having them celebrated with awards programs focusing exclusively on them. There are some characteristics all of these have in common. Awards do not just happen.

Young Readers' Choice Awards

The Pacific Northwest Library Association (PNLA), covering five U.S. states and two Canadian provinces, established the Young Reader's Choice Awards in 1940. It has been presented annually since then. Children in grades four through eight vote to select the winner each year. Their choices are made from a list of ten to fifteen books selected by the group that actually administers the award. Patterns of selection similar to those of PNLA have been followed in many states which have established their own awards. Although the name of the PNLA award is the Young Reader's Choice Award, that term, slightly modified, accurately describes the awards offered in many other regions of the U.S.

One characteristic these awards have in common is the intent to recognize children's books of excellence which also appeal to children as readers. Books may be several years old before they are selected, but that ensures their availability to the young voters. When parents, teachers, and librarians support the awards effectively, they stimulate reading and discussion to help children focus on issues of quality, such as development of characters or writing style, and they encourage children to see beyond their own likes and dislikes to the overall excellence of the book. Almost everyone enjoys having his or her opinion valued, and children have been enthusiastic in their participation in these award programs. When the nominating lists are well chosen, many fine books are brought to the attention of the young readers.

In 1952, Kansas was the first state to establish a young readers' choice award. It was named for William Allen White, the Emporia newspaper editor who achieved international renown for his editorials. At first, the establishment of such awards spread gradually, but more than half the states now have such programs, and it appears likely that there are more to come. Sometimes, regional writers are preferred for such awards, or stories with settings in a given region or state may appear to have an advantage, but the universal appeal of some authors is also recognized. Beverly Cleary, for example, has received at least a dozen such awards, including seven for *Ramona and Her Father*, which was also a Newbery Honor Book.

The names of these awards are part of the picture of the literary scene in the states. Illinois's is named in memory of Rebecca Caudill, an author who resided in Illinois. Other authors honored include Dorothy Canfield Fisher (Vermont), Charlie May Simon (Arkansas), and Mark Twain (Missouri). Some of the names refer to something for which the state is noted: Kentucky Bluegrass, Buckeye (Ohio), Texas Bluebonnet, or Great Stone Face (New Hampshire), while other awards are simply named for the state. The history of these awards programs is still developing and should be interesting for participants and observers alike.

Behind the Scenes with Award Selections

People, usually functioning in committees, select award winners within rules and policies that give both focus and limitations to their decisions. It is always interesting, and can even be fun, to second-guess or even to ridicule or argue their choices. But it is important to keep in mind the context for those choices. Sometimes, rules and policies change. For example, there was a time when Newbery and Caldecott Medals could not be awarded to anyone for a second time unless there was a unanimous vote of the committee. During that period, no author or illustrator received the award twice, and it is possible that some very distinguished books failed to receive the necessary unanimous vote. More recently, policies for at least one of the readers' choice awards were changed in the opposite direction: After one author had received the award several times, the rules were changed to prevent any previous winner from being chosen again. When the partial intent of the awards program is to expand the reading of children, it may indeed make sense to follow such practices in order to assure diversity in the voting list as well as to ensure children that their votes for other authors will have good results.

It can also happen that two or more really wonderful books are published in the same year. Only one can win the award if there is only one award for that year. This kind of thing happens with many kinds of awards. Not long ago, I saw the old film, *The Entertainer*, starring Laurence Olivier. A friend who saw it with me said, "Olivier was great! How did it happen that he didn't win the Academy Award for that performance?" I looked it up later, and discovered that Burt Lancaster won the award that year for his distinguished acting in *Elmer Gantry*. Both performances were exceptional, but only one could win that year. And so it is with the annual children's book awards.

Perhaps especially with books, the most exciting or controversial titles may not be recognized as distinguished when they are new. It is easy to look back and wonder why such books as *Little House in the Big Woods* or *Charlotte's Web* did not win Newbery Medals. But, although it may seem surprising now, many people were vigorously opposed to *Charlotte's Web* as a potential award-winner. Librarians and teachers commented that it failed as a fantasy, and some resented the fact that, since E. B. White was a noted writer for *The New Yorker*, his book received wide support from the New York literary establishment. That was all that was needed to make midwestern members of the committee, for example, oppose its selection. That year, the Newbery Medal went to Ann Nolan Clark for *Secret of the Andes*.

It is naive to think that committees always arrive at the best decisions, and their work and its results can be affected by a chair who pushes them too assertively toward decisions without allowing time for members to speak up for their favorites, or, perhaps worse yet, a chair who allows discussions to drone on so that the process itself distracts from the purpose or outcome. In the real world, both of these kinds of things do happen. In spite of that, awards, if honestly administered, achieve a status, even a luster, which can be shared by the recipients and others associated with the awards process.

Using and Promoting Award Books

A book that wins one of the more prestigious awards is virtually assured a long and respected life. It is likely to stay in print longer than many contemporaneous books, and many libraries maintain collections of such honored books. And yet, no award can ensure popularity. It may even be that some children are intimidated, overwhelmed by the idea of a book's being an award winner. And there is no assurance that a collection of such books provides a well-rounded collection for reading. These books are, quite simply, the ones chosen in a given year as the best within the constraints of the rules and policies governing the award.

It makes sense for teachers, librarians, and parents to become familiar with many of these award books and to encourage children to read them and to appreciate what it means for a book to have been so honored. Although many people may think it is a great idea to study the Newbery Medal books or to feature those that have won the Caldecott Medal in an art unit, that is about equivalent to basing the study of recent American literature on books which have received the Pulitzer Prize.

As has been mentioned, the announcement of awards can be a media event. Schools and libraries may participate in this in their own areas by sponsoring programs about the year's selection, or providing the local news media with comments that children make about the winners. Good public relations is a major reason for the establishment of most awards. It is certainly reasonable to build on these public relations locally and to use the media attention to increase children's awareness of excellence and its rewards, and to develop their tastes for the best of children's books.

Bibliography
Children's Books Cited

CLARK, ANN NOLAN. *Secret of the Andes*. Viking, 1952.
CLEARY, BEVERLY. *Ramona and Her Father*. Morrow, 1977.
WHITE, E. B. *Charlotte's Web*. Harper, 1952.
WILDER, LAURA INGALLS. *Little House in the Big Woods*. Harper, 1932.

Other References

Several sources list awards for children's books, and some include lists of the books which have received the awards. In Appendix D of this book, most are included. Among other references, I have found the following most helpful:

JONES, DOLORES BLYTHE. *Children's Literature Awards and Winners: A Directory of Prizes, Authors, and Illustrators*. Neal-Schuman in association with Gale Research, 1983.

Research in Children's Literature

Kay E. Vandergrift

The world of children's literature is a multifaceted and ever-growing one, which has an almost infinite power to fascinate those who enter into an engagement with it. Part of that fascination is with the questions raised, as well as with those answered, by this literature. Some questions raised by early experiences with children's literature will be answered by continued reading of and about children's books and through discussion with others who share this interest. Other questions can be answered only by more formal and controlled research activities.

One of the difficulties in any kind of literary research is that research is inherently objective; while literary works are subjective compositions, subjectively perceived. If different readers perceive or interpret the same black marks on printed pages differently, how can there be a truly objective analysis of any literary work? It is true that some aspects of literary works and readers' responses to them cannot be objectified, nor would most students of literature want to replace the mystery of the aesthetic composition or the magic of a child's encountering a special book with a kind of scientific puzzle in which all the pieces can be identified, labeled, and assembled to reveal everything that can be known about the literary experience. There are, however, many things about literature that can be studied objectively and the knowledge gained can be used to enhance the magic of that subjective experience between child and book.

Many of the questions stimulated by children's literature have already been addressed by others who have completed research in the field and published the results of their work. For example, at least the initial questions about the reviewing of children's books in the United States just after the Civil War have been answered by Richard L. Darling in *The Rise of Children's Book Reviewing in America, 1865–*

1881. This is not to say that Darling's work may not itself raise additional questions. Serious students will, however, neither proceed in an investigation before completing a thorough search to locate other work on a topic, nor will they assume that all work has been completed if they locate one or more studies in their area of inquiry.

On the other hand, many questions have not yet been addressed and may lead to the design of new research studies. The nature of the questions raised will determine the nature of the research design. Some unanswered questions can be explored by studying children's books themselves in relation to a theoretical construct while others can be answered by looking at situations or events surrounding literary works. For instance, if the question is, "Can one look at children's literature and measure the conformity of the child protagonist's behavior to acceptable ethical standards?" the investigation can proceed in any number of ways; but, in every instance, the primary focus should be on the literary works. If the question is "Has the role of the children's book editor in the creation of picture story books changed from 1930 to 1990?" one will need to analyze publishing archives. Questions about young people's responses to literature will be answered by studying the interactions between children and books and the subsequent activities of those children. Those whose interest has been piqued by children's literature will almost certainly be consumers of research, and many will conduct original research in an attempt to answer intriguing questions or to test emerging theories. Thus, an understanding of the nature of research in this field is essential.

What Is Research?

Whether reading and evaluating the research of others or planning a research study of one's own, one should keep in mind some basic principles. First, a distinction must be made between a research study and other forms of writing and reportage. Informal, or even informed, critical opinions about children's literature and matters relating to that literature can be fascinating reading and valuable sources of information and ideas; but opinions, no matter how informed, are not research. Neither, strictly speaking, are traditional term papers (often called research papers) which identify and extrapolate from a variety of both research and nonresearch sources.

Research begins with a question and the commitment to work toward a verifiable answer to that question. Such questions are usually reformulated as statements or hypotheses to be tested. The analysis of these statements, or hypotheses, singly or in clusters, helps a researcher focus an investigation and select a methodology, the formalized way of examining the hypotheses. Each method has its own set of rules, and it is the rigor with which those rules are applied that most clearly indicates the quality of the research. Of course, this assumes the focus of the research or the problem addressed was significant in the first place. Although the intellectual stimulation and the satisfaction of a task completed can be of value to an individual pursuing even a trivial question, most people who care about children and their literature will look at research activities with a critical eye and ask, "So what?" They want to be able to identify how this particular research benefits the field of children's literature or those involved with that literature.

Evaluating a Research Design

In evaluating a research design, one looks first at the focus of the research or the problem statement to determine if it is clearly stated and if it merits investigation. One then asks several questions. Do the hypotheses grow out of the problem statement and are they testable? Is the methodology clearly identified and described? Is the means of analysis of the data derived from the methodology appropriate? Are the findings reported clearly and accurately, noting distinctions between facts and interpretations, and does the writing style communicate to, rather than confound, readers? In attempting to evaluate a research design using these five steps, one recognizes that it is the logical relationship and progression from one step to another that makes the design work.

In most instances, it is far easier to evaluate someone else's completed research than it is to put your own plan for research to the test. Carefully conceived and evaluated research designs are essential, however, if we are to make significant progress in our understanding of and appreciation for children's literature. There are many sources that will be helpful in the evaluation or design of research studies. Kerlinger's book is a general reference for social science research, and the Thorpe, Kehler, Benton, and Vandergrift volumes are examples of those that focus specifically on literary research. (Full references to these authors appear in "Works Cited in the Text," following this essay.) Books by Haviland, Monson, and Peltola; Lukenbill and Stewart; and Rahn will assist in the identification of previous research. Field and Kellman provide the first level of information about the availability of resources.

From Question to Design

Most questions or problems can be investigated in more than one way. Researchers must guard against selecting the first methodology that comes to mind without thorough consideration of alternative methods and the results that can be derived from each. There is also a danger in becoming too comfortable with one particular methodology and using that method exclusively, regardless of the nature of the questions under consideration. In many instances, it may be possible to combine more than one method in the same investigation. For instance, if you want to know what young people think about a book or an author, the logical first step is to ask them. This seems simple, but whom do you ask and what do you ask? Even more important, how will you deal with their responses? Will you be able to generalize or merely report individual cases?

Interviewing is an appropriate technique, but it requires an interview schedule, that is, a specified series of questions to be used with every child interviewed. The interview schedule is a research instrument that forces the researcher to think through the questions in advance and helps to maintain the focus in the process of the interview. It also provides comparable data that can then be analyzed. An interview schedule, however, may fail to capture some aspects of responses, or the formality of this methodology may inhibit some respondents. Thus, the investigator may decide to include observations of children discussing literature to capture other dimensions of their responses.

In order to analyze the content of children's discussions, these discussions would have to be taped, and a means of analysis of those taped discussions devised. The informality of such discussions, as compared to the more formal responses to an interview schedule, are likely to be much more difficult to categorize. Thus, the investigator will probably need to use research assistants to analyze the tapes. These neutral coders, using a classification system designed by the investigator, will analyze student comments. Of course, if the data collected from interviews and taped discussions are to be meaningful, you will need to know something about the youngsters participating in your study. This may cause you to draw a sample, that is, select the participants based on such variables as age, sex, ethnicity, socioeconomic status, reading scores, or the like. What began as a simple question with an apparent simple means to an answer has become a complex and rigorous methodology.

Types of Literary Research

There are many different ways of categorizing research studies. One of the most common distinctions is that between empirical and nonempirical studies. Literary studies have been classified as intrinsic (looking within the text) or extrinsic (looking outside the text). We might add a third classification to distinguish intertextual studies (within a work), intratextual (among works), or extratextual (beyond the work). The Modern Language Association (MLA) identifies five types of literary research: (1) linguistic, (2) textual, (3) historical, (4) literary criticism, and (5) literary theory.

Literary criticism is not necessarily research-based, but it does provide a useful means of examining various approaches to literary research. Historically, this criticism has been categorized according to four basic approaches or starting points from which one can study literature: (1) the world, (2) the audience, (3) the author, or (4) the literary work itself. This fourfold approach will provide the framework for the subsequent discussion of research in children's literature.

The World

Probably the research studies most familiar to readers are those historical, sociological, or cultural studies that compare the actual world with the created worlds of literature. Such studies go back to the time of Plato and Aristotle and the belief in mimetic theories of literature, that is, the belief that all literature is an imitation of either an ideal world or the actual world. Today's researchers would more likely use the word "reflection" rather than imitation, but many studies of children's literature still focus on the relationship between the work and the world. Historical researchers may attempt to get back to the original context of the literary work to investigate conditions at the time of publication and/or the initial responses of readers. They are more concerned with historical significance than literary worth. Similarly, sociological researchers see literature as a social phenomenon and also seek to identify origins, but they are more concerned with the social milieu than with specific historical events.

Harvey Darton's *Children's Books in England: Five Centuries of Social Life* is a classic example of a general historical approach that identifies landmarks, trends, and influences over an extended period of time. Anne Scott MacLeod's *A Moral Tale: Children's Fiction and American Culture—1820–1860*, and Christa Kamenetsky's *Children's Literature in Hitler's Germany* are examples of studies that demonstrate the relationships between children's literature and the values and concerns of the society that produced that literature in a particular time period. Of course, historical and social events always influence both the literature produced and the kinds of studies that are done of that literature. The social unrest of the 1960s led to increased social awareness in children's books with greater representation of current issues, life-styles, and minority characters. There was also an increase in the number of young adult

problem novels in popular culture and in fantasy. Each of these developments in the literature stimulated related research. Feminist and minority scholars completed many studies that pointed out, and thus challenged, the white, male, middle-class world of children's literature and the subtle, or not so subtle, prejudices in classic stories such as *Doctor Dolittle* as well as in more current works. Investigations of social issues in children's literature continue, for example, in Andree Michel's *Down With Stereotypes*, which was based on studies of sexual roles carried out for UNESCO in countries all over the world. Sadly, these studies confirm the universality of sexual stereotyping around the globe.

Some research studies that compare societal concerns in the actual world with those in the worlds of children's literature seek to trace a particular idea over time while others insert a probe into the literature of a single year to study that same idea. Several studies have examined the portrayal of family life or parental roles as they have changed over time, but one might also examine books published in 1990 to determine the role of the father in stories for young people today. In order to investigate this role, researchers might use content analysis, that is, detailed descriptions of individual works based on a classification schema derived, in this instance, from very specific indicators of the father's role. Although the determination of an objective and reliable classification schema is essential to this type of research, this is not easily accomplished. Sometimes the researcher's bias influences either the design of the schema or the interpretation of results or there is so much emphasis on the schema that the focus of the research shifts to that schema rather than concentrating on what it reveals about the literature.

The Audience

There has been a long tradition of concern with the audience in studying literature. From the days of the earliest storytellers, the tales told served to convey practical information and to pass on the values of the society to listeners. This pragmatic approach to literature has been especially strong among those involved with children's literature. The didacticism that considered children's literature a means of conveying the prevailing morality and social mores or of teaching reading or supplementing other areas of the school curriculum is still seen today in the acts of censors who apparently believe they can control behavior by limiting what is available for young people to read. This same belief is inherent, from another perspective, in those who practice bibliotherapy, which is guidance in the solution of personal problems through selected reading materials.

An obvious reason for this concern with audience among those who do research in children's literature is that adults create, select, and often share books with children. As intermediaries between children and books, parents, teachers, librarians, and other educators and caregivers have always sought more effective means to bring children and books together. Thus, for approximately one hundred years, there have been studies that identify and analyze children's preferences for what they read and hear. Arthur Jordan summarized preference studies from 1897 to 1920 before reporting his own research in *Children's Interests in Reading*. George Norvell's 1958 study is well known for pointing out differences between children's preferences and those of adults. More recently, Ann Terry's *Children's Poetry Preferences: A National Survey of Upper Elementary Grades* confirmed that young people enjoy humorous and story poems but surprised many teachers with evidence that most children in this large sample thoroughly disliked haiku.

Although some studies of children's preferences for literature have been experimental in design, most have been some form of survey or descriptive analysis. In order to compile the necessary data, researchers have used questionnaires, checklists, interviews, observations, written responses, and the analysis of school records or library circulation figures. Less frequently, in-depth analyses of individual readers through case studies have been provided for information about personal preferences. Maureen and Hugh Crago recorded the literary development of their daughter and Dorothy Butler did the same for her granddaughter.

Each of these methods provides a portion of the information on the topic, but the variety of approaches adds substance to the body of research data collected.

Other studies which emphasize audience have examined the effects of violence in children's books or other media on those who hear, read, or view them. There have been many such studies focusing on television or comics, and Bruno Bettelheim's *The Uses of Enchantment: The Meaning of Fairy Tales* discusses the violence in traditional tales as a means of psychological catharsis for children. There is also a body of research which looks at classroom practices with literature, either as a means of enhancing other subject areas, or for the study and teaching of children's literature itself.

Especially in the last decade, there has been an emphasis on research studies based on reader-response or reception theories of literature. Such studies generally concentrate on the reader but also consider the composition of the work as it influences the reader's transaction with that work. Kay Vandergrift's article about Anne McCaffrey's *Dragons of Pern* reports research which tests a model of young people's meaning-making in response to literature; and books by Probst and Protherough discuss classroom practices based on theories of response. The recognition of the power of the reader as an active maker-of-meaning in response to a text has been an important aspect of the research associated with the "whole language" approach to learning now prevalent in many schools. The whole language emphasis on the reading-writing connection suggests many possible research studies to explore the relationships among the literature shared with children, their own writing and the sense of empowerment that leads to personal and academic growth.

The Author

Studies which focus on the author, or, less commonly, on an editor or publisher, are linked to expressive theories of literature which view literary works as expressions or reflections of those who create them. In some instances, researchers have investigated the creative process itself by attempting to identify how writers work. More commonly, literary biographies both satisfy the curiosity of readers about the authors of favorite books and propose relationships between those authors' lives and their work. In order to do so, letters, diaries, drafts of manuscripts, and other documents are studied along with facts about the author's life and historical information about the time, place, and situation in which that person lived. Frequently, these studies move beyond biography to psychology with speculations about a writer's motivations or about influences on the life and work.

A look at the many studies of Horatio Alger and his stories for boys reveals some of the approaches to and problems of literary biography. A 1928 work by Herbert R. Mayes, although intended as a satire of the kind of debunking biographies that discredit well-known authors, was the first "biography" of Alger and was considered the authoritative source on the subject for almost fifty years. Even after the intent of Mayes's work was publicized in a 1974 article by Jack Bales, Mayes's influence on subsequent studies of Alger was evident. Edwin P. Hoyt was aware of Bales's revelation about the "literary hoax" and did go back to original sources for his book, *Horatio's Boys*; but a subtle influence based on Alger's sexual orientation as discussed in the earlier work remains. The well-known scholar and critic Norman Holland based his psychological interpretation of Alger's novels on the Mayes book, as did a whole generation of those who studied this literature.

Even today, one who begins a study of Alger and his stories might discover Mayes's work and a host of others based on it before locating a contradictory source. If that contradictory source does not specifically challenge the inaccuracies in the Mayes biography, the researcher might place more faith in the weight of the "evidence" from the many sources rather than believe in the alternative interpretation. All of this points out both the need for an exhaustive search of the related literature and for the use of primary sources, rather than secondary ones, in designing and conducting research.

Literary biography of an author from an earlier time has both advantages and disadvantages over investigations of the life and work of a living author. Although primary source material about historical figures may be difficult to locate or totally unavailable, the passage of time often gives some perspective to that person's accomplishments and may also have seen the development of a body of secondary source material. On the other hand, a living author may be interviewed, as may family, friends, editors, and others to shed light on the person and the work. The disadvantages of studies of contemporary figures are that (1) their work may not yet be completed; (2) there may be uncertainty about the lasting quality of the work; and (3) the natural human tendency is to write more favorably about one who will actually read the results of your study, either because of a positive relationship established with that person or the fear of legal action against generally negative conclusions. A number of authors of books for young people, including Klein, Lobel, Seuss, Cormier, Kerr, Guy, Mazer, Hinton, and Zindel, have been the subjects of bio-critical studies in Twayne's *U.S. Authors* series. The primary focus of these books is on a critical analysis of the works, but interviews with the authors also serve to introduce the authors as persons as well as to attempt to make connections between the lives and the writings. Neil Philip's *A Fine Anger* is another example of an excellent study of the work of a single author, in this case, Alan Garner.

The Work

Most studies of the literary work itself look at the content of that work, although descriptive bibliographers study books as physical objects. They are concerned with the size and shape of a book, the paper, typography, leading (the space between the lines), margins, editions, presses, and the like. Thus, they are able to distinguish among various versions and variants of a particular work which is essential information for other researchers. Kathleen Horning's study of Caldecott Medal books demonstrates the fact that a work identified as a winner of the Caldecott award does not necessarily mean that it contains the same illustrations that originally won the award. Lyn Lacy's book-length analysis of Caldecott winners looks at design elements in these illustrations. Another fascinating study of visual design in picture books is that of Amy Spaulding who examines the use of comic strip conventions in selected works. Perry Nodelman's *Words About Pictures* is a more comprehensive look at visual narrative in children's books.

Wilbur Stone's *The History of Little Goody-Two-Shoes: An Essay, and a List of Editions*, although dated, is a noteworthy example of textual research that makes a case for Goldsmith's authorship. This might be read in light of Roberts's work on the 1765 edition with its significant textual changes. Betsy Hearne's study of *Beauty and the Beast*, which demonstrates both the verbal and visual transmissions of that tale by authors and illustrators over the years, is another approach to this type of research. Her use of illustrations helps readers see and think through the ideas she is testing. Michael P. Hearn's *The Annotated Wizard of Oz* provides a brief but useful accounting of the publishing history of this classic work.

These studies either concentrate on the book as a physical object, a visual presentation and/or identify variations of both text and illustrations over time. The most familiar forms of text-based scholarship, however, focus on literary ideas or forms. Formalists or "new critics" have studied literary language, elements, imagery, symbolism or the like through a "close reading" of the text. Many researchers have examined the characteristics of a particular genre such as fantasy. Karen Smith's study traces developments in British children's fantasy over almost two hundred years, and C. W. Sullivan investigates the influence of Welsh myth on several modern fantasy writers. Mythic scholars identify more general images and patterns that occur over and over again in the creative products of a culture. A recent emphasis on linguistic, structural, or semiotic analyses of texts in adult literature is also evident in children's literature, as in Shavit's *Poetics of Children's Literature*, and is related to the studies of story schemas or story grammars discussed by Brewer and Lichtenstein.

Of course, many research studies partake of several approaches and methodologies in their design. Allan Cuseo's *A Literary Analysis of the Homosexual in Novels Published for the Young Adult 1969–1982* began with a sociologically based concern for the representation of this minority group in literature read by older children and young adults. Its basic conceptual framework, however, is that of the literary elements of story. An analysis of studies of homosexuality provides a contextual framework, and it is the combination of the two that gives depth to this work. Cuseo also used a panel of experts to select the novels to be studied which adds further credence to his research.

Obstacles to Research

There are numerous obstacles to research in children's literature. Chief among them is the problem of both bibliographic and physical access to primary materials. Children's books have often been considered ephemeral materials that are enjoyed repeatedly by young readers and then discarded when worn. Until recently, there were few collections of historical children's literature and many of those collections had inadequate records of their contents. Today, records of the holdings of the Osborne Collection in Toronto, the children's collection at the Morgan Library in New York, and others provide researchers with precise descriptive bibliographic information. University Microfilms is now making the Opie Collection available in this country; however, many researchers will need to work with the actual items in that collection rather than with the microfilms.

This leads to a second obstacle to research related to the first. Even if bibliographic records are detailed enough to indicate precisely where the items needed for examination are available, such items are often rare and/or fragile and not available for photocopying or loan. Thus, there is a cost factor involved in getting to the materials and staying long enough to complete the research. Certain inquiries into the content of the Opie Collection may be satisfied by University Microfilms, but most scholars will need to visit the actual collection housed at the Bodleian Library in Oxford.

A third barrier to research in children's literature is that of language. There is a substantial body of research which has been conducted around the world as evidenced by the research reports in *Phaedrus* over the years. Most such studies have not been translated so that, unless one has an extraordinary range of language skills, a great deal of information about related research is virtually unavailable. Even *Phaedrus* itself was recently acquired by a Japanese group, and any future publication will be in Japanese with no English summaries.

A fourth and very serious obstacle to research involving children and literature centers around ethical concerns, particularly a child's right to privacy. Teachers, librarians, and others in power over children have sometimes assumed, or granted to another researcher, the right to a child's time and thoughts about literature. Informed consent is a basic requirement of any research using human subjects, and the rights of youngsters not yet of the age to give informed consent must be protected.

A final cluster of obstacles is found in the person of the researcher. These may appear obvious but are often difficult to recognize and eliminate in ones own work. The most important is the lack of objectivity. Too often research is viewed as a means of proving a particular point or justifying a personal belief. A researcher must keep an open mind and avoid skewing the data collection or the interpretation of results to support previously held opinions. Another concern has to do with the role of statistics in research. Two extremes are evident here. Some literary researchers are uncomfortable with statistics and consistently avoid their use while others become so enamored that they attempt to contain all results in statistical forms. It is vital to distinguish those things that are best communicated through statistics and to remember that statistical significance is not necessarily the same as educational or literary significance. Finally, researchers in children's literature, especially those focusing on social issues, need to exercise caution to avoid applying contemporary values and standards to historical periods. One should not, for instance, judge an author of the 1940s or 1950s according to today's standards and label that person as racist or sexist. It may be true

that the person's work appears so today; but many factors, including the collective consciousness of the time, influenced not only the author and the reading public but also the publishing community and thus what could be produced for children.

Although research is a difficult and rigorous activity with many obstacles to overcome, it is also a source of great joy. There is an excitement in the chase for an elusive item or idea; the challenge of a mystery to be solved amidst a sea of seemingly contradictory evidence; and the satisfaction of having shed at least a small spot of light on a topic truly worthy of study. Those who really care about children's literature and get caught up in the enjoyment of this literature ought to accept the challenge of finding answers to some of their most pressing questions through research. All research need not be on a grand scale requiring federal funding or a national sample. Smaller studies, either of literary works themselves or action research involving a particular group of young people, are important in their own right as well as opening possibilities to further research. Research is demanding and time-consuming, but many studies can be done by the practicing teacher or librarian. All that is required is a loving concern for children and their literature, a commitment of time and effort, and an open and inquiring mind. The rewards are in the doing and in communicating interests and ideas to others who share the researcher's love of this special, very important, literature.

Kay E. Vandergrift is an associate professor in the School of Communications, Information and Library Studies, Rutgers University, New Brunswick, New Jersey.

Works Cited in the Text

BALES, JACK. "Herbert R. Mayes and Horatio Alger, Jr.; or, The Story of a Unique Literary Hoax," *Journal of Popular Culture.* Volume 8, pp. 317–319, Fall 1974.

BENTON, MICHAEL. ed. *Approaches to Research in Children's Literature.* The Department of Education, Southampton University, 1980.

BETTELHEIM, BRUNO. *The Uses of Enchantment: The Meaning of Fairy Tales.* Alfred A. Knopf, 1975.

BREWER, W. F., and E. H. LICHTENSTEIN. "Event Schemas, Story Schemas, and Story Grammars," in *Attention and Performance.* edited by J. Long and A. Baddeley. Erlbaum, 1981, pp. 363–379.

BUTLER, DOROTHY. *Cushla and Her Books.* Horn Book, 1980.

CAMPBELL, PATRICIA J. *Presenting Robert Cormier.* 2nd ed. (Twayne's United States Author Series) Twayne/G. K. Hall, 1989.

CRAGO, MAUREEN, and HUGH CRAGO. *Prelude to Literacy: A Preschool Child's Encounter with Picture and Story.* Southern Illinois University Press, 1983.

CUSEO, ALLAN A. "A Literary Analysis of the Homosexual in Novels Published for the Young Adult, 1969–1982." Unpublished dissertation, School of Library Service, Columbia University, 1987. (To be published by Scarecrow Press)

DALY, JAY. *Presenting S. E. Hinton.* (Twayne's United States Authors Series) Twayne/G. K. Hall, 1987.

DARLING, RICHARD L. *The Rise of Children's Book Reviewing in America, 1865–1881.* Bowker, 1968.

DARTON, F. J. HARVEY. *Children's Books in England: Five Centuries of Social Life.* 3rd ed., rev. by Brian Alderson. Cambridge University Press, 1982.

FIELD, CAROLYN E., ed. *Special Collections in Children's Literature.* 2nd ed. American Library Association (ALA), 1982.

FORMAN, JACK JACOB. *Presenting Paul Zindel.* (Twayne's United States Author Series) Twayne/G. K. Hall, 1988.

HAVILAND, VIRGINIA, and others, comps. *Children's Literature: A Guide to Reference Sources.* The Library of Congress, 1966. (plus supplements)

HEARNE, BETSY. *Beauty and the Beast: Visions and Revisions of an Old Tale.* University of Chicago Press, 1989.

HEARN, MICHAEL PATRICK. *The Annotated Wizard of Oz.* Potter, 1973.

HOLLAND, NORMAN N. "Hobbling with Horatio: or The Uses of Literature," *Hudson Review.* Volume 12, pp. 549–557, Winter 1959–60.

HOLTZE, SALLY HOLMES. *Presenting Norma Fox Mazer.* (Twayne's United States Author Series) Twayne/G. K. Hall, 1987.

HORNING, KATHLEEN T. "Are You Sure That Book Won the Caldecott Medal? Variant Printings and Editions of Three Caldecott Medal Books." *Journal of Youth Studies in Libraries.* Volume 1, pp. 173–176, Winter 1988.

HOYT, EDWIN P. *Horatio's Boys: The Life and Works of Horatio Alger, Jr.* Chilton Book Co., 1974.

JORDAN, ARTHUR M. *Children's Interests in Reading.* (Teachers College, Columbia University Contributions to Education, No. 107.) Teachers College, Columbia University, 1921.

KAMENETSKY, CHRISTA. *Children's Literature in Hitler's Germany.* Ohio University Press, 1984.

KEHLER, DOROTHEA. *Problems in Literary Research: A Guide to Selected Reference Works.* Scarecrow, 1987.

KELLMAN, AMY. *A Guide to Children's Libraries and Literature outside the United States.* ALA, 1982.

KERLINGER, FRED. *Foundations of Behavioral Research: Educational and Psychological Inquiry.* 3rd ed. Holt, 1986.

LACY, LYN E. *Art and Design in Children's Picture Books: An Analysis of Caldecott Award-Winning Illustrations.* ALA, 1986.

LUKENBILL, W. BERNARD and SHARON LEE STEWART. *Youth Literature: An Interdisciplinary Annotated Guide to North American Dissertation Research, 1930–1985.* Garland, 1988.

MACDONALD, RUTH K. *Dr. Seuss.* (Twayne's United States Author Series) Twayne/G. K. Hall, 1988.

MACLEOD, ANNE SCOTT. *A Moral Tale: Children's Fiction and American Culture—1820–1860.* Archon Books, 1975.

MAYES, HERBERT R. *Alger: A Biography Without a Hero.* Macy-Masius, 1928.

MICHEL, ANDREE. *Down with Stereotypes: Eliminating Sexism from Children's Literature and School Textbooks.* UNESCO, 1986.

MONSON, DIANNE L., and BETTE J. PELTOLA, comps. *Research in Children's Literature: An Annotated Bibliography.* International Reading Association, 1976.

NILSEN, ALLEN PACE. *Presenting M. E. Kerr.* (Twayne's United States Author Series) Twayne/G. K. Hall, 1986.

NODELMAN, PERRY. *Words about Pictures: The Narrative Art of Children's Picture Books.* The University of Georgia Press, 1988.

NORRIS, JERRIE. *Presenting Rosa Guy.* (Twayne's United States Author Series) Twayne/G. K. Hall, 1988.

NORVELL, GEORGE. *What Boys and Girls Like to Read.* Silver Burdett, 1958.

Phaedrus: An International Annual Incorporating Die Schieffertafel for the History of Children's and Youth Literature. 1973–1988. (with various title changes)

PHILIP, NEIL. *A Fine Anger: A Critical Introduction to the Work of Alan Garner.* Philomel, 1981.

PHY, ALLENE STUART. *Presenting Norma Klein.* (Twayne's United States Author Series) Twayne/G. K. Hall, 1988.

THE PIERPONT MORGAN LIBRARY. *Early Children's Books and Their Illustrators.* The Pierpont Morgan Library, 1975.

PROBST, ROBERT E. *Response and Analysis: Teaching Literature in Junior and Senior High School.* Boynton/Cook Publishers, Heinemann, 1988.

PROTHEROUGH, ROBERT. *Developing Response to Fiction.* Open University Press, 1983.

RAHN, SUZANNE. *Children's Literature: An Annotated Bibliography of the History and Criticism.* Garland Publishing, 1981.

ROBERTS, JULIAN. "The 1765 Edition of Goody Two-Shoes." *British Museum Quarterly.* Volume 29, pp. 67–70, Summer 1965.

SHANNON, GEORGE. *Arnold Lobel.* (Twayne's United States Authors Series) Twayne/G. K. Hall, 1989.

SHAVIT, ZOHAR. *Poetics of Children's Literature.* University of Georgia Press, 1986.

SMITH, KAREN PATRICIA. *The Keys to the Kingdom: From Didacticism to Dynamism in British Children's Fantasy, 1780–1979.* Unpublished Dissertation, Teachers College, Columbia University, 1982. (To be published by Scarecrow)

SPAULDING, AMY E. "Closet Drama for Children: A Study of the Picture Book as Storyboard." Unpublished dissertation, School of Library Service, Columbia University, 1983.

STONE, WILBUR MACEY. *The History of Little Goody-Two-Shoes: An Essay, and a List of Editions.* American Antiquarian Society, 1940.

SULLIVAN, CHARLES WILLIAM, III. *Welsh Celtic Myth in Modern Fantasy.* Greenwood, 1989.

TERRY, ANN. *Children's Poetry Preferences: A National Survey of upper Elementary Grades.* (Research Reports, NCTE. No. 16) National Council of Teachers of English, 1974.

THORPE, JAMES, ed. *The Aims and Methods of Scholarship in Modern Languages and Literature.* 2nd ed. Modern Language Association, 1970.

TORONTO PUBLIC LIBRARY. Osborne Collection. *The Osborne Collection of Early Children's Books, 1566–1910.* Volume 1. Toronto Public Library, 1958.

————. *The Osborne Collection of Early Children's Books, 1476–1910.* Volume 2. Toronto Public Library, 1975.

VANDERGRIFT, KAY E. *Children's Literature: Theory, Research, and Teaching.* Libraries Unlimited, 1990.

————. "Meaning-Making and the Dragons of Pern," *Children's Literature Association Quarterly.* pp. 27–32, Spring 1990.

Appendix A
Book Selection Aids*

A to Zoo: Subject Access to Children's Picture Books, comp. by Carolyn Lima. 3rd ed. Bowker, 1989. More than 12,000 picture books are grouped according to several hundred topics for ready subject access.

Accept Me as I Am: Best Books of Juvenile Nonfiction on Impairments and Disabilities, by Joan Friedberg and others. Bowker, 1985. A useful, selective guide offers perceptive annotations.

Adventuring with Books: A Booklist for Pre-K–Grade 6, ed. by Dianne Monson and a committee of National Council of Teachers of English (NCTE), 1985. This helpful selection tool includes approximately 2500 titles selected for popularity and literary merit, classified by subject.

The Aging Adult in Children's Books and Nonprint Media: An Annotated Bibliography, by Catherine Horner. Scarecrow, 1982. A multimedia list with descriptive annotations but no critical analysis.

Alphabet: A Handbook of ABC Books and Activities for the Elementary Classroom, by Patricia Roberts. Scarecrow, 1984. Descriptive reviews of more than 200 alphabet books come with creative suggestions for classroom use.

Alphabet Books as a Key to Language Patterns: An Annotated Bibliography, by Patricia Roberts. Shoe String, 1987. Bibliographic listings follow a discussion of those elements (accumulation, repetition, refrains, rhythm, etc.) that support the development of language, literacy, and learning skills in young children.

America as Story: Historical Fiction for Secondary Schools, by Elizabeth Howard. American Library Association (ALA), 1988. Annotations are arranged under headings like "The Jazz Age" and "The Depression" with interalphabetized titles, authors, characters, and terms in general use.

American Historical Fiction and Biography for Children and Young People, comp. by Jeanette Hotchkiss. Scarecrow, 1973. Annotations are arranged chronologically and by subject. Symbols are used for reading and interest levels.

Appraisal: Science Books for Young People. Children's Science Book Review Committee. Published three times each year. Around fifty books reviewed in each issue, all rated on a five-point scale by both a librarian and a science specialist.

Best Books for Children: Preschool through the Middle Grades, ed. by John Gillespie and Christine Gilbert. 2nd ed. Bowker, 1981. Contains approximately 13,000 briefly annotated titles, arranged by subject; author/illustrator and title indexes are appended.

The Best in Children's Books: The University of Chicago Guide to Children's Literature, 1979–1984, comp. by Zena Sutherland. Univ. of Chicago Press, 1984. Reviews chosen from the *Bulletin of the Center for Children's Books* are indexed by developmental values, types of literature, reading level, and curricular use as well as conventional indexes.

The Best Science Books for Children: A Selected and Annotated List of Science Books for Children Ages Five through Twelve, comp. by Kathryn Wolff and others. American Association for the Advancement of Science, 1983. A selective listing of more than 1200 science books for children, annotated and indexed.

Beyond Picture Books: A Guide to First Readers, comp. by Barbara Barstow and Judith Riggle. Bowker, 1989. Recommended books, published 1951–1989, for prekindergarten through grade 2 are arranged by author, annotated, and indexed by subject, title, illustrator, readability, and series.

Bibliography of Books for Children, comp. by Bonnie Baron. Assoc. for Childhood Education International, 1977. Annotated list of books for children from preschool through elementary grades, grouped by subject or form in useful categories.

A Bicultural Heritage: Themes for the Exploration of Mexican and Mexican-American Culture in Books for Children and Adolescents, comp. by Isabel Schon. Scarecrow Press, 1978. Hoping to expose students to elements of Mexican and Mexican-American culture and to combat stereotypes, Schon has compiled this annotated bibliography of English fiction and nonfiction titles; recommended books are marked with a special notation.

---

*For additional reading suggestions see the bibliographies accompanying the articles in Part Four.

The Black Experience in Children's Books, prepared by Barbara Rollock, New York Public Library, 1989. An annotated bibliography, classified by age and subject matter about black life in America, in the Islands, in Africa, and in England.

Black Image: Education Copes with Color, ed. by Jean Grambs and John Carr. Wm. C. Brown, 1972. Short essays on the problems of the African-American image in children's books, with evaluations of instructional materials, texts, and some fiction.

The Black World in Literature for Children: A Bibliography of Print and Nonprint Materials, comp. by Joyce White Mills. Atlanta Univ., 1975. Divided by broad age groups and subject areas, this is for children ages 3–13.

The Bookfinder: A Guide to Children's Literature about the Needs and Problems of Youth Aged 2–15, ed. by Sharon Dreyer. American Guidance Service, 1989. A split-page format allows indexes and text to be browsed independently in this critical assessment of fiction touching on upheavals in children's lives. Later editions (up to 1985) are topically expanded.

Booklist. A review journal published by the American Library Association twice monthly save for single issues in July and August. It includes separate sections of books for children and for young adults.

Books for the Chinese-American Child: A Selected List, comp. by Cecilia Mei-Chi Chen. Cooperative Children's Book Center, 1969. A carefully selected list of books, included for their honesty and literary quality.

Books for the Gifted Child by Barbara Holland Baskin and Karen H. Harris. Bowker, 1980. Nearly 150 titles judged stimulating for gifted children, preschool through age 12, are described in critical, detailed annotations.

Books for Today's Young Readers: An Annotated Bibliography of Recommended Fiction for Ages 10–14, comp. by Jeanne Bracken and others. Feminist Press, 1982. Critical evaluations of more than 70 fiction titles whose portrayals of sex, age, and theme are deemed nonstereotypical.

Books for You: A Reading List for Senior High School Students, comp. by NCTE, rev. ed. Washington Square Pr., 1988. An annotated bibliography divided by subject.

Books in Spanish for Children and Young Adults: An Annotated Guide, ed. by Isabel Schon. Scarecrow, 1978. Critical annotations describe Spanish-language titles. A companion volume of the same title (1983) analyzes titles published since 1978.

Books on American Indians and Eskimos: A Selection Guide for Children and Young Adults, comp. by Mary Jo Lass-Woodfin. ALA, 1977. This guide grades the titles, both fiction and nonfiction, and summarizes their contents.

Books to Help Children Cope with Separation and Loss, comp. by Joanne E. Bernstein and Màshà Rudman. Volume 3. Bowker, 1989. An introductory discussion of bibliotherapy, with annotated lists of more than 600 titles grouped by subject headings.

Building Ethnic Collections: An Annotated Guide for School Media Centers and Public Libraries, by Lois Buttlar and Lubomyr Wynar. Libraries Unlimited, 1977. A selection of fiction, nonfiction, reference and audio-visual materials are discussed for over forty minority groups.

Bulletin of the Center for Children's Books, The Univ. of Chicago. Univ. of Chicago Pr. Published monthly except August. Ongoing review of new titles for children and young people, annotated according to whether the book is recommended, acceptable, marginal, not recommended, or for special collections or unusual readers only. The reviews are detailed, and grade levels and prices are given.

Canadian Books for Young People: Livres Canadiens pour la Jeunesse, comp. by Irma McDonough. Univ. of Toronto Pr., 1978. A revised and expanded (titles are now given for children up to the age of 14) version of *Canadian Books for Children,* 1976. Book lists are given in both French and English, arranged under subject headings.

Canadian Children's Literature: A Journal of Criticism and Review. Canadian Children's Press/Canadian Children's Literature Association. Includes articles, reviews, and bibliographies.

Children's Authors and Illustrators: An Index to Biographical Dictionaries, ed. by Adele Sarkissian. 3rd ed. Gale, 1981. A useful finding tool, collating references to biographical sources for information about specific children's authors and illustrators.

Children's Book Review Index, ed. by Gary Tarbert. Gale, 1976. Triannual publication indexing sources of reviews in over 200 periodicals.

Children's Books, comp. by Children's Book Section, U.S. Library of Congress. An annual bibliography, selective and annotated.

Children's Books: Awards and Prizes, comp. and ed. by the Children's Book Council. 8th ed. 1986. A compilation of honors awarded in the children's book field by organizations, schools, publishers, and newspapers. A brief description of each award is followed by a list of all the winners since it was first given.

Children's Books for Times of Stress: An Annotated Bibliography, comp. by Ruth Gillis. Indiana Univ. Pr., 1978. A selective listing of children's books, arranged by subject, which bears on stressful episodes in children's lives.

Children's Books in Print. Bowker, annual. An index to 41,000 books in print at time of publication. This annual has separate author, title, illustrator, and publisher indexes. Prices are given for trade and library bindings, and for paperback editions.

Children's Books of International Interest, ed. by Barbara Elleman. 3rd ed. ALA, 1984. Recommended for international audiences, these children's books published in the U.S. "incorporate universal themes or depict the American way of life."

Children's Books on Africa and Their Authors: An Annotated Bibliography, comp. by Nancy Schmidt. African Bibliography Series, Volume 3. Africana Pub. Co., 1975. Full annotations, no age or reading level assigned. A supplement, also compiled by Schmidt, was issued by Africana in 1979.

Children's Catalog. Wilson. A selected, classified catalog of children's books, arranged with nonfiction first. Classified by Dewey Decimal Classification; followed by fiction, short stories, and the easy books. Five-year cumulations as well as yearly supplements.

Children's Literature Review, ed. by Ann Block and Carolyn Riley. Gale, 1976. A paragraph of information about the author introduces review excerpts relative to specific titles. Cumulative indexes in each volume.

Children's Mathematics Books: A Critical Bibliography, comp. by Margaret Matthias and Diane Thiessen. ALA, 1979. Evaluations of approximately 200 books written for young children.

Children's Periodicals of the United States, by R. Gordon Kelly. Greenwood Press, 1984. An excellent descriptive bibliography, fully annotated and providing publication histories.

Choices: A Core Collection for Young Reluctant Readers, by Carolyn Flemming and Donna Schatt. Burke, 1983. Descriptions of more than 350 books whose reading and interest level makes them likely choices for reluctant readers.

Choosing Books for Children: A Commonsense Guide, by Betsy Hearne. rev. ed. Delacorte, 1990. A lively, personable introduction to aspects of children's literature includes highly selective annotated bibliographies.

Choosing Books for Young People: A Guide to Criticism and Bibliography 1945–1975, comp. by John Ettlinger and Diana Spirt. ALA, 1982. A comprehensive bibliography of English-language book lists for children, with annotations that evaluate entries historically and in terms of their value to contemporary book selectors.

Collective Biographies for Young People, comp. by Karen Breen. 4th ed. Bowker, 1988. Gives access by name, nationality, occupation, and title.

A Comprehensive Guide to Children's Literature with a Jewish Theme, by Enid Davis. Schocken, 1981. More than 450 fiction and nonfiction titles dealing with various aspects of Judaism are arranged in subject categories.

Core Media Collection for Elementary Schools, by Lucy Gregor Brown. Bowker, 1978. A selection guide to nonprint items.

The Elementary School Library Collection: A Guide to Books and Other Media, ed. by Lois Winkel. rev. ed. Brodart, 1988. A standard selection tool, this guide lists more than 13,000 print and nonprint items.

European Historical Fiction and Biography, comp. by Jeanette Hotchkiss. 2nd ed. Scarecrow, 1972. Divided by country and, within that, by period, with brief annotations.

Eyeopeners! How to Choose and Use Children's Books about Real People, Places, and Things, by Beverly Kobrin. Viking, 1988. An excellent guide to nonfiction, with annotations, full bibliographic information, and plenty of sensible advice.

Fantasy for Children: An Annotated Checklist and Reference Guide, by Ruth Nadelman Lynn. 2nd ed. Bowker, 1983. This comprehensive listing of more than 2000 recommended fantasy titles for grade school readers comes with an extensive bibliography of criticism and other professional literature.

Folklore: An Annotated Bibliography and Index to Single Editions, comp. by Elsie Ziegler. Faxon, 1973. Particularly useful because it gives access to single editions.

Folklore of the American Indians: An Annotated Bibliography, comp. by Judith C. Ullom, ill. Library of Congress, 1969. Carefully selected items arranged by culture areas.

For Reading out Loud! A Guide to Sharing Books with Children, by Margaret Mary Kimmel and Elizabeth Segel. rev. ed. Delacorte, 1988. In-depth annotations for child-tested books make this a valuable resource for teachers, librarians, and parents.

Fun for Kids: An Index to Children's Craft Books, comp. by Marion Gallivan. Scarecrow, 1981. A useful index identifies more than 280 craft books suitable for youngsters in preschool through eighth grade.

Gateways to Readable Books, comp. by Dorothy Withrow, Helen Carey, and Bertha Hirzel. Wilson, 1975. An annotated list of titles chosen for the reluctant adolescent reader.

Girls Are People Too! A Bibliography of Nontraditional Female Roles in Children's Books, by Joan E. Newman. Scarecrow, 1982. Books recommended for their unstereotypic female characters are divided into categories representing minority groups.

Good Reading for the Disadvantaged Reader: Multi Ethnic Resources, by George Spache. Garrard, 1975. One-sentence annotations describe books and audiovisual materials suitable for use in the development of self-concept among seven minority groups, including the inner city child.

Good Reading for Poor Readers, comp. by George Spache, rev. ed. Garrard, 1974. Consists primarily of bibliographies: Four chapters discuss children's interests and motives in reading, choosing and using books for children, and estimating readability.

The Great Lakes Region in Children's Books, by Donna Taylor. Green Oak Press, 1980. Includes magazines and is divided by states.

Growing Point, published by Margery Fisher. Belmont, 1962 to date. Nine issues yearly, published in England. Each issue reviews books for parents, teachers, and librarians in the English-speaking world.

Guide to Children's Magazines, Newspapers, Reference Books, prepared by Judy Mathews and Lillian Drag. Assoc. for Childhood Education International, 1974. Revised guide to provide a quick index of available materials.

A Guide to Historical Reading: Nonfiction, comp. by Fred R. Czarra. 11th rev. ed. Heldref, 1983. Annotated listing in the McKinley bibliography series.

A Guide to Nonsexist Children's Books, comp. by Judith Adell and Hilary Klein. Academy Pr., 1976. An annotated bibliography is divided by grade groups: preschool to 3, 3–7, 7–12, and one for all ages. Vol. II, compiled by Denise Wilms and Ilene Cooper, published in 1987, covers subsequently published titles.

Health, Illness, and Disability: A Guide to Books for Children and Young Adults, comp. by Pat Azarnoff. Bowker, 1983. An annotated listing of fiction and nonfiction titles dealing with health, disease, and physical handicaps.

Her Way: A Guide to Biographies of Women for Young People, by Mary-Ellen Siegel. 2nd ed. ALA, 1984. Cites recommended single and collective biographies of more than 1000 notable women throughout history.

High Interest=Easy Reading for Junior and Senior High School Students, ed. by Marian White, rev. ed. NCTE, 1979. Brief annotations describe, but do not critique, high interest/low reading level titles; arrangement is by subject.

A Hispanic Heritage: A Guide to Juvenile Books about Hispanic Peoples and Cultures, by Isabel Schon. Scarecrow, 1980. Critical reviews assess books that faithfully portray various aspects of Hispanic culture; titles are grouped by countries.

The Horn Book Magazine. Horn Book. Published six times a year. A magazine about children's books, authors, illustrators, with a section for reviews.

How to Find Out about Children's Literature, comp. by Alec Ellis. 3rd ed. Pergamon, 1973. Bibliography of bibliographies as well as other useful listings of organizations and collections, both national and international.

Independent Reading, K–3, ed. by Helen Elizabeth Williams with Katharine Mary Gloden. Brodart, 1980. Has cross-referenced subject headings and a reading level index.

Index to Short Biographies: For Elementary and Junior High Grades, comp. by Ellen Stanius. Scarecrow, 1971. Listed by subject and by author, with pages given. Collective biographies only.

An Index to Young Readers' Collective Biographies, comp. by Judith Silverman. 3rd ed. Bowker, 1979. Includes listings for over seven thousand individuals. This volume indexes the contents of some 950 collective biographies. A subject index groups biographies by fields of activity and nationality.

Indian Children's Books, by Hap Gilliland. Montana Council for Indian Education, 1980. Brief evaluations of more than 1650 children's books about native Americans.

Junior High School Library Catalog, ed. by Gary L. Bogart and Richard H. Isaacson. 4th ed. Wilson, 1980. Annual supp. Part 1, the Classified Catalog, is arranged with nonfiction books first, classified according to Dewey Decimal Classification system. Fiction books follow and short stories are next. Part 2 is an author, title, subject, analytical index. Cumulated every five years, with yearly supplements.

Juniorplots #3: A Book Talk Manual for Teachers and Librarians, comp. by John Gillespie and Corinne Naden 1987. Thematic discussions of specific books grouped under eight categories of basic goals of adolescence.

The Kirkus Service. A bimonthly publication: reviews are done from galleys and appear early, but information on illustrations is not always available.

Language Arts. NCTE. Issued monthly, September through May. Besides regular book reviews, this journal has articles on children's reading and related subjects.

Let's Read Together: Books for Family Enjoyment. 4th ed. Association for Library Service to Children. ALA, 1981. Arranged by age levels and also annotated.

Literature by and about the American Indian: An Annotated Bibliography, for Junior and Senior High School Students, comp. by Anna Lee Stensland. 2nd ed. NCTE, 1979. A divided bibliography with study guides and biographies of American Indian authors.

Magazines for Children: A Guide for Parents, Teachers and Librarians, by Selma Richardson. ALA, 1983. Evaluated content, format, and appeal of magazines published for children as well as adult and young adult magazines that children read.

Mexico and Its Literature for Children and Adolescents, comp. by Isabel Schon. Arizona State Univ., 1977. The first annotated guide to Mexican children's books, this volume reflects the compiler's thorough familiarity with the field. Biographical information about authors precedes annotations of their work.

A Multimedia Approach to Children's Literature, ed. by Mary Alice Hunt. 3rd ed. ALA, 1983. Descriptive annotations of films, videocassettes, filmstrips, and sound recordings based on children's books.

The New Read-Aloud Handbook, by Jim Trelease. rev. ed. Penguin, 1989. A detailed discussion of how and why to read aloud is followed by annotations that include other books by the authors.

Notable Children's Books, 1976–1980. ALA, 1986. A reappraisal of ALA's Children's Services Division's annual Notable lists. Short descriptive annotations are given for each title.

Notes from a Different Drummer: A Guide to Juvenile Fiction Portraying the Handicapped, comp. by Barbara Baskin and Karen Harris. Bowker, 1977. An annotated guide to books that have handicapped characters. This guide is prefaced by an analysis of the treatment of the disabled in literature. A companion volume, *More Notes from a Different Drummer* (1984), assesses 450 titles published since 1976.

Periodicals for School Media Programs: A Guide to Magazines, Newspapers, Periodical Indexes, comp. by Selma Richardson. rev. ed. ALA, 1978. A buying guide to periodicals and newspapers for school library purchases. Entries are alphabetical, and each is accompanied by appropriate grade level, name, and address of publisher, frequency of publication, and price. Also included are annotations describing the nature and scope of the publication and possible curricular use.

Popular Reading for Children: A Collection of Booklist Columns, comp. by Barbara Elleman. ALA, 1981. Bibliographies culled from *Booklist* round up titles in perennially popular genres, such as ghost stories, mysteries, and time fantasies.

Reading for Young People: The Great Plains, ed. by Mildred Laughlin. ALA, 1979. One in a series of annotated bibliographies collating fiction and nonfiction pertinent to the states in the regional designation. Other titles include *The Midwest,* ed. by Dorothy Hinman and Ruth Zimmerman (1979); *The Rocky Mountains,* ed. by Mildred Laughlin (1980); *The Middle Atlantic,* ed. by Arabelle Pennypacker (1980); *The Southeast* and *The Southwest,* ed. by Dorothy Heald (1980); and *The Northwest,* ed. by Mary Meacham (1980).

Reading Ladders for Human Relations, ed. by Eileen Tway. 6th ed. Am. Council on Education and NCTE, 1981. This enlarged and revised edition contains an introduction and bibliographies on the role of reading in developing children's self-knowledge and social awareness.

Reference Books for Elementary and Junior High School Libraries, comp. by Carolyn Sue Peterson. Scarecrow, 1970. A very useful annotated bibliography divided into general reference books (dictionaries, atlases, fact books, etc.) and those for subject areas.

Reference Books for Young Readers: Authoritative Evaluations of Encyclopedias, Atlases, and Dictionaries, ed. by Marion Sader. Bowker, 1988. A comprehensive examination of in-print reference books, descriptive and comparative.

Religious Books for Children: An Annotated Bibliography, comp. by Patricia Pearl. Church and Synagogue Library Association, 1983. Annotated listings of books on religious themes are handily organized by subject.

Resources for Middle-Grade Reluctant Readers: A Guide for Librarians, by Marianne Pilla. Libraries Unlimited, 1987. Teachers and parents should also find this useful since it gives, in addition to annotated titles, advice on evaluating books for reluctant readers, and suggestions for ways to decrease the reluctance: programs, use of computers, booktalks, etc.

School Library Journal/SLJ. Bowker. A journal for librarians, published monthly. Approximately 1500 titles are reviewed, sometimes with dissenting opinions. There are also reviews of computer software and audiovisual materials, plus articles on library services, books, and reading for children and young people.

Selecting Materials for Children and Young Adults: A Bibliography of Bibliographies and Review Sources, comp. by the Association for Library Service to Children and Young Adult Services Division. ALA, 1980. Classified by subject, this valuable guide to book selection materials contains both print and nonprint resources.

Senior High School Catalog. Annual supplements. Wilson. Part 1, 1973, the Classified Catalog, is arranged with nonfiction first, classified by Dewey Decimal System; fiction next; and then short stories. Each book is listed under one main entry where full information is given. Part 2 contains an author, title, subject, and analytical index of all the books in the catalog.

Stories to Tell to Children, ed. by Laura E. Cathon, Marion McC. Haushalter, and Virginia A. Russell. 8th ed. Carnegie Library of Pittsburgh, 1974. One of the outstanding bibliographies of folk and fairy literature available for the storyteller. Frequently revised.

Subject Guide to Children's Books in Print. Bowker, annual. A subject index to children's books in 7000 categories.

Subject Index to Poetry for Children and Young People, comp. by Violet Sell and others. Core Collection Books, 1982. Indicates grade level.

VOYA. Voice of Youth Advocates. Published bimonthly, April through February. Contains articles on young adult library services and bibliographies in addition to reviews of films, videotapes, records, and books.

Your Reading: A Book List for Junior High Schools and Middle Schools, ed. by James Davis and the Committee on the Junior High School Book List of the Nat. Council of Teachers of English, 1988. Annotated guide to almost 1300 books.

Appendix B
Adult References*

AFANASYEV, ALEXANDER N. *Russian Fairy Tales*, tr. by Norbert Guterman, ill. by Alexeiff. Pantheon, 1945. See the valuable "Folkloristic Commentary" by Roman Jakobson.

AIKEN, JOAN. *The Way to Write for Children*. St. Martin's, 1983. Guidelines for crafting children's books from a well-established practitioner of the art.

ALDERSON, BRIAN. *Looking at Picture Books 1973*. National Book League, Children's Book Council, 1974. Perceptive and knowledgeable comments on children's book illustration.

ALDISS, BRIAN. *The True History of Science Fiction*, Doubleday, 1973. On the origins of science fiction and its emergence as a genre in the twentieth century.

ALGARIN, JOANNE. *Japanese Folk Literature: A Core Collection and Reference Guide*. Bowker, 1982.

ALMY, MILLIE, and CELIA GENISHI. *Ways of Studying Children*. Teachers College Press, 1979. Chapter Five relates to the use of literature in studying children.

ALTICK, RICHARD D. *Lives and Letters: A History of Literary Biography in England and America*. Knopf, 1965, reprinted by Greenwood Press, 1979. With liberal bibliographical notes for each chapter, the author discusses the achievement and influence of literary biographers from the seventeenth century to today. A thoroughly researched and comprehensive study.

ANDERSON, CELIA, and MARILYN APSELOFF. *Nonsense Literature for Children: Aesop to Seuss*. Shoe String, 1989. Crisp, lively writing makes the depth and sophistication of the analyses eminently enjoyable as well as comprehensible.

ANDERSON, VERNA. *Reading and Young Children*. Macmillan, 1968. A survey of the approaches to the teaching of reading, the problems and the techniques of meeting them, and the use of materials with children.

APPLEBEE, ARTHUR. *The Child's Concept of Story: Ages Two to Seventeen*. Univ. of Chicago Press, 1978. Stories children tell and their responses to stories they hear are used to support this theory of a child's perception of storying.

AQUINO, JOHN. *Fantasy in Literature*. National Education Association (NEA), 1977. A teacher's handbook on curricular use of fantasy.

The Art of Beatrix Potter, with an appreciation by Anne Carroll Moore. Warne, 1956. In a truly beautiful book, landscapes, still life, experimental drawings, and the tiny pictures for her children's classics are reproduced, giving new insight into the versatility of Beatrix Potter.

ASBJÖRNSEN, PETER C., and JÖRGEN MOE. *Norwegian Folk Tales*, tr. by Pat Shaw Iversen and Carl Norman, ill. by Erik Werenskiold and Theodor Kittelson. Viking, 1961. Thirty-six folk tales in an excellent translation which reintroduces the original Asbjörnsen illustrators.

————. *Popular Tales from the Norse*, tr. by Sir George Webbe Dasent. Putnam, 1908. A long and rich introduction by the translator is particularly good on changes from myth to fairy tale.

ASHTON, JOHN. *Chap-Books of the Eighteenth Century*. London: Chatto, 1882. (Facsimile of the original: Singing Tree, 1968.) The author reproduces the stories and some of the pages and illustrations from the old chapbooks.

ASSOCIATION OF HOSPITAL AND INSTITUTION LIBRARIES. *Bibliotherapy: Methods and Materials*. American Library Association (ALA), 1971. Discusses applications of reading as therapy, and provides a guide to children's books of potential usefulness in bibliotherapy.

AUSLANDER, JOSEPH, and FRANK ERNEST HILL. *The Winged Horse: The Story of Poets and Their Poetry*. Doubleday, 1927. Written for older children and young people, this is a thoroughly interesting book for teachers and parents as well. Fine references on ballads and epics.

AUSTIN, MARY, and ESTHER JENKINS. *Promoting World Understanding through Literature, K–8*. Libraries Unlimited, 1983. A program guide and bibliography for cultivating multiethnic awareness.

BADER, BARBARA. *American Picturebooks from Noah's*

Ark to The Beast Within. Macmillan, 1976. A critical and historical study.

BAKER, AUGUSTA, and ELLIN GREENE. *Storytelling: Art and Technique.* 2nd ed. Bowker, 1987. Broad coverage, good organization of material, and clear explanations contribute to a useful guide for storytellers.

BALDWIN, RUTH, comp. *One Hundred Nineteenth-Century Rhyming Alphabets in English.* Southern Ill. Univ. Pr., 1972. Reproductions, some in full color, of alphabets that vary in theme, tone, and degrees of difficulty or didacticism.

BANDURA, ALBERT, and RICHARD H. WALTERS. *Social Learning and Personality Development.* Holt, 1963. The authors deal with the relationships between social learning and the environment, looking at the acquisition of behavior through observational learning.

BARBER, RICHARD. *A Companion to World Mythology.* Delacorte, 1980. Colorful illustrations based on original prototypes embellish this dictionary of world mythological personalities.

BARCHILON, JACQUES, and HENRY PETTIT. *The Authentic Mother Goose Fairy Tales and Nursery Rhymes.* Swallow Pr., 1960. Following a scholarly introduction to the history of Mother Goose and the Perrault fairy tales, there are facsimiles of the complete *Mother Goose's Melody,* and of the 1729 English translation of Perrault's *Tales.*

BARING-GOULD, WILLIAM and CECIL., ed. *The Annotated Mother Goose.* The complete text and illustrations in a fully annotated edition, ill. by Caldecott, Crane, Greenaway, Rackham, Parrish, and historical woodcuts. With chapter decorations by E. M. Simon. Potter, 1962. Mother goose and other rhymes, ditties, and jingles of the nursery run side by side with columns of absorbing historical notes. This impressively large, beautiful book contains over 200 illustrations with a first-line index.

BARRON, NEIL. *Anatomy of Wonder: A Critical Guide to Science Fiction.* 3rd ed. Bowker, 1987. One chapter is devoted to science fiction for children and young adults.

BARRY, FLORENCE V. *A Century of Children's Books.* Doran, 1923; reissued. Singing Tree, 1968. A readable account of early English books for children, with unusually good evaluations.

BATOR, ROBERT, comp. *Signposts to Criticism of Children's Literature.* ALA, 1983. A distinguished roster of contributors is represented in this compendium of previously published essays exploring children's literature from a critical standpoint.

BAUER, CAROLINE FELLER. *This Way to Books.* Wilson, 1982. Potpourri of ideas and activities for introducing books in exciting, imaginative ways.

BAUGHMAN, ERNEST. *A Type and Motif Index of the Folktales of England and North America.* Indiana Univ. Folklore Series, No. 20, 1966. Gives extensive bibliographic references to the well-known folk-tale types.

BAUM, L. FRANK. *The Wizard of Oz,* ed. by Michael Patrick Hearn. Schocken, 1983. Following the text of Baum's classic fantasy are nearly 200 pages of criticism dating from 1900 to the present.

BECHTEL, LOUISE SEAMAN, ed. *Books in Search of Children.* Macmillan, 1969. Speeches and essays by a pioneering editor and critic.

BERRY, THOMAS ELLIOTT, ed. *The Biographer's Craft.* Odyssey, 1967. A textbook with examples of the work of seventeen biographers from Plutarch to contemporary writers, with one-page analyses of the biographers' genres and output. Introductory essay and short additional-reading list.

BETTELHEIM, BRUNO. *The Uses of Enchantment: Meaning and Importance of Fairy Tales.* Knopf, 1976. A defense of the genre and an analysis of some popular fairy tales.

The Bewick Collector. A descriptive catalog of the works of Thomas and John Bewick. . . . The whole described from the originals by Thomas Hugo. M.A., F.R.S.I., etc. London: Lovell Reeve, Volume 1. 1866. Supp., 1868; reissued, Singing Tree, 1968.

BIERHORST, JOHN, ed. *The Monkey's Haircut: And Other Stories Told by the Maya,* ill. by Robert Andrew Parker. Morrow, 1986. A resource collection for students of anthropology and folklore as well as a collection of diverse tales.

————. *The Mythology of Mexico and Central America.* Morrow, 1990. Discusses basic myths (from Aztec and Mayan Civilizations to today) that have influenced life in Central America.

————. *The Mythology of North America.* Morrow, 1985. A guide to the representative gods and heroes of recorded native American mythology, with maps showing tribal locations. Outlines of major myths are included.

————. *The Mythology of South America.* Morrow, 1988. Samplings of stories show how principal myths recur—but with variations—while tribal or regional myths have developed spontaneously.

BILLINGTON, ELIZABETH T., ed. *The Randolph Caldecott Treasury,* with an appreciation by Maurice Sendak. Warne, 1978. A compilation of Caldecott's oeuvre, with meticulous reproductions of many original drawings.

BINGHAM, JANE, ed. *Writers for Children: Critical Studies of the Major Authors since the Seventeenth Century.* Scribner's, 1988. Current authors like Virginia Hamilton and Katherine Paterson are not included; although the title doesn't make it clear, the eighty-four writers included are those who are considered authors of classics. Contributors have supplied bibliographies as well as biographical data and critical commentary.

BLISHEN, EDWARD, ed. *The Thorny Paradise.* Kestrel, 1975. A collection of reflections by authors of children's books on diverse approaches to writing for children.

BLOUNT, MARGARET. *Animal Land: The Creatures of Children's Fiction.* Morrow, 1975. Discusses and analyzes types of animal stories.

BOOSS, CLAIRE, ed. *Scandinavian Folk & Fairy Tales: Tales from Norway, Sweden, Denmark, Finland, Iceland.* Avenel, 1984. More than 200 tales from the five Scandinavian countries constitute a prime storytelling resource.

BOSTON, LUCY M. *Perverse and Foolish: A Memoir of Childhood and Youth.* Atheneum, 1979. Boston's very personal reminiscences of her youth up to the time of her marriage.

BOVA, BENJAMIN. *Through Eyes of Wonder: Science Fiction and Science.* Addison, 1975. An assessment of the contribution of science fiction to scientific knowledge, with some history of the development of the genre.

BOWEN, CATHERINE DRINKER. *Biography: The Craft and the Calling.* Little, 1968. Dealing with the planning, research, and techniques involved, the book analyzes four major biographies, with side excursions for further examples, and provides a good tool for writers in the field.

BRAND, OSCAR. *The Ballad Mongers: Rise of the Modern Folk Song.* Funk, 1962. An excellent survey of the interest in, and development of, the folk music of America.

BREWTON, JOHN E. and SARA W., comps. *Index to Children's Poetry.* Wilson, 1942. First supp., 1954; second supp., 1965; third supp., 1972. Helpful in finding poem sources. Indexed by author, title, subject, and first line. Thorough analysis of book contents, number of poems in a book, and grade placement.

BREWTON, JOHN, and G. MEREDITH and LORRAINE BLACKBURN, comps. *Index to Poetry for Children and Young People 1976–1981.* Wilson, 1984. A title, subject, and first-line index to poetry in age-appropriate collections.

BRIGGS, KATHARINE M. *A Dictionary of British Folk Tales in the English Language.* Indiana Univ. Pr., 1970. Part A, Folk Narratives, Volumes 1 and 2. Part B, Folk Legends, Volumes 1 and 2. Contains complete texts and summaries of all British tales in English with extensive comparative notes.

————. *An Encyclopedia of Fairies: Hobgoblins, Brownies, Bogies, and Other Supernatural Creatures.* Pantheon, 1977. Describes many varieties of fairy people, with references to their appearance in international folklore.

————. *The Personnel of Fairyland: A Short Account of the Fairy People of Great Britain for Those Who Tell Stories to Children.* Bentley, 1954. While this is a shorter treatment than the author's *Encyclopedia,* above, it remains a useful directory to the supernatural beings found in British lore.

BRODERICK, DOROTHY M. *Image of the Black in Children's Fiction.* Bowker, 1973. Limited only by the fact that later titles were chosen from headings assigned by *Children's Catalog,* thus excluding some books with major black characters, this is an incisive and perceptive analysis of issues and attitudes.

BROOKE, HENRY. *Leslie Brooke and Johnny Crow.* Warne, 1982. A warm remembrance by the artist's son tells how the classic Johnny Crow books came to be written.

BROWN, MARCIA. *Lotus Seeds: Children, Pictures, and Books.* Scribner's, 1986. A compilation of Brown's articles and speeches includes comments on books, book people, and book illustration.

BRUNER, JEROME S. *Toward a Theory of Instruction.* Belknap Pr. of Harvard Univ., 1966. A collection of essays concerned with the relationship between the growth and development of the child and the art of teaching.

BULFINCH, THOMAS. *Age of Fable: Or, Stories of Gods and Heroes,* introduction by Dudley Fitts, ill. by Joe Mugnaini. Heritage, 1958. This handsome edition of Bulfinch is almost completely devoted to the Greek and Roman myths, though it does include brief materials from the Norse, Celtic, and Hindu lore.

BUTLER, DOROTHY. *Babies Need Books.* Atheneum, 1980. Stresses the importance of books for young children, both for encouraging the love of reading and for the contribution to language arts skills.

————. *Cushla and Her Books.* Horn Book, 1980. An account of the role books played in the progress of a child with severe handicaps.

BUTLER, FRANCELIA, and RICHARD ROTERT, eds. *Reflections on Literature for Children.* Shoe String/ Library Professional Publications, 1984. A generous sampling of articles from the *Children's Literature* annual.

CADOGAN, MARY, and PATRICIA CRAIG. *You're a Brick, Angela: A New Look at Girls' Fiction from 1839–1975.* London: Gollancz, 1976. Stories for girls are examined as reflections of social history as well as for their place in literary history.

CAMERON, ELEANOR. *The Green and Burning Tree: On the Writing and Enjoyment of Children's Books.* Little, 1969. Critical essays by a writer for children, with a special emphasis on fantasy.

CARLSON, RUTH KEARNEY. *Emerging Humanity: Multi-Ethnic Literature for Children and Adolescents.* Brown, 1972. Describes values of and criteria for multiethnic literature, suggests ways to use it. Separate chapters discuss African- and native-American and Hispanic books.

————. *Enrichment Ideas: Sparkling Fireflies.* Brown, 1970. For the elementary school classroom teacher, suggestions for dramatization, art projects, language games, and ways of using literature to enrich the curriculum. The suggestions for activities are accompanied by selected references for children and selected references for adults.

CARPENTER, HUMPHREY. *Secret Gardens: A Study of the Golden Age of Children's Literature.* Houghton, 1985. A combination of criticism and biographical information scans the work of Late Victorian and Edwardian writers of children's books.

CARPENTER, HUMPHREY, and MARI PRICHARD. *The Oxford Companion to Children's Literature.* Oxford, 1984. A long-awaited and eminently useful reference book containing extensive entries on authors, illustrators, fictional characters, genres, folktales, and other topics.

CARR, JO, ed. *Beyond Fact: Nonfiction for Children and Young People.* ALA, 1982. A stimulating collection of essays focusing on the history of nonfiction, standards for evaluation, discussion of genres, and controversial issues.

CARROLL, LEWIS (pseud.). *The Annotated Alice: Alice's Adventures in Wonderland & Through the Looking Glass,* ill. by John Tenniel. With introduction and notes by Martin Gardner. Potter, 1960. Significant quotations from Carroll biographies and other sources are placed parallel to the story text. An enriching background source for students.

CHALL, JEANNE. *Learning to Read: The Great Debate.* McGraw, 1967. The findings of a three-year study on teaching beginning reading with a sober discussion of conclusions and recommendations.

CHAMBERS, AIDAN. *Introducing Books to Children.* 2nd ed. Horn Book, 1983. Essays on criticism and children's responses to literature by a British author and critic.

CHAMBERS, DEWEY W. *Children's Literature in the Curriculum.* Rand, 1971. A plea to make children's literature an integral part of the elementary school's curriculum and an important factor in the lives of children. The three sections are "The Role of Literature in the Elementary Curriculum," "How Books Can Affect Children," and "Thoughts on Some Controversial Issues in Children's Literature."

————. *Literature for Children: Storytelling and Creative Drama.* Brown, 1970. Recommendations for organizing storytelling and creative drama sessions are accompanied by discussion of educational implications for those activities.

CHAMBERS, NANCY, ed. *The Signal Approach to Children's Books.* Scarecrow, 1981. Noteworthy articles from *Signal,* a British publication on children's literature.

CHAMBERS, ROBERT. *Popular Rhymes of Scotland.* Singing Tree, 1969. First published in 1826, this work has been revised and expanded several times. The 1870 edition is reproduced in this volume.

CHILD, FRANCIS JAMES, ed. *English and Scottish Popular Ballads,* 5 vols. Houghton, 1882–1898. This is a most authoritative source for all English and Scottish traditional ballads. Many variants are given for each ballad, together with copious notes.

Children's Literature Abstracts. Published quarterly by the Children's Library Section of the International Federation of Library Associations. An abstracting service that focuses primarily on articles in English-language journals.

Children's Literature in Education. Human Sciences Press. An international journal, published quarterly, has reviews, interviews, and articles, and is intended for librarians, teachers, writers, and parents.

CHUKOVSKY, KORNEI. *From Two to Five,* tr. and ed. by Miriam Morton. Univ. of Calif. Pr., 1965. A book on the language and comprehension of the very young child written by the dean of Russian children's writers. This text is rich in its insights and observations.

CIANCIOLO, PATRICIA. *Illustrations in Children's Books,* 2nd ed. Brown, 1976. The book deals with art and design as areas of study in the elementary school: styles, techniques, appraisal of illustrations and their use in class. Up-to-date references by chapters, and with bibliography and index.

————. *Picture Books for Children.* 2nd ed. ALA, 1981. This discerning discussion of story themes and artwork surveys hundreds of picture books.

CIONI, ALFRED J., ed. *Motivating Reluctant Readers,* International Reading Association, 1981. A useful book of suggestions for teachers.

CLARK, ANN NOLAN. *Journey to the People,* with introduction by Annis Duff, ill. Viking, 1969. Essays about a lifelong experience with teaching native-American children: Zuni, Navajo, Pueblo, and other tribes of the Southwest, as well as the Dakota Sioux and the Indians of Guatemala and Peru.

CLARKSON, ATELIA, and GILBERT B. CROSS, comps. *World Folktales: A Scribner Resource Collection.* Scribner's, 1980. A substantive, well-documented collection of international folktales, arranged according to story content and tale types.

CLEARY, FLORENCE. *Blueprints for Better Reading: School Programs for Promoting Skill and Interest in Reading.* Wilson, 1970. Offers both inspiration and ideas to teachers and librarians.

COFFIN, TRISTRAM P. *The British Traditional Ballad in North America.* The American Folklore Society, Bibliographic and Special Series II (1950, 1963). Bibliographic listings for all versions of traditional (child) ballads collected in North America.

COGER, LESLIE IRENE, and MELVIN R. WHITE. *Readers Theatre Handbook: A Dramatic Approach to Literature,* 3rd ed. Scott, Foresman, 1982. Provides sample scripts and suggestions for casting and rehearsing Readers Theatre productions.

COLES, ROBERT. *Children of Crisis.* Atlantic, 1964. Based on the author's interviews with black and white people in the South, a long-term study of children, analyzing their drawings as well as their conversation.

COLES, ROBERT, and MARIA PIERS. *Wages of Neglect.* Quadrangle, 1969. An examination of the behavior of young children of the poor, their special hardships, and social and personal anxieties that determine their behavior.

COLUM, PADRAIC, ed. *A Treasury of Irish Folklore.* Crown, 1954. This book gives insight into Irish history and heroism as well as folklore.

COLWELL, EILEEN. *Storytelling.* Bodley Head; dist. by Merrimack Publishers Circle, 1983. A good reference for those comfortable with Colwell's formal approach to storytelling, this also contains practical advice on reaching a handicapped audience and other special situations.

COMENIUS, JOHN AMOS. *The Orbis Pictus of John Amos Comenius.* Singing Tree, 1968. The first children's picture book and the most widely known textbook of the seventeenth and eighteenth centuries, reproduced from an 1887 photographic copy of a 1728 London edition, this volume is of interest to educators and historians alike.

COMMIRE, ANNE. *Something about the Author: Facts and Pictures about Contemporary Authors and Illustrators of Books for Young People.* Vol. I. Gale, 1971. The inclusion of biographical information and lists of writings makes this reference series useful to adults.

————. *Yesterday's Authors of Books for Children.* Gale, 1977. Biographical information for some authors deceased before 1961. Discontinued after publication of two volumes; merged with Commire's *Something about the Author* series.

COODY, BETTY. *Using Literature with Young Children.* 3rd ed. Brown, 1983. A practical literature program for young children at home and in school.

COOK, ELIZABETH. *The Ordinary and the Fabulous: An Introduction to Myths, Legends, and Fairy Tales for Teachers and Storytellers.* Cambridge Univ. Pr., 1969. The author undertakes to show that an adult understanding of life is incomplete without an understanding of myths, legends, and fairy tales and that there are many ways of presenting them.

COTT, JONATHAN. *Pipers at the Gates of Dawn: The Wisdom of Children's Literature.* Random House, 1983. Despite an occasionally intrusive authorial presence, these interviews with Dr. Seuss, Sendak, Steig, Lindgren, P. L. Travers, the Opies, and Chinua Achebe, a Nigerian folklorist, give an invigorating perspective on literary and philosophical themes of the individuals' works.

COUGHLAN, MARGARET, comp. *Folklore from Africa to the United States.* Library of Congress, 1976. A bibliography of African tales with annotations that emphasize sources and patterns of diffusion.

CRAGO, MAUREEN and HUGH. *Prelude to Literacy: A Preschool Child's Encounter with Picture and Story.* Southern Illinois University Press, 1983. Detailed comments about the authors' daughter's reactions to 400-plus children's books she was given between the ages of one and five.

CREIGHTON, HELEN, comp. *Songs and Ballads of Nova Scotia.* Dover, 1966. Includes Scottish and English ballads and folk songs of English and Scottish origin as well as songs native to North America.

CROUCH, MARCUS. *The Nesbit Tradition: The Children's Novel 1945–1970.* Rowman and Littlefield, 1973. A major English critic of children's literature examines, by theme, genre, or setting, the work of contemporary writers of fiction, chiefly British and American.

————. *Treasure Seekers and Borrowers: Children's Books in Britain, 1900–1960.* London: The Library Assoc., 1962. Excellent brief appraisals of authors and books, chiefly British, published during the first sixty years of the twentieth century.

CULLINAN, BERNICE. *Literature and the Child.* Harcourt, 1989. A teaching-oriented examination of literary genres from the child's point of view, with many activity suggestions and profiles of popular authors and illustrators.

————. *Literature for Children: Its Discipline and Content.* Brown, 1971. For elementary classroom teachers, this book is intended to build effective courses in literature. Well constructed and researched with numerous references for each chapter.

CULLINAN, BERNICE, and CAROLYN CARMICHAEL, eds. *Literature and Young Children.* National Council of Teachers of English (NCTE), 1977. Essays relating the education of young children to resources in children's literature, including audiovisual materials.

CURRELL, DAVID. *The Complete Book of Puppetry.* Plays, 1975. A comprehensive book on making and using every kind of puppet.

DARLING, RICHARD L. *The Rise of Children's Book Reviewing in America, 1865–1881.* Bowker, 1968. A scholarly and thorough examination of the publishing and reviewing of children's books, set in the historical context. Thirty-six periodicals are examined, including the most important literary periodicals of the time.

DARLING, HAROLD, and PETER NEUMEYER, eds. *Image & Maker: An Annual Dedicated to the Consideration of Book Illustration.* Green Tiger Press/Star & Elephant, 1984. The first issue of a new annual for the critical study of book illustration, containing an assortment of hand-tipped, full-color reproductions.

DARTON, F. J. H. *Children's Books in England: Five Centuries of Social Life,* 3rd ed. rev. by Brian Alderson. Cambridge Univ. Pr., 1982. A scholarly study of children's books, from the fables to Robert Louis Stevenson. Chapter VII is about John Newbery and the first English books for children.

DEL REY, LESTER. *The World of Science Fiction 1926–1976: The History of a Subculture.* Ballantine, 1979. A literary history of the development of science fiction.

DEUTSCH, MARTIN, and others. *The Disadvantaged Child.* Basic, 1967. Selected papers on the social environment for learning, and on such factors as race, social class, and language in the education of the disadvantaged child.

DEVRIES, LEONARD. *Little Wide-Awake: An Anthology from Victorian Children's Books and Periodicals in the Collection of Anne and Fernand G. Renier,* ill. World, 1967. Interesting examples of what was read by children during the sixty years of Victoria's reign.

DOMAN, GLENN. *How to Teach Your Baby to Read: The Gentle Revolution.* Random, 1983. Work with brain-injured children has led to more complete understanding of how all children learn and the development of a startling reading program.

DONELSON, KENNETH L., and ALLEEN PACE NILSEN. *Literature for Today's Young Adults,* 3rd ed. Scott, Foresman, 1989. Provides an excellent balance among historical, practical, and literary approaches to books for the adolescent reader.

DORSON, RICHARD M. *American Folklore.* Univ. of Chicago Pr., 1959. A very readable general survey of prose forms of oral folklore in the United States. Devotes little attention to folksong.

————. *Buying the Wind, Regional Folklore in the United States.* Univ. of Chicago Pr., 1964. A good selection of authentic folklore texts with useful notes and introduction.

————. ed. *Folktales of the World.* Univ. of Chicago Pr. This most impressive series for the student of folklore has been published under the general editorship of Richard Dorson, a professor of history and director of the Folklore Institute at Indiana University. In each volume, his foreword is learned, informative, and beautifully written. The editor for each volume is a distinguished folklorist in his or her own right. The full notes, index of motifs, glossary, bibliography, and general index in each volume add to their usefulness for the scholar. Each book contains from fifty to one hundred tales; several titles are discussed in Chapter 7.

————. ed. *Folktales Told around the World.* Univ. of Chicago Pr., 1975. Sources are cited for each tale; included are indexes by motif and type, notes on contributors, and a general index.

DOUGLAS, NORMAN. *London Street Games.* Singing Tree, 1968. Greatly expanded from an article published in *English Review* in 1913, this running account of English street life in the early part of the century captures the vocabulary and tone of the children Douglas collected from.

DUFF, ANNIS. *"Bequest of Wings": A Family's Pleasures with Books.* Viking, 1955. A pleasant, anecdotal account of a family and its reading, and some apt generalizations about what books mean to younger children.

————. *"Longer Flight": A Family Grows up with Books.* Viking, 1955. Another pleasant, anecdotal account of a family and its reading, and some apt generalizations about what books mean to children and adolescents.

EASTMAN, MARY HUSE. *Index to Fairy Tales, Myths and Legends.* Faxon, 1926. First supp., 1937; second supp., 1952. Useful for locating various sources in which individual tales may be found. There are geographical and racial groupings and lists for storytellers. See entry for Ireland, Norma.

EASTMAN, MAX. *The Enjoyment of Poetry.* Scribner's, 1921, 1951. This book is an excellent introduction to the pleasures of poetry. Chapter I, "Poetic People," in which he gives his reasons for listing the child as one of the "poetic people," and Chapter V, "Practical Values of Poetry," should be noted.

ECKENSTEIN, LINA. *Comparative Studies in Nursery Rhymes.* London: Duckworth, 1906; reissued, Singing Tree, 1968. A study of the ancient folk origins of the Mother Goose verses and their European counterparts.

EGOFF, SHEILA. *The Republic of Childhood: A Critical Guide to Canadian Children's Literature in English.*

Oxford, 1967. Creative writing for children by Canadian authors between the years of 1950 and 1965.

————, ed. *Thursday's Child: Trends and Patterns in Contemporary Children's Literature.* ALA, 1981. Provocative essays organized by literary genre look at current trends in children's literature.

————. *Worlds Within: Children's Fantasy from the Middle Ages to Today.* ALA, 1988. In tracing the changes in fantasy writing, the author considers how many of them reflect changing societal views of the child, as well as literary aspects of the genre.

————, G. T. STUBBS, and L. F. ASHLEY, eds. *Only Connect: Readings on Children's Literature.* 2nd ed. Oxford, 1980. A popular and lively collection of essays covering literary criticism, standards, and a range of issues in children's books.

ELLIS, ALEC. *A History of Children's Reading and Literature.* Pergamon, 1968. History of schools, educational practice, and library development in England.

ELLIS, ANNE W. *The Family Story in the 1960s.* Archon Books & Clive Bingley, 1970. A survey, with comments on trends, on family stories, almost all of British origin, published during the decade. Good commentary and checklist.

ELLIS, JOHN M. *One Fairy Story Too Many: The Brothers Grimm and Their Tales.* Univ. of Chicago, 1983. An iconoclastic, well-documented reevaluation of the Grimms argues that the brothers intentionally misrepresented their stories as indigenous folklore.

ENGLAND, CLAIRE, and ADELE FASICK. *Childview: Evaluating and Reviewing Materials for Children.* Libraries Unlimited, 1987. Intended as a guide for adults who review materials for children, this keeps children's viewpoints in mind while focusing on the adult point of view.

ERIKSON, ERIK H. *Childhood and Society,* 2nd ed., rev. and enl. Norton, 1964. The noted psychoanalyst's summary of his studies of childhood, emphasizing the importance of early experiences in the development of adult attitudes and actions.

ERNEST, EDWARD, comp., assisted by PATRICIA TRACY LOWE. *The Kate Greenaway Treasury,* ill. World, 1967. A biography of Kate Greenaway, an evaluation of her art, a fine essay about her work by the late Anne Carroll Moore, and an introduction by Ruth Hill Viguers, make this rich collection the definitive study of a beloved children's book illustrator.

ESBENSEN, BARBARA JUSTER. *A Celebration of Bees: Helping Children Write Poetry.* Winston Press, 1975. An informally written guide by an experienced teacher.

EYRE, FRANK. *British Children's Books in the Twentieth Century.* Dutton, 1973. A revised edition of the 1952 title, *20th Century Children's Books,* this historical survey discusses trends and includes an intensive divided bibliography.

FADER, DANIEL N., and ELTON B. MCNEIL. *Hooked on Books: Program and Proof.* Putnam, 1968. A detailed description of a program to get bored and apathetic students to read, accompanied by a description of a research project evaluating the program.

FEAVER, WILLIAM. *When We Were Young: Two Centuries of Children's Book Illustration.* Holt, 1977. Features a potpourri of illustrations from children's books over the past two hundred years, with a concise historical essay.

FELDMAN, EDMUND BURKE. *Becoming Human through Art: Aesthetic Experience in the School,* ill. Prentice, 1970. An interdisciplinary approach to visual education, primarily for teachers and teachers of teachers.

FENWICK, SARA INNIS, ed. *A Critical Approach to Children's Literature.* Univ. of Chicago Pr., 1967. Collected papers from a conference on children's literature, representing a variety of aspects.

FIELD, CAROLYN W., ed. *Special Collections in Children's Literature.* ALA, 1982. Identifies and publicizes special collections of children's literature, especially for those interested in research.

FIELD, ELINOR WHITNEY, comp. *Horn Book Reflections: On Children's Books and Reading.* Selected from eighteen years of *The Horn Book Magazine*—1949–1966. Horn Book, 1969. Contributors are writers, illustrators, teachers, librarians, and parents.

FIELD, LOUISE F. *The Child and His Book: Some Account of the History and Progress of Children's Literature in England.* Singing Tree, 1968. An important scholarly work tracing the history of English books for children from before the Conquest to the nineteenth century, this book is also a social history of England.

FISHER, MARGERY. *Intent upon Reading.* Watts, 1962. A refreshing and critical approach to children's books, both recent and standard selections. Though many of the titles are English publications, a great number are familiar to American readers.

————. *Matters of Fact: Aspects of Nonfiction for Children.* T. Crowell, 1972. An excellent guide to evaluative criteria.

————. *Who's Who in Children's Books.* Holt, 1975. A guide to characters and personalities in children's literature; entries describe the character, the book or books in which the character appeared, and the way the author achieved a successful characterization.

FOLMSBEE, BEULAH. *A Little History of the Horn Book.* Horn Book, 1942. A tiny book, beautifully printed, with a history of hornbooks, in all their variations, both in England and New England.

FORD, PAUL F. *Companion to Narnia,* ill. by Lorinda Bryan Cauley. Harper, 1980. Arranged in dictionary format, this well-researched companion to C. S. Lewis' seven-volume Narnia series comes complete with full-page illustrations and maps.

FORD, PAUL LEICESTER, ed. *The New England Primer.* Dodd, 1897, 1962. The subtitle explains the content: "A history of its origin with a reprint of the unique copy of the earliest known first edition."

FORDYCE, RACHEL. *Children's Theatre and Creative Dramatics: An Annotated Bibliography of Critical Works.* Hall, 1975. A most useful compilation of pertinent articles and books.

FOX, GEOFF, ed. *Writers, Critics and Children.* Agathon, 1976. An anthology of provocative articles from the journal, Children's Literature in Education.

FRASER, JAMES, comp. *Children's Authors and Illustrators: A Guide to Manuscript Collections in United States Research Libraries.* Saur, 1980. Descriptive annotations vary in the amount of information furnished.

FRASER, JAMES H., ed. *Society and Children's Literature.* David R. Godine, 1978. Collected papers from a 1976 symposium on the history of children's literature.

FRAZER, SIR JAMES GEORGE. *The Golden Bough: A Study in Magic and Religion,* 1 volume abr. ed. Macmillan, 1922. First published in 1890, this is a monumental study (originally 13 volumes) in comparative folklore, magic, and religion.

FRIEDMAN, ALBERT B. *The Viking Book of Folk Ballads of the English Speaking World.* Viking, 1956. Contains many ballads, with useful notes.

FRYE, BURTON C., ed. *A St. Nicholas Anthology: The Early Years,* ill. Meredith, 1969. A selection from the years 1870 to 1905 of stories, articles, and poems, as well as illustrations which appeared in this most beloved of all children's magazines.

GERSONI-STAVN, DIANE, ed. *Sexism and Youth.* Bowker, 1974. An anthology of fifty previously published articles.

GESELL, ARNOLD, and FRANCES ILG. *Child Development: an Introduction to the Study of Human Growth.* Harper, 1949. This research study considers child growth in its broadest sense—intellectual, emotional, and social—from infancy through adolescence. Lucid style and revealing case histories make this a readable and essential book for parents and teachers.

GESELL, ARNOLD, and others. *The First Five Years of Life: A Guide to the Study of the Preschool Child.* Harper, 1940. Discusses the nature of mental growth, developmental changes, and such facets of growth as language development and personal-social behavior.

GILLIES, EMILY. *Creative Dramatics for All Children.* ACEI, 1973. Includes suggestions for the use of creative drama in the classroom and means for involving handicapped children.

GODDEN, RUMER. *Hans Christian Andersen: A Great Life in Brief.* Knopf, 1955. "Life itself is the most wonderful fairy tale." So wrote Andersen, and no one could have told his fairy tale more poignantly than Rumer Godden, the English novelist.

GOTTLIEB, GERALD. *Early Children's Books and Their Illustration.* Godine, 1975. Witty and erudite commentary accompanies beautiful reproductions of books in the collection of the Pierpont Morgan Library.

GREEN, PERCY B. *A History of Nursery Rhymes.* Singing Tree, 1968. Detailed explanations of children's games, potentially useful to kindergarten and nursery school teachers as well as parents.

GREEN, PETER. *Kenneth Grahame,* ill. with photos. World, 1959. This very welcome biography is authoritatively and perceptively written. Green's *Beyond the Wild Wood* (1983) is a lavishly illustrated abridgement.

GREEN, ROGER LANCELYN. *Tellers of Tales,* enl. ed. E. Ward, 1953; reissued, Watts, 1965. This is a delightfully written discussion of English authors of children's books. Only twenty pages are devoted to modern writers.

HALLIWELL-PHILLIPPS, JAMES O. *Popular Rhymes and Nursery Tales: A Sequel to the Nursery Rhymes of England.* Singing Tree, 1968. This mid-nineteenth-century book is a collection of material of interest to folklorists as well as teachers and librarians.

HALSEY, ROSALIE V. *Forgotten Books of the American Nursery: A History of the Development of the American Story-Book.* Singing Tree, 1969. A reissue of a book first published at the turn of the century, this volume traces the history of children's books in America from colonial days to the early part of the nineteenth century, with emphasis on the light children's books shed on the social history of the country.

HARDT, ULRICH, ed. *Teaching Reading with the Other Language Arts.* International Reading Association, 1983. Focused on classroom practices, this provides a theoretical foundation for integrating a language arts program.

HARRISON, BARBARA, and GREGORY MAGUIRE, eds. *Innocence & Experience: Essays & Conversations on Children's Literature.* Lothrop, 1987. Compiled from programs at the Simmons College Center for the Study of Children's Literature, this covers a broad range of subjects.

HAVILAND, VIRGINIA. *Children's Literature: A Guide to Reference Sources,* ill. Library of Congress, 1966. The only reference tool of its kind in scope and coverage, this book offers bibliographic guidance to books available today and to the history of children's literature. First supp. 1972. Second supp. 1977.

HAVILAND, VIRGINIA, and MARGARET COUGHLAN, comps. *Yankee Doodle's Literary Sampler of Prose, Poetry, & Pictures.* T. Crowell, 1974. A sampling of writing and illustration drawn from the collection of the Library of Congress.

HAZARD, PAUL. *Books, Children and Men,* tr. by Marguerite Mitchell, 4th ed. Horn Book, 1960. A member of the French Academy and professor of comparative literature both in France and in the United States has written engagingly of the great children's books of many countries.

HEARNE, BETSY. *Beauty and the Beast: Visions and Revisions of an Old Tale.* Univ. of Chicago Press, 1989. An erudite analysis of literary, historical, artistic, and psychological implications of the many versions of a classic tale.

HEARNE, BETSY, and MARILYN KAYE, eds. *Celebrating Children's Books: Essays on Children's Literature in Honor of Zena Sutherland.* Lothrop, 1981. A memorable festschrift, with contributions from twenty-three eminent authors, illustrators, reviewers, and editors.

HEARN, MICHAEL. *The Annotated Wizard of Oz.* Potter, 1973. The text and original drawings for Baum's *The Wonderful Wizard of Oz* are reproduced, illuminated by notes describing the author's life, the history of the Oz books, and the social philosophy of Oz.

HELMS, RANDALL. *Tolkien's World.* Houghton, 1974. A discussion of the relevance of Tolkien's writings as mythic literature.

HENDRICKSON, LINNEA. *Children's Literature: A Guide to the Criticism.* Hall, 1987. Brief notes on critical commentaries are given under names of authors and then under "Subjects, Themes, and Genres."

HEWINS, CAROLINE M. *A Mid-Century Child and Her Books.* Singing Tree, 1969. The autobiography of a pioneer children's librarian who was also the author of many books on children's literature, this book provides a detailed picture of what life was like for a book-loving child in New England in the mid-nineteenth century.

HIGGINS, JAMES E. *Beyond Words: Mystical Fancy in Children's Literature.* Teachers College Pr., 1970. The author discusses the importance of mystical fantasy in the development of the child and its significance as a literary form, with special detailed analysis of the work of such great authors as George Macdonald, W. H. Hudson, Saint-Exupéry, Tolkien, and C. S. Lewis.

HILDICK, WALLACE. *Children and Fiction.* World, 1971. A critical study of the artistic and psychological factors involved in writing fiction for and about children, suggesting the application of high standards in examining children's literature from the literary and sociological points of view.

HIRSCHFELDER, ARLENE B., ed. *American Indian Stereotypes in the World of Children: A Reader and Bibliography.* Scarecrow, 1982. Essays calling attention to stereotypical native American images in children's books are followed by suggested corrective measures to counteract the negative representations.

HODGART, M. J. C. *The Ballads.* Hutchinson's Universal Library, 1950. Useful general discussion of the traditional ballads, stressing the literary approach.

HOFFMAN, MIRIAM, and EVA SAMUELS, eds. *Authors and Illustrators of Children's Books: Writings on Their Lives and Works.* Bowker, 1972. A compilation of articles from magazines gives more depth than many of the briefer entries in other sources, although the coverage is not as broad.

HOLT, JOHN. *How Children Fail,* rev. ed. Delacorte, 1982. An important book, based on records of classroom experience, dealing with the ways children meet or dodge the demands adults make on them, the interaction between fear and failure, the difference between what children are expected to know and what they really know, and finally how the schools fail to meet the real needs of children.

————. *How Children Learn,* rev. ed. Delacorte, 1983. This book, written in journal form about the reactions of various children in games, experiments, reading, talking, and being involved in arts and math, throws light on using their minds effectively and on the relationship between encouragement and progress in learning.

HOLTZE, SALLY HOLMES, ed. *Sixth Book of Junior Authors & Illustrators.* Wilson, 1989. A rich treasury of biographical information about contemporary authors and illustrators.

HOPKINS, LEE BENNETT. *The Best of Book Bonanza.* Holt, 1980. Suggestions for the creative use of children's literature in conjunction with special occasions, seasons, and holidays.

————. *Books Are by People,* ill. Citation, 1969. Human interest interviews with 104 writers and illustrators for children, to be used with children to make their authors "come alive."

——————. *Let Them Be Themselves*. Citation, 1969. Recommendations for enriching the language arts curriculum for all children, but especially the disadvantaged.

——————. *More Books by More People*. Citation, 1974. Interviews with sixty-five children's authors give information about the author's work and his or her personal life.

HUCK, CHARLOTTE S. *Children's Literature in Elementary School*. Holt, 1987. An updated revision of a well-known textbook.

HUDSON, DEREK. *Arthur Rackham: His Life and Work*. London: Heinemann, 1960, 1974. A biography that includes perceptive analysis of Rackham's art, with a fully annotated bibliography.

HUGHES, TED. *Poetry Is*. Doubleday, 1970. Based on a series of BBC talks, a discussion of poetry intended for young writers, but interesting for poetry readers as well.

HUNTER, MOLLIE. *Talent Is Not Enough*. Harper, 1976. A thoughtful exploration of the responsibilities of writing for children. Included is an essay on historical fiction.

HÜRLIMANN, BETTINA. *Picture-Book World*, ed. and tr. by Brian Alderson, ill. World, 1969. Modern picture books for children from twenty-four countries, with introductory chapters on particular countries and with a biobibliographical supplement.

——————. *Three Centuries of Children's Books in Europe*, ed. and tr. by Brian Alderson, ill. World, 1968. A comparative study as well as a history which includes a survey of contemporary books for children in all of the countries of Europe.

HUTCHINS, MICHAEL, ed. *Yours Pictorially: Illustrated Letters of Randolph Caldecott*. Warne, 1977 Caldecott's chatty letters, with companion sketches, give insights into his life, his art, and the world in which he lived.

HUTT, S. J., and CORINNE, eds. *Early Human Development*. Oxford, 1973. A collection of studies on various aspects of early human behavior.

ILG, FRANCES L., and LOUISE BATES AMES. *Child Behavior*. Harper, 1955. Frances Ilg, M.D., and Louise Ames, Ph.D., give direct advice, based on their research at the Gesell Institute, to parents concerning problems of child behavior.

IRELAND, NORMA. *Index to Fairy Tales, 1949–1972: Including Folklore, Legends and Myths in Collections*. Faxon, 1973. A supplement to the Eastman indexes, which indexed fairy tales through 1948. A useful addition, this indexes material in collections, not single tales.

JACOBS, JOSEPH. See listings of his collections of national folklore in the Chapter 7 bibliographies of children's books. They contain significant introductions, and the notes in each appendix are treasures of folklore information.

JACOBS, JOSEPH, comp. *English Fairy Tales: Being the Two Collections English Fairy Tales and More English Fairy Tales*, ill. by Margery Gill. Chatto, Bodley Head, & Jonathan Cape, 1980. Complete versions of the Jacobs classics, first published in the 1890s, with the compiler's original preface, notes, and references.

JACOBS, LELAND B., ed. *Using Literature with Young Children*. Teachers College Pr., 1965. A collection of papers on providing good literature for young children, storytelling, reading aloud, poetry, choral speaking, dramatization, and relating literature to other school experiences.

JAN, ISABELLE. *On Children's Literature*. Schocken, 1974. Extended essays on the appeals of literature to children, focusing on the work of French and British authors. Translated from the French.

JENKINS, GLADYS GARDNER, HELEN S. SCHACTER, and WILLIAM W. BAUER. *These Are Your Children*, 4th ed. Scott, Foresman, 1975. A series of case studies with charts of normal child development and the special needs of children at various ages, enlivened by photographs of children in problem situations or normal activities.

JOHNSON, EDNA, EVELYN SICKELS, and FRANCES CLARKE SAYERS. *Anthology of Children's Literature*, 6th ed. Houghton, 1985. The editors in this latest edition have attempted to hold to the long view, choosing from the present that which gives promise of lasting value and fitting it into the interstices of the proven past.

JOHNSON, FERNE. *Start Early for an Early Start*. ALA, 1976. An analysis of the role of literature and libraries in the child's development, stressing parental involvement.

JONES, DOLORES BLYTHE. *Children's Literature Awards and Winners: A Directory of Prizes, Authors and Illustrators*. 2nd ed. Gale/Neal-Schumann, 1988. Compiles information about awards emanating from English-speaking countries.

JORDAN, ALICE M. *From Rollo to Tom Sawyer*. Horn Book, 1948. Here in beautiful format with decorations by Nora Unwin are twelve little essays on some of the most important nineteenth-century writers for children.

JOSEPH, STEPHEN M., ed. *The Me Nobody Knows: Children's Voices from the Ghetto*. Avon, 1969. Moving and revealing writing by children, mostly African-American and Puerto Rican, in the most impoverished city neighborhoods.

JUSTEN, SUE, ed. *Opening Doors for Preschool Children and Their Parents*. 2nd ed. ALA, 1981.

KIEFER, MONICA. *American Children through Their Books, 1700–1835*, Univ. of Penn. Pr., 1948,

1970. The American child at the beginning of the eighteenth century was too insignificant for physicians to waste time on, the author tells us. She traces the child's developing place in the world through an examination of children's books.

KINGMAN, LEE, ed. *The Illustrator's Notebook.* Horn Book, 1978. A valuable collection of articles by and about children's book illustrators, drawn from the pages of *The Horn Book.*

————, ed. *Newbery and Caldecott Medal Books: 1956–1965.* Horn Book, 1965. A biographical sketch of each author or illustrator, along with his or her acceptance paper and related material from *The Horn Book.*

————, ed. *Newbery and Caldecott Medal Books: 1966–1975,* Horn Book, 1975, and *Newbery and Caldecott Medal Books: 1976–1985,* Horn Book 1986, are companion volumes.

KINGMAN, LEE, JOANNA FOSTER, and RUTH GILES LONTOFT, comps. *Illustrators of Children's Books, 1957–1966,* ill. Horn Book, 1968. This volume, a supplement to *Illustrators of Children's Books, 1744–1945,* and *Illustrators of Children's Books, 1946–1956,* reviews the decade, offers biographies of active illustrators and a bibliography of their works.

KINGMAN, LEE, GRACE HOGARTH, and HARRIET QUIMBY. *Illustrators of Children's Books, 1967–1976.* Horn Book, 1978. Continues the Horn Book series on illustrators.

KINGSTON, CAROLYN. *The Tragic Mode in Children's Literature.* Teachers College Pr., 1974. Discusses tragedy in realistic fiction for ages 8–12, using books published before 1970.

KIRK, GEOFFREY S. *Myth.* Univ. of Calif. Pr., 1970. This text discusses the function of myth in various cultures.

KIRKPATRICK, DANIEL, ed. *Twentieth-Century Children's Writers.* 2nd ed. St. Martin's, 1984. Gives biographical data, critical appraisals, and lists of publications for more than 700 English-language authors.

KITTREDGE, GEORGE LYMAN, ed. *English and Scottish Popular Ballads: Student's Cambridge Edition,* ed. by Helen Child Sargeant. Houghton, 1904. This is the invaluable one-volume edition of the Child collection. It contains the 305 ballads, a few variants of each, brief notes, and the excellent glossary giving the definitions and pronunciations of the difficult ballad words.

KLEMIN, DIANA. *The Art of Art for Children's Books,* ill. Potter, 1966. Examples and commentary on the work of sixty-four illustrators of children's books.

————. *The Illustrated Book: Its Art and Craft,* ill. Potter, 1970. A contemporary survey with examples and commentary on the work of seventy-four artists. A chapter on drawing for reproduction is included, clarifying processes in printing.

KNOX, RAWLE, ed. *The Work of E. H. Shepard.* Schocken, 1980. A well-researched profile of the artist whose illustrations for *Winnie the Pooh* and *Wind in the Willows,* among others, are generally regarded as definitive.

KOCH, KENNETH. *Rose, Where Did You Get that Red?* Random, 1973. Koch explains his own successful approach to teaching adult poetry to children. Includes sample lessons and an anthology of poetry recommended for this use.

————. *Wishes, Lies, and Dreams: Teaching Children to Write Poetry,* ill. with photos. Random, 1971. Working with the children of P.S. 61 in New York City, the author, himself an outstanding poet, has developed ways of getting children to release their ideas and feelings into writing. The book is a collection of their poetry preceded and accompanied by his description of his teaching methods.

KOHL, HERBERT R. *36 Children,* ill. by Robert George Jackson. NAL, 1967. The author's experiences in a sixth-grade Harlem classroom demonstrate the progress that children can make when a good teacher meets their needs.

KREIDER, BARBARA. *Children's Plays in Collection.* Scarecrow, 1972. An interalphabetized author, title, and subject listing. Plays are also listed by cast size; no listings are annotated.

KUJOTH, JEAN SPEALMAN. *Reading Interests of Children and Young Adults.* Scarecrow, 1970. A collection of research findings and observations by teachers, authors, and librarians on reading interests and how they are influenced. Divided by age groups.

LACY, LYN ELLEN. *Art and Design in Children's Picture Books: An Analysis of Caldecott Award-Winning Illustrations.* ALA, 1986. Lacy's approach is through such elements as color, line, shape, and space; the work of each Caldecott Medalist is discussed within these parameters.

LAMME, LINDA LEONARD, and others. *Raising Readers: A Guide to Sharing Literature with Young Children.* Walker, 1980. Spirited advice for bringing books and young readers together.

LANDSBERG, MICHELE. *Reading for the Love of It: Best Books for Young Readers.* Prentice-Hall, 1987. A Canadian author incorporates discussions of individual titles into essays on types of books or book themes.

LANE, MARGARET. *The Magic Years of Beatrix Potter.* Warne, 1978. A close look at the most intensely creative period of Potter's life, before her marriage. During this time the majority of her books for Warne were published, and her talent probably reached its zenith.

LANES, SELMA G. *The Art of Maurice Sendak.* Abrams,

1980. A sumptuously illustrated, comprehensive study of the life and the work of an eminent illustrator.

_____. *Down the Rabbit Hole: Adventures and Misadventures in the Realm of Children's Literature,* ill. Atheneum, 1971. A series of essays, by an editor of children's books, exploring the literary and artistic merits of a particular selection of books. A small bibliography of choice books is appended.

LANG, ANDREW, ed. *Perrault's Popular Tales.* London: Clarendon, 1888. A careful study of Perrault and the tales he edited.

LARKIN, DAVID, ed. *The Art of Nancy Ekholm Burkert.* Harper, 1977. An exquisite volume containing color reproductions of Burkert's work from children's books as well as some previously unpublished paintings, drawings and sculptures. An interpretive essay was written by Michael Danoff.

_____, ed. *Once upon a Time: Some Contemporary Illustrators of Fantasy.* Peacock/Bantam, 1976. The work of fifteen illustrators is pictured here in brilliant color; some pages fold out. The introductory essay suggests that the artist is "emerging as a true author in tales of fantasy where every picture tells a story."

_____, ed. *Somebody Turned on a Tap in These Kids.* Delacorte, 1971. A lively collection of articles on changing the attitudes and expectations of young people toward poetry, with liberal examples of what they like and what they write themselves.

_____. *A Teacher's Guide to Children's Books,* ill. Merrill, 1960. How to stimulate and develop reading interests in the elementary grades, accompanied by extensive bibliographies for the child and the teacher.

LEACH, MARIA, and JEROME FRIED, eds. *Funk and Wagnalls Standard Dictionary of Folklore, Mythology and Legend,* 2 volumes. Funk, 1949. Working with a staff of internationally known folklorists and anthropologists, the editors have compiled an invaluable source on national folklores, characters, and symbols in folklore and mythology.

LEAR, EDWARD. *Lear in the Original: 110 Drawings for Limericks and Other Nonsense.* Kraus, 1975. Facsimile reproductions of Lear's drawings, some previously unpublished, with explanatory notes by Herman Liebert.

LEES, STELLA, ed. *A Track to Unknown Water: Proceedings of the Second Pacific Rim Conference on Children's Literature.* Scarecrow, 1987. A wide range of topics includes essays on minority group leaders, bibliotherapy, trends in contemporary literature, and collecting oral material.

LEONARD, CHARLOTTE. *Tied Together: Topics and Thoughts for Introducing Children's Books.* Scarecrow, 1980. Suggestions of more than sixty themes to use in introducing books to children, with bibliographies and lively ideas for related projects.

LEPMAN, JELLA. *A Bridge of Children's Books,* tr. by Edith McCormick. ALA, 1969. Fascinating autobiographical account of bringing books of all nations to the children of postwar Germany to replace their Nazi-oriented literature.

LEWIS, C. S. *Of Other Worlds: Essays and Stories,* ed. by Walter Hooper. Harcourt, 1966. A posthumous collection which includes essays on fantasy and science fiction, three unpublished short stories, and the first chapters of a novel.

LIEBERT, ROBERT, JOHN NEALE, and EMILY DAVIDSON. *The Early Window: Effects of Television on Children and Youth.* Pergamon, 1973. A survey of studies done on content of programs and their effects on children.

LINDSTROM, MIRIAM. *Children's Art: A Study of Normal Development in Children's Modes of Visualization,* ill. Univ. of Calif. Pr., 1970. Illustrated study of stages of development in expression of visual imagery.

The Lion and the Unicorn. An annual published under the aegis of the Modern Language Association. Each issue is devoted to one facet of children's literature.

LIVINGSTON, MYRA COHN. *When You Are Alone/It Keeps You Capone: An Approach to Creative Writing with Children.* Atheneum, 1973. An insightful discussion by a well-known children's poet.

LIVO, NORMA, and SANDRA RIETZ. *Storytelling: Process and Practice.* Libraries Unlimited, 1966. The style is heavy, but this comprehensive book on the theory and practice of storytelling is impressive in its detail and its coverage. Teachers and parents should find it useful, as well as the librarians for whom it is primarily designed.

LOWNDES, BETTY. *Movement and Creative Drama for Children.* Plays, 1971. A description of the movement and drama work carried on in an infant's school in North London with an emphasis on how both can be used to get children to communicate and to learn with enjoyment.

LUKENBILL, BERNARD, and SHARON LEE STEWART, eds. *An Interdisciplinary, Annotated Guide to North American Dissertation Research, 1930–1985.* Garland, 1988. Contains descriptive citations of over 1500 studies in diverse fields.

LUKENS, REBECCA J. *A Critical Handbook of Children's Literature.* 4th ed. Scott, Foresman, 1990. A concise text focuses on basic literary elements in the context of children's books.

LURIE, ALISON, and JUSTIN SCHILLER, eds. "Classics of Children's Literature 1621–1932," Garland. A series of photo-facsimile editions of hard-to-find books. The 117 titles include books by Bunyan, Edgeworth, Grahame, Goodrich, Lang, Molesworth, and others.

LÜTHI, MAX. *Once upon a Time: On the Nature of Fairy Tales.* Indiana Univ. Press, 1976. Uses familiar tales as examples in probing analyses of the form and content of fairy tales, their style, symbolism, and relationship to legend and primitive tales.

LYSTAD, MARY. *From Dr. Mather to Dr. Seuss: 200 Years of American Books for Children.* G. K. Hall, 1980. An exploration of social values expressed in American children's books since the colonial period. The author uses graphs to measure changes in social values and views of children, based on the sample of books evaluated.

MACCANN, DONNARAE, and OLGA RICHARD. *The Child's First Books.* Wilson, 1973. A discussion of the role of picture books in the history of children's literature.

MACCANN, DONNARAE, and GLORIA WOODWARD, eds. *The Black American in Books for Children: Readings in Racism.* 2nd ed. Scarecrow, 1985. Broad selection of brief essays; notes on contributors.

MACDONALD, MARGARET. *The Storyteller's Sourcebook: A Subject, Title and Motif Index to Folklore Collections for Children.* Gale/Neal-Schuman, 1982.

MCGLATHERY, JAMES, ed. *The Brothers Grimm and Folktales.* Univ. of Illinois Press, 1988. In essays by German and English-language scholars, this presents a sober overview of the work of the Grimms.

MCGUFFEY, WILLIAM HOLMES. *Old Favorites from the McGuffey Readers,* ed. by Harvey C. Minnich. Singing Tree, 1969. Selections from all six of the readers are of special interest to students of educational and social history.

MACLEOD, ANNE SCOTT. *A Moral Tale: Children's Fiction and American Culture 1820–1860.* Archon, 1975. Explores the concepts and the concerns of a period of rapid change as reflected in the stories for children, especially what adults expected of children and wanted for them.

MAHONY, BERTHA E., and ELINOR WHITNEY FIELD, eds. *Newbery Medal Books, 1922–1955.* Horn Book, 1955. Here in one handsome volume are brief biographies of Newbery authors along with their acceptance speeches. See also supplementary volumes by Kingman.

MAHONY, BERTHA E., LOUISE P. LATIMER, and BEULAH FOLMSBEE, comps. *Illustrators of Children's Books, 1744–1945.* Horn Book, 1947. A superb history of illustration in children's books considered as a part of the whole stream of art. Many pictures are reproduced from early books as well as from more recent ones. A major reference. See also supplementary volumes by Viguers and others and by Kingman and others.

MAHONY, BERTHA E., and ELINOR WHITNEY, comps. *Contemporary Illustrators of Children's Books.* Gale, 1978. Originally published in 1930. Includes a directory of children's illustrators with essays on trends in illustrating, as they were perceived in the first quarter of this century.

MAIER, HENRY W. *Three Theories of Child Development: The Contributions of Erik H. Erikson, Jean Piaget and Robert R. Sears, and Their Applications,* rev. ed. Harper, 1969. The expanded psychoanalytic theory of Erikson, Piaget's theories on the development of behavior, and those of Robert Sears are explicated and compared, and the last two chapters deal with how they can be used in working with children. A useful bibliography is appended.

MARTIN, DOUGLAS. *The Telling Line: Essays on Fifteen Contemporary Book Illustrations.* Dell, 1990. Based on interviews with leading British illustrators, this includes a complete chronological bibliography for each artist.

MAYERSON, CHARLOTTE LEON, ed. *Two Blocks Apart: Juan Gonzales and Peter Quinn,* ill. with photos by the Still Photography Workshop Harlem Youth Unlimited. Holt, 1965. Biographies, from tapes, of two boys in New York, living in the same neighborhood, going to the same school, sharing the same religion, one white middle class, the other Puerto Rican, members of two cultures separated by social and economic conditions.

MEACHAM, MARY. *Information Sources in Children's Literature.* Greenwood, 1978. A comprehensive guide to book selection tools, review sources, and reference aids.

MEEK, MARGARET, AIDAN WARLOW, and GRISELDA BARTON, eds. *The Cool Web: The Pattern of Children's Reading.* Atheneum, 1978. Deeply perceptive essays on the nature of the reading process, approaches to writing for children, perspectives on criticism, and suggested areas for further research.

MEIGS, CORNELIA, ANNE EATON, ELIZABETH NESBITT, and RUTH HILL VIGUERS. *A Critical History of Children's Literature,* rev. ed. Macmillan, 1969. Three librarians and an author of children's books have surveyed the field from ancient to recent times. The evaluations of books, authors, illustrators, and trends make this history a valuable reference.

MEYER, SUSAN E. *A Treasury of the Great Children's Book Illustrators.* Abrams, 1982. Replete with stunning art reproductions, this elegantly designed volume features thirteen celebrated nine-teenth- and early twentieth-century illustrators.

MILLAR, SUSANNA. *The Psychology of Play.* Penguin, 1968. Chapter V, "Phantasy, Feeling, and Make-Believe Play."

MILLER, BERTHA MAHONY, and ELINOR WHITNEY FIELD, eds. *Caldecott Medal Books: 1938–1957.* Horn Book, 1957. Stories of artists who won awards for the year's most distinguished picture book, together with their acceptance speeches. An invaluable source for schools and libraries. See also supplementary volume by Kingman.

MONSON, DIANNE, and DAYANN MCCLENATHAN, eds. *Developing Active Readers: Ideas for Parents, Teachers, and Librarians.* IRA, 1979. Each chapter considers means of developing children's responses to literature, some focusing on the experiences of preschool children and others dealing with children on through early adolescence.

MOORE, ANNE CARROLL. *My Roads to Childhood.* Doubleday, 1939. A distinguished librarian and critic of children's books comments on outstanding books up to the year 1938.

MOORE, VARDINE. *The Pleasure of Poetry with and by Children: A Handbook.* Scarecrow, 1981. A practical guide for introducing poetry to children, with examples and suggestions attuned to various age groups.

————. *Pre-School Story Hour.* 2nd ed. Scarecrow, 1972. A discussion of the techniques, programming, and physical arrangements for the story hour, and a chapter on the needs and characteristics of the preschool child is followed by a subject-oriented bibliography and a chapter on games and rhythmic play.

MOORMAN, CHARLES. *Kings & Captains: Variations on a Heroic Theme.* Univ. Press of Kentucky, 1971. A study of the classic hero tales of western civilization.

MOSS, ELAINE. *Part of the Pattern: A Personal Journal through the World of Children's Books 1960–1985.* Greenwillow, 1986. A selection of reviews, articles, lectures and interviews by an English authority on children's books includes biographical information.

MUIR, PERCY. *English Children's Books, 1600 to 1900.* Praeger, 1954, 1969. Muir acknowledges his indebtedness to the books of Darton and the Opies, but his work adds to both. There are excellent indexes and lavish illustrations from the books discussed.

MUNCH, PETER A. *Norse Mythology, Legends of Gods and Heroes,* rev. by Magnus Olsen, tr. by Sigurd B. Hustvedt. American-Scandinavian Foundation, 1926; reissued, Singing Tree, 1968. Authoritative and complete interpretation of sources.

NICHOLSEN, MARGARET. *People in Books: A Selective Guide to Biographical Literature Arranged by Vocations and Other Fields of Reader Interest.* Wilson, 1969. Appended: An index by century and by country; an index to autobiographical books; and an index of persons about whom a book or part of a collective biography is included in the main section.

NODELMAN, PERRY. *Words about Pictures: The Narrative Art of Children's Picture Books.* Univ. of Georgia Press, 1988. An investigation of the interaction of art and words in picture books focuses on that genre as a unique narrative form.

NUDELMAN, EDWARD. *Jessie Wilcox Smith: American Illustrator.* Pelican, 1990. Profusely illustrated by reproductions of the work of an artist who was an important figure in children's book illustration from the turn of the century to the Depression Era.

OPIE, IONA and PETER. *Children's Games in Street and Playground.* Oxford, 1969. This record of the games children play draws its authority from more than 10,000 children in England, Scotland, and Wales.

————, comps. *A Family Book of Nursery Rhymes,* ill. by Pauline Baynes. Oxford, 1964. In addition to the rhymes, this contains excellent notes on origins.

————. *The Lore and Language of Schoolchildren.* Oxford, 1959; Oxford paperbacks, 1967. "The curious lore passing between children about 6–14, which today holds in its spell some 7 million inhabitants" of Great Britain includes rhymes, riddles, childhood customs, and beliefs. Some can be traced back for generations and others are current.

————. *A Nursery Companion.* Oxford, 1980. Fine reproductions of early nineteenth-century booklets containing nursery rhymes and folk tales, with scholarly commentary on their history and use.

————, eds. *The Oxford Dictionary of Nursery Rhymes.* Oxford, 1951. This is the most exhaustive and scholarly study yet made of the origins of the nursery rhymes, their earliest recordings, and variations through the years. Copious illustrations from old plates add to its real interest.

The Original Mother Goose's Melody, as First Issued by John Newbery, of London, about A.D. 1760. Reproduced in facsimile from the Edition as Reprinted by Isaiah Thomas of Worcester, MA, about A.D. 1785, with introductory notes by William H. Whitmore. Singing Tree, 1969. Whitmore's introductory notes discuss the origin, development, and popularity of the Mother Goose rhymes in this reprint.

PAINTER, HELEN W. *Poetry and Children.* International

Reading Association, 1970. An explanatory guide to the use of poetry with children.

PATERSON, KATHERINE. *Gates of Excellence: On Reading and Writing Books for Children*. Elsevier/Nelson, 1981. Speeches, essays, and book reviews by a noted author give challenging insights into children's books.

PELLOWSKI, ANNE. *The Story Vine: A Source Book of Unusual and Easy-to-Tell Stories from around the World*, ill. by Lynn Sweat. Macmillan, 1984. A unique selection of stories whose telling can be accompanied by string figures, nesting dolls, and painting, and other special attention-getters.

PETERSON, LINDA, and MARILYN SOLT, comps. *Newbery and Caldecott Medal and Honor Books: An Annotated Bibliography*. G. K. Hall, 1982. Provocative analyses of plots, artistic merit, and trends of Newbery and Caldecott books.

PFLIEGER, PAT, and HELEN M. HILL, eds. *A Reference Guide to Modern Fantasy for Children*. Greenwood Press, 1984. Descriptive annotations are inter-alphabetized and entered under characters' names, series titles, places, objects, book titles, and so on. A relative index and a list of other books about fantasy are included.

Phaedrus: An International Journal of Children's Literature. Published three times a year by K. G. Saur. Articles and abstracts.

PIAGET, JEAN. *Language and Thought of the Child*, tr. by Marjorie Gabain. London: Routledge and Kegan Paul. 1932. Piaget describes his own observations of children's growth in language and thought.

PIAGET, JEAN, and BARBEL INHELDER. *The Psychology of the Child*, tr. from the French by Helen Weaver. Basic, 1969. A comprehensive summary of Piaget's child psychology, tracing the stages of cognitive development over the entire period of childhood, from infancy to adolescence.

PICKERING, SAMUEL. *John Locke and Children's Books in Eighteenth-Century England*. University of Tennessee Press, 1981. Discusses Locke's philosophy and theories of education and how they influenced others.

PITZ, HENRY C. *Howard Pyle: Writer, Illustrator, Founder of the Brandywine School*. Potter, 1975. A generously illustrated biography of Pyle, following his career as both an author and an artist.

————. *Illustrating Children's Books: History, Technique, Production*. Watson-Guptill, 1963. Detailed and authoritative, profusely illustrated, a book that is particularly useful for its lucid explanations of techniques of art reproduction and how the artist prepares his work.

Plays, the Drama Magazine for Young People. Plays, Inc., 8 Arlington Street, Boston, MA 02116. This useful magazine is published monthly. October through May. Each issue, in addition to providing plays for lower grades, middle grades, and junior and senior high, always has a special feature—a dramatized classic, a radio play, or material for an assembly.

POLETTE, NANCY. *Nancy Polette's E Is for Everybody: A Manual for Bringing Fine Picture Books into the Hands and Hearts of Children*. 2nd ed. Scarecrow, 1982. Activities in the areas of art, drama, and writing are suggested as vehicles for introducing elementary grade children to quality picture books.

————. *Picture Books for Gifted Programs*. Scarecrow, 1981. A practical discussion, augmented with selective bibliographies, of ways to use picture books with gifted youngsters from grade school to junior high.

————, and MARJORIE HAMLIN. *Exploring Books with Gifted Children*. Libraries Unlimited, 1980. An idea-filled manual suggests ways of presenting the works of Konigsburg, L'Engle, Lloyd Alexander, and others to gifted children.

POLKINGHARN, ANNE T., and CATHERINE TOOHEY. *Creative Encounters: Activities to Expand Children's Responses to Literature*, ill. by Lynn Welker. Libraries Unlimited, 1982. Creative springboard activities for stimulating children's excitement about books.

POWER, EFFIE. *Bag O'Tales: A Source Book for Story-Tellers*, ill. by Corydon Bell. Dutton, 1969. Stories for little children, folk tales, myths, and tales of heroes and chivalry, with good lists of source material for the storyteller at the end of each section.

PREISS, BYRON, ed. *The Art of Leo and Diane Dillon*. Ballantine, 1981. A knowledgeable discussion of the styles, media, and techniques used by the Dillons.

PROSTANO, EMANUEL and JOYCE. *The School Library Media Center*. 3rd ed. Libraries Unlimited, 1982. Explores the media center concept as a network serving the school curriculum.

PURVES, ALAN C., and RICHARD BEACH. *Literature and the Reader: Research in Response to Literature, Reading Interests, and the Teaching of Literature*. NCTE, 1972. Each of the three areas is treated separately, with a discussion of the factors, instruments, and quality of studies that have been made, followed by a very extensive bibliography. The citations for Reading Interests run thirty-four pages, for example. A most useful survey.

————, and DIANNE L. MONSON. *Experiencing Children's Literature*. Scott, Foresman, 1984. Aimed at introducing teachers to the world of children's literature, this handbook balances textual assessments with children's responses to the books and authors under consideration.

————, with VICTORIA RIPPERE. *Elements of Writing about a Literary Work: A Study of Response to Literature.* NCTE, 1968. A catalog of elements of literary response, classified as emotional, perception, interpretation, and evaluation responses.

————, and others. *Reading and Literature: American Achievement in International Perspective.* NCTE, 1981. Reports recent international research findings on reading speed, comprehension, word recognition, and literary understanding.

QUIMBY, HARRIET, and MARGARET MARY KIMMEL. *Building a Children's Literature Collection.* 3rd ed. Choice, 1983. *Choice* Bibliographic Essay Series, No. 7. This useful paperback consists of two parts: a suggested reference collection for academic libraries, consisting of guides and background reading for a children's literature collection, and a suggested basic collection of children's books.

RANK, OTTO. *The Myth of the Birth of the Hero: A Psychological Interpretation of Mythology,* tr. by F. Robbins and Smith Ely Jellife. Brunner/Mazel, 1952. A classic exposition of the connection between the form of myths and the unconscious emotions of the child. Studies the myths of the birth of the hero from Moses to Lohengrin, interpreting each myth in terms of the Oedipus complex.

READ, HERBERT. *This Way, Delight.* Pantheon, 1956. An excellent anthology, mentioned here because of its unusual introduction in which the author defines poetry and gives practical suggestions for writing it.

REED, ARTHEA. *Comics to Classics: A Parent's Guide to Books for Teens and Preteens.* IRA, 1988. A discussion of adolescent readers at various stages is followed by an annotated bibliography that indicates reading ranges.

REES, DAVID. *The Marble in the Water.* Horn Book, 1980. A collection of essays on contemporary writers of fiction for children and young adults, by a British critic.

————. *Painted Desert, Green Shade.* Horn Book, 1983. Thought-provoking, often iconoclastic evaluations of thirteen prominent British and American writers.

ROLLOCK, BARBARA. *Black Authors and Illustrators of Children's Books.* Garland, 1988. Brief sketches (one or two paragraphs long) discuss the work of 115 African-American writers and illustrators.

ROSELLE, DANIEL. *Samuel Griswold Goodrich, Creator of Peter Parley: A Study of His Life and Work,* ill. State Univ. of NY, 1968. The Peter Parley books, now largely forgotten, entertained children in the first half of the nineteenth century with caution-

ary tales, instructive fables, and reports of strange lands.

ROSENBACH, ABRAHAM S. W. *Early American Children's Books with Bibliographical Descriptions of the Books in His Private Collection,* foreword by A. Edward Newton. Southworth Pr., Portland, ME, 1933. Dover (paperback), 1971. Facsimile pages and illustrations (many in color) of American children's books published between 1732 and 1836. Probably the greatest and most comprehensive book on juvenile Americana.

ROSENBLATT, LOUISE M. *Literature as Exploration,* rev. ed. Noble, 1969. A probing evaluation of the nature of the literary experience.

RUDDELL, ROBERT B. *Reading Language Instruction: Innovative Practices.* Prentice, 1974. A text about reading instruction which operates from a language development base and includes instruction in language arts, including literature.

RUDMAN, MASHA KABAKOW. *Children's Literature: An Issues Approach.* 2nd ed. Longman, 1984. Issue-oriented discussions of contemporary themes in children's books, accompanied by lists of recommended titles.

————, Anna Pearce, and the editors of CONSUMER REPORT BOOKS. *For Love of Reading: A Parent's Guide to Encouraging Young Readers from Infancy through Age 5.* Consumers Union, 1988. A discussion of types of books is followed by an annotated bibliography.

ST. JOHN, JUDITH. *The Osborne Collection of Early Children's Books 1566–1910: A Catalogue,* introduction by Edgar Osborne. Toronto Public Library, 1958; volume 2, 1976. Descriptive notes on this world-famous collection, illustrated with many facsimiles. Fascinating background material for scholars and students of children's literature.

SALE, ROGER. *Fairy Tales and After: From Snow White to E. B. White.* Harvard Univ. Press, 1978. A highly personalized literary criticism, linking the development of fantasy in children's literature to fairy tales.

SARAFINO, EDWARD P., and JAMES W. ARMSTRONG. *Child and Adolescent Development.* Scott, Foresman, 1980. Good basic coverage of child and adolescent development.

SAWYER, RUTH. *My Spain: A Storyteller's Year of Collecting.* Viking, 1967. Pleasant account of a journey through Spain in search of folk tales.

————. *The Way of the Storyteller.* Viking, 1942, 1962. Informally written in Ruth Sawyer's fine style, this is a contribution both to the art of storytelling and to the history of the old tales.

SAYERS, FRANCES CLARKE. *Summoned by Books: Essays and Speeches by Frances Clarke Sayers,* comp. by Marjeanne Jenson Blinn. Viking, 1965. Essays by an outstanding, influential children's librarian.

SCHOLES, ROBERT, and ERIC S. RABKIN. *Science Fiction: History, Science, Vision.* Oxford Univ. Press, 1977. A literary history of science fiction, with analyses of predominant themes.

SCHOOL LIBRARY JOURNAL/LIBRARY JOURNAL. *Issues in Children's Book Selection.* Bowker, 1973. A broad array of provocative writings on many aspects of book selection.

SCHWAB, GUSTAV. *Gods and Heroes,* tr. by Olga Marx and Ernst Morwitz, ill. with designs from Greek vases. Pantheon, 1946. This large, handsome book is not comprehensive, and the English translation from a German adaptation is not always satisfactory, but it is an excellent source nevertheless.

SCHWARCZ, JOSEPH H. *Ways of the Illustrator: Visual Communication in Children's Literature.* ALA, 1982. An insightful yet demanding examination of the content and meaning of illustrations in children's books and their relationship to the text.

SCOTT, DOROTHEA HAYWARD. *Chinese Popular Literature and the Child.* ALA, 1980. A fine survey of Chinese literature for children, including oral and literary traditions, classic texts, and contemporary Chinese attitudes toward children.

SCOTT, JOHN ANTHONY. *The Ballad of America: The History of the United States in Song and Story.* Grosset, 1966. Chronologically arranged, with musical notation and with substantial comment on the background for each selection.

SEBESTA, SAM L., and WILLIAM J. IVERSON. *Literature for Thursday's Child.* Science Research Associates, 1975. Intended primarily for the classroom teacher, this volume intermingles descriptions of genres in children's literature with suggestions for curricular applications.

SENDAK, MAURICE. *Caldecott & Co: Notes on Books & Pictures.* Farrar, 1988. Essays (some autobiographical), interviews and speeches are thoughtful, perceptive, witty, and often funny.

SHANNON, GEORGE, comp. *Folk Literature and Children: An Annotated Bibliography of Secondary Materials.* Greenwood, 1981. An extensive listing of reference and research materials for studying criticism and scholarship pertaining to children's folklore.

SHAPIRO, JON, ed. *Using Literature & Poetry Affectively.* International Reading Association, 1979. Essays exploring children's reactions to reading, and uses of literature and poetry to stimulate their interest.

SHARP, CECIL J., comp. *English Folk-Songs from the Southern Appalachians,* ed. by Maud Karpeles, rev. and enl., 2 vols. Oxford, 1953. A major contribution by an English collector and musician.

SHAW, JOHN MACKAY. *Childhood in Poetry; A Catalogue, with Biographical and Critical Annotations, of the Books of English and American Poets Comprising the Shaw Childhood in Poetry Collection in the Library of the Florida State University, with Lists of the Poems That Relate to Childhood,* 5 vols. Gale, 1967. Although the price of this work makes it inaccessible to many individuals and small libraries, it is a comprehensive bibliographic guide to English-language children's poetry.

SHEDLOCK, MARIE. *Art of the Story-Teller,* 3rd ed., bibl. by Eulalie Steinmetz. Dover, 1951. Guidance in selection of material, techniques of storytelling, and useful bibliographies are included.

SILBERMAN, CHARLES E. *Crisis in the Classroom: The Remaking of American Education.* Random, 1970. Addressed to laymen and professionals alike, its four parts include: The Educating Society, What's Wrong with the Schools, How the Schools Should Be Changed, and The Education of Educators. A fascinating account based on a three-and-a-half-year study commissioned by the Carnegie Corporation of New York.

SIMS, RUDINE. *Shadow & Substance: Afro-American Experience in Contemporary Children's Fiction.* NCTE, 1982. One hundred and fifty children's books written between 1965 and 1975 form the basis of this intelligent assessment of children's books about African Americans.

SINGER, DOROTHY G., and TRACEY A. REVENSON. *A Piaget Primer: How a Child Thinks.* International Universities Press, Inc., 1978. A lucid clarification of Piaget's theories of child development for the beginning student in psychology, enlivened by passages from children's literature.

SMITH, IRENE. *A History of the Newbery and Caldecott Medals.* Viking, 1957. Excellent historical background material on two major annual awards for distinguished children's books in the United States.

SMITH, LILLIAN. *The Unreluctant Years.* ALA, 1953; reissued, Viking, 1967. A Canadian librarian writes discerningly of children's literature from the standpoint of literary quality only.

SMITH, RUTH, ed. *The Tree of Life,* ill. by Boris Artzybasheff. Viking, 1942. A distinguished text for a comparative study of religious ideas. It is a compilation of the "testaments of beauty and faith from many lands." Excerpts from the expressions of religious ideals of the Navaho Indians, the Norse, Hindu, Buddhist, Confucian, and other religions (including the Hebrew and Christian) make up the content of the book, which is for adolescents or for adults to use with older children.

SOLOMON, JACK and OLIVIA. *Zachary Zan: Childhood Folklore,* ill. by Mark Brewton. Univ. of Alabama Press, 1980. A compilation of folklore found in contemporary children's games and sayings.

SPACHE, GEORGE D. *Parents and the Reading Program.* Garrard, 1965. Suggestions for a program to inform parents on what is involved in teaching pupils to read; a question-and-answer format is used.

SQUIRE, JAMES, ed. *Response to Literature: Dartmouth Seminar Paper No. 6.* NCTE, 1968. Selected papers from the Dartmouth conference discuss various aspects of children's experiences with literature.

————. *The Responses of Adolescents While Reading Four Short Stories.* NCTE, 1964. A report of research which elicited and classified the responses of adolescents to short stories.

STEWART, CHRISTINA. *The Taylors of Ongar: An Analytical Bio-Bibliography,* 2 volumes. Garland, 1975. A superb source of information about the works of the prolific family that included Isaac, Jane, and Ann.

STEWIG, JOHN WARREN. *Children and Literature.* Houghton, 1988. A survey of children's books and related materials.

————. *Read to Write: Using Children's Literature as a Springboard to Writing.* Hawthorn, 1975. A description of a writing program designed to help children improve their ability by becoming conscious of the nature of the writing process.

————, and SAM L. SEBESTA, eds. *Using Literature in the Elementary Classroom.* Rev. ed. NCTE, 1989. A collection of articles discussing means that elementary teachers may use to create interest in and understanding of literature.

STIRLING, NORA. *Who Wrote the Classics?* 2 volumes, ill. Day, 1965, 1968. Short biographies of nineteen English and American writers.

STOTT, JON. *Children's Literature from A to Z: A Guide for Parents and Teachers.* McGraw, 1984. An inter-alphabetized arrangement of brief discussions of the creators of children's books and of types of books is useful for quick reference.

STREET, DOUGLAS, ed. *Children's Novels and the Movies.* Ungar, 1984. A collection of essays reflecting on cinematic adaptations of children's classics as well as contemporary favorites.

SUTCLIFF, ROSEMARY. *Blue Remembered Hills.* Morrow, 1984. A distinguished author relates the story of her childhood and young adulthood with percipience and keen wit.

SUTHERLAND, ZENA. *The Arbuthnot Lectures 1970–1979.* ALA, 1980. The first ten years of a lecture series established by Scott, Foresman, with a brief biography of Mrs. Arbuthnot.

————, ed. *Children in Libraries: Patterns of Access to Materials and Services in School and Public Libraries.* Proceedings of the forty-first conference of the Graduate Library School. Univ. of Chicago, 1981. Proceedings from a conference focusing on children's access to library materials and services.

————, and MYRA COHN LIVINGSTON, eds. *The Scott, Foresman Anthology of Children's Literature.* Scott, Foresman, 1984. This successor to *The Arbuthnot Anthology* offers a discriminating assortment of children's literature, organized by genre. A source book for children's literature classes and also a valuable treasury for use with children of all ages.

SWITZER, ELLEN, and COSTAS. *Gods, Heroes, and Monsters: Their Sources, Their Stories, and Their Meanings.* Atheneum, 1988. Designed as an introduction to the literature of Ancient Greece, this is stronger on citing or retelling stories than on analysis of meanings, but it's a good overview.

TANYZER, HAROLD, and JEAN KARL, eds. *Reading, Children's Books, and Our Pluralistic Society.* International Reading Association, 1972. An array of essays on problems of prejudice in children's books, and the difficulties of providing literature for and about minorities in America.

TARG, WILLIAM, ed. *Bibliophile in the Nursery.* World, 1969. Articles by scholars, collectors, and authors have been combined into a delightful whole, highlighting developments in children's literature and the joys of collecting. Lavishly illustrated.

TAYLOR, JUDY. *Beatrix Potter: Artist, Storyteller and Countrywoman.* Warne, 1986. An affectionate but not adulatory biography is both a tribute to Potter and an informed essay on her work. It is liberally illustrated with the subject's illustrations and with photographs.

————. *That Naughty Rabbit: Beatrix Potter and Peter Rabbit.* Warne, 1987. An intriguing record of the publishing history of Potter's first and best-known book.

Teaching Reading through Children's Literature: Proceedings of the 1971 First Annual Reading Conference, June 21–22. Curriculum Research and Developmental Center, School of Education, Indiana State University, Terre Haute. Articles include "Role Playing in Children's Literature and Its Effect upon the Affective Domain of Children's Thinking," "Teaching Reading through the Use of Films and Children's Literature," and "Reading the Pictures in Children's Books."

TERRY, ANN. *Children's Poetry Preferences: A National Survey of Upper Elementary Grades.* NCTE, 1974. Results of a survey in which students in over 500 classes participated.

THOMAS, JAMES, and RUTH LORING, eds. *Motivating Children and Young Adults to Read.* Oryx, 1980. Articles selected from a variety of journals offer practical suggestions for encouraging children and young adults to read independently; an updated companion volume of the same title was published in 1983.

THOMAS, KATHERINE ELWES. *The Real Personages of Mother Goose.* Lothrop, 1930. Scholarly research into the historical origins of the Mother Goose rhymes as political diatribes, religious philippics, and popular street songs.

THOMAS, REBECCA. *Primaryplots: A Book Talk Guide for Use with Readers Ages 4–8.* Bowker, 1989. Themes (developing a positive self-image, for example), or appeals (humor), or genre (the folktale) are the headings under which titles are given and suggestions for booktalking made.

THOMPSON, STITH. *The Folktale.* Dryden, 1946, 1977. A standard work in the field discusses the nature and forms of folk tales, traces their spread, analyzes types, describes the native-American folk tale in detail, and examines studies of folk tales.

————, comp. *One Hundred Favorite Folktales.* Indiana Univ. Pr., 1968. Tales chosen by a famous folklorist "as the result of more than a half century of almost daily familiarity with these tales." (p. xi)

THWAITE, MARY. *From Primer to Pleasure in Reading,* 2nd ed. London: The Library Assoc., 1972. A history of English children's books from the invention of printing to 1914, with some material on developments in other countries.

TOOZE, RUTH. *Storytelling.* Prentice, 1959. Extensive bibliographies add to the value of this helpful guide for storytellers.

TOWNSEND, JOHN ROWE. *A Sense of Story.* Longman, 1971. An analysis of the work of nineteen writers of children's books, American, British, and Australian, with some notes by the authors on their own writing, and short biographical notes.

————. *A Sounding of Storytellers.* Lippincott, 1979. A companion volume to *A Sense of Story,* above, overlapping but also adding new material.

————. *Written for Children: An Outline of English-Language Children's Literature.* Rev. ed. Lippincott, 1983. Two new chapters, one on older fiction and one on younger fiction, picture books, and poetry, have been added to Townsend's authoritative text on past and present children's books.

TRAVERS, PAMELA L. *About the Sleeping Beauty.* McGraw, 1975. Six versions of the story are accompanied by an essay in which it is analyzed as a part of a discussion of fairy tales.

TRELEASE, JIM. *The Read-Aloud Handbook.* Penguin, 1982. This enthusiastic presentation of good books for reading aloud is complete with extensive annotated bibliographies.

TUCKER, NICHOLAS. *The Child and the Book: A Psychological and Literary Exploration.* Cambridge Univ. Pr., 1981. With a focus on developmental aspects,

this explores the reasons some aspects of books especially appeal to children.

————, ed. *Suitable for Children? Controversies in Children's Literature.* Univ. of California Press, 1976. A selection of excerpts, historic and contemporary, addressing various issues in children's literature.

TUER, ANDREW W. *Pages and Pictures from Forgotten Children's Books: Brought Together and Introduced to the Reader,* ill. Singing Tree, 1969. The introduction offers a description of the various methods used to illustrate children's books published in England in the eighteenth and nineteenth centuries: wood blocks, copper plates, and stone lithographs.

TUROW, JOSEPH. *Getting Books to Children: An Exploration of Publisher-Market Relations.* ALA, 1978. A discussion of children's book publishing for the library and for mass markets, using a case study approach.

VANCE, LUCILLE, and ESTHER TRACEY. *Illustration Index,* 2nd ed. Scarecrow, 1966. A topical index to illustrations in periodicals such as *Life, National Geographic,* and *American Heritage,* ranging from abacus to Zurich.

VANDERGRIFT, KAY E. *Child and Story: The Literary Connection.* Neal-Schuman, 1981. Intelligent and comprehensive, this explores the influence of literary and design factors on the relationship between child and story.

VIGUERS, RUTH HILL, MARCIA DALPHIN, and BERTHA MAHONY MILLER, comps. *Illustrators of Children's Books, 1946–1956.* Horn Book, 1958. An outstanding supplement to *Illustrators of Children's Books, 1744–1945.* Includes art trends, artists' biographies, and a wealth of illustrations from modern children's books.

WAGGONER, DIANA. *The Hills of Faraway: A Guide to Fantasy.* Atheneum, 1978. Types of literary fantasy are analyzed and compared in this imaginative exposition, which includes annotated book lists of fantastic literature.

WAGNER, JOSEPH A. *Children's Literature through Storytelling.* Brown, 1970. Includes suggestions for preparing and using visual aids and puppets as well as guidelines for telling stories.

WARD, MARTHA E., and DOROTHY A. MARQUARDT. *Authors of Books for Young People.* 2nd ed. Scarecrow, 1971. Biographical sketches of authors.

————. *Illustrators of Books for Young People.* Scarecrow, 1970. Biographical information about 370 illustrators of books for children.

WARD, WINIFRED. *Playmaking with Children from Kindergarten through Junior High School.* 2nd ed. Prentice, 1957. Procedures and suggested materials for developing extemporaneous drama.

WEISS, HARRY B. *A Book about Chapbooks: The People's*

Literature of Bygone Times, ill. Singing Tree, 1969. A history of chapbooks, their printers, authors, and salesmen, with reproductions of woodcuts and title pages.

WELSH, CHARLES. *A Bookseller of the Last Century, Being Some Account of the Life of John Newbery, and of the Books He Published with a Notice of the Later Newberys.* London: Griffith, Farran, 1885; reissued, Singing Tree, 1969. A readable history of Newbery, his famous bookshop, and his varied activities.

WHALLEY, JOYCE. *Cobwebs to Catch Flies: Illustrated Books for the Nursery and Schoolroom, 1700–1900.* Univ. of Calif. Pr., 1975. Profusely illustrated, a text that focuses on instructional works.

WHALLEY, JOYCE, and TESSA CHESTER. *The Bright Stream: A History of Children's Book Illustration.* Godline, 1990. Produced in collaboration with John Murray of the Victoria and Albert Museum, this lively history is international in scope, British in emphasis, and profusely illustrated.

WHITE, DOROTHY. *Books before Five,* ill. by Joan Smith. Oxford, 1954. A New Zealand children's librarian's study of her two-year-old daughter's progression in the experience of books over three years, ranging over more than 100 books, from Adams's *First Things* to Tolkien's *The Hobbit.*

WHITE, GABRIEL. *Edward Ardizzone: Artist and Illustrator.* Schocken, 1980. An artistic analysis and biography of a prolific illustrator.

WILKIN, BINNIE TATE. *Survival Themes in Fiction for Children and Young People.* Scarecrow, 1978. Not only life-and-death themes, but also loneliness, fear, and related subjects are presented; an analysis of each topic is supplemented by annotated book lists.

WILSON, BARBARA KER. *Writing for Children: An English Editor and Author's Point of View.* Watts, 1960. Sound comment on writing fiction, nonfiction, and picture books.

WINN, MARIE. *Children without Childhood.* Pantheon, 1983. A clear-thinking investigation of changes in contemporary society that have produced what Winn calls the "unchildlike child."

————. *The Plug-In Drug: Television, Children and the Family.* Viking, 1977. Examines the effects of television-watching on children and their family relationships.

WINTLE, JUSTIN, and EMMA FISHER. *The Pied Pipers.* Paddington, 1975. Interviews in question-and-answer format with American and British writers of children's books.

WITUCKE, VIRGINIA. *Poetry in the Elementary School.* Brown, 1970. An illuminating treatment of strategies for generating interest in poetry, with gener-

ous references and unhackneyed selections of examples, including audiovisual materials.

WYNDHAM, LEE, and ARNOLD MADISON. *Writing for Children and Teen-Agers,* rev. ed. Writer's Digest, 1980. Practical, detailed advice presented in a lively style and covering all phases of writing children's books, marketing them, and seeing them through publication.

Yale French Studies: The Child's Part. Yale Univ. Pr., 1969. A collection of essays exploring children's literature as a vast subspecies, attention to which can illuminate culture, society, literature itself.

YARDLEY, ALICE. *Young Children Thinking.* Citation, 1973. A British educator discusses the mental development of young children, giving suggestions for adding intellectual dimensions to the child's education.

YOLEN, JANE. *Writing Books for Children,* rev. ed. The Writer, 1983. Discusses genres and the children's book market as well as the literary, financial, and legal aspects of writing books.

ZINSSER, WILLIAM, ed. *Worlds of Childhood: The Art and the Craft of Writing for Children.* Essays by Jean Fritz, Jill Krementz, Katherine Paterson, Jack Prelutsky, Maurice Sendak, and Rosemary Wells. Houghton, 1990.

ZIPES, JACK, trans. *Beauties, Beasts and Enchantment: Classical French Fairy Tales.* New American Library, 1989. Prefatory notes and notes on authors add scholarly interest to the stories in an anthology translated in the serious and often elaborate styles of their original versions.

————. *Breaking the Magic Spell: Radical Theories of Folk and Fairy Tales.* Univ. of Texas Pr., 1979. An examination of the sociohistorical forces that influenced the transition from oral folk tales to the literary fairy tale, with a discussion of contemporary theories about both.

————. *The Brothers Grimm: From Enchanted Forests to the Modern World.* Routledge, 1988. A critical study of the work of the Grimms and of the importance of the fairy tale in Germany.

————. *Don't Bet on the Prince: Contemporary Feminist Fairy Tales in North America and England.* Methuen, 1986. In part an anthology, with stories that are for children as well as adults, this text has a scholarly introduction and concludes with a section of essays entitled "Feminist Literary Criticism."

————. *Fairy Tales and the Art of Subversion: The Classical Genre for Children and the Process of Civilization.* London: Heinemann, 1983. A study of the historical development of the fairy tale as a genre and of influences upon it.

Appendix C

Publishers and Their Addresses

ABINGDON. Abingdon Press, 201 Eighth Ave. S., Nashville, TN 37202

ABRAMS. Harry N. Abrams, Inc., 100 Fifth Ave., New York, NY 10011

ACEI. Assoc. for Childhood Education International, 1141 Georgia Ave., Wheaton, MD 20902

ADDISON. Addison-Wesley Pub. Co., Inc., Reading, MA 01867

AFRICANA. Africana Publishing Co., 30 Irving Place, New York, NY 10003

AGATHON. Agathon Press, Inc., 111 Eighth Ave., New York, NY 10011

ALA. American Library Association Pub. Dept., 50 E. Huron St., Chicago, IL 60611

ALADDIN. Aladdin Books. See Macmillan Pub. Co., Inc.

ALDINE. Aldine Pub. Co., 200 Saw Mill River Rd., Hawthorne, NY 10532

ALINDA. Alinda Press, Box 553, Eureka, CA 95502

ALLYN. Allyn & Bacon, Inc., 7 Wells Avenue, Newton, MA 02159

AM. ASSOC. FOR THE ADVANCEMENT OF SCIENCE. 1515 Massachusetts Ave., NW, Washington, DC 20005

AMERICAN COUNCIL ON EDUCATION. One Dupont Circle, NW, Washington, DC 20036

APPLETON. Appleton-Century-Crofts, 25 Van Zant St., East Norwalk, CT 06855

ATHENEUM. Atheneum Publishers. See Macmillan Pub. Co., Inc.

ATHERTON. Lieber-Atherton, Inc., 389 West End Ave., New York, NY 10024

ATLANTIC. Atlantic Monthly Press. See Little, Brown & Co.

AVENEL. See Crown Pub., Inc.

AVON. Avon Books, 105 Madison Ave., New York, NY 10016

BALLANTINE. Ballantine Books, Inc., 201 E. 50th St., New York, NY 10022

BANTAM. Bantam Doubleday Dell Publishing Group, Inc., 666 Fifth Avenue, New York, NY 10103

BARNES. Barnes & Noble Books, 10 E. 53rd St., New York, NY 10022

BASIC. Basic Books, Inc., 10 E. 53rd St., New York, NY 10022

BEHRMAN. Behrman House, Inc., 1261 Broadway, New York, NY 10001

BELKNAP. Belknap Press. See Harvard University Press

BLACK BUTTERFLY. Black Butterfly Children's Books. Box 461, Village Station, New York, NY 10014

BOBBS. Bobbs-Merrill Co., Inc. See Macmillan Pub. Co., Inc.

BOWKER. R. R. Bowker Co., 245 W. 17th St., New York, NY 10011

BRADBURY. Bradbury Press, Inc. See Macmillan Pub. Co., Inc.

BRODART. Brodart Books, 500 Arch St., Williamsport, PA 17705

BROOKLINE. Brookline Books, 460 Broadway, Cambridge, MA 02238

BROWN. William C. Brown Group, 2460 Kerper Blvd., Dubuque, IA 52001

BURGESS. Burgess Pub. Co., 7108 Ohms Lane, Minneapolis, MN 55435

CAMBRIDGE UNIV. PRESS, 32 E. 57th St., New York, NY 10022

CAPE. Jonathan Cape. See Merrimack Publishers' Circle

CAROLRHODA. Carolrhoda Books, Inc., 241 First Ave., N., Minneapolis, MN 55401

CELESTIAL. Celestial Arts, Box 7327, Berkeley, CA 94707

CHATHAM. The Chatham Press. See Devin-Adair Co., Inc.

CHELSEA. Chelsea House Pub. Co., 432 Park Ave., S., New York, NY 10016

CHILDREN'S BOOK COUNCIL, INC., 568 Broadway, New York, NY 10012

CHILDREN'S PRESS, INC., 5440 N. Cumberland Ave., Chicago, IL 60656

CHILTON. Chilton Book Co., Chilton Way, Radnor, PA 19089

CITATION. See Scholastic, Inc.

CLARION. Clarion Books, 215 Park Ave., S., New York, NY 10003

COLLIER. Collier-Macmillan, Inc. See Macmillan Pub. Co., Inc.

CONTEMPORARY. Contemporary Books, Inc., 180 N. Michigan Avenue, Chicago, IL 60601

COPP CLARK. Copp Clark Pitman, 495 Wellington St. W., Toronto, Ont. M5V 1E9, Canada

COWARD. Coward, McCann & Geoghegan. See The

Putnam Publishing Group

CREATIVE EDUCATION, INC., P.O. Box 227, Mankato, MN 56002

CRITERION. Criterion Books, Inc. See Harper & Row

CROWELL. Thomas Y. Crowell Co. See Harper & Row

CROWN. Crown Publishers, Inc., 225 Park Ave., S., New York, NY 10003

DAY. The John Day Co. See Harper & Row

DELACORTE. Delacorte Press, 666 Fifth Ave., New York, NY 10103

DELL. Dell Publishing Co., Inc. See Delacorte Press

DEVIN. Devin-Adair Co., Inc., 143 Sound Beach Ave., Old Greenwich, CT 06870

DIAL. Dial Books. See E. P. Dutton, Inc.

DILLON. Dillon Press, Inc., 242 Portland Ave., S., Minneapolis, MN 55415

DODD. Dodd, Mead & Co., 79 Madison Ave., New York, NY 10016

DOUBLEDAY. Doubleday & Co., Inc. See Delacorte Press

DOVER. Dover Publications, Inc., 31 E. Second St., Mineola, NY 11501

DUFOUR. Dufour Editions, Inc., Box 449, Chester Springs, PA 19425

DUTTON. Children's Books Dutton, Inc., 375 Hudson St., New York, NY 10014

EERDMANS. William B. Eerdmans Pub. Co., 225 Jefferson Ave. SE, Grand Rapids, MI 49503

ELSEVIER. Elsevier/Nelson Pub. Co., Inc., 52 Vanderbilt Ave., New York, NY 10017

ENSLOW. Enslow Publishers, Bloy St. & Ramsey Ave., Box 777, Hillside, NJ 07205

EVANS. M. Evans & Co., Inc., 216 E. 49th St., New York, NY 10017

FABER. Faber & Faber. See Harper & Row

FARRAR. Farrar, Straus & Giroux, Inc., 19 Union Square West, New York, NY 10003

FAXON. The Faxon Co., Inc., 15 Southwest Park, Westwood, MA 02090

FEMINIST. The Feminist Press, Box 334, Old Westbury, NY 11568

FOUR WINDS. Four Winds Press. See Macmillan Pub. Co., Inc.

FUNK. Funk & Wagnalls, Inc., 53 E. 77th St., New York, NY 10021

GALE. Gale Research Co., Book Tower, Detroit, MI 48226

GALLAUDET. Gallaudet University Press, 800 Florida Ave., N.E., Washington, DC 20002

GARLAND. Garland Publishing, Inc., 136 Madison Ave., New York, NY 10016

GARRARD. Garrard Pub. Co., 1607 N. Market St., Champaign, IL 61820

GODINE. David R. Godine Pub., Inc., 300 Massachusetts Ave., Boston, MA 02115

GOLDEN BOOKS. 850 Third Ave., New York, NY 10022

GREEN OAK. Green Oak Press, 9339 Spicer Rd., Brighton, MI 48116

GREEN TIGER. Green Tiger Press, 1061 India St., San Diego, CA 92101

GREENWILLOW. Greenwillow Books. See William Morrow & Co., Inc.

GREENWOOD. Greenwood Press, Box 5007, 88 Post Rd. W., Westport, CT 01890

GROSSET. Grosset & Dunlap, Inc. See the Putnam & Grosset Book Group

GRUNE. Grune & Stratton, Inc., 6277 Sea Harbor Dr., Orlando, FL 32887

GULLIVER. Gulliver Books. See Harcourt Brace Jovanovich, Inc.

HALL. G. K. Hall & Co., 70 Lincoln St., Boston, MA 02111

HARCOURT. Harcourt Brace Jovanovich, Inc., 1250 Sixth Avenue, San Diego, CA 92101

HARPERCOLLINS. Harper Junior Books Group, 10 E. 53rd St., New York, NY 10022

HARVARD. Harvard University Press, 79 Garden St., Cambridge, MA 02138

HASTINGS. Hastings House Pub., Inc., 10 E. 40th St., New York, NY 10016

HAWORTH. Haworth Press, 28 E. 22nd St., New York, NY 10010

HAWTHORN. See E. P. Dutton, Inc.

HEINEMANN. Heinemann Educational Books, 70 Court St., Portsmouth, NH 03801

HILL. Lawrence Hill and Co., Pubs., Inc., 520 Riverside Ave., Westport, CT 06880

HILL & WANG. See Farrar, Straus & Giroux

HOLIDAY. Holiday House, Inc., 425 Madison Ave., New York, NY 10017

HOLT. Henry Holt and Company, Inc., 115 W. 18th St., New York, NY 10011

HORN BOOK. The Horn Book, Inc., 14 Beacon St., Boston, MA 02108

HOUGHTON. Houghton Mifflin Co., One Park St., Boston, MA 02108

HUMANITIES. Humanities Press, Inc., 171 First Ave., Atlantic Highlands, NJ 07716

INDIANA UNIVERSITY PRESS, Tenth and Morton Sts., Bloomington, IN 47405

IRA. International Reading Association, 800 Barksdale Rd., Newark, DE 19714

JALMAR. Jalmar Press, Inc., 45 Hitching Post Dr., Bldg. 2, Rolling Hills Estates, CA 90274

KESTREL. Kestrel Books. See Viking Penguin

KNOPF. Alfred A. Knopf, Inc. See Random House, Inc.

LAWRENCE. Seymour Lawrence, Inc., 2 Lexington Avenue, New York, NY 10010

LERNER. Lerner Publications Co., 241 First Ave., N., Minneapolis, MN 55401

LEXINGTON. Lexington Books, 125 Spring St., Lexington, MA 02173

LIBRARIES. Libraries Unlimited, Inc., Box 263, Littleton, CO 80160

LIBRARY OF CONGRESS, Supt. of Documents, U.S. Government Printing Office, Washington, DC 20402

LIPPINCOTT. See Harper & Row Publishers

LITTLE. Little, Brown & Co., 34 Beacon St., Boston, MA 02106

LIVERIGHT. Liveright Books. See W. W. Norton & Co., Inc.

LODESTAR. See Children's Books Dutton, Inc.

LONGMAN. Longman Trade, 500 N. Dearborn St., Chicago, IL 60610

LOTHROP. Lothrop, Lee & Shepard Co. See William Morrow & Co., Inc.

MCDOUGAL. McDougal, Littell & Co., P.O. Box 1667, Evanston, IL 60204

MCELDERRY. Margaret K. McElderry Books. See Macmillan Pub. Co., Inc.

MCFARLAND. McFarland & Co., Inc., Box 611, Jefferson, NC 28640

MCGRAW. McGraw-Hill, Inc., 1221 Avenue of the Americas, New York, NY 10020

MCKAY. David McKay Co., Inc., 2 Park Ave., New York, NY 10016

MACMILLAN. Macmillan Pub. Co., Inc., 866 Third Ave., New York, NY 10022

MERRILL. Charles E. Merrill Pub. Co., P.O. Box 508, Westerville, OH 43216

MERRIMACK. Merrimack Publishers Circle, 47 Pelham Road, Salem, NH 03079

MESSNER. Julian Messner. 190 Sylvan Ave., Englewood Cliffs, NJ 07632

METHUEN. Methuen, Inc., 733 Third Ave., New York, NY 10017

MORROW. William Morrow & Co., Inc., 105 Madison Ave., New York, NY 10016

NAL. New American Library, Inc., 1633 Broadway, New York, NY 10019

NAT. COUNCIL FOR THE SOCIAL STUDIES, 3501 Newark St., NW, Washington, DC 20016

NAT. COUNCIL OF TEACHERS OF ENGLISH, 1111 Kenyon Rd., Urbana, IL 61801

NATURAL HISTORY PRESS, American Museum of Natural History, Central Park W. at 79th St., New York, NY 10024

NEA. National Education Association, 1201 16th St., NW, Washington, DC 20036

NEAL. Neal-Schuman, 23 Cornelia St., New York, NY 10014

NELSON. Thomas Nelson, Inc., Nelson Pl. at Elm Hill Pike, Nashville, TN 37214

NEW YORK PUBLIC LIBRARY, Fifth Ave. and 42nd St., New York, NY 10018

NOBLE. Bowmar/Noble Pubs., 4563 Colorado Blvd., Los Angeles, CA 90039

NORTON. W. W. Norton & Co., Inc., 500 Fifth Ave., New York, NY 10010

ODYSSEY. See Bobbs-Merrill Co., Inc.

OPEN COURT. Open Court Publishing Co., 315 Fifth St., Peru, IL 61354

ORCHARD. Orchard Books. See Franklin Watts, Inc.

ORYX. The Oryx Press, 2214 N. Central Avenue, Phoenix, AZ 85004

OXFORD. Oxford Univ. Press Inc., 200 Madison Ave., New York, NY 10016

PANTHEON. Pantheon Books. See Random House, Inc.

PARENTS. Parents Magazine Press, 685 Third Ave., New York, NY 10017

PARNASSUS. Parnassus Press. See Houghton Mifflin Co.

PENGUIN. Penguin Books. See Viking/Penguin

PERGAMON. Pergamon Press, Inc., Maxwell House, Fairview Park, Elmsford, NY 10523

PHILLIPS. S. G. Phillips, Inc., P.O. Box 83, Chatham, NY 12037

PHILOMEL. Philomel Books. See Putnam & Grosset Group

PICTURE BOOK STUDIO. 10 Central St., Saxonville, MA 01701

PLATT. Platt & Munk, Inc., 51 Madison Ave., New York, NY 10010

PLAYS. Plays, Inc., Publishers, 120 Boylston St., Boston, MA 02116

POTTER. Clarkson N. Potter, Inc. See Crown Pubs., Inc.

PRAEGER. Praeger Publishers, 521 Fifth Ave., New York, NY 10175

PRENTICE. Prentice-Hall, Inc. See Simon & Schuster, Inc.

PRINCETON. Princeton University Press, 41 Williams St., Princeton, NJ 08540

PROMETHEUS. Prometheus Books, 700 E. Amherst St., Buffalo, NY 14215

PUTNAM. The Putnam & Grosset Book Group, 200 Madison Ave., New York, NY 10016

RAINTREE. Raintree Publishers, Inc., 310 W. Wisconsin Ave., Milwaukee, WI 53203

RAND. Rand, McNally & Co., 8255 Central Park Ave., Skokie, IL 60076

RANDOM. Random House, Inc., 225 Park Ave., S., New York, NY 10003

REGNERY. Regnery Gateway, Inc., 940 N. Shore Dr., Lake Bluff, IL 60044

REVELL. Fleming H. Revell Co., 184 Central Ave.,

Old Tappan, NJ 07675

ROUTLEDGE & KEGAN PAUL, INC., 9 Park St., Boston, MA 02108

ST. MARTIN'S. St. Martin's Press, Inc., 175 Fifth Ave., New York, NY 10010

SAUR. K. G. Saur, Inc., 175 Fifth Ave., New York, NY 10010

SCARECROW. The Scarecrow Press, 52 Liberty St., Metuchen, NJ 08840

SRA. Science Research Associates, Inc., 155 N. Wacker Dr., Chicago, IL 60606

SCHOCKEN. Schocken Books, Inc., 200 Madison Ave., New York, NY 10016

SCHOLASTIC. Scholastic, Inc., 730 Broadway, New York, NY 10003

SCOTT, FORESMAN. Scott, Foresman & Co., 1900 East Lake Avenue, Glenview, IL 60025

SCRIBNER'S. Charles Scribner's Sons. See Macmillan Pub. Co., Inc.

SEABURY. The Seabury Press, Inc. See Winston Press

SHOE STRING. The Shoe String Press, Inc., 995 Sherman Ave., Hamden, CT 06514

SILVER. Silver Burdett Press, Inc., 190 Sylvan Ave., Englewood Cliffs, NJ 07632

SIMON. Simon & Schuster, Inc., 1230 Avenue of the Americas, New York, NY 10020

SINGING TREE. See Gale Research Co.

SMITHSONIAN INST. PRESS, 955 L'Enfant Plaza, Washington, DC 20560

SOUTHERN. Southern Illinois University Press, Box 3697, Carbondale, IL 62901

SOVEREIGN. Sovereign Press, 326 Harris Rd., Rochester, WA 98579

STANFORD. Stanford University Press, Stanford, CA 94305

STEMMER. Stemmer House Publishers, Inc., 2627 Caves Rd., Owing Mills, MD 21117

STERLING. Sterling Pub. Co., Inc., 2 Park Ave., New York, NY 10016

TAPLINGER. Taplinger Pub. Co., Inc., 132 W. 22nd St., New York, NY 10011

TEACHERS. Teachers College Press, Columbia Univ., 1234 Amsterdam Ave., New York, NY 10027

TIME, INC. Time-Life Books, Inc., c/o Silver-Burdett, Box 1226, Westwood, NJ 07675

TROLL. Troll Associates, 100 Corporate Dr., Mahwah, NJ 07430

TUNDRA. Tundra Books, 1434 Ste-Catherine St., W., #303, Montreal, Quebec H3G IR4 Canada

TUTTLE. Charles E. Tuttle Co., Inc., 28 S. Main St., Rutland, VT 05701

UNGAR. Frederick Ungar Pub. Co., Inc., 36 Cooper Square, New York, NY 10013

UNIVERSITY. University Press, 21 East St., Winchester, MA 01890

UNIV. OF ALABAMA PRESS, Box 2877, University, AL 35486

UNIV. OF CALIFORNIA PRESS, 2120 Berkeley Way, Berkeley, CA 94720

UNIV. OF CHICAGO PRESS, 5801 S. Ellis Ave., Chicago, IL 60637

UNIV. OF PENNSYLVANIA PRESS, 3933 Walnut St., Philadelphia, PA 19104

UNIV. OF TENNESSEE PRESS, Knoxville, TN 37996

UNIV. OF TEXAS PRESS, Box 7819, Austin, TX 78712

UNIV. OF TORONTO PRESS, St. George Campus, Toronto, ON M5S 1A6 Canada

VANGUARD. Vanguard Press, Inc., 424 Madison Ave., New York, NY 10017

VAN NOSTRAND. Van Nostrand Reinhold Co., 135 W. 50th St., New York, NY 10020

VIKING. Viking Penguin, Inc., 375 Hudson St., New York, NY 10014

WALKER. Walker & Co., 720 Fifth Ave., New York, NY 10019

WARNE. Frederick Warne & Co., Inc., 375 Hudson St., New York, NY 10014

WARWICK. Warwick/Watts. See Franklin Watts, Inc.

WATTS. Franklin Watts, Inc., 387 Park Ave., S., New York, NY 10016

WESTERN. Western Pub. Co., Inc., 1220 Mound Ave., Racine, WI 53404

WESTERN RESERVE PRESS, 3530 Warrensville Ctr. Rd., Cleveland, OH 44122

WESTMINSTER. The Westminster Press, 925 Chestnut St., Philadelphia, PA 19107

WHITE. David White, Inc., One Pleasant Ave., Port Washington, NY 11050

WHITMAN. Albert Whitman & Co., 5747 W. Howard St., Niles, IL 60648

WILSON. H. W. Wilson Co., 950 University Ave., Bronx, NY 10452

WINDMILL. Windmill Books, Inc. See Simon & Schuster

WINSTON. Winston Press. See CBS Educational Publishing

YALE UNIV. PRESS, 302 Temple St., New Haven, CT 06520

Appendix D
Children's Book Awards

The awards and prizes given in the children's book field by organizations, schools, publishers, and newspapers, in the United States and other countries, have grown to a sizable number. The Newbery and Caldecott Medals, given annually, are the best-known United States awards, and the Hans Christian Andersen Medal, given biennially, the best-known international award. The International Reading Association Children's Book Award is the only award that singles out new authors. The National Council of Teachers of English Award for Excellence in Poetry for Children is the first children's book award given solely for poetry. The Laura Ingalls Wilder Award is given every three years in honor of Wilder. The Carnegie and Kate Greenaway Medals are major British awards for children's books, and the Canadian Library Awards are the most significant given in Canada. In most cases, the awards are given for books published during the preceding year. Following are brief histories of these awards and listings of the winners and runners-up.

The Newbery Medal

Frederic G. Melcher, editor of *Publisher's Weekly Magazine*, donated and named this award as a tribute to John Newbery (1713–1767), the first English publisher of books for children. Beginning in 1922 and every year since, the Newbery Medal has been given by an awards committee of the Children's Services Division of the American Library Association to the author of the most distinguished contribution to literature for children published in the United States during the preceding year. The author must be a citizen or resident of the United States.

1922 *The Story of Mankind* by Hendrik Willem van Loon, Liveright
Honor Books: *The Great Quest* by Charles Hawes, Little; *Cedric the Forester* by Bernard Marshall, Appleton; *The Old Tobacco Shop* by William Bowen, Macmillan; *The Golden Fleece and the Heroes Who Lived before Achilles* by Padraic Colum, Macmillan; *Windy Hill* by Cornelia Meigs, Macmillan

1923 *The Voyages of Doctor Dolittle* by Hugh Lofting, Lippincott

Honor Books: No record

1924 *The Dark Frigate* by Charles Hawes, Atlantic/Little
Honor Books: No record

1925 *Tales from Silver Lands* by Charles Finger, Doubleday
Honor Books: *Nicholas* by Anne Carroll Moore, Putnam; *Dream Coach* by Anne Parrish, Macmillan

1926 *Shen of the Sea* by Arthur Bowie Chrisman, Dutton
Honor Book: *Voyagers* by Padraic Colum, Macmillan

1927 *Smoky, the Cowhorse* by Will James, Scribner's
Honor Books: No record

1928 *Gayneck, The Story of a Pigeon* by Dhan Gopal Mukerji, Dutton
Honor Books: *The Wonder Smith and His Son* by Ella Young, Longmans; *Downright Dencey* by Caroline Snedeker, Doubleday

1929 *The Trumpeter of Krakow* by Eric P. Kelly, Macmillan
Honor Books: *Pigtail of Ah Lee Ben Loo* by John Bennett, Longmans; *Millions of Cats* by Wanda Gág, Coward; *The Boy Who Was* by Grace Hallock, Dutton; *Clearing Weather* by Cornelia Meigs, Little; *Runaway Papoose* by Grace Moon, Doubleday; *Tod of the Fens* by Elinor Whitney, Macmillan

1930 *Hitty, Her First Hundred Years* by Rachel Field, Macmillan
Honor Books: *Daughter of the Seine* by Jeanette Eaton, Harper; *Pran of Albania* by Elizabeth Miller, Doubleday; *Jumping-Off Place* by Marian Hurd McNeely, Longmans; *Tangle-Coated Horse and Other Tales* by Ella Young, Longmans; *Vaino* by Julia Davis Adams, Dutton; *Little Blacknose* by Hildegarde Swift, Harcourt

1931 *The Cat Who Went to Heaven* by Elizabeth Coatsworth, Macmillan
Honor Books: *Floating Island* by Anne Parrish, Harper; *The Dark Star of Itza* by Alida Malkus, Harcourt; *Queer Person* by Ralph Hubbard, Doubleday; *Mountains Are Free* by Julia Davis Adams, Dutton; *Spice and the Devil's Cave* by Agnes Hewes, Knopf; *Meggy Macintosh* by

Elizabeth Janet Gray, Doubleday; *Garram the Hunter* by Herbert Best, Doubleday; *Ood-Le-Uk the Wanderer* by Alice Lide and Margaret Johansen, Little

1932 *Waterless Mountain* by Laura Adams Armer, Longmans
Honor Books: *The Fairy Circus* by Dorothy P. Lathrop, Macmillan; *Calico Bush* by Rachel Field, Macmillan; *Boy of the South Seas* by Eunice Tietjens, Coward; *Out of the Flame* by Eloise Lownsbery, Longmans; *Jane's Island* by Marjorie Allee, Houghton; *Truce of the Wolf and Other Tales of Old Italy* by Mary Gould Davis, Harcourt.

1933 *Young Fu of the Upper Yangtze* by Elizabeth Foreman Lewis, Winston
Honor Books: *Swift Rivers* by Cornelia Meigs, Little; *The Railroad to Freedom* by Hildegarde Swift, Harcourt; *Children of the Soil* by Nora Burglon, Doubleday

1934 *Invincible Louisa* by Cornelia Meigs, Little
Honor Books: *The Forgotten Daughter* by Caroline Snedeker, Doubleday; *Swords of Steel* by Elsie Singmaster, Houghton; *ABC Bunny* by Wanda Gág, Coward; *Winged Girl of Knossos* by Erik Berry, Appleton; *New Land* by Sarah Schmidt, McBride; *Big Tree of Bunlahy* by Padraic Colum, Macmillan; *Glory of the Seas* by Agnes Hewes, Knopf; *Apprentice of Florence* by Anne Kyle, Houghton

1935 *Dobry* by Monica Shannon, Viking
Honor Books: *Pageant of Chinese History* by Elizabeth Seeger, Longmans; *Davy Crockett* by Constance Rourke, Harcourt; *Day on Skates* by Hilda Van Stockum, Harper

1936 *Caddie Woodlawn* by Carol Brink, Macmillan
Honor Books: *Honk, The Moose* by Phil Stong, Dodd; *The Good Master* by Kate Seredy, Viking; *Young Walter Scott* by Elizabeth Janet Gray, Viking; *All Sail Set* by Armstrong Sperry, Winston

1937 *Roller Skates* by Ruth Sawyer, Viking
Honor Books: *Phebe Fairchild: Her Book* by Lois Lenski, Stokes; *Whistler's Van* by Idwal Jones, Viking; *Golden Basket* by Ludwig Bemelmans, Viking; *Winterbound* by Margery Bianco, Viking; *Audubon* by Constance Rourke, Harcourt; *The Codfish Musket* by Agnes Hewes, Doubleday

1938 *The White Stag* by Kate Seredy, Viking
Honor Books: *Pecos Bill* by James Cloyd Bowman, Little; *Bright Island* by Mabel Robinson, Random; *On the Banks of Plum Creek* by Laura Ingalls Wilder, Harper

1939 *Thimble Summer* by Elizabeth Enright, Rinehart
Honor Books: *Nino* by Valenti Angelo, Viking; *Mr. Popper's Penguins* by Richard and Florence Atwater, Little; *"Hello the Boat!"* by Phyllis Crawford, Holt; *Leader by Destiny: George Washington, Man and Patriot* by Jeanette Eaton, Harcourt; *Penn* by Elizabeth Janet Gray, Viking

1940 *Daniel Boone* by James Daugherty, Viking
Honor Books: *The Singing Tree* by Kate Seredy, Viking; *Runner of the Mountain Tops* by Mabel Robinson, Random; *By the Shores of Silver Lake* by Laura Ingalls Wilder, Harper; *Boy with a Pack* by Stephen W. Meader, Harcourt

1941 *Call It Courage* by Armstrong Sperry, Macmillan
Honor Books: *Blue Willow* by Doris Gates, Viking; *Young Mac of Fort Vancouver* by Mary Jane Carr, T. Crowell; *The Long Winter* by Laura Ingalls Wilder, Harper; *Nansen* by Anna Gertrude Hall, Viking

1942 *The Matchlock Gun* by Walter D. Edmonds, Dodd
Honor Books: *Little Town on the Prairie* by Laura Ingalls Wilder, Harper; *George Washington's World* by Genevieve Foster, Scribner's; *Indian Captive: The Story of Mary Jemison* by Lois Lenski, Lippincott; *Down Ryton Water* by Eva Roe Gaggin, Viking

1943 *Adam of the Road* by Elizabeth Janet Gray, Viking
Honor Books: *The Middle Moffat* by Eleanor Estes, Harcourt; *Have You Seen Tom Thumb?* by Mabel Leigh Hunt, Lippincott

1944 *Johnny Tremain* by Esther Forbes, Houghton
Honor Books: *These Happy Golden Years* by Laura Ingalls Wilder, Harper; *Fog Magic* by Julia Sauer, Viking; *Rufus M.* by Eleanor Estes, Harcourt; *Mountain Born* by Elizabeth Yates, Coward

1945 *Rabbit Hill* by Robert Lawson, Viking
Honor Books: *The Hundred Dresses* by Eleanor Estes, Harcourt; *The Silver Pencil* by Alice Dalgliesh, Scribner's; *Abraham Lincoln's World* by Genevieve Foster, Scribner's; *Lone Journey: The Life of Roger Williams* by Jeanette Eaton, Harcourt

1946 *Strawberry Girl* by Lois Lenski, Lippincott
Honor Books: *Justin Morgan Had a Horse* by Marguerite Henry, Rand; *The Moved-Outers* by Florence Crannell Means, Houghton; *Bhimsa, The Dancing Bear* by Christine Weston, Scribner's; *New Found World* by Katherine Shippen, Viking

1947 *Miss Hickory* by Carolyn Sherwin Bailey, Viking
Honor Books: *Wonderful Year* by Nancy Barnes, Messner; *Big Tree* by Mary and Conrad Buff, Viking; *The Heavenly Tenants* by William Maxwell, Harper; *The Avion My Uncle Flew* by Cyrus Fisher, Appleton; *The Hidden Treasure of Glaston* by Eleanor Jewett, Viking

1948 *The Twenty-one Balloons* by William Pène du Bois, Viking
Honor Books: *Pancakes-Paris* by Claire Huchet Bishop, Viking; *Li Lun, Lad of Courage* by Carolyn Treffinger, Abingdon; *The Quaint and Curious Quest of Johnny Longfoot* by Catherine Besterman, Bobbs; *The Cow-Tail Switch, and Other West African Stories* by Harold Courlander, Holt; *Misty of Chincoteague* by Marguerite Henry, Rand

1949 *King of the Wind* by Marguerite Henry, Rand
Honor Books: *Seabird* by Holling C. Holling, Houghton; *Daughter of the Mountains* by Louise Rankin, Viking; *My Father's Dragon* by Ruth S. Gannett, Random; *Story of the Negro* by Arna Bontemps, Knopf

1950 *The Door in the Wall* by Marguerite de Angeli, Doubleday
Honor Books: *Tree of Freedom* by Rebecca Caudill, Viking; *The Blue Cat of Castle Town* by Catherine Coblentz, Longmans; *Kildee House* by Rutherford Montgomery, Doubleday; *George Washington* by Genevieve Foster, Scribner's; *Song of the Pines* by Walter and Marion Havighurst, Winston

1951 *Amos Fortune, Free Man* by Elizabeth Yates, Aladdin
Honor Books: *Better Known as Johnny Appleseed* by Mabel Leigh Hunt, Lippincott; *Gandhi, Fighter Without a Sword* by Jeanette Eaton, Morrow; *Abraham Lincoln, Friend of the People* by Clara Ingram Judson, Follett; *The Story of Appleby Capple* by Anne Parrish, Harper

1952 *Ginger Pye* by Eleanor Estes, Harcourt
Honor Books: *Americans Before Columbus* by Elizabeth Baity, Viking; *Minn of the Mississippi* by Holling C. Holling, Houghton; *The Defender* by Nicholas Kalashnikoff, Scribner's; *The Light at Tern Rock* by Julia Sauer, Viking; *The Apple and the Arrow* by Mary and Conrad Buff, Houghton

1953 *Secret of the Andes* by Ann Nolan Clark, Viking
Honor Books: *Charlotte's Web* by E. B. White, Harper; *Moccasin Trail* by Eloise McGraw, Coward; *Red Sails to Capri* by Ann Weil, Viking; *The Bears on Hemlock Mountain* by Alice Dalgliesh, Scribner's; *Birthdays of Freedom*, Vol. 1 by Genevieve Foster, Scribner's

1954 *. . . and now Miguel* by Joseph Krumgold, T. Crowell
Honor Books: *All Alone* by Claire Huchet Bishop, Viking; *Shadrach* by Meindert DeJong, Harper; *Hurry Home Candy* by Meindert DeJong, Harper; *Theodore Roosevelt, Fighting Patriot* by Clara Ingram Judson, Follett; *Magic Maze* by Mary and Conrad Buff, Houghton

1955 *The Wheel on the School* by Meindert DeJong, Harper
Honor Books: *The Courage of Sarah Noble* by Alice Dalgliesh, Scribner's; *Banner in the Sky* by James Ullman, Lippincott

1956 *Carry on, Mr. Bowditch* by Jean Lee Latham, Houghton
Honor Books: *The Secret River* by Marjorie Kinnan Rawlings, Scribner's; *The Golden Name Day* by Jennie Lindquist, Harper; *Men, Microscopes, and Living Things* by Katherine Shippen, Viking

1957 *Miracles on Maple Hill* by Virginia Sorensen, Harcourt
Honor Books: *Old Yeller* by Fred Gipson, Harper; *The House of Sixty Fathers* by Meindert DeJong, Harper; *Mr. Justice Holmes* by Clara Ingram Judson, Follett; *The Corn Grows Ripe* by Dorothy Rhoads, Viking; *Black Fox of Lorne* by Marguerite de Angeli, Doubleday

1958 *Rifles for Watie* by Harold Keith, T. Crowell
Honor Books: *The Horsecatcher* by Mari Sandoz, Westminster; *Gone-Away Lake* by Elizabeth Enright, Harcourt; *The Great Wheel* by Robert Lawson, Viking; *Tom Paine, Freedom's Apostle* by Leo Gurko, T. Crowell

1959 *The Witch of Blackbird Pond* by Elizabeth George Speare, Houghton
Honor Books: *The Family Under the Bridge* by Natalie S. Carlson, Harper; *Along Came a Dog* by Meindert DeJong, Harper; *Chucaro: Wild Pony of the Pampa* by Francis Kalnay, Harcourt; *The Perilous Road* by William O. Steele, Harcourt

1960 *Onion John* by Joseph Krumgold, T. Crowell
Honor Books: *My Side of the Mountain* by Jean George, Dutton; *America Is Born* by Gerald W. Johnson, Morrow; *The Gammage Cup* by Carol Kendall, Harcourt

1961 *Island of the Blue Dolphins* by Scott O'Dell, Houghton
Honor Books: *America Moves Forward* by Gerald W. Johnson, Morrow; *Old Ramon* by Jack Schaefer, Houghton; *The Cricket in Times Square* by George Selden, Farrar

1962 *The Bronze Bow* by Elizabeth George Speare,

Houghton
Honor Books: *Frontier Living* by Edwin Tunis, World; *The Golden Goblet* by Eloise McGraw, Coward; *Belling the Tiger* by Mary Stolz, Harper

1963 *A Wrinkle in Time* by Madeleine L'Engle, Farrar
Honor Books: *Thistle and Thyme* by Sorche Nic Leodhas, Holt; *Men of Athens* by Olivia Coolidge, Houghton

1964 *It's Like This, Cat* by Emily Cheney Neville, Harper
Honor Books: *Rascal* by Sterling North, Dutton; *The Loner* by Esther Wier, McKay

1965 *Shadow of a Bull* by Maia Wojciechowska, Atheneum
Honor Book: *Across Five Aprils* by Irene Hunt, Follett

1966 *I, Juan de Pareja* by Elizabeth Borten de Trevino, Farrar
Honor Books: *The Black Cauldron* by Lloyd Alexander, Holt; *The Animal Family* by Randall Jarrell, Pantheon; *The Noonday Friends* by Mary Stolz, Harper

1967 *Up a Road Slowly* by Irene Hunt, Follett
Honor Books: *The King's Fifth* by Scott O'Dell, Houghton; *Zlateh the Goat and Other Stories* by Isaac Bashevis Singer, Harper; *The Jazz Man* by Mary H. Weik, Atheneum

1968 *From the Mixed-Up Files of Mrs. Basil E. Frankweiler* by Elaine Konigsburg, Atheneum
Honor Books: *Jennifer, Hecate, Macbeth, William McKinley, and Me, Elizabeth* by Elaine Konigsburg, Atheneum; *The Black Pearl* by Scott O'Dell, Houghton; *The Fearsome Inn* by Isaac Bashevis Singer, Scribner's; *The Egypt Game* by Zilpha Keatley Snyder, Atheneum

1969 *The High King* by Lloyd Alexander, Holt
Honor Books: *To Be a Slave* by Julius Lester, Dial; *When Shlemiel Went to Warsaw and Other Stories* by Isaac Bashevis Singer, Farrar

1970 *Sounder* by William H. Armstrong, Harper
Honor Books: *Our Eddie* by Sulamith Ish-Kishor, Pantheon; *The Many Ways of Seeing: An Introduction to the Pleasures of Art* by Janet Gaylord Moore, World; *Journey Outside* by Mary Q. Steele, Viking

1971 *Summer of the Swans* by Betsy Byars, Viking
Honor Books: *Kneeknock Rise* by Natalie Babbitt, Farrar; *Enchantress from the Stars* by Sylvia Louise Engdahl, Atheneum; *Sing Down the Moon* by Scott O'Dell, Houghton

1972 *Mrs. Frisby and the Rats of NIMH* by Robert C. O'Brien, Atheneum
Honor Books: *Incident at Hawk's Hill* by Allan W. Eckert, Little; *The Planet of Junior Brown* by Virginia Hamilton, Macmillan; *The Tombs of Atuan* by Ursula K. Le Guin, Atheneum; *Annie and the Old One* by Miska Miles, Atlantic/Little; *The Headless Cupid* by Zilpha Keatley Snyder, Atheneum

1973 *Julie of the Wolves* by Jean George, Harper
Honor Books: *Frog and Toad Together* by Arnold Lobel, Harper; *The Upstairs Room* by Johanna Reiss, Crowell; *The Witches of Worm* by Zilpha Keatley Snyder, Atheneum

1974 *The Slave Dancer* by Paula Fox, Bradbury
Honor Book: *The Dark Is Rising* by Susan Cooper, Atheneum/McElderry

1975 *M. C. Higgins, the Great* by Virginia Hamilton, Macmillan
Honor Books: *Figgs & Phantoms* by Ellen Raskin, Dutton; *My Brother Sam Is Dead* by James Lincoln Collier & Cristopher Collier, Four Winds; *The Perilous Gard* by Elizabeth Marie Pope, Houghton; *Philip Hall Likes Me. I Reckon Maybe* by Bette Greene, Dial

1976 *The Grey King* by Susan Cooper, Atheneum/McElderry
Honor Books: *The Hundred Penny Box* by Sharon Bell Mathis, Viking; *Dragonwings* by Laurence Yep, Harper

1977 *Roll of Thunder, Hear My Cry* by Mildred D. Taylor, Dial
Honor Books: *Abel's Island* by William Steig, Farrar; *A String in the Harp* by Nancy Bond, McElderry/Atheneum

1978 *Bridge to Terabithia* by Katherine Paterson, Crowell
Honor Books: *Anpao: An American Indian Odyssey* by Jamake Highwater, Lippincott; *Ramona and Her Father* by Beverly Cleary, Morrow

1979 *The Westing Game* by Ellen Raskin, Dutton
Honor Book: *The Great Gilly Hopkins* by Katherine Paterson, Crowell

1980 *A Gathering of Days: A New England Girl's Journal, 1830–32* by Joan Blos, Scribner's
Honor Book: *The Road from Home: The Story of an Armenian Girl* by David Kherdian, Greenwillow

1981 *Jacob Have I Loved* by Katherine Paterson, Crowell
Honor Books: *The Fledgling* by Jane Langton, Harper; *A Ring of Endless Light* by Madeleine L'Engle, Farrar

1982 *A Visit to William Blake's Inn: Poems for Innocent and Experienced Travelers* by Nancy Willard, Harcourt
Honor Books: *Ramona Quimby, Age 8* by Bever-

ly Cleary, Morrow; *Upon the Head of a Goat* by Aranka Siegel, Farrar

1983 *Dicey's Song* by Cynthia Voigt, Atheneum
Honor Books: *The Blue Sword* by Robin McKinley, Greenwillow; *Dr. De Soto* by William Steig, Farrar; *Graven Images* by Paul Fleischman, ill. by Andrew Glass, Harper; *Homesick: My Own Story* by Jean Fritz, ill. by Margot Tomes, Putnam; *Sweet Whispers, Brother Rush* by Virginia Hamilton, Philomel

1984 *Dear Mr. Henshaw* by Beverly Cleary, Morrow
Honor Books: *The Sign of the Beaver* by Elizabeth George Speare, Houghton; *A Solitary Blue* by Cynthia Voigt, Atheneum; *Sugaring Time* by Kathryn Lasky, Macmillan; *The Wish Giver* by Bill Brittain, Harper

1985 *The Hero and the Crown* by Robin McKinley, Greenwillow
Honor Books: *Like Jake and Me* by Mavis Jukes, Knopf; *The Moves Make the Man* by Bruce Brooks, Harper; *One-Eyed Cat* by Paula Fox, Bradbury

1986 *Sarah, Plain and Tall* by Patricia MacLachlan, Harper
Honor Books: *Commodore Perry in the Land of the Shogun* by Rhoda Blumberg, Lothrop; *Dogsong* by Gary Paulsen, Bradbury

1987 *The Whipping Boy* by Sid Fleischman, Greenwillow
Honor Books: *Volcano: The Eruption and Healing of Mount St. Helens* by Patricia Lauber, Bradbury; *A Fine White Dust* by Cynthia Rylant, Bradbury; *On My Honor* by Marion Dane Bauer, Clarion

1988 *Lincoln: A Photobiography* by Russell Freedman, Clarion/Houghton
Honor Books: *After the Rain* by Norma Fox Mazer, Morrow; *Hatchet* by Gary Paulsen, Bradbury

1989 *Joyful Noise: Poems for Two Voices* by Paul Fleischman, Harper
Honor Books: *In the Beginning: Creation Stories from around the World* by Virginia Hamilton, Harcourt; *Scorpions* by Walter Dean Myers, Harper

1990 *Number the Stars* by Lois Lowry, Houghton
Honor Books: *Afternoon of the Elves* by Janet Taylor Lisle, Orchard; *Shabanu: Daughter of the Wind* by Suzanne Fisher Staples, Knopf; *The Winter Room* by Gary Paulsen, Orchard

The Caldecott Medal

This award is named in honor of Randolph Caldecott (1846–1886), the English illustrator whose pictures still delight children. In 1937, Frederic G. Melcher, the American editor and publisher who had conceived the idea of the Newbery Medal some years earlier, proposed the establishment of a similar award for picture books, and since 1938 the Caldecott Medal has been awarded annually by an awards committee of the American Library Association's Children's Services Division to the illustrator of the most distinguished picture book for children published in the United States during the preceding year. The award is limited to residents or citizens of the United States.

In cases where only one name is given, the book was written and illustrated by the same person.

1938 *Animals of the Bible* by Helen Dean Fish, ill. by Dorothy P. Lathrop, Lippincott
Honor Books: *Seven Simeons* by Boris Artzybasheff, Viking; *Four and Twenty Blackbirds* by Helen Dean Fish, ill. by Robert Lawson, Stokes

1939 *Mei Li* by Thomas Handforth, Doubleday
Honor Books: *The Forest Pool* by Laura Adams Armer, Longmans; *Wee Gillis* by Munro Leaf, ill. by Robert Lawson, Viking; *Snow White and the Seven Dwarfs* by Wanda Gág, Coward; *Barkis* by Clare Newberry, Harper; *Andy and the Lion* by James Daugherty, Viking

1940 *Abraham Lincoln* by Ingri and Edgar Parin D'Aulaire, Doubleday
Honor Books: *Cock-A-Doodle Doo . . .* by Berta and Elmer Hader, Macmillan; *Madeline* by Ludwig Bemelmans, Viking; *The Ageless Story,* by Lauren Ford, Dodd

1941 *They Were Strong and Good* by Robert Lawson, Viking
Honor Books: *April's Kittens* by Clare Newberry, Harper

1942 *Make Way for Ducklings* by Robert McCloskey, Viking
Honor Books: *An American ABC* by Maud and Miska Petersham, Macmillan; *In My Mother's House* by Ann Nolan Clark, ill. by Velino Herrera, Viking; *Paddle-to-the-Sea* by Holling C. Holling, Houghton; *Nothing at All* by Wanda Gág, Coward

1943 *The Little House* by Virginia Lee Burton, Houghton
Honor Books: *Dash and Dart* by Mary and Conrad Buff, Viking; *Marshmallow* by Clare Newberry, Harper

1944 *Many Moons* by James Thurber, ill. by Louis Slobodkin, Harcourt
Honor Books: *Small Rain: Verses from the Bible* selected by Jessie Orton Jones, ill. by Elizabeth Orton Jones, Viking; *Pierre Pigeon* by Lee Kingman, ill. by Arnold E. Bare, Houghton;

The Mighty Hunter by Berta and Elmer Hader, Macmillan; *A Child's Good Night Book* by Margaret Wise Brown, ill. by Jean Charlot, W. R. Scott; *Good Luck Horse* by Chih-Yi Chan, ill. by Plao Chan, Whittlesey

1945 *Prayer for a Child* by Rachel Field, ill. by Elizabeth Orton Jones, Macmillan
Honor Books: *Mother Goose* ill. by Tasha Tudor, Walck; *In the Forest* by Marie Hall Ets, Viking; *Yonie Wondernose* by Marguerite de Angeli, Doubleday; *The Christmas Anna Angel* by Ruth Sawyer, ill. by Kate Seredy, Viking

1946 *The Rooster Crows . . .* (traditional Mother Goose) ill. by Maud and Miska Petersham, Macmillan
Honor Books: *Little Lost Lamb* by Golden MacDonald, ill. by Leonard Weisgard, Doubleday; *Sing Mother Goose* by Opal Wheeler, ill. by Marjorie Torrey, Dutton; *My Mother Is the Most Beautiful Woman in the World* by Becky Reyher, ill. by Ruth Gannett, Lothrop; *You Can Write Chinese* by Kurt Wiese, Viking

1947 *The Little Island* by Golden MacDonald, ill. by Leonard Weisgard, Doubleday
Honor Books: *Rain Drop Splash* by Alvin Tresselt, ill. by Leonard Weisgard, Lothrop; *Boats on the River* by Marjorie Flack, ill. by Jay Hyde Barnum, Viking; *Timothy Turtle* by Al Graham, ill. by Tony Palazzo, Viking; *Pedro, the Angel of Olvera Street* by Leo Politi, Scribner's; *Sing in Praise: A Collection of the Best Loved Hymns* by Opal Wheeler, ill. by Marjorie Torrey, Dutton

1948 *White Snow, Bright Snow* by Alvin Tresselt, ill. by Roger Duvoisin, Lothrop
Honor Books: *Stone Soup* by Marcia Brown, Scribner's; *McElligot's Pool* by Dr. Seuss, Random; *Bambino the Clown* by George Schreiber, Viking; *Roger and the Fox* by Lavinia Davis, ill. by Hildegard Woodward, Doubleday; *Song of Robin Hood* ed. by Anne Malcolmson, ill. by Virginia Lee Burton, Houghton

1949 *The Big Snow* by Berta and Elmer Hader, Macmillan
Honor Books: *Blueberries for Sal* by Robert McCloskey, Viking; *All Around the Town* by Phyllis McGinley, ill. by Helen Stone, Lippincott; *Juanita* by Leo Politi, Scribner's; *Fish in the Air* by Kurt Wiese, Viking

1950 *Song of the Swallows* by Leo Politi, Scribner's
Honor Books: *America's Ethan Allen* by Stewart Holbrook, ill. by Lynd Ward, Houghton; *The Wild Birthday Cake* by Lavinia Davis, ill. by Hildegard Woodward, Doubleday; *The Happy Day* by Ruth Krauss, ill. by Marc Simont,

Harper; *Bartholomew and the Oobleck* by Dr. Seuss, Random; *Henry Fisherman* by Marcia Brown, Scribner's

1951 *The Egg Tree* by Katherine Milhous, Scribner's
Honor Books: *Dick Whittington and His Cat* by Marcia Brown, Scribner's; *The Two Reds* by William Lipkind, ill. by Nicholas Mordvinoff, Harcourt; *If I Ran the Zoo* by Dr. Seuss, Random; *The Most Wonderful Doll in the World* by Phyllis McGinley, ill. by Helen Stone, Lippincott; *T-Bone, the Baby Sitter* by Clare Newberry, Harper

1952 *Finders Keepers* by William Lipkind, ill. by Nicholas Mordvinoff, Harcourt
Honor Books: *Mr. T. W. Anthony Woo* by Marie Hall Ets, Viking; *Skipper John's Cook* by Marcia Brown, Scribner's; *All Falling Down* by Gene Zion, ill. by Margaret Bloy Graham, Harper; *Bear Party* by William Pène du Bois, Viking; *Feather Mountain* by Elizabeth Olds, Houghton

1953 *The Biggest Bear* by Lynd Ward, Houghton
Honor Books: *Puss in Boots* by Charles Perrault, ill. and tr. by Marcia Brown, Scribner's; *One Morning in Maine* by Robert McCloskey, Viking; *Ape in a Cape* by Fritz Eichenberg, Harcourt; *The Storm Book* by Charlotte Zolotow, ill. by Margaret Bloy Graham, Harper; *Five Little Monkeys* by Juliet Kepes, Houghton

1954 *Madeline's Rescue* by Ludwig Bemelmans, Viking
Honor Books: *Journey Cake, Ho!* by Ruth Sawyer, ill. by Robert McCloskey, Viking; *When Will the World Be Mine?* by Miriam Schlein, ill. by Jean Charlot, W. R. Scott; *The Steadfast Tin Soldier* by Hans Christian Andersen, ill. by Marcia Brown, Scribner's; *A Very Special House* by Ruth Krauss, ill. by Maurice Sendak, Harper; *Green Eyes* by A. Birnbaum, Capitol

1955 *Cinderella, or the Little Glass Slipper* by Charles Perrault, tr. and ill. by Marcia Brown, Scribner's
Honor Books: *Books of Nursery and Mother Goose Rhymes*, ill. by Marguerite de Angeli, Doubleday; *Wheel on the Chimney* by Margaret Wise Brown, ill. by Tibor Gergely, Lippincott; *The Thanksgiving Story* by Alice Dalgliesh, ill. by Helen Sewell, Scribner's

1956 *Frog Went A-Courtin'* ed. by John Langstaff, ill. by Feodor Rojankovsky, Harcourt
Honor Books: *Play with Me* by Marie Hall Ets, Viking; *Crow Boy* by Taro Yashima, Viking

1957 *A Tree Is Nice* by Janice May Udry, ill. by Marc Simont, Harper
Honor Books: *Mr. Penny's Race Horse* by Marie

Hall Ets, Viking; *1 Is One* by Tasha Tudor, Walck; *Anatole* by Eve Titus, ill. by Paul Galdone, McGraw; *Gillespie and the Guards* by Benjamin Elkin, ill. by James Daugherty, Viking; *Lion* by William Pène du Bois, Viking

1958 *Time of Wonder* by Robert McCloskey, Viking
Honor Books: *Fly High, Fly Low* by Don Freeman, Viking; *Anatole and the Cat* by Eve Titus, ill. by Paul Galdone, McGraw

1959 *Chanticleer and the Fox* adapted from Chaucer and ill. by Barbara Cooney, T. Crowell
Honor Books: *The House That Jack Built* by Antonio Frasconi, Harcourt; *What Do You Say, Dear?* by Sesyle Joslin, ill. by Maurice Sendak, W. R. Scott; *Umbrella* by Taro Yashima, Viking

1960 *Nine Days to Christmas* by Marie Hall Ets and Aurora Labastida, ill. by Marie Hall Ets, Viking
Honor Books: *Houses from the Sea* by Alice E. Goudey, ill. by Adrienne Adams, Scribner's; *The Moon Jumpers* by Janice May Udry, ill. by Maurice Sendak, Harper

1961 *Baboushka and the Three Kings* by Ruth Robbins, ill. by Nicolas Sidjakov, Parnassus
Honor Book: *Inch by Inch* by Leo Lionni, Obolensky

1962 *Once a Mouse* . . . by Marcia Brown, Scribner's
Honor Books: *The Fox Went Out on a Chilly Night* by Peter Spier, Doubleday; *Little Bear's Visit* by Else Holmelund Minarik, ill. by Maurice Sendak, Harper; *The Day We Saw the Sun Come Up* by Alice E. Goudey, ill. by Adrienne Adams, Scribner's

1963 *The Snowy Day* by Ezra Jack Keats, Viking
Honor Books: *The Sun Is a Golden Earring* by Natalia M. Belting, ill. by Bernarda Bryson, Holt; *Mr. Rabbit and the Lovely Present* by Charlotte Zolotow, ill. by Maurice Sendak, Harper

1964 *Where the Wild Things Are* by Maurice Sendak, Harper
Honor Books: *Swimmy* by Leo Lionni, Pantheon; *All in the Morning Early* by Sorche Nic Leodhas, ill. by Evaline Ness, Holt; *Mother Goose and Nursery Rhymes*, ill. by Philip Reed, Atheneum

1965 *May I Bring a Friend?* by Beatrice Schenk de Regniers, ill. by Beni Montresor, Atheneum
Honor Books: *Rain Makes Applesauce* by Julian Scheer, ill. by Marvin Bileck, Holiday; *The Wave* by Margaret Hodges, ill. by Blair Lent, Houghton; *A Pocketful of Cricket* by Rebecca Caudill, ill. by Evaline Ness, Holt

1966 *Always Room for One More* by Sorche Nic Leodhas, ill. by Nonny Hogrogian, Holt

Honor Books: *Hide and Seek Fog* by Alvin Tresselt, ill. by Roger Duvoisin, Lothrop; *Just Me* by Marie Hall Ets, Viking; *Tom Tit Tot* by Evaline Ness, Scribner's

1967 *Sam, Bangs & Moonshine* by Evaline Ness, Holt
Honor Book: *One Wide River to Cross* by Barbara Emberley, ill. by Ed Emberley, Prentice

1968 *Drummer Hoff* by Barbara Emberley, ill. by Ed Emberley, Prentice
Honor Books: *Frederick* by Leo Lionni, Pantheon; *Seashore Story* by Taro Yashima, Viking; *The Emperor and the Kite* by Jane Yolen, ill. by Ed Young, World

1969 *The Fool of the World and the Flying Ship* by Arthur Ransome, ill. by Uri Shulevitz, Farrar
Honor Book: *Why the Sun and the Moon Live in the Sky* by Elphinstone Dayrell, ill. by Blair Lent, Houghton

1970 *Sylvester and the Magic Pebble* by William Steig, Windmill
Honor Books: *Goggles!* by Ezra Jack Keats, Macmillan; *Alexander and the Wind-Up Mouse* by Leo Lionni, Pantheon; *Pop Corn & Ma Goodness* by Edna Mitchell Preston, ill. by Robert Andrew Parker, Viking; *Thy Friend, Obadiah* by Brinton Turkle, Viking; *The Judge* by Harve Zemach, ill. by Margot Zemach, Farrar

1971 *A Story—A Story* by Gail E. Haley, Atheneum
Honor Books: *The Angry Moon* by William Sleator, ill. by Blair Lent, Atlantic/Little; *Frog and Toad Are Friends* by Arnold Lobel, Harper; *In the Night Kitchen* by Maurice Sendak, Harper

1972 *One Fine Day* by Nonny Hogrogian, Macmillan
Honor Books: *If All the Seas Were One Sea* by Janina Domanska, Macmillan; *Moja Means One: Swahili Counting Book* by Muriel Feelings, ill. by Tom Feelings, Dial; *Hildilid's Night* by Cheli Duran Ryan, ill. by Arnold Lobel, Macmillan

1973 *The Funny Little Woman* retold by Arlene Mosel, ill. by Blair Lent, Dutton
Honor Books: *Anansi the Spider* adapted and ill. by Gerald McDermott, Holt; *Hosie's Alphabet* by Hosea, Tobias, and Lisa Baskin, ill. by Leonard Baskin, Viking; *Snow-White and the Seven Dwarfs* translated by Randall Jarrell, ill. by Nancy Ekholm Burkert, Farrar; *When Clay Sings* by Byrd Baylor, ill. by Tom Bahti, Scribner's

1974 *Duffy and the Devil* by Harve Zemach, ill. by Margot Zemach, Farrar
Honor Books: *Three Jovial Huntsmen* by Susan

Jeffers, Bradbury; *Cathedral: The Story of Its Construction* by David Macaulay, Houghton

1975 *Arrow to the Sun* adapted and ill. by Gerald McDermott, Viking

Honor Book: *Jambo Means Hello* by Muriel Feelings, ill. by Tom Feelings, Dial

1976 *Why Mosquitoes Buzz in People's Ears* retold by Verna Aardema, ill. by Leo and Diane Dillon, Dial

Honor Books: *The Desert Is Theirs* by Byrd Baylor, ill. by Peter Parnall, Scribner's; *Strega Nona* retold and ill. by Tomie dePaola, Prentice

1977 *Ashanti to Zulu: African Traditions* by Margaret Musgrove, ill. by Leo and Diane Dillon, Dial

Honor Books: *The Amazing Bone* by William Steig, Farrar; *The Contest* retold & ill. by Nonny Hogrogian, Greenwillow; *Fish for Supper* by M. B. Goffstein, Dial; *The Golem* by Beverly Brodsky McDermott, Lippincott; *Hawk, I'm Your Brother* by Byrd Baylor, ill. by Peter Parnall, Scribner's

1978 *Noah's Ark* ill. by Peter Spier, Doubleday

Honor Books: *Castle* by David Macaulay, Houghton; *It Could Always Be Worse* retold & ill. by Margot Zemach, Farrar

1979 *The Girl Who Loved Wild Horses* by Paul Goble, Bradbury

Honor Books: *Freight Train* by Donald Crews, Greenwillow; *The Way to Start a Day* by Byrd Baylor, ill. by Peter Parnall, Scribner's

1980 *Ox-Cart Man* by Donald Hall, ill. by Barbara Cooney, Viking

Honor Books: *Ben's Trumpet* by Rachel Isadora, Greenwillow; *The Garden of Abdul Gasazi* by Chris Van Allsburg, Houghton

1981 *Fables* by Arnold Lobel, Harper

Honor Books: *The Bremen-Town Musicians* by Ilse Plume, Doubleday; *The Grey Lady and the Strawberry Snatcher* by Molly Bang, Four Winds; *Mice Twice* by Joseph Low, McElderry/Atheneum; *Truck* by Donald Crews, Greenwillow

1982 *Jumanji* by Chris Van Allsburg, Houghton

Honor Books: *Where the Buffaloes Begin* by Olaf Baker, ill. by Stephen Gammell, Warne; *On Market Street* by Arnold Lobel, ill. by Anita Lobel, Greenwillow; *Outside Over There* by Maurice Sendak, Harper; *A Visit to William Blake's Inn* by Nancy Willard, Harcourt

1983 *Shadow* by Blaise Cendrars, trans. and ill. by Marcia Brown, Scribner's

Honor Books: *When I Was Young in the Mountains* by Cynthia Rylant, ill. by Diane Goode, Dutton; *A Chair for My Mother* by Vera B.

Williams, Greenwillow

1984 *The Glorious Flight: Across the Channel with Louis Bleriot* by Alice and Martin Provensen, Viking

Honor Books: *Ten, Nine, Eight* by Molly Bang, Greenwillow; *Little Red Riding Hood* retold and ill. by Trina Schart Hyman, Holiday House

1985 *St. George and the Dragon* retold by Margaret Hodges, ill. by Trina Schart Hyman, Little, Brown

Honor Books: *Hansel and Gretel* retold by Rika Lesser, ill. by Paul O. Zelinsky, Dodd; *Have You Seen My Duckling?* by Nancy Tafuri, Greenwillow; *The Story of Jumping Mouse* by John Steptoe, Lothrop

1986 *The Polar Express* by Chris Van Allsburg, Houghton

Honor Books: *The Relatives Came* by Cynthia Rylant, ill. by Stephen Gammell, Bradbury; *King Bidgood's in the Bathtub* by Audrey Wood, ill. by Don Wood, Harcourt

1987 *Hey, Al* by Arthur Yorinks, ill. by Richard Egielski, Farrar

Honor Books: *The Village of Round and Square Houses* by Ann Grifalconi, Little; *Alphabatics* by Suse MacDonald, Bradbury; *Rumplestiltskin* adapted and ill. by Paul Zelinsky, Dutton

1988 *Owl Moon* by Jane Yolen, ill. by John Schoenherr, Philomel

Honor Book: *Mufaro's Beautiful Daughters: An African Tale* adapted and ill. by John Steptoe, Lothrop

1989 *Song and Dance Man* by Karen Ackerman, ill. by Stephen Gammell, Knopf

Honor Books: *The Boy of the Three Year Nap* by Allen Say, Houghton; *Free Fall* by David Wiesner, Lothrop; *Goldilocks and the Three Bears* adapted and ill. by James Marshall, Dial; *Mirandy and Brother Wind* by Patricia McKissack, ill. by Jerry Pinkney, Knopf

1990 *Lon Po Po: A Red Riding Hood Story from China* adapted and ill. by Ed Young, Philomel

Honor Books: *Bill Peet: An Autobiography* by Bill Peet, Houghton; *Color Zoo* by Lois Ehlert, Lippincott; *Hershel and the Hanukkah Goblins* by Eric Kimmel, ill. by Trina Schart Hyman, Holiday House; *The Talking Eggs* by Robert D. San Souci, ill. by Jerry Pinkney, Dial

The Laura Ingalls Wilder Award

This prize, administered by the Association for Library Service to Children, was first awarded in 1954. Since 1960 it has been given every five years to an author or illustrator whose books, published in the United States, have made a substantial and lasting contribution to children's literature. It is now given every three years.

1954 Laura Ingalls Wilder
1960 Clara Ingram Judson
1965 Ruth Sawyer
1970 E. B. White
1975 Beverly Cleary
1980 Theodor Geisel (Dr. Seuss)
1983 Maurice Sendak
1986 Jean Fritz
1989 Elizabeth George Speare

International Reading Association Children's Book Award

Given for the first time in 1975, this award is presented annually for a book, published in the preceding year, written by an author "who shows unusual promise in the children's book field." Sponsored by the Institute for Reading Research, the award is administered by the International Reading Association.

1975 *Transport 7-41-R* by T. Degens, Viking
1976 *Dragonwings* by Laurence Yep, Harper
1977 *A String in the Harp* by Nancy Bond, McElderry/Atheneum
1978 *A Summer to Die* by Lois Lowry, Houghton
1979 *Reserved for Mark Anthony Crowder* by Alison Smith, Dutton
1980 *Words by Heart* by Ouida Sebestyen, Atlantic/ Little
1981 *My Own Private Sky* by Delores Beckman, Dutton
1982 *Good Night, Mr. Tom* by Michelle Magorian, Kestrel/Penguin (Great Britain); Harper (U.S.A.)
1983 *The Darkangel* by Meredith Ann Pierce, Atlantic/Little
1984 *Ratha's Creature* by Clare Bell, Atheneum
1985 *Badger on the Barge* by Janni Howker, Greenwillow
1986 *Prairie Songs* by Pam Conrad, Harper
1987 *The Line Up Book* by Marisabina Russo, Greenwillow
1988 *Third Story Cat* by Leslie Baker, Little
1989 For older readers: *Children of the River* by Linda Crew, Delacorte
For younger readers: *No Star Nights* by Anna Egan Smucker, ill. by Steve Johnson, Knopf

National Council of Teachers of English Award for Excellence in Poetry for Children

First presented in the fall of 1977 by the National Council of Teachers of English, the award is given to a living American poet in recognition of his or her aggregate work. After the 1982 award, it was decided to present the award every three years, instead of yearly.

1977 David McCord
1978 Aileen Fisher
1979 Karla Kuskin
1980 Myra Cohn Livingston
1981 Eve Merriam
1982 John Ciardi
1985 Lilian Moore
1988 Arnold Adoff

The Scott O'Dell Award for Historical Fiction

The award was established in 1981 by Mr. O'Dell and is administered by the Advisory Committee of the Bulletin of the Center for Children's Books. The book must be historical fiction, have unusual literary merit, be written by a citizen of the United States, and be set in the New World. It must have been published in the previous year by a United States publisher and must be written for children or young adults. In some years, no award may be given.

1984 *The Sign of the Beaver* by Elizabeth George Speare, Houghton
1985 *The Fighting Ground* by Avi [Wortis], Harper
1986 *Sarah, Plain and Tall* by Paticia MacLachlan, Harper
1987 *Streams to the River, River to the Sea: A Novel of Sacagawea* by Scott O'Dell, Houghton
1988 *Charley Skedaddle* by Patricia Beatty, Morrow
1989 *The Honorable Prison* by Lyll Becerra de Jenkins, Lodestar
1990 *Shades of Gray* by Carolyn Reeder, Macmillan

Coretta Scott King Award

First presented in 1970, this award was "designed to commemorate and foster the life, works and dreams of the late Dr. Martin Luther King, Jr. and to honor Mrs. Coretta Scott King for her courage and determination to work for peace and world brotherhood." The award is given annually to an author for an outstanding inspirational and educational contribution, designed to promote better understanding and appreciation of the culture and contribution of all peoples to the American dream. In 1979 another category was added to this award to honor illustrators. Sponsored by the American Library Association (ALA) Social Responsibilities Roundtable under the Coretta Scott King Task Force.

1970 *Martin Luther King, Jr.: Man of Peace* by Lillie Patterson, Garrard
1971 *Black Troubador: Langston Hughes* by Charlemae Rollins, Rand
1972 *17 Black Artists* by Elton C. Fax, Dodd
1973 *I Never Had It Made* by Jackie Robinson as told to Alfred Duckett, Putnam
1974 *Ray Charles* by Sharon Bell Mathis, T. Crowell
1975 *The Legend of Africania* by Dorothy Robinson, Johnson
1976 *Duey's Tale* by Pearl Bailey, Harcourt
1977 *The Story of Stevie Wonder* by James Haskins, Lothrop
1978 *Africa Dream* by Eliose Greenfield, Day/T. Crowell
1979 Best book: *Escape to Freedom* by Ossie Davis, Viking
Best illustrations: *Something on My Mind* by Nikki Grimes, ill. by Tom Feelings, Dial
1980 Best book: *The Young Landlords* by Walter Dean Myers, Viking
Best illustrations: *Cornrows* by Camille Yarbrough, ill. by Carole Bayard, Coward
1981 Best book: *This Life* by Sidney Poitier, Knopf
Best illustrations: *Beat the Story Drum, Pum-Pum* by Ashley Bryan, Atheneum
1982 Best book: *Sweet Whispers, Brother Rush* by Virginia Hamilton, Philomel
Best illustrations: *Black Child* by Peter Magubane, Knopf
1983 Best book: *Let the Circle Be Unbroken* by Mildred Taylor, Dial
Best illustrations: *Mother Crocodile* by John Steptoe, Delacorte
1984 Best book: *Everett Anderson's Goodbye* by Lucille Clifton, Holt
Best illustrations: *My Mama Needs Me* by Mildred P. Walter, ill. by Pat Cummings, Lothrop
1985 Best book: *Motown and Didi* by Walter Dean Myers, Viking
Best illustrations: No award given
1986 Best book: *The People Could Fly: American Black Folktales* by Virginia Hamilton, Knopf
Best illustrations: *Patchwork Quilt* by Valerie Flourney, ill. by Jerry Pinkney, Dial
1987 Best book: *Justin and the Best Biscuits in the World* by Mildred Pitts Walter, Lothrop
Best illustrations: *Half a Moon and One Whole Star* by Crescent Dragonwagon, ill. by Jerry Pinkney, Macmillan

1988 Best book: *The Friendship* by Mildred Taylor, ill. by Max Ginsburg, Dial
Best illustrations: *Mufaro's Beautiful Daughters: An African Tale* by John Steptoe, Lothrop
1989 Best book: *Fallen Angels* by Walter Dean Myers, Scholastic
Best illustrations: *Mirandy and Brother Wind* by Patricia McKissack, ill. by Jerry Pinkney, Knopf
1990 Best book: *A Long Hard Journey* by Patricia and Frederick McKissack, Walker
Best illustrations: *Nathaniel Talking* by Eloise Greenfield, ill. by Jan Gilchrist, Black Butterfly Press

The Regina Medal

The Regina Medal is given annually by the Catholic Library Association to an author for the body of his or her aggregate work.

1980 Beverly Cleary
1981 Augusta Baker
1982 Theodor Geisel (Dr. Seuss)
1983 Tomie dePaola
1984 Madeleine L'Engle
1985 Jean Fritz
1986 Lloyd Alexander
1987 Betsy Byars
1988 Katherine Paterson
1989 Steven Kellogg

The Carnegie Medal

The Carnegie Medal, established in 1937, is awarded annually by the British Library Association to an outstanding children's book written in English and first published the previous year in the United Kingdom.

1936 *Pigeon Post* by Arthur Ransome, Cape
1937 *The Family from One End Street* by Eve Garnett, Muller
1938 *The Circus Is Coming* by Noel Streatfeild, Dent
1939 *Radium Woman* by Eleanor Doorly, Heinemann
1940 *Visitors from London* by Kitty Barne, Dent
1941 *We Couldn't Leave Dinah* by Mary Treadgold, Penguin
1942 *The Little Grey Men* by B. B., Eyre & Spottiswoode
1943 No Award
1944 *The Wind on the Moon* by Eric Linklater, Macmillan

1945 No Award
1946 *The Little White Horse* by Elizabeth Goudge, Brockhampton Press
1947 *Collected Stories for Children* by Walter de la Mare, Faber
1948 *Sea Change* by Richard Armstrong, Dent
1949 *The Story of Your Home* by Agnes Allen, Transatlantic
1950 *The Lark on the Wing* by Elfrida Vipont Foulds, Oxford
1951 *Nicholas and the Wool-Pack* by Cynthia Harnett, Methuen
1952 *The Borrowers* by Mary Norton, Dent
1953 *A Valley Grows Up* by Edward Osmond, Oxford
1954 *Knight Crusader* by Ronald Welch, Oxford
1955 *The Little Bookroom* by Eleanor Farjeon, Oxford
1956 *The Last Battle* by C. S. Lewis, Bodley Head
1957 *A Grass Rope* by William Mayne, Oxford
1958 *Tom's Midnight Garden* by Philippa Pearce, Oxford
1959 *The Lantern Bearers* by Rosemary Sutcliff, Oxford
1960 *The Making of Man* by I. W. Cornwall, Phoenix
1961 *A Stranger at Green Knowe* by Lucy Boston, Faber
1962 *The Twelve and the Genii* by Pauline Clarke, Faber
1963 *Time of Trial* by Hester Burton, Oxford
1964 *Nordy Banks* by Sheena Porter, Oxford
1965 *The Grange at High Force* by Philip Turner, Oxford
1966 No Award
1967 *The Owl Service* by Alan Garner, Collins
1968 *The Moon in the Cloud* by Rosemary Harris, Faber
1969 *The Edge of the Cloud* by K. M. Peyton, Oxford
1970 *The God Beneath the Sea* by Leon Garfield and Edward Blishen, Kestrel
1971 *Josh* by Ivan Southall, Angus & Robertson
1972 *Watership Down* by Richard Adams, Rex Collings
1973 *The Ghost of Thomas Kempe* by Penelope Lively, Heinemann
1974 *The Stronghold* by Mollie Hunter, Hamilton
1975 *The Machine-Gunners* by Robert Westall, Macmillan
1976 *Thunder and Lightnings* by Jan Mark, Kestrel
1977 *The Turbulent Term of Tyke Tyler* by Gene Kemp, Faber
1978 *The Exeter Blitz* by David Rees, Hamish Hamilton
1979 *Tulku* by Peter Dickinson, Gollancz
1980 *City of Gold* by Peter Dickinson, Gollancz

1981 *The Scarecrows* by Robert Westall, Chatto & Windus
1982 *The Haunting* by Margaret Mahy, Dent
1983 *Handles* by Jan Mark, Kestrel
1984 *The Changeover* by Margaret Mahy, Dent
1985 *Storm* by Kevin Crossley-Holland, Heinemann
1986 *Granny Was a Buffer Girl* by Berlie Doherty, Methuen
1987 *The Ghost Drum* by Susan Price, Faber
1988 *Pack of Lies* by Geraldine McCaughrean, Oxford

The Kate Greenaway Medal

This medal is awarded each year by the British Library Association for the most distinguished work in illustration of a children's book first published in the United Kingdom during the preceding year.

In cases where only one name is given, the book was written and illustrated by the same person.

1956 *Tim All Alone* by Edward Ardizzone, Oxford
1957 *Mrs. Easter and the Storks* by V. H. Drummond, Faber
1958 No Award
1959 *Kashtanka and a Bundle of Ballads* by William Stobbs, Oxford
1960 *Old Winkle and the Seagulls* by Elizabeth Rose, ill. by Gerald Rose, Faber
1961 *Mrs. Cockle's Cat* by Philippa Pearce, ill. by Antony Maitland, Kestrel
1962 *Brian Wildsmith's ABC* by Brian Wildsmith, Oxford
1963 *Borka* by John Burningham, Cape
1964 *Shakespeare's Theatre* by C. W. Hodges, Oxford
1965 *Three Poor Tailors* by Victor Ambrus, Hamilton
1966 *Mother Goose Treasury* by Raymond Briggs, Hamilton
1967 *Charlie, Charlotte & the Golden Canary* by Charles Keeping, Oxford
1968 *Dictionary of Chivalry* by Grant Uden, ill. by Pauline Baynes, Kestrel
1969 *The Quangle-Wangle's Hat* by Edward Lear, ill. by Helen Oxenbury, Heinemann; *Dragon of an Ordinary Family* by Margaret May Mahy, ill. by Helen Oxenbury, Heinemann
1970 *Mr. Gumpy's Outing* by John Burningham, Cape
1971 *The Kingdom Under the Sea* by Jan Piénkowski, Cape
1972 *The Woodcutter's Duck* by Krystyna Turska, Hamilton
1973 *Father Christmas* by Raymond Briggs, Hamilton
1974 *The Wind Blew* by Pat Hutchins, Bodley Head

1975 *Horses in Battle* by Victor Ambrus, Oxford; *Mishka* by Victor Ambrus, Oxford

1976 *The Post Office Cat* by Gail E. Haley, Bodley Head

1977 *Dogger* by Shirley Hughes, Bodley Head

1978 *Each Peach Pear Plum* by Janet and Allan Ahlberg, Kestrel

1979 *The Haunted House* by Jan Piénkowski, Heinemann

1980 *Mr. Magnolia* by Quentin Blake, Jonathan Cape

1981 *The Highwayman* by Alfred Noyes, ill. by Charles Keeping, Oxford

1982 *Long Neck and Thunder Foot*, Kestrel; and *Sleeping Beauty and Other Favorite Fairy Tales*, Gollancz, both ill. by Michael Foreman

1983 *Gorilla* by Anthony Browne, Julia McRae Books

1984 *Hiawatha's Childhood* by Erroll Le Cain, Faber

1985 *Sir Gawain and the Loathly Lady* by Selma Hastings, ill. by Juan Winjngaard, Walker

1986 *Snow White in New York* by Fiona French, Oxford

1987 *Crafty Chameleon* by Adrienne Kennaway, Hodder & Stoughton

1988 *Can't You Sleep, Little Bear?* by Martin Waddell, ill. by Barbara Firth, Walker

The Canadian Library Awards

This award, first presented in June 1947, was established by the Canadian Library Association. It is given annually to a children's book of outstanding literary merit, written by a Canadian citizen. Since 1954 a similar medal has also been awarded yearly to an outstanding children's book published in French.

1947 *Starbuck Valley Winter* by Roderick Haig-Brown, Collins

1948 *Kristli's Trees* by Mabel Dunham, Hale

1949 No Award

1950 *Franklin of the Arctic* by Richard S. Lambert, McClelland & Stewart

1951 No Award

1952 *The Sun Horse* by Catherine Anthony Clark, Macmillan of Canada

1953 No Award

1954 No English Award
Mgr. de Laval by Emile S. J. Gervais, Comité des Fondateurs de l'Eglise Canadienne

1955 No Awards

1956 *Train for Tiger Lily* by Louise Riley, Macmillan of Canada
No French Award

1957 *Glooskap's Country* by Cyrus MacMillan, Oxford
No French Award

1958 *Lost in the Barrens* by Farley Mowat, Little
Le Chevalier du Roi by Béatrice Clément, Les Editions de l'Atelier

1959 *The Dangerous Cove* by John F. Hayes, Copp Clark
Un Drôle de Petit Cheval by Héléne Flamme, Editions Léméac

1960 *The Golden Phoenix* by Marius Barbeau and Michael Hornyansky, Walck
L'Eté Enchanté by Paule Daveluy, Les Editions de l'Atelier

1961 *The St. Lawrence* by William Toye, Oxford
Plantes Vagabondes by Marcelle Gauvreau, Centre de Psychologie et de Pédagogie

1962 No English Award
Les Iles du Roi Maha Maha II by Claude Aubry, Les Editions du Pélican

1963 *The Incredible Journey* by Sheila Burnford, Little
Drôle d'Automne by Paule Daveluy, Les Editions du Pélican

1964 *The Whale People* by Roderick Haig-Brown, William Collins of Canada
Feerie by Cécile Chabot, Librairie Beauchemin Ltée

1965 *Tales of Nanabozho* by Dorothy Reid, Oxford
Le Loup de Noël by Claude Aubry, Centre de Psychologie de Montréal

1966 *Tikta'Liktak* by James Houston, Kestrel
Le Chêne des Tempêtes by Andrée Maillet-Hobden, Fides
The Double Knights by James McNeal, Walck
Le Wapiti by Monique Corriveau, Jeunesse

1967 *Raven's Cry* by Christie Harris, McClelland & Stewart
No French Award

1968 *The White Archer* by James Houston, Kestrel
Légendes Indiennes du Canada by Claude Mélancon, Editions du Jour

1969 *And Tomorrow the Stars* by Kay Hill, Dodd
No French Award

1970 *Sally Go Round the Sun* by Edith Fowke, McClelland & Stewart
Le Merveilleuse Histoire de la Naissance by Lionel Gendron, Les Editions de l'Homme

1971 *Cartier Discovers the St. Lawrence* by William Toye, Oxford University
La Surprise de Dame Chenille by Henriette Major, Centre de Psychologie de Montréal

1972 *Mary of Mile 18* by Ann Blades, Tundra
No French Award

1973 *The Marrow of the World* by Ruth Nichols, Macmillan of Canada

Le Petit Sapin Qui A Poussé Sur Une Étoile by Simone Bussières, Presses Laurentiennes

1974 *The Miraculous Hind* by Elizabeth Cleaver, Holt of Canada
No French Award

1975 *Alligator Pie* by Dennis Lee, Macmillan of Canada
No French Award

1976 *Jacob Two-Two Meets the Hooded Fang* by Mordecai Richler, Knopf
No French Award

1977 *Mouse Woman and the Vanished Princesses* by Christie Harris, McClelland & Stewart
No French Award

1978 *Garbage Delight* by Dennis Lee, Macmillan
No French Award

1979 *Hold Fast* by Kevin Major, Clarke, Irwin
No French Award

1980 *River Runners* by James Houston, McClelland & Stewart
No French Award

1981 *The Violin Maker's Gift* by Donn Kushner, Macmillan of Canada
No French Award

1982 *The Root Cellar* by Janet Lunn, Lester & Orpen Dennys
No French Award

1983 *Up to Low* by Brian Doyle, Groundwood
No French Award

1984 *Sweetgrass* by Jan Hudson, Tree Frog Press
No French Award

1985 *Mama's Going to Buy a Mockingbird* by Jean Little, Penguin
No French Award

1986 *Julie* by Cora Taylor, Western
No French Award

1987 *Shadow in Hawthorne Bay* by Janet Lunn, Lester & Orpen Dennys
No French Award

1988 *A Handful of Time* by Kit Pearson, Penguin
No French Award

1989 *Easy Avenue* by Brian Doyle, Groundwood
No French Award

The Canadian Library Association has awarded the Amelia Frances Howard-Gibbon Medal annually since 1971 for outstanding illustrations in a children's book published in Canada. The illustrator must be a native or resident of Canada.

1971 *The Wind Has Wings,* ed. by Mary Alice Downie and Barbara Robertson, ill. by Elizabeth Cleaver, Oxford

1972 *A Child in Prison Camp* by Shizuye Takashima, Tundra

1973 *Au Dela du Soleil/Beyond the Sun* by Jacques de Roussan, Tundra

1974 *A Prairie Boy's Winter* by William Kurelek, Tundra

1975 *The Sleighs of My Childhood/Les Traineaux de Mon Enfance* by Carlos Italiano, Tundra

1976 *A Prairie Boy's Summer* by William Kurelek, Tundra

1977 *Down by Jim Long's Stage: Rhymes for Children and Young Fish* by Al Pittman, ill. by Pam Hall, Breakwater

1978 *The Loon's Necklace* by William Toye, ill. by Elizabeth Cleaver, Oxford

1979 *A Salmon for Simon* by Betty Waterton, ill. by Ann Blades, Douglas & McIntyre

1980 *The Twelve Dancing Princesses,* retold by Janet Lunn, ill. by Laszlo Gal, Methuen

1981 *The Trouble with Princesses* by Douglas Tait, McClelland & Stewart

1982 *Ytek and the Arctic Orchid: An Inuit Legend* by Heather Woodall, Douglas & McIntyre

1983 *Chester's Barn* by Lindee Climo, Tundra

1984 *Zoom at Sea* by Tim Wynne-Jones, ill. by Ken Nutt, Douglas & McIntyre

1985 *Chin Chian and the Dragon's Dance* by Ian Wallace, Groundwood

1986 *Zoom Away* by Tim Wynn-Jones, ill. by Ken Nutt, Douglas & McIntyre

1987 *Moonbeam on a Cat's Ear* by Marie-Louise Gay, Stoddard

1988 *Rainy Day Magic* by Marie-Louise Gay, Hodder & Stoughton

1989 *Amos's Sweater* by Janet Lunn, ill. by Kim LaFave, Douglas & McIntyre

The Hans Christian Andersen Award

This award was established in 1956 by the International Board on Books for Young People and is given every two years to one living author who, by his or her complete work, has made an important international contribution to children's literature. Since 1966 an artist's medal has also been given. Each national section of the International Board proposes one author and one illustrator as nominees and the final choice is made by a committee of five, each from a different country.

1956 Eleanor Farjeon (Great Britain)
1958 Astrid Lindgren (Sweden)
1960 Erich Kästner (Germany)
1962 Meindert DeJong (U.S.A.)

1964 René Guillot (France)
1966 Author: Tove Jansson (Finland)
     Illustrator: Alois Carigiet (Switzerland)
1968 Authors: James Krüss (Germany)
     Jose Maria Sanchez-Silva (Spain)
     Illustrator: Jiri Trnka (Czechoslovakia)
1970 Author: Gianni Rodari (Italy)
     Illustrator: Maurice Sendak (U.S.A.)
1972 Author: Scott O'Dell (U.S.A.)
     Illustrator: Ib Spang Olsen (Denmark)
1974 Author: Maria Gripe (Sweden)
     Illustrator: Farshid Mesghali (Iran)
1976 Author: Cecil Bødker (Denmark)
     Illustrator: Tatjana Mawrina (U.S.S.R.)
1978 Author: Paula Fox (U.S.A.)
     Illustrator: Otto S. Svend (Denmark)
1980 Author: Bohumil Riha (Czechoslovakia)
     Illustrator: Suekichi Akaba (Japan)
1982 Author: Lygia Bojunga Nunes (Brazil)
     Illustrator: Zbigniew Rychlicki (Poland)
1984 Author: Christine Nostlinger (Austria)
     Illustrator: Mitsumasa Anno (Japan)
1986 Author: Patricia Wrightson (Australia)
     Illustrator: Robert Ingpen (Australia)
1988 Author: Annie M. G. Schmidt (Netherlands)
     Illustrator: Dusan Kallay (Yugoslavia)
1990 Author: Tormod Haugen (Norway)
     Illustrator: Lisbeth Zwerger (Austria)

The Mildred L. Batchelder Award

This award was established in 1966 by the American Library Association in honor of a woman who promoted internationalism and encouraged translations of books from other countries. The award is given annually to a distinguished book first published in a foreign language, translated, and then published in the United States.

1968 *The Little Man* by Erich Kästner, trans. by James Kirkup, ill. by Rick Schreiter, Knopf
1969 *Don't Take Teddy* by Babbis Friis-Baastad, trans. by Lise Somme McKinnon, Scribner's
1970 *Wildcat under Glass* by Alki Zei, trans. by Edward Fenton, Holt
1971 *In the Land of Ur: The Discovery of Ancient Mesopotamia* by Hans Baumann, trans. by Stella Humphries, ill. by Hans Peter Renner, Pantheon

1972 *Friedrich* by Hans Peter Richter, trans. by Edite Kroll, Holt
1973 *Pulga* by Siny Rose Van Iterson, trans. by Alexander and Alison Gode, Morrow
1974 *Petros' War* by Alki Zei, trans. by Edward Fenton, Dutton
1975 *An Old Tale Carved Out of Stone* by Aleksandr M. Linevski, trans. by Maria Polushkin, Crown
1976 *The Cat and Mouse Who Shared a House* written and ill. by Ruth Hurlimann, trans. by Anthea Bell, Walck
1977 *The Leopard* by Cecil Bodker, ill. by Gunnar Poulsen, Atheneum
1978 No Award
1979 *Konrad* by Christine Nostlinger, trans. by Anthea Bell, ill. by Carol Nicklaus, Watts
     Rabbit Island by Jorg Steiner, trans. by Ann Conrad Lammers, ill. by Jorg Muller, Harcourt
1980 *The Sound of Dragon's Feet* by Alki Zei, trans. by Edward Fenton, Dutton
1981 *The Winter When Time Was Frozen* by Els Pelgrom, trans. by Raphael and Maryka Rudnik, Morrow
1982 *The Battle Horse* by Harry Kullman, trans. by George Blecher and Lone Thygesen-Blecher, Bradbury
1983 *Hiroshima no Pika* written and ill. by Toshi Maruki, Lothrop
1984 *Ronia, the Robber's Daughter* by Astrid Lindgren, trans. by Patricia Crampton, Viking
1985 *The Island on Bird Street* by Uri Orlev, trans. from the Hebrew by Hillel Halkin, Houghton
1986 *Rose Blanche* by Christophe Gallaz and Roberto Innocenti, trans. by Martha Coventry and Richard Graglia, ill. by Roberto Innocenti, Creative Education
1987 *No Hero for the Kaiser* by Rudolf Frank, trans. by Patricia Crampton, ill. by Klaus Steffans, Lothrop
1988 *If You Didn't Have Me* by Ulf Nilsson, ill. by Eva Eriksson, trans. by Lone Thygesen-Blecher and George Blecher, McElderry
1989 *Crutches* by Peter Härtling, Lothrop
1990 *Buster's World* by Bjarne Reuter, trans. by Anthea Bell, Dutton

Appendix E
Pronunciation Guide

Symbols used in the pronunciation are as follows: a as in *hat;* ā as in *age;* ã as in *care;* ä as in *father;* e as in *let;* ē as in *see;* ėr as in *term;* i as in *pin;* ī as in *five;* o as in *hot;* ō as in *go;* ô as in *order, all;* oi as in *oil;* ou as in *house;* th as in *thin;* ŧħ as in *then;* u as in *cup;* ů as in *full;* ü as in *rule;* ū as in *use;* zh as in *measure;* ə as in the unaccented syllables of *about, taken, pencil, lemon, circus;* H as in the german *ach;* N as in the French *bon* (not pronounced, but shows that the vowel before it is nasal); œ as in the French *peu* and the German *könig* (pronounced by speaking ā with the lips rounded as for ō); Y as in the French *du* (pronounced by speaking ē with the lips rounded as for ü). All other symbols represent the consonant sounds that they commonly stand for in English spelling.

Aardema   är′de mä
Abrashkin   a brash′kin
Adoff   ā′dof
Afanasyev   ä fä nä′syif
Agle   ā′gůl
Aiken-drum   ā kən drum
Aldis   ôl′dis
Aleichem, Sholem   ə lā′həm,
   shō′ləm
Aliki   ä lē′kī
Almedingen   al′mə ding′ən
Ambrus   ôm′brůsh
Analdas   ə näl′dəs
Anansi   ə nan′si
Ankhsenpaaten   anH′sen pät′en
Anno, Mitsumasa   an ō,
   mit sü mä′sä
Arawn   ä ron′
Ardizzone   är di zō′ni
Arrietty   är i e′tē
Artzybasheff   är tsi ba′shif
Asbjörnsen   äs′byėrn sen

Asimov   as′im ov
Aucassin   ō ka saN′
Averill   ā′və ril
Ayars   ãrz
Baba Yaga   bä′bə yä′gä
Babar   bä bär′
Bacmeister   bok′mī ster
Bandura   ban dur′ä
Banneker   ban′nə kėr
Barbauld   bär′bōld
Barchilon, Jacques
   bär shē yoN′, zhäk
Basho   bä shō
Baudouy, Michel-Aimé
   bô dü ē′, mē shel-e mä′
Baumann   bou′män
Behn   bān
Beim   bīm
Benét   be nā′
Benezet   ben′ə zet′
Beowulf   bā′ə wůlf
Beskow   bes′kō
Bethune, Mary McLeod
   bə thūn′, mak loud′
Bettelheim   be′tl hīm
Bevis   bē′vis
Bewick   bū′ik
Bidpai   bid′pī
Blegvad   bleg′vad
Blos   blōs
Blough   blou
Bolognese   bō lō nā′zē
Bontemps, Arna   bôN tôN′,
   är′nə
Brinsmead, Hesba Fay   hez′bə
Bryson   brī′sən
Bubo   bū′bō
Budulinek   bu dū′lin ek
Bulla   bůl′ə
Burchard   bœr′chärd
Cabeza de Vaca   kä bā′thä
   dā vä′kä
Carigiet, Alois   cä rē zhē ā′,
   al wä′
Caudill   kô′dl
Cavanna   kə van′ə
Cayuse   kī ūs′

Chaga   chä′gä
Chincoteague   ching′kə tēg
Chukovsky, Kornei
   chu kôf′skē, kôr nā′
Chute, Marchette   chüt,
   mär shet′
Chwast   kwäst
Ciardi   chär′dē
Cinderlad, Per, Paal, Espen
   sin′dər-läd, pär, pôl, es′pən
Coblentz   kō′blents
Collodi   kōl lô′dē
Colman, Hila   hī′lä
Colum, Padraic   kol′um,
   pä′drig
Comenius   kə mē′ni us
Contes de Ma Mère l'Oye   kôNt
   də mä mãr lwä
Coombs   kümz
Cormier   kôr′myä
Cowper   kü′pėr
Credle   crā′dəl
Cruikshank   krůk′shangk
Cuchulain   kü kü′lin
Dahl, Roald   däl, rō′äl
Dalgliesh   däl glēsh
D'Amelio   da mēl′ē yō
Dasent   dā′sənt
d'Aulaire   dō lãr′
d'Aulnoy   dōl nwä′
De Angeli   də an′jel ē
De Beaumont, Madame Le
   Prince   də bō môN′,
   ma dam′ lə praNs′
De Brunhoff, Jean   də brün′ôf,
   zhôN
De Gasztold, Carmen Bernos
   də gaz′tōl, bėr′nōs
De Genlis, Madame   də zhôN
   lē′
DeJong, Meindert   də yung′,
   mīn′dėrt
De la Mare   də la mãr′
Demetrius of Phalerum
   də mē′tri-us, fu lėr′əm
De Pareja   dā pə rä′hä
De Regniers   də rān′yä

721

DeRoin də roin′
Des Jarlait dā zhär lä′
De Treviño dā trə vē′nyō
Deucher dü shä′
Deutsch, Babette doich,
  bab et′
Dobry dō′brē
Dodge, Mary Mapes māps
Domanska, Janina dô män′skä,
  yä nē′nä
Doob düb
Douty dü′tē
Du Bois, William Pène dy bwä,
  pen
Duvoisin dy vwä zaN′
Edda ed′ə
Eichenberg ī′ken bėrg
Engdahl əng′dôl
Epaminondas i pam i non′dəs
Farjeon fär′jun
Farquharson fär′kwėr sən
Feagles fē′gləs
Fenians fē ni ənz
Fflewddur Fflam flü′dœr flam
Fiorello fē ō rel′ō
Fjeld fē el/fyel
Forten fôr′tən
Franchere frän′shär
Frascino frə shē′nō
Frasconi, Antonio fras kō′nē,
  än tō′nyō
Frolov, Vadim frō′lof, vädim
Fyleman fīl′man
Gaer gär
Gaetano gä′ä tä nō
Gág gäg
Galdone gal dōn′
Galileo gal ə lē′ō
Galland, Antoine gə läN′,
  än twōn′
Gaudenzia gou den′tsya
Gautama Buddha gô′tə mə
  bủ′də
Geisel gī′z′l
Gengi gən′jē
Gidal gi dal′
Gilgamesh gil′gə mesh
Glubok glü′bok
Gobhai gō bī′
Gottschalk, Fruma gät′shəlk,
  frü′mə
Goudey gou′dē
Gramatky gra mat′kē
Gripe grēpu
Gudbrand gủd′bränd

Guillot, René gē yō, rù nä′
Guion gī′ôn
Guiterman git′ėr mən
Gurgi gœr′jē
Gwydion gwi′dē on
Gylfi gyl′fə
Haas häs
Hader hä′dėr
Haida hī′du
Hakon hô′kən
Hallard hal′lärd
Haugaard hou′gärd
Hautzig hout′zig
Hazard a zär′
Hazeltine hāz′əl tīn′
Heinlein hīn′līn
Hesiod hē′si od
Heumann hoi′män
Heyerdahl, Thor hä′ėr däl, tủr
Heyward, Du Bose dù bōz′
Hidalgo y Costilla ēd häl′go ē
  kōste′yä
Hieatt hi′at
Hitopadesa hi tō pa dā′sha
Hofsinde hof′sin də
Hogrogian, Nonny
  hō grō′gē an, no′nē
Hokusai hō kủ sī
Homily hom′i lē
Hyndman hīnd′man
Ignatow ig nä′tō
Ishi ē shē
Issa is′ə
Jahdu jä′dū
Jancsi yan′sē
Janeczko, Paul Jan es′kō
Jansson, Tove yän′sən, tō′vä
Janosh yä′nōsh
Jarrell jar′rel
Jataka jä′tä kə
Jean-Claude zhôn klōd
Jeanne-Marie zhan′mä rē′
Jenness jen es′
Karana kä rä′nä
Kästner, Erich kest′nər, ä′rik
Katia kä′tyə
Kaula kô lu
Kavaler ka′vủl ėr
Kävik kä′vik
Kenofer ken′o fėr
Kim Van Kieu kēm vən kyū
Kinder und Hausmärchen
  kin′dėr ủnd hous′mär′Hən
Kjelgaard kel′gärd
Konigsburg kō′nigs bėrg

Krakatoa krak ə tō′ə
Kroeber krō′bər
Krylov kril ôf′
Kumin kew′min
Kuskin kus′kin
La Fontaine, Jean de
  lä fon ten′, zhôn də
La Gallienne lə gal′yən
Lakshmi lok′shmē
La Flesche, Susette lä flesh′,
  sü- zet′
Latham lā′thum
Lathrop lā′thrəp
Ledoux lə dy′
Le Guin le gwin′
Le Hibou et la Poussiquette
  lē bü′ ä lä pü si ket′
L'Engle lengl
Lexau lex ô
Liam lē′am
Liddell lid′əl
Liers lirs
Lilliputians lil ə pyü′shəns
Lindgren, Astrid lind grən,
  äs′trid
Lionni lē ō′nē
Lippiza lip′it za
Llyn-Y-Fan Hlin′ə van′
Lobel lō bel′
Lorenzini lô ren tsē′nē
Lueders lwē′dėrs
Lurs lürz
Mafatu ma fa tu
Mahabharata mə hä′bä′rə tə
Mali mä′lē
Manolo män′ō lō
Mari, Iela and Enzo mä′rē,
  ī′la, en zō
Märchen mär′Hən
Mary-Rousselière, Guy
  mä rē-rü se li ä′, gē
Maslow ma′zlō
Massee ma′sē
Massignon mas ē NyōN′
Matthiesen matħ′i sən
Maui mou′ē
Maurois, André mô′rwä,
  än drä′
Mayne mān
Megrimum me′grə məm
Mei Li mā lē
Melendy mə lən′dē
Miers mirz
Miklagard mik′la gärd
Mikolaycak mīk ô lä′chək

Milne   miln

Minarik   min′ə rik

Mizamura, Kazue   mi′zä mü rä,
    kä-zü′ä

Moe, Jörgen   mō ə, ẏr′gən

Momolu   mo′mō lü

Montresor, Beni   mōn′trə sôr,
    bā′nē

Monvel, Boutet de   môN vel′,
    bü- tā′ də

Mordvinoff   mord′vin of

Mosel   mō zəl′

Mowgli   mou′glē

Mulready   múl′red ē

Munari, Bruno   mü nä′rē,
    brü′nō

Nefertiti   ne fèr tē′ti

Nibelungs/Niblungs
    nē′bə lùngz/nē′blùngz

Nic Leodhas, Sorche   nic ly ōs′,
    sôr′ä

Nicolette   nē kô let′

Noguchi, Hideyo   no gu′che,
    hē de yo

Nootka   nùt′kə

Okada, Rokuo   ō ka da, rō kù ō

Olatunji, Michael Babatunde
    o lä- tün′jē, bä bä tün′dē

Orgel   or′gel

Orisha   ôr ē′sha

Orphelines   ôr fel ēnz′

Padre Porko   pä′thre pôrk′ō

Palazzo   pa lat′zō

Panchatantra   pän chə tän′trə

Pandu   pän′dü

Pantaloni   pan tə lō′nē

Papashvily   pa pash vē′lē

Paracelsus   par ə sel′səs

Pecos   pā′kəs

Pelle   pel′lə

Perrault   pe rō′

Petrides, Heidrun   pə trē′dēz,
    hīd′drun

Petry   pē′tri

Pettit   pe tē′

Piaget   pē ä zhä′

Piatti, Celestino   pyät′tē,
    chä läs- tē′nō

Pibroch of Donnel Dhu
    pē′broн, don′-nel dü

Picard, Barbara Leonie
    pi′kärd, lā′ō nē

Planudes   plə nü′dēz

Plasencia   plä sen′thyä

Plouhinec   plü′i nek

Podkayne   pod kän′

Politi   pō lē′tē

Prelutsky   pre lut′skē

Prishvin, Mikhail   prēsh′vin,
    mē на- ēl′

Procyon   prō′si on

Prydain   pri dān′

Pulga   pù′gä

Pwyll and Pyrderi   pü′il,
    pru dä′rē

Quarles   kwôrlz

Rabe   rāb

Ramayana   rä mä′yə nə

Ranke   räng′ke

Rasmussen, Knud   räs′mus ən,
    nùd

Ravielli   rav ē el′li

Repplier   rep′lēr

Rey   rā

Ripopet-Barabas
    rē′pō pä- bä′rä bä

Rocca, Guido   rôk′kō, gwē dō

Roethke   ret′kē

Rojankovsky   rō jan kôf′skē

Rossetti   rō set′ē

Rousseau   rü′sō

Rugh   rü

Rukeyser   rü′kī zèr

Saba   sä′bä

Sadko   säd′kô

Saint Exupéry, Antoine de
    san tāg- zy pä rē, än twän′də

Sasek, Miroslav   sä′sek,
    mī′rō släv

Savigny   säv′in yē

Scheele   shē′lē

Schoenherr   shùn′här

Schweitzer   shvī′tsər

Seignobosc, Françoise
    sängn′yō bosk, fräN swäz′

Sellew   se′lü

Seredy   shär′ə dē

Serraillier   sə räl′yä

Seuss   süs

Shawneen   shä nēn′

Sheftu   shef′tü

Shimin, Symeon   shi′min,
    sim′ē ùn

Shogomoc   shō gō môk

Shulevitz, Uri   shü′lə vitz, ü′rē

Sidjakov   sij′ə kof

Sigurdson   si′gûth son

Singer, Isaac Bashevis
    bə shä′vis

Sita   sē′tä

Slobodkin   slō bod′kin

Smolicheck   smol′i chek

Snegourka   snye gür′kä

Sojo, Toba   sō′jō, to′bä

Sokol   sō′kol

Sonneborn   son′ne born

Soupault   sü pō′

Southall   south′ôl

Spier   spēr

Spyri, Johanna   shpē′rē,
    yō hän′ä

Stahl   stäl

Steig   stīg

Stolz   stōlts

Strachey   strā′chi

Streatfeild, Noel   stret′feld,
    nō′əl

Struwwelpeter   strü′vel pä ter

Sture-Vasa   stùr-vä sä

Sturluson, Snorri   stür′le sôn,
    snôr′ä

Sundiata   sün dē ä′tä

Syme   sīm

Tagore, Rabindranath   tä′gōr,
    rä bēn′drä nät′

Taliesin   tal ē ä′zin

Taran   ta′ran

Tashjian   täs jun

Tenniel   ten′yel

Ter Haar, Jaap   tèr här, yop

Terzian   ter′zian

Thorne-Thomsen, Gudrun
    thôrn-tom′sen, gü′drun

Thorvall, Kerstin   tùr′väl,
    char′stin

Tistou   tē stü′

Tituba   ti′tū bä

Tlingit   tling′git

Tolkien   tôl′ken

Treece   trēs

Tresselt   tre′selt

Tunis   tū′nis

Turska, Krystyna   turs′kä,
    kris- tē′na

Tutankhaten   tüt änн ä′tən

Uchida, Yoshiko   ü chē dä,
    yō shē- kō

Udry   ŭ′dri

Undset, Sigrid   ŭn′set, si′grid

Ungerer, Tomi   un′gœ rœr

Unnerstad   un′nèr stadt

Ushinsky   ù shin′skē

Van Allsburg   vän ôlz′ berg

Vasilisa   va syē′le sa

Vespucci, Amerigo   ves pü′chē,
    a mer ē′gō
Viehmann   vē′män
Viollet   vē ō let′
Viorst   vē ȯrst′
Vivier   viv ē ā′
Volsung   vol′sung
Vulpes   vul′pēz
Watie   wä′tē
Wayah   wä ä
Weisgard   wīs′gärd
Whippety Stourie   wip′ə tē
    stur′ē

Whuppie   wup′ē
Wibberley   wi′ber lē
Weir   wēr
Wiese   vē′zə
Wild, Dortchen   vilt, dôrt′shən
Wodehouse   wud′hous
Wojciechowska, Maia
    woi je hov′-ska, mä′ē ä
Wuorio, Eva-Lis   wur yō,
    ā vä- lēs
Yashima, Taro   yä′shi ma, tä′rō
Yonge   yung

Yonie Wondernose
    yō nē wun′ dər nōz
Yorubaland   yôr u′ba land
Yulya   yü lyä
Zamani   zä mä nē
Zei, Alki   zā′e, al′kē
Zemach   zē′mak
Zhenya   zhä′nyə
Zolotow   zol′ə tou
Zwerger   zver′ger

Subject Index

Author, Illustrator, Title Index

Illustration Acknowledgments

Chapter One

p. 6 Scott Foresman **p. 8** From *Better With Two* by Barbara M. Joosse, illustrated by Catherine Stock. Illustrations copyright © 1988 by Catherine Stock. Reprinted by permission of Harper-Collins Publishers. **p. 10** From *Dream Blocks* by Aileen C. Higgins, illus. by Jessie Willcox Smith. New York: Duffield & Co., 1908. Reprinted with permission of Macmillan Publishing Company from *Told Under the Blue Umbrella*, illustrated by Marguerite Davis. Copyright 1933, renewed 1961 by Macmillan Publishing Company. Illustration by Marjorie Flack reprinted by permission of G. P. Putnam's Sons from *Here, There, and Everywhere* by Dorothy Aldis, copyright 1927, 1928, copyright renewed © 1955, 1956 by Dorothy Aldis. From *Yonie Wondernose* by Marguerite de Angeli. Copyright 1944 by Marguerite de Angeli. Reprinted by permission of Doubleday, a division of Bantam Doubleday Dell Publishing Group, Inc. **p. 11** Illustration from *Hello, Mrs. Piggle-Wiggle* by Betty MacDonald. Drawings by Hillary Knight (J. B. Lippincott). Copyright © 1957 by Betty MacDonald. Reprinted by permission of HarperCollins Publishers. Reprinted by permission of Atheneum Publishers, an imprint of Macmillan Publishing Company, from *Alexander and the Terrible, Horrible, No Good, Very Bad Day* by Judith Viorst. Illustrations by Ray Cruz. Pictures copyright © 1972 by Ray Cruz. From *Ramona and Her Father* by Beverly Cleary. Copyright © 1975, 1977 by Beverly Cleary. Reprinted by permission of William Morrow & Company. From *Hiroshima No Pika* by Toshi Maruki. Copyright © 1980 by Toshi Maruki. Reprinted by permission of Lothrop, Lee & Shepard Books, A Division of William Morrow & Company. **p. 12** From *Ten, Nine, Eight* by Molly Bang. Copyright © 1983 by Molly Garret Bang. Reprinted by permission of Greenwillow Books, A Division of William Morrow & Company. From *Angel Mae: A Tale of Trotter Street* by Shirley Hughes. Copyright © 1989 by Shirley Hughes. Reprinted by permission of Lothrop, Lee & Shepard Books, A Division of William Morrow & Company. From *I Hate English!* by Ellen Levine, illustrated by Steve Björkman. Illustrations copyright © 1989 by Steve Björkman. Reprinted by permission of Scholastic Inc. **p. 15** Scott Foresman **p. 18** From *Like Jake and Me* by Mavis Jukes, illustrated by Lloyd Bloom. Text copyright © 1984 by Mavis Jukes. Illustrations copyright © 1984 by Lloyd Bloom. Reprinted by permission of Alfred A. Knopf, Inc. **p. 19** From *Molly's Pilgrim* by Barbara Cohen, illustrated by Michael J. Deraney. Illustrations copyright © 1983 by Michael J. Deraney. Reprinted by permission of Lothrop, Lee & Shepard, a division of William Morrow & Company. From *Little Navajo Bluebird* by Ann Nolan Clark, illustrated by Paul Lantz. Copyright © 1943 by Ann Nolan Clark & Paul Lantz, renewed 1970 by Ann Nolan Clark. Reprinted by permission of the publisher, Viking Penguin, a division of Penguin Books USA Inc. **p. 22** From *All I See* by Cynthia Rylant. Illustrations copyright © 1988 by Peter Catalanotto. Reprinted by permission of Orchard Books, a division of Franklin Watts, Inc. **p. 24** Illustration by Jill Murphy reprinted by permission of G. P. Putnam's Sons and Walker Books Limited from *Five Minutes' Peace* by Jill Murphy, copyright © 1986 by Jill Murphy. **p. 27** Rick Reil/Realife Photo **p. 28** Illustration from *George and Martha* by James Marshall. Copyright © 1972 by James Marshall. Reprinted by permission of Houghton Mifflin Company. **p. 29** From *The Not-So-Wicked Stepmother* by Lizi Boyd. Copyright © 1987 by Lizi Boyd. Reprinted by permission of the publisher, Viking Penguin, a division of Penguin Books USA Inc.

Chapter Two

p. 39 From *Little House in the Big Woods* by Laura Ingalls Wilder, illustrated by Garth Williams. Pictures copyright 1953 by Garth Williams, renewed 1981 by Garth Williams. Reprinted by permission of HarperCollins Publishers. **p. 41** From *Little Women* by Louisa May Alcott, illustrated by Barbara Cooney (Thomas Y. Crowell). Illustrations copyright © 1955 by Barbara Cooney. Reprinted by permission of HarperCollins Publishers. **p. 42** From *Did You Carry the Flag Today, Charley?* by Rebecca Caudill, illustrated by Nancy Grossman. Text copyright © 1966 by Rebecca Caudill. Illustrations copyright © 1966 by Nancy Grossman. Reprinted by permission of Henry Holt and Company, Inc. **p. 45** Cover illustration from *One-Eyed Cat* by Paula Fox. Copyright © 1984 by Paula Fox. Reprinted by permission of Dell, a Division of Bantam Doubleday Dell Publishing Group, Inc. **p. 47** From *Little Bear* by Else Holmelund Minarik, illustrated by Maurice Sendak. Illustrations copyright © 1957 by Maurice Sendak. Reprinted by permission of HarperCollins Publishers. **p. 48** From *The Secret in the Matchbox* by Val Willis, illustrated by John Shelley. Illustrations copyright © 1988 by John Shelley. Reprinted by permission of Farrar, Straus & Giroux, Inc. **p. 49** From *Spunky Sulks* by William Steig. Copyright © 1988 by William Steig. Reprinted by permission of Farrar, Straus & Giroux, Inc. **p. 50** Cover illustration by Gordon Crabb from *War Comes to Willy Freeman* by James Lincoln Collier and Christopher Collier. Illustration copyright © 1983 by Gordon Crabb. Reprinted by permission of Young Artists Ltd.

Chapter Three

p. 58 New York Public Library, Astor, Lenox and Tilden Foundations. **p. 59** From *Beauty and the Beast*. Anonymous. Ill. Eleanor Vere Boyle. London: Sampson Low, Martsen, Low & Searle, n.d., n.p. **p. 61** Rare Book Department/The Free Library of Philadelphia. **p. 63** Jonathan Swift, *Gulliver's Travels*, illustrated by Louis Rhead. New York: HarperCollins Publishers, 1913. **p. 67** From The English *Struwwelpeter: Or Pretty Stories and Funny Pictures*. London: Routledge & Kegan Paul, Ltd. **p. 70** Illustration by Kay Nielsen and Victor G. Candell, copyright 1914 by Hodder & Stoughton Ltd. From *East of the Sun, West of the Moon* by P. C. Asbjörnesen. Used by permission of Doubleday, a division of Bantam Doubleday Dell Publishing Group, Inc. **p. 72** From *A Child's Garden of Verses* by Robert Louis Stevenson, illus. by J. W. Smith. New York: Scribners (Scribners Illustrated Classics), 1905.

Chapter Four

p. 80 From *Tail Feathers from Mother Goose: The Opie Rhyme Book* by Iona Opie. Illustration copyright © 1988 by Reg Cartwright. Reprinted by permission of Little, Brown and Company. **p. 81** Illustration by Frederick Richardson from *Mother Goose: The Classic Volland Edition*, rearranged and edited by Eulalie Osgood Carver. Copyright © 1971 by Rand McNally & Company. Reprinted by permission. From *An Edward Lear Alphabet*, illustrated by Carol Newsom. Illustrations copyright © 1983 by Carol Newsom. Reprinted by permission of Lothrop, Lee & Shepard Books, a division of William Morrow & Company. **p. 82** "Little Miss Muffet" illustration by Feodor Rojankovsky from *The Tall Book of Mother Goose*. Copyright 1942, copyright renewed 1970 by Western Publishing Company. Reprinted by permission. Illustration for "Humpty Dumpty" from *The Real Mother Goose*, illustrated by Blanche Fisher Wright. Copyright 1916, 1944 Checkerboard Press, Inc. Used with permission. From *London Bridge Is Falling Down!* illustrated by Peter Spier. Copyright © 1967 by Peter Spier. Reprinted by permission of Doubleday, a Division of Bantam Doubleday Dell Publishing Group, Inc. **p. 83** From *Mother Goose* by Brian Wildsmith. Copyright © 1964 by Brian Wildsmith. Reproduced by permission of Franklin Watts, Inc. From *The House That Jack Built: A Mother Goose Nursery*

Rhyme, illustrated by Janet Stevens. Illustrations copyright © 1985 by Janet Stevens. Reprinted by permission of Holiday House.   From *Cakes and Custard* by Brian Alderson, illustrated by Helen Oxenbury. Illustrations copyright © 1984 by Helen Oxenbury. Reprinted by permission of William Morrow & Company.   Illustration by Ed Young reprinted by permission of Philomel Books from *Chinese Mother Goose Rhymes* selected by Robert Wyndham, illustrations © 1968 by Ed Young. **p. 84** Illustration for "Old King Cole" from *Nicola Bayley's Book of Nursery Rhymes*, illustrated by Nicola Bayley. Illustrations copyright © 1975 by Nicola Bayley. Reprinted by permission of Alfred A. Knopf, Inc.   From *Mother Goose: A Collection of Classic Nursery Rhymes* selected and illustrated by Michael Hague. Illustration copyright © 1984 by Michael Hague. Reprinted by permission of Henry Holt and Company, Inc.   Illustration by Tomie dePaola reprinted by permission of G. P. Putnam's Sons from *Tomie dePaola's Mother Goose*, illustrations © 1985 by Tomie dePaola. From *The Orchard Book of Nursery Rhymes* by Zena Sutherland, illustrated by Faith Jaques. Illustrations copyright © 1990 by Faith Jaques. Reprinted by permission of Orchard Books, a division of Franklin Watts, Inc. **p. 85** From *The Random House Book of Mother Goose*, selected and illustrated by Arnold Lobel. Reprinted by permission of Random House, Inc. **p. 87** From *Ape in a Cape*, copyright 1952, 1980 by Fritz Eichenberg. Reproduced by permission of Harcourt Brace Jovanovich, Inc.   Illustration by Wanda Gág reprinted by permission of Coward, McCann & Geoghegan from *The ABC Bunny* by Wanda Gág, copyright 1933 by Wanda Gág, copyright renewed © 1961 by Robert Janssen. From *Aster Aardvark's Alphabet Adventure* by Steven Kellogg. Copyright © 1987 by Steven Kellogg. Reprinted by permission of William Morrow & Company. **p. 88** From *Anno's Alphabet* by Mitsumasa Anno (Thomas Y. Crowell). Copyright © 1974 by Fukuinkan-Shoten Publishers. Reprinted by permission of HarperCollins Publishers.   From *If There Were Dreams to Sell* by Barbara Lalicki, illustrated by Margot Tomes. Illustrations copyright © 1984 by Margot Tomes. Reprinted by permission of Lothrop, Lee & Shepard Books, a division of William Morrow & Company. Illustration from *ABC Americana* by Cynthia Elyce Rubin and National Gallery of Art. Copyright © 1989 by Harcourt Brace Jovanovich, Inc. Reprinted by permission of the publisher. From *The Wildlife ABC: A Nature Alphabet Book* by Jan Thornhill. Copyright © 1988 by Jan Thornhill. Used by permission of the publisher, Simon & Schuster Books for Young Readers, New York, New York 10020. **p. 89** From *The Ark in the Attic Alphabet Adventure*, photographs by Starr Ockenga, text and painted backgrounds by Eileen Doolittle. Photographs © 1987 by Starr Ockenga. Reprinted by permission of David R. Godine, Publisher.   From *A. B. See!* by Tana Hoban. Copyright © 1982 by Tana Hoban. Reprinted by permission of Greenwillow Books, a division of William Morrow & Company, Inc. **p. 91** Illustration by Suse MacDonald from *Alphabatics* by Suse MacDonald. Copyright © 1986 by Suse MacDonald. Reproduced by permission of Bradbury Press, an Affiliate of Macmillan, Inc. **p. 93** From *Anno's Counting Book* by Mitsumasa Anno (Thomas Y. Crowell). Copyright © 1975 by Kodansha (Tokyo). Reprinted by permission of HarperCollins Publishers. **p. 94** From *Counting Wildflowers* by Bruce McMillan. Copyright © 1986 by Bruce McMillan. Reprinted by permission of Lothrop, Lee & Shepard Books, A Division of William Morrow & Company. **p. 95** Photo by Jan Siegieda reprinted by permission of Coward-McCann and Methuen Children's Books from *Let's Look for Shapes* by Bill Gillham and Susan Hulme, photographs copyright © 1984 by Bill Gillham and Jan Siegieda. **p. 96** From *School* by Emily Arnold McCully. Copyright © 1987 by Emily Arnold McCully. Reprinted by permission of HarperCollins Publishers. **p. 100** From *The Angel and the Soldier Boy* by Peter Collington. Reprinted by permission of Alfred A. Knopf, Inc., and Methuen Children's Books. **p. 101** From *Frog and Toad Are Friends* by Arnold Lobel. Copyright © 1970 by Arnold Lobel. Reprinted by permission of HarperCollins Publishers. **p. 102** From *Stanley and Rhoda* by Rosemary Wells. Copyright © 1978 by Rosemary Wells. Reprinted by permission of Dial Books for Young Readers. **p.104** Reprinted with permission of Charles Scribner's Sons, an imprint of Macmillan Publishing Company from "My Goals as an Illustrator" in *Lotus Seeds* by Marcia Brown. Copyright © 1955, 1967, 1986 by Marcia Brown. **p. 105** From *Birthday Presents* by Cynthia Rylant,

pictures by Suçie Stevenson. Illustrations copyright © 1987 by Suçie Stevenson. Reprinted by permission of Orchard Books, a division of Franklin Watts, Inc.   From *Storm in the Night* by Mary Stolz, illustrated by Pat Cummings. Illustrations copyright © 1988 by Pat Cummings. Reprinted by permission of HarperCollins Publishers. **p. 106** From *Annabelle Swift, Kindergartner*, story and pictures by Amy Schwartz. Copyright © 1988 by Amy Schwartz. Reprinted by permission of Orchard Books, a division of Franklin Watts, Inc. **p. 107** From *My Brother Tries to Make Me Laugh* by Andrew Glass. Copyright © 1984 by Andrew Glass. Reprinted by permission of Lothrop, Lee & Shepard Books, A Division of William Morrow & Company. **p. 109** From *A Weekend With Wendell* by Kevin Henkes. Copyright © 1986 by Kevin Henkes. Reprinted by permission of Greenwillow Books, A Division of William Morrow & Company. **p. 110** Illustration by Tejima reprinted by permission of Philomel Books from *Owl Lake* by Tejima, copyright © 1982 by Keizaburo Tejima. **p. 112** From *Charlie Needs a Cloak* by Tomie dePaola. Copyright © 1973 by Tomie dePaola. Used by permission of the publisher, Prentice-Hall, Inc., Englewood Cliffs, NJ.   Illustration by Colin Hawkins reprinted by permission of G.P. Putnam's Sons from *Adding Animals* by Colin Hawkins, copyright © 1983 by Colin Hawkins.

Chapter Five

p. 133 From *Daisy* by Brian Wildsmith. Copyright © 1984 by Brian Wildsmith. Reprinted by permission of Pantheon Books, a division of Random House, Inc., and Oxford University Press. **p. 139** Figure from Cruikshank's *German Popular Stories*, 1823, re-engraved by John Byfield, 1849. **p. 142** From *The House at Pooh Corner* by A.A. Milne, illustrated by E.H. Shepard. Copyright 1928 by E.P. Dutton, renewed 1956 by A.A. Milne. Reproduced by permission of the publisher, Dutton Children's Books, a division of Penguin Books USA, Inc. **p. 144** Illustration from *Little Tim and the Brave Sea Captain* by Edward Ardizzone (Puffin Books, 1955). Copyright © 1955 by Edward Ardizzone. Reprinted by permission of Penguin Books Ltd. **p. 146** From *Louie* by Ezra Jack Keats. Copyright © 1975 by Ezra Jack Keats. Reprinted by permission of Greenwillow Books, A Division of William Morrow & Company. **p. 147** From *Miss Rumphius* by Barbara Cooney. Copyright © 1982 by Barbara Cooney Porter. Reprinted by permission of the publisher, Viking Penguin, a division of Penguin Books USA, Inc. **p. 148** From *The Buck Stops Here* by Alice Provensen (Thomas Y. Crowell). Copyright © 1990 by Alice Provensen. Reprinted by permission of HarperCollins Publishers. **p.149** Reprinted with permission of Charles Scribner's Sons, an imprint of Macmillan Publishing Company from "Integrity and Intuition" in *Lotus Seeds* by Marcia Brown. Copyright © 1955, 1967, 1986 by Marcia Brown. **p. 150** From *Dear Mili* by Wilhelm Grimm, translated by Ralph Manheim, illustrations by Maurice Sendak. Illustrations copyright © 1988 by Maurice Sendak. Reprinted by permission of Farrar, Straus & Giroux, Inc. **p. 152** From *The Tale of the Mandarin Ducks* by Katherine Paterson, illustrated by Leo and Diane Dillon. Text copyright © 1990 by Katherine Paterson. Illustrations copyright © 1990 by Diane and Leo Dillon. Reprinted by permission of Lodestar Books, an affiliate of Dutton Children's Books, a division of Penguin Books USA, Inc. **p. 154** From *On Market Street*, pictures by Anita Lobel, words by Arnold Lobel. Illustrations copyright © 1981 by Anita Lobel. Reprinted by permission of Greenwillow Books, A Division of William Morrow & Company. **p. 155** Reprinted with permission of Macmillan Publishing Company from *The Daywatchers* by Peter Parnall. Copyright © 1984 by Peter Parnall. **p. 156** From *A Child Is Born: The Christmas Story* adapted from The New Testament by Elizabeth Winthrop, illustrated by Charles Ikolaycak. Illustrations copyright © 1983 by Charles Mikolaycak. Reprinted by permission of Holiday House.   From *Geoffrey Chaucer: Canterbury Tales*, selected, translated, and adapted by Barbara Cohen, illustrated by Trina Schart Hyman. Illustrations copyright © 1988 by Trina Schart Hyman. Reprinted by permission of Lothrop, Lee & Shepard Books, A Division of William Morrow & Company.
p. 157 From *Hiawatha* by Henry Wadsworth Longfellow, pictures by Susan Jeffers. Copyright © 1983 by Susan Jeffers. Reprinted

by permission of Dial Books for Young Readers. **p. 158** From *The Adventures of Tom Sawyer* by Mark Twain, illustrated by Barry Moser. Illustrations copyright © 1989 by Barry Moser. Reprinted by permission of Books of Wonder, A Division of William Morrow & Company. **p. 159** Illustration from *Black and White* by David Macaulay. Copyright © 1990 by David Macaulay. Reprinted by permission of Houghton Mifflin Company. **p. 160** Illustration from *Jumanji* by Chris Van Allsburg. Copyright © 1981 by Chris Van Allsburg. Reprinted by permission of Houghton Mifflin Company.   From *Mirandy and Brother Wind* by Patricia McKissack, illustrated by Jerry Pinkney. Text copyright © 1988 by Patricia C. McKissack. Illustrations copyright © 1988 by Jerry Pinkney. Reprinted by permission of Alfred A. Knopf, Inc. **p. 161** From *Iktomi and the Berries: A Plains Indian Story*, retold and illustrated by Paul Goble. Copyright © 1989 by Paul Goble. Reprinted by permission of Orchard Books, a division of Franklin Watts, Inc. **p. 164** Illustration from *The Tale of Two Bad Mice* by Beatrix Potter. Copyright © 1904, 1987 by Frederick Warne & Co. Reprinted by permission of Penguin Books Ltd. **p. 165** Illustration by Arthur Rackham from *Peter Pan in Kensington Gardens* (1906) by James Matthew Barrie. Reprinted by permission of Barbara Edwards.   Washington Irving, *Rip Van Winkle* pictures and decorations by N.C. Wyeth. New York: William Morrow & Company, 1987. **p. 166** From *Tanglewood Tales for Girls and Boys* by Edmund Dulac. Copyright © 1918 by Hodder & Stoughton Ltd., London. Used with permission. **p. 167** From *In the Troll Wood* by John Bauer. Copyright © Albert Bonniers Forlag, Stockholm. Reprinted by permission.   Reprinted with the permission of Charles Scribner's Sons, an imprint of Macmillan Publishing Company, from *The Wind in the Willows* by Kenneth Grahame. Illustrations by Ernest H. Shepard. Illustrations copyright © 1933, 1953,1954 by Charles Scribner's Sons; copyright renewed © 1961 by Ernest H. Shepard; 1981 by Mary Elanor Jessie Knox. **p. 168** From *The Story of Babar* by Jean de Brunhoff. Copyright © 1933 by Random House, Inc. Copyright renewed © 1961 by Random House, Inc. Reprinted by permission of Random House, Inc.   From *The Little Island* by Golden MacDonald, illustrated by Leonard Weisgard. Copyright © 1946 by Doubleday & Company, Inc. Reprinted by permission of Doubleday, a division of Bantam Doubleday Dell Publishing Group.Inc. **p. 169** From *A Tree Is Nice* by Janice May Udry, pictures by Marc Simont. Pictures copyright © 1956 by Marc Simont. Reprinted by permission of HarperCollins Publishers.   From *The Snowy Day* by Ezra Jack Keats. Copyright © 1962 by Ezra Jack Keats. Reprinted by permission of the publisher, Viking Penguin, a division of Penguin Books USA, Inc. **p. 170** From *Where the Wild Things Are*, story and pictures by Maurice Sendak. Copyright © 1963 by Maurice Sendak. Reprinted by permission of HarperCollins Publishers.   From *Song and Dance Man* by Karen Ackerman, illustrated by Stephen Gammell. Illustrations copyright © 1988 by Stephen Gammell. Reprinted by permission of Alfred A. Knopf, Inc.   From *Mr. Gumpy's Motorcar* by John Burningham. Copyright © 1973 by John Burningham. Reprinted by permission of HarperCollins Publishers. **p. 171** Illustration from *Aïda* by Leontyne Price. Illustration copyright © 1990 by Leo and Diane Dillon. Reprinted by permission of Harcourt Brace Jovanovich, Inc.   From *Valentine & Orson* by Nancy Ekholm Burkert. Copyright © 1989 by Nancy Ekholm Burkert. Reprinted by permission of the author. **p. 172** From *The Way Things Work* by David Macaulay. Illustrations copyright © 1988 by David Macaulay. Reprinted by permission of Houghton Mifflin Company. From *Dogger* by Shirley Hughes. Copyright © 1977 by Shirley Hughes. Reprinted by permission of Lothrop Lee & Shepard Books, a division of William Morrow & Company., Inc., and The Bodley Head. **p. 173** From *Flying* by Donald Crews. Copyright © 1986 by Donald Crews. Reprinted by permission of Greenwillow Books, a division of William Morrow & Company. From *Carousel* by Brian Wildsmith. Copyright © 1988 by Brian Wildsmith. Reprinted by permission of Alfred A. Knopf, Inc., and Oxford University Press. **p. 174** From *Free Fall* by David Wiesner. Copyright 1988 by David Wiesner. Reprinted by permission of Lothrop, Lee & Shepard Books, a division of William Morrow & Company.   From *Swan Lake* by Mark Helprin, illustrated by Chris Van Allsburg. Illustrations copyright © 1989 by Chris Van Allsburg. Reprinted by permission of Houghton Mifflin Company.   Illustration by Ed Young reprinted by permission

of Philomel Books from *Lon Po Po: A Red-Riding Hood Story from China*. Copyright © 1989 by Ed Young. **p. 175** From *The Mountains of Tibet* by Mordicai Gerstein. Copyright © 1987 by Mordicai Gerstein. Reprinted by permission of HarperCollins Publishers.   From *The Land of Narnia* by Brian Sibley, illustrated by Pauline Baynes. Illustrations copyright © 1989 by Pauline Baynes. Reprinted by permission of HarperCollins Publishers. **p. 176** From *Oh, Brother* by Arthur Yorinks, pictures by Richard Egielski. Pictures copyright © 1989 by Richard Egielski. Reprinted by permission of Farrar, Straus & Giroux, Inc.   From *Mufaro's Beautiful Daughters* by John Steptoe. Copyright © 1987 by John Steptoe. Reprinted by permission of Lothrop, Lee & Shepard Books, a division of William Morrow & Company. **p. 177** Illustration from *In the Beginning: Creation Stories from Around the World* by Virginia Hamilton, illustrated by Barry Moser. Copyright © 1988 by Harcourt Brace Jovanovich, Inc. Reprinted by permission of the publisher.   Illustration from *Heckedy Peg* by Audrey Wood. Copyright © 1987 by Don Wood. Reprinted by permission of Harcourt Brace Jovanovich, Inc. **p. 178** From *The Devil with the Three Golden Hairs* by Nonny H. Kherdian. Copyright © 1983 by Nonny H. Kherdian. Reprinted by permission of Alfred A. Knopf, Inc.   From *The Water of Life: A Tale from the Brothers Grimm*, retold by Barbara Rogasky, illustrated by Trina Schart Hyman. Illustrations copyright © 1986 by Trina Schart Hyman. Reprinted by permission of Holiday House.   From *The Talking Eggs* by Robert D. San Souci, illustrated by Jerry Pinkney. Illustrations copyright © 1989 by Jerry Pinkney. Reprinted by permission of the publisher, Dial Books for Young Readers. **p. 179** From *Rumpelstiltskin* by Paul O. Zelinsky. Copyright © 1986 by Paul O. Zelinsky. Reprinted by permission of the publisher, Dutton Children's Books, a division of Penguin Books USA, Inc.   From *The White Cat* by Robert D. San Souci, illustrated by Gennady Spirin. Illustrations copyright © 1990 by Gennady Spirin. Reprinted by permission of Orchard Books, a division of Franklin Watts, Inc.

Chapter Six

p. 183 Illustration by Ed Young reprinted by permission of Philomel Books from *Yeh-Shen: A Cinderella Story from China* retold by Ai-Ling Louie, illustrated by Ed Young, illustrations copyright © 1982 by Ed Young. **p. 186** From *Little Red Cap* by the Brothers Grimm, illustrated by Lisbeth Zwerger, translated from the German by Elizabeth D. Crawford. English translation copyright © 1983 by William Morrow & Company. Reprinted by permission of the publisher. **p. 187** Illustration from *The Three Sillies*, copyright © 1986 by Kathryn Hewitt. Reprinted by permission of Harcourt Brace Jovanovich, Inc. **p. 191** From *Rumpelstiltskin*, retold from the Brothers Grimm and illustrated by Donna Diamond. Copyright © 1983 by Donna Diamond. Reprinted by permission of Holiday House. **p. 193** From *Rapunzel* from The Brothers Grimm, retold by Barbara Rogasky. Illustrations copyright © 1982 by Trina Schart Hyman. Reprinted by permission of Holiday House. **p. 195** Illustration from *The Three Billy Goats Gruff*, copyright © 1987 by Janet Stevens. Reprinted by permission of Harcourt Brace Jovanovich, Inc. **p. 196** From *Alan Garner's Book of British Fairy Tales*, illustrations by Derek Collard. Illustrations copyright © 1984 by Derek Collard. Reprinted by permission of William Collins Publishers. **p. 198** From *Hansel and Gretel* illustrated by Anthony Browne. Illustrations © Anthony Browne 1981. Reprinted by permission of Alfred A. Knopf, Inc. **p. 201** From *Little Brother and Little Sister* by Barbara Cooney. Copyright © 1982 by Barbara Cooney Porter. Used by permission of Doubleday, a division of Bantam Doubleday Dell Publishing Group, Inc.   From *The Juniper Tree and Other Tales from Grimm*, selected by Lore Segal and Maurice Sendak, translated by Lore Segal, pictures by Maurice Sendak. Illustration copyright © 1973 by Maurice Sendak. Reprinted by permission of Farrar, Straus & Giroux, Inc. **p. 202** From *Great Swedish Fairy Tales*, translated by Holger Lundberg, illustrated by John Bauer. English translation copyright © 1973 by Dell Publishing Co., Inc. Reprinted by permission of Delacorte Press/Seymour Lawrence, a division of Bantam Doubleday Dell Publishing Group, Inc. **p. 204** From *Duffy and the Devil* by Harve Zemach, illustrated by Margot Zemach. Copyright © 1973 by Farrar, Straus & Giroux, Inc. Reprinted by permission. **p. 205** From *The Adventures of*

Spider: West African Folk Tales retold by Joyce Cooper Arkhurst with illustrations by Jerry Pinkney. Copyright © 1964 by Barker/Black Studio, Inc. Reprinted by permission of Little, Brown and Company. **p. 206** From *The Rumor of Pavel and Paali* by Carole Kismaric, illustrated by Charles Mikolaycak. Illustrations copyright © 1988 by Charles Mikolaycak. Reprinted by permission of HarperCollins Publishers. **p. 207** Illustration by Fritz Eichenberg from *Padre Porko* by Robert Davis. Copyright 1939 by Robert Davis. Reproduced by permission of Holiday House. **p. 208** From *The People Could Fly*, retold by Virginia Hamilton, illustrated by Leo & Diane Dillon. Text copyright © 1985 by Virginia Hamilton. Illustrations copyright © 1985 by Leo & Diane Dillon. Reprinted by permission of Alfred A. Knopf, Inc. **p. 210** From *Paul Bunyan*, retold and illustrated by Steven Kellogg. Copyright © 1984 by Steven Kellogg. Reprinted by permission of Morrow Junior Books, A Division of William Morrow & Company.

Chapter Seven

p. 228 From *The Fables of India* by Joseph Gaer, with illustrations by Randy Monk. Copyright 1955 by Joseph Gaer; copyright © renewed 1983 by Fay Gaer. Reprinted by permission of Little, Brown and Company. **p. 229** From "Chanticleer and the Fox" in *Canterbury Tales* by Geoffrey Chaucer, illustrated by Barbara Cooney. Copyright © 1958 by Thomas Y. Crowell Company, Inc. Reprinted by permission of HarperCollins Publishers. **p. 231** From *Persephone and the Springtime* by Margaret Hodges with illustrations by Arvis Stewart. Illustrations copyright © 1973 by Arvis Stewart. Reprinted by permission of Little, Brown and Company. **p. 234** Illustration by Laszlo Gal. From *Iduna and the Magic Apples* by Marianna Mayer. Illustration copyright © 1988 by Laszlo Gal. Reproduced by permission of Macmillan Publishing Company. **p. 235** From *Norse Gods and Giants* by Ingri & Edgar Parin d'Aulaire. Copyright © 1967 by Ingri & Edgar Parin d'Aulaire. Used by permission of Doubleday, a division of Bantam Doubleday Dell Publishing Group, Inc. **p. 238** Illustration by N.C. Wyeth from *The Boy's King Arthur* by Sidney Lanier is used with the permission of Charles Scribner's Sons. Copyright 1917 Charles Scribner's Sons, copyright renewed 1945 N.C. Wyeth. **p. 239** From *Sir Gawain and the Loathly Lady*, retold by Selina Hastings, illustrations by Juan Wijngaard. Illustrations copyright © 1985 by Juan Wijngaard. Reprinted by permission of Lothrop, Lee & Shepard Books, A Division of William Morrow & Company. **p. 240** Illustration taken from p. 35 of *The Story of Prince Rama* by Brian Thompson (Viking Kestrel, 1980). Copyright © Brian Thompson, 1980, illustrations copyright © Jeroo Roy, 1980. Reprinted by permission of Penguin Books Ltd. From *Tales From the Mabinogion* by Gwyn Thomas and Kevin Crossley-Holland, illustrated by Margaret Jones. Copyright © 1984 by Welsh Arts Council. Published by the Overlook Press, Lewis Hollow Road, Woodstock, New York 12498. Reprinted by permission. **p. 241** From *Legend of the Milky Way*, retold and illustrated by Jeanne M. Lee. Copyright © 1982 by Jeanne M. Lee. Reprinted by permission of Henry Holt and Company, Inc.

Chapter Eight

p. 250 Illustration from *The Little Mermaid* retold by Katie Thamer Treherne. Illustration copyright © 1989 by Katie Thamer Treherne. Reprinted by permission of Harcourt Brace Jovanovich, Inc. **p. 251** Illustration by Wanda Gág reprinted by permission of Coward-McCann from *Millions of Cats* by Wanda Gág, copyright 1928 by Wanda Gág, copyright renewed © 1956 by Robert Janssen. **p. 252** Illustration by Michael Hague from *The Hobbit* by J.R.R. Tolkien. Illustrations copyright © 1984 by Oak, Ash, and Thorn, Ltd. Reprinted by permission of Houghton Mifflin Company. **p. 258** Illustration from *The Borrowers* by Mary Norton, copyright 1953, 1952 and renewed 1981, 1980 by Mary Norton, Beth and Joe Krush. Reprinted by permission of Harcourt Brace Jovanovich, Inc. **p. 259** From *The Stones of Green Knowe* by L. M. Boston, illustrated by Peter Boston. Illustrations copyright © 1976 by Peter Boston. Reprinted by permission of The Bodley Head, London. **p. 261** From *Outside Over There* by Maurice Sendak. Copyright © 1981 by Maurice Sendak. Reprinted by permission of HarperCollins Publishers. **p. 263** From *The Devil's Other Storybook* by Natalie Babbitt. Copyright © 1987 by Natalie Babbitt. Reprinted by permission of Farrar, Straus &

Giroux, Inc. From *Peter Pan*, illustrated by Greg Hildebrandt, story by J.M. Barrie. Artwork © 1987 by Greg Hildebrandt. Reprinted by permission of The Unicorn Publishing House. **p. 265** From *Just So Stories* by Rudyard Kipling. Illustrated by Safaya Salter. Illustrations copyright © 1987 by Safaya Salter. Reprinted by permission of Henry Holt and Company, Inc. **p. 267** From *Charlotte's Web* by E.B. White, illustrated by Garth Williams. Copyright 1952 by E.B. White. Text copyright renewed © 1980 by E.B. White. Illustrations copyright renewed © 1980 by Garth Williams. Reprinted by permission of HarperCollins Publishers. **p. 268** Illustration by Zena Bernstein. From *Mrs. Frisby and the Rats of NIMH* by Robert C. O'Brien. Copyright © 1971 by Robert C. O'Brien. Reproduced by permission of Atheneum, an imprint of Macmillan Publishing Company. **p. 269** From *Abel's Island* by William Steig. Copyright © 1976 by William Steig. Reprinted by permission of Farrar, Straus & Giroux, Inc. **p. 271** Illustration from *The Little House* by Virginia Lee Burton. Copyright 1942 by Virginia Lee Demetrios. Copyright © renewed 1969 by George Demetrios. Reprinted by permission of Houghton Mifflin Company. **p. 272** From *Amy's Eyes* by Richard Kennedy, illustrated by Richard Egielski. Copyright © 1985 by Richard Kennedy. Reprinted by permission of HarperCollins Publishers. Illustration from *The Lady Who Put Salt in Her Coffee* by Lucretia Hale. Illustration copyright © 1989 by Amy Schwartz. Reprinted by permission of Harcourt Brace Jovanovich, Inc. **p. 273** From *The Cat in the Hat* by Dr. Seuss. Copyright © 1957 by Dr. Seuss. Copyright renewed 1985 by Theodore S. Geisel & Audrey S. Geisel. Reprinted by permission of Random House, Inc. **p. 274** From *Imogene's Antlers* by David Small. Copyright © 1985 by David Small. Reprinted by permission of Crown Publishers, Inc. **p. 275** From *Dr. Dredd's Wagon of Wonders* by Bill Brittain, illustrated by Andrew Glass. Illustrations copyright © 1985 by Andrew Glass. Reprinted by permission of HarperCollins Publishers. **p. 279** From *The Trouble on Janus* by Alfred Slote, illustrated by James Watts (J.B. Lippincott). Illustrations copyright © 1985 by James Watts. Reprinted by permission of HarperCollins Publishers. **p. 280** From *The Wizard of Oz* by L. Frank Baum, illustrated by Michael Hague. Illustrations copyright © 1982 by Michael Hague. Reprinted by permission of Henry Holt and Company, Inc.

Chapter Nine

p. 297 Illustration for "Eletelephony" by Richard Egielski from *Sing a Song of Popcorn: Every Child's Book of Poems,* selected by Beatrice Schenk de Regniers et al. Illustration copyright © 1988 by Richard Egielski. Reprinted by permission of Scholastic Inc. **p. 298** From *Brats* by X.J. Kennedy, illustrations by James Watts (Atheneum, 1986). Illustrations copyright © 1986 by James Watts. Reprinted by permission of James Watts. **p. 300** Illustration for "Firefly" by Eric Carle reprinted by permission of Philomel Books from *Animals, Animals*, illustrations © 1989 by Eric Carle. **p. 302** Illustration from *Tam Lin*, retold by Jane Yolen. Illustration copyright © 1990 by Charles Mikolaycak. Reprinted by permission of Harcourt Brace Jovanovich, Inc. **p. 303** Illustration by Tomie dePaola from *The Night Before Christmas* by Clement Moore. Copyright © 1980 by Tomie dePaola. Reprinted by permission of Holiday House. **p. 304** From *The Microscope* by Maxine Kumin. Pictures by Arnold Lobel. Pictures copyright © 1984 by Arnold Lobel. Reprinted by permission of HarperCollins Publishers. **p. 307** From *Consider the Lemming* by Jeanne Steig, illustrations by William Steig. Illustrations copyright © 1988 by William Steig. Reprinted by permission of Farrar, Straus & Giroux, Inc. **p. 308** Illustration by Nancy Tafuri from *If I Had a Paka* by Charlotte Pomerantz. Copyright © 1982 by Charlotte Pomerantz. Reprinted by permission of Greenwillow Books, A Division of William Morrow & Company. **p. 313** From *A Child's Garden of Verses* by Robert Louis Stevenson. Illustrated by Tasha Tudor. Illustration copyright © 1981 by Macmillan, Inc. Reproduced by permission of Macmillan Publishing Company. **p. 314** From *The Voice: A Sequence of Poems by Walter de la Mare*, chosen and illustrated by Catherine Brighton. Illustrations copyright © 1986 by Catherine Brighton. Used by permission of Dell Books, a Division of Bantam Doubleday Dell Publishing Group, Inc. **p. 315** Illustration for "Stopping By Woods on a Snowy Evening" by Marcia Brown from *Sing a Song of Popcorn: Every Child's Book* *of Poems,* selected by Beatrice Schenk de Regniers et al. Illustration copyright © 1988 by Marcia Brown. Reprinted by permission of Scholastic Inc. **p. 319** From *Every Time I Climb a Tree* by David McCord, illustrated by Marc Simont. Illustrations copyright © 1967 by Marc Simont. Reprinted by permission of Little, Brown and Company. **p. 321** From *Don't You Turn Back* by Langston Hughes, illustrated by Ann Grifalconi. Illustrations copyright © 1969 by Ann Grifalconi. Reprinted by permission of Alfred A. Knopf, Inc. **p. 324** From *You Read to Me, I'll Read to You* by John Ciardi. Drawings by Edward Gorey. Copyright © 1962 by John Ciardi. Reprinted by permission of HarperCollins Publishers. **p. 325** From *The Covered Bridge House and Other Poems* by Kaye Starbird Jennison, illustrations by Jim Arnosky. Copyright © 1979 by Kaye Starbird Jennison. Reprinted by permission of Scholastic Inc. **p. 326** From *Blackberry Ink* by Eve Merriam, pictures by Hans Wilhelm. Illustrations copyright © 1985 by Hans Wilhelm. Reprinted by permission of William Morrow & Company. **p. 328** From *A Tune Beyond Us,* edited by Myra Cohn Livingston, illustrated by James J. Spanfeller. Copyright © 1968 by Harcourt Brace Jovanovich, Inc. Reprinted by permission of the publisher.   From *Chocolate Dreams,* Poems by Arnold Adoff, illustrated by Turi MacCombie. Illustrations copyright © 1989 by Turi MacCombie. Reprinted by permission of Lothrop, Lee & Shepard Books, A Division of William Morrow & Company. **p. 329** From *Song in Stone: City Poems,* selected by Lee Bennett Hopkins. Photographs by Anna Held Audette. Illustrations copyright © 1983 by Anna Held Audette. Reprinted by permission of HarperCollins Publishers. **p. 330** From *Out and About* by Shirley Hughes. Copyright © 1988 by Shirley Hughes. Reprinted by permission of Lothrop, Lee & Shepard Books, A Division of William Morrow & Company.   From *Joyful Noise: Poems for Two Voices* by Paul Fleischman. Illustrated by Eric Beddows. Illustrations copyright © 1988 by Eric Beddows. Reprinted by permission of HarperCollins Publishers. **p. 332** From *Turtle in July* by Marilyn Singer. Illustrations copyright © 1989 by Jerry Pinkney. Reproduced by permission of Macmillan Publishing Company.

Chapter Ten

p. 346 Illustration by Elsa Beskow from *Pelle's New Suit* (New York: Harper & Row, Publishers, Inc., 1929). Reprinted by permission of Bonnier Juveniles International, Stockholm. **p. 348** From *The Hating Book* by Charlotte Zolotow. Pictures by Ben Shecter. Pictures copyright © 1969 by Ben Shecter. Reprinted by permission of HarperCollins Publishers. **p. 349** From *Russell and Elisa* by Johanna Hurwitz, illustrated by Lilian Hoban. Illustrations copyright © 1989 by Lilian Hoban. Reprinted by permission of Morrow Junior Books, A Division of William Morrow & Company. **p. 350** From *The Two of Them* by Aliki. Illustrations copyright © 1979 by Aliki Brandenberg. Reprinted by permission of Greenwillow Books, A Division of William Morrow & Company. **p. 352** Illustration from *The Hundred Dresses* by Eleanor Estes and illustrated by Louis Slobodkin. Copyright 1944 by Harcourt Brace Jovanovich, Inc. and renewed 1971 by Eleanor Estes and Louis Slobodkin. Reprinted by permission of the publisher. **p. 353** Illustration by Paul O. Zelinsky from *Dear Mr. Henshaw* by Beverly Cleary. Copyright © 1983 by Beverly Cleary. Reprinted by permission of Morrow Junior Books, A Division of William Morrow & Company. **p. 354** From *The House of Sixty Fathers* by Meindert DeJong. Pictures by Maurice Sendak. Copyright © 1955 by Meindert DeJong. Reprinted by permission of HarperCollins Publishers. **p. 355** From *The Family Under the Bridge* by Natalie Savage Carlson. Illustrated by Garth Williams. Pictures copyright © 1958 by Garth Williams. Reprinted by permission of HarperCollins Publishers. **p. 358** From *Harriet the Spy* by Louise Fitzhugh. Copyright © 1964 by Louise Fitzhugh. Reprinted by permission of HarperCollins Publishers. **p. 359** From *Zeely* by Virginia Hamilton. Copyright © 1967 by Virginia Hamilton. Reproduced by permission of the publisher. **p. 362** From *The Cybil War* by Betsy Byars, illustrated by Gail Owens. Illustrations copyright © 1984 by Viking Penguin Inc. Reprinted by permission of the publisher, Viking Penguin, a division of Penguin Books USA Inc. **p. 364** From *Bridge to Terabithia* by Katherine Paterson. Illustrated by Donna Diamond (Thomas Y. Crowell). Copyright © 1977 by Katherine Paterson. Reprinted by permission of HarperCollins Publishers. **p. 365**

Jacket illustration by Diane deGroat from *Anastasia Has the Answers* by Lois Lowry. Copyright © 1986 by Lois Lowry. Reprinted by permission of Houghton Mifflin Company. **p. 367** Jacket art by Stephen Marchesi reprinted by permission of Philomel Books from *The Broccoli Tapes* by Jan Slepian. Jacket art © 1989 by Stephen Marchesi. **p. 368** From *Arthur, For the Very First Time* by Patricia MacLachlan. Illustrations by Lloyd Bloom. Illustrations copyright © 1980 by Lloyd Bloom. Reprinted by permission of HarperCollins Publishers. **p. 369** Cover illustration from *M.E. and Morton* by Sylvia Cassedy. Copyright © 1987 by Sylvia Cassedy. Reprinted by permission of HarperCollins Publishers. **p. 372** From *Julie of the Wolves* by Jean Craighead George. Illustrated by John Schoenherr. Illustrations copyright © 1972 by John Schoenherr. Reprinted by permission of HarperCollins Publishers. **p. 376** Cover illustration from *Going Backwards* by Norma Klein. Copyright © 1986 by Norma Klein. Reprinted by permission of Scholastic Inc. **p. 378** From the painting "The Corner Seat" by Robert Vickrey, in the collection of Mrs. Robert Vickrey. **p. 379** Cover illustration from *Scorpions* by Walter Dean Myers. Copyright © 1988 by Walter Dean Myers. Reprinted by permission of HarperCollins Publishers. **p. 383** Drawing by Carl Burger from *The Incredible Journey* by Shelia Burnford. Copyright © 1960, 1961 by Shelia Burnford. Reprinted by permission of Knox Burger. **p. 384** From *Red-Hot Hightops* by Matt Christopher with illustrations by Paul D. Mock. Illustrations copyright © 1987 by Paul D. Mock. Reprinted by permission of Little, Brown and Company. **p. 387** From *The Whipping Boy* by Sid Fleischman, illustrated by Peter Sis. Illustrations copyright © 1986 by Peter Sis. Reprinted by permission of Greenwillow Books, A Division of William Morrow & Company.

Chapter Eleven

p. 414 From *The Fighting Ground* by Avi. Frontispiece by Ellen Thompson (J. B. Lippincott). Frontispiece copyright © 1984 by Ellen Thompson. Reprinted by permission of HarperCollins Publishers. **p. 417** From *A Lion to Guard Us* by Clyde Robert Bulla. Illustrated by Michele Chessare. Illustrations copyright © 1981 by Michele Chessare. Reprinted by permission of HarperCollins Publishers. **p. 418** From *Harald and the Great Stag* by Donald Carrick. Copyright © 1988 by Donald Carrick. Reprinted by permission of Ticknor & Fields, a Houghton Mifflin Company. **p. 419** From *Zekmet, the Stone Carver: A Tale of Ancient Egypt* by Mary Stolz. Illustrations copyright © 1988 by Deborah Nourse Lattimore. Reprinted by permission of Harcourt Brace Jovanovich, Inc. **p. 420** From *The Door in the Wall* by Marguerite de Angeli. Copyright 1949 by Marguerite de Angeli. Reprinted by permission of Doubleday, a division of Bantam Doubleday Dell Publishing Group, Inc. **p. 421** Illustration by Tomie dePaola reprinted by permission of Coward, McCann & Geoghegan from *Can't You Make Them Behave, King George?* by Jean Fritz. Illustrations © 1977 by Tomie dePaola. **p. 423** From *My Prairie Year* by Brett Harvey, illustrated by Deborah Kogan Ray. Illustrations copyright © 1986 by Deborah Kogan. Reprinted by permission of Holiday House. **p. 424** From *Granny Reardun* by Alan Garner, illustrated by Michael Foreman. Illustrations copyright © 1977 by Michael Foreman. Reprinted by permission of Michael Foreman. **p. 426** Illustration by Leo and Diane Dillon from *Hakon of Rogen's Saga* by Erik Christian Haugaard. Copyright © 1963 by Erik Christian Haugaard. Reprinted by permission of Houghton Mifflin Company. **p. 429** From *Beyond the Weir Bridge* by Hester Burton. Illustrated by Victor G. Ambrus. Copyright © 1969 by Hester Burton. Reprinted by permission of HarperCollins Publishers. **p. 432** Illustration by Lynd Ward from *Johnny Tremain* by Esther Forbes. Copyright 1943 by Esther Forbes Hoskins. Copyright © renewed 1971 by Linwood M. Erskine, Jr. Reprinted by permission of Houghton Mifflin Company. **p. 433** From *Wayah of the Real People* by William O. Steele, illustrated by Isa Barnett (Williamsburg, Virginia: Colonial Williamsburg, Inc., 1964). Reprinted by permission of Mary Q. Steele. **p. 434** Jacket illustration by Ted Lewin from *Streams to the River, River to the Sea* by Scott O'Dell. Copyright © 1986 by Scott O'Dell. Reprinted by permission of Houghton Mifflin Company. **p. 438** From *Children of the Fox* by Jill Paton Walsh, pictures by Robin Eaton. Copyright © 1978 by Farrar, Straus and Giroux, Inc. Reprinted by permission of Farrar, Straus and Giroux, Inc.

Chapter Twelve

p. 454 From *Anthony Burns: The Defeat and Triumph of a Fugitive Slave* by Virginia Hamilton, illustrated by Leo and Diane Dillon. Illustration copyright © 1988 by Leo and Diane Dillon. Reprinted by permission of Alfred A. Knopf, Inc. **p. 456** Nebraska State Historical Society. **p. 461** University of Oklahoma, Western History Collections. **p. 462** From *The One Bad Thing About Father* by F.N. Monjo. Illustrations by Rocco Negri. Illustrations copyright © 1970 by Rocco Negri. Reprinted by permission of HarperCollins Publishers. Illustration by Ed Young reprinted by permission of G.P. Putnam's Sons from *The Double Life of Pocahontas* by Jean Fritz. Illustrations copyright © 1983 by Ed Young. **p. 464** From *Abraham Lincoln* by Ingri and Edgar d'Aulaire. Copyright 1939, 1957 by Doubleday, a division of Bantam Doubleday Dell Publishing Group, Inc. Used by permission of the publisher. **p. 465** From *Shoes for Everyone: A Story About Jan Matzeliger* by Barbara Mitchell, illustrated by Hetty Mitchell. Copyright © 1986 by Carolrhoda Books, 241 First Avenue North, Minneapolis, MN 55401. Used by permission of the publisher. **p. 466** From *Peter the Great* by Diane Stanley. Copyright © 1986 by Diane Stanley Vennema. Reproduced by permission of Four Winds Press, an Imprint of Macmillan Publishing. **p. 467** Illustration by Ati Forberg from *Jeanne d'Arc* by Aileen Fisher. Illustrations copyright © 1970 by Ati Forberg. Reproduced by permission. **p. 469** Illustration from *Bill Peet: An Autobiography* by Bill Peet. Copyright © 1989 by William Peet. Photos © 1989 by William Peet. Drawings of scenes and characters from Disney Films © 1989 The Walt Disney Company. Reprinted by permission of Houghton Mifflin Company. **p. 470** From *The King's Day: Louis XIV of France* by Aliki (Thomas Y. Crowell). Copyright © 1989 by Aliki Brandenberg. Reprinted by permission of HarperCollins Publishers. **p. 474** Illustration by John O'Hara Cosgrave, II, from *Carry On, Mr. Bowditch* by Jean Latham. Copyright © 1955 by Jean Lee Latham and John O'Hara Cosgrave, II. Copyright © renewed 1983 by Jean Lee Latham. Reprinted by permission of Houghton Mifflin Company. **p. 481** Photo courtesy of The United Nations. **p. 482** From *A Girl of Yamhill* by Beverly Cleary. Copyright © 1988 by Beverly Cleary. Reprinted by permission of Morrow Junior Books, A Division of William Morrow & Company.

Chapter Thirteen

p. 503 Brent Ashabranner/Paul Conklin. **p. 505** From *Journey into a Black Hole* by Franklyn M. Branley. Illustrated by Marc Simont (Thomas Y. Crowell). Illustrations copyright © 1986 by Marc Simont. Reprinted by permission of HarperCollins Publishers. **p. 506** From *The Blacksmiths* by Leonard Everett Fisher. Copyright © 1976 by Leonard Everett Fisher. Reprinted by permission of the publisher, Franklin Watts, Inc. **p. 507** Museum of the American Indian, The Heye Foundation. From *One Day in the Prairie* by Jean Craighead George. Illustrated by Bob Marstall (Thomas Y. Crowell). Illustrations copyright © 1986 by Bob Marstall. Reprinted by permission of HarperCollins Publishers. **p. 509** Illustration from *Paddle-to-the-Sea* by Holling C. Holling. Copyright 1941 and copyright © renewed 1969 by Holling C. Holling. Reprinted by permission of Houghton Mifflin Company. **p. 510** From *Get Ready for Robots!* by Patricia Lauber. Illustrated by True Kelley. Illustrations copyright © 1987 by True Kelley. Reprinted by permission of HarperCollins. **p. 511** From *Lili: A Giant Panda of Sichuan* by Robert M. McClung, illustrated by Irene Brady. Illustrations © 1988 by Irene Brady. Reprinted by permission of Morrow Jr. Books, A Division of William Morrow & Company. **p. 513** From *Follow a Fisher* by Laurence Pringle. Illustrated by Tony Chen (Thomas Y. Crowell). Illustrations copyright © 1973 by Tony Chen. Reprinted by permission of HarperCollins Publishers. **p. 515** From *Heartbeats: Your Body, Your Heart* by Dr. Alvin and Virginia B. Silverstein. Illustrated by Stella Ormai (J.B. Lippincott). Illustration copyright © 1983 by Stella Ormai. Reprinted by permission of HarperCollins Publishers. **p. 516** From *Storms* by Seymour Simon. Copyright © 1989 by Seymour Simon. Reprinted by permission of Morrow Junior Books, A Division of William Morrow & Company. **p. 518** From *Shelters: From Tepee to Igloo* by Harvey Weiss (Thomas Y. Crowell). Copyright © 1988 by Harvey Weiss. Reprinted by permission of HarperCollins Publishers. **p. 520** From *From Flower to Fruit* by Anne Ophelia Dowden (Thomas Y. Crowell). Copyright © 1984 by Anne Ophelia Dowden. Reprinted by permission of HarperCollins Publishers. **p. 521** From *Koko's Kitten* by Dr. Francine Patterson, photographs by Dr. Ronald H. Cohn. Photographs copyright © Ronald Cohn/The Gorilla Foundation/National Geographic Society. Reprinted by permission of Scholastic Inc. **p. 522** Illustration by Gen Shimada from *The First Travel Guide to the Bottom of the Sea* by Rhoda Blumberg. Copyright © 1983 by Gen Shimada. Reprinted by permission of Lothrop, Lee & Shepard Books, a division of William Morrow & Company. **p. 524** Illustration by Mitsumasa Anno reprinted by permission of Philomel Books from *Anno's Math Games II* by Mitsumasa Anno. Copyright © 1982 by Kuso Kobo. **p. 525** From *The Invisible World of the Infrared* by Jack R. White, illustrations by Valerie Temple. Copyright © 1984 by Jack R. White. Reprinted by permission of Dodd, Mead & Company, publishers. **p. 526** Reprinted with permission of Charles Scribner's Sons, an imprint of Macmillan Publishing Company from *Digging to the Past: Excavations in Ancient Lands* by W. John Hackwell. Copyright © 1986 by W. John Hackwell. **p. 527** From *A Tournament of Knights*, written and illustrated by Joe Lasker (Thomas Y. Crowell). Copyright © 1986 by Joe Lasker. Reprinted by permission of HarperCollins Publishers. **p. 528** Courtesy of the National Food and Drug Administration. **p. 529** From *Jerusalem, Shining Still* by Karla Kuskin. Illustrations by David Frampton. Illustrations copyright © 1987 by David Frampton. Reprinted by permission of G.P. Putnam's Sons from *Michelangelo's World* by Piero Ventura. Copyright © 1988 by Arnoldo Mondadori Editore, Milan. Reprinted by permission. **p. 532** Illustration from *City* by David Macaulay. Copyright © 1974 by David Macaulay. Reprinted by permission of Houghton Mifflin Company. **p. 533** From *The Fun of Cooking* by Jill Krementz. Copyright © 1985 by Jill Krementz. Reprinted by permission of Alfred A. Knopf, Inc. **p. 534** From *Gobs of Goo* by Vicki Cobb. Illustrated by Brian Schatell (J.B. Lippincott). Illustrations copyright © 1983 by Brian Schatell. Reprinted by permission of HarperCollins Publishers. **p. 535** From *Linnea's Windowsill Garden* by Christina Björk and Lena Anderson, translated by Joan Sandin. Pictures copyright © 1978 by Lena Anderson. Reprinted by permission of Raben & Sjogren Bokforlag and Lena Anderson.

Chapter Fourteen

p. 566 ScottForesman **p. 571** ScottForesman **p. 577** ScottForesman **p. 578** Elizabeth Crews **p. 579** ScottForesman

Chapter Fifteen

p. 586 ScottForesman **p. 596** Elizabeth Crews **p. 602** ScottForesman **p. 605** Dawn Murray

Chapter Sixteen

p. 618 From *Doctor De Soto*, written and illustrated by William Steig. Copyright © 1982 by William Steig. Reprinted by permission of Farrar, Straus & Giroux, Inc. **p. 620** From *The True Story of the Three Little Pigs* by Jon Scieszka, illustrated by Lane Smith. Illustrations copyright © 1989 by Lane Smith. Reprinted by permission of the publisher, Viking Penguin, a division of Penguin Books USA Inc. **p. 621** Illustration by Tomie dePaola reprinted by G.P. Putnam's Sons from *The Legend of the Bluebonnet* by Tomie dePaola. Copyright © 1983 by Tomie dePaola. **p. 623** Illustration for "Jumping Rope" from *Where the Sidewalk Ends* by Shel Silverstein. Copyright © 1974 by Snake Eye Music, Inc. Reprinted by permission of HarperCollins Publishers. **p. 626** Illustration by Maurice Sendak, reprinted with permission of Macmillan Publishing Company from *The Bat-Poet* by Randall Jarrell. Copyright © Macmillan Publishing Company, 1963, 1964. **p. 628** From *Ragtime Tumpie* by Alan Schroeder with illustrations by Bernie Fuchs. Copyright © 1989 by Bernie Fuchs. Reprinted by permission of Little, Brown and Company. **p. 629** Jacket photo from *Number the Stars* by Lois Lowry. Copyright © 1989 by Lois Lowry. Reprinted by permission of Houghton Mifflin Company. **p. 630** From *Handtalk Birthday: A Number & Story Book in Sign Language* by Remy Charlip and Mary Beth Miller. Photographs copyright © 1987 by George Ancona. Reprinted by permission of James K. Ross.